Psychology

The Science of Mind and Behavior

Psychology

The Science of Mind and Behavior **Third Edition**

Michael W. Passer
University of Washington

Ronald E. Smith
University of Washington

Boston Burr Ridge, IL Dubuque, IA Madison, WI New York
San Francisco St. Louis Bangkok Bogotá Caracas Kuala Lumpur
Lisbon London Madrid Mexico City Milan Montreal New Delhi
Santiago Seoul Singapore Sydney Taipei Toronto

The *McGraw·Hill* Companies

Mc Graw Hill **Higher Education**

PSYCHOLOGY: THE SCIENCE OF MIND AND BEHAVIOR, Third Edition
Published by McGraw-Hill, an imprint of The McGraw-Hill Companies, Inc., 1221 Avenue of
the Americas, New York, NY, 10020. Copyright © 2007, 2004, 2001 by The McGraw-Hill
Companies, Inc. All rights reserved. No part of this publication may be reproduced or distributed in any form or by any means, or stored in a database or retrieval system, without the
prior written consent of The McGraw-Hill Companies, Inc., including, but not limited to, in
any network or other electronic storage or transmission, or broadcast for distance learning.

Some ancillaries, including electronic and print components, may not be available to
customers outside the United States.

This book is printed on acid-free paper.

1 2 3 4 5 6 7 8 9 0 WCK/WCK 0 9 8 7 6 5

ISE-13: 978-0-07-110715-0
ISE-10:   0-07-110715-0

About the Authors

MICHAEL W. PASSER, PH.D.

Michael Passer coordinates the introductory psychology program at the University of Washington, which enrolls about 2,500 students per year, and also is the faculty coordinator of training for new teaching assistants (TAs). He received his bachelor's degree from the University of Rochester and his PhD in Psychology from the University of California, Los Angeles, with a specialization in social psychology. Dr. Passer has been a faculty member at the University of Washington since 1977. A former Danforth Foundation Fellow and University of Washington Distinguished Teaching Award finalist, Dr. Passer has had a career-long love of teaching. Each academic year he teaches introductory psychology twice and a required pre-major course in research methods. Dr. Passer developed and teaches a graduate course on the Teaching of Psychology, which prepares students for careers in the college classroom, and has also taught courses in social psychology and attribution theory. He has published more than 20 scientific articles and chapters, primarily in the areas of attribution, stress, and anxiety, and has taught the introductory psychology course for almost 20 years.

RONALD E. SMITH, PH.D.

Ronald E. Smith is Professor of Psychology at the University of Washington, where he has served as Director of Clinical Psychology Training and as Head of the Social Psychology and Personality area. He received his bachelor's degree from Marquette University and his PhD from Southern Illinois University, where he had dual specializations in clinical and physiological psychology. His major research interests are in anxiety, stress and coping, and in performance enhancement research and intervention. Dr. Smith is a Fellow of the American Psychological Association. He received a Distinguished Alumnus Award from the UCLA Neuropsychiatric Institute for his contributions to the field of mental health. He has published more than 140 scientific articles and book chapters in his areas of interest and has authored or coauthored 21 books on introductory psychology, human performance enhancement, and personality, including *Introduction to Personality: Toward an Integration*, with Walter Mischel and Yuichi Shoda (Wiley, 2004). An award-winning teacher, he has more than 15 years of experience in teaching the introductory psychology course.

To Bev and Kay, for their endless love and support.

Brief Contents

Contents

CHAPTER 2

Studying Behavior Scientifically 28

CHAPTER 3

Biological Foundations of Behavior:
Evolution, Genes, and Brain 61

CHAPTER 4

Sensation and Perception 105

CHAPTER 5

States of Consciousness 149

CHAPTER 6

Learning and Adaptation: The Role of Experience 191

CHAPTER 7

Memory 232

CHAPTER 8

Language and Thinking 273

CHAPTER 9

Intelligence 312

CHAPTER 10

Motivation and Emotion 348

CHAPTER 11

Development over the Life Span 395

CHAPTER 12

Personality 440

CHAPTER 13

Adjusting to Life: Stress, Coping, and Health 485

CHAPTER 14

Psychological Disorders 528

CHAPTER 15

Treatment of Psychological Disorders 572

CHAPTER 16

Social Thinking and Behavior 613

Preface

Psychology: The Science of Mind and Behavior (3rd Edition)
—**Michael W. Passer and Ronald E. Smith**
University of Washington

Mind and behavior: There is nothing more fascinating in all the universe, but we didn't recognize this when we entered college. In fact, the study of psychology wasn't on either of our radar screens. Michael planned to major in physics, Ron in journalism. Then something unexpected occurred. Each of us took an introductory psychology course, and suddenly our life paths changed. Because of instructors who brought psychology to life, we were hooked, and that initial enthusiasm has never left us.

Now, through this textbook, we have the pleasure and privilege of sharing our enthusiasm with today's instructors and a new generation of students. We've endeavored to create a thoughtfully integrated book and multimedia package of uncompromising student friendliness and scientific integrity—a teaching tool that introduces students to psychology as a science while highlighting its relevance to their lives and to society. We want students to experience, as we did, the intellectual excitement of studying the mind and behavior. We also seek to help students sharpen their critical-thinking skills and dispel commonly held myths. All of this is done within a simple conceptual framework that emphasizes relations between biological, psychological, and environmental levels of analysis.

We are particularly excited about the unique way in which our textbook is integrated with its supplements. This integration results in a learning package that "uses science to teach science." Specifically, we have taken note of research (e.g., Hamilton, 1985; Moreland et al., 1997; Thiede & Anderson, 2003) showing that recall of textual material is significantly enhanced by asking students to summarize material they have just read and by presenting focus questions and learning objectives that serve as retrieval cues and help students identify important information. Marginal Focus Questions integrated into each chapter of this textbook serve these purposes and help students assess their mastery of the material. But well beyond that, these Focus Questions provide a comprehensive learning framework for the supplements.

What you will find throughout the supplements is a carefully developed integration of the in-text Focus Questions with Learning Objectives. Instructors and students alike will be guided by the Learning Objectives, as they form the cornerstone of the Instructor's Manual, Online Learning Center, Instructor's Resource CD-ROM, student Study Guide, In-Psych*plus* CD-ROM including exclusive Discovery Channel™ video clips, and Test Banks. Items in the three Test Banks are keyed specifically to the Focus Questions and Learning Objectives. Students who are guided by the Focus Questions and Learning Objectives should be well prepared for questions taken from the test banks and should achieve at a high level.

Let's take a closer look at the features of our third edition.

THE BIG PICTURE: A SIMPLE UNIFYING FRAMEWORK THAT EASILY ADAPTS TO THE INSTRUCTOR'S PREFERENCES

Psychology is a vibrant but sprawling discipline, and the tremendous diversity of issues covered in the introductory course can lead students to perceive psychology as a collection of unrelated topics. To reduce this tendency and also help students become more sophisticated in their everyday understanding of behavior, we present a simple unifying framework that is applied throughout the book. This framework, called *Levels of Analysis* (LOA), emphasizes how psychologists examine *biological, psychological, and environmental factors* in their quest to understand behavior. The parsimonious LOA framework is easy for students to understand and remember; is consistently applied in every chapter; accurately portrays the focus of modern psychology; supports critical thinking; and also helps students understand how biological, psychological, and environmental factors are related to one another.

Although we carry the LOA framework throughout the book in textual discussion and schematics, we are careful to apply it selectively so that it does not become overly repetitious for students or confining for instructors. Indeed, one of the beauties of the LOA framework is that it stands on its own and thus instructors can easily adapt it to their personal teaching preferences. For example, some adopters of the book have told us that they never bring up the LOA framework explicitly in class. Instead, they emphasize their own preferred theoretical perspective in lectures while resting assured that, behind the scenes, each textbook chapter illustrates for students how behavior can be studied from multiple angles, that is, from different levels of analysis. Other instructors consistently incorporate a levels-of-analysis approach into their lectures. Finally, as we do in our own courses, instructors can explicitly bring the LOA framework into their lectures only for selected topics, once again knowing that for other topics the textbook will round out their students' conceptual exposure.

READABILITY, RIGOR, AND RELEVANCE

A textbook has long-term educational value only if students read it, understand its content, and find that content to be worthwhile. We have worked diligently to develop a narrative that will excite students and draw them into to the fascinating world of mind and behavior. We have made every attempt to use clear prose, careful explanations, engaging examples, and supporting artwork to make the book and multimedia accessible to a wide range of students. At the same time, we portray psychology as the rigorous and keenly relevant discipline that it is. The following elements support these goals.

- **Focus on Scientific Psychology:** Throughout the narrative we portray *psychology as a contemporary science* without becoming excessively formal or terminological. And because we live in an era in which students (along with everyone else) are bombarded with scientific information and misinformation, we focus not only on principles derived from research, but also on how good research is done.

- **Focus on Personal and Societal Applications:** Everyday examples are used throughout the narrative not only to illustrate psychological principles and concepts, but also to engage students and personalize their learning experience. We also highlight numerous ways in which psychological knowledge has been used to enhance the welfare of society.

- **Focus on Relations between Basic Science and Application:** Whether in the context of their personal lives or of larger societal issues, we emphasize that many questions studied from a basic science perspective are inspired by real-world questions and issues, and that basic research findings often guide solutions to individual and societal problems.

- **Focus on Helping Students to Think Critically and Dispel Misconceptions:** In diverse ways, we strongly emphasize critical thinking as a skill for students to learn and practice. In the general narrative throughout the text, we repeatedly address basic critical-thinking issues, such as the importance of identifying alternative explanations and recognizing that correlation does not establish causation. We emphasize that many faulty inferences—in everyday life as well as in science—are made by failing to pay attention to basic critical-thinking principles.

- **Highlighted Features That Support the General Narrative's Scientific, Applied, and Critical-Thinking Emphases:**
  - **Levels of Analysis:** The book's basic LOA framework and schematics emphasize how psychologists carefully study behavior from diverse angles, reinforce the core concept that behavior typically has multiple causes, and encourage students to be wary of overly simplistic explanations.

- **Research Close-Ups:** In each chapter, this feature uses a scientific-journal format to provide students with an inside look at a research study and engage students in a process of critical thinking about the research question.

- **Applying Psychological Science:** In each chapter, this feature brings a key concept into the realm of personal or societal real-life application. Six of these *Applying Psychological Science* (APS) boxes throughout the book focus on important skills that can enhance students' learning and performance. In Chapter 1, this feature discusses good study habits and other ways that students can enhance their learning. In Chapter 6, it focuses on behavioral self-regulation and breaking bad study habits. Other APS features emphasize memory enhancement (Chapter 7), enhancing meta-comprehension (Chapter 8), systematic goal setting (Chapter 12), and stress management (Chapter 13).

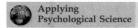

Applying Psychological Science   Being Happy: Guidelines from Psychological Research

As research has accumulated on factors that relate to happiness, psychologists have been able to offer advice based on data rather than intuition (Seligman, 2002). Most psychologists believe that happiness, like a good marriage, is something that one must work at (Seligman & Peterson, 2004). Here, then, are some suggestions that may help you maintain and enhance personal happiness.

- *Spend time with other people, and work to develop close relationships.* Research consistently suggests that good relationships provide the strongest basis for life satisfaction. Even if you tend to be introverted, form at least a few close relationships and nurture them. Make time for social interactions.
- *Look for ways to be helpful to others, and reach out to the less fortunate.* Try to make a positive difference in the lives of others. Doing so will increase your sense of self-worth, add meaning to your life, and deepen relationships with those whose lives you touch. It will also help put your own problems in perspective and direct your energies away from self-absorption. There's a lot to be said for the proposition that we receive by giving.
- *Seek meaning and challenge in work.* Enjoying one's work is a prime ingredient of happiness. If you feel stuck doing something that provides little gratification, be it your job or your major, consider looking for something more satisfying. Everyone has to make a living, but many people spend their lives doing things they don't derive satisfaction or meaning from—hardly a recipe for a happy life. Even if you love your work, strive for balance between work and personal pursuits. People on their death beds rarely, if ever, express the wish that they had spent more time at the office.
- *Set meaningful personal goals for yourself, and make progress toward them.* Whether in work, school, or relationships, engaging in goal-directed activity and seeing yourself

moving toward your goals will provide a basis for life satisfaction and foster feelings of being in greater control of your life. Many people find that spiritual development (religiously based or not) confers meaning in their life.
- *Make time for enjoyable activities.* One of the benefits of time-management skills is the ability to schedule everyday activities that provide pleasure around school, work, and other obligations. Make time for a hobby, reading, and recreational activities.
- *Nurture physical well-being.* Many studies show that even moderate physical exercise contributes to emotional well-being (Morgan, 1997). Such activities provide a temporary respite from life stressors. When done in a social context, they add the benefits of social interaction as well. People who exercise, get sufficient sleep, and practice good dietary habits tend to be more stress resistant and satisfied with themselves and their lives (Taylor, 2006).
- *Be open to new experiences.* Some of our most pleasurable experiences can occur when we try new things. It's easy to fall into a rut, so whether it's traveling, developing a new hobby, or taking a college course on a new subject, be open to doing something you haven't done before.
- *Cultivate optimism, and count your blessings.* As we've seen, cognitive appraisals influence emotions, and an upbeat, optimistic approach to life is linked with subjective well-being. Try to look on the positive side of things, to see demanding events as challenges and opportunities rather than threats. Learn to appreciate and be grateful for even the mundane, average day in which nothing bad happens to you. There is a Buddhist saying: "Happiness is a day without a toothache." All of us are gifted in ways that we may take for granted. Perhaps we should focus more often on these typically ignored aspects of good fortune.

- **Beneath the Surface** discussions and **What Do You Think?** exercises challenge students to think critically in evaluating popular truisms, scientific and pseudo-scientific claims, and psychology's relevance to their own lives.

Beneath the Surface   Older but Wiser?

In many traditional cultures around the world, elderly adults are esteemed for their wisdom. Common sense says that as we progress through adulthood, we become "older but wiser," but is this true?

THE NATURE OF WISDOM

Wisdom represents a system of knowledge about the meaning and conduct of life. To quickly refresh your memory, in Chapter 8 we described several major components of wisdom identified by psychologist Paul Baltes and his coworkers (2002, 2004), which included:

- Rich factual knowledge about life (e.g., about human nature and social relationships)
- Rich procedural knowledge about life (e.g., strategies for making decisions, handling conflict, giving advice)
- An understanding of life-span contexts (e.g., family, friends, work; past, present, future)
- An awareness that values and priorities differ across people and societies
- An ability to recognize and manage uncertainty (e.g., "the future cannot be fully known")

AGING AND WISDOM

Does age bring greater wisdom? To find out, Baltes and other researchers presented participants of different ages with various life problems (e.g., a 15-year-old girl wants to get married right away; an adult realizes that she hasn't achieved major goals) and asked them what the hypothetical person should do. Experts blind to the participants' ages then scored their solutions, using the five criteria of wisdom described above.

What did they find? Older teens gave wiser solutions than younger teens, adults in their early 20s gave still wiser solutions, and older adults—on average—showed no greater or lesser wisdom. As these findings suggest, wisdom seems to rise steadily from age 13 to 25 and then remain relatively stable through age 75 (Baltes & Staudinger, 2000; Pasupathi et al., 2001). Beyond that, wisdom may decline, but the researchers were able to study relatively few people older than 75.

Let's turn, however, to a different type of task. Read the story below, then answer the question that follows.

> A burglar who has just robbed a shop is making his getaway. As he is running home, a policeman on his beat sees him drop his glove. He doesn't know the man is a burglar, he just wants to tell him he dropped his glove. But when the policeman shouts out to the burglar, "Hey, you! Stop!" the burglar turns round, sees the policeman, and gives himself up. *Question:* Why did the burglar do that? (Happé et al., 1998, p. 362)

Did you find this task easy? A good answer would be that the burglar mistakenly assumed that the officer knew he had robbed the shop and didn't realize that the officer was only trying to return the dropped glove. This task measures how well you understand "what someone else is thinking" based on their behavior. This type of social wisdom comes into play when we need to infer what people must have been thinking to have acted as they did or need to predict how others will behave based on what is "going on in their head." Francesca Happé and coworkers (1998) found that on such tasks, younger adults (average age 21 years) generally gave good responses, but older adults (average age 73 years), on average, displayed superior social reasoning. Several other researchers also have found superior performance among older adults on various reasoning tasks.

As a critical thinker, you should recognize that all of the studies just mentioned are cross-sectional; that is, they compare people from different age groups. Asking whether 75-year-olds are wiser than 25-year-olds is not quite the same as asking whether the same young adults will become wiser as they age. Only longitudinal and sequential studies can answer that question.

At present, then, research suggests that "older but wiser" may apply only up to a point, beyond which "older but at least as wise" is more appropriate. Of course, these are averages. Some older adults—even into their 80s—display greater wisdom than many young adults. To stereotype elderly adults as "wise," however, is just as inappropriate as to stereotype them as "senile." Erik Erikson (Erikson et al., 1986) emphasized that old age brings with it only the *potential* for wisdom. And even in traditional cultures where elders are revered, such as among the Inuit of the Canadian Arctic, members readily acknowledge that not everyone ages successfully.

development of personality (Lewis, previously wide gulf between psychotheories and other psychological perspectives starting to narrow, due largely to the development of new methods for studying unmental processes.

The psychodynamic perspective offer insights into Charles Whitman's personal eventual eruption into violence? Although into a family of means and showered material goods, Whitman grew up within a home environment. His father was a self-brutal man who ruled his house with an fist, frequently beat his wife. He tolerated less from his sons and viciously belittled any perceived failures. Whitman was to his mother and deeply resented his treatment of her, which, according to

that he had frequent fantasies about "going up on the tower with a deer rifle and shooting people," but the psychiatrist did not take them seriously because of his nonviolent history (Lavergne, 1997, p. 137).

What Do You Think?

HOW SERIOUSLY SHOULD WE TAKE PEOPLE'S VIOLENT FANTASIES?

What are we to make of people's reports of violent fantasies? Should Whitman's report of his violent fantasies have alerted the psychiatrist about his penchant for violence and caused the psychiatrist to contact authorities? What would you have done? Think about it, then read the discussion on page 484.

- **Integrated and Featured Coverage of Cultural and Gender Issues:** Cultural and gender issues are at the forefront of contemporary psychology, and rather than isolating this material within dedicated chapters, we integrate it throughout the text. Our levels-of-analysis approach conceptualizes culture as an environmental factor and also as a psychological factor that reflects the internalization of cultural influences. In addition to coverage of cultural and gender issues throughout the narrative, these topics are addressed via features such as the *Research Close-Ups* and *What Do You Think?* exercises. Notable in this regard are sections in Chapter 9 (Intelligence) on sex differences in cognitive abilities and the effects of stereotypes on math performance, in Chapter 13 (Adjusting to Life: Stress, Coping, and Health) on possible reasons why women live longer than men, and in Chapter 15 (Treatment of Psychological Disorders) on cultural and gender issues in psychotherapy.

- **Thorough, Up-To-Date Coverage:** To portray our discipline with accuracy, we have made every effort to be the most current book on the market. As in our past editions, our emphasis on new research is balanced with thorough coverage of classic studies.

- **Additional Pedagogical Features:** A textbook should inspire students and help them master the material at hand. Our book incorporates many pedagogical features to accomplish these goals.
  - *Multiple brief summaries within each chapter*: To facilitate student understanding and instructor flexibility of assignments, chapters feature main (first-level) sections that are largely self-contained. At the end of each major section, an interim *In Review* summary helps to break the content into more manageable segments.
  - *Chapter-opening vignettes* present interesting stories that capture students' attention, draw them into the material, and are used later in the chapter to reinforce important points.
  - *Focus Questions* appear in the margins of the book adjacent to important material. These are designed to function as study guides, retrieval cues, and self-tests.

- **Running key terms with definitions:** Key terms are presented in the text in boldface, followed by italicized definitions. This in-context presentation serves as an *integrated glossary,* supplementing the list of key terms at chapter's end and the comprehensive glossary in the back of the book.

SOMATOFORM DISORDERS

Somatoform disorders *involve physical complaints or disabilities that suggest a medical problem but that have no known biological cause and are not produced voluntarily by the person* (Finell, 1997). In **hypochondriasis,** *people become unduly alarmed about any physical symptom they detect and are convinced that they have or are about to have a serious illness.* People with **pain disorder** *experience intense pain that either is out of proportion to whatever medical condition they might have or for which no physical basis can be found.*

▶ **Focus 14**
Describe three kinds of somatoform disorders. What causal factors might be involved?

- **Chapter outlines,** an end-of-chapter list of **key terms and concepts,** and a brief discussion of the critical-thinking **What Do You Think?** exercises round out the pedagogical features in each chapter.

CHAPTER OUTLINE

STRESS AND WELL-BEING
Stressors
The Stress Response: A Mind-Body Link
Effects of Stress on Well-Being
WHAT DO YOU THINK? Do Stressful Events Cause Psychological Distress?
RESEARCH CLOSE-UP How Does Stress Affect the Immune System?
Factors That Influence Stress-Health Relations

COPING WITH STRESS
Effectiveness of Coping Strategies
Controllability and Coping Efficacy
Trauma Disclosure and Emotional Release
Bottling Up Feelings: The Hidden Costs of Emotional Constraint

PAIN AND PAIN MANAGEMENT
Biological Mechanisms of Pain
Cultural and Psychological Influences on Pain
APPLYING PSYCHOLOGICAL SCIENCE Psychological Techniques for Controlling Pain and Suffering

HEALTH PROMOTION AND ILLNESS PREVENTION
How People Change: The Transtheoretical Model
Increasing Behaviors That Enhance Health
Reducing Behaviors That Impair Health
BENEATH THE SURFACE College-Age Drinking: Harmless Fun or Russian Roulette?
Relapse Prevention: Maintaining Positive Behavior Change
A Concluding Thought

KEY TERMS AND CONCEPTS

Each term has been boldfaced and defined in the chapter on the page indicated in parentheses.

abnormal behavior (p. 533)	dissociative disorders (p. 544)	phobia (p. 537)
agoraphobia (p. 537)	dissociative identity disorder (DID; p. 545)	positive symptoms (p. 556)
antisocial personality disorder (p. 561)	dopamine hypothesis (p. 557)	posttraumatic stress disorder (PTSD; p. 539)
anxiety (p. 536)	dysthymia (p. 546)	
anxiety disorders (p. 536)	expressed emotion (p. 558)	psychogenic amnesia (p. 544)
attention deficit/hyperactivity disorder (ADHD; p. 568)	generalized anxiety disorder (p. 537)	psychogenic fugue (p. 544)
	hallucinations (p. 555)	regression (p. 558)
autistic disorder (p. 568)	hypochondriasis (p. 543)	reliability (p. 533)
bipolar disorder (p. 547)	insanity (p. 535)	schizophrenia (p. 554)
borderline personality disorder (BPD; p. 565)	learned helplessness theory (p. 551)	social causation hypothesis (p. 559)
	major depression (p. 546)	social drift hypothesis (p. 559)
catatonic schizophrenia (p. 555)	mania (p. 547)	social phobia (p. 537)

? **What Do You Think?**

HOW SERIOUSLY SHOULD WE TAKE PEOPLE'S VIOLENT FANTASIES? (PAGE 449)

In some cases, critical thinking requires the balancing of competing demands. In the case of Charles Whitman, the psychiatrist who interviewed him needed to balance the competing demands of traditional patient confidentiality and public safety. In hindsight, we might conclude that the therapist should have sacrificed confidentiality and warned university security personnel. But the issue is clouded by the fact that, in general, mental health professionals have a very poor record of success in predicting violent behavior (Monahan, 1992).

In 1966 when the Whitman incident occurred, it was solely up to the therapist to decide whether a breach of confidentiality was warranted. Following the Whitman tragedy, a formal inquiry was held, and although many professionals questioned his judgment in not alerting authorities, the psychiatrist who saw Whitman was exonerated of professional misconduct. But three years later, at the University of California, a college student murdered his estranged girlfriend after telling his therapist he intended to do so. Although the therapist notified campus police, who released the assailant after questioning him, the victim's family sued the university and the therapist, claiming that he should also have warned the victim and her family. The family won the case. Thereafter, most jurisdictions passed laws requiring mental health professionals to violate confidentiality and report threats of violence in order to protect potential victims. The "duty to protect" is granted precedence over the seal of confidentiality. Had today's standards existed in 1966, the tragedy in Texas might have been averted. Still, legal man-

dates call for the therapist to exercise professional judgment as to whether a given client and a given set of circumstances constitute a clear and present danger. Therapists are hesitant to break the seal of confidentiality unless they are confident in their judgment of imminent danger to the community. In Whitman's case, a professional who didn't know about Whitman's earlier aggressive acts may well have concluded that his stated fantasies were not a compelling danger signal. Thus it is part of a psychologist's professional responsibility to have the training and expertise to make such judgments.

IS SELF-ACTUALIZATION A USEFUL SCIENTIFIC CONSTRUCT? (PAGE 453)

Self-actualization is a centerpiece of some humanistic theories, but it is troublesome from a scientific perspective. Some critics believe that it is impossible to define an individual's actualizing tendency except in terms of the behavior that it supposedly produces. This would be an example of circular reasoning: Why did the person achieve such success? Because of self-actualization. How do we know self-actualization was at work? Because the person achieved great success.

Unless a construct can be operationally defined in a manner independent of the phenomena it is supposed to cause, it is not scientifically useful. A construct must also be measurable. While it is true that concepts related to the self-actualization motive (such as people's beliefs that they are fulfilling their potential) could potentially be measured, most psychologists suggest that rather than being a scientific construct, self-actualization is better considered a philosophical concept.

- **Multimedia Integration with the Text and Instructional Materials:** The Instructor's Manual, In-Psych CD-ROM, Test Banks, and other supplements are built to support this book; in turn, the book supports them with the Focus Questions and multimedia icons that appear in its margins. The Focus Questions are streamlined from the Learning Objectives on which the Instructor's Manual is built, making it easy for instructors to use them in whatever way best supports their course and to access Test Bank questions covering whichever Focus Questions they wish to emphasize. In addition, each multimedia segment—including McGraw-Hill's exclusive Discovery Channel™ video clips, additional videos, animation, and interactivities—has been chosen to support one or more Learning Objectives, is accompanied by its own pedagogy, and has Test Bank items and Instructor's Manual commentary associated with it. Further details about these multimedia materials appear below under "Supplements."

FIGURE 13.3
Stressful life events can vary from catastrophic ones, such as 2005's Hurricane Katrina, to microstressors, or daily hassles. Both classes of stressor take their toll on physical and psychological well-being.

- **New Art:** Approximately 25 percent of the photographs are new to this edition, and the line art program has been revised for improved conceptual clarity and visual appeal.

- **Updated coverage:** Our third edition is rich in discussions of research and new references—hundreds of the book's citations are from the years 2000 and beyond, and many are from the years 2004 to 2006.

NEW TO THIS EDITION: *LANGUAGE AND THINKING,* AND *INTELLIGENCE,* ARE NOW COVERED IN SEPARATE CHAPTERS

Teaching the introductory course often necessitates difficult decisions about content coverage. In our first two editions, we covered the topics of language, thinking, and intelligence in a single chapter. This approach resonated with many adopters who, due to time pressures or personal preferences, skipped all of these topics in their course or wanted only brief coverage of one or more of these topics. A far greater number of instructors, however, expressed a preference for splitting these topics into two chapters so that they could be covered in more depth and breadth. After taking a long hard look at the pros and cons, we have decided to cover language and thinking in one chapter and intelligence in its own chapter. Together, the chapters now provide students with a more complete picture of the intriguing issues that surround the psychological study of language, thinking, and intelligence. Instructors who do not cover all three topics will find it easy to focus their students' reading, as Chapter 8 is organized into two main sections, one on language and the other on thinking. The section below details some of the major content changes in these and all of the other chapters.

CONTENT CHANGES IN INDIVIDUAL CHAPTERS

CHAPTER 1: THE SCIENCE OF PSYCHOLOGY

- A modified section now called *Psychology's Broad Scope: A Levels-of-Analysis Framework* briefly introduces the LOA framework before rather than after the discussion of psychology's major historical perspectives. The framework is illustrated with two short examples—a common event (eating) and a rare event (voodoo death). As in past editions, later in the chapter a more detailed example of depression integrates the LOA framework with the major perspectives.

- A new subsection on *Mind-Body and Nature-Nurture Interactions* condenses the discussion of these issues from earlier editions, links them to the LOA framework, and highlights the nature-nurture theme before rather than after discussing the historical perspectives.

- Object relations theory is now explicitly mentioned in the section on *Modern Psychodynamic Theory* and a brief subsection on *Cognitive Behaviorism* is now called out within the broader discussion of the behavioral perspective.

- The section on *Origins of the Cognitive Perspective* has been streamlined, and the field of cognitive psychology is now mentioned and defined explicitly in the section on *The Modern Cognitive Perspective*.

- The last major section of the chapter, which describes the science and profession of contemporary psychology, has been reorganized and expanded. Now titled *Psychology Today,* existing material on subfields, careers, and personal application has been organized into two new subsections—*A Global Science and Profession* and *Psychology and Your Life*—and a new section on *Psychology and Public Policy* has been added.

CHAPTER 2: STUDYING BEHAVIOR SCIENTIFICALLY

- The discussion of *Gathering Evidence: Steps in the Scientific Process* now addresses how scientists communicate their research findings to the larger scientific community.

- The section on *Ethical Principles in Research* has been placed earlier in the chapter and immediately follows the opening discussion of general scientific principles. Thus specific research methods are now discussed after broad scientific and ethical principles have been presented. The modular nature of these sections, however, easily enables instructors to alter the sequence of topics if they wish.

- Limitations of survey research are discussed more fully.

- A simple, engaging section on *Analyzing and Interpreting Data* has been added. It emphasizes being a critical consumer of statistics, describes basic descriptive and inferential statistical concepts, and includes a brief discussion of meta-analysis.

CHAPTER 3: BIOLOGICAL FOUNDATIONS OF BEHAVIOR: EVOLUTION, GENES, AND BRAIN

- The treatment of natural selection and brain evolution, including the critical-thinking element on limits of evolutionary explanations, has been updated.

- The section on behavior genetics has been updated and includes new findings summarized by Bouchard (2004) and Plomin & Spinath (2004).

- A new section on heritability coefficients and their interpretation has been added.

- A preview of how nerve impulses occur now introduces the section on the electrical activity of neurons to frame the process.

- The explanation of resting, action, and graded potentials is now clearer and less detailed.

- A new *What Do You Think?* feature invites students to critically think about pop psychology depictions of Sperry's split brain work and its educational implications.

- The section on neurogenesis in the human brain and neural stem cell research has been updated.

CHAPTER 4: SENSATION AND PERCEPTION

- A new section reviews recent work on inattentional blindness.

- New material on the role of early experience on color perception has been added.

CHAPTER 5: STATES OF CONSCIOUSNESS

- A new chapter-opening vignette on visual agnosia replaces the vignette on Hofmann's discovery of LSD and is better integrated into subsequent sections of the chapter.

- Coverage of normal waking consciousness has been significantly expanded. New sections include:
  - *Unconscious Perception and Influence*, which covers visual agnosia and blindsight, explains the concept of

priming, and incorporates existing material on the emotional unconscious.

- *Why Do We Have Consciousness?* describes adaptive functions of consciousness.
- *The Neural Basis of Consciousness* presents new material on the neuroscience of consciousness and discusses the view of consciousness as a global workspace.
- The rigorous treatment of sleep, dreaming, drugs, and hypnosis has been retained, but coverage has been streamlined slightly.
- A discussion of cross-cultural differences in normal sleep patterns has been added.

CHAPTER 6: LEARNING AND ADAPTATION: THE ROLE OF EXPERIENCE

- A new table summarizes key differences between classical and operant conditioning.
- A new figure provides 10 common examples of negative reinforcement.
- Coverage of biological constraints and cognitive factors in conditioning (*Crossroads of Conditioning*) now immediately follows the sections on classical and operant conditioning, rather than coming in the last section of the chapter.
- Bandura's *social cognitive theory* (formerly known as *social learning theory*) is now discussed explicitly in the section on observational learning.
- A new section on *Applications of Observational Learning* includes a new *Research Close-Up* illustrating how social cognitive theory is being used to tackle global societal problems, such as the AIDS crisis.
- The discussion of *The Adaptive Brain* has been expanded and now ends the chapter.

CHAPTER 7: MEMORY

- The topics of *Encoding: Entering Information*, *Storage: Retaining Information*, and *Retrieval: Accessing Information* have been moved from secondary headings into their own primary headings, improving the overall structure of the chapter and making it easier to identify subtopics within these keys sections.
- The discussion of working memory has been expanded to include Baddeley's updated four-component model, with more examples and a figure added to help students understand the various components.
- A new subsection on *Arousal, Emotion, and Memory* describes research on how arousal boosts memory and how emotionality for autobiographical memory events typically fades over time.
- The feature *Beneath the Surface: Do We Really Remember It Like It Was Yesterday?* provides expanded coverage of flashbulb memory research on the terrorist attacks of 9/11.

- The explanation of neural network models has been clarified and expanded.
- The topic of *Amnesia* has been divided into subsections to improve organization, with substantially expanded coverage of dementia and Alzheimer's disease.
- Coverage of brain regions underlying working memory has been expanded, and to enhance organization, new subheads have been added throughout the section on *Memory and the Brain*.

CHAPTER 8: LANGUAGE AND THINKING

- Coverage of language, thinking, and intelligence is now split into two chapters. In this chapter the discussion of language and thinking is expanded, updated, and organized into separate modules. Instructors who wish to assign only one of these topics will find it easy to do so.
- Discussion of the adaptive functions, basic properties, and structure of language has been reorganized.
- A new section on *Understanding and Producing Language* discusses the role of bottom-up and top-down processes, as well as pragmatics. A new *What Do You Think?* critical-thinking feature on *The Sleeping Policeman* highlights the importance of pragmatics.
- The section on *Can Animals Acquire Human Language?* and its embedded critical-thinking component have been expanded.
- The section on *Bilingualism* has been reorganized and expanded. It includes updated coverage of whether a second language is represented in the same parts of the brain as the native language and whether learning a second language might influence other cognitive abilities.
- A new *Beneath the Surface* feature critically examines the assumption that there is a developmental critical period for learning a second language.
- Before addressing the topics of *Reasoning* and *Problem Solving and Decision Making*, a new section on *Thought, Brain, and Mind* describes an intriguing brain-computer interface study to introduce the module on *Thinking*.
- A new section on *Knowledge, Expertise, and Wisdom* expands previous coverage of expertise and adds coverage of knowledge and wisdom.
- A new section on *Mental Imagery* examines whether mental images are more closely tied to visual perception or to language.
- A section on *Metacognition* is added and includes a new *Research Close-Up* titled "Why Did I Get That Wrong?" *Improving College Students' Awareness of Whether They Understand Text Material*.
- A new *Levels of Analysis* graphic summarizes the section on *Thinking* and complements the existing *Levels of Analysis* graphic on *Language*.

CHAPTER 9: INTELLIGENCE

- The *Intelligence in Historical Perspective* section has been expanded and describes Army Alpha/Beta and other group intelligence tests and the growth of the intelligence-testing industry.

- A simplified description of factor analysis is presented to help students understand the rationale underlying factor analytic attempts to identify general and specific mental skills.

- Carroll's three-stratum model is presented as an attempt to define the structure of intellect in terms of general and specific abilities, using factor analysis to reanalyze data from many data sets.

- Treatment of multiple intelligences and emotional intelligence has been expanded.

- Treatment of intelligence testing, including theory-based tests and dynamic testing procedures, has been expanded.

- The latest research on the relations of intelligence to academic and job performance, income, well-being, and longevity is presented.

- New material on the Flynn effect (population increases in IQ over time) and its implications for intelligence testing is included.

- A new section on assessing intelligence in non-Western cultures with culture-specific tests and dynamic testing has been added.

- Coverage of genetic factors, shared environment, unique environment, and their contributions to IQ in childhood and adulthood has been expanded and updated.

- A new *Applying Psychological Science* feature focuses on early-childhood interventions and their impact on intellectual growth.

- A new *Beneath the Surface* feature presents recent evidence that, relative to genetic factors, environmental factors become more important determinants of IQ as we age.

- Updated treatment of ethnic and sex differences in cognitive skills illustrates the interaction of biological and environmental factors.

- A new *What Do You Think?* feature invites students to critically evaluate the proposition that gifted children tend to be maladjusted.

- Treatment of mental retardation, its causes, and its educational and adaptive implications has been updated.

CHAPTER 10: MOTIVATION AND EMOTION

- A new section on the behavioral activation and behavioral inhibition systems has been added.

- The section on humanistic approaches to motivation has been expanded and features Deci and Ryan's self-determination theory.

- A new section on *Achievement Goal Theory* covers ego and mastery goal orientations and motivational climates.

- Familial and cultural factors that influence the development of achievement-related motives are summarized.

- Updated research on situational, cognitive, physiological, and behavioral components of emotional responses has been added.

- Coverage of Ambady's research on cultural "dialects" in emotional display rules has been added.

- Coverage of the somatic and cognitive appraisal models of emotion has been included.

CHAPTER 11: DEVELOPMENT OVER THE LIFE SPAN

- Coverage of *Infancy and Childhood* has been reduced slightly, and the sections on *Adolescence* and *Adulthood* have been expanded slightly to bring them into better balance. Respectively, they represent 49 percent and 41 percent of the chapter. Developmental research designs and prenatal development are also discussed.

- Brain development receives more explicit coverage in new subsections on *The Young Brain, The Adolescent Brain,* and *The Adult Brain.*

- The information-processing approach to cognitive development receives greater attention in the sections on childhood, adolescence, and adulthood.

- A new section on *Understanding the Physical World* focuses on violation-of-expectancy experiments as a method for examining very young infants' conceptual understanding of physical objects and "numbers." This section complements existing theory of mind coverage.

- A new section on *The Transition to Adulthood* addresses a question likely to be of special interest to most college students: "How do you know when you're an adult?"

- A new subsection on *Cognitive Impairment in Old Age,* which expands coverage of senile dementia, is added to the discussion of adult cognitive development.

CHAPTER 12: PERSONALITY

- The chapter has been reorganized to conform with most instructors' preferred sequence. Psychodynamic and phenomenological-humanistic theories now precede trait, biological, and social cognitive perspectives.

- Recent research on relations of adult attachment styles to emotional distress has been added.

- A new section on Kelly's theory of personal constructs, including a description of the Rep test, has been added.

- A new *Research Close-Up* features a recent study on how, despite general tendencies toward self-enhancement, low-self-esteem people maintain their negative self-evaluations.

- An expanded section on evolutionary personality theory discusses strategic pluralism as a mechanism for the selection of seemingly opposite traits within different environments.
- A new section on temperament as a biological foundation for some personality traits has been included.

CHAPTER 13: ADJUSTING TO LIFE: STRESS, COPING, AND HEALTH

- New research addressing the long-term effects of unemployment on subjective well-being even after reemployment is described.
- New data on the importance of flexibility in emotional expression and inhibition have been included.
- A new *Research Close-Up* features a recent meta-analytic study of stressor effects on natural and specific immune functions.
- New studies on the beneficial effects of giving social support and general sociability on health and longevity have been included.
- New research on "goodness of fit" between coping strategies and situational controllability is discussed.
- In-depth treatment of a recent study on Pennebaker's trauma disclosure approach has been added.
- New findings on the role of spinal glial cells and cytokines in pain add to the discussion of spinal gate mechanisms.
- Watkins/Maier's work on how stress hormones increase sensory neurons' pain excitability has been included.
- Statistics on epidemiological and behavioral health factors and on behavioral interventions for health-enhancing and health-impairing behaviors have been updated.

CHAPTER 14: PSYCHOLOGICAL DISORDERS

- New sections on borderline personality disorder and autistic disorder have been added.
- A new *Research Close-Up* describes the classic Schachter-Latané study of emotional arousal and avoidance learning in psychopaths.
- Content on anxiety disorders, mood disorders, schizophrenia, and antisocial personality disorder has been updated.
- All other disorders have been thoroughly updated.

CHAPTER 15: TREATMENT OF PSYCHOLOGICAL DISORDERS

- New sections on behavioral activation treatment for depression and dialectical behavior therapy for borderline personality disorder have been added.

- A new section discusses the controversial topic of empirically supported treatments.
- A new *Beneath the Surface* feature discusses increasing concerns about the effectiveness and side effects of antidepressant medications.
- Coverage of cultural and gender issues in therapy has been expanded and updated.
- The treatment of community-based prevention programs has been expanded.

CHAPTER 16: SOCIAL THINKING AND BEHAVIOR

- The discussion of interpersonal attraction includes a new subsection on judging facial beauty, titled *Facial Attractiveness: Is "Average" Beautiful?*
- In discussing sex differences in attraction and short-term mating strategies, the fact that the sexual strategies model is not universally accepted even among evolutionary psychologists is pointed out more explicitly.
- A new subsection on *Ostracism: Rejection Hurts* covers recent studies on the psychological consequences of ostracism and findings regarding the presence of social rejection as a risk factor in school shootings.
- The section on *Explicit and Implicit Prejudice* now notes the physiological approach to measuring implicit prejudice and describes how reaction-time measures have detected implicit racial biases missed by explicit measures of prejudice.
- Coverage of *Reducing Prejudice* is expanded and includes recent research on decreasing college students' stereotype threat and police officers' race-based "shooting bias."
- The *Beneath the Surface* feature on *Do Violent Video Games Promote Aggression?* replaces previous material on the history of warfare with new material that stimulates students' critical thinking with regard to drawing causal conclusions from correlational data.
- The *What Do You Think?* discussion on *Does Pure Altruism Really Exist?* incorporates recent brain-imaging findings regarding the degree of correspondence between feeling our own pain and empathizing with someone else's pain. Students are asked to think about this finding in terms of the "negative state relief" versus "empathy-altruism" models of helping.

SUPPLEMENTS

New to our third-edition supplements package is an innovative set of media-rich PowerPoint slides prepared by Mike Atkinson of the University of Western Ontario, who is known for his highly successful approach to teaching a 1,200-student lecture course. A more detailed description of the PowerPoint slides is given below.

Another new feature that will excite students is Sylvius, Special Edition for McGraw-Hill Psychology. This interactive brain anatomy dictionary is found on the student side of the Online Learning Center at http://www.mhhe.com/passer3.

As with our second edition, a key feature of our third-edition supplements package is the comprehensive chapter-by-chapter list of Learning Objectives linked to the Focus Questions in the margins of the textbook. The Learning Objectives form the cornerstone of not only the Instructor's Manual, but also the Test Banks, Online Learning Center, and student Study Guide. Instructors may use the Learning Objectives as a guide to structuring the content of their courses and to preparing lectures, class activities, quizzes and exams. Students may use them to focus on key concepts before, during, and after reading the chapter, as well as to review and test their knowledge.

FOR THE INSTRUCTOR

Instructor's Manual

Written by Kevin Larkin of West Virginia University, this invaluable 500-page guide (ISBN 0-07-321415-9) contains a wealth of material that you can tailor to your teaching preferences and goals. For new instructors, it offers a master blueprint for organizing and structuring the introductory psychology course. Learning Objectives for each section of a chapter expand on the Focus Questions found in the textbook's margins and serve as the foundation on which all instructor resources are built. These resources include: pre-class student assignments, material for lecture enhancement, in-class demonstrations and activities, suggestions for class discussions, a list of images available either as overhead transparencies or in digital formats, recommended guest presentations, an extensive array of handouts, and a complete list of the technology resources relevant to that portion of the text. Recommended strategies for evaluating student progress on mastery of the Learning Objectives cap off each section of a chapter. The Instructor's Manual incorporates the **In-Class Activities Manual for Instructors of Introductory Psychology,** written by the Illinois State University team of Patricia Jarvis, Cynthia Nordstrom, and Karen Williams.

New to the third-edition Instructor's Manual are contributions from NiCole Buchanan of Michigan State University (**Focus on Diversity**) and Jay Brophy-Ellison of the University of Central Florida (**Promoting Student Engagement**). These added features will make the Instructor's Manual even more versatile and useful for instructors in a wide variety of schools and situations.

Three Test Banks Featuring over 7,200 Items

McGraw-Hill's EZ Test is a flexible and easy-to-use electronic testing program. The program allows instructors to create tests from book-specific items. It accommodates a wide range of question types, and instructors may add their own questions. Multiple versions of the test can be created, and any test can be exported for use with course management systems such as WebCT, BlackBoard, or PageOut. EZ Test Online is a new service that gives you a place to easily administer your EZ Test–created

exams and quizzes online. The program is available for Windows and Macintosh environments.

Consonant with the integrative nature of our supplements package, all Test Bank questions are written to support the Learning Objectives and can be customized for instructor control and convenience.

- **Test Bank 1,** by Adriel Boals of Duke University, includes not only fact- and application-based questions, but also more challenging conceptual items (over 25%). This comprehensive resource offers more than 3,500 items in all, including multiple-choice, true-false, fill-in, matching, and essay questions.

- **Test Bank 2,** by Walter Cegelka of St. Thomas University and Anita Rosenfield of Yavapai College, comprises more than 2,500 multiple-choice items, of which more than a third are conceptual in nature.

- **Test Bank 3,** by Carolyn Kaufman of Columbus State Community College, offers 40 conceptual questions per chapter (640 in all). This unique resource is especially appealing to instructors who wish to challenge their students to think more conceptually.

McGraw-Hill Media Resources for Teaching Psychology

McGraw-Hill and The Discovery Channel^{TM} have formed an exclusive partnership to bring you video segments and interactivities for use in your psychology course. Forty-eight video segments and 17 interactivities were chosen especially to support the Learning Objectives and are fully described in the Instructor's Manual. The majority of the video segments are timed at 5 minutes or less; the longest runs 12 minutes. They are available either as a DVD and CD-ROM set (ISBN 0-07-293885-4) or as a set of two VHS videocassettes and CD-ROM (ISBN 0-07-293884-6).

Visual Asset Database ("VAD")

Jasna Jovanovic, University of Illinois—Urbana-Champaign

McGraw-Hill's password-protected Visual Asset Database offers hundreds of multimedia resources for use in classroom presentations, including original video clips, audio clips, photographs, and illustrations—all designed to bring to life concepts in developmental psychology. In addition to providing ready-made multimedia presentations for every stage of the lifespan, the VAD search engine and unique "My Modules" program allows instructors to select from the database's resources to create customized presentations, or "modules." Instructors can save these customized presentations in specially marked "module" folders on the McGraw-Hill site, and then run presentations directly from VAD to the Internet-equipped classroom. Contact your McGraw-Hill representative for a password to this valuable resource.

Online Learning Center for Instructors

The instructor side of the Passer & Smith *Psychology* 3rd edition Web site at http://www.mhhe.com/passer3 contains the

Instructor's Manual and other valuable material to help you design your course. Ask your local McGraw-Hill representative for your password.

- **PowerWeb** This unique online reader provides readings; *New York Times* news feeds; weekly updates; curriculum-based materials; refereed Web links; tools for research, study, and assessment; and interactive exercises. You will be excited by this powerful tool for helping keep your lectures up-to-date and timely.

- **Annual Editions: Psychology 06/07** By Karen Duffy of SUNY–Geneseo, this annually updated reader is a compilation of carefully selected articles from magazines, newspapers, and journals. This title is supported by Dushkin Online, a student Web site that provides study support and tools and links to related sites. An Instructor's Manual and Using Annual Editions in the Classroom are available as support materials for instructors.

- **Sources: Notable Selections in Psychology, 3e** Edited by Terry Pettijohn of Ohio State University, this book includes over 40 book excerpts, classic articles, and research studies that have shaped the study of psychology and our contemporary understanding of it.

- **Taking Sides: Clashing Views on Controversial Psychological Issues, 14e** By Brent Slife of Brigham Young University, this debate-style reader is designed to introduce students to controversial viewpoints on the field's most crucial issues. Each issue is carefully framed for the student, and the pro and con essays represent the arguments of leading scholars and commentators in their fields.

- **Course Management Systems:**
  - **WebCT** and **Blackboard** Popular **WebCT** and **Blackboard** course cartridges are available for FREE upon adoption of a McGraw-Hill textbook. Contact your McGraw-Hill sales representative for details.
  - **PageOut** Build your own course Web site in less than an hour. You don't have to be a computer whiz to create a Web site, especially with an exclusive McGraw-Hill product called PageOut. Best of all, it's FREE! Visit us at www.pageout.net to find out more.
  - **Knowledge Gateway** McGraw-Hill service is second to none. We offer help at a special Web site called Knowledge Gateway. For more information, call 1-888-851-2372. For larger adoptions, if hands-on training is necessary, we have a team of experts ready to train you on campus. This FREE service is available to support PageOut, WebCT, and BlackBoard users.
  - **Image Gallery** These files include all of the figures, tables, and photos from this textbook (more than 150 images in all) for which McGraw-Hill holds copyright.

- **Classroom Performance System (CPS) by eInstruction** This revolutionary system brings ultimate interactivity to the lecture hall or classroom. It is a wireless electronic response system that gives the instructor and students immediate feedback from the entire class. CPS is a superb way to give interactive quizzes, maximize student participation in class discussions, and take attendance.

Instructor's Resource CD-ROM

This CD-ROM (ISBN 0-07-321416-7) conveniently contains the Instructor's Manual, Test Banks and EZ Test system. Here you will also find the new **PowerPoint presentations** for Passer & Smith's third edition. Created by Mike Atkinson of the University of Western Ontario, these innovative presentations include video clips, photographs, and other multimedia elements to enliven the classroom experience, especially in large lecture courses. Built around a theme for each chapter, the PowerPoints provide a turnkey resource for the instructor wishing to energize and engage students at a deep level.

Film Clips from Films for the Humanities and Social Sciences Based on adoption size, you may qualify for FREE videos from this resource. View their more than 700 psychology-related videos at http://www.films.com.

As a full service publisher of quality educational products, McGraw-Hill does much more than just sell textbooks to your students. We create and publish an extensive array of print, video, and digital supplements to support instruction on your campus. Orders of new (versus used) textbooks help us defray the cost of developing such supplements, which is substantial. We have a broad range of other supplements in psychology that you may wish to tap for your introductory psychology course. Ask your local McGraw-Hill representative about the availability of these and other supplements that may help you with your course design.

FOR THE STUDENT

In-Psych Student CD-ROM

This important study tool, written by Kristin Lazarova of Northeast State Community College, is packaged FREE with every new copy of the textbook. Each CD-ROM icon in the margin of the textbook guides students to the corresponding multimedia item on the CD-ROM. Each multimedia segment includes an introductory overview with pre-test and post-test questions. In-Psych also includes Web resources, chapter quizzes, a student research guide, and an interactive timeline that puts events, key figures, and research in psychology in historical perspective. Teachers may choose to test students on any of these items.

 Find out more about infant attachment by watching the "Attachment Theory" video in Chapter 11 of your CD.

Study Guide

The Study Guide (ISBN 0-07-321414-0), written by Dianne Leader of Georgia Technical University, is built on the same list of chapter-by-chapter Learning Objectives that forms the cornerstone of many of the instructor supplements, encouraging students to focus on the same key concepts that they are learning from the textbook and in class lectures and activities. Critical thinking is promoted by the essay questions at the end of each chapter, which challenge students to apply concepts from the chapter to issues of ethics, social policy, and their own personal lives; and by the *Analyze This* feature, in which students examine an assertion based on information in the text by using a series of critical-thinking questions.

Online Learning Center for Students

Written by Jay Brophy-Ellison of the University of Central Florda, the Passer & Smith, *Psychology* third edition Online Learning Center at www.mhhe.com/passer3 gives students access to the Learning Objectives that form the cornerstone of other supplements such as the Test Banks and Instructor's Manual. In addition, this useful study tool offers chapter outlines, practice quizzes, key term flashcards, interactive exercises, Web Links to relevant psychology sites, and more.

New to this edition of the Passer and Smith Online Learning Center is Sylvius, Special Edition for McGraw-Hill Psychology. This unique visual quick reference guide to human nervous system structure is based on the line of Sylvius neuroanatomical reference tools (www.sylvius.com) widely used by medical schools and neuroscience training programs. For the major nervous system structures and terms, Sylvius allows the user to quickly view high-resolution images, read brief descriptions of location and function, hear an audio pronunciation, take notes directly in the interface, and take a quiz on the material. Sylvius presents the essentials of human brain structure in an intuitive and visually compelling format, giving students a valuable tool to assist in the mastery of the biological foundations of human behavior. This state-of-the-art interactive brain anatomy dictionary is found on the student side of the Online Learning Center in the Coursewide Content menu.

PowerWeb

A PowerWeb passcard is included FREE with each new copy of the book. Students should be sure to save it so that they can benefit from this unique online reader. Here they will find readings; *New York Times* news feeds; weekly updates; curriculum-based materials; refereed Web links; tools for research, study, and assessment; and interactive exercises.

ACKNOWLEDGMENTS

A project having the scope of an introductory psychology text is truly a team enterprise, and we have been the fortunate recipients of a great team effort. We wish to thank and acknowledge the contributions of the many people who made this book possible, beginning with Steve Rutter and Beth Mejia, McGraw-Hill Higher Education's publishers for Psychology. We are indebted to Steve and Beth for their strong faith in this project and their unwavering support for putting together the best introductory

psychology textbook package in the market. We are also grateful to our editor, John Wannemacher, for his invaluable guidance throughout the past year and a half. We have been blessed with superlative developmental editors. Elsa Peterson helped shape the textbook in many important ways and coordinated numerous aspects of this project. Marion Castellucci provided great assistance during the editing of the drafts, and Sylvia Shepherd provided extraordinarily valuable input regarding organizational and topical development. Similarly, our copy editor, Andrea McCarrick, was splendid, and her input went well beyond the normal call of duty.

On the production end, thanks go to our project manager, Diane Folliard, for coordinating the endless production details; to Laurie Entringer, our design manager, for creating the fabulous cover and attractive layout of the book; and to Emma Ghiselli, our art editor. David Tietz, our photo researcher, worked diligently to acquire many of the excellent and unique photos in this edition. We also thank Melissa Caughlin, our marketing manager, who has worked tirelessly to create an imaginative marketing program.

In today's competitive market, outstanding supplements are a critical element in the success of any textbook, but our supplement authors have gone beyond excellence in implementing the total integration of the supplements with the text. We are in great debt to Kevin Larkin (West Virginia University) for developing an absolutely first-class Instructor's Manual that not only includes a wealth of useful material for novice and experienced instructors alike, but also coordinates outstanding audio/visual and electronic resources with the content of the textbook. Our third-edition Instructor's Manual is further enriched by Focus on Diversity materials by NiCole Buchanan (Michigan State University) and Engage Your Students activities by Jay Brophy-Ellison (University of Central Florida). Mike Atkinson (University of Western Ontario) developed a highly innovative set of media-rich PowerPoint slides that instructors can use to spark their lectures. For students, Kristin Lazarova (Northeast State Community College) prepared the invaluable In-Psych CD-ROM, Jay Brophy-Ellison (University of Central Florida) created the exciting Online Learning Center, and Dianne Leader (Georgia Technical University) did a stellar job of revising the Student Study Guide for this edition. Finally, Adriel Boals (Duke University), Walter Cegelka (St. Thomas University), and Carolyn Kaufman (Columbus State Community College) did an excellent job revising the three Test Banks that are second to none in quality and breadth.

We also owe special thanks to the distinguished corps of colleagues who provided review feedback—on both the textbook and its supplements—as we prepared *Psychology: The Science of Mind and Behavior,* third edition. Many of the improvements in the book are the outgrowth of their comments about what they want in an introductory psychology textbook for their courses. In this regard, we sincerely appreciate the time and effort contributed by the following instructors:

Bill Adler, *Collin County Community College–Plano*

Ronald Baenninger, *Temple University*

David R. Barkmeier, *Northeastern University*

Robert S. Baron, *University of Iowa–Iowa City*

Pam Birrell, *University of Oregon*

Adriel Boals, *Duke University*

Edward Brady, *Southwestern Illinois College*

Angela Bragg, *Mt. Hood Community College*

Cody Brooks, *Denison University*

Josh Burk, *College of William and Mary*

Walter Cegelka, *St. Thomas University*

Michael Clump, *Marymount University*

Perry L. Collins, *Wayland Baptist University*

Laura Da Costa, *University of Illinois–Springfield*

Joan Doolittle, *Anne Arundel Community College*

Tracy Dunne, *Boston University*

Amanda Emo, *University of Cincinnati*

Phil Finney, *Southeast Missouri State University*

Perry Fuchs, *University of Texas–Arlington*

Glenn Geher, *State University of New York, Albany University*

Tresmaine Grimes, *Iona College*

Michelle Haney, *Berry College*

Dwight Hennessy, *Buffalo State College*

Jennifer Hodges, *Louisiana Tech University*

Steven W. Horowitz, *Central Connecticut State University*

Charles Huffman, *James Madison University*

Timothy B. Jay, *Massachusetts College of Liberal Arts*

Rosalie Kern, *Michigan Technological University*

Mark Krause, *University of Portland*

Cynthia D. Kreutzer, *Georgia Perimeter College–Lawrenceville*

Holly Krueger, *University of Oregon*

Gert Kruger, *University of Johannesburg*

Kristin Lazarova, *Northeast State Technical Community College*

Dianne Leader, *Georgia Technical University*

Christopher W. LeGrow, *Marshall University*

Ting Lei, *Borough of Manhattan Community College*

Paul Lipton, *Boston University*

Mary Livingston, *Louisiana Technical University*

Mark Ludorf, *Stephen F. Austin State University*

Derek Mace, *Penn State University–Erie*

Kim MacLin, *University of Northern Iowa*

Stephen Madigan, *University of Southern California*

Brian Malley, *University of Michigan*

Gregory Manley, *University of Texas–San Antonio*

David McDonald, *University of Missouri at Columbia*

Mary Meiners, *San Diego Miramar College*

David B. Mitchell, *Loyola University–Chicago*

Nancy Olson, *Mt. Hood Community College*

Phil Pegg, *Western Kentucky University*

Edison Perdomo, *Central State University*

Brady Phelps, *South Dakota State University*

Richard Pisacreta, *Ferris State University*

Deborah Podwika, *Kankakee Community College*

Daren S. Protolipac, *St. Cloud State University*

Lauretta Reeves, *University of Texas–Austin*

Melani Russell, *Louisiana Tech University*

Catherine Sanderson, *Amherst College*

Jennifer Stevens, *College of William and Mary*

Carla Strassle, *York College*

Jim Stringham, *University of Georgia–Athens*

Cheryl Terrance, *University of North Dakota*

Robert Tigner, *Truman State University*

Meral Topcu-LaCroix, *Ferris State University*

Lisa Valentino, *Seminole Community College*

Kristin Vermillion, *Rose State College*

Thomas J. Weatherly, *Georgia Perimeter College–Clarkston*

Mark Wessinger, *University of Nevada at Reno*

Leonard J. Williams, *Rowan University*

Fred W. Whitford, *Montana State University–Bozeman*

John W. Wright, *Washington State University*

Karen Yanowitz, *Arkansas State University*

We also wish to thank the distinguished colleagues who provided review assistance for our first and second editions:

Mark D. Alicke, *Ohio University*

Susan Baillet, *University of Portland*

Jeffrey Baker, *Rochester Institute of Technology*

Ute J. Bayen, *University of North Carolina–Chapel Hill*

Mark Brechtel, *University of Florida*

David Burrows, *Beloit College*

James F. Calhoun, *University of Georgia*

Marc Carter, *Hofstra University*

P. Niels Christensen, *San Diego State University*

Betty Davenport, *Campbell University*

M. Catherine DeSoto, *University of Northern Iowa*

Rochelle Diogenes, *Montclair, NJ*

William Fabricius, *Arizona State University*

Barry Fritz, *Quinnipiac University*

Dean E. Frost, *Portland State University*

Ray Fuller, *Trinity College of Dublin*

Janet Gebelt, *University of Portland*

Andrew Getzfeld, *New Jersey City University*

Shepard B. Gorman, *Nassau Community College*

Gary J. Greguras, *Louisiana State University*

Carlos Grijalva, *University of California–Los Angeles*

Michelle Haney, *Berry College*

Jason W. Hart, *Indiana University of Pennsylvania*

Robert A. Johnston, *College of William and Mary*

Deana Julka, *University of Portland*

Robert Kaleta, *University of Wisconsin–Milwaukee*

Rick Kasschau, *University of Houston*

Gary King, *Rose State College*

Pat King, *Del Mar College*

Karen Kopera-Frye, *Buchtel College of Arts and Sciences*

F. Scott Kraly, *Colgate University*

Kevin Larkin, *West Virginia University*

Estevan R. Limon, *Hunter College, City University of New York*

Alan J. Lipman, *Georgetown University*

Laura Madson, *New Mexico State University*

Kathleen Malley-Morrison, *Boston University*

David McDonald, *University of Missouri*

Mary Meiners, *San Diego Miramar College*

Kevin Moore, *De Pauw University*

Joseph Morrissey, *State University of New York–Binghamton*

Donald J. Polzella, *University of Dayton*

Gary Poole, *Simon Fraser University*

J. T. Ptacek, *Bucknell University*

Jacqueline T. Ralston, *Columbia College*

Janice L. Rank, *Portland Community College*

Scott Ronis, *University of Missouri*

Richard Sandargas, *University of Tennessee*

Stephen Saunders, *Marquette University*

William G. Shadel, *University of Pittsburgh*

Rebecca Shiner, *Colgate University*

Jennifer Siciliani, *University of Missouri–St. Louis*

Alice H. Skeens, *University of Toledo*

Steven M. Smith, *Texas A&M University*

Sheldon Solomon, *Skidmore College*

Mary Hellen Spear, *Prince George's Community College*

Dawn L. Strongin, *California State University–Stanislaus*

David Thomas, *Oklahoma State University*

David M. Todd, *University of Massachusetts–Amherst*

Joseph Troisi, *Saint Anselm College*

David Uttal, *Northwestern University*

Kristin Vermillion, *Rose State College*

Lori Van Wallandael, *University of North Carolina–Charlotte*

Dennis Wanamaker, *Bellevue College*

Paul J. Watson, *University of Tennessee*

Clemens Weikert, *Lund University*

Alan S. W. Winton, *Massey University–Palmerston North*

Tricia Yurak, *Rowan University*

CHAPTER ONE

The Science of Psychology

Perhaps the most fascinating and mysterious universe of all is the one within us.

—CARL SAGAN

A young woman appeared in the emergency room of Baltimore City Hospital three days before her 23rd birthday, pleading for help. The story she told was a strange one indeed. She and two other girls had been delivered by the same midwife in Georgia's Okefenokee Swamp on a Friday the 13th. The midwife, a member of a voodoo cult, had placed a curse on all three babies. She proclaimed that the first would die before her 16th birthday, the second before her 21st birthday, and the third (the patient) before her 23rd birthday.

True to the midwife's prediction, the first died in an auto accident when she was 15 years old. The second was killed during a shooting in a nightclub where she was celebrating her 21st birthday. Now the third woman waited in fear for her own death.

The emergency-room psychiatrist admitted her for observation and reassured the terrified woman that no harm would come to her in the hospital. Still, the woman believed that she was doomed. The next morning, two days before her 23rd birthday, she was found dead in her hospital bed. Doctors were unable to determine a physical cause for her death (Seligman, 1975).

■ ■ ■ ■ ■

Waiting in line at the theater, Ray put his arms around Kira and playfully kissed her cheek. "Remember that party where we met last year?" he asked. "You caught my eye the moment you walked into the room." "Sure," Kira laughed, "but you were so shy. Your friends practically had to drag you over to talk to me! You're lucky I'm so outgoing."

Ray knew he was shy, especially around women, yet he wasn't sure why. He had been too nervous to enjoy the few dates he had gone on in high school. During his first semester at college he met a few women he really liked but was afraid to ask them out. He didn't make many male friends either, and by winter the loneliness was getting to him. He became mildly depressed, he couldn't sleep well, and his schoolwork suffered.

After a good visit with his family during spring break, Ray turned things around. He studied hard, did well on his tests, and made friends with some guys in the dorm. His mood improved, and toward the end of the semester he met Kira. Attracted to Ray and sensing both his shyness and his interest, Kira asked Ray out. Now dating Kira for a year and doing well in school, Ray is happy and self-confident. He and Kira have even talked about getting married after they graduate.

▶ Focus 1
What is psychology's focus? In science and daily life, what does critical thinking involve, and why is it important? (These focus questions will help you identify key concepts as you read, study, and review; they also tie in with the "Learning Objectives" in the Online Learning Center and other supplements.)

THE NATURE OF PSYCHOLOGY

Why are some individuals shy and others outgoing? What causes people, such as Kira and Ray, to become attracted to one another and fall in love? Can we predict which relationships will last? Why is it that we remember a first date from long ago yet forget information during a test that we studied for only hours before? Where in the brain are memories stored? Why did Ray become depressed? Was it his lack of a social life, or was something else going on? And in the case of the "cursed" woman, is it possible that a psychological factor—a culturally based belief in voodoo—could have affected her biological functioning and actually brought about her death?

Welcome to psychology, the discipline that studies all of these questions and countless more. We can define **psychology** as *the scientific study of behavior and the mind*. The term *behavior* refers to actions and responses that we can directly observe, whereas the term *mind* refers to internal states and

2

processes—such as thoughts and feelings—that cannot be seen directly and that must be inferred from observable, measurable responses. For example, we cannot see Ray's feeling of loneliness directly. Instead, we must infer how Ray feels based on his verbal statement that he is lonely.

Because behavior is so complex, its scientific study poses special challenges. As you become familiar with the kinds of evidence necessary to validate scientific conclusions, you will become a better-informed consumer of the many claims made in the name of psychology. For one thing, this course will teach you that many widely held beliefs about behavior are inaccurate. Can you distinguish the valid claims from the invalid ones in Table 1.1?

Perhaps even more important than the concepts you learn in this course will be the habits of thought that you acquire—habits that involve *critical thinking*. Critical thinking involves taking an active role in understanding the world around you, rather than merely receiving information. It's important to reflect on what that information means, how it fits in with your experiences, and its implications for your life and society. Critical thinking also means evaluating the validity of something presented to you as fact. For example, when someone tells you a new "fact," ask yourself the following questions:

What exactly are you asking me to believe?

How do you know? What is the evidence?

Are there other possible explanations?

What is the most reasonable conclusion?

We hope that after completing this course you will be more cautious about accepting psychological claims and less likely to form simplistic judgments about why people behave and think as they do. These critical-thinking skills will serve you well in many areas of your life.

In this book we hope to share with you our enthusiasm about psychology. As you will see, psychology relates to virtually every aspect of your life. Psychological research provides us with a greater understanding of ourselves and with powerful tools to improve our lives and promote human welfare.

PSYCHOLOGY AS A BASIC AND APPLIED SCIENCE

Science involves two types of research: **basic research,** *which reflects the quest for knowledge purely for its own sake,* and **applied research,** *which is designed to solve specific, practical problems.* For psychologists, most basic research examines how and

TABLE 1.1 Widely Held Beliefs about Behavior: Fact or Fiction?

***Directions:* Decide whether each statement is true or false.**

1. Most people with exceptionally high IQs are well adjusted in other areas of their life.
2. In romantic relationships, opposites usually attract.
3. Overall, married adults are happier than adults who aren't married.
4. In general, we only use about 10 percent of our brain.
5. A person who is innocent of a crime has nothing to fear from a lie detector test.
6. People who commit suicide usually have signaled to others their intention to do so.
7. If you feel that your initial answer on a multiple-choice test is wrong, leave it alone; students usually lose points by changing answers.
8. On some types of mental tasks, people perform better when they are 70 years old than when they are 20 years old.
9. Usually, it is safe to awaken someone who is sleepwalking.
10. A schizophrenic is a person who has two or more distinct personalities, hence the term *split personality.*

Answers: Items 1, 3, 6, 8, and 9 are supported by psychological research. The remaining items are false. (If you correctly answered 9 or 10 of these items, you've done significantly better than random guessing.)

why people behave, think, and feel the way they do. Basic research may be carried out in laboratories or real-world settings, with human participants or other species. Psychologists who study other species usually attempt to discover principles that ultimately will shed light on human behavior, but some study animal behavior for its own sake. In applied research, psychologists often use basic scientific knowledge to design, implement, and assess intervention programs. Consider the following example.

Robber's Cave and the Jigsaw Classroom

How does hostility and prejudice develop between groups, and what can be done to reduce it? In today's multicultural world, where religious and ethnic groups often clash, this question has great importance.

To provide an answer, psychologists conduct basic research on factors that increase and reduce intergroup hostility. In one experiment, researchers divided 11-year-old boys into two groups when the boys arrived at a summer camp in Robber's Cave, Oklahoma (Sherif et al., 1961). The groups, named the "Eagles" and "Rattlers," lived in separate cabins but did all other activities together. Initially, they got along well.

To test the hypothesis that competition would breed intergroup hostility, the researchers began

► **Focus 2**
How do basic and applied research differ? Explain how knowledge from basic research helps solve practical problems.

to pit the Eagles and Rattlers against one another in athletic and other contests. As predicted, hostility soon developed between the groups. Next the researchers examined whether conflict could be reduced by having the two groups share enjoyable activities, such as watching movies together. Surprisingly, these activities only bred more taunting and fighting. The researchers then created several small emergencies to test a final hypothesis—that placing hostile groups in situations requiring cooperation to attain important, common goals would reduce intergroup conflict. In one "emergency," a heavy truck bringing food to the hungry boys supposedly stalled, forcing the Eagles and Rattlers to pool their strength and tow it with a rope to get it started. This and other cooperative experiences gradually reduced hostility between the groups, and many new friendships developed.

The Robber's Cave study, which has since become a classic (that is, an older but widely known and influential study), represents basic research because its goal was to discover general principles of intergroup conflict, not to solve some preexisting problem. Prejudice between the Eagles and Rattlers did not exist from the outset; rather, the researchers created it. They showed that hostility could be bred by competition and reduced by making hostile groups dependent on one another to reach a common goal. But could this principle, derived from basic research, also be applied to real-life situations?

▶ **Focus 3**
Identify the major goals of psychology. Describe the levels-of-analysis framework.

Years later, during a stormy desegregation of public schools in Texas, psychologist Elliot Aronson and his coworkers (1978) developed and evaluated a classroom procedure called the "jigsaw program." This program, which is now widely used to foster cooperation among children, involves creating multiethnic groups of five or six children who are assigned to prepare for an upcoming test on, for example, the life of Abraham Lincoln. Within the groups, each child is given a piece of the total knowledge to be learned. One child has information about Lincoln's childhood, another about his political career, and so on. To pass the test, group members must fit their knowledge pieces together as if working on a jigsaw puzzle. Each child must teach the others his or her piece of knowledge. Like the children at Robber's Cave, students learn that to succeed they must work together (Figure 1.1).

The jigsaw technique and other *cooperative learning programs* have been evaluated in hundreds of classrooms, with encouraging results (Johnson, 2000). Children's liking for one another generally increases, prejudice decreases, and self-esteem and school achievement improve. Cooperative learning programs show how basic research, such as the Robber's Cave experiment, provide a foundation for designing intervention programs. We will see many other examples of how basic research provides knowledge that not only satisfies our desire to understand our world but also can be applied to solve practical problems.

THE GOALS OF PSYCHOLOGY

As a science, psychology has five central goals:

1. To *describe* how people and other species behave
2. To *understand* the causes of these behaviors
3. To *predict* how people and animals will behave under certain conditions
4. To *influence* behavior through the control of its causes
5. To *apply* psychological knowledge in ways that enhance human welfare

In the Robber's Cave study, the researchers carefully observed the boys' behavior under various conditions (description). They believed that competition would cause intergroup hostility and that cooperation could reduce it (tentative understanding). To test whether their understanding was correct, they predicted that competition would create hostility between the Eagles and Rattlers and that cooperation would reduce this conflict (prediction).

FIGURE 1.1

The jigsaw classroom, designed by psychologist Elliot Aronson, was inspired by basic research that showed how mutual dependence and cooperation among hostile groups can reduce intergroup hostility. Aronson's applied research had similar positive effects within racially integrated classrooms.

Next they controlled the camp setting, first by pitting the Eagles and Rattlers against one another in contests and then by arranging situations that forced the groups to cooperate (influence). As predicted, competition produced hostility and cooperation reduced it, suggesting that the researchers' understanding was correct. Later, when Aronson and his coworkers sought to reduce racial hostility within newly integrated schools, they had a scientific basis for predicting what might work. They were able to apply their knowledge successfully in the form of the jigsaw program (application).

PSYCHOLOGY'S BROAD SCOPE: A LEVELS-OF-ANALYSIS FRAMEWORK

The scope of modern psychology stretches from the borders of medicine and the biological sciences to those of the social sciences (Figure 1.2). Because we are biological creatures living in a complex social world, psychologists study an amazing array of factors to understand why people behave, think, and feel as they do. At times, this diversity of factors may seem a bit overwhelming, but we would like to provide you with a framework that will greatly simplify matters. We call it *levels of analysis:* behavior and its causes can be examined at the *biological level* (e.g., brain processes, genetic influences), the *psychological level* (e.g., our thoughts, feelings, and motives), and the *environmental level* (e.g., past and current physical and social environments to which we are exposed).

Here are two brief examples of how the levels-of-analysis framework can be applied. First, consider a behavior that you engage in every day: eating (Figure 1.3). At the biological level of analysis, various chemicals, neural circuits, and structures in your brain respond to bodily signals and help regulate whether you feel hungry or full. At the psychological level of analysis, your moods, food preferences, and motives affect eating. Do you ever eat when you're not hungry, perhaps because you feel stressed or bored? The environmental level of analysis calls attention to specific stimuli (such as the appearance or aroma of different food) that may trigger eating and to cultural customs that influence our food preferences. Does the aroma of freshly baked treats ever make your stomach growl? How about the sight of duck feet or a mound of fish gills on a plate? To most Westerners, duck feet and fish gills may not be appetizing, but during a stay in China we discovered that our hosts considered them delicious.

Now let's apply the levels-of-analysis framework to a rare and seemingly mysterious event: the case of voodoo death described earlier. How

FIGURE 1.2

Psychology as a scientific hub. Psychology links with and overlaps many sciences.

can we explain voodoo death without invoking supernatural powers?

Voodoo is practiced in several regions of the world, including parts of the United States. Decades ago, physiologist Walter Cannon (1942) suggested a possible mechanism for death by "magic curses." Cannon drew on his own research on severe stress responses in animals, as well as eyewitness reports by cultural anthropologists of deaths by magic curses. One such account described the practice of "boning," the placing of a death curse by pointing a sacred bone at the victim:

> The man who discovers that he is being boned by any enemy is, indeed, a pitiable sight. . . . His cheeks blanch and his eyes become glassy. . . . His body begins to tremble and the muscles twitch involuntarily . . . soon after he writhes as if in mortal agony. Unless help is forthcoming in the shape of a countercharm administered by the . . . medicine-man, his death is only a matter of a comparatively short time. (Basedow, 1925, pp. 178–179)

Cannon noted that in cases of death by magic curses, the victim firmly believed that he or she was doomed. For the victim, this belief represents the psychological level of analysis. At the environmental level, this belief was supported by the victim's family, friends, enemies, and culture. At the biological level of analysis, Cannon speculated that the victim's beliefs triggered a profound and persistent stress response—a flood of stress hormones

The Biological Level

The Psychological Level

The Environmental Level

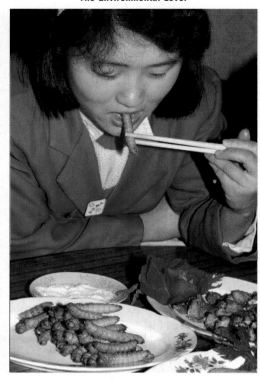

FIGURE 1.3

(*left*) **Biological level.** This rat weighs about triple the weight of a normal rat. As we (or rats) eat, hunger decreases as certain brain regions regulate the sensation of becoming full. Those regions in this rat's brain have been damaged, causing it to overeat and become obese. (*center*) **Psychological level.** At times we may eat out of habit, stress, or boredom. With candy bar in hand and other candies lined up, this student is ready for some autopilot munching. (*right*) **Environmental level.** Does a plateful of big, juicy insect larvae sound appetizing to you? Grubs, traditionally eaten by Australian Aboriginal peoples, are also served in some restaurants. Cultural norms influence food preferences.

(chemicals released by glands in the body)—sending the victim into physiological shock. Cannon's research had shown that one aspect of such shock is a rapid and often fatal drop in blood pressure as stress hormones allow fluid to leak out of veins and capillaries. He noted that normal autopsy procedures would not detect this mechanism of death, making it appear, as in the case of the young woman, that there was no natural cause.

Mind-Body and Nature-Nurture Interactions

Cannon's hypothesis is a plausible alternative to supernatural explanations and is consistent with research showing that negative thoughts about a stressful situation can quickly trigger the secretion of stress hormones (Borod, 2000). This work illustrates what traditionally have been called *mind-body interactions*—the relations between mental processes in the brain and the functioning of other bodily systems. Mind-body interactions focus our attention on the fascinating interplay between the psychological and biological levels of analysis. This topic has a long history within psychology, and, as you will see throughout the textbook, it remains one of psychology's most exciting frontiers.

The levels-of-analysis framework also addresses an issue that has been debated since antiquity: Is our behavior primarily shaped by nature (our biological endowment) or by nurture (our environment and learning history)? The pendulum has swung toward one end or the other at different times in history, but today growing interest in cultural influences and advances in genetics and brain research keep the nature-nurture pendulum in a more balanced position.

Perhaps most important, modern research increasingly reveals that nature and nurture interact (Jaffee et al., 2003). Just as our biological capacities affect how we behave and experience the world, our experiences influence our biological capacities. For humans and rats alike, continually depriving a newborn of physical contact, or providing a newborn with an enriched environment in which to grow, can influence its brain functioning and biological development (Rosenzweig, 1984). Thus, while it may be tempting to take sides, "nature *or* nurture?" usually is the wrong question. As the levels-of-analysis framework implies, nature, nurture, and psychological factors must all be taken into account to gain the fullest understanding of behavior.

Later in the chapter we'll provide a more detailed example of how looking at behavior from multiple levels enhances our understanding. For now, in concluding our discussion of psychology's scope, we'd like you to think critically about Cannon's mind-body explanation for voodoo death.

THE CASE OF VOODOO DEATH

Based on Cannon's hypothesis, why did the woman cursed by voodoo die? Do you believe that this hypothesis is reasonable? Can you think of other explanations for her death? (Think about it, then see page 27.)

IN REVIEW

■ Psychology is the scientific study of behavior and the mind. The term *behavior* refers to actions and responses that can be observed and measured directly. In contrast, mental processes such as thoughts and feelings must be inferred from directly observable responses.

■ Basic research reflects the quest for knowledge for its own sake. Applied research focuses on solving practical problems.

■ The primary goals of psychological science are to describe, understand, predict, and influence behavior and to apply psychological knowledge to enhance human welfare.

■ To understand more fully why people act, think, and feel as they do, psychologists examine behavior at the biological, the psychological, and the environmental levels of analysis.

PERSPECTIVES ON BEHAVIOR

The fact that psychologists study biological, psychological, and environmental factors that influence behavior is not new; it has been an integral part of psychology's history. But just how did psychology's scope become so broad? In part, it happened because psychology has roots in such varied disciplines as philosophy, medicine, and the biological and physical sciences. As a result, different ways of viewing people, called *perspectives,* became part of psychology's intellectual traditions. (Figure 1.4).

If you have ever met someone who views the world differently from the way you do, you know that perspectives matter. Perspectives serve as lenses through which psychologists examine and interpret behavior. In science, new perspectives are an engine of progress. Advances occur as existing beliefs are challenged, a debate ensues, and scientists seek new evidence to resolve the debate. Sometimes, the best-supported elements of contrasting perspectives are merged into a new framework, which in turn will be challenged by still newer viewpoints.

Psychology's major perspectives guide us through its intellectual traditions and address timeless questions about human nature. To better understand how these perspectives evolved, let's briefly examine psychology's roots.

PSYCHOLOGY'S INTELLECTUAL ROOTS

Humans have long sought to understand themselves, and at the center of this quest lies an issue that has tested the best minds of the ages, the so-called *mind-body problem.* Is the mind—the inner agent of consciousness and thought—a spiritual entity separate from the body, or is it a part of the body's activities?

Many early philosophers held a position of **mind-body dualism,** *the belief that the mind is a spiritual entity not subject to physical laws that govern the body.* But if the mind is not composed of physical matter, how could it become aware of bodily sensations, and how could its thoughts exert control over bodily functions? French philosopher, mathematician, and scientist René Descartes (1596–1650) proposed that the mind and body interact through the tiny pineal gland in the brain. Although Descartes placed the mind within the brain, he maintained that the mind was a spiritual, nonmaterial entity. Dualism implies that no amount of research on the physical body (including the brain) could ever hope to unravel the mysteries of the nonphysical mind.

An alternative view, **monism** (from the Greek word *monos,* meaning "one"), *holds that mind and body are one and that the mind is not a separate spiritual entity.* To monists, mental events are simply a product of physical events in the brain, a position advocated by English philosopher Thomas Hobbes (1588–1679). Monism helped set the stage for psychology because it implied that the mind could be studied by measuring physical processes within the brain. The stage was further set by John Locke (1632–1704) and other philosophers from the school of **British empiricism,** *which held that all ideas and knowledge are gained empirically—that is, through the senses.* According to the empiricists, observation is a more valid approach to knowledge than is reason, because reason is fraught with the potential for error. This idea bolstered the development of modern science, whose methods are rooted in empirical observation.

Discoveries in physiology (an area of biology that examines bodily functioning) and medicine also paved the way for psychology's emergence. By 1870 European researchers were electrically stimulating the brains of laboratory animals and mapping the surface areas that controlled various

FIGURE 1.4

Youth and beauty? Or maturity and wisdom? What we perceive depends on our perspective. If you examine this drawing, you will see either a young woman or an old one. Now try changing your perspective. The ear and necklace of the young woman are the left eye and mouth of the old woman.

▶ **Focus 4**
Discuss psychology's philosophical and scientific roots, earliest schools of thought, and founders.

To learn more about the historical approaches to studying human behavior and treating mental illness, watch the video in Chapter 1 of your CD, "History of Mental Illness."

FIGURE 1.5

At the University of Leipzig in 1879, Wilhelm Wundt (*far right*) established the first laboratory of experimental psychology to study the structure of the mind.

FIGURE 1.6

William James, a leader of functionalism, helped establish psychology in North America. His multivolume book *Principles of Psychology* (1890/1950), greatly expanded the scope of psychology.

▶ **Focus 5**
Describe the psychodynamic perspective. Contrast Freud's psychoanalytic theory with modern psychodynamic theories.

body movements. During this same period, medical reports linked damage in different areas of patients' brains with various behavioral and mental impairments. For example, damage to a specific region on the brain's left side impaired people's ability to speak fluently.

Mounting evidence of the relation between brain and behavior supported the view that empirical methods of the natural sciences could also be used to study mental processes. Indeed, by the mid-1800s, German scientists were measuring people's sensory responses to many types of physical stimuli (for example, how the perceived loudness of a sound changes as its physical intensity increases). Their experiments established a new field called *psychophysics,* the study of how psychologically experienced sensations depend on the characteristics of physical stimuli.

Around this time, Charles Darwin's (1809–1882) theory of evolution generated shock waves that are still felt today. His theory, which we will discuss later, was vigorously opposed because it seemed to contradict philosophical and religious beliefs about the exalted nature of human beings. Evolution implied that the human mind was not a spiritual entity but rather the product of a biological continuity between humans and other species. Moreover, Darwin's theory implied that scientists might gain insight about human behavior by studying other species. By the late 1800s, a convergence of intellectual forces provided the impetus for psychology's birth.

EARLY SCHOOLS: STRUCTURALISM AND FUNCTIONALISM

The infant science of psychology emerged in 1879, when Wilhelm Wundt (1832–1920) established the first experimental psychology laboratory at the University of Leipzig in Germany. Wundt, who helped train the first generation of scientific psychologists, wanted to model the study of the mind after the natural sciences (Figure 1.5). He believed that the mind could be studied by breaking it down into its basic components, as a chemist might do in studying a complex chemical compound. One of his graduate students, Englishman Edward Titchener (1867–1927), later established a psychology laboratory in the United States at Cornell University. Like Wundt, Titchener attempted to identify the basic building blocks, or structures, of the mind. Wundt and Titchener's approach came to be known as **structuralism,** *the analysis of the mind in terms of its basic elements.*

In their experiments, structuralists used the method of *introspection* ("looking within") to study

sensations, which they considered the basic elements of consciousness. They exposed participants to all sorts of sensory stimuli—lights, sounds, tastes—and trained them to describe their inner experiences. Although this method of studying the mind was criticized and died out after a few decades, the structuralists left an important mark on the infant field of psychology by establishing a scientific tradition for the study of cognitive processes.

In the United States, structuralism eventually gave way to **functionalism,** *which held that psychology should study the functions of consciousness rather than its structure.* Here's a rough analogy to explain the difference between structuralism and functionalism: Consider your arms and hands. A structuralist would try to explain their movement by studying how muscles, tendons, and bones operate. In contrast, a functionalist would ask, "Why do we have arms and hands? How do they help us adapt to our environment?" The functionalists asked similar questions about mental processes and behavior. In part, they were influenced by Darwin's evolutionary theory, which stressed the importance of adaptation in helping organisms survive and reproduce in their environment. Functionalists did much of the early research on learning and problem solving.

William James (1842–1910), a leader in the functionalist movement, was a "big-picture" person who taught courses in physiology, psychology, and philosophy at Harvard University (Figure 1.6). James's broad functionalist approach helped widen the scope of psychology to include the study of various biological processes, mental processes, and behaviors. Like Wundt, James helped train psychologists who went on to distinguished careers. Among them was Mary Whiton Calkins (1863–1930), who became the first female president of the American Psychological Association in 1905 (Figure 1.7).

Although functionalism no longer exists as a school of thought within psychology, its tradition endures in two modern-day fields: *cognitive psychology,* which studies mental processes, and *evolutionary psychology,* which emphasizes the adaptiveness of behavior.

THE PSYCHODYNAMIC PERSPECTIVE: THE FORCES WITHIN

Have you ever been mystified by why you behaved or felt a certain way? Recall the case of Ray, the student described at the beginning of the chapter who could not understand why he was so shy. The **psychodynamic perspective** *searches for the causes of behavior within the inner workings of our personality (our unique pattern of traits, emotions, and motives),*

emphasizing the role of unconscious processes. Sigmund Freud (1856–1939) developed the first and most influential psychodynamic theory (Figure 1.8).

Psychoanalysis: Freud's Great Challenge

Late in the 19th century, as a young physician in Vienna, Freud was intrigued by the workings of the brain. He was confronted with patients who experienced physical symptoms such as blindness, pain, or paralysis without any apparent bodily cause. Over time he treated patients who had other problems, such as *phobias* (intense unrealistic fears). Because no disease or bodily malfunction could explain these conditions, Freud reasoned that the causes must be psychological. Moreover, if his patients were not producing their symptoms consciously, Freud reasoned that the causes must be hidden from awareness—they must be unconscious. At first Freud treated his patients by using hypnosis. Later he used a technique called *free association,* in which the patient expressed any thoughts that came to mind. To Freud's surprise, his patients eventually described painful and long-"forgotten" childhood experiences, often sexual in nature. Often, after recalling and figuratively reliving these traumatic childhood experiences, the patients' symptoms improved.

Freud became convinced that an unconscious part of the mind profoundly influences behavior, and he developed a theory and a form of psychotherapy called **psychoanalysis**—*the analysis of internal and primarily unconscious psychological forces.* He also proposed that humans have powerful inborn sexual and aggressive drives and that because these desires are punished in childhood, we learn to fear them and become anxious when we are aware of their presence. This leads us to develop **defense mechanisms,** *which are psychological techniques that help us cope with anxiety and the pain of traumatic experiences. Repression,* a primary defense mechanism, protects us by keeping unacceptable impulses, feelings, and memories in the unconscious depths of the mind. All behavior, whether normal or "abnormal," reflects a largely unconscious and inevitable conflict between the defenses and internal impulses. This ongoing psychological struggle between conflicting forces is dynamic in nature, hence the term *psychodynamic.* To explain Ray's extreme shyness around women, Freud might have explored whether Ray is unconsciously afraid of his sexual impulses and therefore avoids putting himself into dating situations where he would have to confront those hidden impulses.

Freud's theory became a lightning rod for controversy. Some of his own followers strongly disagreed with aspects of the theory, especially its heavy emphasis on childhood sexuality. Other psychologists viewed the theory as difficult to test. Indeed, Freud opposed laboratory research on psychoanalytic theory, believing that his clinical observations were more valid. Nevertheless, Freud's ideas did stimulate research on topics such as dreams, memory, aggression, and mental disorders. A scholarly review of more than 3,000 scientific studies examining Freud's ideas found support for some aspects of his theory, whereas other aspects were unsupported or contradicted (Fisher & Greenberg, 1996). But even where Freud's theory was not supported, the research it inspired led to important discoveries. In addition, Freud's work forever broadened the face of psychology to include the study and treatment of psychological disorders.

Modern Psychodynamic Theory

Modern psychodynamic theories continue to explore how unconscious and conscious aspects of personality influence behavior. However, they downplay the role of hidden sexual and aggressive motives and focus more on how early family relationships, other social factors, and our sense of "self" shape our personality (Kohut, 1977). For example, psychodynamic **object relations theories** *focus on how early experiences with caregivers shape the views that people form of themselves and others* (Kernberg, 1984, 2000). In turn, these views unconsciously influence a person's relationships with other people throughout life. To explain Ray's shyness, a modern psychodynamic psychologist might examine Ray's conceptions of himself and his parents. Ray's shyness may stem from a fear of rejection of which he is unaware. This fear may be based on conceptions that he developed of his parents as being rejecting and disapproving, views that now unconsciously shape his expectations of how relationships with women and men will be.

The psychodynamic perspective dominated thinking about personality, mental disorders, and psychotherapy for the first half of the 20th century, and it continues to influence applied and academic psychology. Among American psychologists who provide therapy, a large group—20 to 30 percent—report their orientation as being psychodynamic. Psychoanalysis also remains a major force in European psychology (Tuckett, 2005).

Links with psychodynamic concepts can be found within several areas of psychological science. For example, biologically oriented psychologists have identified brain mechanisms that can produce emotional reactions of which we are consciously unaware (LeDoux, 2000), and cognitive scientists

FIGURE 1.7

Mary Whiton Calkins founded a psychology laboratory at Wellesley College, where she taught for over 30 years. She studied memory and dreams, and in 1905 became the first female president of the American Psychological Association.

FIGURE 1.8

Sigmund Freud founded psychoanalysis. For more than 50 years, he probed the hidden recesses of the mind.

have shown that many aspects of information processing occur outside of awareness (Chartrand & Bargh, 2002). Thus, while most contemporary psychological scientists reject Freud's version of the unconscious mind, many support the concept that behaviors can be triggered by nonconscious processes.

THE BEHAVIORAL PERSPECTIVE: THE POWER OF THE ENVIRONMENT

The **behavioral perspective** *focuses on the role of the external environment in governing our actions.* From this perspective, our behavior is jointly determined by habits learned from previous life experiences and by stimuli in our immediate environment.

Origins of the Behavioral Perspective

The behavioral perspective is rooted in the philosophical school of British empiricism, which held that all ideas and knowledge are gained through the senses. According to the early empiricist John Locke, at birth the human mind is a *tabula rasa*—a "blank tablet" or "slate"—upon which experiences are written. In this view, human nature is shaped purely by the environment.

In the early 1900s, experiments by Russian physiologist Ivan Pavlov (1849–1936) revealed one way in which the environment shapes behavior: through the association of events with one another. Pavlov found that dogs automatically learned to salivate to the sound of a new stimulus, such as a tone, if that stimulus was repeatedly paired with food. Meanwhile, in the United States, Edward Thorndike (1874–1949) examined how organisms learn through the consequences of their actions. According to Thorndike's (1911) *law of effect,* responses followed by satisfying consequences become more likely to recur, and those followed by unsatisfying consequences become less likely to recur. Thus learning is the key to understanding how experience molds behavior.

Behaviorism

Behaviorism, *a school of thought that emphasizes environmental control of behavior through learning,* began to emerge in 1913. John B. Watson (1878–1958), who led the new movement, strongly opposed the "mentalism" of the structuralists, functionalists, and psychoanalysts (Figure 1.9). He argued that the proper subject matter of psychology was observable behavior, not unobservable inner consciousness. Human beings, he said, are products of their learning experiences. So passionately did Watson hold this position that in 1924 he issued the following challenge:

> Give me a dozen healthy infants, well-formed, and my own specialized world to bring them up in and I'll guarantee you to take any one of them at random and train him to become any type of specialist I might select—doctor, lawyer, artist, merchant-chief and, yes, even beggar-man and thief, regardless of his talents, penchants, tendencies, abilities, vocations, and race of his ancestors. (p. 82)

Behaviorists sought to discover the laws that govern learning, and in accord with Darwin's theory of evolution, they believed that the same basic principles of learning apply to all organisms. B. F. Skinner (1904–1990) was the leading modern figure in behaviorism (Figure 1.10). Although Skinner did not deny that thoughts and feelings occur within us, he maintained that "No account of what is happening inside the human body, no matter how complete, will explain the origins of human behavior" (1989b, p. 18). Skinner believed that the real causes of behavior reside in the outer world and insisted that "A person does not act upon the world, the world acts upon him" (1971, p. 211). His research, based largely on studies of rats and pigeons under controlled laboratory conditions, examined how behavior is shaped by the rewarding and punishing consequences that it produces.

In the case of our college student, Ray, a behaviorist might explain Ray's shyness around women by examining his past dating experiences. In high school, the first time Ray invited a girl to a dance he was turned down. Later, he had a crush on a girl and they went out once, after which she turned him down. Though nervous, he asked out

► Focus 6
What are the behavioral perspective's origins and focus? Contrast radical behaviorism with cognitive behaviorism.

FIGURE 1.9

John B. Watson founded the school of behaviorism. He published *Psychology as a Behaviorist Views It* in 1913.

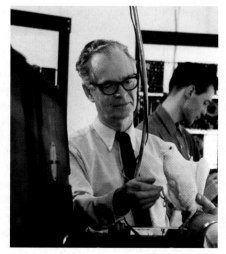

FIGURE 1.10

B. F. Skinner, a leading behaviorist, argued that mentalistic concepts were not necessary to explain behavior and that learning principles could be used to enhance human welfare.

a few girls after that but was turned down each time. Such punishing consequences decreased the likelihood that Ray would ask someone out in the future. Fortunately, Kira asked Ray out, and the positive consequences they experienced on their first date reinforced their behavior, increasing the odds that they would go out again.

Skinner believed that society could harness the power of the environment to change behavior in beneficial ways and that the chief barrier to creating a better world through "social engineering" is an outmoded conception of people as free agents. Skinner's approach, known as *radical behaviorism*, was considered extreme by many psychologists, but he was esteemed for his scientific contributions and for focusing attention on how environmental forces could be used to enhance human welfare. In the 1960s behaviorism inspired powerful techniques known collectively as *behavior modification*. These techniques, aimed at decreasing problem behaviors and increasing positive behaviors by manipulating environmental factors, are still used widely today (Silverman et al., 2005).

Behaviorism's insistence that psychology should focus only on observable stimuli and responses resonated with many who wanted this young science to model itself on the natural sciences. Behaviorism dominated North American research on learning into the 1960s, challenged psychodynamic views about the causes of psychological disorders, and led to highly effective treatments for some disorders. But radical behaviorism's influence waned after the 1970s as interest in studying mental processes expanded (Robins et al., 1999). Nevertheless, behaviorists continue to make important contributions to basic and applied psychology, and their discovery of basic laws of learning was one of the greatest contributions made by American psychology in the 20th century.

Cognitive Behaviorism

In the 1960s and 1970s, a growing number of psychologists showed that cognitive processes such as attention and memory could be rigorously studied by using sophisticated experiments. This led some behaviorists to challenge radical behaviorism's view that mental life was off-limits as a topic for scientific study. They developed a modified view called **cognitive behaviorism,** *which proposes that learning experiences and the environment influence our expectations and other thoughts, and in turn our thoughts influence how we behave* (Bandura, 1969, 2002). Cognitive behaviorism remains an influential viewpoint to this day (Figure 1.11).

A cognitive behaviorist might say that Ray's past dating rejections were punishing and led him to expect that further attempts at romance would be doomed. In turn, these expectations of social rejection inhibited him from asking women out and even from making male friends. While at home for spring break, family discussions helped Ray think about his situation in a new light. This helped Ray modify his behavior, become more outgoing, and improve his social relationships.

What Do You Think?

ARE THE STUDENTS LAZY?
Imagine that you are a high school teacher. Whenever you try to engage your students in a class discussion, they gaze into space and hardly say anything. You start to think that they're just a bunch of lazy kids. From a radical behavioral perspective, is your conclusion reasonable? How might you improve the situation? (Think about it, then see page 27).

THE HUMANISTIC PERSPECTIVE: SELF-ACTUALIZATION AND POSITIVE PSYCHOLOGY

In the mid-20th century, as the psychodynamic and behavioral perspectives vied for intellectual dominance within psychology, a new viewpoint arose to challenge them both. Known as the **humanistic perspective** (or **humanism**), *it emphasized free will, personal growth, and the attempt to find meaning in one's existence.*

Humanists rejected psychodynamic concepts of humans as being controlled by unconscious forces. They also denied behaviorism's view of humans as reactors molded by the environment. Instead, humanistic theorists such as Abraham Maslow (1908–1970) proposed that each of us has an inborn force toward *self-actualization*, the reaching of one's individual potential (Figure 1.12). When the human personality develops in a supportive environment, the positive inner nature of a person emerges. In contrast, misery and pathology occur when environments frustrate our innate tendency toward self-actualization. Humanists emphasized the importance of personal choice and responsibility, personality growth, and positive feelings of self-worth. They insisted that the meaning of our existence resides squarely in our own hands.

Thinking about Ray's shyness and loneliness, a humanist might say that no matter how many rejections Ray has had in the past, he must take personal responsibility for turning things around. A humanist also might wonder whether, in his freshman year,

FIGURE 1.11

Albert Bandura has played a key role in developing cognitive behaviorism, which merges the behavioral and cognitive perspectives.

▶ **Focus 7**
How does humanism's conception of human nature differ from that advanced by psychodynamic theory and behaviorism?

FIGURE 1.12

The humanistic perspective emphasizes the human ability to surmount obstacles in the drive toward self-actualization.

▶ **Focus 8**
Describe the focus and the origins of the cognitive perspective and some areas of modern cognitive science.

Ray's happiness and sense of self-worth were resting too heavily on his hope for a good romantic relationship. By focusing on building a few friendships, Ray wisely found another way to satisfy what Maslow (1954) called "belongingness," our basic human need for social acceptance and companionship.

Few early humanists were scientists and, historically, humanism has had a more limited impact on mainstream psychological science than have other perspectives. Still, it has inspired important areas of research. Humanist Carl Rogers (1902–1987) pioneered the scientific study of psychotherapy. In the 1940s and 1950s his research group was the first to audiotape counseling sessions and analyze their content. Rogers (1967) identified key processes that led to constructive changes in clients. As another example, psychologists have conducted many studies of self-concept over the past 25 years, and much of this work incorporates humanistic ideas (Verplanken & Holland, 2002).

Humanism's focus on self-actualization and growth is also seen in today's growing **positive psychology movement,** *which emphasizes the study of human strengths, fulfillment, and optimal living* (Diener & Seligman, 2004). In contrast to psychology's long-standing focus on "what's wrong with our world" (e.g., mental disorders, conflict, prejudice), positive psychology examines how we can nurture what is best within ourselves and society to create a happy and fulfilling life.

THE COGNITIVE PERSPECTIVE: THE THINKING HUMAN

Derived from the Latin word *cogitare* ("to think"), the **cognitive perspective** *examines the nature of the mind and how mental processes influence behavior.* In this view, humans are information processors whose actions are governed by thought.

Origins of the Cognitive Perspective

As discussed earlier, structuralism and functionalism arose as two of psychology's earliest schools of thought. The structuralists attempted to identify the basic elements, or structure, of consciousness by using the method of introspection. In contrast, functionalists explored the purposes of consciousness. Other pioneering cognitive psychologists, such as Hermann Ebbinghaus (1850–1909) studied memory.

By the 1920s German scientists had formed a school of thought known as **Gestalt psychology,** *which examined how elements of experience are organized into wholes.* The word *gestalt* may be translated roughly as "whole" or "organization." Instead of trying to break consciousness down into its elements, Gestalt psychologists argued that our perceptions are organized so that "the whole is greater than the sum of its parts." Consider the painting in Figure 1.13. Many people

FIGURE 1.13

This painting illustrates the Gestalt principle that the whole is greater than the sum of its parts. The individual elements are sea creatures, but the whole is perceived as a portrait of a face. *The Water,* by Arcimboldo, from Kunsthistorisches Museum, Vienna.

initially perceive it as a whole—as a portrait of a strange-looking person—rather than as a mosaic of individual sea creatures. Gestalt psychology stimulated interest in cognitive topics such as perception and problem solving.

Structuralism, functionalism, and Gestalt psychology eventually disappeared as scientific schools. As behaviorism and its antimentalistic stance rose in the 1920s and 1930s to become the dominant perspective guiding North American research, the study of the mind was relegated to the back burner.

Renewed Interest in the Mind

In the 1950s several factors contributed to a renewed interest in studying cognitive processes. In part, this interest stemmed from psychologists' involvement during World War II in designing information displays, such as gauges in airplane cockpits, that enabled military personnel (e.g., pilots) to recognize and interpret that information quickly and accurately. Increasingly, psychologists began to conduct experiments that reflected an information-processing approach.

Computer technology, which was in its infancy at that time, provided new information-processing concepts and terminology that psychologists began to adapt to the study of memory and attention (Broadbent, 1958). A new metaphor was developing—the mind as a system that processes, stores, and retrieves information. The information-processing approach to studying the mind continues to be influential.

On another front in the 1950s, a heated debate arose between behaviorists and linguists about how children acquire language. The behaviorists, led by B. F. Skinner, claimed that language is acquired through basic principles of learning. The linguists, led by Noam Chomsky (b. 1928), argued that humans are biologically "preprogrammed" to acquire language and that children come to understand language as a set of "mental rules." This debate convinced many psychologists that language was too complex to be explained by behavioral principles and that it needed to be examined from a more cognitive perspective.

Interest in cognition also grew in other areas. For example, a theory developed by Swiss psychologist Jean Piaget (1896–1980), which explained how children's thinking processes become more sophisticated with age, gained widespread recognition in North America (Figure 1.14). Overall, psychologists' interest in mental processes swelled by the 1960s and 1970s—a period that sometimes is referred to as the "cognitive revolution."

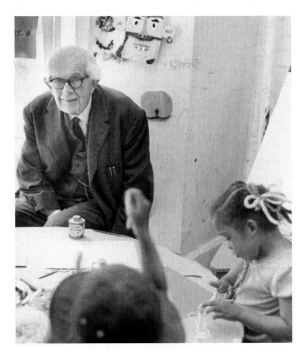

FIGURE 1.14

Swiss psychologist Jean Piaget was a master of observation. Many of his conclusions about cognitive development came from carefully watching children solve problems.

The Modern Cognitive Perspective

Cognitive psychology, *which focuses on the study of mental processes,* embodies the cognitive perspective. Cognitive psychologists study the processes by which people reason and make decisions, devise solutions to problems, form perceptions and mental images, and produce and understand language. They study the nature of knowledge and expertise. Some, such as Elizabeth Loftus (b. 1944), have greatly expanded our understanding of memory and of factors that distort it (Figure 1.15). Cognitive psychologists continue to explore the nature of attention and consciousness and have increasingly become interested in how nonconscious processes influence behavior.

Cognitive neuroscience, *which uses sophisticated electrical recording and brain-imaging techniques to examine brain activity while people engage in cognitive tasks,* is a rapidly growing area that represents the intersection of cognitive psychology and the biological perspective within psychology. Cognitive neuroscientists seek to determine how the brain goes about its business of learning language, acquiring knowledge, forming memories, and performing other cognitive activities (Rajah & McIntosh, 2005).

Social constructivism, an influential cognitive viewpoint, *maintains that what we consider "reality" is largely our own mental creation,* the product of a shared way of thinking among members

FIGURE 1.15

Cognitive psychologist Elizabeth Loftus studies the nature of memory and how memories become distorted.

of social groups (Gergen, 2000). Constructivists would maintain, for example, that the long-standing conflict between Israeli Jews and Palestinian Arabs reflects immense differences in how they perceive God's plan for them and how they interpret the history of the land where they live (Rouhana & Bar-Tal, 1998).

From a cognitive perspective, we might examine Ray's shyness in terms of how he pays attention to and processes information, his perceptions, and his memory. The few times that he went on dates, Ray's nervousness may have caused him to focus on even the slightest things that weren't going well, while failing to notice other cues that suggested his date was having a good time. Ray's interpretation of his past dating failures may also be based on faulty reasoning. Ray believes he was rejected because of his personal qualities ("I'm not attractive or interesting enough") and therefore expects that future dating attempts will also be unsuccessful. If Ray correctly attributed the rejections to some temporary or situational factor ("Clarissa was already interested in someone else"), then he would not necessarily expect other women to reject him in the future. A cognitive psychologist also might ask whether Ray's memories of his past dating experiences are accurate or have become distorted over time. Ray may be remembering those events as much more unpleasant than they actually were.

THE SOCIOCULTURAL PERSPECTIVE: THE EMBEDDED HUMAN

Humans are social creatures. Embedded within a culture, each of us encounters ever changing social settings that shape our actions and values, our sense of identity, our very conception of reality. The **sociocultural perspective** *examines how the social environment and cultural learning influence our behavior, thoughts, and feelings.*

Cultural Learning and Diversity

Culture *refers to the enduring values, beliefs, behaviors, and traditions that are shared by a large group of people and passed from one generation to the next.* All cultural groups develop their own social **norms,** *which are rules (often unwritten) that specify what behavior is acceptable and expected for members of that group.* Norms exist for all types of social behaviors, such as how to dress, respond to people of higher status, or act as a woman or man (Figure 1.16). For culture to endure, each new generation must internalize, or adopt, the norms and values of the group as their own. **Socialization** *is the process by which culture is transmitted to new members and internalized by them.*

In word if not in deed, psychologists have long recognized culture's impact in shaping who we are. Two influential behaviorists, Neil Miller and John Dollard, noted in 1941 that

> no psychologist would venture to predict the behavior of a rat without knowing [where in a maze] the feed or the shock is placed. It is no easier to predict the behavior of a human being without knowing the conditions of his "maze," i.e., the structure of his social environment. Culture . . . is a statement of the design of the human maze, of the type of reward involved, and of what responses are to be rewarded. (p. 5)

Yet despite acknowledging culture's importance, throughout much of the 20th century psychological research largely ignored non-Western groups.

▶ **Focus 9**
Explain the sociocultural perspective. What are culture, norms, socialization, and individualism-collectivism?

FIGURE 1.16

Social norms differ across cultures and over time within cultures. The idea of women engaging in aggressive sports or military combat is unthinkable in many cultures. Several generations ago, it was also unthinkable in the United States.

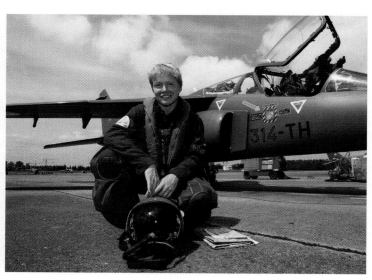

Such cross-cultural work usually was left to anthropologists. Even within Western societies, for decades participants in psychological research typically were white and came from middle- or upper-class backgrounds. This situation was so common that in 1976, African American psychologist Robert Guthrie published a book titled *Even the Rat Was White: A Historical View of Psychology.* There were important exceptions, however, such as research by Kenneth Clark (1914–2005) and Mamie Clark (1917–1983) and others, examining how discrimination and prejudice influenced the personality development of African American children (Clark & Clark, 1947; Figure 1.17).

Over time, psychologists increasingly began to study diverse ethnic and cultural groups. Today the growing field of **cultural psychology** (sometimes called *cross-cultural psychology*) *explores how culture is transmitted to its members and examines psychological similarities and differences among people from diverse cultures.*

One important difference among cultures is the extent to which they emphasize *individualism* versus *collectivism* (Triandis & Suh, 2002). Most industrialized cultures of northern Europe and North America promote **individualism,** *an emphasis on personal goals and self-identity based primarily on one's own attributes and achievements.* In contrast, many cultures in Asia, Africa, and South America nurture **collectivism,** *in which individual goals are subordinated to those of the group and personal identity is defined largely by the ties that bind one to the extended family and other social groups.* This difference is created by social learning experiences that begin in childhood and continue in the form of social customs. In school, for example, Japanese children more often work in groups on a common assignment, whereas American children more often work alone on individual assignments.

Thinking about Ray's lonely first year in college, the sociocultural perspective leads us to ask how his cultural upbringing and other social factors contributed to his shy behavior. Throughout his teen years, cultural norms for male assertiveness may have put pressure on Ray. His shyness may have evoked teasing and other negative reactions from his high school peers, increasing his feelings of inadequacy by the time he reached college. As for Ray and Kira's relationship, we might examine how norms regarding courtship and marriage differ across cultures.

In each chapter of this book, a "Research Close-Up" provides you with a highly condensed, in-depth look at an important study, paralleling the format of research articles published in psychological journals. We give you background information about the study, describe its method and key results, and discuss (evaluate) key aspects of the study. Our first "Research Close-Up" examines cross-cultural attitudes about love and marriage.

FIGURE 1.17

Psychologists Kenneth B. Clark and Mamie P. Clark studied the development of racial identity among African American children. Kenneth Clark also wrote books on the psychological impact of prejudice and discrimination.

▶ **Focus 10**
How does the "Research Close-Up" illustrate cultural psychology's goals and importance?

 Research Close-Up   **Love and Marriage in Eleven Cultures**

SOURCE: ROBERT LEVINE, SUGURU SATO, TSUKASA HASHIMOTO, and JYOTI VERMA (1995). Love and marriage in eleven cultures. *Journal of Cross-Cultural Psychology*, 26, 554–571.

INTRODUCTION

Would you marry someone you did not love? According to one theory, people in individualistic cultures are more likely to view romantic love as a requirement for marriage because love is a matter of personal choice (Goode, 1959). In collectivistic cultures, concern for the extended family plays a larger role in marriage decisions.

Psychologist Robert Levine and his colleagues (1995) examined college students' views about love and marriage. Whereas previous research focused on American students, these authors studied students from 11 countries. They also examined whether students from collectivistic and economically poorer countries would be less likely to view love as a prerequisite to marriage.

METHOD

The researchers administered language-appropriate versions of the same questionnaire to 1,163 female and male college students from 11 countries. The key question was, "If someone had all the other qualities you desired, would you marry this person if you were not in love with him/her?" The students responded "No," "Yes," or "Not Sure." The researchers determined each country's economic status and collectivistic versus individualistic orientation from data gathered by previous cross-cultural investigators.

RESULTS

Within each country, the views of female and male students did not differ significantly. In contrast, beliefs across countries varied strongly (Table 1.2). In India, Thailand, and Pakistan, most students said they would marry or at least consider marrying

Continued

| TABLE 1.2   Love and Marriage in Eleven Cultures |

If someone had all the other qualities you desired, would you marry this person if you were not in love with him/her?

Country	Percentage		
	No	Yes	Not Sure
India	24	49	27
Thailand	34	19	47
Pakistan	39	50	11
Philippines	64	11	25
Japan	64	2	34
Hong Kong	78	6	16
Australia	80	5	15
Mexico	83	10	7
England	84	7	9
Brazil	86	4	10
United States	86	4	10

SOURCE: Levine et al., 1995.

someone they did not love. In the Philippines and Japan, a sizable minority—just over a third—felt the same way. In contrast, students from the other countries overwhelmingly rejected the notion of marrying somebody they did not love. Overall, students from collectivistic and economically poorer countries were less likely to view love as a prerequisite to marriage.

DISCUSSION

Among most of our own students, the notion that you marry someone you love is a truism. They are surprised—as perhaps you are—that many students in other countries would consider marrying someone they did not love. This study reminds us that as members of a particular culture, it is easy to mistakenly assume that "our way" is the "normal way."

As in all research, we must interpret the results carefully. For example, among those students who said they would marry someone without being in love, would it be accurate to conclude that they view love as irrelevant to marriage? Not necessarily, because other research has found that "mutual attraction/love" is viewed across most cultures as a desirable quality in a mate (Buss, 1989). Thus the results of the Levine et al. study suggest only that in some cultures love is not viewed as an *essential prerequisite* to enter into marriage.

THE BIOLOGICAL PERSPECTIVE: THE BRAIN, GENES, AND EVOLUTION

▶ **Focus 11**
Describe the biological perspective and the focus of behavioral neuroscience and behavior genetics.

The **biological perspective** *examines how brain processes and other bodily functions regulate behavior.* Biological psychology has always been a prominent part of the field, but its influence has increased dramatically over recent decades.

Behavioral Neuroscience

Ray and Kira are in love. They study and eat together. They hold hands and kiss. Yet a year earlier, Ray was afraid to ask women out and became depressed. What brain regions, neural circuits, and brain chemicals enable us to feel love, pleasure, fear, and depression? To read, study, and feel hunger? How do hormones influence behavior? These questions are the province of **behavioral neuroscience** (also called *physiological psychology*), *which examines brain processes and other physiological functions that underlie our behavior, sensory experiences, emotions, and thoughts* (Robinson et al., 2005).

The study of brain-behavior relations was in its infancy as psychology entered the 20th century. Two pioneers of biological psychology, American Karl Lashley (1890–1958) and Canadian Donald O. Hebb (1904–1985), studied the brain's role in learning. Lashley trained rats to run mazes and

then measured how surgically produced lesions (damage) to various brain areas affected the rats' learning and memory. His research inspired other psychologists to map the brain regions involved in specific psychological functions (Figure 1.18).

Hebb (1949) proposed that changes in the connections between nerve cells in the brain provide the biological basis for learning, memory, and perception. His influential theory inspired much research, continuing to this day, on how the brain's neural circuitry changes as we learn, remember, and perceive. This research led to the discovery of **neurotransmitters,** *which are chemicals released by nerve cells that allow them to communicate with one another.* The study of neurotransmitters' role in normal behavior and mental disorders represents an important area of current neuroscience research.

Because behavioral neuroscience focuses on processes that are largely invisible to the naked eye, its development has depended on technological advancements. Today, using computer-based brain-imaging techniques and devices that record brain waves, psychologists can watch activity in specific brain areas as people experience emotions, perceive stimuli, and perform tasks (Figure 1.19). These advances have led to new areas of study that forge links between various psychological perspectives. For example, cognitive

FIGURE 1.18

Karl Lashley was a pioneer of physiological psychology (behavioral neuroscience). He examined how damage to various brain regions affected rats' ability to learn and remember.

FIGURE 1.19

Behavioral neuroscientists use positron-emission tomography (PET) scans to measure brain activity as people perform various tasks. Viewed from above, each image pictures a horizontal slice of the brain with the front of the brain at the top. Yellow and red indicate regions of greatest activity: (*top left*) visual task, (*top center*) auditory task, (*top right*) cognitive task, (*bottom left*) memory task, and (*bottom right*) motor task.

neuroscience—the study of brain processes that underlie attention, reasoning, problem solving, and so forth—represents an intersection of cognitive psychology and behavioral neuroscience. As a whole, however, behavioral neuroscience is broader than cognitive neuroscience. Behavioral neuroscientists, for example, also study the biology of hunger, thirst, sex, body-temperature regulation, emotion, movement, and sensory processes such as vision, hearing, and taste.

Behavior Genetics

Psychologists have had a long-standing interest in **behavior genetics,** *the study of how behavioral tendencies are influenced by genetic factors* (DiLalla, 2004). As we all know, animals can be selectively bred for physical traits (Figure 1.20). But they can also be bred for behavioral traits such as aggression and intelligence. This is done by allowing highly aggressive or very bright males and females to mate with one another over generations. In Thailand, where gambling on fish fights is a national pastime, the selective breeding of winners has produced the highly aggressive Siamese fighting fish. The male of this species will instantly attack his own image in a mirror.

Human behavior also is influenced by genetic factors. Identical twins, who result from the splitting of a fertilized egg and therefore have the same genetic makeup, are far more similar to one another on many behavioral traits than are frater-nal twins, who result from two different fertilized eggs and therefore are no more similar genetically than are nontwin siblings. This greater degree of similarity is found even when the identical twins have been reared in different homes and dissimilar environments (Plomin & Caspi, 1999).

Thinking about Ray, a behavior geneticist would consider the extent to which heredity contributes to differences in shyness among people. Some infants display an extremely shy, inhibited emotional style that seems to be biologically based and persists through childhood into adulthood (Kagan, 1989; Newman et al., 1997). Perhaps Ray inherited a tendency to be shy, and dating rejections in high school reinforced his natural reluctance to ask women out.

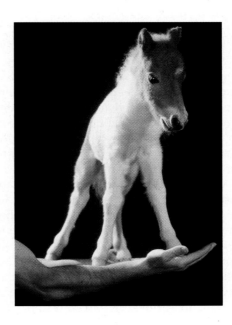

FIGURE 1.20

Selective breeding can produce physical and behavioral characteristics. This tiny horse was produced by selectively breeding very small horses over a number of generations.

Evolutionary Psychology

Charles Darwin published his theory of evolution in 1859 (Figure 1.21). He was not the first to suggest that organisms evolve, but his theory was the best documented. His ideas were stimulated by a five-year voyage aboard a British research vessel that explored coastal regions around the globe. Darwin was struck by the numerous differences between seemingly similar species that lived in different environments. He began to view these differences as ways in which each species had adapted to its unique environment.

Darwin noted that the individual members of given species differ naturally in many ways. Some possess specific traits to a greater extent than other members do. Through a process he called **natural selection,** *if an inherited trait gives certain*

▶ **Focus 12**
What is natural selection? Explain the focus of evolutionary psychology.

FIGURE 1.21

Charles Darwin, a British naturalist, formulated a theory of evolution that revolutionized scientific thinking.

FIGURE 1.22

Natural selection pressures result in physical changes. The peppered moth's natural color is that of the lighter insect. However, over many generations, peppered moths who live in polluted urban areas have become darker, not from the pollution but because moths who inherited slightly darker coloration blended better into their grimy environment. Thus they were more likely to survive predators and pass their "darker" genes on to their offspring. However, a trip into the countryside to visit their light-colored relatives could easily prove fatal for these darker urban insects.

members an advantage over others (such as increasing their ability to attract mates, escape danger, or acquire food), *these members will be more likely to survive and pass these characteristics on to their offspring.* In this way, species evolve as the presence of adaptive traits increases within the population over generations. In contrast, traits that put certain members at a disadvantage tend to become less common within a species over time because members having these traits will be less likely to survive and reproduce.

As the environment changes, the adaptiveness of a trait may increase or decrease. Thus through natural selection, a species' biology evolves in response to environmental conditions (Figure 1.22). Darwin assumed that the principle of natural selection could be applied to all living organisms, including humans.

Evolutionary psychology *is a growing discipline that seeks to explain how evolution shaped modern human behavior* (Buss, 2005). Evolutionary psychologists stress that through natural selection, human mental abilities and behavioral tendencies evolved along with a changing body (Tooby & Cosmides, 1992). Consider how the brain evolved over millions of years, with the greatest growth occurring in brain regions involving higher mental processes.

According to one theory, as our humanlike ancestors developed new physical abilities (such as the ability to walk upright, thus freeing the use of the arms and hands), they began to use tools and weapons and to hunt and live in social groups (Pilbeam, 1984). Certain psychological abilities—memory, thought, language, and the capacity to learn and solve problems—became more important to survival as our ancestors had to adapt to new ways of living.

Within any generation, genetically based variations in brain structure and functioning occur among individuals. Ancestors whose brain characteristics better supported adaptive mental abilities were more likely to survive and reproduce. Thus through natural selection, adaptations to new environmental demands contributed to the development of the brain, just as brain growth contributed to the further development of human behavior.

Evolutionary psychologists also attempt to explain the evolution of human social behaviors. For example, recall that Ray and Kira are contemplating marriage. As a species, why have we evolved to seek out a long-term bond with a mate? And why is it that across the world, on average, men desire a younger mate and attach greater importance than women to a potential mate's physical attractiveness, whereas women

tend to seek an older mate and attach more importance than men to a potential mate's ambition? As we'll discuss more fully in Chapter 10, whereas sociocultural psychologists argue that socialization and gender inequality in job opportunities cause most sex differences in mate preferences, some evolutionary psychologists propose that through natural selection men and women have become biologically predisposed to seek somewhat different qualities in a mate (Buss, 1989, 2005).

IN REVIEW

- Psychology's intellectual roots lie in philosophy, biology, and medicine. Several major perspectives have shaped psychology's scientific growth. In the late 1800s Wundt and James helped found psychology. Structuralism, which examined the basic components of consciousness, and functionalism, which focused on the purposes of consciousness, were psychology's two earliest schools of thought.

- The psychodynamic perspective calls attention to unconscious motives, conflicts, and defense mechanisms that influence our personality and behavior. Freud emphasized how unconscious sexual and aggressive impulses and childhood experiences shape personality. Modern psychodynamic theories focus more on how early family relationships and our sense of self unconsciously influence our current behavior.

- The behavioral perspective emphasizes how the external environment and learning shape behavior. Behaviorists such as Watson and Skinner believed that psychology should only study observable stimuli and responses, not unobservable mental processes. Behaviorists discovered basic laws of learning through controlled research with laboratory animals and applied these principles to enhance human welfare. Cognitive behaviorists believe that learning experiences influence our thoughts, which in turn influence our behaviors.

- The humanistic perspective emphasizes personal freedom and choice, psychological growth, and self-actualization. Humanism has contributed to research on the self, the process of psychotherapy, and today's positive psychology movement.

- The cognitive perspective, embodied by the field of cognitive psychology, views humans as information processors who think, judge, and solve problems. Its roots lie in the early schools of structuralism, functionalism, and Gestalt psychology. Cognitive neuroscience examines the brain processes that occur as people perform mental tasks. Social constructivism maintains that much of what we call reality is a creation of our own mental processes.

■ The sociocultural perspective examines how the social environment and cultural learning influence our behavior and thoughts. Cultural psychologists study how culture is transmitted to its members and examine similarities and differences among people from various cultures. An orientation toward individualism versus collectivism represents one of many ways in which cultures vary.

■ With roots in physiology, medicine, and Darwin's theory of evolution, the biological perspective examines how bodily functions regulate behavior. Behavioral neuroscientists study brain and hormonal processes that underlie our behavior, sensations, emotions, and thoughts. Behavior geneticists study how behavior is influenced by our genetic inheritance. Evolutionary psychologists examine the adaptive functions of behaviors and seek to explain how evolution has biologically predisposed modern humans toward certain ways of behaving.

USING LEVELS OF ANALYSIS TO INTEGRATE THE PERSPECTIVES

As summarized in Table 1.3, psychology's major perspectives (presented in the order we have discussed them) provide us with differing conceptions of human nature. Fortunately, we can distill the essence of these perspectives into the simple three-part framework that we briefly introduced earlier in the chapter: Behavior can be understood at biological, psychological, and environmental levels of analysis.

First, we can analyze behavior and its causes in terms of brain functioning and hormones, as well as genetic factors shaped over the course of evolution. This is the *biological level of analysis*. The biological level can tell us much, but not everything. For example, we may know that certain thoughts and emotions are associated with activity in particular brain regions, but this does not tell us what those thoughts are. Thus we must also examine the *psychological level of analysis*. Here we might look to the cognitive perspective and analyze how thought, memory, and planning influence behavior. Borrowing from the psychodynamic and humanistic perspectives, we also can examine how certain motives and personality traits

influence behavior. Finally, we must also consider the *environmental level of analysis*. Here we can use the behavioral and sociocultural perspectives to examine how stimuli in the physical and social environment shape our behavior, thoughts, and feelings.

Realize that a full understanding of behavior often moves us back and forth between these three levels. Consider Ray and Kira. When we describe aspects of the culture in which they were raised, such as its religious values and social customs, we are operating at the environmental level of analysis. However, once Ray and Kira adopted those cultural values as their own, those values became an essential part of their identities, which represent the psychological level of analysis. Similarly, we might describe a family environment as highly abusive, but an abused child's tendency to worry and feel anxious—and the chemical changes in the brain that underlie this anxiety—move us to the psychological and biological levels of analysis.

AN EXAMPLE: UNDERSTANDING DEPRESSION

To appreciate how the levels-of-analysis framework can help us understand behavior, let's examine a common but complex psychological problem in our culture: depression. Most people experience sadness, grief, or the blues at some time in their lives. Recall that Ray was lonely during his first year at college and became mildly depressed for a short time. These feelings often are normal responses to significant negative events or losses that we have experienced. However, when these emotions are intense, persist over a long period, and are accompanied by thoughts of hopelessness and an inability to experience pleasure, we have crossed the boundary between a normal reaction and clinical depression.

To better understand depression, let's begin at the biological level of analysis. First, genetic factors appear to predispose some people toward developing depression (Neumeister et al., 2004). In one study, relatives of people who had developed major depression before age 20 were 8 times more likely to become depressed at some point than were relatives of nondepressed people (Weissman et al., 1984).

Biochemical factors also play a role. Recall that neurotransmitters are chemicals that transmit signals between nerve cells within the brain. For many depressed people, certain neurotransmitter systems do not operate normally, and the most effective antidepressant drugs restore neurotransmitter activity to more normal levels.

From an evolutionary perspective, ancestors who developed effective ways to cope with

▶ **Focus 13**
Use the three-level framework to integrate psychology's perspectives and discuss causes of depression.

How would you apply the three levels of analysis to another psychological condition, an eating disorder? Consider this question as you watch the video in Chapter 1 of your CD, "Bulimia Nervosa."

TABLE 1.3	Comparison of Six Major Perspectives on Human Behavior					
	Psychodynamic	**Behavioral**	**Humanistic**	**Cognitive**	**Sociocultural**	**Biological**
Conception of human nature	The human as controlled by inner forces and conflicts	The human as reactor to the environment	The human as free agent, seeking self-actualization	The human as thinker	The human as social being embedded in a culture	The human animal
Major causal factors in behavior	Unconscious motives, conflicts, and defenses; early childhood experiences and unresolved conflicts	Past learning experiences and the stimuli and behavioral consequences that exist in the current environment	Free will, choice, and innate drive toward self-actualization; search for personal meaning of existence	Thoughts, anticipations, planning, perceptions, attention, and memory processes	Social forces, including norms, social interactions, and group processes in one's culture and social environment	Genetic and evolutionary factors; brain and biochemical processes
Predominant focus and methods of discovery	Intensive observations of personality processes in clinical settings; some laboratory research	Study of learning processes in laboratory and real-world settings, with an emphasis on precise observation of stimuli and responses	Study of meaning, values, and purpose in life; study of self-concept and its role in thought, emotion, and behavior	Study of cognitive processes, usually under highly controlled laboratory conditions	Study of behavior and mental processes of people in different cultures; experiments examining people's responses to social stimuli	Study of brain-behavior relations; role of hormones and biochemical factors in behavior; behavior genetics research

environmental threats increased their chances of surviving and passing on their genes. At times, the psychological and physical ability to withdraw and conserve one's resources was undoubtedly the most adaptive defense against an environmental stressor, such as an unavoidable defeat or personal loss. Some evolutionary theorists view depression (and its accompanying disengagement and sense of hopelessness) as an exaggerated form of this normally adaptive, genetically based withdrawal process (Gilbert, 2001).

Moving to a psychological level of analysis, we find that depression is associated with a thinking style in which the person interprets events pessimistically (Seligman & Isaacowitz, 2000). Depressed people can find the black cloud that surrounds every silver lining. They tend to blame themselves for negative things that occur and take little credit for the good things that happen in their lives; they generally view the future as bleak and may have perfectionistic expectations that make them overly sensitive to how other people evaluate them (Bieling et al., 2004).

Are some personality patterns more prone to depression than others? Many psychodynamic theorists believe that severe losses, rejections, or traumas in childhood help create a personality style that causes people to overreact to setbacks, setting the stage for future depression. In support of this notion, studies show that depressed people are more likely than nondepressed people to have experienced parental rejection, sexual abuse, or the loss of a parent through death or separation during childhood (Bowlby, 2000a).

Finally, at the environmental level of analysis, behaviorists propose that depression is a reaction to a nonrewarding environment. A vicious cycle begins when the environment provides fewer rewards for the person. As depression intensifies, some people feel so badly that they stop doing things that ordinarily give them pleasure, which decreases environmental rewards still further. To make things worse, depressed people may complain a lot and seek excessive support from others. These behaviors eventually begin to alienate other people, causing them to shy away from the depressed person. The net result is a worsening environment with fewer rewards, reduced support from others, and hopeless pessimism (Lewinsohn et al., 1985; Nezlek et al., 2000).

Sociocultural factors also affect depression. As noted above, abusive family environments and other traumatic social experiences increase children's risk for depression later in life. Moreover, although depression is found in virtually all cultures, its symptoms, causes, and prevalence may reflect cultural differences (Kleinman, 2004). For reasons still unknown, in the United States, Canada, and other Western nations, women are about twice as likely as men to report feeling depressed; no such sex difference is found in developing countries (Culbertson, 1997).

Figure 1.23 organizes causal factors in depression into three classes: biological, psychological, and environmental. Keep in mind, however, that the specific causes of depression and the way in which they combine or interact may differ from case to case. **Interaction** *means that the way in*

LEVELS OF ANALYSIS   **Factors Related to Depression**

Biological
- Genetic predisposition, as shown in identical vs. fraternal twin rates
- Chemical factors within brain, influenced by antidepressant drugs
- Possible exaggerated form of adaptive withdrawal mechanism shaped by evolution

Psychological
- Negative thought patterns and distortions, which may trigger depression
- Pessimistic personality style
- Susceptibility to loss and rejection, possibly linked to early life experiences

Environmental
- Previous life experiences of loss, rejection, deprivation
- Current decreases in pleasurable experiences and/or increases in life stress
- Loss of social support due to own behaviors
- Cultural factors, including sex roles and cultural norms for reacting to negative events and expressing unhappiness

Depression

FIGURE 1.23

Levels of analysis: Factors related to depression.

which one factor influences behavior depends on the presence of another factor. For example, someone who experiences a minor setback in life may become depressed if she or he has a strong biological predisposition for depression. The same setback might barely faze a person with a weak biological predisposition for depression; only a catastrophic loss might cause this other person to become depressed. Thus the intensity of life stress and strength of biological predisposition would interact to influence behavior. Just as boiling water softens celery and hardens an egg, the same environment can affect two people differently.

SUMMARY OF MAJOR THEMES

Our excursion through psychology's major perspectives and levels of analysis reveals several principles that you will encounter repeatedly as we explore the realm of behavior:

- As a science, psychology is empirical. It favors direct observation over pure intuition or reasoning as a means of attaining knowledge about behavior.

- Although committed to studying behavior objectively, psychologists recognize that our personal experience of the world is subjective.

- Behavior is determined by multiple causal factors, including our biological endowment ("nature"), the environment and our past learning experiences ("nurture"), and psychological factors that include our thoughts and motives.

- Behavior is a means of adapting to environmental demands; capacities have evolved during each species' history because they facilitated adaptation and survival.

- Behavior and cognitive processes are affected by the social and cultural environments in which we develop and live.

► **Focus 14**
Discuss five major themes identified in this chapter.

Beneath the Surface   What Did You Expect?

We'd like you to reflect for a moment on a simple question: What have you learned thus far about psychology that differs from your initial expectations? We ask you this question because, up to now, we've focused on what psychology is. We would now like to point out what psychology *isn't*.

Perhaps like many of our own students you may have equated psychology with counseling or therapy. If so, then

you have already seen that psychology is much more. Many students do not expect psychologists to study brain processes and genetics; others are surprised at the overlap between psychology and disciplines such as sociology and anthropology.

Perhaps you did not expect the rich diversity of theoretical perspectives within psychology. You may have heard of
Continued

Sigmund Freud and psychoanalysis, or possibly of B. F. Skinner and behaviorism. Indeed, in popular cartoons, psychologists are often stereotyped as therapists who analyze patients lying on couches, or as researchers in white lab coats studying rats in a maze. Now you know that other major perspectives are important parts of psychology's past and present.

Given psychology's theoretical diversity, perhaps you did not expect how environmental, psychological, and biological factors intertwine to influence behavior. And, with regard to influencing behavior, we hasten to dispel the notion that psychology is about mind control. Psychology's goal is not to control people's minds in the sense that *control* means inducing people to think or do things against their will. Rather, psychologists conduct basic research to learn how people behave, think, and feel; many also apply that knowledge to promote positive changes for individuals, groups, and society as a whole.

We've observed that some students mistakenly expect psychology to be just plain common sense. After all, each of us has spent much of our lives interacting with other people,

and we all form notions about human behavior and why people act as they do. For many reasons (which we'll explore in later chapters), our common sense often misleads us. For example, we usually don't subject our commonsense notions to a careful test. Perhaps when you took the true-false test in Table 1.1 you found that some of your commonsense answers were not consistent with the scientific findings.

Finally, we have found that many students underestimate the amount of work required to succeed in this course and therefore mistakenly expect introductory psychology to be easy. However, because of the breadth of topics and the nature of the concepts and information covered in this course, you may find that it takes a lot more effort than you anticipated to gain a true understanding of the material.

In the coming chapters, you will read about many research findings that are likely to contradict your expectations and many popular misconceptions about behavior. We look forward to helping you explore our exciting and important branch of science.

IN REVIEW

- Factors that influence behavior can be organized into three broad levels of analysis. The biological level examines how brain processes, hormonal and genetic influences, and evolutionary adaptations underlie behavior. The psychological level focuses on mental processes and psychological motives and how they influence behavior. The environmental level examines physical and social stimuli, including cultural factors, that shape our behavior and thoughts.

- To understand behavior, we often move back and forth between these levels of analysis. For example, when as children we are first exposed to cultural norms, those norms reflect a characteristic of our environment. However, once we adopt norms as our own, they become a part of our worldview and now represent the psychological level of analysis.

- Biological, psychological, and environmental factors contribute to depression. These factors can also interact. A mild setback may trigger depression in a person who has a strong biological predisposition toward depression, whereas a person who has a weak biological predisposition may become depressed only after suffering a severe setback.

PSYCHOLOGY TODAY

▶ **Focus 15**
Describe some of psychology's major subfields and professional organizations.

To many people, when you say the word *psychologist*, the first image that comes to mind is that of a therapist. This is understandable, as a large

number of psychologists are indeed *clinical psychologists*, who diagnose and treat people with psychological problems in clinics, hospitals, and private practice. Yet many clinical psychologists also are scientists who conduct research on the causes of mental disorders and the effectiveness of various kinds of treatment. Moreover, there are many other types of psychologists who have no connection with therapy and instead work as basic or applied researchers.

A GLOBAL SCIENCE AND PROFESSION

As a science and profession, psychology today is more diversified and robust than ever before. Because of psychology's enormous breadth, no psychologist can be an expert on all aspects of behavior. As in other sciences, many areas of specialization have emerged. Table 1.4 describes some of psychology's major subfields, but realize that psychological research often cuts across subfields. For example, developmental, social, clinical, and physiological psychologists might all study the causes of antisocial behavior among children.

Modern psychology also is geographically, ethnically, and gender diversified. A century ago, psychological research was conducted almost entirely in Europe, North America, and Russia by White males. Today these regions remain scientific powerhouses, but you will find women and men from diverse backgrounds conducting psychological research and providing psychological services around the globe. Founded in 1951 to support psychology worldwide, the International Union of Psychological Science consists of major psychological organizations from 70 countries (IUPsyS, 2005). Moreover, across the world, college students are eagerly studying psychology. In the United States, psychology ranks among the top five disciplines in the number of undergraduate degrees and doctoral degrees awarded annually (National Center for Education Statistics, 2001).

The American Psychological Association (APA), founded in 1892, is the largest individual psychological association in the world. Its 150,000 members and 53 divisions represent not only the subfields shown in Table 1.4 but also areas that focus on psychology's relation to the arts, religion, the military, the environment, sports, social policy issues, the law, and the media (APA, 2005). The American Psychological Society (APS), a newer organization consisting primarily of researchers, has grown to 12,000 members in just two decades (APS, 2005). Both APA and APS have international members in dozens of countries.

A career in most of the subfields described in Table 1.4 requires a doctoral degree based on four to six years of training beyond the bachelor's degree. Graduate training includes broad exposure to knowledge in psychology, concentrated study in one or more subfields, and extensive training in research methods. In some areas, such as clinical, counseling, school, and industrial/organizational psychology, additional supervised practical experience in a hospital, clinic, school, or workplace setting is generally required. Please note, however, that psychologists who perform mental health services are not the same as psychiatrists. *Psychiatrists* are medical doctors who, after completing their general training in medicine, receive additional training in diagnosing and treating mental disorders.

Besides its fascinating subject matter, psychology attracts many people with its rich variety of career options. Figure 1.24 shows the major settings in which psychologists work. Many psychologists teach, engage in research, or apply psychological principles and techniques to help solve personal or social problems. For more information on careers in psychology, visit the Online Learning Center (OLC) that accompanies this book.

PSYCHOLOGY AND PUBLIC POLICY

Modern society faces a host of complex social problems. Psychology, as a science and profession, is poised to help solve them. Through basic research, psychologists provide fundamental knowledge about behavior. In applied research, they use this knowledge to design, implement,

TABLE 1.4	Major Specialty Areas within Psychology
Specialty	**Major Focus**
Animal behavior (comparative)	Study of nonhuman species in natural or laboratory environments; includes genetics, brain processes, social behavior, evolutionary processes
Behavioral neuroscience	Examination of brain and hormonal processes that underlie behavior; behavior genetics and evolutionary psychology are sometimes grouped under behavioral neuroscience
Clinical	Diagnosis and treatment of psychological disorders; research on causes of disorders and treatment effectiveness
Cognitive	Study of mental processes such as memory, problem solving, planning, consciousness, and language (psycholinguistics)
Counseling	Consultation with clients on issues of personal adjustment; vocational and career planning; interest and aptitude testing
Cultural/cross-cultural	Study of cultural transmission, psychological similarities and differences among people from different cultures
Developmental	Study of physical, mental, emotional, and social development across the entire life span
Educational	Study of psychological aspects of the educational process; curriculum and instructional research; teacher training
Experimental	Research (typically laboratory experiments, often with non-humans) on basic processes such as learning, perception, and motivation
Industrial/organizational	Examination of behavior in work settings; study of factors related to employee morale and performance; development of tests to select job applicants; development of machines and tasks to fit human capabilities
Personality	Study of individual differences in personality and their effects on behavior; development of personality tests
Social	Examination of how the social environment—the presence of other people—influences an individual's behavior, thoughts, and feelings
Quantitative	Measurement issues and data analysis; development of mathematical models of behavior

and assess intervention programs. Together, basic research and applied research are pillars for *evidence-based public policies* that affect the lives of millions of people.

Increasingly, psychologists are being called on to tackle social issues and shape public policy. Consider three of many examples:

- *Education:* From grade school through college, how can we best teach students? In 2002 psychologist Grover Whitehurst became the first director of the U.S. Institute for Education Sciences, a new research unit within the U.S. Department of Education. The Institute's goal is to transform education "into an evidence-based field in which decision makers routinely seek out the best available research and data before adopting programs or practices" (Institute of Education Sciences, 2005).

► **Focus 16**
How does psychology help shape public policy?

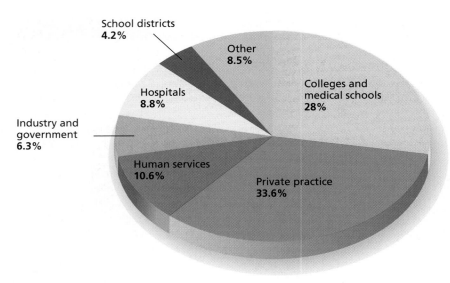

School districts
4.2%

Other
8.5%

Colleges and
medical schools
28%

Hospitals
8.8%

Industry and
government
6.3%

Human services
10.6%

Private practice
33.6%

FIGURE 1.24

Work settings of psychologists.
Source: Adapted from data in Table 4,
American Psychological Association
Research Office, 2001.

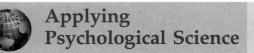

▶ **Focus 17**
Describe scientifically-based
strategies that can enhance
students' learning and academic
performance.

- *Violence prevention:* Based on decades of aggression research, the APA and other organizations are conducting a program to provide children with nonviolent role models and to improve the violence-prevention skills of teachers, parents, and other caregivers. Training sessions are held in local communities, and almost 170,000 antiviolence public-service announcements aired on television and radio nationwide within the program's first two years (Farberman, 2002).
- *Mental health:* When research indicated that college students needed greater access to on-campus mental health care, the APA

crafted the Campus Care and Counseling Act to help meet this need. Some provisions of this act were incorporated into legislation that was passed by the U.S. Congress in 2004.

Psychologists also influence national policy by helping politicians craft legislation dealing with a host of other social issues, from preventing AIDS and obesity to enhancing child care and homeland security. Moreover, their influence is not limited to the United States. School bullying, for example, is a serious problem in several countries. Norwegian psychologist Dan Olweus, a leading researcher on bullying, developed a prevention program that the Norwegian government makes available to all of its public schools (Olweus, 2004). Some American schools also have adopted it.

PSYCHOLOGY AND YOUR LIFE

We're biased, of course, but to us psychology is the most fascinating subject around, and we hope that some of this enthusiasm rubs off on you. We also hope that as you learn new concepts in your psychology course, you will reflect on how they relate to your own experiences. Psychological principles can not only help solve societal problems but also enhance your own life. For example, research by behavioral, cognitive, and educational psychologists on learning and memory provides guidelines that can improve your academic performance. To conclude this chapter, our first "Applying Psychological Science" feature describes some of these guidelines.

Applying Psychological Science   How to Enhance Your Academic Performance

College life presents many challenges, and working smart can be as important for meeting those challenges as working hard. The following strategies can help you increase your learning and academic performance (Figure 1.25).

EFFECTIVE TIME MANAGEMENT

If you efficiently allocate the time needed for study, you will have a clear conscience when it's time for recreational activities and relaxation. First, *develop a written schedule.* This forces you to decide how to allocate your time and increases your commitment to the plan. Begin by writing down your class meetings and other responsibilities. Then block in periods of study, avoiding times when you are likely to be tired.

Distribute study times throughout the week, and schedule some study times immediately before enjoyable activities, which you can use as rewards for studying.

Second, *prioritize your tasks* (Lakein, 1973). Most of us tend to procrastinate by working on simple tasks while putting off the toughest tasks until later. This can result in never getting to the major tasks (such as writing a term paper or studying for an exam) until too little time remains. Ask yourself, each day, "What is the most important thing to get done?" Do that task first, then move to the next most important task, and so on.

Third, *break large tasks into smaller parts* that can be completed at specific times (Catrambone, 1998). Important tasks often are too big to complete all at once, so break them down and define each part in terms of a specific but realistic goal

FIGURE 1.25

Improving academic performance. Academic performance-enhancement methods include strategies for managing time, studying more effectively, preparing for tests, and taking tests.

(e.g., number of pages to be read or amount of material to be studied). Successfully completing each goal is rewarding, strengthens your study skills, and increases your feelings of mastery.

STUDYING MORE EFFECTIVELY

After planning your study time, use that time effectively. *Choose a study place where there are no distractions and where you do nothing but study,* say, a quiet library rather than a busy cafeteria. In time, you will learn to associate that location with studying, and studying there will become even easier (Watson & Tharp, 1997).

How you study is vital to your academic success. Don't read material passively and hope that it will just soak in. Instead, *use an active approach to learning* (Glaser & Bassok, 1989). For example, when reading a textbook chapter, first look over the chapter outline, which will give you a good idea of the information you are going to be processing. As you read the material, think about how it applies to your life or how it relates to other information that you already know.

USE FOCUS QUESTIONS TO ENHANCE ACTIVE LEARNING

You can also increase active learning by using the focus questions that appear in the margins of this book. These questions call attention to major concepts and facts. Use them to help you anticipate key points before you read a section, and use them again after you have read each section to test your understanding of the material. This will require you to stop and think about the content. Research shows that responding to these types of questions promotes better recall (Moreland et al., 1997).

Realize that these questions focus on only a portion of the important material. We could have written more questions,

but just because some sections don't have focus questions doesn't mean that you can skip the material. In fact, you will learn even more if you supplement our questions with ones of your own—especially for sections that do not already have focus questions. Answering the focus questions and writing questions of your own will require more effort than passive reading does, but it will result in better learning (Estes & Vaughn, 1985; Hamilton, 1985).

PREPARING FOR TESTS

Contrary to what many students believe, introductory psychology is not an easy course. It covers a lot of diverse material, and many new concepts must be mastered. Many students who are new to college don't realize that the academic demands far exceed those of high school. Moreover, many students don't realize how hard high achievers actually work. In one study, researchers found that failing students spent only one third as many hours studying as did A-students (who studied about two hours for every hour spent in class). Yet the failing students *thought* they were studying as much as anyone else, and many wondered why they were not doing well (Watson & Tharp, 1997).

As we noted earlier, a written study schedule helps spread your test preparation over time and helps avoid last-minute cramming. Cramming is less effective because it is fatiguing, taxes your memory, and may increase test anxiety, which interferes with learning and test performance (Sarason & Sarason, 1990). Ideally, as the exam day nears, you should already understand the material. Then use the time before the test to refine your knowledge. Using the focus questions can pay big dividends in the final days before an exam.

TEST-TAKING STRATEGIES

Some students are more effective test takers than others. They know how to approach different types of tests (e.g., multiple choice or essay) to maximize their performance. Such skills are called *testwiseness* (Fagley, 1987). Here are some strategies that testwise students use:

- Use time wisely. Check your progress occasionally during the test. Answer the questions you know first (and, on essay exams, the ones worth the most points). Do not get bogged down on a question you find difficult. Mark it and come back to it later.

- On essay exams, outline the points you want to make before you begin writing, then cover the key points in enough detail to communicate what you know.

- On multiple-choice tests, read each question and try to answer it before reading the answer options. If you find your answer among the alternatives, that alternative is probably the correct one. Still, read all the other alternatives to make sure that you choose the best one.

Continued

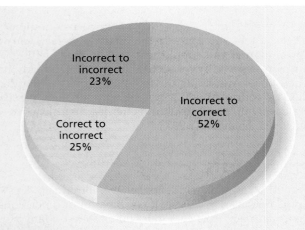

FIGURE 1.26

Changing answers on multiple-choice tests. Researchers analyzed the eraser marks on 6,412 exams taken by introductory psychology students. Contrary to popular wisdom, changing one's answer was twice as likely to result in gaining points rather than losing points. SOURCE: Based on Kruger et al., 2005.

- Many students believe that they should not change answers on multiple-choice tests because the first guess is most likely to be correct. Eighty years of research shows that this belief is false (Kruger et al., 2005). As Figure 1.26 shows, changing an answer is far more likely to result in a wrong answer becoming a correct one than vice versa. Don't be reluctant to change an answer if you are fairly sure that the alternative is better.

- Some multiple-choice questions have "all of the above" as an alternative. If one of the other answers is clearly incorrect, eliminate the "all of the above" option; if you are sure that at least two of the other answers are correct but are not sure about the third, choose "all of the above."

Time management, study skills, test-preparation strategies, and testwiseness are not acquired overnight; they require effort and practice. Look ahead to the "Applying Psychological Science" and "Research Close-Up" features in the following chapters; they discuss additional principles that can help you enhance your academic performance:

Chapter 6: modifying your study behavior (page 216)

Chapter 7: improving memory (page 269)

Chapter 8: solving problems creatively (page 300)

Chapter 8: recognizing whether you understand textbook material (page 306)

Chapter 12: setting goals (page 470)

IN REVIEW

- Psychologists today conduct research and provide services around the globe.

- Psychologists specialize in various subfields and work in many settings. They teach, conduct research, perform therapy and counseling, and apply psychological principles to solve personal and social problems.

- You can use principles derived from psychological science to enhance your learning and increase your likelihood of performing well on tests. These include time-management principles, strategies for studying more effectively, test-preparation strategies, and techniques for taking tests.

KEY TERMS AND CONCEPTS

Each term has been boldfaced and defined in the chapter on the page indicated in parentheses.

applied research (p. 3)
basic research (p. 3)
behavioral neuroscience (p. 16)
behavioral perspective (p. 10)
behavior genetics (p. 17)
behaviorism (p. 10)
biological perspective (p. 16)
British empiricism (p. 7)
cognitive behaviorism (p. 11)
cognitive neuroscience (p. 13)
cognitive perspective (p. 12)
cognitive psychology (p. 13)
collectivism (p. 15)

cultural psychology (p. 15)
culture (p. 14)
defense mechanisms (p. 9)
evolutionary psychology (p. 18)
functionalism (p. 8)
Gestalt psychology (p. 12)
humanistic perspective
  (humanism; p. 11)
individualism (p. 15)
interaction (p. 20)
mind-body dualism (p. 7)
monism (p. 7)
natural selection (p. 17)

neurotransmitters (p. 16)
norms (p. 14)
object relations theory (p. 9)
positive psychology movement (p. 12)
psychoanalysis (p. 9)
psychodynamic perspective (p. 8)
psychology (p. 2)
social constructivism (p. 13)
socialization (p. 14)
sociocultural perspective (p. 14)
structuralism (p. 8)

? What Do You Think?

THE CASE OF VOODOO DEATH (PAGE 7)

According to Cannon's hypothesis, the woman's belief in voodoo and knowledge that she had been "cursed" caused her to experience persistent, excessive stress. She became increasingly terrified as her 23rd birthday neared, and her stress response eventually triggered a fatal drop in blood pressure, producing shock and causing death.

Does this explanation seem reasonable to you? In forming your answer, one issue to consider is whether any good evidence supports Cannon's explanation. Cannon's research with animals suggested that a persistent, intense stress response could cause death in a way that would not be easily detectable upon autopsy, and more recent psychological and medical research points to negative effects that stress (caused by fear, worry, or other factors) can have on bodily functioning. However, we also need to consider other possible explanations for the woman's death.

First, in many cases, even ones that Cannon described, voodoo victims refuse all food and drink after they have been cursed, and prolonged severe dehydration may be the cause of death (Barber, 1961). However, in other documented cases, food and drink restriction can be ruled out. Had the woman in our example been severely dehydrated, it seems unlikely that the hospital medical staff would have failed to notice this.

Second, voodoo victims often seem to surrender psychologically; they feel helpless and hopeless, believing that there is no place to hide from impending death (Cohen, 1985). Some scientists argue that this hopelessness increases victims' susceptibility to disease, which then leads to death (Lester, 1972). Others propose that this hopelessness has a more direct effect, triggering bodily responses that eventually decrease one's heart rate and cause death (Richter, 1957). Realize that all of these explanations, although different from Cannon's, still illustrate mind-body interactions, and they support the general point that psychological beliefs can trigger responses that—one way or another—impair health.

Finally, even without the voodoo curse, perhaps the woman would have died that night anyway. Sudden death at such a young age is rare, and the timing would have been an amazing coincidence, but we can't completely rule out the possibility that the woman suffered from a life-threatening medical condition that the physicians did not detect.

In our opinion, Cannon's explanation seems plausible, but as a critical thinker, you should keep the bottom line in mind: We can't say for sure why the woman died. For obvious ethical reasons, researchers don't expose people to voodoo curses in controlled experiments to carefully examine whether and how they die! Instead, scientists obtain clues from natural cases of voodoo death and from research on stress and mind-body interactions and then try to formulate the most plausible explanation.

ARE THE STUDENTS LAZY? (PAGE 11)

It may be tempting to blame the students' unresponsiveness on laziness, but a radical behaviorist would not focus on internal mental states to explain their inaction. First, to say that students are unresponsive *because* they're lazy doesn't explain anything. Consider this reasoning: How do we know that the students are lazy? Answer: because they are unresponsive. Therefore, if we say that students are lazy because they're unresponsive and then turn around and conclude that students are unresponsive because they are lazy, all we are really saying is that "students are unresponsive because they are unresponsive." This is not an explanation at all but rather an example of circular reasoning.

From a behavioral perspective, people's actions are shaped by the environment and learning experiences. Put yourself in the hypothetical role of the high school teacher: You may not realize it, but when students sit quietly, you smile and seem more relaxed. When students participate in class discussions, you are quick to criticize their ideas. In these ways you may have taught your students to behave passively.

To change their behavior, you can modify their educational environment so that they will learn new responses. Reward behaviors that you want to see (raising hands, correctly answering questions, and so on). For example, praise students not only for giving correct answers but also for participating. If an answer is incorrect, point this out in a nonpunitive way while still reinforcing the student's participation.

Modifying the environment to change behavior is often not as easy as it sounds, but this example illustrates one way a behaviorist might try to rearrange the environmental consequences rather than jump to the conclusion that the situation is hopeless.

CHAPTER TWO

Studying Behavior Scientifically

> *I have no special talents. I am only passionately curious.*
>
> —ALBERT EINSTEIN

Winter was around the corner, and Teryl's Sunday-morning drive to Oregon City was about to take an unexpected twist. The pickup truck in front of her hit a slick spot, veered off the road, and went over the edge. Teryl, who has paralyzed legs and only partial use of her arms, stopped her minivan, lowered herself into her wheelchair, and headed to the crash site. She then got out of her wheelchair, slid down the wet embankment, crawled to reach the bleeding, dazed driver, and administered first aid until the paramedics arrived. Said Teryl, "I think anybody would have done that. You see a car go down a ditch, and I can't imagine not stopping to help" (*Seattle Times*, 1997). Yet three decades earlier, the unimaginable had indeed occurred.

■■■■■

In March of 1964, 28-year-old Kitty Genovese was stabbed repeatedly and raped by a knife-wielding assailant as she returned from work to her New York City apartment at about 3 A.M. The attack lasted about 30 minutes, during which time her screams and pleas for help were heard by at least 38 neighbors. Many went to their windows to find out what was happening. Yet nobody assisted her, and by the time anyone called the police, she had died. The incident drew international attention from a shocked public, and commentators expressed outrage over "bystander apathy" and people's refusal to "get involved."

Science frequently has all the mystery of a good detective story. Consider the psychological puzzle of bystander intervention. If you were in trouble and needed help from bystanders, would you receive it? Ordinary citizens like Teryl often act decisively to help someone in need (Figure 2.1). But, as the Kitty Genovese murder and similar tragedies illustrate, people do not always come to the aid of others. Why do bystanders sometimes risk injury and death to assist a stranger yet at other times fail to intervene—even when helping or calling the police entails little personal risk? We will return to this puzzle shortly.

In this chapter we explore principles and methods that form the foundation of psychological science. These principles also promote a way of thinking—critical thinking—that can serve you well in many aspects of your life.

SCIENTIFIC PRINCIPLES IN PSYCHOLOGY

Science is about discovery. At its core, science is an approach to asking and answering questions about the universe around us. Certainly, there are other ways we learn about our world and ourselves: through philosophy and reason; religion and spirituality; art, music, and literature; the teachings of family, friends, and others; and intuition and common sense. What distinguishes science from these approaches is a process guided by certain principles.

SCIENTIFIC ATTITUDES

Curiosity, skepticism, and open-mindedness are driving forces behind scientific inquiry. Like a child who constantly asks "Why?" the good scientist has an insatiable curiosity. And like a master detective, the good scientist is an incurable skeptic. Each claim is met with the reply, "Show me your evidence." Scientists also must remain open-minded to conclusions that are supported by facts, even if those conclusions refute their own beliefs.

Following the Kitty Genovese murder, two psychology professors in New York City, John Darley of New York University and Bibb Latané of Columbia University, met for dinner. They were so curious about how 38 people could witness a violent crime and not even call the police that they decided to investigate further. Darley and Latané also were skeptical of the "bystander apathy" explanation offered by the media; they believed it was unlikely that every

FIGURE 2.1

What determines whether a bystander will help a victim?

29

one of the 38 bystanders could have been apathetic. As social psychologists, they understood that the social environment powerfully influences behavior, even though people may be unaware of its influence. They noted that the bystanders could see that other neighbors had turned on their lights and were looking out their windows. Each bystander might have been concerned about Kitty Genovese's plight but assumed that someone else surely would help or call the police.

Darley and Latané reasoned that the presence of multiple bystanders produced a *diffusion of responsibility,* a psychological state in which each person feels decreased personal responsibility for intervening. They performed several experiments to test their explanation but had to remain open-minded to the possibility that the findings would not support their point of view.

GATHERING EVIDENCE: STEPS IN THE SCIENTIFIC PROCESS

Figure 2.2 shows how scientific inquiry often proceeds. Curiosity sparks the first step: Scientists observe something noteworthy and ask a question about it. Darley and Latané observed that nobody helped Kitty Genovese and then asked the question "Why?"

At the second step, scientists examine whether any studies, theories, and other information already exist that might help answer their question, and then they formulate a tentative explanation. Noting that many bystanders had been present and that each one probably knew that others were witnessing Genovese's plight, Darley and Latané combined these clues to arrive at a possible explanation: A diffusion of responsibility reduced the likelihood that any one bystander would feel responsible for helping. This tentative explanation is then translated into a **hypothesis,** *a specific prediction about some phenomenon* that often takes the form of an "If-Then" statement: "In an emergency, IF multiple bystanders are present, THEN the likelihood that any one bystander will intervene is reduced."

The third step is to test the hypothesis by conducting research. Darley and Latané (1968) staged an "emergency" in their laboratory and observed people's responses. Undergraduate participants were told that they would be discussing "personal problems faced by college students." They were also told that to ensure privacy, they would be in separate rooms and communicate through an intercom system and that the experimenter would not listen to their conversation. Partici-

STEPS IN THE SCIENTIFIC PROCESS

1. Initial Observation or Question

Kitty Genovese incident. Why did no one help?

2. Gather Information and Form Hypothesis

A diffusion of responsibility may have occurred. Hypothesis: IF multiple bystanders are present, THEN each bystander's likelihood of intervening will decrease.

3. Test Hypothesis (Conduct Research)

• Create "emergency" in controlled setting.
• Manipulate perceived number of bystanders.
• Measure helping.

4. Analyze Data and Draw Tentative Conclusion

Helping decreases as the perceived number of bystanders increases. The hypothesis is supported. (If data do not support the hypothesis, revise and retest.)

5. Report Findings to Scientific Community

Researchers submit report to a scientific journal. If expert reviewers favorably evaluate the study, it is published. Fellow scientists learn about the research and may challenge, support, or expand on it.

6. Further Research and Theory Building

Additional studies support the hypothesis. A Theory of Social Impact is developed based on these and other findings.

7. New Hypotheses Derived from Theory

The theory is tested directly by deriving new hypotheses and conducting new research.

FIGURE 2.2

The scientific process. This sequence represents one common path to scientific understanding. In other cases, scientists begin with an observation or question, gather background information, and proceed directly to research without testing hypotheses or trying to build theories.

pants understood that they would take turns speaking for several rounds. In each round, a participant would have 2 minutes to speak, during which time the others would be unable to interrupt or be heard, because their microphones would be turned off.

As the discussion began over the intercom, a speaker described his difficulties adjusting to college life and disclosed that he suffered from seizures. During the next round of conversation, this same speaker began to gasp and stammer, saying: "'. . . Could somebody-er-er—help . . . [choking sounds] . . . I'm gonna die-er-er—I'm

FIGURE 2.3

Helping in an emergency. Participants who believed that they were the only bystander who could hear a seizure victim's plea for help were more likely to take action than were participants who believed that either one or four additional bystanders were listening. SOURCE: Data from Darley & Latané, 1968.

gonna die-er—help . . . seizure' [chokes, then silence]" (Darley & Latané, 1968, p. 379).

Unbeknownst to the participants, they were actually listening to a tape recording. This ensured that all of them were exposed to the identical "emergency." To test how the number of bystanders influences helping, Darley and Latané manipulated the number of other people that each participant believed to be present and listening over the intercom. Participants were assigned to one of three conditions on a random basis. Each participant actually was alone but was led to believe that (1) they were alone with the victim, (2) there was another listener present, or (3) there were four other listeners present. Participants believed that the seizure was real and serious. But did they help?

At the fourth step of scientific inquiry, researchers analyze the information (called *data*) they collect and draw tentative conclusions. As Figure 2.3 shows, Darley and Latané found that all participants who thought they were alone with the victim helped within 3 minutes of the seizure. As the number of presumed bystanders increased, the proportion of actual participants who helped decreased, and those who helped took longer to respond. These findings support the diffusion-of-responsibility explanation and illustrate how research can contradict commonsense adages such as "There's safety in numbers." As you will see throughout this book, many commonsense beliefs have not survived the cutting edge of psychological research.

At the fifth step, scientists communicate their findings to the scientific community. Using the same general format that you see in our "Research Close-Up" features, Darley and Latané submitted an article describing their research to a scientific journal. Expert reviewers favorably evaluated the quality and importance of their bystander research, so the journal published the article. Scientists may also present their research at professional conferences and in books. Disseminating research is essential to scientific progress. It allows fellow scientists to learn about new ideas and findings, to scrutinize the research, and to challenge or expand on it.

At the sixth step, scientists conduct more research. As additional evidence comes in, scientists attempt to build theories. A **theory** *is a set of formal statements that explains how and why certain events are related to one another.* Theories are broader than hypotheses. For example, dozens of experiments revealed that diffusion of responsibility occurred across a range of situations. Latané then combined the principle of diffusion of responsibility with other principles of group behavior to develop a broader *theory of social impact,* which he and others have since used to explain a variety of human social behaviors (Latané & Bourgeois, 2001).

Finally, at the seventh step, scientists use the theory to develop new hypotheses, which are then tested by conducting additional research and gathering new evidence. In this manner the scientific process becomes self-correcting. If research consistently supports the hypotheses derived from the theory, confidence in the theory becomes stronger. If the predictions made by the theory are not supported, then it will need to be modified or, ultimately, discarded.

TWO APPROACHES TO UNDERSTANDING BEHAVIOR

Humans have a strong desire to understand why things happen. Why do scientists favor the preceding step-by-step approach to understanding behavior over the approach typically involved in everyday commonsense: hindsight?

Hindsight (After-the-Fact Understanding)

Many people erroneously believe that psychology is nothing more than common sense. "I knew that all along!" or "They had to do a study to find that out?" are common responses to some psychological research. For example, decades ago a *New York Times* book reviewer criticized a report titled *The American Soldier* (Stouffer et al., 1949a, 1949b), which summarized the results of a study of the attitudes and behavior of U.S. soldiers during

▶ **Focus 3**
Explain the major drawback of hindsight understanding. What approach to understanding do scientists prefer? Why?

World War II. The reviewer blasted the government for spending a lot of money to "tell us nothing we don't already know."

Consider the following statements. How would you account for each of them?

1. Compared to White soldiers, Black soldiers were less motivated to become officers.

2. During basic training, soldiers from rural areas had higher morale and adapted better than soldiers from large cities.

3. Soldiers in Europe were more motivated to return home while the fighting was going on than they were after the war ended.

You should have no difficulty explaining these results. Typical reasoning might go something like this: (1) Due to widespread prejudice, Black soldiers knew that they had little chance of becoming officers. Why should they torment themselves wanting something that was unattainable? (2) It's obvious that the rigors of basic training would seem easier to people from farm settings, who were used to hard work and rising at the crack of dawn. (3) Any sane person would have wanted to go home while bullets were flying and people were dying.

Did your explanations resemble these? If so, they are perfectly reasonable. There is one catch, however. The results of the actual study were the *opposite* of the preceding statements. In fact, Black soldiers were more motivated than White soldiers to become officers, city boys had higher morale than farm boys during basic training, and soldiers were more eager to return home after the war ended than during the fighting. When told these actual results, our students quickly find explanations for them. In short, it is easy to arrive at reasonable after-the-fact explanations for almost any result.

In everyday life, *hindsight* (after-the-fact explanation) is probably our most common method of trying to understand behavior. The Danish philosopher Søren Kierkegaard noted, "Life is lived forwards, but understood backwards." The major limitation of relying solely on hindsight is that past events usually can be explained in many ways, and there is no sure way to know which—if any—of the explanations is correct. Despite this drawback, after-the-fact understanding can provide insights and is often the foundation on which further scientific inquiry is built. For example, Darley and Latané's diffusion-of-responsibility explanation was initially based on after-the-fact reasoning about the Kitty Genovese murder.

▶ **Focus 4**
Describe some characteristics of a good theory.

Understanding through Prediction, Control, and Theory Building

Whenever possible, scientists prefer to test their understanding of "what causes what" more directly. If we truly understand the causes of a given behavior, then we should be able to predict the conditions under which that behavior will occur in the future. Furthermore, if we can control those conditions (e.g., in the laboratory), then we should be able to produce that behavior.

Darley and Latané's research illustrates this approach. They predicted that due to a diffusion of responsibility, the presence of multiple bystanders during an emergency would reduce individual helping. Next, they carefully staged an emergency and controlled participants' beliefs about the number of bystanders present. Their prediction was supported. Understanding through prediction and control is a scientific alternative to after-the-fact understanding.

Theory building is the strongest test of scientific understanding, because good theories generate an integrated network of predictions. A good theory has several important characteristics.

- It incorporates existing knowledge within a broad framework; that is, it organizes information in a meaningful way.

- It is testable. It generates new hypotheses whose accuracy can be evaluated by gathering new evidence (Figure 2.4).

- The predictions made by the theory are supported by the findings of new research.

- It conforms to the *law of parsimony:* If two theories can explain and predict the same phenomenon equally well, the simpler theory is the preferred one.

Even when a theory is supported by many successful predictions, it is never regarded as an absolute truth. It is always possible that some future observation will contradict it or that a newer and more accurate theory will take its place. The displacement of old beliefs and theories by newer ones is the essence of scientific progress.

Finally, although scientists use prediction as a test of "understanding," this does not mean that prediction requires understanding. Based on experience, even a child can predict that thunder will follow lightning without knowing why it does so. But prediction based on understanding (i.e., theory building) has advantages: It satisfies our curiosity and generates principles that can be applied to new situations that we have not yet directly experienced.

"IT MAY VERY WELL BRING ABOUT IMMORTALITY, BUT IT WILL TAKE FOREVER TO TEST IT."

FIGURE 2.4

Is the scientist's claim of discovering an eternal life potion a testable hypothesis? Yes, because it is possible to show the hypothesis to be false. If people drink it but still die at some point, then we have refuted the hypothesis. Therefore it is testable. It is, however, impossible to absolutely prove true. If a person drinks the potion, then no matter how long she or he lives—even a million years—she or he might die the next day. Thus we cannot prove that the potion can make you live forever. Copyright © 2004 by Sidney Harris. ScienceCartoonsPlus.com. Reprinted with permission.

DEFINING AND MEASURING VARIABLES

Psychologists study variables and the relations among them. A **variable,** quite simply, *is any characteristic or factor that can vary.* Gender is a variable: Some people are female, others male. People's age, grade point average, and typing speed are variables, as are concepts such as intelligence and stress. There were three major variables in Darley and Latané's bystander experiment: (1) the number of other bystanders that the real participants thought were present, (2) whether a participant helped the victim or not, and (3) for those who helped, how many seconds passed before they responded.

Because any variable (such as stress) may mean different things to different people, scientists must define their terms clearly. When conducting research, scientists do this by defining variables operationally. An **operational definition** *defines a variable in terms of the specific procedures used to produce or measure it.* Operational definitions translate abstract terms into something observable and measurable.

For example, suppose we want to study the relation between stress and academic performance among college students. How shall we operationally define our concepts? "Academic performance" could mean a single test score, a course grade, or one's overall grade point average. So, for our study, let's define it as students' final exam scores in an introductory chemistry course. As for "stress," before or during the exam we could measure students' levels of muscle tension or stress hormones, or ask them to report how worried they feel. During the test we might observe their frequency of nail biting. We also could define stress in terms of environmental conditions, such as whether the exam questions and grading scale are easy or difficult. Figure 2.5 summarizes how we might operationally define exam stress at the biological, psychological, and environmental levels.

► **Focus 5**
Why are operational definitions important? Identify four major ways to measure behavior and explain a limitation of each one.

FIGURE 2.5

Levels of analysis: Measuring exam stress.

LEVELS OF ANALYSIS   Measuring Exam Stress

Biological	Psychological	Environmental
• Stress-hormone levels measured at rest and during an exam • Measures of heart rate and respiration rate • Physiological measures of muscle tension and sweating	• General achievement anxiety measured by self-report personality test • Preexam questionnaire ratings of worry, tension, and anxiety • Behavioral observations of "nervous habits" during exam (e.g., fingernail biting, foot wiggling, hair pulling)	• Aspects of immediate environment that create stress (e.g., difficulty of exam, time pressure, noise and heat levels) • Easy or difficult course grading standards set by instructor • Achievement expectations set by parents or instructor

Exam Stress

(a)

(b)

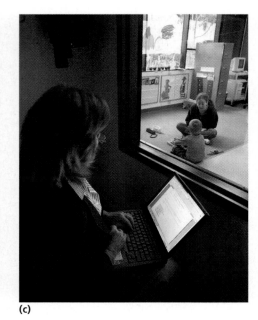

(c)

FIGURE 2.6

(a) Self-report, (b) physiological, and (c) behavioral measures are important scientific tools for psychologists.

To define a concept operationally, we must be able to measure it. Measurement is challenging because psychologists study incredibly varied and complex processes. Some processes are directly observable, but others are not. Fortunately, psychologists have numerous measurement techniques at their disposal (Figure 2.6).

Self-Reports and Reports by Others

Self-report measures ask people to report on their own knowledge, attitudes, feelings, experiences, or behavior. This information can be gathered in several ways, such as through interviews or questionnaires. The accuracy of self-reports hinges on people's ability and willingness to respond honestly. Especially when questions focus on sensitive topics, such as sexual habits or drug use, self-reports may be distorted by *social desirability bias,* the tendency to respond in a socially acceptable manner rather than according to how one truly feels or behaves. Researchers try to minimize this bias by establishing rapport with participants and allowing them to respond confidentially or anonymously. Questionnaires can also be designed to reduce social desirability bias.

We also can get information about someone's behavior by obtaining *reports made by other people,* such as parents, spouses, and teachers who know the person. College students might be asked to rate their roommates' personality traits, and job supervisors might be asked to rate a worker's competence. As with self-reports, researchers try to maximize participants' honesty in reporting about other people.

Observations of Behavior

Another measurement approach is to *observe and record overt (i.e., directly visible) behavior.* In an animal learning experiment, we might measure how often a rat follows the correct path in a maze. In Darley and Latané's (1968) bystander emergency experiment, they recorded whether college students helped a seizure victim. Psychologists also develop *coding systems* to record different categories of behavior. If we observe how a parent behaves while a child performs a task, we might code each instance of parental behavior into categories such as "praises child," "assists child," "criticizes child," and so forth. Once a coding system is developed, observers are trained to use it properly so that their measurements will be *reliable* (i.e., consistent). If two observers watching the same behaviors repeatedly disagree in their coding (e.g., one says the parent "praised" and another says the parent "assisted"), then the data are unreliable and of little use.

Humans and other animals may behave differently when they know they are being observed. To counter this problem, researchers may camouflage themselves or use **unobtrusive measures,** *which record behavior in a way that keeps participants unaware that they are being observed.* For example, scientists from the Centers for Disease Control assessed the effects of a "safer sex" program by counting the number of used condoms that turned up in a Baltimore sewage treatment plant before and after the program was begun. (We never said that science is always glamorous.)

Psychologists also gather information about behavior by using **archival measures,** *which are records or documents that already exist.* For example, researchers assessing a program to reduce drunk driving could examine police records to measure how many people were arrested for driving while intoxicated before and after the program was implemented.

Psychological Tests

Psychologists develop and use specialized tests to measure many types of variables. For example, *personality tests,* which assess people's personality traits, often contain series of questions that ask how a person typically feels or behaves (e.g., "True or False: I prefer to be alone rather than in social gatherings."). In essence, such tests are specialized self-reports. Other personality tests present a series of ambiguous stimuli (e.g., pictures that could have different meanings), and personality traits are judged based on how a person interprets these stimuli.

Other psychological tests consist of performance tasks. For example, *intelligence tests* may ask people to assemble objects or solve arithmetic problems. *Neuropsychological tests* help diagnose normal and abnormal brain functioning by measuring how well people perform mental and physical tasks, such as recalling lists of words or manipulating objects (Holtzer et al., 2005). As you will learn in Chapter 9, developing a good psychological test takes a tremendous amount of technical work.

Physiological Measures

Although psychologists use self-reports to measure people's subjective experiences, they also record physiological responses to assess what people are experiencing. Measures of heart rate, blood pressure, respiration rate, hormonal secretions, and electrical and biochemical processes in the brain have long been the mainstay of researchers working within the biological perspective, but these measures have become increasingly important in many other areas of psychology.

Physiological responses can have their own interpretive problems, the main one being that we don't always understand what they mean. For example, if a person shows increased heart rate and brain activity in a particular situation, what emotion or thought is being expressed? The links between specific patterns of physiological activity and particular mental events are far from being completely understood.

In sum, psychologists can measure behavior in many ways, each with advantages and disadvantages. To gain greater confidence in their findings, researchers may use several types of measures within a single study.

IN REVIEW

■ Curiosity, skepticism, and open-mindedness are key scientific attitudes. The scientific process proceeds through several steps: (1) asking questions based on some type of observation, (2) formulating a tentative explanation and a testable hypothesis, (3) conducting research to test the hypothesis, (4) analyzing the data and drawing a tentative conclusion, (5) reporting one's findings to the scientific community, (6) building a theory, and (7) using the theory to generate new hypotheses, which are tested by more research.

■ In everyday life we typically use hindsight to explain behavior. Hindsight is flawed because there may be many possible explanations and no way to assess which is correct. Psychologists prefer to test their understanding through prediction, control, and theory building.

■ A good theory organizes known facts, gives rise to additional hypotheses that are testable, is supported by the findings of new research, and is parsimonious.

■ An operational definition defines a concept or variable in terms of the specific procedures used to produce or measure it.

■ To measure behavior, psychologists obtain people's self-reports and reports from others who know the participants, directly observe behavior, use unobtrusive measures, analyze archival data, administer psychological tests, and measure physiological responses.

ETHICAL PRINCIPLES IN RESEARCH

When conducting research, scientists must weigh the knowledge and possible applications to be gained against potential risks to research participants. To safeguard the rights of participants,

FIGURE 2.7

Ethical standards are designed to protect the welfare of both humans and nonhumans in psychological research.

▶ **Focus 6**
Identify major ethical issues in human and animal research.

researchers must adhere to ethical standards set by government regulations and national psychological organizations (Figure 2.7). Animal subjects must also be treated in accord with established ethical guidelines. At academic and research institutions, special committees review the ethical issues involved in research proposals. If a proposed study is considered ethically questionable, it must be modified or the research cannot be conducted.

The *Ethics Code* of the American Psychological Association (APA) was first published in 1953. The current code (APA, 2002) also builds on work by international and national commissions charged with developing ethical guidelines for biomedical and behavioral research. The APA code sets forth five broad ethical principles that represent ideals toward which psychologists should strive in their professional roles, including their role as researchers. These principles include:

- *Beneficence:* seeking to benefit other people
- *Responsibility:* performing professional duties with utmost care
- *Integrity:* being honest and accurate
- *Justice:* enhancing all people's access to the benefits of psychological knowledge
- *Respect:* respecting people's dignity and rights to confidentiality and self-determination (APA, 2002)

ETHICAL STANDARDS IN HUMAN RESEARCH

The APA's *Ethics Code* also provides dozens of specific guidelines for psychological activities,

including research. According to the ethical standard of **informed consent,** *before people agree to participate in research they should be informed about:*

- *the study's purpose and procedures;*
- *the study's potential benefits;*
- *potential risks to participants;*
- *the right to decline participation and withdraw at any time without penalty;*
- *whether responses will be confidential and, if not, how privacy will be safeguarded.*

When children, seriously disturbed mental patients, or other people who cannot give true informed consent are involved, consent must be obtained from their parents or guardians. To safeguard a participant's right to privacy, researchers typically gather and report data in ways that keep participants' identity anonymous or confidential.

Deception, which occurs when participants are misled about the nature of a study, is controversial. Consider the Darley and Latané (1968) bystander experiment. Participants were not told that the study was going to examine how they would respond to an emergency, nor were they informed that the procedure (someone presumably having a seizure) might cause them stress.

Deception violates the principle of informed consent, but its proponents argue that when studying certain types of behaviors, deception is the only way to obtain natural, spontaneous responses from participants. Darley and Latané's participants, for example, had to believe that the emergency was significant and real.

Guidelines currently permit deception only when no other feasible alternative is available and the study has scientific, educational, or applied benefits that clearly outweigh the ethical costs of deceiving participants. When deception is used, the true purpose of the study should be explained to participants after it is over. The overwhelming majority of psychological studies do not involve deception.

ETHICAL STANDARDS IN ANIMAL RESEARCH

According to the APA's Committee on Animal Research and Ethics (CARE, 2005), animals are subjects in perhaps 7 to 8 percent of psychological studies. This includes research done in the wild and in more controlled settings. Rodents and birds comprise 90 percent of the animals studied; nonhuman primates comprise another 5 percent.

Some psychologists study animals to discover principles that shed light on human behavior, and some do so to learn more about other species. National surveys find that the vast majority of psychologists and college psychology majors believe that animal research is necessary for scientific progress in psychology (Plous, 1996a, 1996b). As in medical research, however, some studies expose animals to conditions considered too hazardous for humans.

APA and federal government guidelines require that animals be treated humanely and that the potential importance of the research clearly justify the risks to which they are exposed. This determination, however, is not always easy to make, and people of good will can disagree. For example, should researchers be allowed to inject a drug into an animal in order to learn whether that drug might permanently impair memory? Before animal research can be conducted, it must be reviewed and approved by panels that often include nonscientists.

Animal research is debated both outside and within the psychological community (Herzog, 2005). Psychologists agree that it is morally wrong to subject animals to needless suffering. Many scientists, however, do not agree with the former head of the American Anti-Vivisection Society who maintained that animals should never be used in research "which is not for the benefit of the animals involved" (Goodman, 1982, p. 61). Proponents point to numerous important medical and psychological advances made possible by animal research. For example, had Louis Pasteur not subjected some dogs to suffering, he could not have developed the rabies vaccine, which has saved the lives of count-

less humans as well as animals. They ask, "Does the prospect of finding a cure for cancer or of identifying harmful drug effects or the causes of psychological disorders justify exposing some animals to harm?"

Proponents also point to examples of how animal research has benefited animals themselves. For example, using learning principles discovered in studies with dogs, researchers have changed the behavior of coyotes, bears, and other wild animals that were endangering humans or livestock, thereby sparing those wild animals from being shot and killed (Gustavson & Gustavson, 1985).

Although animal research has declined slightly in recent decades, the ethical questions remain as vexing as ever. What is most encouraging is that the welfare of animals in research is receiving the careful attention it deserves.

IN REVIEW

- Psychological research follows extensive ethical guidelines. In human research, key issues are the use of informed consent, the participants' right to privacy, potential risks to participants, and the use of deception.

- Ethical guidelines require that animals be treated humanely and that the risks to which they are exposed be justified by the potential importance of the research. As in human research, before animal research can be conducted it must be reviewed and approved, often by ethics review boards that include nonscientists.

METHODS OF RESEARCH

Like detectives searching for clues to solve a case, psychologists conduct research to gather evidence about behavior and its causes. The research method chosen depends on the problem being studied, the investigator's objectives, and ethical principles.

DESCRIPTIVE RESEARCH: RECORDING EVENTS

The most basic goal of science is to describe phenomena. In psychology, **descriptive research** *seeks to identify how humans and other animals behave, particularly in natural settings.* It provides valuable information about the diversity of behavior, can be

▶ **Focus 7**
Discuss three types of descriptive research, and explain the advantages and disadvantages of each.

used to test hypotheses, and may yield clues about potential cause-effect relations that are later tested experimentally. Case studies, naturalistic observation, and surveys are common descriptive methods.

Case Studies: The Hmong Sudden Death Syndrome

A **case study** *is an in-depth analysis of an individual, group, or event.* By studying a single case in great detail, the researcher typically hopes to discover principles of behavior that hold true for people or situations in general. Data may be gathered through observation, interviews, psychological tests, physiological recordings, or task performance.

One advantage of a case study is that when a rare phenomenon occurs, this method enables scientists to study it closely. A second advantage is that a case study may challenge the validity of a theory or widely held scientific belief. Perhaps the biggest advantage of a case study is that it can be a vibrant source of new ideas that may subsequently be examined using other research methods. Consider the following example.

Vang is a former Hmong (Laotian) soldier who resettled in Chicago in 1980 after escaping the ravages of war in Laos. Vang had traumatic memories of wartime destruction and severe guilt about leaving his brothers and sisters behind when he fled with his wife and child (Figure 2.8). The culture shock created by moving from rural Laos to urban Chicago increased Vang's stress. According to a mental health team, Vang experienced problems almost immediately:

> [He] could not sleep the first night in the apartment, nor the second, nor the third. After three days . . . Vang came to see his resettlement worker . . . Moua Lee. Vang told Moua that the first night he woke suddenly, short of breath, from a dream in which a cat was sitting on his chest. The second night . . . a figure, like a large black dog, came to his bed and sat on his chest . . . and he grew quickly and dangerously short of breath. The third night, a tall, white-skinned female spirit came into his bedroom . . . and lay on top of him. Her weight made it increasingly difficult for him to breathe. . . . After 15 minutes, the spirit left him and he awoke, screaming. (Tobin & Friedman, 1983, p. 440)

Vang's report attracted scientific interest because about 25 Laotian refugees in the United States had died of what was termed the "Hmong sudden death syndrome." The cases were similar to Vang's: A healthy person died in his or her

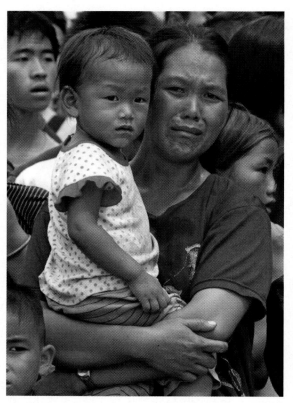

FIGURE 2.8

Many Hmong refugees who escaped the ravages of war in their homeland experienced great stress and guilt when they resettled in North America. This stress, combined with cultural beliefs about angry spirits, may have contributed to the Hmong sudden death syndrome, which eventually claimed more than 40 lives.

sleep after exhibiting labored breathing, screaming, and frantic movements. The U.S. Centers for Disease Control investigated these deaths and, unable to find a physical cause, concluded that the deaths were triggered by a combination of the stress of resettlement, guilt over abandoning family in Laos, and the Hmong's cultural beliefs about angry spirits.

The authors of Vang's case study concluded that he might have been a survivor of the sudden death syndrome. The role of cultural beliefs is suggested by what happened next. Vang went for treatment to a Hmong woman regarded as a shaman (a person, acting as both doctor and priest, who is believed to work with spirits and the supernatural). She told him his problems were caused by unhappy spirits and performed ceremonies to release the spirits. Vang's nightmares and breathing problems during sleep ceased.

Vang's case study—like the case of "voodoo death" described in Chapter 1—suggests that cultural beliefs and stress may profoundly influence physical well-being. This work was followed by other studies of Hmong immigrants and stimulated interest in the relation between cultural beliefs and health (Miller & Rasco, 2004).

The major limitation of a case study is that it is a poor method for determining cause-effect relations. In most case studies, explanations of behavior occur after the fact and there is little opportunity to rule out alternative explanations. The fact that Vang's symptoms ended after seeing a shaman might not have had anything to do with his cultural beliefs; it could have been pure coincidence, or other changes in Vang's life could have been responsible.

A second potential drawback concerns the *generalizability* of the findings: Will the principles uncovered in a case study hold true for other people or in other situations? The question of generalizability pertains to all research methods, but drawing broad conclusions from a case study can be particularly risky. The key issue is the degree to which the case under study is representative of other people or situations.

A third drawback is the possible lack of objectivity in the way data are gathered and interpreted. Such bias can occur in any type of research, but case studies can be particularly worrisome because they are often based largely on the researcher's subjective impressions. In science, a skeptical attitude requires that claims based on case studies be followed up by more comprehensive research methods before they are accepted. In everyday life we should adopt a similar skeptical view. When you encounter claims based on case examples or anecdotes, keep in mind that the case may be atypical or that the person making the claim may be biased. Try to seek out other evidence to support or refute the claim.

Naturalistic Observation: Chimpanzees, Tool Use, and Cultural Learning

In **naturalistic observation,** *the researcher observes behavior as it occurs in a natural setting.* Naturalistic observation is used extensively to study animal behavior (Figure 2.9). British researcher Jane Goodall gained fame for her observations of African chimpanzees in the wild. Goodall (1986) and other researchers found that chimpanzees display behaviors, such as making and using tools, that were formerly believed to lie only within the human domain.

Swiss researcher Christophe Boesch (1991) has observed a "hammer/anvil" tool-use technique among wild African chimpanzees. A chimp places a nut on a hard surface (the anvil) and then hammers it several times with a stone or a fallen

FIGURE 2.9

Researcher Jane Goodall uses naturalistic observation to study the behavior of wild chimpanzees.

branch until it cracks. Some nuts with hard shells are tricky to open, and it may take several years for chimps to perfect their hammering. Especially fascinating is Boesch's observation that mothers seem to intentionally teach their young how to use this technique. Consider this interaction between a chimp named Ricci and her 5-year-old daughter, Nina:

> Nina . . . tried to open nuts with the only available hammer, which was of an irregular shape. As she struggled unsuccessfully . . . Ricci joined her and Nina immediately gave her the hammer. . . . Ricci, in a very deliberate manner, slowly rotated the hammer into the best position with which to pound the nut effectively. . . . With Nina watching her, she then proceeded to use the hammer to crack 10 nuts . . . then Ricci left and Nina resumed cracking. Now, by adopting the same hammer grip as her mother, she succeeded in opening four nuts in 15 min. . . . In this example the mother corrected an error in her daughter's behaviour. (Boesch, 1991, p. 532)

For evolutionary and cultural psychologists, such naturalistic observations can provide clues about the possible origins of human behavior. As in human cultures, these chimpanzees developed a method for using tools and appeared to teach it to their young. These findings support the view that the mechanisms by which human cultures are formed—such as the intentional transmission of information across generations—may have an evolutionary basis (McGrew, 2002).

The excerpt about Ricci and Nina illustrates how naturalistic observation can provide a rich description of behavior. Numerical data, such as the frequency of various behaviors, may be recorded and analyzed. Naturalistic observation is also used to study human behavior. For example, developmental psychologists observe children in

FIGURE 2.10

Surveys and sampling. A representative sample possesses the important characteristics of the population in the same proportions. Data from a representative sample are more likely to generalize to the larger population than are data from an unrepresentative sample.

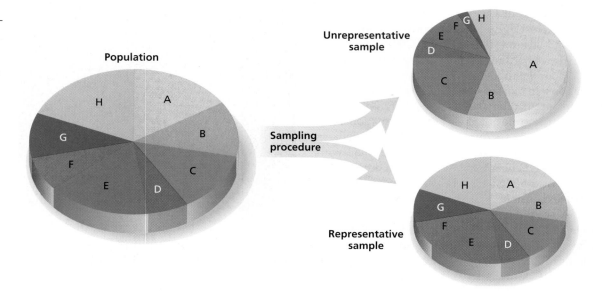

Population

Sampling procedure

Unrepresentative sample

Representative sample

► Focus 8
What is random sampling and why do survey researchers use it? What problems can occur when conducting surveys?

natural settings to learn about their cooperative play, aggression, and friendships.

Like case studies, naturalistic observation does not permit clear conclusions about the causal relations between variables. In the real world, many variables simultaneously influence behavior, and they cannot be disentangled with this research technique. There also is the possibility of bias in the way that researchers interpret the behaviors they observe. Finally, observers must try to avoid influencing the participants being studied. Even the mere presence of a human observer may disrupt a person's or animal's behavior, at least initially. As time passes, people and other animals typically adapt to and ignore the presence of an observer. This adaptation process is called *habituation*.

Survey Research: How Well Do You Sleep?

In **survey research,** *information about a topic is obtained by administering questionnaires or interviews to many people.* Surveys typically ask about participants' attitudes, opinions, and behaviors. For example, do you ever have difficulty falling or staying asleep? Are you ever so sleepy during the day that it interferes with your activities? The National Sleep Foundation (2002) conducted a nationwide survey of American adults' sleep problems. Almost 60 percent of the participants reported experiencing symptoms of insomnia a few nights or more per week, and 37 percent reported that daytime sleepiness interfered with their daily activities at least a few times a month. This survey studied 1,010 Americans, ages 18 and older, who were interviewed by telephone. How is it possible to make an accurate estimate of the

sleep problems of almost 200 million adults based on these data?

Two key concepts in survey research are population and sample. A **population** *consists of all the individuals that we are interested in drawing a conclusion about,* such as "American adults" in the sleep survey example. Because it is often impractical to study the entire population, we would administer the survey to a **sample,** *which is a subset of individuals drawn from the larger population.*

To draw valid conclusions about a population from the results of a single survey, the sample must be representative: A **representative sample** *is one that reflects the important characteristics of the population* (Figure 2.10). A sample composed of 80 percent males would not be representative of the student body at a college where only 50 percent of the students are men. To obtain a representative sample, survey researchers typically use a procedure called **random sampling,** *in which every member of the population has an equal probability of being chosen to participate in the survey.* A common variation of this procedure, called *stratified random sampling,* is to divide the population into subgroups based on characteristics such as gender or ethnic identity. Suppose the population is 55 percent female. In this case, 55 percent of the spaces in the sample would be allocated to women and 45 percent to men. Random sampling is then used to select the individual women and men who will be in the survey.

When a representative sample is surveyed, we can be confident (though never completely certain) that the findings closely portray the population as a whole. This is the strongest advantage of survey research. Modern political opinion polls typically use such excellent sampling procedures that, just prior to elections, they can reasonably predict from a sample of about 1,000 people who will win or—as we saw in the 2004 U.S. presidential election—whether a race is too close to call.

In contrast, unrepresentative samples can produce distorted results. It is better to have a smaller representative sample than a larger, unrepresentative one. In 1936, a mail survey of almost 2 million voters by *Literary Digest* magazine predicted that Republican presidential candidate Alf Landon would easily defeat Democratic candidate Franklin Roosevelt. When the election took place, Roosevelt won in a landslide!

How could a prediction based on 2 million people be wrong? The answer is that the sample selected for the poll was unrepresentative of the population that voted in the election. The researchers obtained names and addresses from telephone directories, automobile registration lists, and magazine subscription lists. In 1936 most poorer Americans did not have telephones, cars, or magazine subscriptions. Thus the sample underrepresented poorer socioeconomic groups and overrepresented wealthier people. Bad sample, bad prediction. In sum, always consider the nature of the sample when interpreting survey results.

In scientific research, surveys are an efficient method for collecting a large amount of information about people's opinions and lifestyles, and they can reveal changes in people's beliefs and habits over many years. For example, the 2002 National Sleep Foundation survey found a 12-percent increase in the number of people who reported having sleep problems as compared with a similar survey conducted in 1999.

There are several major drawbacks to surveys. First, survey data cannot be used to draw conclusions about cause and effect. Second, surveys rely on participants' self-reports, which can be distorted by factors such as social desirability bias, interviewer bias, or people's inaccurate perceptions of their own behavior. Third, unrepresentative samples can lead to faulty generalizations about how an entire population would respond. And finally, even when surveys use proper random sampling procedures, once in a while—simply by chance—a sample that is randomly chosen will turn out not to be representative of the larger population. In most good professional and scientific surveys this happens less than 5 percent of the time . . . but it does happen. Thus for several reasons even well-crafted surveys can yield inaccurate estimates.

What Do You Think?

SHOULD YOU TRUST INTERNET AND POP MEDIA SURVEYS?
Tom fills out a political-attitude survey posted on the Internet. Claire mails in a marital-satisfaction survey that came in a fashion magazine to which she subscribes. Sam responds to a local TV news phone-in survey on a tax issue ("Call our number, press '1' to agree, '2' to disagree"). For each survey, can the results be trusted to reflect the general public's attitudes? Think about it, then see page 60.

CORRELATIONAL RESEARCH: MEASURING ASSOCIATIONS BETWEEN EVENTS

What factors distinguish happily married couples from those headed for divorce? Do firstborn children differ in personality from later-born children? Is monetary wealth related to happiness? These and countless other psychological questions ask about associations between naturally occurring events or variables. To examine such relationships, scientists typically conduct **correlational research,** which in its simplest form has three components:

1. The researcher *measures one variable (X),* such as people's age.

2. The researcher *measures a second variable (Y),* such as self-reported daytime sleepiness.

3. The researcher *statistically determines whether X and Y are related.*

Keep in mind that correlational research involves measuring variables, not manipulating them.

Naturalistic observation and surveys are often used not only to describe events but also to study associations between variables. For example, the National Sleep Foundation survey examined the relation between age and daytime sleepiness (Table 2.1). Other types of studies also fall under the correlational umbrella, as our "Research Close-Up" illustrates.

▶ **Focus 9**
Describe three components of correlational research and how they are illustrated by the study of very happy people.

TABLE 2.1	Age and Daytime Sleepiness

Percentage of people who report that daytime sleepiness interferes with their daily activities at least a few days per month:

Age Group	Percentage
18- to 29-year-olds	44
30- to 64-year-olds	38
65 years and older	23

SOURCE: National Sleep Foundation, 2002.

Research Close-Up   Very Happy People

SOURCE: ED DIENER and MARTIN E. P. SELIGMAN (2002). Very happy people. *Psychological Science, 13*, 81–84.

INTRODUCTION

What characteristics distinguish very happy people from other people? Thousands of studies have examined depressed, anxious, or otherwise unhappy people. Yet according to psychologists Ed Diener and Martin Seligman, this study is the first to explore factors correlated with high happiness. In the spirit of critical thinking, let's test your common sense. Which of the following statements do you expect to be true?

In college, compared to students who experience average happiness, the happiest students

- worry less about things in general.
- have more satisfying close friendships, family relationships, and romantic relationships.
- generally are more outgoing.
- have more money.
- have higher grades.
- are more physically attractive.

METHOD

At a midwestern American university, 222 students completed questionnaires and psychological tests measuring their general level of positive and negative emotions, personality traits, social relationships, satisfaction with life, and other characteristics. People who knew the students rated how often the students experienced positive and negative emotions. For 51 days, students also recorded their daily emotions in a diary.

Based on these measures, the researchers identified the 10 percent of students who consistently were the happiest, the 10 percent who consistently were the unhappiest, and a group (27 percent) that displayed average happiness.

RESULTS

Compared to the other participants, very happy students reported spending the greatest amount of time socializing with people and having the most satisfying social relationships with close friends, family, and romantic partners. Ratings from other people also indicated that very happy students had the most satisfying social relationships. Conversely, the unhappiest students reported the least satisfying social relationships and spent the most time alone.

Very happy students also were more outgoing and agreeable and worried less about things in general. However, compared to average-happiness peers, the happiest students did not differ in how much money they said they had. College transcripts revealed that, overall, they did not have a higher grade point average, nor did independent observers rate them as being more physically attractive.

DISCUSSION

Although strong social relationships were related to greater happiness, they did not guarantee happiness; some unhappy students also had satisfying social relationships. Diener and Seligman found a similar pattern for the other variables in their study and concluded that "there appears to be no single key to high happiness that automatically produces this state" (p. 83). Instead, high levels of happiness seem to involve a combination of social and psychological factors.

Were all of your predictions accurate? As you might imagine, had the results shown that the happiest students had more money and higher grades and were more physically attractive, many people would likely say "Big deal, that's just common sense." But the findings did not support these conclusions, illustrating why scientists gather data—rather than rely solely on intuition—to answer the questions they pose.

This study also illustrates basic characteristics of correlational research. The researchers measured several variables— happiness, social relationships, and so on—and then examined whether these variables were statistically related to one another. In contrast to experiments, correlational studies only *measure* variables that occur naturally. Diener and Seligman did not *manipulate* any variables; they didn't try to influence people's happiness or relationships. As we will now discuss, the correlational approach has advantages and limitations.

▶ **Focus 10**
Explain why scientists cannot draw causal conclusions from correlation research. Discuss an example.

Correlation and Causation

As just described, Diener and Seligman (2002) found that very happy people had stronger, more satisfying social relationships than unhappy people (Figure 2.11a). It is tempting to conclude from these findings that stronger social relationships cause people to be happier, but as Diener and Seligman point out, correlational research does not allow us to draw such a conclusion. First, the direction of causality could be just the opposite. Perhaps being happy causes people to have stronger social relationships. For example, maybe happiness makes a person more receptive to going out and forming relationships, or perhaps it makes it easier to attract other people who are looking to form relationships. In correlational research, you must consider the possibility that

(a) Social relationships and happiness are correlated

(b) Bidirectionality problem

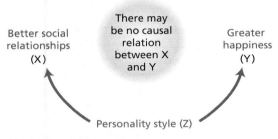

(c) Third-variable problem

FIGURE 2.11

Correlation and causation. (a) Students who have better social relationships are happier. But why does this association occur? (b) Good social relationships could cause people to become happier, or, conversely, being a happier person could make it easier to form good social relationships. This is the bidirectionality problem. (c) There may be no causal link between social relationships and happiness. Other variables, such as personality traits (e.g., having a more outgoing, agreeable disposition), may be part of the true common origin of better social relationships and of happiness. This is the third-variable problem.

variable X (social relationships) has caused variable Y (happiness), that Y has caused X, or that both variables have influenced each other. This interpretive problem is called the *bidirectionality* (i.e., *two-way causality*) *problem* (Figure 2.11b).

Second, the association between social relationships and happiness may be artificial, or what scientists call *spurious* (not genuine). Although social relationships and happiness are statistically related, it may be that neither variable has any causal effect on the other. A third variable, Z, may really be the cause of why some people have better social relationships and also why those people are happier. For example, Z might be a certain personality style. Recall that very happy people in Diener and Seligman's study were, in general, more outgoing and agreeable and tended to worry less. Perhaps this personality style makes it easier for people to establish good social relationships. At the same

time, this style may help people soak up more joy from life and therefore feel happier. Thus on the surface it looks as if social relationships and happiness are causally linked, but in reality this may only be due to Z (in this case, personality style).

This interpretive problem is called the *third-variable problem:* Z is responsible for what looks like a relation between X and Y (Figure 2.11c). As Z varies, it causes X to change. As Z varies, it also causes Y to change. The net result is that X and Y change in unison, but this is caused by Z—not by any direct effect of X or Y on each other. In sum, we cannot draw causal conclusions from correlational data, and this is the major disadvantage of correlational research.

What Do You Think?

DOES EATING ICE CREAM CAUSE PEOPLE TO DROWN?
Nationally, ice cream consumption and drownings are positively correlated. Over the course of the year, on days when more ice cream is consumed, there tend to be more drownings. Are these two variables causally related? What causal possibilities should you consider? Think about it, then see page 60.

The Correlation Coefficient

A **correlation coefficient** *is a statistic that indicates the direction and strength of the relation between two variables.* Variables can be correlated either positively or negatively. A **positive correlation** *means that higher scores on one variable are associated with higher scores on a second variable.* Thus social relationships and happiness are positively correlated such that more satisfying relationships are associated with higher levels of happiness. Similarly, people's height and weight are positively correlated (i.e., in general, taller people tend to weigh more), as are hours of daylight and average daily temperature (overall, the longer days of spring and summer have higher average temperatures than do the shorter days of fall and winter).

A **negative correlation** *occurs when higher scores on one variable are associated with lower scores on a second variable.* Job satisfaction and job turnover are negatively correlated, which means that workers who are more satisfied with their jobs tend to have lower rates of turnover (e.g., quitting, being fired). Likewise, students' test anxiety and exam performance are negatively correlated (students with higher levels of test anxiety tend to perform more poorly on exams), as are hours of daylight and time spent indoors (overall, on the longer days of the year, we spend less time indoors).

▶ **Focus 11**
Explain positive and negative correlation coefficients and scatterplots. How does correlation facilitate prediction?

FIGURE 2.12

Scatterplots depicting correlations. A scatterplot depicts the correlation between two variables. The horizontal axis represents variable X, the vertical axis variable Y. Each data point represents a specific pair of X and Y scores, such as the number of hours a week a student studies (X) and that student's grade point average (Y). The three scatterplots show (a) a strong positive correlation, (b) a zero correlation (0.00), and (c) a strong negative correlation for hypothetical sets of data.

(a) A positive correlation

(b) Zero correlation

(c) A negative correlation

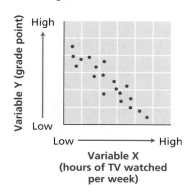

Correlation coefficients range from values of +1.00 to −1.00. The plus or minus sign tells you the direction of a correlation (i.e., whether the variables are positively or negatively correlated). The absolute value of the statistic tells you the strength of the correlation. The closer the correlation is to +1.00 (a perfect positive correlation) or −1.00 (a perfect negative correlation), the more strongly the two variables are related. Therefore a correlation of −.59 indicates a stronger association between X and Y than does a correlation of +.37. A zero correlation (0.00) means that X and Y are not related statistically: As scores on X increase or decrease, scores on Y do not change in any orderly fashion. Figure 2.12 illustrates three **scatterplots,** *graphs that show the correlation between two variables.* (For more detailed information about the correlation coefficient, see the Appendix that follows Chapter 16.)

Correlation as a Basis for Prediction

Why conduct correlational research if it does not permit clear cause-effect conclusions? One benefit is that correlational research can help establish whether relations found in the laboratory generalize to the outside world. For example, suppose that laboratory experiments show that talking on a telephone while operating a driving simulator causes people to get into more simulated crashes. Correlational studies, while not demonstrating cause-effect, can at least establish whether there is a real-world association between driver cell-phone usage and automobile accident rates. (By the way, there is.) A second benefit is that correlational research can be conducted before experiments to discover associations that can then be studied under controlled laboratory conditions. Third, for practical or ethical reasons some questions cannot be studied with experiments but can be examined correlationally. We cannot experimentally manipulate how religious someone is, but we can mea-

sure people's religiousness and determine if it is associated with other variables, such as personality traits.

Another benefit is that correlational data allow us to make predictions. If two variables are correlated, either positively or negatively, knowing the score of one variable helps us estimate the score on the other variable. For example, students who apply to college in North America typically take a national test that assesses academic aptitude and skills, such as the SAT. Scores on these tests help admissions officers estimate how well a student is likely to do in college, as the scatterplot in Figure 2.13 shows.

You can see that higher SAT scores are associated with higher first-year grade point averages (GPAs). The scatterplot also shows that this positive correlation is not perfect. Some students who do well on the SAT end up having an average or poor GPA; conversely, others have low SAT scores but excel in college. Still, even a moderate

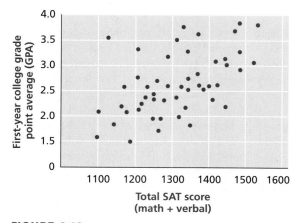

FIGURE 2.13

Correlation of SAT scores with first-year college GPAs. This scatterplot represents data for a hypothetical sample of 50 students. The horizontal axis represents variable X, SAT scores. The vertical axis represents variable Y, these same students' overall grade point averages for their first year in college. Variables X and Y are moderately correlated.

SAT-GPA correlation is useful to admissions officers, especially when SAT scores are used with other variables—such as high school GPAs—that also help estimate college performance. Remember, we are not saying that higher SAT scores *cause* better first-year performance, only that they help predict it. Similarly, business, government, and military organizations spend millions of dollars developing screening tests that correlate with work performance and therefore help predict how well applicants will do on the job.

EXPERIMENTS: EXAMINING CAUSE AND EFFECT

In contrast to descriptive and correlational methods, experiments are a powerful tool for examining cause-and-effect relations. Suppose we conduct an experiment to examine whether noise influences college students' ability to learn new information. Each student is placed alone in a room, has 30 minutes to study five pages of textbook material, and then takes a 20-item multiple-choice test.

An **experiment** has three essential characteristics:

1. The researcher *manipulates one or more variables.* In the noise example, the researcher manipulates (i.e., controls) one variable—the amount of noise in the room. Some students (participants) are placed in a noisy room; others are placed in a quiet room. These would represent the groups (conditions) of the experiment (i.e., noise condition, no-noise condition).

2. The researcher *measures whether this manipulation influences other variables* (i.e., variables that represent the participants' responses). In the noise experiment, the researcher uses the multiple-choice test to measure whether the amount of learning differs in the noise condition versus the no-noise condition. We might find, for example, that participants in the noise condition perform more poorly on the multiple-choice test than do participants in the no-noise condition.

3. The researcher *attempts to control extraneous factors that might influence the outcome of the experiment.* For example, we would not want one group to do better because it had easier textbook material or test questions. So every participant will read the same material and take the same test. The room temperature and lighting will be kept constant, and the researcher will be courteous to everyone.

The logic behind this approach is straightforward:

- Start out with equivalent groups of participants.
- Treat them equally in all respects except for the variable that is of particular interest (in this case, noise).
- Isolate this variable and manipulate it (creating the presence or absence of noise).
- Measure how the groups respond (in this case, the amount they learn).

If the groups respond differently, then the most likely explanation is that these differences were caused by the manipulated variable (Figure 2.14).

Independent and Dependent Variables

The term **independent variable** *refers to the factor that is manipulated by the experimenter.* In our example, noise is the independent variable. The **dependent variable** *is the factor that is measured by the experimenter and may be influenced by the independent variable.* In this experiment, the amount of learning is the dependent variable.

▶ **Focus 12**
What is the major advantage of experiments? Identify the key characteristics and logic of experiments.

▶ **Focus 13**
What are independent and dependent variables? Experimental and control groups?

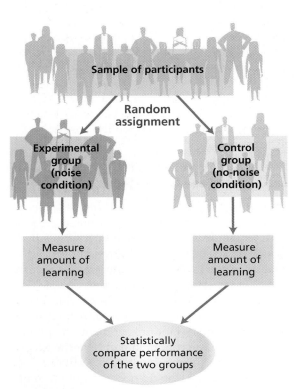

FIGURE 2.14

The logic of designing an experiment. The experimenter manipulates the amount of noise to which participants are exposed, measures their learning, and attempts to treat them equally in every other way. This creates an experimental group and a control group.

An easy way to keep this distinction clear is to remember that the dependent variable depends on the independent variable. Presumably, students' learning will depend on whether they were in a noisy or quiet room. The independent variable is the cause, and the dependent variable is the effect.

We have described the independent and dependent variables at a general level, but recall that when doing research we must also define our variables operationally. "Noise" could mean many things, from the roar of a jet engine to the annoying drip of a faucet. "Learning" could mean anything from memorizing a list of words to acquiring the skill to ride a bicycle. In our experiment, we could operationally define our variables as follows:

▶ Focus 14
How and why are random assignment and counter-balancing used to design experiments?

	Independent Variable (cause)	Dependent Variable (effect)
Conceptual Level	Noise	Learning
Operational Level	Recording of street sounds played at 60 decibels for 30 minutes (versus quiet room)	Number of multiple-choice questions, based on five pages of text, answered correctly

Our noise experiment thus far has only one dependent variable, but we could have many. We could measure how quickly participants read the material, their stress during the task, and so on. This way, we could gain more knowledge about how noise affects people. To test your understanding, identify the independent and dependent variables in Darley and Latané's bystander experiment (pages 30–31). See the answer in the margin on page 50.

Experimental and Control Groups

The terms *experimental group* and *control group* are often used when discussing experiments. An **experimental group** *is the group that receives a treatment or an active level of the independent variable.* A **control group** *is not exposed to the treatment or receives a zero-level of the independent variable.* The purpose of the control group is to provide a standard of behavior to which the experimental group can be compared. In our experiment, the participants in the noise condition represent the experimental group (or experimental condition), and the participants in the no-noise condition represent the control group (or control condition).

Experiments often include several experimental groups. In our study on noise, we could play the recording of street sounds at three different volume levels, creating high-noise, moderate-noise, and low-noise experimental conditions. The no-noise condition would still represent the control group. In some experiments, however, the concept of a control group does not apply. For example, in a taste-test experiment in which participants taste and then rate how much they like Coca-Cola versus Pepsi, each drink represents an experimental condition, and participants simply make a direct comparison between the two drinks.

Two Basic Ways to Design an Experiment

One common way to design an experiment is to have different participants in each condition. To draw meaningful conclusions, the various groups of participants must be equivalent at the start of the study. For example, suppose that in our experiment the noise group performed substantially worse on the multiple-choice test than the no-noise group. If the students in the noise group, on average, happened to be poorer readers or more anxious than the students in the no-noise group, then these factors—not the noise—might have been why they performed more poorly.

To address this issue, researchers typically use **random assignment,** *a procedure in which each participant has an equal likelihood of being assigned to any one group within an experiment.* Thus a participant would have a 50 percent chance of being in the noise group and a 50 percent chance of being in the no-noise group; that determination would be made randomly. This procedure does not eliminate the fact that participants differ from one another in reading ability, anxiety, or other characteristics. Instead, random assignment is used to balance these differences across the various conditions of the experiment. It increases our confidence that, at the start of an experiment, participants in the various conditions are equivalent overall.

A second way to design experiments is to expose each participant to all the conditions. We could measure how much the same people learn when exposed to noise and when placed in a quiet room. By doing so, factors such as the participants' reading ability and general anxiety are held constant across the no-noise and noise conditions, and therefore we can rule them out as alternative explanations for any results we obtain. However, this approach creates problems if not used properly.

For one thing, it would make little sense to have our participants read the same textbook pages and take the same multiple-choice questions twice. Instead, we would have to develop two equally difficult reading tasks and have participants perform each task only once. Most important, suppose that every participant were exposed to the no-noise

How was the experimental method used to measure people's level of acceptance of authority? To find out, watch the video, "Obedience to Authority," in Chapter 2 of your CD.

Watch the "Conformity" video in Chapter 2 of your CD to see another classic study using the experimental method.

FIGURE 2.15

At birth, rat pups from several litters were randomly assigned to experimental and control groups. This photo illustrates the enriched environment of the experimental group, with toys and playmates. Control-group pups were raised alone in standard laboratory cages. In this experiment, the difference in the environmental conditions represented the independent variable. Brain development was the main dependent variable.

condition first. If they then learned more poorly in the noise condition, what would be the cause? The noise? Perhaps. But perhaps the participants were bored or fatigued by the time they performed the second task. To avoid this problem, researchers use **counterbalancing,** *a procedure in which the order of conditions is varied so that no condition has an overall advantage relative to the others.* Half the participants would be exposed to the no-noise condition first and the noise condition second. For the remaining participants, this order would be reversed.

Manipulating One Independent Variable: Effects of Environmental Stimulation on Brain Development

In a Miami hospital, a massage therapist gently strokes a tiny premature baby who was exposed to cocaine while in its mother's womb. This procedure is repeated several times each day. Why is the infant receiving this treatment?

The answer partially lies in landmark experiments by physiological psychologist Mark Rosenzweig (1984) and his coworkers, who manipulated the degree of environmental stimulation to which infant rats (called "pups") were exposed. This independent variable—environmental stimulation—was operationally defined by creating two conditions: an experimental condition in which some pups lived in a stimulating environment containing toys and other pups with whom they could interact, and a control condition in which other pups lived alone in standard cages (Figure 2.15). The pups came from several litters, so

to create equivalent groups at the outset the researchers randomly assigned some pups from each litter to the enriched and standard environments.

After the rats had lived in these environments for several months, the dependent variable—brain development—was measured. Brain development was operationally defined by several measures, such as the weight of the rats' brains and the concentrations of brain chemicals involved in learning. The rats raised in the enriched environment were superior on each measure and performed better on learning tasks than did the control-group rats. Years later, researchers found that other types of environmental stimulation, such as physical stroking and touch, also enhanced rats' brain development and performance on learning tasks (Meaney et al., 1991).

Developmental psychologist Tiffany Field and other researchers have found that, like the rat pups, newborn human infants benefit from stimulation (Field, 2001). In one experiment, the researchers manipulated one independent variable, randomly assigning premature infants either to receive three daily massage sessions for 10 days or to receive standard care and contact (Wheeden et al., 1993). The researchers measured several dependent variables and found that the massaged infants had fewer health problems, more mature movement patterns, and greater weight gain (Figure 2.16). Because massage enhances their health, premature infants can leave the hospital sooner, reducing heath-care costs. Full-term infants also benefit from massage. They display better development than infants who are simply held and rocked for the same amount of time.

These areas of research helped revolutionize thinking about how experience affects brain development. They also show, once again, how basic research—including animal experiments—can have human applications.

FIGURE 2.16

Experiments by psychologist Tiffany Field and others reveal that massage therapy improves the health and enhances the physical development of premature infants. It also shortens their hospital stay, thus reducing medical costs. Field (2001) estimates that if all premature infants received massage therapy, the national savings would be nearly $5 billion.

Manipulating Two Independent Variables: Effects of Alcohol and Expectations on Sexual Arousal

▶ Focus 15
Explain the advantage of manipulating two independent variables in the same experiment.

To better capture the complexity of behavior, researchers often study several causal factors within a single experiment by manipulating two or more independent variables simultaneously. They assess the separate influence of each variable on behavior and also examine whether combinations of variables produce distinct effects.

Consider that many men and women report that alcohol enhances their sexual arousal. Why might this be? Perhaps alcohol's chemical properties directly influence sexual arousal. Or maybe the cause is psychological—that is, if people simply believe that alcohol will enhance their sexual arousal, then perhaps this expectation by itself can bring about increased sexual responsiveness.

How can we separate the purely physiological effects of drinking from the psychological ones? The answer emerged in an ingenious procedure developed more than 25 years ago (Rohsenow & Marlatt, 1981). The researchers created two drinks that people could not tell apart by taste: one with tonic water and a squirt of lime juice, the other with vodka added to this mix. Then they designed an experiment with two independent variables. The first independent variable manipulated participants' expectations: They were told either that their drink contained alcohol or that it didn't. The second independent variable was whether participants received the alcoholic or nonalcoholic drink.

As Figure 2.17a shows, when these two independent variables are combined within the same experiment, four different conditions are created. Condition 1 is expect alcohol/receive alcohol. This is the normal state of affairs when people drink; they expect that they are drinking alcohol and actually are. Changes in sexual arousal that occur in this condition could reflect either the chemical effects of alcohol, psychological expectations, or a combination of both. Condition 2 is expect no alcohol/receive alcohol. This condition assesses physiological effects alone. Because participants believe they are not receiving alcohol, changes in sexual arousal would presumably be due to alcohol's chemical effects. Condition 3 is expect alcohol/receive no alcohol. Because no alcohol is consumed, changes in sexual arousal, if any, would have to be caused by participants' expectations about drinking alcohol. Finally, Condition 4 is expect no alcohol/receive no alcohol. This condition creates a control group having neither alcohol nor alcohol expectations.

Participants in the four conditions are then shown identical sexually stimulating materials (e.g., slides or films) or are led to anticipate that they will be viewing such materials. The dependent variable, sexual arousal, may be assessed by self-report ratings on questionnaires or by physiological measures.

Most researchers have studied men, in part due to an interest in the issue of alcohol consumption and rape, which primarily is committed by men. (We will discuss the findings with

FIGURE 2.17

Alcohol, expectations, and sexual arousal. (a) Simultaneously manipulating two independent variables—participant's expectation and actual drink content—creates four conditions in this design. (b) In one experiment, male participants in these four conditions were shown sexually explicit films. The dependent variable, sexual arousal, was measured by a device that recorded changes in the size of each man's penis. Regardless of what they actually drank, men who believed they had consumed alcohol became more aroused than men who believed they had not consumed alcohol. Among men who believed they drank alcohol, those who drank only tonic were just as aroused as those who actually drank alcohol. Source: Data adapted from Wilson & Lawson, 1976.

(a)

(b)

TABLE 2.2 An Overview of Research Methods

Method	Primary Features	Main Advantages	Main Disadvantages
Case study	An individual, group, or event is examined in detail, often using several techniques (e.g., observations, interviews, psychological tests).	Provides rich descriptive information, often suggesting hypotheses for further study. Can study rare phenomena in depth.	Poor method for establishing cause-effect. The case may not be representative. Often relies on the researcher's subjective interpretations.
Naturalistic observation	Behavior is observed in the setting where it naturally occurs.	Can provide detailed information about the nature, frequency, and context of naturally occurring behaviors.	Poor method for establishing cause-effect relations. Observer's presence, if known, may influence participants' behavior.
Survey	Questions or tests are administered to a sample drawn from a larger population.	A properly selected, representative sample typically yields accurate information about the broader population.	Unrepresentative samples may yield misleading results. Interviewer bias and social desirability bias can distort the findings.
Correlational study	Variables are measured and the strength of their association is determined. (Naturalistic observation and surveys are often used to examine associations between variables.)	Correlation allows prediction. May help establish how well findings from experiments generalize to more natural settings. Can examine issues that cannot be studied ethically or practically in experiments.	Correlation does not imply causation, due to the bidirectionality problem and the third-variable problem (which creates a confounding of variables).
Experiment	Independent variables are manipulated, and their effects on dependent variables are measured.	Optimal method for examining cause-effect relations. Ability to control extraneous factors helps rule out alternative explanations.	Confounding of variables, demand characteristics, placebo effects, and experimenter expectancies can threaten the validity of causal conclusions.

women later.) Overall, as Figure 2.17b shows, men who believe that they have consumed low to moderate doses of alcohol—regardless of whether they actually drank alcohol—feel more aroused and show greater physiological arousal to sexual stimuli than men who believe that they have consumed only tonic water (Seto & Barbaree, 1995). Among men, the *mere expectation* that one is drinking alcohol also weakens sexual inhibitions and impairs judgment in recognizing coercive sexual behavior toward women (Gross et al., 2001).

Thus at low to moderate doses that produce blood-alcohol levels of about .04 or less, men's expectations about alcohol contribute to their enhanced sexual arousal. But at higher doses, the chemical effects of alcohol take over and decrease—yes, decrease—men's sexual arousal and ability to reach orgasm (Kelly, 2004). Alcohol is a depressant drug; it suppresses neural activity.

This research illustrates how studying several independent variables simultaneously can help unravel some of the complexity of behavior. It also reinforces one of our main themes: Behavior (in this case, sexual arousal) results from an interplay of factors that are psychological (beliefs and expectations), environmental (the presence of sexual stimuli), and physiological (chemical effects of alcohol at certain doses).

Table 2.2 summarizes key features of the research methods we have discussed, as well as some limitations of experiments, which we will discuss next.

IN REVIEW

- Descriptive research describes how organisms behave, particularly in natural settings. Case studies involve the detailed study of a person, group, or event. They often suggest ideas for further research, but are a poor method for establishing cause-effect relations.

- Naturalistic observation gathers information about behavior in real-life settings. It can yield rich descriptions of behavior and allows the examination of relations between variables. Researchers must avoid influencing the participants that they observe.

- Surveys involve administering questionnaires or interviews to many people. Most surveys study a sample that is randomly drawn from the larger population the researcher is interested in. Representative samples allow for reasonably accurate estimates of the opinions or behaviors of the entire population. Unrepresentative samples can lead to inaccurate estimates. Interviewer bias and bias in participants' self-reports can distort survey results.

■ Correlational research measures the relation between naturally occurring variables. A positive correlation means that higher scores on one variable are associated with higher scores on a second variable. A negative correlation occurs when higher scores on one variable are associated with lower scores on a second variable.

■ Causal conclusions cannot be drawn from correlational data. Variable X may cause Y, Y may cause X, or some third variable (Z) may be the true cause of both X and Y. Nevertheless, if two variables are correlated, then knowing the scores of one variable will help predict the scores of the other.

■ A well-designed experiment is the best way to examine cause-effect relations. Experiments have three essential characteristics: (1) one or more variables are manipulated, (2) their effects on other variables are measured, and (3) extraneous factors are eliminated or reduced so that cause-effect conclusions can be drawn.

■ Manipulated variables are called independent variables. Dependent variables are measured, not manipulated. The independent variable is viewed as the cause, the dependent variable as the effect. The experimental group receives a treatment or an active level of the independent variable, whereas the control group does not.

■ In some experiments different participants are randomly assigned to each condition. In other experiments the same participants are exposed to all the conditions, but the order in which the conditions are presented is counterbalanced.

■ Researchers can study several causal factors within one experiment by simultaneously manipulating two or more independent variables. They assess the separate influence of each variable on behavior and examine whether combinations of variables produce distinct effects.

THREATS TO THE VALIDITY OF RESEARCH

▶ **Focus 16**
What is internal validity? Why do confounding of variables and demand characteristics decrease internal validity?

Although the experimental approach is a powerful tool for examining causality, researchers must avoid errors that can lead to faulty conclusions. **Internal validity** *represents the degree to which an experiment supports clear causal conclusions.* For example, because Darley and Latané's bystander experiment had proper controls, we can be confident that it was the independent variable (i.e., the

number of bystanders) that caused the differences in the dependent variable (i.e., whether a bystander helped the victim). Thus the experiment had high internal validity. However, if an experiment contains important flaws it will have low internal validity because we can no longer be sure what caused the differences in the dependent variable.

CONFOUNDING OF VARIABLES

Consider a fictitious experiment in which Dr. Starr examines how listening to different types of music influences people's feelings of relaxation. The independent variable is the type of music: new age, country, or rock. Sixty college students are randomly assigned to listen to one of the three types of music for 20 minutes. Afterward, they rate how relaxed they feel on a questionnaire.

Dr. Starr believes that the experiment will be more realistic if the new age music is played at a low volume, the country music at a moderate volume, and the rock music at a loud volume. The results show that students who listened to the new age music felt most relaxed, while those who listened to the rock music felt least relaxed. Dr. Starr concludes that, of the three types of music, new age music is the most relaxing.

What is wrong with Dr. Starr's conclusion that the type of music caused the differences in how relaxed students felt? Stated differently, can you identify another major factor that could have produced these results? Perhaps students who listened to new age music felt most relaxed because their music was played at the lowest, most soothing volume. Had they listened to it at a high volume, maybe they would have felt no more relaxed than the students who listened to the rock music. We now have two variables that, like the strands of a rope, are intertwined: the independent variable (the type of music) that Dr. Starr really was interested in and a second variable (the volume level) that Dr. Starr was not interested in but foolishly did not keep constant.

Confounding of variables *means that two variables are intertwined in such a way that we cannot determine which one has influenced a dependent variable.* In this experiment the music's volume level is called a *confound* or a *confounding variable.*

	Group 1	Group 2	Group 3
Independent Variable (type of music)	New age	Country	Rock
Confounding Variable (volume level)	Low	Moderate	High

The key point to remember is that this confounding of variables prevents Dr. Starr from drawing clear causal conclusions, thereby ruining the internal validity of the experiment. Dr. Starr can eliminate this problem by keeping the volume level constant across the three music conditions.

Confounding, by the way, is a key reason why causal conclusions cannot be drawn from correlational research. Recall the "third-variable" problem (see page 43). If variables X (e.g., level of happiness) and Y (e.g., quality of social relationships) are correlated, a third variable, Z (e.g., personality style) may be mixed up with X and Y, so we cannot tell what has caused what. Thus Z is just another type of confounding variable.

DEMAND CHARACTERISTICS

In unfamiliar situations, it is natural for us to search for clues about how we are expected to act. **Demand characteristics** *are cues that participants pick up about the hypothesis of a study or about how they are supposed to behave* (Orne, 1962). Consider the experiments on alcohol and sexual arousal discussed earlier. Some participants are told that they are drinking alcohol but in reality are given nonalcoholic drinks. Suppose that after a few drinks a participant does not feel intoxicated and concludes that the drinks are nonalcoholic. At this point the researchers' statement that the drinks are alcoholic is a cue—a demand characteristic—that may tip off the participant about the hypothesis being tested ("Hmm, maybe they're trying to see how I behave if I simply believe I'm drinking alcohol.") This damages the experiment's internal validity because it can distort participants' true responses. Most people want to be good participants and may respond in ways that they think the experimenter wants (Figure 2.18).

Skilled researchers try to anticipate demand characteristics and design studies to avoid them. For example, if careful procedures are used, participants given nonalcoholic drinks can be convinced that they have consumed moderate to high amounts of alcohol (MacDonald et al., 2000).

PLACEBO EFFECTS

In medical research, the term **placebo** *refers to a substance that has no pharmacological effect.* In experiments testing the effectiveness of new drugs for treating diseases, one group of patients—the *treatment group*—receives the actual drug (e.g., through pills or injections). A second group, the *placebo control group,* only receives a placebo (e.g., pills composed of inactive ingredients or injections of

"WHAT IT COMES DOWN TO IS YOU HAVE TO FIND OUT WHAT REACTION THEY'RE LOOKING FOR, AND YOU GIVE THEM THAT REACTION."

FIGURE 2.18

Demand characteristics provide participants with clues about how they "should" behave during a study. This may cause participants to alter their natural responses, thereby ruining the internal validity of the experiment. Copyright © by Sidney Harris. ScienceCartoonsPlus.com. Reprinted with permission.

saline). Typically, participants are told that they will be given either a drug or a placebo, but they are not told which one.

The rationale for using placebos is that patients' symptoms may improve solely because they expect that a drug will help them. If 40 percent of patients receiving the actual drug improve but 37 percent of the placebo control patients show similar improvement, then we have evidence of a **placebo effect:** *People receiving a treatment show a change in behavior because of their expectations, not because the treatment itself had any specific benefit* (Figure 2.19).

Placebo effects decrease internal validity by providing an alternative explanation for why responses change after exposure to a treatment. This problem applies to evaluating all types of treatments, not just those that test the effectiveness of drugs. For example, suppose that depressed patients improve (i.e., become less depressed) while receiving psychotherapy. Is this due to the specific procedures and content of the psychotherapy itself, or might it merely be a placebo effect resulting from their positive expectations that the therapy would help them? Experiments that include the proper control groups can examine this question, as we will discuss in Chapter 15.

EXPERIMENTER EXPECTANCY EFFECTS

Researchers typically have a strong commitment to the hypothesis they are testing. In psychology,

FIGURE 2.19

Throughout history, placebo effects have fostered the commercial success of many products that had no proven physiological benefit. Herbal medicines are one of today's health crazes. Do they really work? If so, is it because of placebo effects or the herbs' chemical properties? The best way to answer this question is through experiments that include placebo control groups.

▶ **Focus 17**

What are placebo effects and experimenter expectancy effects? How can they be minimized?

the term **experimenter expectancy effects** *refers to the subtle and unintentional ways researchers influence their participants to respond in a manner that is consistent with the researcher's hypothesis.* Scientists can take several steps to avoid experimenter expectancy effects. For example, researchers who interact with participants in a study or who record participants' responses are often kept blind to (i.e., not told about) the hypothesis or the specific condition to which a participant has been assigned. This makes it less likely that these researchers will develop expectations about how participants "should" behave.

The **double-blind procedure,** *in which both the participant and experimenter are kept blind as to which experimental condition the participant is in,* simultaneously minimizes participant placebo effects and experimenter expectancy effects. In research testing drug effects, each participant receives either a real drug or a placebo but does not know which. People who interact with the participants (e.g., those who dispense the drugs or measure participants' symptoms) also are kept unaware of which participants receive the drug or placebo. This procedure minimizes the likelihood that the researchers will behave differently toward the two groups of participants, and it reduces the chance that participants' own expectations will influence the outcome of the experiment (Figure 2.20).

▶ **Focus 18**
What is external validity? Why is replication important? Apply these concepts to paranormal claims.

"IT WAS MORE OF A 'TRIPLE-BLIND' TEST. THE PATIENTS DIDN'T KNOW WHICH ONES WERE GETTING THE REAL DRUG, THE DOCTORS DIDN'T KNOW, AND I'M AFRAID, NOBODY KNEW"

FIGURE 2.20

The double-blind procedure is useful, but scientists try to avoid the infamous "triple-blind procedure." Copyright © 2000 by Sidney Harris. ScienceCartoonsPlus.com.

REPLICATING AND GENERALIZING THE FINDINGS

Let's return to our finding that college students in a noisy room learned textbook material more poorly than did students in a quiet room. Because our study was done properly, it has high internal validity and thus we are confident that the noise, and not some other factor, caused students to perform more poorly. There remain, however, other questions that we must ask. Would the results be similar with other types of participants (e.g., children, adults not in college) or with different tasks (e.g., learning music or sports skills)? Does noise impair learning in real-world settings?

These questions focus on **external validity,** *which is the degree to which the results of a study can be generalized to other populations, settings, and conditions.* Judgments about external validity typically do not focus on the exact responses of the participants. For example, the fact that students in noisy versus quiet rooms correctly answered, say, 48 percent versus 83 percent of the questions is not the issue. Rather, *we are concerned about the external validity of the underlying principle:* Does noise decrease learning?

To determine external validity, either we or other scientists will need to replicate our experiment. **Replication** *is the process of repeating a study to determine whether the original findings can be duplicated.* If our findings are successfully replicated—especially in experiments that study other types of participants (e.g., children), noise (e.g., airplanes flying overhead), and learning tasks (e.g., learning a sports skill)—we become more confident in concluding that noise impairs learning. For example, researchers in Canada, Israel, Japan, and the United States attempted to replicate Darley and Latané's (1968) findings on bystander helping. Some studies took place in subways, Internet chat rooms, and other real-life settings. Different types of helping behavior were measured, and women and men were studied. The vast majority of experiments replicated the original finding (Latané & Nida, 1981; Markey, 2000).

Increasingly, psychologists are paying more attention to *cross-cultural replication.* For example, German Posada and his coworkers (2002) studied interactions between mothers and their infant girls and boys. Middle-class families from Denver (United States) and Bogotá (Colombia) participated. In both samples, infants showed a closer emotional bond to mothers who were more sensitive and responsive to their baby's needs (Figure 2.21). Because this study was correlational, it does not demonstrate cause-effect relations. Still, replicating the findings across two cultural groups increases our confidence in the generalizability of a *potential* causal association between sensitive caregiving and infant attachment.

Research findings that fail to replicate often lead to important discoveries. For example, we have seen that men's belief that they have consumed a few alcoholic drinks (even if the drinks are nonalcoholic) increases their sexual arousal to explicit sexual materials. But experiments have found that women's expectation of having consumed a few alcoholic drinks does not increase their sexual responsiveness (Crowe & George, 1989; Norris, 1994). Scientists are still exploring why this gender difference occurs.

In contrast, studies that consistently fail to replicate the original results of earlier research suggest that the original study may have been flawed or that the finding was a fluke. Even so, the scientific process has done its job and prevented us from getting caught in a blind alley. To see why replication is such an important component of the scientific process, let's look at the following "Beneath the Surface."

FIGURE 2.21

Cross-cultural replications help establish the generalizability of psychological principles. Among families in Denver (United States) and Bogotá (Colombia), sensitive maternal caregiving is associated with closer emotional bonding by infants. Source: Posada et al., 2002.

Beneath the Surface   Science, Psychics, and the Paranormal

Do you believe—or know people who believe—in psychic phenomena, such as mental telepathy (transmitting thoughts between individuals) and precognition (foretelling the future; Figure 2.22)? Surveys around the world reveal widespread public belief in the paranormal (Alcock, 2003). Adopting a scientific attitude means we should approach this issue with open-minded skepticism; that is, we should apply rigorous standards of evaluation, as we do to all phenomena (Cardeña et al., 2000). The ability of independent investigators to replicate initial research findings is one of those standards.

When tested under controlled conditions in well-designed experiments and replications, claim after claim of psychic ability has evaporated. In 1976 the Committee for the Scientific Investigation of Claims of the Paranormal was formed. It consists of psychologists, other scientists, philosophers, and magicians expert in the art of fakery. To conclude that a phenomenon is psychic, the committee requires that presently known natural physical or psychological explanations be ruled out. To date, it has not judged any psychic claims to be valid.

What about paranormal demonstrations by self-proclaimed psychics, such as using mental powers to bend spoons? About 30 years ago, James Randi, a magician and expert in the art of psychic fraud, began offering $10,000 to anyone who could demonstrate paranormal ability under his scrutiny. Today the offer is $1 million, and still no one has

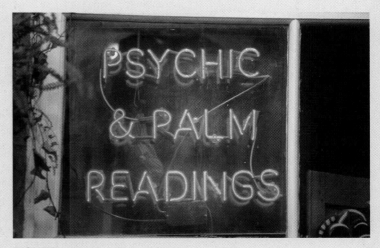

FIGURE 2.22

Many people believe in the paranormal, despite an overwhelming lack of reliable scientific evidence.

collected. Predictions made by leading psychics in national newspapers also yield dismal results (Emery Jr., 2001).

In the 1990s a report in a major scientific journal provided evidence of mental telepathy from 11 studies using the *ganzfeld*

Continued

procedure (Bem & Honorton, 1994). In this approach, a participant (the "receiver") listens to a hissing sound played through earphones and sees red light through translucent goggles. Parapsychologists believe this procedure makes the receiver more sensitive to mental telepathy signals. In another shielded room, the "sender" concentrates on one of four different visual forms presented in random order. In these studies, the receivers reported the correct form on 32 percent of the trials, a statistically significant increase above the chance level of 25 percent.

Does the ganzfeld procedure—which involves many rigorous controls—provide the first solid evidence of a psychic phenomenon? Some scientists suggest that the original ganzfeld studies may not have fully prevented the receivers from detecting extremely subtle cues that could have influenced their responses (Hyman, 1994). Although several parapsychology researchers have reported successful replications (Parker, 2000), psychologists Julie Milton and Richard Wiseman (1999) analyzed 30 ganzfeld studies conducted by seven independent laboratories and concluded that "the ganzfeld technique *does not* at present offer a replicable method for producing ESP in the laboratory" (p. 387, italics added). As newer studies and reviews are published, scientists continue to debate the status of the ganzfeld findings (Palmer, 2003).

Critical thinking requires us to have a reasoned skepticism that demands solid scientific evidence, but not a blind skepticism that rejects the unknown as impossible. In our opinion, at present there is no generally accepted scientific evidence to support the existence of paranormal phenomena. Research continues, and while the burden of proof lies with those who believe in the paranormal, evaluations of their claims should be based on scientific evidence rather than on preconceived positive or negative expectations.

IN REVIEW

- An experiment has high internal validity when it is designed well and permits clear causal conclusions.

- Confounding occurs when the independent variable becomes mixed up with an uncontrolled variable. This ruins internal validity because we can no longer tell which variable caused the changes in the dependent variable.

- Internal validity is weakened by (1) demand characteristics, which are cues that tip off participants as to how they should behave; (2) placebo effects, in which the mere expectation of receiving a treatment produces a change in behavior; and (3) experimenter expectancy effects, which are the subtle ways a researcher's behavior influences participants to behave in a manner consistent with the hypothesis being tested.

- The double-blind procedure prevents placebo effects and experimenter expectancy effects from biasing research results.

- External validity is the degree to which the findings of a study can be generalized to other populations, settings, and conditions. By replicating (repeating) a study under other circumstances, researchers can establish its external validity.

▶ **Focus 19**
What are some things you can do to be a critical consumer of statistics?

ANALYZING AND INTERPRETING DATA

Around election time, do you feel like you're swimming in a sea of statistics from endless voter polls and political advertisements? As a student, you live in a world of grade point averages. And in newspapers and TV shows that cover sports and finances, you'll find loads of statistics about athletes, teams, the economy, and stock prices.

Statistics are woven into the fabric of modern life, and they are integral to psychological research. We'll explain why statistics are important by focusing on a few basic concepts. The Appendix that follows Chapter 16 provides more information about these and other concepts.

BEING A SMART CONSUMER OF STATISTICS

Suppose that a neighborhood group wants your support for a new crime-watch program. To convince you, the group quotes statistics from a nearby town, showing that this program will reduce your chance of being robbed by a whopping 50 percent. Sounds impressive, but would you be impressed if you learned that in 2006 this town had two robberies and that after adopting the crime-watch program in 2007 they had only one? Because the number of robberies was so low to begin with, this percentage change doesn't mean much. In everyday life, it helps to ask about the number of cases or observations that stand behind percentages.

Now consider a fictitious consumer study that asked 1,000 people to taste three cola drinks from competing companies and choose the one they liked best. The two *bar graphs* in Figure 2.23 show the same results but make a different visual impression. It's always wise to look at the fine print, including the scale of measurement, that accompany graphs and charts.

Lastly, imagine that you apply for a consulting job at Honest Al's Consulting Firm. You ask Al how

Percentage of people in taste test who prefer each cola

(a)

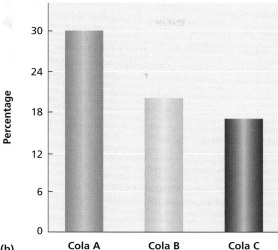

(b)

FIGURE 2.23

Manipulating visual impressions of data. Of 1,000 taste testers, suppose that 33 percent had no preference (thus their results are not placed in the graph), 30 percent preferred Cola A, 20 percent preferred Cola B, and 17 percent preferred Cola C. Look at the Y-axis (the vertical axis) of each graph. The left-hand graph (a), where the Y-axis scale goes from 0 to 100 percent, makes this difference seem small. The right-hand graph (b), with a Y-axis scale of 0 to 30 percent, makes this difference seem substantial. As the marketing director for Cola A, which graph would you put in your advertisements?

much money his consultants make. Al replies, "Our consultants' average salary is $75,000." "Wow," you think to yourself. Now look at the list of 10 salaries in Table 2.3. Is the job still as attractive to you? This is another example of why it is important to think critically about statistics. Honest Al was indeed being honest, but as you will now see, by asking questions about a few other statistics, you come away with a more accurate understanding of the situation.

USING STATISTICS TO DESCRIBE DATA

In contrast to the information in Table 2.3, psychological research often involves a large number of measurements. Typically it is difficult to make much sense out of the *data* (i.e., the information collected) by examining the individual scores of each participant. **Descriptive statistics** *allow us to summarize and describe the characteristics of a set (or distribution) of data.* You are already familiar with one descriptive statistic—the correlation coefficient, which we discussed on pages 43–44. Now we'll introduce two other types of descriptive statistics.

Measures of Central Tendency

Given a set of data, *measures of central tendency* address the question, "What's the typical score?" One measure, the **mode,** *is the most frequently occurring score in a distribution.* At Honest Al's the modal salary is $263,000. While the mode is easy to identify, it may not be the most representative score. Clearly, $263,000 is not the typical salary of the 10 consultants.

A second measure of central tendency is the **median,** *the point that divides a distribution of scores in half when those scores are arranged in order from lowest to highest.* Half of the scores lie above the median, half below it. In Table 2.3, because there is an even number of scores, the median is $28,500— the point halfway between employee 5 ($29,000) and employee 6 ($28,000).

Finally, the **mean** *is the arithmetic average of a set of scores.* To determine the mean you simply add up all the scores in a distribution and divide by the number of scores. The $75,000 average that Honest Al quoted was the mean salary.

Be aware that the mean has a disadvantage: It is affected by extreme scores. The $263,000 salaries of Al's brother and sister inflate the mean, making it less representative of the typical salary.

▶ **Focus 20**
Describe three measures of central tendency and two measures of variability.

TABLE 2.3	Salaries of 10 Consultants at Honest Al's Consulting Firm
Consultant	**Annual Salary**
1. Al's brother	$263,000 ⎤ mode
2. Al's sister	263,000 ⎦ ᵃmost frequent score ᵇ
3. Johnson	30,500
4. Rodriguez	29,500
5. Jones	29,000
6. Chen	28,000 ⎤ median
7. Brown	27,500 ⎦ ᵃmiddle score: $28,500 ᵇ
8. Carter	27,500
9. Mullins	26,500
10. Watson	26,000
Mean (average salary)	= $\frac{\$750,000}{10 \text{ scores}}$ = $75,000

The median, in contrast, is not affected by extreme scores. Changing the top salary to $1 million does not change the median but further inflates the mean. Still, the mean has a key advantage over the median and mode: It captures information from every score. In Table 2.3, if Johnson and Rodriguez each received a $50,000 salary increase, the median and mode would not change. However, the mean would increase and reflect the fact that Honest Al was now paying some of his employees a better salary.

Because the mean takes all the information in a set of scores into account, it is the most commonly used measure of central tendency in research, and perhaps in everyday life as well. But keep in mind that extreme scores will distort the mean. When you go for that job interview, also ask about the median and modal salaries.

Measures of Variability

To describe a set of data, we want to know not only the typical score, but also whether the scores cluster together or vary widely. *Measures of variability* capture the degree of variation, or spread, in a distribution of scores. Look at Table 2.4, which lists Honest Al's salaries alongside those of 10 consultants from Claire's Consulting Firm. The mean salary is the same at both firms, but notice how Claire's salaries are closer to one another—less variable—than are Al's. The simplest but least informative measure of variability is the **range,** *which is the difference between the highest and lowest scores in a distribution.* At Honest Al's, the salary range is $237,000; at Claire's the range is only $11,000.

▶ **Focus 21**
What is the purpose of inferential statistics? What is statistical significance?

A more important statistic, the **standard deviation,** *takes into account how much each score in a distribution differs from the mean.* At Honest Al's, the standard deviation is $94,009; at Claire's it's only $3,000. We need not be concerned here with how the standard deviation is calculated. Rather, the key point is that it uses information from every score, whereas the range only takes into account the highest and lowest scores.

USING STATISTICS TO MAKE INFERENCES

Descriptive statistics allow researchers to efficiently summarize data, but researchers typically want to go beyond mere description and draw *inferences* (conclusions) from their data. To illustrate, let's return to our experiment examining how noise affects students' learning. Suppose that 80 college students agree to participate in our study. We randomly assign 40 students to the noise condition and 40 to the quiet condition. They study the identical textbook material for 30 minutes and then take a 20-item multiple-choice test. We find that, on average, students in the noisy room perform more poorly (mean = 8.20 correct answers) than students in the quiet room (mean = 12.50).

At this point we would like to make a general inference: Noise impairs students' learning of textbook material. However, we must first wrestle with a key issue: Even if our experiment had all the proper controls and there were no confounding variables, perhaps the noise really had no effect on performance, and our findings were merely a chance outcome. Perhaps, for example, just by random chance we happened to end up with 40 students in the noisy room who would have performed this poorly anyway, even if they had been in a quiet room.

For all types of research, **inferential statistics** *tell us how likely it is that our findings are merely a chance occurrence.* In our case, they help determine the probability that we would obtain similar results if our experiment were repeated over and over with other samples drawn from the same population of college students. Inferential statistics tell researchers whether their findings are *statistically significant.* **Statistical significance** *means that it is very unlikely that a particular finding occurred by chance alone.* Psychologists typically consider results to be statistically significant only if the results could have occurred by chance alone fewer than 5 times in 100.

TABLE 2.4 Annual Salaries of Ten Consultants at Two Consulting Firms		
Honest Al's Firm		**Claire's Firm**
$263,000		$81,000
263,000		78,000
30,500		76,000
29,500		76,000
29,000		76,000
28,000		75,000
27,500		73,000
27,000		73,000
26,500		72,000
26,000		70,000
$75,000	Mean	$75,000
$237,000	Range	$11,000
$94,009	Standard deviation	$3,000

Keep in mind that *statistical significance* does not mean that a finding is scientifically or socially important. If thousands of students took our 20-item test in either a noisy or quiet room, and if the variability (the standard deviation) within each condition was small, then even a tiny difference between the average test performance of these groups might be statistically significant but trivial for practical purposes. Yet a psychological technique that helps athletes run or swim faster by one hundredth of a second might make the difference between winning the gold medal or no medal at the Olympics. Statistical significance only means it is unlikely that the results of study are due to chance. The scientific or social significance of the findings must be judged within a broader context.

META-ANALYSIS: COMBINING THE RESULTS OF MANY STUDIES

As research on a topic accumulates, scientists must reach overall conclusions about how variables are related. Often experts on a topic will review the number and quality of studies that support, or fail to support, a particular relation and then draw conclusions that they believe are best supported by the facts.

Increasingly, these expert reviews are being supplemented by **meta-analysis,** *a statistical procedure for combining the results of different studies that examine the same topic.* In a typical research study, the responses of each participant are analyzed. In a meta-analysis, however, each study is treated as a "single participant," and its overall results are analyzed with those of other studies. A meta-analysis will tell researchers about the direction and statistical strength of the relation between two variables.

For example, would you expect that exercising during the day helps people sleep better at night? One meta-analysis combined the results of 38 studies and concluded that the overall relation is weak (Youngstedt et al., 1997). On average, people slept only about 10 minutes longer when they had exercised that day, and they fell asleep only about 1 minute faster.

Researchers who use meta-analysis must decide which studies to include and describe their common limitations. The authors of the meta-analysis on exercise and sleep cautioned that most studies only examined young adults who slept well. Many researchers consider meta-analysis to be the most objective way to integrate the findings of multiple studies and reach overall conclusions about behavior.

IN REVIEW

- Statistics can be misleading if they are based on very few observations or are distorted by extreme scores. Understanding basic statistical concepts can help you be a smarter citizen and consumer.

- Descriptive statistics summarize the characteristics of a set of data.

- Measures of central tendency identify the typical score in a distribution. The mode is the most frequent score. The median is the halfway point in a distribution of scores arranged in numerical order; half of the scores are above and half are below. The mean is the arithmetic average of the scores.

- Measures of variability assess whether scores are clustered together or spread out. The range is the difference between the highest and lowest scores. The standard deviation takes into account how much each score differs from the mean.

- Inferential statistics allow researchers to determine whether their findings reflect a chance occurrence. The term *statistical significance* means that it is very unlikely that a particular finding occurred by chance alone.

- Meta-analysis statistically combines the results of many studies that examine the same variables. It calculates the direction and strength of the overall relation between those variables.

▶ **Focus 22**
Describe the purpose of meta-analysis.

CRITICAL THINKING IN SCIENCE AND EVERYDAY LIFE

In today's world we are exposed to a great deal of information about human behavior—some of which is accurate and much of which is not. Especially in the popular media, we encounter oversimplifications, overgeneralizations, and *pseudoscientific misinformation*—bunk and psychobabble that is made to sound scientific. To be an informed consumer, you must be able to critically evaluate research and identify factors that limit the validity of conclusions. Critical-thinking skills can also help you avoid being misled by claims made in everyday life, such as those in advertisements. Thus, enhancing your critical-thinking skills is an important benefit that you can derive from your psychology course.

▶ **Focus 23**
What critical thinking questions can be used to evaluate claims made in everyday life?

Throughout this chapter you have seen how critical thinking, a healthy dose of skepticism, and the scientific method help scientists solve puzzles of mind and behavior. As critical thinkers, we should recognize that our beliefs and emotions can act as psychological blinders that allow us to accept inadequate evidence uncritically, especially when this evidence supports our current views. This does not mean that we should be so skeptical of everything that we end up believing nothing at all. Rather, we need to balance open-mindedness with a healthy skepticism and evaluate evidence for what it is worth (Figure 2.24).

FIGURE 2.24

Modern society bombards us with scientific and pseudoscientific claims. Critical thinking often can help us tell good science from junk science. This journal, which promotes healthy skepticism and critical thinking, is published by the Committee for the Scientific Investigation of Claims of the Paranormal. Another organization, the Skeptics Society, publishes *Skeptic*. You can find the Web sites for these organizations at the Online Learning Center for this textbook. After reaching the OLC, go to Chapter 2.

 Applying Psychological Science   **Evaluating Claims in Research and Everyday Life**

To exercise your critical-thinking skills, read the following descriptions of a research study, an advertisement, and a newspaper article. Have some fun and see if you agree with the claims made.

Write down your answers and compare them with the answers provided at the end of the box. You can facilitate critical thinking by asking yourself the following questions:

1. What claim is being made?
2. What evidence is being presented to support this claim?
3. What is the quality of the evidence? Are there any other plausible explanations for the conclusions being drawn?
4. What additional evidence would be needed to reach a clearer conclusion?
5. What is the most reasonable conclusion to draw?

SOME INTERESTING CLAIMS

Example 1: A Lot of Bull

Deep inside the brain of humans and other mammals is a structure called the *caudate nucleus*. Years ago, a prominent researcher hypothesized that this part of the brain is responsible for turning off aggressive behavior. The scientist was so confident in his hypothesis that he bet his life on it. A microelectrode was implanted inside the caudate nucleus of a large, aggressive bull. The researcher stood before the bull

and, like a Spanish matador, waved a cape to incite the bull to charge. As the bull thundered toward him, the researcher pressed a button on a radio transmitter that he held in his other hand. This sent a signal that caused the microelectrode to stimulate the bull's caudate nucleus. Suddenly, the bull broke off its charge and stopped. Each time this sequence was repeated, the bull stopped its charge. The researcher concluded that the caudate nucleus was the "aggression-off" center of the brain.

Stimulating the caudate nucleus caused the bull to stop charging, but does this demonstrate that the caudate nucleus is an aggression-off center? Why or why not? (*Hint:* What other bodily functions might the caudate nucleus help regulate that would cause the bull to stop charging?)

Example 2: Vacations and Burglaries

A newspaper advertisement appeared in several American cities. The headline "While You're on Vacation, Burglars Go to Work" was followed by this statement: "According to FBI statistics, over 26 percent of home burglaries take place between Memorial Day and Labor Day" (U.S. holidays in late May and early September). The ad then offered a summer sale price for a home security system. In sum, the ad implied that burglaries are particularly likely to occur while people are away on summer vacation. How do you feel about this claim and its supporting evidence?

Example 3: Will Staying up Late Cause You to Forget What You Have Studied?

The headline of a newspaper article read, "Best Way to Retain Complex Information? Sleep on It, Researcher Says." The article began, "Students who study hard Monday through Friday and then party all night on weekends may lose much of what they learned during the week, according to a sleep researcher." The researcher was then quoted as saying, "It appears skewing the sleep cycle by just two hours can have this effect. Watching a long, late movie the night following a class and then sleeping in the next morning will make it so you're not learning what you thought. You'll not lose it all—just about 30 percent."

Next, the experiment was described. College students learned a complex logic game and then were assigned to one of four sleep conditions. Students in the control condition were allowed to have a normal night's sleep. Those in Condition 2 were not allowed to have any sleep, whereas students in Conditions 3 and 4 were awakened only when they went into a particular stage of sleep. (We'll learn about sleep stages in Chapter 5.) A week later everyone was tested again. Participants in Conditions 3 and 4 performed 30 percent worse than the other two groups.

Reexamine the experimental conditions, then identify what's wrong with the claims in the first paragraph.

CRITICAL ANALYSES OF THE CLAIMS

Analysis 1: A Lot of Bull

Perhaps the caudate nucleus plays a role in vision, memory, or movement, and stimulating it momentarily caused the bull either to become blind, to forget what it was doing, or to alter its movement. Perhaps the bull simply became dizzy or experienced pain. These are all possible explanations for why the bull stopped charging. In fact, the caudate nucleus helps regulate movement; it is not an aggression-off center in the brain.

Analysis 2: Vacations and Burglaries

First, how much is "over 26 percent"? We don't know for sure but can assume that it is less than 27 percent, because it would be to the advertiser's advantage to state the highest number possible. The key problem is that the time period between Memorial Day and Labor Day typically represents between 26 and 29 percent of the days of the year. Therefore about 26 percent of burglaries occur during about 26 percent of the year. Wow! Technically the ad is correct: Burglars do go to work in the summer while you're on vacation. But the ad also may have misled people. Burglars seem to be just as busy at other times of the year.

Analysis 3: Will Staying up Late Cause You to Forget What You Have Studied?

It could be true that going to bed and waking up later than usual might cause you to forget more of what you have studied. However, the article does not provide evidence for this claim. Look at the four conditions carefully. To test this claim, an experiment would need to include a condition in which participants went to bed later than usual, slept through the night, and then awakened later than usual. But in this experiment, the control group slept normally, and the three experimental conditions examined only the effects of getting no sleep or losing certain types of sleep.

When you read newspaper or magazine articles, look beyond the headlines and think about whether the claims are truly supported by the evidence. Were you able to pick out some flaws in these claims before you read the analyses? Critical thinking requires practice, and you will get better at it if you keep asking yourself the five critical-thinking questions listed earlier.

IN REVIEW

- Critical thinking is an important life skill. We should also be open-minded to new ideas that are supported by solid evidence.

- In science and everyday life, critical thinking can prevent us from developing false impressions about how the world operates and from being duped in everyday life by unsubstantiated claims.

- When someone presents you with a claim, you should consider the quality of the evidence, whether there are other plausible explanations for the conclusions being drawn, and whether additional evidence is needed to reach a clearer conclusion. Then ask yourself whether the claim is the most reasonable conclusion to draw.

KEY TERMS AND CONCEPTS

Each term has been boldfaced and defined in the chapter on the page indicated in parentheses.

archival measures (p. 35)
case study (p. 38)

confounding of variables (p. 50)
control group (p. 46)

correlational research (p. 41)
correlation coefficient (p. 43)

counterbalancing (p. 47)

demand characteristics (p. 51)

dependent variable (p. 45)

descriptive research (p. 37)

descriptive statistics (p. 55)

double-blind procedure (p. 52)

experiment (p. 45)

experimental group (p. 46)

experimenter expectancy effects (p. 52)

external validity (p. 52)

hypothesis (p. 30)

independent variable (p. 45)

inferential statistics (p. 56)

informed consent (p. 36)

internal validity (p. 50)

mean (p. 55)

median (p. 55)

meta-analysis (p. 57)

mode (p. 55)

naturalistic observation (p. 39)

negative correlation (p. 43)

operational definition (p. 33)

placebo (p. 51)

placebo effect (p. 51)

population (p. 40)

positive correlation (p. 43)

random assignment (p. 46)

random sampling (p. 40)

range (p. 56)

replication (p. 52)

representative sample (p. 40)

sample (p. 40)

scatterplot (p. 44)

standard deviation (p. 56)

statistical significance (p. 56)

survey research (p. 40)

theory (p. 31)

unobtrusive measures (p. 34)

variable (p. 33)

❓ What Do You Think?

SHOULD YOU TRUST INTERNET AND POP MEDIA SURVEYS? (PAGE 41)

Recall the *Literary Digest* survey we just discussed. Even with 2 million people responding, the survey was inaccurate because the sample did not represent the overall population.

Typical Internet, magazine, and phone-in surveys share two major problems. First, people who choose to respond are entirely *self-selected* (rather than selected by the researcher), and the resulting samples likely do not even represent the entire population of people who use the Internet, subscribe to that magazine, or watch that TV show, respectively. Perhaps those who respond are more motivated, have a more helpful personality, or differ in some other important way from those who don't respond.

Second, it is unlikely that samples of Internet users, magazine subscribers, and TV news viewers represent the population at large (e.g., American adults). For example, at the time one massive Internet study was conducted, about 25 percent of Americans were Black or Latino. Yet just under 5 percent of the people who participated in the study were Black or Latino (Gosling et al., 2004). Do you think that the readers of *Cosmopolitan, Playboy, Guns & Ammo,* or any magazine typify the general population? In sum, because Internet and pop media surveys do not use random sampling, they are likely to generate samples that are not representative of the broader population.

Surely, many news organizations sponsor high-quality surveys conducted by professional pollsters. The key is that these surveys, such as political polls, use appropriate random sampling procedures to obtain representative samples.

Finally, be aware that some psychologists—especially those who study people's personality and social behaviors—are increasingly using the Internet to collect research data. As users surf the Web, they may find a site that invites them to participate in an experiment or take a psychological test. These studies are not surveys that critically depend on having representative samples of the broader population. Rather, they typically examine relations among variables and underlying psychological principles. Some researchers question the validity of such Internet-based studies, but proponents have shown that most of these concerns are unfounded. More research is needed, but thus far it seems that Internet-based studies of this type yield findings that are consistent with those obtained from more traditional types of methods (Best et al., 2001; Gosling et al., 2004).

DOES EATING ICE CREAM CAUSE PEOPLE TO DROWN? (PAGE 43)

Just because two variables are correlated, we cannot conclude that they are causally related. First, consider the bidirectionality problem. We don't see any likely way that drownings could cause the rest of the public to eat more ice cream, so let's rule that out. Can we conclude, then, that more ice cream consumption causes more drownings? We suppose that in a few cases gorging on ice cream soon before swimming might enhance the risk of drowning. But nationally, how often is this likely to happen?

Now consider the third-variable problem. What other factors might cause people to eat more ice cream and also lead to an increase in drownings? The most obvious third variable is "daily temperature" (or "month of the year"). Summer months bring hotter days, and people eat more ice cream in hot weather. Likewise, on hotter days drownings increase simply because so many more people go swimming. In short, the most reasonable conclusion is that the ice cream–drowning correlation is due to a third variable.

CHAPTER THREE

Biological Foundations of Behavior:

Evolution, Genes, and Brain

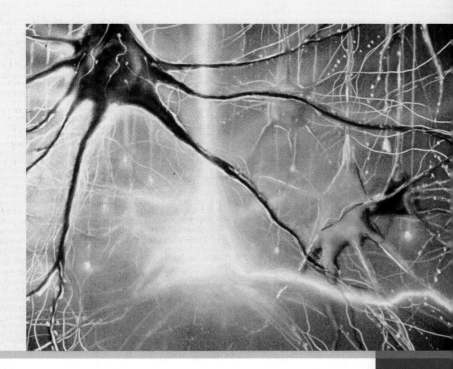

CHAPTER OUTLINE

The brain is the last and grandest biological frontier, the most complex thing we have yet discovered in our universe. It contains hundreds of billions of cells interlinked through trillions of connections. The brain boggles the mind.

—JAMES WATSON, NOBEL PRIZE RECIPIENT

FIGURE 3.1

Jim Springer and Jim Lewis are identical twins who were separated when 4 weeks old and raised in different families. When reunited in adulthood, they showed striking similarities in personality, interests, and behavior. They both favored poodles as pets and had erected circular benches around trees in their yards.

 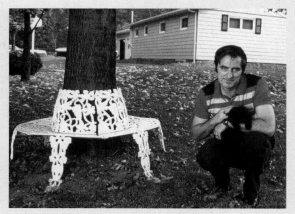

FIGURE 3.2

The brain damage suffered by Phineas Gage seemed to change him into a new person. The red image shows the path of the spike that shot through Gage's brain.

I dentical twins Jim Springer and Jim Lewis met for the first time when they were 39 years old. They discovered each other through a landmark University of Minnesota study of twins who had been separated shortly after birth and raised by different adoptive parents. Although they had been raised in different families, the two Jims found that they had many things in common. Both had been married twice, and each had a son named James. Both men smoked Salem cigarettes and preferred Miller Lite beer. Both worked part-time as sheriffs, suffered from the same kind of headache symptoms when under stress, and bit their fingernails. Both twins were the only people in their neighborhoods to have built a circular bench around a tree in their front yards (Figure 3.1). When given a series of psychological tests, they were strikingly similar in intelligence and personality traits (Tellegen et al., 1988).

■ ■ ■ ■ ■

T he year was 1848. As the Vermont winter approached, a railroad construction crew hurried to complete its work on a new track. The men could not know that they were about to witness one of the most celebrated incidents in the annals of neuroscience.

As a blasting crew prepared its charges, the dynamite accidentally exploded. A 13-pound spike more than 3 feet long was propelled through the head of Phineas Gage, a 25-year-old foreman. The spike entered through the left cheek, passed through the brain, and emerged through the top of the skull (Figure 3.2). Dr. J. M. Harlow, who treated Gage, described the incident:

> The patient was thrown upon his back by the explosion, and gave a few convulsive motions of the extremities, but spoke in a few minutes. He . . . seemed perfectly conscious, but was becoming exhausted from the hemorrhage, . . . the blood pouring from the top of his head. . . . He bore his sufferings with firmness, and directed my attention to the hole in his cheek, saying, "the iron entered there and passed through my head." (1868, pp. 330–332)

Miraculously, Gage survived. Or did he?

> His physical health is good, and I am inclined to say that he has recovered. Has no pain in his head, but says it has a queer feeling that he is not able to describe. . . . His contractors, who regarded him

as the most efficient and capable foreman in their employ previous to his injury, considered the change in his mind so marked that they could not give him his place again. The equilibrium or balance, so to speak, between his intellectual faculties and animal propensities, seems to have been destroyed. He is fitful, irreverent, indulging at times in the grossest profanity (which was not previously his custom), manifesting but little deference for his fellows, impatient of restraint or advice when it conflicts with his desires . . . devising many plans of future operations, which are no sooner arranged than they are abandoned in turn for others. . . . His mind is radically changed, so decidedly that his friends and acquaintances say that he is "no longer Gage." (pp. 339–340)

How can we explain the behavioral similarities in Jim Springer and Jim Lewis? The Minnesota researchers found that the adoptive families of the "Jim twins" differed in important ways. What the Jims did have in common, however, were their identical genes. Although their behavioral commonalities could be coincidental, the Minnesota researchers found that other identical-twin pairs separated early in life also showed striking similarities. When a pair of twin housewives from England met one another in Minneapolis, they found to their amazement that each was wearing seven rings, two bracelets on one wrist, and a watch and bracelet on the other. Another pair of men, one raised in Germany and the other in the Caribbean, shared a host of unusual behaviors, such as reading magazines from back to front, flushing toilets before using them, and dipping buttered toast in their coffee. Whether raised together or apart, the identical twins were far more similar in personality and intelligence test scores than were nontwins and fraternal twins raised in the same families (Tellegen et al., 1988). For psychologists, the connections between the twins' biological and behavioral similarities raise fascinating questions that may be answered by examining the biological foundations of behavior.

The tragic story of Phineas Gage poses different questions. Physical damage to Gage's brain changed his thinking and behavior so radically that he became, psychologically, a different person. Is our personal identity so thoroughly locked within our skull? Is who we are and what we do reducible to the electrochemical activities of the nervous system?

It has been said that each of us is (1) what all humans are, (2) what some other humans are, and (3) what no other human in the history of the world has been, is, or will be (Kluckhohn & Murray, 1953). In this chapter we will explore biological factors that underlie the behavioral commonalities and differences among humans. First, we will explore the role of evolutionary forces, which forged some of what you are millions of years before your birth. Second, we will consider the role of the genes, passed on to you at

conception. As we will see, genetic factors influence many of your psychological characteristics and behaviors. Finally, we will enter the realm of neuroscience, where we focus on the brain and other physiological systems whose functions underlie your every thought, feeling, and behavior. These systems were shaped in part by ancient evolutionary forces and passed on to you by genetic programming. In each instance, whether considering evolutionary, genetic, or neural functions, we will see that neither biological nor environmental factors act in isolation; rather, they interact with one another in complex ways.

As we shall see throughout the book, the biological level of analysis provides us with key insights into behavior and its causes. The knowledge gained in this chapter will give you the background needed to understand many behaviors in the chapters that follow.

EVOLUTION AND BEHAVIOR: INFLUENCES FROM THE DISTANT PAST

In the misty forests and verdant grasslands of past eons, our early human ancestors faced many environmental challenges as they struggled to survive. If even one of your ancestors had not behaved adaptively enough to survive and reproduce, you would not be here to contemplate your existence. In this sense, each of us is an evolutionary success story. As descendants of those successful forebears, we carry within us genes that contributed to their adaptive and reproductive success.

The vast majority (99.9 percent) of genes we share with all other humans creates the "human nature" that makes us like all other people. We enter the world with **biologically based mechanisms** *that enable and predispose us to behave, to feel, and even to think in certain ways* (Stearns & Hoekstra, 2005). In humans, these inborn capacities allow us to learn, remember, speak a language, perceive certain aspects of our environment at birth, respond with universal emotions, and bond with other humans.

Cartoon by Don Wright, © 2001. Tribune Media Services. Reprinted with permission.

Most scientists view these biological characteristics as products of an evolutionary process. Evolutionary theorists also believe that important aspects of social behavior, such as aggression, altruism, sex roles, protecting kin, and mate selection are influenced by biological mechanisms that have evolved during the development of our species.

EVOLUTION OF ADAPTIVE MECHANISMS

▶ **Focus 1**
Define evolution and explain how genetic variation and natural selection produce adaptations.

Evolution *is a change over time in the frequency with which particular genes—and the characteristics they produce—occur within an interbreeding population.* As particular genes become more or less frequent in a population, so do the characteristics they influence. Some genetic variations arise in a population through *mutations,* random events and accidents in gene reproduction during the division of cells. If mutations occur in the cells that become sperm and egg cells, the altered genes will be passed on to offspring. Mutations help create variation within a population's physical characteristics. It is this variation that makes evolution possible.

Natural Selection

Long before Charles Darwin published his theory of evolution in 1859, people knew that animals and plants could be changed over time by breeding members of a species that shared desired traits. Just as plant and animal breeders "select" for certain characteristics, so, too, does nature. According to Darwin's principle of **natural selection,** *characteristics that increase the likelihood of survival and ability to reproduce within a particular environment will be more likely to be preserved in the population and therefore will become more common in the species over time.* As environmental changes

produce new and different demands, some different characteristics may contribute to survival and the ability to pass on one's genes (Barrow, 2003). In this way natural selection acts as a set of filters, allowing certain characteristics of survivors to become more common. Conversely, characteristics of nonsurvivors become less common and, perhaps, even extinct over time. The filters also allow neutral variations that neither facilitate nor impede fitness to be preserved in a population. These neutral variations, sometimes called *evolutionary noise,* could conceivably become important in meeting some future environmental demand. For example, people differ in their ability to tolerate radiation (Vral et al., 2002). In today's world, these variations are of limited importance, but they could clearly affect survivability if a future nuclear war were to increase levels of radioactivity around the world. As those who could tolerate higher levels of radiation survived and those who could not perished, the genetic basis for high-radiation tolerance would become increasingly more common in the human species. Thus for natural selection to work, there must be individual variation in a species characteristic that influences survival or the ability to reproduce.

Evolutionary Adaptations The products of natural selection are called **adaptations,** *physical or behavioral changes that allow organisms to meet recurring environmental challenges to their survival, thereby increasing their reproductive ability.* In the final analysis, the name of the natural selection game is to pass on one's genes, either personally or through kin who share at least some of them. Some evolutionary psychologists believe this is why animals and humans may risk or even sacrifice their lives to protect their kin and the genes they carry.

Let us apply these concepts to theoretical accounts of human evolution. We begin with the notion that an organism's biology determines its behavioral capabilities and that its behavior (including its mental abilities) determines whether or not it will survive. In this manner, successful human behavior evolved along with a changing body (Buss, 1995; Tooby & Cosmides, 1992).

One theory is that when dwindling vegetation in some parts of the world forced apelike animals down from the trees and required that they hunt for food on open, grassy plains, chances for survival were greater for those capable of *bipedal locomotion* (walking on two legs). By freeing the hands, bipedalism fostered the development and use of tools and weapons that could kill at a distance (Lewin, 1998). Hunting in groups encouraged social organization, which required the development of specialized social roles (such as "hunter and protector" in the male and "nurturer of children" in the female) that still exist in most cultures. It also favored the development of language, which enhanced social communication and the transmission of knowledge.

Brain Evolution Tool use, bipedal locomotion, and social organization put new selection pressures on many parts of the body. These included the teeth, the hands, and the pelvis, all of which changed over time in response to the new dietary and behavioral demands. But the greatest pressure was placed on the brain structures involved in the abilities most critical to the emerging way of life: attention, memory, language, and thought. These mental abilities became important to survival in an environment that required quick learning and problem solving. In the evolutionary progression from *Australopithecus* (an early human ancestor who lived about 4 million years ago) through *Homo erectus* (1.6 million to 100,000 years ago) to the human subspecies Neandertal of 75,000 years ago, the brain tripled in size, and the most dramatic growth occurred in the parts of the brain that are the seat of the higher mental processes (Figure 3.3). Thus, evolved changes in behavior seem to have contributed to the development of the brain, just as the growth of the brain contributed to evolving human behavior (Striedter, 2005).

Surprisingly, perhaps, today's human brain does not differ much from the Stone Age brain of our ancient ancestors. In fact, Neandertal had a slightly larger brain than we have. Yet the fact that we perform mental activities that could not have been imagined in those ancient times tells us that human capabilities are not solely determined by the brain; cultural evolution is also important in the development of adaptations. From an evolutionary perspective, culture provides important environmental inputs to evolutionary mechanisms. The creation of new environments through our own behavior is another important part of the evolutionary equation (Boyd & Richerson, 2005).

? What Do You Think?

NATURAL SELECTION AND GENETIC DISEASES
If Darwin was right about natural selection, then why do we have so many harmful genetic disorders? Consider, for example, cystic fibrosis, a hereditary disorder of European origin that clogs one's lungs with mucus and prevents digestion, or sickle cell anemia, which causes early deaths in many people of African descent. Can you reconcile the existence of such disorders with "survival of the fittest"? Think about it, then see page 103.

An Evolutionary Snapshot of Human Nature

To evolutionary psychologists, human nature consists of inborn biological tendencies that have evolved through natural selection. We now consider a sampling of common aspects of human behavior that will be discussed in greater detail throughout the book.

- Infants are born with an innate ability to acquire any language spoken in the world (see Chapter 8). The specific language(s) learned depends on which ones they are exposed to. Deaf children have a similar innate ability to acquire any sign language, and their language acquisition pattern parallels the learning of spoken language. Language is central to human thought and communication.

- Newborns are prewired to perceive specific stimuli (see Chapter 4). For example, they are more responsive to pictures of human

▶ **Focus 2**
Describe examples of human behavior that suggest innate evolved mechanisms. Differentiate between remote and proximate causal factors.

FIGURE 3.3

An evolving brain. The human brain evolved over a period of several million years. The greatest growth occurred in those areas concerned with the higher mental processes, particularly attention, memory, language, and thought.

Australopithecus
(4 million years ago)

The brain capacity ranges from 450 to 650 cubic centimeters (cc).

Homo erectus
(1.6 million to 100,000 years ago)

Further development of the skull and jaw are evident, and brain capacity is 900 cc.

Neandertal
(75,000 years ago)

The human skull has now taken shape: the skull case has elongated to hold a complex brain of 1,450 cc.

Homo sapiens

The deeply convoluted brain reflects growth in areas concerned with higher mental processes.

FIGURE 3.4

The human smile seems to be a universal expression of positive emotion and is universally perceived in that way. Evolutionary psychologists believe that expressions of basic emotions are hardwired biological mechanisms that have adaptive value as methods of communication.

faces than to pictures of the same facial features arranged in a random pattern (Fantz, 1961). They are also able to discriminate the odor of their mother's milk from that of other women (McFarlane, 1975). Both adaptations improve human bonding with caregivers.

- At one week of age, human infants show primitive mathematical skills, successfully discriminating between two and three objects. These abilities improve with age in the absence of any training. The brain seems designed to make "greater than" and "less than" judgments, which are clearly important in decision making (Geary, 1995).

- According to Robert Hogan (1983), establishing cooperative relationships with a group was critical to the human species' survival and reproductive success. Thus humans seem to have a need to belong and strongly fear being ostracized from the group (see Chapter 10). Social anxiety (fear of social disapproval) may be an adaptive mechanism to protect against doing things that will prompt group rejection (Baumeister & Tice, 1990).

- As a species, humans tend to be altruistic and helpful to one another, especially to children and relatives (see Chapter 16). Research shows that altruism increases with degree of relatedness. People are also more likely to help younger people than older ones (Burnstein et al., 1994). Evolutionary theorists suggest that helping family members and relatives increases the likelihood that they will be able to pass on the genes they share with you. Likewise, from a species perspective, younger people have

more reproductive value than do older people.

- As we will see in Chapter 10, there is much evidence for a set of basic emotions that are universally recognized (Ekman, 1973). Smiling, for example, is a universal expression of happiness and goodwill that typically evokes positive reactions from others (Figure 3.4). Emotions are important means of social communication that evoke psychological mechansims in others (Ketellar, 1995).

- In virtually all cultures, males are more violent and more likely to kill others (particularly other males) than are females. Across many cultures, male-male killings outnumber female-female killings by about 30 to 1 (Daly & Wilson, 1988). Evolutionary researchers suggest that male-male violence is rooted in hunting, dominance hierarchies, and competition for mates, all of which enhance personal and reproductive survival.

Some Caveats Concerning Evolutionary Theory

Adaptations are forged over a long period of time—perhaps thousands of generations—and we cannot go back to prehistoric times and determine with certainty what the environmental demands were. For this reason, evolutionary theorists are often forced to infer the forces to which our ancestors adapted, leading to after-the-fact speculation that is difficult to prove or disprove. A challenge for evolutionary theorists is to avoid the logical fallacy of circular reasoning:

"Why does behavioral tendency X exist?"

"Because of environmental demand Y."

"How do we know that demand Y existed?"

"Because otherwise behavior X would not have developed."

Evolutionary theorists also remind us that it is fallacious to attribute every human characteristic to natural selection (Clark & Grunstein, 2005; Lloyd & Feldman, 2002). In the distant past, as in the present, people created environments that shape behavior, and those behaviors are often passed down through cultural learning instead of through natural selection. Likewise, a capability that evolved in the past for one reason may now be adaptive for something else. For example, the ability to discern shapes was undoubtedly advantageous for prehistoric hunters. Today, however, few humans in our culture need to hunt in order to survive, but those shape-discriminating capabilities are critical in perceiving letters and learning to read.

Evolutionary theorists have sometimes been accused of giving insufficient weight to cultural learning factors, and many debates about evolutionary explanations center around this issue (Regal, 2005). To an increasing degree, modern evolutionary theorists acknowledge the role of both *remote causes* (including past evolutionary pressures that may have prompted natural selection) and *proximate* (more recent) *causes,* such as cultural learning and the immediate environment, that influence current behavior. Human culture evolves as both a cause and an effect of brain and behavioral evolution (Boyd & Richerson, 2005). Figure 3.5 shows how remote and proximate biological and environmental factors interact with one another as determinants of behavior—from the distant evolutionary past to the present.

Finally, in thinking about behavior from an evolutionary point of view, it is important to avoid two fallacies. The first is that evolution is purposive, or "has a plan." There is, in fact, no plan in evolutionary theory; there is only adaptation to environmental demands and the natural selection process that results. Second, it makes no sense to conclude that because something in nature (such as male violence) is influenced by our genes, it is either unavoidable, natural, or right. In many cases, what we consider to be self-control or morality requires that we override our biological, or natural, inclinations. Our ability to regulate our own behavior and to exercise moral control is often just as important to our survival (i.e., as adaptive) as are our biological tendencies.

IN REVIEW

■ Evolutionary psychology focuses on biologically based mechanisms sculpted by evolutionary forces as solutions to the problems of adaptation faced by species. Some of these genetically based mechanisms are general (e.g., the ability to learn from the consequences of our behavior), but many are domain-specific, devoted to solving specific problems (e.g., mate selection).

■ Evolution is a change over time in the frequency with which particular genes—and the characteristics they produce—occur within an interbreeding population. Evolution represents an interaction between biological and environmental factors.

■ The cornerstone of Darwin's theory of evolution is the principle of natural selection. According to this principle, biologically based characteristics that contribute to survival and reproductive success increase in the population over time because those who lack the characteristics are less likely to pass on their genes.

■ Critical thinking helps counter circular reasoning about evolutionary causes and effects. We should also recognize that harmful genetically based behavior tendencies can be overridden by human decision and self-control.

FIGURE 3.5

Nature and nurture. Biological and environmental factors interact and influence one another as both remote and proximate causes of behavior. From evolution to the immmediate environment, we see the interaction of nature and nurture.

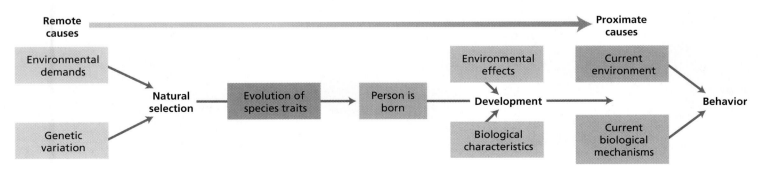

GENETIC INFLUENCES ON BEHAVIOR: FROM THEN TO NOW

Our species' evolutionary history has played a role in what humans are today. Evolution can only operate through genetic transmission across generations. For each of us, however, a more proximate influence is the genes we inherited at conception. Our physical development, including the development of the nervous system, is in large part directed by an elaborate genetic blueprint passed on to us by our parents.

Since antiquity, humans have wondered how physical characteristics are passed on from parents to their offspring. The answer was provided by Gregor Mendel, an Austrian monk whose research with garden peas in the 1860s marked the beginning of modern genetic theory. Mendel showed that heredity involves the passing on of specific organic factors, not a simple blending of the parents' characteristics. These specific factors might produce visible characteristics in the offspring, or they might simply be carried for possible transmission to another generation. In any case, the offspring of one set of parents do not all inherit the same traits, as is evident in the differences we see among brothers and sisters.

Early in the 20th century, geneticists made the important distinction between **genotype,** *the specific genetic makeup of the individual,* and **phenotype,** *the individual's observable characteristics.* A person's genotype is like the commands in a computer software program. Some of the directives are used on one occasion, some on another. Some are never used at all, either because they are contradicted by other genetic directives or because the environment never calls them forth. For example, geneticists discovered that chickens have retained the genetic code for teeth (Kollar & Fisher, 1980). Yet because the code is prevented from being expressed phenotypically, there's not a chicken anywhere that can sink its teeth into a mailman. Genotype is present from conception, but phenotype can be affected both by other genes and by the environment.

CHROMOSOMES AND GENES

The union of two cells—the egg from the mother and the sperm from the father—is called a *zygote.* Like all other cells in the body except red blood cells, which have no nucleus, the egg and sperm carry within their nuclei the material of heredity in the form of rodlike units called *chromosomes.* A **chromosome** *is a double-stranded and tightly coiled molecule of deoxyribonucleic acid (DNA).* All of the information of heredity is encoded in the various combinations of four chemical bases—adenine, thymine, guanine, and cytosine—that occur throughout the chromosome. The specific arrangement of these ATGC bases on the chromosome creates the specific commands for every feature and function of your body. The ordering of 99.9 percent of these bases is exactly the same in all people.

The DNA portion of the chromosome carries the **genes,** *the biological units of heredity* (Figure 3.6). The average gene has about 3,000 ATGC bases, but sizes vary greatly; the largest gene has 2.4 million bases. Each gene carries the codes for manufacturing specific proteins somewhere in the body. These proteins can take infinite forms, and they underlie every bodily structure and chemical process. It is estimated that about half of all genes target brain structure and functions (Kolb & Whishaw, 2003). Every moment of every day, the strands of DNA silently transmit their detailed instructions for cellular functioning.

With one exception, every cell in the human body with a nucleus has 46 chromosomes. The

▶ **Focus 3**
Differentiate between genotype and phenotype. How do genes regulate biological structures and functions?

FIGURE 3.6

The ladder of life. Chromosomes consist of two long, twisted strands of DNA, the chemical that carries genetic information. Except for red blood cells, every cell in the body carries within its nucleus 23 pairs of chromosomes, each containing numerous genes that regulate every aspect of cellular functioning.

Each chromosome contains numerous **genes**, segments of DNA that contain instructions to make proteins—the building blocks of life.

One **chromosome** of every pair is from each parent.

Each nucleus contains 46 **chromosomes**, arranged in 23 pairs.

Each human cell (except red blood cells) contains a **nucleus.**

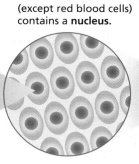

The human body contains 100 trillion **cells.**

exception is the *sex cell* (the egg or sperm), which has only 23. At conception, the 23 chromosomes from the egg combine with the 23 corresponding chromosomes from the sperm to form a new cell containing 46 chromosomes. Within each chromosome, the corresponding genes received from each parent occur in matched pairs.

Dominant, Recessive, and Polygenic Effects

Genotype and phenotype are not identical because some genes are dominant and some are recessive. If a gene in the pair received from both the mother and father is *dominant,* the particular characteristic that it controls will be displayed. If, however, a gene received from one parent is *recessive,* the characteristic will not show up unless the partner gene inherited from the other parent is also recessive. In humans, for example, brown eyes are dominant over blue eyes. A child will have blue eyes only if both parents have contributed recessive genes for blue eyes. However, even if the blue-eyed trait remains hidden (as would occur if one parent has brown eyes), the recessive gene for blue eyes will be passed on to offspring by the brown-eyed child.

In a great many instances, *a number of gene pairs combine their influences to create a single phenotypic trait. This is known as* **polygenic transmission,** and it complicates the straightforward picture that would occur if all characteristics were determined by one pair of genes. It also magnifies the number of possible variations in a trait that can occur. It is estimated that the union of sperm and egg can result in about 70 trillion potential genotypes, accounting for the great diversity of characteristics that occurs even in siblings.

At present our knowledge of phenotypes greatly exceeds our understanding of the underlying genotype, but that may soon change. In 1990 geneticists began the Human Genome Project, a coordinated effort to map the DNA, including all the genes of the human organism. The genetic structure in every one of the 23 chromosome pairs has now been mapped by methods that allow the investigators to literally disassemble the genes on each chromosome and study their specific sequence of substances (A, T, G, and C; see Figure 3.6).

The first results of the genome project provided a surprise: The genome consists of approximately 30,000 genes rather than the 100,000 previously estimated (Human Genome Project, 2004). That result told geneticists that gene interactions are even more complex than formerly believed and that it's highly unlikely that manipulating a single gene could solve a complex problem such

as anorexia or schizophrenia. Even given this reduced number of genes, the 3.1 billion ATGC combinations in the entire human genome, if printed consecutively, would add about 150,000 pages to this book.

The "book of life" revealed by the Human Genome Project has given us greater knowledge of which specific genes or gene combinations are involved in normal and abnormal characteristics (McGuffin et al., 2005). The location and structure of more than 80 genes that contribute to hereditary diseases have already been identified through gene mapping (Human Genome Project, 2005). On another front, behavioral scientists are exploring the gene combinations that underlie behavior and, in some cases, are modifying those genes.

BEHAVIOR GENETICS

Researchers in the field of **behavior genetics** *study how heredity and environment interact to influence psychological characteristics.* Whereas evolutionary psychologists are interested in the commonalities among people, behavior geneticists focus on the potential role of genetic factors in accounting for differences among people.

Degree of relatedness to one another tells us how genetically similar people are. Recall that children get half of their genetic material from each parent. Thus the probability of sharing any particular gene with one of your parents is 50 percent, or .50. Brothers and sisters also have a .50 probability of sharing the same gene with one another, since they get their genetic material from the same parents. And what about a grandparent? Here, the probability of a shared gene is .25 because, for example, your maternal grandmother passed half of her genes on to your mother, who passed half of hers on to you. Thus the likelihood that you inherited a specific gene from your grandmother is .50 × .50, or .25. The probability of sharing a gene is also .25 for half siblings, who share half their genes with the common biological parent but none with the other parent. If you have a first cousin, you share 12.5 of your genes with him or her. Theoretically, an adopted child has an entirely different genotype from those of his or her adoptive parents, and the same is true for unrelated people. These facts about genetic similarity give us a basis for studying the role of genetic factors in physical and behavioral characteristics. If a characteristic has higher **concordance,** or *co-occurrence,* in people who are more closely related to one another, this points to a possible genetic contribution, particularly if the people have lived in different environments.

▶ **Focus 4**
Describe dominant, recessive, and polygenic influences on phenotype.

▶Focus 5

How are adoption and twin studies are used to estimate genetic and environmental determinants of behavior?

Family, Adoption, and Twin Studies

Knowing the level of genetic similarity among family and kin provides a basis for estimating the relative contributions of heredity and environment to a physical or psychological characteristic. As discussed earlier, family members and relatives differ in the percentages of genes they share. Many studies have shown that the more similar people are genetically, the more similar they are likely to be psychologically, although this level of similarity differs depending on the characteristic in question.

One research method used to estimate the influence of genetic factors is the **adoption study**, *in which people who were adopted early in life are compared on some characteristic with both their biological parents, with whom they share genetic endowment, and with their adoptive parents, with whom they share no genes.* If adopted people are more similar to a biological parent (with whom they share 50 percent of their genes) than to an adoptive parent (with whom they share a common environment but no genes), a genetic influence on that trait is indicated. If they're more similar to their adoptive

parents, environmental factors are judged to be more important for that particular characteristic. For example, Seymour Kety and coworkers (1978) identified adoptees who were diagnosed with schizophrenia in adulthood. They then examined the backgrounds of the biological and adoptive parents and relatives to determine the rate of schizophrenia in the two sets of families. The researchers found that 12 percent of biological family members had also been diagnosed with schizophrenia, compared with a concordance rate of only 3 percent of adoptive family members, suggesting a hereditary link.

Twin studies, *which compare trait similarities in identical and fraternal twins,* are one of the more powerful techniques used in behavior genetics. Because *monozygotic,* or identical, twins develop from the same fertilized egg, they are genetically identical (Figure 3.7). Approximately 1 in 250 births produces identical twins. *Dizygotic,* or fraternal, twins develop from two fertilized eggs, so they share 50 percent of their genetic endowment, like any other set of brothers and sisters. Approximately 1 in 150 births produces fraternal twins.

FIGURE 3.7

Two kinds of twins. Identical (*monozygotic*) twins come from a single egg and sperm as a result of a division of the zygote. They have all of their genes in common. Fraternal (*dizygotic*) twins result from two eggs fertilized by two sperm. They share only half of their genes. Source: (a, c) Smith, 1998.

Identical twins (1 in 250 births)

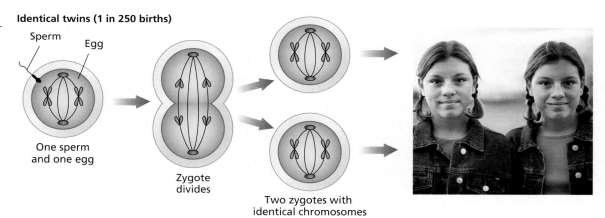

Sperm
Egg

One sperm
and one egg

Zygote
divides

Two zygotes with
identical chromosomes

Fraternal twins (1 in 150 births)

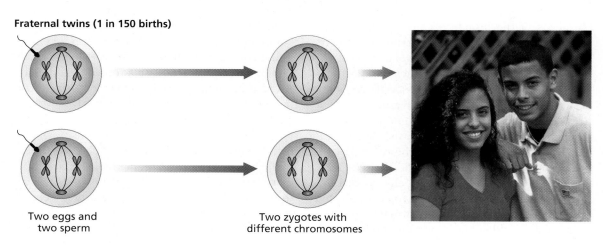

Two eggs and
two sperm

Two zygotes with
different chromosomes

Twins, like other siblings, are usually raised in the same familial environment. Thus we can compare concordance rates or behavioral similarity in samples of identical and fraternal twins, assuming that if the identical twins are far more similar to one another than are the fraternal twins in a specific characteristic, a genetic factor is likely to be involved. Of course, the fly in this ointment is the possibility that because identical twins are more similar to one another in appearance than fraternal twins are, they are treated more alike and therefore share a more similar environment. This could partially account for greater behavioral similarity in identical twins.

To rule out this environmental explanation, behavior geneticists have adopted an even more elegant research method. Sometimes, as in the University of Minnesota study in which the Jim twins participated, researchers are able to find and compare sets of identical and fraternal twins who were separated very early in life and raised in *different* environments (Bouchard et al., 1990). By eliminating environmental similarity, this design permits a better basis for evaluating the respective contributions of genes and environment.

Many (but not all) psychological characteristics, including intelligence, personality traits, and certain psychological disorders, have a notable genetic contribution (Bouchard, 2004). Adopted children are typically found to be more similar to their biological parents than to their adoptive parents on these measures, and identical twins tend to be more similar to one another than are fraternal twins, even if they were separated early in life and reared in different environments (Loehlin, 1992; Lykken et al., 1992; Plomin & Spinath, 2004). On the other hand, identical twins reared together still tend to be more similar than identicals reared apart, indicating that the environment also makes a difference.

Heritability: Estimating Genetic Influence

A **heritability coefficient** *estimates the extent to which the differences, or variation, in a specific characteristic within a group of people can be attributed to genetic factors.* Heritability estimates can be computed in different ways. One common method is to double the absolute difference between correlation coefficients derived from identical and fraternal twins on a particular characteristic. For example, twin studies have shown that the correlation of IQ scores in sets of identical twins is around .85 and around .50 in sets of fraternal twins (Plomin & Spinath, 2004). The difference of .35 between those correlations is multiplied by 2 to give

Trait	Heritability Estimate
Height	.80
Weight	.60
Intelligence (IQ)	.70
School achievement	.40
Personality	
Extraversion	.36
Conscientiousness	.28
Agreeableness	.28
Neuroticism	.31
Temperament	
Emotional reactivity	.40
Activity level	.25
Sociability	.25
Impulsivity	.45

TABLE 3.1 Heritability Estimates for Various Human Characteristics

SOURCES: Bouchard et al., 1990; Dunn & Plomin, 1990; Tellegen et al., 1988.

us a heritability estimate of .70 for intelligence. Table 3.1 shows the range of heritability found for various human physical and psychological characteristics.

This heritability coefficient of .70 for intelligence in Table 3.1 indicates that 70 percent of the amount of variation in *that sample's* IQ scores can be attributed to genetic differences among its members. Note carefully that it does *not* mean that 70 percent of a particular person's intelligence is due to genetic factors and the rest to the environment. It is important to remember that heritability applies only to differences within groups (and estimates can vary, depending on the group).

Even while they try to estimate the contributions of genetic factors, behavior geneticists realize that genes and environment are not really separate determinants of behavior. Instead, they operate as a single, integrated system. Gene expression is influenced on a daily basis by the environment. For example, two children of equal intellectual potential may have differences in IQs as great as 15 to 20 points if one is raised in an impoverished environment and the other in an enriched one. And high or low environmental stress can be responsible for turning on or off genes that regulate the production of stress hormones. We will have occasion to view gene-environment interactions in virtually every chapter of this book.

▶ **Focus 6**
Define heritability. How are heritability coefficients estimated?

► **Focus 7**
Describe some of the gene-modification methods used to study causes of behavior.

Gene Manipulation

Until recently, genetics researchers had to be content with studying genetic phenomena occurring in nature. Aside from selectively breeding plants and animals for certain characteristics or studying the effects of genetic mutations, they had no ability to influence genes directly. Today, however, technological advances have enabled scientists not only to map the human genome but also to duplicate and modify the structures of genes themselves (Aldridge, 1998).

In one gene-manipulation approach, researchers use certain enzymes (proteins that create chemical reactions) to cut the long threadlike molecules of genetic DNA into pieces, combine it with DNA from another organism, and insert it into a host organism, such as a bacterium. Inside the host, the new DNA combination continues to divide and produce many copies of itself. Researchers can also insert new genetic material into viruses that can infiltrate the brain and modify the genetic structure in brain tissue.

Recent gene-modification research by psychologists has focused on processes such as learning, memory, emotion, and motivation. One procedure done with animals (typically mice) is to alter a specific gene in a way that prevents it from carrying out its normal function. This is called a *knockout procedure* because that particular function of the gene is knocked out, or eliminated. The effects on behavior are then observed. For example, psychologists can insert genetic material that will prevent neurons from responding to a particular neurotransmitter. They can then measure whether the animal's ability to learn or remember is subsequently affected. This can help psychologists determine the importance of particular transmitter substances in relation to the behaviors of interest (Jang et al., 2003; Thomas & Palmiter, 1997). Researchers can also use a *knockin procedure* to insert a new gene into an animal during the embryonic stage and study its impact on behavior. Gene-modification techniques may one day enable us to alter genes that contribute to psychological disorders, such as depression and schizophrenia (McGuffin et al., 2005).

Why are neurons critical to our thinking and behavior? To discover the answer, watch the video, "Neurons and How They Work," in Chapter 3 of your CD.

phenotype (outward appearance) are not identical, in part because some genes are dominant while others are recessive. Many characteristics are polygenic in origin, that is, they are influenced by the interactions of multiple genes.

■ Behavior geneticists study how genetic and environmental factors contribute to the development of psychological traits and behaviors. Adoption and twin studies are the major research methods used to disentangle hereditary and environmental factors. Especially useful is the study of identical and fraternal twins who were separated early in life and raised in different environments. Identical twins are more similar on a host of intellectual and personality characteristics, even when reared apart. Many psychological characteristics have appreciable heritability.

■ Genetic manipulation allows scientists to duplicate and alter genetic material or, potentially, to repair dysfunctional genes. These procedures promise groundbreaking advances in understanding genetic mechanisms and in treating physical and psychological disorders.

NEURAL MECHANISMS OF MIND AND BEHAVIOR

The evolutionary history of our species, the genes you inherited from your parents, and your life experiences have shaped who you are. From a psychological perspective, your most important physical organ is your brain, a grapefruit-sized mass of tissue that feels like jelly and has the gnarled appearance of a grayish walnut. One of the true marvels of nature, the brain has been termed "our three-pound universe," for every experience is represented within our skull (Hooper & Teresi, 1986). To understand how the brain controls our experience and behavior, we must first understand how its individual cells function and how they communicate with one another.

NEURONS

Specialized cells called **neurons** *are the basic building blocks of the nervous system.* The estimated 100 billion nerve cells in your brain and spinal cord are linked together in circuits, not unlike the electrical circuits in a computer. Each neuron has three main parts: a cell body, dendrites, and an axon (Figure 3.8). The cell body, or *soma,* contains the biochemical structures needed to keep the neuron

► **Focus 8**
Name and describe the functions of the three main parts of the neuron. What do glial cells do?

IN REVIEW

■ Hereditary potential is carried in the genes, whose commands trigger the production of proteins that control body structures and processes. Genotype (genetic structure) and

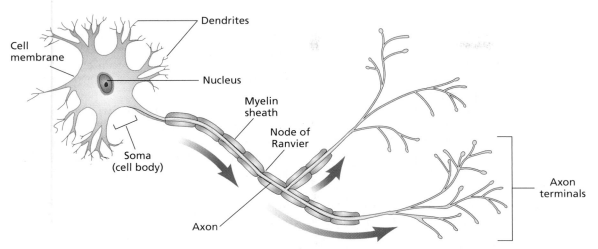

FIGURE 3.8

The neuron and its structural elements. Stimulation received by the dendrites or soma (cell body) may trigger a nerve impulse, which travels down the axon to stimulate other neurons, muscles, or glands. Some axons have a fatty myelin sheath interrupted at intervals by the nodes of Ranvier. The myelin sheath helps increase the speed of nerve conduction.

alive, and its nucleus carries the genetic information that determines how the cell develops and functions. Emerging from the cell body are branchlike fibers called **dendrites** (from the Greek word meaning "tree"), *specialized receiving units like antennae that collect messages from neighboring neurons and send them on to the cell body.* There, the incoming information is combined and processed. The many branches of the dendrites can receive input from 1,000 or more neighboring neurons. The surface of the cell body also has receptor areas that can be directly stimulated by other neurons. All parts of a neuron are covered by a protective membrane that controls the exchange of chemical substances between the inside and outside of the cell. These exchanges play a critical role in the electrical activities of nerve cells.

Extending from one side of the cell body is a single **axon,** *which conducts electrical impulses away from the cell body to other neurons, muscles, or glands.* The axon branches out at its end to form a number of *axon terminals*—as many as several hundred in some cases. Each axon terminal may connect with dendrites from numerous neurons, making it possible for a single neuron to pass messages to as many as 50,000 other neurons (Kolb & Whishaw, 2003). Given the structure of the dendrites and axons, it is easy to see how there can be trillions of interconnections in the brain, making it capable of performing the complex activities that are of interest to psychologists.

Neurons can vary greatly in size and shape. Researchers using electron microscopes have viewed more than 200 different types of nerve cells (Nolte, 1998). A neuron with its cell body in your spinal cord may have an axon that extends several feet to one of your fingertips, whereas a neuron in your brain may be no more than a thousandth of an inch long. Regardless of their shape or size, neurons have been exquisitely sculpted by

nature to perform their function of receiving, processing, and sending messages.

Neurons are supported in their functions by *glial cells* (from the Greek word meaning "glue"). Glial cells do not send or receive nerve impulses, but they surround neurons and hold them in place. The glial cells also manufacture nutrient chemicals that neurons need, and they absorb toxins and waste materials that would damage or kill neurons. During prenatal brain development, as new neurons are being formed through cell division, glial cells send out long fibers that guide newly divided neurons to their targeted places in the brain (Filogamo, 1998). Within the brain, glial cells outnumber neurons about 10 to 1.

THE ELECTRICAL ACTIVITY OF NEURONS

Neurons do two important things. Like tiny batteries, they generate electricity that creates nerve impulses. They also release chemicals that allow them to communicate with other neurons and with muscles and glands.

Let's first consider how nerve impulses occur. Nerve activation involves three basic steps:

1. At rest, the neuron has an electrical *resting potential* due to the distribution of positively and negatively charged chemical ions inside and outside the neuron.

2. When stimulated, a flow of ions in and out through the cell membrane reverses the electrical charge of the resting potential, producing an *action potential*, or nerve impulse.

3. The original ionic balance is restored, and the neuron is again at rest.

Let's now flesh out the details of this remarkable process. Like other cells, neurons are

► **Focus 9**
What chemical actions create the neuron's resting potential? What chemical changes cause the action potential?

Why are neurotransmitters critical to our ability to experience stress, relaxation, pain, and pleasure? To find out, watch the video, "Functions of Neurotransmitters," in Chapter 3 of your CD.

surrounded by body fluids and separated from this liquid environment by a protective membrane. This cell membrane is a bit like a selective sieve, allowing certain substances in the body fluid to pass through *ion channels* into the cell while refusing or limiting passage to other substances.

The chemical environment inside the neuron differs from its external environment in significant ways, and the process whereby a nerve impulse is created involves the exchange of electrically charged atoms called *ions*. In the salty fluid outside the neuron are positively charged sodium ions (Na^+) and negatively charged chloride ions (Cl^-). Inside the neuron are large negatively charged protein molecules (*anions*, or A^-) and positively charged potassium ions (K^+). The high concentration of sodium ions in the fluid outside the cell, together with the negatively charged protein ions inside, results in an uneven distribution of positive and negative ions that makes the interior of the cell negative compared to the outside (Figure 3.9a). *This internal difference of around 70 millivolts (mV) is called the neuron's* **resting potential.** At rest, the neuron is said to be in a state of *polarization*.

Nerve Impulses: The Action Potential

In research that won them the 1963 Nobel Prize, neuroscientists Alan Hodgkin and Andrew Huxley found that if they stimulated the neuron's axon with a mild electrical stimulus, the interior voltage differential shifted instantaneously from −70 millivolts to +40 millivolts. *This electrical shift, which lasts about a millisecond (1/1,000 of a second), is called the* **action potential,** *or nerve impulse.*

What happens in the neuron to cause the action potential? Hodgkin and Huxley found that the key mechanism was the action of sodium and potassium ion channels in the cell membrane. Figure 3.9 shows what happens. In a resting state, the neuron's sodium and potassium channels are closed, and the concentration of Na^+ ions is 10 times higher outside the neuron than inside it (see Figure 3.9a). But when a neuron is stimulated sufficiently, nearby sodium channels open up. Attracted by the negative protein ions inside, positively charged sodium ions flood into the axon, creating a state of *depolarization* (see Figure 3.9b). In an instant, the interior now becomes positive (by about 40 millivolts) in relation to the outside, creating the action potential. In a reflex action to restore the resting potential, the cell closes its sodium channels, and positively charged potassium ions flow out through their channels, restoring the negative resting potential (see Figure 3.9c). Eventually, the excess sodium

▶ **Focus 10**
What is the nature and importance of the myelin sheath? Which disorder results from damage to it?

ions flow out of the neuron, and the escaped potassium ions are recovered. The resulting voltage changes are shown in Figure 3.9d.

Once an action potential occurs at any point on the membrane, its effects spread to adjacent sodium channels, and the action potential flows down the length of the axon to the axon terminals. Immediately after an impulse passes a point along the axon, however, there is a recovery period as the K^+ ions flow out of the interior. During this **absolute refractory period,** *the membrane is not excitable and cannot discharge another impulse.* This places an upper limit on the rate at which nerve impulses can occur. In humans, the limit seems to be about 300 impulses per second (Kolb & Whishaw, 2003).

It's All or Nothing   One other feature of the action potential is noteworthy. In accordance with the so-called **all-or-none law,** *action potentials occur at a uniform and maximum intensity, or they do not occur at all.* Like firing a gun, which requires that a certain amount of pressure be placed on the trigger, the negative potential inside the axon has to be changed from −70 millivolts to about −50 millivolts (the *action potential threshold*) by the influx of sodium ions into the axon before the action potential will be triggered. *Changes in the negative resting potential that do not reach the −50 millivolt action potential threshold are called* **graded potentials.** Under certain circumstances, graded potentials caused by several neurons can add up to trigger an action potential in the postsynaptic neuron.

For a neuron to function properly, sodium and potassium ions must enter and leave the membrane at just the right rate. Drugs that alter this transit system can decrease or prevent neural functioning. For example, local anesthetics such as Novocain and Xylocaine attach themselves to the sodium channels, stopping the flow of sodium ions into the neurons. This stops pain impulses from being sent by the neurons (Ray & Ksir, 2002).

The Myelin Sheath   Many axons that transmit information throughout the brain and spinal cord are covered by a tubelike **myelin sheath,** *a whitish, fatty insulation layer derived from glial cells during development.* Unmyelinated axons are gray in color, hence the term, *gray matter*. Myelinated fibers are sometimes called *white matter*.

Because the myelin sheath is interrupted at regular intervals by the *nodes of Ranvier*, where the myelin is either extremely thin or absent, myelinated axons look a bit like sausages placed end to end (see Figure 3.8). In axons lacking the myelin sheath, the action potential travels down the axon length in a point-to-point fashion like a burning

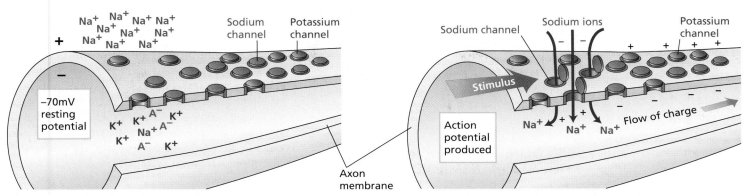

(a) The 10:1 concentration of sodium (Na^+) ions outside the neuron and the negative protein (A^-) ions inside contribute to a resting potential of –70mV.

(b) If the neuron is sufficiently stimulated, sodium channels open and sodium ions flood into the axon. Note that the potassium channels are still closed.

(c) Sodium channels that were open in (b) have now closed and potassium channels behind them are open, allowing potassium ions to exit and restoring the resting potential at that point. Sodium channels are opening at the next point as the action potential moves down the axon.

(d)

FIGURE 3.9

Nerve impulses: From resting potential to action potential. When a neuron is not being stimulated, a difference in electrical charge of about −70 millivolts (mV) exists between the interior and the surface of the neuron. (a) This resting potential is caused by the uneven distribution of positively and negatively charged ions, with a greater concentration of positively charged sodium ions kept outside the cell by closed sodium channels and the presence of negatively charged protein (A^-) ions inside the cell. In addition, the action of sodium-potassium pumps helps maintain the negative interior by pumping out three sodium (Na^+) ions for every two positively charged potassium (K^+) ions drawn into the cell. (b) Sufficient stimulation of the neuron causes an action potential. Sodium channels open for an instant and Na^+ ions flood into the axon, reversing the electrical potential from −70 mV to +40 millivolts. (c) Within a millisecond, the sodium channels close and many K^+ ions flow out of the cell through open potassium channels, helping to restore the interior negative potential. As adjacent sodium channels are opened and the sequence in (b) and (c) is repeated, the action potential moves down the length of the axon. (d) Shown here are the changes in electrical potential that would be recorded from a particular point on the axon. After a brief absolute refractory period during which the neuron cannot be stimulated, another action potential can follow.

fuse. But in myelinated axons, the nodes of Ranvier are close enough to one another so that depolarization at one node can activate the next node, allowing electrical conduction to jump from node to node at higher speeds.

The myelin sheath is most commonly found in the nervous systems of higher animals. In many neurons, the myelin sheath is not completely formed until some time after birth. The resulting efficiency of neural transmission is partly responsible for the gains that infants exhibit in muscular coordination and cognitive functioning as they grow older (Cabeza et al., 2005).

Damage to the myelin coating can have tragic effects. In people afflicted with multiple sclerosis, the person's own immune system attacks the myelin sheath, disrupting the delicate timing of nerve impulses to the muscles. The result is

▶ **Focus 11**
Describe five important steps in neurotransmitter function. How do transmitters produce excitation and inhibition? How are they deactivated?

FIGURE 3.10

A synapse between two neurons. The action potential travels to the axon terminals, where it stimulates the release of transmitter molecules from the synaptic vesicles. (a) These molecules travel across the synaptic space and bind to specially keyed receptor sites on the cell body or dendrite of the postsynaptic neuron. (b) The lock-and-key nature of neurotransmitters and receptor sites means that only transmitters that fit the receptor sites will influence membrane potentials. (c) The sequence of neurotransmitter activity moves from synthesis to deactivation. If the neurotransmitter has an excitatory effect on the neuron, the chemical reaction that occurs creates a graded or an action potential. If the transmitter substance is inhibitory, it increases the negative potential inside the neuron and makes it more difficult to fire it.

increasingly jerky and uncoordinated movements and, in the final stages, paralysis (Olek, 2005).

We've now seen how nerve impulses are created. However, the activity of a single neuron means little unless it can communicate its message to other neurons. This is where the chemical activities of neurons come into play.

HOW NEURONS COMMUNICATE: SYNAPTIC TRANSMISSION

The nervous system operates as a giant communications network, and its action requires the transmission of nerve impulses from one neuron to another. Early in the history of brain research, scientists thought that the tip of the axon made physical contact with the dendrites or cell bodies of other neurons, passing electricity directly from one neuron to the next. With the advent of the electron microscope, however, researchers discovered a **synaptic space,** *a tiny gap between the axon terminal and the next neuron.* This discovery raised new and perplexing questions: If neurons do not physically touch the other neurons to which they send signals, how does communication occur? If the action potential does not cross the synapse, what does? What carries the message?

Neurotransmitters

We now know that in addition to generating electricity, neurons produce **neurotransmitters,** *chemical substances that carry messages across the synaptic space to other neurons, muscles, or glands.* This process of chemical communication involves five steps: synthesis, storage, release, binding, and deactivation. In the *synthesis* stage, the transmitter molecules are formed inside the neuron. The molecules are then *stored* in **synaptic vesicles,** *chambers within the axon terminals.* When an action potential comes down the axon, these vesicles move to the surface of the axon terminal and the molecules are *released* into the fluid-filled space between the axon of the *presynaptic* (sending) neuron and the membrane of the *postsynaptic* (receiving) neuron. The molecules cross the synaptic space and *bind* themselves to **receptor sites,** *large protein molecules embedded in the receiving neuron's cell membrane.* Each receptor site has a specially shaped surface that fits a specific transmitter molecule, just as a lock accommodates a single key (Figure 3.10).

When a transmitter molecule binds to a receptor site, a chemical reaction occurs. This reaction can have two different effects on the receiving neuron. When an *excitatory* transmitter is at work, the chemical reaction causes the postsynaptic neuron's

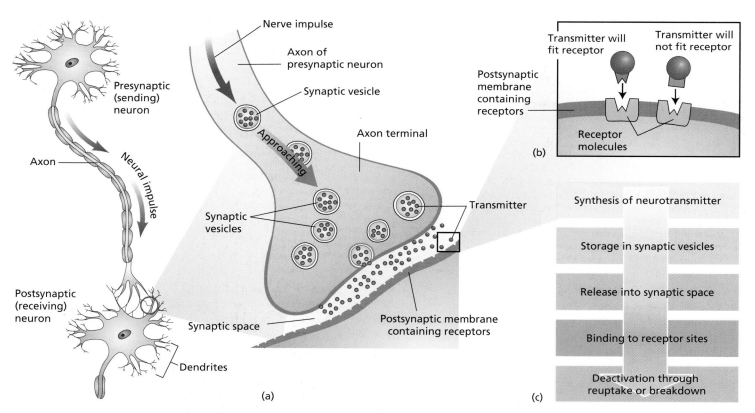

(a)   (b)   (c)

sodium channels to open. As sodium ions flood into the cell and depolarize it, they create either a graded potential or an action potential as just described. An *inhibitory* neurotransmitter will do the opposite. It may cause positive potassium ions to flow out of the neuron or negative chloride ions from the exterior to flow into it through chloride channels in the membrane, increasing the neuron's negative potential and making it harder to fire the neuron. The action of an inhibitory neurotransmitter from one presynaptic neuron may prevent the postsynaptic neuron from firing an action potential even if it is receiving excitatory stimulation from other neurons at the same time.

If the nervous system is to function properly, it must maintain a fine-tuned balance between excitation and inhibition. Even such a simple act as bending your arm requires excitation of your biceps muscles and simultaneous inhibition of your triceps so those muscles can relax.

Once a neurotransmitter molecule binds to its receptor, it continues to excite or inhibit the neuron until it is *deactivated,* or shut off. This occurs in two major ways (Fain, 1999). Some transmitter molecules are deactivated by other chemicals located in the synaptic space that break them down into their chemical components. In other instances, the deactivation mechanism is **reuptake,** *in which the transmitter molecules are taken back into the presynaptic axon terminals.* Some antidepressant medications inhibit reuptake of the excitatory transmitter serotonin, allowing serotonin to continue to excite neurons and thereby reduce depression.

Specialized Transmitter Systems

Through the use of chemical transmitters, nature has found an ingenious way of dividing up the brain into systems that are uniquely sensitive to certain messages. There is only one kind of electricity, but there are many shapes that can be assumed by transmitter molecules. Because the various systems in the brain recognize only certain chemical messengers, they are immune to cross talk from other systems.

There are many different neurotransmitter substances, some of which can coexist within the same neuron. A given neuron may use one transmitter at one synapse and a different one at another synapse. Moreover, different transmitters can be found within the same axon terminal or in the same synapse, adding another layer of complexity (Kolb & Whishaw, 2003). Each substance has a specific excitatory or inhibitory effect on certain neurons. Some neurotransmitters (for example, norepineph-

rine) can have either excitatory or inhibitory effects, depending on which receptor sites they bind to.

Table 3.2 lists several of the more important neurotransmitters that have been linked to psychological phenomena. We'll encounter all of these substances in this and future chapters. For the moment, we'll focus on **acetylcholine (ACh),** *a neurotransmitter involved in muscle activity and memory,* to illustrate the diversity of neurotransmitter mechanisms.

Underproduction of ACh is an important factor in Alzheimer's disease, a degenerative brain disorder that afflicts 5 to 10 percent of people over 65 years of age (Morris & Becker, 2005). Reductions in ACh weaken or deactivate neural circuitry that stores memories, creating profound memory impairments. ACh is also an excitatory transmitter at the synapses where neurons activate muscle cells, helping to account for the severe motor impairments found in the later stages of Alzheimer's disease.

Drugs that block the action of ACh can prevent muscle activation and cause paralysis. One example occurs in botulism, a serious type of food poisoning that can result from improperly canned food. The toxin formed by the botulinum bacteria blocks the release of ACh from the axon terminal, resulting in a potentially fatal paralysis of the muscles, including those of the respiratory system. A mild form of the toxin, known as Botox, is used cosmetically to remove skin wrinkles by paralyzing the muscles whose contraction causes them.

The opposite effect on ACh occurs with the bite of the black widow spider. The spider's venom triggers a torrent of ACh, resulting in violent muscle contractions, convulsions, and possible death. Some chemical agents, such as the deadly sarin gas released into the Tokyo subway system by terrorists in 1995, also raise havoc by allowing ACh to run wild in the nervous system. Sarin and similar nerve gas agents prevent the activity of an enzyme that normally degrades ACh at the synapse. The result is uncontrolled seizures and convulsions that can kill.

Most neurotransmitters have their excitatory or inhibitory effects only on specific neurons that have receptors for them. Others, called **neuromodulators,** *have a more widespread and generalized influence on synaptic transmission.* These substances circulate through the brain and either increase or decrease (i.e., modulate) the sensitivity of thousands, perhaps millions, of neurons to their specific transmitters. The best known neuromodulators are the *endorphins,* which travel through the brain's circulatory system and inhibit pain transmission while enhancing neural activity that produces

▶ **Focus 12**
Describe the roles played by acetylcholine and the consequences that occur when its functioning is disrupted.

TABLE 3.2 Some Neurotransmitters and Their Effects

Neurotransmitter	Major Function	Disorders Associated with Malfunctioning	Additional Discussion
Acetylcholine (ACh)	Excitatory at synapses involved in muscular movement and memory	Memory loss in Alzheimer's disease (undersupply); paralysis (absence); violent muscle contractions and convulsions (oversupply)	Chapters 3, 7
Norepinephrine	Excitatory and inhibitory functions at various sites, involved in neural circuits controlling learning, memory, wakefulness, and eating	Depression (undersupply); stress and panic disorders (overactivity)	Chapters 3, 5, 13
Serotonin	Inhibitory or excitatory; involved in mood, sleep, eating, and arousal, and may be an important transmitter underlying pleasure and pain	Depression; sleeping and eating disorders (undersupply). Obsessive-compulsive disorder (overactivity)	Chapters 5, 12, 14, 15
Dopamine	Excitatory; involved in voluntary movement, emotional arousal, learning, memory, and experiencing pleasure or pain	Parkinson's disease and depression (undersupply); schizophrenia (overactivity)	Chapters 3, 5, 14, 15
GABA (gamma-aminobutyric acid)	Inhibitory transmitter in motor system	Destruction of GABA-producing neurons in Huntington's disease produces tremors and loss of motor control, as well as personality changes	Chapter 5
Endorphin	Inhibits transmission of pain impulses (a neuromodulator)	Insensitivity to pain (oversupply); pain hypersensitivity, immune problems (undersupply)	Chapters 4, 5, 13

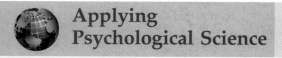

▶ **Focus 13**
How do agonist and antagonist functions underlie the neural and behavioral effects of psychoactive drugs?

pleasurable feelings. We'll examine the endorphins in greater detail in Chapter 4. Other neuromodulators play important roles in functions such as eating, sleeping, and coping with stress.

Knowledge about neurotransmitter systems has many important applications. For one thing, it helps us understand the mechanisms that underlie the effects of **psychoactive drugs,** *chemicals that produce alterations in consciousness, emotion, and behavior.* The following "Applying Psychological Science" feature focuses on mechanisms of drug effects within the brain.

Applying Psychological Science   Understanding How Drugs Affect Your Brain

Drugs affect consciousness and behavior by influencing the activity of neurons. If you've had a soft drink or a cup of coffee, taken an aspirin, or smoked a cigarette, you've ingested a drug. A survey of 55,000 students at 132 colleges in the United States revealed that in the prior year, 47 percent had used tobacco; 84 percent, alcohol; 33.6 percent, marijuana; and 5 to 10 percent, cocaine, amphetamines, hallucinogenic drugs such as LSD, and designer drugs such as Ecstasy (Core Institute, 2002). Countless students ingest caffeine in coffee, chocolate, cocoa, and soft drinks. Perhaps

you have wondered exactly how these drugs exert their diverse effects.

Most psychoactive drugs produce their effects by either increasing or decreasing the synthesis, storage, release, binding, or deactivation of neurotransmitters. An **agonist** *is a drug that increases the activity of a neurotransmitter.* Agonists may (1) enhance a neuron's ability to synthesize, store, or release neurotransmitters; (2) mimic the action of a neurotransmitter by binding with and stimulating postsynaptic receptor sites; (3) bind with and stimulate postsynaptic receptor sites; or (4) make it more difficult for neurotransmitters to be deactivated, such as by inhibiting reuptake.

An **antagonist** *is a drug that inhibits or decreases the action of a neurotransmitter.* An antagonist may (1) reduce a neuron's ability to synthesize, store, or release neurotransmitters; or (2) prevent a neurotransmitter from binding with the post-synaptic neuron by fitting into and blocking the receptor sites on the postsynaptic neuron.

With the distinction between agonist and antagonist functions in mind, let us consider how some commonly used drugs work within the brain. We will discuss drug effects on consciousness and behavior in greater detail in Chapter 5.

Alcohol is a depressant drug having both agonist and antagonist effects. As an agonist, it stimulates the activity of the inhibitory transmitter GABA, thereby depressing neural activity. As an antagonist, it decreases the activity of gluta-mate, an excitatory transmitter (Gonzalez & Jaworski, 1997). The double-barreled effect is a neural slowdown that inhibits normal brain functions, including clear thinking, emotional control, and motor coordination. Sedative drugs, including barbiturates and tranquilizers, also increase GABA activity, and taking them with alcohol can be deadly when their depressant effects on neural activity are combined with those of alcohol.

Caffeine is a stimulant drug that increases the activity of neurons and other cells. It is an antagonist for the transmitter adenosine. Adenosine inhibits the release of excitatory trans-mitters. By reducing adenosine activity, caffeine helps pro-duce higher rates of cellular activity and more available energy. Although caffeine is a stimulant, it is important to note that contrary to popular belief, caffeine does *not* coun-teract the effects of alcohol and sober people up. What your drunken friend needs is a ride home with a driver who is sober—not a cup of coffee.

Nicotine is an agonist for the excitatory transmitter acetylcholine. Its chemical structure is similar enough to ACh to allow it to fit into ACh binding sites and create action potentials. At other receptor sites, nicotine stimulates dopamine activity, which seems to be an important chemical mediator of energy and pleasure. This may help account for nicotine's powerful addictive properties. Researchers are work-ing to develop medications that could wean people off ciga-rettes and other tobacco products by blocking or occupying the specific receptor sites that trigger dopamine release.

Amphetamines are stimulant drugs that boost arousal and mood by increasing the activity of the excitatory neuro-transmitters dopamine and norepinephrine. They do so in two major ways. First, they cause presynaptic neurons to release greater amounts of these neurotransmitters. Second, they inhibit reuptake, allowing dopamine and norepinephrine to keep stimulating postsynaptic neurons (Diaz, 1997).

Cocaine produces excitation, a sense of increased muscu-lar strength, and euphoria. Like amphetamines, cocaine

FIGURE 3.11

Partying can alter brain activity in several ways. Nicotine from cigarette smoke activates acetylcholine and dopamine neurons, increasing neural excitation. Alcohol stimulates the activity of the inhibitory transmitter GABA and decreases the activity of an excitatory transmitter, glutamate, thus depressing brain functions. The possibility of a drink having been spiked with one of the powerful and potentially deadly date-rape sedative drugs could place a partygoer at great risk.

increases the activity of norepinephrine and dopamine, but it does so in only one major way: It blocks their reuptake. Thus amphetamines and cocaine have different mechanisms of action on the dopamine and norepinephrine transmitter sys-tems, but both drugs produce highly stimulating effects on mood, thinking, and behavior.

We should comment on two other drugs that, unfortu-nately, are also found on college campuses. Rohypnol (fluni-trazepam, known as "roofies" or "rope") and GHB (gamma hydroxybutyrate, known as "easy lay") are so-called date-rape drugs. Partygoers sometimes add these drugs to punch and other drinks in hopes of lowering drinkers' inhibitions and facilitating nonconsensual sexual conquest. The drugs are powerful sedatives that suppress general neural activity by enhancing the action of the inhibitory transmitter GABA (Lobina et al., 1999). Rohypnol is about 10 times more potent than Valium. At high doses or when mixed with alcohol or other drugs, these substances may lead to respiratory depres-sion, loss of consciousness, coma, and even death. Rohypnol also attacks neurotransmission in areas of the brain involved in memory, producing an amnesia effect that may prevent users from remembering the circumstances under which they ingested the drug or what happened to them afterwards. GHB, which makes its victim appear drunk and helpless, is now a restricted drug, and slipping it into someone's drink is a criminal act. The bottom line is that these drugs are good neither to give nor to receive (Figure 3.11). Increasingly, women are being advised against accepting an opened drink from a fellow reveler or leaving their own drink unattended at parties.

▶ **Focus 14**
What are the three major types of neurons in the nervous system? What are their functions?

FIGURE 3.12

Structural organization of the nervous system.

IN REVIEW

■ Each neuron has dendrites, which receive nerve impulses from other neurons; a cell body, which controls the vital processes of the cell; and an axon, which conducts nerve impulses to adjacent neurons, muscles, and glands.

■ Neural transmission is an electrochemical process. The nerve impulse, or action potential, is a brief reversal in the electrical potential of the cell membrane from negative to positive as sodium ions from the surrounding fluid flow into the cell through sodium ion channels. The action potential obeys the all-or-none law, firing completely or not at all. The myelin sheath increases the speed of neural transmission.

■ Passage of the impulse across the synapse is mediated by chemical transmitter substances. Neurons are selective in the neurotransmitters that can stimulate them. Some neurotransmitters excite neurons, whereas others inhibit firing of the postsynaptic neuron. The nervous system requires a delicate balance of excitation and inhibition of neurons. Agonists can mimic or increase the action of neurotransmitters, whereas antagonists inhibit or decrease the action of neurotransmitters.

THE NERVOUS SYSTEM

The nervous system is the body's control center. Three major types of neurons carry out the system's input, output, and integration functions. **Sensory neurons** *carry input messages from the sense organs to the spinal cord and brain.* **Motor neurons** *transmit output impulses from the brain and spinal cord to the body's muscles and organs.* Finally, there are neurons that link the input and output functions. These **interneurons,** which far outnumber sensory and motor neurons, *perform connective or associative functions within the nervous system.* For example, interneurons would allow us to recognize a friend by linking the sensory input from the visual system with the memory of that person's characteristics stored elsewhere in the brain. The activity of interneurons makes possible the complexity of our higher mental functions, emotions, and behavioral capabilities.

The nervous system can be broken down into several interrelated subsystems (Figure 3.12). The two major divisions are the peripheral and central nervous systems.

THE PERIPHERAL NERVOUS SYSTEM

The **peripheral nervous system** *contains all the neural structures that lie outside of the brain and*

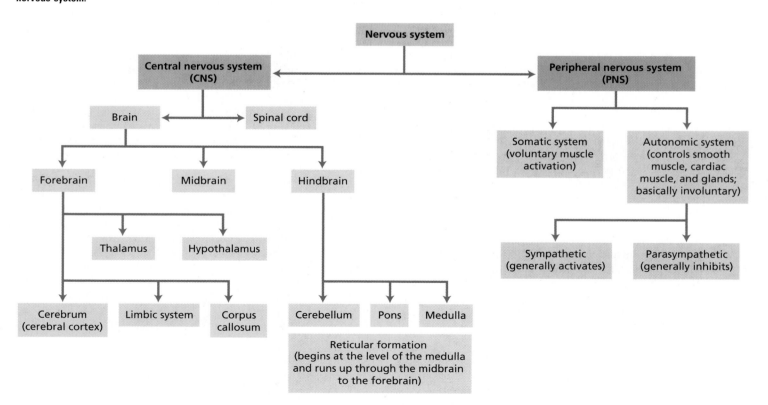

spinal cord. Its specialized neurons help carry out (1) the input functions that enable us to sense what is going on inside and outside our bodies and (2) the output functions that enable us to respond with our muscles and glands. The peripheral nervous system has two major divisions, the somatic nervous system and the autonomic nervous system.

The Somatic Nervous System

The **somatic nervous system** *consists of sensory neurons that are specialized to transmit messages from the eyes, ears, and other sensory receptors, and motor neurons that send messages from the brain and spinal cord to the muscles that control our voluntary movements.* The axons of sensory neurons group together like many strands of a rope to form *sensory nerves,* and motor-neuron axons combine to form *motor nerves.* As you read this page, sensory neurons in your eyes are sending impulses into a complex network of specialized visual tracts that course through your brain. (Inside the brain and spinal cord, nerves are called *tracts.*) At the same time, motor neurons are stimulating the eye movements that allow you to scan the lines

of type and turn the pages. The somatic system thus allows you to sense and respond to your environment.

The Autonomic Nervous System

The body's internal environment is regulated largely through the activities of the **autonomic nervous system,** *which senses the body's internal functions and controls the glands and the smooth (involuntary) muscles that form the heart, the blood vessels, and the lining of the stomach and intestines.* The autonomic system is largely concerned with involuntary functions, such as respiration, circulation, and digestion; it is also involved in many aspects of motivation, emotional behavior, and stress responses. It consists of two subdivisions, the *sympathetic nervous system* and the *parasympathetic nervous system* (Figure 3.13). Typically, these two divisions affect the same organ or gland in opposing ways.

The **sympathetic nervous system** *has an activation or arousal function, and it tends to act as a total unit.* For example, when you encounter a stressful situation, your sympathetic nervous system helps you confront the stressor in several

▶ **Focus 15**
Name the two divisions of the peripheral nervous system. How does the autonomic system maintain homeostasis?

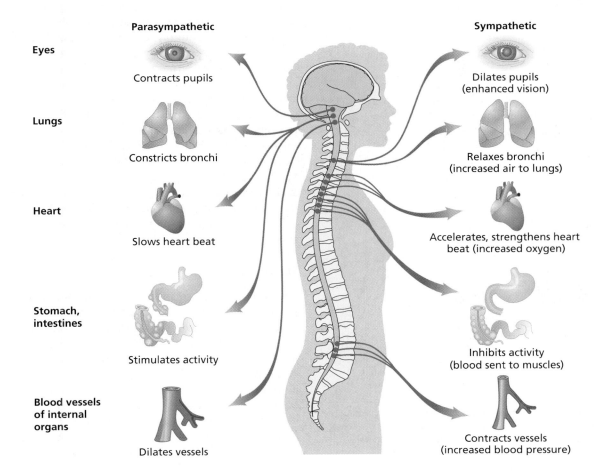

Parasympathetic

Sympathetic

Eyes
Contracts pupils
Dilates pupils (enhanced vision)

Lungs
Constricts bronchi
Relaxes bronchi (increased air to lungs)

Heart
Slows heart beat
Accelerates, strengthens heart beat (increased oxygen)

Stomach, intestines
Stimulates activity
Inhibits activity (blood sent to muscles)

Blood vessels of internal organs
Dilates vessels
Contracts vessels (increased blood pressure)

FIGURE 3.13

Autonomic nervous system. The sympathetic branch of the autonomic nervous system arouses the body and speeds up its vital processes. It tends to act in a nonspecific fashion, activating many organs at the same time. The parasympathetic division, which is more specific in its opposing actions, slows down body processes. The two divisions work in concert to maintain an equilibrium within the body.

▶ **Focus 16**
What are the two main structures in the central nervous system?

ways. It speeds up your heart rate so that it can pump more blood to your muscles, dilates your pupils so that more light can enter the eye and improve your vision, slows down your digestive system so that blood can be transferred to the muscles, increases your rate of respiration so that your body can get more oxygen, and, in general, mobilizes your body. This is sometimes called the *fight-or-flight response.*

Compared with the sympathetic branch, which tends to act as a unit, the **parasympathetic nervous system** *is far more specific in its opposing actions, affecting one or a few organs at a time. In general, it slows down body processes and maintains a state of tranquility.* Thus your sympathetic system speeds up your heart rate; your parasympathetic system slows it down. By working together to maintain equilibrium in our internal organs, the two divisions can maintain **homeostasis,** *a delicately balanced or constant internal state.* In addition, sympathetic and parasympathetic activities sometimes coordinate to enable us to perform certain behaviors. For example, sexual function in the male involves penile erection (through parasympathetic dilation of blood vessels) followed by ejaculation (a primarily sympathetic function; Masters et al., 1988).

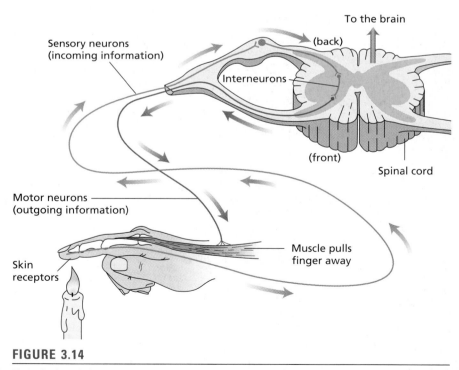

FIGURE 3.14

The spinal cord. A cross section of the spinal cord. Sensory and motor nerves enter and exit the spinal cord on both sides of the spinal column. Interneurons within the H-shaped spinal gray matter can serve a connective function, as shown here, but in many cases, sensory neurons can also synapse directly with motor neurons. At this level of the nervous system, reflex activity is possible without involving the brain.

THE CENTRAL NERVOUS SYSTEM

More than any other system in our body, the central nervous system distinguishes us from other creatures. This **central nervous system** *contains the brain and the spinal cord, which connects most parts of the peripheral nervous system with the brain.*

The Spinal Cord

Most nerves enter and leave the central nervous system by way of the spinal cord, a structure that in a human adult is 16 to 18 inches long and about 1 inch in diameter. The vertebrae (bones of the spine) protect the spinal cord's neurons. When the spinal cord is viewed in cross section (Figure 3.14), its central portion resembles an H or a butterfly. The H-shaped portion consists largely of gray-colored neuron cell bodies and their interconnections. Surrounding the gray matter are white-colored myelinated axons that connect various levels of the spinal cord with each other and with the higher centers of the brain. Entering the back side of the spinal cord along its length are sensory nerves. Motor nerves exit the spinal cord's front side.

Some simple stimulus-response sequences, known as *spinal reflexes,* can be triggered at the level of the spinal cord without any involvement of the brain. For example, if you touch something hot, sensory receptors in your skin trigger nerve impulses in sensory nerves that flash into your spinal cord and synapse inside with interneurons. The interneurons then excite motor neurons that send impulses to your hand, so that it pulls away (see Figure 3.14). Other interneurons simultaneously carry the "Hot!" message up the spinal cord to your brain. But it is a good thing that you don't have to wait for the brain to tell you what to do in such emergencies. Getting messages to and from the brain takes slightly longer, so the spinal cord reflex system significantly reduces reaction time and, in this case, potential tissue damage.

The Brain

The three pounds of protein, fat, and fluid that you carry around inside your skull is the real you. It is also the most complex structure in the known universe and the only one that can wonder about itself. As befits this biological marvel, your brain is the most active energy consumer of all your body organs. Although your brain accounts for only about 2 percent of your total body weight, it consumes about 25 percent of your body's oxygen and 70 percent of its glucose. Moreover, the brain never rests; its rate of energy metabolism is relatively constant day and night. In fact, when you dream, the brain's metabolic rate actually increases slightly (Hobson, 1996).

How can this rather nondescript blob of grayish tissue discover the principle of relativity, build the Hubble Space Telescope, and produce great works of art, music, and literature? Answering such questions requires the ability to study the brain and how it functions. To do so, neuroscientists use a diverse set of tools and procedures.

Unlocking the Secrets of the Brain

Because of scientific and technical advances, more has been learned about the brain in the past four decades than was known throughout all the preceding ages. Neuroscientists use a number of methods to study the brain's structures and activities.

Neuropsychological Tests   Psychologists have developed a variety of *neuropsychological tests* to measure verbal and nonverbal behaviors of people who may have suffered brain damage through accident or disease (Lezak, 1995). They are also important research tools. For example, Figure 3.15 shows a portion of a Trail Making Test, used to test memory and planning. Scores on the test give an indication of a person's type and severity of brain damage. Neuropsychological tests of this kind have provided much information about brain-behavior relations. They are also used to assess learning disabilities and developmental disorders.

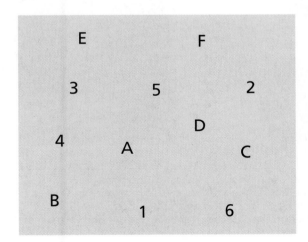

FIGURE 3.15

A neuropsychological test. The Trail Making Test is used by psychologists to assess brain functioning. It consists of randomly scattered numbers and letters. On this timed test, the patient must connect the numbers and letters consecutively with a continuous line, or "trail" (i.e., A to 1 to B to 2 to C to 3 and so on). People with certain kinds of brain damage have trouble alternating between the numbers and letters because they cannot retain a plan in memory long enough.

Destruction and Stimulation Techniques   Experimental studies are another useful method of learning about the brain. Researchers can produce brain damage (lesions) in which specific nervous tissue is destroyed with electricity, with cold or heat, or with chemicals. They can also surgically remove some portion of the brain and study the consequences. Most experiments of this kind are performed on animals, but humans can also be studied when accident or disease produces a specific lesion or when abnormal brain tissue must be surgically removed.

An alternative to destroying neurons is chemically or electrically stimulating them, which typically produces effects opposite to destruction. In chemical stimulation, a tiny tube, or *cannula*, is inserted into a precise area of the brain so that chemicals, including neurotransmitters, can be delivered directly and their effects on behavior studied. A specific region of the brain can also be stimulated by a mild electric current. Electrodes can be permanently implanted so that the region of interest can be stimulated repeatedly. Some electrodes are so tiny that they can stimulate individual neurons.

In a recent electrical-stimulation study, placement of electrodes on a specific region of the brain's outer surface above the right ear produced a surprising effect. The woman experienced herself as floating in the air above her body (Blanke et al., 2002). Neuroscientists wonder if the researchers may have accidentally discovered a neural basis for "near death" and other so-called paranormal out-of-body experiences that have been reported by many people.

Electrical Recording   Because electrodes can record brain activity as well as stimulate it, scientists can eavesdrop on the electrical "conversations" occurring within the brain. Neurons' electrical activity can be measured by inserting small electrodes in particular areas of the brain or even in individual neurons.

In addition to measuring individual "voices," scientists can tune in to "crowd noise." The **electroencephalograph (EEG)** *measures the activity of large groups of neurons through a series of large electrodes placed on the scalp* (Figure 3.16 a, b). Although the EEG is a rather nonspecific measure that taps the electrical activity of thousands of neurons in many parts of the brain, specific EEG patterns correspond to certain states of consciousness, such as wakefulness and sleep. Clinicians also use the EEG to detect abnormal electrical patterns that signal the presence of brain disorders.

▶ **Focus 17**
Describe four methods used to study brain-behavior relations.

To discover how brain researchers are harnessing the power of new technologies to better understand how the brain functions, view the video, "Brain Structures and Imaging Methods," in Chapter 3 of your CD.

FIGURE 3.16

Measuring brain activity. (a) The electroencephalogram (EEG) records the activity of large groups of neurons in the brain through a series of electrodes attached to the scalp. (b) The results appear on an EEG readout. (c) Various brain scanning machines, such as the one shown here, produce a number of different images. (d) The CT scan uses narrow beams of X-rays to construct a composite picture of brain structures. (e) MRI scanners produce vivid pictures of brain structures. (f) Functional MRI (fMRI) procedures take images in rapid succession, showing neural activity as it occurs. (g) PET scans record the amount of radioactive substance that collects in various brain regions to assess brain activity.

▶ **Focus 18**
How are CAT scans, PET scans, and MRIs produced, and what kinds of information does each provide?

Brain Imaging   The newest tools of discovery are imaging techniques that permit neuroscientists to peer into the living brain (Figure 3.16c). The most important of these are *CT scans, PET scans, MRIs* and *fMRIs*. CT scans and MRIs are used to visualize brain structure, whereas PET scans and

fMRIs allow scientists to view brain activity (Bremner, 2005).

Developed in the 1970s, **computerized axial tomography (CT,** or **CAT) scans** *use X-ray technology to study brain structures*. A highly focused beam of X-rays takes pictures of narrow slices of the brain. A computer analyzes the X-rayed slices and creates pictures of the brain's interior from many different angles (Figure 3.16d). Pinpointing where deterioration or injuries have occurred helps clarify relations between brain damage and psychological functioning. CT scans are 100 times more sensitive than standard X-ray procedures, and the technological advance was so dramatic that its developers, Allan Cormack and Godfrey Hounsfield, were awarded the 1979 Nobel Prize for medicine.

Magnetic resonance imaging (MRI) *creates images based on how atoms in living tissue respond to a magnetic pulse delivered by the device.* When the magnetic field is shut off, the magnetic energy absorbed by the atoms in the tissue emits a small electrical voltage that is relayed to a computer for analysis. MRI provides color images of the tissue and can make out details one tenth the size of those detected by CT scans (Figure 3.16e).

Whereas CT scans and MRIs provide pictures of brain structures, **positron-emission tomography (PET) scans** *measure brain activity, including metabolism, blood flow, and neurotransmitter activity.* Glucose, a natural sugar, is the major nutrient of neurons, so when neurons are active, they consume more glucose. To prepare a patient for a PET scan, a radioactive (but harmless) form of glucose is injected into the bloodstream and travels to the brain, where it circulates in the blood supply. The PET scan measures the energy emitted by the radioactive substance, and the data, fed into a computer, produce a color picture of the brain on a display screen (Figure 3.16g). If the patient is performing a reasoning task, for example, a researcher can tell by the glucose-concentration pattern which parts of the brain are most heavily activated.

The conventional MRI yields pictures taken several minutes apart. An important advance in MRI technology is **functional MRI (fMRI),** *which can produce pictures of blood flow in the brain taken less than a second apart.* Researchers can now, quite literally, watch live presentations as different regions of the brain light up when participants perform various tasks (Figure 3.16f). Active brain tissue uses more oxygen; thus scanning the oxygen concentration of blood in the brain provides a vivid picture of brain activity without the need to inject a radioactive substance into the brain (Huettel et al., 2005).

Advances in brain research represent an important frontier of psychology. Driven by its intense desire to "know thyself," the brain is beginning to yield its many secrets. Yet many important questions remain. This should not surprise us, for as one observer noted, "If the brain were so simple that we could understand it, we would be so simple that we couldn't" (Pugh, 1977).

IN REVIEW

■ The nervous system contains sensory neurons, motor neurons, and interneurons. Its two major divisions are the central nervous system, consisting of the brain and spinal cord, and the peripheral nervous system. The peripheral system is divided into the somatic system (which is responsible for sensory and motor functions) and the autonomic nervous system (which directs the activity of the body's internal organs and glands).

■ The autonomic nervous system consists of sympathetic and parasympathetic divisions. The sympathetic system has an arousal function and tends to act as a unit. The parasympathetic system slows down body processes and is more specific in its actions. Together, the two divisions maintain a state of homeostasis, or internal balance.

■ The spinal cord contains sensory neurons and motor neurons. Interneurons inside the spinal cord serve a connective function between the two. Simple stimulus-response sequences can occur as spinal reflexes.

■ Neuropsychological tests, destruction and stimulation techniques, electrical recording, and brain imaging have facilitated discoveries about brain-behavior relations. Recently developed methods for producing computer-generated pictures of structures and processes within the living brain include the CT scan, PET scan, MRI, and fMRI.

THE HIERARCHICAL BRAIN: STRUCTURES AND BEHAVIORAL FUNCTIONS

In an evolutionary sense, your brain is far older than you are, for it represents perhaps 500 million years of evolutionary development and fine-tuning. The human brain is like a living archaeological site, with the more recently developed structures built atop structures from the distant evolutionary past (Striedter, 2005). The structures at the brain's core, which we share with all other vertebrates, govern the basic physiological functions that keep us alive, such as breathing and heart rate. Built upon these basic structures are newer systems that involve progressively more complex functions—sensing, emoting, wanting, thinking, reasoning. Evolutionary theorists believe that as genetic variation sculpted these newer structures over time, natural selection favored their retention because animals who had them were more likely

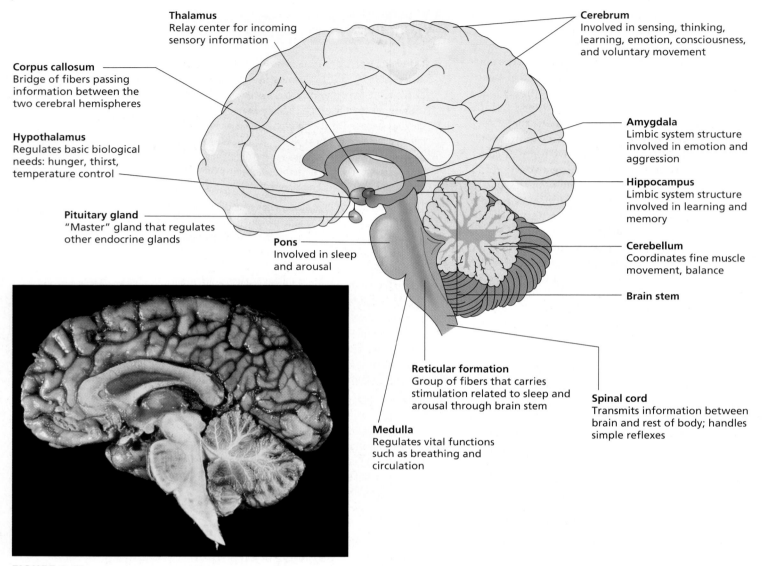

Thalamus
Relay center for incoming sensory information

Cerebrum
Involved in sensing, thinking, learning, emotion, consciousness, and voluntary movement

Corpus callosum
Bridge of fibers passing information between the two cerebral hemispheres

Amygdala
Limbic system structure involved in emotion and aggression

Hypothalamus
Regulates basic biological needs: hunger, thirst, temperature control

Hippocampus
Limbic system structure involved in learning and memory

Pituitary gland
"Master" gland that regulates other endocrine glands

Pons
Involved in sleep and arousal

Cerebellum
Coordinates fine muscle movement, balance

Brain stem

Reticular formation
Group of fibers that carries stimulation related to sleep and arousal through brain stem

Spinal cord
Transmits information between brain and rest of body; handles simple reflexes

Medulla
Regulates vital functions such as breathing and circulation

FIGURE 3.17

Interior of the brain. The photograph shows the human brain sectioned at its midline. The drawing shows the brain structures as they would appear if the left side of the brain were transparent, permitting a view to the midline.

▶ **Focus 19**
Which behavioral functions are controlled by the medulla, the pons, and the cerebellum? What is the consequence of damage to these structures?

to survive in changing environments. The crowning feature of brain development is the *cerebral cortex,* the biological seat of Einstein's scientific genius, Mozart's creativity, Saddam Hussein's brutality, Mother Teresa's compassion, and that which makes you a unique human being.

The major structures of the human brain, together with their psychological functions, are shown in Figure 3.17. The brain has traditionally been viewed as having three major subdivisions: the hindbrain; the midbrain, which lies above the hindbrain; and the forebrain.

THE HINDBRAIN

The **hindbrain** *is the lowest and most primitive level of the brain.* As the spinal cord enters the brain, it enlarges to form the structures that compose the stalk-

like brain stem. Attached to the brain stem is the other major portion of the hindbrain, the *cerebellum.*

The Brain Stem: Life-Support Systems

The structures of the **brain stem** *support vital life functions.* Included are the *medulla* and the *pons.* The 1.5-inch-long medulla is the first structure above the spinal cord. Well developed at birth, the **medulla** *plays an important role in vital body functions such as heart rate and respiration.* Because of your medulla, these functions occur automatically. Damage to the medulla usually results in death or, at best, the need to be maintained on life-support systems. Suppression of medulla activity can occur at high levels of alcohol intoxication, resulting in death by heart or respiratory failure (Blessing, 1997).

The medulla is also a two-way thoroughfare for all the sensory and motor nerve tracts coming up from the spinal cord and descending from the brain. Most of these tracts cross over within the medulla, so the left side of the brain receives sensory input from and exerts motor control over the right side of the body, and the right side of the brain serves the left side of the body. Why this crossover occurs is one of the unsolved mysteries of brain function.

The **pons** (meaning "bridge" in Latin) *lies just above the medulla and carries nerve impulses between higher and lower levels of the nervous system.* The pons also has clusters of neurons that help regulate sleep. Like the medulla, the pons helps control vital functions, especially respiration, and damage to it can produce death.

The Cerebellum: Motor-Coordination Center

Attached to the rear of the brain stem, the cerebellum ("little brain" in Latin) does indeed look like a miniature brain. Its wrinkled *cortex*, or covering, consists mainly of gray cell bodies (gray matter). The **cerebellum** *is concerned primarily with muscular movement coordination, but it also plays a role in learning and memory.*

Specific motor movements are initiated in higher brain centers, but their timing and coordination depend on the cerebellum (Thatch et al., 1992). The cerebellum regulates complex, rapidly changing movements that require precise timing, such as those of a ballet dancer or a competitive diver. Within the animal kingdom, cats have an especially well developed cerebellum, helping to account for their ability to move gracefully (Altman & Bayer, 1996).

The motor-control functions of the cerebellum are easily disrupted by alcohol, producing the coordination difficulties that police look for in roadside sobriety tests. Intoxicated people may be unable to walk a straight line or touch their nose with their index finger (Figure 3.18). Physical damage to the cerebellum results in severe motor disturbances characterized by jerky, uncoordinated movements, as well as an inability to perform habitual movements such as walking.

THE MIDBRAIN

Lying just above the hindbrain, the **midbrain** *contains clusters of sensory and motor neurons.* The sensory portion of the midbrain contains important relay centers for the visual and auditory systems. Here, nerve impulses from the eyes and ears are organized and sent to forebrain structures involved in visual and auditory perception (Nolte, 1998). The midbrain also contains motor neurons that control eye movements.

Cerebellum

FIGURE 3.18

Balance and coordination. The cerebellum's movement-control functions are easily disrupted by alcohol, providing the neural basis for the sobriety tests administered by police officers.

The Reticular Formation: The Brain's Gatekeeper

Buried within the midbrain is a finger-shaped structure that extends from the hindbrain up into the lower portions of the forebrain. This structure receives its name from its resemblance under a microscope to a *reticulum,* or net. The **reticular formation** *acts as a kind of sentry, both alerting higher centers of the brain that messages are coming and then either blocking those messages or allowing them to go forward.* The reticular formation has an *ascending* part, which sends input to higher regions of the brain to alert it, and a *descending* portion, through which higher brain centers can either admit or block out sensory input.

The reticular formation plays a central role in consciousness, sleep, and attention. Without reticular stimulation of higher brain regions, sensory messages do not register in conscious awareness even though the nerve impulses may reach the appropriate higher areas of the brain. It is as if the brain is not awake enough to notice them. In fact, some general anesthetics work by deactivating neurons of the ascending reticular formation so that sensory impulses that ordinarily would be experienced as pain never register in the sensory areas of the brain (Derogatis, 1986).

The reticular formation also affects sleep and wakefulness. In a classic series of experiments in the late 1940s, researchers discovered that electrical stimulation of different portions of the reticular formation can produce instant sleep in a wakeful cat and sudden wakefulness in a sleeping animal (Marshall & Magoun, 1997). Severe damage to the reticular formation can produce a permanent coma (Roland, 1997).

▶ **Focus 20**
Describe the roles played by the ascending and descending reticular formation. What occurs with damage to this structure?

Attention is an active process during which only important or meaningful sensory inputs get through to our consciousness. Other inputs have to be toned down or completely blocked out or we'd be overwhelmed by stimulation. The descending reticular formation plays an important part in this process, serving as a kind of gate through which some inputs are admitted while others are blocked out by signals coming down from higher brain centers (Van Zomeren & Brouwer, 1994).

THE FOREBRAIN

The **forebrain** *is the brain's most advanced portion from an evolutionary standpoint.* Its major structure, the **cerebrum,** *consists of two large hemispheres, a left side and a right side,* that wrap around the brain stem as the two halves of a cut grapefruit might wrap around a large spoon. The outer portion of the forebrain has a thin covering, or cortex. Within are a number of important structures buried in the central regions of the hemispheres.

► **Focus 21**
Describe the structural characteristics and functions of the thalamus and the hypothalamus.

The Thalamus: The Brain's Sensory Switchboard

The *thalamus* is located above the midbrain. It resembles two small footballs, one within each cerebral hemisphere. The **thalamus** *has sometimes been likened to a switchboard that organizes inputs from sensory organs and routes them to the appropriate areas of the brain.* The visual, auditory, and body senses (balance and equilibrium) all have major relay stations in the thalamus.

Because the thalamus plays such a key role in routing sensory information to higher brain regions, individuals with disrupted functioning in the thalamus often experience a highly confusing world. In research at the National Institutes of Mental Health (NIMH) carried out by Nancy Andreason and her coworkers (1994), MRIs from 39 schizophrenic men were compared with those of 47 normal male volunteers. The brain images showed specific abnormalities in the thalamus of the schizophrenic brains, suggesting that the thalamus may have been sending garbled sensory information to the higher regions of the brain and creating the confusing sensory experiences and hallucinations reported by many patients.

The Hypothalamus: Motivation and Emotion

The *hypothalamus* (literally, "under the thalamus") consists of tiny groups of neuron cell bodies that lie at the base of the brain, above the roof of the mouth. The **hypothalamus** *plays a major role in many aspects of motivation and emotion, including sexual behavior, temperature regulation, sleeping, eating, drinking, and aggression.* Damage to the hypothalamus can disrupt all of these behaviors. For example, destruction of one area of a male's hypothalamus results in a complete loss of sex drive; damage to another portion produces an overwhelming urge to eat that results in extreme obesity.

The hypothalamus has important connections with the *endocrine system,* the body's collection of hormone-producing glands (discussed later in this chapter). Through its connection with the nearby *pituitary gland* (the master gland that exerts control over the other glands of the endocrine system), the hypothalamus directly controls many hormonal secretions that regulate sexual development and sexual behavior, metabolism, and reactions to stress.

The hypothalamus is also involved in our experiences of pleasure and displeasure. The discovery of this fact occurred quite by accident. In 1953 psychologist James Olds was conducting an experiment to study the effects of electrical stimulation in a rat's midbrain reticular formation. One of the electrodes missed the target and was mistakenly implanted in the hypothalamus. Olds noticed that whenever this rat was stimulated, it repeated whatever it had just done, as if it had been rewarded for that behavior. Olds then implanted electrodes in the hypothalamus of other animals and exposed them to a variety of learning situations. He found that they also learned and performed behaviors in order to receive what was clearly an electrical reward. In fact, some of the rats pressed a pedal up to 5,000 times in an hour until they dropped from exhaustion. Stimulation of other nearby areas produced just the opposite effect—a tendency to stop performing any behavior that was followed by stimulation, as if the animal had been punished. Olds and other researchers who replicated his work concluded that they had discovered what they called "reward and punishment areas" in the brain, some of which were in the hypothalamus. The reward areas are rich in neurons that release dopamine, which seems to be an important chemical mediator of pleasure (Kolb & Whishaw, 2003).

Humans who have had electrodes implanted in their brains to search for abnormal brain tissue have reported experiencing pleasure when these reward regions were electrically stimulated. One patient reportedly proposed marriage to the experimenter while being so stimulated (Heath, 1972). Thus a misplaced electrode in James Olds's

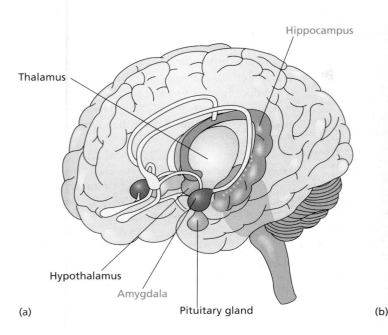

(a)

Thalamus

Hippocampus

Hypothalamus

Amygdala

Pituitary gland

(b)

FIGURE 3.19

Limbic system structures. (a) The amygdala and hippocampus are major structures of the limbic system (indicated by red type). The hippocampus is important in the establishment of memories. (b) Electrical stimulation of the amygdala, which organizes emotional responses, can evoke an immediate aggressive response.

▶ **Focus 22**
What roles do the hippocampus and amygdala play in psychological functions?

laboratory led to a discovery that neural events occurring in the hypothalamus and adjacent areas have important roles in motivation.

The Limbic System: Memory, Emotion, and Goal-Directed Behavior

As we continue our journey up through the brain, we come to the *limbic system,* a set of structures lying deep within the cerebral hemispheres (Figure 3.19). The **limbic system** *helps coordinate behaviors needed to satisfy motivational and emotional urges that arise in the hypothalamus. It is also involved in memory.*

Two key structures in the limbic system are the *hippocampus* and the *amygdala.* The **hippocampus** *is involved in forming and retrieving memories.* Damage there can result in severe memory impairment for recent events (Isaacson, 2002). The **amygdala** (from the Greek word for "almond") *organizes motivational and emotional response patterns, particularly those linked to aggression and fear* (LeDoux, 1998). Electrically stimulating certain areas of the amygdala causes animals to snarl and assume aggressive postures (see Figure 3.19b), whereas stimulation of other areas results in a fearful inability to respond aggressively, even in self-defense. For example, a normally aggressive and hungry cat will cower in fear from a tiny mouse placed in its cage. The amygdala can also produce emotional responses without the higher centers of the brain "knowing" that we are emotionally aroused, providing a possible explanation for unconscious emotional responses (LeDoux, 1998).

The amygdala is a key part of a larger control system for anger and fear that also involves other brain regions (Siegel, 2005). It has important interconnections with the hippocampus, and amygdala stimulation is important in the hippocampus's creation of emotional memories. Without amygdala activity, emotional memories are not well established. One patient whose amygdala was removed could not recall emotional scenes from movies seen a day earlier, although he was able to remember the nonemotional scenes.

Finally, like the hypothalamus, the limbic system contains reward and punishment areas that have important motivational functions. Certain drugs, such as cocaine and marijuana, seem to induce pleasure by stimulating limbic reward areas that use dopamine as their neurotransmitter (LeMoal, 1999).

The Cerebral Cortex: Crown of the Brain

The **cerebral cortex,** *a 1/4-inch-thick sheet of gray (unmyelinated) cells that form the outermost layer of the human brain,* is the crowning achievement of brain evolution. Fish and amphibians have no cerebral cortex, and the progression from more primitive to more advanced mammals is marked by a dramatic increase in the proportion of cortical tissue. In humans, the cortex constitutes fully 80 percent of brain tissue (Nolte, 1998).

The cerebral cortex is not essential for physical survival in the way that the brain stem structures are, but it is essential for human functioning. How much so is evident in this description of patients who, as a result of an accident during prenatal development, were born without a cerebral cortex:

> Some of these individuals may survive for years, in one case of mine for twenty years. From these cases, it appears that the human [lacking a cortex] sleeps and wakes; . . . reacts to hunger, loud sounds, and crude visual stimuli by movement of eyes, eyelids, and facial muscles; . . . may see and hear, . . . may be able to taste and smell, to reject the unpalatable and accept such food as it likes. . . . [They can] utter crude sounds, can cry and smile, showing displeasure when hungry and pleasure, in a babyish way, when being sung to; [they] may be able to perform spontaneously crude [limb] movements. (Cairns, 1952, p. 109)

Because the cortex is wrinkled and convoluted, like a wadded-up piece of paper, a great amount of cortical tissue is compressed into a relatively small space inside the skull. If we could remove the cortex and smooth it out, the tissue would cover an area roughly the size of a pillowcase. Perhaps 75 percent of the cortex's total surface area lies within its *fissures,* or canyonlike folds. Three of these fissures are important landmarks. One large fissure runs lengthwise across the top of the brain, dividing it into a right and a left hemisphere. Within each hemisphere, a *central fissure* divides the cerebrum into front and rear halves, and a third fissure runs from front to rear along the side of the brain. On the basis of these landmarks, neurologists have divided each hemi-

sphere into four lobes: *frontal, parietal, occipital,* and *temporal.* A fist made with your right hand (with the side of your thumb facing you) can serve as a rough orientation to these lobes. The bend in your fingers represents the frontal lobe, your knuckles the parietal lobe, your wrist area the occipital lobe, and your thumb the temporal lobe of the left hemisphere.

As shown in Figure 3.20, each of the cerebral lobes is associated with particular sensory and motor functions, as well as with speech understanding and speech production. The large areas in Figure 3.20 that are not associated with sensory or motor functions (about three fourths of the cortex) make up the *association cortex,* involved in mental processes such as thought, memory, and perception. (We will discuss the association cortex in more detail shortly.)

The Motor Cortex The **motor cortex** *controls the 600 or more muscles involved in voluntary body movements.* It lies at the rear of the frontal lobes adjacent to the central fissure. Because the nerve tracts from the motor cortex cross over at the level of the medulla, each hemisphere governs movement on the opposite side of the body. Thus severe damage to the right motor cortex would produce paralysis in the left side of the body. The left side of Figure 3.21 shows the relative organization of function within the motor cortex. As you can see, specific body areas are represented in upside-down fashion within the motor cortex, and the amount of

▶ **Focus 23**
Describe the locations of the four lobes of the brain and the organization of the motor, sensory, and association cortexes.

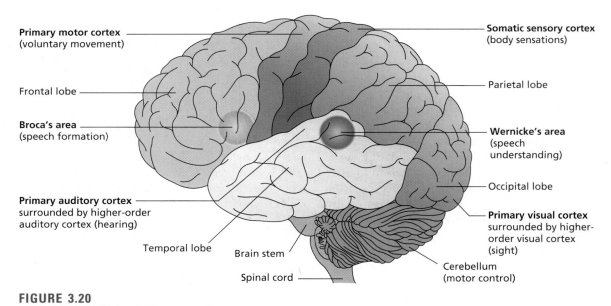

Primary motor cortex (voluntary movement)

Frontal lobe

Broca's area (speech formation)

Primary auditory cortex surrounded by higher-order auditory cortex (hearing)

Temporal lobe

Brain stem

Spinal cord

Somatic sensory cortex (body sensations)

Parietal lobe

Wernicke's area (speech understanding)

Occipital lobe

Primary visual cortex surrounded by higher-order visual cortex (sight)

Cerebellum (motor control)

FIGURE 3.20

Lobes of the brain. Division of the brain into frontal (blue), parietal (green), occipital (purple), and temporal (yellow) lobes, showing localization of sensory, motor, and some important language functions in the cortex. The remainder is primarily association cortex, consisting of interneurons involved in complex psychological functions, such as perception and reasoning.

cortex devoted to each area depends on the complexity of the movements that are carried out by the body part. For example, the amount of cortical tissue devoted to your fingers is far greater than that devoted to your torso, even though your torso is much larger. If we electrically stimulate a particular point on the motor cortex, movements occur in the muscles governed by that part of the cortex.

The Sensory Cortex Specific areas of the cortex receive input from our sensory receptors. With the exception of taste and smell, at least one specific area in the cortex has been identified for each of the senses.

The **somatic sensory cortex** *receives sensory input that gives rise to our sensations of heat, touch, and cold and to our senses of balance and body movement (kinesthesis).* It lies at the front portion of the parietal lobe just behind the motor cortex, separated from it by the central fissure. As in the case of the motor system, each side of the body sends sensory input to the opposite hemisphere. Like the motor area next to it, the somatic sensory area is basically organized in an upside-down fashion, with the feet being represented near the top of the brain. Likewise, the amount of cortex devoted to each body area is directly proportional to that region's sensory sensitivity. The organization of the sensory cortex is shown on the right side of Figure 3.21, as is the proportion of cortex devoted to each body area. As far as your sensory cortex is con-

cerned, you are mainly fingers, lips, and tongue. Notice also that the organization of the sensory cortex is such that the body structures it serves lie side by side with those in the motor cortex, an arrangement that enhances sensory-motor interactions in the same body area.

The senses of hearing and sight are well represented in the cortex. As shown in Figure 3.20, the auditory area lies on the surface of the temporal lobe at the side of each hemisphere. Each ear sends messages to the auditory areas of both hemispheres, so the loss of one temporal lobe has little effect on hearing. The primary sensory area for vision lies at the rear of the occipital lobe. Here, messages from the eyes are analyzed, integrated, and translated into sight. As in the auditory system, each eye sends input to both hemispheres.

Within each sensory area, neurons respond to particular aspects of the sensory stimulus; they are tuned in to specific aspects of the environment. Thus certain cells in the visual cortex fire only when we look at a particular kind of stimulus, such as a vertical line or a corner (Hubel & Wiesel, 1979). In the auditory cortex, some neurons fire only in response to high tones, whereas others respond only to tones having some other specific frequency. Many of these neuronal responses are present at birth, suggesting that we are prewired to perceive many aspects of our sensory environment (Noback et al., 2005). Nonetheless, the sensory

FIGURE 3.21

Cortical organization. Both the motor cortex and the somatic sensory cortex are highly specialized so that every site is associated with a particular part of the body. The amount of cortex devoted to each body part is proportional to the sensitivity of that area's motor or sensory functions. Both the motor cortex and somatic sensory cortex are arranged in an upside-down fashion and serve the opposite side of the body.

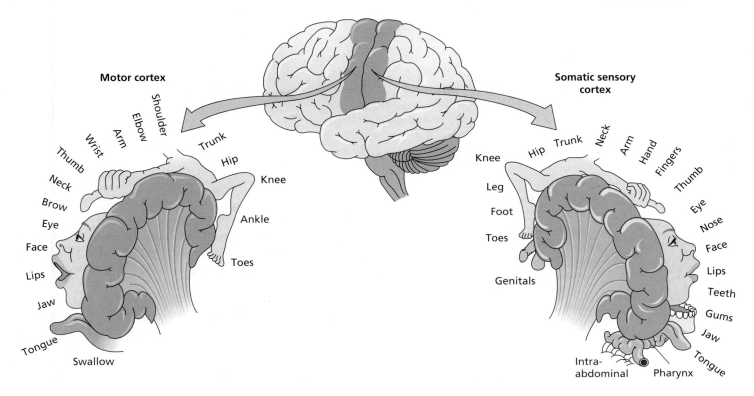

cortex, like other parts of the brain, is also sensitive to experience. For example, when people learn to read Braille, the area in the sensory cortex that receives input from the fingertips increases in size, making the person more sensitive to the tiny sets of raised dots (Pool, 1994).

Speech Comprehension and Production   Two specific areas that govern the understanding and production of speech are also located in different lobes of the left hemisphere (see Figure 3.20). **Wernicke's area,** *in the temporal lobe, is primarily involved in speech comprehension.* Damage to this cortical region leaves patients unable to understand written or spoken speech. **Broca's area,** *in the frontal lobe, is mainly involved in the production of speech through its connections with the motor cortex region that controls the muscles used in speech.* Damage to this area leaves patients with the ability to comprehend speech but not to express themselves in words or sentences. These two speech areas normally work in concert when you are conversing with another person. They allow you to comprehend what the other person is saying and to express your own thoughts.

Association Cortex   The **association cortex** *is involved in many important mental functions, including perception, language, and thought.* These areas are sometimes referred to as "silent areas" because electrically stimulating them does not give rise to either sensory experiences or motor responses. Damage to specific parts of the association cortex causes disruption or loss of functions such as speech, understanding, thinking, and problem solving. As we might expect, if the association cortex is involved in higher mental processes, the amount of association cortex increases dramatically as we move up the brain ladder from lower animals to human beings. It constitutes about 75 percent of the human cerebral cortex and accounts for people's superior cognitive abilities. One scientist has described our mass of association cortex as "evolution's missing link" (Skoyles, 1997). He suggests that its flexibility and learning capacity have allowed us to acquire new mental skills specific to our human way of life, such as reading and mathematics, far more quickly than could have occurred through natural selection alone.

The importance of the association cortex is demonstrated in people who suffer from *agnosia*, the inability to identify familiar objects. One such case is described by the neurologist Oliver Sacks (1985):

> Dr. P. [one of Sacks's patients] was a talented and accomplished musician whose behavior was quite normal except for one glaring exception: Although his vision was perfect, he often had difficulty recognizing familiar people and objects. Thus, he would chat with pieces of furniture and wonder why they did not reply, or pat the tops of fire hydrants, thinking they were children. One day, while visiting Sacks's office for an examination, Dr. P. looked for his hat as he was ready to depart. He suddenly reached out and grabbed his wife's head, trying to lift it. He had mistaken his wife for his hat! His wife smiled tolerantly; she had become accustomed to such actions on his part.

Dr. P. had suffered brain damage that left him unable to connect the information sent to the visual cortex with information stored in other cortical areas that concerned the nature of objects. The associative neurons responsible for linking the two types of information no longer served him.

The Frontal Lobes: The Human Difference   Some neuroscientists suggest that the entire period of human evolutionary existence could well be termed the "age of the frontal lobe" (Krasnegor et al., 1997). This brain region hardly exists in mammals such as mice and rats. The frontal lobes compose about 3.5 percent of the cerebral cortex in the cat, 7 percent in the dog, and 17 percent in the chimpanzee. In a human, the frontal lobes constitute 29 percent of the cortex. The frontal lobes—the site of such human qualities as self-awareness, planning, initiative, and responsibility—are in some respects the most mysterious and least understood part of the brain.

Much of what we know about the frontal lobes comes from detailed studies of patients who have experienced brain damage. Frontal-lobe damage results not so much in a loss of intellectual abilities as in an inability to plan and carry out a sequence of actions, even when patients can verbalize what they should do. This can result in an inability to correct actions that are clearly erroneous and self-defeating (Shallice & Burgess, 1991).

The frontal cortex is also involved in emotional experience. In people with normal brains, PET scans show increased activity in the frontal cortex when people are experiencing feelings of happiness, sadness, or disgust (Lane et al., 1997). In contrast, patients with frontal-lobe damage often exhibit attitudes of apathy and lack of concern. They simply don't seem to care about anything.

A region of the frontal lobe has received increasing attention in recent years. The **prefrontal cortex,** *located just behind the forehead, is the seat of the so-called executive functions.* Executive functions are mental abilities—such as goal setting, judgment,

---

▶ **Focus 24**
Where are Wernicke's and Broca's areas? How are they involved in speech?

▶ **Focus 25**
Describe the role of the frontal cortex in higher mental (including executive) functions.

strategic planning, and impulse control—that allow people to direct their behavior in an adaptive fashion. Deficits in executive functions seem to underlie a number of problem behaviors. People with prefrontal-cortex disorders seem oblivious to the future consequences of their actions and seem to be governed only by immediate consequences (Raine et al., 1997). As you may have guessed by now, Phineas Gage, the railroad foreman described in our chapter-opening case, suffered massive prefrontal damage when the spike tore through his brain (see Figure 3.2). Thereafter he exhibited classic symptoms of disturbed executive functions, becoming behaviorally impulsive and losing his capacity for future planning.

A more ominous manifestation of prefrontal dysfunction—the capacity to kill—was recently discovered by researchers using PET-scan technology. We describe this landmark study in the following "Research Close-Up."

Research Close-Up   Inside the Brain of a Killer

SOURCE: JACQUELINE STODDARD, ADRIAN RAINE, SUSAN BIHRLE, and MONTE BUCHSBAUM (1997). Prefrontal dysfunction in murderers lacking psychosocial deficits. In A. Raine, P. A. Brennan, D. P. Farrington, and S. A. Mednick (Eds.), *Biosocial bases of violence* (pp. 301–305). New York: Plenum.

INTRODUCTION

What stops us from impulsively killing an irritating neighbor, a disloyal friend, or a total stranger wearing a coat we'd like to own? The answer may lie, at least in part, in our frontal lobes. Much of what makes you a civilized person—self-control, judgment, foresight, reasoning, delaying gratification—is regulated by the executive functions of your prefrontal cortex. As seen in the case of Phineas Gage, damage in this region of the brain can reduce those civilizing inhibitions.

Until recently, researchers could only infer that impulsively violent people without obvious brain damage had reduced prefrontal activity, for they could not look directly into the brain and see how it was functioning. That changed with the development of brain-imaging procedures, particularly the PET scan. In this study, Jacqueline Stoddard and her coworkers applied PET technology to examine brain functioning in a group of people who had committed savage acts of violence. They also examined the possible contribution of environmental factors in this violence-prone population.

METHOD

The researchers studied 41 individuals (39 men and 2 women) who had been tried for murder or manslaughter in California. All had pleaded not guilty by reason of insanity or were judged mentally incompetent to stand trial. Each killer was paired with a nonviolent control participant matched for age, sex, and ethnicity. A radioactive glucose substance was injected into the participants, and this nutrient traveled to the brain. PET scans were then taken to assess brain activity while the participants worked on a mental performance task that is known to require frontal-lobe involvement.

To assess the potential role of environmental factors that might foster violent tendencies, the records of the murderers were independently reviewed by two raters for degree of psychosocial deprivation. "Deprivation" was defined as histories of physical or sexual abuse, severe family conflict, neglect, or being raised in a broken home. There was high agreement between the two raters, who knew nothing about the murderers' PET data.

RESULTS

On the basis of the psychosocial history ratings, the murderers were divided into a deprived group, numbering 26, who clearly had grown up under adverse circumstances, and a second group of 12 whose histories showed no evidence of deprivation. (The other 3 murderers had only minor deprivation and were not included in the comparisons.) These groups were compared with the nonviolent controls in glucose metabolic rates, which measure the activity of neurons in the brain. The glucose recordings from the prefrontal areas of the left and right hemispheres are shown in Figure 3.22.

The murderers with no history of psychosocial deprivation differed significantly from their nonviolent controls, the lower glucose readings indicating reduced activity in the prefrontal area. Although their prefrontal readings were also lower, the murderers with adverse environmental histories did not differ significantly from the nonviolent controls.

DISCUSSION

This study illustrates the value of brain-imaging techniques for studying brain-behavior relations. Prior research using PET technology had suggested that violent individuals have reduced prefrontal activity (Raine et al., 1997), and other

Continued

FIGURE 3.22

Prefrontal cortical activity. Prefrontal cortical activity was measured by PET scans in (a) murderers with no history of psychosocial conditions predictive of aggressive behavior, (b) murderers with a history of psychosocial deprivation, and (c) a nonviolent control group. Murderers with no history of deprivation showed notable prefrontal dysfunction. Source: Data from Stoddard et al., 1997.

research using fMRI with nonviolent participants showed that the prefrontal cortex lit up when people were made to feel guilty or embarrassed, suggesting the role of this structure in the inhibition of unacceptable behavior (Takahashi et al., 2004).

The study by Stoddard and her coworkers is particularly significant because it took into account not only brain functioning but also environmental effects known to be associated with the development of violent behavior. The researchers reasoned that both biological and environmental factors can prime people to become violent. In the absence of being raised in an environment that would be expected to foster impulsive violence, a brain abnormality that affected the executive functions of the prefrontal cortex would be a likely biological suspect. In accord with the researchers' hypothesis, the murderers who did not have a history of adverse environmental experiences were the ones who showed the greatest prefrontal dysfunction.

Other questions remain, however. First, the 41 murderers were not only violent people, but they were also psychologically disturbed enough to plead not guilty by reason of insanity. Although these people are obviously an important and dangerous subset of murderers, the findings can be applied to differences only between disturbed murderers and nonviolent populations who are not psychologically disturbed. In this study, it would have been ideal to have a second control group that was nonviolent but psychologically disturbed so that we could be more certain that the group differences were related to violent tendencies and not simply to mental illness. Also needed to flesh out the links between brain and violence are future studies of prefrontal functioning in other populations that engage in impulsive, poorly planned violence, such as certain types of juvenile delinquents or violent children. However, no single study can address all of these questions, and this study is an excellent start toward understanding brain mechanisms responsible for violence and how they might interact with environmental factors.

HEMISPHERIC LATERALIZATION: THE LEFT AND RIGHT BRAINS

▶ **Focus 26**
What is hemispheric lateralization, and what functions are localized in the left and right hemispheres?

The left and right cerebral hemispheres are connected by a broad white band of myelinated nerve fibers. The **corpus callosum** *is a neural bridge consisting of white myelinated fibers that acts as a major communication link between the two hemispheres and allows them to function as a single unit* (see Figure 3.17). Despite the fact that they normally act in concert, however, there are important differences between the psychological functions of the two cerebral hemispheres (Hugdahl & Davidson, 2005). **Lateralization** *refers to the relatively greater localization of a function in one hemisphere or the other.*

Medical studies of patients who suffered various types of brain damage provided the first clues that certain complex psychological functions were lateralized on one side of the brain or the other. The deficits observed in people with damage to either the left or right hemisphere

suggested that for most people, verbal abilities and speech are localized in the left hemisphere, as are mathematical and logical abilities (Springer, 1997). When Broca's or Wernicke's speech areas in the left hemisphere are damaged, the result is **aphasia,** *the partial or total loss of the ability to communicate.* Depending on the location of the damage, the problem may lie in recognizing the meaning of words, in communicating verbally with others, or in both functions. We should note, however, that women are less likely to suffer aphasia when their left hemisphere is damaged, suggesting that for women, language is represented in both hemispheres to a greater extent than for men (Rossell et al., 2002).

When the right hemisphere is damaged, the clinical picture is quite different. Language functions are not ordinarily affected, but the person has great difficulty perceiving spatial relations. A patient may have a hard time recognizing faces and may even forget a well-traveled route or, as in the case of Dr. P., mistake his wife for a hat (Sacks, 1985). It appears that mental imagery, musical and artistic abilities, and the ability to perceive and understand spatial relations are primarily right-hemisphere functions (Ornstein, 1997).

The two hemispheres differ not only in the cognitive functions that reside there but also in their links with positive and negative emotions. EEG studies have shown that the right hemisphere is relatively more active when negative emotions such as sadness and anger are being experienced. Positive emotions such as joy and happiness are accompanied by relatively greater left-hemisphere activation (Marshall & Fox, 2000).

The Split Brain: Dividing the Hemispheres

Despite the lateralization of specific functions in the two cerebral hemispheres, the brain normally functions as a unified whole because the two hemispheres communicate with one another through the corpus callosum. But what would happen if this communication link were cut? Would we, in effect, produce two different and largely independent minds in the same person? A series of Nobel Prize–winning studies by Roger Sperry (1970) and his associates addressed this question. Sperry and his coworkers studied people whose corpus callosa had been severed to stop epileptic seizures from spreading throughout the brain.

Split-brain research was made possible by the way in which our visual input to the brain is organized. To illustrate, extend your two hands straight out in front of you, separated by about one foot. Now focus on the point between them. You'll find that you can still see both hands in your peripheral vision and that you have a unified view of the scene. It therefore might surprise you to know that your left hand is being "seen" only by your right hemisphere and your right hand only by your left hemisphere. To see how this occurs, examine Figure 3.23, which shows that some of the fibers of the optic nerve from each eye cross over at the *optic chiasma* and travel to the opposite brain hemisphere.

Despite this arrangement, we experience a unified visual world (as you did when you looked at your hands), rather than two half-worlds, because our hemispheres' visual areas are connected by the corpus callosum. When the corpus callosum is cut, however, visual input to only one hemisphere can be accomplished by projecting the stimulus to either the right side of the visual field, in which case the image goes only to the left hemisphere, or to the left side of the visual field, which sends it to the right hemisphere.

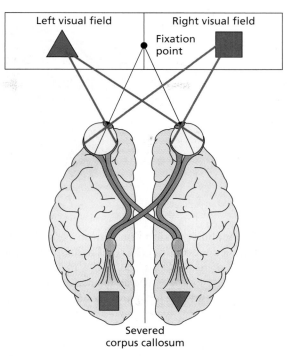

FIGURE 3.23

The split brain. The visual system's anatomy made studies of split-brain subjects possible. Images entering the eye are reversed by the lens, so that light waves from the right visual field fall on the left side of the retina and those from the left visual field fall on the right side of the retina. Optic nerve fibers from the inner portion of the retina (toward the nose) cross over at the optic chiasma, whereas the fibers from the outer portion of the retina do not. As a result, the right side of the visual field projects to the visual cortex of the left hemisphere, whereas the left visual field projects to the right hemisphere. When the corpus callosum is cut, the two hemispheres no longer communicate with each other. By presenting stimuli to either side of the visual fixation point, researchers can control which hemisphere receives the information.

In Sperry's experiments, split-brain patients basically did what you did with your hands: They focused on a fixation point, a dot on the center of a screen, while slides containing visual stimuli (words, pictures, and so on) were flashed to the right or to the left side of the fixation point (Figure 3.24).

Sperry found that when words were flashed to the right side of the visual field, resulting in their being sent to the language-rich left hemisphere, patients could verbally describe what they had seen. They could also write what they had seen with their right hand (which is controlled by the left hemisphere). However, if words were flashed to the left side of the visual field and sent on to the right hemisphere, the patients could not describe what they had seen on the screen. This pattern of findings indicates that the right hemisphere does not have well-developed verbal-expressive abilities.

Picture of hairbrush
flashed on screen

(a)

"What did you see?"

"I don't know."

(b)

"With your left hand, select the object you
saw from those behind the screen."

(c)

FIGURE 3.24

A split-brain patient. A split-brain patient focuses on the fixation point in the center of the screen. (a) A picture of a hairbrush is briefly projected to the left side of the visual field, thus sending the information to the right hemisphere. (b) The patient is asked to report what she saw. She cannot name the object. (c) She is then asked to select the object she saw and quickly finds it with her left hand. What would happen if the object were to be transferred to her right hand or if the word were to be projected to the right side of the visual field? In either case, the information would be sent to the language-rich left hemisphere, and she would be able to name the object.

The inability to describe stimuli verbally did not mean, however, that the right hemisphere was incapable of recognizing them. If a picture of an object (e.g., a hairbrush) was flashed to the right hemisphere and the left hand (controlled by the right hemisphere) was allowed to feel different objects behind the screen, the person's hand would immediately select the brush. As long as the person continued to hold the brush in the left hand, sending sensory input about the object to the "nonverbal" right hemisphere, the person was unable to name it. However, if the brush was transferred to the right hand, the person could immediately name it. In other words, until the object was transferred to the right hand, the left hemisphere had no knowledge of what the right hemisphere was experiencing.

Later research showed the right hemisphere's definite superiority over the left in the recognition of patterns. In one study, three split-brain patients were presented with photographs of similar-looking faces projected in either the left or right visual fields. On each trial, they were asked to select

the photo they had just seen from a set of 10 cards. On this task, the spatially oriented right hemisphere was far more accurate than the linguistic left hemisphere in correctly identifying the photos (Figure 3.25). Apparently, the faces were too similar to one another to be differentiated very easily by left-hemisphere verbal descriptions, but the pattern-recognition abilities of the right hemisphere allowed discrimination among them (Gazzaniga & Smylie, 1983). Split-brain research firmly established the different abilities of the two hemispheres.

? What Do You Think?

TWO MINDS IN ONE BRAIN?
Sperry's split-brain studies caused a sensation in neuroscience and in the popular press. Soon *left brain* and *right brain* became part of the popular vernacular, and educational programs were proposed to unearth the unrealized potential of the right brain. Do you believe that this left brain/right brain concept and programs based on it are justified by Sperry's findings? How can you explain the fact that the split-brain patients were able to function in daily life? Think critically about these questions, then see the discussion on page 103.

FIGURE 3.25

Facial-recognition accuracy by the left and right hemispheres of three split-brain patients. Patients show greater accuracy when information is flashed to the right hemisphere, which has stronger pattern-recognition abilities. SOURCE: Data from Gazzaniga & Smylie, 1983.

IN REVIEW

- The brain is divided structurally into the hindbrain, the midbrain, and the forebrain. This organization reflects the evolution of increasingly more complex brain structures related to behavioral capabilities.

- Major structures within the hindbrain include the medulla, which monitors and controls vital body functions; the pons, which contains important groups of sensory and motor neurons; and the cerebellum, which is concerned with motor coordination.

- The reticular formation, located in the midbrain, plays a vital role in consciousness, attention, and sleep. Activity of the ascending reticular formation excites higher areas of the brain and prepares them to respond to stimulation. The descending reticular formation acts as a gate, determining which stimuli enter into consciousness.

■ The forebrain consists of two cerebral hemispheres and a number of subcortical structures. The cerebral hemispheres are connected by the corpus callosum.

■ The thalamus acts as a switchboard through which impulses originating in sense organs are routed to the appropriate sensory-projection areas. The hypothalamus plays a major role in many aspects of motivational and emotional behavior. The limbic system seems to be involved in organizing the behaviors involved in motivation and emotion.

■ The cerebral cortex is divided into frontal, parietal, occipital, and temporal lobes. Some areas of the cerebral cortex receive sensory input, some control motor functions, and others (the association cortex) are involved in higher mental processes in humans. The frontal lobes are particularly important in such executive functions as planning, voluntary behavior, and self-awareness.

■ Although the two cerebral hemispheres ordinarily work in coordination with one another, they appear to have different functions and abilities. Studies of split-brain patients, whose corpus callosa have been cut, indicate that the left hemisphere commands language and mathematical abilities, whereas the right hemisphere has well-developed spatial abilities but a generally limited ability to communicate through speech. Positive emotions are linked to relatively greater left-hemisphere activation and negative emotions to relatively greater right-hemisphere involvement. Despite hemispheric localization, however, most behaviors involve interactions between both hemispheres; the brain normally operates as a highly integrated system.

PLASTICITY IN THE BRAIN: THE ROLE OF EXPERIENCE AND THE RECOVERY OF FUNCTION

Learn to walk, acquire speech, begin to read, fall in love, and your brain changes in ways that make you a different person from who you were before. Learning and practicing a mental or physical skill may change the size or number of brain areas involved and alter the neural pathways used in the skill (Adams & Cox, 2002). This process of brain alteration begins in the womb and continues throughout life. It is governed in important ways by genetic factors but is also strongly influenced by the environment.

Neural plasticity *refers to the ability of neurons to change in structure and function* (Huttenlocher, 2002). Two aspects of neural plasticity—the effects of early experience on brain development and recovery from brain damage—are at the forefront of current research.

How Experience Influences Brain Development

Brain development is programmed by complex commands from our genes, but how these genetic commands express themselves can be powerfully affected by the environment in which we develop, including the environment we are exposed to in the womb (Filogamo, 1998). Consider the following research findings:

• For the fetus in the womb, exposure to high levels of alcohol ingested by the pregnant mother can disrupt brain development and produce the lifelong mental and behavioral damage seen in fetal alcohol syndrome. Drinking during the first weeks of pregnancy—sometimes before a woman is even aware that she's pregnant—is particularly risky in this regard (Streissguth et al., 1985).

• Compared with those of normally reared rats, the brains of rat pups raised in a stimulating environment weighed more and had larger neurons, more dendritic branches, and greater concentrations of acetylcholine, a neurotransmitter involved in motor control and in memory (Rosenzweig, 1984).

• Prematurely born human infants who were caressed and massaged on a regular basis showed faster neurological development than did those given normal care and human contact (Field et al., 1986).

• MRI recordings revealed that experienced violinists and other string-instrument players who do elaborate movements on the strings with their left hands had a larger right-hemisphere somatosensory area devoted to these fingers than did nonmusicians. The corresponding left-hemisphere (right-hand) cortical areas of the musicians and nonmusicians did not differ. The earlier in life the musicians had started playing their instruments, the greater the cortical differences (Elbert et al., 1995).

► **Focus 27**
What is neural plasticity? How do age, environment, and behavior affect plasticity?

- Chronic alcoholism inhibits the production of new neural connections in the hippocampus, thereby impairing learning, memory, and other cognitive functions. After weeks of abstinence, the process of neural regeneration is reinstated (Nixon & Crews, 2004).

- Some theorists believe that life stress has a similar negative effect on neuron formation in the brain, thereby causing or maintaining clinical depression. Antidepressant medications increase serotonin action in the brain, and serotonin increases neuron production in the brain (Jacobs, 2004).

- Cultural factors may affect brain development as well. For example, the Chinese language uses complex pictorial images (rather than words) to represent objects or concepts. Because pictorial stimuli are processed in the right hemisphere, we might expect less left-hemisphere lateralization of language among speakers of Chinese than among people who speak English or other alphabet-based languages. There is evidence to support this hypothesis in the areas of reading and writing (Tzeng et al., 1979).

These and other findings show that in a very real sense, each person's brain goes through its own personal evolutionary process. The brain changes and adapts as it is sculpted by life experiences.

Studies using the electron microscope help explain why such plasticity is possible early in life. The 1- to 2-year-old child has about 50 percent more brain synapses than mature adults do (Huttenlocher, 1979). This greater availability of synapses may help explain why children can recover from brain damage more quickly and completely than adults. But, sadly, the days of synaptic riches don't last forever. Unused or weaker synapses deteriorate with age, so that the brain loses some of its plasticity (Huttenlocher, 2002). Moreover, cell death is programmed into every neuron by its genes, and what some neuroscientists refer to as the neuron's "suicide apparatus" is activated by a lack of stimulation from other neurons and by many other factors that are not yet known. As a result, adults actually have fewer synapses than do children, despite their more advanced cognitive and motor capabilities. However, the remaining neurons form new connections in response to experiences and the formation of new memories.

Healing the Nervous System

When nerve tissue is destroyed or neurons die as part of the aging process, surviving neurons can restore functioning by modifying themselves either structurally or biochemically. They can alter their structure by sprouting enlarged networks of dendrites or by extending axons from surviving neurons to form new synapses (Shepherd, 1997). Surviving neurons may also make up for the loss by increasing the volume of neurotransmitters they release (Robinson, 1997). Moreover, research findings have disproved the long-standing assumption of brain scientists that dead neurons cannot be replaced in the mature brain (McMillan et al., 1999). *The production of new neurons in the nervous system is called* **neurogenesis.** Neurogenesis occurs in both the immature and the adult brain. In the adult brain, the birth of new cells has been established only in the hippocampus so far, but it may occur in other areas as well. The study of neurogenesis is an exciting research frontier.

One revolutionary neurogenesis technique involves the transplantation into the brain of **neural stem cells,** *immature "uncommitted" cells that can mature into any type of neuron or glial cell needed by the brain.* These cells, found in both the developing and adult nervous systems, can be put into a liquid medium and injected directly into the brain. Once in the brain, they can travel to any of its regions, especially developing or degenerating areas. There they can detect defective or genetically impaired cells and somehow convert themselves into healthy forms of the defective cells. Stem cells have been successfully transplanted into the spinal cords of injured animals, where they have taken hold and organized themselves into neural networks (Tzeng, 1997). This success may herald an eventual ability to do what has never before been possible: repair the severed spinal cord.

The fact that transplanted stem cells can apparently go anywhere in the brain and become any kind of cell suggests the possibility of revolutionary treatments for diseases involving neural degeneration and dysfunction. These include Alzheimer's disease, multiple sclerosis, strokes, mental disorders, and genetically based birth defects, all of which have serious psychological consequences (Wernig & Brustle, 2002). Stem cells may also hold the key to countering the effects of aging on brain functioning. In one study, human stem cells transplanted into the brains of aged rats migrated to the hippocampus and cortex. Four weeks later, these rats showed improved performance in a water-maze task, suggesting improved learning and memory ability (Qu et al., 2001). Much more research is needed, but, at long last, we may be on the threshold of being able to heal the damaged brain and restore lost psychological functions (Brazel & Rao, 2004).

▶ **Focus 28**
Describe the ways in which neural function can be restored following damage.

Beneath the Surface   Do We Really Use Only Ten Percent of Our Brain Capacity?

How often have you heard that we only use 10 percent of our brain capacity? Is there any truth to this notion?

Let's apply what we've learned in this chapter to critically evaluate that statement. One principle of critical thinking is to test an idea by trying to find evidence against it. The reason is that we can find something to support almost any statement, even if it's false. In contrast, one disconfirming piece of evidence tells us the statement is not true as is.

First, let's consider what we know about brain activity from PET and fMRI imaging studies. Do they show that only 10 percent of the brain is active at any time? Certainly not. Instead, the brain exhibits widespread activity even during sleep. Although certain functions may use only a small part of the brain at one time, any sufficiently complex set of activities or thought patterns involves many parts of the brain. For any given activity, such as eating, watching television, walking, or reading this book, you may use a few specific parts of your brain. Over the course of a whole day, however, just about all of the brain is used at one time or another. Thus, brain activity data fly in the face of the 10-percent truism.

Next, we might consider what we know about brain damage. Does the 10-percent principle mean that we would be just fine if 90 percent of our brain were removed? Hardly. It is well known that damage to a relatively small area of the brain, such as that caused by a stroke, can cause devastating disabilities. Yet the damage caused by such a condition is far less than what would occur if 90 percent of the brain were removed. As a prominent neurologist told us, "If a surgeon tells you he or she is going to remove the 90 percent of the brain you don't need, run like hell."

We might also apply what we've learned about neural development, particularly the "use it or lose it" principle. The process of brain development involves pruning synapses that are not used, thereby fine-tuning brain functioning. Many studies have shown that if the input to a particular neural system is eliminated, then neurons in this system will not function properly. If we were really using only 10 percent of the brain, we could expect the other 90 percent to atrophy over time.

Where did the 10-percent idea come from in the first place? Perhaps it was inspired in part by the work of psychologist Karl Lashley in the 1920s and 1930s. Lashley removed large areas of the cerebral cortex in rats and found that these animals could still relearn specific tasks. This did not mean, however, that other functions were not severely affected. But psychics and other "human potential" marketeers found the idea intriguing and have kept it alive over the decades. After all, if we use only 10 percent of our brain, imagine the untapped psychic abilities that lie dormant, just waiting to be released using their methods. Psychics often attribute their special, if fraudulent, gifts to the release of neural potential that other people have not accessed.

This does not mean that we don't have untapped potentials; it's just that if realized, they would be represented in the form of new synapses within brain tissue that you're already using. A final reason why the myth persists is that it's been repeated so often over the years in the mass media that it's become a part of popular culture, an unquestioned factoid that's taken on a life of its own. However, there's no question that the 10-percent principle is a myth without scientific foundation.

IN REVIEW

- Neural plasticity refers to the ability of neurons to change in structure and function. Environmental factors, particularly early in life, have notable effects on brain development. There are often periods during which environmental factors have their greatest (or only) effects on plasticity.

- A person's ability to recover from brain damage depends on several factors. Other things being equal, recovery is greatest early in life and declines with age.

- When neurons die, surviving neurons can alter their structure and functions to recover the ability to send and receive nerve impulses. Neurons can also increase the amount of neurotransmitters they release. Recent findings suggest that the brains of mature primates and humans are capable of producing new neurons (neurogenesis).

- Current advances in the treatment of neurological disorders include experiments on neurogenesis and the injection of neural stem cells into the brain, where they find and replace diseased or dead neurons.

THE NERVOUS SYSTEM INTERACTS WITH THE ENDOCRINE AND IMMUNE SYSTEMS

The nervous system interacts with two other communication systems within the body, namely, the endocrine and immune systems. These interactions have major influences on behavior and on psychological and physical well-being.

INTERACTIONS WITH THE ENDOCRINE SYSTEM

▶ **Focus 29**
How does the endocrine system differ from the nervous system? How do hormones affect development and behavior?

The **endocrine system** *consists of numerous hormone-secreting glands distributed throughout the body* (Figure 3.26). Like the nervous system, the endocrine system's function is to convey information from one area of the body to another. Rather than using nerve impulses, however, the endocrine system conveys information in the form of **hormones,** *chemical messengers that are secreted from its glands into the bloodstream.* Just as neurons have receptors for certain neurotransmitters, cells in the body (including neurons) have receptor molecules that respond to

specific hormones from the endocrine glands. Many of the hormones secreted by these glands affect psychological development and functioning.

Endocrine messages trigger responses in the brain, and mental processes within the brain can affect endocrine functioning. For example, negative thoughts about a stressful situation can quickly trigger the secretion of stress hormones within the body (Borod, 2000).

The nervous system transmits information rapidly, with the speed of nerve impulses. In contrast, the endocrine system is much slower because the delivery of its messages depends on the rate of blood flow. Nonetheless, hormones travel throughout the body in the bloodstream and can reach billions of individual cells. Thus when the brain has important information to transmit, it has the choice of sending it quickly and directly in the form of nerve impulses to a relatively small number of neurons or indirectly by means of hormones to a large number of cells. Often both communication networks are used, resulting in both immediate and prolonged stimulation.

Hormones begin to influence our development, capacities, and behavior long before we're born. In the third to fourth month of pregnancy, genetically programmed releases of sex hormones in the fetus determine sex organ development, as well as differences in the structure and function of several parts of the nervous system, including the hypothalamus. One area of the hypothalamus affected in this manner continues to influence hormonal release in later life, such as the cyclic pattern of hormonal release during the female menstrual cycle.

Aside from reproductive structures and sexual behaviors, prenatal hormones affect a variety of other characteristics including sex differences in aggressiveness and longevity; males tend to be more aggressive than females, and females live longer than men (Nelson & Luciana, 2001). Prenatal hormones also produce differences in brain structures in males and females. Females have a greater density of neurons in language-relevant areas of the temporal lobe, which may contribute to the small overall superiority they manifest in verbal skills (Collins & Kimura, 1997). They also tend to have a relatively larger corpus callosum than males, which may help account for the fact that language functions are less localized in the left hemisphere in females (Rossell et al., 2002). These sex differences will be discussed in greater detail in Chapter 8.

Of special interest to psychologists are the **adrenal glands,** *twin structures perched atop the kidneys that serve, quite literally, as hormone factories, producing and secreting about 50 different hormones that regulate many metabolic processes within the*

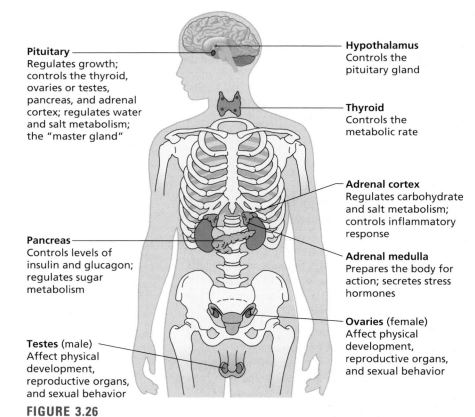

Pituitary
Regulates growth; controls the thyroid, ovaries or testes, pancreas, and adrenal cortex; regulates water and salt metabolism; the "master gland"

Pancreas
Controls levels of insulin and glucagon; regulates sugar metabolism

Testes (male)
Affect physical development, reproductive organs, and sexual behavior

Hypothalamus
Controls the pituitary gland

Thyroid
Controls the metabolic rate

Adrenal cortex
Regulates carbohydrate and salt metabolism; controls inflammatory response

Adrenal medulla
Prepares the body for action; secretes stress hormones

Ovaries (female)
Affect physical development, reproductive organs, and sexual behavior

FIGURE 3.26

The endocrine system. This illustration shows the location of the glands that comprise the endocrine system and the effects of their hormones on bodily functions.

brain and other parts of the body. The adrenals produce the neurotransmitter dopamine, as well as several stress hormones. In an emergency, the adrenal glands are activated by the sympathetic branch of the autonomic nervous system. Stress hormones are then secreted into the bloodstream, mobilizing the body's emergency response system. Because hormones remain in the bloodstream for some time, the action of these adrenal hormones is especially important under conditions of prolonged stress. If not for the long-term influence of hormones, the autonomic nervous system would have to produce a constant barrage of nerve impulses to the organs involved in responding to stress.

INTERACTIONS INVOLVING THE IMMUNE SYSTEM

The nervous and endocrine systems interact not only with one another but also with the immune system. A normal, healthy immune system is a wonder of nature. At this moment, microscopic soldiers patrol every part of your body, including your brain. They are on a search-and-destroy mission, seeking out biological invaders that could disable or kill you. Programmed into this legion of tiny defenders is an innate ability to recognize which substances belong to the body and which are foreign and must be destroyed. Such recognition occurs because *foreign substances known as* **antigens** (meaning *anti*body *gen*erators) *trigger a biochemical response from the immune system.* Bacteria, viruses, abnormal cells, and many chemical molecules with antigenic properties start the wars that rage inside our bodies every moment of every day (Figure 3.27).

The immune system has a remarkable memory. Once it has encountered one of the millions of

FIGURE 3.27

An immune-system cell reaches out to capture bacteria, shown here in yellow. The bacteria that have already been pulled to the surface of the cell will be engulfed and devoured.

different antigens that enter the body, it will recognize the antigen immediately in the future and produce the biochemical weapons, or *antibodies,* needed to destroy it (Nossal & Hall, 1995). This memory is the basis for developing vaccines to protect people and animals from some diseases; it is also the reason we normally catch diseases such as mumps and chicken pox only once in our lives. Unfortunately, though the memory may be perfect, our body's defenses may not be. Some bacteria and viruses evolve so rapidly that they can change just enough over time to slip past the sentinels in our immune system and give us this year's cold or flu.

The immune system, like the nervous system, has an exquisite capacity to receive, interpret, and respond to specific forms of stimulation. It senses, learns, remembers, and reacts; in other words, it behaves. Despite these similarities, research on the nervous and immune systems proceeded along independent paths for many years, with only a few visionaries suggesting that the two systems might be able to communicate and influence each others' activities. We now know that the nervous, endocrine, and immune systems are all parts of a communication network that so completely underlies our every mental, emotional, and physical action that neuroscientist Candace Pert (1986), one of the pioneers in this area of research, has dubbed this network "bodymind."

Pieces of this communication puzzle began to fall into place with several key discoveries. First, researchers found that electrical stimulation or destruction of certain sites in the hypothalamus and cerebral cortex resulted in immediate increases or decreases in immune-system activity. Conversely, activating the immune system by injecting antigens into the body resulted in increased electrical activity in several brain regions (Saphier, 1992). Clearly, the nervous and immune systems were communicating with and influencing one another.

Later research showed that the nervous and immune systems are chemically connected as well. Immune-system cells contain receptors keyed to specific neurotransmitter substances, meaning that the action of immune cells can be directly influenced by chemical messengers from the brain (Maier & Watkins, 1999). An equally startling discovery was that immune cells can actually produce hormones and neurotransmitters, allowing them to directly influence the brain and endocrine system (Felton & Maida, 2000). In sum, the brain, endocrine glands, and immune system form a complete communication loop, with each having sensory and motor functions and each influencing and being influenced by one another.

▶ **Focus 30**
What evidence exists that the nervous, endocrine, and immune systems communicate with and influence one another?

FIGURE 3.28

Levels of analysis: Factors related to immune-system functioning.

Inspired by these findings, many researchers began to study psychological influences on the immune system. Scientific investigations soon revealed a host of psychosocial factors that can increase or decrease immunity. For example, chronic stress, depression, and pessimistic thinking reduce immune functioning, whereas stress-management skills, an optimistic outlook, a sense of humor, and social support help preserve immunity (Kiecolt-Glaser et al., 2002; Segerstrom & Miller, 2004). As Figure 3.28 shows, immune functioning is now being studied at biological, psychological, and environmental levels of analysis. We will examine these findings and their applied implications in greater depth in Chapter 13.

IN REVIEW

■ The nervous, endocrine, and immune systems have extensive neural and chemical means of communication, and each is capable of affecting and being affected by the others.

■ The endocrine system secretes hormones into the bloodstream. These chemical messengers affect many body processes, including those associated with the central and autonomic nervous systems. Because of the adrenal glands' relation to functions of the nervous system, they are of particular interest to psychologists. Hormonal effects in the womb may produce brain differences in males and females that influence sex differences in certain psychological functions.

■ The immune system interacts extensively with the central and autonomic nervous systems and with the endocrine system. As a behaving entity, the immune system has the capacity to sense, interpret, and respond to specific forms of stimulation.

SOME FINAL REFLECTIONS

We've considered three aspects of biological foundations of behavior. First, evolutionary forces have forged the development of innate biological mechanisms that underlie human capabilities and behavioral tendencies. Second, genetic factors help determine not only the characteristics that we have in common with other humans but also important mental, emotional, and behavioral aspects of our individual identities. Third, we've considered the biological structures and functions that compose the nervous, endocrine, and immune systems. In each instance, we've seen that biological and environmental factors affect one another and combine to influence development and behavior.

Reflecting on the many ways that biological and environmental factors interact at the evolutionary, genetic, and nervous-system levels helps bring perspective to our understanding of behavior and its causes: Discovering the nature and extent of biological and environmental influences for various behaviors is a major frontier in psychology. The manner in which the brain, mind, and world interact to cause behavior is the basis for psychology's use of the biological, psychological, and environmental levels of analysis that we feature throughout this book.

KEY TERMS AND CONCEPTS

Each term has been boldfaced and defined in the chapter on the page indicated in parentheses.

absolute refractory period (p. 74)
acetylcholine (ACh; p. 77)
action potential (p. 74)
adaptations (p. 64)
adoption studies (p. 70)
adrenal glands (p. 100)
agonist (p. 78)
all-or-none law (p. 74)
amygdala (p. 89)
antagonist (p. 79)
antigens (p. 101)
aphasia (p. 94)
association cortex (p. 92)
autonomic nervous system (p. 81)
axon (p. 73)
behavior genetics (p. 69)
biologically based mechanisms (p. 63)
brain stem (p. 86)
Broca's area (p. 92)
central nervous system (p. 82)
cerebellum (p. 87)
cerebral cortex (p. 89)
cerebrum (p. 88)
chromosome (p. 68)
computerized axial tomography
  (CT, or CAT) scan (p. 84)
concordance (p. 69)

corpus callosum (p. 94)
dendrites (p. 73)
electroencephalograph (EEG; p. 83)
endocrine system (p. 100)
evolution (p. 64)
forebrain (p. 88)
functional MRI (fMRI; p. 85)
genes (p. 68)
genotype (p. 68)
graded potentials (p. 74)
heritability coefficient (p. 71)
hindbrain (p. 86)
hippocampus (p. 89)
homeostasis (p. 82)
hormones (p. 100)
hypothalamus (p. 88)
interneurons (p. 80)
lateralization (p. 94)
limbic system (p. 89)
magnetic resonance imaging (MRI; p. 85)
medulla (p. 86)
midbrain (p. 87)
motor cortex (p. 90)
motor neurons (p. 80)
myelin sheath (p. 74)
natural selection (p. 64)
neural plasticity (p. 97)

neural stem cells (p. 98)
neurogenesis (p. 98)
neuromodulators (p. 77)
neurons (p. 72)
neurotransmitters (p. 76)
parasympathetic nervous system (p. 82)
peripheral nervous system (p. 80)
phenotype (p. 68)
polygenic transmission (p. 69)
pons (p. 87)
positron-emission tomography (PET)
  scan (p. 85)
prefrontal cortex (p. 92)
psychoactive drugs (p. 78)
receptor sites (p. 76)
resting potential (p. 74)
reticular formation (p. 87)
reuptake (p. 77)
sensory neurons (p. 80)
somatic nervous system (p. 81)
somatic sensory cortex (p. 91)
sympathetic nervous system (p. 81)
synaptic space (p. 76)
synaptic vesicles (p. 76)
thalamus (p. 88)
twin studies (p. 70)
Wernicke's area (p. 92)

? What Do You Think?

NATURAL SELECTION AND GENETIC DISEASES (PAGE 65)

Genetics research shows that in most cases, there's not a one-to-one relation between a particular gene and a particular trait. Most traits involve the influence of many genes, and a given gene can contribute to many traits. Traits, therefore, come in packages, with some of the traits in the package being adaptive and others maladaptive. In fact, cystic fibrosis (CF) is one such example. CF is the most commonly inherited disorder among people of European descent. Why would such a damaging genetic trait survive in the gene pool? Geneticists have found that people with CF also have a trait that slows the release of salts into the intestine. Some scientists believe that this related trait might have helped save carriers from severe dehydration and death from the diarrheal diseases that killed 7 out of every 10 newborns in medieval Europe. Perhaps CF was preserved in the population because another part of the trait package made carriers more likely to survive and pass on their genes.

Let's consider sickle cell anemia. Many people of African descent suffer from this genetically caused blood disorder that lowers one's life expectancy. Why would a disorder that decreases survival be preserved in a population? The answer may be that despite its negatives, the sickle cell gene has an important redeeming quality: It makes people more resistant to malaria, the most lethal disease in the African environment. Because it enhanced survival from malaria, the sickle cell trait became more common among Africans and can therefore be seen as a product of natural selection. This example shows us that we should be careful not to oversimplify the concept of adaptation and assume that any trait that survives, whether physical or psychological, is of immediate benefit to the species.

TWO MINDS IN ONE BRAIN? (PAGE 96)

Let's consider the second question first. How is it that the split-brain patients could function in everyday life? Would

Continued

not two independent minds get in the way of one another? It appears that in daily life, the split-brain patients could function adequately because they had learned to compensate for their disconnected hemispheres. For example, they could scan the visual environment so that input from both the left and right visual fields got into both hemispheres. Where personal identity was concerned, the linguistic left hemisphere seemed to connect present and future with the past in a manner that prevented two different personalities from emerging and tripping over one another. Some "psychologists" have suggested that what we call the conscious self resides in the left hemisphere, because consciousness is based on our ability to verbalize about the past and present (Ornstein, 1997).

The exotic "split-mind" phenomena shown in Sperry's laboratory emerged because patients with a rare biological feature were tested under experimental conditions that were specifically designed to isolate the functions of the two hemispheres. Nonetheless, the results of split-brain research were so dramatic that they led some people (and even some scientists) to promote a conception of brain functions as being highly localized and restricted to one hemisphere or the other. Even today, we hear about education programs directed at developing the "untapped potentials of the right brain." Certainly, there is some degree of localization of brain functions, but a far more important principle is that in the normal brain, most functions involve many areas (and both hemispheres) of the brain working together. The brain is an exquisitely integrated system, not a collection of isolated functions.

Sensation and Perception

CHAPTER OUTLINE

> *All our knowledge has its origins in our perceptions.*
>
> —LEONARDO DA VINCI

Sometimes, it is true, a sense of isolation enfolds me like a cold mist as I sit alone and wait at life's shut gate. Beyond, there is light, and music, and sweet companionship; but I may not enter. Fate, silent, pitiless, bars the way. . . . Silence sits immense upon my soul. (Keller, 1955, p. 62)

So wrote Helen Keller, deprived of both vision and hearing by an acute illness she suffered at the age of 19 months (Figure 4.1). For those of us who enjoy and take for granted the use of these senses, it is hard to imagine what it would be like to sink into a dark and silent universe, cut off from all sight and sound. Helen Keller was saved from this abyss by her teacher, Anne Sullivan, who tried day after day to communicate with her by tapping signs onto the little girl's palm. One day, Anne tapped *water* onto Helen's palm as she placed the child's hand under the gushing spout of a pump.

That living word awakened my soul, gave it light, hope, joy, set it free! That was because I saw everything with a strange new sight that had come to me. . . . It would have been difficult to find a happier child than I was. (p. 103)

Helen Keller went on to write her celebrated book *The Story of My Life* while an undergraduate at Radcliffe College. She became an inspiration and advocate for people with disabilities.

■ ■ ■ ■ ■

Nature gives us a marvelous set of sensory contacts with our world. If our sense organs are not defective, we experience light waves as brightnesses and colors, air vibrations as sounds, chemical substances as odors or tastes, and so on. However, such is not the case for people with a rare condition called **synesthesia,** *which means, quite literally, "mixing of the senses"* (Cytowic, 2002; Harrison & Baron-Cohen, 1997). Individuals with synesthesia may experience sounds as colors, or tastes as touch sensations of different shapes.

Russian psychologist A. R. Luria (1968) studied a highly successful writer and musician whose life was a perpetual stream of mixed-up sensations. On one occasion, Luria asked him to report on his experiences while listening to electronically generated musical tones. In response to a medium-pitched tone, the man experienced a brown strip with red edges, together with a sweet and sour flavor. A very high-pitched tone evoked the following sensation: "It looks something like a fireworks tinged with a pink-red hue. The strip of color feels rough and unpleasant, and it has an ugly taste—rather like that of a briny pickle. . . . You could hurt your hand on this." Mixed sensations like these frequently occurred in the man's daily life, and they were sometimes disconcerting. On one occasion, the man asked an ice cream vendor what flavors she sold. "But she answered in such a tone that a whole pile of coals, of black cinders, came bursting out of her mouth, and I couldn't bring myself to buy any ice cream after she answered that way."

Sensory-impaired people like Helen Keller and those who experience synesthesia provide glimpses into different aspects of how we sense and understand our world. These processes, previewed in Figure 4.2, begin when specific types of stimuli activate specialized sensory receptors. Whether the stimulus is light, sound waves, a chemical molecule, or pressure, your sensory receptors must translate the information into the only language your nervous system understands: the language of nerve impulses. Once this translation occurs, specialized neurons break down and analyze the specific features of the stimulus. At the next stage, these numerous stimulus features are reconstructed into a neural representation that is then compared with previously stored information, such as our knowledge of how particular objects look, smell, or feel. This matching of a new stimulus with our internal storehouse of knowledge allows us to recognize the stimulus and give it meaning. We then consciously experience a perception.

Helen Keller could not detect light waves or sound waves, the stimuli for sight and hearing. But for her, the sense of touch helped make up for this deficit, giving her a substitute window to her world. In contrast, in the mysterious condition of synesthesia, something goes wrong at the level of either feature detection or the recombining of the elements of a stimulus so that light waves might give rise to an experience of a sound or texture (Cytowic, 2002).

In some ways, sensation and perception blend together so completely that they are difficult to separate, for the stimulation we receive through our sense organs is instantaneously organized and transformed into the experiences that we refer to as perceptions. Nevertheless, psychologists do distinguish between them. **Sensation** *is the stimulus-detection process by which our sense organs respond to and translate environmental stimuli into nerve impulses that are sent to the brain.* **Perception**—*making "sense" of what our senses tell us—is the active process of organizing this stimulus input and giving it meaning* (Goldstein, 2005; Pashler & Yantis, 2002).

Because perception is an active and creative process, the same sensory input may be perceived in different ways at different times. For example, read the two sets of symbols in Figure 4.3. The middle symbols in both sets are exactly the same, and they sent identical input to your brain, but you probably perceived them differently. Your interpretation, or perception, of the characters was influenced by their context—that is, by the characters that preceded and followed them and by your learned expectation of what normally follows the letter A and the number 12. This is a simple illustration of how perception takes us a step beyond sensation.

SENSORY PROCESSES

Locked within the silent, dark recesses of your skull, your brain cannot "understand" light waves, sound waves, or the other types of stimuli that make up the language of the environment. Contact with the outer world is possible only because certain neurons have developed into specialized sensory receptors that can transform these energy forms into the code language of nerve impulses.

As a starting point, we might ask how many senses there are. Certainly there appear to be more than the five classical senses: vision, audition (hearing), gustation (taste), olfaction (smell), and touch. For example, there are senses that provide information about balance and body position. Also, the sense of touch can be subdivided into separate senses of pressure, pain, and temperature. Receptors deep within the brain monitor the chemical composition of our blood. The immune system also has sensory functions that allow it to detect foreign invaders and to receive stimulation from the brain.

Like those of other organisms, human sensory systems are designed to extract from the environment the information that we need to function and survive. Although our survival does not depend on having eyes like eagles or owls, noses like bloodhounds, or ears as sensitive as those of the worm-hunting robin, we do have specialized sensors that can detect many different kinds of stimuli with considerable sensitivity. The scientific area of **psychophysics,** *which studies relations between the physical characteristics of stimuli and sensory capabilities,* is concerned with two kinds of sensitivity. The first concerns the absolute limits of sensitivity. For example, what is the dimmest light, the faintest sound, or the weakest salt solution that humans can detect? The second kind of sensitivity has to do with

FIGURE 4.3

Context and perception. Quickly read these two lines of symbols out loud. Did your perception of the middle symbol in each line depend on the symbols that surrounded it?

▶ **Focus 1**
Describe the six stages in the sensory processing and perception of information. Differentiate between sensation and perception.

Sensation

Stimulus is received by sensory receptors

Receptors translate stimulus properties into nerve impulses (transduction)

Feature detectors analyze stimulus features

Stimulus features are reconstructed into neural representation

Neural representation is compared with previously stored information in brain

Matching process results in recognition and interpretation of stimulus

Perception

FIGURE 4.2

Sensation becomes perception. Sensory and perceptual processes proceed from the reception and translation of physical stimuli into nerve impulses. Then occurs the active process by which the brain receives the nerve impulses, organizes and confers meaning on them, and constructs a perceptual experience.

 What do researchers know about how perception occurs? Watch the "Sensory Processes and Brain Integration" video in Chapter 4 of your CD to find out.

differences between stimuli. What is the smallest difference between two tones that we can detect?

STIMULUS DETECTION: THE ABSOLUTE THRESHOLD

▶ **Focus 2**
Define the absolute threshold from traditional and signal-detection perspectives.

How intense must a stimulus be before we can detect its presence? Researchers answer this question by systematically presenting stimuli of varying intensities to people and asking whether they can detect them. Researchers designate the **absolute threshold** *as the lowest intensity at which a stimulus can be detected 50 percent of the time.* Thus the lower the absolute threshold, the greater the sensitivity. From studies of absolute thresholds, we can estimate the general limits of human sensitivity for the five major senses. Some examples are presented in Table 4.1. As you can see, many of our absolute thresholds are surprisingly low. Yet some other species have sensitivities that far surpass those of humans. For example, a female silkworm moth who is ready to mate needs to release only a billionth of an ounce of an attractant chemical molecule per second to attract every male silkworm moth within a mile's radius.

SIGNAL DETECTION THEORY

Perhaps you can remember lying in bed as a child after seeing a horror movie, straining your ears to detect any unusual sound that might signal the presence of a monster in the house. Your vigilance may have caused you to detect faint and ominous sounds that would have probably gone unnoticed had you just watched a comedy or a romantic movie.

At one time scientists thought that although some people have greater sensory acuity than others, each person has a more or less fixed level of sensitivity for each sense. But psychologists who study stimulus detection found that an individual's apparent sensitivity can fluctuate quite a bit. The concept of a fixed absolute threshold is inaccurate because there is no single point on the intensity scale that

FIGURE 4.4

Signal-detection research. This matrix shows the four possible outcomes in a signal-detection experiment in which participants decide whether a stimulus has been presented or not presented. The percentages of responses that fall within each category can be affected by both characteristics of the participants and the nature of the situation.

separates nondetection from detection of a stimulus. There is instead a range of uncertainty, and people set their own **decision criterion,** *a standard of how certain they must be that a stimulus is present before they will say they detect it.* The decision criterion can also change from time to time, depending on such factors as fatigue, expectation (e.g., having watched a horror movie), and the potential significance of the stimulus. **Signal detection theory** *is concerned with the factors that influence sensory judgments.*

In a typical signal-detection experiment, participants are told that after a warning light appears, a barely perceptible tone may or may not be presented. Their task is to tell the experimenter whether or not they hear the tone. Under these conditions, there are four possible outcomes, as shown in Figure 4.4. When the tone is in fact presented, the participant may say "yes" (a hit) or "no" (a miss). When no tone is presented, the participant may also say "yes" (a false alarm) or "no" (a correct rejection).

At low stimulus intensities, both the participant's and the situation's characteristics influence the decision criterion (Methot & Huitema, 1998; Pitz & Sachs, 1984). Bold participants who frequently say "yes" have more hits, but they also have more false alarms than do conservative participants. Researchers can influence participants to become bolder or more conservative by manipulating the rewards and costs for giving correct or incorrect responses. Increasing the rewards for hits or the costs for misses results in lower detection thresholds (more "yes" responses at low intensities). Thus a Navy radar operator may be more likely to notice a faint blip on her screen during a wartime mission—when a miss could have disastrous consequences—than during a peacetime voyage. Conversely, like physicians who will not perform a risky medical procedure without strong evidence to support their diagnosis, participants become more conservative

TABLE 4.1 Some Approximate Absolute Thresholds for Humans	
Sensory Modality	**Absolute Threshold**
Vision	Candle flame seen at 30 miles on a clear, dark night
Hearing	Tick of a watch under quiet conditions at 20 feet
Taste	1 teaspoon of sugar in 2 gallons of water
Smell	1 drop of perfume diffused into the entire volume of a large apartment
Touch	Wing of a fly or bee falling on a person's cheek from a distance of 1 centimeter

Source: Based on Galanter, 1962.

in their "yes" responses as costs for false alarms are increased, resulting in higher detection thresholds (Irwin & McCarthy, 1998). Signal-detection research shows us that perception is, in part, a decision.

SUBLIMINAL STIMULI: CAN THEY AFFECT BEHAVIOR?

A **subliminal stimulus** *is one that is so weak or brief that although it is received by the senses, it cannot be perceived consciously.* There is little question that subliminal stimuli can register in the nervous system (Kihlstrom, 1999; MacLeod, 1998). But can such stimuli affect attitudes and behavior without our knowing it? The answer appears to be yes—to a limited extent.

In the late 1950s, James Vicary, a public relations executive, arranged to have subliminal messages flashed on a theater screen during a movie. The messages urged the audience to drink Coca-Cola and eat popcorn. Vicary's claim that the subliminal messages increased popcorn sales by 50 percent and soft drink sales by 18 percent aroused a public furor. Consumers and scientists feared the possible abuse of subliminal messages to covertly influence the buying habits of consumers; they were concerned such messages might be used for mind-control and brainwashing purposes. The National Association of Broadcasters reacted by outlawing subliminal messages on American television.

The outcries were, in large part, false alarms. Several attempts to reproduce Vicary's results under controlled conditions failed, and many other studies conducted in laboratory settings, on TV and radio, and in movie theaters indicated that there is little reason to be concerned about significant or widespread control of consumer behavior through subliminal stimulation (Dixon, 1981; Drukin, 1998). Years later, Vicary admitted that his study was a hoax designed to revive his floundering advertising agency. Nonetheless, his false report stimulated a great deal of useful research on the power of subliminal stimuli to influence behavior. Where consumer behavior is concerned, the conclusion is that persuasive stimuli above the perceptual threshold are far more influential than subliminal attempts to sneak into our subconscious mind.

Although subliminal stimuli cannot control consumer behavior, research suggests that such stimuli do affect more subtle phenomena, such as perceptions and attitudes (Greenwald & Banaji, 1995). In one study, college students who were exposed to subliminal presentations of aggressively toned words like "hit" and "attack" later judged ambiguous behaviors of others as more aggressive. They also were more likely to behave aggressively than were participants who had been exposed to subliminal nonaggressive words (Todorov & Bargh, 2002). Although the original fears about brainwashing with subliminal stimuli may be unfounded, there is little doubt that subliminal stimuli can have subtle effects on attitudes, judgments, and behavior. Many people believe that they can also be a means to self-improvement. The following "Beneath the Surface" feature discusses this issue.

► **Focus 3**
How do subliminal stimuli affect consumer behavior, attitudes, and self-improvement outcomes?

Beneath the Surface   **Are Subliminal Self-Help Products Effective?**

Consumers spend millions of dollars on subliminal audiotapes and CDs that promise to help them lose weight, stop smoking, conquer fears, feel better about themselves, and achieve other self-improvement goals. But do these aids work?

In fact, many people believe they do. Why are these products effective? Do they program the subconscious mind to make changes? Or is it possible that people make changes because they believe in the tapes? Can you think of a way to test these two possibilities?

Let's suppose you have a research group of people who want to change in one of two ways. Some want to improve their memory, and others want to increase their self-esteem. You then pretest them on both a memory task and a psychological test measuring self-esteem so that you can determine later whether they've improved. You're now ready for your critical experiment.

You've purchased two commercial subliminal tapes: one for memory improvement, the other to increase self-esteem. Each person who comes for memory improvement is given a tape labeled "memory improvement" and told to use it once a day for a month. What they won't know is that half of the memory-improvement participants will actually be given the self-esteem-improvement tape. Similarly, the self-esteem seekers are each given a tape labeled "self-esteem improvement," but half of them will actually receive the tape containing subliminal memory-improvement messages. This experimental design lets you control for participants' expectations.

A month later you bring the people back and retest them on the memory and self-esteem measures. Theoretically, if change is being produced by the subliminal messages, people should improve only in the area addressed by the tape they actually heard. What do you expect to find?

Continued

Social psychologist Anthony Greenwald and coworkers (1991) conducted an experiment exactly like this. They found that people generally improved in both self-esteem and memory, regardless of which tape they heard. More significantly, self-esteem improvement was actually greater for those who listened to the memory-improvement tape, and those who listened to the self-esteem tape improved more in memory than they did in self-esteem. Thus the power of an expectancy, or a placebo effect, explains the results better than does the power of subliminal programming of the unconscious mind. And the bottom line is that while subliminal products may appeal to some people as a relatively effortless way to bring about change, they remain unproven scientifically, especially in comparison with other behavior-change methods. Personally, we have much greater faith in the effectiveness of the techniques presented in this book's "Applying Psychological Science" features, because they're backed by scientific evidence.

THE DIFFERENCE THRESHOLD

Distinguishing between stimuli can sometimes be as important as detecting stimuli in the first place. When we try to match the colors of paints or clothing, small stimulus differences can be very important. Likewise, a slight variation in taste might signal that food is tainted or spoiled. Professional wine tasters and piano tuners make their living by being able to make subtle discriminations.

The **difference threshold** *is defined as the smallest difference between two stimuli that people can perceive 50 percent of the time*. The difference threshold is sometimes called the *just noticeable difference (jnd)*. German physiologist Ernst Weber discovered in the 1830s that there is some degree of lawfulness in the range of sensitivities within our sensory systems. **Weber's law** *states that the difference threshold, or jnd, is directly proportional to the magnitude of the stimulus with which the comparison is being made* and can be expressed as a *Weber fraction*. For example, the jnd value for weights is a Weber fraction of approximately 1/50 (Teghtsoonian, 1971). This means that if you lift a weight of 50 grams, a comparison weight must be at least 51 grams in order for you to be able to judge it as heavier. If the weight were 500 grams, a second weight would have to be at least 510 grams (i.e., 1/50 = 10g/500g) for you to discriminate between them.

Although Weber's law breaks down at extremely high and low intensities of stimulation, it holds up reasonably well within the most frequently encountered range, thereby providing a useful barometer of our abilities to discern differences in the various sensory modalities. Table 4.2 lists Weber fractions for the various senses. The smaller the fraction, the greater the sensitivity to differences. As highly visual creatures, humans show greater sensitivity in their visual sense than they do in, for example, their sense of smell. Undoubtedly many creatures who depend on their sense of smell to track their prey would show quite a different order of sensitivity. Weber fractions

► Focus 4
What is the difference threshold? What is Weber's law, and why is it important?

TABLE 4.2 Weber Fractions for Various Sensory Modalities	
Sensory Modality	**Weber Fraction**
Audition (tonal pitch)	1/333
Vision (brightness, white light)	1/60
Kinesthesis (lifted weights)	1/50
Pain (heat produced)	1/30
Audition (loudness)	1/20
Touch (pressure applied to skin)	1/7
Smell (India rubber)	1/4
Taste (salt concentration)	1/3

SOURCE: Based on Teghtsoonian, 1971.

also show that humans are highly sensitive to differences in the pitch of sounds but far less sensitive to loudness differences.

SENSORY ADAPTATION

From a survival perspective, it's important to know when some new development requires your attention. If you were relaxing outdoors, you would want to be aware of the whine of an approaching mosquito. Because changes in our environment are usually noteworthy, sensory systems are finely attuned to changes in stimulation (Rensink, 2002). Sensory neurons are engineered to respond to a constant stimulus by decreasing their activity, and *the diminishing sensitivity to an unchanging stimulus is called* **sensory adaptation.**

Adaptation (sometimes called *habituation*) is a part of everyday experience. After a while, monotonous background sounds are largely unheard. The feel of your wristwatch against your skin recedes from awareness. When you dive into a swimming pool, the water may feel cold at first because your body's sensors respond to the change in temperature. Over time, however, you become used to the water temperature.

Adaptation occurs in all sensory modalities, including vision. Indeed, were it not for tiny involuntary eye movements that keep images moving about the retina, stationary objects would simply fade from sight if we stared at them. In an ingenious demonstration of this type of adaptation, R. M. Pritchard (1961) attached a tiny projector to a contact lens worn by each participant (Figure 4.5a). This procedure guaranteed that visual images presented through the projector would maintain a constant position on the retina, even when the eye moved. When a stabilized image was projected through the lens onto the retina, participants reported that the image appeared in its entirety for a time and then began to vanish and reappear as parts of the original stimulus (Figure 4.5b).

Although sensory adaptation may reduce our overall sensitivity, it is adaptive, for it frees our senses from the constant and the mundane, allowing them to pick up informative changes in the environment that could be important to our well-being or survival.

IN REVIEW

■ Sensation is the process by which our sense organs receive and transmit information, whereas perception involves the brain's processing and interpretation of the information.

■ Psychophysics is the scientific study of how the physical properties of stimuli are related to sensory experiences. Sensory sensitivity is concerned in part with the limits of stimulus detectability (absolute threshold) and the ability to discriminate between stimuli (difference threshold). The absolute threshold is the intensity at which a stimulus is detected 50 percent of the time. Signal detection theory is concerned with factors that influence decisions about whether or not a stimulus is present.

■ Research indicates that subliminal stimuli, which are not consciously perceived, can influence perceptions and behavior in subtle ways, but not strongly enough to justify concerns about the subconscious control of behavior through subliminal messages. The use of subliminal self-help materials sometimes results in positive behavior changes that may be a product of expectancy factors rather than the subliminal messages themselves.

■ The difference threshold, or just noticeable difference (jnd), is the amount by which two stimuli must differ for them to be perceived as different 50 percent of the time. Studies of the jnd led to

(a)

(b)

Original image | Perceptions

FIGURE 4.5

Demonstrating visual adaptation. (a) To create a stabilized retinal image, a person wears a contact lens to which a tiny projector has been attached. Despite tiny eye movements, images are cast on the same region of the retina. (b) Under these conditions, the stabilized image is clear at first and then begins to fade and reappear in meaningful segments as the receptors fatigue and recover. Source: adapted from Pritchard, 1961.

Weber's law, which states that the jnd is proportional to the intensity of the original stimulus and is constant within a given sense modality.

■ Sensory systems are particularly responsive to changes in stimulation, and adaptation occurs in response to unchanging stimuli.

THE SENSORY SYSTEMS

The particular stimuli to which different animals are sensitive vary considerably. The sensory equipment of any species is an adaptation to the environment in which it lives. Many species have senses that humans lack altogether. Carrier pigeons, for example, use the earth's magnetic field to find their destination on cloudy nights when they can't navigate by the stars. Sharks sense electric currents leaking through the skins of fish hiding in undersea crevices, and rattlesnakes find their prey by detecting infrared radiation given off by small rodents. Whatever the source of stimulation, its energy must be converted into nerve impulses, the only language the nervous system understands. **Transduction** *is the process whereby the characteristics of a stimulus are converted*

10^{-3}	10^{-1}	10^{1}	10^{3}	10^{5}	10^{7}	10^{9}	10^{11}	10^{13}	10^{15}
Gamma rays	X-rays	Ultra-violet rays	Infra-red rays	Radar		FM radio	TV AM radio		AC circuits

Ultraviolet · **Infrared**

Wavelength (nanometers): 400 · 500 · 600 · 700

FIGURE 4.6

Light energy. Of the full spectrum of electromagnetic radiation, only the narrow band between 400 and 700 nanometers (nm) is visible to the human eye. One nanometer equals one 1,000,000,000th of a meter.

into nerve impulses. We now consider the range of stimuli to which humans and other mammals are attuned and the manner in which the various sense organs carry out the transduction process.

VISION

The normal stimulus for vision is electromagnetic energy, or light waves, which are measured in nanometers (nm), or one billionth of a meter. In addition to that tiny portion of light waves that humans can perceive, the electromagnetic spectrum encompasses X-rays, television and radio signals, and infrared and ultraviolet rays (Figure 4.6). Bees are able to see ultraviolet light, and rattlesnakes, as mentioned above, can detect infrared energy. Our visual system is sensitive only to wavelengths extending from about 700 nanometers (red) down to about 400 nanometers (blue-violet). (You can remember the order of the spectrum, from higher wavelengths to lower ones, with the name ROY G. BIV—red, orange, yellow, green, blue, indigo, and violet.)

The Human Eye

▶ **Focus 5**
How does the lens affect visual acuity, and how does its dysfunc-tion cause myopia and hyperopia?

Light waves enter the eye through the *cornea,* a transparent protective structure at the front of the eye (Figure 4.7). Behind the cornea is the *pupil,* an adjustable opening that can dilate or constrict to control the amount of light that enters the eye. The pupil's size is controlled by muscles in the colored *iris* that surrounds the pupil. Low levels of illumination cause the pupil to dilate, letting more light into the eye to improve optical clarity; bright light makes the pupil constrict.

Behind the pupil is the **lens,** *an elastic structure that becomes thinner to focus on distant objects and thicker to focus on nearby objects.* Just as the lens of a camera focuses an image on a photosensitive material (film), so the lens of the eye focuses the visual image on the **retina,** *a multilayered light-sensitive tissue at the rear of the fluid-filled eyeball.* As seen in Figure 4.7a, the lens reverses the image from right to left and top to bottom when it is projected upon the retina, but the brain reverses the visual input into the image that we perceive.

The ability to see clearly depends on the lens's ability to focus the image directly onto the retina (Pedrotti & Pedrotti, 1997). If you have good vision for nearby objects but have difficulty seeing faraway objects, you probably suffer from *myopia* (nearsightedness). In nearsighted people, the lens focuses the visual image in front of the retina (or too near the lens), resulting in a blurred image for faraway objects. This condition generally occurs because the eyeball is longer (front to back) than normal. In contrast, some people have excellent distance vision but have difficulty seeing close-up objects clearly. *Hyperopia* (farsightedness) occurs when the lens does not thicken enough and the image is therefore focused on a point behind the retina (or too far from the lens). Eyeglasses and contact lenses are designed to correct for the natural lens's inability to focus the visual image directly onto the retina.

Photoreceptors: The Rods and Cones

The retina, with its specialized sensory neurons, is actually an extension of the brain (Bullier, 2002). It contains two types of light-sensitive receptor cells, called *rods* and *cones* because of their shapes (see Figure 4.7b). There are about 120 million rods and 6 million cones in the human eye.

The **rods,** *which function best in dim light, are primarily black-and-white brightness receptors.* They are about 500 times more sensitive to light than are the cones, but they do not give rise to color sensations. The retinas of some nocturnal creatures, such as owls, contain only rods, giving them exceptional vision in very dim light but no color vision (Dossenbach & Dossenbach, 1998). The **cones,** *which are color receptors, function best in bright illumination.* Some creatures that are active only during the day, such as pigeons and chipmunks, have only cones in their retinas, so they see the world in living color but have very poor night vision (Dossenbach & Dossenbach, 1998). Animals that

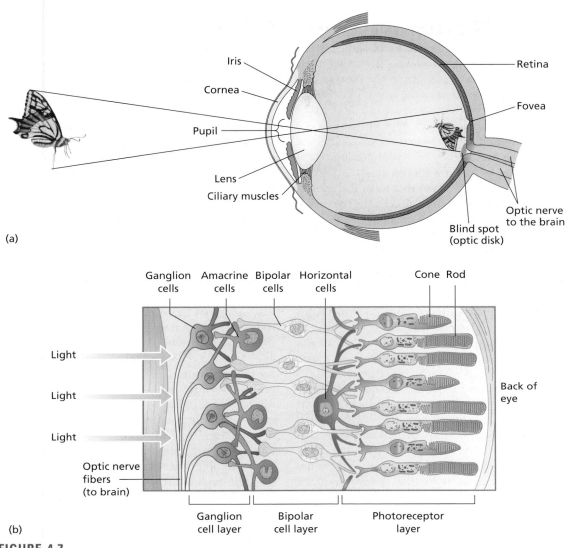

FIGURE 4.7

The human eye. (a) This cross section shows the major parts of the human eye. The iris regulates the size of the pupil. The ciliary muscles regulate the shape of the lens. The image entering the eye is reversed by the lens and cast on the retina, which contains the rod and cone photoreceptor cells. The optic disk, where the optic nerve exits the eye, has no receptors and produces a blind spot, as demonstrated in Figure 4.8. (b) Photoreceptors in the retina, the rods and cones, synapse with bipolar cells, which in turn synapse with ganglion cells whose axons form the optic nerve. The horizontal and amacrine cells allow sideways integration of retinal activity across areas of the retina.

are active both day and night, as humans are, have a mixture of rods and cones. In humans, rods are found throughout the retina except in the **fovea,** *a small area in the center of the retina that contains no rods but many densely packed cones.* Cones decrease in concentration the farther away they are from the center of the retina, and the periphery of the retina contains mainly rods.

Rods and cones send their messages to the brain via two additional layers of cells. The rods and cones have synaptic connections with *bipolar cells,* which, in turn, synapse with a layer of about 1 million *ganglion cells, whose axons are collected into a bundle to form the* **optic nerve.** Thus input from

more than 126 million rods and cones is eventually funneled into only 1 million traffic lanes leading out of the retina toward higher visual centers. Figure 4.7b shows how the rods and cones are connected to the bipolar and ganglion cells. One interesting aspect of these connections is the fact that the rods and cones not only form the rear layer of the retina, but their light-sensitive ends actually point away from the direction of the entering light so that they receive only a fraction of the light energy that enters the eye.

The manner in which the rods and cones are connected to the bipolar cells accounts for both the greater importance of rods in dim light and

▶ **Focus 6**

How are the rods and cones distributed in the retina, and how do they contribute to brightness perception, color vision, and visual acuity?

our greater ability to see fine detail in bright illumination, when the cones are most active. Typically, many rods are connected to the same bipolar cell. They can therefore combine, or funnel, their individual electrical messages to the bipolar cell, where the additive effect of the many signals may be enough to fire it. That is why we can more easily detect a faint stimulus, such as a dim star, if we look slightly to one side so that its image falls not on the fovea but on the peripheral portion of the retina, where the rods are packed most densely.

Like the rods, the cones that lie in the periphery of the retina share bipolar cells. In the fovea, however, the densely packed cones each have their own "private line" to a single bipolar cell. As a result, our **visual acuity,** *or ability to see fine detail,* is greatest when the visual image projects directly onto the fovea. Such focusing results in the firing of a large number of cones and their private-line bipolar cells. Some birds of prey, such as eagles and hawks, are blessed with two foveas in each eye, contributing to a visual acuity that allows them to see small prey on the ground as they soar hundreds of feet above the earth (Tucker, 2000).

The optic nerve formed by the axons of the ganglion cells exits through the back of the eye not far from the fovea, producing a blind spot where there are no photoreceptors. You can demonstrate the existence of your blind spot by following the directions in Figure 4.8. Ordinarily, we are unaware of the blind spot because our perceptual system fills in the missing part of the visual field (Rolls & Deco, 2002).

Visual Transduction: From Light Waves to Nerve Impulses

Rods and cones translate light waves into nerve impulses through the action of protein molecules called **photopigments** (Stryer, 1987; Wolken, 1995). The

absorption of light by the photopigments produces a chemical reaction that changes the rate of neurotransmitter release at the receptor's synapse with the bipolar cells. The greater the change in transmitter release, the stronger the signal passed on to the bipolar cell and, in turn, to the ganglion cells whose axons form the optic nerve. If a stimulus triggers nerve responses at each of the three levels (rod or cone, bipolar cell, and ganglion cell), the message is instantaneously on its way to the visual relay station in the thalamus and then on to the visual cortex of the brain.

Brightness Vision and Dark Adaptation

As noted earlier, rods are far more sensitive than cones under conditions of low illumination. Nonetheless, the sensitivity of both the rods and the cones to light intensity depends in part on the wavelength of the light. Research has shown that rods have a much greater sensitivity than cones throughout the color spectrum except at the red end, where rods are relatively insensitive. Cones are most sensitive to low illumination in the greenish-yellow range of the spectrum. These findings have prompted many cities to change the color of their fire engines from the traditional red (to which rods are insensitive) to a greenish yellow in order to increase the vehicles' visibility to both rods and cones in dim lighting.

Although the rods are by nature sensitive to low illumination, they are not always ready to fulfill their function. Perhaps you have had the embarrassing experience of entering a movie theater on a sunny day, groping around in the darkness, and finally sitting down in someone's lap. Although one can meet interesting people this way, most of us prefer to stand in the rear of the theater until our eyes adapt to the dimly lit interior.

Dark adaptation *is the progressive improvement in brightness sensitivity that occurs over time under conditions of low illumination.* After absorbing light, a photoreceptor is depleted of its pigment molecules for a period of time. If the eye has been exposed to conditions of high illumination, such as bright sunlight, a substantial amount of photopigment will be depleted. During dark adaptation, the photopigment molecules are regenerated and the receptor's sensitivity increases greatly.

Vision researchers have plotted the course of dark adaptation as people move from conditions of bright light into darkness (Carpenter & Robson, 1999). By focusing light flashes of varying wavelengths and brightness on the fovea (which contains only cones) or on the periphery of the retina (where rods reside), they discovered the two-part curve

▶ **Focus 7**
How does the transduction process occur in the photoreceptors of the eye?

▶ **Focus 8**
What is the physiological basis for dark adaptation and for the two components of the dark adaptation curve?

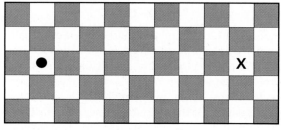

FIGURE 4.8

Find your blind spot. Close your left eye and, from a distance of about 12 inches, focus steadily on the dot with your right eye as you slowly move the book toward your face. At some point the image of the X will cross your optic disk (blind spot) and disappear. It will reappear after it crosses the blind spot. Note how the checkerboard remains wholly visible even though part of it falls on the blind spot. Your perceptual system fills in the missing information.

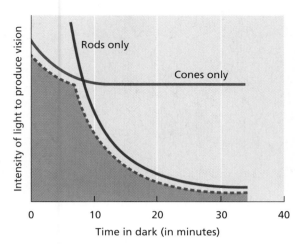

FIGURE 4.9

Adapting to the dark. The course of dark adaptation is graphed over time. The curve has two parts, one for the cones and one for the rods. The cones adapt completely in about 10 minutes, whereas the rods continue to increase their sensitivity for another 20 minutes.

FIGURE 4.10

Working in red light keeps the rods in a state of dark adaptation because rods are quite insensitive to that wavelength. Therefore they retain high levels of photopigment and remain sensitive to low illumination.

shown in Figure 4.9. The first part of the curve is due to dark adaptation of the cones. As you can see, the cones gradually become sensitive to fainter lights as time passes, but after about 5 to 10 minutes in the dark, their sensitivity has reached its maximum. The rods, whose photopigments regenerate more slowly, do not reach their maximum sensitivity for about half an hour. It is estimated that after complete adaptation, rods are able to detect light intensities 1/10,000 as great as those that could be detected before dark adaptation began (Stryer, 1987).

During World War II, psychologists familiar with the process of dark adaptation provided a method for enhancing night vision in pilots who needed to take off on a moment's notice and see their targets under conditions of low illumination. Knowing that the rods are important in night vision and relatively insensitive to red wavelengths, they suggested that fighter pilots either wear goggles with red lenses or work in rooms lit only by red lights while waiting to be called for a mission. Because red light stimulates only the cones, the rods remain in a state of dark adaptation, ready for immediate service in the dark. That highly practical principle continues to be useful to this day (Figure 4.10).

Color Vision

We are blessed with a world rich in color. The majesty of a glowing sunset, the rich blues and greens of a tropical bay, the brilliant colors of fall foliage are all visual delights. Human vision is finely attuned to color; our difference thresholds for light wavelengths are so small that we are able

to distinguish an estimated 7.5 million hue variations (Backhaus et al., 1998). Historically, two different theories of color vision have tried to explain how this occurs.

The Trichromatic Theory Around 1800 it was discovered that any color in the visible spectrum can be produced by some combination of the wavelengths that correspond to the colors blue, green, and red in what is known as additive color mixture (Figure 4.11a). This fact was the basis for an important trichromatic (three-color) theory of color vision advanced by Thomas Young, an English physicist, and Hermann von Helmholtz, a German physiologist. According to the **Young-Helmholtz trichromatic theory,** *there are three types of color receptors in the retina.* Although all cones can be stimulated by most wavelengths to varying degrees, individual cones are most sensitive to wavelengths that correspond to either blue, green, or red (Figure 4.12). Presumably, each of these receptor classes sends messages to the brain, based on the extent to which they are activated by the light energy's wavelength. The visual system then combines the signals to recreate the original hue. If all three cones are equally activated, a pure white color is perceived (see the center of Figure 4.11a).

Although the Young-Helmholtz theory was consistent with the laws of additive color mixture, there are several facts that did not fit the theory. Take our perception of yellow, for example. According to the theory, yellow is produced by the activity of red and green receptors. Yet certain people with red-green color blindness, who are unable to perceive either color, are somehow able to experience yellow. A second phenomenon that posed problems for the trichromatic theory was the color afterimage, in which an image in a different color appears after a color stimulus has been viewed steadily and then withdrawn. To experience an afterimage,

▶ **Focus 9**
Summarize the trichromatic, opponent-process, and dual-process theories of color vision. What evidence supports each theory?

(a)   (b)

FIGURE 4.11

Two kinds of color mixture. Additive and subtractive color mixture are different processes. (a) In additive color mixture, a beam of light of a specific wavelength directed onto a white surface is perceived as the color that corresponds to that wavelength on the visible spectrum. If beams of light that fall at certain points within the blue, green, or red color range are directed together onto the surface in the correct proportions, a combined, or additive, mixture of wavelengths will result, with the possibility of producing any color in the visible spectrum (including white at the point where all three colors intersect). The Young-Helmholtz trichromatic theory of color vision assumes that color perception results from the additive mixture of impulses from cones that are sensitive to blue, green, and red. (b) In subtractive color mixture, mixing pigments or paints produces new colors by subtraction—that is, by removing (i.e., absorbing) other wavelengths. Paints absorb (subtract) colors different from themselves while reflecting their own color. For example, blue paint mainly absorbs wavelengths that correspond to nonblue hues. Mixing blue paint with yellow paint (which absorbs wavelengths other than yellow) will produce a subtractive mixture that emits wavelengths between yellow and blue (i.e., green). Theoretically, certain wavelengths of the three primary colors of blue, yellow (not green, as in additive mixture), and red can produce the whole spectrum of colors by subtractive mixture. Thus in additive color mixture, the primary colors are blue, green, and red; in subtractive color mixture, they are blue, yellow, and red.

FIGURE 4.12

Two classic theories of color vision. The Young-Helmholtz trichromatic theory proposed three different receptors, one for blue, one for green, and one for red. The ratio of activity in the three types of cones yields our experience of a particular hue, or color. Hering's opponent-process theory also assumed that there are three different receptors: one for blue-yellow, one for red-green, and one for black-white. Each of the receptors can function in two possible ways, depending on the wavelength of the stimulus. Again, the pattern of activity in the receptors yields our perception of the hue.

follow the instructions for Figure 4.13. Trichromatic theory cannot account for what you'll see.

Opponent-Process Theory A second influential color theory, formulated by Ewald Hering in 1870, also assumed that there are three types of cones. **Hering's opponent-process theory** *proposed that each of the three cone types responds to two different wavelengths.* One type responds to blue or yellow, another to red or green, and a third to black or

white. For example, a red-green cone responds with one chemical reaction to a green stimulus and with its other chemical reaction (opponent process) to a red stimulus (see Figure 4.12). You have experienced one of the phenomena that support the existence of opponent processes if you did the exercise in Figure 4.13. The afterimage that you saw in the blank space contains the colors specified by opponent-process theory: The green portion of the flag appeared as red; the black, as white; and the yellow, as blue. According to opponent-process theory, as you stared at the green, black, and yellow colors, the neural processes that register those colors became fatigued. Then when you cast your gaze on the white surface, which reflects all wavelengths, a rebound opponent reaction occurred as each receptor responded with its opposing red, white, or blue reactions.

Dual Processes in Color Transduction Which theory—the trichromatic theory or the opponent-process theory—is correct? Two centuries of research have yielded verifying evidence for each theory. Today's **dual-process theory** *combines the trichromatic and opponent-process theories to account for the color transduction process* (Knoblauch, 2002).

The trichromatic theorists Young and Helmholtz were right about the cones. The cones do indeed contain one of three different protein photopigments that are most sensitive to wavelengths roughly corresponding to the colors blue, green,

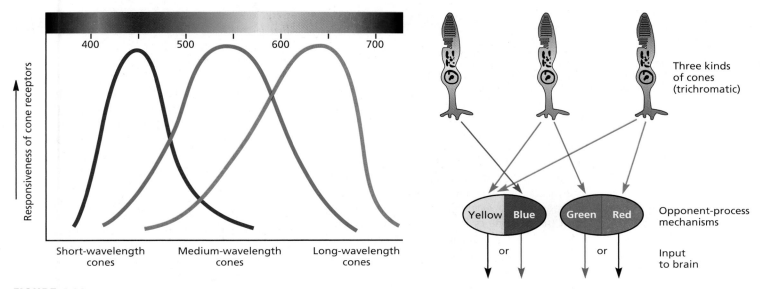

FIGURE 4.14

Dual color vision processes. Color vision involves both trichromatic and opponent processes that occur at different places in the visual system. Consistent with trichromatic theory, three types of cones are maximally sensitive to short (blue), medium (green), and long (red) wavelengths, respectively. However, opponent processes occur further along in the visual system, as opponent cells in the retina, visual relay stations, and the visual cortex respond differentially to blue versus yellow, red versus green, and black versus white stimuli. Shown here are the inputs from the cones that produce the blue-yellow and red-green opponent processes.

and red (Abramov & Gordon, 1994). Different ratios of activity in the blue-, green-, and red-sensitive cones can produce a pattern of neural activity that corresponds to any hue in the spectrum (Backhaus et al., 1998). This process is similar to that which occurs on your TV screen, where color pictures (including white hues) are produced by activating combinations of tiny blue, green, and red dots in a process of additive color mixture.

Hering's opponent-process theory was also partly correct, but opponent processes do not occur at the level of the cones, as he maintained. When researchers began to use microelectrodes to record from single cells in the visual system, they discovered that ganglion cells in the retina, as well as neurons in visual relay stations and the visual cortex, respond in an opponent-process fashion by altering their rate of firing (Knoblauch, 2002). For example, if a red light is shone on the retina, an opponent-

process ganglion cell may respond with a high rate of firing, but a green light will cause the same cell to fire at a very low rate. Other neurons respond in a similar opponent fashion to blue and yellow stimuli.

The red-green opponent processes are triggered directly by input from the red- or green-sensitive cones in the retina (Figure 4.14). The blue-yellow opponent process is a bit more complex. Activity of blue-sensitive cones directly stimulates the blue process further along in the visual system. And yellow? The yellow opponent process is triggered not by a yellow-sensitive cone, as Hering proposed, but rather by simultaneous input from the red- and green-sensitive cones (Abramov & Gordon, 1994).

Color-Deficient Vision People with normal color vision are referred to as *trichromats*. They are sensitive to all three systems: blue-yellow, red-green, and

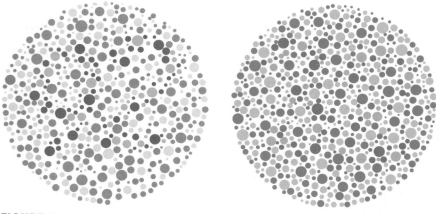

FIGURE 4.15

Test your color vision. These dotted figures are used to test for color-deficient vision. The left one tests for blue-yellow color blindness, the right one for red-green color blindness. Because the dots in the picture are of equal brightness, color is the only available cue for perceiving the numbers in the circles. Can you see them?

▶ **Focus 10**
What kinds of feature detectors exist in the visual system? What is parallel processing of sensory information?

black-white. However, about 7 percent of the male population and 1 percent of the female population have a deficiency in the blue-yellow system, the red-green system, or both. This deficiency is caused by an absence of hue-sensitive photopigment in certain cone types. A *dichromat* is a person who is color-blind in only one of the systems (blue-yellow or red-green). A *monochromat* is sensitive only to the black-white system and is totally color-blind. Most color-deficient people are dichromats and have their deficiency in the red-green system. Color-blindness tests typically employ sets of colored dots such as those in Figure 4.15. Depending on the type of deficit, a color-blind person cannot discern the number embedded in one of the two circles.

Analysis and Reconstruction of Visual Scenes

Once the transformation of light energy to nerve impulses occurs, the process of combining the messages received from the photoreceptors into the perception of a visual scene begins. As you read this page, nerve impulses from countless neurons are being analyzed and the visual image that you perceive is being reconstructed. Moreover, you know what these black squiggles on the page mean. How does this occur?

From the retina, the optic nerve sends impulses to a visual relay station in the thalamus, the brain's sensory switchboard. From there, the input is routed to various parts of the cortex, particularly the primary visual cortex in the occipital lobe at the rear of the brain. Microelectrode studies have shown that there is a point-to-point correspondence between tiny regions of the retina and groups of neurons in the visual cortex. As you might expect, the fovea, where the one-to-one synapses of cones with bipolar cells produce high

visual acuity, is represented by a disproportionately large area of the visual cortex. Somewhat more surprising is the fact that there is more than one cortical map of the retina; there are at least 10 duplicate mappings. Perhaps this is nature's insurance policy against damage to any one of them, or perhaps the duplicate maps are somehow involved in the integration of visual input (Bullier, 2002).

Groups of neurons within the primary visual cortex are organized to receive and integrate sensory nerve impulses originating in specific regions of the retina. Some of these cells, known as **feature detectors,** *fire selectively in response to visual stimuli that have specific characteristics* (Kanwisher, 1998). Discovery of these feature detectors won David Hubel and Torsten Wiesel of Harvard University the 1981 Nobel Prize. Using tiny electrodes to record the activity of individual cells of the visual cortex of animals (Figure 4.16), Hubel and Wiesel found that certain neurons fired most frequently when lines of certain orientations were presented. One neuron might fire most frequently when a horizontal line was presented; another neuron in response to a line of a slightly different orientation; and so on "around the clock." For example, the letter A could be constructed from the response of feature detectors that responded to three different line orientations: /, \, and −. Within the cortex, this information is integrated and analyzed by successively more complex feature-detector systems to produce our perception of objects (Palmer, 2002).

Other classes of feature detectors respond to color, to depth, or to movement (Livingstone &

FIGURE 4.16

A partially anesthetized monkey views an image projected on the screen while an electrode embedded in its visual cortex records the activity of a single neuron. This research by Hubel and Wiesel led to the discovery of feature detectors that analyze visual stimulus features such as contours and shapes, movement, and color.

Neuron's Electrical Response

Hubel, 1994). These feature-detector "modules" subdivide a visual scene into its component dimensions and process them simultaneously. Thus, as a red, white, and green beach ball sails toward you, separate but overlapping modules within the brain are simultaneously analyzing its colors, shape, distance, and movement by engaging in parallel processing of the information and constructing a unified image of its properties (Hubel & Wiesel, 2005). The final stages in the process of constructing a visual representation occur when the information analyzed and recombined by the primary visual cortex is routed to other cortical regions known as the *visual association cortex,* where features of the visual scene are combined and interpreted in light of our memories and knowledge (Grossberg et al., 2005). If all goes correctly, a process that began with nerve impulses from the rods and cones now ends with our recognizing the beach ball for what it is and catching it. Quite another conscious experience and response would probably occur if we interpreted the oncoming object as a water balloon.

Recently, scientists have discovered that neurons in the brain respond selectively not only to basic stimulus characteristics like corners and colors, but also to complex stimuli that have acquired special meaning through experience. For example, brain scientists at the University of California, Los Angeles who were recording from single neurons in the amygdala of a brain-damaged patient found a neuron that responded electrically to only 3 of 50 visual scenes. All of the 3 scenes involved former president Bill Clinton, but they differed considerably. One was a portrait, another a group picture that included Clinton, and the third was a cartoonist's representation of the president. Pictures of other celebrities, animals, landscapes, and geometric forms evoked no response (Figure 4.17). This neuron was likely part

of a neural circuit that was created within the brain to register this particular celebrity (Koch, 2004).

IN REVIEW

■ The senses may be classified in terms of the stimuli to which they respond. Through the process of transduction, these stimuli are transformed into the common language of nerve impulses.

■ The normal stimulus for vision is electromagnetic energy, or light waves. Light-sensitive visual receptor cells are located in the retina. The rods are brightness receptors, and the less numerous cones are color receptors. Light energy striking the retina is converted into nerve impulses by chemical reactions in the photopigments of the rods and cones. Dark adaptation involves the gradual regeneration of photopigments that have been depleted by brighter illumination.

■ Color vision is a two-stage process having both trichromatic and opponent-process components. The first stage involves the reactions of cones that are maximally sensitive to blue, green, and red wavelengths. In the second stage, color information from the cones is coded through an opponent-process mechanism further along in the visual system.

■ Visual stimuli are analyzed by feature detectors in the primary visual cortex, and the stimulus elements are reconstructed and interpreted in light of input from the visual association cortex.

AUDITION

The stimuli for our sense of hearing are sound waves, a form of mechanical energy. What we call *sound* is actually pressure waves in air, water, or

FIGURE 4.17

A Bill Clinton feature detector?
Single-neuron electrical recording in a patient's amygdala (which receives extensive visual input) revealed a neuron that responded to depictions of Bill Clinton but not to 47 other pictures showing other presidents, celebrities (e.g., Michael Jordan, *far right*), objects, landscapes, and geometric shapes. This neuron was apparently part of a neuronal network that had learned to recognize and represent the former president. SOURCE: Koch, 2004.

▶ **Focus 11**
Describe the two physical characteristics of sound waves and their relation to auditory experience.

FIGURE 4.18

Auditory stimuli. Sound waves are a form of mechanical energy. As the tuning fork vibrates, it produces successive waves of compression and expansion of air molecules. The number of maximum compressions per second (cycles per second) is its frequency, measured in hertz (Hz). The height of the wave above zero air pressure represents the sound's amplitude. Frequency determines pitch; amplitude determines loudness, measured in decibels (dB).

TABLE 4.3	**Decibel Scaling of Common Sounds**	
Level in Decibels (dB)	**Common Sounds**	**Threshold Levels**
140	50-horsepower siren at a distance of 100 feet, jet fighter taking off 80 feet away	Potential damage to auditory system
130	Boiler shop	
120	Air hammer at position of operator, rock-and-roll band, jet aircraft at 500 feet overhead	Human pain threshold
110	Trumpet automobile horn at 3 feet	
100	Crosscut saw at position of operator	
90	Inside subway car	Hearing damage with prolonged exposure
80	Train whistle at 500 feet	
70	Inside automobile in city	
60	Downtown city street (Chicago), average traffic	
50	Restaurant, business office	
40	Classroom, church	
30	Hospital room, quiet bedroom	
20	Recording studio	Threshold of hearing (young men)
10		
0		Minimum threshold of hearing

NOTE: The decibel scale relates a physical quantity—sound intensity—to the human perception of that quantity—sound loudness. It is a logarithmic scale—that is, each increment of 10 dB represents a tenfold increase in loudness. The table indicates the decibel ranges of some common sounds as well as thresholds for hearing, hearing damage, and pain. Prolonged exposure at 150 dB causes death in laboratory rats.

some other conducting medium. When a stereo's volume is high enough, you can actually see cloth speaker covers moving in and out. The resulting vibrations cause successive waves of compression and expansion among the air molecules surrounding the source of the sound. These sound waves have two characteristics: frequency and amplitude (Figure 4.18).

Frequency *is the number of sound waves, or cycles, per second.* The **hertz (Hz)** *is the technical measure of cycles per second; 1 hertz equals 1 cycle per second.* The sound waves' frequency is related to the pitch that we perceive; the higher the frequency (hertz), the higher the perceived pitch. Humans are capable of detecting sound frequencies from 20 to 20,000 hertz (about 12,000 hertz in older people). Most common sounds are in the lower frequencies. Among musical instruments, the piano can play the widest range of frequencies, from 27.5 hertz at the low end of the keyboard to 4,186 hertz at the high end. An operatic soprano's voice, in comparison, has a range of only about 250 to 1,100 hertz (Aiello, 1994).

Amplitude *refers to the vertical size of the sound waves—that is, the amount of compression and expansion of the molecules in the conducting medium.* The sound wave's amplitude is the primary determinant of the sound's perceived loudness. Differences in amplitude are expressed as **decibels (dB),** *a measure of the physical pressures that occur at the eardrum.* The absolute threshold for hearing is arbitrarily designated as 0 decibels, and each increase of 10 decibels represents a tenfold increase in loudness. Table 4.3 shows various sounds scaled in decibels.

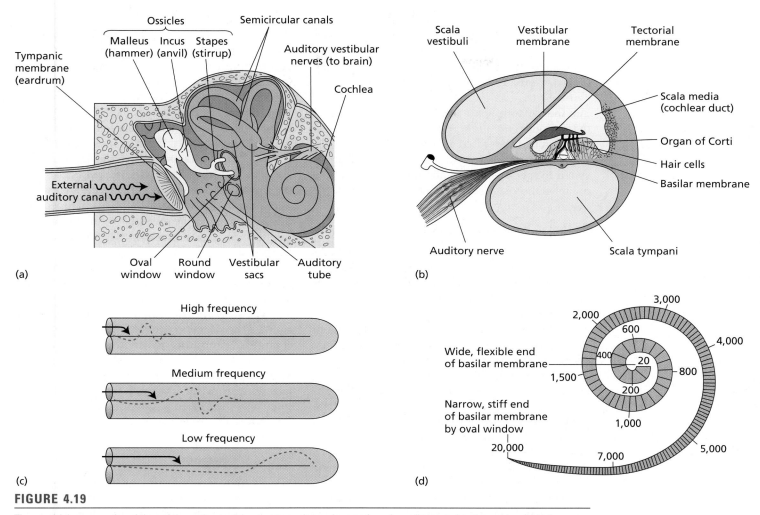

FIGURE 4.19

The ear. (a) A cross section of the ear shows the structures that transmit sound waves from the auditory canal to the cochlea. (b) In the cochlea, sound waves are translated into fluid waves that stimulate hair cells in the organ of Corti. The resulting nerve impulses reach the brain via the auditory nerve. The semicircular canals and vestibular sacs of the inner ear contain sense organs for equilibrium. (c) Fluid waves are created by different sound frequencies. (d) Varying frequencies maximally stimulate different areas of the basilar membrane. High-frequency waves peak quickly and stimulate the membrane close to the oval window.

Auditory Transduction: From Pressure Waves to Nerve Impulses

The transduction system of the ear is made up of tiny bones, membranes, and liquid-filled tubes designed to translate pressure waves into nerve impulses (Figure 4.19). Sound waves travel into an auditory canal leading to the *eardrum,* a membrane that vibrates in response to the sound waves. Beyond the eardrum is the *middle ear,* a cavity housing three tiny bones (the smallest in the body, in fact). The vibrating activity of these bones—the *hammer (malleus), anvil (incus),* and *stirrup (stapes)*—amplifies the sound waves more than 30 times. The first bone, the hammer, is attached firmly to the eardrum, and the stirrup is attached to another membrane, the *oval window,* which forms the boundary between the middle ear and the inner ear.

The inner ear contains the **cochlea,** *a coiled, snail-shaped tube about 3.5 centimeters (1.4 inches) in length that is filled with fluid and contains the* **basilar membrane,** *a sheet of tissue that runs its length.* Resting on the basilar membrane is the **organ of Corti,** *which contains thousands of tiny hair cells that are the actual sound receptors.* The tips of the hair cells are attached to another membrane, the *tectorial membrane,* that overhangs the basilar membrane along the entire length of the cochlea. The hair cells synapse with the neurons of the auditory nerve, which in turn send impulses via an auditory relay station in the thalamus to the temporal lobe's auditory cortex.

When sound waves strike the eardrum, pressure created at the oval window by the hammer,

▶ **Focus 12**
Describe how the middle and inner ear structures are involved in the auditory transduction process.

anvil, and stirrup of the middle ear sets the fluid inside the cochlea into motion. The fluid waves that result vibrate the basilar membrane and the tectorial membrane, causing a bending of the hair cells in the organ of Corti (see Figure 4.19b). This bending of the hair cells triggers the release of neurotransmitters into the synaptic space between the hair cells and the neurons of the auditory nerve, resulting in nerve impulses that are sent to the brain. Within the auditory cortex are feature-detector neurons that respond to specific kinds of auditory input, much as occurs in the visual system (Goldstein, 2002).

Coding of Pitch and Loudness

▶ **Focus 13**
Describe the frequency and place theories of pitch perception. In what sense are both theories correct?

The auditory system transforms the sensory qualities of wave amplitude and frequency (experienced by us as loudness and pitch) into the language of nerve impulses (Syka & Merzenich, 2005). In the case of intensity, high-amplitude sound waves cause the hair cells to bend more and release more neurotransmitter substance at the point where they synapse with auditory nerve cells, resulting in a higher rate of firing within the auditory nerve. Also, certain receptor neurons have higher thresholds than others, so that they will fire only when the hair cells bend considerably in response to an intense sound. Thus what we experience as loudness is coded in terms of both the rate of firing in the axons of the auditory nerve and the specific hair cells that are sending messages (Carney, 2002).

The coding of wave frequency that produces our perception of pitch also involves two different processes, one for frequencies below about 1,000 hertz (two octaves below the top of the piano keyboard) and another for higher frequencies. Historically, as in the case of color vision, two competing theories were advanced to account for pitch perception. According to the **frequency theory of pitch perception,** *nerve impulses sent to the brain match the frequency of the sound wave.* Thus a 30-hertz (30 cycles per second) sound wave from a piano should send 30 volleys of nerve impulses per second to the brain.

Unfortunately, frequency theory encounters a major problem. Because neurons are limited in their rate of firing, individual impulses or volleys of impulses fired by groups of neurons cannot produce high enough frequencies of firing to match sound-wave frequencies above 1,000 hertz. How then do we perceive higher frequencies, such as a 4,000-hertz note from the same piano? Experiments conducted by Georg von Bekesy (1957) uncovered a second mechanism for coding pitch that earned him the 1961 Nobel Prize. Bekesy cut tiny holes in the cochleas of guinea pigs and human cadavers and observed through a microscope what happened inside the fluid-filled cochlea when he stimulated the eardrum with tones of varying frequencies. He found that high-frequency sounds produced an abrupt fluid wave (Figure 4.19c) that peaked close to the oval window, whereas lower-frequency vibrations produced a slower fluid wave that peaked farther down the cochlear canal. Bekesy's observations supported a **place theory of pitch perception,** *suggesting that the specific point in the cochlea where the fluid wave peaks and most strongly bends the hair cells serves as a frequency coding cue* (Figure 4.19d). Researchers later found that similar to the manner in which the retina is mapped onto the visual cortex, the auditory cortex has a tonal-frequency map that corresponds to specific areas of the cochlea. By analyzing the specific location of the cochlea from which auditory nerve impulses are being received, the brain can code pitches like our 4,000-hertz piano note (Carney, 2002).

Thus, like trichromatic and opponent-process theories of color vision, which were once thought to contradict one another, frequency and place theories of pitch perception both proved applicable in their own ways. At low frequencies, frequency theory holds true; at higher frequencies, place theory provides the mechanism for coding the frequency of a sound wave.

Sound Localization

Have you ever wondered why you have two ears, one located on each side of your head? As is usually the case in nature's designs, there is a good reason. Our very survival can depend on our ability to locate objects that emit sounds. The nervous system uses information concerning the time and intensity differences of sounds arriving at the two ears to locate the source of sounds in space (Luck & Vecera, 2002).

Sounds arrive first and loudest at the ear closest to the sound. When the source of the sound is directly in front of us, the sound wave reaches both ears at the same time and at the same intensity, so the source is perceived as being straight ahead. Our binaural (two-eared) ability to localize sounds is amazingly sensitive. For example, a sound 3 degrees to the right arrives at the right ear only 300 millionths of a second before it arrives at the left ear, and yet we can tell which direction the sound is coming from (Yin & Kuwada, 1984).

Other animals have even more exotic sound-localization systems. For example, the barn owl comes equipped with ears that are exquisitely tailored for pinpoint localization of its prey during night hunting. Its right ear is directed slightly upward, its left ear slightly downward. This allows it to localize sounds precisely in both the vertical and horizontal planes and thereby to zero in on its prey with deadly accuracy.

⁇ What Do You Think?

NAVIGATING IN FOG: PROFESSOR MAYER'S TOPOPHONE
The device shown in Figure 4.20 is called a *topophone.* It was used in the late 1880s to help sailors locate sounds while navigating in thick fog. Based on what you've learned about the principles of sound localization, can you identify two features of this instrument that would assist sailors in detecting and locating sounds? Think about it, then see page 148.

FIGURE 4.20

An early "hearing aid." The topophone, used in the late 1800s by sailors to increase their ability to locate sounds while navigating in thick fog, assisted in two ways. Can you identify the relevant principles?

Hearing Loss

If you had to make the unwelcome choice of being blind or being deaf, which impairment would you choose? When asked this question, most of our students say that they would rather be deaf. Yet hearing loss can have more devastating social consequences than blindness does. Helen Keller, who was both blind and deaf, considered deafness to be more socially debilitating. She wrote, "Blindness cuts people off from things. Deafness cuts people off from people."

In the United States alone, more than 20 million people suffer from impaired hearing. Of these, 90 percent were born with normal hearing (Sataloff & Thayer, 2006). They suffer from two major types of hearing loss. **Conduction deafness** *involves problems with the mechanical system that transmits sound waves to the cochlea.* For example, a punctured eardrum or a loss of function in the tiny bones of the middle ear can reduce the ear's capacity to transmit vibrations. Use of a hearing aid, which amplifies the sounds entering the ear, may correct many cases of conduction deafness.

An entirely different matter is **nerve deafness,** *caused by damaged receptors within the inner ear or damage to the auditory nerve itself.* Nerve deafness cannot be helped by a hearing aid because the problem does not lie in the transmission of sound waves to the cochlea. Although aging and disease can produce nerve deafness, exposure to loud sounds is one of its leading causes. Repeated exposure to loud sounds of a particular frequency (as might be produced by a machine in a factory) can eventually cause the loss of hair cells at a particular point on the basilar membrane, thereby causing hearing loss for that frequency.

Extremely loud music can also take a serious toll on hearing (West & Evans, 1990). Figure 4.21 shows the devastating results of a guinea pig's exposure to a sound level approximating that of loud rock music heard through earphones. As shown in Table 4.3, even brief exposure to sounds exceeding 140 decibels can cause irreversible damage to the receptors in the inner ear, as can more continuous sounds at lower decibel levels. In 1986, a rock concert by The Who reached 120 decibels at a distance of 164 feet from the speakers. Although this earned The Who a place in the Guinness Book of Records for the all-time loudest concert, it inflicted severe and permanent damage to many in the audience. The Who's lead guitarist, Pete Townshend, eventually suffered severe hearing loss from prolonged noise exposure.

▶ **Focus 14**
What are the two kinds of deafness, and how can they be treated?

FIGURE 4.21

Danger! Hearing loss. Exposure to loud sounds can destroy auditory receptors in the inner ear. These pictures, taken through an electron microscope, show the hair cells of a guinea pig before (*left*) and after (*right*) exposure to 24 hours of noise comparable to that of a loud rock concert. SOURCE: Micrographs by Robert E. Preston, courtesy of Professor J. E. Hawkins, Kresge Hearing Research Institute, University of Michigan.

TASTE AND SMELL: THE CHEMICAL SENSES

Gustation, *the sense of taste,* and **olfaction,** *the sense of smell,* are chemical senses; their receptors are sensitive to chemical molecules rather than to some form of energy. These senses are so intertwined that some scientists consider them a "common chemical sense" (Halpern, 2002). Enjoying a good meal usually depends on the simultaneous activity of taste and odor receptors, as becomes apparent when we have a stuffy nose and our food tastes bland. People who lose their sense of smell typically believe they have lost their sense of taste as well (Beauchamp & Bartoshuk, 1997).

Gustation: The Sense of Taste

▶ **Focus 15**
Describe the stimuli and the receptors involved in gustation and olfaction.

People who consider themselves gourmets are frequently surprised to learn that their sense of taste responds to only four qualities: sweet, sour, salty, and bitter. Every other taste experience combines these qualities and those of other senses, such as smell, temperature, and touch. For example, part of the taste of popcorn includes its complex texture, its crunchiness, and its odor. In addition to its chemical receptors, the tongue is richly endowed with tactile (touch) and temperature receptors.

Taste buds *are chemical receptors concentrated along the tip, edges, and back surface of the tongue* (Figure 4.22). Each taste bud is most responsive to one or two of the basic taste qualities but responds weakly to the others as well. An additional taste

sensation, called *umani,* increases the intensity of other taste qualities. This sensory response is activated by certain proteins, as well as by monosodium glutamate, a substance used by some restaurants for flavor enhancement.

Humans have about 9,000 taste buds, each one consisting of several receptor cells arranged like the segments of an orange. A small number of receptors are also found in the roof and back of the mouth, so that even people without a tongue can taste substances. Hairlike structures project from the top of each cell into the taste pore, an opening to the outside surface of the tongue. When a substance is taken into the mouth, it interacts with saliva to form a chemical solution that flows into the taste pore and stimulates the receptor cells. A taste results from complex patterns of neural activity produced by the four types of taste receptors (Halpern, 2002).

The sense of taste not only provides us with pleasure but also has adaptive significance in discriminating between nutrients and toxins (Scott, 1992). Our response to some taste qualities is innate. For example, newborn infants respond positively to sugar water placed on the tongue and negatively to bitter substances such as quinine (Davidson & Fox, 1988). Many poisonous substances in nature have bitter tastes, so this emotional response seems to be hardwired into our physiology. In nature, sweet substances are more likely to occur in high-calorie (sugar-rich) foods. Unfortunately, many humans now live in an environment that is different from the food-scarce environment in which preferences for sweet substances evolved (Scott & Giza, 1993). As a result, people in affluent countries overconsume sweet foods that are good for us only in small quantities.

Olfaction: The Sense of Smell

Humans are visually oriented creatures, but the sense of smell (olfaction) is of great importance for many species. Bloodhounds, for example, have poor eyesight but a highly developed olfactory sense that is about 2 million times more sensitive than ours (Thomas, 1974). A bloodhound can detect a person's scent in a footprint that is four days old, something no human could do. Yet people who are deprived of other senses often develop a highly sensitive olfactory sense. Helen Keller, though blind and deaf, exhibited a remarkable ability to smell her environment. With uncanny accuracy, she could tell when a storm was brewing by detecting subtle odor changes in the air. She could also identify people (even those who bathed regularly and did not wear perfumes or colognes) by their distinctive odors (Keller, 1955).

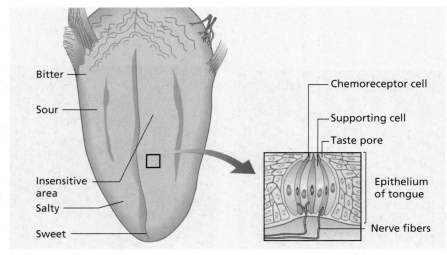

FIGURE 4.22

Taste organs. The receptors for taste are specialized cells located in the tongue's taste buds. The tongue's 9,000 taste buds are found on the tip, back, and sides of the tongue. As this figure shows, certain areas of the tongue are especially sensitive to chemical stimuli that produce particular taste sensations. However, these different sensitivities are a matter of degree, as all kinds of taste buds are found in most areas of the tongue. The center of the tongue is relatively insensitive to chemical stimuli for taste.

The receptors for smell are long cells that project through the lining of the upper part of the nasal cavity and into the mucous membrane. Humans have about 40 million olfactory receptors, dogs about 1 billion. Unfortunately, our ability to discriminate among different odors is not well understood. The most popular current theory is that olfactory receptors recognize diverse odors individually rather than by mixing the activity of a smaller number of basic receptors, as occurs in taste (Wilson et al., 2004). Olfactory receptors have structures that resemble neurotransmitter binding sites on neurons. Any of the thousands of potential odor molecules can lock into sites that are tailored to fit them (Buck & Axel, 1991). The receptors that fire send their input to the **olfactory bulb,** *a forebrain structure immediately above the nasal cavity.* Each odorous chemical excites only a limited portion of the olfactory bulb, and odors are apparently coded in terms of the specific area of the olfactory bulb that is excited (Dalton, 2002).

The social and sexual behavior of animals is more strongly regulated by olfaction than is human behavior (Alcock, 2002). For example, many species use urine to mark their territories; we humans find other ways, such as erecting fences or spreading our belongings over the table we are using in the library. Nonetheless, like animals, we have special receptors in the nose that send impulses to a separate olfactory area in the brain that connects with brain structures involved in social and reproductive behavior. Some researchers believe that **pheromones,** *chemical signals found in natural body scents,* may affect human behavior in subtle ways (Beauchamp & Bartoshuk, 1997).

One interesting phenomenon known as **menstrual synchrony** *is the tendency of women who live together or are close friends to become more similar in their menstrual cycles.* Psychologist Martha McClintock (1971) tested 135 college women and found that during the course of an academic year, roommates moved from a mean of 8.5 days apart in their periods to 4.9 days apart. Another study of 51 women who worked together showed that close friends had menstrual onsets averaging 3.5 to 4.3 days apart, whereas those who were not close friends had onsets that averaged 8 to 9 days apart (Weller et al., 1999). Are pheromones responsible for synchrony? In one experiment, 10 women with regular cycles were dabbed under the nose every few days with underarm secretions collected from another woman. After 3 months, the recipients' cycles began to coincide with the sweat donor's cycles. A control group of women who were dabbed with an alcohol solution rather than sweat showed no menstrual synchrony with a partner (Preti et al., 1986). In other studies, however, menstrual synchrony was not found for cohabiting lesbian couples or for Bedouin women who spent most of their time together, indicating that prolonged and very intensive contact may not be conducive to menstrual synchrony (Weller et al., 1999; Weller & Weller, 1997).

Do odors make us sexually attractive? The marketers of various "pheromone" perfumes tell us they do. And, if you have ever owned a dog or cat that went into heat, you can attest to the effects of such odors in animals. However, researchers have yet to find any solid evidence to back the claims of commercial products promising instant sexual attraction. For humans, it appears that a pleasant personality and good grooming are a better bet than artificially applied pheromones when it comes to finding a mate.

THE SKIN AND BODY SENSES

The skin and body senses include the senses of touch, kinesthesis (muscle movement), and equilibrium. The last two are called *body senses* because they inform us of the body's position and movement. They tell us, for example, if we are running or standing still, lying down or sitting up.

The Tactile Senses

Touch is important to us in many ways. Sensitivity to extreme temperatures and to pain enables us to escape external danger and alerts us to disorders within our body. Tactile sensations are also a source of many of life's pleasures, including sexual orgasm. As discussed in Chapter 2, massage enhances newborn babies' development (Cigales et al., 1997; Field, 2000). Conversely, it has been shown that a lack of tactile contact with a caretaking adult retards physical, social, and emotional development (Harlow, 1958).

Humans are sensitive to at least four tactile sensations: pressure (touch), pain, warmth, and cold. These sensations are conveyed by receptors in the skin and in our internal organs. Mixtures of these four sensations form the basis for all other common skin sensations, such as itch.

Considering the importance of our skin senses, surprisingly little is known about how they work. The skin, a multilayered elastic structure that covers 2 square yards and weighs between 6 and 10 pounds, is the largest organ in our body. As shown in Figure 4.23, it contains a variety of receptor structures, but their role in specific sensations is less clear than for the other senses. Many sensations probably depend on specific patterns of

▶ **Focus 16**
Describe the receptors and processing mechanisms for the tactile senses.

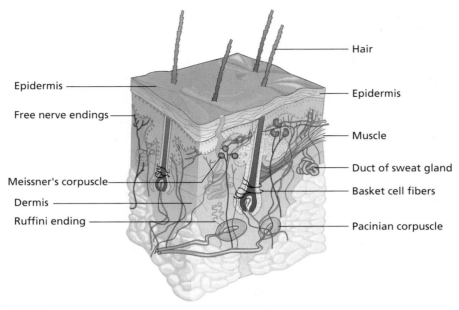

FIGURE 4.23

Skin receptors. A variety of sensory receptors in the human skin and internal tissues allow us to sense touch and temperature. Basket cell fibers around hair follicles detect bending of the hair in light touch, and Meissner's corpuscles provide the same information in hairless areas. Pacinian corpuscles and Ruffini endings provide deeper touch sensations, and the free nerve endings respond to temperature and painful stimuli.
SOURCE: Adapted from Smith, 1998.

► **Focus 17**
What are the two major body senses? Where are their receptors?

► **Focus 18**
What sensory principles underlie sensory prosthetics for the blind and the hearing impaired?

activity in the various receptors (Goldstein, 2002). We do know that the primary receptors for pain and temperature are the *free nerve endings,* simple nerve cells beneath the skin's surface that resemble bare tree branches (Gracely et al., 2002). *Basket cell fibers* situated at the base of hair follicles are receptors for touch and light pressure (Heller & Schiff, 1991).

The brain can locate sensations because skin receptors send their messages to the point in the somatosensory cortex that corresponds to the area of the body where the receptor is located. As we saw in Chapter 3, the amount of cortex devoted to each area of the body is related to that part's sensitivity. Our fingers, lips, and tongue are well represented, accounting for their extreme sensitivity to stimulation (Figure 4.24; see also Figure 3.21).

Sometimes the brain "locates" sensations that cannot possibly be present. This occurs in the puzzling phantom-limb phenomenon, in which amputees experience vivid sensations coming from the missing limb (Warga, 1987). Apparently an irritation of the nerves that used to originate in the limb fools the brain into interpreting the resulting nerve impulses as real sensations. Joel Katz and Ronald Melzack (1990) studied 68 amputees who insisted that they experienced pain from the amputated limb that was as vivid and real as any pain they had ever felt. This pain was not merely a recollection of what pain used to feel like in the limb; it was actually ex-

perienced in the present. The phantom-limb phenomenon can be quite maddening. Imagine having an intense itch that you never can scratch or an ache that you cannot rub. When amputees are fitted with prosthetic limbs and begin using them, phantom pain tends to disappear (Gracely et al., 2002).

Pain is one of the most intriguing of the skin senses. The sensory and perceptual aspects of pain are topics of great theoretical and research interest to psychologists (Pappagallo, 2005; Watkins & Maier, 2003). Because of pain's relevance to stress and health, we will focus on this sensory modality in greater detail in Chapter 13.

The Body Senses

We would be totally unable to coordinate our body movements were it not for the sense of **kinesthesis,** *which provides us with feedback about our muscles' and joints' positions and movements.* Kinesthetic receptors are nerve endings in the muscles, tendons, and joints. The information this sense gives us is the basis for making coordinated movements. Cooperating with kinesthesis is the **vestibular sense,** *the sense of body orientation, or equilibrium* (Figure 4.25).

The vestibular receptors are located in the vestibular apparatus of the inner ear (see Figure 4.19). One part of the equilibrium system consists of three semicircular canals, which contain the receptors for head movement. Each canal lies in a different plane: left-right, backward-forward, or up-down. These canals are filled with fluid and lined with hairlike cells that function as receptors.

FIGURE 4.24

World-renowned percussionist Evelyn Glennie became deaf many years ago. She now uses her tactile sense to detect distinct vibrations that correspond with individual tones. Though deaf, she is capable of perfect tonal discrimination.

When the head moves, the fluid in the appropriate canal shifts, stimulating the hair cells and sending messages to the brain. The semicircular canals respond only to acceleration and deceleration; when a constant speed is reached (no matter how high), the fluid and the hair cells return to their normal resting state. That's why airplane takeoffs and landings give a sense of movement whereas cruising along at 500 miles per hour does not. Located at the base of the semicircular canals, the vestibular sacs also contain hair cells that respond to the position of the body and tell us whether we are upright or tilted at an angle. These structures form the second part of the body-sense system.

You have now learned a considerable amount about the principles underlying stimulus detection and transduction. As the following "Applying Psychological Science" section shows, these principles have not only informational value for understanding how our sensory systems operate, but also applied value in helping people with sensory impairments.

FIGURE 4.25

Kinesthesis and the vestibular sense are especially well developed in some people—and essential for performing actions like this one.

Applying Psychological Science

Sensory Prosthetics: "Eyes" for the Blind, "Ears" for the Hearing Impaired

Millions of people suffer from blindness and deafness, living in sightless or soundless worlds. A promising development combines psychological research on the workings of the sensory systems with technical advances in bioengineering. The result is **sensory prosthetic devices** *that provide sensory input that can, to some extent, substitute for what cannot be supplied by the person's sensory receptors.* In considering these devices, we should remind ourselves that we don't see with the eyes, hear with the ears, or taste with the taste buds; we see, hear, and taste with our brain. The nerve impulses sent from the retina or the organ of Corti or the taste buds are no different from those sent from anywhere else in the body. Sight, hearing, or taste is simply the brain's adaptation to the input it receives.

SEEING WITH THE EARS

One device, known as a Sonicguide, provides new "eyes" through the ears, capitalizing on principles of auditory localization (Kay, 1982). The Sonicguide (Figure 4.26) works on the same principle as *echolocation*, the sensory tool used by bats to navigate in total darkness. A headset contains a transmitter that emits high-frequency sound waves beyond the range of human hearing. These waves bounce back from objects in the environment and are transformed by the Sonicguide into sounds that can be heard through earphones. Different sound

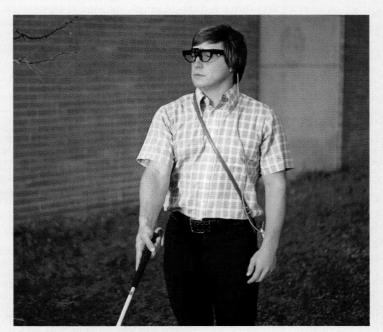

FIGURE 4.26

The Sonicguide allows a blind person to perceive the size, distance, movement, shape, and texture of objects through sound waves that represent the visual features of objects.

Continued

qualities match specific features of external objects, and the wearer must learn to interpret the sonic messages. For example, the sound's pitch tells the person how far away an object is; a low pitch signals a nearby object and becomes higher as the distance to the object increases. The loudness of the sound tells how large the object is, and the clarity of the sound (ranging from a static-like sound to a clear tone) signals the texture of the object, from very rough to very smooth. Finally, the sound-localization principle described earlier tells the person where the object is located in the environment by means of differences in the time at which sounds arrive at the two ears.

In the first laboratory tests of the Sonicguide, psychologists Stuart Aitken and T. G. R. Bower (1982) used the apparatus with 6 blind babies who ranged in age from 5 to 16 months. Within hours or days, all of the babies using the Sonicguide could reach for objects, walk or crawl through doorways, and follow the movement of their hands and arms as they moved them about. Moreover, abilities such as reaching for objects, recognizing favorite toys, and reaching out to be picked up when mother (but not someone else) approached seemed to occur on the same developmental timetable as in sighted children. Aitken and Bower concluded that blind infants can extract the same information from sonic cues as sighted babies do from visual cues.

Older children and adults can learn to use the device too, but not as easily as babies can. Older children trained with the device can easily find objects, such as water fountains and specific toys. They can thread their way through crowded school corridors and can even play hide-and-seek. The Sonicguide is now being used by visually impaired children in schools and other natural settings, as well as by adults (Hill et al., 1995).

THE SEEING TONGUE

At the University of Wisconsin, Paul Bach-y-Rita has developed a tactile tongue-based, electrical input sensor as a sub-stitute for visual input. The tongue seems an unlikely substitute for the eye, hidden as it is in the dark recess of the mouth. Yet in many ways it may be the second-best organ for providing detailed input, for it is densely packed with tactile receptors, thus allowing the transmission of high-resolution data. Moreover, its moist surface is a good conducting medium for electricity, meaning that minimum voltage is required to stimulate the receptors.

Researchers have built an experimental prototype of a device that eventually will be small enough to be invisibly attached directly to the teeth. The current stimulator, shown in Figure 4.27a, receives digital data from a camera and provides patterns of stimulation to the tongue through a 144-electrode array. The array can transmit shapes that correspond to the main features of the visual stimulus. Initial trials with blindfolded sighted people and blind people show that with about 9 hours of training, users can "read" the letters of a Snellen eye chart with an acuity of 20/430, a modest but noteworthy beginning (Simpaio et al., 2001).

With continued development, a miniature camera in an eyeglass will transmit wireless data to a more densely packed electrode array attached to a dental retainer. Bach-y-Rita believes the device also might have both military and civilian applications. For example, it could help soldiers locate objects in pitch-black environments, such as caves, where night-vision devices are useless; it could also aid firefighters as they search smoke-filled buildings for people to rescue.

CORTICAL IMPLANTS

A different approach to a visual prosthesis is being perfected at the University of Utah, where researchers have developed a device to stimulate the visual cortex directly (Normann et al., 1999). When cells in the visual cortex are stimulated electrically, discrete flashes of light called *phosphenes* are experienced by both sighted and blind people. Because sensory neurons in the visual cortex are arranged in a manner

FIGURE 4.27

Two approaches to providing artificial vision for the blind.
(a) Bach-y-Rita's device converts digitized stimuli from a camera to a matrix of electrodes, which stimulate tactile receptors in the tongue to communicate spatial information to the brain. (b) Tiny electrodes implanted into individual neurons in the visual cortex produce patterns of phosphenes that correspond to the visual scene observed through the video camera and encoder. Note how the cortical image is reversed as in normal visual input.

(a)

(b)

Skin

External coil

Internal coil

Cochlea contains implanted electrodes

Receiver circuitry

Input cable to cochlea

Eardrum

To microphone and sound processor

FIGURE 4.28

Cochlear implants. Cochlear implants provide direct stimulation of the auditory nerve in people whose hair cells are too damaged to respond to fluid waves in the cochlea. Sound enters a microphone and is sent to a processor that breaks the sound down into its principal frequencies and sends electrical signals to external and internal coils. The receiver circuitry stimulates electrodes implanted in cochlear areas associated with particular frequencies.

that corresponds to the organization of the retina, a specific pattern of stimulation applied to individual neurons in the cortex can form a phosphene pattern that conforms to the shapes of letters or objects. The acuity of the pattern depends on the area of the visual cortex that is stimulated (the portion receiving input from the densely packed fovea produces greatest acuity) and on the number of stimulating electrodes in the array.

Building on this approach, researchers have developed the device shown in Figure 4.27b. The Utah Intracortical Electrode Array consists of a silicon strip containing thousands of tiny stimulating electrodes that penetrate directly into individual neurons in the visual cortex, where they can stimulate phosphene patterns. Eventually, a tiny television camera mounted in specially designed eyeglasses will provide visual information to a microcomputer that will analyze the scene and then send the appropriate patterns of electrical stimulation through the implanted electrodes to produce corresponding phosphene patterns in the visual cortex. The researchers have shown that sighted participants who wear darkened goggles that produce phosphene-like patterns of light flashes like those provided by cortical stimulation can quickly learn to navigate through complex environments and are able to read text at about two thirds their normal rate (Normann et al., 1996, 1999). Blind people who have had the stimulating electrodes implanted in their visual cortex have also been able to learn a kind of cortical braille for reading purposes. Although still experimental, a commercially available intracortical prosthetic device should appear in the near future.

COCHLEAR IMPLANTS

People with hearing impairments have also been assisted by the development of prosthetic devices. The cochlear implant, a device that can restore hearing in people suffering from nerve deafness, has helped many. Instead of amplifying sound like a conventional hearing aid (people with nerve deafness cannot be helped by mere sound amplification), the cochlear implant sorts out useful sounds and converts them into electrical impulses, bypassing the disabled hair cells in the cochlea and stimulating the auditory nerve directly (Figure 4.28). With a cochlear implant, patients can hear everyday sounds such as sirens, and many of them can understand speech (Meyer et al., 1998; Parkinson et al., 1998). But because sounds heard with currently developed implants tend to be muffled, patients who expect the device to restore normal hearing are invariably disappointed. Electrical recording of cortical responses to sounds revealed that hearing-impaired people provided with a cochlear implant show a more widespread pattern of neural activity in the auditory cortex than do people with normal hearing, perhaps helping to account for their poorer sound discrimination (Ito et al., 2004).

Sensory prosthetics illustrate the ways in which knowledge about sensory phenomena such as phosphenes, the organization of the visual cortex, sound localization, and the place theory of pitch perception can provide the information needed to take advantage of new technological advances. Yet even with all our ingenuity, prosthetic devices are not substitutes for our normal sensory systems, a fact that should increase our appreciation for what nature has given us.

IN REVIEW

- Sound waves, the stimuli for audition, have two characteristics: frequency, measured in terms of cycles per second, or hertz (Hz); and amplitude, measured in terms of decibels (dB). Frequency is related to pitch, amplitude to loudness. The receptors for hearing are hair cells in the organ of Corti of the inner ear.

- Loudness is coded in terms of the number and types of auditory nerve fibers that fire. Pitch is coded in two ways. Low-frequency tones are coded in terms of corresponding numbers of nerve impulses in individual receptors or by volleys of impulses from a number of receptors. Frequencies above 4,000 hertz are coded according to the region of the basilar membrane that is displaced most by the fluid wave in the cochlear canal.

- Hearing loss may result from conduction deafness, produced by problems involving the structures of the ear that transmit vibrations to the cochlea, or from nerve deafness, in which the receptors in the cochlea or the auditory nerve are damaged.

- The receptors for taste and smell respond to chemical molecules. Taste buds are responsive to four basic qualities: sweet, sour, salty, and bitter. The receptors for smell (olfaction) are long cells in the upper nasal cavity. Natural body odors produced by pheromones appear to account for a menstrual synchrony that sometimes occurs among women who live together or are close friends.

- The skin and body senses include touch, kinesthesis, and equilibrium. Receptors in the skin and body tissues are sensitive to pressure, pain, warmth, and cold. Kinesthesis functions by means of nerve endings in the muscles, tendons, and joints. The sense organs for equilibrium are in the vestibular apparatus of the inner ear.

- Principles derived from the study of sensory processes have been applied in developing sensory prosthetics for the blind and the hearing impaired. Examples include the Sonicguide, which uses auditory input; a device that provides visual information through tactile stimulation of the tongue; direct electrical stimulation of the visual cortex; and cochlear implants.

PERCEPTION: THE CREATION OF EXPERIENCE

▶ **Focus 19**
Compare bottom-up and top-down processing of sensory information.

Sensory systems provide the raw materials from which experiences are formed. Our sense organs do not select what we will be aware of or how we will experience it; they merely transmit as much information as they can through our nervous system. Yet our experiences are not simply a one-to-one reflection of what is external to our senses. Different people may experience the same sensory information in radically different ways, because perception is an active, creative process in which raw sensory data are organized and given meaning.

To create our perceptions, the brain carries out two different kinds of processing functions (Figure 4.29). In **bottom-up processing,** *the system takes in individual elements of the stimulus and then combines them into a unified perception.* Your visual system operates in a bottom-up fashion as you read. Its feature detectors analyze the elements in each letter of every word and then recombine them into your visual perception of the letters and words. In **top-down processing,** *sensory information is interpreted in light of existing knowledge, concepts, ideas, and expectations.* Top-down processing is occurring as you interpret the words and sentences constructed by the bottom-up process. Here you make use of higher-order knowledge, including what you have learned about the meaning of words and sentence construction. Indeed, a given sentence may convey a different personal meaning to you than to another person if you relate its content to some unique personal experiences. Top-down processing accounts for many psychological influences on perception, such as the roles played by our motives, expectations, previous experiences, and cultural learning.

FIGURE 4.29

Perceptual processing. Bottom-up perceptual processing builds from an analysis of individual stimulus features to a unified perception. Top-down processing begins with a perceptual whole, such as an expectation or an image of an object, then determines the degree of fit with the stimulus features.

Bottom-up processing
Combination and interpretation of "whole"
↑
Breakdown/analysis of stimuli (e.g., feature detection)
↑
Detection of individual stimulus elements

Top-down processing
Concept, expectation
↓
Guides analysis (Yes? No?)
↓
Interpretation of incoming stimuli

PERCEPTION IS SELECTIVE: THE ROLE OF ATTENTION

As you read these words, 100 million sensory messages may be clamoring for your attention. Only a few of these messages register in awareness; the rest you perceive either dimly or not at all. But you can shift your attention to one of those unregistered stimuli at any time. (For example, how does the big toe of your right foot feel right now?) Attention, then, involves two processes of selection: (1) focusing on certain stimuli and (2) filtering out other incoming information (Luck & Vecera, 2002).

These processes have been studied experimentally through a technique called *shadowing*. Participants wear earphones and listen simultaneously to two messages, one sent through each earphone. They are asked to repeat (or shadow) one of the messages word for word as they listen. Most participants can do this quite successfully, but only at the cost of not remembering what the other message was about. Shadowing experiments demonstrate that we cannot attend completely to more than one thing at a time. But we can shift our attention rapidly back and forth between the two messages, drawing on our general knowledge to fill in the gaps (Bonnel & Hafter, 1998; Sperling, 1984).

Inattentional Blindness

Electrical recording and brain-imaging studies have shown that unattended stimuli register in the nervous system but do not enter into immediate experience (Itti & Rees, 2005). In the visual realm, scientists have coined the term **inattentional blindness** *to refer to the failure of unattended stimuli to register in consciousness* (Mack, 2003). We can look right at something without "seeing" it if we are attending to something else. In one study, several experienced pilots training on flight simulators were so intent on watching the landing instruments, such as the airspeed indicator on the plane's windshield, that they directed their plane onto a runway containing another aircraft (Haines, 1991). In another instance, research participants who were counting the number of passes made during a videotaped basketball game did not notice a man wearing a gorilla suit who stopped to thump his chest as he walked across the court, even though he remained in clear sight for more than 5 seconds (Simons & Chabris, 1999). Inattentional blindness is surely relevant to findings that cell phone conversations significantly reduce driving performance in experimental studies (e.g., Golden et al., 2003). It's a bad idea to drive and yack at the same time.

Environmental and Personal Factors in Attention

Attention is strongly affected by both the nature of the stimulus and by personal factors. Stimulus characteristics that attract our attention include intensity, novelty, movement, contrast, and repetition. Advertisers use these properties in their commercials and packaging (Figure 4.30). Internal factors, such as our motives and interests, act as powerful filters and influence which stimuli in our environment we will notice. For example, when we are hungry, we are especially sensitive to food-related cues. A botanist walking through a park is especially attentive to the plants; a landscape architect attends primarily to the layout of the park.

People are especially attentive to stimuli that might represent a threat to their well-being, a tendency that would clearly have biological survival value (Izard, 1989; Oehman et al., 2001). A study by Christine and Ranald Hansen (1988) illustrates this tendency. They presented slides showing groups of nine people. In half of the pictures, all of the people looked either angry or happy. In the other half, there was one discrepant face, either an angry face in a happy crowd or a happy face in an angry crowd. Participants were asked to judge as quickly as possible whether there was a discrepant face in the crowd, then press "yes" or "no" buttons attached to electrical timers. The dependent variable was the length of time required to make this judgment, measured in milliseconds (thousandths of a second).

▶ **Focus 20**
What two complementary processes occur in attention? What is inattentional blindness? What kinds of external and internal factors influence attention?

 We each interpret incoming stimuli based on previous experiences and associations. Thus, while individuals may have very similar sensory experiences, their perceptual experiences differ. Consider this as you view the "Perceptual Integration" video in Chapter 4 of your CD.

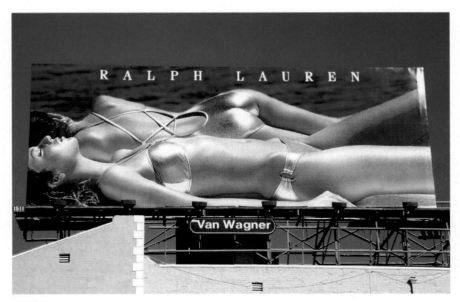

FIGURE 4.30

Advertisers use attention-attracting stimuli in their advertisements. Personal characteristics of potential customers are also important. What kinds of individuals do you suppose would be most attentive to this ad?

FIGURE 4.31

Primed to perceive threat.
Perceptual vigilance to threatening stimuli is shown in the finding that people required less time to detect an angry face in a happy crowd than to detect a happy face in an angry crowd or to determine if there was any discrepant face in a happy or an angry crowd. Source: Based on Hansen & Hansen, 1988.

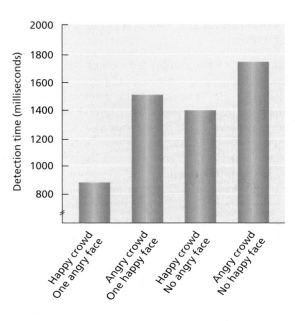

The results, summarized in Figure 4.31, showed that participants were much faster at detecting a single angry face in an otherwise happy crowd than at finding a happy face in an angry crowd. It was as if the angry face, which the experimenters assumed to have threat value, jumped out of the crowd when the stimuli were scanned. Swedish psychologist Ulf Dimberg (1997) also believes that humans are biologically programmed to detect threatening faces, and he has shown via high-speed photography that emotional facial responses to such stimuli occur in observers within one third of a second. Attentional processes are thus based both on innate biological factors and on past experiences that make certain stimuli important or meaningful to us.

Advertisers are adept at using attention-getting stimuli to attract potential customers to their products. Sometimes, however, the process backfires, as in the following case.

> A famous model glides down a staircase, removing articles of clothing as she goes. Once inside the car being promoted in this British advertisement, she removes her panties and flings them out the window. The only problem with this wildly popular ad? An informal survey by a Welsh psychologist revealed that the visual image was so compelling that virtually no one remembered the brand of car being advertised. (Clay, 2002, p. 38)

PERCEPTIONS HAVE ORGANIZATION AND STRUCTURE

▶ **Focus 21**
Which Gestalt psychology principles and laws underlie perceptual organization?

Have you ever stopped to wonder why we perceive the visual world as being composed of distinct objects? After all, the information sent by the

retina reflects nothing but an array of varying intensities and frequencies of light energy. The light rays reflected from different parts of a single object have no more natural "belongingness" to one another than those coming from two different objects. Yet we perceive scenes as involving separate objects, such as trees, buildings, and people. These perceptions must be a product of an organization imposed by our nervous system (Jenkin & Harris, 2005; Tarr & Vuong, 2002). This top-down process of perceptual organization occurs so automatically that we take it for granted. But Dr. Richard, a prominent psychologist who suffered brain damage in an accident, no longer does.

> There was nothing wrong with his eyes, yet the input he received from them was not put together correctly. Dr. Richard reported that if he saw a person, he sometimes would perceive the separate parts of the person as not belonging together in a single body. But if all the parts moved in the same direction, Dr. Richard then saw them as one complete person. At other times, he would perceive people in crowds wearing the same color clothes as "going together" rather than as separate people. He also had difficulty putting sights and sounds together. Sometimes, the movement of the lips did not correspond to the sounds he heard, as if he were watching a badly dubbed foreign movie. Dr. Richard's experience of his environment was thus disjointed and fragmented. (Sacks, 1985, p. 76)

Another, more extreme example of perceptual organization gone awry is synesthesia, which we described at the beginning of this chapter. What, then, are the processes whereby sensory nonsense becomes perceptual sense?

Gestalt Principles of Perceptual Organization

Early in the 20th century, psychologists from the German school of Gestalt psychology set out to discover how we organize the separate parts of our perceptual field into a unified and meaningful whole. *Gestalt* is the German term for "pattern," "whole," or "form." Gestalt theorists were early champions of top-down processing, arguing that the wholes we perceive are often more than (and frequently different from) the sum of their parts. Thus your perception of the photo in Figure 4.32 is likely to be more than people on a field.

The Gestalt theorists emphasized the importance of **figure-ground relations,** *our tendency to organize stimuli into a central or foreground figure and a background.* In vision, the central figure is usually in front of or on top of what we perceive

FIGURE 4.32

As Gestalt psychologists emphasized, what we perceive (in this case, the name spelled out by the band) is more than simply the sum of its individual parts.

FIGURE 4.33

What do you see? Figure-ground relations are important in perceptual organization. Here the artist Bev Doolittle has created great similarity between figure and ground in this representation of natural camouflage, yet enough figural cues remain to permit most people to detect the ponies. *Pintos,* by Bev Doolittle, 1979. The Greenwich Workshop, Trumbull, Connecticut.

as background. It has a distinct shape and is more striking in our perceptions and memory than the background. We perceive borders or contours wherever there is a distinct change in the color or brightness of a visual scene, but we interpret these contours as part of the figure rather than background. Likewise, we tend to hear instrumental music as a melody (figure) surrounded by other chords or harmonies (ground).

Separating figure from ground can be challenging (Figure 4.33), yet our perceptual systems are usually equal to the task. Sometimes, however, what's figure and what's ground is not completely obvious, and the same stimulus can give rise to two different perceptions. Consider Figure 4.34, for example. If you examine it for a while, two alternating but equally plausible perceptions will emerge, one based on the inner portion and the other formed by the two outer portions. When the alternative perception occurs, what was previously the figure becomes the background.

In addition to figure-ground relations, the Gestalt psychologists were interested in how separate stimuli come to be perceived as parts of larger wholes. They suggested that people group and interpret stimuli in accordance with four **Gestalt laws of perceptual organization:** *similarity, proximity, closure, and continuity.* These organizing principles are illustrated in Figure 4.35.

What is your perception of Figure 4.35a? Do you perceive 16 unrelated dots or two triangles formed by different-sized dots? If you see triangles, your perception obeys the Gestalt *law of similarity,* which says that when parts of a configuration are perceived as similar, they will be perceived as be-

longing together. The *law of proximity* says that elements that are near each other are likely to be perceived as part of the same configuration. Thus most people perceive Figure 4.35b as three sets of two lines rather than six separate lines. Illustrated in Figure 4.35c is the *law of closure,* which states that people tend to close the open edges of a figure or fill in gaps in an incomplete figure, so that their identification of the form (in this case, a circle) is more complete than what is actually there. Finally, the *law of continuity* holds that people link individual elements together so they form a continuous line or pattern that makes sense. Thus Figure 4.35d is far more likely to be seen as combining components a-b and c-d rather than a-d and c-b, which have poor continuity. Or consider Fraser's spiral, shown in Figure 4.36, which is not really a spiral at all! (To demonstrate, trace one of the circles with a pencil.) We perceive the concentric circles as a spiral because, to our nervous system, a spiral gives better continuity between individual elements than does a set of circles. The spiral is created by us, not by the stimulus.

FIGURE 4.34

One stimulus, two perceptions. This reversible figure illustrates alternating figure-ground relations. It can be seen as a vase or as two people facing one another. Whichever percept exists at the moment is seen as figure against background.

(a) Similarity   (b) Proximity   (c) Closure   (d) Continuity

FIGURE 4.35

Gestalt perceptual laws. Among the Gestalt principles of perceptual organization are the laws of (a) similarity, (b) proximity, (c) closure, and (d) continuity. Each principle causes us to organize stimuli into wholes that are greater than the sums of their parts.

FIGURE 4.36

A spiral that isn't. Fraser's spiral illustrates the Gestalt law of continuity. If you follow any part of the "spiral" with a pencil, you will find that it is not a spiral at all but a series of concentric circles. The "spiral" is created by your nervous system because that perception is more consistent with continuity of the individual elements.

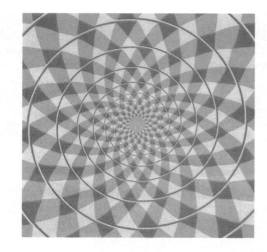

▶ **Focus 22**

What roles do perceptual schemas and perceptual sets play in our sensory interpretations?

PERCEPTION INVOLVES HYPOTHESIS TESTING

Recognizing a stimulus implies that we have a **perceptual schema**—*a mental representation or image containing the critical and distinctive features of a person, object, event, or other perceptual phenomenon.* Schemas provide mental templates that allow us to classify and identify sensory input in a top-down fashion.

Imagine, for example, that a person approaches you and calls out your name. Who is this person? If the stimuli match your internal schemas of your best friend's appearance and voice closely enough, you identify the person as your friend (McAdams & Drake, 2002). Many political cartoonists have an uncanny ability to capture the most noteworthy facial features of famous people so that we can easily recognize the person represented by even the simplest line sketch.

Perception is, in this sense, an attempt to make sense of stimulus input, to search for the best interpretation of sensory information we can arrive at based on our knowledge and experience. Likening perception to the scientific process described in Chapter 2, Richard L. Gregory (1966, 2005) suggested that each of our perceptions is essentially a hypothesis about the nature of the object or, more generally, the meaning of the sensory information. The perceptual system actively searches its gigantic library of internal schemas for the interpretation that best fits the sensory data.

An example of how effortlessly our perceptual systems build up descriptions or hypotheses that best fit the available evidence is found in the comic strips created by Gustave Verbeek in the early 1900s. The Sunday *New York Herald* told Verbeek that his comic strip had to be restricted to 6 panels. Verbeek wanted 12 panels, so he ingeniously created 12-panel cartoons in only 6 panels by drawing pictures like that shown in Figure 4.37a. The reader viewed the first 6 panels, then turned the newspaper upside down to read the last 6 and finish the story. Try this yourself on the panel shown in the figure, and you will find that a bird story becomes a fish story! The point is that you do not see an upside-down bird; you see an entirely different picture because the stimuli created by the new orientation match other perceptual schemas.

In some instances, sensory information fits two different internal representations, and there is not enough information to permanently rule out one of them in favor of the other. For example, examine the Necker cube, shown in Figure 4.37b. If you stare at the cube for a while, you will find that it changes before your very eyes as your nervous system tries out a new perceptual hypothesis.

FIGURE 4.37

Reversible perceptions. Here are two examples of how the same stimulus can give rise to different perceptions. (a) After viewing this comic strip panel by Gustave Verbeek, turn it upside down for a different spin on the story. (b) Stare at this Necker cube for a while; the front of the cube will suddenly become the back, and it will appear as if you're viewing the cube from a different angle.

(a)

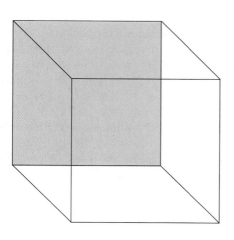

(b)

PERCEPTION IS INFLUENCED BY EXPECTATIONS: PERCEPTUAL SETS

On July 3, 1988, the warship USS *Vincennes* was engaged in a pitched battle with several speedy Iranian gunboats. Suddenly, the *Vincennes*'s advanced radar system detected an aircraft taking off from a military-civilian airfield in Iran and heading straight toward the American vessel. Radar operators identified the plane as an Iranian F-14 fighter, known to carry lethal missiles used earlier in a damaging attack on another U.S. warship. Repeated requests to the plane to identify itself yielded no response. The plane was now only 10 miles from the ship and, according to the crewmen watching the radar, descending toward the *Vincennes* on an attack course. As a final warning evoked no response, the *Vincennes*'s captain gave the command to fire on the plane. Two surface-to-air missiles streaked into the sky. Moments later, all that remained of the plane was a shower of flaming debris.

The jubilation and relief of the *Vincennes*'s crew was short-lived. Soon the awful truth was known. The plane they had shot down was not an attacking F-14 warplane but a commercial airliner carrying 290 passengers, all of whom died when the aircraft was destroyed. Moreover, videotape recordings of the electronic information used by the crew to identify the plane and its flight pattern showed conclusively that the aircraft was not an F-14 and that it had actually been climbing rather than descending toward the ship.

How could such a tragic error have been made by a well-trained and experienced crew with access to the world's most sophisticated radar equipment? At a congressional hearing on the incident, several prominent perception researchers reconstructed the psychological environment that could have caused the radar operators' eyes to lie.

Clearly, the situation was stressful and dangerous. The *Vincennes* was already under attack by Iranian gunboats, and other attacks could be expected. It was easy for the radar operators, observing a plane taking off from a military field and heading toward the ship, to interpret this as a prelude to an air attack. The *Vincennes*'s crew was determined to avoid the fate of the other American warship, producing a high level of vigilance for any stimuli that suggested an impending attack. Fear and expectation thus created a psychological context within which the sensory input from the computer system was interpreted in a top-down fashion. The perception that the aircraft was a warplane and that it was descending toward the ship fit the crew's expectations and fears, and it became the reality that they experienced. They had a **perceptual set**—*a readiness to perceive stimuli in a particular way.* Sometimes, believing is seeing.

STIMULI ARE RECOGNIZABLE UNDER CHANGING CONDITIONS: PERCEPTUAL CONSTANCIES

When a closed door suddenly swings open, it casts a different image on our retina, but we still perceive it as a door. Our perceptual hypothesis remains the same. Were it not for **perceptual constancies,** *which allow us to recognize familiar stimuli under varying conditions,* we would have to literally rediscover what something is each time it appeared under different conditions. Thus you can recognize a tune even if it is played in a different octave, as long as the relations among its notes are maintained. You can detect the flavor of a particular spice even when it occurs in foods having very different tastes.

In vision, several constancies are important. *Shape constancy* allows us to recognize people and other objects from many different angles, as in the case of the swinging door. Perhaps you have had the experience of sitting up front and off to one side of the screen in a crowded movie theater. At first the picture probably looked distorted, but after a while your visual system corrected for the distortion and objects on the screen looked normal again.

Because of *brightness constancy*, the relative brightness of objects remains the same under different conditions of illumination, such as full sunlight and shade. Brightness constancy occurs because the ratio of light intensity between an object and its surroundings is usually constant. The actual brightness of the light that illuminates an object does not matter, as long as the same light intensity illuminates both the object and its surroundings.

When we take off in an airplane, we know that the cars on the highway below are not shrinking and becoming the size of ants. *Size constancy* is the perception that the size of objects remains relatively constant even though images on our retina change in size with variations in distance. Thus a man who is judged to be 6 feet tall when standing 5 feet away is not perceived to be 3 feet tall at a distance of 10 feet, even though the size of his image on the retina is reduced to half its original size (Figure 4.38).

▶ **Focus 23**
What factors account for shape, brightness, and size constancy in vision?

FIGURE 4.38

Who's bigger? Size constancy based on distance cues causes us to perceive the person in the background as being of normal size. When the same stimulus is seen in the absence of the distance cues, size constancy breaks down. The two men no longer look similar in size, nor do the photographic images of the man in the blue shirt.

What Do You Think?

WHY DOES THAT RISING MOON LOOK SO BIG?

Just before bedding down for the night on a backpacking trip, a friend of ours poked his head outside of his tent and gasped to his wife, "Look at the moon! Just look at that moon!" Indeed, a bright-red full moon had just come over the horizon, and it was so enormous that it dwarfed the mammoth peaks surrounding them. The couple gazed at it in wonder for a few minutes and then retired into their tent. Later that night, they looked outside again and were puzzled to see a rather small, ordinary full moon approaching the zenith.

You too may have exclaimed over the size of a rising moon, only to notice later that the moon, well above the horizon, seemed to have shrunk. What can explain this phenomenon? Think about it, then see page 148.

IN REVIEW

■ Perception involves both bottom-up processing, in which individual stimulus fragments are combined into a perception, and top-down processing, in which existing knowledge and perceptual schemas are applied to interpret stimuli.

■ Attention is an active process in which we focus on certain stimuli while blocking out others. We cannot attend completely to more than one thing at a time, but we are capable of rapid attentional shifts. Inattentional blindness refers to a failure to perceive certain stimuli when attending to other stimulus elements. Attentional processes are affected by the nature of the stimulus and by personal factors such as motives and interests. The perceptual system appears to be especially vigilant to stimuli that denote threat or danger.

■ Gestalt psychologists identified a number of principles of perceptual organization, including figure-ground relations and the laws of similarity, proximity, closure, and continuity. Gregory suggested that perception is essentially a hypothesis about what a stimulus is, based on previous experience and the nature of the stimulus.

■ Perceptual sets involve a readiness to perceive stimuli in certain ways, based on our expectations, assumptions, motivations, and current emotional state.

■ Perceptual constancies allow us to recognize familiar stimuli under changing conditions. In the visual realm, there are three constancies: shape, brightness, and size.

PERCEPTION OF DEPTH, DISTANCE, AND MOVEMENT

The ability to adapt to a spatial world requires that we make fine distinctions involving distances and the movement of objects within the environment. Humans are capable of great precision in making such judgments. Consider, for example, the perceptual task faced by a baseball batter (Figure 4.39). A fastball thrown by the pitcher at 90 miles per hour from 60 feet will reach the batter who is trying to hit it in about 42/100 of a second. A curveball thrown at 80 miles per hour will reach the hitting zone in 47/100 of a second, a difference of only 5/100 of a second, but a world of difference for timing and hitting the pitch. Within the first 6 to 8 feet of a ball's flight from the pitcher's hand (an interval of about 25/1,000 of a second), the batter must correctly judge the speed, spin, and location of the pitch. If any of the judgments are wrong, the hitter will probably be unable to hit a fair ball, for the ball will be in the bat's contact zone for only 2/1,000 of a second

FIGURE 4.39

The demands faced by a batter in judging the speed, distance, and movements of a pitched baseball within thousandths of a second underscore the capabilities of the visual perceptual system.

FIGURE 4.40

Patterns of light and shadow can serve as monocular depth cues, as shown in *Drawing Hands*, by M. C. Escher.

(Adair, 1990). The perceptual demands of such a task are imposing indeed—as are the salaries earned by those who can perform this task consistently. How does the visual perception system make such judgments?

DEPTH AND DISTANCE PERCEPTION

One of the more intriguing aspects of visual perception is our ability to perceive depth. The retina receives information in only two dimensions (length and width), but the brain translates these cues into three-dimensional perceptions. It does this by using both **monocular depth cues,** *which require only one eye,* and **binocular depth cues,** *which require both eyes.*

Monocular Depth Cues

Judging the relative distances of objects is one important key to perceiving depth. When artists paint on a flat canvas, they depend on a variety of monocular cues to create perceptions of depth in their pictures. One such cue is *patterns of light and shadow.* The 20th-century artist M. C. Escher skillfully used light and shadow to create the three-dimensional effect shown in Figure 4.40. The depth effect is as powerful if you close one eye as it is when you use both.

Another cue, *linear perspective,* refers to the perception that parallel lines converge, or angle toward one another, as they recede into the distance. Thus if you look down railroad tracks, they appear to angle toward one another with increased distance, and we use this as a depth cue. The same occurs with the edges of a highway or the sides of

an elevator shaft. *Interposition,* in which objects closer to us may cut off part of our view of more distant objects, provides another cue for distance and depth.

An object's *height in the horizontal plane* provides another source of information. For example, a ship 5 miles offshore appears in a higher plane and closer to the horizon than does one that is only 1 mile from shore. *Texture* is a fifth cue, because the texture or grain of an object appears finer as distance increases. Likewise, *clarity* can be an important cue for judging distance; we can see nearby hills more clearly than ones that are far away, especially on hazy days.

Relative size is yet another basis for distance judgments. If we see two objects that we know to be of similar size, then the one that looks smaller will be judged to be farther away. For example, this cue may figure prominently in the moon illusion.

None of these monocular cues involve movement of the object(s), but a final monocular cue, *motion parallax,* tells us that if we are moving, nearby objects appear to move faster in the opposite direction than do faraway ones. Like the other monocular cues, motion provides us with information that we can use to make judgments about distance and therefore about depth.

Figure 4.41 illustrates all of the monocular cues just described, with the exception of motion parallax.

Binocular Depth Cues

The most dramatic perceptions of depth arise with binocular depth cues, which require the use of both eyes. For an interesting binocular effect, hold your two index fingers about 6 inches in front of

▶ **Focus 24**
Describe the major monocular and binocular depth/distance cues, as well as the bases for movement perception.

FIGURE 4.41

In this mural, painted on the Mississippi River flood wall at Cape Girardeau, Missouri, the artist has skillfully used seven monocular depth cues to create a striking 3-dimensional depth effect. (1) Linear perspective is produced by the converging lines of the plank. (2) The people and objects in the background are smaller than those in the foreground (relative size). (3) The background is in a higher horizontal plane than the foreground. (4, 5) The objects in the background are less detailed than the "closer" ones (texture and clarity). (6) The people and objects in the foreground cut off parts of those "behind" them in the background (interposition). (7) Light and shadow are also used to create a depth effect.

your eyes with their tips about 1 inch apart. Focus on your fingers first, then focus beyond them across the room. Doing so will produce the image of a third finger between the other two. This third finger will disappear if you close either eye.

Most of us are familiar with the delightful depth experiences provided by View-Master slides and 3-D movies watched through special glasses. These devices make use of the principle of **binocular disparity,** *in which each eye sees a slightly different image.* Within the brain, the visual input from the two eyes is analyzed by feature detectors that are attuned to depth (Howard, 2002; Livingstone & Hubel, 1994). Some of the feature detectors respond only to stimuli that are either in front of or behind the point on which we are fixing our gaze. The responses of these depth-sensitive neurons are integrated to produce our perception of depth (Goldstein, 2002).

A second binocular distance cue, **convergence,** *is produced by feedback from the muscles that turn your eyes inward to view a close object.* You can experience this cue by holding a finger about 1 foot in front of your face and then moving it slowly toward you. Messages sent to your brain by the eye muscles provide it with a depth cue.

PERCEPTION OF MOVEMENT

The perception of movement is a complex process, sometimes requiring the brain to integrate information from several different senses. To demonstrate, hold a pen in front of your face. Now, while holding your head still, move the pen back and forth. You will perceive the pen as moving. Now hold the pen still and move your head back and forth at the same rate of speed. In both cases, the image of the pen moved across your retina in about the same way. But when you moved your head, your brain took into account input from your kinesthetic and vestibular systems and concluded that you were moving but the pen was not.

The primary cue for perceiving motion is the movement of the stimulus across the retina (Sekuler et al., 2002). Under optimal conditions, a retinal image need move only about one fifth the diameter of a single cone for us to detect movement (Nakayama & Tyler, 1981). The relative movement of an object against a structured background is also a movement cue (Gibson, 1979). For example, if you fixate on a bird in flight, the relative motion of the bird against its background is a strong cue for perceived speed of movement.

The illusion of smooth motion can be produced if we arrange for the sequential appearance of two or more stimuli. Gestalt psychologist Max Wertheimer (1912) demonstrated this in his studies of **stroboscopic movement,** *illusory movement produced when a light is briefly flashed in darkness and then, a few milliseconds later, another light is flashed nearby.* If the timing is just right, the first light seems to move from one place to the other in a manner indistinguishable from real movement.

Stroboscopic movement (termed the "phi phenomenon" by Wertheimer) has been used commercially in numerous ways. For example, think of the strings of successively illuminated lights on theater marquees that seem to move endlessly around the border or that spell out messages in a moving script. Stroboscopic movement is also the principle behind motion pictures, which consist of a series of still photographs, or frames, that are projected on a screen in rapid succession with dark intervals in between (Figure 4.42). The rate at which the frames are projected is critical to our perception of smooth movement. Early movies, such as the silent films of the 1920s, projected the stills at only 16 frames per second, and the movements appeared fast and jerky. Today the usual speed is 24 frames per second, which more perfectly produces an illusion of smooth movement. Television presents at 30 images per second.

FIGURE 4.42

Stroboscopic movement is produced in moving pictures as a series of still photographs projected at a rate of 24 per second.

(a)

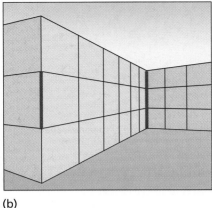

(b)

FIGURE 4.43

Two examples of the Ponzo illusion. Which lines in (a) and (b) are longer? Measure them and see. The distance cues provided by the converging railroad tracks and the walls affect size perception and disrupt size constancy.

ILLUSIONS: FALSE PERCEPTUAL HYPOTHESES

Our analysis of perceptual schemas, hypotheses, sets, and constancies allows us to understand some interesting perceptual experiences known as **illusions,** *compelling but incorrect perceptions.* Such perceptions can be understood as erroneous perceptual hypotheses about the nature of a stimulus. Illusions are not only intriguing and sometimes delightful visual experiences, but they also provide important information about how our perceptual processes work under normal conditions (Gregory, 2005).

Ironically, most visual illusions can be attributed to perceptual constancies that ordinarily help us perceive more accurately (Frisby, 1980). For example, size constancy results in part from our ability to use distance cues to judge the size of objects. But as we saw in the discussion of the moon illusion, distance cues can sometimes fool us. In the Ponzo illusion, shown in Figure 4.43a, the depth cues of linear perspective (the tracks converging) and height of the horizontal plane provide distance cues that make the upper bar appear farther away than the lower bar. Because it seems farther away, the perceptual system concludes that the bar in the background must be larger than the bar in the foreground, despite the fact that the two bars cast retinal images of the same size. The same occurs in the vertical arrangement seen in Figure 4.43b.

Distance cues can be manipulated to create other size illusions. To illustrate this, Adelbert Ames constructed a special room. Viewed through a peephole with one eye, the room's scene presents a startling size reversal (Figure 4.44a). Our

▶ **Focus 25**
What is an illusion? How are constancies and context involved in visual illusions?

FIGURE 4.44

A size illusion. (a) The Ames Room produces a striking size illusion because it is designed to appear rectangular. (b) The room, however, is actually trapezoidal, and the figure on the left is actually much farther away from the viewer than the one on the right and thus appears smaller. We perceive the boy as if he were the purple figure, making him appear very large.

(a)

(b)

The long lines are actually parallel, but the small lines make them appear crooked.

FIGURE 4.45

Context-produced geometric illusions.

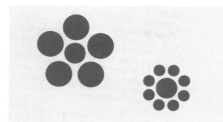

Which inner circle is larger? Check and see.

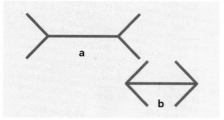

The Müller-Lyer illusion. Which line, a or b, is longer? Compare them with a ruler.

perceptual system assumes that the room has a normal rectangular shape because, in fact, most rooms do. Monocular depth cues do not allow us to see that, in reality, the left corner of the room is twice as far away as the right corner (Figure 4.44b). As a result, size constancy breaks down, and we base our judgment of size on the sizes of the retinal images cast by the two people.

The study of perceptual constancies shows that our perceptual hypotheses are strongly influenced by the context, or surroundings, in which a stimulus occurs. Figure 4.45 shows some examples of how context can produce illusory perceptions.

Some of the most intriguing perceptual distortions are produced when monocular depth cues are manipulated to produce a figure or scene whose individual parts make sense but whose overall organization is "impossible" in terms of our existing perceptual schemas. Figure 4.46 shows three impossible figures. In each case, our brain extracts information about depth from the individual features of the objects, but when this information is put together and matched with our existing schemas, the percept that results simply doesn't make sense. The "devil's tuning fork," for example, could not exist in our universe. It is a two-dimensional image containing paradoxical depth cues. Our brain, however, automatically interprets it as a three-dimensional object and matches it with its internal schema of

a fork—a bad fit indeed. The never-ending staircase provides another compelling example of an impossible scene that seems perfectly reasonable when we focus only on its individual elements.

Illusions are not only personally and scientifically interesting, but they can have important real-life implications. Our "Research Close-Up" describes one scientist's search for an illusion having life-and-death implications.

 ### What Do You Think?

EXPLAIN THIS STRIKING ILLUSION

We'd like you to experience a truly interesting illusion. To do so, all you need is a piece of fairly heavy paper and a little patience.

Fold the piece of paper lengthwise down the middle and set it on a table with one of the ends facing you like an open tent. Close one eye and, from slightly above the object, stare at a point midway along the top fold of the paper. At first the object looks like a tent, but after a while the paper will suddenly "stand up" and look like a corner viewed from the inside. When this happens, gently move your head back and forth while continuing to view with one eye. The movement will produce a striking perception. Can you explain what you now see? For a discussion of this illusion, see page 148.

FIGURE 4.46

Things that couldn't be. Monocular depth cues are cleverly manipulated to produce an impossible triangle, a never-ending staircase, and the "devil's tuning fork."

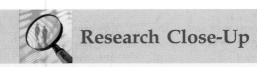

Research Close-Up　　Stalking a Deadly Illusion

SOURCE: CONRAD L. KRAFT (1978). A psychophysical contribution to air safety: Simulator studies of illusions in night visual approaches. In H. L. PICK, JR., H. W. LEIBOWITZ, J. E. SINGER, A. STEINSCHNEIDER, and H. W. STEVENSON (Eds.), *Psychology: From research to practice.* New York: Plenum.

INTRODUCTION

When the Boeing Company introduced the 727 jet airliner in the mid-1960s, it was the latest word in aviation technology. The plane performed well in test flights, but four fatal crashes soon after it was placed in service raised fears that there might be a serious flaw in its design.

The first accident occurred as a 727 made its approach to Chicago over Lake Michigan on a clear night. The plane plunged into the lake 19 miles offshore. About a month later, another 727 glided in over the Ohio River to land in Cincinnati. Unaccountably, it struck the ground about 12 feet below the runway elevation and burst into flames. The third accident occurred as an aircraft approached Salt Lake City over dark land. The lights of the city twinkled in the distance, but the plane made too rapid a descent and crashed short of the runway. Months later, a Japanese airliner approached Tokyo at night. The flight ended tragically as the plane, its landing gear not yet lowered, struck the waters of Tokyo Bay 6 miles from the runway.

Analysis of these four accidents, as well as others, suggested a common pattern. All occurred at night under clear weather conditions, so the pilots were operating under visual flight rules rather than performing instrument landings. In each instance, the plane was approaching city lights over dark areas of water or land. In all cases, the lights in the background terrain sloped upward to varying degrees. Finally, all of the planes crashed short of the runway. These observations led a Boeing industrial psychologist, Conrad L. Kraft, to suspect that the cause of the crashes might be pilot error based on some sort of visual illusion.

METHOD

To test this possibility, Boeing engineers constructed an apparatus to simulate night landings (Figure 4.47). It consisted of a cockpit and a miniature lighted city named Nightertown. The city moved toward the cockpit on computer-controlled rollers, and it could be tilted to simulate various terrain slopes. The pilot could control simulated air speed and rate of climb and descent, and the Nightertown scene was controlled by the pilot's responses just as a true visual scene would be.

The participants were 12 experienced Boeing flight instructors who made virtual-reality landings at Nightertown under systematically varied conditions created by the computerized simulator. All of their landings were visual landings so as to be able to test whether a visual illusion was occurring. Every aspect of their approach and the manner in which they controlled the aircraft were measured precisely.

FIGURE 4.47

Conrad Kraft, a Boeing psychologist, created an apparatus to study how visual cues can affect the simulated landings of airline pilots. Pilots approached Nightertown in a simulated cockpit. The computer-controlled city could be tilted to reproduce the illusion thought to be responsible for fatal air crashes.

RESULTS

The flight instructors' landings were nearly flawless until Kraft duplicated the conditions of the fatal crashes by having the pilots approach an upward-sloping distant city over a dark area. When this occurred, the pilots were unable to detect the upward slope, assumed that the background city was flat, and consistently overestimated their approach altitude. On a normal landing, the preferred altitude at 4.5 miles from the runway is about 1,240 feet. As Figure 4.48 shows, the pilots approached at about this altitude when the simulated city was in a flat position. But when it was sloped upward, 11 of the 12 experienced pilot instructors crashed about 4.5 miles short of the runway.

CRITICAL DISCUSSION

This study, considered a classic by many psychologists, shows the value of studying behavior under highly controlled conditions and with precise measurements. By simulating the conditions under which the fatal crashes had occurred, Kraft identified the visual illusion that was the source of pilot error. He showed that the perceptual hypotheses of the flight instructors, like those of the pilots involved in the real crashes, were tragically incorrect. It would have been ironic if one of the finest jetliners ever built had been removed from service because of presumed mechanical defects while other aircraft remained aloft and at risk for tragedy.

Continued

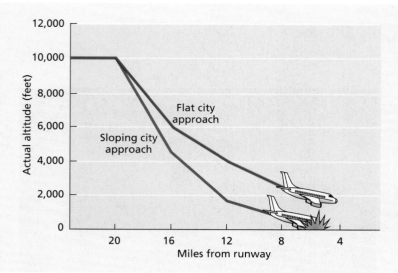

Kraft's research not only saved the 727 from months—or perhaps years—of needless mechanical analysis but, more important, it also identified a potentially deadly illusion and the precise conditions under which it occurred. On the basis of Kraft's findings, Boeing recommended that pilots attend carefully to their instruments when landing at night, even under perfect weather conditions. Today, commercial airline pilots are required to make instrument landings not only at night but also during the day.

FIGURE 4.48

Misperceptions of experienced pilots. The illusion created by upward-sloping city lights caused even highly experienced pilots to overestimate their altitude, and 11 of the 12 flight instructors crashed short of the runway. When the lights were flat, all the pilots made perfect approaches. SOURCE: Based on Kraft, 1978.

IN REVIEW

■ Monocular cues to judge distance and depth include linear perspective, relative size, height in the horizontal plane, texture, and clarity. Depth perception also occurs through the monocular cues of light and shadow patterns, interposition, and motion parallax.

■ Binocular disparity occurs as slightly different images are viewed by each eye and acted on by feature detectors for depth. Convergence of the eyes provides a second binocular cue.

■ The basis for perception of movement is absolute movement of a stimulus across the retina or relative movement of an object in relation to its background. Stroboscopic movement is illusory.

■ Illusions are erroneous perceptions. They may be regarded as incorrect perceptual hypotheses. Perceptual constancies help produce many illusions, including the moon illusion and a variety of other context-produced illusions.

EXPERIENCE, CRITICAL PERIODS, AND PERCEPTUAL DEVELOPMENT

Development of sensory and perceptual systems results from the interplay of biological and experiential factors. Genes program biological development, but this development is also influenced by environmental experiences. For example, if you were to be blinded in an accident and later learned to read braille, the area of the somatosensory cortex that is devoted to the fingertips would enlarge over time as it borrowed other neurons to increase its sensitivity (Pool, 1994). By the time they are old enough to crawl, children placed on a "visual cliff" formed by a glass-covered table that suddenly drops off beneath the glass will not ordinarily venture over the edge (Figure 4.49). This aversion may result from the interaction of innate depth-perception abilities and previous experience (Gibson & Walk, 1960).

What might a lifetime of experience in a limited environment do to perceptual abilities that seem innate? Sometimes, conditions under which people live create natural experiments that help provide answers. For example, the Ba Mbuti pygmies, who live in the rain forests of Central Africa, spend their lives in a closed-in green world of densely packed trees without open spaces. The anthropologist C. M. Turnbull (1961) once brought a man named Kenge out of the forest to the edge of a vast plain. A herd of buffalo grazed in the distance. To Turnbull's surprise, Kenge remarked that he had never seen insects of that kind. When told that they were buffalo, not insects, Kenge was deeply offended and felt that Turnbull was insulting his intelligence. To prove his point, Turnbull drove Kenge in his jeep toward the animals. Kenge stared in amazement as the "insects" grew into buffalo before his eyes. To explain his perceptual experience to himself, he concluded that witchcraft was being used to fool him. Kenge's misperception occurred as a failure in size constancy. Having lived in an environment without open spaces, he had no experience in judging the size of objects at great distances.

As noted earlier, when light passes through the lens of the eye, the image projected on the

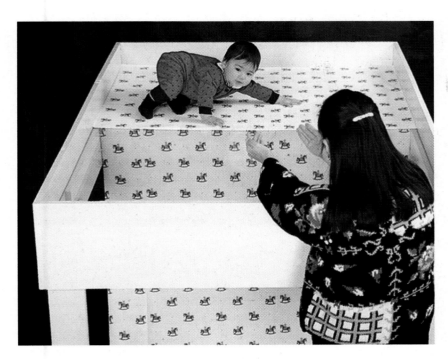

FIGURE 4.49

Eleanor Gibson and Richard Walk constructed this "visual cliff" with a glass-covered drop-off to determine whether crawling infants and newborn animals can perceive depth. Even when coaxed by their mothers, young children refuse to venture onto the glass over the cliff. Newborn animals also avoid the cliff.

retina is reversed, so that right is left and up is down. What would happen if you were to wear a special set of glasses that undid this natural reversal of the visual image and created a world like that in Figure 4.50? In 1896 perception researcher George Stratton did just that, possibly becoming the first human ever to have a right-side-up image on his retina while standing upright. Reversing how nature and a lifetime of experience had fashioned his perceptual system disoriented Stratton at first. The ground and his feet were now up, and he had to put on his hat from the bottom up. He had to reach to his left to touch something he saw on his right. Stratton suffered from nausea and couldn't eat or get around for several days. Gradually, however, he adapted to his inverted world, and by the end of 8 days he was able to successfully reach for objects and walk around. Years later, people who wore inverting lenses for longer periods of time did the same. Some were able to ski down mountain slopes or ride motorcycles while wearing the lenses, even though their visual world remained upside down and never became normal for them. When they removed the inverting lenses, they had some initial problems but soon readapted to the normal visual world (Dolezal, 1982).

CROSS-CULTURAL RESEARCH ON PERCEPTION

As far as we know, humans come into the world with the same perceptual abilities regardless of where they are born. From that point on, however,

the culture they grow up in helps determine the kinds of perceptual learning experiences they have. Cross-cultural research can help identify which aspects of perception occur in all people, regardless of their culture, as well as perceptual differences that result from cultural experiences (Deregowski, 1989). Although there are far more perceptual similarities

▶ **Focus 26**
What evidence shows that cultural factors can influence perceptual interpretations, constancies, and susceptibility to illusions?

FIGURE 4.50

A challenging world. Inverted vision would create a world that looks like this. How would you make your way around in this upside-down environment where right is left and left is right? Adaptation to such a world is possible but challenging.

(a)

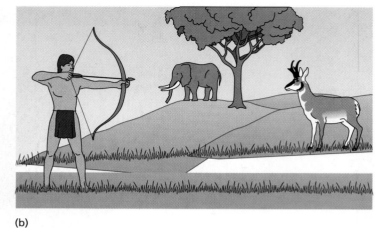

(b)

FIGURE 4.51

Does culture influence perception? (a) What is the object above the woman's head? East Africans had a far different answer than did North Americans and Europeans. (b) Cultural differences also occurred when people were asked which animal the archer was about to shoot. SOURCES: (a) Adapted from Gregory & Gombrich, 1973; (b) Adapted from Hudson, 1960.

than differences among the peoples of the world, the differences that do exist show us that perception can indeed be influenced by experience.

Consider the perception of a picture that depends on both the nature of the picture and characteristics of the perceiver. In Figure 4.51a, what is the object above the woman's head? In one study, most North Americans and Europeans instantly identified it as a window. They also tended to see the family sitting inside a dwelling. But when the same picture was shown to East Africans, nearly all perceived the object as a basket or box that the woman was balancing on her head. To them, the family was sitting outside under a tree (Gregory & Gombrich, 1973). These interpretations were more consistent with their own cultural experiences.

In our earlier discussion of monocular depth cues, we used paintings such as the one in Figure 4.41 to illustrate monocular depth perception. In Western culture, we have constant exposure to two-dimensional pictures that our perceptual system effortlessly turns into three-dimensional perceptions. Do people who grow up in cultures where they are not exposed to pictures have the same perceptions? When presented with the picture in Figure 4.51b and asked which animal the hunter was about to shoot, tribal African people answered that he was about to kill the "baby elephant." They did not use the monocular cues that cause Westerners to perceive the man as hunting the antelope and to view the elephant as an adult animal in the distance (Hudson, 1960).

Illusions occur when one of our common perceptual hypotheses is in error. Earlier we showed you the Müller-Lyer illusion (see Figure 4.45), in which a line appears longer when the V-shaped lines at its ends radiate outward rather than inward. Westerners are very susceptible to this illusion. They have learned that in their "carpentered" envi-

ronment, which has many corners and square shapes, inward-facing lines occur when corners are closer and outward-facing lines occur when they are farther away (Figure 4.52). But when people from other cultures who live in more rounded environments are shown the Müller-Lyer stimuli, they are more likely to correctly perceive the lines as equal in length (Segall et al., 1966). They do not fall prey to a perceptual hypothesis that normally is correct in an environment like ours that is filled with sharp corners but wrong when applied to the lines in the Müller-Lyer illusion (Deregowski, 1989).

Cultural learning affects perceptions in other modalities as well. Our perceptions of tastes, odors, and textures are strongly influenced by our cultural experiences. A taste that might produce nausea in one culture may be considered delicious in another. The taste and gritty texture experienced when chewing a large raw insect or the rubbery texture of a fish eye may appeal far less to you than it would to a person from a culture in which that food is a staple.

FIGURE 4.52

Which vertical line is longer? Perceptual experiences within our "carpentered" environment make us susceptible to the Müller-Lyer illusion (see Figure 4.45), which appears here in vertical form. Again, the vertical lines are the same physical length.

CRITICAL PERIODS: THE ROLE OF EARLY EXPERIENCE

The examples in the preceding section suggest that experience is essential for the development of perceptual abilities. For some aspects of perception, there are also **critical periods** *during which certain kinds of experiences must occur if perceptual abilities and the brain mechanisms that underlie them are to develop normally.* If a critical period passes without the experience occurring, it is too late to undo the deficit that results.

Earlier we saw that the visual cortex has feature detectors composed of neurons that respond only to lines at particular angles. What would happen if newborn animals grew up in a world in which they saw some angles but not others? In a classic experiment, British researchers Colin Blakemore and Grahame Cooper (1970) created such a world for newborn kittens. The animals were raised in the dark except for a 5-hour period each day during which they were placed in round chambers that had either vertical or horizontal stripes on the walls. Figure 4.53a shows one of the kittens in a vertically striped chamber. A special collar prevented the kittens from seeing their own bodies while they were in the chamber, guaranteeing that they saw nothing but stripes.

When the kittens were 5 months old, Blakemore and Cooper presented them with bars of light at differing angles and used microelectrodes to test the electrical responses of individual feature-detector cells in their visual cortex. The results for the kittens raised in the vertically striped environment are shown in Figure 4.53b. As you can see, the kittens had no cells that fired in response to horizontal stimuli, resulting in visual impairments. They also acted as if they could not see a pencil when it was held in a horizontal position and moved up and down in front of them. However, as soon as the pencil was rotated to a vertical position, the animals began to follow it with their eyes as it was moved back and forth.

As you might expect, the animals raised in the horizontally striped environment showed the opposite effect. They had no feature detectors for vertical stimuli and did not seem to see them. Thus the cortical neurons of both groups of kittens developed in accordance with the stimulus features of their environments.

Other visual abilities also require early exposure to the relevant stimuli. Yoichi Sugita (2004) raised infant monkeys in rooms illuminated with only monochromatic light. As adults, these monkeys were clearly deficient in color perception. They had particular difficulty with color con-

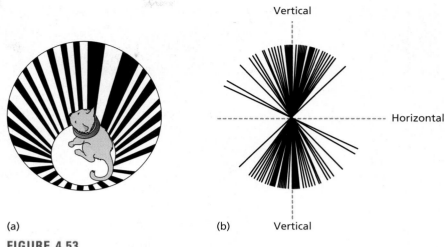

(a)   (b)

FIGURE 4.53

Effects of visual deprivation. (a) Kittens raised in a vertically striped chamber such as the one shown here lacked cortical cells that fired in response to horizontal stimuli. (b) The kittens' perceptual "holes" are easily seen in this diagram, which shows the orientation angles that triggered nerve impulses from feature detectors. SOURCE: Adapted from Blakemore & Cooper, 1970.

stancy, being unable to recognize the same colors under changing brightness conditions.

Some perceptual abilities are influenced more than others by restricted stimulation. In other research, monkeys, chimpanzees, and kittens were raised in an environment devoid of shapes. The animals distinguished differences in size, brightness, and color almost as well as normally reared animals do, but for the rest of their lives they performed poorly on more complex tasks, such as distinguishing different types of objects and geometric shapes (Riesen, 1965).

RESTORED SENSORY CAPACITY

Suppose it had been possible to restore Helen Keller's vision when she reached adulthood. What would she have seen? Could she have perceived visually the things that she had learned to identify through her other senses?

Unfortunately, it was not possible to provide Helen Keller with the miracle of restored vision. However, scientists have studied the experiences of other visually impaired people who acquired the ability to see later in life. For example, people born with cataracts grow up in a visual world without form. The clouded lenses of their eyes permit them to perceive light but not patterns or shapes. One such person was Virgil, who had been almost totally blind since childhood. He read braille, enjoyed listening to sports on the radio and conversing with other people, and had adjusted quite well to his disability. At the urging of his fiancée, Virgil agreed to undergo surgery to remove his thick cataracts. The day after the surgery,

▶ **Focus 27**
How do studies of restricted stimulation and restored vision illustrate the role of critical periods in perceptual development?

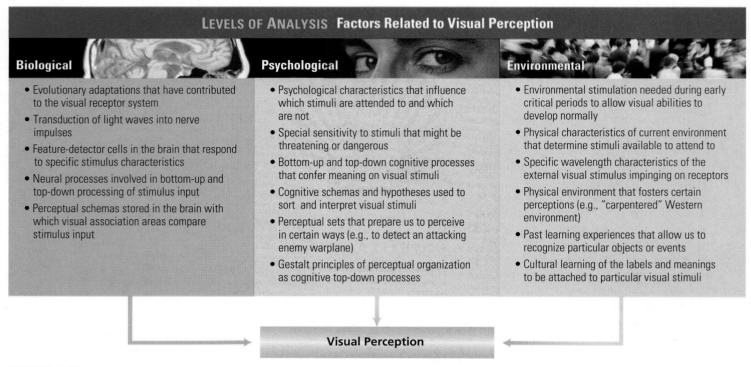

LEVELS OF ANALYSIS Factors Related to Visual Perception

Biological

- Evolutionary adaptations that have contributed to the visual receptor system
- Transduction of light waves into nerve impulses
- Feature-detector cells in the brain that respond to specific stimulus characteristics
- Neural processes involved in bottom-up and top-down processing of stimulus input
- Perceptual schemas stored in the brain with which visual association areas compare stimulus input

Psychological

- Psychological characteristics that influence which stimuli are attended to and which are not
- Special sensitivity to stimuli that might be threatening or dangerous
- Bottom-up and top-down cognitive processes that confer meaning on visual stimuli
- Cognitive schemas and hypotheses used to sort and interpret visual stimuli
- Perceptual sets that prepare us to perceive in certain ways (e.g., to detect an attacking enemy warplane)
- Gestalt principles of perceptual organization as cognitive top-down processes

Environmental

- Environmental stimulation needed during early critical periods to allow visual abilities to develop normally
- Physical characteristics of current environment that determine stimuli available to attend to
- Specific wavelength characteristics of the external visual stimulus impinging on receptors
- Physical environment that fosters certain perceptions (e.g., "carpentered" Western environment)
- Past learning experiences that allow us to recognize particular objects or events
- Cultural learning of the labels and meanings to be attached to particular visual stimuli

Visual Perception

FIGURE 4.54

Levels of analysis: Factors related to visual perception.

his bandages were removed. Neurologist Oliver Sacks (1999) recounts what happened next.

> There was light, there was color, all mixed up, meaningless, a blur. Then out of the blur came a voice that said, "Well?" Then, and only then . . . did he finally realize that this chaos of light and shadow was a face—and, indeed, the face of his surgeon. . . . His retina and optic nerve were active, transmitting impulses, but his brain could make no sense of them. (p. 132)

Virgil was never able to adjust to his new visual world. He had to touch objects in order to identify them. He had to be led through his own house and would quickly become disoriented if he deviated from his path. Eventually, Virgil lost his sight once again. This time, however, he regarded his blindness as a gift, a release from a sighted world that was bewildering to him.

Virgil's experiences are characteristic of people who have their vision restored later in life. A German physician, Marius von Senden (1960), compiled data on patients born with cataracts who were tested soon after their cataracts were surgically removed in adulthood. These people were immediately able to perceive figure-ground relations, to scan objects visually, and to follow moving targets with their eyes, indicating that such abilities are innate. However, they could not visually identify objects, such as eating utensils, that they were familiar with through touch; nor were they able to distinguish simple geometric figures without counting the corners or tracing the figures with their fingers.

After several weeks of training, the patients were able to identify simple objects by sight, but their perceptual constancies were very poor. Often they were unable to recognize the same shape in another color, even though they could discriminate between colors. Years later, some patients could identify only a few of the faces of people they knew well. Many also had great difficulty judging distances. Apparently, no amount of subsequent experience could make up for their lack of visual experience during the critical period of childhood.

All of these lines of evidence—cross-cultural perceptual differences, animal studies involving visual deprivation, and observations of congenitally impaired people whose vision has been restored—suggest that biological and experiential factors interact in complex ways. Some of our perceptual abilities are at least partially present at birth, but experience plays an important role in their normal development. How innate and experiential factors interact promises to be a continued focus of perception research. Thus, perception is very much a biopsychological process whose mysteries are best explored by examining them from biological, psychological, and environmental levels of analysis (Figure 4.54).

IN REVIEW

- Perceptual development involves both physical maturation and learning. Some perceptual abilities are innate or develop shortly after birth, whereas others require particular experiences early in life in order to develop.

- Cultural factors can influence certain aspects of perception, including picture perception and susceptibility to illusions. However, many aspects of perception seem constant across cultures.

- Visual-deprivation studies, manipulation of visual input, and studies of restored vision have shown that the normal biological development of the perceptual system depends on certain sensory experiences at early periods of development.

SOME FINAL REFLECTIONS

Suppose someone were to be born cut off not only from sight and sound, as Helen Keller was, but from all internal and external sensory stimulation. What would that person's conscious life be like? With the brain deprived of all sensory input from world and body, what mental processes could exist? What knowledge could accrue? What memories could form? Would the brain itself atrophy as it was deprived of the sensory input needed for neuronal development and synaptic network formation?

As far as we know, such a scenario has never occurred. However, imagining such a condition does bring home the vital role our sensory and perceptual systems play in being a functioning organism. Leonardo da Vinci was indeed correct when he proclaimed, "All knowledge has its origin in our perceptions." Nature has given us specialized sensors that allow the brain to convert the many kinds of energy into the common language of nerve impulses through the process of transduction, and it has given us a brain that can take all of this input—often from more than one sense—and construct our perceptual experiences.

Sensation and perception are the basis for our existence as sentient, conscious creatures. In the next chapter, we will explore in greater detail the varieties of consciousness. As we do so, reflect back occasionally on what you've learned in this chapter and ask yourself what sensory and perceptual building blocks underlie such phenomena as sleep and wakefulness, drug- and hypnotically produced alterations in conscious experience, and other aspects of our conscious life.

KEY TERMS AND CONCEPTS

Each term has been boldfaced and defined in the chapter on the page indicated in parentheses.

absolute threshold (p. 108)
amplitude (p. 120)
basilar membrane (p. 121)
binocular depth cues (p. 137)
binocular disparity (p. 138)
bottom-up processing (p. 130)
cochlea (p. 121)
conduction deafness (p. 123)
cones (p. 112)
convergence (p. 138)
critical periods (p. 145)
dark adaptation (p. 114)
decibel (dB; p. 120)
decision criterion (p. 108)
difference threshold (p. 110)
dual-process theory (p. 116)
feature detectors (p. 118)
figure-ground relations (p. 132)
fovea (p. 113)
frequency (p. 120)
frequency theory of pitch perception (p. 122)

Gestalt laws of perceptual organization (p. 133)
gustation (p. 124)
Hering's opponent-process theory (p. 116)
hertz (Hz; p. 120)
illusion (p. 139)
inattentional blindness (p. 131)
kinesthesis (p. 126)
lens (p. 112)
menstrual synchrony (p. 125)
monocular depth cues (p. 137)
nerve deafness (p. 123)
olfaction (p. 124)
olfactory bulb (p. 125)
optic nerve (p. 113)
organ of Corti (p. 121)
perception (p. 107)
perceptual constancies (p. 135)
perceptual schema (p. 134)
perceptual set (p. 135)
pheromones (p. 125)

photopigments (p. 114)
place theory of pitch perception (p. 122)
psychophysics (p. 107)
retina (p. 112)
rods (p. 112)
sensation (p. 107)
sensory adaptation (p. 110)
sensory prosthetic devices (p. 127)
signal detection theory (p. 108)
stroboscopic movement (p. 138)
subliminal stimulus (p. 109)
synesthesia (p. 106)
taste buds (p. 124)
top-down processing (p. 130)
transduction (p. 111)
vestibular sense (p. 126)
visual acuity (p. 114)
Weber's law (p. 110)
Young-Helmholtz trichromatic theory (p. 115)

148   CHAPTER 4

? What Do You Think?

NAVIGATING IN FOG: PROFESSOR MAYER'S TOPOPHONE (PAGE 123)

The device shown in Figure 4.20 made use of two principles of sound localization. First, because the two ear receptors were much larger than human ears, they could capture more sound waves and funnel them to the sailor's ears. Second, the wide spacing between the two receptors increased the time difference between the sound's arrival at the two human ears, thus increasing directional sensitivity.

WHY DOES THAT RISING MOON LOOK SO BIG? (PAGE 136)

To begin with, let's emphasize the obvious: The moon is not actually larger when it's on the horizon. Photographs show that the size of the image cast on the retina is exactly the same in both cases. So what psychologists call the moon illusion must be created by our perceptual system. Though not completely understood, the illusion seems to be a false perception caused by cues that ordinarily contribute to maintaining size constancy. The chief suspect is apparent distance, which figures importantly in our size judgments. One theory holds that the moon looks bigger as it's rising over the horizon because we use objects in our field of vision, such as trees, buildings, and landscape features to estimate its distance. Experiments have shown that objects look farther away when viewed through filled spaces than they do when viewed through empty spaces (such as the sky overhead). Filled space can make objects look as much as 2.5 to 4 times farther away. According to the theory, the perceptual system basically says, "If the size of the retinal image is the same but it's farther away, then it must be bigger."

This explanation can't be the whole story, however, because some people perceive the moon on the horizon as being closer, rather than farther away. If something the same size seems closer, it will look larger even though it isn't. It may be that there are individual differences in the size-judgment processes that cause the illusion, so that no single explanation applies to everybody.

EXPLAIN THIS STRIKING ILLUSION (PAGE 140)

To analyze your experience, it is important to understand that both the "tent" and the "corner" cast identical images on your retina. After perceiving the tent for a while, your brain shifted to the second perceptual hypothesis, as it did in response to the Necker cube shown in Figure 4.37. When the object looked like a tent, all the depth information was consistent with that perception. But when you began to see it as a corner and then moved your head slowly back and forth, the object seemed to twist and turn as if it were made of rubber. This occurred because when you moved, the image of the near point of the fold moved across your retina faster than the image of the far point. This is the normal pattern of stimulation for points at different depths and is known as motion parallax. Thus when you were seeing a tent, the monocular cue of motion parallax was consistent with the shape of the object. But when the object was later seen as standing upright, all the points along the fold appeared to be the same distance away, yet they were moving at different rates of speed! The only way your brain could maintain its "corner" perception in the face of the motion parallax cues was to see the object as twisting and turning. Again, as in other illusions, forcing all of the sensory data to fit the perceptual hypothesis produced an unusual experience.

CHAPTER FIVE

States of Consciousness

CHAPTER OUTLINE

Our normal waking consciousness is but one special type of consciousness, whilst all about it, parted from it by the filmiest of screens, there lie potential forms of consciousness entirely different.

—WILLIAM JAMES

T hree unrelated people, whom we'll call Sondra, Jason, and Ellen, sought treatment for an unusual problem: eating while asleep. They would rise from bed several times each night and sleepwalk to the kitchen. Sondra would

> consume cat food or salt sandwiches, buttered cigarettes and odd concoctions prepared in a blender. . . . She frequently binged on large quantities of peanut butter, butter, salt and sugar. . . . Once she awakened while struggling to open a bottle of ammonia cleaning fluid, which she was prepared to drink on account of being thirsty. (Schenck et al., 1991, p. 430)

While sleepwalking, Jason and Ellen also consumed odd foods (such as raw bacon), and sometimes Jason spoke coherently with his wife. Upon awakening, they couldn't remember their experiences, but empty packages and half-eaten food indicated that something was amiss.

After evaluation by sleep specialists, Sondra was treated with medication and Jason was referred to his primary physician. Neither drugs nor psychotherapy helped Ellen, so a new plan was tried: locking the kitchen door before turning in, putting the key in a hard-to-find location, and placing crackers and a pitcher of water by the bed. Usually, when Ellen awakens in the morning, the crackers and water are gone, and she has no memory of having consumed them (Whyte & Kavey, 1990).

■ ■ ■ ■ ■

A t age 34, D. F. lost consciousness and suffered brain damage from carbon-monoxide exposure. As psychologist Melvin Goodale (2000) describes, when D. F. regained consciousness,

> she was unable to recognize the faces of her relatives and friends or identify the visual form of common objects. In fact, she could not even tell the difference between simple geometric shapes such as a square and a triangle. At the same time, she had no difficulty recognizing people from their voices or identifying objects placed in her hands; her perceptual problems appeared to be exclusively visual. (p. 367)

D. F.'s condition is called **visual agnosia**, *an inability to visually recognize objects*. Visual agnosia is not blindness. D. F. can see, and brain imaging has revealed that her primary visual cortex is largely undamaged. Rather, regions that are damaged have "left her unable to perceive the size, shape, and orientation of objects" (Goodale, 2000).

But how, then, is D. F. able to walk across a room while easily avoiding obstacles? And if she can't consciously perceive the difference in shape and size between, say, a spoon and a glass, how does she know to open her hand to the proper width to grasp objects? On a laboratory task, how is D. F. able to insert an object into a tilted rectangular slot when, just moments before, she could not consciously recognize the slot's orientation (see Figure 5.1)?

Sondra, Jason, and Ellen's sleepeating and D. F.'s visual agnosia are clear departures from our normal state of conscious awareness. Yet their experiences contain features that are not as far removed from our daily existence as we might think.

How can someone be asleep yet find the kitchen and prepare food? Well, consider this: Why don't you fall out of bed at night? You are not consciously aware of your many postural shifts when you are sound asleep, yet a part of you somehow

FIGURE 5.1

Perception without conscious awareness. A rectangular slot was rotated to different angles on a series of trials. When asked simply to hold and tilt a rectangular card to match the slot's angle, D. F. performed poorly. She could not consciously recognize the orientation of the slot. Despite this, when asked to rapidly insert the card into the slot, as illustrated here, she performed well. SOURCE: Goodale, 1995.

(a)

(b)

FIGURE 5.2

(a) During a Sufi religious ceremony in Istanbul, Turkey, whirling dervishes perform a spinning dance—a prayer in motion—that induces an altered state of consciousness. (b) Buddhists believe that meditation produces inner peace, facilitates insight and enlightenment, and opens the path to different dimensions of consciousness.

knows where the edge of the bed is. And what of D. F.'s ability, while awake, to avoid obstacles and grasp objects without conscious awareness of their shape or size? Again, consider this: Have you ever spaced out while driving because you were deeply engrossed in thought? Suddenly you snap out of it, with no memory of the miles you've just driven. While you were consciously focused inward, some part of you—without conscious awareness—kept track of the road and controlled your hand movements at the wheel.

Philosopher David Chalmers (1995) notes that consciousness "is at once the most familiar thing in the world and the most mysterious." As we now explore, its mysteries range from normal waking states to sleep and dreams, drug-induced experiences, and beyond (Figure 5.2).

THE PUZZLE OF CONSCIOUSNESS

What is consciousness, and how does it arise within our brain? When psychology was founded in the late 1800s, its "great project" was to unravel some of the puzzles of consciousness (Natsoulas, 1999). This interest waned during behaviorism's mid-20th century dominance, but a resurgence of the cognitive and biological perspectives has led us to rethink long-standing conceptions about the mind.

CHARACTERISTICS OF CONSCIOUSNESS

In psychology, **consciousness** *is often defined as our moment-to-moment awareness of ourselves and our environment.* Among its characteristics, consciousness is:

- *subjective and private:* Other people cannot directly know what reality is for you, nor can you enter directly into their experience.

- *dynamic (ever changing):* We drift in and out of various states throughout each day. Moreover, though the stimuli of which we are aware constantly change, we typically experience consciousness as a continuously flowing stream of mental activity, rather than as disjointed perceptions and thoughts (James, 1890/1950).

- *self-reflective and central to our sense of self:* The mind is aware of its own consciousness. Thus no matter what your awareness is focused on—a lovely sunset or an itch on your back—you can reflect on the fact that you are the one who is conscious of it.

Finally, consciousness is *intimately connected with the process of selective attention*, discussed in Chapter 4. William James noted that "the mind is at every stage a theatre of simultaneous possibilities. Consciousness consists in. . . . the selection of some, and the suppression of the rest by the . . . agency of Attention" (1879, p. 13). **Selective attention** *is the process that focuses awareness on some stimuli to the exclusion of others.* If the mind is a theater of mental activity, then consciousness reflects whatever is illuminated at the moment—the bright spot on the stage—and selective attention is the spotlight or mechanism behind it (Baars, 1997).

MEASURING STATES OF CONSCIOUSNESS

Scientists who study consciousness must operationally define private inner states in terms of measurable responses. *Self-report measures* ask

▶ **Focus 1**
Describe the basic characteristics of consciousness. How are states of consciousness measured?

FIGURE 5.3

Gordon Gallup (1970) exposed 4 chimps to a mirror. By day 3 they used it to inspect hard-to-see parts of their own bodies and began making odd faces at themselves in the mirror. To further test whether the chimps knew the mirror image was their own reflection, Gallup anesthetized them and put a red mark on each of their foreheads. Later, with no mirror, the chimps rarely touched the red mark. But upon seeing it when a mirror was introduced, they touched the red spot on their forehead almost 30 times in 30 minutes, suggesting that the chimps had some self-awareness. Using a similar test in which a red mark was placed on the tip of infants' noses, researchers found that infants begin to recognize themselves in a mirror around 18 months of age.

people to describe their inner experiences. They offer the most direct insight into a person's subjective experiences but are not always verifiable or possible to obtain. While asleep, most of us (thankfully) do not speak; nor can we fill out self-report questionnaires.

Behavioral measures record, among other things, performance on special tasks. By examining D. F.'s performance on the card-slot task under different conditions (see Figure 5.1), researchers concluded that despite being unable to consciously perceive the slot's orientation, her brain nonetheless processed this information. Behavioral measures are objective, but they require us to infer the person's state of mind. Figure 5.3 illustrates another clever behavioral measure.

Physiological measures establish the correspondence between bodily processes and mental states. Through electrodes attached to the scalp, the electroencephalograph (EEG) measures brain-wave patterns that reflect the ongoing electrical activity of large groups of neurons. Different patterns correspond to different states of consciousness, such as whether you are alert, relaxed, or in light or deep sleep. Brain-imaging techniques

allow scientists to more specifically examine brain regions and activity that underlie various mental states. Physiological measures cannot tell us what a person is experiencing subjectively, but they have been invaluable for probing the inner workings of the mind.

LEVELS OF CONSCIOUSNESS

Much of what occurs within your brain is beyond conscious access. You don't consciously perceive the brain processes that lull you to sleep, awaken you, or regulate your body temperature. You're aware of your thoughts but not of how your brain creates them. What else lies outside of conscious awareness?

The Freudian Viewpoint

A century ago Sigmund Freud (1900/1953) proposed that the human mind consists of three levels of awareness. The *conscious* mind contains thoughts and perceptions of which we are currently aware. *Preconscious* mental events are outside current awareness but can easily be recalled

► **Focus 2**
Contrast the psychodynamic and cognitive views of the mind, and controlled versus automatic processing.

under certain conditions. For instance, you may not have thought about a friend for years, but when someone mentions your friend's name, you become aware of pleasant memories. *Unconscious* events cannot be brought into conscious awareness under ordinary circumstances. Freud proposed that some unconscious content—such as unacceptable sexual and aggressive urges, traumatic memories, and threatening emotional conflicts—is *repressed;* that is, it is kept out of conscious awareness because it would arouse anxiety, guilt, or other negative emotions.

Behaviorists roundly criticized Freud's ideas. After all, they sought to explain behavior without invoking conscious mental processes, much less unconscious ones. Cognitive psychologists and many contemporary psychodynamic psychologists also take issue with specific aspects of Freud's theory. As psychodynamic psychologist Drew Westen (1998) notes, "Many aspects of Freudian theory are indeed out of date, and they should be. Freud died in 1939, and he has been slow to undertake further revisions" (p. 333). However, as we will see, research supports Freud's general premise that unconscious processes can affect behavior.

The Cognitive Viewpoint

Cognitive psychologists reject the notion of an unconscious mind driven by instinctive urges and repressed conflicts. Rather, they view conscious and unconscious mental life as complementary forms of information processing that work in harmony (Reisberg, 2001). To illustrate, consider how we perform everyday tasks.

Many activities, such as planning a vacation or studying, require **controlled (conscious) processing,** *the conscious use of attention and effort.* Other activities involve **automatic (unconscious) processing** *and can be performed without conscious awareness or effort.*

Automatic processing occurs most often when we carry out routine actions or very well-learned tasks, particularly under familiar circumstances (Ouellette & Wood, 1998). In everyday life, learning to write, drive, and type on a computer keyboard all involve controlled processing; at first you have to pay a lot of conscious attention to what you are doing as you learn. With practice, performance becomes more automatic and certain brain areas involved in conscious thought become less active (Jansma et al., 2001). Through years of practice, athletes and musicians program themselves to execute highly complex skills with a minimum of conscious thought.

Automatic processing, however, has a key disadvantage because it can reduce our chances of finding new ways to approach problems (Langer, 1989). Controlled processing is slower than automatic processing, but it is more flexible and open to change. Still, many well-learned behaviors seem to be performed faster and better when our mind is on autopilot, with controlled processing taking a backseat. The baseball player Yogi Berra captured this idea in his classic statement, "You can't think and hit at the same time." At tasks ranging from putting a golf ball to playing video games, experiments suggest that too much self-focused thinking can hurt task performance and cause people to choke under pressure (Beilcock & Carr, 2001).

Automatic processing also facilitates **divided attention,** *the capacity to attend to and perform more than one activity at the same time.* We can talk while we walk, type as we read, and so on. Yet divided attention has limits and is more difficult when two tasks require similar mental resources. For example, we cannot fully attend to separate messages delivered simultaneously through two earphones.

UNCONSCIOUS PERCEPTION AND INFLUENCE

The concept of unconscious information processing is widely accepted among psychologists today, but this was not always the case. It has taken painstaking research to demonstrate that stimuli can be perceived without conscious awareness and in turn can influence how we behave or feel. Let's look at some examples.

Visual Agnosia

Studies of people with brain damage can provide scientists with important insights into how the mind works. Recall that D. F., the woman with visual agnosia, could not consciously perceive the shape, size, or orientation of objects, yet she had little difficulty performing a card-insertion task and avoiding obstacles when she walked across a room. In order to perform these tasks so easily, her brain must have been processing accurate information about the shape, size, and angles of objects. And if she professed no conscious awareness of these properties, then this information processing must have occurred at an unconscious level (Goodale, 2000).

There are many types of visual agnosia. For example, people with *prosopagnosia* can visually recognize objects but not faces. When some of

 According to Freud, dreams are a key to the unconscious. Watch the video, "Freudian Interpretation of Dreams," in Chapter 5 of your CD to learn more about this theory.

▶ **Focus 3**
How do visual agnosia, blindsight, and priming illustrate unconscious processing?

these patients look in the mirror, they do not recognize their own faces. Despite this lack of conscious awareness, in laboratory tests these patients display different patterns of brain activity, autonomic arousal, and eye movements when they look at familiar rather than unfamiliar faces (Bauer & Verfaellie, 1988). In other words, their brain is recognizing and responding to the difference between familiar and unfamiliar stimuli, but this recognition does not reach the level of conscious awareness.

Blindsight

People with agnosia are not blind, but those with a rare condition called **blindsight** *are blind in part of their visual field yet in special tests respond to stimuli in that field despite reporting that they can't see those stimuli* (Kentridge et al., 2004; Weiskrantz, 2002). For example, due to left-hemisphere damage from an accident or disease, a blindsight patient may be blind in the right half of the visual field. A stimulus (e.g., a horizontal line) is flashed on a screen so that it appears in one of several locations within the patient's blind visual field. On trial after trial, the patient reports seeing nothing, but when asked to point to where the stimulus was, she or he guesses at rates much higher than chance.

On other tasks, different colors or photographs of facial expressions are projected to the blind visual field. Again, despite saying that they can't see anything, patients guess the color or facial expression at rates well above chance. On some tasks, guessing accuracy may reach 80 to 100 percent (Weiskrantz, 2002).

Priming

Here's a simple task. Starting with the two letters *ho_____* (this is called a *word stem*), what is the first word that comes to your mind? Was it *hot, how, home, house, hope, hole,* or *honest*? Clearly, you had these and many other words to choose from.

Now imagine that just before completing this word stem you had looked at a screen on which the word *hose* (or perhaps a picture of a hose) was presented *subliminally* (it was displayed so rapidly or weakly that it was below your threshold for conscious perception).

Suppose we conduct an experiment with many participants and many word stems (e.g., *ho_____, gr_____, ma_____,* etc.). We find that compared to people who are not exposed to subliminal words such as *hose, gripe,* and *manage,* people who are subliminally exposed are more likely to complete the word stems with those particular

words. This provides evidence of a process called **priming:** *Exposure to a stimulus influences (i.e., primes) how you subsequently respond to that same or another stimulus.* Thus even without consciously seeing *hose,* the subliminal word or image primes people's response to *ho_____*.

Subliminal stimuli can prime more than our responses to word stems. For example, when people are shown photographs of a person, the degree to which they evaluate that person positively or negatively is influenced by whether they have first been subliminally exposed to pleasant images (e.g., smiling babies) or unpleasant images (e.g., a face on fire; Krosnick et al., 1992). Likewise, being subliminally exposed to words with an aggressive theme causes people to judge another person's ambiguous behavior as being more aggressive (Todorov & Bargh, 2002).

The Emotional Unconscious

Modern psychodynamic psychologists emphasize that beyond the types of unconscious processing we've just discussed, emotional and motivational processes also operate unconsciously and influence behavior (Westen, 1998). At times these hidden processes can cause us to feel and act in ways that mystify us. Consider the case of a 47-year-old amnesia patient who could not remember new personal experiences. One day, as Swiss psychologist Edouard Claparède (1911) shook this woman's hand, he intentionally pricked her hand with a pin hidden between his fingers. Later, Claparède extended his hand to shake hers again. The woman could not consciously recall the pinprick or even having met Claparède, but despite her amnesia, she suddenly withdrew her hand. Apparently, an unconscious memory of the painful experience influenced her behavior.

Numerous experiments support the view that unconscious processes can have an emotional and motivational flavor (LeDoux, 2000). For example, have you ever been in a bad or a good mood and wondered why you were feeling that way? Perhaps it is because you were influenced by events in your environment of which you were not consciously aware.

In one study, Tanya Chartrand and her colleagues (2002) subliminally presented college students with nouns that were either strongly negative (e.g., *cancer, cockroach*), mildly negative (e.g., *Monday, worm*), mildly positive (e.g., *parade, clown*), or strongly positive (e.g., *friends, music*). Later, students rated their mood on psychological tests. Although not consciously aware of seeing the nouns, students shown the strongly negative words reported the saddest mood, whereas those who had seen the strongly positive words reported the happiest mood.

WHY DO WE HAVE CONSCIOUSNESS?

Given our brain's capacity to process information unconsciously, why have we evolved into conscious beings? What functions does consciousness serve? Surely the subjective richness of your life might evaporate if you lost the ability to consciously reflect on nature's beauty or on your feelings, thoughts, and memories. But what about survival? How does consciousness help us adapt to, and survive in, our environment?

In his book *The Quest for Consciousness*, Christof Koch (2004) notes that, "evolution gave rise to organisms with subjective feelings. These convey significant survival advantages, because consciousness goes hand-in-hand with the ability to plan, to reflect upon many possible courses of action, and to choose one" (p. 205).

Koch suggests that consciousness serves a summarizing function. At any instant, your brain is processing numerous external stimuli (e.g., sights, sounds, etc.) and internal stimuli (e.g., bodily sensations). Conscious awareness provides a summary—a single mental representation—of what is going on in your world at each moment, and it makes this summary available to brain regions involved in planning and decision making. Other scientists agree that consciousness facilitates the distribution of information to many areas of the brain (Baars, 2002).

On another front, a lack of self-awareness would compromise your ability to override potentially dangerous behaviors governed by impulses or automatic processing. Without the capacity to reflect, you might lash out after every provocation. Without the safety net of consciousness, Sondra almost drank ammonia during a sleepwalking episode. Under the control of unconscious, autopilot processing, other sleepwalkers have fallen down stairs or have cooked foods and then burned themselves severely while grabbing red-hot pans.

Unconscious processing also is poorly equipped to deal with novelty, such as when we have to learn new tasks or figure out how to handle new situations. Consciousness allows us to deal flexibly with novel situations and helps us plan responses to them (Koch, 2004; Langer, 1989). Self-awareness—coupled with communication— also enables us to express our needs to other people and coordinate actions with them.

THE NEURAL BASIS OF CONSCIOUSNESS

Within our brains, where does consciousness arise? And if no individual brain cell is conscious (as far as we know), then how does brain activity produce consciousness? Psychologists and other scientists who study the brain are in hot pursuit of answers to these difficult questions.

Windows to the Brain

Some researchers have examined the brain functioning of patients who have visual agnosia, blindsight, or other disorders that impair conscious perception. Let's return to the case of D. F. Brain imaging revealed that D. F.'s primary visual cortex was largely undamaged from carbon-monoxide exposure. Why then, could she not consciously recognize objects and faces?

The answer builds on prior research in which psychologists discovered multiple brain pathways for processing visual information (Ungerleider & Mishkin, 1982). One pathway, extending from the primary visual cortex to the parietal lobe, carries information to support the unconscious guidance of movements (Milner & Dijkerman, 2001). A second pathway, extending from the primary visual cortex to the temporal lobe, carries information to support the conscious recognition of objects (Figure 5.4). Consistent with this view, imaging of D. F.'s brain indicated that parts of this second visual pathway were badly damaged (Goodale, 2000). Although other parts of D. F.'s brain were also damaged, studies of humans and monkeys with more localized brain damage

▶ **Focus 4**
What are some adaptive functions of consciousness?

▶ **Focus 5**
How do scientists identify brain pathways involved in conscious versus unconscious processing? Describe the global-workspace view of consciousness.

FIGURE 5.4

Action and perception. The neural pathway shown in red is sometimes called the *vision-for-action pathway* because it carries information used in the visual control of movement, such as reaching for and grasping something or inserting a card into a slot. The pathway shown in green is sometimes called the *vision-for-perception pathway* because it carries information that helps us recognize objects (Koch, 2004; Milner & Dijkerman, 2001). Both pathways ultimately make connections to the prefrontal cortex.

(a) UNMASKED STIMULUS
The angry face is shown alone for 30 milliseconds.

Stimulus

↓

People are aware of seeing the angry face.

(b) MASKED STIMULUS
The angry face is shown for 30 milliseconds. The neutral face follows immediately for 45 milliseconds.

Stimulus   Mask

↓

People are aware of seeing the neutral face. They do not consciously perceive the angry face.

FIGURE 5.5

An example of masking. (a) If a picture of an angry face is flashed on a screen for 30 milliseconds, people report seeing it. In this case, the picture is not masked. (b) If the angry face is immediately followed by a photo of a neutral face shown for a longer time (e.g., 45 milliseconds), people report seeing the neutral face but not the angry face. In this approach—called *backward masking*—the presentation of the second photo masks the conscious perception of the first photo. Masking works with many types of stimuli, not just photos of faces. SOURCE: Adapted from Morris & Dolan, 2001.

support the existence of these different visual pathways.

Scientists have also studied the neural basis of consciousness in other creative ways. Some have explored conscious perceptions that are created when specific brain areas are electrically stimulated, while others have tried to determine how consciousness is lost when patients are put under anesthesia (Flohr, 2000). Still others have used a procedure called *masking* (Figure 5.5) to control whether people perceive a stimulus consciously or unconsciously. In experiments, participants undergo brain imaging while exposed to masked and unmasked stimuli. This enables scientists to assess how brain activity differs depending on whether the same stimuli (e.g., photos of angry faces) are consciously or unconsciously perceived.

Building on this technique, neuroscientists have found that emotionally threatening stimuli are processed consciously and unconsciously through different neural pathways. The pathway that produces conscious recognition involves the prefrontal cortex and several other brain regions that are bypassed in the pathway for unconscious processing (Morris & Dolan, 2001).

Consciousness as a Global Workspace

Neuroscience research has led many investigators to the same conclusion: There appears to be no single place in the brain that gives rise to

consciousness. Instead, they view the mind as a collection of largely separate but interacting information-processing modules that perform tasks related to sensation, perception, memory, movement, planning, problem solving, emotion, and so on. The modules process information in parallel—that is, simultaneously and largely independently. However, there also is cross talk between them, as when the output from one module is carried by neural circuits to provide input for another module. For example, a formula recalled from memory can become input for problem-solving modules that allow you to compute answers during a math exam.

According to this view, consciousness is a *global workspace* that represents the unified activity of multiple modules in different areas of the brain (Baars, 2002; Dehaene & Naccache, 2001). In essence, of the many brain modules and connecting circuits that are active at any instant, a particular subset becomes joined in unified activity that is strong enough to become a conscious perception or thought (Dehaene & Naccache, 2001; Koch, 2004). The specific modules and circuits that make up this dominant subset can vary as our brain responds to changing stimuli—sights, sounds, smells, and so on—that compete for conscious attention.

Subjectively, of course, we experience consciousness as unitary, rather than as a collection of modules and circuits. This is somewhat akin to listening to a choir sing. We are aware of the integrated, harmonious sound of the choir rather than the voice of each individual member. As we now see, many factors influence these modules and, in so doing, alter our consciousness.

IN REVIEW

■ *Consciousness* refers to our moment-to-moment awareness of ourselves and the environment. It is subjective, dynamic, self-reflective, and central to our sense of identity.

■ Scientists use self-report, behavioral, and physiological measures to define states of consciousness operationally.

■ Freud believed that the mind has conscious, preconscious, and unconscious levels. He viewed the unconscious as a reservoir of unacceptable desires and repressed experiences. Cognitive psychologists view the unconscious mind as an information-processing system and distinguish between controlled and automatic processing.

■ Research on visual agnosia, blindsight, and priming reveals that information processed unconsciously can influence people's responses. Emotional and motivational processes also can operate unconsciously and influence behavior.

- Consciousness enhances our ability to adapt to our environment. It makes information available to brain regions involved in planning and decision making. It also helps us cope with novel situations and override impulsive and autopilot behaviors.

- Brain-imaging studies of healthy and brain-damaged people have discovered separate neural circuits for conscious versus unconscious information processing.

- Many theorists propose that the mind consists of separate but interacting information-processing modules. Global-workspace models propose that consciousness arises from the unified, coordinated activity of multiple modules located in different brain areas.

CIRCADIAN RHYTHMS: OUR DAILY BIOLOGICAL CLOCKS

Like other animals, humans have adapted to a world with a 24-hour day-night cycle. Every 24 hours our body temperature, certain hormonal secretions, and other bodily functions undergo a rhythmic change that affects our alertness and readies our passage back and forth between waking consciousness and sleep (Figure 5.6). These *daily biological cycles are called* **circadian rhythms.**

KEEPING TIME: BRAIN AND ENVIRONMENT

As Figure 5.7 shows, *most circadian rhythms are regulated by the brain's* **suprachiasmatic nuclei (SCN),** located in the hypothalamus. SCN neurons have a genetically programmed cycle of activity and inactivity, functioning like a biological clock. They link to the tiny pineal gland, which secretes **melatonin,** *a hormone that has a relaxing effect on the body.* SCN neurons become active during the daytime and reduce the pineal gland's secretion of melatonin, raising body temperature and heightening alertness. At night SCN neurons are inactive, allowing melatonin levels to increase and promoting relaxation and sleepiness (Zhdanova & Wurtman, 1997).

Our circadian clock is biological, but environmental cues such as the day-night cycle help keep SCN neurons on a 24-hour schedule. Your eyes have neural connections to the SCN, and after a night's sleep, the light of day increases SCN activ-

FIGURE 5.6

Circadian rhythms. (a) Changes in our core body temperature, (b) levels of melatonin in our blood, and (c) degrees of alertness are a few of the bodily functions that follow a cyclical 24-hour pattern called a *circadian rhythm.* Humans also have longer and shorter biological cycles, such as the 28-day female menstrual cycle and a roughly 90-minute brain activity cycle during sleep. SOURCE: Adapted from Monk et al., 1996.

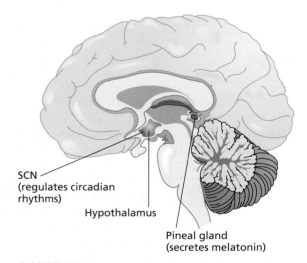

FIGURE 5.7

The master circadian clock. The suprachiasmatic nuclei (SCN) are the brain's master circadian clock. Neurons in the SCN have a genetically programmed cycle of activity and inactivity, but daylight and darkness help regulate this cycle. The optic nerve links our eyes to the SCN, and SCN activity affects the pineal gland's secretion of melatonin. In turn, melatonin influences other brain systems governing alertness and sleepiness.

▶ **Focus 6**
How do the brain and environment regulate circadian rhythms? What are free-running circadian rhythms?

ity and helps reset your 24-hour biological clock. What would happen, then, if you lived in a laboratory or underground cave without clocks and could not tell whether it was day or night outside? In experiments in which people did just that, most participants drifted into a natural wake-sleep cycle, called a *free-running circadian rhythm*, that is longer than 24 hours (Hillman et al., 1994).

For decades, research suggested that our free-running rhythm was about 25 hours long. In these studies, however, the bright room lights that participants kept on artificially lengthened their circadian rhythms. Under more controlled conditions, the free-running rhythm averages around 24.2 hours (Lavie, 2000). Yet even this small deviation from the 24-hour day is significant. If you were to follow your free-running rhythm, two months from now you would be going to bed at noon and awakening at midnight.

Early Birds and Night Owls

Circadian rhythms also influence our tendency to be a morning person or a night person (Duffy et al., 2001). Compared to night people ("night owls"), morning people ("early birds") go to bed and rise earlier, and their body temperature, blood pressure, and alertness peak earlier in the day. As Figure 5.8 shows, a study of college students found that early birds are more likely than night owls to enroll in and perform better in early (8 A.M.) classes.

Cultures may differ in their overall tendency toward "morningness." Carlla Smith and her coworkers (2002) used questionnaires to measure the degree of morningness among college students

TABLE 5.1	Morningness among College Students from Six Countries
Country	**Morningness Score**
Colombia	42.4
India	39.4
Spain	33.9
England	31.6
United States	31.4
Netherlands	30.1

NOTE: Scores can range from 13 ("extreme evening type") to 55 ("extreme morning type").
SOURCE: Smith et al., 2002.

from six countries. They predicted and found that students from Colombia, India, and Spain—regions with warmer annual climates—exhibited greater morningness than students from England, the United States, and the Netherlands (Table 5.1).

What Do You Think?

EARLY BIRDS, CLIMATE, AND CULTURE
Is this cross-cultural study of morningness correlational or experimental? Why might people from warmer regions display greater morningness? What factors other than climate might explain these results? Think about it, then see page 189.

ENVIRONMENTAL DISRUPTIONS OF CIRCADIAN RHYTHMS

Our circadian rhythms are vulnerable to disruption by both sudden and gradual environmental changes. Jet lag is a sudden circadian disruption caused by flying across several time zones in one day. Flying east, you lose hours from your day; flying west extends your day to more than 24 hours. Jet lag, which often causes insomnia and decreased alertness, is a significant concern for businesspeople, athletes, airline crews, and others who frequently travel across many time zones (Ariznavarreta et al., 2002). The body naturally adjusts about one hour or less per day to time-zone changes. Typically, people adjust faster when flying west, presumably because lengthening the travel day is more compatible with our natural free-running circadian cycle (Kimble, 1992).

Night-shift work, affecting millions of full-time workers around the globe, is the most problematic circadian disruption for society. Imagine having to begin an 8-hour work shift at 11 P.M. or midnight, a

▶ **Focus 7**
Describe environmental disruptions of circadian rhythms.

FIGURE 5.8

Course grades of early birds and night owls. In a study of 454 University of Kansas students, "night owls" struggled in their 8 A.M. classes, as compared with "early birds." In later classes the two groups performed more similarly. Stated differently, early birds did slightly better in their earliest class than in later classes, whereas night owls did better in their later classes rather than their earliest class. SOURCE: Based on Guthrie et al., 1995.

time when your biological clock is promoting sleepiness. After work you head home in morning daylight, making it harder to alter your biological clock. Like many night workers, if you turn into bed in the late morning or early afternoon, you may get only 2 to 4 hours of sleep (Kogi, 1985). Over time you may become fatigued, stressed, and more accident-prone (Garbarino et al., 2002). On your days off, reverting to a typical day-night schedule to spend time with family and friends will disrupt any hard-earned circadian adjustments you have made. And, if you work for a company that requires employees to rotate shifts every few days or weeks, then after adapting to night work, you'll have to switch to a day or evening shift and readjust your biological clock once again.

These circadian disruptions, combined with fatigue from poor daytime sleep, can be a recipe for disaster. Job performance errors, fatal traffic accidents, and engineering and industrial disasters peak between midnight and 6 A.M. (Akerstedt et al., 2001). In some cases, night operators at nuclear power plants have been found asleep at the controls. On-the-job sleepiness is also a major concern among long-distance truck drivers, airline crews, doctors and nurses, and others who work at night.

Seasonal affective disorder (SAD) *is a cyclic tendency to become psychologically depressed during certain seasons of the year*. Some people become depressed in spring and summer; however, in the vast majority of cases, SAD begins in fall or winter, when there is less daylight, and then lifts in spring (Rosenthal & Wehr, 1987). The circadian

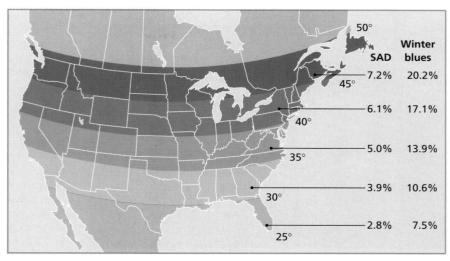

FIGURE 5.9

The latitude puzzle. In North America, the rates of winter SAD and milder depression ("winter blues") increase at more northerly latitudes, where the hours of daylight diminish more severely in late fall and winter. Yet European studies report lower winter SAD rates and a weaker SAD–latitude relation. In fact, most studies in Sweden, Norway, Finland, and Iceland report winter SAD rates similar to those in the southern United States. The reason for this discrepancy is not clear. SOURCES: Data adapted from Mersch et al., 1999. Map graphic from *The New York Times*, 29 December 1993, p. B7; copyright © 1993 The New York Times.

rhythms of SAD sufferers may be particularly sensitive to light, so as sunrises occur later in winter, the daily onset time of their circadian clocks may be pushed back to an unusual degree. On late-fall and winter mornings, when many people must arise for work and school in darkness, SAD sufferers remain in sleepiness mode long after the morning alarm clock sounds (Figure 5.9).

▶ **Focus 8**
Describe ways to minimize circadian disruptions involved in jet lag, night-shift work, and SAD.

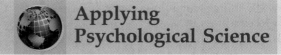

Applying Psychological Science   **Outsmarting Jet Lag, Night-Work Disruptions, and Winter Depression**

Circadian research provides important insights on the nature of consciousness. It also offers several treatments for circadian disruptions affecting millions of people.

CONTROLLING EXPOSURE TO LIGHT

Reducing Jet Lag

When you fly east across time zones, your body's internal clock falls behind the time at your destination. Exposure to outdoor light in the morning—and avoiding light late in the day—moves the circadian clock forward and helps it catch up to local time. (Think of morning light as jump-starting your circadian clock at a time when you would be asleep back home.) Flying west, your body clock moves ahead of local time. So to reduce jet lag, you want to delay your circadian cycle by avoiding bright light in the morning and exposing yourself to light in the afternoon or early evening. These are general rules, but the specific timing and length of exposure to light depend on the number of time zones crossed (Houpt et al., 1996). For jet travelers, spending time outside (even on cloudy days) is the easiest way to get the needed exposure to light.

Adjusting to Night Work

When night employees go home after work, their circadian adjustment can be increased by (1) keeping the bedroom dark and quiet to foster daytime sleep and (2) maintaining a schedule of daytime sleep even during days off (Boulos, 1998). Day sleepers are advised to install light-blocking window shades, unplug the phone, and use earplugs.

Continued

FIGURE 5.10

For many people, the depression from SAD can be reduced by daily exposure to bright fluorescent lights.

Treating SAD

Many experts believe that phototherapy, which involves properly timed exposure to specially prescribed bright artificial lights, is the best treatment for SAD and milder winter blues (Leppämäki et al., 2002). Several hours of daily phototherapy, especially in the early morning, can shift circadian rhythms by as much as 2 to 3 hours per day (Neumeister, 2004). The fact that phototherapy effectively treats SAD is the strongest evidence that SAD is triggered by winter's lack of sunlight rather than by its colder temperatures (Figure 5.10).

MELATONIN TREATMENT: USES AND CAUTIONS

The hormone melatonin is a key player in the brain's circadian clock. Melatonin also exists in pill or capsule form; it is a prescription drug in some countries and is unavailable to the public in others. In the United States it is a nonprescrip-tion dietary supplement. Depending on when it is taken, oral melatonin can shift some circadian cycles forward or backward by as much as 30 to 60 minutes per day of use. Melatonin treatment has been used with some success to decrease jet lag, help employees adapt to night-shift work, and alleviate SAD (Arendt et al., 1997).

But there is reason for caution. Doses of 0.1 to 0.5 milligrams are often sufficient to produce circadian shifts, but tablet doses are often 3 to 5 milligrams, producing melatonin levels in the blood that are over 10 times the normal concentration (Sack et al., 1997). Melatonin use is supervised during research, but individuals who self-administer it may do themselves more harm than good. Taking melatonin at the wrong time can backfire and make circadian adjustments more difficult. Daytime use may decrease alertness (Graw et al., 2001). Some experts are also concerned that millions of people are using melatonin tablets as a nightly sleeping aid even though possible side effects of long-term use have not been adequately studied.

REGULATING ACTIVITY SCHEDULES

Properly timed physical exercise may help shift the circadian clock (Mistlberger et al., 2000). For example, compared to merely staying up later than normal, exercising when you normally go to bed may help push back your circadian clock, as you would want to do when flying west (Baehr, 2001). To reduce jet lag, you can also begin synchronizing your biological clock to the new time zone in advance. To do so, adjust your sleep and eating schedules by 30 minutes to 1 hour per day, starting several days before you leave. Schedule management can also apply to night-shift work. For workers on rotating shifts, circadian disruptions can be reduced by a forward-rotating shift schedule—moving from day to evening to night shifts—rather than a schedule that rotates backward from day to night to evening shifts (Knauth, 1996). The forward schedule takes advantage of our free-running circadian rhythms. When work shifts change, it is easier to extend the waking day than to compress it.

IN REVIEW

- Circadian rhythms are 24-hour biological cycles that help regulate many bodily processes and influence our alertness and readiness for sleep. The suprachiasmatic nuclei (SCN) are the brain's master circadian clock.

- Our free-running circadian rhythm is roughly 24.2 hours, but environmental factors such as the day-night cycle help reset our daily clocks to a 24-hour schedule.

- Circadian rhythms influence our tendency to be either a morning person or a night person, but cultural factors may also play a role.

- In general, our alertness is lowest in the early morning hours between 12 A.M. and 6 A.M. Job performance errors, major industrial accidents, and fatal auto accidents peak during these hours.

- Jet lag, night-shift work, and seasonal affective disorder (SAD) involve environmental disruptions of circadian rhythms. Treatments include controlling one's exposure to light, taking oral melatonin, and regulating one's daily activity schedule.

1 EEG (brain waves)

2 Right eye movements

3 Left eye movements

4 Muscle tension

FIGURE 5.11

The sleep laboratory. In a modern sleep laboratory, people sleep while their physiological responses are monitored. Electrodes attached to the scalp record the person's EEG brain-wave patterns. Electrodes attached beside the eyes record eye movements during sleep. Electrodes attached to the jaw record muscle tension. A neutral electrode is attached to the ear.

SLEEP AND DREAMING

Sweet, refreshing, mysterious sleep. We spend much of our lives in this altered state, relinquishing conscious control of our thoughts, entering a world of dreams, and remembering so little of it upon awakening. Yet sleep, like other behaviors, can be studied at biological, psychological, and environmental levels.

STAGES OF SLEEP

Circadian rhythms promote a readiness for sleep by decreasing alertness, but they do not regulate sleep directly. Instead, roughly every 90 minutes while asleep, we cycle through different stages in which brain activity and other physiological responses change in a generally predictable way (Dement, 1974; Kleitman, 1963).

Sleep research is often carried out in specially equipped laboratories where sleepers' physiological responses are recorded (Figure 5.11). EEG recordings of your brain's electrical activity would show a pattern of **beta waves** *when you are awake and alert*. Beta waves have a high frequency (of about 15 to 30 cycles per second, or cps) but a low amplitude, or height (Figure 5.12). As you close your eyes, *feeling relaxed and drowsy, your brain waves slow down and* **alpha waves** occur at about 8 to 12 cps.

Stage 1 through Stage 4

As sleep begins, your brain-wave pattern becomes more irregular, and slower *theta waves* (3.5 to

7.5 cps) increase. You are now in *stage 1*, a form of light sleep from which you can easily be awakened. You'll probably spend just a few minutes in stage 1, during which time some people experience dreams, vivid images, and sudden body jerks. As sleep becomes deeper, *sleep spindles*—periodic 1- to 2-second bursts of rapid brain-wave activity (12 to 15 cps)—begin to appear. Sleep spindles indicate that you are now in *stage 2* (see Figure 5.12). Your muscles are more relaxed, breathing and heart rate are slower, dreams may occur, and you are harder to awaken.

▶ **Focus 9**
What brain-wave patterns distinguish waking states and the stages of sleep? Describe the characteristics of REM sleep.

Awake/alert — Beta waves
Relaxed/drowsy — Alpha waves
Stage 1 — Theta waves
Stage 2 — Sleep spindle
Stage 3 — Delta waves
Stage 4 — Delta waves
REM sleep

FIGURE 5.12

Stages of sleep. Changing patterns of brain-wave activity help define the various stages of sleep. Note that brain waves become slower as sleep deepens from stage 1 through stage 4. Source: Based on Hauri, 1982.

FIGURE 5.13

Cycling through a night's sleep. This graph shows a record of a night's sleep. The REM stages are shown in blue. People typically average four to five REM periods during the night, and these tend to become longer as the night wears on. On this night, the REM 5 period has been cut short because the person awakened.

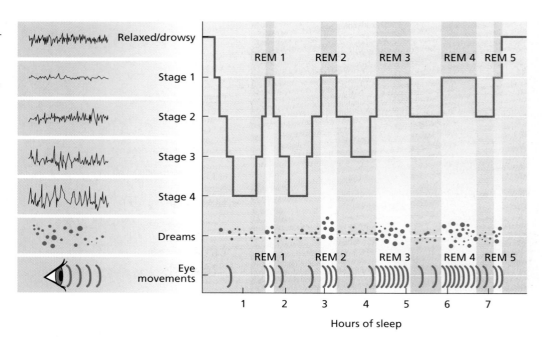

Sleep deepens as you move into *stage 3*, marked by the regular appearance of *very slow (0.5 to 2 cps) and large* **delta waves.** As time passes, they occur more often, and when delta waves dominate the EEG pattern, you have reached *stage 4. Together, stage 3 and stage 4 are often referred to as* **slow-wave sleep.** Your body is relaxed, activity in various parts of your brain has decreased, you are hard to awaken, and you may have dreams. After 20 to 30 minutes of stage-4 sleep, your EEG pattern changes as you go back through stages 3 and 2, spending a little time in each. Overall, within 60 to 90 minutes of going to sleep, you have completed a cycle of stages: 1-2-3-4-3-2. At this point, a remarkably different sleep stage ensues.

REM Sleep

In 1953 Eugene Aserinsky and Nathaniel Kleitman of the University of Chicago struck scientific gold when they identified a unique sleep stage called **REM sleep,** *characterized by rapid eye movements (REM), high arousal, and frequent dreaming.* They found that every half minute or so during REM sleep, bursts of muscular activity caused sleepers' eyeballs to vigorously move back and forth beneath their closed eyelids. Moreover, sleepers awakened from REM periods almost always reported a dream—including people who swore they "never had dreams." At last, scientists could examine dreaming more closely. Wait for REM, awaken the sleeper, and catch a dream.

During REM sleep, physiological arousal may increase to daytime levels. The heart rate quickens, breathing becomes more rapid and irregular, and brain-wave activity resembles that of active wakefulness. Regardless of dream content (most dreams are not sexual), men have penile erections and women experience vaginal lubrication. The brain also sends signals making it more difficult for voluntary muscles to contract. As a result, muscles in the arms, legs, and torso lose tone and become relaxed. These muscles may twitch, but in effect you are paralyzed, unable to move. This state is called *REM sleep paralysis,* and because of it REM sleep is sometimes called *paradoxical sleep:* Your body is highly aroused, yet it looks like you are sleeping peacefully because there is so little movement.

Although each cycle through the sleep stages takes an average of 90 minutes, Figure 5.13 shows that as the hours pass, stage 4 and then stage 3 drop out and REM periods become longer.

GETTING A NIGHT'S SLEEP: FROM BRAIN TO CULTURE

The brain steers our passage through sleep, but it has no single "sleep center." Various brain mechanisms control different aspects of sleep, such as falling asleep and REM sleep. Moreover, falling asleep is not just a matter of turning off brain systems that keep us awake. There are separate systems that turn on and actively promote sleep.

Certain areas at the base of the forebrain (called the *basal forebrain*) and within the brain stem regulate our falling asleep. Other brain stem

What is the function of REM sleep? View the video, "REM Sleep," in Chapter 5 of your CD to explore a REM-sleep debate among researchers and theorists.

▶ **Focus 10**
What factors regulate nightly sleep and differences in people's sleep behavior? How does sleep change with age?

The Brain During REM-Sleep

Primary motor cortex

Prefrontal lobe

Association areas near primary visual cortex

Thalamus

Amygdala, hypothalamus

▬ Regional cerebral blood flow increases during REM sleep

▬ Regional cerebral blood flow decreases during REM sleep

FIGURE 5.14

Brain activity during REM sleep. As compared to the waking brain, during REM sleep several brain regions display markedly decreased (blue) and increased (rust) activity. Note the decreased activation in certain prefrontal lobe regions and increased activity in parts of the amygdala and hypothalamus, thalamus, primary motor cortex, and association areas near the primary visual cortex in the occipital lobe. SOURCE: Schwartz & Maquet, 2002.

areas—including where the reticular formation passes through the pons (called the *pontine reticular formation*)—play a key role in regulating REM sleep (Hobson et al., 2000). This region contains neurons that periodically activate other brain systems, each of which controls a different aspect of REM sleep, such as eye movement and muscular paralysis.

Brain images taken during REM sleep reveal intense activity in limbic system structures, such as the amygdala that regulate emotions—a pattern that may reflect the emotional nature of many REM-sleep dreams (Figure 5.14). The primary motor cortex is active, but its signals for movement are blocked and don't reach our limbs. Association areas near the primary visual cortex are active, which may reflect the processing of visual dream images. In contrast, decreased activity occurs in regions of the prefrontal cortex involved in high-level mental functions, such as planning and logical analysis. This may indicate that our sleeping mind does not monitor and organize its mental activity as carefully as when awake, enabling dreams to be illogical and bizarre (Hobson et al., 2000).

Environmental factors, such as changes in season, also affect sleep. In fall and winter, most people sleep about 15 to 60 minutes longer per night. Shift work, stress at work and school, and nighttime noise can decrease sleep quality (Bronzaft et al., 1998).

Several aspects of sleep, such as its timing and length, vary across cultures. One study of 818 Japanese and Slovak adolescents found that, on average, the Japanese teenagers went to sleep later at night and slept for a shorter time than their Slovak peers (Iwawaki & Sarmany-Schuller, 2001). Many people, particularly those living in cultures in tropical climates, enjoy the traditional ritual of a 1- to 2-hour midday nap and reduce the length of nighttime sleep (Kribbs, 1993).

Cultural norms also influence several behaviors related to sleep. Do you sleep on a cushioned bed? In some cultures people sleep on floors or suspended in hammocks (Figure 5.15). *Co-sleeping*, in which children sleep with their parents in the same bed or room, is not common in the United States, as children's sleeping alone is seen as a way to foster independence. But in most cultures, cosleeping is the norm (Rothrauff et al., 2004).

HOW MUCH DO WE SLEEP?

The question seems simple enough, as does the answer for many of us: not enough! In reality, the

FIGURE 5.15

In warmer regions of the Americas, the use of hammocks for sleeping has been common among various indigenous peoples for centuries. This photo shows a Mayan family in the Yucatan, Mexico.

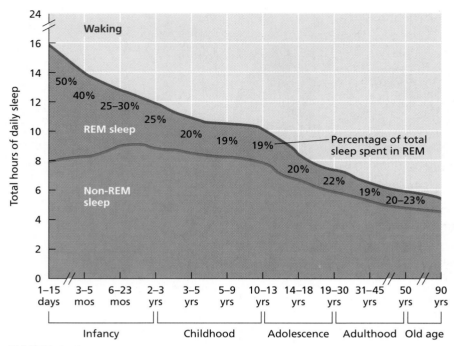

FIGURE 5.16

Aging and sleep. Daily total sleep time and the percentage of sleep time in REM and non-REM sleep change with age. Source: Adapted from Roffwarg, H. P., Muzio, J. N., & Dement, W. C. (1966). Ontogenic development of human dream-sleep cycle. *Science, 152,* 604, figure 1. Copyright © American Association for the Advancement of Science. Reprinted with permission.

▶ **Focus 11**
How do different types of sleep deprivation affect mood and behavior?

issue is complex. First, Figure 5.16 reveals that there are substantial differences in how much people sleep at various ages. Newborn infants average 16 hours of sleep a day, and almost half of their sleep time is in REM. But as we age, three important changes occur:

- We sleep less; 19- to 30-year-olds average around 7 to 8 hours of sleep a night, and elderly adults average just under 6 hours.

- REM sleep decreases dramatically during infancy and early childhood but remains relatively stable thereafter.

- Time spent in stages 3 and 4 declines. By old age we get relatively little slow-wave sleep.

Second, individual differences in the amount of sleep occur at every age. Sleep surveys indicate that about two thirds of young adults sleep between 6.5 and 8.5 hours a night (Webb, 1992). About 1 percent sleep more than 10 hours a night and 1 percent less than 5 hours.

Do We Need Eight Hours of Nightly Sleep?

Sleep surveys, of course, describe how much sleep people believe they get, not how much they need. Still, it appears that the old adage, "everyone needs 8 hours of sleep a night," is not true

(Monk et al., 2001). Indeed, laboratory studies reveal that a few people function well on very little sleep. Researchers in London examined a healthy, energetic 70-year-old woman who claimed to sleep less than 1 hour a night (Meddis et al., 1973). Over five consecutive nights at the sleep lab, she averaged 67 minutes of sleep a night and showed no ill effects. Such extreme short-sleepers, however, are rare.

What accounts for differences in how much we sleep? Part of the answer appears to reside in our genes. Surveys of thousands of twins in Finland and Australia reveal that identical twins have more similar sleep lengths, bedtimes, and sleep patterns than do fraternal twins (Heath et al., 1990). Using selective breeding, researchers have developed some genetic strains of mice that are long- versus short-sleepers, other strains that spend more or less time in REM, and still others that spend more or less time in slow-wave sleep (Ouyang et al., 2004).

The twin studies indicate that differences in sleep length and sleep patterns are also affected by nongenetic factors. Working day versus night jobs, having low-key versus high-pressure lifestyles, and sleeping in quiet versus noisy environments are among the many factors contributing to the variability in people's sleep.

SLEEP DEPRIVATION

Sleep deprivation is a way of life for many college students and other adults (National Sleep Foundation, 2002). June Pilcher and Allen Huffcutt (1996) meta-analyzed 19 studies in which participants underwent either "short-term total sleep deprivation" (up to 45 hours without sleep), "long-term total sleep deprivation" (more than 45 hours without sleep), or "partial deprivation" (being allowed to sleep no more than 5 hours a night for one or more consecutive nights). The researchers measured participants' mood (e.g., irritability) and responses on mental tasks (e.g., logical reasoning, word memory) and physical tasks (e.g., manual dexterity, treadmill walking).

What would you predict? Would all types of deprivation affect behavior, and which behaviors would be affected the most? In fact, all three types of sleep deprivation impaired functioning. Combined across all studies, the typical sleep-deprived person functioned only as well as someone in the bottom 9 percent of nondeprived participants. Overall, mood suffered most, followed by cognitive and then physical performance, although sleep loss significantly impaired *all three* behaviors.

But what about students who pull all-nighters or cut back their sleep, claiming they still perform as well as ever? June Pilcher & Amy Walters (1997) found that college students deprived of one night's sleep performed more poorly on a critical-thinking task than students allowed to sleep—yet they incorrectly perceived that they had performed better. The authors concluded that students underestimate the negative effects of sleep loss on performance.

Most total-sleep-deprivation studies with humans last less than 5 days, but 17-year-old Randy Gardner set a world record (since broken) of staying awake for 11 days for his 1964 high school science-fair project in San Diego. Grateful sleep researchers received permission to study him (Gulevich et al., 1966). Contrary to a popular myth that Randy suffered few negative effects, at times during the first few days he became irritable, forgetful, and nauseated. By the fifth he had periods of disorientation and mild hallucinations. Over the last 4 days he developed finger tremors and slurred speech. Still, in his final day without sleep he beat sleep researcher William Dement 100 consecutive times at a pinball-type game. When Randy finally went to bed, he slept almost 15 hours the first night and returned to his normal amount of sleep within a week. In general, it takes several nights to recover from extended sleep deprivation, and we do not make up all the sleep time that we have lost.

WHY DO WE SLEEP?

Given that we spend almost a third of our lives sleeping, it must serve an important purpose. But what might that purpose be?

Sleep and Bodily Restoration

According to the **restoration model,** *sleep recharges our run-down bodies and allows us to recover from physical and mental fatigue* (Hess, 1965). Sleep-deprivation research strongly supports this view, indicating that we need sleep to function at our best.

If the restoration model is correct, activities that increase daily wear on the body should increase sleep. Evidence is mildly supportive. A study of 18- to 26-year-old ultramarathon runners found that they slept much longer and spent a greater percentage of time in slow-wave sleep on the two nights following their 57-mile run (Shapiro et al., 1981). For the rest of us mere mortals, a meta-analysis of 38 studies found that we tend to sleep longer by about 10 minutes on days we have exercised (Youngstedt et al., 1997).

What is it that gets restored in our bodies while we sleep? Are vital chemicals depleted during the day and replenished at night? Does waking activity produce toxins that are purged during sleep? We don't have precise answers, but many researchers believe that a cellular waste product called *adenosine* plays a role (Alanko et al., 2004). Like a car's exhaust emissions, adenosine is produced as cells consume fuel. As adenosine accumulates, it inhibits brain circuits responsible for keeping us awake, thereby signaling the body to slow down because too much cellular fuel has been burned. During sleep, however, our adenosine levels decrease.

Sleep as an Evolved Adaptation

Evolutionary/circadian sleep models *emphasize that sleep's main purpose is to increase a species' chances of survival in relation to its environmental demands* (Webb, 1974). Our prehistoric ancestors had little to gain—and much to lose—by being active at night. Hunting, food gathering, and traveling were accomplished more easily and safely during daylight. Leaving the protection of one's shelter at night would have served little purpose other than to become dinner for nighttime predators.

Over the course of evolution, each species developed a circadian sleep-wake pattern that was adaptive in terms of its status as predator or prey, its food requirements, and its methods of defense from attack. For small prey animals such as mice and squirrels, which reside in burrows or trees safely away from predators, spending a lot of time asleep is adaptive. For large prey animals such as horses, deer, and zebras, which sleep in relatively exposed environments and whose safety from predators depends on running away, spending a lot of time asleep would be hazardous (Figure 5.17). Sleep may also have evolved as a mechanism for conserving energy. Our body's overall metabolic rate during sleep is about 10 to 25 percent slower than during waking rest (McGinty, 1993). The restoration and evolutionary theories highlight complementary functions of sleep, and both contribute to a two-factor model of why we sleep (Webb, 1994).

Sleep and Memory Consolidation

Do specific sleep stages have special functions? To answer this question, imagine volunteering for a sleep-deprivation study in which we will awaken you only when you enter REM sleep; you will be undisturbed through the other sleep stages. How will your body respond? First, on successive nights, we will have to awaken you more often,

▶ **Focus 12**
Explain the restoration, evolutionary/circadian, and memory-consolidation models of sleep.

FIGURE 5.17

Daily hours of sleep. The average daily hours of sleep vary across species.

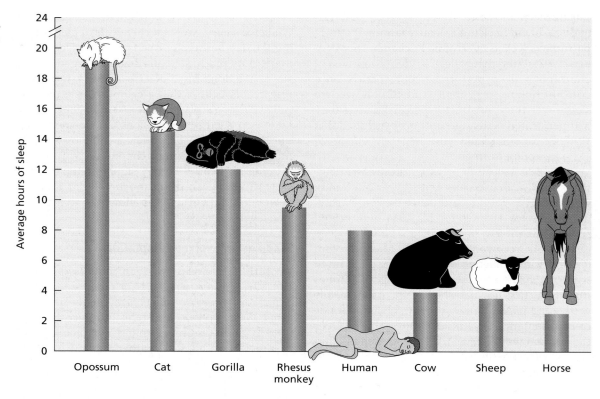

because your brain will fight back to get REM sleep (Figure 5.18a). Second, when the study ends, for the first few nights you probably will experience a *REM-rebound effect*, a tendency to increase the amount of REM sleep after being deprived of it (Figure 5.18b).

This suggests that the body needs REM sleep (similar effects are found for slow-wave sleep). But for what purpose? Many theorists believe that the high level of brain activity in REM sleep helps us remember important events by enhancing **memory consolidation**, *a gradual process by which the brain transfers information into long-term memory* (Smith et al., 2004; Winson, 1990). There have been many experiments on this topic, including brain-imaging studies, but despite much supportive evidence, the issue remains controversial (Vertes & Eastman, 2003). For example, the consolidation hypothesis is contradicted by the fact that although many antidepressant drugs greatly suppress or nearly eliminate REM sleep, patients taking these drugs for long periods of time do not show impaired abilities to remember new information or experiences.

In contrast to the memory-consolidation view, some researchers argue that the function of REM sleep is purely biological. The periodic high activation of REM sleep keeps the brain healthy

FIGURE 5.18

REM-sleep deprivation. (a) In REM-sleep-deprivation studies, participants start to go into REM periods more times with each passing night, as the brain tries to get REM sleep. (b) After REM deprivation ends, the sleeper spends more time than usual in REM sleep for a few nights. This is the REM-rebound effect. SOURCE: Adapted from Agnew et al., 1967.

during sleep and offsets the periods of low brain arousal during restful slow-wave sleep (Vertes & Eastman, 2003). At present, the unique functions of REM and other sleep stages are still debated.

SLEEP DISORDERS

As the sleepeating cases of Sondra, Jason, and Ellen illustrate, the processes that regulate sleep are complex and can go wrong in many ways. Almost 75 percent of American adults feel that they have some type of sleep problem (National Sleep Foundation, 2002).

Insomnia

True or False: Someone who falls asleep easily can still have insomnia. The statement is true because **insomnia** *refers to chronic difficulty in falling asleep, staying asleep, or experiencing restful sleep.* If you occasionally have trouble getting a good night's sleep, don't worry. Almost everyone does. People with true insomnia have frequent and persistent sleep troubles.

Many people with insomnia overestimate how much sleep they lose and how long it takes them to fall asleep. To some, 20 minutes of lying awake may seem like an hour. Still, insomnia is the most common sleep disorder, experienced by 10 to 40 percent of the population of various countries (Ohayon & Lemoine, 2004). Some people, however, display *pseudoinsomnia*; they complain of insomnia but sleep normally when examined in the laboratory (McCall & Edinger, 1992).

Some people are genetically predisposed toward insomnia. Moreover, medical conditions, mental disorders such as anxiety and depression, and many drugs can disrupt sleep, as can general worrying, stress at home and work, poor lifestyle habits, and circadian disruptions such as jet lag and night-shift work.

Psychologists have pioneered many nondrug treatments to reduce insomnia and improve sleep quality. One treatment, called *stimulus control*, involves conditioning your body to associate stimuli in your sleep environment (such as your bed) with sleep, rather than with waking activities and sleeplessness (Bootzin, 2002). For example, if you are having sleep difficulties, do not study, watch TV, or snack in your bedroom. Use your bed only for sleeping. If you cannot fall asleep within 10 minutes, get up and leave the bedroom. Do something relaxing until you feel sleepy, then return to bed. Table 5.2 contains more guidelines from sleep experts for reducing insomnia and achieving better sleep.

TABLE 5.2   How to Improve the Quality of Your Sleep
Sleep experts recommend a variety of procedures to reduce insomnia and improve the general quality of sleep.   • Maintain a regular sleep-wake pattern to establish a stable circadian rhythm.   • Get the amount of sleep you need during the week, and avoid sleeping in on weekends, as doing so will disrupt your sleep rhythm. Even if you sleep poorly or not at all one night, try to maintain your regular schedule the next.   • If you have trouble falling asleep at night, avoid napping if possible. Evening naps should be especially avoided because they will make you less sleepy when you go to bed.   • Avoid stimulants. This includes not just tobacco products and coffee but also caffeinated soft drinks and chocolate (sorry), which contains caffeine. It can take the body 4 to 5 hours to reduce the amount of caffeine in the bloodstream by 50 percent.   • Avoid alcohol and sleeping pills. As a depressant, alcohol may make it easier to go to sleep, but it disrupts the sleep cycle and interferes with REM sleep. Sleeping pills also impair REM sleep, and their constant use can lead to dependence and insomnia.   • Try to go to bed in a relaxed state. Muscle-relaxation techniques and meditation can reduce tension, remove worrisome thoughts, and help induce sleep.   • Avoid physical exercise before bedtime because it is too stimulating. If you are unable to fall asleep, do not use exercise to try and wear yourself out.   • If you are having sleep difficulties, avoid performing nonsleep activities in your bedroom.   Sources: Bootzin, 2002; King et al., 2001.

Narcolepsy

About 1 out of every 2,000 people suffers not from an inability to sleep but from an inability to stay awake (Ohayon et al., 2002). **Narcolepsy** *involves extreme daytime sleepiness and sudden, uncontrollable sleep attacks that may last from less than a minute to an hour.* No matter how much they rest at night, individuals with narcolepsy may experience sleep attacks at any time.

When a sleep attacks occurs, they may go right into a REM stage. People with narcolepsy also may experience attacks of *cataplexy*, a sudden loss of muscle tone often triggered by excitement and other strong emotions. In severe cases, the knees buckle and the person collapses, conscious but unable to move for a few seconds to a few minutes. Cataplexy is an abnormal version of the normal muscular paralysis that takes place during nighttime REM sleep, and some experts view narcolepsy as a disorder in which REM sleep intrudes into waking consciousness.

Narcolepsy can be devastating. People with narcolepsy are more prone to accidents, feel that their quality of life is impaired, and may be misdiagnosed by doctors as having a mental disorder rather than a sleep disorder (Kryger et al., 2002).

Some people may be genetically predisposed toward developing narcolepsy. It can be selectively

► **Focus 13**
Describe the symptoms, causes, and treatment of major sleep disorders.

FIGURE 5.19

This dog lapses suddenly from alert wakefulness into a limp sleep while being held by sleep researcher William Dement. Using selective breeding, researchers at Stanford's Sleep Disorders Center have established a colony of narcoleptic canines.

bred in dogs (Figure 5.19). In humans, if one identical twin has narcolepsy, the other has a 30-percent chance of developing it (Mignot, 1998). At present there is no cure for narcolepsy, but stimulant drugs and daytime naps often reduce daytime sleepiness, and antidepressant drugs (which suppress REM sleep) can decrease attacks of cataplexy.

REM-Sleep Behavior Disorder

Kaku Kimura and his colleagues in Japan (1997) reported the case of a 72-year-old woman who, during a night in a sleep laboratory, repeatedly sang and waved her hands during REM sleep. One episode lasted 3 minutes. She was experiencing **REM-sleep behavior disorder (RBD),** *in which the loss of muscle tone that causes normal REM-sleep paralysis is absent.* If awakened, RBD patients often report dream content that matches their behavior, as if they were acting out their dreams: "A 67-year-old man . . . was awakened one night by his wife's yelling as he was choking her. He was dreaming of breaking the neck of a deer he had just knocked down" (Schenck et al., 1989, p. 1169).

RBD sleepers may kick violently, throw punches, or get out of bed and move about wildly, leaving the bedroom in shambles. Many RBD patients have injured themselves or their sleeping partners. Research suggests that brain abnormalities may interfere with signals from the brain stem that normally inhibit movement during REM sleep, but in many cases the causes of RBD are unknown (Zambelis et al., 2002).

Sleepwalking

Unlike RBD, sleepwalking typically occurs during a stage-3 or stage-4 period of slow-wave sleep (Guilleminault et al., 2001). Sleepwalkers often stare blankly and are unresponsive to other people. Many seem vaguely conscious of the environment as they navigate around furniture, yet they can injure themselves accidentally, such as by falling down stairs. Some go to the bathroom or—like Sondra, Jason, and Ellen—find something to eat. The pattern, however, is variable. Recall that Jason, while eating during his sleepwalking episodes, could have intelligible conversations with his wife. People who sleepwalk often return to bed and awaken in the morning with no memory of the event.

About 10 to 30 percent of children sleepwalk at least once, but less than 5 percent of adults do. If you did not sleepwalk as a child, the odds are less than 1 percent that you will do so as an adult (Hublin et al., 1997).

A tendency to sleepwalk may be inherited, and daytime stress, alcohol, and certain illnesses and medications can increase sleepwalking (Hublin et al., 2001). Treatments may include psychotherapy, hypnosis, and awakening children before the time they typically sleepwalk (Frank et al., 1997). But for children, the most common approach is simply to wait for the child to outgrow it while creating a safe sleep environment to prevent injury. Contrary to common belief, awakening people who sleepwalk is not harmful, although they may be confused for a few minutes.

Nightmares and Night Terrors

Nightmares are bad dreams, and virtually everyone has them. Like all dreams, they occur more often during REM sleep. Arousal during nightmares typically is similar to levels experienced during pleasant dreams.

Night terrors *are frightening dreams that arouse the sleeper to a near-panic state.* In contrast to nightmares, night terrors are most common during slow-wave sleep (stages 3 and 4), are more intense, and involve greatly elevated physiological arousal; the heart rate may double or triple. In some cases the terrified sleeper may suddenly sit up, let out a scream, or flee the room—as if trying to escape from something. Come morning the sleeper usually has no memory of the episode. If brought to full consciousness during an episode—which is hard to do—the person may report a sense of having been choked, crushed, or attacked (Fisher et al., 1974).

Up to 6 percent of children, but only 1 to 2 percent of adults, experience night terrors (Ohayon et al., 1999). In most childhood cases, treatment is simply to wait for the night terrors to diminish with age.

Sleep Apnea

People with **sleep apnea** *repeatedly stop and restart breathing during sleep.* Stoppages usually last 20 to 40 seconds but can continue for 1 to 2 minutes. In severe cases they occur 400 to 500 times a night. Sleep apnea is most commonly caused by an obstruction in the upper airways, such as sagging tissue as muscles lose tone during sleep. The chest and abdomen keep moving, but no air gets through to the lungs. Finally, reflexes kick in and the person gasps or produces a loud, startling snore, followed by a several-second awakening. The person typically falls asleep again without remembering having been awake.

About 1 to 5 percent of people have some form of sleep apnea, and the obstructive type is most common among overweight, middle-aged males (Ip et al., 1998). Surgery may be performed to remove the obstruction, and sleep apnea sometimes is treated by having the sleeper wear a mask that continuously pumps air to keep the air passages open (Sage et al., 2001). It is often the partner of a person with sleep apnea—repeatedly awakened by the gasps, loud snores, and jerking body movements—who encourages the person to seek treatment.

THE NATURE OF DREAMS

Dreams play a key role in the social fabric of many traditional cultures, such as the Timiar (Senoi) of Malaysia (Greenleaf, 1973). To the Timiar, dreams provide a link to the spirit world, and dream interpretation, particularly when performed by shamans, is highly valued. Although Western societies attach less importance to dreams than do many cultures, dreams remain a source of endless curiosity in everyday life.

When Do We Dream?

Mental activity occurs throughout the sleep cycle. Some of our students say they experience vivid images soon after going to bed and ask if this is unusual. It isn't. When Jason Rowley and his colleagues (1998) awakened college students merely 45 seconds after sleep onset, about 25 percent of the students reported that they had been experiencing visual hallucinations (visual images that seemed real). As this *hypnagogic state*—the transitional state from wakefulness through early stage-2

sleep—continued, mental activity became less "thoughtlike" and more "dreamlike." By 5 minutes after sleep onset, visual hallucinations were reported after 40 percent of awakenings.

Throughout the night we dream most often during REM sleep, when activity in many brain areas is highest. Awaken a REM sleeper and you have about an 80- to 85-percent chance of catching a dream. In contrast, people awakened from non-REM (NREM) sleep report dreams about 15 to 50 percent of the time. Also, our REM dreams are more likely to be vivid, bizarre, and storylike than NREM dreams. Some researchers attribute this to the fact that REM dreams typically are longer, allowing more time for vivid content to unfold (Domhoff, 1999). But like the proverbial chicken and the egg, other researchers argue that it is the greater richness of REM dreams that causes them to be longer (Hobson et al., 2000).

Despite these REM-NREM differences, don't believe the fallacy (often reinforced by the popular media) that dreaming only happens during REM sleep. Figure 5.20 shows an analysis of 1,576 reports collected from 16 college students awakened from various sleep stages (Fosse et al., 2001). Even during NREM sleep, hallucinatory images were more common than non-dreamlike thoughts. By some estimates, about 25 percent of the vivid dreams we have each night actually occur during NREM periods (Solms, 2002).

▶ **Focus 14**
When do dreams occur, and what are common characteristics of dream content? How can science explain "psychic" dreams?

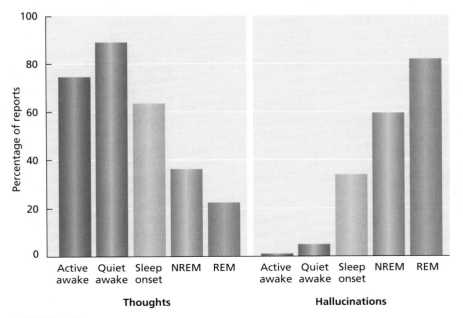

FIGURE 5.20

Mental activity during sleep. This graph shows the percentage of verbal reports that reflected thoughts and visual hallucinations recorded during active and quiet wakefulness and when awakened during sleep onset, REM sleep, and NREM sleep. Source: Adapted from Fosse et al., 2001.

What Do We Dream About?

Much of our knowledge about dream content derives from 40 years of research using a coding system developed by Calvin Hall and Robert Van de Castle (1966). Analyzing 1,000 dream reports (mostly from college students), they found that although some dreams certainly are bizarre, overall dreams are not nearly as strange as they are stereotyped to be. Most take place in familiar settings and often involve people we know.

Given the stereotype of "blissful dreaming," it may surprise you that most dreams contain negative content. In their research, Hall and Van de Castle (1966) found that 80 percent of dream reports involved negative emotions, almost half contained aggressive acts, and a third involved some type of misfortune. They also found that women dreamt almost equally about male and female characters, whereas about two thirds of

men's dream characters were male. Although the reason for this gender difference is not clear, a similar pattern has been found across several cultures and among teenagers and preadolescents.

Our cultural background, life experiences, and current concerns can shape dream content (Domhoff, 2001). Pregnant women, for example, have dreams with many pregnancy themes, and Palestinian children living in violent regions of the Gaza Strip dream about persecution and aggression more often than do their peers living in nonviolent areas (Punamäki & Joustie, 1998). In the weeks following the September 11, 2001, terrorist attacks, a study of 1,000 residents of Manhattan found that 1 in 10 experienced distressing dreams about the attacks (Galea et al., 2002). Overall, it appears that up to half of our dreams contain some content reflecting our recent experiences (Harlow & Roll, 1992).

Beneath the Surface   When Dreams Come True

"Last summer, I had a dream that my sister was hurt in an accident. A week later, she was seriously injured in a bicycle crash! Why does this happen? Are some dreams psychic?"

Have you ever had a dream that came true? Many of our students say they have, and they often ask us whether this has some special meaning. As critical thinkers, let's consider a few issues. First, what are we being asked to believe? Two things really: (1) that a dream foretold the future and (2) that this signifies something special or psychic.

Second, what's the evidence? Well, the evidence is that a dream supposedly came true. So let's think about this. Did the dream really come true? In the example above, what type of accident did the dream involve? A car, train, plane, boat, home, sports, or work accident? If it wasn't a bicycle accident, then the dream really didn't come true.

"Come on," you might say, "that's being too picky. After all, the dream was 'close'—the main theme was that the sister was injured." Well, in that case, suppose you picked a number from 1 to 1,000, we bet you $500 that we could guess it, and we guessed 625. You actually picked 638, but we said, "Our prediction came true. We were very close." Would you agree and pay us $500? If not, then why set a sloppy standard for accuracy when it comes to deciding whether a

dream comes true? Nonetheless, for the sake of argument let's assume that the dream did involve a bicycle accident and came true a week later.

Third, what is the most plausible explanation? Given all the dreams that we recall, some of them are bound to come true simply by sheer coincidence. If you consider how many dreams you have had that *did not* come true, you will realize this. By some estimates we have dozens of dreams nightly, most of which we forget; but let's suppose we remember one dream every two nights. Between the ages of 15 and 75 we'll have almost 11,000 opportunities for a remembered dream to come true the same day, 77,000 opportunities for a remembered dream to come true within a week, and so on. Thus a good number of our dreams should come true simply by coincidence. Collectively, if you consider that hundreds of millions of people may recall a dream each day, the odds are that someone, somewhere, by sheer coincidence will have had a recent dream come true. This is especially true given that ongoing events or issues in our lives can influence the content of our dreams.

In short, we don't need to resort to mystical phenomena to explain why some dreams come true. Rather, we need only consider the likelihood that certain events will occur periodically by chance and coincidence alone.

► **Focus 15**
Contrast the psychoanalytic, activation-synthesis, and cognitive dream theories.

Why Do We Dream?

Questions about the purpose and meaning of dreams have intrigued humankind for ages. Let's examine a few viewpoints.

Freud's Psychoanalytic Theory Sigmund Freud (1900/1953) believed that the main purpose of dreaming is **wish fulfillment,** *the gratification of our unconscious desires and needs*. These desires include sexual and aggressive urges that are too unacceptable to be consciously acknowledged and fulfilled in real life. Freud distinguished between (1) a dream's *manifest content*, the surface story that the dreamer reports and (2) its *latent content*, which is its disguised psychological meaning. Thus a dream about being with a stranger on a train that goes through a tunnel (manifest content) might represent a hidden desire for sexual intercourse with a forbidden partner (latent content).

Dream work was Freud's term for the process by which a dream's latent content is transformed into the manifest content. It occurs through symbols (e.g., train = penis; tunnel = vagina) and by creating individual dream characters who combine features of several people in real life. This way, unconscious needs can be fulfilled, and because they are disguised within the dream, the sleeper does not become anxious and can sleep peacefully.

Although dreams often reflect ongoing emotional concerns, many researchers reject the specific postulates of Freud's theory. They find little evidence that dreams have disguised meaning or that their general purpose is to satisfy forbidden, unconscious needs and conflicts (Domhoff, 1999). Critics of dream analysis say that it is highly subjective; the same dream can be interpreted differently to fit the particular analyst's point of view.

Activation-Synthesis Theory Is it possible that dreams serve no special purpose? In 1977, J. Allan Hobson and Robert McCarley proposed a physiological theory of dreaming.

According to the **activation-synthesis theory,** *dreams do not serve any particular function—they are merely a by-product of REM neural activity.* When we are awake, neural circuits in our brain are activated by sensory input—sights, sounds, tastes, and so on. The cerebral cortex interprets these patterns of neural activation, producing meaningful perceptions. During REM sleep the brain stem bombards our higher brain centers with random neural activity (the activation component). Because we are asleep,

this neural activity does not match any external sensory events, but our cerebral cortex continues to perform its job of interpretation. It does this by creating a dream—a perception—that provides the best fit to the particular pattern of neural activity that exists at any moment (the synthesis component). This helps to explain the bizarreness of many dreams, as the brain is trying to make sense out of random neural activity. Our memories, experiences, desires, and needs can influence the stories that our brain develops, and therefore dream content may reflect themes pertaining to our lives. In this sense, dreams can have meaning, but they serve no special function (McCarley, 1998).

Critics claim that activation-synthesis theory overestimates the bizarreness of dreams and pays too little attention to NREM dreaming (Solms, 2002). Nevertheless, this theory revolutionized dream research by calling attention to a physiological basis for dreaming, and it remains a dominant dream theory (Hobson et al., 2000).

Cognitive Theories According to **problem-solving dream models,** *because dreams are not constrained by reality they can help us find creative solutions to our problems and ongoing concerns* (Cartwright, 1977). Self-help books and numerous Web sites promote this idea, and history offers some intriguing examples of inventors, scientists, and authors who allegedly came upon creative ideas or solutions to problems in a dream (Figure 5.21). But critics argue that because so many of our dreams don't focus on personal problems, it's difficult to see how problem solving can be the broad underlying reason for *why* we dream. They also note that just because a problem shows up in a dream does not mean that the dream involved an attempt to solve it. Moreover, we may think consciously about our dreams after awakening and obtain important new insights; in this sense dreams may indeed help us work through ongoing concerns. However, this is not the same as solving problems *while* dreaming (Squier & Domhoff, 1998).

FIGURE 5.21

Dreams and problem solving. In 1846 American inventor Elias Howe patented a sewing machine that could sew 250 stitches per minute. He had struggled unsuccessfully for years to figure out how to get a machine to stitch using a needle with the threading hole in the back (blunt) end—as in a traditional hand-held needle. Allegedly, one night he had a dream that he was being pursued by spear-throwing tribesmen. In the dream he saw that each spearhead had a hole in it. When Howe awoke, he recognized that for a sewing machine to work, the threading hole needed to be at the front (sharp) end of the needle, as it had been on the spears.

Hand-held needle

Spears in Howe's dream

Sewing machine needle

Cognitive-process dream theories *focus on the process of how we dream and propose that dreaming and waking thought are produced by the same mental systems in the brain* (Foulkes, 1982). For example, research indicates that there is more similarity between dreaming and waking mental processes than was traditionally believed (Domhoff, 2001). Consider that one reason many dreams appear bizarre is because their content shifts rapidly. "I was dreaming about an exam and all of a sudden, the next thing I knew, I was in Hawaii on the beach." (Don't we wish!) Yet if you reflect on the contents of your waking thoughts—your stream of consciousness—you will realize they also shift suddenly. About half of REM dream reports involve rapid content shifts, but when people are awake and placed in the same environmental conditions as sleepers (a dark, quiet room), about 90 percent of their reports involve rapid content shifts (Antrobus, 1991). Thus rapid shifting of attention is a process common to dreaming and waking mental activity.

Toward Integration Although there is no agreed-on model of why or even of how we dream, theorists are developing models that integrate several perspectives. In general, these models propose that dreaming involves an integration of perceptual, emotional, motivational, and cognitive processes performed by various brain modules. For example, *neurocognitive models* (such as the activation-synthesis model) bridge the cognitive and biological perspectives by attempting to explain how various subjective aspects of dreaming correspond to the physiological changes that occur during sleep (Hobson et al., 2000). And as noted earlier, these models allow for the possibility that motivational factors—our needs and desires—can influence how the brain goes about its business of attaching meaning to the neural activity that underlies our dreams.

DAYDREAMS AND WAKING FANTASIES

Our dreams and fantasy lives are not restricted to the nocturnal realm. Daydreams are a significant part of waking consciousness, providing stimulation during periods of boredom and letting us experience a range of emotions (Hartmann et al., 2001). In *The Secret Life of Walter Mitty*, author James Thurber portrayed the fictional Mitty as a person who transformed his humdrum existence into an exhilarating fantasy world of adventure. Like Mitty, people who have a **fantasy-prone personality** *often live in a vivid, rich fantasy world that they control*, and most are female. In one study, about three quarters of fantasy-prone people were able to achieve sexual orgasm merely by fantasizing about sex, and all could experience fantasies "as real as real" in each of the five senses (Wilson & Barber, 1982).

Daydreams typically involve greater visual imagery than other forms of waking mental activity but tend to be less vivid, emotional, and bizarre than nighttime dreams (Kunzendorf et al., 1997). There also is surprising similarity in the themes of daydreams and nighttime dreams, suggesting once again that nocturnal dreams may be an extension of daytime mental activity (Beck, 2002). Figure 5.22

▶ **Focus 16**
What functions do daydreams serve? How are they different from and similar to nighttime dreams?

FIGURE 5.22

Levels of analysis: Factors related to sleep and dreaming.

LEVELS OF ANALYSIS   Factors Related to Sleep and Dreaming

Biological	Psychological	Environmental
• Circadian rhythms that affect sleepiness and alertness	• Learned sleep habits that facilitate or impair a sound night's sleep	• Day-night cycle and time cues that help regulate circadian rhythms and sleep readiness
• Evolution of sleep-wake cycle that is adaptive for each species	• Worries and stress that may hinder falling asleep	• Events that disrupt circadian rhythms and impair sleep
• Brain regions and neural activity that regulate sleep and dreaming	• Cognitive activity during sleep (e.g., dreams, thoughts, images)	• Nighttime stimuli that affect sleep quality (e.g., quiet or noisy room)
• Genetic and age-related processes that influence sleep length and patterns	• Ongoing problems or concerns that may show up in dream content	• Events and experiences from waking life that show up in dream content
• Genetic factors that predispose some people toward developing sleep disorders		• Cultural norms that influence sleep-related behaviors (e.g., co-sleeping) and the meaning attached to dreams

Sleep and Dreaming

summarizes some of the biological, psychological, and environmental factors that contribute to our understanding of sleep and dreaming.

IN REVIEW

- Sleep has five main stages. Stages 1 and 2 are lighter sleep, and stages 3 and 4 are deeper, slow-wave sleep. High physiological arousal and periods of rapid eye movement characterize the fifth stage, REM sleep.

- Several brain regions regulate sleep, and the amount we sleep changes as we age. Genetic, psychological, and environmental factors affect sleep duration and quality.

- Sleep deprivation negatively affects mood and performance. The restoration model proposes that we sleep to recover from physical and mental fatigue. Evolutionary/circadian models state that each species developed a sleep-wake cycle that maximized its chance of survival.

- Insomnia is the most common sleep disorder, but less common disorders such as narcolepsy, REM-sleep behavior disorder, and sleep apnea can have serious consequences. Sleepwalking typically occurs during slow-wave sleep, whereas nightmares most often occur during REM sleep. Night terrors create a near-panic state of arousal and typically occur in slow-wave sleep.

- Dreams occur throughout sleep but are most common during REM periods. Unpleasant dreams are common. Our cultural background, current concerns, and recent events influence what we dream about.

- Freud proposed that dreams fulfill unconscious wishes that show up in disguised form within our dreams. Activation-synthesis theory regards dreaming as the brain's attempt to fit a story to random neural activity. Cognitive-process dream theories emphasize that dreaming and waking thought are produced by the same mental systems.

- Daydreams and nocturnal dreams often share similar themes. People with fantasy-prone personalities have especially vivid daydreams.

DRUG-INDUCED STATES

Like sleep and dreaming, drug-induced states have mystified humans for ages. Three thousand years ago, the Aztecs considered hallucinogenic mushrooms to be a sacred substance for communicating with the spirit world. Today drugs are a cornerstone of medical practice and, as Figure 5.23 shows, a pervasive part of social life. They alter consciousness by modifying brain chemistry, but drug effects are also influenced by psychological, environmental, and cultural factors (Julien, 2005).

DRUGS AND THE BRAIN

Like any cell, a neuron is essentially a fragile bag of chemicals, and it takes a delicate chemical balancing act for neurons to function properly. Drugs work their way into the bloodstream and are carried throughout the brain by an extensive network of small blood vessels called capillaries.

FIGURE 5.23

Drug use among college students. This graph illustrates nonmedical drug use among American college students who are 1 to 4 years beyond high school. These data are based on a nationally representative survey of 1,270 students. Source: Johnston et al., 2004.

(a) SYNTHESIS, STORAGE, RELEASE

AGONISTIC DRUGS

Drug causes neuron to synthesize more transmitter molecules, store them more safely, or release them.

(b) BINDING

Neurotransmitter molecule

Agonistic drug molecule

Receptor binding site

Postsynaptic neuron

Drug and neurotransmitter have similar structure. Drug binds with receptor site and activates it.

(c) REUPTAKE

Reuptake blocked by drug

Drug blocks reuptake. More transmitter molecules remain in synapse, available to activate receptor sites.

ANTAGONISTIC DRUGS

Leakage

Drug impairs neuron's ability to synthesize, store, or release transmitter. Molecules may leak and degrade prematurely.

Neurotransmitter molecule

Antagonistic drug molecule

Receptor binding site

Postsynaptic neuron

Drug binds with receptor site but is not similar enough to transmitter to activate site. Blocks transmitter from activating site.

FIGURE 5.24

How drugs affect neurotransmitters. (*top*) Agonistic drugs increase the activity of a neurotransmitter. (*bottom*) Antagonistic drugs decrease the activity of a neurotransmitter.

▶ **Focus 17**
Describe several ways in which agonist and antagonist drugs influence synaptic transmission.

These capillaries contain a **blood-brain barrier,** *a special lining of tightly packed cells that lets vital nutrients pass through so neurons can function.* The blood-brain barrier screens out many foreign substances, but some, including various drugs, can pass through. Once inside they alter consciousness by facilitating or inhibiting synaptic transmission (Julien, 2005).

How Drugs Facilitate Synaptic Transmission

Recall from Chapter 3 that synaptic transmission involves several basic steps. First, neurotransmitters are synthesized inside the presynaptic (sending) neuron and stored in vesicles. Next, neurotransmitters are released into the synaptic space, where they bind with and stimulate receptor sites on the postsynaptic (receiving) neuron. Finally, neurotransmitter molecules are deactivated by enzymes or by reuptake.

An **agonist** *is a drug that increases the activity of a neurotransmitter.* Figure 5.24 shows that agonists may

- enhance a neuron's ability to synthesize, store, or release neurotransmitters;

- bind with and stimulate postsynaptic receptor sites (or make it easier for neurotransmitters to stimulate these sites);

- make it more difficult for neurotransmitters to be deactivated, such as by inhibiting reuptake.

Consider two examples. First, *opiates* (such as morphine and codeine) are effective pain relievers. Recall that the brain contains its own chemicals, endorphins, which play a major role in pain relief. Opiates have a molecular structure similar to that of endorphins. They bind to and activate receptor sites that receive endorphins. To draw an analogy, think of trying to open a lock with a key. Normally an endorphin molecule acts as the key, but due to its similar shape, an opiate molecule can fit into the lock and open it.

Second, *amphetamines* boost arousal and mood by causing neurons to release greater amounts of dopamine and norepinephrine and by inhibiting reuptake. During reuptake, neurotransmitters in the synapse are absorbed back into presynaptic neurons through special channels. As shown in Figure 5.24c, amphetamine molecules block this process. Therefore, dopamine and nor-epinephrine remain in the synaptic space longer and keep stimulating postsynaptic neurons.

How Drugs Inhibit Synaptic Transmission

An **antagonist** *is a drug that inhibits or decreases the action of a neurotransmitter.* As Figure 5.24 shows, an antagonist may

- reduce a neuron's ability to synthesize, store, or release neurotransmitters; or
- prevent a neurotransmitter from binding with the postsynaptic neuron, such as by fitting into and blocking the receptor sites on the postsynaptic neuron.

Consider the action of drugs called *antipsychotics* used to treat *schizophrenia*, a severe psychological disorder whose symptoms may include hallucinations (e.g., hearing voices) and delusions (clearly false beliefs, such as believing you are Joan of Arc). These symptoms are often associated with overactivity of the dopamine system. To restore dopamine activity to more normal levels, pharmaceutical companies have developed drugs with a molecular structure similar to dopamine, but not too similar. Returning to the lock-and-key analogy, imagine finding a key that fits into a lock but won't turn. The key's shape is close enough to the real key to get in but not to open the lock. Similarly, antipsychotic drugs fit into dopamine receptor sites but not well enough to stimulate them. While they occupy the sites, dopamine released by presynaptic neurons is blocked and cannot get in, and the schizophrenic symptoms usually decrease.

DRUG TOLERANCE AND DEPENDENCE

When a drug is used repeatedly, the intensity of effects produced by the same dosage level may decrease over time. This *decreasing responsivity to a drug is called* **tolerance.** As it develops, the person must take increasingly larger doses to achieve the same physical and psychological effects. Tolerance stems from the body's attempt to maintain a state of optimal physiological balance, called *homeostasis.* If a drug changes bodily functioning in a certain way, say by increasing heart rate, the brain tries to restore balance by producing **compensatory responses,** *which are reactions opposite to that of the drug* (e.g., reactions that decrease heart rate).

What happens when drug tolerance develops and the person suddenly stops using the drug? The body's compensatory responses may con-tinue and, no longer balanced out by the drug's effects, the person can experience strong reactions opposite to those produced by the drug. This *occurrence of compensatory responses after discontinued drug use is known as* **withdrawal.** For example, in the absence of alcohol's sedating and relaxing effects, a chronic drinker may experience anxiety and hypertension.

Learning, Drug Tolerance, and Overdose

Tolerance for various drugs depends partly on the familiarity of the drug setting. Figure 5.25 illustrates how environmental stimuli associated with repeated drug use begin to elicit compensatory responses through a learning process called *classical conditioning.* As drug use continues, the physical setting triggers progressively stronger compensatory responses, increasing the user's tolerance. This helps explain why drug addicts often experience increased cravings when they enter a setting associated with drug use. The environmental stimuli trigger compensatory responses that, without drugs to mask their effect, cause the user to feel withdrawal symptoms (Duncan et al., 2000).

There is a hidden danger in this process, particularly for experienced drug users. Compensatory responses serve a protective function by physiologically countering part of the drug's effects. If a user takes his or her usual high dose in a familiar environment, the body's compensatory responses are at full strength—a combination of compensatory reactions to the drug itself and also to the familiar, conditioned environmental stimuli. But in an *unfamiliar* environment, the conditioned compensatory responses are weaker, and

▶ **Focus 18**
How are tolerance, compensatory responses, withdrawal, and dependence related? How does learning affect tolerance?

Conditioned Drug Responses

1. Take drug → Body produces compensatory responses.

2. Repeatedly take drug in a particular setting → Compensatory responses.

3. Setting alone → *now produces* → Conditioned compensatory response.

4. Take same dose of drug in unfamiliar setting → Compensatory responses not at full strength. Drug produces stronger reaction. "Overdose" more likely.

FIGURE 5.25

Conditioned drug responses and overdose. Environmental stimuli that are repeatedly paired with the use of a drug can eventually trigger compensatory responses on their own. If the same drug dose is now taken in a new setting, compensatory responses will not be at full strength, thereby increasing the risk of an "overdose" reaction.

the drug has a stronger physiological net effect than usual (Siegel et al., 2000).

Shepard Siegel (1984) interviewed people addicted to heroin who experienced near-fatal overdoses. He found that in most cases they had not taken a dose larger than their customary one. Rather, they had injected a normal dose in an unfamiliar environment. Siegel concluded that the addicts were not protected by their usual compensatory responses, resulting in an "overdose" reaction.

Drug Addiction and Dependence

Drug addiction, which is formally called **substance dependence,** *is a maladaptive pattern of substance use that causes a person significant distress or substantially impairs that person's life.* Substance dependence is diagnosed as occurring with *physiological dependence* if drug tolerance or withdrawal symptoms have developed. The term *psychological dependence* is often used to describe situations in which people strongly crave a drug because of its pleasurable effects, even if they are not physiologically dependent. However, this is not a diagnostic term, and some drug experts feel it is misleading. Drug cravings do have a physical basis; they are rooted in patterns of brain activity (Sun & Rebec, 2005).

Misconceptions About Substance Dependence

Many people mistakenly believe that if a drug does not produce tolerance or withdrawal, one cannot become dependent on it. In reality, neither tolerance nor withdrawal is needed for a diagnosis of substance dependence.

The popular media image of a shaking alcoholic desperately searching for a drink or a heroin junkie looking for a fix reinforces another misconception, namely that the motivation to avoid or end withdrawal symptoms is the primary cause of addiction. Such physiological dependence contributes powerfully to drug dependence, but consider these points:

- People can become dependent on drugs, such as cocaine, that produce only mild withdrawal (Kampmann et al., 2002). The drug's pleasurable effects—often produced by boosting dopamine activity—play a key role in causing dependence.

- Many drug users who quit and make it through withdrawal eventually start using again, even though they are no longer physiologically dependent.

- Many factors influence drug dependence, including genetic predispositions, personality traits, religious beliefs, family and peer influences, and cultural norms.

DEPRESSANTS

Depressants *decrease nervous system activity.* In moderate doses, they reduce feelings of tension and anxiety and produce a state of relaxed euphoria. In extremely high doses, depressants can slow down vital life processes to the point of death.

Alcohol

Alcohol is the most widely used recreational drug in many cultures. A national survey of American college students found that 66 percent had consumed alcohol within the previous month, with 41 percent bingeing (five or more drinks at one time) within the previous two weeks (Johnston et al., 2004). Tolerance develops gradually and can lead to physiological dependence.

Alcohol dampens the nervous system by increasing the activity of GABA, the brain's main inhibitory neurotransmitter, and by decreasing the activity of glutamate, a major excitatory neurotransmitter (Anton, 2001). Why, then, if alcohol is a depressant drug, do many people initially seem less inhibited when they drink and report getting a high from alcohol? In part, the weakening of inhibitions occurs because alcohol's neural slowdown depresses the action of inhibitory control centers in the brain. As for the subjective high, alcohol boosts the activity of several neurotransmitters, such as dopamine, that produce feelings of pleasure and euphoria (Lewis, 1996; Tupala & Tiihonen, 2004). At higher doses, however, the brain's control centers become increasingly disrupted, thinking and physical coordination become disorganized, and fatigue may occur as blood alcohol level (BAL) rises (Table 5.3).

► **Focus 19**
How do depressants affect the brain? How does alcohol intoxication affect decisions about drinking and driving?

TABLE 5.3   Behavioral Effects of Alcohol

BAL	Hours to Leave Body	Behavioral Effects
.03	1	Decreased alertness, impaired reaction time in some people
.05	2	Decreased alertness, impaired judgment and reaction time, good feeling, release of inhibitions
.10	4	Severely impaired reaction time, motor function, and judgment; lack of caution
.15	10	Gross intoxication, worsening impairments
.25	?	Extreme sensory and motor impairment, staggering
.30	?	Stuporous but conscious, cannot comprehend immediate environment
.40	?	Lethal in over 50 percent of cases

1 glass of wine = 1 shot of whiskey = 1 bottle of beer

Number of drinks in a 2-hour period

Caution: some impairment
BAL up to .05

Definite impairment: legally drunk
in some areas
BAL .05 to .09

Marked impairment: legally drunk
in all areas
BAL .10 or more

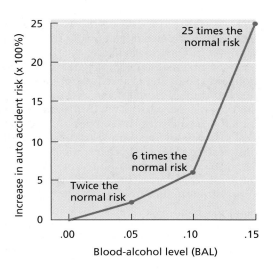

FIGURE 5.26

Drinking, driving, and accident risk. At .08 to 0.10 BAL, the legal definition of intoxication in most American states and Canadian provinces, the risk of having an auto accident is about 6 times greater than at 0.00, and the risk climbs to 25 times higher at a BAL of 0.15. SOURCE: Based on National Safety Council, 1992.

The *blood-alcohol level (BAL)* is a measure of alcohol concentration in the body. Elevated BALs impair reaction time, coordination, and decision making and also increase risky behaviors (Figure 5.26). About 40 percent of American and Canadian traffic accident deaths involve alcohol (National Highway Traffic Safety Administration, 2002).

Why do intoxicated people often act in risky ways that they wouldn't when sober? It is not simply a matter of lowered inhibitions. Alcohol also produces what Claude Steele and Robert Josephs (1990) call **alcohol myopia,** *shortsighted thinking caused by the inability to pay attention to as much information as when sober*. People who drink start to focus only on aspects of the situation (cues) that stand out. In the absence of strong cautionary cues (such as warnings) to inhibit risky behavior, they don't think about long-term consequences of their actions as carefully as when they are sober. Our "Research Close-Up" illustrates this effect.

Research Close-Up — Drinking and Driving: Decision Making in Altered States

SOURCE: TARA K. MACDONALD, MARK P. ZANNA, and GEOFFREY T. FONG (1995). Decision making in altered states: Effects of alcohol on attitudes toward drinking and driving. *Journal of Personality and Social Psychology, 68*, 973–985.

INTRODUCTION

Most people have negative attitudes about drunk driving and say they would not do it. They realize that the cons (e.g., risk of accident, injury, death, and police arrest) far outweigh the pros (e.g., not having to ask someone for a lift). Why, then, do so many people decide to drive after becoming intoxicated?

Based on alcohol-myopia principles, Tara MacDonald and her colleagues reasoned that when intoxicated people decide whether to drive, they may focus on the pros or the cons but do not have the attentional capacity to focus on both. If a circumstance that favors driving (a *facilitating cue*) is called to the intoxicated person's attention (e.g., "It's only a short distance"), she or he will latch onto it and fail to consider the cons. But in general situations that do not contain facilitating cues, intoxicated people's feelings about driving should remain as negative as when they were sober.

The authors made two predictions. First, intoxicated and sober people will have equally negative *general attitudes* and intentions toward drinking and driving. Second, intoxicated people will have less negative attitudes and greater intentions toward drinking and driving than sober people in situations that contain a facilitating cue.

METHOD

Laboratory Experiment

Fifty-seven male introductory psychology students, all regular drinkers who owned cars, participated. They were randomly assigned to either the sober condition, in which they received no alcohol, or the alcohol condition, in which they received three alcoholic drinks within an hour (the average

Continued

BAL was .074 percent, just below the .08 percent legal driving limit in Ontario, Canada).

Participants then completed a drinking-and-driving questionnaire. Some items asked about general attitudes and intentions (e.g., "I will drink and drive the next time that I am out at a party or bar with friends"). Other items contained a facilitating cue, a special circumstance that suggested a possible reason for drinking and driving ("If I had only a short distance to drive home . . . / If my friends tried to persuade me to drink and drive . . . I would drive while intoxicated."). Participants rated each item on a 9-point scale (1 = "strongly disagree"; 9 = "strongly agree").

Party/Bar Diary Study

Fifty-one male and female college students recorded a telephone diary while at a party or bar where they were going to drink alcohol. Some were randomly assigned to record the diary when they first arrived; others, just before they left. To record the diary, participants opened up a packet containing the same drinking-and-driving questionnaire described above, called a number on the packet, and recorded their responses on the researchers' answering machine. Based on participants' descriptions of how much alcohol they had consumed, the researchers estimated their BAL and identified two groups: "sober participants" (average BAL .01) and "intoxicated participants" (average BAL .11).

RESULTS

The findings from both studies supported the predictions. Sober participants and intoxicated participants both expressed negative general attitudes about drinking and driving and indicated they would not drive when intoxicated. But, as Figure 5.27 shows, when the questions presented a special circumstance, intoxicated participants expressed more favorable attitudes and a greater intention to drive than sober participants.

DISCUSSION

This study nicely illustrates how a person's physiological state (sober versus intoxicated) and an environmental factor (general situation versus special circumstance) interact to influence psychological functioning (attitudes and decision making). However, let's think critically about the results. Was it really narrowed attention—leading to a failure to consider negative consequences—that caused the results? The authors anticipated two alternative explanations. First, perhaps people who drink do not realize how intoxicated they are. Second, perhaps intoxicated people overestimate their driving ability, a

FIGURE 5.27

Intoxicated and sober people's attitudes toward drinking and driving. When general attitudes and intentions toward drinking and driving are measured, intoxicated and sober participants have similar negative reactions. But when questioned about situations involving special circumstances (facilitating cues), intoxicated participants have more favorable attitudes and greater intentions to drive after drinking than do sober participants. Source: MacDonald et al., 1995.

belief called *drunken invincibility*. The authors tested and ruled out these explanations. Intoxicated participants believed they were *more* intoxicated than they actually were and also estimated that they would drive *more poorly* than the average person.

Is it possible that the findings were caused by participants' expectations about alcohol rather than its chemical effects? The authors conducted a placebo control experiment in which some participants were convincingly misled to believe they were intoxicated. Results showed that the alcohol-myopia effect occurred only for participants who truly had consumed alcohol. It was not caused by participants' expectations.

What practical value do these findings have? The researchers suggest that a sign saying "Drinking and Driving Kills," or a large photograph of a police officer administering a breathalyzer test, be made highly visible near the exit of a bar. Alcohol myopia should cause intoxicated people to narrow their focus of attention to these *inhibiting cues*, causing them to rethink any decision to drink and drive. In subsequent research, MacDonald and coworkers (2003) found that making strong inhibiting cues salient did indeed lead intoxicated people to behave more cautiously.

Barbiturates and Tranquilizers

Physicians prescribe barbiturates (sleeping pills) and tranquilizers (antianxiety drugs, such as Valium) as sedatives and relaxants. Like alcohol, they depress the nervous system by increasing the activity of the inhibitory neurotransmitter GABA (Nishino et al., 2001).

Mild doses are effective as sleeping pills but are highly addictive. As tolerance builds, addicted people may take up to 50 sleeping pills a day. At high doses, barbiturates trigger initial excitation, followed by slurred speech, loss of coordination, depression, and memory impairment. Overdoses, particularly when taken with alcohol, may cause unconsciousness, coma, and even death. Barbiturates and tranquilizers are widely overused, and tolerance and physiological dependence can occur. Users often don't recognize that they have become dependent until they try to stop and experience serious withdrawal symptoms, such as anxiety, insomnia, and possibly seizures.

STIMULANTS

Stimulants *increase neural firing and arouse the nervous system.* They increase blood pressure, respiration, heart rate, and overall alertness. While they can elevate mood to the point of euphoria, they also can heighten irritability.

Amphetamines

Amphetamines are powerful stimulants prescribed to reduce appetite and fatigue, decrease the need for sleep, and reduce depression. Unfortunately, they are widely overused to boost energy and mood (Anthony et al., 1997).

Amphetamines increase dopamine and norepinephrine activity. Tolerance develops, and users may crave their pleasurable effects. Eventually, many heavy users start injecting large quantities, producing a sudden surge of energy and rush of intense pleasure. With frequent injections, they may remain awake for a week, their bodily systems racing at breakneck speed. Injecting amphetamines greatly increases blood pressure and can lead to heart failure and cerebral hemor-

rhage (stroke); repeated high doses may cause brain damage (Diaz, 1997).

There is an inevitable crash when heavy users stop taking the drug. They may sleep for 1 to 2 days, waking up depressed, exhausted, and irritable. This crash occurs because the neurons' norepinephrine and dopamine supplies have become depleted. Amphetamines tax the body heavily.

Cocaine

Cocaine is a powder derived from the coca plant, which grows mainly in western South America. Usually inhaled or injected, it produces excitation, a sense of increased muscular strength, and euphoria. Cocaine increases the activity of norepinephrine and dopamine by blocking their reuptake.

At various times in history, cocaine has been hailed as a wonder drug and branded as a menace. It was once widely used as a local anesthetic in eye, nose, and throat surgery. Novocain, a synthetic form of cocaine, is still used in dentistry as an anesthetic. Due to its stimulating effects, cocaine found its way into potions sold to the public to enhance health. In 1885 John Pemberton developed Coca Cola by mixing cocaine with the kola nut and syrup (Figure 5.28).

In large doses, cocaine can produce vomiting, convulsions, and paranoid delusions (Boutros et al., 2002). A depressive crash may occur after a cocaine high. Tolerance develops to many of cocaine's effects, and chronic use has been associated with an increased risk of cognitive impairments and brain

▶ **Focus 20**
How do amphetamines, cocaine, and Ecstasy affect the brain? Why can their use lead to a "crash"?

FIGURE 5.28

(a) When Coca-Cola was first produced, there was a clear reason why it "relieved fatigue": It contained cocaine. (b) Before it was made illegal, cocaine was found in a variety of medicinal products.

(a)

(b)

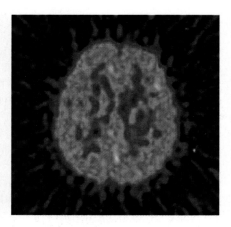

FIGURE 5.29

Frequent Ecstasy use and the brain. (*left*) This PET-scan image shows the brain of a person who never used Ecstasy. (*right*) This image shows the brain of a person who used Ecstasy 70 times or more over a period of at least 1.5 years but who stopped using the drug for several weeks before these images were taken. Areas of lighter color indicate a higher density of special proteins (called *transporters*) necessary for normal serotonin reuptake. The darker image of the brain on the right suggests that there is damage to the serotonin reuptake system. SOURCE: McCann et al., 1998.

▶ **Focus 21**
Describe the major effects and dangers of opiates, hallucinogens, and marijuana.

damage (Franklin et al., 2002). Crack is a chemically converted form of cocaine that can be smoked, and its effects are faster and more dangerous. Overdoses can cause sudden death from cardiorespiratory arrest.

Ecstasy (MDMA)

Ecstasy, also known as MDMA (methylenedioxymethamphetamine), is artificially synthesized and has a chemical structure that partly resembles both methamphetamine (a stimulant) and mescaline (a hallucinogen). Ecstasy produces feelings of pleasure, elation, empathy, and warmth. In the brain, it primarily increases serotonin functioning, which boosts one's mood but may cause agitation. After the drug wears off, users often feel sluggish and depressed—a rebound effect partly due to serotonin depletion (Travers & Lyvers, 2005). They may have to take increasingly stronger doses to overcome tolerance to Ecstasy.

Ecstasy is called a *rave drug* because it is used at nightclubs and rave parties. In experiments with laboratory rats, Ecstasy has produced long-lasting damage to the axon terminals of neurons that release serotonin (Mechan et al., 2002). Human studies of habitual Ecstasy users suggest a similar possibility (Figure 5.29), but it is not clear whether such damage is permanent. In the long run, Ecstasy may produce consequences that are anything but pleasurable. Continued use has been associated with impaired memory, sleep difficulties, and a diminished capacity to experience sexual pleasure (Parrott, 2001).

OPIATES

Opium is a product of the opium poppy. *Opium and drugs derived from it, such as morphine, codeine, and heroin, are called* **opiates.** Opiates have two major effects: they provide pain relief and cause mood changes, which may include euphoria. Opiates stimulate receptors normally activated by endorphins, thereby producing pain relief. Opiates also increase dopamine activity, which may be one reason they induce euphoria (Bardo, 1998).

In medical use, opiates are the most effective agents known for relieving intense pain. Heroin was developed in 1889 by the Bayer company (which today produces aspirin). Initially thought to be a nonaddictive painkiller, heroin is, like other opiates, highly addictive. In the 1920s it was made illegal in the United States.

Heroin users feel an intense rush within several minutes of an injection, but they often pay a high price for this transient pleasure. High doses may lead to coma, and overdoses can cause death (Julien, 2005).

HALLUCINOGENS

Hallucinogens *are powerful mind-altering drugs that produce hallucinations.* Many are derived from natural sources; mescaline, for example, comes from the peyote cactus. Natural hallucinogens have been considered sacred in many tribal cultures because of their ability to produce unearthly states of consciousness and contact with spiritual forces (Figure 5.30). Other hallucinogens, such as LSD (lysergic acid diethylamide, or "acid") and phencyclidine ("angel dust") are synthetic.

Hallucinogens distort sensory experience and can blur the boundaries between reality and

FIGURE 5.30

In some cultures, hallucinogenic drugs are thought to have spiritual powers. Under the influence of peyote, this Indian shaman prepares to conduct a religious ceremony.

fantasy. Users may speak of having mystical experiences and of feeling exhilarated. They may also experience violent outbursts, paranoia, and panic and have flashbacks after the trip has ended. The mental effects of hallucinogens are always unpredictable, even if they are taken repeatedly. This unpredictability constitutes their greatest danger.

LSD is a powerful hallucinogen that causes a flooding of excitation in the nervous system. Tolerance develops rapidly but decreases quickly. It increases the activity of serotonin and dopamine at certain receptor sites, but scientists still do not know precisely how LSD produces its effects (Nichols & Sanders-Bush, 2002).

MARIJUANA

Marijuana, a product of the hemp plant (*Cannabis sativa*), is the most widely used and controversial illegal drug in the United States (Figure 5.31). **THC (tetrahydrocannabinol)** *is marijuana's major active ingredient*, and it binds to receptors on neurons throughout the brain. But why does the brain have receptor sites for a foreign substance such as marijuana? The answer is that the brain produces its own THC-like substances called *cannabinoids* (Devane et al., 1992). With chronic use, THC may increase GABA activity, which slows down neural activity and produces relaxing effects (Diaz, 1997). THC also increases

dopamine activity, which may account for some of its pleasurable subjective effects (Maldonado & Rodriguez de Fonseca, 2002).

Misconceptions about Marijuana

One misconception about marijuana is that chronic use causes people to become unmotivated and apathetic toward everything, a condition called *amotivational syndrome*. Another misconception is that marijuana causes people to start using more dangerous drugs. Neither statement is supported by scientific evidence (Diaz, 1997; Rao, 2001). A third misconception is that using marijuana has no significant dangers. In fact, marijuana smoke contains more cancer-causing substances than does tobacco smoke. At high doses, users may experience negative changes in mood, sensory distortions, and feelings of panic and anxiety. While users are high, marijuana can impair their reaction time, thinking, memory, learning, and driving skills (Lane et al., 2005).

Another misconception is that users can't become dependent on marijuana. Actually, repeated marijuana use produces tolerance, and at typical doses, some chronic users may experience mild withdrawal symptoms, such as restlessness. People who use chronically high doses and suddenly stop may experience vomiting, disrupted sleep, and irritability. About 5 to 10 percent of people who use marijuana develop dependence (Coffey et al., 2002).

FROM GENES TO CULTURE: DETERMINANTS OF DRUG EFFECTS

Table 5.4 summarizes some typical drug effects, but a user's reaction depends on more than the drug's chemical structure.

Biological Factors

Animal research indicates that genetic factors influence sensitivity and tolerance to drugs' effects (Boehm et al., 2002). The most extensive research has focused on alcohol. Rats and mice can be genetically bred to inherit a strong preference for drinking alcohol instead of water. Even in their first exposure to alcohol, these rats show greater tolerance than normal rats.

Among humans, identical twins have a higher concordance rate for alcoholism than do fraternal twins (Heath et al., 1997). Scientists have also identified a gene that is found more often among alcoholics and their children than among nonalcoholics and their offspring (Noble, 1998). No one claims that this is an "alcoholism gene";

▶ **Focus 22**
Explain how drug reactions depend on biological, psychological, and environmental factors.

FIGURE 5.31

Marijuana is illegal in the United States at the federal level, but some jurisdictions have legalized marijuana use for certain medical purposes. Although the U.S. Supreme Court ruled against the medical legalization of marijuana in 2005, the issue remains hotly debated.

TABLE 5.4   Effects of Some Major Drugs

Class	Typical Effects	Risks of High Doses and/or Chronic Use
Depressants		
Alcohol	Relaxation, lowered inhibition, impaired physical and psychological functioning	Disorientation, unconsciousness, possible death at extreme doses
Barbiturates, tranquilizers	Reduced tension, impaired reflexes and motor functioning, drowsiness	Shallow breathing, clammy skin, weak and rapid pulse, coma, possible death
Stimulants		
Amphetamines, cocaine, Ecstasy	Increased alertness, pulse, and blood pressure; elevated mood; suppressed appetite; agitation; sleeplessness	Hallucinations, paranoid delusions, convulsions, long-term cognitive impairments, brain damage, possible death
Opiates		
Opium, morphine, codeine, heroin	Euphoria, pain relief, drowsiness, impaired motor and psychological functioning	Shallow breathing, convulsions, coma, possible death
Hallucinogens		
LSD, mescaline, phencyclidine	Hallucinations and visions, distorted time perception, loss of contact with reality, nausea	Psychotic reactions (delusions, paranoia), panic, possible death
Marijuana	Mild euphoria, relaxation, enhanced sensory experiences, increased appetite, impaired memory and reaction time	Fatigue, anxiety, disorientation, sensory distortions, possible psychotic reactions, exposure to carcinogens

rather, it may influence how the brain responds to alcohol.

People who grow up with alcoholic versus nonalcoholic parents respond differently to drinking alcohol under laboratory conditions. Adults who had alcoholic parents typically display faster hormonal and psychological reactions as blood-alcohol levels rise, but these responses drop off more quickly as blood-alcohol levels decrease (Newlin & Thomson, 1997). Compared with other people, they must drink more alcohol over the course of a few hours to maintain their feeling of intoxication. Overall, many scientists see evidence for a genetic role in determining responsiveness and addiction to alcohol (Knopik et al., 2004).

Psychological Factors

At the psychological level, people's beliefs and expectancies can influence drug reactions (George et al., 2000). Experiments show that people may behave as if drunk if they simply think they have consumed alcohol but actually have not. If a person's fellow drinkers are happy and gregarious, he or she may feel it's expected to respond the same way. Personality factors also influence drug reactions and usage. People who have difficulty adjusting to life's demands or whose contact with reality is marginal may be particularly vulnerable to severe and negative drug reactions and to drug addiction (Ray & Ksir, 2004).

Environmental Factors

The physical and social setting in which a drug is taken can strongly influence a user's reactions. As noted earlier, merely being in a familiar drug-use setting can trigger compensatory physiological responses and cravings. Moreover, the behavior of other people who are sharing the drug experience provides important cues for how to respond, and a hostile environment may increase the chances of a bad trip with drugs such as LSD (Palfai & Jankiewicz, 1991).

Cultural learning also affects how people respond to a drug (Bloomfield et al., 2002). In many Western cultures, increased aggressiveness and sexual promiscuity are commonly associated with drunken excess. In contrast, members of the Camba culture of Bolivia customarily drink large quantities of a 178-proof beverage, remaining cordial and nonaggressive between episodes of passing out. In the 1700s, Tahitians introduced to alcohol by European sailors reacted at first with pleasant relaxation when intoxicated, but after witnessing the violent aggressiveness exhibited by drunken sailors, they too began behaving aggressively (MacAndrew & Edgerton, 1969).

Cultural factors also affect drug consumption. Traditionally, members of the Navajo tribe do not consider drinking any amount of alcohol to be normal, whereas drinking wine or beer is central to social life in some European countries

LEVELS OF ANALYSIS Factors Related to the Effects of Drugs

Biological

- Agonistic or antagonistic effects on neurotransmission
- Neural pathways and brain centers affected by drug action
- Compensatory responses and tolerance to drug intake
- Genetic factors that influence biological reactivity to specific drugs

Psychological

- Attitudes toward the drug and drug use
- Expectations concerning drug effects
- Individual's level of personal adjustment, which can influence the likelihood of a negative response

Environmental

- Cultural norms and experiences that affect user expectations
- Physical setting and presence of conditioned compensatory stimuli
- Social context and behavior of other drug users who are present

Drug-Induced States of Consciousness

FIGURE 5.32

Levels of analysis: Factors related to the effects of drugs.

(Tanaka-Matsumi & Draguns, 1997). In some cultures, hallucinogenic drugs are feared and outlawed, whereas in others they are used in medicinal or religious contexts to seek advice from spirits. Figure 5.32 summarizes some of the biological, environmental, and psychological factors that may influence drug experiences.

IN REVIEW

- Drugs alter consciousness by modifying neurotransmitter activity. Agonists increase the activity of a neurotransmitter, whereas antagonists decrease it.

- Tolerance develops when the body produces compensatory responses to counteract a drug's effects. When drug use is stopped, compensatory responses continue and produce withdrawal symptoms.

- Substance dependence is a maladaptive pattern of drug use. It can occur with or without physiological dependence.

- Depressants, such as alcohol, barbiturates, and tranquilizers, decrease neural activity. The weakened inhibitions often associated with low alcohol doses partly occur because alcohol depresses inhibitory brain centers.

- Amphetamines and cocaine are stimulants that increase arousal and boost mood. Ecstasy produces elation but can also cause agitation. A depressive crash can occur after these drugs wear off. Repeated use may produce serious negative psychological effects and bodily damage.

- Opiates increase endorphin activity, producing pain relief and mood changes that may include euphoria. Opiates are important in medicine but are highly addictive.

- Hallucinogens, such as LSD, powerfully distort sensory experience and can blur the line between reality and fantasy.

- Marijuana produces relaxation at low doses but can cause anxiety and sensory distortions at higher doses. It can impair thinking and reflexes.

- A drug's effect depends on its chemical actions, the physical and social setting, cultural norms and learning, as well as the user's genetic predispositions, expectations, and personality.

HYPNOSIS

In 18th-century Vienna, physician Anton Mesmer gained fame for using magnetized objects to cure patients. He claimed that illness was caused by blockages of an invisible bodily fluid and that his technique of "animal magnetism" (later named *mesmerism* in his honor) would restore the fluid's normal flow. A scientific commission discredited mesmerism, but its use continued. Decades later, Scottish surgeon James Braid investigated the fact that mesmerized patients often went into a trance in which they seemed oblivious to their surroundings. Braid concluded that mesmerism was a state of "nervous sleep" produced by concentrated attention, and he renamed it *hypnosis*, after Hypnos, the Greek god of sleep.

► Focus 23
Evaluate claims that hypnosis can produce involuntary behavior, amazing feats, pain relief, and altered memory.

THE SCIENTIFIC STUDY OF HYPNOSIS

Hypnosis *is a state of heightened suggestibility in which some people are able to experience imagined situations as if they were real.* Hypnosis draws great interest because many therapists use it in treating mental disorders. In the United States, about 25 percent of psychology Ph.D. programs offer a course in hypnosis (Walling et al., 1998). Basic scientists, exploring whether hypnosis is a unique state of altered consciousness, put its claims to rigorous test.

Hypnotic induction is the process by which one person (a researcher or hypnotist) leads another person (the subject) into hypnosis. A hypnotist may ask the subject to sit down and gaze at an object on the wall, and then, in a quiet voice, suggest that the subject's eyes are becoming heavy. The goal is to relax the subject and increase her or his concentration.

Contrary to popular belief, people cannot be hypnotized against their will. Even when people want to be hypnotized, they differ in how susceptible (i.e., responsive) they are to hypnotic suggestions. **Hypnotic susceptibility scales** *contain a standard series of pass-fail suggestions that are read to a subject after a hypnotic induction* (Table 5.5). The subject's score is based on the number of passes. About 10 percent of subjects are completely nonresponsive, 10 percent pass all or nearly all of the items, and the rest fall in between (Hilgard, 1977).

HYPNOTIC BEHAVIORS AND EXPERIENCES

Does hypnosis alter people's psychological functioning and behavior? Let's examine some claims.

Involuntary Control and Behaving against One's Will

Hypnotized people *subjectively experience* their actions to be involuntary (Kirsch, 2001). For example, look at the second item in Table 5.5. To hypnotized subjects, it really feels like their hands are being pushed apart by a mysterious force, rather than by their conscious control.

If behavior seems involuntary under hypnosis, then can a hypnotist make people perform acts that are harmful to themselves or others? Martin Orne and Frederick Evans (1965) found that hypnotized subjects could be induced to dip their hands briefly in a foaming solution they were told was acid and then to throw the "acid" in another person's face. This might appear to be a striking example of the power of hypnosis to get people to act against their will. However, Orne and Evans tested a control group of subjects who were asked to simply pretend that they were hypnotized. These subjects were just as likely as hypnotized subjects to put their hands in the "acid" and throw it at someone.

In Chapter 16 you will learn about experiments in which researchers induced hundreds of "normal" adults to keep giving what they believed were extremely painful electric shocks to an innocent man with a heart condition who begged them to stop (Milgram, 1974). Not one participant was hypnotized; they were simply following the researcher's orders. Hypnosis does not involve a unique power to get people to behave against their will (Kirsch & Braffman, 2001). A legitimate authority figure can induce people to commit out-of-character and dangerous acts whether they are hypnotized or not.

TABLE 5.5	Sample Test Items from the Stanford Hypnotic Susceptibility Scale, Form C	
Item	**Suggested Behavior**	**Criterion for Passing**
Lowering Arm	Right arm is held out; subject is told arm will become heavy and drop	Arm is lowered by 6 inches in 10 seconds
Moving Hands Apart	With hands extended and close together, subject is asked to imagine a force pushing them apart	Hands are 6 or more inches apart in 10 seconds
Mosquito Hallucination	It is suggested that a mosquito is buzzing nearby and lands on subject	Any grimace or acknowledgment of mosquito
Posthypnotic Amnesia	Subject is awakened and asked to recall suggestions after being told under hypnosis that he or she will not remember the suggestions	Three or fewer items recalled before subject is told, "Now you can remember everything."

Source: Based on Weitzenhoffer & Hilgard, 1962.

FIGURE 5.33

The human-plank demonstration, a favorite of stage hypnotists, seems to demonstrate the power of hypnosis. Are you convinced?

Amazing Feats

Have you seen or heard about stage hypnotists who get an audience member to perform an amazing physical feat, such as the "human plank" (Figure 5.33)? A subject, usually male, is hypnotized and lies outstretched between two chairs. He is told that his body is rigid and then, amazingly, another person successfully stands on the subject's legs and chest.

Similarly, hypnosis can have striking physiological effects. Consider a classic experiment involving 13 people who were strongly allergic to the toxic leaves of a certain tree (Ikemi & Nakagawa, 1962). Five of them were hypnotized, blindfolded, and told that a leaf from a harmless tree to which they were not allergic was touching one of their arms. In fact, the leaf really was toxic, but 4 out of the 5 hypnotized people had no allergic reaction. Next, the other arm of each hypnotized person was rubbed with a leaf from a harmless tree, but he or she was falsely told that the leaf was toxic. All 5 people responded to the harmless leaf with allergic reactions.

Should we attribute the human-plank feat and the unusual responses of the allergic people to unique powers of hypnosis? Here is where a healthy dose of critical thinking is important.

What Do You Think?

HYPNOSIS AND AMAZING FEATS
In the case of the human plank and in the allergy experiment, what additional evidence do you need to determine whether these amazing feats and responses really are caused by hypnosis? How could you gather this evidence? Think about it, then see page 190.

FIGURE 5.34

This patient is having her appendix removed with hypnosis as the sole anesthetic. Her verbal reports that she feels no pain are being recorded.

Pain Tolerance

Scottish surgeon James Esdaile performed more than 300 major operations in the mid-1800s using hypnosis as the sole anesthetic (Figure 5.34). Experiments confirm that hypnosis often increases pain tolerance and that this is not due to a placebo effect (Montgomery et al., 2000). For patients who experience chronic pain, hypnosis can produce relief that lasts for months or even years (Patterson, 2004). Brain-imaging research reveals that hypnosis modifies neural activity in brain areas that process painful stimuli, but nonhypnotic techniques, such as mental imagery and performing distracting cognitive tasks, also alter neural functioning and reduce pain (Petrovic & Ingvar, 2002).

We do not know exactly how hypnosis produces its painkilling effects. It may influence the release of endorphins, decrease patients' fear of pain, distract patients from their pain, or somehow help them separate the pain from conscious experience (Barber, 1998).

Hypnotic Amnesia

You may have seen TV shows or movies in which hypnotized people are given a suggestion that they will not remember something (such as a familiar person's name), either during the session itself (*hypnotic amnesia*) or after coming out of hypnosis (*posthypnotic amnesia*). A reversal cue also is given, such as a phrase ("You will now remember everything") that ends the amnesia once the person hears it. Is this Hollywood fiction?

Research indicates that about 25 percent of hypnotized college students can be led to experience amnesia (Kirsch, 2001). Although researchers agree that hypnotic and posthypnotic amnesias occur, they debate the causes. Some feel it results from voluntary attempts to avoid thinking about certain information, and others believe it is caused by an altered state of consciousness that weakens normal memory systems (Kihlstrom, 1998; Spanos, 1986).

Hypnosis, Memory Enhancement, and Eyewitness Testimony

In contrast to producing forgetting, can hypnosis enhance memory? Law enforcement agencies sometimes use hypnosis to aid the memory of eyewitnesses to crimes. In a famous 1977 case in California, a bus carrying 26 children and its driver disappeared without a trace. The victims, buried underground in an abandoned trailer truck by three kidnappers, were later found alive. After the rescue, a police expert hypnotized the bus driver and asked him to recall the ordeal. The driver formed a vivid image of the kidnappers' white van and could "read" all but one digit on the van's license plate. This information allowed the police to track down the kidnappers.

Despite occasional success stories like this one, controlled experiments find that hypnosis does not reliably improve memory. In some experiments, participants watch videotapes of simulated bank robberies or other crimes. Next, while hypnotized or not, they are questioned by police investigators or criminal lawyers. Hypnotized people display better recall than nonhypnotized people in some studies but no better recall in others (Lynn et al., 2001). In still other experiments, hypnotized participants perform more poorly than nonhypnotized controls; they recall more information, but much of that extra recall is inaccurate (Burgess & Kirsch, 1999).

Another concern is that some memories recalled under hypnosis may be *pseudomemories*, false memories *created* during hypnosis by statements or leading suggestions made by the examiner. In some experiments, hypnotized and nonhypnotized subjects are intentionally exposed to false information about an event (e.g., about a bank robbery). Later, after the hypnotized subjects have been brought out of hypnosis, all participants are questioned. Highly suggestible people who have been hypnotized are most likely to report the false information as being a true memory and

often are confident that their false memories are accurate (Sheehan et al., 1992).

Although some psychologists are exploring ways to minimize hypnosis-induced memory errors, at present, many courts have banned or limited testimony obtained under hypnosis (Wagstaff et al., 2004). The increased suggestibility of hypnotized people makes them particularly susceptible to memory distortion caused by leading questions, and they may honestly come to believe facts that never occurred (Scoboria et al., 2002). Similarly, if a therapist uses hypnosis to help patients recall long-forgotten memories of sexual abuse, what shall we conclude? Are the horrible memories real, or are they pseudomemories created during therapy? We explore this issue in Chapter 7.

THEORIES OF HYPNOSIS

Hypnos may have been the Greek god of sleep, but studies of brain physiology reveal that hypnosis definitely *is not* sleep. What is hypnosis, and how does it produce its effects?

Dissociation Theories

Several researchers propose **dissociation theories** *that view hypnosis as an altered state involving a division (dissociation) of consciousness.* Ernest Hilgard (1977, 1991) proposed that hypnosis creates a division of awareness in which the person simultaneously experiences two streams of consciousness that are cut off from one another. One stream responds to the hypnotist's suggestions, while the second stream—the part of consciousness that monitors behavior—remains in the background but is aware of everything that goes on. Hilgard refers to this second part of consciousness as the *hidden observer*.

Suppose a hypnotized subject is given a suggestion that she will not feel pain. Her arm is lowered into a tub of ice-cold water for 45 seconds, and every few seconds she reports the amount of pain. In contrast to nonhypnotized subjects, who find this experience moderately painful, she probably will report feeling little pain. But suppose the procedure is done differently. Before lowering the subject's arm, the hypnotist says, "Perhaps there is another part of you that is more aware than your hypnotized part. If so, would that part of you report the amount of pain." In this case, the subject's other stream of consciousness, the hidden observer, will report a higher level of pain (Figure 5.35).

▶ **Focus 24**
Contrast dissociation and social-cognitive theories of hypnosis. What does research on the hypnotized brain reveal?

For Hilgard, this dissociation explained why behaviors that occur under hypnosis seem involuntary or automatic. Given the suggestion that "your arm will start to feel lighter and will begin to rise," the subject intentionally raises his or her arm, but only the hidden observer is aware of this. The main stream of consciousness that responds to the command is blocked from this awareness and perceives that the arm is rising all by itself.

Social-Cognitive Theories

To other theorists, hypnosis does not represent a special state of dissociated consciousness. Instead, **social-cognitive theories** *propose that hypnotic experiences result from expectations of people who are motivated to take on the role of being hypnotized* (Kirsch, 2001; Spanos, 1991). Most people believe that hypnosis involves a trancelike state and responsiveness to suggestions. People motivated to conform to this role develop a readiness to respond to the hypnotist's suggestions and to perceive hypnotic experiences as real and involuntary.

In a classic study, Martin Orne (1959) illustrated the importance of expectations about hypnosis. During a classroom demonstration, college students were told that hypnotized people frequently exhibit spontaneous stiffening of the muscles in the dominant hand. (Actually, this rarely occurs.) An accomplice of the lecturer pretended to be hypnotized and, sure enough, he "spontaneously" exhibited hand stiffness. When students who had seen the demonstration were later hypnotized, 55 percent of them exhibited stiffening of the hand without any suggestion from the hypnotist. Control-group participants saw a demonstration that did not mention or display hand stiffening. Not one of these students exhibited hand stiffening when they were hypnotized.

Does social-cognitive theory imply that hypnotized people are faking or playacting? Not at all. Role theorists emphasize that when people immerse themselves in the hypnotic role, their responses are completely real and may indeed represent altered experiences (Kirsch, 2001). Our expectations strongly influence how the brain organizes sensory information. Often we literally see what we expect to see. According to social-cognitive theory, many effects of hypnosis represent an extension of this principle. The hypnotized subject whose arm automatically rises in response to a suggestion genuinely perceives the behavior to be involuntary because this is what

(a)   (b)

FIGURE 5.35

Hypnosis and the hidden observer. (a) This hypnotized woman's hand is immersed in painfully cold ice water. Placing his hand on her shoulder, Ernest Hilgard contacts her dissociated hidden observer. (b) This graph shows pain-intensity ratings given by a woman when she is not hypnotized, when she is under hypnosis, and by her hidden observer in the same hypnotic state. The hidden observer reports more pain than the hypnotized woman but less than the subject when she is not hypnotized. Source: Based on Hilgard, 1977.

the subject expects and because attention is focused externally on the hypnotist and the hypnotic suggestion.

THE HYPNOTIZED BRAIN

Can peering inside the brain help us determine the nature of hypnosis? To find out, take a look at the colored drawing and the gray-scale drawing in Figure 5.36. Now, do two simple tasks:

1. Look at the colored drawing again, form a mental image of it, and try to drain the color out of it. In other words, try to visualize it as if it were a gray-scale figure.

2. Next, look at the gray-scale drawing, form a mental picture of it, and try to add color to it. In other words, visualize it as if it were a colored figure.

Stephen Kosslyn and coworkers (2000) identified 8 people who scored high in hypnotic susceptibility and who reported they could successfully drain away or add color to their mental images of such drawings. Subjects then performed these tasks (in varying order) while inside a PET scanner. On some trials they were hypnotized, and on other trials they were not hypnotized.

FIGURE 5.36

Color perception and the hypnotized brain. These color and grayscale drawings are similar to the ones used by Kosslyn and his colleagues (2000).

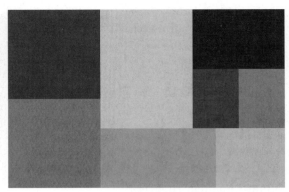

The PET scans revealed that whether subjects were hypnotized or not, an area in the right hemisphere that processes information about color was more active when subjects visualized the gray drawing as having color (Task 2) than when they visualized the color drawing as gray (Task 1). In other words, this right-hemisphere region actually responded to mental images involving color, and subjects didn't need to be hypnotized for this brain activity to occur. In the left hemisphere, however, visualizing the gray drawing as having color increased brain activation in one particular region only when the subjects were hypnotized. As the researchers noted, "The right hemisphere appeared to respond to imagery per se, whereas the left required the additional boost provided by hypnosis" (Kosslyn et al., 2000, p. 1283).

The results of brain-imaging studies converge with other physiological findings in leading to an important conclusion: Hypnotized people are not faking it but rather are experiencing an altered state of brain activation that matches their verbal reports (Raz & Shapiro, 2002). In this study, when hypnotized subjects mentally added color to the drawing and drained color from it, their brain activity changed in ways beyond those brought about by mental imagery in a nonhypnotized state. Likewise, other studies reveal that giving hypnotized subjects pain-reducing suggestions not only decreases their subjective report of pain but also decreases activity in several brain regions that process pain signals (Petrovic & Ingvar, 2002). But do these findings indicate that hypnosis is an altered state of dissociation?

Social cognitive theorists would argue that these findings do not resolve the issue (Kirsch, 2001). They note that hypnotic experiences are subjectively real, and the fact that brain activity patterns under hypnosis differ from those of simple mental imagery does not contradict their position that people's expectations are what lead them to become hypnotized in the first place. In sum, cognitive neuroscience is providing us with fascinating insights into the hypnotized brain, but it will take more research to resolve the debate about hypnosis.

I'M INTOXICATED, NO MATTER WHAT YOU SAY!

To close our discussion of hypnosis and altered states, consider the behavior of a college student in the "Research Close-Up" experiment on drinking and driving. (Nobody was hypnotized in this study.) This student consumed three nonalcoholic drinks, but through taste and smell cues, he was convincingly led to believe that they were alcoholic. Prior to taking a Breathalyzer test, he estimated his blood-alcohol level to be .07, just below the .08 legal driving limit where he lived. He felt intoxicated, and when told the drinks were nonalcoholic, he argued that there had to be a mistake. When shown his true Breathalyzer result of .000, he claimed it was rigged and refused to drive home until the effects of his drinks wore off (MacDonald et al., 1995).

This example, along with topics previously covered (e.g., voodoo spells, placebo effects), suggests that we have a remarkable capacity to alter our own state of consciousness without being aware that we ourselves are responsible for causing the change. The popular belief is that a hypnotist places the subject under a mysterious spell or into a trance, but this is a myth (Kirsch, 2001; Raz & Shapiro, 2002). Rather, like a guide on a wilderness hike, the hypnotist may point the way, but the subject is doing the actual mental work and ultimately altering her or his own state of consciousness.

IN REVIEW

■ Hypnosis involves an increased receptiveness to suggestions. Hypnotized people experience their actions as involuntary, but hypnosis has no unique power to make people behave against their will, alter their physiological reactions, or perform amazing feats. Hypnosis increases pain tolerance, as do other psychological techniques.

■ Some people can be led to experience hypnotic amnesia and posthypnotic amnesia. The use of hypnosis to improve memory is controversial. Hypnosis increases the danger that people will develop distorted memories about events in response to leading questions asked by a hypnotist or examiner.

■ Dissociation theories view hypnosis as an altered state of divided consciousness. Social-cognitive theories state that hypnotic experiences occur because people have strong expectations about hypnosis and are highly motivated to enter a hypnotized role.

■ Brain imaging reveals that hypnotized people display changes in neural activity consistent with their subjectively reported experiences. This supports the view that hypnosis involves an altered state, but whether it is a dissociated state and the extent to which people's expectations bring about this state are still unclear.

KEY TERMS AND CONCEPTS

Each term has been boldfaced and defined in the chapter on the page indicated in parentheses.

activation-synthesis theory (p. 171)
agonist (p. 174)
alcohol myopia (p. 177)
alpha waves (p. 161)
antagonist (p. 175)
automatic (unconscious) processing (p. 153)
beta waves (p. 161)
blindsight (p. 154)
blood-brain barrier (p. 174)
circadian rhythms (p. 157)
cognitive-process dream theories (p. 171)
compensatory responses (p. 175)
consciousness (p. 151)
controlled (conscious) processing (p. 153)
delta waves (p. 162)
depressants (p. 176)

dissociation theories (of hypnosis; p. 186)
divided attention (p. 153)
evolutionary/circadian sleep
  models (p. 165)
fantasy-prone personality (p. 172)
hallucinogens (p. 180)
hypnosis (p. 184)
hypnotic susceptibility scales (p. 184)
insomnia (p. 167)
melatonin (p. 157)
memory consolidation (p. 166)
narcolepsy (p. 167)
night terrors (p. 168)
opiates (p. 180)
priming (p. 154)
problem-solving dream models (p. 171)

REM sleep (p. 162)
REM-sleep behavior disorder (RBD; p. 168)
restoration model (p. 165)
seasonal affective disorder (SAD; p. 159)
selective attention (p. 151)
sleep apnea (p. 169)
slow-wave sleep (p. 162)
social-cognitive theories (of hypnosis; p. 187)
stimulants (p. 179)
substance dependence (p. 176)
suprachiasmatic nuclei (SCN; p. 157)
THC (tetrahydrocannabinol; p. 181)
tolerance (p. 175)
visual agnosia (p. 150)
wish fulfillment (p. 170)
withdrawal (p. 175)

❓ What Do You Think?

EARLY BIRDS, CLIMATE, AND CULTURE (page 158)

As a critical thinker, it's important to keep in mind that correlation does not establish causation. This is a correlational study, not an experiment. The major variables (climate of country, students' degree of morningness) were not manipulated; they were only measured. The association between climate and morningness suggests the possibility of a causal relation, but we must consider other possible explanations.

First, why might climate affect morningness? The researchers (who were from India, Spain, Wales, and the United States) hypothesized that to avoid performing daily activities during the hottest part of the day, people who live in warmer climates adapt to a pattern of rising early in the morning, a finding consistent with a prior study that revealed strong tendencies toward morningness among Brazilians (Benedito-Silva et al., 1989).

Second, as the authors note, these results could be due to factors other than climate. The Netherlands, England, and the United States share a northern-European heritage, and perhaps some aspect of this common background predisposes people toward less morningness. Yet, say the authors, India's cultural traditions are distinct from those of Spain and Colombia, so it's difficult to apply the "common cultural heritage" argument to explain the greater morningness

Continued

found among students from these countries. If not cultural heritage, perhaps the greater industrialization and use of air-conditioned environments in the Netherlands, England, and the United States to avoid summer heat reduce the necessity for residents to adapt circadian cycles to local climatic conditions. Strip away the air-conditioning from homes, workplaces, food markets, shopping centers, and cars, buses, and trains, and it would be interesting to see whether people would gradually shift toward greater morningness in hot weather. Aware of the limitations of the study, the authors suggest that climate may be just one of several factors that contribute to cross-cultural differences in morningness.

HYPNOSIS AND AMAZING FEATS (page 185)

No matter what the claim, as critical thinkers, it's always important to think about the concept of control groups. Thus, you should keep this question in mind: What would have happened anyway, even without this special treatment or intervention, or condition? Applied to hypnosis, the key question is whether people can exhibit these same amazing feats when they are not hypnotized. When a stage hypnotist gets someone to perform the human plank, the audience indeed attributes this feat to the hypnotic trance. What the audience doesn't know is that an average man suspended in this manner can support 300 pounds on his chest with little discomfort and no need of a hypnotic trance. Indeed, Figure 5.33 shows The Amazing Kreskin, a professional performer and self-proclaimed "mentalist," standing on someone who is not hypnotized.

As for the allergy experiment, the findings are impressive, but we must ask whether allergic people might show the same reactions if they were not hypnotized. For this reason, the researchers properly designed their experiment to measure the responses of 8 nonhypnotized control participants (Ikemi & Nakagawa, 1962). When blindfolded and exposed to a toxic leaf but misled to believe that it was harmless, 7 out of the 8 nonhypnotized people did not show an allergic response. Conversely, when their arm was rubbed with a harmless leaf but they were falsely told it was toxic, all 8 had an allergic reaction. In short, the nonhypnotized people responded the same way as the hypnotized subjects.

Other research shows that under hypnosis, vision in nearsighted people can be improved, warts can be cured, and stomach acidity can be increased. However, well-controlled studies show that nonhypnotized subjects can exhibit these same responses (Spanos & Chaves, 1988). As we have already seen when discussing placebo effects and other mind-body interactions, people's beliefs and expectations can produce real physiological effects.

CHAPTER SIX

Learning and Adaptation:
The Role of Experience

CHAPTER OUTLINE

A man who carries a cat by the tail learns something he can learn in no other way.

—MARK TWAIN

T hanks to six sessions of psychotherapy, Carol's life is normal again. She is now free from the intense fear of something most of us take for granted: riding in a car. Carol was severely injured in a car crash and hospitalized for months. A year later, she described to a therapist how the fear began when her husband came to take her home from the hospital.

> As we walked toward the new car he had bought, I began to feel uneasy. I felt nervous all the way home. It started to get worse after that. I found myself avoiding riding in the car, and couldn't drive it at all. I stopped visiting friends and tried to get them to come to our house. . . . After a while, even the sight of a car started to make me nervous. . . . You know, this is the first time I've left the house in about four months.

To help Carol, the therapist used a highly successful procedure based, in part, on century-old principles of learning discovered in laboratory investigations of salivating dogs.

■ ■ ■ ■ ■

O utside a Las Vegas casino, a woman volunteers her time soliciting donations for a local charity. Though hot and tired, she remains upbeat and thanks each person who drops money in her collection can. Inside, exhausted and down to his last dollar, a man has been playing the slot machines for 36 hours. A casino guard mutters to a cocktail waitress, "I'll never understand what keeps these guys going."

■ ■ ■ ■ ■

A judge in New York City prohibited two teenage brothers from watching professional wrestling on television because they were becoming too violent. The boys vigorously practiced body slams and choke holds, repeatedly injuring one another. Their frightened mother reported that her 13-year-old son tried to apply a "sleeper hold" on her as she was cooking in the kitchen. Fortunately, she broke free before losing consciousness. The judge told the mother that either she had to prohibit the boys from watching wrestling or he would have the family's TV set removed and might place the boys in foster homes (*Sporting News*, 1985).

▶ **Focus 1**
What is learning? Contrast the behavioral and ethological approaches.

Although vastly different, the behaviors in these examples share an important characteristic: They are all learned. Our genetic endowment creates the potential for these behaviors to occur, but we are not biologically programmed to fear cars, solicit donations, play slot machines, or wrestle people by applying sleeper holds.

Reflect for a moment on how much of your behavior is learned: telling time, getting dressed, driving, reading, using money, playing sports and music, and so on. Beyond such skills, learning affects our emotional reactions, perceptions, and physiological responses. Through experience, we learn to think, act, and feel in ways that contribute richly to our individual identity.

Learning *is a process by which experience produces a relatively enduring change in an organism's behavior or capabilities*. The term *capabilities* highlights a distinction made by many theorists: "knowing how" versus "doing." For example, experience may provide us with immediate knowledge (e.g., the boys *learned how* to apply a choke hold when they watched a wrestling match on TV), but in science we must measure learning by actual changes in *performance* (e.g., later that day they began applying choke holds to each other).

In this chapter we explore four basic learning processes. The first and simplest, *habituation*, involves a change in behavior that results merely from repeated exposure to a stimulus. Next, we look in depth at two types of *conditioning*, which involves learning associations between events. *Classical conditioning* occurs when two stimuli become associated with one another (say, being inside a car and being severely burned) such that one stimulus (being in a car) now triggers a response (intense fear) that previously was triggered by the other stimulus (being burned). In *operant conditioning*, organisms learn to associate their responses with specific consequences (e.g., asking for a charitable donation leads to a monetary gift). Lastly, we consider *observational learning*, in which observers imitate the behavior of a model (e.g., children imitate choke holds performed by wrestlers on TV).

This chapter focuses on how environmental experiences modify behavior, but you will see that biological and cognitive factors also play important roles in learning. You will also find many examples of how psychologists have creatively applied learning principles to enhance human welfare.

ADAPTING TO THE ENVIRONMENT

We encounter changing environments from the moment we are born, each with its unique challenges. Some challenges, such as acquiring food and shelter, affect survival. Others, such as deciding where to go on a date, do not. But no matter what the challenge, learning makes it possible for us to adapt to it. In fact, we can view learning as a process of *personal adaptation* to the circumstances of our lives.

HOW DO WE LEARN? THE SEARCH FOR MECHANISMS

For a long time, the study of learning proceeded along two largely separate paths, guided by two different perspectives on behavior: *behaviorism* and *ethology* (Bolles & Beecher, 1988). Within psychology, behaviorism dominated learning research from the early 1900s through the 1960s. Behaviorists assumed that there are laws of learning that apply to virtually all organisms. For example, each species they studied—whether birds, reptiles, rats, monkeys, or humans—responded in predictable ways to patterns of reward or punishment.

Behaviorists treated the organism as a *tabula rasa*, or "blank tablet," on which learning experiences were inscribed. Most of their research was conducted with nonhuman species in controlled laboratory settings. Behaviorists explained learning solely in terms of directly observable events and avoided speculating about an organism's unobservable mental state. The learning principles they discovered are a major focus of this chapter.

WHY DO WE LEARN? THE SEARCH FOR FUNCTIONS

While behaviorism flourished in early- to mid-20th-century America, a specialty area called *ethology* arose in Europe within the discipline of biology (Lorenz, 1937; Tinbergen, 1951). Ethologists focused on animal behavior in the natural environment and noted striking differences among species, not so much in how they learned but in what they learned in order to survive. Ethologists viewed the organism as anything but a blank tablet, arguing that because of evolution, every species comes into the world biologically prepared to act in certain ways. Ethologists focused on the *functions* of behavior, particularly its **adaptive significance,** *how a behavior influences an organism's chances of survival and reproduction in its natural environment.*

Consider how newly hatched herring gulls beg for food by pecking at a red mark on their parents' bills. Parents respond by regurgitating food, which the chicks ingest. Seeing the red mark and long shape of a parent's bill automatically triggers the chicks' pecking. This behavior is so strongly prewired that chicks will peck just as much at long inanimate models or objects with red dots or stripes (Figure 6.1). Ethologists call this instinctive behavior a **fixed action pattern,** *an unlearned response automatically triggered by a particular stimulus.*

Herring gull

Inanimate releaser stimuli
(Model of gull face, rod)

FIGURE 6.1

Releaser stimuli. A herring gull hatchling will peck most frequently at objects that are long and have red markings, even if they are inanimate models or do not look like adult gulls. This fixed action pattern is present from birth and does not require learning. The stimuli that trigger a fixed action pattern, such as the red markings on the inanimate objects and on the beak of the real herring gull shown here, are called *releaser stimuli.* SOURCE: Adapted from Hailman, 1969.

FIGURE 6.2

People in each culture learn specific behaviors in order to adapt to their environment. Even the same general skill will take on different forms depending on unique environmental demands.

As ethology grew, several things became clear. First, some fixed action patterns are modified by experience. Unlike herring gull hatchlings, older chicks have learned what an adult gull looks like and will not peck at an inanimate object unless it resembles the head of an adult (Hailman, 1967). Second, in many cases what appears to be instinctive behavior actually involves learning. For example, the indigo bunting is a songbird that migrates between North and Central America. As if by pure instinct, it knows which direction to fly by using the North Star to navigate. (The North Star is the only stationary star in the Northern Hemisphere that maintains a fixed compass position.) Experiments show, however, that although the indigo bunting is genetically prewired to navigate by a fixed star, it has to learn through experience which specific star in the nighttime sky is stationary (Emlen, 1975).

LEARNING, CULTURE, AND EVOLUTION

The separate paths of behaviorism and ethology have increasingly converged (Papini, 2002), reminding us that the environment shapes behavior in two fundamental ways: through *personal adaptation* and through *species adaptation*. Our personal adaptation to life's circumstances occurs through the laws of learning that the behaviorists and other psychologists have examined, and it results from our interactions with immediate and past environments.

When you drive or go out on a date, your behavior is influenced by the immediate environment (e.g., traffic, your date's smiles) and by capabilities you acquired through past experiences (e.g., driving skills, social skills). Because culture plays an ongoing role in shaping our present and past experiences, it strongly affects what we learn. Cultural socialization influences our beliefs and perceptions, our social behavior and sense of

identity, the skills that we acquire, and countless other characteristics (Figure 6.2).

The environment also influences species adaptation. Over the course of evolution, environmental conditions faced by each species help shape its biology. This does not occur directly. Learning, for example, does not modify an organism's genes, and therefore learned behaviors do not pass genetically from one generation to the next. But through natural selection, genetically based characteristics that enhance a species' ability to adapt to the environment—and thus to survive and reproduce—are more likely to be passed on to the next generation. Eventually, as physical features (e.g., the red mark on the adult gull's beak) and behavioral tendencies (e.g., the chick's pecking the mark) influenced by those genes become more common, they become a part of a species' very nature.

Theorists propose that as the human brain evolved, it acquired adaptive capacities that enhanced our ability to learn and solve problems (Chiappe & MacDonald, 2005; Cosmides & Tooby, 2002). In essence, we have become prewired to learn. Of course, so have other species. Because all species face some common adaptive challenges, we might expect some similarity in their library of learning mechanisms. Every environment is full of events, and each organism must learn

- which events are, or are not, important to its survival and well-being;
- which stimuli signal that an important event is about to occur;
- whether its responses will produce positive or negative consequences.

As we will see, each learning process examined in this chapter helps us respond to one or more of these adaptive challenges. Consider, for example, a learning process known as *habituation*.

► **Focus 2**

Discuss the relation of culture and evolution to learning. Describe habituation and its adaptive significance.

HABITUATION

Imagine that you are a participant in an experiment. You're sitting alone in a quiet laboratory when suddenly (as part of the experiment) a loud sound startles you. Your body jerks slightly, you become aroused, and you look toward the source of the sound. Over time, as you hear it again and again, your startle response diminishes until eventually you ignore the sound.

Habituation *is a decrease in the strength of response to a repeated stimulus.* It may be the simplest form of learning and occurs across species ranging from humans to dragonflies to sea snails. Touch the skin of a sea snail in a certain location, and it will reflexively contract its gill. With repeated touches, this response habituates. Habituation serves a key adaptive function. If an organism responded to every stimulus in its environment, it would rapidly become overwhelmed and exhausted. By learning not to respond to uneventful familiar stimuli, organisms conserve energy and can attend to other stimuli that are important.

Habituation also plays an important role in enabling scientists to study behavior. Whether observing animal behavior in the wild or children's behavior in a classroom, the mere presence of a researcher may initially disrupt participants' natural responses. Thus before collecting data, observers often allow the people or animals they are studying to habituate to their presence.

IN REVIEW

- Learning is a process by which experience produces a relatively enduring change in an organism's behavior or capabilities. Learning is measured by changes in performance.

- Learning involves adapting to the environment. Historically, behaviorists focused on the processes by which organisms learn, and ethologists focused on the adaptive significance of learning.

- The environment influences adaptation in two major ways: personal adaptation, which occurs through the laws of learning that the behaviorists examined, and species adaptation, which occurs through natural-selection pressures that guide evolution.

- Habituation is a decrease in the strength of a response to a repeated stimulus. It may be the simplest form of learning and allows organisms to attend to other stimuli that are more important.

CLASSICAL CONDITIONING: ASSOCIATING ONE STIMULUS WITH ANOTHER

Life is full of interesting associations. Do you ever hear songs on the radio or find yourself in places that instantly make you feel good because they're connected to special times you've had? When you smell the aroma of popcorn or freshly baked cookies, does your mouth water or your stomach growl? These examples illustrate a learning process called **classical conditioning**, *in which an organism learns to associate two stimuli* (e.g., a song and a pleasant event), *such that one stimulus* (the song) *comes to elicit a response* (feeling happy) *that originally was elicited only by the other stimulus* (the pleasant event).

Like habituation, classical conditioning is a basic form of learning that occurs across numerous species. Its discovery dates back to the late 1800s and an odd twist of fate.

PAVLOV'S PIONEERING RESEARCH

In the 1860s, Ivan Pavlov was studying theology in a Russian seminary when his plans to join the priesthood unexpectedly changed. A new government policy allowed the translation of Western scientific publications into Russian. Pavlov read Darwin's theory of evolution and other works, which sparked a strong interest in the sciences (Windholz, 1997). Pavlov became a renowned physiologist, conducting research on digestion in dogs that won him the Nobel Prize in 1904.

To study digestion, Pavlov presented food to dogs and measured their salivary response (Figure 6.3). As often occurs in science, Pavlov made an accidental but important discovery. He noticed that with repeated testing, the dogs began to salivate before the food was presented, such as when they heard the footsteps of the approaching experimenter.

Further study by Pavlov's (1923/1928) research team confirmed this observation. Dogs have a natural reflex to salivate to food but not to tones. Yet when a tone or other stimulus that ordinarily did not cause salivation was presented just before food powder was squirted into a dog's mouth, soon the sound of the tone alone made the dog salivate. This process of learning by association came to be called *classical*, or *Pavlovian*, *conditioning*. Many psychologists regard Pavlov's discovery as one of the most important in psychology's history (Wills, 2005). But why all the fuss about dogs salivating to tones?

▶ **Focus 3**
Describe Pavlov's research and how a classically conditioned response is acquired. Explain spontaneous recovery and extinction.

(a)

(b)

FIGURE 6.3

Pavlov's method of measuring salivation in dogs. (a) Ivan Pavlov (*with the white beard*) is shown here with colleagues and one of his canine subjects. (b) In his early research, Pavlov measured salivation using a simple device similar to the one shown here. In later research, a collection tube was inserted directly into the salivary gland.

This question raises a widely misunderstood point about basic scientific research: It is the *underlying principle*—not the specific findings—that is paramount. Classical conditioning is a basic learning process that performs a key adaptive function: It alerts organisms to stimuli that signal the impending arrival of an important event. As Pavlov noted, if salivation could be conditioned,

so might bodily processes that affect diseases and mental disorders.

BASIC PRINCIPLES

What factors influence the acquisition and persistence of conditioned responses? Let's examine some basic principles of conditioning.

Acquisition

Acquisition refers to the period during which a response is being learned. Suppose we wish to condition a dog to salivate to a tone. Sounding the tone initially may cause the dog to perk up its ears but not to salivate. At this time, the tone is a *neutral stimulus* because it does not elicit salivation (Figure 6.4). If, however, we place food in the dog's mouth, the dog will salivate. This salivation response to food is *reflexive*—it's what dogs do by nature. Because no learning is required for food to produce salivation, the food is an **unconditioned stimulus (UCS),** *a stimulus that elicits a reflexive or innate response (the UCR) without prior learning.* Salivation is an **unconditioned response (UCR),** *a reflexive or innate response that is elicited by a stimulus (the UCS) without prior learning.*

Next the tone and the food are paired—each pairing is called a *learning trial*—and the dog salivates. After several learning trials, if the tone is presented by itself, the dog salivates even though there is no food. The tone has now become a **conditioned stimulus (CS),** *a stimulus that, through association with a UCS, comes to elicit a conditioned response similar to the original UCR.* Because the dog is now salivating to the tone, salivation has become a **conditioned response (CR),** *a response elicited by a conditioned stimulus.* Notice that when the dog salivates to food, this

FIGURE 6.4

The classical conditioning process. In classical conditioning, after a neutral stimulus such as a tone is repeatedly associated with food (unconditioned stimulus), the tone becomes a conditioned stimulus capable of eliciting a salivation response (conditioned response).

FIGURE 6.5

Acquisition, extinction, and spontaneous recovery. The strength of the CR (salivation) increases during the acquisition phase as the CS (tone) and the UCS (food) are paired on each trial. During the extinction phase, only the CS is presented, and the strength of the CR decreases and finally disappears. After a rest period following extinction, presentation of the CS elicits a weaker CR (spontaneous recovery) that extinguishes more quickly than before.

natural (unconditioned) reflex is called a UCR. But when it salivates to a tone, this learned (conditioned) response is called a CR.

During acquisition, a CS typically must be paired multiple times with a UCS to establish a strong CR (Figure 6.5). Pavlov also found that a tone became a CS more rapidly when it was followed by greater amounts of food. Indeed, when the UCS is intense and aversive—such as an electric shock or a traumatic event—conditioning may require only one CS-UCS pairing (Richard et al., 2000). Carol's car phobia illustrates this *one-trial (single-trial) learning.* As she explains to the therapist, her automobile accident was very traumatic:

> My car went out of control. It crashed into a light pole, rolled over, and began to burn. I . . . couldn't get out . . . I'm sorry, doctor, but even thinking about it is horrible. I had a broken pelvis and third-degree burns over half my body.

In Carol's example, a stimulus (riding in or seeing a car) became a CS after only one pairing with an intense UCS (an extremely painful crash). Fear was the UCR, and it became a CR triggered by the sight of cars (Figure 6.6).

The sequence and time interval of the CS-UCS pairing also affect conditioning. Learning usually occurs most quickly with a *forward short-delay pairing:* The CS (tone) appears first and is still present when the UCS (food) appears. In *forward trace pairing,* the tone sounds and then stops, and afterward the food is presented. In forward pairing, it is often optimal for the CS to appear no more than 2 or 3 seconds before the UCS (Klein & Mowrer, 1989). Forward pairing has adaptive value because the CS signals the impending arrival of the UCS. Typically, presenting the CS and UCS at the same time *(simultaneous pairing)* produces less rapid conditioning, and learning is slowest when the CS is presented after the UCS *(backward pairing).*

FIGURE 6.6

Classical conditioning and Carol's car phobia. It is likely that Carol's phobia of cars was acquired through classical conditioning.

Once a CR is established, it may persist for a long time. In one study, hospitalized Navy veterans who had seen combat aboard ships in World War II showed strong physiological responses to the sound of a call-to-battle-stations gong, even though 15 years had passed since this gong had been associated with danger. Hospitalized Army veterans who had not served on ships had weaker reactions to the gong (Edwards, 1962). Similarly, after her horrible accident, Carol's fear of cars persisted for months despite the fact that she was in no further crashes.

To summarize, classical conditioning usually is strongest when (1) there are repeated CS-UCS pairings, (2) the UCS is more intense, (3) the sequence involves forward pairing, and (4) the time interval between the CS and UCS is short.

Extinction and Spontaneous Recovery

If classical conditioning is to help organisms adapt to their environment, there must be a way to eliminate the CR when it is no longer appropriate. Indeed, there is. **Extinction** *is a process in which the CS is presented repeatedly in the absence of the UCS, causing the CR to weaken and eventually disappear.* Each occurrence of the CS without the UCS is called an *extinction trial.* When Pavlov repeatedly presented the tone without the food, the dogs eventually stopped salivating to the tone (see Figure 6.5). Occasional re-pairings of the CS (e.g., tone) and the UCS (e.g., food) usually are required to maintain a CR.

Perhaps it seems inconsistent to you that Pavlov's dogs would eventually stop salivating to the tone if food no longer was presented with it, whereas Carol's phobia of cars persisted for months even though she was not in any additional crashes. How can we explain this?

What Do You Think?

WHY DID CAROL'S CAR PHOBIA PERSIST?
Reread the definition of extinction carefully. In Carol's case, identify the CS, UCS, and CR. Can you explain why her fear of cars did not extinguish on its own? Think about it, then see page 230.

Even when a CR extinguishes, not all traces of it are necessarily erased. Suppose we condition a dog to salivate to a tone. Then we repeatedly present the tone without food, and the dog eventually stops salivating to the tone. Later, if we present the tone alone, the dog may salivate once again. This is called **spontaneous recovery,** *the reappearance of*

▶ Focus 4
Explain stimulus generalization, discrimination, higher-order conditioning, and their adaptive significance.

a previously extinguished CR after a rest period and without new learning trials. As Figure 6.5 shows, the spontaneously recovered CR usually is weaker than the initial CR and extinguishes more rapidly in the absence of the UCS.

Generalization and Discrimination

Thus far we have explained Carol's car phobia as a case of one-trial conditioning in which being in a car was paired with a traumatic experience. But why would Carol fear other cars when it was her old car—now long gone—that was in the accident?

Pavlov found that once a CR is acquired, the organism often responds not only to the original CS but also to stimuli that are similar to it. The greater the stimulus similarity, the greater the chance that a CR will occur. A dog that salivates to a medium-pitched tone is more likely to salivate to a new tone slightly different in pitch than to a very low- or high-pitched tone. Learning theorists call this **stimulus generalization:** *Stimuli similar to the initial CS elicit a CR* (Figure 6.7).

Stimulus generalization serves critical adaptive functions. An animal that ignores the sound of rustling bushes and then is attacked by a hidden predator will (assuming it survives) become alarmed by the sound of rustling bushes in the future. If stimulus generalization did not occur, then the next time the animal heard rustling it would become alarmed only if the sound was identical to the rustling that preceded the earlier attack. This would be of little value to the animal's survival. Through stimulus generalization, however, the animal develops an alarm response to a range of rustling sounds. Some will be false alarms, but safe is better than sorry.

FIGURE 6.7

Stimulus generalization. An animal will salivate most strongly to the CS that was originally paired with the UCS. Progressively weaker conditioned responses occur as stimuli become less similar to the CS, as seen here with tones of lower or higher frequencies (pitch).

Unfortunately, maladaptive responses can occur when generalization spreads too far. The car involved in Carol's crash was gone, but after leaving the hospital her fear immediately generalized to the new car her husband bought. Over time, stimulus generalization continued, though the fear was weaker:

Carol: After a while, even the sight of a car started to make me nervous.

Therapist: As nervous as riding in one?

Carol: No, but still nervous. It's so stupid. I'd even turn off the TV during scenes involving car crashes.

To prevent stimulus generalization from running wild, organisms must be able to discriminate between irrelevant stimuli and those that may signal danger. An animal that became alarmed at every sound it heard would exhaust itself from stress. In classical conditioning, **discrimination** *is demonstrated when a CR* (such as an alarm reaction) *occurs to one stimulus* (a sound) *but not to others.* Carol's fear of cars was widespread, but it did not occur when she saw bicycles, trains, or airplanes.

When my mother was a girl a large dog bit her several times. From then on, she was afraid of dogs. Years later, when my brother wanted a dog, my mother would have none of it. But he pleaded endlessly. How could our family satisfy my brother's wish yet not trigger my mother's fear? The solution: get a dog as dissimilar as possible to the large dog that bit her, in hopes that my mother's fear would display stimulus discrimination. So we adopted a tiny Chihuahua puppy, and the plan was half-successful. My mother was not afraid and adored the dog. Alas, my brother's fondness for big dogs failed to generalize to Chihuahuas, and he repeatedly called it a "yippity oversized rat."

Higher-Order Conditioning

Imagine that we expose a dog to repeated tone-food pairings and the tone becomes a CS that elicits a strong salivation response. Next, suppose that we present a neutral stimulus, such as a black square, and the dog does not salivate. Now, we present the black square just prior to the tone, but do not present any food. After repeated square-tone pairings, the square will become a CS and elicit salivation by itself (Figure 6.8). This process is called **higher-order conditioning**: *A neutral stimulus becomes a CS after being paired with an already established CS.* Typically, a higher-order CS produces a CR that is weaker and extinguishes more rapidly than the original CR: The dog will salivate less to the black square than to the tone,

Before higher-order conditioning

Black square → No salivation

(neutral stimulus)

During higher-order conditioning

Black square + (tuning fork) → Salivation (CR)

(CS₁)

After higher-order conditioning

Black square → Salivation (CR)

(CS₂)

FIGURE 6.8

Higher-order conditioning. Once a tone has become a conditioned stimulus that triggers salivation, we can now use it to condition a salivation response to a new neutral stimulus: a black square. The tone is the CS₁. The black square becomes the CS₂.

and its response to the square will extinguish sooner.

Higher-order conditioning greatly expands the influence of conditioned stimuli and can affect what we come to value, fear, like, or dislike (Gerwitz & Davis, 2000). For example, political candidates try to get voters to like them by associating themselves with patriotic symbols, cuddly babies, famous people, and other conditioned stimuli that already trigger positive emotional reactions.

APPLICATIONS OF CLASSICAL CONDITIONING

Pavlov's belief that salivation was merely the tip of the classical conditioning iceberg has proven correct. Conditioning principles discovered in laboratory research—much of it with nonhuman species—help us understand diverse human behaviors and problems.

Acquiring and Overcoming Fear

Building on Pavlov's discoveries, pioneering behaviorist John B. Watson challenged Freud's view of the causes of mental disorders, such as phobias. To explain Carol's car phobia, no assumptions about hidden unconscious conflicts or repressed traumas are needed. Instead, from the behaviorist viewpoint, cars have become a fear-triggering CS due to a one-trial pairing with the UCS (crash) and subsequent stimulus generalization.

▶ **Focus 5**
How is classical conditioning relevant to fear acquisition and treatment, attraction and aversion, and health?

TABLE 6.1   Using Exposure Training to Reduce Fear

This table lists 10 of the 17 steps Mary Cover Jones used to eliminate Peter's fear of rabbits.

Step	Peter's Progress
1.	Rabbit anywhere in room triggers fear.
2.	Rabbit 12 feet away tolerated.
4.	Rabbit 3 feet away tolerated.
5.	Rabbit close in cage tolerated.
6.	Rabbit free in room tolerated.
8.	Rabbit touched when free in room.
10.	Rabbit allowed on tray of high chair.
12.	Holds rabbit on lap.
16.	Fondles rabbit affectionately.
17.	Lets rabbit nibble his fingers.

SOURCE: Adapted from Jones, 1924.

Does this explanation seem reasonable? It may, but almost any explanation can seem plausible in hindsight. Therefore, John B. Watson and Rosalie Rayner (1920) set out to obtain stronger evidence that fear could be conditioned. They studied an 11-month-old infant named Albert. One day, as Little Albert played in a hospital room, Watson and Rayner showed him a white rat. Albert displayed no sign of fear. Later, knowing that Albert was afraid of loud noises, they hit a steel bar with a hammer, making a loud noise as they showed Albert the rat. The noise scared Albert and made him cry. After several rat-noise pairings, the sight of the white rat alone made Albert cry.

To examine stimulus discrimination and generalization, Watson and Rayner exposed Albert to other test stimuli several days later. Albert displayed no fear when shown colored blocks, but furry white or gray objects, such as a rabbit and a bearded Santa Claus mask, made him cry (Figure 6.9). By the time Albert's mother took him from the hospital, he had not been exposed to any treatment designed to extinguish his fear. Unfortunately, we do not know what became of Albert after that.

Two other sources of evidence suggest that at least some fears are conditioned. First, laboratory experiments convincingly show that animals become afraid of neutral stimuli that are paired with electric shock (Ayres, 1998). Second, in humans, behavioral treatments partially based on classical conditioning principles are among the most effective psychotherapies for phobias (Wolpe & Plaud, 1997). The key assumption is that if phobias are learned, they can be unlearned.

In 1924 psychologist Mary Cover Jones successfully treated a boy named Peter who had a strong fear of rabbits. Jones gradually extinguished Peter's fear using the procedure shown in Table 6.1. Her approach was a forerunner of current behavior therapies, discussed in Chapter 15. Collectively, they are called **exposure thera-**

pies, *in which a patient is exposed to a stimulus (CS) that arouses an anxiety response (such as fear) without the presence of the UCS, allowing extinction to occur.* In reality, the origin of a patient's phobia is often unknown, and psychologists debate whether all phobias are learned. But, even so, in most cases, exposure treatments are effective.

Mental imagery, real-life situations, or both can be used to present the phobic stimulus. In one approach called *systematic desensitization*, the patient learns muscle-relaxation techniques and then is gradually exposed to the fear-provoking stimulus (Wolpe, 1958). Another approach, sometimes called *flooding*, immediately exposes the person to the phobic stimulus (Nesbitt, 1973). In Carol's case, her therapist extinguished the car phobia in six sessions of flooding. He asked her to imagine vivid scenes in which she drove in freeway traffic and traveled at high speeds on narrow mountain roads. As Carol's initially strong anxiety decreased, she was able to sit in her car and eventually drive it. Exposure therapies are highly effective and represent one of behaviorism's important applied legacies (Taylor, 2004).

? What Do You Think?

WAS THE "LITTLE ALBERT" STUDY ETHICAL?
Review boards that oversee research ethics did not exist in the 1920s. Would you have approved Watson and Rayner's request to conduct the Little Albert study? Why or why not? Think about it, then see page 230.

Attraction and Aversion

Classical conditioning influences what attracts and pleasurably arouses us. Consider sexual arousal. The comment, "It really turns me on when you wear that," reflects how a garment or scent of a partner's cologne can become a CS for arousal. People, fish, birds, and rats become more sexually aroused to originally neutral stimuli after those stimuli have been paired with a naturally arousing UCS (Domjan, 2000b).

Classical conditioning also can decrease our arousal and attraction to stimuli. This principle is used in **aversion therapy,** *which attempts to condition an aversion (a repulsion) to a stimulus that triggers unwanted behavior by pairing it with a noxious UCS.* To treat pedophiles (child molesters), a therapist may pair pictures of children with strong electric shock, and to reduce an alcoholic's attraction to alcohol, the patient may be given a drug that induces severe nausea when alcohol is consumed (Nathan, 1985). Aversion therapies yield mixed results, often producing short-term changes that extinguish over time.

Conditioned attraction and aversion also influence our attitudes. By repeatedly pairing a CS with pleasant or unpleasant stimuli, we may develop a favorable or unfavorable attitude toward that CS. Advertising executives carefully link products to attractive and famous people, humor, and pleasurable interactions with family, friends, and the opposite sex (Figure 6.10). Marketing experiments show that the products become conditioned stimuli that elicit favorable consumer attitudes (Priluck & Till, 2004).

Sickness and Health

Through classical conditioning, our bodies can learn to respond in ways that either promote or harm our health. Let's look at three examples.

Allergic Reactions   Classical conditioning often can account for the appearance of physical symptoms that do not seem to have a medical cause. For example, by consistently pairing a neutral stimulus (e.g., a distinct odor) with a substance that naturally triggers an allergic reaction, the odor can become a CS that elicits a similar allergic response (Irie et al., 2001). Also consider the case of an asthma patient who experienced wheezing attacks whenever she saw goldfish. To confirm this, doctors showed her a live goldfish in a bowl: "Under our eyes she developed a severe asthmatic attack with loud wheezing. . . . During the next experiment the goldfish was replaced by a plastic toy fish which was easily recognized as such . . . but a fierce attack resulted" (Dekker and Groen, 1956, p. 62). For the asthma patient, goldfish appear to be conditioned stimuli that

trigger wheezing attacks, and her response to the plastic fish indicates stimulus generalization.

Anticipatory Nausea and Vomiting   Chemotherapy and radiation therapy save countless lives in the fight against cancer but often cause nausea and vomiting. Many cancer patients eventually develop **anticipatory nausea and vomiting (ANV);** *they become nauseated and may vomit anywhere from minutes to hours* before *a treatment session.*

ANV is a classically conditioned response (Stockhorst et al., 2000). Initially neutral stimuli, such as hypodermic needles, the hospital room, or even the sight of a hospital, become associated with the treatment (the UCS) and act as conditioned stimuli that trigger nausea and vomiting (the UCR). Fortunately, like conditioned fear, psychological treatments can help patients unlearn the ANV response (Edser, 2002). The patient may first be taught how to physically relax, and then the conditioned stimuli that trigger ANV are paired with relaxation and pleasant mental imagery.

The Immune System   As psychologist Robert Ader (2001; Ader & Cohen, 1975) discovered decades ago, even the immune system can be classically conditioned, affecting susceptibility to disease and fatal illness. As Figure 6.11 shows, when rats drink

FIGURE 6.11

The immune system can be classically conditioned. After being paired with an immune-suppressant drug, sweet water becomes a CS that triggers a reduced immune response.

sweetened water (a neutral stimulus) that is paired with injections of a drug (the UCS) that suppresses immune activity (the UCR), the sweetened water becomes a CS that suppresses immune activity.

Conversely, conditioning can also increase immune functioning (DeMoranville et al., 2000). German researchers gave sweet sherbet to an experimental group of volunteers, along with an injection of epinephrine (i.e., adrenaline), which increases the activity of immune-system cells that attack tumors. Compared with control groups, people receiving the sherbet-epinephrine pairings subsequently reacted to the sherbet alone with a stronger immune response (Buske-Kirschbaum et al., 1992, 1994).

Can classical conditioning help fight disease? One experiment involved mice suffering from a normally fatal illness that caused their immune systems to attack their own bodies (Ader & Cohen, 1982). By classically conditioning a sweet taste (CS) to trigger immune suppression (CR), the researchers reduced the mice's mortality rate. Later, a similar conditioning procedure was used along with drug therapy to successfully treat an 11-year-old-girl who had a life-threatening disease in which her immune system was overactive (Olness & Ader, 1992).

► Focus 6
Describe how Thorndike and Skinner pioneered the study of operant conditioning.

IN REVIEW

- Classical conditioning involves pairing a neutral stimulus with an unconditioned stimulus (UCS) that elicits an unconditioned response (UCR). Through repeated pairing, the neutral stimulus becomes a conditioned stimulus (CS) that evokes a conditioned response (CR) similar to the original UCR.

- The acquisition phase involves pairing the CS with the UCS. Extinction, the disappearance of the CR, occurs when the CS is presented repeatedly in the absence of the UCS. Sometimes spontaneous recovery occurs after a rest period, and the CS will temporarily evoke a response even after extinction has taken place.

- Stimulus generalization occurs when a CR is evoked by a stimulus similar to the original CS. Discrimination occurs when a CR occurs to one stimulus but not another.

- In higher-order conditioning, once a stimulus (e.g., a tone) becomes a CS, it can be used in place of the original UCS (food) to condition other neutral stimuli.

- A wide range of bodily and psychological responses can be classically conditioned, including fears, sexual attraction, and positive and negative attitudes. Techniques based on classical conditioning are highly successful in treating fears and phobias.

- Cancer patients may develop anticipatory nausea and vomiting (ANV) to stimuli that are paired with their chemotherapy. ANV is a classically conditioned response. Classical conditioning also can increase or decrease immune-system responses.

OPERANT CONDITIONING: LEARNING THROUGH CONSEQUENCES

For all its power to affect our emotions, attitudes, physiology, and health, classical conditioning cannot explain how a dog learns to sit on command. Nor can it account for how we learn to drive cars, use computers, or make friends. Unlike salivating to a tone, these are not *elicited responses* automatically triggered by some stimulus. Rather, they are *emitted (voluntary) responses*, and they are learned in a different way.

THORNDIKE'S LAW OF EFFECT

While Pavlov was studying classical conditioning, American psychology student Edward L. Thorndike (1898) was exploring how animals learn to solve problems. He built a special cage, called a *puzzle box*, that could be opened from the inside by pulling a string or stepping on a lever (Figure 6.12). Thorndike placed a hungry animal, such as a cat, inside the box. Food was put outside, and to get it the animal had to learn how to open the box. The cat scratched and pushed the bars, paced, and tried to dig through the floor. By chance, it eventually stepped on the lever, opening the door. Performance slowly improved with repeated trials, and over time the cat learned to press the lever soon after the door was shut.

Because performance improved slowly, Thorndike concluded that the animals did not attain *insight* into the solution. Rather, with trial and error, they gradually eliminated responses that failed to open the door and became more likely to perform the actions that worked. Thorndike (1911) called this process *instrumental learning* because an organism's behavior is instrumental in bringing about certain outcomes. He also proposed the **law of effect**, *which states that in a given situation, a response followed by a satisfying*

FIGURE 6.12

Thorndike's puzzle box. Through trial and error, a cat eventually learns to open Thorndike's puzzle box in order to obtain food. Source: Based on Thorndike, 1898, 1911.

consequence will become more likely to occur and a response followed by an annoying consequence will become less likely to occur.

SKINNER'S ANALYSIS OF OPERANT CONDITIONING

Harvard psychologist B. F. Skinner, who built on and expanded Thorndike's work, was America's leading proponent of behaviorism throughout much of the 20th century. Skinner coined the term *operant behavior*, meaning that an organism *operates* on its environment in some way.

Operant conditioning *is a type of learning in which behavior is influenced by the consequences that follow it* (Skinner, 1938, 1953). Skinner designed what has come to be known as a **Skinner box,** *a special chamber used to study operant conditioning experimentally.* A lever on one wall is positioned above a small cup. When the lever is depressed, a food pellet automatically drops into the cup. As

shown in Figure 6.13, a hungry rat is put into the chamber and, as it moves about, it accidentally presses the lever. A food pellet clinks into the cup, and the rat eats it. We record the rat's behavior on a cumulative recorder, which shows that the rat presses the bar more frequently over time.

Skinner identified several types of consequences. For now, we will focus on two: *reinforcement* and *punishment.* With **reinforcement,** *a response is strengthened by an outcome that follows it.* Typically, the term *strengthened* is operationally defined as an increase in the frequency of a response. The outcome (a stimulus or event) that increases the frequency of a response is a called a *reinforcer.* Food pellets are reinforcers because they increase the rat's frequency of lever pressing. Once a response becomes established, reinforcers maintain it: The rat keeps pressing the lever because it continues to receive food.

In contrast to reinforcement, **punishment** *occurs when a response is weakened by outcomes that*

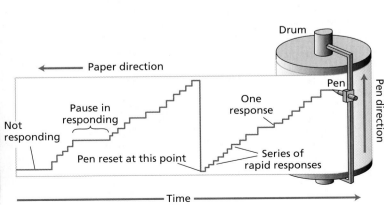

FIGURE 6.13

Measuring and reinforcing an operant response. With B. F. Skinner watching, a rat raises up and presses a lever in an operant experimental chamber (Skinner box). This turns on a light inside the chamber. (Notice the silver lever just below the rat's front paws, and the orange light to the left of its paws.) A food reinforcer is automatically delivered by the apparatus to the left of the box, and the rat's performance is displayed on a cumulative recorder.

▶ **Focus 7**

Contrast classical and operant conditioning. Why are antecedent stimuli important in operant conditioning?

follow it. Take our lever-pressing rat. Suppose we change things so that pressing the lever delivers a brief electric shock rather than food. If lever pressing decreases (which it will), then the electric shock represents a *punisher*, a consequence that weakens the behavior. Notice that reinforcers and punishers are defined in terms of their observable effects on behavior. If the food doesn't increase lever pressing, then it is not a reinforcer for this rat at this time.

Following Darwin's notion of natural selection, which applies to species adaptation, Skinner viewed operant conditioning as a type of natural selection that facilitates an organism's personal adaptation to the environment. Through operant conditioning, organisms generally learn to increase behaviors that are followed by favorable consequences and reduce behaviors that are followed by unfavorable consequences, a pattern consistent with Thorndike's law of effect.

Skinner's analysis of operant behavior involves three kinds of events that form a three-part contingency: (1) *antecedents*, which are stimuli that are present before a behavior occurs, (2) *behaviors* that the organism emits, and (3) *consequences* that follow the behaviors. Thus

> IF antecedent stimuli are present (IF I say, "Sit!")
>
> AND behavior is emitted (AND my dog Jessie sits),
>
> THEN consequences will occur (THEN Jessie will receive a treat).

The relation between the behavior and the consequence is called a *contingency*. After I say, "Sit!" the consequence of receiving food is contingent on Jessie's response of sitting.

Distinguishing Operant from Classical Conditioning

Despite accurately learning all of the terms involved in classical and operant conditioning, some students still have difficulty distinguishing between these two types of learning. As we explore operant conditioning more closely, keep in mind these differences between classical and operant conditioning:

- Classical conditioning focuses on *elicited* behaviors: The conditioned response (e.g., salivation) is triggered involuntarily, almost like a reflex, by the conditioned stimulus (e.g., a tone). Operant conditioning focuses on *emitted* behaviors: In a given situation, the organism generates responses (e.g., pressing a lever) that are under its physical control.

- In classical conditioning, learning occurs through CS-UCS pairings. In other words, one stimulus (e.g., a tone) becomes associated with another stimulus (e.g., food). In operant conditioning, behavior changes when responses made by the organism (e.g., pressing a lever) become associated with certain consequences (e.g., receiving food).

- In classical conditioning the CS (e.g., tone) occurs before the CR (e.g., salivation) and triggers it. In operant conditioning, the reinforcing or punishing consequences occur *after* a response is made. Table 6.2 summarizes these differences.

Also realize that, although classical and operant conditioning are different processes, many learning situations involve both. Have you ever had a teacher who squeaked chalk when writing on a blackboard? One of your authors had a high

---

TABLE 6.2   Some Differences between Classical and Operant Conditioning

Question	Classical Conditioning	Operant Conditioning
What type of behavior is involved?	Elicited: CR is a reflex-like response (e.g., salivation, fear) triggered by CS (e.g., tone, sight of cars)	Emitted: response (e.g., lever pressing, sitting down) operates on the environment and is under the organism's control
How does learning occur?	Through CS-UCS pairings, one stimulus (CS; tone) is associated with another stimulus (UCS; food)	Organism's responses are associated with reinforcing, punishing, or neutral consequences
What is the sequence of events?	The CS occurs *before* the CR and triggers it (e.g., tone triggers salivation; sight of car triggers fear)	Consequences *follow* an organism's response (e.g., food is delivered after a lever is pressed); antecedent stimuli may set the occasion for emitting certain responses

school teacher who was a pro at this. Soon the mere sight of him raising the chalk to the board became a CS that automatically triggered a CR of shivers up the spine. It also was a signal for the students to put their fingers in their ears (an operant response), which was reinforced by the consequence of reducing the squeaking sound. Thus one stimulus (raising the chalk) can have classical as well as operant functions.

ANTECEDENT CONDITIONS: IDENTIFYING WHEN TO RESPOND

In operant conditioning, the antecedent may be a general situation or a specific stimulus. Let's return to our lever-pressing rat. At present, simply being in the Skinner box is the antecedent condition. In this situation, the rat will press the lever. Suppose we place a light on the wall above the lever. When the light is on, pressing the lever dispenses food, but when the light is off, no food is given. The rat will soon learn to press the lever only when the light is on. The light becomes a

discriminative stimulus, *a signal that a particular response will now produce certain consequences*. Discriminative stimuli set the occasion for operant responses. The sight of the teacher raising chalk to the blackboard was—in operant conditioning terms—a discriminative stimulus signaling it was time for the students to put their fingers in their ears.

Discriminative stimuli guide much of your everyday behavior. Food on your plate, classroom bells, the words people speak to you, and the sight of a friend's face are all discriminative stimuli that set the occasion for you to make certain responses.

CONSEQUENCES: DETERMINING HOW TO RESPOND

Behavior is governed by its consequences. Two major types of reinforcement strengthen responses, and two major types of punishment weaken them. Operant behavior also is weakened by extinction. Figure 6.14 shows these processes.

PROCESS	BEHAVIOR	CONSEQUENCE	RESULT
REINFORCEMENT			
Positive reinforcement	Response occurs → (Rat presses a lever)	A stimulus is presented → (Food pellets appear)	Response increases (Lever pressing increases)
Negative reinforcement	Response occurs (Person takes aspirin)	An aversive stimulus is removed → (Headache pain goes away)	Response increases (Increased tendency to take aspirin for headache relief)
OPERANT EXTINCTION			
	Response occurs → (Rat presses a lever)	A stimulus that was reinforcing the behavior no longer appears → (No food pellets)	Response decreases (Lever pressing decreases)
PUNISHMENT			
Aversive punishment (also called **positive punishment**)	Response occurs → (Two siblings fight over a toy)	An aversive stimulus is presented → (Parents scold or spank them)	Response decreases (Fighting decreases)
Response cost (also called **negative punishment**)	Response occurs → (Two siblings fight over a toy)	A stimulus is removed → (No TV for 1 week)	Response decreases (Fighting decreases)

FIGURE 6.14

Five major operant processes.

▶ Focus 8
Explain and illustrate positive and negative reinforcement, operant extinction, aversive punishment, and response cost.

Positive Reinforcement

Positive reinforcement *occurs when a response is strengthened by the subsequent presentation of a stimulus.* A rat receives food pellets when it presses a lever and eventually begins to press the lever more often. A new employee, praised by her boss for completing a small project quickly, begins to complete more of her projects on time. The stimulus that follows and strengthens the response is called a *positive reinforcer.* Food, drink, comforting physical contact, attention, praise, and money are common positive reinforcers. In our chapter-opening vignette, the volunteer's behavior of soliciting money for charity is positively reinforced by each donation, by the praise of fellow workers at the charity, and by her feeling of pride in helping people.

The term *reward* is often misused as a synonym for the term *positive reinforcer.* Behaviorists prefer *positive reinforcer* because it focuses on how consequences affect behavior. In many instances rewards do not function as positive reinforcers. Parents may give a child a reward (such as a new toy) for cleaning her room, but if the child does not clean her room in the future, then the toy was not a positive reinforcer for that behavior.

Primary and Secondary Reinforcers Psychologists distinguish between two broad types of positive reinforcers: **Primary reinforcers** *are stimuli, such as food and water, that an organism naturally finds reinforcing because they satisfy biological needs.* **Secondary (conditioned) reinforcers** *are stimuli that acquire reinforcing properties through their association with primary reinforcers.* Money is a conditioned reinforcer. Similarly, chimpanzees learn to value, work for, and even hoard tokens (a secondary

reinforcer) that they can place into a vending machine to obtain raisins.

Secondary reinforcers illustrate how behavior often depends on both classical and operant conditioning. Consider dog training. Correct responses, such as sitting on command, initially are operantly reinforced with food. But just before delivering food, the trainer enthusiastically says, "Good Dog!" At first the phrase "Good Dog!" is just meaningless sounds to the dog. But by repeatedly pairing "Good Dog!" with food each time the dog sits, "Good Dog!" becomes a classically conditioned stimulus that elicits excitement (salivation, tail wagging). Now the trainer can use the phrase "Good Dog!" as a secondary reinforcer, instead of always having to carry and provide food.

Negative Reinforcement

B. F. Skinner noted that when a response pays off, it is more likely to occur in the future. In everyday life, our behaviors pay off not only when they lead to the presentation of praise, money, and so on, but also when they enable us to get rid of or avoid something we find aversive. For example, taking aspirin pays off because it relieves a headache. This process is called **negative reinforcement:** *A response is strengthened by the subsequent removal (or avoidance) of an aversive stimulus* (see Figure 6.14). The aversive stimulus that is removed (e.g., the headache) is called a *negative reinforcer* (Hill, 1963). Figure 6.15 presents other examples of negative reinforcement.

Do not confuse negative reinforcement with punishment. Punishment weakens a response. Reinforcement—whether positive or negative—strengthens a response (or maintains it once it has reached full strength). When it comes to the terms

FIGURE 6.15

Negative reinforcement in everyday life. Here are some common examples of negative reinforcement. In each case, the consequence strengthens the behavior. There are countless other examples. Can you think of a few?

SITUATION (aversive stimulus is present)	BEHAVIOR	CONSEQUENCE (removal, reduction, or avoidance of aversive stimulus)
• Muscles ache	Take hot bath	Muscle ache decreases
• Sunlight is uncomfortably bright	Put on sunglasses	Discomfort is reduced
• You feel hungry, thirsty	Eat, drink something	Hunger, thirst decrease
• Neighbor's music is too loud	Ask neighbor to lower music	Music is less disruptive
• It starts to pour	Open an umbrella	Rain stops falling on you
• Alarm clock rings	Hit the off button	Annoying ringing stops
• You worry about getting sunburned	Put on sunscreen	Worry is reduced; sunburn is avoided
• Parent nags child to clean room	Child cleans room	Nagging stops
• Seat belt buzzer comes on	Put on seat belt	Annoying buzzer stops
• You feel chilly	Put on more clothes	You no longer feel cold

positive reinforcement and *negative reinforcement*, the adjectives *positive* and *negative* do not mean "good" or "bad." Rather they refer to procedures: *Positive* refers to presenting a stimulus; *negative* refers to removing a stimulus.

Negative reinforcement plays a key role in helping us learn to escape from and avoid aversive situations. While showering, have you ever heard someone flush a toilet, only to have your shower water turn scalding hot? Your response of backing away is negatively reinforced—strengthened—by the escape from (i.e., removal of) the scalding water. Soon the mere sound of the flush becomes a signal—a discriminative stimulus—for you to back away. You successfully avoid the scalding water, which negatively reinforces your response of backing away as soon as you hear the flush.

Operant Extinction

Operant extinction *is the weakening and eventual disappearance of a response because it is no longer reinforced.* When previously reinforced behaviors no longer pay off, we are likely to abandon and replace them with more successful ones. If pressing a lever no longer results in food pellets, the rat will eventually stop making this response.

The degree to which nonreinforced responses persist is called *resistance to extinction*. Nonreinforced responses may stop quickly (low resistance), or they may keep occurring hundreds or thousands of times (high resistance). People who solicit charitable donations, like the woman in Las Vegas, do not stop just because 100 passersby in a row fail to give money. As we explain later, resistance to extinction is strongly influenced by the pattern of reinforcement that has previously maintained the behavior.

Operant extinction often provides a good alternative to punishment as a method for reducing undesirable behaviors. Consider the case of "Pascal the Rascal" (author's files):

Mrs. Adams sought help at a child guidance clinic because her 4-year-old son, Pascal, delighted in misbehaving. She had tried to reason with him. Then she resorted to yelling. When that failed, Mrs. Adams began spanking Pascal. Even that did not work.

The intended punishments failed because they actually reinforced Pascal with what he wanted most: attention. The psychologist told Mrs. Adams that as difficult as it might be at times, she needed to ignore Pascal when he misbehaved, thereby depriving him of attention. Mrs. Adams was also told to reinforce Pascal's desirable behaviors by paying attention to him when he acted accordingly. Soon thereafter, Pascal was no longer a rascal.

Aversive Punishment

Like reinforcement, punishment comes in two forms. One involves actively *applying* aversive stimuli, such as painful slaps, electric shock, and verbal reprimands. This is called **aversive punishment** (also called **positive punishment**, or **punishment by application**): *A response is weakened by the subsequent presentation of a stimulus.* Spanking and scolding a child for misbehaving are obvious examples, but so is a child's touching a hot stovetop burner. The pain delivered by the burner makes it less likely that the child will touch it in the future. Likewise, a high school student wears a new blouse, her friends' facial expressions say "ugh," and she tosses the blouse into the back of her closet.

Aversive punishment can produce rapid results, an important consideration when it is necessary to stop a particularly dangerous behavior, such as an animal or person attacking someone. Although aversive punishment often works, the use of spanking and other forms of physical punishment for disciplinary purposes is controversial. Let's explore this issue.

▶ **Focus 9**
Discuss the corporal punishment debate and some limitations of punishment and reinforcement.

Beneath the Surface   Spare the Rod, Spoil the Child?

As a child, were you spanked for misbehaving? And, as someone who may one day become a parent or may already be one, do you believe that there are times when parents should spank their children? If you grew up in the United States, odds are high that your answer to both questions is yes. In one national survey of American parents, 94 percent reported that by the time their children reached the age of 4, they had spanked them (Straus & Stewart, 1999). Yet your answers would likely be different if you grew up in Sweden, which banned corporal (i.e., physical) punishment of

Continued

children in 1979. Other countries, including Austria, Denmark, and Norway have since passed similar bans.

THE CORPORAL PUNISHMENT DEBATE

Should parents physically punish children's misbehavior? Newspapers, magazines, and TV shows frequently raise this issue, so let's probe beneath the surface.

What's the claim? Conventional wisdom says that sparing the rod spoils the child. What's the evidence? Psychologist Elizabeth Gershoff (2002a) of Columbia University meta-analyzed 88 studies on parental use of corporal punishment, involving about 36,000 participants. Five of these studies examined whether corporal punishment was effective in temporarily suppressing children's misbehavior. Overall the answer was yes, but Gershoff cautioned that this result was inconsistent because it was found in only 3 of the 5 studies.

In contrast, the other major outcomes that Gershoff studied consistently showed unfavorable associations with child corporal punishment. These outcomes, based almost entirely on correlational studies, included

- decreased quality of the parent-child relationship;
- poorer internalization of moral standards during childhood;
- increased aggressive behavior during childhood and, later, during adulthood;
- increased delinquent and antisocial behavior (e.g., truancy, stealing) during childhood and adulthood;
- poorer mental health during childhood and adulthood;
- increased childhood risk of physical abuse;
- increased risk, upon becoming an adult, of physically abusing one's own children or spouse.

Gershoff (2002a) emphasizes that these findings "do not imply that all children who experience corporal punishment turn out to be aggressive or delinquent. . . . Corporal punishment may make certain behaviors more likely but clearly not inevitable" (p. 551). Remember, most people who are spanked do not grow up to be violent or antisocial adults.

What are the alternative explanations? As a critical thinker, recall that correlation does not prove causation. To see why, let's examine the association between corporal punishment and child aggression. Before reading further, can you identify three possible causal explanations for this correlation? (If you have trouble, refer back to Figure 2.11 on page 43.)

One possibility is that corporal punishment causes children to behave more aggressively. Many psychologists have expressed this concern because physical punishment amounts to control by aggression and may send a message to the child that aggression is appropriate and effective.

Moreover, laboratory experiments indicate that children learn aggressive behaviors by watching aggressive adult models (Bandura, 1965).

We also must consider the bidirectionality problem. Perhaps children who are more aggressive cause their parents to be more physically punitive. Thus greater misbehavior may lead to greater punishment. And finally, we must consider the third-variable problem. Maybe something else—an inherited or environmental factor—causes children to behave more aggressively and also causes parents to punish more aggressively (i.e., physically), making it seem like aggression and corporal punishment are directly related when in fact they are not.

What additional evidence would be helpful? After child corporal punishment was banned in Sweden, did new generations of children grow up to become poorly socialized teenagers? Examining national statistics from 1975 through 1996, Joan Durrant (2000) found that after the corporal punishment ban, teenage rates of theft, rape, narcotics trafficking, drug use, and suicide all declined. Durrant points out that economic, social, and other national factors likely influenced these results, so we cannot conclude that banning corporal punishment caused these changes. Yet whatever the cause, the direction of the findings runs counter to "spare the rod, spoil the child." As Durrant notes, "Swedish youth have not become more unruly, undersocialized, or self-destructive following the . . . ban. In fact, most measures demonstrated a substantial improvement in youth well-being" (p. 451).

What should we conclude? The study of Swedish youth and Gershoff's meta-analysis converge on the same point: Causality is unclear, but the direction of the association runs counter to common folklore: it appears that using the rod—rather than sparing it—may be associated with poorer child-development outcomes. Still, some psychologists cite evidence that mild to moderate spanking has its place, such as a backup technique when other types of discipline fail with young children who have behavior problems (Baumrind et al., 2002).

WOULD YOU BAN CORPORAL PUNISHMENT?

Decisions about banning child corporal punishment involve more than scientific evidence. University of Texas psychologist George Holden (2002) notes, "Parents' belief in their entitlement to use corporal punishment is deeply embedded in American history, beliefs about the privacy of the family and personal freedoms, and attitudes about children and how to rear them" (p. 594). Indeed, in almost half of the states in the United States, even schoolteachers are allowed to discipline misbehaving children physically (Gershoff, 2002b).

After examining the preceding evidence, what are your thoughts about the appropriateness of spanking?

Response Cost

A parent recently told us, "Just because you don't spank doesn't mean you have to let your kids have their own way all the time. You can still set limits." Indeed, groundings, loss of privileges, and monetary fines represent another approach to modifying behavior. They take away something that an individual finds satisfying. In **response cost** (also called **negative punishment,** or **punishment by removal**), *a response is weakened by the subsequent removal of a stimulus* (i.e., "that'll cost you"). A child who misbehaves may be punished with a time-out, in which he or she has to sit quietly (possibly in isolation) for a period of time; this temporarily removes opportunities to play, watch TV, or participate in other enjoyable activities. Response cost, of course, is not limited to disciplining children or teenagers, as any automobile driver who has paid a fine for speeding knows (that'll *really* cost you). And even adults can receive a time-out (Figure 6.16).

Many psychologists and therapists who counsel parents on modifying children's behavior favor using time-out as a punishment technique (Baumrind et al., 2002). Still, as disciplinary techniques, aversive punishment and response cost have limitations. They suppress behavior but do not cause an organism to forget how to make the response. Because they tell us what not to do but don't necessarily help us learn what to do, it is important to use positive reinforcement to strengthen desirable alternative responses directly. Finally, punishment of any type may arouse negative emotions, such as fear and anger, that can produce dislike and avoidance of the person delivering the punishment.

Skinner (1953) believed that punishing behavior was not an effective way to produce long-term change. Yet research indicates that under the proper conditions, punishment can promote enduring changes in behavior (Domjan, 2000a). As psychologist George Holden (2002) notes, "To be effective, it must occur after every transgression, be immediate, be intense at least for the first transgression, and not be signaled by a discriminative stimulus," (p. 591) such as a threat or warning. Unfortunately, as Holden also notes, "These conditions represent a tall order for parents; in fact, it is likely parents are destined to fail on all four counts." For example, parents cannot always be present when children transgress.

Reinforcing desired responses and operantly extinguishing misbehavior often provide good alternatives to punishment (recall the case of Pascal the Rascal). But these approaches also have limits. Reinforced behaviors may extinguish or fail to generalize (as when children act politely when parents

FIGURE 6.16

In ice hockey, misbehavior can earn a time-out in the penalty box.

are present but not when parents are absent), and attempts to operantly extinguish misbehavior may fail. Thus, in practice, many psychologists believe that punishment must remain a disciplinary option.

Immediate, Delayed, and Reciprocal Consequences

In general, a consequence that occurs immediately after a behavior has a stronger effect than when it is delayed. Training animals typically requires immediate reinforcement so that they associate the correct response, rather than a subsequent behavior, with the reinforcer.

Because humans can imagine future consequences, our behavior is less rigidly controlled by the timing of consequences than that of other species. Still, the power of immediate reinforcement helps explain why many people continue to engage in behaviors with maladaptive long-term consequences. Chronic drug users usually find it difficult to stop because the immediate reinforcing consequences of the drug override the delayed benefits of not using the drug (e.g., being healthier, living longer). With many drugs, such as cocaine, use is positively reinforced by feelings of pleasure that seem to result from enhanced dopamine activity (Julien, 2005). Powerful negative reinforcers also play a role. Chronic cigarette smokers experience increased tension as the nicotine level in their blood drops after their last cigarette. When they smoke again, the tension decreases. Thus smoking is negatively reinforced by the removal of unpleasant tension.

▶ **Focus 10**

How do immediate, delayed, and reciprocal consequences affect learning?

Finally, realize that in everyday life, learning frequently is a reciprocal process—a two-way street involving a sequence of responses between organisms. Whether it's friends hanging out or a tiger chasing a gazelle, each response by one organism may reinforce, punish, help extinguish, or classically condition the other organism's behavior.

? What Do You Think?

CAN YOU EXPLAIN THE "SUPERMARKET TANTRUM"?
At the market, a child asks his dad to buy candy. He refuses. The child screams and won't stop. Soon the father can't stand it, buys the candy, and the child's tantrum ends. A week later this scene repeats, but the father gives in as soon as the tantrum starts. The next time the child asks for candy, the father just says, "ok." Use concepts of reinforcement and punishment to explain this sequence of events. Then, see page 231.

SHAPING AND CHAINING: TAKING ONE STEP AT A TIME

Mark is a 4-year-old who attends preschool. He doesn't play much with other children, rarely engages in physical activity, and during outdoor recess spends most of his time sitting in the sandbox. His teachers and parents would like him to be more active. How can we use operant conditioning to change Mark's behavior?

First, let's set a specific goal: getting Mark to play on the monkey bars. Second, let's select a positive reinforcer: attention. Now, all we need to do is reinforce Mark with attention when he plays on the monkey bars. The problem is, we'll be waiting a long time because Mark rarely displays this behavior.

Fortunately, Skinner discovered a powerful process for overcoming this problem. We begin by reinforcing Mark with attention every time he stands up in the sandbox. This is the first approximation toward our final goal. Once this response is established, we reinforce him only if he stands up and walks from the sandbox toward the monkey bars. This is the second approximation. Then we reinforce him only when he stands next to the bars, and finally only when he is on the bars and moving. This process, known as **shaping** (also called the *method of successive approximations*), *involves reinforcing successive approximations toward a final response*. Using a shaping procedure similar to the one just described, researchers took little time to get Mark playing on the monkey bars (Johnston et al., 1966).

Even when behaviors can be learned through trial and error—such as a rat learning to press a lever for food—shaping can speed up the process. By reinforcing successive approximations—such as standing near the lever, raising a front paw, touching the lever, and finally depressing the lever—acquisition time is reduced.

Another procedure, **chaining,** *is used to develop a sequence (chain) of responses by reinforcing each response with the opportunity to perform the next response.* For example, suppose that a rat has learned to press a lever when a light is on to receive food. Next we place a bell nearby. By accident, the rat eventually bumps into and rings the bell, which turns on the light. Seeing the light, the rat runs to and presses the lever. Over time, the rat will learn to ring the bell because this response is reinforced by the light turning on, which provides the opportunity to press the lever for food. As in this example, chaining usually begins with the final response in the sequence and works backward toward the first response (Catania, 1998). Figure 6.17 shows another example.

The behaviors that we display in everyday life often develop through shaping and chaining. Recall the father who initially refused his child's request for candy, then gave in after a lengthy tantrum, then gave in as soon as a tantrum started, and finally just said okay to the request. In essence, his response of agreeing immediately was shaped. Instructors who teach musical, athletic, and academic skills often shape their students' performance by starting with a simple response and reinforcing progressively closer approximations to the complex response that is ultimately desired.

GENERALIZATION AND DISCRIMINATION

As in classical conditioning, operant responses may generalize to similar antecedent situations. A dog taught by its owner to "Sit" will likely start sitting when other people give the command. A young child who touches a hot stovetop burner learns to avoid touching not only that burner but other hot burners as well. Thus in **operant generalization,** *an operant response occurs to a new antecedent stimulus or situation that is similar to the original one.*

Through experience, we also learn to discriminate between antecedent conditions. Children learn to raid the cookie jar only when the parents are not in the kitchen. We learn to board buses and trains marked by specific symbols (79: Express) and avoid otherwise identical vehicles with different symbols (78: Local). **Operant discrimination** *means that an*

▶ **Focus 11**
Explain how behaviors develop through shaping and chaining. Describe operant generalization and discrimination.

FIGURE 6.17

Chaining a sequence of responses. Through chaining, this rat has learned to climb a ladder to reach a string, pull on the string to raise the ladder, and then climb the ladder again to reach food at the top. Typically, you begin this training with the last step in the chain. Then, working backward, each prior step in the chain is reinforced by the opportunity to perform the next step.

operant response will occur to one antecedent stimulus but not to another. These antecedent stimuli—parents' presence or absence, bus markings—are discriminative stimuli. *A behavior that is influenced by discriminative stimuli is said to be under* **stimulus control.** The sight of a police car exerts stimulus control over most people's driving behavior.

The concept of operant discrimination gives science a powerful tool for examining the perceptual and cognitive abilities of human infants and nonhuman species. We can't ask infants and animals to tell us if they can distinguish between different colors, sounds, faces, and so on. But by using a procedure called *operant discrimination training,* we can teach an organism, for example, that pressing a lever when a red light is on produces a food reinforcer. Now all we have to do is change the color of the light and not reinforce any response when that light is on. If the organism learns to respond to one color and not the other, we infer that it can discriminate between them.

SCHEDULES OF REINFORCEMENT

In daily life, reinforcement comes in different patterns and frequencies. These patterns, called *schedules of reinforcement,* have strong and predictable effects on learning, extinction, and performance (Ferster & Skinner, 1957). The most basic distinction is between continuous and partial reinforcement. With **continuous reinforcement,** *every response of a particular type is reinforced.* Every press of the lever results in food pellets. Every $1.25

deposit in the soda machine results in a can of cool, bubbly drink. With **partial (intermittent) reinforcement,** *only a portion of the responses of a particular type are reinforced.* (Hereafter, when discussing reinforcement schedules, we will simply use the term *response* to refer to the particular behavior of interest.)

Partial reinforcement schedules can be categorized along two important dimensions. The first is ratio versus interval schedules. On *ratio schedules,* a certain percentage of responses are reinforced. For example, we might decide to reinforce only 50 percent of the rat's lever presses with food. The key factor is that ratio schedules are based on the number of responses: more responses, more reinforcement. On *interval schedules,* a certain amount of time must elapse between reinforcements, regardless of how many responses might occur during that interval. We might reinforce lever pressing only once per minute, whether the rat presses the lever 5, 10, or 60 times. The key factor is that interval schedules are based on the passage of time.

The second dimension is fixed versus variable schedules. On a *fixed schedule,* reinforcement always occurs after a fixed number of responses or after a fixed time interval. On a *variable schedule,* the required number of responses or the time interval between them varies at random around an average. Combining these two dimensions creates four types of reinforcement schedules (Figure 6.18).

Fixed-Ratio Schedule

On a **fixed-ratio (FR) schedule,** *reinforcement is given after a fixed number of responses.* For example,

▶ **Focus 12**
Describe and illustrate schedules of reinforcement. How do they affect performance, learning rates, and extinction?

FIGURE 6.18

Partial reinforcement schedules affect performance. Each type of positive reinforcement schedule produces a typical cumulative response curve. The hash marks indicate the delivery of a reinforcer. Ratio schedules produce a high rate of responding, as shown in the steep slopes of the curves. Variable schedules typically produce a steadier rate of responding than fixed schedules. Notice the prominent scalloped pattern in the fixed-interval schedule; responding decreases immediately after reinforcement and then increases as the time for the next reinforcement approaches.

FR-3 means that reinforcement occurs after every third response, regardless of how long it takes for those responses to occur.

If we told you that you would receive $1 every 3 times you pressed a lever, would you work hard? Skinner found that fixed-ratio schedules produce high rates of responding. That is one reason why some businesses prefer paying employees' wages based on a set number of items produced. If the ratio is gradually increased over time, many responses can be obtained with relatively few reinforcements. Pigeons in a Skinner box have been known to wear down their beaks pecking a disc on an FR-20,000 schedule (one reinforcer per 20,000 responses).

FR schedules have a second characteristic effect. As shown in Figure 6.18, the organism may pause briefly after each reinforcement, perhaps because the next response (or responses) is never reinforced.

Variable-Ratio Schedule

On a **variable-ratio (VR) schedule,** *reinforcement is given after a variable number of responses, all centered around an average.* A VR-3 schedule means that, *on average,* 3 responses are required for reinforcement. For example, for the first 12 responses, reinforcement might occur after responses 2, 3, 6, and 11.

VR schedules, like FR schedules, produce a high rate of responding. But because reinforcement is less predictable (the next response *might* be reinforced), there often is less pausing after reinforcement and a steadier rate of responding, as shown in Figure 6.18. VR schedules also are highly resistant to extinction because the organism learns that long periods of no payoff will eventually be followed by reinforcement.

Gambling activities are maintained by VR schedules (Figure 6.19). For example, the gambler in our opening vignette plays a slot machine programmed to pay off an average of every 20 pulls (VR-20). After 8 pulls, he receives a 10-coin jackpot. After 2 more attempts, he hits a 15-coin jackpot. But then, after 30 more attempts, nothing. He's frustrated but still hooked by the VR schedule. That next attempt just might be the one that pays off, so he plays again . . . and again.

Fixed-Interval Schedule

On a **fixed-interval (FI) schedule,** *the first response that occurs after a fixed time interval is reinforced.* Suppose a rat is pressing a lever on an FI-3 (3-minute) schedule. After a lever press is reinforced, for the next 3 minutes it makes no difference how many more times the rat responds. There will be no further reinforcement. Once these 3 minutes elapse, the next lever press is reinforced. The FI schedule's characteristic response pattern is shown in Figure 6.18. Notice the pronounced scalloping after each reinforcement. Responding slows after reinforcement and becomes more frequent as the time for the next reinforcement draws near.

In college, many instructors give exams at equal (or nearly equal) intervals, perhaps one exam every 3 or 4 weeks. Does your study behavior resemble the scalloped pattern shown in Figure 6.18, reflecting little studying immediately following each exam and cramming just before the next one? This uneven performance rate is typical of FI schedules (Figure 6.20).

Variable-Interval Schedule

On a **variable-interval (VI) schedule,** *reinforcement is given for the first response that occurs after a variable time interval, centered around an average.* A VI-3 schedule means that, *on average,* there is a 3-minute interval between opportunities to obtain reinforcement. Sometimes, responses a few seconds apart may be reinforced; at other times the interval may be many minutes. As Figure 6.18 shows, because the availability of reinforcement is less predictable than on an FI schedule, the VI schedule produces a steadier response rate.

FIGURE 6.19

Gambling is reinforced on a variable-ratio schedule. The ratio component means that the frequency of reinforcement is based on the amount of performance. On average, you will receive more payoffs when you play 100 times than when you play only 10 times. The variable component means that you never know when the next jackpot might occur.

FIGURE 6.20

As some of us know all too well, procrastination can lead to a heavy burden of cramming before an assignment is due. This pattern often results when assignments and tests occur on a fixed-interval schedule. SOURCE: Copyright © Zits Partnership. Reprinted with special permission of King Features Syndicate.

Pop quizzes represent a VI schedule. A course might average a quiz every week, but the unpredictable timing will likely produce a steadier approach to studying than regularly scheduled quizzes. Random drug testing and roadside speed traps also reflect VI schedules. They reinforce desired behaviors (staying drug-free, driving within the speed limit) by appearing at unpredictable intervals. Of course, they also punish undesired behaviors with suspensions and fines!

Reinforcement Schedules, Learning, and Extinction

Continuous reinforcement has an important advantage over partial reinforcement: It produces more rapid learning because the association between a behavior and its consequences is easier to perceive. However, it also has a disadvantage: Continuously reinforced responses extinguish more rapidly, because the shift to no reinforcement is sudden and easier to perceive.

Partial reinforcement produces behavior that is learned more slowly but is more resistant to extinction. Especially when reinforcement has been unpredictable in the past, it takes longer to learn that it is gone forever. People do not continue to drop coins into a soda machine that doesn't deliver, because vending machines are supposed to operate on a continuous schedule. But it would take many pulls on a slot machine to recognize that it had stopped paying off completely. To sum up, the best way to promote fast learning and high resistance to extinction is to begin reinforcing a desired behavior on a continuous schedule until the behavior is well established and then shift to a partial (preferably variable) schedule that is gradually made more demanding.

ESCAPE AND AVOIDANCE CONDITIONING

Behavior often involves escaping from or avoiding aversive situations. Escape occurs when we take medications to relieve pain or put on more clothes when we are cold. Avoidance occurs when we put on sunscreen to prevent sunburn or obey traffic laws to avoid tickets. You can probably think of many more examples.

In **escape conditioning,** *the organism learns a response to terminate an aversive stimulus.* Escape behaviors are acquired and maintained through negative reinforcement. If you're cold, putting on a sweater is negatively reinforced by the desirable consequence that you no longer shiver. Taking a pain reliever is negatively reinforced by the reduction of pain. In **avoidance conditioning,** *the organism learns a response to avoid an aversive stimulus.* We learn to dress warmly to avoid feeling cold in the first place.

Escape and avoidance conditioning can be demonstrated experimentally (Solomon & Wynne, 1953; Van der Borght et al., 2005). For example, researchers may place an animal in a *shuttlebox*, a rectangular chamber divided into two compartments and connected by a doorway (Figure 6.21). The floor is a grid through which electric shock can be delivered to either compartment. When the animal receives a shock in its compartment, it attempts to escape. Eventually, it runs through the door and into the other compartment. When shock is delivered to that compartment, the animal can escape by running back to the original side. Running through the door removes the shock, which negatively reinforces this escape

▶ **Focus 13**
Describe and illustrate escape and avoidance conditioning. Explain the two-factor theory of avoidance learning.

FIGURE 6.21

A shuttlebox. Researchers use the shuttlebox to study escape and avoidance learning.

behavior. Over a few trials, the animal learns to escape as soon as the shock is administered.

To study avoidance conditioning experimentally, researchers introduce a discriminative stimulus—a warning signal such as a light—that precedes the shock by a few seconds. After a few trials, the animal learns that the light signals impending shock. It runs to the other compartment as soon as it sees the light and thereby avoids being shocked.

Once this avoidance response is learned, it often is hard to extinguish, even when the animal no longer experiences any shock after the light is turned on. We saw the same situation with Carol's car phobia. She continued to avoid cars even though the intense pain from her accident was no longer experienced. What makes avoidance so resistant to extinction?

According to one model, the **two-factor theory of avoidance learning,** *both classical and operant conditioning are involved in avoidance learning* (Mowrer, 1947; Rescorla & Solomon, 1967). For our rat, the warning light is initially a neutral stimulus paired with a shock (UCS). Through classical conditioning, the light becomes a CS that elicits fear. Now operant conditioning takes over. Fleeing from the light is negatively reinforced by the termination of fear. This strengthens and maintains the avoidance response. Now if we permanently turn off the shock, the avoidance response prevents extinction from taking place. Seeing the light come on, the animal will not hang around long enough to learn that the shock no longer occurs.

In similar fashion, Carol's fear of cars was classically conditioned. The mere sight of a car (like the light for the rat) elicits fear and she flees, thereby avoiding riding in or driving the car. This avoidance is negatively reinforced by fear reduction, so it remains strong (Figure 6.22). Extinction is difficult because Carol doesn't give herself the opportunity to be in the car without experiencing

physical pain and trauma. This is why exposure therapies for phobias are so effective. By preventing avoidance responses, they provide the key ingredient for extinction: exposure to the CS (car) in the absence of the UCS (pain, trauma).

The two-factor theory helps us understand how many avoidance behaviors develop (Baron & Perone, 2001). However, it has trouble explaining some aspects of avoidance, such as why people and other animals develop phobic avoidance to some stimuli (e.g., snakes) more easily than to others (e.g., flowers). As we shall explore later, other factors also regulate our avoidance responses.

APPLICATIONS OF OPERANT CONDITIONING

In his best-selling books *Walden Two* (1948) and *Beyond Freedom and Dignity* (1971), Skinner set forth his utopian vision of how a "technology of behavior" based on positive reinforcement could end war, improve education, and solve other social problems. To his critics, Skinner's ideas conjured up images of people being manipulated like rats. But Skinner's point was that social influence is a natural part of human existence. Parents and children influence each other, as do employees and employers, teachers and students, friends, and romantic partners. To behaviorists, individual and societal problems are created by the all-too-common *haphazard* use of reinforcement and overreliance on punishment (Catania, 2001).

Education and the Workplace

Walk into your local computer store, and you likely will find shelves of educational software, teaching everything from math to foreign languages. The effectiveness of computerized instruction rests on two principles championed by Skinner: *immediate performance feedback* and *self-paced learning.*

Skinner was deeply concerned about the inefficiency of traditional instructional methods (1968, 1989b). Long before the advent of personal computers, he developed mechanical teaching machines. Each machine presented material, quizzed the student, and provided immediate feedback. Students who did not learn the material the first time could repeat steps; those who did could advance to the next set of information. Today, personal computers have made Skinner's vision an educational reality. Computer-assisted instruction also is found in business, industry, and the military (Parchman et al., 2000).

Skinner's work also increased society's attention to the broad issue of motivation. A key behaviorist assumption is that poor performance should

▶ **Focus 14**
How have operant principles been applied to education, the workplace, animal training, and solving problem behaviors?

FIGURE 6.22

Two-factor theory of avoidance learning. The two-factor theory of avoidance learning would account for Carol's car phobia in terms of two sets of learning processes: classical conditioning of a fear response and the negative reinforcement of avoidance of cars through fear reduction.

Factor 1: Classical conditioning of fear

Car (CS) + Traumatic car accident (UCS) → Conditioned fear response to cars (CR)

Factor 2: Operant conditioning of avoidance
Avoidance of cars is negatively reinforced

Avoid cars → Fear is reduced → Tendency to avoid cars is strengthened

FIGURE 6.23

(*left*) A trainer uses a laser to point out an object for the monkey to pick up. (*right*) Because of injuries suffered in an accident, this woman cannot move her arms or legs. The monkey has been operantly trained to assist her with basic chores, such as eating.

not be attributed to laziness or a bad attitude. Instead, we should assume that the environment is not providing the proper consequences to reinforce the desired behaviors. Many corporations invest heavily in training programs designed to enhance managers' effectiveness in reinforcing desired worker behaviors. Incentive systems—from stock options to bonuses for meeting performance goals—are now common in business and professional sports.

Token economies, *in which desirable behaviors are quickly reinforced with tokens* (e.g., points, gold stars) *that are later turned in for tangible rewards* (e.g., prizes, recreation time), have been used to enhance academic and job performance. In one study, a token economy reduced the number of work injuries among open-pit mine workers (Fox et al., 1987). Miners received stamp awards for making safety suggestions and avoiding injuries, and they lost stamps for unsafe behaviors. Stamps were later traded in for tangible reinforcers. The program cost money, but far less than the cost of worker absenteeism due to accidents.

Specialized Animal Training

Through shaping and chaining, animals can learn to perform some truly remarkable behaviors. Some are trained to be TV, movie, or circus performers, whereas others learn to assist people with disabilities (Figure 6.23). Police dogs assist officers on routine patrol, and other dogs learn to use their sense of smell to help locate hidden bombs, illegal drugs, and missing persons. The U.S. Navy trains sea lions to dive and retrieve sunken test weapons, and dolphins learn to patrol waters around nuclear submarine bases and search for underwater intruders (Morrison, 1988). Operantly trained dolphins also patrolled the waters around some U.S. ships during the Vietnam and Persian Gulf Wars.

Modifying Problem Behaviors

Operant conditioning research gave rise to a field called **applied behavior analysis,** *which combines a behavioral approach with the scientific method to solve individual and societal problems* (Kazdin, 1975). Essentially, applied behavior analysts design and implement a program to change behavior, and they measure its effectiveness objectively by gathering data before and after the program is in place (Figure 6.24). The procedures (e.g., reinforcement,

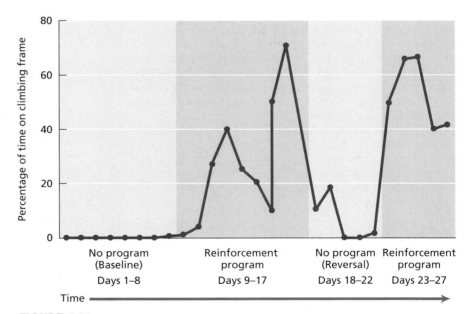

FIGURE 6.24

Behavior modification: Increasing a child's physical activity. Mark, a 4-year-old, was observed for 8 days (baseline) under natural circumstances. He spent virtually no time on the climbing frame (monkey bars). During Days 9 to 17 he was reinforced with attention for climbing on the frame, and his behavior changed. During Days 18 to 22 the program was withdrawn (reversal) and his climbing decreased. It increased again when reinforcement was reintroduced. This pattern provides reasonable evidence that the reinforcement caused his behavior to change. Ultimately, the researchers shifted to a partial reinforcement schedule and reinforced him for climbing on other equipment. Mark remained physically active. Source: Adapted from Johnston et al., 1966.

shaping) that are used to change behavior are collectively known as *behavior modification.*

Applied behavior analysis has reduced an incredible range of behavior problems, from chronic hair pulling to drivers' failure to use seat belts (Byrd et al., 2002). It has improved students' academic performance and social skills, increased employee productivity, reduced worker injuries and accidents, increased energy conservation, and reduced children's tendency to play with real guns that they discover (Himle et al., 2004).

Operant conditioning demonstrates the environment's power in shaping behavior. But this does not mean we are at its mercy. The following "Applying Psychological Science" describes how you can use your knowledge of learning principles to gain greater control over your own behavior.

▶ **Focus 15**
Describe the five main steps in a behavioral self-regulation program.

Applying Psychological Science   Using Operant Principles to Modify Your Behavior

People often blame the inability to overcome bad habits or maladaptive behaviors on vague concepts such as poor willpower and lack of self-control. Behaviorists prefer the more optimistic assumption that we can acquire *self-regulation,* which means using learning principles to change our behavior (Kanfer & Goldstein, 1991). This approach has helped people overcome addictions, lose excess weight, reduce their risk of heart disease, and improve their lives in many other ways. Let's examine how a college student could use self-regulation principles to increase the amount and effectiveness of studying.

STEP 1: SPECIFY THE PROBLEM

The first step in a self-regulation program is to pinpoint the behaviors you want to change (Watson & Tharp, 1997). This may be more challenging than it sounds, because we often use vague words to describe our problems. Here's how one of our students described her study problem: "I'm just not motivated to study hard." With a little help, she redefined her problem in more specific behavioral terms: "Between 7 and 10 P.M. I don't spend enough time at my desk reading and outlining my textbook."

Whenever possible, design your program to positively reinforce desirable behaviors (i.e., studying) rather than punish undesirable ones (i.e., not studying). Therefore we define this student's *target behavior* (the specific goal) as follows: "Four nights a week, between 7 and 10 P.M., spend $2\frac{1}{2}$ hours studying."

STEP 2: COLLECT BASELINE DATA

The next step is to collect *baseline (preintervention) data* on your behavior. Baseline data provide information about how frequently the target behavior currently occurs. Without it, you have no way of measuring how much you change after starting your program. The most effective approach is to plot data on a graph. Figure 6.25 shows data collected by one of our students.

STEP 3: IDENTIFY ANTECEDENTS AND CONSEQUENCES

While you collect baseline data, try to identify *antecedent* factors that disrupt study behavior, such as friends calling or

FIGURE 6.25

Using self-reinforcement to increase study time. This student graphed the amount of time he spent in the study environment and the time he actually spent studying. Study time increased when he began to self-reinforce study behavior in the second week.

stopping by (Watson & Tharp, 1997). Also focus on the *consequences* of your behavior. Does studying produce outcomes that are satisfying?

STEP 4: DEVELOP A PLAN TO MODIFY THE ANTECEDENTS AND CONSEQUENCES

Once you have identified key antecedents and consequences, you are in position to modify either or both.

Altering the Antecedents

You can modify the environment so that different stimuli control your behavior. To increase studying, select a specific place where you do nothing but study. If your attention wanders, get up and leave the study area. Your objective is to condition yourself to study in response to the stimuli present in the study area. B. F. Skinner used this technique throughout his own career: He did all of his writing at a particular desk and did nothing else there.

Altering the Consequences

Consequences determine whether a behavior will be repeated. Fortunately, we have the power to arrange many of our own consequences. Self-administered *positive reinforcement* should be the cornerstone of most programs. Find an effective reinforcer that you can control, and make it available only if you engage in the desired behavior. Almost any activity or object you enjoy can serve as a reinforcer, but it must be potent enough to maintain the desired behavior. Awarding yourself a penny for each hour of study time is unlikely to modify your behavior, whereas a 30-minute credit toward a recreational activity might be very effective. After selecting a reinforcer, decide how to use it. Draw up and sign a contract with yourself. The contract should precisely state

- how often or how long you must perform the target behavior (or refrain from performing it if the goal is to reduce an undesirable behavior);
- the kind and amount of reinforcement you will receive for specific achievements.

Use Reinforcers Effectively

Immediately reinforce the target behavior whenever possible. If your reinforcer cannot be available immediately, use tokens that can later be converted into a reinforcer. One student who wanted to increase her study time awarded herself 1 point per 15 minutes of study time. Points were redeemed for rewards that varied in their reinforcement value. For example, 1 point was worth 15 minutes of TV viewing, but 15 points earned the right to "do anything I want to, all day." Behavior analysts have used token economies successfully with workers, children, patients in mental hospitals, prison inmates, and other groups (Swain & McLaughlin, 1998). If it works for them, it can work for you.

Use Shaping

If you collect good baseline data, you will know the level at which you currently perform your target behavior. Begin at this level or slightly beyond it and move *slowly* toward your final goal, reinforcing yourself at each step. For example, begin by reinforcing yourself for each 10-minute increase in study time. If you have trouble, reduce the size of your steps. Attaining each small goal along the way can be reinforcing and provides motivation to continue (Locke & Latham, 2002). The goal is to bring about gradual change while enjoying plenty of reinforcers, as well as the satisfaction that comes from increasing self-mastery. *The way you arrange reinforcement contingencies is the most critical determinant of whether you will achieve your goal.*

STEP 5: IMPLEMENT THE PROGRAM AND KEEP MEASURING BEHAVIOR

Most people experience occasional setbacks or plateaus when progress seems to stop. If this happens repeatedly, it is not a sign of weak willpower but rather a need to modify the program. Yes, self-regulation programs can fail, but failure calls for resourcefulness rather than despair. If need be, change the terms of your contract, but always operate under a specific contract. Keep recording and graphing the target behavior. This is the only way to identify your progress accurately.

This five-step process is one of several behavioral approaches to gaining greater control of our lives. Psychologists continue to design and test methods to increase self-regulation, adding new meaning to the phrase "Power to the people."

IN REVIEW

- Thorndike's law of effect states that responses followed by satisfying consequences will be strengthened, whereas those followed by annoying consequences will be weakened.

- Skinner analyzed operant conditioning in terms of relations between antecedents, behaviors, and consequences. Discriminative stimuli are antecedents that signal the likely consequences of particular behaviors in a given situation.

- Reinforcement occurs when a response is strengthened by an outcome (a reinforcer) that follows it. With positive reinforcement, a response is strengthened by the presentation of a stimulus that follows it. With negative reinforcement, a response is strengthened by the removal of an aversive stimulus.

- Operant extinction is the weakening and eventual disappearance of a response because it no longer is reinforced.

- Punishment occurs when a behavior is weakened by an outcome (a punisher) that follows it. With aversive punishment, the behavior becomes weaker when it is followed by the presentation of an aversive stimulus. With response cost, the behavior becomes weaker when it is followed by the removal of a stimulus.

- The use of corporal punishment with children is controversial and is correlated with several negative outcomes for children's development.

- Shaping, which uses the method of successive approximations, involves reinforcing behaviors that increasingly resemble the final desired behavior. Chaining is used to develop a sequence of responses by reinforcing each response with the opportunity to perform the next response.

■ Operant generalization occurs when behavior changes in one situation due to reinforcement or punishment, and the new response then carries over to similar situations. In contrast, operant discrimination occurs when an operant response is made to one discriminative stimulus but not to another.

■ On a continuous reinforcement schedule, every response is reinforced. Partial reinforcement may occur on a ratio schedule, in which a certain percentage of responses are reinforced, or on an interval schedule, in which a certain amount of time must pass before a response gets reinforced. In general, ratio schedules produce higher rates of performance than interval schedules.

■ On a fixed-ratio schedule, reinforcement occurs after a fixed number of responses; on a fixed-interval schedule, it occurs after a fixed time interval. On variable schedules, the required number of responses or interval of time between them varies around some average.

■ Escape conditioning and avoidance conditioning result from negative reinforcement. According to the two-factor theory, fear is created through classical conditioning. This fear motivates escape and avoidance, which are then negatively reinforced by fear reduction.

■ Operant conditioning principles can enhance human performance in educational and work settings, reduce a wide array of behavior problems, and help people self-regulate their behavior. Animals can be operantly trained to perform many specialized tasks.

CROSSROADS OF CONDITIONING

Behaviorists built much of the foundation on which our knowledge of learning principles rests, and behaviorism remains influential today (Leslie, 2002). Over the years, however, psychologists who viewed behavior from biological and cognitive perspectives enriched our understanding of learning by challenging some of behaviorism's key assumptions.

BIOLOGICAL CONSTRAINTS: EVOLUTION AND PREPAREDNESS

Behaviorists never suggested that a rat could learn to fly, but for decades they assumed that they could condition virtually any behavior an organism was physically capable of performing. Yet evidence mounted that "conditioned" animals did not always respond as they were supposed to. The behaviorist assumption was wrong because it ignored a key principle discussed at the outset of this chapter: Behavior is influenced by an organism's evolutionary history, and this places biological constraints on learning.

Martin Seligman's (1970) concept of *preparedness* captures this idea. **Preparedness** *means that through evolution, animals are biologically predisposed (prewired) to learn some associations more easily than others.* In general, behaviors related to a species' survival are learned more easily than behaviors contrary to an organism's natural tendencies. Let's consider some examples.

Constraints on Classical Conditioning: Learned Taste Aversions

Imagine eating or drinking something, then becoming sick to your stomach and throwing up. Perhaps it is a case of the flu, or it could be food poisoning. When a food is associated with nausea or vomiting, that particular food can become a CS that triggers a **conditioned taste aversion,** *a conditioned response in which the taste (and sometimes the sight and smell) of a particular food becomes disgusting and repulsive* (Garcia et al., 1985). The very thought of it may even make us feel queasy, and we learn to avoid it. During pregnancy many women experience nausea and vomiting, and they may develop aversions to foods associated with these symptoms (Bayley et al., 2002). Cancer patients may develop aversions to foods they eat before chemotherapy or radiation therapy sessions even when they know that the food did not cause their posttreatment stomach upset. Like other conditioned responses, the aversion develops involuntarily.

Psychologist John Garcia pioneered numerous taste-aversion experiments that challenged two basic assumptions of classical conditioning. First, behaviorists had assumed that the CS-UCS time interval had to be relatively short: usually a few seconds. Garcia showed that animals learned taste aversions even though the food (CS) was consumed up to several hours—or even a day—before they became ill (in this case, the UCS).

▶ **Focus 16**
How does research on learned taste aversions and fear conditioning support the concept of biological preparedness?

Stage 1: All Rats
When rats touch the drinking tube, sweet water is delivered and a light and buzzer turn on.

Stage 2

Illness condition	Fear condition

Group 1 rats get nause-ating X-rays when they drink.

Group 2 rats get electric shocks when they drink.

Stage 3

Group 1 rats avoid the sweet water and prefer the plain water with the light and buzzer.

Group 2 rats still drink the sweet water, but avoid the plain water with the light and buzzer.

FIGURE 6.26

Biological preparedness in classical conditioning. This figure illustrates the design and main results of Garcia and Koelling's (1966) aversion experiment.

Second, in a classic experiment, Garcia illustrated how biological preparedness influences learned aversions (Garcia & Koelling, 1966). Whenever rats licked a drinking tube, they were simultaneously exposed to three neutral stimuli: sweet-tasting water, a bright light, and a buzzer (Figure 6.26). The rats were then divided into two conditions. In one condition, the rats were exposed to X-rays upon drinking the water, which later made them ill (UCS). Would the rats develop an aversion to all three neutral stimuli? No, they avoided the sweet water but not the light or buzzer. Why did only the sweet taste become a CS? Because rats are biologically primed to form taste-illness associations, which means that in nature they most easily identify poisonous or bad food by its taste (or smell). In nature, sounds and lights don't make rats sick.

When rats in the second condition licked the tube, the light, buzzer, and sweet taste were all paired with an electric shock. Would these rats learn to fear all three neutral stimuli? No, they avoided the light and buzzer but kept drinking the sweet water. This also makes adaptive sense. In nature, sights and sounds—but not how food and drink taste—signal fear-provoking situations (e.g., a cat about to pounce).

The same principle applies to humans. When a food makes us violently sick, we may develop an aversion to it but not to the friends we ate with. Further, seeing the food again may repulse us but not make us afraid.

Psychologists have applied knowledge about conditioned aversions to save animals' lives. To prevent coyotes from killing ranchers' sheep, scientists (Gustavson et al., 1974) laced pieces of meat with lithium chloride, a nausea-inducing drug. They wrapped the meat in sheep hide and left it out for coyotes to eat. The coyotes ate it, became ill, and developed an aversion to the meat, thereby becoming less likely to kill sheep. This saved the lives of sheep—and also of the coyotes, who otherwise would have been shot by the ranchers. Figure 6.27 illustrates nature's own wildlife management based on learned taste aversions.

Applying taste-aversion principles to children with cancer, psychologists gave young patients an unusual-tasting candy before their chemotherapy sessions (Broberg & Bernstein, 1987). As hypothesized, the candy acted as a scapegoat and protected the children from developing aversions to their normal foods. Thus the candy—rather than their normal food—became the aversive CS.

FIGURE 6.27

A conditioned aversion in nature. This blue jay has never eaten a monarch butterfly but doesn't pass up an easy meal. Soon, toxins in the butterfly cause food poisoning. The jay feels discomfort, vomits, and develops a conditioned aversion triggered by the sight of the monarch's brightly patterned wings. From now on, it will leave monarchs alone. Source: Photos courtesy of Lincoln P. Brower.

Are We Biologically Prepared to Fear Certain Things?

Seligman (1971) proposes that like other animals, humans are biologically prepared to acquire certain fears more readily than others. In one case, a 4-year-old girl saw a snake in a park but wasn't frightened by it (Marks, 1977). Soon thereafter she returned to the family car and accidentally smashed her hand in the car door. She subsequently developed a phobia not of car doors or automobiles, but of snakes!

In the laboratory, Swedish psychologists showed people pictures of various stimuli, flashing each picture on a screen and pairing it with electric shock (the UCS). Next, they measured people's physiological responses when those stimuli were presented alone (Öhman & Soares, 1998). When the pictures showed snakes, spiders, or angry faces, people quickly acquired conditioned fear responses to these stimuli, even when the pictures were flashed too briefly to be consciously perceived. But participants who received shocks while looking at slides of flowers, houses, or happy faces displayed much weaker fear conditioning.

Humans develop phobias to many stimuli, but most often we fear things that seem to have greater evolutionary significance: snakes, spiders, and potentially dangerous animals and places (Hofmann et al., 2004). Is this the result of evolution-based biological preparedness, or might it be due to learning experiences that teach us to expect that some stimuli can be dangerous? Multiple factors may affect human fear conditioning, but one thing is clear: As with taste aversions, fear can be conditioned much more easily to some stimuli than to others.

Constraints on Operant Conditioning: Animals That "Won't Shape Up"

▶ Focus 17
How does instinctive drift illustrate preparedness, and why is it important?

Two of B. F. Skinner's students, Keller and Marian Breland (1961, 1966), became famous animal trainers. They successfully used shaping and chaining to train thousands of animals for circuses, TV shows, and movies, but sometimes the animals simply refused to behave according to the laws of operant conditioning.

On one occasion, the Brelands tried to train a chicken to play baseball. A small ball would roll toward home plate, and the chicken would pull a chain to swing a small metal bat. If the ball was hit, a bell would ring and the chicken was supposed to run to first base to get a food reinforcer. The Brelands easily trained the chicken to pull the chain that swung the bat and to run to first base when it heard the bell. But when the ball was introduced into the game, utter chaos ensued. If the chicken hit the ball, instead of running to first base it chased the ball all over the field, pecking at it furiously and flapping its wings. Try as they might, the Brelands could not extinguish these behaviors. End of training and end of the chicken's baseball career. This and other similar cases suggest that in operant conditioning (as in classical conditioning), organisms are biologically prepared to learn some types of associations more readily than others.

The Brelands also found that once a particular stimulus came to represent food, animals began to act as if it were food. The chicken pecked at the ball as if it were something to eat. In another case, raccoons had learned to deposit tokens into a box to receive a food reinforcer. But soon, instead of depositing the tokens, the raccoons kept rubbing them as if they were washing real food. This washing behavior was so deeply rooted that it simply overrode the conditioning procedure. The Brelands called this **instinctive drift,** *the tendency for a conditioned response to drift back toward instinctive behavior.*

Research provides other evidence of instinctive drift. For example, wild rats trained to press a lever for food will often drift back to instinctive behaviors and instead scratch and bite the lever (Powell & Curley, 1976).

Instinctive drift also has practical importance. People who adopt wild animals as pets or who train them for circuses face some personal risk no matter how hard they try to domesticate these animals. An acquaintance of ours once rescued a baby raccoon and raised it lovingly for nearly a year, at which time the raccoon unexpectedly reverted to its more instinctive, aggressive behavior. Our friend, now known as "Three Fingers," returned his pet to the wild.

COGNITION AND CONDITIONING

Early behaviorists believed that learning involves the relatively automatic formation of bonds between stimuli and responses. This viewpoint came to be known as *S-R (stimulus-response) psychology.* Behaviorists opposed explanations of learning that went beyond observable stimuli and responses. They did not deny that people had thoughts and feelings but argued that behavior could be explained without referring to such mentalistic concepts (Skinner, 1953, 1990).

THE FAR SIDE® BY GARY LARSON

"Stimulus, response! Stimulus, response! Don't you ever *think?*"

FIGURE 6.28

Some psychologists who challenged behaviorism's S-R model argued that to best explain human and animal behavior (though, obviously, not the activity of amoebae), the organism's cognitive representations must be taken into account.

Even in psychology's early years, some learning theorists challenged the S-R model, arguing that in between stimulus and response there is something else: the organism's (O) cognitive representation of the world (Figure 6.28). This came to be known as the *S-O-R,* or *cognitive, model of learning.* Today the cognitive perspective represents an important force in learning theory.

Early Challenges to Behaviorism: Insight and Cognitive Maps

In the 1920s, German psychologist Wolfgang Köhler (1925) challenged Thorndike's behaviorist assumption that animals learn to perform tasks only by trial and error. Köhler exposed chimpanzees to novel learning tasks and concluded that they were able to learn by **insight,** *the sudden perception of a useful relationship that helps to solve a problem.* Figure 6.29 shows how one of his apes solved the problem of how to retrieve bananas that were dangling beyond reach. Köhler emphasized that the apes often spent time staring at the bananas and available tools, as if they were contemplating the problem, after which the solution suddenly appeared.

Behaviorists argued that insight actually represents the combining of previously learned responses (Epstein et al., 1984). Imagine a pigeon placed inside a chamber where a miniature model of a banana dangles from the ceiling, out of reach. A small box sits in the corner of the chamber. Similar to Köhler's apes, the pigeon looks around, goes to the box, moves it under the banana by pushing it with its beak, then stands on the box and pecks the banana. Without knowing the pigeon's behavioral history (just as we don't know the entire behavioral history of Köhler's apes), we might conclude that this is a novel behavior reflecting remarkable insight. But instead, the pigeon has simply combined several independent behaviors (e.g., pushing a box, stepping onto a box) that researchers had operantly conditioned using reinforcement. Although the debate about insight continues to this day, Köhler's work nevertheless helped place the cognitive learning viewpoint on the map.

▶ **Focus 18**
Discuss how research on insight and cognitive maps challenged behaviorist views of learning.

FIGURE 6.29

Sultan seems to study the hanging bananas that are out of reach. After looking around, Sultan suddenly grabs some crates, stacks them, and obtains his tasty reward.

FIGURE 6.30

Cognitive maps in rats. (a) Rats first learned to run the simple maze. (b) When the maze was switched, many rats chose the fourth path to the right of the original route. Tolman proposed that the rats had developed a cognitive map of the maze. SOURCE: Adapted from Tolman, 1948.

(a)   Start

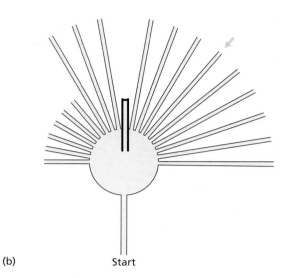

(b)   Start

▶ **Focus 19**

Describe the role of cognition in classical and operant conditioning. How did Tolman illustrate latent learning?

Another cognitive pioneer, American learning theorist Edward Tolman, studied spatial learning in rats. Look at the maze in Figure 6.30a. A rat runs to an open circular table, continues across, and follows the only path available to a goal box containing food. After 12 trials, the rat easily negotiates the maze. Next, the maze is changed. The rat runs its usual route and reaches a dead end (Figure 6.30b). What will the rat do?

Tolman found that rats returned to the table, briefly explored most of the 18 new paths for just a few inches, and then chose one. By far, the largest number—36 percent—chose the fourth path to the right of their original route, which took them closest to where the goal box had been. In short, the rats behaved as you would, given your advantage of seeing the maps.

Tolman (1948) argued that reinforcement theory could not explain this behavior but that he could: The rats had developed a **cognitive map,** *a mental representation of the spatial layout.* The concept of cognitive maps supported Tolman's belief that learning does not merely "stamp in" stimulus-response connections. Rather, learning provides knowledge, and based on their knowledge, organisms develop an expectancy, a cognitive representation, of "what leads to what."

Behaviorists disagreed with Tolman's interpretations and, as with insight, the debate over cognitive maps continues. Nevertheless, Tolman's concept of expectancy remains a cornerstone of today's cognitive approaches to classical and operant conditioning.

Cognition in Classical Conditioning

Early American behaviorists believed that classical conditioning created a direct reflexlike connection between the CS (e.g., tone) and CR (e.g., salivation). Interestingly, Pavlov held a different view, proposing that a neural bond is formed between the CS and the UCS. Thus for Pavlov's dogs, the tone triggered an association with food, which then triggered salivation.

Cognitive learning theorists also believe that classical conditioning forms a CS-UCS link. In cognitive terminology, the link is an expectancy that the CS will be followed by the UCS (Hollis, 1997). This *expectancy model* states that the most important factor in classical conditioning is not how often the CS and the UCS are paired, but how well the CS predicts (i.e., signals) the appearance of the UCS (Rescorla & Wagner, 1972).

Robert Rescorla (1968) tested this principle in a fear-conditioning experiment. Rats in one condition received electric shocks (UCS), and each shock was preceded by a tone. As usual, the tone soon became a CS that elicited a fear response when presented alone. In a second condition, rats received the same number of tone-shock pairings as the first group, but they also received as many shocks that were not preceded by the tone. Would the tone become a CS for fear? According to traditional learning theory, the answer should be yes, because the number of tone-shock pairings was the same as in the first group. But the expectancy model predicts no, because the tone does not reliably predict when the shock will occur. The results supported Rescorla's hypothesis: The tone did not elicit a fear response for the second group.

CS-UCS inconsistency also explains why we don't become conditioned to all the neutral stimuli that are present just before a UCS appears. For example, when Pavlov's dogs were presented with tone-food pairings, there was light in the room. Why didn't the dogs learn to salivate whenever they saw light? The key is that when the room was lit, the dogs often were *not* receiving food. When a neutral stimulus does not consistently predict the arrival of the UCS, it is less likely to become a CS. This is highly adaptive; if it were not the case, you and I (along with Pavlov's dogs) would be twitching, salivating, and exhibiting all sorts of reflexive responses to so many stimuli that it would be difficult to function.

Other evidence supports the expectancy model. For example, recall that forward pairing (e.g., a tone followed by food) typically produces the strongest learning, whereas backward pairing (e.g., food followed by a tone) produces the weakest learning. This makes sense based on the expectancy model. In forward pairing, the tone predicts the imminent arrival of the food; it is a signal that something meaningful is about to happen. In backward pairing, the tone has no predictive value because the food has already arrived. In sum, the expectancy model has been highly influential and provides good evidence that cognition plays a role in classical conditioning (Siegel & Allan, 1996).

Cognition in Operant Conditioning

S-O-R theorists believe that cognitive processes also play a key role in operant conditioning. Let's examine three issues.

The Role of Awareness   To demonstrate operant conditioning to an introductory psychology class, an instructor sent a student, Kyle, out of the room and instructed another student in how to shape the response of flicking a light switch on and off, using small chocolate candies as the reinforcer. When Kyle returned, he was given a piece of chocolate first for looking at the wall that held the light switch, then for approaching the wall, and so on. After 25 minutes of shaping, Kyle was flicking the switch and chomping one piece of chocolate after another.

At this point, another student asked if she could serve as experimenter. A new participant, Jeff, left the room while the class decided that he should be shaped to erase the blackboard. When Jeff returned, the new experimenter said, "Jeff, if you'll erase the blackboard immediately, I'll give you this whole bag of candy." This time, it took all of 5 seconds to produce the desired behavior.

Cognitive theorists emphasize that organisms develop an *awareness,* or *expectancy,* of the relations between their responses and probable consequences. From this viewpoint, Kyle and Jeff developed an expectation that flicking the light switch and erasing the blackboard would produce a delicious consequence. Similarly, suppose I ask you to make up 10 sentences and recite them to me. As you speak, I say "good" or "mmm-hmm" every time a sentence contains a noun that refers to humans (e.g., *boy, woman, people*), and I measure whether your usage of human nouns changes. In an actual experiment, only those participants who received praise *and* who became aware of the reinforcement contingency increased their usage of human nouns (Spielberger & DeNike, 1966). Those who received praise but were unaware of why it was given performed no differently than a control group receiving no praise.

The concept of awareness implies that the best predictor of behavior is the perceived contingency, not the actual one (Figure 6.31). Often the two are identical, but sometimes people perceive contingencies that do not actually exist. One example is *superstitious behavior.* In cognitive terms, the organism misperceives that a specific behavior produces favorable consequences or helps avoid bad ones. Humans often engage in superstitious behaviors to gain a sense of control over environmental events (Keinan, 2002). One traveler we know eats ice cream prior to taking any trip on a train because this supposedly will guarantee a safe journey. This superstitious behavior, of course, has been reinforced each time by a safe arrival.

Latent Learning   Tolman's research illustrated in Figure 6.30 suggested that the rats developed cognitive maps when they were reinforced with food for running a maze. Tolman also believed that cognitive maps could be learned without reinforcement, posing an even greater challenge to the behaviorist viewpoint. In one experiment, three

"Boy, have I got this guy conditioned! Every time I press the bar down, he drops in a piece of food."

FIGURE 6.31

Perception versus reality.
SOURCE: Cartoon by H. Masseo & P. Gardner (1951) from *Columbia Jester.* Reprinted with permission of *Jester of Columbia,* Columbia University.

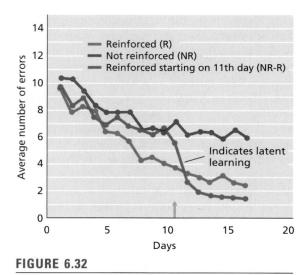

FIGURE 6.32

Tolman's demonstration of latent learning. Rats had one trial in the maze per day. Group R was reinforced with food every time they reached the end of the maze. Group NR never received reinforcement. The critical group, NR-R, received food reinforcement on Day 11. Their immediate performance improvement suggested that they had learned the maze prior to the introduction of reinforcement. SOURCE: Tolman & Honzik, 1930.

groups of rats learned the correct path through a complex maze (Tolman & Honzik, 1930). Rats in the first group found food each time they reached the goal box. Rats in the second group found the goal box empty each time they reached it. Rats in the third group found no food at the end of the maze for the first 10 days but did find food in the goal box starting on the eleventh day.

The results are shown in Figure 6.32, and the key finding is this: On Day 11, the rats in the third group discovered food in the goal box for the first time. By the very next day, they were performing just as well as the first group, which had been reinforced all along. What could explain this significant, sudden performance improvement? According to Tolman, during Days 1 to 10, rats in the third group were learning the spatial layout of the maze as they wandered about. They were not being reinforced by food, but they gained knowledge and developed their cognitive maps. This learning remained *latent* (hidden) until the rats discovered a good reason on Day 11 to get to the goal box quickly; it was then immediately displayed in performance the next day. Tolman's experiments support the concept of **latent learning,** *which refers to learning that occurs but is not demonstrated until later, when there is an incentive to perform* (Blodgett, 1929). In other words, we may learn how to do something at one time but not display that knowledge until we perform a task at a future time.

Self-Evaluations as Reinforcers and Punishers Students called him "Holy Hubert," and he visited our college campus for over 10 years. His fire-and-brimstone warnings to repent often evoked amusement, insults, and ridicule. One could hardly imagine less positive consequences for an evangelist. One day, we asked Hubert why he continued to preach when students reacted so negatively. He answered, "I don't care what they say. When I know I'm doing the Lord's work, I feel so good."

Hubert's persistence illustrates that external reinforcement and punishment are not the only consequences controlling behavior. We often feel pride for doing something even if others do not know or approve of our deeds. We may also disapprove of ourselves for failing to live up to our own standards. These *cognitive self-evaluations* represent important internal reinforcers and punishers (Scott & Cervone, 2002). Think back to the woman in Las Vegas who solicits charitable donations. Her strong belief that she is doing something valuable may be all the positive reinforcement she needs.

IN REVIEW

■ An organism's evolutionary history prepares it to learn certain associations more easily than others, and this places biological constraints on learning. Thus organisms show faster classical conditioning when a CS has evolutionary significance.

■ It is difficult to operantly condition animals to perform behaviors that are contrary to their evolved natural tendencies. Instinctive drift occurs when a conditioned behavior is abandoned in favor of a more natural response.

■ Köhler's studies of animal insight and Tolman's research on cognitive maps suggested that cognition plays a role in learning. Tolman emphasized that learning is based on knowledge and an expectation of "what leads to what."

■ Cognitive interpretations of classical conditioning propose that organisms learn an expectancy that the CS will be followed by the UCS.

■ Cognitive learning theorists view operant conditioning as the development of an expectancy that certain behaviors will produce certain consequences under certain conditions. Research on latent learning indicates that learning can occur without reinforcement.

■ In humans, cognitive self-evaluations (e.g., pride and shame) can function as reinforcers and punishers.

OBSERVATIONAL LEARNING: WHEN OTHERS SHOW THE WAY

How did you learn to write, dance, and drive a car, or even to spread peanut butter and jelly across a piece of bread rather than piling it up in the center? Reinforcement certainly was involved, but so was **observational learning,** *the learning that occurs by observing the behavior of a model.* Teachers, parents, and coaches often help us learn by intentionally modeling skills, but observational learning extends beyond such contexts. We also learn fears, prejudices, likes and dislikes, and social behaviors by watching others (Olsson & Phelps, 2004). Through observation we may learn desirable responses, or like the two boys in our opening vignette who overzealously emulated their TV wrestling heroes, we may acquire undesirable behaviors. When parents who swear in front of their children complain to one another, "Where did our kids learn that damn language?" the answer should be apparent.

Observational learning can be highly adaptive. By observing others, an organism can learn which events are important, which stimuli signal that such events are about to occur, and which responses are likely to produce positive or negative consequences. For example, hens may learn which other hens they can reasonably pick a fight with and which ones they should avoid by observing the hens that emerge as victors and losers in battles (Hogue et al., 1996). And monkeys may learn adaptive fears—such as a fear of snakes—by observing other monkeys react with fear (Öhman & Mineka, 2001).

Humans' capacity to learn by observation, which is also called *modeling,* far outstrips that of other creatures. It helps us bypass the potentially time-consuming and dangerous process of trial and error. For example, we wouldn't want each new generation of brain surgeons or airline pilots to learn their craft only through trial and error!

BANDURA'S SOCIAL-COGNITIVE THEORY

As you've seen, research on biological preparedness and cognitive factors in conditioning challenged behaviorism's S-R view of learning. Psychologist Albert Bandura's pioneering research and theorizing on observational learning also helped carry the S-O-R challenge to behaviorism's gate. Bandura's **social-cognitive theory,** also known by its former name **social-learning theory,** *emphasizes that people learn by observing the behavior*

of models and acquiring the belief that they can produce behaviors to influence events in their lives *(Bandura, 1969, 2004).*

The Modeling Process and Self-Efficacy

Bandura views modeling as a four-step process that includes several cognitive factors:

- *Attention:* First, we must pay attention to the model's behavior.
- *Retention:* Second, we must retain that information in memory so that it can be recalled when needed.
- *Reproduction:* Third, we must be physically capable of reproducing the model's behavior or something similar to it.
- *Motivation:* Fourth, we must be motivated to display the behavior.

According to Bandura, **self-efficacy,** *which represents people's belief that they have the capability to perform behaviors that will produce a desired outcome,* is a key motivational factor in observational learning. Recall that at the beginning of the chapter we defined learning as a change in an organism's behavior or capabilities based on experience. According to Bandura, the knowledge or capability to perform a behavior may be acquired at one time but not displayed until a later time when the motivational conditions are favorable.

Tolman's research on latent learning in rats demonstrated this point, and a classic experiment by Bandura (1965) on modeling demonstrated the learning-versus-performance distinction in humans. In this experiment, children watched a film in which a model acted aggressively toward a "Bobo doll" (an inflatable plastic clown), punching, kicking, and hitting it with a mallet. One group saw the model rewarded with praise and candy, a second group saw the model reprimanded for aggression, and a third group saw no consequences for the model. After the film, each child was placed in a room with various toys, including a Bobo doll (Figure 6.33).

Children who saw the model punished performed fewer aggressive actions toward the Bobo doll than did children in the other two groups. Does this mean that this group failed to learn how to respond aggressively? To find out, the experimenter later offered the children attractive prizes if they could do what the model had done. All of the children quickly reproduced the model's aggressive responses. Note that just as Tolman showed that rats apparently learned the layout of a maze while they were not receiving reinforcement, Bandura demonstrated that regardless of whether the

► **Focus 20**
What is the adaptive significance of observational learning? Describe Bandura's theory and the four steps in the modeling process.

"Why Are We Violent?" This video in Chapter 6 of your CD presents a landmark researcher's view on this question.

FIGURE 6.33

In Bandura's (1965) experiment, most children who watched an aggressive model attack a Bobo doll later imitated that behavior. These photos show only one of several specific actions that the children spontaneously imitated.

model was reinforced or punished, children had indeed learned the model's behavior.

Imitation of Aggression and Prosocial Behavior

Bandura's work helped stir a societal controversy that was brewing in the 1960s and continues to this day: What effect does viewing aggressive models on TV or in movies have on our attitudes and behavior? We will discuss this issue, along with violent video games, more fully in Chapter 16. In brief, research strongly suggests that viewing media violence

- decreases viewers' concerns about the suffering of victims;
- habituates us to the sight of violence;
- provides aggressive models that increase viewers' tendency to act aggressively (Eron, 2000; Huesmann et al., 2003).

If watching media violence can enhance our tendency to act aggressively, might watching prosocial models (models who do good deeds) increase our tendency to help others? Psychologist Joyce Sprafkin and her colleagues (1975) conducted one of the first experiments on this issue. They found that by exposing children to a TV show in which an action hero helps save a young puppy, the children became more likely to help what they believed were real puppies in danger, even though helping meant giving up the opportunity to win prizes at a game. Many studies similarly indicate that exposure to prosocial models enhances people's helping behavior (Hearold, 1986).

APPLICATIONS OF OBSERVATIONAL LEARNING

In everyday life we learn many skills from observing models. Elementary school teachers model how to write, pronounce, and use words. In college, foreign-language instructors do the same. Parents, teachers, business managers, and athletic coaches model how to solve problems and perform tasks. If you play sports or video games, you may have picked up strategies or moves by watching other players.

Psychologists have also used observational learning to enhance prosocial behavior. For example, researchers showed high school students an audiovisual program that featured models (other students) who donated blood; donations to a blood bank subsequently increased by 17 percent (Sarason et al., 1991).

More ambitiously, observational learning has been used to address global social problems. Miguel Sabido, a vice president in charge of research at Mexico's largest media company, used Bandura's theory to help develop the first project of its kind in 1975 (Smith, 2002). When a national literacy program in Mexico failed to draw a good turnout, Sabido created a TV soap opera to give the literacy program a boost. The popular soap opera aired for a year and featured a literate female character who, as part of the national program, organized a self-study group for teenagers and adults who struggled with illiteracy.

Sabido hoped that the soap opera characters' learning to read would provide viewers with positive role models, increase viewers' self-efficacy that they could learn to read, and motivate viewers to enroll in the literacy program. His hope bore fruit. After one episode in which viewers were directly asked to enroll, "about 25,000 people descended on the distribution center in Mexico City to get their reading materials" (Bandura, 2002, p. 224). New annual enrollments in the literacy program jumped from 100,000 in the previous year to over 900,000 in the year the soap opera aired and decreased to about 400,000 the year after the soap opera ended.

Mass media programs incorporating social-cognitive learning principles have since tackled social problems in South America, Africa, India, and Asia. Our "Research Close-Up" describes an experiment that implemented and evaluated one of these programs.

▶ **Focus 21**
Describe applications of social-cognitive theory to solve global problems.

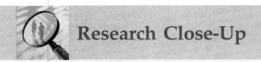

Research Close-Up

Using Social-Cognitive Theory to Prevent AIDS: A National Experiment

SOURCE: PETER W. VAUGHAN, EVERETT M. ROGERS, ARVIND SINGHAL, and RAMADHAN M. SWALEHE (2000). Entertainment-education and HIV/AIDS prevention: A field experiment in Tanzania. *Journal of Health Communication, 5*, 81–100.

INTRODUCTION

In the 1990s, the African nation of Tanzania, like many countries, faced a growing AIDS crisis that was fueled by risky sexual practices and widespread misinformation about HIV transmission. Many Tanzanians believed that HIV was spread by mosquitos or the lubricant on condoms. Some men believed that AIDS could be cured by having sex with a virgin (Bandura, 2002). HIV/AIDS was widely spread through heterosexual contact between truck drivers and prostitutes who frequented the areas where truckers made stops.

To combat this crisis and other societal problems, the Tanzanian government and Radio Tanzania produced and aired 208 episodes of a radio soap opera over several years. The content of this series was carefully designed by educators, government officials, members of the clergy, and other consultants to take advantage of principles from social-cognitive theory. In this 5-year study, Peter Vaughan and his colleagues (2000) measured the effects of the radio program on listeners' attitudes and sexual practices.

METHOD

The soap opera featured three types of role models. Positive role models were knowledgeable about HIV/AIDs, minimized risky sex, and ultimately attained rewarding social outcomes. Transitional role models began by acting irresponsibly but eventually adopted safer sexual practices. Negative role models, such as a major character named Mkwaju, engaged in risky sex that led to punishing outcomes. Mkwaju was a promiscuous, married truck driver who had unprotected sex with many girlfriends and ignored warnings about HIV/AIDS. During the series his wife, fearing infection, leaves him. Later, Mkwaju contracts HIV and dies of AIDS.

The program's content was designed to (1) make listeners realize that they were at risk for contracting HIV/AIDS, (2) increase listeners' self-efficacy by showing them how to control the risk, and (3) get listeners to reduce their number of sexual partners and use condoms when having sex.

This prime-time soap opera was broadcast twice weekly to six geographic regions (e.g., the experimental regions) of Tanzania for 5 years. A seventh geographic region served as a control region for the first 3 years and received the radio program for only the final 2 years. Each year interviewers gathered information about participants' attitudes, sexual behaviors, and personal characteristics. One or more family members from roughly 2,750 randomly chosen households participated.

RESULTS

Just over half of the participants living in the six experimental regions listened to the soap opera, a remarkably high figure given that many Tanzanians did not own radios. The typical listener heard 108 of the 204 episodes, and about 80 percent said that the program helped them learn about preventing HIV/AIDS. Compared to people who were not exposed to the program, those who tuned in became more likely to believe that they were at risk for contracting HIV/AIDS but could control this risk through safer sexual practices. Listeners identified with the soap opera's positive role models, spoke more often with their partners about HIV/AIDS, reduced their number of sexual partners, and increased their use of condoms. These findings were replicated in the seventh geographic region after it was switched from being a control group to an experimental group.

DISCUSSION

This study illustrates how a scientific theory can guide the development of a treatment program that addresses a major societal problem. The project had several features of an experiment. There was an independent variable (exposure/no exposure to the program) and many dependent variables (participants' attitudes and sexual behaviors). By cleverly turning the comparison region into an experimental region after 3 years, the researchers were able to test whether their initial findings would replicate.

Still, conducting large-scale research in the real world presents difficult challenges that can threaten a study's internal validity. Within each experimental region, the researchers could not control who tuned in to the radio programs. Indeed, listeners and nonlisteners differed in several ways (e.g., listeners were somewhat better educated and wealthier). To minimize the chance that such factors would distort the results, the researchers statistically adjusted for these factors when they analyzed the data.

The study also relied heavily on participants' self-reports. One drawback to self-reports is that especially when answering sensitive questions, participants may distort their answers in a socially desirable way. However, by gathering some objective data, such as increases in the number of condoms distributed in these regions, the researchers were able to corroborate some of the self-report measures. In sum, this project was an ambitious attempt to change people's attitudes and behavior on a national level.

IN REVIEW

- Observational learning occurs by watching the behavior of a model.

- Bandura's social-cognitive theory proposes that modeling involves four steps: attention, retention, reproduction, and motivation. Observing successful models can increase people's self-efficacy and thus motivate them to perform the modeled behavior.

- Children can learn aggressive and prosocial behaviors by watching models. Even when viewing an aggressive model who is punished, children may learn the behavior and display it at a later time.

- Modeling is often a key instructional technique in everyday skill-learning situations. Psychologists have applied modeling concepts to increase people's prosocial behavior.

- Social-cognitive theory has helped stimulate intervention programs to address social problems, such as illiteracy and HIV/AIDS, around the globe.

THE ADAPTIVE BRAIN

We began this chapter by noting that learning represents your personal adaptation to the circumstances you encounter throughout your life. To close the chapter, we'd like to emphasize that your ability to learn and adapt depends not only on networks of brain structures and circuits, but also on the brain's own ability to adapt—to modify its structure and functioning—in response to experience.

No single part of the brain controls learning. For example, the hypothalamus and neural pathways involving dopamine play a key role in regulating our ability to experience reward (Olds, 1958; Rolls, 2000). Humans report pleasure when specific areas of the hypothalamus are electrically stimulated, and both humans and rats will learn to repeatedly press a button or lever to receive these electrical reinforcers. The cerebellum plays an important role in acquiring some classically conditioned movements, such as conditioned eyeblink responses, whereas the amygdala is centrally involved in acquiring conditioned fears (Schafe & LeDoux, 2002). We'll take a closer look at brain processes that underlie learning when we discuss memory in the next chapter.

Biology affects learning, but learning also influences brain functioning (Fanselow & Poulos, 2005). As we noted in the last chapter, as you

▶ **Focus 22**
How does learning influence the brain? Summarize biological, psychological, and environmental factors involved in learning.

Before practice   After practice

FIGURE 6.34

While learning a computer game, the brain of a novice player is highly active and uses a lot of energy, as indicated by the large yellow and red areas in the left PET scan. As the right scan shows, energy consumption decreases with experience.

make the transition at a new task from inexperienced novice to experienced master, your brain is able to rely less on conscious processing and instead process more information nonconsciously. Highly trained athletes and musicians can execute incredibly complex skills with a minimum of conscious thought. No doubt you can think of skills that seem almost automatic to you now (perhaps driving a car or typing on a keyboard) but which required considerable effort when you first learned them. As we gain experience at novel tasks, the brain's frontal lobes—the seat of executive functions such as decision making and planning—tend to exercise less control and become less active (Eliassen et al., 2003). Indeed, notice in Figure 6.34 how a video-game player's brain activity generally decreased after practicing the game.

Learning also etches its imprints on the brain's physical structure. During countless hours of practice and performance, a violinist makes continuous, precise movements with the fingers of his or her left hand while the right hand moves the bow (Figure 6.35). This constant fingering of the strings provides a great deal of sensory stimulation to the somatosensory cortex of the right hemisphere. By using brain imaging, researchers found that the area in this brain region that is devoted to representing the fingers was larger among string-instrument musicians (who averaged almost 12 years of experience) than among nonmusicians. Moreover, the earlier in life that the musicians had started to play their instruments, the greater the size of this brain area. In contrast, the left-hemisphere somatosensory area representing the right-hand fingers of the musicians and nonmusicians did not differ (Elbert et al., 1995).

FIGURE 6.35

The precise, constant left-hand movements involved in fingering the strings provides a great deal of sensory stimulation to this violinist's right-hemisphere somatosensory cortex.

Because these findings are correlational, they can't clearly establish cause and effect. Perhaps it wasn't playing music that caused the brain differences. Maybe it was the other way around: Preexisting brain differences helped these individuals become musicians. Yet controlled experiments with animals do indeed show that learning

leaves its mark not only on the somatosensory cortex but on other parts of the brain as well. For example, when monkeys and rats learn skilled movements that require them to use their fingers and paws, respectively, the representations of these body parts in their motor cortex change (Kleim et al., 2002).

Learning's effects on the brain occur throughout the life cycle. Compared to newborn rats that grow up in standard cages, litter mates that grow up in enriched environments—with toys and greater opportunities to learn—develop heavier brains whose neurons have more dendrites and synapses and greater concentrations of various neurotransmitters (Rosenzweig, 1984). In turn, this increased brain development enables animals to perform better on subsequent learning tasks (Meaney et al., 1991). And in humans, exposure to stimulating environments and new learning opportunities during late adulthood seems to slow declines in brain functioning, as measured by better performance on intellectual and perceptual tasks (Goldstein et al., 1997; Schaie, 2005). In a sense, then, every day you are alive your brain adapts and continues its own personal evolution; its neural networks and patterns of activity are affected not only by your genetic endowment but by your learning experiences as well.

In closing, Figure 6.36 summarizes some of the environmental, psychological, and biological factors that play key roles in learning. As you study the learning concepts we've covered, try to apply them to your own behavior. Think about the roles that classical conditioning, operant conditioning, and observational learning play in developing and maintaining important behaviors in your life.

FIGURE 6.36

Levels of analysis: Factors related to learning.

LEVELS OF ANALYSIS   Factors Related to Learning

Biological	Psychological	Environmental
• Adaptive significance of behavior	• Knowledge: Insight, cognitive maps, and latent learning	• Classical conditioning experiences
• Evolution-based preparedness to learn certain associations	• Expectancies concerning CS-UCS associations	• Operant conditioning experiences
• Brain regions and neurotransmitters that regulate learning	• Awareness of reinforcement contingencies	• Live and media models who demonstrate behavior
• Changes in brain activity and neural circuits as a result of experience	• Self-evaluative standards and reinforcers (e.g., pride, shame)	• Cultural norms and socialization processes that affect what we learn

Learning

KEY TERMS AND CONCEPTS

Each term has been boldfaced and defined in the chapter on the page indicated in parentheses.

adaptive significance (p. 193)
anticipatory nausea and
   vomiting (ANV; p. 201)
applied behavior analysis (p. 215)
aversion therapy (p. 201)
aversive punishment (positive
   punishment, punishment by
   application; p. 207)
avoidance conditioning (p. 213)
chaining (p. 210)
classical conditioning (p. 195)
cognitive map (p. 222)
conditioned response (CR; p. 196)
conditioned stimulus (CS; p. 196)
conditioned taste aversion (p. 218)
continuous reinforcement (p. 211)
discrimination (classical
   conditioning; p. 199)
discriminative stimulus (p. 205)
escape conditioning (p. 213)
exposure therapies (p. 200)

extinction (classical conditioning; p. 198)
fixed action pattern (p. 193)
fixed-interval (FI) schedule (p. 212)
fixed-ratio (FR) schedule (p. 211)
habituation (p. 195)
higher-order conditioning (p. 199)
insight (p. 221)
instinctive drift (p. 220)
latent learning (p. 224)
law of effect (p. 202)
learning (p. 192)
negative reinforcement (p. 206)
observational learning (p. 225)
operant conditioning (p. 203)
operant discrimination (p. 210)
operant extinction (p. 207)
operant generalization (p. 210)
partial (intermittent) reinforcement (p. 211)
positive reinforcement (p. 206)
preparedness (p. 218)
primary reinforcers (p. 206)

punishment (p. 203)
reinforcement (p. 203)
response cost (negative punishment,
   punishment by removal; p. 209)
secondary (conditioned)
   reinforcers (p. 206)
self-efficacy (p. 225)
shaping (p. 210)
Skinner box (p. 203)
social-cognitive theory (social-learning
   theory; p. 225)
spontaneous recovery (p. 198)
stimulus control (p. 211)
stimulus generalization (p. 198)
token economy (p. 215)
two-factor theory of avoidance
   learning (p. 214)
unconditioned response (UCR; p. 196)
unconditioned stimulus (UCS; p. 196)
variable-interval (VI) schedule (p. 212)
variable-ratio (VR) schedule (p. 212)

? What Do You Think?

WHY DID CAROL'S CAR PHOBIA PERSIST? (PAGE 198)

We can't know for sure why Carol's anxiety reaction failed to extinguish, but a strong possibility is that she was not exposed to sufficient extinction trials. The key to extinction is the presentation of the CS (car) without the UCS (events of the crash). If Carol avoided cars after her accident, then there was little opportunity for the CS to occur without the UCS. This is the unfortunate irony of phobias: People avoid the stimulus they fear, thereby depriving themselves of extinction trials. Thus, the key ingredient to extinction is not the mere passage of time but repeated presentation of the CS without the UCS.

Applying this same principle, can you explain why the Navy veterans who heard the battle gong automatically

showed a strong alarm reaction 15 years after the war's end? Again, we can't know for sure, but once the combat ended, the sailors likely had insufficient opportunities to experience extinction trials. In other words, the way to extinguish their fear would be to sound the battle gong (CS) repeatedly without the associated danger of manning battle stations and preparing for combat (UCS).

WAS THE "LITTLE ALBERT" STUDY ETHICAL? (PAGE 200)

In forming your judgment, did you consider the ethical criteria discussed in Chapter 2 (pages 35–37)? With those criteria in mind, let's imagine that we are reviewing this research proposal in the early 1900s.

(1) If you initially thought that you would not approve a study like this, then consider the following:

- Suppose the experimenters promise to obtain informed consent from Albert's parents and keep everyone's identity confidential.

- Although Albert will experience some short-term stress, consider the enormous potential benefits of this study. If we can classically condition phobias in humans, this may revolutionize thinking about how phobias develop and could lead to faster, more effective treatments. These treatments could benefit countless people with phobias.

- Suppose that the experimenters promise to use procedures based on learning theory to extinguish Albert's phobia after the study, so that he will not suffer any negative long-term consequences.

Under these conditions and with these issues in mind, would you now approve the study?

(2) If your initial judgment (or new judgment) is that you would approve this study, then consider the following:

- Would it be ethical to proceed with the study if the parents did not give informed consent?

- Based on learning theory, isn't there a risk that the phobia will generalize to other stimuli? Consider the short-term and long-term psychological risks associated with this possibility if Albert's phobia persists.

- If a phobia is successfully conditioned, what about the treatment to eliminate it? What steps are in place to guarantee that Albert will receive this treatment? Has the treatment been scientifically tested with humans? What is the failure rate? If there already is good evidence that the treatment is effective, then why conduct this study?

Applying today's ethical standards to the "Little Albert" study, we believe it clearly would have been rejected. Even with informed consent and a secure system in place to guarantee that an infant would receive treatment afterward, the risks would have been considered too high. At the time of the actual experiment, there was insufficient evidence to clearly support the effectiveness of the extinction treatment with humans. An alternative, ethical research approach would have been to study whether learning-based treatments are effective with patients who already have phobias.

CAN YOU EXPLAIN THE "SUPERMARKET TANTRUM"? (PAGE 210)

The father's initial refusal to buy candy is followed by an aversive stimulus (the tantrum). This punishes the father's response, and after two tantrums he no longer refuses the request. When the father eventually gives in, this removes the aversive stimulus (the tantrum), which negatively reinforces (strengthens) the response of giving in. Thus the father's response of refusing to buy candy is weakened by punishment, and the response of giving in is strengthened by negative reinforcement. Just as important, the child has learned that throwing a tantrum pays off. The tantrum was positively reinforced by the consequence of getting candy.

CHAPTER SEVEN

Memory

> *The charm, one might say the genius of memory, is that it is choosy, chancy, and temperamental.*
>
> —ELIZABETH BOWEN

Some people are famous for their extraordinary remembering; others, for their extraordinary forgetting. Consider Rajan Mahadevan, who at age 5 sauntered outside his home in India one day while his parents entertained about 40 to 50 guests at a party. Rajan studied the guests' parked cars, returned to the party, and then recited all the license plate numbers from memory, matching each to the proper guest in the order they had parked. While in college, Rajan set a world record by flawlessly recalling the first 31,811 digits of pi. He averaged 3.5 digits per second!

How does Rajan perform such amazing feats? When memory researchers at Kansas State University (where Rajan attended graduate school in psychology) asked him this very question, he said "that being asked to describe how he learned numbers was like being asked to describe how he rode a bicycle. He knew how to do both tasks, but he found it difficult to describe either process" (Thompson et al., 1993, p. 13).

In most other ways, Rajan's memory is ordinary. Indeed, he uses a grocery list to remember what to buy at the market. As he notes, "Unless I put my glasses, wallet and keys together near the door before I leave to start my day, I will surely forget them" (Harris, 2002).

■■■■■

You are about to meet H. M., who at age 27 had most of his hippocampus and surrounding brain tissue surgically removed to reduce his severe epileptic seizures. The operation succeeded, but it unexpectedly left H. M. with *amnesia,* or memory loss.

When you talk with H. M., he can discuss his childhood, teens, and early 20s, for those memories are intact. Indeed, for the most part, at age 27 H. M.'s amnesia did not rob him of his past. Rather, it robbed him of his future.

H. M. lost the ability to form new memories that he can consciously recall. Typically, once an experience or fact leaves his immediate train of thought, he cannot remember it. Spend the day with H. M., depart and return minutes later, and he will not recall having met you. He reads magazines over and over as if he has never seen them before. A favorite uncle has died, but H. M. cannot remember. Thus every time H. M. asks how his uncle is, he experiences shock and grief as though it were the first time he learned of his uncle's death.

H. M.'s surgery took place in 1953, and researchers have studied him for over 50 years (Skotko et al., 2004). No matter how many years pass, H. M.'s memory for events contains little after 1953. Even his sense of identity is frozen in time. H. M. recalls himself looking like a young man but cannot remember the aging image of himself that he sees in the mirror.

Memory *refers to the processes that allow us to record, store, and later retrieve experiences and information.* Memory adds richness and context to our lives, but even more fundamentally, it allows us to learn from experience and thus adapt to changing environments. From an evolutionary standpoint, without the capacity to remember we would not have survived as a species.

As the cases of Rajan and H. M. illustrate, memory is complex. How did Rajan remember

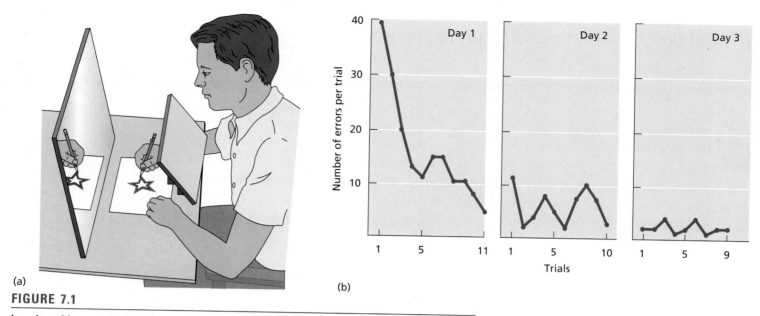

FIGURE 7.1

Learning without consciously remembering. (a) On this complex task, a participant traces a pattern while looking at its mirror image, which also shows the writing hand moving in the direction opposite to its actual movement. (b) H. M.'s performance on this task rapidly improved over time—he made fewer and fewer errors—indicating that he had retained a memory of how to perform the task. Yet each time he performed it, he stated that he had never seen the task before and had to have the instructions explained again. SOURCE: Adapted from Milner, 1965.

over 31,000 digits of pi? Why is it, as Figure 7.1 shows, that H. M. can remember the skilled movements needed to perform a new task yet swear each time he encounters the task that he has never even seen it before (Milner, 1965)? In this chapter we explore the fascinating nature of memory.

MEMORY AS INFORMATION PROCESSING

► Focus 1
What is memory, and how is it like an information-processing system?

Psychological research on memory has a rich tradition, dating back to late-19th-century Europe. By the 1960s, computer advances and the cognitive revolution in psychology led to a new metaphor that continues to guide memory research: the mind as a processing system that encodes, stores, and retrieves information. **Encoding** *refers to getting information into the system by translating it into a neural code that your brain processes.* This is a little like what happens when you type on a computer keyboard, as your keystrokes are translated into an electrical code that the computer can understand and process. **Storage** *involves retaining information over time.* Once in the system, information must be filed away and saved, as happens when a computer stores information temporarily in RAM (random access memory) and more permanently on a hard

drive. Finally, **retrieval** *refers to processes that access stored information.* On a computer, retrieval occurs when you give a software command (e.g., "open file") that transfers information from the hard drive back to RAM and the screen, where you can scroll through it. Keep in mind, however, that this analogy between human and computer is crude. For one thing, people routinely forget and distort information and sometimes "remember" events that never occurred (Loftus & Bernstein, 2005). Human memory is highly dynamic, and its complexity cannot be fully captured by any existing information-processing model.

Encoding, storage, and retrieval represent what our memory system does with information. Before exploring these processes more fully, let's examine some basic components of memory.

A THREE-STAGE MODEL

The model in Figure 7.2, developed by Richard Atkinson and Richard Shiffrin (1968) and subsequently modified, depicts memory as having three major components: sensory memory, working (short-term) memory, and long-term memory. Other models have been proposed, but this three-stage framework has been the most influential.

FIGURE 7.2

The three-stage model of memory. In this model, memory has three major components: (1) sensory memory, which briefly holds incoming sensory information; (2) working (short-term) memory, which processes certain information received from sensory memory and information retrieved from long-term memory; and (3) long-term memory, which stores information for longer periods of time. Source: Adapted from Atkinson & Shiffrin, 1968.

Sensory Memory

Sensory memory *briefly holds incoming sensory information*. It comprises different subsystems, called *sensory registers*, which are the initial information processors. Our visual sensory register is called the *iconic store*, and in 1960 George Sperling conducted a classic experiment to assess how long it holds information. On one task, Sperling arranged 12 letters in three rows and four columns, like those in Figure 7.3. He flashed the array on a screen for $\frac{1}{20}$ of a second, after which participants immediately recalled as many letters as they could. Typically, they were able to recall only 3 to 5 letters.

Why was recall so poor? Did participants have too little time to scan all the letters, or had they seen the whole array, only to have their iconic memory fade before they could report all the letters? To find out, Sperling conducted another experimental condition. This time, just as the letters were flashed off, participants heard either a high-, medium-, or low-pitched tone, which signaled them to report either the top, middle, or bottom row of letters.

In this case, participants often could report all 4 letters in whichever row was signaled. Their not knowing which row would be signaled ahead of time implies that their iconic memory had stored an image of the whole array, and they now had time to "read" their iconic image of any one line before it rapidly disappeared. If this logic is correct, then participants should have done poorly if the signaling tone was delayed. Indeed, with just a 1-second delay, performance was no better than without the tone. As Figure 7.4 illustrates, it is difficult, perhaps impossible, to retain complete information in purely visual form for more than a fraction of a second. In contrast, our auditory sensory register, called the *echoic store*, can hold information about the precise details of a sound for several seconds (Winkler et al., 2002).

Working/Short-Term Memory

Most information in sensory memory rapidly fades away. But according to the original three-stage model, through selective attention some information enters **short-term memory**, *a memory*

▶ **Focus 2**
Describe sensory memory. How long does information remain in iconic memory, and how did Sperling determine this?

▶ **Focus 3**
Discuss the limits of short-term/working memory. What are four major components of working memory?

Fixation

Display (1/20 sec.) plus tone

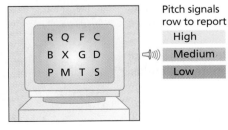

Pitch signals row to report
High
Medium
Low

R Q F C
B X G D
P M T S

Report

B X G D

FIGURE 7.3

Sperling's classic study of iconic memory. After a participant fixates on a screen, a matrix of letters is flashed for $\frac{1}{20}$ of a second. In one condition, participants do not hear any tone and must immediately report as many letters as they can. In another condition, a high-, medium-, or low-pitched tone signals the participant to report either the top, middle, or bottom row. If the tone occurs just as the letters are flashed off, participants typically can report 3 or all 4 letters, no matter which row is signaled.

FIGURE 7.4

The arc of light that you see traced by a twirling fiery baton or sparkler or the lingering slash that you see after observing a lightning bolt results from the brief duration of information in iconic memory. Because your iconic memory stores complete information for only a fraction of a second, the image quickly vanishes.

store that temporarily holds a limited amount of information.

Memory Codes Once information leaves sensory memory, it must be represented by some type of code if it is to be retained in short-term memory. For example, the words that someone just spoke to you ("I like your new haircut") must somehow become represented in your mind. **Memory codes** *are mental representations of some type of information or stimulus,* and they can take various forms. We may try to form mental images (*visual codes*), code something by sound (*phonological codes*), or focus on the meaning of a stimulus (*semantic codes*). For physical actions, such as learning sports or playing musical instruments, we code patterns of movement (*motor codes*).

The form of a memory code often does not correspond to the form of the original stimulus. As you read these words (visual stimuli) you are probably not storing images of the way the letters look. Rather, you are likely forming phonological codes (as you say the words silently) and semantic codes (as you think about their meaning). Thus when people are presented with lists of words or letters and asked to recall them immediately, they often make phonetic errors. They might mistak-

enly recall a *V* as a *B* because of the similarity in how the letters sound (Conrad, 1964).

Capacity and Duration Short-term memory can hold only a limited amount of information at a time. Depending on the stimulus, such as a series of unrelated numbers or letters, most people can hold no more than five to nine meaningful items in short-term memory, leading George Miller (1956) to set the capacity limit at "the magical number seven, plus or minus two." To demonstrate this, try administering the digit-span test in Table 7.1 to some people you know.

If short-term memory capacity is so limited, how can we remember and understand sentences as we read? For a partial answer, read the letters below (one per second); then cover them up and write down as many letters as you can remember, in the order presented.

B I R C D E R Y K A E U Q S A S A W T I

Did you have any trouble? Now, with the order of the letters reversed (and a few spaces added), try to remember all 20 letters.

IT WAS A SQUEAKY RED CRIB

No doubt you found the second task much easier. The limit on short-term storage capacity concerns the number of meaningful *units* that can be recalled, and the 20 letters have been combined into 6 meaningful units (words). *Combining individual items into larger units of meaning is called* **chunking,** which aids recall.

Short-term memory is limited in duration as well as capacity. Have you ever been introduced to someone and then, moments later, realized that

TABLE 7.1 Digit-Span Test

Directions: Starting with the top sequence, read these numbers at a steady rate of one per second. Immediately after saying the last number in each series, signal the person to recall the numbers in order. Most people can recall a maximum sequence of 5 to 9 digits.

8 3 5 2
4 3 9 3 1
7 1 4 9 3 7
5 4 6 9 2 3 6
1 5 2 4 8 5 8 4
9 3 2 6 5 8 2 1 4
6 8 1 3 1 9 4 7 3 5
4 2 4 6 9 5 2 1 7 4 3
3 7 9 8 4 6 1 7 2 4 9 5

FIGURE 7.5

Rapid forgetting of nonrehearsed information in working memory. Participants who were prevented from rehearsing three-letter syllables in working memory showed almost no recall of the letters within 18 seconds, illustrating the rapid forgetting of information in working memory. SOURCE: Based on Peterson & Peterson, 1959.

you've forgotten her or his name? Without rehearsal, information in short-term memory generally has a shelf life of up to 20 seconds (Figure 7.5; Peterson & Peterson, 1959). However, by rehearsing information—such as when you look up a telephone number and keep saying it to yourself while waiting to use a phone—you can extend its duration in short-term memory.

Putting Short-Term Memory to Work The original three-stage model viewed short-term memory as a temporary holding station along the route from sensory to long-term memory. Information that remained in short-term memory long enough presumably was transferred into more permanent storage. Cognitive scientists now reject this view as too passive. Instead, they view short-term memory as **working memory,** *a limited-capacity system that temporarily stores and processes information* (Baddeley, 2002). In other words, working memory is a mental workspace that stores information, actively manipulates it, and supports other cognitive functions such as problem solving and planning.

Components of Working Memory According to one influential model, working memory has several components, as shown in Figure 7.6 (Baddeley, 2002; Baddeley & Hitch, 1974). One component, the *phonological loop*, briefly stores mental repre-

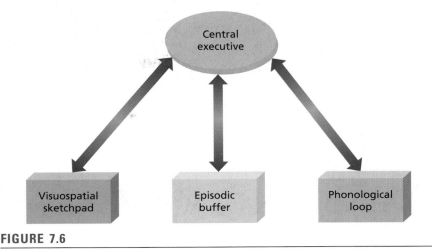

FIGURE 7.6

Components of working memory. According to Baddeley's most recent model, working memory has four components. SOURCE: Adapted from Baddeley, 2002.

sentations of sounds. The phonological loop is active when you listen to a spoken word or when you sound out a word to yourself as you read. Silently repeating the name of person to whom you're being introduced will briefly refresh the acoustic codes stored in the phonological loop.

A second component, the *visuospatial sketchpad*, briefly stores visual and spatial information, as occurs when you form a mental image of someone's face or of the spatial layout of your bedroom. Note that the phonological loop and visuospatial sketchpad can be active simultaneously. For example, you can silently repeat the word *sunset* while at the same time holding a mental image of a sunset or, for that matter, of an elephant.

A third component, called the *episodic buffer*, provides a temporary storage space where information from long-term memory and from the phonological and/or visuospatial subsystems can be integrated, manipulated, and made available for conscious awareness (Baddeley, 2002). For example, after reading or hearing me say "How much is 87 plus 36?" your phonological loop initially maintains the acoustic codes for the sounds of 87 and 36 in working memory. Your visuospatial sketchpad also might maintain a mental image of the numbers. But to do this task, the rules for performing addition must be retrieved from your long-term memory and temporarily stored in the episodic buffer, where they are integrated with (i.e., applied to) information from the phonological and visuospatial subsystems. This creates the ingredients for the conscious perceptions that you experience as you perform the mental addition (e.g., "7 + 6 = 13, carry the 1 . . . ").

The episodic buffer also comes into play when you chunk information. British psychologist

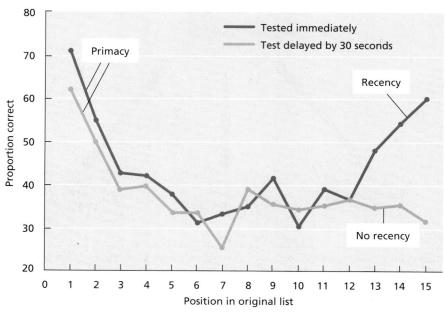

FIGURE 7.7

The serial position effect. Immediate recall of a word list produces a serial position curve, where primacy and recency effects are both evident. However, even a delay of 15 to 30 seconds in recall (during which rehearsal is prevented) eliminates the recency effect, indicating that the later items in the word list have disappeared from short-term memory. SOURCE: Adapted from Glanzer & Cunitz, 1966.

Alan Baddeley (2002) notes that despite the phonological loop's very limited acoustic storage capacity, people can routinely listen to and then repeat novel sentences that are 15 or 16 words long. It is within the episodic buffer, he proposes, that groups of words are chunked into meaningful phrases and stored (and phrases can be further chunked into sentences), enabling us to recall relatively long sections of prose.

The fourth component of working memory, called the *central executive,* directs the overall action. When solving arithmetic problems, for example, the central executive doesn't store the numbers or rules of addition. Instead, it plans and controls the sequence of actions that need to be performed, divides and allocates attention to the other subsystems, and integrates information within the episodic buffer. It also may monitor the progress as interim steps are completed (DeStefano & LeFevre, 2004).

Long-Term Memory

Long-term memory *is our vast library of more durable stored memories.* Perhaps there have been times in your life, such as periods of intensive study during final exams, when you have felt as if there is no room for storing so much as one more new fact inside your brain. Yet as far as we know, long-term storage capacity essentially is unlim-

▶ **Focus 4**
Describe long-term memory and its limits. Based on the three-stage model, why does the serial position effect occur?

ited, and once formed, a long-term memory can endure for up to a lifetime.

Are short-term and long-term memory really distinct? Case studies of amnesia victims like H. M. suggest so. If you told H. M. your name or some fact, he could remember it briefly but could not form a long-term memory of it. Experiments in which people with normal memory learn lists of words also support this distinction. Suppose that we present you with a series of 15 unrelated words, one word at a time. Immediately after seeing or hearing the last word, you are to recall as many words as you can, in any order you wish. As Figure 7.7 illustrates, most experiments find that words at the end and beginning of a list are the easiest to recall. This U-shaped pattern is called the **serial position effect,** *meaning that the ability to recall an item is influenced by the item's position in a series.* The serial position effect has two components: a *primacy effect*, reflecting the superior recall of the earliest items, and a *recency effect*, representing the superior recall of the most recent items.

What causes the primacy effect? According to the three-stage model, as the first few words enter short-term memory, we can quickly rehearse them and transfer them into long-term memory. However, as the list gets longer, short-term memory rapidly fills up and there are too many words to keep repeating before the next word arrives. Therefore, beyond the first few words, it is harder to rehearse the items and they are less likely to get transferred into long-term memory. If this hypothesis is correct, then the primacy effect should decrease if we are prevented from rehearsing the early words, say by being presented the list at a faster rate. Indeed, this is what happens (Glanzer, 1972).

As for the recency effect, the last few words still linger in short-term memory and have the benefit of not being bumped out by new information. Thus if we try to recall the list immediately, all we have to do is recite the last words from short-term memory before they decay (i.e., fade away). In sum, according to the three-stage model, the primacy effect is due to the transfer of early words into long-term memory, whereas the recency effect is due to the continued presence of information in short-term memory.

If this explanation is correct, then it must be possible to wipe out the recency effect—but not the primacy effect—by eliminating the last words from short-term memory. This happens when the recall test is delayed, even for as little as 15 to 30 seconds, *and* we are prevented from rehearsing the last words. To prevent rehearsal, we might be asked to briefly count a series of numbers immediately after the last word is presented (Glanzer & Cunitz, 1966; Postman & Phillips, 1965). Now by the time we try to recall the last words, they will have faded from short-term memory or been bumped out by the numbers task (6 . . . 7 . . . 8 . . . 9 . . .). Figure 7.7 shows that under delayed conditions, the recency effect disappears while the primacy effect remains.

Having examined some basic components of memory, let us now explore more fully how information is encoded, stored, and retrieved.

IN REVIEW

- Memory involves three main processes (encoding, storage, and retrieval) and three components (sensory memory, working/short-term memory, and long-term memory).
- Sensory memory briefly holds incoming sensory information. Some information reaches working memory and long-term memory, where it is mentally represented by visual, phonological, semantic, or motor codes.
- Working memory actively processes a limited amount of information and supports other cognitive functions. It has phonological, visuospatial, episodic, and executive (coordinating) components.
- Long-term memory stores large amounts of information for up to a lifetime. Research on amnesia and on the serial position effect support the distinction between working- and long-term memory.

ENCODING: ENTERING INFORMATION

The holdings of your long-term memory, like those of a library, must be organized if they are to be available when you wish to retrieve them. The more effectively we encode material into long-term memory, the greater the likelihood of retrieving it (Figure 7.8). Let's explore two basic types of encoding and then examine some ways to optimize encoding quality.

EFFORTFUL AND AUTOMATIC PROCESSING

Think of the parade of information that you have to remember every day: names, meeting times, and mountains of schoolwork. Remembering it all involves *effortful processing,* encoding that is initi-

FIGURE 7.8

Ineffective encoding can have practical as well as theoretical significance. SOURCE: Copyright © The New Yorker Collection 1983 Ed Fisher. All rights reserved. Used with permission from cartoonbank.com.

"The matters about which I'm being questioned, Your Honor, are all things I should have included in my long-term memory but which I mistakenly inserted in my short-term memory."

ated intentionally and requires conscious attention (Hasher & Zacks, 1979). When you rehearse information, make lists, and take notes, you are engaging in effortful processing.

In contrast, have you ever been unable to answer an exam question and thought, "I should know this! I can even picture the diagram on the upper corner of the page!" In this case, you have apparently transferred information about the diagram's location on the page (which you were not trying to learn) into your long-term memory through *automatic processing,* encoding that occurs without intention and requires minimal attention. Information about the frequency, spatial location, and sequence of events is often encoded automatically (Jimenez & Mendez, 2001).

LEVELS OF PROCESSING: WHEN DEEPER IS BETTER

Imagine that you are participating in a laboratory experiment and are about to be shown a list of words, one at a time. Each word will be followed by a question, and all you have to do is answer yes or no. Here are three examples:

1. POTATO "Is the word in capital letters?"
2. HORSE "Does the word rhyme with *course*?"
3. TABLE "Does the word fit in the sentence, 'The man peeled the _____'?"

Each question requires effort but differs from the others in an important way. Question 1 requires

► **Focus 5**
Contrast effortful and automatic processing, and discuss the levels-of-processing model.

superficial *structural encoding,* as you only have to notice how the word looks. Question 2 requires a little more effort. You must engage in *phonological* (also called *phonemic*) *encoding* by sounding out the word to yourself and then judging whether it matches the sound of another word. Question 3 requires *semantic encoding* because you must pay attention to what the word means.

Like the three examples above, the words you are about to be presented with in this experiment will be followed by a question that requires either structural, phonological, or semantic encoding. Unexpectedly, you will then be given a memory test in which you will be shown a list of words and asked to identify which words were presented earlier. Which group of words will you recognize most easily? Those processed structurally, phonologically, or semantically?

According to the concept of **levels of processing,** *the more deeply we process information, the better we will remember it* (Craik & Lockhart, 1972). Thus you should best remember those words that you processed semantically, as shown in Figure 7.9. Merely perceiving the structural properties of the words (e.g., uppercase versus lowercase) involves shallow processing, and phonemically encoding words is intermediate. Semantic encoding, however, involves the deep-

est processing because it requires us to focus on the meaning of information.

Although many experiments have replicated this finding, at times depth of processing can be difficult to measure. If some students prepare for an exam by creating hierarchical outlines while others create detailed flashcards, which method involves deeper processing? If the first group performs better, should we assume that they processed the information more deeply? To do so, warns Alan Baddeley (1990), is to fall into a trap of circular reasoning. Still, the levels-of-processing model has stimulated much research (Clifford, 2004). There are situations where few would argue with at least a broad distinction between shallow and deep processing. Here is one of them.

EXPOSURE AND REHEARSAL

Years ago one of our students sought advice after failing an exam. He said that he had been to all the lectures and read each chapter three times. Yet not a word in his textbook had been underlined or highlighted. When asked whether he took notes as he read the text or paused to reflect on the information, he said no. Instead, he read and reread each chapter quickly, much like a novel, and assumed that the information would somehow sink in.

Unfortunately, mere exposure to a stimulus without focusing on it represents shallow processing. To demonstrate, try drawing from memory a picture of the smallest-value coin in your country (e.g., a U.S. penny), accurately locating all the markings. Few people can do this. Even thousands of shallow exposures to a stimulus do not guarantee long-term retention.

Rehearsal goes beyond mere exposure. When we rehearse information, we are thinking about it. But not all rehearsals are created equal. Have you ever seen a live performance of a play and been amazed at the actors' flawless recall of volumes of material in front of live audiences? You may picture the actors reading the script and saying the words over and over, day after day, until they've memorized their lines. This approach, called **maintenance rehearsal,** *involves simple, rote repetition,* and some students rely on it to learn their course material.

Maintenance rehearsal keeps information active in working memory, as when someone tells you a phone number and you repeat it to yourself as you place the call. However, rote memorization usually is not an optimal method to transfer information into long-term memory.

What, then, is a better method? Professional actors begin not by memorizing but by studying

▶ **Focus 6**
Contrast maintenance and elaborative rehearsal. Describe ways to use organization and imagery to enhance encoding.

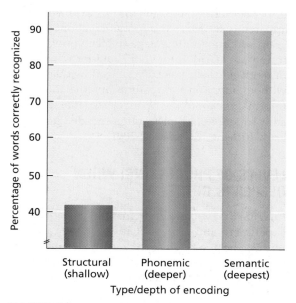

FIGURE 7.9

Depth of processing and memory. Participants were shown words and asked questions that required (1) superficial structural processing, (2) somewhat deeper phonemic processing, or (3) deeper semantic processing of each word. Depth of processing increased later recognition of the words in a larger list. SOURCE: Based on Craik & Tulving, 1975.

the script in great depth, trying to get into the mindset of their characters. Based on detailed research, psychologists Tony and Helga Noice (2002a) note that actors, "before they gave any thought to memorization, stressed the notion of understanding the ideas behind the utterances, and the reasons the characters used those words to express those ideas" (p. 9). The techniques actors use are examples of **elaborative rehearsal,** *which involves focusing on the meaning of information or expanding (i.e., elaborating) on it in some way.*

If your study habits include (1) organizing and trying to understand the material rather than just memorizing it, (2) thinking about how it applies to your own life, and (3) relating it to concepts or examples you already know, then you are using elaboration. According to Craik and Lockhart (1972), elaborative rehearsal involves deeper processing than maintenance rehearsal, and experiments show that it is more effective in transferring information into long-term memory (Benjamin & Bjork, 2000).

ORGANIZATION AND IMAGERY

J. C. is an awe-inspiring restaurant waiter. Perhaps you would like a filet mignon, medium-rare, a baked potato, and Thousand Island dressing on your salad? Whatever you order, it represents only 1 of over 500 options (7 entrees × 5 serving temperatures × 3 side dishes × 5 salad dressings) available at the restaurant where J. C. works. Yet you and 20 of your friends can place your selections with J. C., and he will remember them perfectly without writing them down.

Psychologists K. Anders Ericsson and Peter Polson (1988) studied J. C. and found that he invented an organizational scheme to aid his memory. He divided customers' orders into four categories (entree, temperature, side dish, dressing) and used a different system to encode the orders in each category. For example, he encoded dressings by their initial letter, so orders of Thousand Island, oil and vinegar, blue cheese, and oil and vinegar would become *TOBO*. Organizational schemes are an excellent way to enhance memory.

Hierarchies and Chunking

Organizing material in a *hierarchy* takes advantage of the principle that memory is enhanced by associations between concepts (Bower et al., 1969). A logical hierarchy enhances our understanding of how individual items are related; as we proceed from top to bottom, each category serves as a cue that triggers our memory for the items below it. Because hierarchies have a visual organization, imagery can be used as a supplemental memory code. The hierarchy in Figure 7.10, for example, may help you remember some concepts about encoding.

As noted earlier, chunking refers to combining individual items into larger units of meaning. To refresh your memory, read the letters below (one per second), then try to recall as many as you can in the same sequence.

I R S Y M C A I B M C I A F B I

If you recalled 5 to 9 letters in order, you did well. Now let's reorganize these 16 letters into 5 larger, more meaningful chunks: IRS, YMCA, IBM, CIA, and FBI. These chunks are easier to rehearse, keep active in working memory, and transfer into long-term memory. When learning a new telephone number (e.g., 123-456-7890), you probably encode it in chunks.

FIGURE 7.10

Meaningful hierarchical organization enhances memory. Placing information into a meaningful hierarchy enhances encoding and memory. This hierarchy could be developed further by adding a fifth level of boxes under "Organization" labeled *Hierarchies, Chunking, Acronyms,* and *Rhymes.* A box labeled *Method of Loci* could be added under "Imagery," although it also organizes information.

Visual Imagery

What did your sixth-grade classmates look like? To answer this question, you might construct mental images in your working memory, based on information that you draw out of long-term memory.

Allan Paivio (1969) proposes that information is stored in long-term memory in two forms: verbal codes and visual codes. According to his **dual coding theory,** *encoding information using both verbal and visual codes enhances memory because the odds improve that at least one of the codes will be available later to support recall.* Dual coding, however, is harder to use with some types of stimuli than it is with others. Try to construct a mental image of (1) a fire truck and (2) jealousy. You probably found the second task more difficult because jealousy represents an abstract concept rather than a concrete object (Paivio et al., 2000).

Memory experts recommend using imagery to dual-code information. The ancient Greeks developed the **method of loci** (*loci* is Latin for "places"), *a memory aid that associates information with mental images of physical locations.* To use this technique, imagine a place that has distinct locations, such as your campus. Next, link each location with an item you are trying to remember. For example, to remember the components of working memory, imagine walking to the administration building (central executive), an art studio (visuospatial sketchpad), a music room (phonological loop), and the campus newspaper room (episodic buffer). It may take some practice to use this imagery technique effectively, but many studies support its effectiveness (Wang & Thomas, 2000).

Other Mnemonic Devices

The term *mnemonics* (*nee-MON-iks*) refers to the art of improving memory, and a **mnemonic device** *is a memory aid.* Mnemonic devices reorganize information into more meaningful units and provide extra cues to help retrieve information from long-term memory. Hierarchies, chunking, visual imagery, and the method of loci are mnemonic devices. So are *acronyms*, which combine one or more letters (usually the first letter) from each piece of information you wish to remember. For example, many students learn the acronym ROY G. BIV to help remember the hues in the visible spectrum (the colors of the rainbow: red, orange, yellow, green, blue, indigo, violet).

Even putting information in a rhyme may enhance memory. As memory researcher Paul

► **Focus 7**
How do schemas affect encoding? What role do schemas and mnemonic devices play in expertise and exceptional memory?

Whalen (2003) humorously noted: "I once had the greatest difficulty remembering the name of a woman I had met named Gisa, until it later occurred to me that her name rhymed with both a leaning tower and a credit card" (p. 240). Some of our students use rhyming when they study, and advertisers often include rhyming jingles in their messages. In one experiment, adults listened to a 10-minute radio program into which researchers had inserted an advertisement for a fictitious mouth rinse (Cavoloss). The advertisement either contained a rhyme ("Toss the floss, use Cavoloss") or presented the same information without a rhyme. Tested 1 week later, participants exposed to the rhyme remembered more product information and showed better brand-name recall (Smith & Phillips, 2001).

HOW PRIOR KNOWLEDGE SHAPES ENCODING

Can you recall the paragraph you just read word for word? Typically, when we read, listen to someone speak, or experience some event, we do not precisely encode every word, sentence, or moment. Rather, we usually encode the *gist*—the general theme (e.g., "rhymes can enhance memory")—of that information or event.

Schemas: Our Mental Organizers

The themes that we extract from events and encode into memory are often organized around *schemas.* A **schema** *is a mental framework—an organized pattern of thought—about some aspect of the world* (Bartlett, 1932; Koriat et al., 2000). For example, the concepts "dog," "shopping," and "love" serve as schemas that help you organize your world. To see more clearly what a schema is and how it can influence encoding, read the following paragraph.

> The procedure is actually quite simple. First you arrange things into different groups. Of course, one pile may be sufficient depending on how much there is to do. If you have to go somewhere else due to lack of facilities, that is the next step; otherwise you are pretty well set . . . it is better to do too few things at once than too many. In the short run this might not seem important, but complications can easily arise. A mistake can be expensive as well. . . . After the procedure is completed, one arranges the materials into different groups again. Then they can be put into their appropriate places. Eventually they will be used once more, and the whole

cycle will have to be repeated. (Bransford & Johnson, 1972, p. 722)

Asked to recall the details of the preceding paragraph, you would probably have trouble. However, suppose we tell you that the paragraph is about a common activity: washing clothes. Now if you read the paragraph again, you will find that the abstract and seemingly unrelated details suddenly make sense. Thus, your schema for "washing clothes" helps you organize and encode these details as a meaningful pattern and thus remember more of them.

Schemas, Encoding, and Expertise

When most people look at a musical score, they see sheets of uninterpretable information. In contrast, musicians see organized patterns that they can easily encode. In music, as in other fields, acquiring *expertise* is a process of developing schemas that help encode information into meaningful patterns (Boschker et al., 2002).

William Chase and Herbert Simon (1973) demonstrated this point in an intriguing study. Three chess players—an expert ("master"), an intermediate player, and a beginner—were allowed 5 seconds to look at a chessboard containing about 25 pieces. Then they looked away and, on an empty board, attempted to reconstruct the placement of the pieces from memory. This was repeated over several trials, each with a different arrangement of pieces. On some trials, the chess pieces were arranged in *meaningful positions* that

actually might occur in game situations. With only a 5-second glance, the expert typically recalled 16 pieces, the intermediate player 8, and the novice only 4. But when the pieces were in *random positions*, each player did poorly, accurately recalling only 2 or 3 pieces.

How would you explain these results? We have to reject the conclusion that the expert had better overall memory than the other players, because he performed no better than they did with the random arrangements. But the concepts of schemas and chunking do explain the findings (Gobet & Simon, 2000). When the chess pieces were arranged in meaningful positions, the expert could apply well-developed schemas to recognize patterns and group pieces together. For example, he would treat as a unit all pieces that were positioned to attack the king. The intermediate player and especially the novice, who did not have well-developed chess schemas, could not construct the chunks and had to try to memorize the position of each piece.

However, when the pieces were not in positions that would occur in a real game, they were no more meaningful to the expert than to the other players. When that happened, the expert lost the advantage of schemas and had to approach the task on a piece-by-piece basis just as the other players did. Similarly, football coaches show much better recall than novices do after looking at diagrams of football plays (patterns of Xs and Os), but only when the plays are logical (Figure 7.11).

FIGURE 7.11

Schemas, expertise, and memory. Diagrams of football plays were shown to football coaches (experts) and to people who had played football but were not coaches (novices). Given 5 seconds to see each play, coaches displayed excellent memory—but only when the plays were logical. Their well-developed football schemas were of little use when the patterns of Xs and Os were illogical. These findings are similar to those obtained when expert, intermediate, and novice chess players tried to reproduce meaningful and random arrangements of chess pieces. SOURCE: Based on Garland & Barry, 1991.

How does a mnemonist develop superior memory abilities? View the video, "Mnemonic Strategies in Memory," in Chapter 7 of your CD to find out.

ENCODING AND EXCEPTIONAL MEMORY

A **mnemonist** (or **memorist**) *is a person who displays extraordinary memory skills*, and it's tempting to assume that mnemonists like the waiter J. C. or pi-master Rajan Mahadevan have an innate, photographic memory. But K. Anders Ericsson and his colleagues (1982, 2004) argue that exceptional memory is a highly learned skill that involves prior knowledge, meaningful associations, efficient storage and retrieval, and extensive practice.

Mnemonists take advantage of basic memory principles. Many create visual images or stories to help them encode information. They often chunk information into larger units, combine smaller chunks into larger ones, and elaborate on the material by associating chunks with other meaningful information. Thus, 194473862001 might become "1944=World War II; 73 and 86=two old people; 2001=famous movie." Combining techniques like these with 190 hours of practice, a college student with average memory became capable of remembering strings of up to 80 numbers on a digit-span test (Ericsson et al., 1980).

How, then, did Rajan learn 31,811 digits of pi? Rajan said that he did not have a photographic memory, and psychologists Charles Thompson and coworkers (1993), who studied Rajan intensively, agreed. Instead, they found that Rajan used chunking; the mathematical tables of pi that he studied grouped digits in chunks of 10, so Rajan did the same. But surprisingly, Rajan did not associate the chunks with meaningful material. Rather, beyond basic chunking, Rajan relied primarily on the brute force of rote memorization and extensive practice. How much practice? Thompson and coworkers estimated that it took Rajan over a year to learn the digits of pi.

Realize that just because rote memorization can transfer information into long-term memory, it's not necessarily the best way. Mnemonists (including the person who broke Rajan's record by recalling 42,195 digits of pi) often use elaborative rehearsal. Moreover, rote memorization is better suited to learning a string of numbers than to learning material that has meaning. When Rajan applied his rote strategy to memory tasks that involved meaningful stimuli (e.g., written stories), he performed more poorly or no better than college students in a control group.

So, is exceptional memory a learned skill? After a year of practice, could the average person really remember 32,000 digits of pi? Thompson and coworkers (1993) believe that in memory, as in sports and music, endless skilled practice will not enable most people to rise to the top unless they also have the requisite innate ability. Yet Ericsson and coworkers (1993, 2004) disagree, arguing that "many characteristics once believed to reflect innate talent are actually the result of intense practice" (1993, p. 363).

What Do You Think?

WOULD PERFECT MEMORY BE A GIFT OR A CURSE?
If you could have a perfect memory, would you want it? What might be the drawbacks? Think about it, then see page 271.

IN REVIEW

- Effortful processing involves intentional encoding and conscious attention. Automatic processing occurs without intention and requires minimal effort.

- Deep processing enhances memory. Elaborative rehearsal provides deeper processing than maintenance rehearsal. Hierarchies, chunking, dual coding that includes visual imagery, and other mnemonic devices facilitate deeper encoding.

- Schemas are mental frameworks that shape how we encode information. As we become experts in any given field, we develop schemas that allow us to encode information into memory more efficiently.

- People who display exceptional memory take advantage of sound memory principles and mnemonic devices.

STORAGE: RETAINING INFORMATION

At a moment's notice you can recall an incredible wealth of information, from the name of Russia's capital to how you spent your most recent vacation. This ability to rapidly access diverse facts, concepts, and experiences has influenced many cognitive models of how information is stored and organized in memory.

MEMORY AS A NETWORK

We noted that memory is enhanced by forming associations between new information and other items already in memory. The general principle that memory involves associations goes to the heart of the *network* approach.

▶ **Focus 8**
Contrast associative network models and neural network models of memory, and explain priming.

Associative Networks

One group of theories proposes that long-term memory can be represented as an **associative network,** *a massive network of associated ideas and concepts* (Collins & Loftus, 1975). Figure 7.12 shows what a tiny portion of such a network might be like. In this network, each concept or unit of information—"fire engine," "red," and so on—is represented by a *node* somewhat akin to each knot in a huge fishing net. The lines in this network represent associations between concepts, with shorter lines indicating stronger associations. For simplicity, Figure 7.12 shows only a few connections extending from each node, but there could be hundreds or more. Notice that items within the same category—types of flowers, types of fruit, colors, and so on—generally have the strongest associations and therefore tend to be clustered closer together. In essence, an associative network is a type of schema; it is a mental framework that represents how we have organized information and how we understand the world (Roediger & McDermott, 2000).

Alan Collins and Elizabeth Loftus (1975) theorize that when people think about a concept, such as "fire engine," there is a *spreading activation* of related concepts throughout the network. For example, when you think about a "fire engine," related concepts such as "truck," "fire," and "red" should be partially activated as well. The term **priming** *refers to the activation of one concept (or one unit of information) by another.* Thus "fire engine" primes the node for "red," making it more likely that our memory for this color will be accessed (Chwilla & Kolk, 2002).

The notion that memory stores information in an associative network helps explain how hints and mnemonic devices stimulate recall (Reisberg, 1997). For example, when you hear "Name the colors of the rainbow," the nodes for "color" and "rainbow" jointly activate the node for "ROY G. BIV," which in turn primes your recall for "red," "orange," "yellow," and so forth.

Neural Networks

Neural network models take a different approach to explain why spreading activation and priming occur (Chappell & Humphreys, 1994). Neural network models are computer models whose programming incorporates principles taken from the operation of the nervous system. A neural network has nodes (often called *units*) that are linked to each other, but unlike the nodes in associative network models, each node in a neural network model does not contain an individual unit of information.

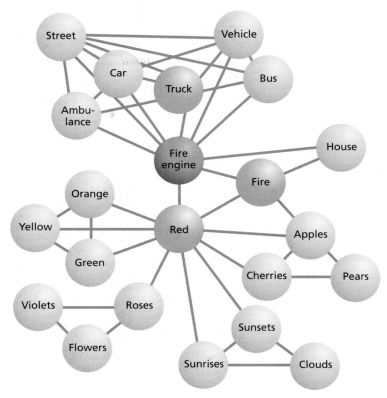

FIGURE 7.12

Semantic networks. Each node in this semantic network represents a concept. The lines represent associations between concepts, with shorter lines indicating stronger associations. SOURCE: Adapted from Collins & Loftus, 1975.

There is no single node for "red," no single node for "fire engine," and so on. Instead, each node in a neural network is more like a small information-processing unit. As an analogy, think of each neuron in your brain as a node. A neuron processes inputs and sends outputs to other neurons, but as far as we know, the concepts of "red" and "fire engine" are not stored within any single neuron.

Recall that in the brain, neurons have synaptic connections with many other neurons, receive and send signals that can be excitatory (increasing the likelihood that a neuron will fire) or inhibitory (decreasing the likelihood of firing), and will fire if the overall input they receive moves their electrical potential to a certain threshold point (see pages 73 to 75). Similarly, nodes in neural network models have connections with many other nodes, are programmed to receive and transmit excitatory or inhibitory signals, and become activated when the input they receive reaches a certain threshold strength. Just as learning experiences modify the brain's neural circuitry, in computer simulations neural networks "gain experience" by processing different bits of information, such as sounds or visual patterns. As they do, connections

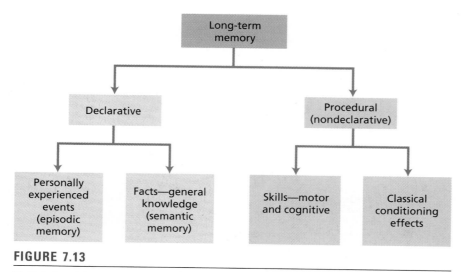

FIGURE 7.13

Multiple long-term memory systems. Some theorists propose that we have separate but interacting declarative and procedural memory systems. Episodic and semantic memories are declarative; their contents can be verbalized. Procedural memory is nondeclarative; its contents cannot readily be verbalized.

▶ **Focus 9**
Contrast and illustrate declarative versus procedural memory and explicit versus implicit memory.

among various nodes become stronger or weaker (reflected by changes in the mathematical weight assigned to each connection) and the network learns to recognize and distinguish between different types of stimuli (e.g., images of faces, spoken words, and so on).

In trying to model how memory operates, if concepts such as "red" and "fire engine" are not stored in their own individual nodes, then where are they stored? In **neural network (connectionist) models,** *each memory is represented by a unique pattern of interconnected and simultaneously activated nodes.* When node 4 is activated simultaneously (i.e., in parallel) with nodes 95 and 423, the concept "red" comes to mind. But when node 4 is simultaneously activated with nodes 78 and 901, the concept of "fire engine" enters our thoughts.

As we look across the entire neural network, various nodes *distributed* throughout the network fire in parallel at each instant and simultaneously spread their activation to other nodes. In this manner, certain nodes prime other nodes, and concepts and information are retrieved. For this reason, *neural network (connectionist) models are often called* **parallel distributed processing (PDP) models** (Rumelhart et al., 1986). Increasingly, scientists in many fields are using the neural network approach to model learning, memory, and other cognitive processes such as perception and decision making (Vogel, 2005).

TYPES OF LONG-TERM MEMORY

Research with amnesia patients, brain-imaging studies, and animal experiments indicate that the brain houses several long-term memory systems (Park & Gutchess, 2005). Think back, for example, to H. M.'s amnesia. Once new facts or new personal experiences leave his immediate train of thought, he is unable to consciously remember them. Yet with practice, H. M. can retain the skills needed to perform new tasks even though he cannot recall having seen the tasks before (Milner, 1965).

Declarative and Procedural Memory

Declarative memory *involves factual knowledge* and includes two subcategories (Figure 7.13). **Episodic memory** *is our store of knowledge concerning personal experiences: when, where, and what happened in the episodes of our lives.* Your recollections of childhood friends, a favorite movie, and what you ate this morning represent episodic memories. **Semantic memory** *represents general factual knowledge about the world and language, including memory for words and concepts.* You know that Mount Everest is the world's tallest peak and that $e=mc^2$. Episodic and semantic memories are called *declarative* because to demonstrate our knowledge, we typically have to declare it: We tell other people what we know.

H. M.'s brain damage impaired both components of his declarative memory. He could not remember new personal experiences, nor could he remember new general facts. For example, H. M. retained good memory for words that he had learned growing up (Kensinger et al., 2001). Yet no matter how many times he was told their definition, he could not remember the meaning of new words (e.g., *Xerox, biodegradable*) that entered the English language in the years after his operation. In contrast, some brain-injured children cannot remember their daily personal experiences but can remember new factual knowledge, enabling them to learn language and attend mainstream schools (Vargha-Khadem et al., 1997).

Procedural (nondeclarative) memory *is reflected in skills and actions* (Gupta & Cohen, 2002). One component of procedural memory consists of skills that are expressed by doing things in particular situations, such as typing or riding a bicycle. H. M. formed a new procedural memory when he learned how to perform the mirror-tracing task.

Classically conditioned responses also reflect procedural memory. After a tone was repeatedly paired with a puff of air blown toward H. M.'s eye, he began to blink involuntarily to the tone alone (Woodruff-Pak, 1993). Although H. M. could not consciously remember undergoing this procedure (i.e., he did not form a declarative memory), his brain stored a memory for the tone–air puff association, and thus he blinked when subsequently exposed to the tone alone (i.e., he formed a procedural memory).

Explicit and Implicit Memory

Many researchers distinguish between *explicit* and *implicit memory*. **Explicit memory** *involves conscious or intentional memory retrieval, as when you consciously recognize or recall something. Recognition* requires us to decide whether a stimulus is familiar, as when an eyewitness is asked to pick out a suspect from a police lineup or when students take multiple-choice tests. In recognition tasks, the target stimuli (possible suspects or answers) are provided to you. *Recall* involves spontaneous memory retrieval, in the sense that you must retrieve the target stimuli or information on your own. This occurs when you are briefly shown a list of words and then asked to recall them. With *cued recall*, hints are given to stimulate memory. If you cannot recall the word *hat* from the list, we might say, "It rhymes with *bat*." As a student, you are no doubt familiar with test items that involve recall or cued recall, such as essay, short-answer, and fill-in-the-blank questions.

Implicit memory *occurs when memory influences our behavior without conscious awareness* (May et al., 2005). H. M. was able to form a procedural memory for performing the mirror-tracing task, although he had no conscious awareness of having learned it. His memory for the task (in this case, procedural memory) was implicit. In Chapter 5 we encountered another amnesia patient, whose hand Edouard Claparède (1911) intentionally pricked with a pin during a handshake. Shortly thereafter the patient could not consciously recall this incident, but despite her amnesia, she showed implicit memory of their encounter by withdrawing her hand when Claparède offered to shake it again.

In less dramatic ways, each of us demonstrates memory without conscious awareness. Riding a bicycle, driving, or performing any well-learned skill are common examples. Bicycling to class, you may be consciously thinking about an upcoming exam while your implicit, procedural memory enables you to keep pedaling and maintain your balance.

Consider another example of implicit memory. Suppose that as part of an experiment you read a list of words (one word per second) that includes *kitchen, moon,* and *defend*. Days, weeks, or even a year later, you participate in another, seem-ingly unrelated study. The experimenter rapidly shows you many word stems, some of which might be *KIT—*, *MO—*, and *DE—*, and asks you to complete each stem to form a word. You are not aware that this is a memory test, but compared with people not given the original list of words, you will be more likely to complete the stems with words on the original list (e.g., *MOon*, rather than *MOther* or *MOney*). This represents one of many types of *priming tasks:* The word stems have activated, or primed, your stored mental representations of the original complete words. This suggests that information from the original list is still in your memory and is implicitly influencing your behavior even though you may have no explicit, conscious recall of the original words (Schacter, 1992).

IN REVIEW

- Associative network models view long-term memory as a network of associated nodes, with each node representing a concept or unit of information.

- Neural network models propose that each piece of information in memory is represented not by a single node but by multiple nodes distributed throughout the brain. Each memory is represented by a unique pattern of simultaneously activated nodes.

- Declarative long-term memories involve factual knowledge and include episodic memories (knowledge concerning personal experiences) and semantic memories (facts about the world and language). In contrast, procedural memory is reflected in skills and actions.

- Explicit memory involves conscious or intentional memory retrieval, whereas implicit memory influences our behavior without conscious awareness.

RETRIEVAL: ACCESSING INFORMATION

Storing information is useless without the ability to retrieve it. A **retrieval cue** *is a stimulus, whether internal or external, that activates information stored in long-term memory.* If I ask you, "Have you seen Sonia today?" the word *Sonia* is intended to serve as a retrieval cue. Likewise, a yearbook picture can act as a retrieval cue that triggers memories of a

▶ **Focus 10**
How do retrieval cues assist memory? What is the benefit of having multiple, self-generated cues and distinctive cues?

classmate. Priming is another example of how a retrieval cue (*MO—*) can trigger associated elements (*MOon*) in memory, presumably via a process of spreading activation (Chwilla & Kolk, 2002).

THE VALUE OF MULTIPLE CUES

Experiments by Timo Mäntylä (1986) vividly show the value of having multiple retrieval cues. In one, Swedish college students were presented with a list of 504 words. Some students were asked to think of and write down one association for each word, while others produced three associations per word. To illustrate, what three words come to your mind when I say *banana*? Perhaps you might think of *peel, fruit,* and *ice cream*.

The students had no idea that their memory would be tested, and after finishing the association task they were given an unexpected recall test for 252 of the original words. For some words, students were first shown the one or three associations they had just generated. As a control, for other words they were first shown one or three associations another participant had generated. Then they tried to recall the original word.

The results were remarkable. When the associations (i.e., retrieval cues) were self-generated, students shown one cue recalled 61 percent of the words and those shown three cues recalled 91 percent. In contrast, when students were shown cues that someone else had generated, recall with one cue dropped to 11 percent and with three cues to 55 percent. Further, when given another surprise recall test 1 week later on the remaining 252 words, students still remembered 65 percent of the words when they were first provided with three self-generated retrieval cues.

Why does having multiple, self-generated retrieval cues maximize recall? On the encoding side, generating your own associations involves deeper processing than does being presented with associations generated by someone else. Similarly, generating three associations involves deeper processing than generating only one. On the retrieval side, these self-generated associations become cues that have personal meaning. And with multiple cues, if one fails, another may activate the memory. The implication for studying academic material is clear. Think about the material you are studying, and draw one or (preferably) more links to ideas, knowledge, or experiences that have meaning for you.

THE VALUE OF DISTINCTIVENESS

To demonstrate a simple point, here is a brief self-test. A list of words appears below. Say each word

▶ **Focus 11**
Are emotionally arousing events, including those that produce flashbulb memories, remembered differently from other events? How are confidence and memory accuracy related?

to yourself (one per second); then when you see the word *WRITE*, look away and write down as many words as you can recall, in any order. Here's the list:

> sparrow, eagle, nest, owl, feather, goose, crow, artichoke, rooster, fly, robin, parrot, chirp, hawk, pigeon, WRITE.

If you are like most of our own students, you probably recalled *artichoke* even though it appeared in the middle of the list. The other words all relate to birds, but *artichoke* is a food: It's distinctive. In general, distinctive stimuli are better remembered than nondistinctive ones (Ghetti et al., 2002).

In school, when all the material starts looking the same, you can make it more distinctive by associating it with other information that is personally meaningful to you. According to Mäntylä (1986), this is one reason why students who generated their own three-word associations remembered almost all of the original 504 words. The associations formed a distinctive set of cues.

Distinctive events stand a greater chance of etching long-term memories that seem vivid and clear. In one study, college students listed their three clearest memories (Rubin & Kozin, 1984). Distinctive events such as weddings, romantic encounters, births and deaths, vacations, and accidents were among the most frequently recalled. In another study, college students watched a videotape of a guest lecturer who engaged in some distinctive, atypical behaviors (e.g., ate potato chips, burped) and some typical ones (e.g., sat down, took off jacket). On a memory test a week later, students correctly remembered about 80 percent of all the lecturer's behaviors, but they were more likely to report having a clear image of the distinctive ones (Neuschatz et al., 2002).

AROUSAL, EMOTION, AND MEMORY

Many experiences in our lives, such as romantic encounters, deaths, graduations, accidents, and local or world events may be better remembered not only because they were distinctive, but also because they stirred up our emotions and aroused us (Figure 7.14). In experiments, people shown arousing and neutral stimuli (e.g., pictures of happy, fearful, or neutral faces; violent or neutral film scenes) typically remember the arousing stimuli best, even when tested several weeks later (Matlin & Stang, 1978; Putman et al., 2004).

Why do emotionally arousing stimuli wind their way more deeply into memory? By physiologically monitoring people during these tasks, researchers have found that arousing stimuli

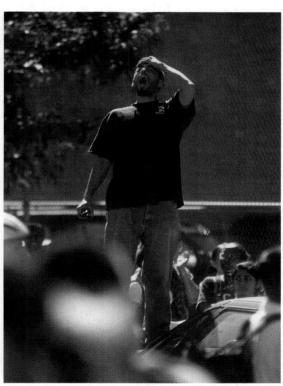

FIGURE 7.14

A memory of an emotionally arousing, distinctive event can seem so vivid and clear that we feel we can picture it as if it were a snapshot of a moment in time. Researchers call this a *flashbulb memory.*

trigger the release of stress hormones. This causes neurotransmitters to increase activation of the amygdala, a brain structure that helps encode the emotional aspects of experiences into longer-term memories (McGaugh & Roozendaal, 2002). Injecting rats with drugs that stimulate or inhibit stress-hormone activity will, respectively, boost or impair the rats' ability to remember responses that they are learning or have recently learned.

Outside the laboratory, researchers have found that emotional arousal enhances **autobiographical memories,** *recollections of personally experienced events that make up the stories of our lives* (Schaefer & Philippot, 2005). When people are asked to record their unique daily experiences in a diary and rate the emotional pleasantness and intensity of each event (e.g., say, on a 7-point scale ranging from "extremely unpleasant" to "extremely pleasant"), it typically is the more intense events that they recall most vividly when tested days, months, or years later. Over time, however, the emotionality of most pleasant and unpleasant memories may fade a bit, as Richard Walker and his colleagues (1997) found when they asked college students to (1) remember diary events that were experienced during the prior month or year and (2) rate how pleasant or unpleasant each event "feels to you now."

Interestingly, even though the students originally rated their pleasant and unpleasant events as equally arousing when the events happened, the intensity of memories for the pleasant events faded a little less rapidly over time. This slower emotional fading of positive memories, combined with cross-cultural findings that most people express positive life satisfaction, led Walker and his colleagues (2003) to proclaim that "life is pleasant—and memory helps to keep it that way!" (p. 203). Of course, as they emphasize, life surely is not pleasant for everyone, and some people don't exhibit these memory effects. They found, for example, that among mildly depressed students, the intensity of pleasant and unpleasant memories faded at the same rate (Walker et al., in press). Moreover, some people's memories of traumatic experiences may remain emotionally intense for years.

Overall, then, distinctive and emotionally arousing events are recalled most easily or vividly over time. But just because a memory seems vivid doesn't guarantee its accuracy. In the experiment where a guest lecturer ate chips, burped, and performed other odd behaviors, some students vividly remembered events (e.g., the lecturer zipped up his pants) that actually never occurred. Do similar errors occur when we retrieve memories of even more distinctive, dramatic real-world events—events that we seemingly remember like it was just yesterday? Let's take a look in the following "Beneath the Surface" segment.

Beneath the Surface   Do We Really Remember It Like It Was Yesterday?

Can you picture the tragic moment on September 11, 2001, when you first heard or saw that jetliners had crashed into the World Trade Center and the Pentagon? Perhaps you can picture the moment when you learned that the space shuttle Columbia had disintegrated upon reentering Earth's atmosphere, or that a massive tsunami had struck Southeast Asia. Your authors, like others of our generation, can vividly recall the moment over 40 years ago when we heard that President John F. Kennedy had been assassinated.

Flashbulb memories *are recollections that seem so vivid, so clear, that we can picture them as if they were snapshots of moments in time.* They are most likely to occur for distinctive events that evoke strong emotional reactions and that are repeatedly recalled in conversations with other people (Brown & Kulik, 1977).

FLASHBULB MEMORIES: FOGGING UP THE PICTURE?

Because flashbulb memories seem vivid and are easily recalled, we often feel confident of their accuracy. But are they accurate? In 1986 the space shuttle Challenger exploded shortly after takeoff, killing all on board. It was a horrific event, watched live on TV by a huge audience that was expecting the shuttle to successfully carry America's first civilian and other crew members into space. The American public was shocked. The next day, Ulric Neisser and Nicole Harsch (1993) asked college students to describe how they learned of the disaster, where they were, who they were with, and so on. Reinterviewed 3 years later, about half of the students remembered some details correctly but recalled other details inaccurately. One fourth of the students completely misremembered all the major details and were astonished at how inaccurate their memories were after reading their original descriptions.

Throughout much of 1995, the televised and racially charged murder trial of O. J. Simpson—a famous African American athlete and celebrity who was accused of murdering his ex-wife—dominated the news. To a captivated public, the jury's not-guilty verdict seemed to be an unforgettable moment. Was it? Three days later researchers asked college undergraduates how, when, with whom, and where they had learned of the verdict (Schmolck et al., 2000). Students reported whether they agreed with the verdict and how emotional they felt about it. When some students' memory was retested 15 months later, only 10 percent made major mistakes in recalling the event. Over time, however, the flashbulb seemed to fade. Among other students retested 32 months after the verdict, 43 percent misremembered major details. Here's how one student's memory changed:

[3 days after the verdict] I was in the Commuter Lounge at Revelle [College] and saw it on TV . . . more and more people came into the room. We kept having to turn up the volume, but it was kind of cool.

[32 months after the verdict] I first heard it while I was watching TV. At home in my living room. My sister and father were with me . . . eating and watching. (p. 41)

Memory accuracy was not related to whether students had originally agreed or disagreed with the verdict, but those who reported a stronger emotional reaction in 1995 displayed better memory 32 months later.

CONFIDENCE AND MEMORY ACCURACY

If people are highly confident in their memory, is it likely to be accurate? Three years after the O. J. Simpson verdict, almost all the students who had accurate memories displayed high confidence. But one of the most striking findings was that among students with grossly inaccurate recall, 61 percent also were highly confident of their memories.

After a car crash killed Princess Diana in 1997, a study in England found that 44 percent of participants said that they had seen a videotape on the TV news showing the crash take place. No such tape was ever shown, yet they were as confident in their memory as people who said they never saw such a tape (Ost et al., 2002). Similarly, a few weeks after the 9/11 terrorist attacks, Kathy Pezdek (2003) asked students attending college in New York City (Manhattan), Southern California, and Hawaii: "On September 11, did you see the videotape on television of the first plane striking the first tower?" Overall, 73 percent of the students said yes. Yet this was impossible, because a videotape of the first plane crashing was not broadcast until after September 11. Moreover, students who incorrectly responded yes were more confident in their memory than the students who correctly said no!

Indeed, one day after 9/11, Jennifer Talarico and David Rubin (2003) asked Duke University students to report the personal details (e.g., where were you, who were you with) for two events: (1) the moment they learned about the 9/11 terrorist attacks and (2) a typical college event of their choice that they had recently experienced (e.g., a party, sports event, studying). A week, 6 weeks, and 32 weeks later, the students did not display any more accurate autobiographical memory for 9/11 than for the everyday personal event, even though they rated 9/11 as a more emotionally intense event. As Figure 7.15a shows, students' recall for both events, though still good, became less accurate (i.e., less consistent with their original reports) over time. The key difference: For the everyday event, over time students said that they were less confident in their memory and that it was less vivid, but not so for 9/11. After 32 weeks, students were as confident in their memory and said it was as vivid (e.g., "I

FIGURE 7.15

Flashbulb memories of 9/11.
(a) During the 32 weeks following the terrorist attacks of 9/11, students' recall of personal details for 9/11 (e.g., where they were, who they were with) and for an everyday event became less consistent with their initial reports made on September 12. (b) Despite this decrease in memory accuracy, students continued to report a vivid memory of 9/11, whereas the memory of the everyday event became progressively less vivid. SOURCE: Talarico and Rubin, 2003.

feel as though I am reliving the experience") as the day after the attacks happened (Figure 7.15b). Similarly, another study asked people to report personal details surrounding 9/11 within 2 days after the attacks; over the next year, respondents remained highly confident of their memories despite the fact that those memories actually became less accurate (Weaver & Krug, 2004).

Memory researchers have studied the relation between confidence and accuracy with children and adults, inside and outside the laboratory, and for many types of events. Overall, confidence and accuracy are weakly related (Busey et al., 2000). People accurately recall many events—even after years pass—and typically are very confident when they do. But people often swear by inaccurate memories. In general, distinctive and emotionally arousing events in our lives have a memory advantage. However, even for such events, a memory can feel like it happened just yesterday when, in truth, it's foggy.

THE EFFECTS OF CONTEXT, STATE, AND MOOD ON MEMORY

Our ability to retrieve a memory is influenced not only by the nature of the original stimulus (such as its distinctiveness) but also by environmental, physiological, and psychological factors. Years ago, two Swedish researchers reported the case of a young woman who was raped while out for a jog (Christianson & Nilsson, 1989). When found by a passerby, she was in shock and could not remember the assault. Over the next 3 months, the police took her back to the crime scene several times. Although she could not recall the rape, she became emotionally aroused, suggesting implicit memory of the event. While jogging one day shortly thereafter, she consciously recalled the rape.

Why did her memory return? One possibility is based on the **encoding specificity principle,** *which states that memory is enhanced when conditions present during retrieval match those that were present during encoding* (Tulving & Thomson, 1973). When stimuli associated with an event become encoded as part of the memory, they may later serve as retrieval cues.

Context-Dependent Memory: Returning to the Scene

Applying the encoding specificity principle to *external* cues leads us to **context-dependent memory:** *It typically is easier to remember something in the same environment in which it was originally encoded.* Thus visiting your high school or old neighborhood may trigger memories of teachers, classmates, and friends. As with the Swedish jogger, police detectives may take an eyewitness or crime victim back to the crime scene, hoping to stimulate the person's memory.

In a classic experiment, Duncan Godden and Alan Baddeley (1975) asked scuba divers to learn some lists of words underwater and some on dry land. When the divers were later retested in both environments, lists learned underwater were recalled better underwater and those learned on land were better recalled on land (Figure 7.16). Other studies, spanning diverse environments, have replicated this finding (Smith and Vela, 2001).

Consider the relevance of context-dependent memory to college life. In one experiment, when randomly assigned college students studied

▶ **Focus 12**
Describe and illustrate encoding specificity, context- and state-dependent memory, and mood-congruent recall.

FIGURE 7.16

Context-dependent memory.
Scuba divers who learned lists of words while under water later recalled them best while under water, whereas words they learned on land were best recalled on land. Recall was poorer when the learning and testing environments were mismatched. SOURCE: Adapted from Godden & Baddeley, 1975.

material in either a quiet or noisy room, they later displayed better memory on short-answer and multiple-choice questions when tested in a similar (quiet or noisy) environment (Grant et al., 1998). Thus if you take exams in quiet environments, try to study in a quiet environment.

State-Dependent Memory: Arousal, Drugs, and Mood

Moving from external to internal cues, the concept of **state-dependent memory** *proposes that our ability to retrieve information is greater when our internal state at the time of retrieval matches our original state during learning.* The Swedish jogger who was raped consciously remembered her assault for the first time while jogging. In her case, both context-dependent cues (similar environment) and state-dependent cues (arousal while jogging) may have stimulated her memory.

Diverse experiments support this effect. Many students at the campus gym read course materials while exercising on a bicycle, treadmill, or stair-climber machine. Christopher Miles and Elinor Hardman (1998) found that material learned while we are aroused during aerobic exercise is later recalled more effectively if we are once again aerobically aroused, rather than at rest. Conversely, material learned at rest is better recalled at rest.

Many drugs produce physiological effects that directly impair memory, but state-dependent memory also explains why events experienced in a drugged state may be difficult to recall later while in a drug-free state (Figure 7.17). Experiments examining alcohol, marijuana, amphetamines, and other drugs have often found that information recall is poorer when there is a mismatch between the person's states during

learning and testing (Carter & Cassaday, 1998). This *does not* mean, by the way, that drugs improve memory relative to not taking drugs during initial learning.

Does state-dependent memory extend to mood states? Is material learned while we are in a happy mood or a sad mood better recalled when we are in that mood again? Inconsistent findings suggest that such *mood-dependent memory* is not a reliable phenomenon. Instead, there is more consistent evidence of **mood-congruent recall:** *We tend to recall information or events that are congruent with our current mood* (Fiedler et al., 2001). When happy we are more likely to remember positive

FIGURE 7.17

State-dependent memory. In the film *City Lights*, a drunken millionaire befriends and spends the evening partying with Charlie Chaplin after Chaplin saves his life. The next day, in a sober state, the millionaire doesn't remember Chaplin and considers him an unwanted pest. After getting drunk again, he remembers Chaplin and treats him like a good buddy.

LEVELS OF ANALYSIS   Factors Related to Remembering

Biological

- Evolutionary adaptiveness of memory
- Brain regions involved in sensory, working, and long-term memory
- Changes in brain activity during encoding and retrieval
- Stress hormones and biological states (e.g., emotion- or drug-induced) that affect memory

Psychological

- Memory codes (visual, phonological, semantic, motor)
- Working memory, maintenance and elaborative rehearsal
- Schemas and expertise
- Memory as a network of associations
- Emotional arousal at time of event; mood at time of retrieval

Environmental

- Amount and rate of information
- Order of information (serial position effect)
- Stimulus characteristics (e.g., distinctiveness, hierarchical structure, pleasant/unpleasant events)
- Retrieval cues and context-dependent memory

Remembering

FIGURE 7.18

Levels of analysis: Factors related to remembering.

events, and when sad we tend to remember negative events.

Thus far we have focused on how information is remembered, and Figure 7.18 summarizes some of the factors involved. We'll have more to say about the brain's role later, but first, in the next two sections we will examine why we forget and why we sometimes remember events that never occurred.

IN REVIEW

- ■ Retrieval cues activate information stored in long-term memory. Memory retrieval is more likely to occur when we have multiple cues, self-generated cues, and distinctive cues.

- ■ We experience flashbulb memories as vivid and clear snapshots of an event and are confident of their accuracy. However, over time many flashbulb memories become inaccurate. Overall, memory accuracy and memory confidence are only weakly related.

- ■ The encoding specificity principle states that memory is enhanced when cues present during retrieval match cues that were present during encoding. Typically it is easier to remember a stimulus when we are in the same environment (context-dependent memory) or same internal state (state-dependent memory) as when the stimulus was originally encoded.

- ■ Mood states provide an exception to encoding specificity. In general, we tend to recall stimuli that are congruent with our current mood.

FORGETTING

Some very bright people are legendary for their memory failures. The eminent French writer Voltaire began a passionate letter, "My Dear Hortense," and ended it, "Farewell, my dear Adele." The splendid absentmindedness of English nobleman Canon Sawyer once led him, while welcoming a visitor at a railroad station, to board the departing train and disappear (Bryan, 1986). Indeed, how we forget is as interesting a scientific question as how we remember.

THE COURSE OF FORGETTING

German psychologist Hermann Ebbinghaus (1885/1964) pioneered the study of forgetting by testing only one person—himself (Figure 7.19).

▶ **Focus 13**
Describe Ebbinghaus's research, its value, and its limitations.

FIGURE 7.19

Hermann Ebbinghaus was a pioneering memory researcher.

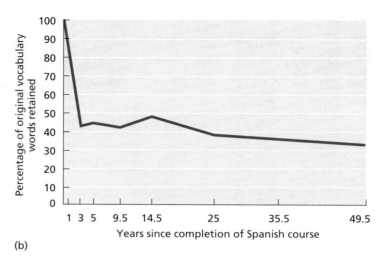

(a) Retention interval

(b) Years since completion of Spanish course

FIGURE 7.20

Forgetting over time. (a) Hermann Ebbinghaus's forgetting curve shows a rapid loss of memory for nonsense syllables at first and then a more gradual decline. The rapid decline is probably due to the meaningless nature of the nonsense syllables. (b) The forgetting of vocabulary from high school Spanish language classes follows a similar curve, except that the time frame is in years, not days. SOURCES: Based on (a) Ebbinghaus, 1885/1964, and (b) Bahrick, 1984.

▶ **Focus 14**
Explain why we forget based on concepts of encoding failure, decay, and interference.

He created over 2,000 *nonsense syllables*, meaningless letter combinations (e.g., *biv, zaj, xew*), to study memory with minimal influence from prior learning, as would happen if he used actual words. In one study, Ebbinghaus performed over 14,000 practice repetitions trying to memorize 420 lists of nonsense syllables.

Ebbinghaus typically measured memory by using a method called *relearning* and then computing a savings percentage. For example, if it initially took him 20 trials to learn a list but only half as many trials to relearn it a week later, then the savings percentage was 50 percent. In one series of studies, he retested his memory at various time intervals after mastering several lists of nonsense syllables. As Figure 7.20a shows, forgetting occurred rapidly at first and slowed noticeably thereafter.

Do we indeed forget most of what we learn so quickly? Ebbinghaus studied so many lists of non-

sense syllables that his ability to distinguish among them undoubtedly suffered. If you learned just a few lists, the shape of your forgetting curve might resemble Ebbinghaus's, but the amount you forgot would likely be less. Moreover, when material is meaningful (unlike nonsense syllables), we are likely to retain more of it over time (Bahrick, 2005).

Consider the forgetting curve in Figure 7.20b, based on a study examining the vocabulary retention of people who had studied Spanish in school anywhere from 3 to 50 years earlier and then rarely used it (Bahrick, 1984). Once again, forgetting occurred more rapidly at first, but notice that the Spanish-retention study employed a time frame of years rather than hours and days as in Ebbinghaus's studies.

WHY DO WE FORGET?

If some memories last a lifetime, why do we forget so much? Explanations for normal memory loss emphasize difficulties in encoding, storage, and retrieval.

Encoding Failure

Many memory failures result not from forgetting information that we once knew, but from failing to encode the information into long-term memory in the first place. Perhaps you had the radio or TV on this morning while eating breakfast, but chances are you can recall only those songs or stories that you found especially interesting. Much of what we sense simply is not processed deeply enough to commit to memory.

We noted earlier that few people can accurately draw a coin from memory. Even when the task is made easier by requiring only recognition, as in Figure 7.21, most people cannot identify the

FIGURE 7.21

Which coin portrays a real penny? If you want to try your skill at picking it out, do it before reading further. Most people have difficulty choosing the correct one because they have never bothered to encode all of the features of a real penny. The correct penny is (d). SOURCE: Adapted from Nickerson & Adams, 1979.

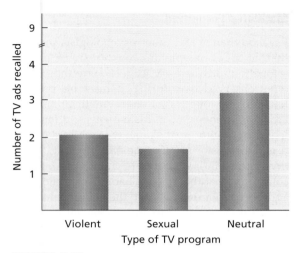

FIGURE 7.22

Violence, sex, and memory for TV commercials. In one study, TV viewers who watched programs with violent or sexual content recalled fewer commercials than viewers who watched a neutral program. SOURCE: Based on Bushman & Bonacci, 2002.

correct coin (Nickerson & Adams, 1979). Can you? The details of a coin's appearance are not meaningful to most of us, and we may not notice them, no matter how often we see coins.

We may notice information but fail to encode it deeply because we turn our attention to something else. Brad Bushman and Angelica Bonacci (2002) randomly assigned 328 adults to watch either a sexually explicit, violent, or neutral TV program. Nine commercial advertisements (e.g., for snacks, cereal, laundry detergent) appeared during each program. Immediately afterward and again a day later, the researchers tested viewers' memory for the ads. At both times, viewers who watched the sexually explicit and violent programs remembered the fewest number of ads (Figure 7.22). Several factors might account for this, and as the researchers proposed, one of them is encoding failure: All the viewers clearly saw the ads, but those watching the sexually explicit and violent programs likely were the most preoccupied with thoughts about the content of the shows.

Decay of the Memory Trace

Information in sensory memory and short-term memory decays quickly as time passes. Do long-term memories also decay? One early explanation for forgetting was **decay theory,** *which proposed that with time and disuse the long-term physical memory trace in the nervous system fades away.* Decay theory soon fell into disfavor because scientists could not locate physical memory traces nor

measure physical decay. In recent decades, however, scientists have begun to unravel how neural circuits change when a long-term memory is formed. This has sparked new interest in examining how these changes might decay over time (Villarreal et al., 2002).

Unfortunately, decay theory's prediction—the longer the time interval of disuse between learning and recall, the less should be recalled—is problematic. Some professional actors display perfect memory for words they had last spoken on stage 2 years earlier—this despite having moved on to new acting roles and scripts (Noice & Noice, 2002b). Moreover, when research participants learn a list of words or a set of visual patterns and are retested at two different times, they sometimes recall material during the second testing that they could not remember during the first. This phenomenon, called *reminiscence,* seems inconsistent with the concept that a memory trace decays over time (Greene, 1992). In sum, scientists still debate the validity of decay theory.

Interference

According to *interference theory,* we forget information because other items in long-term memory impair our ability to retrieve it (Postman & Underwood, 1973). Figure 7.23 illustrates two major types of interference. **Proactive interference** *occurs when material learned in the past interferes with recall of newer material.* Suppose that Kim changes residences, gets a new phone number, and memorizes it. That night, when a friend asks Kim for her new number, she can recall only three digits and instead keeps remembering her old phone number. Memory of her old phone

FIGURE 7.23

Interference and forgetting. Interference is a major cause of forgetting. With proactive interference, older memories interfere with the retrieval of newer ones. With retroactive interference, newer memories interfere with the retrieval of older ones.

▶ Focus 15
Why is motivated forgetting a controversial concept? Describe some types and causes of amnesia and the nature of prospective memory.

number is interfering with her ability to retrieve the new one.

Retroactive interference *occurs when newly acquired information interferes with the ability to recall information learned at an earlier time.* Suppose Kim has now had her new phone number for two months and recalls it perfectly. If we ask her, "What was your old number?" Kim may have trouble recalling it, perhaps mixing up the digits with her new number. In general, the more similar two sets of information are, the more likely it is that interference will occur. Kim (or you) would probably experience little interference in recalling highly dissimilar material, such as her new phone number and French vocabulary.

Why does interference occur? It takes time for the brain to convert short-term memories into long-term memories, and some researchers propose that when new information is entered into the system, it can disrupt (i.e., retroactively interfere with) the conversion of older information into long-term memories (Wixted, 2005). Others believe that once long-term memories are formed, retroactive and proactive interference are caused by competition among retrieval cues (Anderson & Neely, 1996). When different memories become associated with similar or identical retrieval cues, confusion can result and accessing a cue may call up the wrong memory. Retrieval failure also can occur because we have too few retrieval cues or the cues may be too weak.

Almost all of us have experienced a retrieval problem called the **tip-of-the-tongue (TOT) state,** *in which we cannot recall something but feel that we are on the verge of remembering it.* When Bennett Schwartz (2002) asked 56 college students to record a diary for 4 weeks, he found that they averaged just over one TOT experience per week. Most often, TOT states aroused emotion and were triggered by the inability to remember the name of an acquaintance, famous person, or object. Sooner or later, the answer often popped into the mind spontaneously, but in many cases students had to consult a book or another person.

? What Do You Think?

IS IT REALLY ON THE TIP OF YOUR TONGUE?
Suppose you're having a TOT experience. Should you assume that it's a retrieval problem? What else might explain your inability to come up with an answer? Think about it, then see page 272.

Motivated Forgetting

Psychodynamic and other psychologists propose that, at times, people are consciously or unconsciously motivated to forget. Sigmund Freud often observed that during therapy, his patients remembered long-forgotten traumatic or anxiety-arousing events. One of his patients suddenly remembered with great shame that while standing beside her sister's coffin she had thought, "Now my brother-in-law is free to marry me." Freud concluded that the thought had been so shocking and anxiety arousing that the woman had *repressed* it—pushed it down into her unconscious mind, there to remain until it was uncovered years later during therapy. **Repression** *is a motivational process that protects us by blocking the conscious recall of anxiety-arousing memories.*

The concept of repression is controversial. Some evidence supports it, and other evidence does not (Karon, 2002). People certainly do forget unpleasant events—even traumatic ones—yet they also forget very pleasant events. If a person cannot remember a negative experience, is this due to repression or to normal information-processing failures (Epstein & Bottoms, 2002)? Overall, it has been difficult to demonstrate experimentally that a special process akin to repression is the cause of memory loss for anxiety-arousing events (Holmes, 1990). We will return to this topic shortly.

FORGETTING TO DO THINGS: PROSPECTIVE MEMORY

Have you ever forgotten to mail a letter, turn off the oven, keep an appointment, or purchase something at the market? In contrast to *retrospective memory,* which refers to memory for past events, **prospective memory** *concerns remembering to perform an activity in the future.* That people forget to do things as often as they do is interesting, because prospective memories typically involve little content. Often we need only recall that we must perform some event-based task ("Remember, on your way out, mail the letter.") or time-based task ("Remember, take your medication at 4 P.M."). Successful prospective memory, however, draws on other cognitive abilities, such as planning and allocating attention while performing other tasks.

During adulthood, do we become increasingly absentminded about remembering to do things, as a common stereotype suggests? Numerous laboratory experiments support this view (Vogels et al., 2002). Typically, participants perform a task that requires their ongoing attention while trying to remember to signal the experimenter at certain time intervals or whenever specific events take place. Older adults generally display poorer prospective memory, especially when signaling is time-based. However, when prospective memory is tested outside the laboratory using tasks such as simulated pill-taking, healthy adults in their 60s to 80s often perform as well as or better than adults in their 20s (Rendell & Thomson, 1999). Perhaps older adults are more motivated to remember in such situations, or they rely more on habit and setting up a standard routine (Anderson & Craik, 2000).

AMNESIA

As H. M.'s case illustrates, the most dramatic instances of forgetting occur in amnesia. The term *amnesia* commonly refers to memory loss due to special conditions, such as brain injury, illness, or psychological trauma. However, as we'll see shortly, there is one type of amnesia that all of us experience.

Retrograde and Anterograde Amnesia

Amnesia takes several forms. **Retrograde amnesia** *represents memory loss for events that took place sometime in life before the onset of amnesia.* For example, H. M.'s brain operation, which took place at age 27, caused him to experience mild memory loss for events in his life that had occurred during the preceding year or two (i.e., when he was 25 to 26 years old). Football players experience retrograde amnesia when they are knocked out by a concussion, regain consciousness, and cannot remember the events just before being hit.

Anterograde amnesia *refers to memory loss for events that occur after the initial onset of amnesia.* H. M.'s brain operation, and particularly the removal of much of his hippocampus, produced severe anterograde amnesia and robbed him of the ability to consciously remember new experiences and facts. Similarly, the woman whose hand was pinpricked by Swiss psychologist Edouard Claparède during a handshake also suffered from anterograde amnesia; moments later she could not consciously remember the episode. Unlike H. M.'s anterograde amnesia, hers was caused by *Korsakoff's syndrome,* which can result from chronic alcoholism and may also cause severe retrograde amnesia.

Dementia and Alzheimer's Disease

Dementia *refers to impaired memory and other cognitive deficits that accompany brain degeneration and interfere with normal functioning.* There are more than a dozen types and causes of dementia, and although it can occur at any point in life, dementia is most prevalent among elderly adults.

Alzheimer's disease (AD) *is a progressive brain disorder that is the most common cause of dementia among adults over the age of 65,* accounting for about 50 to 60 percent of such cases. Overall, 2 to 4 percent of elderly adults are estimated to have AD.

The early symptoms of AD, which worsen gradually over a period of years, include forgetfulness, poor judgment, confusion, and disorientation. Often, memory for recent events and new information is especially impaired. By itself, forgetfulness is not necessarily a sign that a person is developing AD. However, memory is the first psychological function affected, as AD initially attacks subcortical temporal lobe regions—areas near the hippocampus and then the hippocampus itself—that help convert short-term memories into long-term ones.

Alzheimer's disease spreads across the temporal lobes and to the frontal lobes and other cortical regions (Figure 7.24). As German physician Alois Alzheimer first noticed a century ago, patients with this disease have an abnormal amount of plaques and tangles in their brain. *Plaques* are clumps of protein fragments that build up on the outside of neurons, whereas *tangles* are fibers that get twisted and wound together within neurons (Cattabeni et al., 2004). Neurons become damaged and die, brain tissue shrinks, and communication between neurons is impaired as AD disrupts

The Progression of Alzheimer's Disease

Preclinical AD   Mild to moderate AD   Severe AD

Blue indicates areas affected at various stages of AD.

FIGURE 7.24

The progression of Alzheimer's disease. SOURCE: National Institutes of Health, 2002.

several neurotransmitter systems, especially the acetylcholine system. Acetylcholine plays a key role in synaptic transmission in several brain areas involved in memory, and drugs that help maintain acetylcholine functioning have had some temporary success in improving AD patients' cognitive functioning (Ritchie et al., 2004).

Working memory and long-term memory worsen as AD progresses. If you read a list of just 3 words to healthy 80-year-old adults and then test their recall after a brief time delay, they will typically remember 2 or all 3 words. Patients with AD, however, typically recall either no words or 1 word (Chandler et al., 2004). Anterograde and retrograde amnesia become more severe, and procedural, semantic, episodic, and prospective memory can all be affected. Patients may lose the ability to learn new tasks or remember new information or experiences, forget how to perform familiar tasks, and have trouble recognizing even close family members.

What causes AD and its characteristic plaques and tangles? Scientists have identified several genes that contribute to early-onset AD, an inherited form of the disease that develops before the age of 65 (and as early as age 30) but accounts for only 5 to 10 percent of Alzheimer's cases (Cattabeni et al., 2004). The precise causes of the more typical, late-onset AD remain elusive, but researchers have identified one genetic risk factor. This gene helps direct the production of proteins that carry cholesterol in the blood plasma, and high cholesterol and other risk factors for cardiovascular disease may likewise increase the risk of developing AD. Indeed, a recent study found that even healthy elderly adults who carried this particular gene, as compared to peers who did not, performed more poorly on a prospective memory task (Driscoll et al., 2005).

If you know someone who has AD, then you're aware that it involves much more than memory loss. Patients experience language problems, disorganized thinking, and mood and personality changes. Ultimately, they may lose the ability to speak, walk, and control bladder and bowel functions. We'll have more to say about the psychological, physical, and social aspects of dementia and aging in Chapter 11.

Infantile (Childhood) Amnesia

There is one type of amnesia that almost all of us encounter: an inability to remember personal experiences from the first few years of our lives. Even though infants and preschoolers can form long-term memories of events in their lives (Peterson & Whalen, 2001), as adults we typically are unable to recall these events consciously. *This memory loss for early experiences is called* **infantile amnesia** (also known as *childhood amnesia*). Our memories of childhood typically do not include events that occurred before the age of 3 or 4, although some adults can partially recall major events (e.g., the birth of a sibling, hospitalization, or a death in the family) that happened before the age of 2 (Eacott & Crawley, 1998).

What causes infantile amnesia? One hypothesis is that brain regions that encode long-term episodic memories are still immature in the first years after birth. Another is that we do not encode our earliest experiences deeply and fail to form rich retrieval cues for them. Additionally, because infants lack a clear self-concept, they do not have a personal frame of reference around which to organize rich memories (Harley & Reese, 1999).

IN REVIEW

- Forgetting tends to occur most rapidly soon after initial learning, but the time frame and degree of forgetting can vary widely depending on many factors.

- We often cannot recall information because we never encoded it into long-term memory in the first place. Decay theory proposes that physical memory traces in long-term memory deteriorate with disuse over time.

- Proactive interference occurs when material learned in the past impairs recall of newer material. Retroactive interference occurs when newly acquired material impairs the ability to recall information learned at an earlier time.

- Psychodynamic theorists propose that we may forget anxiety-arousing material through repression, an unconscious process of motivated forgetting.

- Whereas retrospective memory refers to memory for past events, prospective memory refers to our ability to remember to perform some activity in the future.

- Retrograde amnesia is memory loss for events that occurred before the onset of amnesia. Anterograde amnesia refers to memory loss for events that occur after the initial onset of amnesia. Alzheimer's disease produces both types of amnesia and is the leading cause of dementia among elderly adults. Infantile amnesia is our inability to remember experiences from the first few years of our lives.

MEMORY AS A CONSTRUCTIVE PROCESS

Retrieving information from long-term memory is not like viewing a digital replay. Our memories are often incomplete or sketchy. We may literally *construct* (or, as some say, *reconstruct*) a memory by piecing together bits of stored information in a way that seems real and accurate. Yet, as our discussion of flashbulb memories illustrated, we may be highly confident of memories that in fact are inaccurate.

Memory construction can be amusing at times. Many of us have a tendency to recall the world through slightly rosy glasses, which helps us feel good about ourselves. For example, when college students in one study recalled their high school grades, the worse the grade was, the less often students remembered it accurately. Students correctly recalled almost all of their As, but only a third of their Ds (Figure 7.25). Most important, errors were positively biased; students usually misremembered their Bs as having been As, their Cs as Bs, and their Ds as Cs (Bahrick et al., 1996). As we will see, however, memory construction also can have serious personal and societal consequences.

MEMORY DISTORTION AND SCHEMAS

Decades ago, Sir Frederick Bartlett (1932) asked residents of Cambridge, England, to read stories and then retell them days or months later. One story, a Pacific Northwest Indian tale called "The War of the Ghosts," describes two young men who go down to a river to hunt seals. While there, warriors in canoes come up the river, and one of the young men agrees to join them for a raid on a town. During the raid, the man discovers that his companions are ghosts, and later he dies a mysterious death.

Bartlett's participants were 20th-century residents of England, not 18th-century Native

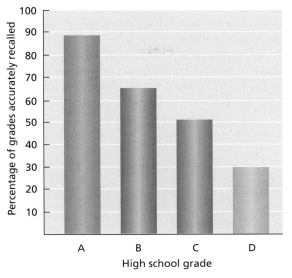

FIGURE 7.25

Rosy recall of high school grades. The lower the grade, the less likely students were to accurately recall it. When students incorrectly recalled a grade, they almost always overestimated how well they did. SOURCE: Adapted from Bahrick et al., 1996.

Americans. When they retold the story, they partly reconstructed it in a way that made sense to them. A day after reading the story, one participant shortened it by almost half, described the hero as fishing rather than as hunting seals, and substituted the word *boat* for *canoe*. Bartlett found that the longer the time interval between the reading and retelling of the story, the more the story changed to fit English culture.

Bartlett, who coined the term *schema*, believed that people have generalized ideas (schemas) about how events happen, which they use to organize information and construct their memories. Recall, for example, the clothes-washing description. Schemas, however, often distort our memories by leading us to encode or retrieve information in ways that make sense and fit in with our preexisting assumptions about the world.

Quite literally, memory construction extends to how we visualize the world (Intraub, 2002). As Figure 7.26 illustrates, when college students in

▶ **Focus 16**
Discuss examples of memory construction, and explain how schemas influence this process.

(a)

(b)

FIGURE 7.26

Boundary extension: What you see . . . what you remember. Helene Intraub and her colleagues (1996) have found that when people (a) briefly look at close-up pictures, such as this one of a teddy bear, and then (b) draw the pictures from memory, they unknowingly convert the image into a wide-angle scene in which the size of the main object shrinks. This effect is less likely to occur if the original picture is already a wide-angle scene. SOURCE: Images courtesy of Helene Intraub.

▶ **Focus 17**

How did the "Research Close-Up" studies investigate false memories? What might have caused the false memories?

one study looked at photographs that had a main object within a scene and then drew what they saw from memory, they consistently displayed *boundary extension;* they remembered the scene as more expansive (in this case, wider-angled) than it really was (Intraub et al., 1996). In real life, objects usually occur against an expansive back-ground, creating a schema for how we expect scenes to look. Thus when we remember close-up images, our schemas lead us to recall a broader scene than the one we saw. The following "Research Close-Up" offers some insight into how schemas can lead us to remember things that never happened.

 Research Close-Up   **Memory Illusions: Remembering Things That Never Occurred**

STUDY 1: COLLEGE STUDENTS REMEMBERING WORD LISTS

SOURCE: HENRY L. ROEDIGER III and KATHLEEN MCDERMOTT (1995). Creating false memories: Remembering words not presented in lists. *Journal of Experimental Psychology: Learning, Memory, and Cognition, 21,* 803–814.

Introduction

In this famous experiment, Henry Roediger III and Kathleen McDermott examined how often false memories occurred while people performed a simple task: remembering lists of words. They also investigated whether people experience false memories as being vivid and clear.

Method

Building on previous research (Deese, 1959), the researchers created lists of 15 words. Each list contained words that, to varying degrees, were associated with a central organizing word. To illustrate, look at the following list:

> sour, candy, sugar, bitter, good, taste, tooth, nice, honey, soda, chocolate, heart, cake, tart, pie

The word *sweet* doesn't occur in the list, yet it is associated with these items. The central word (*sweet*) is called a *critical lure.*

Thirty-six college students each listened to 16 lists. For some lists, students' recall was measured as soon as each list ended. Then, after hearing all 16 lists, students performed a recognition task. They were given a sheet of paper with 96 words, half of which actually had been on the lists. The other words were critical lures and filler items. Students identified whether each word had been on the lists they heard. If they selected a word, they also reported whether they had a vivid memory of having heard it or, instead, were sure that they had heard it but lacked a vivid memory.

Results

Students correctly recalled 62 percent of the real words but falsely recalled almost as many (55 percent) of the critical lures. On the recognition task, they correctly identified 62 percent of the actual words but falsely identified 72 percent of the critical lures. And in just over half of the cases where students falsely recognized a critical lure, they reported having a vivid memory of it.

Discussion

Although critical lures were never presented, students falsely recalled them half the time and falsely recognized them almost three quarters of the time. Moreover, students often reported having a clear memory of the nonexistent critical lure. Many researchers have replicated this finding.

What causes these false memories? Roediger and McDermott (1995, 2000) argue that hearing the words activates an associative network—a schema—for the critical lure. For some people, the words *sour, candy, sugar,* etc. may consciously trigger a thought of "sweet." For others, spreading activation from the words unconsciously primes the concept of "sweet." Either way, the critical lure is activated, so that during retrieval people may misinterpret the source of activation and falsely remember the lure as being on the list (Figure 7.27a).

In your view, are these findings relevant to memory in the real world? Critics argue that the research context—college students learning word lists—may have little relevance to situations involving memory for important events. Yet Roediger and McDermott argue that this context makes the findings more impressive. Students knew it was a memory test and that inaccurate memories would be spotted. Further, memory was tested soon after hearing each list. If people can be confident of their false memories in this straightforward situation, then what might happen in real-world contexts where conditions for remembering events are more complex and not as optimal?

STUDY 2: PEOPLE REPORTING ABDUCTION BY ALIENS

SOURCE: SUSAN A. CLANCY, RICHARD J. MCNALLY, DANIEL L. SCHACTER, MARK F. LENZEWEGER, and ROGER K. PITMAN (2002). Memory distortion in people reporting abduction by aliens. *Journal of Abnormal Psychology, 111,* 455–461.

Introduction

Is there a relation between false memories on the word-list task in Study 1 and false memories for significant events in

(a)

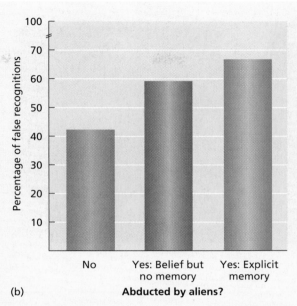

(b)

Abducted by aliens?

FIGURE 7.27

Memory illusion. (a) After listening to a list of related words, people often remember hearing a critical lure (*sweet*) that was never presented. (b) This graph shows the degree of false recognition of critical lures among three groups of participants. SOURCE: Based on Clancy et al., 2002.

real life? To examine this question, Susan Clancy and coworkers recruited three groups of participants through newspaper advertisements: a control group of 13 people who said they had never been abducted by aliens, 9 people who were sure they had been abducted by aliens but who had no explicit memory of it, and 11 people who said that, for a time, they had forgotten that they had been abducted but then had a clear memory of the abduction gradually return to them. Why study people claiming to be alien abductees? Because, say the researchers, these individuals are reporting a major traumatic event that we can assume is unlikely to have occurred.

Method and Results

Participants listened to word lists of varying lengths, based on the lists used in Study 1. The three groups did not differ in how accurately they recalled and recognized words that actually had been on the lists. However, the two abductee groups falsely recalled and falsely recognized more critical lures than the control group, and those with explicit memories of abduction made the most recognition errors (Figure 7.27b).

Discussion

The findings indicate a relation between how prone people are to display false memories both inside and outside the laboratory. The researchers speculated that both types of false memories may share a common basis: a confusion over the source of the memory. In the lab, spreading activation caused by the word lists is mistakenly attributed to a false source: the presence of a critical lure that actually was not on the list. A similar type of confusion could occur, for example, when "an individual might watch a movie about alien abductions as a child and then—years later—come to believe that the events in the movie actually occurred because he or she has forgotten the actual source of the memory" (p. 460).

MISINFORMATION EFFECTS AND EYEWITNESS TESTIMONY

If memories are constructed, then information that occurs *after* an event may shape that construction process. This **misinformation effect,** *the distortion of a memory by misleading postevent information,* has frequently been investigated in relation to mistaken eyewitness testimony. In one celebrated case, Father Bernard Pagano, a Roman Catholic priest, was positively identified by seven eyewitnesses as the perpetrator of a series of armed robberies in the Wilmington, Delaware, area. He was saved from almost certain conviction when the true robber, dubbed the "gentleman bandit" because of his politeness and concern for his victims, confessed to the crimes. You can see in Figure 7.28 that there was little physical resemblance between the two men.

Two key factors may have distorted the witnesses' memory. First, the polite manner of the robber is consistent with the schema many people have of priests. Second, before presenting pictures of suspects to the eyewitnesses, the police let it be known that the suspect might be a priest. Father Pagano was the only suspect wearing a clerical collar (Tversky & Tuchin, 1989).

Even one or two words can produce a misinformation effect while questioning an eyewitness. Imagine that after witnessing a two-car crash, a police officer takes your statement and asks you, "About how fast were the cars going when they *contacted* each other?" In one experiment,

▶ **Focus 18**
Describe the misinformation effect, why it occurs, and how it affects memory accuracy in children and adults.

FIGURE 7.28

Seven eyewitnesses to armed robberies committed by Ronald Clouser (*left*) mistakenly identified Father Bernard Pagano (*right*) as the robber, probably as a result of information from police that influenced their memory reconstructions.

 Watch the video, "When Eyes Deceive," in Chapter 7 of your CD to see a research experiment illustrating the unreliability of eyewitness testimony.

college students viewed films of car accidents and then judged how fast the cars were going. As Figure 7.29 shows, the judged speed increased by up to 33 percent when the word *contacted* was changed to *hit, bumped into, collided with,* or *smashed into* (Loftus & Palmer, 1974).

Source Confusion

Misinformation effects also occur because of **source confusion** (also called *source monitoring error*), *our tendency to recall something or recognize it as familiar but to forget where we encountered it.* Suppose an eyewitness to a crime looks through a series of mug shots and reports that none of the individuals is the perpetrator. Several days later, the eyewitness is brought back to view a live lineup and is asked to identify the person who committed the crime. In reality, none of the people in the lineup did, but one suspect was pictured in a mug shot that the eyewitness had seen earlier. "That's the person," says the eyewitness. Source confusion occurs because the eyewitness recognizes the individual's face but fails to re-

member that this recognition stems from the mug shot. Instead, the witness mistakenly assumes that he or she saw the familiar-looking suspect committing the crime.

In an experimental analog to this situation, 29 percent of participants who witnessed a staged event and later viewed mug shots misidentified *innocent* suspects as having been involved in the event because of source confusion (Brown et al., 1977). Source confusion also occurs when people witness an event (e.g., a video of an unarmed home burglar) and then are exposed to misleading, suggestive statements about it (e.g., that the burglar had a gun). They may forget that the source of the misinformation was a question or statement made by someone else and then come to believe it was part of the event they had witnessed (Mitchell & Zaragoza, 2001).

Researchers have begun to use brain-imaging techniques to study the neural activity that occurs when false memories are created by misinformation (Okado & Stark, 2005), but the debate over whether misinformation permanently alters a witness's original memory is far from resolved. Still, researchers overwhelmingly agree that misinformation can distort eyewitness reports. Results like these have raised concerns about the reliability of eyewitness testimony not only from adults but also from children in cases of alleged physical and sexual abuse.

THE CHILD AS EYEWITNESS

In cases of alleged child sexual abuse, there is often no conclusive corroborating medical evidence and the child is usually the only witness (Bruck et al., 1998). If the charges are true, failing to convict the abuser and returning the child to an abusive environment is unthinkable. Conversely, if the charges are false, the consequences of convicting an innocent person are equally distressing.

Accuracy and Suggestibility

A single instance of suggestive questioning can distort some children's memory, but suggestive questioning most often leads to false memories when it is repeated. Young children are typically

FIGURE 7.29

A misinformation effect. College students' memory of how fast two cars were moving just before an accident varied significantly depending on how the question was phrased. Source: Adapted from Loftus & Palmer, 1974.

How fast were the two cars going when they _____ each other?	
Words	**Perceived speed**
smashed into	41 mph
collided with	39 mph
bumped into	38 mph
hit	34 mph
contacted	31 mph

more susceptible to misleading suggestions than older children (Ceci et al., 2000).

In one experiment by Michelle Leichtman and Stephen Ceci (1995), 3- to 6-year-old children were told about a man named Sam Stone. Over several weeks, some children were repeatedly told stories that portrayed Sam as clumsy. Later Sam visited their classroom, was introduced, and behaved innocuously. The next day, the children were shown a ripped book and soiled teddy bear, things for which Sam was not responsible. Over the next 10 weeks they were interviewed several times, and some were asked suggestive questions about Sam (e.g., "When Sam Stone tore the book, did he do it on purpose, or was he being silly?"). Two weeks later a new interviewer asked all the children to describe Sam's visit to the classroom.

Children who had heard suggestive information about Sam—whether before, after, or especially before *and* after Sam's appearance—made more false reports about Sam's behavior than a control group that had never heard suggestive information. One child stated that after soaking the teddy bear in the bath, Sam smeared it with a crayon. These findings are troubling, because during many sexual-abuse investigations, the child initially denies being abused, but then after repeated suggestive questioning during therapy or police interviewing, the child acknowledges the abuse (Bruck et al., 1998). Was the child understandably reluctant to open up at first, or did suggestive questions produce a false allegation?

Recall of Traumatic Events   How well do children remember traumatic events? Elaine Burgwyn-Bailes and coworkers (2001) interviewed 3- to 7-year-olds a few days, 6 weeks, and 1 year after the children underwent emergency plastic surgery for facial lacerations. At each interview, children accurately remembered most of the details of their operations, but they also mistakenly agreed with about 15 percent of leading questions ("Did the doctor's helper use any needles?") and suggestive questions ("The lady took off your watch, didn't she?") about events that never occurred. Compared to older children, younger children remembered fewer true details and agreed more often to leading and suggestive questions.

True Versus False Reports: Can Professionals Tell Them Apart?

Can professionals reliably distinguish between children's accurate and false reports? The answer appears to be no, at least when false reports are caused by repeated, suggestive questioning. Mental health workers, social workers, prosecutors, and judges shown videotapes of children's reports in the Sam Stone experiment often rated false reports as highly credible. Perhaps many children who make false reports are credible because they are not intentionally lying; rather, they believe their memories are accurate. After suggestive questioning, children are as confident of their false memories as they are of their accurate ones (Roebers, 2002).

What should society do? Like adults, young children accurately remember a lot, but they also misremember and are susceptible to repeated suggestive questioning. Thanks to psychological research, law enforcement officials, mental health workers, and legal professionals are now paying more attention to how children's admissions of abuse are elicited, and training programs are helping practitioners minimize suggestive interviewing techniques (Sternberg et al., 2002). The goal is not to discredit children's allegations of abuse. To the contrary, the hope is that by minimizing the risk of false allegations, nonsuggestive interviewing will elicit allegations judged as even more compelling, thereby helping to ensure that justice is done.

THE RECOVERED MEMORY CONTROVERSY

In 1997 a woman from Illinois settled a lawsuit against two psychiatrists and their hospital for $10.6 million. She alleged that her psychiatrists used hypnosis, drugs, and other treatments that led her to develop false memories of having been a high priestess in a sexually abusive satanic cult (*APA Monitor*, 1997). Yet only years earlier, there had been a wave of cases in which adults—usually in the course of psychotherapy—began to remember long-forgotten childhood sexual abuse and sued their parents, other family members, and former teachers for the alleged trauma (Figure 7.30).

The scientific controversy over the validity of recovered memories of childhood trauma involves two issues. First, when a recovered memory of sexual abuse occurs, is it accurate? Second, if the abuse really happened, what caused the memory to be forgotten—repression or another psychological process? Let's briefly examine the second issue. Many scientists and therapists question Freud's concept of repression. Repression implies a special psychological mechanism that actively pushes traumatic memories into the unconscious mind, and we have already noted that researchers have had difficulty demonstrating it experimentally.

▶ **Focus 19**
Discuss the recovered memory controversy, the two key issues involved, and relevant evidence.

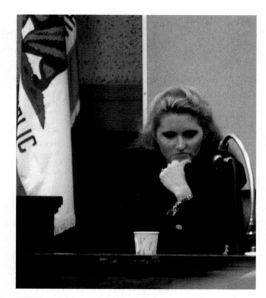

FIGURE 7.30

In a famous 1990 case, George Franklin was convicted of the 1969 murder of 8-year-old Susan Nason. Franklin's 28-year-old daughter Eileen (*shown here*), who had been Susan's childhood friend, provided the key evidence. During therapy Eileen recovered memories of her father sexually assaulting and killing Susan. A judge overturned the conviction after learning that Eileen's memories had been recovered under hypnosis. The details of the case that Eileen recalled had been published in the newspapers, creating the possibility of source confusion in her memory. Eileen also had other recovered memories that were proven to be untrue, such as those of her father killing two other girls.

▶ **Focus 20**
Illustrate how culture influences memory construction.

Recovered memories of childhood sexual abuse or other traumas cannot be taken as automatic evidence of repression. Memory loss may have occurred because of ordinary sources of forgetting or because the victim intentionally avoided thinking about the abuse or reinterpreted the trauma to make it less upsetting (Epstein & Bottoms, 2002). But beyond these factors, other researchers and many therapists believe that repression is a valid concept (Brewin, 2004). This controversy will not be resolved soon.

What about the more basic question? Can someone forget childhood sexual abuse, by whatever psychological mechanism, and then recover that memory as an adult? Indeed, some survivors of natural disasters, children who witness the violent death of a parent, victims of rape, combat veterans, and victims of sexual and physical abuse have shown limited or no memory of their traumas (Epstein & Bottoms, 2002). Some victims of documented child sexual abuse do not recall their trauma when they are adults, and accurate memories of the abuse can indeed return after many years of posttrauma forgetting (Kluft, 1999). Yet memory loss after psychological trauma is usually far shorter, with memory returning over

weeks, months, or perhaps a few years. In many cases of trauma, the victim's primary problem is not memory loss but rather an *inability* to forget, which may involve involuntary nightmares or flashbacks (Berntsen, 2001).

Experiments reveal that when exposed to suggestive questioning, American college students developed false memories of personal childhood events that never happened (e.g., being hospitalized overnight), and residents of Moscow developed false memories for fictitious details (e.g., the presence of injured animals) of a 1999 terrorist bombing in their city (Nourkova et al., 2004). Such studies may not tap the intense trauma of directly experiencing sexual abuse, and for ethical reasons experimenters do not test whether false memories of sexual abuse can be implanted. Nevertheless, say many researchers and clinicians, add these findings to everything science has taught us about forgetting and constructive memory, and the conclusion is that we should not take the accuracy of recovered memories at face value (Pickrell et al., 2003). They are especially concerned that in recovered-memory therapy, therapists repeatedly suggest the possibility of abuse to people who are already emotionally vulnerable.

The message from science is not that all claims of recovered traumatic memories should be dismissed. Rather, it is to urge caution in unconditionally accepting those memories, particularly when suggestive techniques are used to recover the memories (Brandon et al., 1998). Some day it may be scientifically possible to separate true memories from false ones; researchers have begun to examine whether some types of true versus false memories are associated with different patterns of brain activity. But at present, these findings cannot be used to determine reliably whether any individual memory is true or false (Pickrell et al., 2003).

CULTURE AND MEMORY CONSTRUCTION

Culture and memory have a reciprocal relation. On the one hand, cultural survival depends on transmitting knowledge and customs from one generation to the next. Without our capacity to remember events and information, culture simply could not exist (nor could we, as a species).

At the same time, culture influences memory. Our cultural upbringing shapes the schemas that we acquire and use to perceive ourselves and the world. For example, as we discussed in Chapter 1, most people living in northern Europe and North America learn to view the world through a relatively *individualistic* lens in which self-identity is

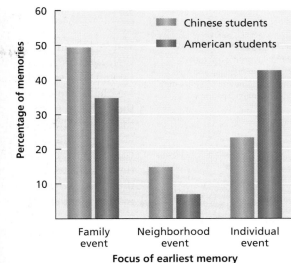

FIGURE 7.31

Culture and our earliest memories. What is your earliest memory? In one study, Chinese students recalled events that, overall, were more family and neighborhood oriented than events recalled by American students. How else might our cultural upbringing and world-view influence memory? SOURCE: Based on Wang, 2001.

based primarily on one's own attributes and achievements. People living in many Asian, African, and South American cultures tend to see the world through a more *collectivistic* framework in which personal identity is defined largely by ties to the extended family and other social groups. If cultural socialization influences our schemas and our schemas influence how we encode and reconstruct events, then people from different cultures may recall events in somewhat distinct ways.

Let's consider an example: our earliest memories. In one study, Qi Wang (2001) asked over 200 college students from Harvard University and Beijing University to describe their earliest memories (Figure 7.31). He predicted and found that the Americans were more likely than their Chinese counterparts to recall events that focused on individual experiences and self-determination (e.g., "I was sorting baseball cards when I dropped them. As I reached down to get them, I knocked over a jug of iced tea."). In contrast, Chinese students were more likely than American students to recall memories that involved family or neighborhood activities (e.g., "Dad taught me ancient poems. It was always when he was washing vegetables that he would explain a poem to me.").

Wang also found that American college students dated their earliest personal memory back to the time when they were, on average, $3\frac{1}{2}$ years old. Students in China, however, reported memories that, on average, dated to the time they were almost 4 years old. Although the reason isn't clear, it may relate to American students' greater tendency to report earliest memories of single, distinctive events that involved greater emotionality, whereas Chinese students were more likely than Americans to report more routine events that

involved collective activity. Other researchers also have found cross-cultural differences in age of earliest memories. When Shelley MacDonald and coworkers (2000) studied New Zealand European, New Zealand Asian, New Zealand Maori, and Chinese adults, they found that Maori adults—whose traditional culture strongly values the past—recalled the earliest personal memories.

IN REVIEW

- Our schemas may cause us to misremember events in ways that fit with our preexisting concepts about the world; they also may lead us to recall events that never occurred.

- Misinformation effects occur when our memory is distorted by misleading postevent information, and they often occur because of source confusion—our tendency to recall something or recognize it as familiar but to forget where we encountered it.

- Like adults, children experience misinformation effects. Vulnerability is greatest among younger children and when suggestive questions are asked repeatedly. Experts cannot reliably tell when children are reporting accurate memories versus sincerely believed false memories.

- Psychologists debate whether recovered memories of child abuse are accurate and whether they are forgotten through repression or other psychological processes. Concern about the possibility of false memory has led many experts to urge caution in unconditionally accepting the validity of recovered memories.

MEMORY AND THE BRAIN

▶ **Focus 21**
Describe brain structures involved in memory and how changes in neural circuitry may underlie memory formation.

Where in your brain are memories located? How were they formed? The quest for answers has taken some remarkable twists. Psychologist Karl Lashley spent decades searching for the *engram*—the physical trace that presumably was stored in the brain when a memory was formed. Lashley (1950) trained animals to perform tasks, such as running mazes, and later removed or damaged (lesioned) specific regions of their cortexes to see if they would forget how to perform the task. No matter what small area was lesioned, memories remained intact. Lashley never found the engram and concluded that a memory is stored throughout the brain.

Perhaps most striking was James McConnell's (1962) discovery of "memory transfer." He classically conditioned flatworms to a light that was paired with electric shock, eventually causing the worms to contract to the light alone. Next he chopped them up and fed the RNA (ribonucleic acid) from their cells to untrained worms. Amazingly, the untrained worms showed some conditioning to the light, suggesting that RNA might be a memory molecule that stores experiences. Some scientists replicated these findings, but others were unable to, and McConnell eventually gave up on the idea (Rilling, 1996). Yet despite the inevitable dead ends, scientists have learned a great deal about memory processes in the brain.

WHERE ARE MEMORIES FORMED AND STORED?

To answer this question, scientists examine how damage to different brain regions affects the memory of human patients and laboratory animals; they also peer into the healthy human brain as research participants perform various memory tasks. These lines of research reveal that memory involves many interacting brain regions. Figure 7.32 shows a few of the major regions.

Sensory and Working Memory

Sensory memory depends on our visual, auditory, and other sensory systems to detect stimulus information (e.g., the sounds of "Hi, my name is Carlos"), transform it into neural codes, and send it to the brain, where sensory areas of the cerebral cortex initially process it. As working memory becomes involved in different types of tasks—remembering a person's name and face, recalling a list of numbers, or learning and rehearsing a concept in your textbook—a network of cortical areas located across different lobes of the brain becomes more active (Zhang et al., 2004). For example, using visuospatial working memory to form a mental image of an object will activate some of the same areas of the visual cortex and other brain regions that become more active when looking at the actual object (Ganis et al., 2004).

The frontal lobes—especially the prefrontal cortex—play key roles in working memory. The frontal lobes generally become more active during tasks that place greater demands on working memory. In one brain-imaging experiment, students had to pay attention to the meaning of words (i.e., deep, semantic encoding) or to whether the words were in capital or lowercase letters (i.e., shallow, perceptual encoding). Deeper encoding produced better memory for the words and, as Figure 7.33 shows, also produced greater activity in specific areas of the left prefrontal cortex (Gabrieli et al., 1996). Other imaging studies have found that spatial working-memory tasks produce somewhat greater activation in the right prefrontal cortex than verbal tasks do (Walter et al., 2003).

The frontal lobes seem to be particularly important in supporting central-executive functions, such as allocating attention to the other components of working memory. This does not mean, however, that the central executive resides exclusively within the frontal lobes. Frontal-lobe damage often—but not always—impairs central-executive functions of working memory. Moreover, patients with intact frontal lobes but damage in other brain areas may

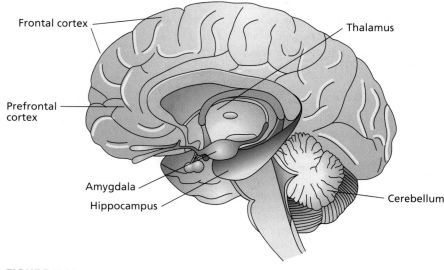

Frontal cortex

Prefrontal cortex

Amygdala

Hippocampus

Thalamus

Cerebellum

FIGURE 7.32

Some brain regions involved in memory. Many areas of the brain, such as the regions shown here, play key roles in memory.

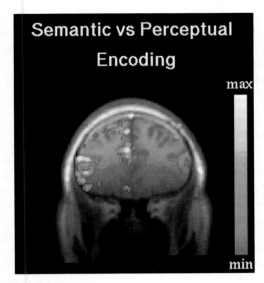

FIGURE 7.33

Depth of processing and the prefrontal lobes. Four participants in one experiment performed shallow perceptual (i.e., structural) encoding and deep (semantic) encoding tasks while undergoing functional magnetic resonance imaging (fMRI). The results, shown here for one participant, revealed that semantic encoding was accompanied by greater neural activity in specific regions of the left prefrontal cortex. SOURCE: Photo courtesy of John Gabrieli.

exhibit central-executive impairments (Adrés, 2003). Thus even the "master control" executive functions of working memory depend on a network of neural activity that connects regions across the brain.

Long-Term Memory

Where are long-term memories formed and stored? Once again, multiple brain areas are involved, but the hippocampus and its adjacent areas appear to play important roles in encoding certain types of long-term memories (Squire et al., 2004).

Declarative Memory Like H. M., many patients with extensive hippocampal damage retain the use of their short-term memory but cannot form new, explicit long-term declarative memories—memories for new personal experiences and facts. For example, one patient could recall the names of presidents elected before his brain injury occurred but not the names of presidents elected after his injury (Squire, 1987). The hippocampus does not seem to be the site where long-term declarative memories are permanently stored, which explains why H. M. retained his long-term memories acquired earlier in life. Rather, it helps to gradually convert short-term memories into permanent ones.

According to one view, the diverse components of an experience—where something happened, what the scene or people looked like, sounds we heard, the meaning of events or information, and so on—are processed initially in different regions of the cortex and then gradually bound together in the hippocampus (Squire & Zola-Morgan, 1991). *This hypothetical and gradual binding process is called* **memory consolidation.** Once a memory for a personal experience is consolidated, its various components appear to be stored across wide areas of the cortex, although we retrieve and reintegrate these components as a unified memory. Semantic memories (factual information) also appear to be stored across wide-ranging areas of the brain. As John Gabrieli (1998) notes, "knowledge in any domain [e.g., for pictures or words] . . . is distributed over a specific, but extensive, neural network that often extends over several lobes" (p. 94). Several brain regions, including portions of the prefrontal cortex and hippocampus, appear to be involved in consciously retrieving declarative memories (LePage et al., 1998; Tulving, 2002).

Although we have focused on the frontal lobes and hippocampus, memory formation also depends on other brain areas. For example, damage to the thalamus—the brain's major sensory relay station—can impair both the encoding of new memories and the retrieval of old ones (Van Der Werf et al., 2003). In one famous case, a young U.S. Air Force technician named N. A. was injured in a freak accident (Squire, 1987). While his roommate was practicing thrusts with a miniature fencing foil, N. A. suddenly turned around in his seat and was stabbed through the right nostril, piercing his brain and damaging a portion of his thalamus. The damage permanently limited his ability to form new declarative memories. In many cases, thalamic damage also can cause permanent retrograde amnesia.

The amygdala encodes emotionally arousing aspects of stimuli and plays an important role in helping us form long-term memories for events that stir our emotions (McGaugh, 2004). As we discussed earlier, in laboratory experiments, most people remember emotionally arousing stimuli (e.g., film clips, slides) better than neutral ones. Damage to the amygdala eliminates much of this "memory advantage" from arousing stimuli (LaBar & Phelps, 1998).

Procedural Memory Along with other parts of the brain, the cerebellum plays an important role in forming procedural memories. This helps explain why H. M., whose cerebellum was not damaged by the operation, showed improved performance at various hand-eye coordination tasks (e.g., mirror tracing) even though he was unable to consciously remember having performed the tasks.

Richard Thompson (1985) and coworkers have examined another type of procedural memory. Studying rabbits, they repeatedly paired a tone (CS) with a puff of air to the eyes (UCS), and soon the tone alone caused the rabbits to blink. As the rabbits learned this conditioned response, electrical recordings revealed increased activity in the cerebellum. Later Thompson found that removing a tiny portion of the cerebellum completely abolished the memory for the *conditioned* eyeblink but did not affect the rabbits' general (unconditioned) eyeblink response. Similarly, eyeblink conditioning fails to work with human patients who have a damaged cerebellum (Green & Woodruff-Pak, 2000).

HOW ARE MEMORIES FORMED?

How does the nervous system form a memory? The answer appears to lie in chemical and physical changes that take place in the brain's neural circuitry.

Synaptic Change and Memory

Eric Kandel (2001) and his coworkers have studied a marine snail, *Aplysia californica,* for over 25 years—work for which Kandel received a Nobel Prize in 2000. *Aplysia* is no mental giant, but it can learn, form memories, and has only about 20,000 neurons (compared with our 100 billion) that are larger and easier to study than ours. For example, *Aplysia* retracts its gill slightly in self-defense when a breathing organ atop the gill is gently squirted with water. But if a squirt is paired with electric shock to its tail, *Aplysia* covers up its gill with a protective flap of skin. After repeated pairings, *Aplysia* acquires a classically conditioned response and will cover its gill with the protective flap when the water is squirted alone. In other words, *Aplysia* forms a simple procedural memory.

Kandel and his coworkers have traced the formation of this procedural memory to a series of biochemical events that occur between and within various sensory neurons and motor neurons. How long these events last seems to be one key in determining whether short-term memories become long-term ones. If a single shock is paired with the squirt of water, certain chemical reactions shut off after a brief period and no permanent memory is formed. But with repeated pairings, these chemical reactions persist and a long-term memory forms. Days later, a squirt of water will still trigger a conditioned response.

During the conditioning procedure, various sensory neurons become densely packed with neurotransmitter release points, and postsynaptic motor neurons (which cause the protective flap to cover the gill) develop more receptor sites. These structural changes result in a greater ease of synaptic transmission that may be the basis for memory consolidation (Abel & Kandel, 1998).

Long-Term Potentiation

A different line of research, involving rats and other species with more complex nervous systems, supports the hypothesis that synaptic changes may be the basis for memory consolidation. Here, researchers try to mimic (albeit very crudely) a process of long-term memory formation by stimulating specific neural pathways with rapid bursts of electricity (say, 100 impulses per second for several seconds). They find that once this rapid stimulation ends, the neural pathway becomes stronger—synaptic connections are activated more easily—for days or even weeks (Martinez et al., 1998). *This enduring increase in synaptic strength is called* **long-term potentiation (LTP).** LTP has been studied most extensively in regions of the hippocampus where neurons send and receive using glutamate, the most abundant neurotransmitter in the brain.

For LTP to occur, complex biochemical events must take place inside and between these neurons. Administering drugs that inhibit these events will block LTP. Moreover, mice can be genetically bred to be deficient in certain proteins required for LTP. These mice not only have impaired long-term potentiation but also display memory deficits on a variety of learning tasks (Schimanski & Nguyen, 2005).

How, then, does LTP occur? At least in some cases, it appears that when neural pathways are sufficiently stimulated, the postsynaptic neurons alter their structure so that they become more responsive to glutamate. For example, postsynaptic neurons may change the shape of some receptor sites, or they may increase the number of receptor sites by developing additional tiny branches (spines) on their dendrites. This means that in the future, presynaptic neurons will not need to release as much glutamate in order to stimulate postsynaptic neurons to fire. In sum, the formation of a long-term memory seems to involve long-lasting changes in synaptic efficiency that result from new or enhanced connections between presynaptic and postsynaptic neurons (Kandel, 2001).

In closing, we hope that this chapter has piqued your interest in understanding why we remember, forget, and sometimes misremember. Figure 7.34 summarizes some factors involved in forgetting and memory distortion. We also hope

LEVELS OF ANALYSIS   Factors Related to Forgetting and Memory Distortion

Biological
- Evolutionary adaptiveness of forgetting
- Inadequate brain chemical activity
- Memory not consolidated in hippocampus
- Brain damage that produces amnesia

Psychological
- Failure to encode information (e.g., inadequate rehearsal)
- Weak retrieval cues and interference
- Mental schemas distort information
- Motivated forgetting of anxiety-arousing information

Environmental
- Stimulus overload
- Information lacks distinctiveness, meaning, or organization
- Mismatch between learning and recall environments
- Misinformation effects: postevent stimuli distort information

Forgetting and Memory Distortion

FIGURE 7.34

Levels of analysis: Factors related to forgetting and memory distortion.

that the chapter has applied value for you. Following the "In Review" summary, our "Applying Psychological Science" feature describes some ways to enhance your own memory and academic learning.

IN REVIEW

- Memory involves numerous interacting brain regions. Sensory memory depends on input from our sensory systems and sensory areas of the cortex that initially process this information.

- Working memory involves a network of brain regions. The frontal lobes play a key role in performing the executive functions of working memory.

- The hippocampus helps consolidate long-term declarative memories. The cerebral cortex stores declarative memories across distributed sites.

- The amygdala encodes emotionally arousing aspects of events, and the cerebellum helps form procedural memories. Damage to the thalamus can produce severe amnesia.

- Research with sea snails and studies of long-term potentiation in other species indicate that as memories form, complex chemical and structural changes that enhance synaptic efficiency occur in neurons.

► Focus 22
Identify practical principles for enhancing memory.

Applying Psychological Science   Improving Memory and Academic Learning

There are no magical or effortless ways to enhance memory, but psychological research offers many principles that you can put to your advantage. Memory-enhancement strategies fall into three broad categories:

- *external aids,* such as shopping lists, notes, and appointment calendars
- *general memory strategies,* such as organizing and rehearsing information
- *formal mnemonic techniques,* such as acronyms, the method of loci, and other systems that take practice to be used effectively

Memory researchers strongly recommend using external aids and general strategies to enhance memory (Park et al., 1990). Of course, during closed-book college exams, external aids may land you in the dean's office! The following principles can enhance memory.

USE ELABORATIVE REHEARSAL TO PROCESS INFORMATION DEEPLY

Elaborative rehearsal—focusing on the meaning of information—enhances deep processing and memory (Benjamin & *Continued*

Bjork, 2000). Put simply, *if you are trying to commit information to memory, make sure that you understand what it means.* You may think we're daffy for stating such an obvious point, but many students try to learn material by rote memorization rather than by making an effort to understand it. Students who find material confusing sometimes try to bypass their confusion with rote memorization—an approach that often fails—whereas they should be seeking assistance to have the material explained. The learning objectives and practice tests that appear in the Online Learning Center (OLC) can help you process the course material more deeply by helping you focus on and think about key points.

LINK NEW INFORMATION TO EXAMPLES AND ITEMS ALREADY IN MEMORY

Once you understand the material, process it more deeply by associating it with information you already know. This creates memory "hooks" onto which you can hang new information. Because you already have many memorable life experiences, *make new information personally meaningful by relating it to your life.*

Pay attention to examples, even if they are unrelated to your own experiences. In one study, participants read a 32-paragraph essay about a fictitious African nation. Each paragraph contained a topic sentence stating a main theme, along with zero, one, two, or three examples illustrating that theme. The greater the number of examples, the better the participants recalled the themes (Palmere et al., 1983).

ORGANIZE INFORMATION

Organizing information keeps you actively thinking about the material and makes it more meaningful. Before reading a chapter, look at its outline or headings to determine how the material is logically developed. When studying, take notes from a chapter and use outlining to organize the information. This hierarchical structure forces you to arrange main ideas above subordinate ones, and it becomes an additional retrieval cue that facilitates recall (Bower et al., 1969).

USE IMAGERY

As dual coding theory predicts, images provide a splendid additional "cognitive hook" on which to hang and retrieve information (Paivio et al., 2000). Instead of writing down customers' orders, some restaurant waiters and waitresses form images, such as visualizing a man who has ordered a margarita as turning light green. As one waitress remarked, "After a while, customers start looking like drinks" (Bennett, 1983, p. 165). Be creative. For example, to help you remember that flashbulb memories often are less accurate than people think, imagine a camera flashbulb with a big red X through it.

OVERLEARN THE MATERIAL

Overlearning *refers to continued rehearsal past the point of initial learning, and it significantly improves performance on memory tasks* (Driskell et al., 1992). Moreover, much of this memory boost persists for a long time after overlearning ends. In short, just as elite athletes keep practicing their already-honed skills and professional actors continue to rehearse scripts they already know, keep studying material after you have first learned it (Noice & Noice, 2002a).

DISTRIBUTE LEARNING OVER TIME AND TEST YOURSELF

You have finished the readings and organized your notes for an upcoming test. Now it's time to study and review. Are you better off with *massed practice*, a marathon session of highly concentrated learning, or with *distributed practice*, several shorter sessions spread out over a few days? Research indicates that you will retain more information with distributed practice and that periodically testing yourself on the material before an exam can further enhance learning (Cull, 2000). Distributed practice can reduce fatigue and anxiety, both of which impair learning. Testing yourself ahead of time (e.g., using practice items, if available, or questions such as those in the margins of this textbook) helps you to further rehearse the material and to identify content that you don't understand.

MINIMIZE INTERFERENCE

Distributed practice is effective because rest periods between study sessions reduce interference from competing material. However, when you need to study for several exams on the same or consecutive days, there really are few rest periods. There is no simple solution to this problem. Suppose you have a psychology exam on Thursday and a sociology exam on Friday. Try to arrange several sessions of distributed practice for each exam over the preceding week. On Wednesday, limit your studying to psychology if possible. Once your psychology exam is over, return your attention to studying sociology. This way, the final study period for each course will occur as close as possible to test time and minimize interference from other cognitive activities.

Studying before you go to sleep may enhance retention by temporarily minimizing interference, but if you are carrying a typical college course load, you will likely have to contend with interference much of the time. This is why you are advised to study the material beyond the point where you feel you have learned it.

KEY TERMS AND CONCEPTS

Each term has been boldfaced and defined in the chapter on the page indicated in parentheses.

Alzheimer's disease (AD; p. 257)
anterograde amnesia (p. 257)
associative network (p. 245)
autobiographical memory (p. 249)
chunking (p. 236)
context-dependent memory (p. 251)
decay theory (p. 255)
declarative memory (p. 246)
dementia (p. 257)
dual coding theory (p. 242)
elaborative rehearsal (p. 241)
encoding (p. 234)
encoding specificity principle (p. 251)
episodic memory (p. 246)
explicit memory (p. 247)
flashbulb memories (p. 250)
implicit memory (p. 247)
infantile amnesia (p. 258)
levels of processing (p. 240)

long-term memory (p. 238)
long-term potentiation (LTP; p. 268)
maintenance rehearsal (p. 240)
memory (p. 233)
memory codes (p. 236)
memory consolidation (p. 267)
method of loci (p. 242)
misinformation effect (p. 261)
mnemonic device (p. 242)
mnemonist (memorist; p. 244)
mood-congruent recall (p. 252)
neural network (connectionist)
  model (p. 246)
overlearning (p. 270)
parallel distributed processing (PDP)
  model (p. 246)
priming (p. 245)
proactive interference (p. 255)

procedural (nondeclarative) memory
  (p. 246)
prospective memory (p. 256)
repression (p. 256)
retrieval (p. 234)
retrieval cue (p. 247)
retroactive interference (p. 256)
retrograde amnesia (p. 257)
schema (p. 242)
semantic memory (p. 246)
sensory memory (p. 235)
serial position effect (p. 238)
short-term memory (p. 235)
source confusion (p. 262)
state-dependent memory (p. 252)
storage (p. 234)
tip-of-the-tongue (TOT) state (p. 256)
working memory (p. 237)

? What Do You Think?

WOULD PERFECT MEMORY BE A GIFT OR A CURSE? (PAGE 244)

No doubt, perfect memory would have advantages, but were you able to think of any liabilities? Russian newspaper reporter S. V. Shereshevski—arguably the most famous mnemonist in history—had a remarkable capacity to remember numbers, poems in foreign languages, complex mathematical formulas, nonsense syllables, and sounds. Psychologist Aleksandr Luria (1968), who studied "S." for decades, describes how S. was tyrannized by his seeming inability to forget meaningless information. Almost any stimulus might unleash a flood of trivial memories that dominated his consciousness and made it difficult for him to concentrate or think abstractly.

S.'s experience may have been atypical, but perfect memory could indeed clutter up our thinking with trivial information. Moreover, perfect memory would deprive us of one of life's blessings: the ability to forget unpleasant experiences from our past. As illustrated in this chapter, imperfect memory allows us to view our past through slightly rosy glasses (Bahrick et al., 1996).

Would a perfect memory help you perform better on exams? On test questions calling only for definitions, formulas, or facts, probably so. But on questions asking you to apply concepts, synthesize ideas, analyze issues, and so forth, perfect memory might be of little benefit unless you also understood the material. In his graduate school classes,

Rajan had a tendency to try to commit the reading assignments to memory and reproduce them on tests. The strategy . . . is counterproductive in graduate courses where students are asked to apply their knowledge and understanding to new situations. . . . When taking tests, Rajan would write furiously . . . in hopes that the correct answer was somewhere in his response. . . . As he progressed in our graduate program, he tended to rely less on the strategy of memorizing everything and more on trying to understand and organize the information (Thompson et al.,1993, p. 15).

Rajan's extraordinary memory for numbers did not extend to reading or visual tasks, but even if yours did, it still might tempt you to focus too heavily on sheer memorization and cause you to neglect paying attention to the meaning of the material. In sum, although imperfect memory can be frustrating and have serious consequences (as when eyewitnesses identify the wrong suspect), we should also appreciate how our memory system is balanced between the adaptiveness of remembering and the benefits of forgetting.

(By the way, in case you're curious, the current record for recalling pi is 42,195 digits. In 1999, Sim Pohann of Malaysia recalled 67,053 digits, but, alas, he made 15 errors. To put this feat in perspective, imagine the next 12 pages of this textbook filled up with nothing but numbers!)

Continued

IS IT REALLY ON THE TIP OF YOUR TONGUE? (PAGE 256)

Please try to answer the following questions:

- What is the name of the only kind of living reptile that flies?

- What is the name of the only type of cat native to Australia?

- What is the name of the planet Mercury's moon?

Did you feel like the answer to any of these questions was on the tip of your tongue? If you didn't, that's okay. We just want to illustrate some of the questions that Bennett Schwartz (1998) asked college students in a clever TOT study.

Schwartz asked students 100 questions, but 20 of them—like the ones above—were unanswerable (e.g., Mercury has no moon). If there was no correct answer, then students could not have a true retrieval problem, because there was no stored information to retrieve. Yet nearly one fifth of the time students felt that the answer was on the tip of their tongue when they were contemplating these questions. Schwartz obtained similar findings in another experiment.

Schwartz calls these experiences "illusory TOT states": People feel that the answer is on the tip of their tongue when it can't possibly be. Illusory TOT states raise complex issues about the nature of memory, but for the moment, let's just focus on a simple point. Sometimes, when we feel that an answer is on the tip of our tongue, the cause may not be an inability to retrieve information stored in long-term memory, but rather it may be that the information never got stored in the first place. In other words, whether due to encoding failure (we've encountered the information but didn't process it adequately) or some other reason, we really may not know the answer, although we think we do. This may help explain why we never resolve some of our TOT states and often turn to other people or reference books to help find an answer.

If you're curious, try reading the three questions above to several friends (give them time to think about each question). Don't expect to trigger a lot of illusory TOT states, but even eliciting one or two would provide an interesting demonstration. Afterward, be sure to let them know that the questions are unanswerable (so they won't keep thinking about them!), and explain the purpose of the exercise.

CHAPTER EIGHT

Language
and Thinking

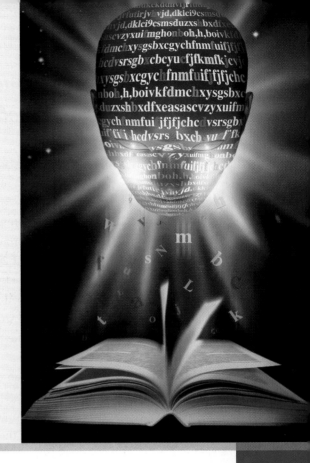

CHAPTER OUTLINE

Let language be the divining rod that finds the sources of thought.

—Karl Krauss

FIGURE 8.1

The successful landing of United Airlines Flight 118 was a tribute to the power of human reasoning, language, and problem solving.

For the crew and passengers of United Airlines Flight 118, the skies over Hawaii were about to become the scene of a terrifying test of human resourcefulness, with survival at stake. On a routine flight 20,000 feet above the Pacific Ocean, the unthinkable happened. With an explosive popping of rivets and a shriek of tearing metal, part of the surface at the front of the plane suddenly ripped away from the rest of the aircraft, exposing the flight deck and forward passenger compartments to the air. Inside, terrified passengers and flight attendants quite literally hung on for dear life as gale-force winds swirled through the cabin and the plane threatened to spin out of control.

The sudden change in the aerodynamics of the plane meant that it could not be flown normally. The captain, an experienced pilot, needed to develop a mental model of the plane in its altered form to keep it from plunging into the ocean. Thanks to his flight experience and his knowledge of the principles under which the aircraft normally responded to its controls, the captain quickly recognized what needed to be done and formulated a plan for doing it.

Yet formulating the plan wasn't enough. The captain needed his copilot's help to execute the appropriate actions. Under normal circumstances this would pose no problem: The captain would simply use spoken language to describe his thoughts, convey the plan, and tell the copilot what to do. But in a torn-open jetliner flying at several hundred miles per hour, the noise of the engines and the roar of the wind rendered speech useless, so the captain and the copilot switched to hand signals to communicate their thoughts and coordinate their activities. Through perfect teamwork, they landed the aircraft safely at an auxiliary airfield (Figure 8.1), a feat described by one aeronautical engineer as "astonishing."

Incidents like this one illustrate the power of human communication, reasoning, and problem solving—cognitive skills that underlie adaptive behavior. Yet as we shall see, the basic communication procedures and mental operations these aviators used to deal with this life-and-death challenge were really no different from many of the linguistic, reasoning, and problem-solving activities that we engage in each day.

We humans are physically puny and relatively defenseless in comparison with some other species, but we dominate our world because we communicate more effectively and think better than other animals do. Humans have a remarkable ability to create *mental representations* of the world and to manipulate them in the forms of language, thinking, reasoning, and problem solving (Simon, 1990). **Mental representations** *include images, ideas, concepts, and principles.* At this very moment, through the printed words you are reading,

mental representations are being transferred from our minds to yours. Indeed, the process of education is all about transferring ideas and skills from one mind to another.

LANGUAGE

Language has been called "the jewel in the crown of cognition" (Pinker, 2000) and "the human essence" (Chomsky, 1972). Much of our thinking, reasoning, and problem solving involves the use of language. In turn, these advanced cognitive processes build on the large store of knowledge that resides in memory, and they provide a foundation for intelligent behavior.

Language *consists of a system of symbols and rules for combining these symbols in ways that can generate an infinite number of possible messages and meanings.* To most of us, using our native language comes as naturally as breathing, and we give it about as much thought. Yet using language actually involves a host of complex skills. **Psycholinguistics** *is the scientific study of the psychological aspects of language,* such as how people understand, produce, and acquire language. Before delving into some of these topics, let's consider some adaptive functions and characteristics of language.

ADAPTIVE FUNCTIONS OF LANGUAGE

According to anthropologists who have studied the skulls of prehistoric humans, the brain probably achieved its present form some 50,000 years ago (Pilbeam, 1984). Yet it took another 35,000 years before lifelike paintings began to appear on cave walls and another 12,000 years after that before humans developed a way to store knowledge outside the brain in the form of writing (Kottak, 2000). These time lags tell us that human thought and behavior depend on more than the physical structure of the brain; although the structure of the brain may not have evolved much over the past 50,000 years, human cognitive and linguistic skills clearly have.

Over the course of evolution, humans adopted a more socially oriented lifestyle that helped them survive and reproduce (Flinn, 1997). Some evolutionary theorists believe that the use of language evolved as people gathered to form larger social units. As the social environment became more complex, new survival problems emerged: the need to create divisions of labor and cooperative social systems, to develop social customs and communicate thoughts, and to pass on knowledge and wisdom. The development of language made it easier for humans to adapt to these environmental demands (Bjorklund & Pellegrini, 2002).

It is no coincidence, then, that every human culture, no matter how isolated or geographically remote, has developed one or more languages. Nor is it a coincidence that the human brain seems to have an inborn capacity to acquire any of the roughly 5,000 to 6,000 languages spoken across the globe. Humans have evolved into highly social creatures who need to communicate with one another and have the physical characteristics (e.g., a highly developed brain, a vocal tract) that allow them to do so in the most flexible way known: through language (Figure 8.2).

Language underlies so much of what we do that it is almost impossible to imagine functioning without it. Our conscious thinking usually takes the form of self-talk, or inner speech. Through lan-

"GOT IDEA. TALK BETTER. COMBINE WORDS. MAKE SENTENCES."

FIGURE 8.2

According to many theorists, the development of language was a major milestone in human evolution. SOURCE: Copyright © 2004 by Sidney Harris. ScienceCartoonsPlus.com. Reprinted with permission.

▶ **Focus 1**
What are some adaptive functions of language?

guage, we are also able to share our thoughts, feelings, goals, intentions, desires, needs, and memories with other people and thus interact socially in rich and diverse ways that would not otherwise be possible.

In ways small and big, language also is an extremely powerful learning mechanism. To get to a friend's house for the first time, you don't have to drive or walk all over the area (trial-and-error learning) or wait until someone shows up to lead the way (observational learning). Instead, you simply ask for directions or read a map. More broadly, in oral and written form—through storytelling, books, instruction, mass media, and the Internet—language puts the customs and knowledge accrued over generations at your fingertips.

PROPERTIES OF LANGUAGE

What is it that first captures your attention when someone uses a foreign language that you don't speak? Perhaps it is how different that language sounds or looks when written, or simply how incomprehensible it seems to you. Yet what is truly striking about the world's languages is not their differences but the underlying features that they share.

As we noted earlier, language is a system of symbols and rules for combining these symbols in ways that can generate an infinite number of messages and meanings. This definition encompasses four properties that are essential to any language: symbols, structure, meaning, and generativity. We will also describe a fifth property: displacement.

▶ **Focus 2**
Describe key properties of language.

Language Is Symbolic and Structured

Language uses sounds, written characters, or some other system of symbols (e.g., hand signs) to represent objects, events, ideas, feelings, and actions. Moreover, the symbols used in any given language are arbitrary. Figure 8.3, for example, lists the words used to represent "dog" in several languages. None of these written words looks like a dog, and when spoken, there is nothing about how any one of these words sounds that makes it an intrinsically correct choice for representing the concept of "dog." In English, *gerk, kreg, woof, zog, professor,* or countless other words could be used to represent what we call a *dog.* But they aren't. (Even though "No Professors Allowed on the Lawn" has a certain ring.) Regardless of how the word *dog* came into being, it has an agreed-on meaning to people who speak English. The same holds true for all the other words we use.

Language also has a rule-governed structure. A language's **grammar** *is the set of rules that dictate how symbols can be combined to create meaningful units of communication.* Thus if we ask you whether *zpflrovc* is an English word, you will almost certainly say that it is not. Why? Because it violates the rules of the English language; z is not to be followed by *pf*, and five consonants (*z, p, f, l, r*) cannot be put in an unbroken sequence. Likewise, if we ask you whether "Bananas have sale for I" is an appropriate English sentence, you will shake your head and say "No. It should read: 'I have bananas for sale.'" In this case, "Bananas have sale for I" violates a portion of English grammar called **syntax,** *the rules that govern the order of words.*

You may not be able to verbalize the formal rules of English that are violated in these examples, but you know them implicitly because they are part of the language you speak. The grammars of all languages share common functions, such as providing rules for how to change present tense ("I am walking the dog") into the past tense ("I walked the dog") or a negative ("I didn't walk the dog"). Yet just as symbols (e.g., words) vary across languages, so do grammatical rules. In English, for example, we say "green salad" and "big river," which follow the rule that adjectives almost always come before the noun they modify.

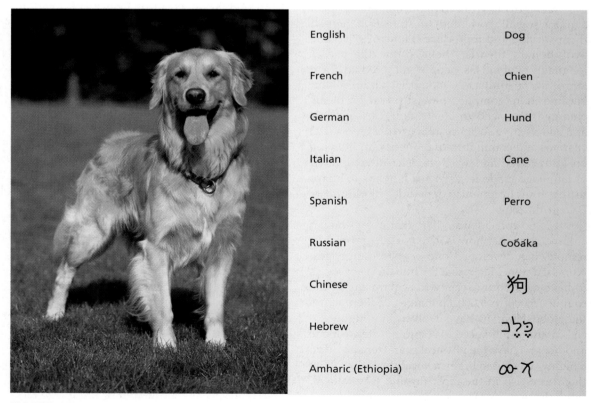

English	Dog
French	Chien
German	Hund
Italian	Cane
Spanish	Perro
Russian	Собáka
Chinese	狗
Hebrew	כֶּלֶב
Amharic (Ethiopia)	∞ϒ

FIGURE 8.3

The symbols used in a language are arbitrary. As a symbol to represent the animal pictured here, none of these words is inherently better or more appropriate than the others.

In French and Spanish, however, adjectives often follow nouns ("salade verte," "rio grande"). Although language changes over time, with new words appearing regularly, new words and new phrases need to conform to the basic rules of that language.

Language Conveys Meaning

No matter the arbitrary symbols or grammatical rules used, once people learn those symbols and rules, they are able to form and then transfer mental representations to the mind of another person. Thus you can talk with a friend about your courses, your favorite foods, how you feel, and so on. Based in part on the words you use and how they are organized, both you and your friend will extract meaning—and, it is hoped, the correct or intended meaning—from what is being said. But understanding **semantics,** *the meaning of words and sentences,* actually is a tricky business. For example, when you ask a friend "How did you do on the test?" and the reply is "I nailed it," you know that your friend is not saying "I hammered the test to the desk with a nail." Someone who is familiar with English knows from experience not to interpret this expression literally; someone just beginning to learn English might find this expression perplexing.

Language Is Generative and Permits Displacement

Generativity *means that the symbols of language can be combined to generate an infinite number of messages that have novel meaning.* The English language, for example, has only 26 letters, but they can be combined into over half a million words, which in turn can be combined to create a virtually limitless number of sentences. Thus you can create and understand a sentence like "Why is that sparrow standing underneath my pancake?" even though you are unlikely to have heard anything like it before.

Displacement *refers to the fact that language allows us to communicate about events and objects that are not physically present.* In other words, language frees us from being restricted to focusing on events and objects that are right before us in the present. You can discuss the past and the future, as well as people, objects, and events that currently exist or are taking place elsewhere. You can even discuss completely imaginary situations, such as a sparrow standing underneath a pancake.

THE STRUCTURE OF LANGUAGE

Psycholinguists describe language as having a *surface structure* and a *deep structure.* They also examine the hierarchical structure of language, in which smaller elements are combined into larger ones. Let's look at both of these issues.

Surface Structure and Deep Structure

When you read, listen to, or produce a sentence, its **surface structure** *consists of the symbols that are used and their order.* As noted earlier, the syntax of a language provides the rules for ordering words properly. In contrast, a sentence's **deep structure** *refers to the underlying meaning of the combined symbols,* which brings us back to the issue of semantics.

Sentences can have different surface structures but the same deep structure. Consider these examples:

1. Sam ate the cake.
2. The cake was eaten by Sam.
3. Eaten by Sam the cake was.

Each sentence conveys the underlying meaning: that the cake ended up in Sam's stomach. Notice that the syntax of the third sentence is incorrect. English isn't spoken this way, except, perhaps, by the fictional *Star Wars* character Yoda. Still, in this case its meaning is clear enough.

Sometimes, a single surface structure can give rise to two deep structures, as happens when people speak or write ambiguous sentences. Consider this example:

> The police must stop drinking after midnight.

On the one hand, this sentence could mean that police officers need to enforce a curfew designed to prevent citizens from drinking alcohol after midnight. On the other hand, it could mean that if police officers go out for a few drinks after work, they need to wrap up their drinking by midnight.

In everyday life, when you read or hear speech, you are moving from the surface structure to deep structure: from the way a sentence looks or sounds to its deeper level of meaning. After time you may forget the precise words used in the sentence, but you're likely to recall its essential meaning. In contrast, when you express your thoughts to other people, you must transform deep structure (the meaning that you want to communicate) into a surface structure that others

▶ **Focus 3**
Differentiate between surface and deep structure. Describe the hierarchy of language.

FIGURE 8.4

This grave marker in Boothill Graveyard illustrates an interesting relation between surface structure and deep structure.

can understand. Eloquent speakers and writers have the ability to convert their deep-structure meanings into clear and pleasing surface-structure expressions.

What Do You Think?

DISCERNING SURFACE AND DEEP STRUCTURES OF LANGUAGE

Figure 8.4 shows a grave marker in the Boothill Graveyard in Tombstone, Arizona, where many notorious outlaws and gunfighters are buried. Analyze the marker carefully in relation to what you have learned about surface structure and deep structure, and then come up with two possible meanings for the inscription. Think about it, then see page 311.

The Hierarchical Structure of Language

Human language has a hierarchical structure, and its most elementary building block is the **phoneme,** *the smallest unit of sound that is recognized as separate in a given language.* Linguists have identified about 100 phonemes that humans can produce, including the clicking sounds used in some African languages, but no language uses all of these sounds. The world's languages vary considerably in phonemes, some employing as few as 15 and others more than 80. English uses about 40 phonemes, consisting of the various vowel and consonant sounds, as well as certain letter combi-

nations such as *th* and *sh*. Thus sounds associated with *th*, *a*, and *t* can be combined to form the three-phoneme word *that*.

Phonemes have no inherent meaning, but they alter meaning when combined with other elements. For example, the phoneme *d* creates a different meaning from the phoneme *l* when it precedes *og* (i.e., *dog* versus *log*). At the next level of the hierarchy, phonemes are combined into **morphemes,** *the smallest units of meaning in a language.* Thus *dog*, *log*, and *ball* are all morphemes, as are prefixes and suffixes such as *pre-*, *un-*, *-ed*, and *-ous*. Notice in Figure 8.5 that morphemes are not always syllables. For example, in English *s* is not a syllable, but the final *s* on a noun is a morpheme that means "plural." Thus the word *fans* has one syllable, but two morphemes; *players* has two syllables but three morphemes. In every language, rules determine how phonemes can be combined into morphemes. English's 40 phonemes can be combined into more than 100,000 morphemes.

Morphemes, in turn, are the stuff of which words are formed. English morphemes can be combined into over 500,000 words, words into countless phrases, and phrases into an infinite number of sentences. Thus from the humble phoneme to the elegant sentence, we have a five-step language hierarchy (see Figure 8.5). Beyond this basic hierarchy lies the sixth and most comprehensive level, that of **discourse,** *in which sentences are combined into paragraphs, articles, books, conversations, and so forth.*

FIGURE 8.5

The hierarchical structure of language. Human language is structured hierarchically, with phonemes being the most basic unit. The row of phonemes contains symbols used by linguists to denote particular sounds.

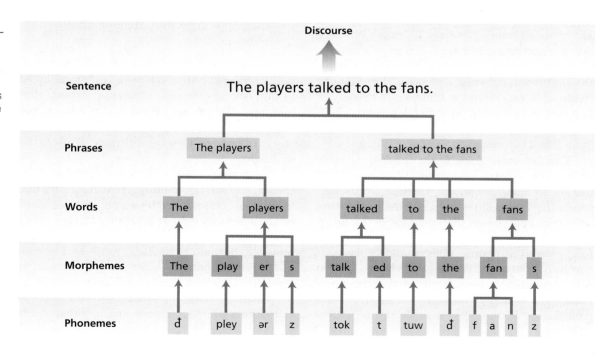

UNDERSTANDING AND PRODUCING LANGUAGE

One day after a class discussion on language, a student told us about a humorous incident that had happened the evening before. Her husband answered a phone call, listened for 5 seconds, and hung up. "It was a prerecorded telemarketing call," he said. "Some company called Pressgrits." "Pressgrits. That's a really weird name," she said. And then it dawned on her. She was expecting an automated call from a company called Express Scripts to confirm an order. Later, she found out that this had indeed been the confirmation call.

How can a voice on the phone produce the words *Express Scripts* and her husband hear it as "Pressgrits"? Did he need to clean out his ears? Hardly. He simply failed to perceive the morpheme *Ex,* which left *Press* for the first word. And by saying both words rapidly, as the prerecorded voice did (try it 5 times, fast), you'll realize that phonetically, *pressscripts* and *pressgrits* are not that far apart. Most importantly, her husband had no context for interpreting the message. Later on, when our student listened to a callback of the same message, she heard "Express Scripts" because she knew what to expect. Context, as you'll see, plays a key role in understanding language.

The Role of Bottom-Up Processing

To understand language, your brain must recognize and interpret patterns of stimuli—the sounds of speech, shapes of letters, movements that create hand signs, or tactile patterns of dots used in braille—that are detected by your sensory systems. And just like other perceptual tasks, extracting information from linguistic stimuli involves the joint influence of bottom-up and top-down processing (concepts that you may recall from Chapter 4). In **bottom-up processing,** *individual elements of a stimulus are analyzed and then combined to form a unified perception.* Analyzing the hierarchical structure of spoken language as a set of building blocks that involve the use of phonemes to create morphemes and the combination of morphemes to create words reflects a bottom-up approach.

Likewise, as you read this sentence, specialized cell groups in your brain are (1) analyzing the basic elements (e.g., contours, angles of lines) of the visual patterns that are right before your eyes and (2) feeding this information to other cell groups that lead you to perceive these patterns as letters. We then recognize words either directly by perceiving the visual patterns of letters or indirectly by first translating those visual patterns into auditory codes, as happens when you sound out in your head the phonemes and morphemes created by the letter sequences (Bernstein & Carr, 1996). Words and their grammatical sequence then become the building blocks for sentences, and sentences the building blocks for discourse. But at every step in this bottom-up sequence, including pattern recognition, our understanding of language also is influenced by top-down processing.

The Role of Top-Down Processing

In a Seattle farmers' market, there used to be a store called The Bead Store, which sold beads for making jewelry. Tourists would often walk by and ask "Where's the bread?" The store's sign said *Bead,* but these patrons literally perceived the word as *Bread,* a function perhaps of their mental set (i.e., a perceptual expectation) that they were in a farmers market that sold food. It got so bad for the merchants that they eventually put up a sign saying "We Don't Sell Bread."

In **top-down processing,** *sensory information is interpreted in light of existing knowledge, concepts, ideas, and expectations.* In Chapter 4 we discussed how people's unconscious expectations (i.e., mental sets) literally shape what they visually perceive. As the Bead Store example illustrates, people looked at a stimulus pattern on a store sign that said *Bead,* but *Bread* is what they saw.

Language by its very nature involves top-down processing, because the words you write, read, speak, or hear activate and draw upon your knowledge of vocabulary, grammar, and other linguistic rules that are stored in your long-term memory. That's why if we write "Bill g_ve th_ pe_cil to h_s fr__nd," you can probably interpret the words with little difficulty ("Bill gave the pencil to his friend"), despite the absence of several bottom-up elements.

Let's consider another example of top-down processing. Have you ever listened to someone speak a foreign language in which you aren't fluent and found that it was difficult to tell where one word ended and the next began? Even if you have studied that language for a semester or two in school, native speakers may seem to talk so quickly that you can't distinguish the individual words they are saying. Conversely, they would have the same problem listening to you speak English. Despite all the sophistication of modern computers and software, many still struggle with human voice recognition.

▶ **Focus 4**
Explain the role of bottom-up and top-down processes in language. Use speech segmentation and pragmatics as examples.

How is it, then, that in your native language this process of **speech segmentation**—*perceiving where each word within a spoken sentence begins and ends*—seems to occur automatically? When you read a sentence, the spaces between words make segmentation easy. But when people speak, they don't pause in between each pair of words. In fact, when psycholinguists measure the sound energy produced as people utter sentences, they find that the decreases in energy output between words often are smaller than the decreases between segments within the same words. To illustrate, say "We hope you have a nice day" out loud and at a normal speech rate. Did you distinctly segment each whole word, creating a sound energy break between each one? Or were your segments more like "We ho pew ha va nice day"? Moreover, in English about 40 percent of words consist of two or more syllables that are vocally stressed (i.e., emphasized) when spoken (Mattys, 2000). Thus in these and other words, the auditory breaks that we hear in speech often do not correspond well to the physical breaks produced by the spaces in written sentences.

Psycholinguists have discovered that we use several cues to tell when one spoken word ends and another begins (Mattys, 2004). For example, through experience we learn that certain sequences of phonemes are unlikely to occur within the same words, so when we hear these sounds in sequence we are more likely to perceive them as the ending or beginning of an adjacent word.

We also use the context provided by the other words in a sentence to interpret the meaning of any individual word. In two classic experiments, Irwin Pollack and J. M. Pickett (1964) recorded the conversations of four female college students and text passages spoken by four adult men. The researchers then played back 1-, 2-, 3-, or 4-word segments taken from these recordings to 38 college students. For example, from the words " . . . of the world was covered in ice," the researchers created the segments "of," "of the," "of the world," and "of the world was" and asked participants to identify the first word in the segment. Remarkably, when participants listened to 1-word excerpts, and thus had to identify a word based on its sound alone, they could do so on average only 35 to 62 percent of the time, depending on the voice of the particular speaker. When participants listened to the 4-word segments, they were able to identify the initial word between 70 to 100 percent of the time, depending on the speaker. In sum, the availability of context made the job of identifying individual words much easier.

Pragmatics: The Social Context of Language

Suppose that you call up a friend and someone else answers the phone. You ask "Is Bill there?" The person says "Hang on" and goes to get Bill. Or imagine that a passerby asks you "Do you have the time?" You say "10:20" and part ways. In these cases, the questions really are shorthand for "Is Bill there, and if so, please go get him and tell him to pick up the phone" and "I'm not wearing a watch, so please tell me what time it is right now." You wouldn't expect the person who answered the phone to merely say "Yes" and then wait until you gave more instructions ("Uh, okay, would you please go get him!"). Nor would you respond to someone's request "Do you have the time?" merely by saying "Yes, I do" and then walking away.

Instead, you and the other people involved in these communications understand the social context and rules for how to respond. Likewise, if a friend says "I need you to explain this material to me. Do you have the time?" you wouldn't say "10:20" and walk away. In this context, you understand that "Do you have the time?" means "Can you take a few minutes to help me?"

These examples illustrate that it takes more than having a vocabulary and arranging words grammatically to understand language and communicate effectively with others. It also involves **pragmatics,** *a knowledge of the practical aspects of using language* (Cummings, 2005). Language occurs in a social context, and pragmatic knowledge not only helps you understand what other people are really saying, it helps you make sure that other people get the point of what you're communicating. In essence, pragmatics is another example of how top-down processing influences language use.

Psycholinguists have identified social rules that guide communication between people (Grice, 1975). One rule states that messages should be as clear as possible (Figure 8.6). Thus, depending on whether you are speaking with an adult who is proficient in your language, a 5-year-old-child, or a foreign visitor who speaks little English, you usually adjust your rate of speech, choice of words, and the complexity of your sentences.

Pragmatics also depend on other aspects of the social context. For example, when you write a term paper or go for a job interview, you normally would use a more formal tone than when writing an e-mail or speaking to friends. Thus when a college student sent an e-mail to her instructor (it wasn't to one of us) that read "I can't find tomorrow's assignment could you pleeeeez send it to me pleeeeez, could ya, could ya?" the instructor

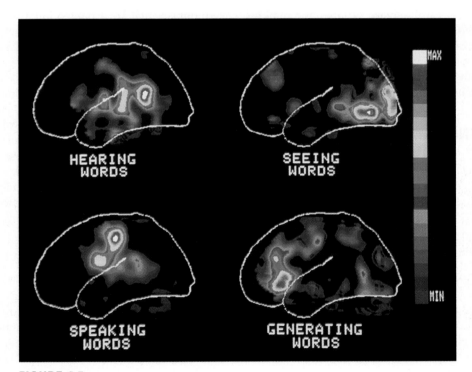

FIGURE 8.6

A breakdown of pragmatics. Although most of us might understand the underlying meaning of "Can I see you again," it seems that in this case our suitor made an error in his choice of words. SOURCE: Copyright © Jim Toomey. Reprinted with special permission of King Features Syndicate.

sternly let the student know about her violation of pragmatics, namely, that the style of the message was completely inappropriate for the context.

? What Do You Think?

THE SLEEPING POLICEMAN

You're on vacation in England, driving to a countryside bed-and-breakfast to spend the night. You stop in a small town to get directions. A storekeeper tells you to take a left turn a mile up the road, drive "until you come to the sleeping policeman," and then take a right. What do you imagine "the sleeping policeman" (or "The Sleeping Policeman") might be? Think about it, then see page 311.

Language Functions, the Brain, and Sex Differences

Language functions are distributed in many areas of the brain, but the regions shown in Figure 8.7 are especially significant. As discussed in Chapter 3, Broca's area, located in the left hemisphere's frontal lobe, is most centrally involved in word production and articulation (lower-right brain scan). Wernicke's area, in the rear portion of the temporal lobe, is more centrally involved in speech comprehension (upper-left scan). People with

FIGURE 8.7

Brain areas involved in various aspects of language. In these PET scans, regions of white, red, and yellow show the greatest activity. Notice in the upper-left image that Wernicke's area (in the temporal lobe) is especially active when we hear words, and in the lower-right image that Broca's area (located in the frontal lobe) is especially active when we generate words. (See also Figure 3.20.)

► **Focus 5**
What sex differences exist in the brain's language processing?

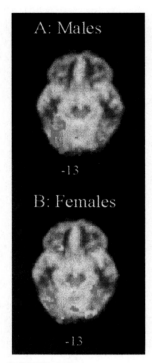

FIGURE 8.8

Brain activation, as recorded by fMRI, is shown in the red areas. For males, the left hemisphere is more active than the right hemisphere during this language task. Females' activation patterns are distributed in corresponding areas of both the left and right hemispheres, indicating less lateralization of language functions than in the males' brains. The yellow activation patterns occurred in response to a control (nonlanguage) task. SOURCE: Rossell et al., 2002.

► **Focus 6**
How do biological factors influence language acquisition?

► **Focus 7**
How do social learning factors influence language acquisition?

damage in one or both areas typically suffer from **aphasia,** *an impairment in speech comprehension and/or production* that can be permanent or temporary (LaPointe, 2005). The visual area of the cortex is also involved in recognizing written words.

Years ago scientists noted that men who suffer left-hemisphere strokes are more likely than women to show severe aphasic symptoms. In female stroke victims with left-hemisphere damage, language functions are more likely to be spared, suggesting that more of their language function is shared with the right hemisphere.

Recent brain-imaging research by Susan Rossell and coworkers (2002) supports this hypothesis. In their study, men and women engaged in a language task in which words and nonwords were presented on each side of a computer screen. Participants had to identify which was the real word as quickly as possible by pressing one of two computer keys. Functional MRIs (fMRIs) were recorded during the task and during a nonlanguage control task. As the image in Figure 8.8 shows, men exhibited greater left-hemisphere activation (red areas) during the language task, whereas women's brain activation occurred in both the left and right hemispheres. Maximum activation occurred in regions corresponding to Broca's area and Wernicke's area. Neural systems involved in several aspects of language may be organized differently in women than in men, but because this finding has been successfully replicated in some studies but not others, more research is needed to sort out why these inconsistencies occur (Démonet et al., 2005).

ACQUIRING A FIRST LANGUAGE

Language acquisition is one of the most striking events in human cognitive development. It represents the joint influences of biology (nature) and environment (nurture). Many language experts believe that humans are born linguists, inheriting a biological readiness to recognize and eventually produce the sounds and structure of whatever language they are exposed to (Chomsky, 1965; Pinker 2000).

Biological Foundations

Several facts suggest a biological basis for language acquisition. First, human children, despite their limited thinking skills, begin to master language early in life without any formal instruction. Moreover, despite their differences at the phoneme level, all adult languages throughout the world—including sign languages for the deaf that developed independently in different parts of the world—seem to have common underlying structural characteristics. Language acquisition thus represents the unfolding of a biologically primed process within a social learning environment (Aitchison, 1998; Chomsky, 1987).

Whether born in Toledo, Taiwan, or Tanzania, young infants vocalize the entire range of phonemes found in the world's languages. At about 6 months of age, however, they begin to make only those sounds that are specific to their native tongue and abandon those of other languages. For example, Japanese children lose the ability to distinguish between the *r* and *l* sounds because their language does not make this phonetic distinction, but children exposed to English continue to discriminate these sounds as they mature. Likewise, Japanese-speaking children learn the syntactic rule to put the object before the verb ("Ichiro the ball hit"), whereas English-speaking children learn the syntactic rule that the verb comes before the object ("Ichiro hit the ball").

The linguist Noam Chomsky (1987) proposed that humans are born with a **language acquisition device (LAD),** *an innate biological mechanism that contains the general grammatical rules (which he terms "universal grammar") common to all languages.* Among the principles inherent in LAD are that languages contain such things as noun phrases and verb phrases that are arranged in particular ways, such as subjects, predicates, and adjectives. Chomsky likened LAD to a huge electrical panel with banks of linguistic switches that are thrown as children hear the words and syntax of their native language. For example, for a child learning to speak English, the "switch" that indicates whether to insert a pronoun before a verb (as in "*I* want") is set to yes. But in Spanish, the same switch is set to no, because the applicable verb (in this case, *deseo*) already includes the first-person singular and inserting a pronoun is not necessary. In this manner, universal grammar becomes calibrated to the grammar and syntax of one's native tongue.

Social Learning Processes

Given the required biological foundation, social learning plays a central role in acquiring a language (Kramsch, 2003). Early on, mothers and fathers attract their children's attention and maintain their interest by conversing with them in what has been termed *child-directed speech,* a high-pitched intonation that seems to be used all over the world (Fernald et al., 1989). Parents also teach their children words by pointing out objects and naming them, by reading aloud to them, and by responding to the never-ending question "What dat?" (Figure 8.9).

As this point also shows, much of children's language is very different from that of their parents, and thus it can't be explained simply as an imitative process. Nonetheless, social learning is a crucial contributor to language acquisition, and the interplay between biological and environmental factors is a given for most modern theorists. Psychologist Jerome Bruner (1983) proposed the term **language acquisition support system (LASS)** *to represent factors in the social environment that facilitate the learning of a language.* One could say that when LAD and LASS interact in a mutually supportive fashion, normal language development occurs.

Developmental Timetable and Sensitive Periods

As biological factors (including the maturation of speech-production mechanisms) and experiential factors combine their influences, language acquisition proceeds according to a developmental timetable that is common to all cultures. As shown in Table 8.1, children progress from reflexive

 In the video, "Language Ability at Age 2," in Chapter 8 of your CD, a child demonstrates several essential components of language.

FIGURE 8.9

Language development depends not only on the brain's biological programming device but also on exposure to one's language. Childhood is an important sensitive period for such exposure.

The behaviorist B. F. Skinner (1957) developed an operant conditioning explanation for language acquisition. His basic premise was that children's language development is strongly governed by adults' positive reinforcement of appropriate language and nonreinforcement or correction of inappropriate verbalizations. However, most modern psycholinguists doubt that operant learning principles alone can account for language development. For one thing, children learn so much so quickly. By 30 months of age, they already have learned several hundred words. By age 6, children are learning an average of more than 15 words per day, and their vocabularies have grown to between 8,000 and 14,000 words (Carey, 1977). Moreover, observational studies have shown that parents do *not* typically correct their children's grammar as language skills are developing. Rather, parents' corrections focus primarily on the "truth value" (or deep structure) of what the child is trying to communicate. Thus they are less likely to correct a young child who says "I have two foots" than they are to correct one who says "I have four feet," even though the latter statement is grammatically correct (Brown, 1973).

TABLE 8.1	Course of Normal Language Development in Children
Age	**Speech Characteristics**
1–3 months	Infant can distinguish speech from nonspeech sounds and prefers speech sounds (phonemes). Undifferentiated crying gives way to cooing when happy.
4–6 months	Babbling sounds begin to occur. These contain sounds from virtually every language. Child vocalizes in response to verbalizations of others.
7–11 months	Babbling sounds narrow to include only the phonemes heard in the language spoken by others in the environment. Child moves tongue with vocalizations ("lalling"). Child discriminates between some words without understanding their meaning and begins to imitate word sounds heard from others.
12 months	First recognizable words typically spoken as one-word utterances to name familiar people and objects (e.g., *da-da* or *block*).
12–18 months	Child increases knowledge of word meanings and begins to use single words to express whole phrases or requests (e.g., *out* to express a desire to get out of the crib); primarily uses nouns.
18–24 months	Vocabulary expands to between 50 and 100 words. First rudimentary sentences appear, usually consisting of two words (e.g., *more milk*) with little or no use of articles (*the, a*), conjunctions (*and*), or auxiliary verbs (*can, will*). This condensed, or telegraphic, speech is characteristic of first sentences throughout the world.
2–4 years	Vocabulary expands rapidly at the rate of several hundred words every 6 months. Two-word sentences give way to longer sentences that, though often grammatically incorrect, exhibit basic language syntax. Child begins to express concepts with words and to use language to describe imaginary objects and ideas. Sentences become more correct syntactically.
4–5 years	Child has learned the basic grammatical rules for combining nouns, adjectives, articles, conjunctions, and verbs into meaningful sentences.

crying at birth through stages of cooing, babbling, and one-word utterances. By 2 years of age, children are uttering sentences called *telegraphic speech* that at first consist of a noun and a verb (e.g., "Want cookie"), with nonessential words left out as in a telegraph message. Soon, additional words may be added (e.g., "Daddy go car"). From that point on, speech development accelerates as vocabulary increases and sentences become more grammatically correct. In the short span of 5 years, an initially nonverbal creature has come to understand and produce a complex language.

In Chapter 4 we saw how the normal development of perceptual abilities requires certain kinds of sensory input early in life. Some linguists are convinced there is also a sensitive period from infancy to puberty during which the brain is most responsive to language input from the environment. Support for a sensitive period comes from studies of children who lived by themselves in the wild or who were isolated from human contact by deranged parents. One such child, found when she was 6 years old, immediately received language training and seemed to develop normal language abilities (Brown, 1958). In contrast, language-deprived children who were found when they were past puberty seemed unable to acquire normal language skills despite extensive training (Clarke & Clarke, 2000; Curtiss, 1977).

The importance of early language exposure applies to any language, not just spoken language. Because sign languages share the deep-structure characteristics of spoken languages, deaf children who learn sign language before puberty develop normal linguistic and cognitive abilities even though they never hear a spoken word (Marschark & Mayer, 1998). In contrast, deaf people who are not exposed to sign language before age 12 show a distinct language-learning deficit even when they reach age 30 (Meier, 1991).

Can Animals Acquire Human Language?

► Focus 8
Does evidence support the view that apes can acquire human language? Why or why not?

Nonhuman species communicate in diverse ways. Chimpanzees grunt, bark, scream, and make gestures to other chimps. Dolphins make clicking sounds and high-pitched vocalizations (Figure 8.10). Many species use special calls to warn of predators and to attract mates (Alcock, 2002).

Communication also abounds in the insect world. Honeybees use a repertoire of body movements—so-called dances—to communicate. When a honeybee discovers nectar, it returns to the hive and performs a turning "waggle dance" (von Frisch, 1974). The dance's pattern and duration convey information about the nectar's loca-

"Although humans make sounds with their mouths and occasionally look at each other, there is no solid evidence that they actually communicate with each other."

FIGURE 8.10

Human scientists debate whether dolphins and other animals use language. Could the opposite also be occurring? Source: Copyright © 2004 by Sidney Harris. ScienceCartoonsPlus.com. Reprinted with permission.

tion, which other bees receive by sensing vibrations as they stay in contact behind the dancer. Using this information and odor cues, they can zero in on the food source. Honeybees also vibrate their bodies from side to side in a "grooming invitation dance" that signals other bees to come by and help clean them (Land & Seeley, 2004).

In some species, communication shows interesting parallels to human language. Just as humans have different languages, each songbird species has its own songs. Remarkably, some songbirds also have local dialects, as humans do (Catchpole & Rowell, 1993). Thus experts can tell whether a male white-crowned sparrow lives in certain areas north, south, or east of San Francisco by how it sings. And just as humans have a sensitive period in childhood for language acquisition, some songbirds will not sing normally in adulthood unless they hear the songs of their species while growing up (Marler, 1970).

Although other species can communicate in intriguing and sophisticated ways, the capacity to use full-fledged language has long been regarded as the sole province of humans. Several decades ago, some scientists attempted to challenge this assumption by teaching apes to use human language.

Washoe: Early Signs of Success At first, investigators tried to teach chimpanzees to speak verbally, but chimps lack a vocal system that would permit humanlike speech. A breakthrough came in 1966 when Allen Gardner and Beatrice Gardner (1969) took advantage of chimps' hand and finger dexterity and began teaching American Sign Language to a 10-month-old chimp named Washoe. They *cross-fostered* Washoe: They raised her at home and treated her like a human child. By age 5, Washoe had learned 160 signs. More important, at times she combined signs (e.g., "more fruit," "you tickle Washoe") in novel ways. For example, when a researcher showed Washoe a baby doll inside a cup and signed "What that?" Washoe signed back "Baby in my drink." Other researchers also had success. A gorilla named Koko learned over 600 signs (Bonvillian & Patterson, 1997), and a chimp named Lana learned to communicate via visual symbols on a specially designed keyboard (Rumbaugh, 1990).

Project Nim: Dissent from Within

At Columbia University, behaviorist Herbert Terrace (1979) taught sign language to a chimp he named Nim Chimpsky—a play on the name of linguist Noam Chomsky. But after years of work and videotape analysis of Nim's "conversations," Terrace concluded that when Nim combined symbols into longer sequences, he was either imitating his trainer's previous signs or "running on" with his hands until he got what he wanted. Moreover, Nim spontaneously signed only when he wanted something, which is not how humans use language. Terrace concluded that Nim had not learned language.

Not surprisingly, some ape-language researchers disputed Terrace's conclusions. They agreed that although apes signed mainly to request things, other types of communication also occurred. For example, Chantek, an orangutan who had been taught a symbol for "dirty" in regard to feces and urine, spontaneously began applying the symbol to spilled food, soiled objects, and toilets (Miles et al., 1996). At Central Washington University, Roger Fouts and Deborah Fouts continued working with Washoe and other cross-fostered chimps. They intentionally refrained from signing in front of Loulis, Washoe's adopted son, and found that Loulis acquired over 50 signs by observing other chimps communicate (Fouts et al., 1989). The chimps also signed with each other when humans were not present, and signing occurred across various contexts, such as when they were playing, feeding, and fighting (Cianelli and Fouts, 1998).

Kanzi: Chimp versus Child

Sue Savage-Rumbaugh of Georgia State University has worked extensively with a chimpanzee species called the *bonobo* (Figure 8.11). At age $1\frac{1}{2}$, a bonobo named Kanzi spontaneously showed an interest in using plastic geometric symbols that were associated with words. By age 4, with only informal training during social interactions, Kanzi had learned more than 80 symbols and produced a number of two- and three-word communications. Kanzi typically

(a)

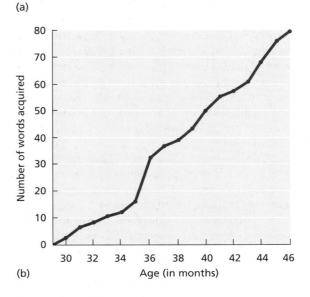

(b)

FIGURE 8.11

Can a chimpanzee acquire language? (a) Using complex symbols, a bonobo communicates with psychologist Sue Savage-Rumbaugh. (b) This graph shows the rate of Kanzi's symbol acquisition over 17 months of informal training. SOURCE: Adapted from Savage-Rumbaugh et al., 1986.

combined gestures and symbols that he pointed to on a laminated board or typed on a specially designed keyboard. For example, Kanzi created the combinations "Person chase Kanzi," "Kanzi chase person," and "Person chase person" to designate who should chase whom during play. Kanzi also responded readily to spoken English commands.

Savage-Rumbaugh and her coworkers (1993) also tested Kanzi's ability to understand unfamiliar spoken sentences under controlled conditions. For example, when told "Give the doggie a shot," Kanzi picked up a toy dog, grabbed a toy hypodermic needle, and gave the dog a shot. Kanzi also appeared to understand syntax. Given slightly different requests, such as "Make the [toy] snake bite the [toy] doggie" and "Make the doggie bite the snake," Kanzi responded appropriately. For comparison, one of the researcher's daughters, Alia, was tested under the same conditions between the ages of 2 and $2\frac{1}{2}$. Kanzi correctly responded to 74 percent of the novel requests and Alia to 65 percent. In short, Kanzi was comprehending speech at the level of a human toddler.

Is It Language? What should we conclude about apes' language abilities? Recall that human language (1) is symbolic, (2) is structured, (3) conveys meaning, (4) is generative, and (5) permits displacement. Evidence is strongest for the first and third criteria. Apes, undisputedly, are capable of communicating with symbols and hand signs, and they can learn a small vocabulary of several hundred words. However, whether the apes perceive the symbols and signs as words in the sense that humans do is still unclear. As for conveying meaning, realize that just as toddlers can convey meaning by using one- or two-word utterances, apes can convey meaning by using one- or two-symbol communications (e.g., "banana" or "give banana"), and they have also produced longer symbol strings that, at least some of the time, convey meaning. As for structure, both sides can point to examples of how apes follow—and violate—rules of grammar. Lastly, the evidence for generativity and displacement is limited and controversial.

Critics—even those impressed by Kanzi's feats—are not persuaded. Some believe that ambiguous ape communications are interpreted as language because the researchers erroneously assume what must be going on inside the apes' minds. Conversely, proponents believe the data show that great apes can acquire rudimentary language skills (Taglialatela et al., 2003). If it were anatomically possible, argues Sue Savage-Rumbaugh, Kanzi would be speaking.

At present, neither side in the debate has convinced the other. If nothing else, this intriguing scientific work should remind us to appreciate something that we often take for granted, namely the seemingly natural ease with which humans acquire a native language.

BILINGUALISM

▶ **Focus 9**
Is there a critical (or sensitive) period for acquiring a second language? Discuss the evidence.

For those of us trying to learn a second language, there are models to inspire us. M. D. Berlitz, inventor of the well-known system for teaching foreign languages, spoke 58 of them. Sir John Bowring, a former British governor of Hong Kong, could speak 100 languages and read 100 more. And some sort of record must be held by the Jesuit missionary Benjamin Schulze (1699–1760), who could recite the Lord's Prayer in 215 languages (Bryan, 1986).

Bilingualism, *the use of two languages in daily life,* is common throughout the world (Fabbro, 2001). Many Europeans, for example, routinely speak two or more languages. In North America, Canada officially is a bilingual country. French is

▶ **Focus 10**
Discuss the relation between bilingualism and other cognitive abilities. How does the brain process two languages?

TABLE 8.2	Most Commonly Spoken Languages at Home in the United States*
Language	**Number of Homes**
1. English	215,424,000
2. Spanish**	28,101,000
3. French**	2,097,000
4. Chinese	2,022,000
5. German	1,383,000
6. Tagalog***	1,224,000
7. Vietnamese	1,010,000
8. Italian	1,008,000
9. Korean	894,000
10. Russian	706,000
11. Polish	667,000
12. Arabic	615,000
13. Portuguese**	565,000
14. Japanese	478,000
15. Greek	365,000

*Includes Americans who are at least 5 years old.

**Includes people who speak a Spanish, French, or Portuguese creole. A *creolized* language is a version of an original language (say, French) that has been blended with some characteristics of another language (say, English) and that evolves into the native language of people living in a certain area.

***Tagalog is native to the Philippines.

SOURCE: U.S. Census Bureau, 2003a, 2003b.

the official language of the province of Quebec, English is the official language elsewhere, and the federal government promotes both languages. But individually, only about 18 percent of Canadians (including 41 percent of those living in Quebec) report that they speak both English and French (Statistics Canada, 2002).

English is the sole official language in the United States, but as in Canada and other countries, a history of immigration means that many languages and bilingual combinations are spoken. For example, of the 47 million Americans who speak a language at home other than English, the vast majority also speak English well or very well (U.S. Census Bureau, 2003a, 2003b). Table 8.2 shows the 15 most commonly spoken languages in the United States.

Does Bilingualism Affect Other Cognitive Abilities?

In childhood, does learning a second language influence the development of other cognitive abilities or affect acquisition of one's native language?

Beneath the Surface   Learning a Second Language: Is Earlier Better?

Given that children are language sponges, it seems obvious that a second language would be learned best and spoken most fluently when acquired early in life. Some psycholinguists believe that there is a critical period for learning a second language that ends in childhood or possibly in the early teens. If this is the case, it would not be possible for people who begin to learn a second language in high school or college, or after emigrating as late teens or adults to a foreign country, to achieve the fluency of native speakers. What do you think about this hypothesis?

In one sense, it does appear that the earlier one learns a second language, the better. If you start to learn a second language in childhood, then by the time you reach age 25 to 30, let's say, you will have had many more years of exposure to that language than if you had first started to learn it in your late teens. Thus "age of acquisition" can easily be confounded with "years of exposure and practice." As a critical thinker, realize that to test the biologically based critical-period hypothesis, researchers must try to compare the proficiency of people who are "early" versus "late" second-language learners yet who also have had a similar amount of overall exposure to that second language.

In one well-known study, Jacqueline Johnson and Elissa Newport (1989) studied university students and faculty members who had emigrated from Korea or China to the United States when they were either 3 to 16 years old ("early arrivals") or 17 to 39 years old ("late arrivals"). Overall, the early- and late-arrival groups had nearly identical years of exposure to English since coming to the United States. Johnson and Newport presented these individuals with 276 English sentences that were either grammatically correct (e.g., "Every Friday our neighbor washes her car.") or incorrect (e.g., "Two mouses ran into the house this morning."). The participants were asked to judge the correctness of each sentence. A sample of native-born Americans also took this grammar test.

The findings strongly supported the critical-period hypothesis. Overall, the early arrivals performed far better than the late arrivals. Moreover, even among the early arrivals, those who had arrived by age 7 mastered English grammar just as well as native-born Americans, whereas immigrants who had arrived between the ages of 8 to 10 and between 11 to 16 did progressively worse on the grammar test (Figure 8.12). The 17- to 39-year olds showed the poorest understanding of grammar and, within this age group, breaking the data down by age subgroups made little difference: Immigrants who had arrived after age 30 performed as well, for example, as those who had arrived in their late teens (Johnson & Newport, 1989). These findings suggest that because late arrivals had missed a critical period for learning a second language, it mattered little at what age they started to acquire English.

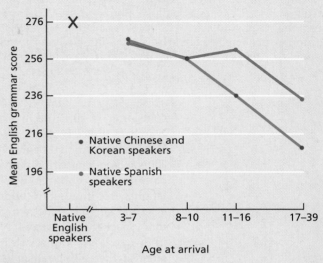

FIGURE 8.12

Age and proficiency of learning a second language. The X represents the grammar score of native-born Americans. The blue line shows the relation between age of arrival in the United States by Korean and Chinese individuals and their scores on a 276-item test of English grammar, compared with native-born Americans. The red line shows the relation between age of arrival in the United States by native Spanish speakers and their scores on a 274-item version of the same grammar test. SOURCES: Based on data from Johnson & Newport, 1989; Birdsong & Molis, 2001.

Other findings, however, complicate the picture. David Birdsong and Michelle Molis (2001) used the same grammar test in a study of native Spanish speakers who had emigrated to America at different ages and were now either faculty members, students, or employees at a university. Once again, despite having a similar amount of overall exposure to English, early-arriving immigrants (i.e., arrival by age 16) performed much better than late-arriving immigrants (i.e., arrival after age 16). But unlike the previous study, performance among early arrivals generally remained high all the way through age 16 (see Figure 8.12). And among the late arrivals, age did make a difference. It was not as if some biological second-language acquisition switch got completely turned off by the end of childhood or even by the late teens. Overall, immigrants who arrived in their twenties, though not as proficient as early arrivals, still performed better than those who arrived in their thirties or forties.

Differences in the patterns of findings across studies have led researchers to debate whether there is a biologically based critical period for second-language acquisition and, if so, at what age range it ends. Moreover, some studies suggest that to speak a second language with the fluency and accent of a native speaker people must begin to

Continued

acquire that language in childhood. Other studies find that even after mid-adolescence, some second-language learners acquire the proficiency (if not quite the perfect accent) of native speakers (Bialystok, 2001; Birdsong & Molis, 2001).

The issue of whether earlier is better—or, more precisely, whether earlier is biologically better—is far from resolved. One study, for example, found that the better grammar proficiency of early- versus late-arriving immigrants to America seemed to be due not to a biological critical period but to the greater amount of formal education in English that the early arrivals had received (Flege et al., 1999). Still, the two studies discussed above, along with most others, support the general principle that it is more difficult to learn a second language in adulthood than in childhood. Overall, at present, the data suggest that there may at least be a *sensitive* (rather than a *critical*) period for learning a second language that extends through mid-adolescence.

Causation is difficult to establish because researchers typically don't get to randomly assign children to bilingual or monolingual classrooms. Thus, when comparing native-born monolingual children (i.e., children who speak only a first language) to immigrant children who are learning a second language, the two groups may differ on many background factors. Nevertheless, studies in Switzerland, South Africa, Israel, and Canada suggest that bilingualism is at least correlated with greater thinking flexibility and higher performance on nonverbal intelligence tests. However, such associations are not likely to appear until both languages are well learned (Lambert et al., 1993).

Bilingual children also perform better than monolingual children on perceptual tasks that require them to inhibit attention to an irrelevant feature of an object and pay attention to another feature (Bialystok & Martin, 2004). For example, suppose you sit in front of a computer screen like the one shown in Figure 8.13. There's a box in the lower-left corner with a red square above it and a box in the lower-right corner with a blue circle above it. Next, a stimulus appears at the top of the screen—either a blue square or a red circle. At first, your task is to place the stimulus into the box that has the same color. If a blue square appears, you hit the letter O on the keyboard to drop it into the lower-right box. If a red circle appears, you hit the X key to drop it into the lower-left box. After several trials, however, we switch the rule. Now your task is to sort each stimulus by its shape, not by its color: Drop blue squares into the left box and red circles into the right box. This new rule requires you to ignore the color of each stimulus, which just a moment ago was foremost in your mind, and instead to selectively focus your attention on the shape of the stimulus.

According to Canadian psychologist Ellen Bialystok (2001), bilingual children perform better on tasks like this because in learning a second language, they gain continuous experience in using selective attention to inhibit one set of responses while making other responses. For example, while speaking in their second language, they must inhibit their tendency to use the more familiar words of their first language.

Learning a second language also may help children better perceive the unique grammar of their native language and help them realize that the words used to label objects are arbitrary. However, at least in the case of non-English-speaking immigrant children, it appears that they perform best in bilingual educational settings that provide instruction in both their native language and in English. Compared with similar children who are placed in English-only classrooms and left to struggle, those in bilingual classes develop higher self-esteem and exhibit better academic performance and English fluency (Thomas & Collier, 1997).

The Bilingual Brain

Is a second language represented in the same parts of the brain as the native language? One intriguing set of findings comes from studies of bilingual people who experience a brain trauma (e.g., from a tumor or stroke) and subsequently develop an aphasia. In some bilingual patients, the same linguistic

FIGURE 8.13

Measuring your ability to ignore irrelevant details. This figure shows one of the attention-inhibition tasks used by Bialystok & Martin (2004).

ability—such as understanding the meaning of words—may be impaired to different degrees in each language, or impaired in one language and not the other (Fabbro, 2001). Moreover, when brain damage produces similar impairments in both languages, patients may experience some simultaneous recovery in both languages, or recovery in one language but not the other. These findings suggest that there is variability among people in how bilingual abilities are represented in the brain, but also that in some cases, each language is represented by at least partially distinct neural networks.

Brain-imaging studies shed further light on this issue. At the University of Milan, Daniela Perani and her coworkers (1998) used PET scans to measure cortical activation patterns in the brains of English-speaking Italians as they listened to stories read aloud in Italian and in English. People who were highly proficient in English and who had learned this second language before the age of 10 showed representation of the two languages in the same cortical areas. The two languages had, in a sense, become one, accounting for the fluent participants' ability to use the languages interchangeably. In contrast, less fluent Italians who had learned English later in life showed brain activity in different areas depending on whether they listened to stories in Italian or English.

In general, it appears that when people acquire a second language early in life or learn it to a high degree of proficiency later in life, both languages use a common neural network (Démonet et al., 2005). Yet even within this common network, some brain regions become more active when fluent bilinguals use the language to which they have been less extensively exposed (usually the second language). Thus, despite fluency in both languages, this may suggest that the person has to exert more conscious effort to process the less dominant language (Marian et al., 2003). In contrast, people who learn a second language only moderately well later in life show more variability in their patterns of neural activation; at least in certain cases, some of the specific brain areas that process each language are distinct.

LINGUISTIC INFLUENCES ON THINKING

Although many politicians throughout history have demonstrated that a well-developed larynx bears little relation to the capacity for sound thinking, a relation between language and thinking has long been assumed. The linguist Benjamin Lee Whorf (1956) took an extreme position on this matter, contending in his **linguistic relativity hypothesis** *that language not only influences but also determines what we are capable of thinking.*

Was Whorf's position overstated? If the linguistic relativity hypothesis is correct, then people whose cultures have only a few words for colors should have greater difficulty in perceiving the spectrum of colors than do people whose languages have many color words. To test this proposition, Eleanor Rosch (1973) studied the Dani of New Guinea, who have only two color words in their language, one for bright warm colors and the other for dark cool ones. She found that contrary to what strict linguistic determinism would suggest, the Dani could discriminate among and remember a wide assortment of hues in much the same manner as can speakers of the English language, which contains many color names.

A more recent study, however, comparing English children and Himba children from Africa, suggests that color categories in a given language have a greater influence on color perception than Rosch's study of the Dani suggested (Davidoff, 2004). The English language contains 11 basic color terms, whereas the Himba language has only 5. Himba children made fewer distinctions among colored tiles than did English children. For example, Himba children categorized under the color term *zoozu* a variety of dark colors, such as dark shades of blue, green, brown, purple, red, and the color black. English children distinguished among these colors and remembered the different hues better when retested on which ones they had seen earlier.

Still, most linguists do not agree with Whorf's strong assertion that language *determines* how we think. They would say instead that language can *influence* how we think, how efficiently we can categorize our experiences, and perhaps how much detail we attend to in our daily experience (Hunt & Agnoli, 1991). Language can also color our perceptions, the decisions we make, and the conclusions we draw (Figure 8.14). Consider, for example, the ability of sexist language to evoke

► **Focus 11**
How does language influence thinking?

FIGURE 8.14

Sexist language influences our perceptions, our decisions, and the conclusions we draw. Which of these people would you assume is the chairperson of this committee? Might you consider the question differently if we said "Which of these people would you assume is the *chairman* of the committee?"

LEVELS OF ANALYSIS   Factors Related to Language

Biological

- Biological maturation of language-relevant brain structures
- Brain areas involved in understanding and producing language
- Biologically based sensitive periods for language acquisition
- Possible hemispheric lateralization differences between males and females
- Brain modifications created by learning native and new languages at various ages

Psychological

- Cognitive processes involved in learning a language's symbols and grammatical rules
- Bottom-up and top-down processes that influence language recognition
- Ways in which language influences thinking, problem solving, and adaptive behavior
- Relations between deep structure and surface structure in discourse
- Association between bilingualism and cognitive task performance

Environmental

- Early caretaker behaviors in teaching language to children
- Social learning and operant conditioning processes in children's language acquisition
- Effects of cultural variables on language acquisition
- Formal educational experiences that facilitate language development
- Exposure to a monolingual versus bilingual language environment

Language

FIGURE 8.15

Levels of analysis: Factors related to language.

gender stereotypes. In one study, college students read one of the following statements about psychology:

> The psychologist believes in the dignity and worth of the individual human being. He is committed to increasing man's understanding of himself and others.

> Psychologists believe in the dignity and worth of the individual human being. They are committed to increasing people's understanding of themselves and others.

The students then were asked to rate the attractiveness of a career in psychology for men and women. Those who had read the first statement rated psychology as a less attractive profession for women than did the students who read the second statement, written in gender-neutral language (Briere & Lanktree, 1983). Apparently, the first statement implied that psychology is a male profession (when, actually, the majority of psychology doctorates awarded over the past decade went to women). In such ways, language can help create and maintain stereotypes.

Language not only influences *how* we think but also may influence *how well* we think in certain domains. For example, English-speaking children consistently score lower than children from Asian countries in mathematical skills such as counting, addition, and subtraction (Geary, 1995). One reason may be the words and symbols the languages use to represent numbers. Asian languages make it far easier to learn the base-10 number system, particularly the numbers between 10 and 100. For example, in Chinese, the number 11 is "ten-one," 12 is "ten-two," and 13 is "ten-three." In contrast, English speakers struggle with such words as *eleven, twelve,* and *thirteen,* which bear little conceptual relation to a base-10 mode of thinking. Regardless of their counting proficiency, American and British children fail to grasp the base-10 system by age 5; in contrast, by age 5 many Chinese children understand this concept, enabling them to do addition and subtraction with greater ease (Miller & Stigler, 1987). In this manner, the English language appears to hamper the development of skills in using numbers, whereas Asian languages seem to facilitate the development of mathematical skills.

In sum, language provides the foundation of many human behaviors and capabilities, and in this chapter we have touched on only a few of its complexities. As a central topic of psychological research, it continues to be studied vigorously at the biological, psychological, and environmental levels of analysis (Figure 8.15).

IN REVIEW

■ Human languages across the globe share the same underlying features. Language is symbolic and structured, conveys meaning, is generative, and permits displacement. Language has many adaptive functions, such as facilitating cooperative social systems and allowing people to transmit knowledge to one another. Scientists believe that humans have evolved an innate capacity for acquiring language.

■ The surface structure of a language refers to how symbols are combined; the deep structure refers to the underlying meaning of the symbols. Language elements are hierarchically arranged: from phoneme to morpheme to words, phrases, and sentences. Discourse involves higher-level combinations of sentences.

■ Understanding and producing language— including pattern recognition of words and the hierarchical structure of language—involve bottom-up and top-down processing.

■ In infancy, babies emit all the phonemes that exist in all the languages of the world. At about 6 months of age, babbling sounds narrow to include only the sounds specific to their native tongue. By ages 4 to 5, most children have learned the basic grammatical rules for combining words into meaningful sentences.

■ Language development seems to depend heavily on innate mechanisms that permit the learning and production of language, provided that the child is exposed to an appropriate linguistic environment during a sensitive period that extends from early childhood to puberty.

■ Some researchers have attempted to teach apes to use hand signs or keyboard symbols to communicate in language-like fashion. At best, apes are capable of learning, combining, and communicating with symbols at a level similar to that of a human toddler. Skeptics question, however, whether they can learn syntax and generate novel ideas.

■ Although research findings are not entirely consistent, it appears that a second language is most easily mastered and fluently spoken if it is learned during a sensitive period that ranges from early childhood possibly through mid-adolesence. Bilingual children tend to perform better than monolingual children on a variety of cognitive tasks.

■ In general, it appears that when people acquire a second language early in life or learn it to a high degree of proficiency later in life, both languages share a common neural network.

■ Language influences what people think and how effectively they think. Expansion of vocabulary allows people to encode and process information in more sophisticated ways.

THINKING

Can pure thought move mountains? Perhaps not yet, but pure thought can play a video game. In a scene that could be taken right out of a science-fiction movie, 19-year-old Tristan Lundemo looks at a video screen located next to his hospital bed and, without speaking a word or lifting a finger, makes a red electronic cursor (similar to the paddle in the video game *Pong*) move up, down, to the left, or to the right, merely by thinking it (Paulson, 2004). In this literal mind game, Lundemo tries to move the cursor quickly enough to strike rectangular targets that pop up and then disappear from random locations on the video screen.

THOUGHT, BRAIN, AND MIND

Lundemo is a patient with epilepsy who agreed to participate in a brain-computer interface study while undergoing diagnostic tests at Seattle's Harborview Medical Center (Figure 8.16a). During a session, the researchers attach 72 electrodes to Lundemo's scalp to record his brain's electrical activity. A computer analyzes the patterns and intensity of these brain signals and uses that information to control the movement of the cursor on the video screen. It's not quite that simple, however, as computer and human essentially have to adapt to each other and learn the precise patterns of thought that will make the cursor move. Lundemo was a fast study (as was the computer), and in two days he mastered the task. Electric mind over electronic matter.

As Lundemo notes, now "I just think up, up, up or over left, left, left and it moves" (Paulson, 2004, A15). Figure 8.16b shows that several brain regions become most active when Lundemo's thought moves the cursor in a particular direction. The pattern of brain activity changes when he has a thought that moves the cursor in different direction. Researchers hope that this technology eventually will improve the lives of people who have lost limbs or are paralyzed.

As we discussed in Chapter 5, according to some neuroscientists, conscious thought arises from the unified activity of different brain areas. In essence, of the many brain regions and connecting circuits that are active at any instant, a particular subset becomes joined in unified activity that is strong enough to become a conscious thought or perception (Dehaene & Naccache, 2001; Koch, 2004). The specific pattern of brain activity that composes this

(a)

(b)

FIGURE 8.16

The power of pure thought. (a) With electrodes attached to his scalp underneath the bandage, Tristan Lundemo uses his thoughts to control the movement of a cursor on a video screen. (b) Various brain regions become active when Lundemo moves the cursor in a particular direction.

dominant subset varies from moment to moment as we experience different thoughts and respond to changing stimuli. Even altering one's thought from "move up" to "move down," "move left," or "move right" produces a different pattern of brain activity. Although we're still far from understanding exactly how the brain produces thought, it is clear that from a biological level of analysis, thought exists as patterns of neural activity.

▶ **Focus 12**
What are concepts, and how do they enter into propositions? How are prototypes involved in concept formation?

Subjectively, at the psychological level, thinking may seem to be the internal language of the mind—somewhat like "inner speech"—but it actually includes several mental activities. One mode of thought does indeed take the form of verbal sentences that we say or hear in our minds. This is called **propositional thought** *because it expresses a proposition, or statement,* such as "I'm hungry" or "It's almost time for dinner." Another thought mode, **imaginal thought,** *consists of images that we can see, hear, or feel in our mind.* A third mode, **motoric thought,** *relates to mental representations of mo-*

tor movements, such as throwing an object. All three modes of thinking enter into our abilities to reason, solve problems, and engage in many forms of intelligent behavior. In this chapter, however, we'll focus on propositional and imaginal thought.

CONCEPTS AND PROPOSITIONS

Much of our thinking occurs in the form of **propositions,** *statements that express ideas.* All propositions consist of concepts combined in a particular way. For example, "college students are intelligent people" is a proposition in which the two concepts "college students" and "intelligent people" are linked by the verb *are* (Figure 8.17). **Concepts** *are basic units of semantic memory—mental categories into which we place objects, activities, abstractions* (such as "liberal" and "conservative"), *and events that have essential features in common.* Every psychological term you are learning in this course is a concept. Concepts can be acquired through explicit instruction or through our own observations of similarities and differences among various objects and events.

Many concepts are difficult to define explicitly. For example, you are quite familiar with the concept "vegetable," yet you might have difficulty coming up with an explicit definition of what a vegetable is. However, you can quickly think of a good example of a vegetable, such as broccoli or carrots. According to Eleanor Rosch (1977), many concepts are defined by **prototypes,** *the most typical and familiar members of a category, or class.* Rosch suggests that we often decide which category something belongs to by its degree of resemblance to the prototype.

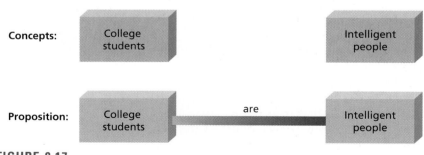

Concepts: College students   Intelligent people

Proposition: College students ——are—— Intelligent people

FIGURE 8.17

Concepts are building blocks of thinking and reasoning. Concepts can be combined into propositions to create simple and complex thoughts, and the propositions can serve as the basis for reasoning and discourse.

Consider the following questions:

Is an eagle a bird?

Is a penguin a bird?

Is a bat a bird?

According to the prototype view, you should have come to a quicker decision on the first question than on the last two. Why? Because an eagle fits most people's "bird" prototype better than does a penguin (which is a bird, though it lacks some essential prototypic features, such as the ability to fly) or a bat (which is not a bird, even though it flies). Experiments measuring how quickly participants responded yes or no to the preceding questions have found that it does indeed take most people longer to decide whether penguins or bats are birds (Rips, 1997).

The use of prototypes is perhaps the most elementary method of forming concepts. It requires that we note *only* similarities among objects. Thus children's early concepts are based on prototypes of the objects and people they encounter personally. They then decide if new objects are similar enough to the prototype to be a "Mommy," a "cookie," a "doggie," and so on (Smith & Zarate, 1992). Because prototypes may differ as a result of personal experience, there is considerable room for arbitrariness and individual differences in prototypic concepts. Thus one person's "terrorist" can be another person's "freedom fighter."

How we state propositions can influence how we try to solve a problem, reason through to a decision, or make a judgment (Anderson, 1991). For example, in one study, college students who were told that a cancer treatment had a 50 percent success rate judged the treatment to be significantly more effective and expressed a greater willingness to have it administered to a family member than did participants who were told that it had a 50 percent failure rate (Kahneman & Tversky, 1979). Representing outcomes in terms of positives or negatives has this effect because people tend to assign greater costs to negative outcomes (such as losing $100) than they assign value to an equivalent positive outcome (finding $100). The proposition that "there is a 50 percent chance of failure" evokes thoughts about the patient's dying and causes the 50-50 treatment to appear riskier (Slovic et al., 1988). Thus differences in how we verbally represent choices and goals can make a difference in our perceptions and decisions.

REASONING

One aspect of intelligent thinking is the ability to reason and think logically. Such thinking helps us acquire knowledge, make sound decisions, and solve problems. Reasoning helps us avoid the hazards and time-consuming efforts of trial and error. Most of the time, people solve problems by developing solutions in their minds before applying them in the external world. For example, if you decide to build a bookcase, you are unlikely to nail or screw boards together at random in the hope that the finished product will serve your purposes. Instead, you will develop mental representations to guide your efforts, such as a visual image of the finished product and general principles for its successful construction (e.g., "build from the bottom up").

Deductive Reasoning

Two types of reasoning underlie many of our attempts to make decisions and solve problems (Figure 8.18). In **deductive reasoning,** *we reason from the top down, that is, from general principles to a conclusion about a specific case.* When people reason deductively, they begin with a set of *premises* (propositions assumed to be true) and determine what the premises imply about a specific situation. Deductive reasoning is the basis of formal mathematics and logic. Logicians regard it as the strongest and most valid form of reasoning because the conclusion *cannot be false* if the premises (factual statements) are true. More formally, the underlying deductive principle may be stated: Given the general proposition "if X then Y," if X occurs, then you can infer Y. Thus, to use a classic deductive argument, or *syllogism,*

> *If* all humans are mortal (first premise), and
>
> *if* Socrates is a human (second premise),
>
> *then* Socrates must be mortal (conclusion).

 In the video, "Categorizing Pictures at Age 4," in Chapter 8 of your CD, a child uses prototypes and concepts to identify and classify pictures he is shown.

▶ **Focus 13**

Distinguish between deductive reasoning and inductive reasoning. How do irrelevant information and belief bias affect reasoning?

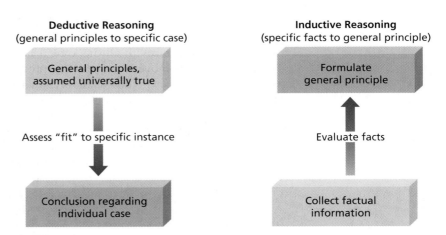

Deductive Reasoning
(general principles to specific case)

General principles, assumed universally true

Assess "fit" to specific instance

Conclusion regarding individual case

Inductive Reasoning
(specific facts to general principle)

Formulate general principle

Evaluate facts

Collect factual information

FIGURE 8.18

A comparison of deductive and inductive reasoning.

Inductive Reasoning

In **inductive reasoning,** *we reason from the bottom up, starting with specific facts and trying to develop a general principle.* Scientists use induction when they discover general principles, or laws, as a result of observing a number of specific instances of a phenomenon. After Ivan Pavlov observed repeatedly that the dogs in his laboratory began to salivate when approached by the experimenter who fed them, he began to think in terms of a general principle that eventually became the foundation of classical conditioning (repeated CS-UCS pairings produce a CR). A college student who experiences repeated negative consequences when she gets drunk may eventually conclude that binge drinking is a high-risk behavior to be avoided.

An important difference between deductive and inductive reasoning lies in the certainty of the results. Deductive conclusions are certain to be true *if* the premises are true, but inductive reasoning leads to likelihood rather than certainty. Even if we reason inductively in a flawless manner, the possibility of error always remains because some new observation may disprove our conclusion. Thus you may observe that every person named Jordan you have ever met has blue eyes, but it would obviously be inaccurate to reason that, therefore, all people named Jordan have blue eyes.

In daily life and in science, inductive and deductive reasoning may be used at different points in problem solving and decision making. For example, psychologists often make informal observations (e.g., hearing about crime victims like Kitty Genovese who do not receive help when many bystanders are present). These specific observations may prompt them to construct an initial explanation (e.g., diffusion of responsibility) for the observed phenomenon. This is inductive reasoning, so the explanation could be wrong even if it is consistent with all the known facts. Therefore scientists move to a deductive process in which they design experiments to formally test specific *if-then* hypotheses, moving now from a general explanatory principle to a specific observation (the experiment's results). If the results of these experimental tests do *not* support their hypotheses, they conclude that their explanation or theory cannot be correct and needs to be revised or discarded.

Stumbling Blocks in Reasoning

The ability to reason effectively is a key factor in critical thinking, in making sound decisions, and in solving problems. Unfortunately, several factors may prevent us from selecting the information needed to draw sound conclusions.

Distraction by Irrelevant Information   Distinguishing relevant from irrelevant information can be challenging. Consider the following problem. As you solve it, analyze the mental steps you take, and do not read on until you have decided on an answer.

> Your drawer contains 19 black socks and 13 blue socks. Without turning on the light, how many socks do you have to pull out of the drawer to have a matching pair?

As you solved the problem, what information entered into your reasoning? Did you take into account the fact that there were 19 black socks and 13 blue ones? If so, you're like many of Robert Sternberg's (1988) Yale University students who did the same thing, thereby making the problem much more difficult than it should be. In this case, all that matters is how many *colors* of socks there are. It wouldn't matter if there were 1,000 socks of each color; once you have selected any 3 of them, you are bound to have at least 2 of the same color. People often fail to solve problems because they simply don't focus on the *relevant* information. Instead, they take into account irrelevant information that leads them astray.

Belief Bias   **Belief bias** *is the tendency to abandon logical rules in favor of our own personal beliefs.* To illustrate, let us consider an experiment in which college students were asked to judge whether conclusions followed logically from syllogisms like the following:

> All things that are smoked are good for one's health.
>
> Cigarettes are smoked.
>
> Therefore cigarettes are good for one's health.

What do you think? Is the logic correct? Actually, it is. If we accept (for the moment) that the premises are true, then the conclusion *does* follow logically from the premises. Yet students in one study frequently claimed that the conclusion was not logically correct because they disagreed with the first premise that all things smoked are good for one's health. In this case, their beliefs about the harmful effects of smoking got in the way of their logic. When the same syllogism was presented with a nonsense word such as *ramadians* substituted for *cigarettes*, the errors in logic were markedly reduced (Markovits & Nantel, 1989). Incidentally, we agree that the conclusion that cigarettes are good for one's health is factually false. However, it is false because the first premise is false, not because the logic is faulty. Unfortunately, many people confuse factual correctness with logical correctness. The two are not at all the same.

PROBLEM SOLVING AND DECISION MAKING

Humans have an unmatched ability to solve problems and adapt to the challenges of their world. As illustrated in our chapter-opening vignette, the remarkable problem-solving abilities of the pilot and copilot of Flight 118 enabled them to rapidly implement and execute a plan for successfully flying their badly mangled jetliner and saving the lives of the terrified passengers.

Steps in Problem Solving

In accomplishing their astonishing feat, the pilot and copilot had to rapidly gain an understanding of the problem they were facing, generate a solution, test that solution, and then evaluate the results. Problem solving typically proceeds through four stages (Figure 8.19). How well we carry out each of these stages determines our success in solving the problem.

Understanding, or Framing, the Problem   Most of us have had the experience of feeling totally frustrated in our attempts to solve a problem. We may even think that the problem is unsolvable. Then someone suggests a new way of looking at the problem, and the solution suddenly becomes obvious. How we mentally represent, or *frame*, a problem can make a huge difference. Consider the following problem (illustrated in Figure 8.20):

> Train A leaves Baltimore for its 50-mile trip to Washington, DC, at a constant speed of 25 mph. At the same time, train B leaves Washington, bound for Baltimore at the same speed of 25 mph. The world's fastest crow leaves Baltimore at the same time as train A, flying above the tracks toward Washington at a speed of 60 mph. When the crow encounters train B, it turns and flies back to train A, then instantly reverses its direction and flies back to train B. The supercharged bird continues this sequence until trains A and B meet midway between Baltimore and Washington. Try to solve this problem before reading on: What is the total distance the bird will have traveled in its excursions between trains A and B?

Many people approach the problem as a distance problem, which is quite natural because the question is stated in terms of distance. They try to compute how far the bird will fly during each segment of its flight between trains A and B, sometimes filling up several pages with increasingly frenzied computations in the process. But suppose you approach the problem by asking not how far the bird will fly but *how long* it will take the trains to meet. The crow will have flown the same period of time at 60 mph. Now that you have reframed it as a time problem, the problem becomes much easier to solve. (Check your solution against the answer given on page 310.)

As you can see, our initial understanding of a problem is a key step toward a successful solution. If we frame a problem poorly, we can easily be led into a maze of blind alleys and ineffective solutions. If we frame it optimally, we at least have a chance to generate an effective solution. A knack for framing problems in effective ways that differ from conventional expectations has been called *outside-the-box thinking*; it is a prized ability in many academic and work environments.

Generating Potential Solutions   Once we have interpreted the problem, we can begin to formulate potential solutions or explanations. Ideally, we might proceed in the following fashion:

1. Determine which procedures and explanations will be considered.

2. Determine which solutions are consistent with the evidence that has so far been observed. Rule out any solutions that do not fit the evidence.

Stage 1
Interpret (frame) and understand the problem

Stage 2
Generate hypotheses or possible solutions

Stage 3
Test the solutions or hypotheses, seeking to disconfirm one or more of them

Stage 4
Evaluate results and, if necessary, revise step 1, 2, or 3

FIGURE 8.19

The stages of problem solving.

▶ **Focus 14**
Summarize the four major stages of problem solving. Why are problem framing and mental sets important?

Baltimore ◀━━━━━━━━▶ Washington
50 miles
60 mph
25 mph
25 mph

FIGURE 8.20

The crow-and-trains problem. (The answer appears on page 310.)

FIGURE 8.21

Luchins's water jugs problems.
Using containers A, B, and C with the capacities shown in the table, how would you measure out the volumes indicated in the right-hand column? You may discover a general problem-solving schema that fits all seven problems.

	Given jugs of these sizes			Measure out this much water
Problem	**A**	**B**	**C**	
1	21	127	3	100
2	14	46	5	22
3	18	43	10	5
4	7	42	6	23
5	20	57	4	29
6	23	49	3	20
7	15	39	3	18

▶ **Focus 15**
What are problem-solving schemas? Distinguish between algorithms and heuristics. Describe the means-ends and subgoal analysis heuristics.

Testing the Solutions Consider the possible solutions that remain. If a solution requires you to choose between specific explanations, ask if there is any test that should give one result if one explanation is true and another result if a different explanation is true. If so, evaluate the explanations again in light of the evidence from that test. In essence, this is what scientists do when they design experiments.

Let us consider a common difficulty in the process of discovering and applying solutions to problems. Consider problem 1 in Figure 8.21:

> You have a 21-cup jug, a 127-cup jug, and a 3-cup jug. Drawing and discarding as much water as you like, how will you measure out exactly 100 cups of water?

Try to solve all seven problems in Figure 8.21 in order, and write down your calculations for each one before reading on. Does a common solution emerge? If so, can you specify what it is?

As you worked the problems, you probably discovered that they are all solvable by the same formula, namely $B - A - (2 \times C) =$ desired amount. In problem 1, for example, $127 - 21 - (2 \times 3) = 100$. If you discovered this, it gave you a logical formula that you could apply to the rest of the problems. And it worked, didn't it? However, by applying this successful formula to problems 6 and 7, you may have missed even easier solutions for these last two problems, namely $A - C$ for problem 6 and $A + C$ for problem 7.

Abraham Luchins (1942) developed the water jugs problems to demonstrate the manner in which a **mental set**—*the tendency to stick to solutions that have worked in the past*—can result in less-effective problem solving. Luchins found that most people who worked on problems 6 and 7 were blinded by the mental set they had developed by working the first five problems. In contrast, people who had not worked on problems 1 through 5 almost always applied the simple solutions to problems 6 and 7. Studies of mental set show how easy it is to become rigidly fixated on one particular approach that has been successful in the past.

Evaluating Results The final stage of problem solving is to evaluate the solutions. As we saw in the water jugs problems, even solutions that prove successful may not be the easiest or the best. Thus after solving a problem, we should ask ourselves, "Would there have been an easier or more effective way to accomplish the same objective?" This can lead to the development of additional problem-solving principles that may be applicable to future problems.

The Role of Problem-Solving Schemas

In solving problems, people often learn to employ shortcut methods that apply to specific situations (Rips, 1997). **Problem-solving schemas** *are like mental blueprints or step-by-step scripts for selecting information and solving specialized classes of problems.* We have all learned a great many of them, from schemas for cooking dinner to schemas for studying and mastering academic course content (Figure 8.22). Once we master them, we seem to know what to do without having

FIGURE 8.22

Experienced snowboarders and skiers learn schemas for various types of snow, and the discriminations made possible by these schemas can affect planning and decision making. This boarder might approach a slope covered with "powder" differently than one covered with "corn" or "hardpack" because of their different effects on the board and potentially on the boarder's safety.

to engage in step-by-step formal problem-solving procedures.

Algorithms and Heuristics   *Algorithms* and *heuristics* are two important strategies for problem solving. **Algorithms** *are formulas or procedures that automatically generate correct solutions.* Mathematical and chemical formulas are algorithms; if you use them correctly, you will always get the correct answer. Consider another example of an algorithm. If the letters of a word are scrambled in random order to produce an anagram like *teralbay,* we can identify the word by using a process in which we rearrange the eight letters in all possible combinations—all 40,320 combinations, that is. As you can see, using algorithms can be very time-consuming. You might therefore decide to use some rule-of-thumb strategy, such as trying out only consonants in the first and last positions, because you know that more words begin and end in consonants than in vowels. When we adopt rule-of-thumb approaches like this, we are using heuristics.

Heuristics *are general problem-solving strategies that we apply to certain classes of situations.* Means-ends analysis is one example of a heuristic (Newell & Simon, 1972). In **means-ends analysis,** *we identify differences between the present situation and the desired state, or goal, and then make changes that will reduce these differences.* Assume, for example, that you have a 30-page paper due at the end of the term and have not begun working on it yet. The present situation is no pages written; the desired end state is a 30-page paper. What, specifically, needs to be done to reduce that discrepancy, and how are you going to do it?

You would be foolish to decide, "There are 30 days until the paper is due, so all I have to do is write 1 page a day." This approach is likely to result in a 30-page paper, but it is unlikely to result in one that will earn a passing grade. Instead, you would be wise to use another heuristic known as **subgoal analysis,** *formulating subgoals, or intermediate steps, toward a solution.* In this case, your expertise as a student will likely lead you to break down the task of writing a paper into subgoals, such as (1) choosing a topic, (2) doing library and Internet research on the topic to get the facts you need, (3) organizing the facts within a general outline of the paper, (4) writing a first draft or specific sections of the paper, (5) reorganizing and refining the first draft, and so on. In so doing, a huge task becomes a series of smaller and more manageable tasks, each with a subgoal that leads you toward the ultimate goal of a quality 30-page paper.

FIGURE 8.23

The Tower-of-Hanoi problem. The object is to move the rings one at a time from peg 1 to peg 3 in no more than seven moves. Only the top ring on a peg can be moved, and a larger ring can never be placed on top of a smaller one. (The answer appears on page 310.)

The value of setting subgoals can be seen in the tower-of-Hanoi problem, which is explained in Figure 8.23. Breaking this task into subgoals helps us solve the problem. The first subgoal is to get ring C to the bottom of peg 3. The second subgoal is to get ring B over to peg 3. With these two subgoals accomplished, the final subgoal of getting ring A to peg 3 is quite easy. The solution requires planning (hypothesis formation), checking, and revising hypotheses. The correct seven-step sequence of moves appears on page 310.

Heuristics enter not only into problem-solving strategies but also into a wide range of decisions and judgments, from judgments about other people to judgments about our own health to decisions about buying products (Katapodi et al., 2005). As we shall see, heuristics can also contribute to errors in judgment.

Uncertainty, Heuristics, and Decision Making

Few decisions in everyday life can be made with the absolute certainty that comes from applying some mathematical formula or other algorithm. Typically, the best we can hope for is a decision that has a high probability of a positive outcome. Because we seldom know what the exact probabilities are (for example, how likely it is that the stock market will be up or down when you need your money in the future, or how probable it is that a new dating relationship will become permanent), we tend to apply certain heuristics to form judgments of likelihood.

In daily life, we routinely make decisions about what other people are like. Suppose, for

▶ **Focus 16**
What role do uncertainty and heuristics play in decision making? How do the representativeness and availability of heuristics distort probability judgments?

example, you are given the following description of a young woman:

> Linda is 31 years old, single, outspoken, and very bright. She majored in philosophy. As a student, she was deeply concerned with issues of discrimination and social justice, and she also participated in anti-nuclear demonstrations.

Now rate the likelihood that each of the following hypotheses is true. Use 1 to indicate the most likely statement, 8 to indicate the least likely statement, and any number between 2 and 7 to indicate the likelihood of the second most likely statement.

_____ Hypothesis A: Linda is active in the feminist movement.

_____ Hypothesis B: Linda is a bank teller.

_____ Hypothesis C: Linda is active in the feminist movement and is a bank teller.

Cognitive psychologists Daniel Kahneman and Amos Tversky (1982) used this problem in a series of experiments that studied the role of heuristics in judgment and decision making. They showed that certain heuristics underlie much of our inductive decision making (drawing conclusions from facts) and that their misuse results in many of our thinking errors. Let us examine how that occurs.

The Representativeness Heuristic "What does it look (or seem) like?" This is probably the first decision faced by our perceptual system when it processes incoming stimuli. Earlier, we discussed the importance of prototypes in concept formation. We use the **representativeness heuristic** *to infer how closely something or someone fits our prototype for a particular concept, or class, and therefore how likely it is to be a member of that class.* In essence, we are asking, "How likely is it that this [person, object, event] *represents* that class?" In this case, does Linda seem like a feminist? This is a perfectly logical question to ask ourselves. Sometimes, however, our use of representativeness can cause us to make decisions that fly in the face of logic.

For example, what was your order of likelihood judgments concerning Linda? Figure 8.24 shows the mean likelihood estimates that college students attached to each statement (a low number indicating greater likelihood). First of all, there is a clear tendency to favor hypothesis A (Linda is a feminist). This is not surprising; the description does make her sound like a feminist. However, the significant finding is that hypothesis C (Linda is a feminist bank teller) was favored over hypothesis B (Linda is a bank teller). But this

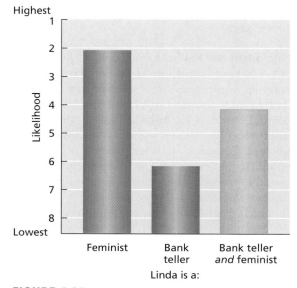

FIGURE 8.24

Illogical judgments. This graph shows the mean likelihood judgments made by participants on the basis of the description of Linda (top left column). Overall, people judge it to be more likely that Linda is a bank teller and a feminist rather than just a bank teller. Logically, this is impossible. SOURCE: Based on Tversky & Kahneman, 1982.

cannot possibly be correct. Why not? Because everyone who is both a feminist and a bank teller is also *simply* a bank teller. Furthermore, there are many bank tellers who are not feminists, and Linda could be one of them. Stated differently, any person is more likely to be simply a bank teller than to be a bank teller *and* a feminist—or, for that matter, a bank teller and anything else. People who say that hypothesis C is more likely than hypothesis B (and about 85 percent of people given this problem do so) violate the logical principle that the combination of two events cannot be more likely than either event alone.

Tversky and Kahneman believe that the reason people make this sort of error is that they confuse representativeness with probability. Linda represents our prototype for a feminist bank teller better than she fits our prototype for a bank teller. Therefore, we erroneously think the former is more likely than the latter. Notice how this argument fits with the ideas about memory discussed in Chapter 7. The description of Linda as "outspoken" and "concerned with issues of discrimination and social justice" serves a *priming* function, activating the elements in memory that are associated with the concept of "feminist," so it is hard to think of Linda without thinking of a feminist. On the other hand, there is nothing in Linda's description that would activate the concept of "bank teller." Thus if Linda is to be a bank teller at all, we think she must be a feminist bank teller.

The Availability Heuristic Another heuristic that can sometimes lead us astray is the **availability heuristic,** *which causes us to base judgments and decisions on the availability of information in memory.* We tend to remember events that are most important and significant to us. Usually that principle serves us well, keeping important information at the forefront in our memories, ready to be applied. But if something easily comes to mind, we may exaggerate the likelihood that it could occur. For example, consider each of the following pairs and choose the more likely cause of death:

- murder or suicide?
- botulism or lightning?
- asthma or tornadoes?

When Paul Slovic and coworkers (1988) asked people to make these judgments, 80 percent chose murder over suicide as the more likely cause of death, 63 percent chose botulism over lightning, and 43 percent chose tornadoes over asthma. In actuality, public health statistics show that people are 25 percent less likely to be murdered than to kill themselves, that lightning kills 53 times more people than botulism does, and that death by asthma is 21 times more likely than death as a result of a tornado. Yet murder, botulism, and tornados are more highly and dramatically publicized when they do occur and thus are more likely to come to mind.

A recent memorable event can increase people's belief that they may suffer a similar fate. After the terrorist hijackings of September 11, 2001, airline bookings and tourism declined dramatically within the United States for a significant period. Demand for office space in landmark high-rise buildings also declined, and many businesses sought space in less conspicuous suburban settings. Similarly, in the summer of 1975, when Steven Spielberg's movie *Jaws* burned into people's memories graphic images of a great white shark devouring swimmers at a New England seaside town, beach attendance all over the country decreased. In fact, *Jaws* was blamed for a drop in tourism on the New England coast so dramatic that in the summer of 1976 many beachfront resorts nearly went bankrupt. The images available in memory—even though the movie was clearly fiction—increased people's perceived likelihood that they, too, could become shark bait.

Thus at times the representativeness and availability heuristics can lead us astray by distorting our estimates of how likely an event really is. In other words, they can blind us to the *base rates,* or actual frequencies, at which things occur.

In general, it's always best to find out what the actual probabilities are and make judgments on that basis; that's the strategy that allows insurance companies to flourish.

Confirmation Bias and Overconfidence

Sometimes one of the most challenging tasks is obtaining new evidence to test a hypothesis or solution. But what's the best type of evidence? Here is a principle that may seem puzzling to you: The best thing we can do to test our ideas is to seek evidence that will *disconfirm* them, rather than look for evidence that supports them. Why? Because the most informative piece of evidence we can obtain is one that rules out a hypothesis or idea. Disconfirming evidence proves conclusively that our idea *cannot* be true in its current form. In contrast, confirming evidence only supports our idea. It doesn't prove it with certainty, for it is possible that some future observation will disconfirm it or that another explanation fits the facts even better. Especially in the area of causal beliefs, you can be absolutely sure when you're wrong about something, but you can't be absolutely sure when you're right because there might be a better explanation or an impending observation that calls your belief into question.

Following this disconfirmation principle is easier said than done, because people are often unwilling to challenge their cherished beliefs. Instead, they are prone to fall into a trap called **confirmation bias,** *tending to look for evidence that will confirm what they currently believe rather than looking for evidence that could disconfirm their beliefs.* Many studies have shown that if people have strong beliefs about something, they are very selective in the kinds of information they expose themselves to. They seek out like-minded people and compatible mass media sources and Internet sites. Likewise, when people are given the choice of what kinds of feedback they would like to have about themselves, they have a strong tendency to seek out and recall feedback from others that confirms their beliefs about themselves. They tend to avoid and forget evidence that disconfirms these self-beliefs (Swann et al., 1992). The fact that people find it difficult or even upsetting to test and challenge their ideas, particularly those to which they are strongly committed, can be a major obstacle to getting the evidence needed to make a correct decision.

Confirmation bias often contributes to a distorted sense of how correct our opinions and beliefs are. **Overconfidence,** *the tendency to overestimate one's correctness in factual knowledge, beliefs, and*

▶ **Focus 17**
When making decisions, why is disconfirming evidence important? How does overconfidence contribute to confirmation bias?

FIGURE 8.25

Displaying overconfidence.
Overconfidence is illustrated in the discrepancy between the accuracy with which students predicted that specific events would occur to them during the coming academic year and the degree of confidence that they had in their predictions. Overall, accuracy was considerably lower than confidence level, even for those events for which the students expressed complete certainty. SOURCE: Based on Vallone et al., 1990.

▶ **Focus 18**
Discuss some factors that inhibit and facilitate creative problem solving.

decisions, is another reason people do not challenge their beliefs. This tendency, like confirmation bias, is widespread. In one study, college students were asked at the beginning of the academic year to make predictions about how likely it was (from 0 percent to 100 percent) that they would experience any of a long list of personal events, such as drop-ping a course, breaking up with a romantic partner, or joining a fraternity or sorority. They also indicated how confident they were in their probability estimates (i.e., how likely it was that they would be correct). At the end of the following semester and at the end of the academic year, they indicated which events had in fact occurred. As shown in Figure 8.25, confidence exceeded accuracy overall, and the difference between the two was equally great when the students were originally 100 percent confident in their predictions (Vallone et al., 1990). Similar overconfidence effects have been found in studies involving investment professionals, military strategists, weather forecasters, and other populations. It apparently stems from people's need to see themselves as knowledgeable and competent (Blanton et al., 2001).

Overconfidence and confirmation bias can be potent adversaries in our search for correct predictions and decisions. When we're confident in the correctness of our views and reluctant to seek evidence that could prove them wrong, we can easily be blinded to the truth.

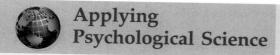

Applying Psychological Science   Guidelines for Creative Problem Solving

Creativity *is the ability to produce something that is both new and valuable.* The product may be virtually anything, from a creative painting to a novel approach to solving a problem. In this case, we will be concerned with creative problem solving.

Research on reasoning offers insights into how effective and creative problem solvers think and how they approach problems. In some ways, as experts so often demonstrate, there is no substitute for experience, for it teaches us useful heuristics and problem-solving schemas. Yet one of the marks of creativity is the ability to break out of conventional schemas when the occasion demands it and to engage in **divergent thinking,** *the generation of novel ideas that depart from the norm* (Guilford, 1959). In part, this means being able to apply concepts or propositions from one domain to another unrelated domain in a manner that produces a new insight (Chi, 1997). It also means refusing to be constrained by traditional approaches to a problem. Creative people are, in this respect, intellectual rebels. The constraints created by the tried-and-true can be difficult to overcome.

Consider, for example, the nine-dot problem in Figure 8.26. Many people have difficulty solving this problem. Did you? If so, it is probably because you imposed a traditional but unnecessary constraint on yourself and tried to stay within the boundary formed by the dots. But nothing in the statement of the problem forced you to do so. To solve the problem, you have to think outside the box.

FIGURE 8.26

The nine-dot problem. Without lifting your pencil from the paper, draw no more than four straight lines that will pass through all nine dots. (The answer appears on page 310.)

Creative problem solvers are often able to ask themselves questions like the following to stimulate divergent thinking (Simonton, 1999):

- What would work instead?
- Are there new ways to use this? How else could it be used if I modified it in some way? By adding, subtracting, or rearranging parts, or by modifying the sequence in which things are done, could I make it more useful?
- Do the elements remind me of anything else? What else is like this?

FIGURE 8.27

The candlestick problem. Using these objects, find a way to mount the candle on a wall so it functions like a lamp. (The answer appears on page 310.)

Use some of these questions when trying to solve the candlestick problem illustrated in Figure 8.27.

Solving the problem requires using some of the objects in unconventional ways. Many people, however, are prevented from doing so because of **functional fixedness**, *the tendency to be so fixed in their perception of the proper function of an object or procedure that they are blinded to new ways of using it.*

Sometimes creative solutions to problems seemingly appear out of the blue, suddenly popping into our mind in a flash of insight after we have temporarily given up and put the problem aside. **Incubation** *is the name given to this phenomenon; it is as if the problem is incubating and being worked on at a subconscious level* (Cattell, 1971). Sometimes the best approach when we are stymied by a problem is to put it aside for a while and gain a bit of psychological distance from it. Perhaps this causes mental sets and other biases to dissipate somewhat, allowing a new idea to emerge (Anderson, 1985). In addition, as time passes, new internal or external stimuli may activate a different perspective on the problem, aiding its solution (Bastik, 1982).

As you can see, creative problem solving involves many of the principles discussed earlier in the chapter. We see the operation of means-ends reasoning, the testing of hypotheses, and the need to overcome biases that may cause us to overestimate or underestimate the likelihood of certain outcomes. Here are some other general problem-solving guidelines:

1. When you encounter a new problem you haven't solved before, ask yourself if it is similar to other problems you've solved. Maybe the schema for solving a problem with similar features can be modified to solve this one. Take advantage of the storehouse of knowledge in long-term memory.
2. Make a true effort to test your ideas. Try to find evidence that would disconfirm your ideas, not evidence that would confirm what you already believe. For example, if you are asked to accept statement X as true, see if you can imagine situations in which X would be false. Beware of the human tendency toward confirmation bias.
3. Be careful not to confuse representativeness with probability. The bird you see that looks too big to be a sparrow but just the right size to be a rare Patagonian warbler is probably . . . a big sparrow; the odds are overwhelmingly in favor of its being a sparrow because there are so many more sparrows (even big ones) than Patagonian warblers.
4. Make use of the means-ends problem-solving heuristic. Ask yourself what you are trying to accomplish, what the present state of affairs is, and what means you have for reducing the discrepancy.
5. Don't be afraid to use pencil and paper. Orderly notes and schematics can substitute for our rather limited working memory and allow us to have more information at hand to work with.

KNOWLEDGE, EXPERTISE, AND WISDOM

Knowledge forms a foundation for expertise and wisdom, and knowledge acquisition comes in many forms. At times it may involve little more than memorizing facts or the procedures to perform simple skills. At other times it involves learning concepts and principles, discovering "personal truths," and acquiring the ability to perform complex cognitive or physical skills. Each culture passes down its knowledge and worldview from one generation to the next through language, instruction, and socialization. This vast library of knowledge, shaped by cultural learning and by other environmental experiences (including trial-and-error learning), also supports the reasoning, decision-making, and problem-solving skills that we have been discussing in this chapter.

Acquiring Knowledge: Schemas and Scripts

We can also think of knowledge acquisition as a process of building schemas. Most broadly, a **schema** *is a mental framework, an organized pattern of thought about some aspect of the world.* Concepts and categories represent types of schemas, and together they help you build a mental framework of your world, such as "interesting versus dull people" or "easy versus hard exams." Algorithms and heuristics also are types of schemas—problem-solving schemas—that provide you

▶ **Focus 19**
What roles do schemas play in knowledge acquisition and expertise?

with mental frameworks for solving certain types of problems.

Another type of schema, called a **script,** *is a mental framework concerning a sequence of events that usually unfolds in a regular, almost standardized order.* For example, if we tell you that "John and Linda went to the movies," these mere seven words convey a lot of information because "going to the movies" is a fairly standardized (i.e., scripted) activity. You can reasonably assume that John and Linda got to the theater, waited in the ticket line and bought tickets (or bought them online), entered the theater where someone checked their tickets, bought a snack, found seats, and so on. The scripts that you learn—"attending class," "shopping," "driving," and so on—provide knowledge to guide and interpret actions. In sum, your knowledge grows as you acquire new scripts, concepts, and other types of schemas; as your existing schemas become more complex; and as you form connections between schemas.

The Nature of Expertise

Schemas help explain what it means to be an expert. Masters and grand masters in chess can glance at a chessboard and quickly plan strategies and make adjustments in the heat of competition. The world's best players can store in memory as many as 50,000 board configurations, together with the locations of the individual pieces (Chase & Simon, 1973). For years, world chess champion Gary Kasparov's sophisticated schemas enabled him to regularly defeat chess-playing computers that used logical rules, even those capable of logically analyzing up to 100,000 moves per second. It took Deep Blue, a 1.4-ton behemoth capable of calculating at a rate of 200 million positions and 200,000 moves per second, to finally defeat the schemas within Kasparov's 3-pound brain (Figure 8.28).

Expert athletic coaches, surgeons, military leaders, and political consultants all rely on the schemas they have developed from experience. Training world-class athletes, performing medical operations, planning military strategies, and running political campaigns are very different activities. Nevertheless, researchers have found a common factor underlying expertise: Experts have developed many schemas to guide problem solving in their field, and just as critically, they are much better than novices at recognizing when each schema should be applied (Montgomery et al., 2005). Applying the correct mental blueprint provides a proven route to solving a problem quickly and effectively.

Expert Schemas and Memory

Consider what the ability to flexibly apply schemas means in terms of what we know about human memory and pattern recognition. As you learned in Chapter 7, schemas reside in long-term memory. Because they rely on learned schemas, experts take advantage of their spacious long-term memory. They can quickly analyze a problem deductively, select the retrieval cues needed to pull the appropriate schema from memory, and apply the schema to solve the problem at hand (Horn & Masunaga, 2000). In contrast, novices who haven't yet learned specialized schemas must use general problem-solving methods in working memory, the space-limited blackboard of the mind (Newell & Simon, 1972). In so doing, they tax their working memory—the weakest link in the human mind.

When people develop expertise, their brain functioning changes in ways that increase processing efficiency. This occurs even in animals. Thus as macaque monkeys in one study became experts in categorizing objects, brain recordings revealed quicker and stronger activity in the specific neurons that responded to the stimulus features of importance in categorizing the stimuli (Sigala & Logothetis, 2002). These feature detectors were referred to as "expert neurons" (Hasegawa & Myashita, 2002).

What Is Wisdom?

Anthropologist Peter Collings (2001) notes that, as in many cultures, the Inuit living in the Arctic of western Canada accord their elders special status and great respect (Figure 8.29). Young and old Inuit alike regard wisdom as a key component of aging successfully. To them, wisdom reflects "the individual's function as a repository of cultural knowledge and his or her involvement in community life by interacting with younger people and talking to them, teaching them about 'traditional' cultural values" (p. 146).

FIGURE 8.28

Chess master Gary Kasparov has developed chess schemas that make him a worthy opponent for even the most sophisticated computers, including IBM's Deep Blue.

Does the Inuit conception of wisdom coincide with yours? If not, how would you define wisdom? Until the past 20 years, relatively few psychologists explored this issue, but their interest in studying wisdom has grown considerably since then (Sternberg, 1998). To German psychologist Paul Baltes and his colleagues, **wisdom** *represents a system of knowledge about the meaning and conduct of life* (Baltes & Kunzmann, 2004). What, then, are the components—the types of schemas—that make up this system of knowledge? One way to answer this question would be to study the characteristics of people who are widely esteemed for their wisdom. Yet, say Baltes and Kunzmann, this approach is not ideal, because "Wise persons are approximations to wisdom, but they are not wisdom" (2004, p. 290). Instead, Baltes and his colleagues took another approach, pouring over numerous cultural, historical, philosophical, religious, and psychological views of wisdom (Baltes & Staudinger, 2000). They concluded that wisdom has five major components:

1. *Rich factual knowledge about life.* This includes knowledge about human nature and human development, social norms and social relationships, major life events, and how one's own well-being is interrelated with the well-being of other people.

2. *Rich procedural knowledge about life.* Such procedural knowledge includes strategies for making decisions, handling conflict, giving advice, and weighing the importance of life goals.

3. *An understanding of lifespan contexts.* This understanding includes an awareness that life involves many contexts, such as family, friends, work, and leisure. It also involves an awareness that these contexts need to be viewed from a broad temporal perspective that includes the past, present, and future.

4. *An awareness of the relativism of values and priorities.* This includes recognizing that values and priorities differ across people and societies.

5. *The ability to recognize and manage uncertainty.* This ability stems from an awareness that the future cannot be fully known and that there are inherent limitations in the ways humans gather and process information.

Wisdom versus Expertise

You can readily see from this discussion that expertise and wisdom, though they may partly intersect, are not the same. To achieve wisdom, a person does not have to possess the expertise that scientists, physicians, electricians, chefs, or other people attain in their specific domains of life. Conversely, being an expert does not guarantee the breadth of qualities and knowledge that comprise wisdom.

True wisdom, say Baltes and Staudinger, is hard to achieve, for it combines extraordinary scope with "a truly superior level of knowledge, judgment, and advice . . . used for the good or well-being of oneself and that of others" (2000, p. 123). Indeed, throughout history, stories and other accounts of wise people, such as sages, have often incorporated the theme that wise people "know that they are not wise" (Baltes & Kunzmann, 2004, p. 293).

MENTAL IMAGERY

Having spent most of this chapter discussing language and the types of thought that primarily involve what we subjectively experience as inner speech, let's turn to another mode of thought: *mental imagery.* A **mental image** *is a representation of a stimulus that originates inside your brain, rather than from external sensory input.* Nighttime dreams are among the most common forms of mental imagery. During daydreaming, people may intentionally create and manipulate mental images to get a break from reality or relieve boredom. Many elite athletes receive psychological training in how to effectively use mental imagery to rehearse

FIGURE 8.29

Among the Inuit of the Canadian Arctic, wisdom involves extensive cultural knowledge, involvement in community life, and teaching young people about cultural values.

▶ **Focus 20**
What are some components of wisdom? How do wisdom and expertise differ?

FIGURE 8.30

Mental rotation. (a, b, c) These are three of the many pairs of objects used in Shepard and Metzler's (1971) mental rotation study. (d) This graph shows the average number of seconds it took participants to decide that the two objects in each pair were similar, as a function of the initial angle of rotation. Factoring in the time that it took to make a physical response, participants' speed of mental rotation was approximately 60 degrees per second.

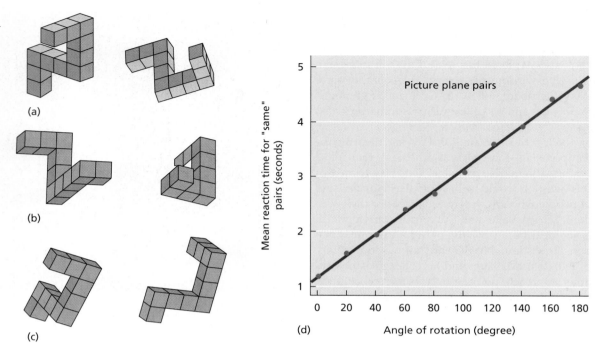

(a)

(b)

(c)

(d)

skills, and people from all walks of life may use mental imagery to help solve problems. By using mental imagery to conduct experiments in their minds, Sir Isaac Newton and Albert Einstein gained insights that led to the discovery of several laws of physics. In a daydream at age 16:

> Einstein imagined himself running alongside a light beam and asked himself the fateful question: what would the light beam look like. Like Newton visualizing throwing a rock until it orbited the earth like the moon, Einstein's attempt to imagine such a light beam would yield deep and surprising results. (Kaku, 2004, p. 43)

Although people have mental images that subjectively involve sounds, tastes, smells, and so on, visual mental images are the most common and most thoroughly researched. Thus, we'll focus on them here.

Mental Rotation

Take a look at the objects shown in Figure 8.30. In each pair, are the two objects different, or are they the same object that has simply been rotated to a different orientation? This activity is called a *mental rotation task*. Typically, people rotate one object in their mind's eye until it lines up sufficiently with the other object to permit a same-different judgment. (By the way, in pairs (a) and (b) the objects are the same. In pair (c) they are different.)

In 1971 the journal *Science* published an experiment by psychologists Roger Shepard and Jacqueline Metzler that helped place the study of mental imagery on the scientific map. At a time when cognitive psychology was still in its infancy and emerging from under the shadow of behaviorism's half-century-long dominance, this elegant experiment demonstrated that mental images could be studied by gathering objective data, rather than by relying exclusively on people's subjective self-reports.

Shepard and Metzler presented each participant in their study with 1,600 pairs of rotated objects, including the objects shown in Figure 8.30. Upon seeing each pair, participants pulled one of two levers to signal whether the two objects were the same or different, and their speed of response was measured. In 800 of the pairs, the objects within the pair were identical and were rotated from each other at angle of either 0, 20, 40, 60, 80, 100, 120, 140, 160, or 180 degrees. The two objects in pair (a) and pair (b) in Figure 8.30, for example, are rotated 80 degrees from one another. Because the two objects in pair (c) differ from one another, the concept of angle of rotation does not apply.

Subjectively, the participants reported that they were able to mentally rotate the objects as if the objects existed physically in three-dimensional space (i.e., they could rotate the objects vertically, horizontally, and from front to back) but that the

► **Focus 21**
Why was Shepard and Metlzer's mental rotation study important? What did they find?

speed of this mental rotation process was limited. Shepard and Metzler's key finding concerned the pairs in which the two objects were the same. On these trials, the greater the difference in rotation between the two pictured objects, the longer it took participants to reach their decision. Moreover, as Figure 8.30d shows, this relation was linear. Shepard and Metzler (1971) concluded that "If we can describe this process as some sort of 'mental rotation in three-dimensional space,' then . . . the average rate at which these particular objects can be thus 'rotated' is roughly 60° per second"(p. 703).

Are Mental Images Pictures in the Mind?

Many researchers believe that mental images, while not literally pictures in the mind, function in ways analogous to actual visual images and are represented in the brain as a type of perceptual code. If this is the case, then mental images should have qualities similar to those that occur when we perceive objects and scenes in the real world. For example, if the objects portrayed in Figure 8.30 were real objects, you would be able to physically rotate them in three-dimensional space. Shepard and Metzler's (1971) experiment revealed that mental images likewise can be rotated within mental space.

Mental Imagery as Perception   Based on studies by Stephen Kosslyn, a leading researcher in the field of mental imagery, let's consider two other examples that illustrate the perceptual nature of mental imagery. For the first example, take a look at the island shown in Figure 8.31, and notice that it contains seven landmarks (e.g., a hut, lake, hill, beach), each of which is marked by a red dot. Suppose that after giving you time to memorize this map, we ask you to close your eyes and focus on a mental image of the map. Next, we ask you to (1) focus on a particular landmark (say, the beach), (2) scan the map until you come to the hill, and (3) press a button (which measures your response time) when you find the hill. On another trial, we might ask you to start at the tree and scan the map until you come to the lake. In total, you will end up taking 21 of these mental trips as you scan once between every possible pair of locations. In the real world, visually scanning between two objects takes longer when they are farther apart. When Stephen Kosslyn and his colleagues (1978) conducted the actual experiment, they found that the greater the distance between the two locations on the mental image of the map, the longer it took participants

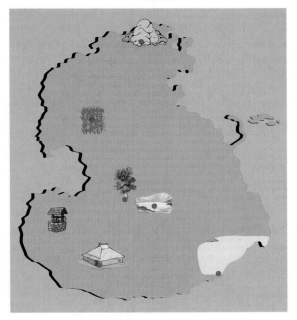

FIGURE 8.31

Imagine an island. This island is similar to one used in Kosslyn et al.'s (1978) mental imagery scanning study.

▶ **Focus 22**
Does research, including brain research, support the view that mental images are perceptual in nature? Explain.

to scan and find the second location. This supports the view that mental images involve a spatial representation.

For the second example, create a mental image of a brick wall that is far enough away so that you can see the entire wall in your image. Now slowly walk toward it until you are about a foot away. What happens to your image? In the real world, as you walk toward the wall, it would look bigger and bigger, and at some point the edges of the wall would move beyond the boundaries of your visual image. Moreover, as you moved closer, you would see more details (e.g., the marks on the bricks). Kosslyn (1978) conducted experiments (involving mental images of animals rather than walls) that indicated that the size and level of detail of mental images can be changed in ways that correspond to perceiving actual objects.

Mental Imagery as Language   Some researchers challenge the view that mental images originate from visual codes that are stored in the brain. Instead, they argue that mental imagery is more closely tied to language than to visual perception (Pylyshyn, 2003). According to this view, for example, when you create a mental image of a brick wall, you are not pulling a visual code that represents a brick wall directly out of your long-term memory. Rather, you may subjectively

► **Focus 23**
What is metacognition? Identify two types of metacognition, and provide examples.

experience a mental image of a brick wall that seems visual, but in reality "brick wall" is being represented by linguistic concepts that are brought together to form propositions ("brick," "bonded with," "mortar," "stacked," "vertical," "spread," "horizontal").

Mental Imagery and the Brain

If mental imagery is rooted in perception, then people who experience brain damage that causes perceptual difficulties might also be expected to show similar impairments in forming mental images. In most instances this seems to be the case, but there are exceptions. For example, some patients who have damage on one side of the brain (usually, the right hemisphere) suffer from a condition called *visual neglect:* They fail to visually perceive objects on the other side (e.g., the left side) of their visual field. If you showed patients who have left-side visual neglect the picture of the island in Figure 8.31 and asked them to draw a copy, they would draw the right side of the island but fail to copy the left side. However, in some cases, if you were to ask the patients to draw the picture from memory (by calling up a mental image of the picture of the island) rather than to copy it (which relies on direct visual perception), they would be able to draw the entire island (Halligan et al., 2003). Most often, however, damage to brain regions involved in perception also disrupts people's ability to form mental images.

Brain-imaging studies of healthy people reveal that many brain regions that become more active when people perceive actual objects also become more active when people form mental images of those objects (Ganis et al., 2004). Moreover, in Chapter 4 we described a study in which researchers, during a medical procedure to help treat patients with epilepsy, had the unique opportunity to show patients photographs and drawings and measure how single neurons in the temporal lobe responded. The researchers also compared how single neurons responded to real stimuli versus mental images of those stimuli (Kreiman et al., 2000). They found evidence of neurons, which they called *imagery neurons,* that fired in response to a particular stimulus regardless of whether it was visual (a photo of a baseball) or imagined (a mental image of a baseball). Altogether, studies of brain functioning suggest that while mental imagery and visual perception do not map onto all of the same neural components, there is a lot of overlap between these two processes.

METACOGNITION: KNOWING YOUR OWN COGNITIVE ABILITIES

Have you ever had a friend or classmate say to you after an exam, "I don't understand why I got this question wrong?" or "I don't understand how I got such a low grade? I thought I really knew this stuff." Have you ever felt that way?

Recognizing What You Do and Don't Know

To cognitive psychologists, the term **metacognition** *refers to your awareness and understanding of your own cognitive abilities.* For example, *comprehension* has to do with understanding something, such as a concept that you just read about. You may *think* you understand the concept, but in actuality you may or may not understand it. Metacognition has to do with truly knowing whether you do or do not understand the concept. The particular component of metacognition that we're discussing in this case is *metacomprehension.* In other words, people who display good metacomprehension are accurate in judging what they do or don't know, whereas people with poor metacomprehension have difficulty judging what they actually do and don't understand. They may typically think they understand things that, in fact, they don't, or they may often think they don't understand things that they actually do.

Metacomprehension is only one aspect of metacognition. Another component, called *metamemory,* represents your awareness and knowledge of your memory capabilities. For example, suppose that you try to memorize a list of definitions or facts. Your ability to accurately judge how well you will be able to remember those items for an upcoming test reflects one aspect of metamemory. (Note that being able to remember material, as in the case of rote memorization, does not necessarily mean that you understand it.) Your awareness of how to use various memory strategies (e.g., mnemonic devices) to improve your memory also constitutes part of your metamemory. In this discussion, however, we'll focus on metacomprehension.

As a student, your ability to effectively monitor what you do and don't know is an important ingredient in studying efficiently (Koriat & Bjork, 2005; Son & Metcalfe, 2000). Some students excel at this. Unfortunately, many studies have found that when it comes to reading text material, students, overall, are only mildly to moderately accurate in judging how well they understand what they are reading. Our "Research Close-Up" examines one technique for improving students' metacomprehension.

Research Close-Up

"Why Did I Get That Wrong?" Improving College Students' Awareness of Whether They Understand Text Material

SOURCE: KEITH W. THEIDE and MARY C. M. ANDERSON (2003). Summarizing can improve metacomprehension accuracy. *Contemporary Educational Psychology, 28,* 129–160.

INTRODUCTION

Previous studies had shown that students' understanding of text material can be improved by asking them to summarize the material after reading it. These studies, however, did not examine students' metacomprehension. According to psychologists Keith Theide and Mary Anderson, this study is the first to examine whether students' metacomprehension for text material can be enhanced by requiring them to write summaries of that material. Based on other metacognition research, Theide and Anderson hypothesized that students who write delayed summaries of passages of text material will show better metacomprehension than students who write immediate summaries or no summaries. Presumably, the task of writing delayed rather than immediate summaries taps more powerfully into students' long-term memory and provides them with a better opportunity to assess whether they truly understand what they have read.

METHOD

Ethnically diverse samples of 75 and 90 college students taking introductory psychology participated, respectively, in Experiment 1 and Experiment 2. The students in each experiment read six passages of text material, with each passage focusing on a different topic (e.g., black holes, global warming, genetics, intelligence, Norse settlements). In Experiment 1 the passages were each about 220 words long, whereas in Experiment 2 they were much longer (1,100 to 1,600 words) and more similar in style to material presented in textbooks.

Students in each experiment were randomly assigned to one of three groups. In the no-summary group (control group), they read all six passages and then rated their comprehension of each passage ("How well do you think you understood the passage") on a scale ranging from 1 ("very poorly") to 7 ("very well"). In the immediate-summary group, students summarized each passage immediately after they read it and then, after finishing all six summaries, rated their comprehension of each one. In the delayed-summary group, students read all six passages before summarizing each one and then rating their comprehension of each passage.

All students, after rating their comprehension, took a multiple-choice comprehension test for each passage that included both factual and conceptual questions. These tests enabled Theide and Anderson to measure how well students' *beliefs* about their comprehension (measured by the rating scales) correlated with their actual comprehension (measured by their test scores).

FIGURE 8.32

Writing summaries helps us recognize what we do and don't know. Students who wrote delayed summaries of text material showed far better metacomprehension than did students who wrote immediate summaries or no summaries.

RESULTS

In all three conditions, there was a positive correlation between students' comprehension ratings and comprehension scores, but in the no-summary and immediate-summary groups, this correlation was only weak to moderate. The critical finding was that in both experiments, students in the delayed-summary group were much more accurate than the other students in judging whether they knew or didn't know the material. In other words, the correlation between their comprehension ratings and their comprehension test scores was much stronger (Figure 8.32).

The data also revealed that, overall, the three groups did not differ in their comprehension ratings or in their test performance. In other words, students in the delayed-summary group did not feel that they knew the material better, and in fact they didn't. Rather, summarizing the passages after a time delay helped them become more accurate in distinguishing the material they did know from the material they didn't.

DISCUSSION

Both experiments supported the researchers' hypothesis: Students' ability to accurately determine how well they understood passages of text improved greatly when they summarized that material after a time delay. Because the delayed-summary group did not rate their comprehension higher or perform better on the comprehension tests than the other groups, we want

Continued

to take special care in making sure that you do *not* reach the wrong conclusion of "So what if metacomprehension improved; the students didn't do better on the test."

Realize that the students in this experiment were not allowed to go back and study the text passages again before taking the comprehension tests. Therefore, students in the delayed-summary group did not have the opportunity to act on their superior metacognitive knowledge (i.e., to bone up on the material that they accurately felt they didn't know). But in real-world test situations, students who are better at recognizing what they know and don't know can indeed put that information to efficient use in the days and hours before a test. They can allocate more time to studying the material they have found difficult and less time to the material that they already understand. Students with poor metacomprehension may end up allocating their study time less efficiently, ignoring material that they think they know but truly don't. Indeed, Theide and Anderson found in Experiment 2 that when all the students were asked to identify which passages of text, hypothetically, they would select to restudy for an exam, students in the delayed-summary group were the most likely to accurately select the passages that they had learned least well.

▶ Focus 24
Based on the "Research Close-Up" and other research, describe some ways to enhance metacomprehension.

Further Advice on Improving Metacomprehension

In Chapter 1's "Applying Psychological Science" feature we discussed several study strategies that can enhance your academic performance. As a student, you also want to be able to accurately assess your understanding of how well you know the material *before* it's time to take a test. One way to do this is to take advantage of practice tests, such as those found in study guides. Trying to memorize specific questions and answers from practice tests—as some students do—will do little to help you assess your broader understanding of the material. Instead, seriously study the material first and then try to answer the questions. For each question, rate how confident you are that your answer is right; this may help you develop a better sense of whether your metacomprehension is good.

The "Research Close-Up" study found that writing delayed summaries improved students' metacomprehension, and other research finds that writing summaries boosts actual comprehension of text material (Winne & Hadwin, 1998). Many college textbooks provide preview questions or review questions in each chapter. In this textbook there are focus questions in the margins of each chapter. Use these focus, preview, or review questions as the

FIGURE 8.33

Levels of analysis: Factors related to human thought.

LEVELS OF ANALYSIS   Factors Related to Human Thought

Biological
- Patterns of neural activity, integrated across brain areas, that underlie our conscious thoughts at any particular moment
- Development of expertise, which alters brain functioning in ways that improve processing efficiency
- Brain damage that disrupts visual perception and, often, visual imagery
- General correspondence of brain activation during imagery and visual perception

Psychological
- Concepts and propositions that underlie propositional thought
- Deductive/inductive reasoning and factors such as belief bias that impair reasoning
- Framing a problem and the use of problem-solving schemas
- Heuristics, confirmation bias, and overconfidence, which can influence decision making and problem solving
- Schemas that underlie the acquisition of knowledge, expertise, and wisdom
- Use of mental imagery to plan and to solve problems
- Metacognitive abilities, such as metacomprehension and metamemory

Environmental
- Problems requiring solution presented by the environment
- Cultural and educational experiences that teach problem solving and foster expertise and wisdom
- Presence of irrelevant stimuli that can impair reasoning
- Resemblance of stimuli to prototypes, prompting use or misuse of representativeness heuristic
- Dramatic and vivid events that can increase likelihood of future similar events through availability heuristic

Thinking

basis for writing brief summaries of the text. It's not magic. It takes time and effort. But in writing these summaries, if you find yourself struggling to remember the material or if you have a hard time articulating the main concepts, then you have gained the knowledge that you need to restudy this material or seek assistance in trying to understand it.

In closing this chapter, Figure 8.33 provides a levels-of-analysis summary of some of the aspects of thinking that we have discussed.

IN REVIEW

- At the level of the brain, thoughts are patterns of neural activity. At the level of the mind, thoughts are propositional, imaginal, or motoric mental representations.

- Concepts are mental categories, or classes, that share certain characteristics. Many concepts are based on prototypes, the most typical and familiar members of a class. How much something resembles the prototype determines whether the concept is applied to it. Propositional thought involves the use of concepts in the form of statements.

- In deductive reasoning, we reason from general principles to a conclusion about a specific case. Inductive reasoning involves reasoning from a set of specific facts or observations to a general principle. Deduction is the strongest and most valid form of reasoning because the conclusion cannot be false if the premises are true. Inductive reasoning cannot yield certainty.

- Unsuccessful deductive reasoning can result from (1) failure to select relevant information, (2) failure to apply the appropriate deductive-reasoning rules, particularly in novel situations, and (3) belief bias, the tendency to abandon logical rules in favor of personal beliefs.

- Problem solving proceeds through several steps: (1) understanding the nature of the problem, (2) establishing initial hypotheses or potential solutions, (3) testing the solutions against existing evidence, and (4) evaluating the results of these tests.

- People use several types of problem-solving schemas. Algorithms are formulas or procedures that guarantee correct solutions. Heuristics are general strategies that may or may not provide correct solutions. Means-ends analysis is a common heuristic. The representativeness heuristic is the tendency to judge evidence according to whether it is consistent with an existing concept or schema. The availability heuristic is the tendency to base conclusions and probability judgments on what is readily available in memory.

- Humans exhibit confirmation bias, a tendency to look for facts to support hypotheses rather than to disprove them. They also suffer from overconfidence, a tendency to overestimate their knowledge, beliefs, and decisions.

- In some situations, divergent thinking is needed for generating novel ideas or variations on ideas. Functional fixedness can blind us to new ways of using an object or procedure, thereby interfering with creative problem solving. Sometimes, a period of incubation permits problem solving to proceed on a subconscious level while giving the problem solver psychological distance from the problem.

- Knowledge acquisition can be viewed as a process of building schemas, which are mental frameworks. Scripts, which are one type of schema, provide a framework for understanding sequences of events that usually unfold in a regular, almost standardized order.

- Experts rely heavily on schemas that they have developed from experience. Compared to novices, experts have more schemas to guide problem solving in their field and are much better at recognizing when each schema should be applied. Schemas also enable experts to take greater advantage of long-term memory.

- Wisdom represents a system of knowledge about the meaning and conduct of life. According to one model, wisdom has five major components: rich factual knowledge, rich procedural knowledge, an understanding of lifespan contexts, an awareness of the relativism of values and priorities, and the ability to recognize and manage uncertainty.

- A mental image is a representation of a stimulus that originates inside the brain, rather than from external sensory input. The objective, quantifiable study of mental imagery received a huge boost from research examining people's ability to mentally rotate objects.

- Mental images of objects seem to have properties that are analogous to the properties of actual objects (e.g., you can rotate them, visually scan them). Thus one viewpoint holds that mental images are basically perceptual in nature. A second viewpoint proposes that mental images actually are based on language. Overall, brain research offers more support to the imagery-as-perception view.

Answers to Problems in the Text

Figure 8.20   Baltimore and Washington are 50 miles apart. The trains are traveling at the same speed (25 mph). Hence they will meet at the halfway point, which is 25 miles, after 1 hour of travel time. Since the crow is flying at 60 mph, it will have flown a total of 60 miles when the trains meet.

Figure 8.23   Sequence of moves: A to 3, B to 2, A to 2, C to 3, A to 1, B to 3, A to 3.

Figure 8.26   Here are two solutions to the nine-dot problem. Both require you to think outside the box, literally.

Figure 8.27   Solution to the candlestick problem:

KEY TERMS AND CONCEPTS

Each term has been boldfaced and defined in the chapter on the page indicated in parentheses.

algorithms (p. 297)
aphasia (p. 282)
availability heuristic (p. 299)
belief bias (p. 294)
bilingualism (p. 286)
bottom-up processing (p. 279)
concept (p. 292)
confirmation bias (p. 299)
creativity (p. 300)
deductive reasoning (p. 293)
deep structure (p. 277)
discourse (p. 278)
displacement (p. 277)
divergent thinking (p. 300)
functional fixedness (p. 301)
generativity (p. 277)
grammar (p. 276)

heuristics (p. 297)
imaginal thought (p. 292)
incubation (p. 301)
inductive reasoning (p. 294)
language (p. 274)
language acquisition device (LAD; p. 282)
language acquisition support system (LASS; p. 283)
linguistic relativity hypothesis (p. 289)
means-ends analysis (p. 297)
mental image (p. 303)
mental representations (p. 274)
mental set (p. 296)
metacognition (p. 306)
morpheme (p. 278)
motoric thought (p. 292)
overconfidence (p. 299)

phoneme (p. 278)
pragmatics (p. 280)
problem-solving schemas (p. 296)
proposition (p. 292)
propositional thought (p. 292)
prototype (p. 292)
psycholinguistics (p. 275)
representativeness heuristic (p. 298)
schema (p. 301)
script (p. 302)
semantics (p. 277)
speech segmentation (p. 280)
subgoal analysis (p. 297)
surface structure (p. 277)
syntax (p. 276)
top-down processing (p. 279)
wisdom (p. 303)

? What Do You Think?

DISCERNING SURFACE AND DEEP STRUCTURES OF LANGUAGE (PAGE 278)

The final words on the grave marker ("No Les No More") consist of a single surface structure with two possible deep structures. First, given the preceding words on the tombstone, the phrase "No Les No More" could be a play on words, which in this case is meant to represent the expression "No Less, No More." In other words, Lester Moore was killed by exactly 4 bullets, no less, no more. Alternatively, the deep structure of "No Les No More" can be interpreted simply as meaning that Lester is no longer among the living. Thus, like the sentence "The police must stop drinking after midnight," the inscription on this tombstone has an ambiguous deep structure.

Sometimes, interpreting ambiguous sentences literally can yield humorous results. For example, in a restaurant washroom you might see the sign "Employees must wash hands." Should you therefore go back into the restaurant to find an employee who will wash your hands? Similarly, there are signs at the entrances to the escalators in the London subway that read, "Dogs Must Be Carried." Should you conclude that unless you are carrying a dog in your arms, you cannot use the escalator? These examples may strike you as a bit silly, but they illustrate how the existence of ambiguity in language highlights the need to make a distinction between surface and deep structure.

THE SLEEPING POLICEMAN (PAGE 281)

This sequence of events actually happened to me when I was traveling in England. It illustrates how top-down processing and pragmatics affect our ability to understand language. First, I did not take the storekeeper's words literally; that is, I did not expect to see a police officer sleeping on the side of the road, and you probably made a similar assumption.

Second, if you haven't been to England (or Ireland or Scotland), let me inform you that the pubs (i.e., taverns) there often have wonderfully colorful names: The Drunken Duck, The Black Swan, The Gun and Hound, and so on. Given this knowledge about the names of English pubs, would it change your interpretation of "sleeping policeman"? Indeed, I assumed that the storekeeper was referring to a physical landmark—a pub or perhaps a restaurant—and I interpreted his spoken words as "The Sleeping Policeman."

Unfortunately, as I drove along the road, I saw nothing but farmland and homes. So I returned to the town and specifically asked the storekeeper, "When you say 'Sleeping Policeman,' are you referring to a pub?" He chuckled and said, "Oh no, no. You know . . . it's that long thing in the road . . . the thing that slows you down." "Ah," I replied, "at home we call them speed bumps!"

My assumption that the storekeeper's words referred to a pub illustrates how knowledge acts as a top-down processing filter that shapes our understanding of language. Such top-down processing usually serves us well, but at times it can lead to misinterpretation.

When I later asked some English friends if they had heard of the term *sleeping policeman*, they said no. Thus the storekeeper made an erroneous assumption as well, namely, that visitors would have the background knowledge to understand the meaning of the local idiom *sleeping policeman*. This reflects a breakdown in pragmatics, namely, a violation of the rule of clarity. Can you think of idioms (e.g., "biggest bang for the buck," "give me a hand," "that's cool") that are obvious in meaning to you but which may have a literal interpretation that could confuse a foreign visitor?

Intelligence

CHAPTER OUTLINE

Many highly intelligent people are poor thinkers. Many people of average intelligence are skillful thinkers. The power of a car is separate from the way the car is driven.

—EDWARD DE BONO

We know that you highly esteem the kind of learning taught in those colleges. . . . But you, who are wise, must know that different nations have different conceptions of things: and you will not therefore take it amiss, if our ideas of this kind of education happen not to be the same with yours. We have had some experience of it; several of our young people were formerly brought up at the colleges of the Northern provinces; they were instructed in all your sciences; but, when they came back to us, they were bad runners, ignorant of every means of living in the woods, unable to bear either cold or hunger, knew neither how to build a cabin, take a deer, nor kill an enemy, spoke our language imperfectly, were therefore neither fit for hunters, warriors, nor counselors; they were totally good for nothing. . . .

We are, however not the less obligated by your kind offer, though we decline accepting it; and to show our grateful sense of it, if the gentlemen of Virginia will send us a dozen of their sons, we will take care of their education, instruct them in all we know, and make men of them. (A Native American leader quoted in Benjamin Franklin, *Remarks Concerning the Savage of North America* [1784])

This response to a well-intentioned offer by American colonists to provide Native American boys with access to European educational opportunities reminds us that people have different conceptions of what it means to be smart. In Western cultures, being smart is typically thought of as having good mental skills that are instrumental to succeeding in school and in higher-level jobs and occupations. As we shall see, people with good mental skills do indeed do better in school and on the job in our culture. But if we view intelligence in broader perspective as the ability to respond adaptively to the demands of a particular environment, we can understand why the Native American leader was less impressed with the products of Anglo-Saxon education than were the colonists. It's important to remember, then, that intelligence is not something that has concrete existence; it is, instead, a socially constructed concept (Sternberg, 2004; Figure 9.1).

In previous chapters, we have explored general principles of human learning, memory, thinking, reasoning, and problem solving. In all of these areas, we have seen that people differ widely in how effectively they learn, remember, think, and behave. Is it therefore the case that

some people are generally more intelligent than others? If so, can we measure these differences and use the measures to predict success and failure in real-life settings? What is the nature of intelligence, and what factors account for the differences we observe in people's cognitive, emotional, and behavioral skills? Attempts to answer these questions have influenced our culture enormously. Today, there exists a multibillion-dollar intelligence-testing industry. Programs such as No Child Left Behind demand that we assess the aptitudes and learning outcomes of children in a search for educational accountability. You yourself have undoubtedly taken mental ability tests for educational or occupational reasons. In fact, your results on one or more college entrance examinations may have played an important role in your admission to college.

As we shall see, however, even after more than a century of research and theory development, there are still sharp disagreements about what intelligence is. In our discussion, we use the following definition, which accommodates most viewpoints: **Intelligence** *is the ability to acquire knowledge, to think and reason effectively, and to deal adaptively with the environment.*

▶ **Focus 1**
What is our working definition of intelligence?

313

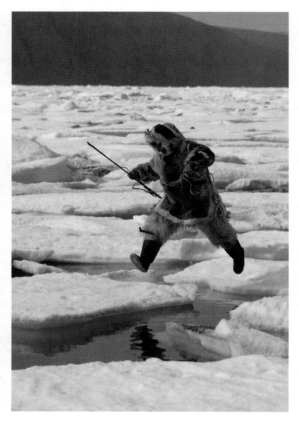

FIGURE 9.1

The skills required to adapt successfully to environmental demands may differ from culture to culture, suggesting to some theorists that what constitutes intelligence may be somewhat culture-specific.

▶ **Focus 2**
How did Galton and Binet differ in their approaches to measuring mental abilities?

FIGURE 9.2

Sir Francis Galton pioneered the study of intelligence with his studies of hereditary genius.

INTELLIGENCE IN HISTORICAL PERSPECTIVE

Historically, two scientists with entirely different agendas played seminal roles in the study and measurement of mental skills. The contributions of Sir Francis Galton and Alfred Binet set the stage for later attempts to measure intelligence and discover its causes.

SIR FRANCIS GALTON: QUANTIFYING MENTAL ABILITY

Sir Francis Galton was a cousin of Charles Darwin and was strongly influenced by Darwin's theory of evolution (Figure 9.2). In his book *Hereditary Genius* (1869), Galton showed through the study of family trees that eminence and genius seemed to occur within certain families. No intellectual slouch himself, young Francis wrote a childhood letter to his sister that contained the following: "My dear Adele, I am 4 years old, and I can read any English book. I can say all of the Latin sub-

stantives and adjectives and active verbs besides 52 lines of Latin poetry."

Galton's research convinced him that eminent people had "inherited mental constitutions" that made them more fit for thinking than their less successful counterparts. Exhibiting his own belief bias, Galton dismissed the fact that the more successful people he studied almost invariably came from privileged environments.

Galton then attempted to demonstrate a biological basis for eminence by showing that people who were more socially and occupationally successful would also perform better on a variety of laboratory tasks thought to measure the "efficiency of the nervous system." He developed measures of reaction speed, hand strength, and sensory acuity. He even measured the size of people's skulls, believing that skull size reflected brain volume and hence intelligence.

In time, Galton's approach to mental skills measurement fell into disfavor because his measures of nervous-system efficiency proved unrelated to socially relevant measures of mental ability, such as academic and occupational success.

Nonetheless, Galton's work created an interest in the measurement of mental abilities, setting the stage for the pioneering work of Alfred Binet.

ALFRED BINET'S MENTAL TESTS

The modern intelligence-testing movement began at the turn of the 20th century, when the French psychologist Alfred Binet was commissioned by France's Ministry of Public Education to develop the test that was to become the forerunner of all modern intelligence tests (Figure 9.3). Unlike Galton, with whom he had trained, Binet was interested in solving a practical problem rather than supporting a theory. Certain children seemed unable to benefit from normal public schooling. Educators wanted an objective way to identify these children as early as possible so that some form of special education could be arranged for them.

In developing his tests, Binet made two assumptions about intelligence: First, mental abilities develop with age. Second, the rate at which people gain mental competence is a characteristic of the person and is fairly constant over time. In other words, a child who is less competent than expected at age 5 should also be lagging at age 10.

To develop a measure of mental skills, Binet asked experienced teachers what sorts of problems children could solve at ages 3, 4, 5, and so on, up through the school years. He then used their answers to develop a standardized interview in which an adult examiner posed a series of questions to a child to determine whether the child was performing at the correct mental level for his or her age (Table 9.1). The result of the testing was a score called the *mental age*. For instance, if an 8-year-old child could solve problems at the level of the average 10-year-old, the child would be said to have a mental age of 10. For the French school system, the practical implication was that educational attainment could be enhanced if placement in school were based at least in part on the child's mental age. An 8-year-old child with a mental age of 6 could hardly be expected to cope with the academic demands of a normal classroom for 8-year-olds.

The concept of mental age was subsequently expanded by the German psychologist William Stern to provide a relative score—a common yardstick of intellectual attainment—for people of different chronological ages. Stern's **intelligence quotient (IQ)** *was the ratio of mental age to chronological age, multiplied by 100: IQ = (mental age/chronological age) × 100.* Thus a child who was performing at exactly his or her age level would

have an IQ of 100. In our previous example, the child with a mental age of 10 and a chronological age of 8 would have an IQ of (10/8) × 100 = 125. A 16-year-old with a mental age of 20 would also have an IQ of 125, so the two would be comparable in intelligence even though their ages differed.

Today's tests no longer use the concept of mental age. Although the concept works pretty well for children, many of the basic skills measured by intelligence tests are acquired by about age 16 through normal life experiences and schooling, so that Stern's quotient is less useful for adults. Moreover, some intellectual skills show an actual decline at advanced ages. If we applied Stern's definition of IQ to a 20-year-old who performed at the typical level of an 80-year-old, we would have to say that the 20-year-old's IQ was 400! To deal with these problems, today's intelligence tests provide an "IQ" score that is not a quotient at all. Instead, it is based on a person's performance relative to the scores of other people the same age, with a score of 100 corresponding to the average performance of that age group.

FIGURE 9.3

Alfred Binet developed the first intelligence test to assess the mental skills of French school children. His test launched the modern intelligence-testing movement.

▶ **Focus 3**
Why do today's intelligence tests no longer use the concept of mental age? How is IQ now defined?

TABLE 9.1	Sample Problems from the Stanford-Binet Intelligence Test That Should Be Answered Correctly at Particular Ages	
Age 3—Child should be able to:	Point to objects that serve various functions such as "goes on your feet." Name pictures of objects such as *chair, flag*. Repeat a list of 2 words or digits such as *car, dog*.
Age 4—Child should be able to:	Discriminate visual forms such as squares, circles, and triangles. Define words such as *ball* and *bat*. Repeat 10-word sentences. Count up to 4 objects. Solve problems such as "In daytime it is light; at night it is . . ."
Age 6—Child should be able to:	State the differences between similar items such as *bird* and *dog*. Count up to 9 blocks. Solve analogies such as "An inch is short; a mile is . . ."
Age 9—Child should be able to:	Solve verbal problems such as "Tell me a number that rhymes with tree." Solve simple arithmetic problems such as "If I buy 4 cents' worth of candy and give the storekeeper 10 cents, how much money will I get back?" Repeat 4 digits in reverse order.
Age 12—Child should be able to:	Define words such as *muzzle*. Repeat 5 digits in reverse order. Solve verbal absurdities such as "Bill's feet are so big he has to pull his trousers over his head. What is foolish about that?"

SOURCE: Terman & Merrill, 1972.

FIGURE 9.4

Lewis Terman imported the intelligence test developed by Binet to the United States and revised it as the Stanford-Binet Scale. The Stanford-Binet became the standard for future individually administered intelligence tests and is still used today.

► **Focus 4**
What was Wechsler's concept of intelligence? How do the Wechsler scales reflect this concept?

BINET'S LEGACY: AN INTELLIGENCE-TESTING INDUSTRY EMERGES

Lewis Terman (Figure 9.4), a professor at Stanford University, was intrigued by Binet's work. He revised Binet's test for use in the United States, translating it into English and rewriting some of its items to improve their relevance to American culture. Terman's revised test became known as the *Stanford-Binet*. By the mid-1920s, it had become widely accepted in North America as the gold standard for measuring mental aptitude. The Stanford-Binet contained mostly verbal items, and it yielded a single IQ score.

At about the time that the Stanford-Binet test was introduced in 1916, the United States entered World War I. One of Terman's students at Stanford, Arthur Otis, had been working on a group-administered test of intellectual ability. This test became the prototype for the *Army Alpha*, a verbally oriented test that was used to screen large numbers of U.S. Army recruits for intellectual fitness. Because some recruits were unable to read, a nonverbal instrument using mazes, picture-completion problems, and digit-symbol tasks was also developed and given the name *Army Beta*. Before the war's end, more than 1.7 million men had been screened for intelligence using these tests.

Inspired by the success of the Army Alpha and Beta for measuring the intelligence of large numbers of people in a group setting, educators clamored for similar instruments to test groups of children. New group tests of intelligence, such as the Lorge-Thorndike Intelligence Test and the Otis-Lennon School Ability Test, soon appeared and became an important part of educational reform and policy. Many school districts use these or similar tests routinely, and you are likely to have taken one or more of them during your earlier school years.

Two decades after Terman introduced the American version of Binet's test, psychologist David Wechsler developed a major competitor to the Stanford-Binet. Wechsler believed that the Stanford-Binet relied too much on verbal skills. He thought that intelligence should be measured as a group of distinct but related verbal *and* nonverbal abilities. He therefore developed intelligence tests for adults and for children that measured both verbal and nonverbal intellectual skills. In 1939 the Wechsler Adult Intelligence Scale (WAIS) appeared, followed by the Wechsler Intelligence Scale for Children (WISC) in 1955 and the Wechsler Preschool and Primary Scale of Intelligence (WPPSI) in 1967. The Wechsler scales have undergone several revisions. Today, the Wechsler tests (WAIS-III and WISC-IV) are the most popular individually administered

intelligence tests in the United States (Newmark, 2005). Following Wechsler's lead, the Stanford-Binet has also been revised to measure a wider range of mental abilities. Later in the chapter, we'll have a closer look at the Wechsler tests, as well as other measures that assess various classes of mental skills.

Intelligence has long been a major focus of psychological research, much of which has been inspired by questions that, even after a century of research, continue to evoke disagreement and controversy (Bartholomew, 2005). Should we regard intelligence as a single aptitude or as many specific abilities? Is intelligence an innate mental capacity, or is it a product of our upbringing? What kinds of brain processes underlie mental skills? Are there actually multiple intelligences, including some that may have little to do with mental skills? These and other questions have inspired a fascinating odyssey of scientific discovery. We begin with the most basic question of all: Just what is this attribute we call *intelligence?*

IN REVIEW

■ Intelligence is the ability to acquire knowledge, to think and reason effectively, and to deal adaptively with the environment. Because cultural environments differ in the skills most important for adaptation, cultural conceptions of intelligence may differ markedly.

■ Galton's studies of hereditary genius and Binet's methods for measuring differences in children's mental skills were important historical milestones in the study of intelligence.

THE NATURE OF INTELLIGENCE

Psychologists have used two major approaches in the study of intelligence (Sternberg et al., 2003). The *psychometric approach* attempts to map the structure of intellect and to discover the kinds of mental competencies that underlie test performance. The *cognitive processes approach* studies the specific thought processes that underlie those mental competencies.

THE PSYCHOMETRIC APPROACH: THE STRUCTURE OF INTELLECT

Psychometrics *is the statistical study of psychological tests.* The psychometric approach to intelligence tries to identify and measure the abilities that underlie individual differences in performance; in essence, it tries to provide a measurement-based map of the mind.

Factor Analysis

Psychometric researchers have long sought to identify the mental abilities of the human mind. How many are there? Are there dozens, or are there perhaps only one or a few basic abilities that underlie performance across diverse tasks? What is the nature of these abilities?

To answer questions like these, researchers administer diverse measures of mental abilities and then correlate them with one another. They reason that if certain tests are correlated highly with one another—if they "cluster" mathematically—then performance on these tests probably reflects the same underlying mental skill. Further, if the tests within a cluster correlate highly with one another but much less with tests in other clusters, then these various test clusters probably reflect different mental abilities. Thus researchers hope to determine the number of test clusters and to use this information to infer the nature of the underlying abilities.

When large numbers of tests are correlated with one another, many correlation coefficients result, and it is difficult to determine by visual examination the actual patterning of the test scores. Fortunately, a statistical technique called **factor analysis** *reduces a large number of measures to a smaller number of clusters, or factors, with each cluster containing variables that correlate highly with one another but less highly with variables in other clusters.* A factor allows us to infer the underlying characteristic that presumably accounts for the links among the variables in the cluster.

To illustrate with a highly simplified example the kind of clustering of tests that we are interested in, consider the small correlation matrix in Table 9.2, based on only 6 different mental ability tests. (There might be as many as 10 to 15 tests in an actual study.) Examination of Table 9.2 reveals two clusters of tests. Tests 1, 2, and 3 correlate highly with one another. Tests 4, 5, and 6 also show high positive correlations with one another. But tests 1, 2, and 3 do not correlate highly with tests 4, 5, and 6. This indicates that the two sets of tests are measuring different abilities. A factor analysis would tell us that there are two different factors.

But what are these two sets of tests measuring? The factor analysis cannot answer this question; it can only identify the clusters for us. It's now up to us to examine the nature of the tests

within each cluster and decide what the underlying factors might be. Suppose that test 1 is a measure of vocabulary, test 2 measures reading comprehension, and test 3 requires respondents to complete sentences with missing words. Because all three tasks involve the use of words, we might decide to call the underlying factor "verbal ability." Inspection of tests 4, 5, and 6 might reveal that all of them involve the use of numbers or mathematical word problems. We might therefore decide to name this factor "mathematical reasoning." What matters is that we have now reduced six variables to two variables, based on the correlations among them, and we have arrived at some idea of what the underlying abilities might be.

We should note, however, that the two clusters of tests we've identified are not totally unrelated to one another. The verbal and mathematical scores are also correlated with one another, though at a much lower level than within the clusters. This fact suggests that although the verbal and mathematical factors are clearly distinct from one another, they also share something in common, perhaps some more general mental ability that cuts across both verbal and mathematical abilities. This pattern of results anticipates one of the major controversies in the field of intelligence: Is intelligence a general mental capacity, or does it consist of separate and specific mental abilities?

The *g* Factor: Intelligence as General Mental Capacity

The psychometric argument for intelligence as a general ability was first advanced by the British psychologist Charles Spearman (1923). He observed that school grades in different subjects, such as English and mathematics, were almost always positively correlated but not perfectly. Spearman found the same to be true for different types of Stanford-Binet intelligence test items, such as vocabulary questions, arithmetic reasoning problems, and the ability to solve puzzles. Were he to

▶ **Focus 5**
How is factor analysis used in the study of intelligence?

▶ **Focus 6**
What kinds of evidence supported the existence of Spearman's *g* factor?

TABLE 9.2	Correlations among Six Cognitive Ability Tests					
Test	**1**	**2**	**3**	**4**	**5**	**6**
1	1.00	.84	.79	.46	.39	.43
2		1.00	.87	.51	.48	.54
3			1.00	.47	.50	.48
4				1.00	.88	.91
5					1.00	.82
6						1.00

TABLE 9.3   Thurstone's Primary Mental Abilities

Ability Name	Description
S—Space	Reasoning about visual scenes
V—Verbal comprehension	Understanding verbal statements
W—Word fluency	Producing verbal statements
N—Number facility	Dealing with numbers
P—Perceptual speed	Recognizing visual patterns
M—Rote memory	Memorization
R—Reasoning	Dealing with novel problems

SOURCE: Thurstone, 1938.

▶ **Focus 7**
What led Thurstone to view intelligence as specific mental abilities?

look at the correlation matrix in Table 9.2, he would be impressed by the fact that the verbal-ability cluster and mathematical-reasoning cluster are correlated with one another at about the .40 to .50 level. He would regard these correlations as evidence that verbal and mathematical abilities, while clearly different, also reflect a more basic or general mental capacity that contributes to them.

Spearman concluded that intellectual performance is determined partly by a *g* **factor,** *or general intelligence*, and partly by whatever special abilities might be required to perform that particular task. Spearman contended that because the general factor—the *g* factor—cuts across virtually all tasks, it constitutes the core of intelligence. Thus Spearman would argue that your performance in a mathematics course would depend mainly on your general intelligence but also on your specific ability to learn mathematics.

Today, many theorists continue to believe that the *g* factor is the core of what we call *intelligence*. Moreover, *g* matters a great deal as a predictor of both academic and job performance. Nathan Kuncel and coworkers (2004) performed a meta-analysis of 127 studies involving 20,352 participants in numerous educational and work settings. They concluded that the same general mental ability is significantly related to success in both areas of life. Taking this argument a step further, Frank Schmidt and John Hunter (2004) concluded that measures of the *g* factor predict job success even better than do measures of specific abilities tailored to individual jobs. Summarizing the research evidence, David Lubinski, a prominent intelligence researcher, concluded: "*g* is clearly the most important dimension uncovered in the study of cognitive abilities to date" (2004, p. 100).

Intelligence as Specific Mental Abilities

Spearman's conclusion about the centrality of the *g* factor was soon challenged by L. L. Thurstone of the University of Chicago. While Spearman had been impressed by the fact that scores on different mental tasks are correlated, Thurstone was impressed by the fact that the correlations are far from perfect. Thurstone therefore concluded that human mental performance depends not on a general factor but rather on seven distinct abilities, which he called *primary mental abilities* (Table 9.3). Thus Thurstone would focus on the two clusters of test scores shown in Table 9.2 and attach special significance to the high correlations within each cluster. He would expect that performance on a given verbal or mathematical task would be influenced more by the specific skills represented in the relevant cluster than by any *g* factor.

Following Thurstone's lead, other investigators claimed to have found many more specific cognitive factors. One prominent theorist maintained that there are more than 100 distinct and measurable mental abilities (Guilford, 1967). Other theorists suggest fewer abilities but maintain that intelligence is more complex than a single *g* factor.

For practical reasons, educators tend to find the specific-abilities notion of intelligence more attractive and useful than the general mental ability model (Mayer, 2000). They are more interested in identifying the specific mental skills involved in learning subjects such as reading, mathematics, and science. They are also interested in helping children increase the specific mental abilities that are needed for success in various subjects. For such purposes, general mental ability measures such as an overall IQ are less useful than are measures of specific cognitive abilities that can point to a student's areas of strength and weakness. Additionally, it may appear more feasible to enhance specific mental skills than to raise general intelligence. This brings us to a question we'd like you to consider.

? What Do You Think?

IS INTELLIGENCE FIXED OR MALLEABLE?
Consider at this point your personal conception of intelligence. Do you view intelligence to be relatively fixed and unchanging, or do you think it can be changed significantly? How might your position on this issue influence your view of your own intellectual potential and your approach to achievement situations? Think about it, then see page 346.

Crystallized and Fluid Intelligence

Raymond Cattell (1971) and John Horn (1985) proposed a new model of intelligence (Figure 9.5). They broke down Spearman's general intelligence into two distinct but related subtypes of g (with a correlation of about .50). **Crystallized intelligence (g_c)** *is the ability to apply previously acquired knowledge to current problems.* Vocabulary and information tests are good measures of crystallized intelligence. Crystallized intelligence, which is the basis for expertise, depends on the ability to retrieve previously learned information and problem-solving schemas from long-term memory (Horn & Masunaga, 2000; Hunt, 1997). It is dependent on previous learning and practice.

Cattell and Horn's second general factor is **fluid intelligence (g_f),** *defined as the ability to deal with novel problem-solving situations for which personal experience does not provide a solution.* It involves inductive reasoning and creative problem-solving skills like those discussed in the previous chapter. Fluid intelligence is dependent primarily on the efficient functioning of the central nervous system rather than on prior experience and cultural context. People high in fluid intelligence can perceive relations among stimulus patterns and draw inferences from relationships. The tower-of-Hanoi and nine-dot problems you worked on in the previous chapter are fluid-intelligence tasks.

Fluid intelligence requires the abilities to reason abstractly, think logically, and manage information in working (short-term) memory so that new problems can be solved on the blackboard of the mind (Hunt, 1997). Thus long-term memory contributes strongly to crystallized intelligence, whereas fluid intelligence is particularly dependent on efficient working memory.

The g_c-g_f model is based in part on what has been learned about intellectual development in adulthood (Berg, 2000). Cattell and Horn concluded that over our life span, we progress from using fluid intelligence to depending more on crystallized intelligence. Early in life, we encounter many problems for the first time, so we need fluid intelligence to figure out solutions. As experience makes us more knowledgeable, we have less need to approach each situation as a new problem. Instead, we simply call up appropriate information and schemas from long-term memory, thereby utilizing our crystallized intelligence. This is the essence of wisdom (Kunzman & Baltes, 2003).

Because long-term memory remains strong even as we age, performance on tests of crystallized intelligence improves during adulthood and remains stable well into late adulthood. In contrast, performance on tests of fluid intelligence begins to decline as people enter late adulthood (Cattell, 1998; Schaie, 1998). The fact that aging affects the two forms of intelligence differently is additional evidence that they represent different classes of mental abilities (Horn & Noll, 1997; Weinert & Hany, 2003).

Carroll's Three-Stratum Model: A Modern Synthesis

In their attempts to specify the nature of intellect, psychometric researchers have been administering measures of mental abilities for over a century. The many tasks they have used have probably left no cognitive stone unturned. In an attempt to synthesize the results of prior research, John B. Carroll (1993) used factor analysis to reanalyze more than 460 different sets of data obtained by researchers around the world between 1935 and 1980. Carroll's analysis resulted in an integrative model of intelligence that contains elements of Spearman's, Thurstone's, and Cattell-Horn's models. The **three-stratum theory of cognitive abilities** *establishes three levels of mental skills—general, broad, and narrow—arranged in a hierarchical model.* As shown in Figure 9.6, at the top, or third stratum, of the model is a g factor thought to underlie most mental activity. Below g at the second stratum are eight broad intellectual factors arranged from left to right in terms of the extent to which they are influenced by (or correlated with) g. Fluid intelligence is most strongly related to (or "saturated with") g, and crystallized intelligence is next, indicating the importance of the

▶ **Focus 8**
Differentiate between crystallized and fluid intelligence, and indicate their relation to aging and types of memory.

▶ **Focus 9**
Describe Carroll's three-stratum psychometric model and how it originated. How does it relate to the previously discussed models?

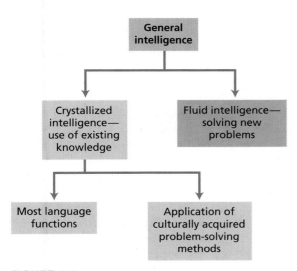

FIGURE 9.5

Crystallized and fluid intelligence. Raymond Cattell and John Horn made an important distinction between crystallized and fluid intelligence. Crystallized intelligence is based more strongly on previous learning and experience, whereas fluid intelligence is a more creative type of intelligence.

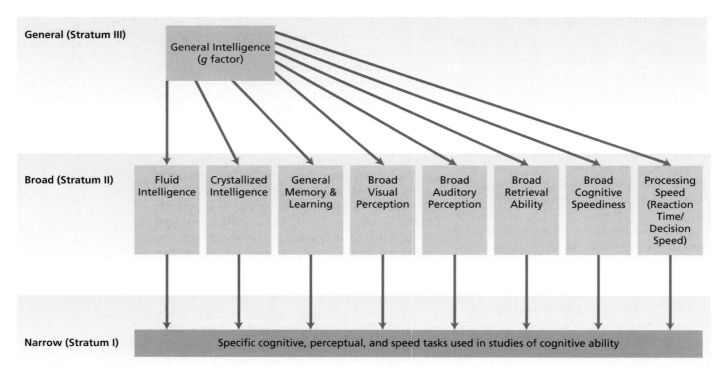

General (Stratum III)

General Intelligence (*g* factor)

Broad (Stratum II)

| Fluid Intelligence | Crystallized Intelligence | General Memory & Learning | Broad Visual Perception | Broad Auditory Perception | Broad Retrieval Ability | Broad Cognitive Speediness | Processing Speed (Reaction Time/ Decision Speed) |

Narrow (Stratum I)

Specific cognitive, perceptual, and speed tasks used in studies of cognitive ability

FIGURE 9.6

A modern model of intellect. John B. Carroll's three-stratum model of cognitive skills is based on a reanalysis of more than 400 data sets. The model builds upward from specific skills to a *g* factor at its apex. The lengths of the arrows from Stratum III to Stratum II represent the contribution of the *g* factor to each Stratum II ability. Source: Adapted from Carroll, 1993.

Cattell-Horn factors. The other broad abilities at the second stratum involve basic cognitive functions such as memory and learning, perceptual abilities, and speed of mental functioning, some of which resemble Thurstone's primary mental abilities. Finally, at the first stratum of the model are nearly 70 highly specific cognitive abilities that feed into the broader second-stratum factors. On average, these specific ability measures tend to correlate around .30 with one another, reflecting the common *g* factor at the top of the model. Carroll believes that the three-stratum model encompasses virtually all known cognitive abilities and provides the most complete and detailed map of the human intellect derived from the psychometric approach to intelligence.

COGNITIVE PROCESS APPROACHES: THE NATURE OF INTELLIGENT THINKING

Psychometric theories of intelligence are statistically sophisticated ways of describing *how* people differ from one another. What psychometric theories don't explain is *why* people vary in these mental skills. **Cognitive process theories** *explore the specific information-processing and cognitive processes that underlie intellectual ability*. Recall that this was

the logic behind Galton's early attempts to relate thinking ability to speed of reaction and sensory acuity. Robert Sternberg (1988, 2004) is a leading proponent of the cognitive processes approach to intelligence. His **triarchic theory of intelligence** *addresses both the psychological processes involved in intelligent behavior and the diverse forms that intelligence can take*. Sternberg's theory divides the cognitive processes that underlie intelligent behavior into three specific components (Figure 9.7).

Metacomponents *are the higher-order processes used to plan and regulate task performance*. They include problem-solving skills such as identifying problems, formulating hypotheses and strategies, testing them logically, and evaluating performance feedback. Sternberg believes that metacomponents are the fundamental sources of individual differences in fluid intelligence. He finds that intelligent people spend more time framing problems and developing strategies than do less intelligent people, who have a tendency to plunge right in without sufficient forethought.

Performance components *are the actual mental processes used to perform the task*. They include perceptual processing, retrieving appropriate memories and schemas from long-term memory,

▶ **Focus 10**
Differentiate between psychometric and cognitive process approaches to intelligence.

and generating responses. Finally, **knowledge-acquisition components** *allow us to learn from our experiences, store information in memory, and combine new insights with previously acquired information.* These abilities underlie individual differences in crystallized intelligence. Thus Sternberg's theory addresses the processes that underlie the distinction made by Cattell and Horn between fluid and crystallized intelligences.

Sternberg believes that there is more than one kind of intelligence. He suggests that environmental demands may call for three different classes of adaptive problem solving and that people differ in their intellectual strengths in these areas:

1. *Analytical intelligence* involves the kinds of academically oriented problem-solving skills measured by traditional intelligence tests.

2. *Practical intelligence* refers to the skills needed to cope with everyday demands and to manage oneself and other people effectively.

3. *Creative intelligence* comprises the mental skills needed to deal adaptively with novel problems.

Sternberg has shown that these forms of intelligence, while having a modest underlying g factor, are also distinct from one another. Consider, for example, the relation between academic and practical skills. In one study, adolescents in Kenya were given one set of analytical tests measuring traditional academic knowledge and another set measuring their knowledge of natural herbal medicines used to treat illnesses, a kind of practical knowledge viewed by villagers as important to their survival. The results indicated that the practical intelligence measure of herbal knowledge was unrelated to (and sometimes negatively correlated with) the academic measures (Sternberg et al., 2001). Sternberg also found that Brazilian street children were very proficient at the math required to carry on their street businesses, despite the fact that many of them had failed mathematics in school (Sternberg, 2004).

Sternberg believes that educational programs should teach all three classes of skills, not just analytical-academic skills. In studies with elementary school children, he and his colleagues have shown that a curriculum that also teaches practical and creative skills results in greater mastery of course material than does a traditional analytic, memory-based approach to learning course content (Sternberg et al., 1998). As Sternberg's work illustrates, cognitive science is leading us to a focus on understanding and enhancing the mental processes that underlie intelligent behavior.

Types of Intellectual Competence

Analytical intelligence | Practical intelligence | Creative intelligence

Metacomponents
Plan and regulate task behavior

Performance components
Execute strategies specified by metacomponents

Knowledge-acquisition components
Encode and store information

Underlying Cognitive Processes

FIGURE 9.7

Sternberg's triarchic theory. Sternberg's theory includes three different types of intelligence and three classes of cognitive processes that underlie each type of intelligence.

BROADER CONCEPTIONS OF INTELLIGENCE: BEYOND MENTAL COMPETENCIES

Traditionally, intelligence has been viewed as *mental competence.* Some psychologists think this is too limited a definition to capture the range of human adaptations. They believe that intelligence may be more broadly conceived as relatively *independent intelligences* that relate to different adaptive demands.

Gardner's Multiple Intelligences

Harvard psychologist Howard Gardner (2003) is one of the strongest proponents of this view. Inspired by his observations of how specific human abilities are affected by brain damage, Gardner advanced a theory of multiple intelligences. The number of intelligences has varied as Gardner's work has progressed; he currently defines eight distinct varieties of adaptive abilities, and a possible ninth variety (Gardner, 2000):

1. *Linguistic intelligence:* the ability to use language well, as writers do.

2. *Logical-mathematical intelligence:* the ability to reason mathematically and logically.

3. *Visuospatial intelligence:* the ability to solve spatial problems or to succeed in a field such as architecture.

4. *Musical intelligence:* the ability to perceive pitch and rhythm and to understand and produce music.

5. *Bodily-kinesthetic intelligence:* the ability to control body movements and skillfully

▶ **Focus 11**
What three classes of psychological processes and forms of intelligence are found in Sternberg's triarchic theory?

▶ **Focus 12**
What kinds of abilities are included in Gardner's multiple intelligences?

FIGURE 9.8

According to Howard Gardner, these people's abilities exemplify forms of intelligence that are not measured by traditional intelligence tests. Ray Charles possessed high musical intelligence, whereas Andre Agassi and Oprah Winfrey exhibit high bodily-kinesthetic and interpersonal intelligence, respectively.

manipulate objects, as demonstrated by a highly skilled dancer, athlete, or surgeon.

6. *Interpersonal intelligence:* the ability to understand and relate well to others.

7. *Intrapersonal intelligence:* the ability to understand oneself.

8. *Naturalistic intelligence:* the ability to detect and understand phenomena in the natural world, as a zoologist or meteorologist might.

In recent writings, Gardner (2000) has also speculated about a ninth possible intelligence, which he calls *existential intelligence,* a philosophically oriented ability to ponder questions about the meaning of one's existence, life, and death.

Gardner's first three intelligences are measured by existing intelligence tests, but the others are not. Indeed, some of Gardner's critics insist that these other abilities are not really part of the traditional concept of intelligence at all and that some of them are better regarded as talents. However, Gardner replies that the form of intelligence that is most highly valued within a given culture depends on the adaptive requirements of that culture. In Gardner's view, the abilities exhibited by Albert Einstein, Tiger Woods, and a street-smart gang leader exemplify different forms of intelligence that are highly adaptive within their respective environments (Figure 9.8). Gardner further suggests that these different classes of abilities require the functioning of separate but interacting modules in the brain. Gardner's approach, though provocative, remains controversial because it goes far beyond traditional conceptions of intelligence as mental skills.

Emotional Intelligence

Another form of adaptive ability lies within the emotional realm, and some theorists believe that emotional competence is a form of intelligence. According to John Mayer and Peter Salovey, **emotional intelligence** *involves the abilities to read others' emotions accurately, to respond to them appropriately, to motivate oneself, to be aware of one's own emotions, and to regulate and control one's own emotional responses* (Mayer et al., 2004).

According to Mayer and Salovey, emotional intelligence includes four components, or branches, as shown in Figure 9.9. The Mayer-Salovey-Caruso

Branch 1
Perceiving emotions

Branch 2
Using emotions to facilitate thought

EI

Branch 3
Understanding emotions

Branch 4
Managing emotions

FIGURE 9.9

The structure of emotional intelligence. Four specific classes of emotion-detection and control abilities are assumed to underlie emotional intelligence. Source: Based on Mayer et al., 2004.

Emotional Intelligence Test (MSCEIT) includes specific tasks to measure each branch. *Perceiving emotions* is measured by people's accuracy in judging emotional expressions in facial photographs, as well as the emotional tones conveyed by different landscapes and designs. *Using emotions to facilitate thought* is measured by asking people to identify the emotions that would best enhance a particular type of thinking, such as how to deal with a distressed coworker or plan a birthday party. To measure *understanding emotions,* people are asked to specify the conditions under which their emotions change in intensity or type; another task measures people's understanding of which basic emotions blend together to create subtle emotions, such as envy or jealousy. Finally, *managing emotions* is measured by asking respondents to indicate how they can change their own or others' emotions to facilitate success or increase interpersonal harmony.

The scoring method for the MSCEIT tasks yields high reliability among expert scorers; it produces scores for each branch, as well as a total emotional-intelligence score. Mayer and Salovey view these tasks as ability measures in the same sense that a Wechsler scale measures mental abilities. As in the case of mental intelligence, it seems important to measure what people can actually do rather than simply asking them how competent they are. Other measures of emotional intelligence, which ask people how competent they are in emotional areas, tend not to correlate highly with the MSCEIT or predict competent behaviors as well (Mayer et al., 2004).

Proponents of emotional intelligence point to the important adaptive advantages of emotional skills in meeting the challenges of daily life, and they believe that the ability to read, respond to, and manage emotions has evolutionary roots. Emotionally intelligent people, they suggest, form stronger emotional bonds with others; enjoy greater success in careers, marriage, and child-rearing; modulate their own emotions so as to avoid strong depression, anger, or anxiety; and work more effectively toward long-term goals by being able to control impulses for immediate gratification. In the end, some people who are high in emotional intelligence may enjoy more success in life than do others who surpass them in mental intelligence (Salovey & Pizzaro, 2003).

As is the case with Gardner's multiple intelligences, emotional intelligence has its critics. Some psychologists believe that the concept of intelligence is being stretched too far from its original focus on mental ability (e.g., Matthews

et al., 2004). They would prefer a different term, such as *emotional competence*, to distinguish this concept from the traditional mental-skills concept of intelligence. But emotional-intelligence proponents respond that if we regard intelligence as adaptive abilities, we ought not limit ourselves to the purely cognitive realms of human ability. The debate concerning multiple intelligence continues to rage and promises to do so into the future.

So far we have explored the nature of intelligence. Let's now examine more closely how individual differences in intelligence are measured.

▶ **Focus 13**
Describe the four branches of emotional intelligence and how they are measured.

IN REVIEW

- The psychometric approach to intelligence attempts to map the structure of intellect and establish how many different classes of mental ability underlie test performance. A newer approach, the cognitive processes approach, focuses on the specific thought processes that underlie mental competencies.

- Factor analysis can be applied to correlations among test scores to identify clusters of measures that correlate highly with one another and therefore are assumed to have a common underlying factor, such as verbal ability or mathematical reasoning.

- Spearman believed that intelligence is determined both by specific cognitive abilities and by a general intelligence (*g*) factor that constitutes the core of intelligence. Thurstone disagreed, viewing intelligence as a set of specific abilities. Thurstone's position is best supported by observed distinctions between verbal and spatial abilities.

- Cattell and Horn differentiated between crystallized intelligence, the ability to apply previously learned knowledge to current problems, and fluid intelligence, the ability to deal with novel problem-solving situations for which personal experience does not provide a solution. They argued that over our life span, we show a progressive shift from using fluid intelligence to using crystallized intelligence as we attain wisdom.

- Carroll's three-stratum model is based on reanalyses of hundreds of data sets. Mental abilities are represented at three levels, with general intelligence (*g*) at the apex and highly specific cognitive and perceptual skills at its base. Carroll's model may be the most accurate psychometric representation of human cognitive abilities.

- Cognitive process theories of intelligence focus on the elementary information-processing abilities

► Focus 14
How is Wechsler's view of intelligence reflected in the Wechsler tests? What kinds of scores do they provide?

FIGURE 9.10

The Wechsler Adult Intelligence Scale. These sample items resemble those found on subscales of the Wechsler Adult Intelligence Scale (WAIS-III). SOURCE: Simulated items similar to those in the Wechsler Adult Intelligence Scale, third edition. Copyright © 2005 by Harcourt Assessment, Inc. Reproduced with permission. All rights reserved.

that contribute to intelligence. Sternberg's triarchic theory of intelligence includes a components subtheory that addresses the specific cognitive processes that underlie intelligent behavior.

■ Sternberg and Gardner maintain that there are distinct forms of intelligence beyond the traditional concept. Sternberg differentiates between analytical, practical, and creative intelligence, and Gardner proposes nine different kinds of intelligence. The theory of emotional intelligence refers to people's ability to read and respond appropriately to others' emotions, to motivate themselves, and to be aware of and in control of their emotions.

THE MEASUREMENT OF INTELLIGENCE

Today, the Wechsler tests (WAIS-III and WISC-IV) are the most popular individually administered intelligence tests in the United States (Groth-Marnat, 1999). They provide a good illustration of how intelligence is assessed.

Recall that Wechsler believed that intelligence tests should measure a wide array of different mental abilities. His tests reflect that conviction. The WAIS-III consists of a series of subtests that fall into two classes: verbal and performance (Figure 9.10). A psychologist can therefore plot a profile based on

Wechsler Adult Intelligence Scale (WAIS-III)

Subtest	Description	Example
Verbal Scales		
Information	Taps general range of knowledge	What is steam made of?
Comprehension	Tests understanding of social conventions and ability to evaluate past experience	What is the advantage of keeping money in a bank?
Arithmetic	Tests arithmetic reasoning through verbal problems	Three women divided eighteen golf balls equally among themselves. How many golf balls did each person receive?
Similarities	Asks in what way certain objects or concepts are similar; measures abstract thinking	In what way are an hour and a week alike?
Letter-number Sequencing	Tests attention and ability to retain and manipulate information in memory; the alternating numbers and letters are presented orally and the subject must repeat first the numbers and then the letters in order of magnitude and alphabetical order, respectively (Alternative to the Digit Span subtest)	Item: 5-J-4-A-1-S Response: 1-4-5-A-J-S
Vocabulary	Tests ability to define increasingly difficult words	What does "formidable" mean?
Performance Scales		
Digit Symbol	Tests speed of learning through timed coding tasks in which numbers must be associated with drawings of various shapes	Shown: / Fill in appropriate symbol:
Picture Completion	Tests visual alertness and visual memory through presentation of an incompletely drawn figure; the missing part must be discovered and named	What is missing in this picture?
Block Design	Tests ability to perceive and analyze patterns by presenting designs that must be copied with blocks	Assemble blocks to match this design:
Picture Arrangement	Tests understanding of social situations through a series of comic-strip-type pictures that must be arranged in the right sequence to tell a story	Put the pictures in the correct order:
Object Assembly	Tests ability to deal with part/whole relationships by presenting puzzle pieces that must be assembled to form a complete object	Assemble the pieces into a complete object:

Note: Sample items courtesy of The Psychological Corporation, 2005.

the scores on each of the subtests to assess a person's pattern of intellectual strengths and weaknesses. The test yields three summary scores: a *Verbal IQ* based on the sum of the verbal subtests; a *Performance IQ* based on the performance subtests; and a *Full-Scale IQ* based on all of the subtests. For some purposes, it is useful to examine differences between the Verbal IQ and the Performance IQ. For example, individuals from an impoverished environment with little formal schooling might score higher on the performance subtests than on the verbal subtests, suggesting that their overall IQ might be an underestimate of their intellectual potential. Sometimes, too, various types of brain damage are reflected in large discrepancies between certain subtest scores (Goldstein, 2000).

INCREASING THE INFORMATIONAL YIELD FROM INTELLIGENCE TESTS

Revisions of both the Stanford-Binet and the Wechsler scales have been responsive to advances in the understanding of the mental processes that underlie intelligence. The original Stanford-Binet yielded a single IQ score based mainly on verbal items, but today's test samples a wider range of abilities and provides, in addition to a composite IQ score, separate scores for Verbal Reasoning, Abstract/Visual Reasoning, Quantitative Reasoning, and Short-Term Memory. The WISC-IV, used to assess children between ages 6 and 11, provides, in addition to its Full-Scale IQ, separate scores for Verbal Comprehension, Perceptual Organization, Freedom from Distractibility, and Processing Speed. These scores make the tests more useful for understanding test takers' intellectual strengths and weaknesses and possibly planning educational interventions for them. Many other tests of specific cognitive skills are currently in use, providing many tools for assessing both children and adults (Bartholomew, 2005; Groth-Marnat, 1999).

THEORY-BASED INTELLIGENCE TESTS

Advances in the theory of intelligence have stimulated the development of new instruments to test the specific abilities dictated by the theories. For example, the Cattell-Horn distinction between crystallized and fluid intelligence has had a strong impact on the field of intelligence testing. Several recently developed tests, such as the Kaufman Adolescent and Adult Intelligence Test and the Woodcock-Johnson Psycho-Educational Battery, are specifically designed to measure fluid and crystallized abilities separately (Kaufman & Kaufman, 1997; Woodcock, 1997). The Kaufman test has three crystallized-ability subscales and three fluid-ability scales, and test results yield separate g_c and g_f IQs, as well as a composite, or full-scale, IQ. The crystallized-intelligence scales require respondents to define words, listen to and answer questions about a detailed news story, and study two sets of words, such as "*animal* and *vampire*" and "*baseball* and *stick*" and then produce a word that relates to both, such as *bat*. The fluid-intelligence subtests require respondents to break mystery codes, solve logic problems, and associate words with complex drawings and then "read" sentences composed only of the drawings. The Kaufman and Woodcock-Johnson tests have become quite popular in educational, job-screening, and clinical settings.

Sternberg's triarchic model of intelligence has inspired the development of a new test as well. The Sternberg Triarchic Ability Test (STAT) measures the three forms of intelligence identified in his model—analytic, practical, and creative. This test can be useful in identifying students' levels of each of the three types of intelligence so that school curricula can be individualized to capitalize on their strengths and thereby optimize learning and school performance.

APTITUDE OR ACHIEVEMENT?

Using written tests for selection purposes highlights an issue that Binet faced and that continues to plague test developers today: Should we test a person's abstract "aptitude for learning," or should we test what a person already knows? Consider an example. In selecting applicants for college, we could give students either an **achievement test** *designed to find out how much they have learned so far in their lives*, or we could present them with an **aptitude test** *containing novel puzzle-like problems that presumably go beyond prior learning and are thought to measure the applicant's potential for future learning and performance*.

The argument for achievement testing is that it is usually a good predictor of future performance in a similar situation. If a student learned a lot of academic material in high school (and therefore scored well on the test), he or she is likely to also learn a lot in college. The argument against achievement testing is that it assumes that everyone has had the same opportunity to learn the material being tested. In college selection, for example, a given applicant's test score could depend on whether that person went to a good school rather than on his or her ability to learn in college.

The argument for aptitude testing is that it is fairer because it supposedly depends less on prior

▶ **Focus 15**
How have theories of intelligence influenced recently developed tests?

▶ **Focus 16**
Describe the controversy involving aptitude versus achievement tests in relation to the measurement of intelligence.

Watch the video, "Intelligence Testing," in Chapter 9 of your CD to evaluate arguments about how well standardized tests predict future performance.

knowledge than on a person's ability to react to the problems presented on the test. The argument against aptitude testing is that it is difficult to construct a test that is independent of prior learning. Further, such a test may require an ability to deal with puzzles that is not relevant to success in situations other than the test itself.

In fact, most intelligence tests measure a combination of aptitude and achievement, reflecting both native ability and previous learning (Lubinski, 2004). This has raised major scientific and social issues concerning the meaning of test scores, the extent to which improvement can be fostered by educational experiences, and the usefulness of the measures for describing mental competence and predicting performance in nontest situations.

Tests of mental skills have become a staple of Western societies. They are used to make important educational, occupational, and clinical decisions, as well as to set social policy. These measures also have become important scientific tools for cognitive psychologists who study the development, stability, operation, and modification of cognitive functions. We will now consider the scientific standards required for psychological tests.

PSYCHOMETRIC STANDARDS FOR INTELLIGENCE TESTS

A **psychological test** *is a method for measuring individual differences related to some psychological concept, or construct, based on a sample of relevant behavior in a scientifically designed and controlled situation.* In the case of intelligence testing, intelligence is the *construct* and scores obtained on the test are its *operational definition.* To design a test, we need to decide which specific behaviors serve as indicators

▶ **Focus 17**
Define the three types of test reliability.

of intellectual abilities. Then we need to devise test items that allow us to assess individual differences in those behaviors. We will, of course, need evidence that our sample of items (a sample, because we can't ask every conceivable question) actually measures the abilities we are assessing. As in designing an experiment (see Chapter 2), we want to collect *a sample of relevant behavior* under standardized conditions, attempting to control for other factors that could influence responses to the items. To understand how psychologists meet these requirements, we must examine three key measurement concepts: *reliability, validity,* and *standardization.* We should note that these standards apply to all psychological tests, not just intelligence measures.

Reliability

Reliability *refers to consistency of measurement.* As shown in Table 9.4, reliability can take several forms when applied to psychological tests. It can refer to consistency of measurement over time, consistency of measurement by the items within the test itself, or consistency in scores assigned by different examiners.

One of the most important is consistency over time. If you step on your bathroom scale five times in a row, you should expect it to register the same weight each time unless you have a very unusual metabolism. Likewise, if we assume that intelligence is a relatively stable trait (and virtually all psychologists do), then scores on our measure should be stable, or consistent, over time. Where psychological tests are concerned, this type of measurement stability over time is defined as **test-retest reliability,** *which is assessed by administering the measure to the same group of participants on two (or more) separate occasions and correlating the two (or more) sets of scores.*

After about age 7, scores on intelligence tests show considerable stability, even over many years (Gregory, 1998). Over a short interval (2 to 12 weeks), the test-retest correlation of adult IQs on the WAIS-III is .96, or nearly perfect (Tulsky et al., 2003). Correlations between IQs at age 9 and age 40 are in the .70 to .80 range (Plomin & Spinath, 2004), indicating a high degree of stability. In a Scottish national sample, scores on a test of general intelligence administered at age 11 correlated .66 with scores on the same test at age 80 (Deary et al., 2004). Thus, *relative to his or her age group,* a person who achieves an above-average IQ at age 9 or 11 is very likely to also be above the average for 40- or 80-year-olds when he or she reaches those ages. Even while children's cognitive

TABLE 9.4	Types of Reliability and Validity in Psychological Testing
Types of Reliability	**Meaning and Critical Questions**
Test-retest reliability	Are scores on the measure stable over time?
Internal consistency	Do all of the items on the measure seem to be measuring the same thing, as indicated by high correlations among them?
Interjudge reliability	Do different raters or scorers agree on their scoring or observations?
Types of Validity	
Construct validity	To what extent is the test actually measuring the construct of interest (e.g., intelligence)?
Content validity	Do the questions or test items relate to all aspects of the construct being measured?
Criterion-related validity	Do scores on the test predict some present or future behavior or outcome assumed to be affected by the construct being measured?

skills are developing rapidly during middle childhood, IQs are quite stable, with test-retest coefficients around .90 (Canivez & Watkins, 1998).

Another form of reliability, **internal consistency,** *has to do with consistency of measurement within the test itself.* For example, if a Wechsler subtest is internally consistent, all of its items are measuring the same skill, as evidenced by high correlations among the items. In accord with this requirement, the individual items within the Wechsler subtests correlate substantially with one another (Gregory, 1998).

Finally, **interjudge reliability** *refers to consistency of measurement when different people observe the same event or score the same test.* Ideally, two psychologists who independently score the same test will assign exactly the same scores. To attain high interjudge reliability, the scoring instructions must be so explicit that trained professionals will use the scoring system in the same way.

Validity

As a general concept, **validity** *refers to how well a test actually measures what it is designed to measure.* As in the case of reliability, there are several types of validity (see Table 9.4).

As noted earlier, intelligence is a concept, or mental construct. **Construct validity** *exists when a test successfully measures the psychological construct it is designed to measure, as indicated by relations between test scores and other behaviors that it should be related to.* If an intelligence test had perfect construct validity, individual differences in IQs would be due to differences in intelligence and nothing else. In reality, this ideal is never attained, for other factors such as motivation and educational background also influence test scores.

Two other kinds of validity contribute to construct validity. **Content validity** *refers to whether the items on a test measure all the knowledge or skills that are assumed to underlie the construct of interest.* For example, if we want the Arithmetic subtest of the WAIS-III to measure general mathematical reasoning skills, we would not want to have only addition problems; we would want the items to sample other relevant mathematical abilities as well, such as subtraction, division, and fractions.

If an intelligence test is measuring what it is assumed to measure, the IQ it yields should allow us to predict other behaviors that are assumed to be influenced by intelligence, such as school grades or job performance. These outcome measures are called *criterion measures,* and **criterion-related validity** *refers to the ability of test scores to correlate with meaningful criterion measures.* A criti-

cal issue for intelligence tests is the extent to which they predict the kinds of outcomes we would expect intelligence to influence, such as school and job performance. Let us examine this aspect of validity.

Intelligence and Academic Performance   Intelligence tests were originally developed to predict academic and other forms of achievement. How valid are they for this purpose? Actually, they do fairly well. Correlations of IQ with school grades are in the .60 range for high school students and in the .30 to .50 range for college students (Kuncel et al., 2004). In general, then, people who score well on the tests tend to do well academically. Likewise, the college entrance examination you took while in high school is designed to predict the criterion of grades in college by assessing verbal and mathematical abilities. In fact, SAT scores do predict college grades, with correlations slightly below .50 (Willingham et al., 1990). This correlation, which is about the same magnitude as the correlation between people's height and weight, is high enough to justify using the tests for screening purposes but low enough to necessitate the use of other predictors (such as high school grades) in combination with SAT scores.

Another measure of general intelligence used in selecting graduate students, the Miller Analogies Test, successfully predicts a variety of performance criteria, including grades, faculty ratings, comprehensive examination scores, and number of years required to attain the advanced degree, with validity coefficients ranging from .35 to .58 (Kuncel et al., 2004). There is little doubt that measures of intelligence successfully predict academic performance.

Job Performance, Income, and Longevity   Intelligence test scores also predict military and job performance. General mental ability predicts both occupational level and performance within one's chosen occupation (Schmidt & Hunter, 2004). Intelligent individuals are far more likely to attain prestigious occupations. One study followed siblings raised together, thereby controlling for home background. When the siblings were in their late 20s, mental ability measures collected during young adulthood were related to their annual adult incomes. Siblings with IQs of 120 or more were, on average, earning $18,000 more than siblings of average intelligence (Murray, 1998). Intelligence correlates .50 to .70 with the level of socioeconomic status that people attain (Lubinski, 2004).

People with higher intelligence perform better on their jobs, and the more complex the job, the

► **Focus 18**
What is validity? Describe three kinds of test validity.

► **Focus 19**
How well do IQ scores predict academic, job, and other life outcomes?

more strongly intelligence is related to performance (Hunter & Hunter, 1984). The relation is particularly striking during the job-training period, when the superior learning ability of highly intelligent people helps them shine (Schmidt & Hunter, 2004). Furthermore, intelligence predicts job performance better than does job experience, specific abilities, or personality traits (Schmidt & Hunter, 2004).

FIGURE 9.11

Does intelligence predict life span? This graph shows the relation between IQ assessed at age 11 and survival at ages 50 and 76 in women followed in the Scottish Mental Survey. SOURCE: Data from Whalley & Deary, 2001.

▶ **Focus 20**
What are the two meanings of standardization?

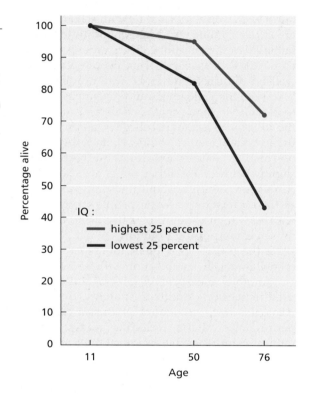

Intelligence predicts other life outcomes as well. In fact, it literally predicts life and death. In 1932 every child in Scotland who had been born in 1921 was administered an intelligence test. These children and another similar-age cohort of children tested in 1947 were followed as their lives unfolded (Deary et al., 2004). Higher childhood intelligence was associated with significantly greater survival to age 76 in both men and women, but the results were particularly striking for women (Figure 9.11).

How shall we account for these results? Is it possible that cognitive ability is a reflection of general fitness to survive? The researchers suggest the possibility that lower childhood intelligence may in some cases be influenced by prenatal or postnatal events that also impair later health. Or perhaps good brain development is related to optimal development of other bodily organs as well. But it is also possible that intelligent people are more likely to engage in healthy behaviors and to avoid unhealthy ones, or that higher intelligence allows people to live and work in safer physical environments or to enjoy better nutrition, thereby helping them live longer and healthier lives.

Standardization

The third measurement requirement, **standardization,** *has two meanings: (1) the development of norms and (2) rigorously controlled testing procedures.* The first meaning of standardization is especially important in providing a meaningful IQ score. It involves the collection of **norms,** *test scores derived from a large sample that represents particular age segments of the population.* These normative scores provide a basis for interpreting a given individual's score, just as the distribution of scores in a course exam allows you to determine how well you did relative to your classmates. Normative data also allow us to recalibrate the distribution of test scores so that an IQ of 100 will remain the "average" score even if the general population's test performance changes over time.

When norms are collected for mental skills (and for many other human characteristics), the scores usually form a **normal distribution,** *a bell-shaped curve with most scores clustering around the center of the curve.* On intelligence tests, the center of the distribution for each age group from childhood to late adulthood is assigned an IQ score of 100. Because the normal distribution has known statistical properties, we can specify what percentage of the population will score higher than a given score. Thus, as Figure 9.12 shows, an IQ score of 100 cuts the distribution in half, with an equal percentage of the population scoring above

FIGURE 9.12

The bell curve of intelligence. When administered to large groups of people, intelligence tests yield a normal, or bell-shaped, distribution of IQ scores that has known statistical properties. The mean of the distribution is set at 100. It is possible to specify for any given score which percentage of the standardization group achieved higher or lower scores. Common descriptive labels are shown relative to the bell-shaped distribution. The range of scores from 90 to 110 is labeled average and includes nearly half of the population.

and below this midpoint. The farther we move from this average score of 100 in either direction, the fewer people attain the higher or lower scores. The figure also shows the percentage of people who score above certain IQ levels. On modern intelligence tests, this method of assigning an IQ score has replaced the original formula of mental age divided by chronological age.

The Flynn Effect: Are We Getting Smarter?

The relative nature of the IQ allows its meaning to be preserved even if performance changes within the population. A notable discovery by New Zealand researcher James Flynn (1987, 1998) suggests that much of the world's population is scoring progressively higher on intelligence tests. This "rising-curve" phenomenon (also called the *Flynn effect*) has resulted in IQ increases of 28 points in the United States since 1910 and a similar increase in Britain since 1942. On average, IQs in the West have increased about 3 points per decade, meaning that today's average IQ would be about 115 if the tests were scored according to the norms used in 1955. The increase seems to be occurring to the same degree for both men and women and for different ethnic groups (Truscott & Frank, 2001).

The reasons underlying the Flynn effect are not clear, but several possibilities have been suggested (Flynn, 1998; Neisser et al., 1998). One possibility is that better nutrition has helped fuel the IQ increase. Height has also increased dramatically over the past century, and it, like increased brain functioning, may be due to nutritional gains. Other explanations focus on the environment. Richer and more complex learning environments that require more complex coping may have increased mental abilities. Likewise, technological advances may have helped shape the kinds of analytical and abstract reasoning skills that boost performance on intelligence tests. Whatever the reasons, however, the rising-curve phenomenon means that the intelligence score distribution has to be recalibrated upward periodically if the average IQ is to remain at 100, the traditional midpoint of the intelligence range.

Testing Conditions: Static and Dynamic Testing

Test instructions and procedures are designed to create a well-controlled, or standardized, environment for administering the intelligence test so that other uncontrolled factors will not influence scores. Tests like the Stanford-Binet and Wechsler scales have very detailed instructions that must be closely adhered to, even to the point of reading the instructions and items to the person being tested (Figure 9.13). The goal is to make sure that

FIGURE 9.13

When administering intelligence tests, psychologists use consistently applied instructions and procedures in order to create a standardized testing environment.

all testees are responding to as similar a stimulus situation as possible so that their scores will be solely a reflection of their ability. *This traditional approach to testing is called* **static testing.**

Some theorists suggest that the static approach to testing may reveal an incomplete picture of a person's abilities by measuring only the products of previous learning. In **dynamic testing,** *the standard testing is followed up with an interaction in which the examiner gives the respondent guided feedback on how to improve performance and observes how the person utilizes the information.* This part of the session provides a window to the individual's ability to profit from instruction and improve performance and may disclose cognitive capacities not revealed by static testing.

Let's look in on a dynamic testing session with a 5-year-old child who is being tested for educational purposes. Daniel is impulsive in the classroom, and the teacher wants to know how best to instruct him. The child has been asked to draw a picture of a person (a task common to several intelligence tests) and has hurriedly scribbled a poorly formed figure that merits a low score. The examiner wants to see how much Daniel can improve with feedback:

> Wow, Daniel. I can really tell that that's a boy. I see a head, two arms, and two legs. He even looks like he could be running, because his legs are kind of bent. Now we're going to work together to see if we can get this picture to look more like a boy. I think we need to think real hard about some more parts that people have and just

▶ **Focus 21**
What is the Flynn effect? What explanations have been suggested?

▶ **Focus 22**
Explain the nature and value of dynamic testing.

▶ **Focus 23**
How is intelligence assessed in non-Western cultures?

where they need to go. I also noticed that you did this really fast, and that made this look kind of wobbly. So I'm going to help you slow down a bit so you can make this boy stand really straight. (Lidz, 1997, p. 283)

By testing the limits of Daniel's competencies and his ability to profit from various kinds of feedback, the dynamic tester may gain a fuller picture of his mental skills and may be able to make better educational recommendations. Dynamic testing can be particularly useful when people have not had equal learning opportunities, as occurs in disadvantaged groups. Equally important is the fact that dynamic feedback tends to improve test scores, and these new scores often relate more highly to educational outcomes than do the original test scores (Lidz, 1997). Dynamic testing can be particularly useful and revealing when testing people from cultures that are not accustomed to taking Western-style tests (Sternberg, 2004).

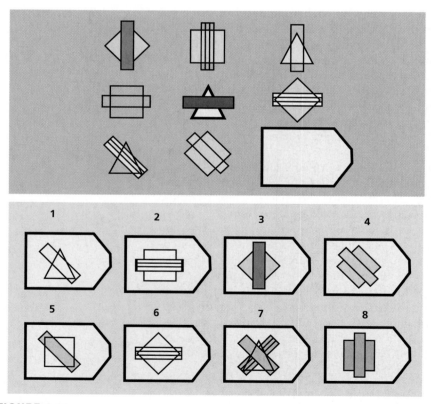

FIGURE 9.14

Culture-fair measurement? This problem is similar to those on the Raven Progressive Matrices test. This nonverbal measure tests fluid-intelligence ability, requiring subjects to perceive relationships and decipher the rules underlying the pattern of drawings in the rows and columns of the upper figure and then to select the figure that is the missing entry from the eight alternatives below. (The answer appears on page 332.)
SOURCE: Carpenter et al., 1990.

ASSESSING INTELLIGENCE IN NON-WESTERN CULTURES

Special challenges await the psychologist who wishes to assess intelligence in non-Western cultures. Traditional intelligence tests such as the WAIS and the Stanford-Binet draw heavily on the cognitive skills and learning that are needed to succeed in Western educational and occupational settings. They tend to have strong verbal content and to rely on the products of Western schooling. Taken into a cultural context where *smart* is defined in different ways and requires other kinds of adaptive behavior, such tests cannot hope to measure intelligence in a valid fashion. For example, the WAIS does not measure the ability to create herbal medicines, construct shelters, or navigate in the open sea. Robert Sternberg (2004) has advanced a *theory of successful intelligence* in which intelligence is whatever is required to meet the adaptive demands of a given culture. Sternberg believes that fundamental mental skills (the metacomponents described earlier) are required for successful behavior in any culture. These include the ability to mentally represent problems in a way that facilitates their solution, to develop potential solutions and to choose successfully among them, to utilize mental resources wisely, and to evaluate the effects of one's action plans. What differs is the kinds of problems to which these basic intellectual skills are applied. People from different cultures may think about the same problem in very different ways (Nisbett, 2003).

Two main approaches have been taken to meet the challenges of cross-cultural intelligence assessment. One is to choose reasoning problems that are not tied to the knowledge base of any culture but that reflect the ability to process and evaluate stimulus patterns. The problem shown in Figure 9.14 resembles one on the Raven Progressive Matrices, a test that is frequently used to measure fluid intelligence (Raven, 1962). On this nonverbal task, you must detect relationships and then decipher the rules underlying the pattern of drawings in the rows and columns of the upper figure. Finally, you must use this information to select the figure that is the missing entry from the eight alternatives below. The Raven test has been used in many cultures and measures a general mental capacity that is also measured by traditional intelligence tests in our culture (Jensen, 1998). Scores on the Raven correlate positively with measures of IQ derived from traditional tests, yet they seem to be more "culture fair."

A second and more challenging approach is to create measures that are tailored to the kinds of knowledge and skills that are valued in the particular culture. Such tests may measure how smart an individual is in terms of the practical skills and adaptive behaviors within that culture. Scores may be unrelated or even negatively correlated with other measures of intelligence, yet, they may predict successful functioning within that culture (Sternberg, 2004). If intelligence is defined as the ability to engage in culture-specific adaptive behavior, then who is to say that the culture-specific measure is not a valid measure of intelligence in that context?

GALTON RESURRECTED: INTELLIGENCE AND NEURAL EFFICIENCY

The scientific study of intelligence began with Sir Francis Galton's attempts to develop measures of nervous system efficiency that might underlie mental skills. As noted earlier, these attempts fell into disfavor because scores on his measures were unrelated to one another and to external criteria of success. As tools for directly measuring brain functions become more sophisticated, however, Galton's legacy lives on in current attempts to relate IQ to brain functioning (Garlick, 2002; Posthuma et al., 2001). For example, one line of evidence comes from studies of brain metabolism. PET scans of people's brains taken while they engage in problem-solving tasks have shown lower levels of glucose consumption in people of high intelligence than in those of average or low intelligence, suggesting that intelligent brains work more efficiently and expend less energy (Haier et al., 1993). Whether these findings herald a new way of measuring intelligence is an unanswered question. The critical issue will be the ability of such measures to predict external achievement and performance criteria, as traditional intelligence tests do.

The brain is clearly the locus of intellectual activities. For a brain to operate more efficiently, it makes sense that having more neurons, or more connections among them, might be advantageous, especially in the areas most involved in processing information. This notion has spurred attempts to relate brain size with intelligence. As noted in Chapter 3, evolutionary evidence indicates a progressive increase in brain size as humanoid species evolved over the ages, particularly in the parts of the brain involved in higher mental functions, such as the cerebral cortex and frontal lobes (Kolb & Whishaw, 2002). Not suprisingly, therefore, scientists have revisited Galton's original hypothesis that individual differences in brain size might be related to intellectual competency.

One intriguing way of testing this hypothesis might be to study the brains of dead geniuses to see if they differ from the brains of less brilliant people and, if so, how. After Albert Einstein's death in 1955, a Missouri physician removed and preserved his brain. The brain has undergone several analyses by neuroscientists over the years. The examinations have shown that Einstein's brain was not larger than average overall; in fact, it was actually smaller than average in some regions. But it was indeed bigger in some ways. His parietal lobes were densely packed with neurons and glial cells (which produce nutrients for neurons and support them) to such an extent that some major fissures were no longer visible. Significantly, this area of the brain is involved in mathematical thinking and visuospatial functions—precisely the kinds of abilities that seemed to underlie Einstein's creative genius (Witelson et al., 1999).

These findings are intriguing, but are you ready to conclude that the larger your brain is, the more intelligent you're likely to be? If so, consider these points: Women and men have virtually identical mean IQs, but women's brains are smaller on average (Ankney, 1992). Other research, beginning with Galton's, indicates that brain size is only weakly related to intelligence, and it's not clear whether larger brain mass causes intelligence, whether lots of "intelligent" interactions with the environment facilitate brain growth (as in the environmental enrichment studies with rats described in Chapter 2), or whether some other factor(s) influences both brain mass and intelligence. It's not how large your brain is, but how efficiently it functions, and it is the efficiency question that drives today's research. Indeed, we can be thankful that brain size does not determine intelligence, for Neandertals, ancient humans hardly known for their intellectual brilliance, had slightly larger brains than we do (Kolb & Whishaw, 2002).

Dennis Garlick (2002) of the University of Sydney proposes that individual differences in *brain plasticity*—the ability of the brain to change by forming new connections among neurons in response to environmental input—may be the key neural factor underlying differences in intelligence. The ability to quickly establish new neural networks would increase processing speed and efficiency, and people with brains capable of greater plasticity would develop better intellectual skills. Garlick believes that there is a critical period for the growth of new neural circuits that ends at about age 16, the same age by which crystallized intelligence seems to be established. To this point, however, no methods have been developed to measure neural circuitry with the detail and precision that would allow a direct test of this provocative theory.

▶ **Focus 24**
What evidence exists that neural efficiency and brain size underlie high intelligence?

Answer to the problem in Figure 9.14:
The correct choice is geometric form
number 5. Can you specify why?

▶ **Focus 25**
What evidence supports a genetic contribution to intelligence,
and how much IQ group variation
is accounted for?

IN REVIEW

- Most modern intelligence tests, such as the Wechlser scales, measure an array of different mental abilities. In addition to a global, or full-scale, IQ, they provide scores for each subtest and summary scores for broader abilities, such as verbal and performance IQs. Some recent tests are derived directly from theories of intelligence. The Kaufman scale provides separate scores for crystallized and fluid intelligence, and Sternberg's STAT measures analytical, practical, and creative intelligence.

- Achievement tests measure what has already been learned, whereas aptitude tests are assumed to measure potential for future learning and perfor-mance. Most intelligence tests measure combina-tions of achievement and aptitude, for it is difficult to separate past learning and future learning potential.

- Three important standards for psychological tests are reliability (consistency of measurement over time, within tests, and across scorers), validity (successful measurement of the construct and acceptable relations with relevant criterion mea-sures), and standardization (development of norms and standard testing conditions).

- IQ scores successfully predict a range of aca-demic, occupational, and life outcomes, including how long people live. Such findings indicate that intelligence tests are measuring important adap-tational skills.

- The Flynn effect refers to the notable rise in intelli-gence test scores over the past century, possibly due to better living conditions, more schooling, or more complex environments.

- In dynamic testing, standard test administration is followed by feedback and suggestions from the examiner and a retaking of the test, thus allowing an assessment of how well the person profits from feedback and how intellectual skills might be coached in the future. Dynamic testing provides information that static testing does not, and retest scores sometimes relate more strongly to crite-rion measures.

- Intelligence testing in non-Western cultures is a challenge. One approach is to use tests that are not tied to any culture's knowledge base. Another approach is to devise tests of the abilities that are important to adaptation in that culture. These culture-specific abilities may bear little relation to the mental skills assessed by Western intelli-gence tests.

- Recent physiological evidence suggests that the brains of intelligent people may function more effi-ciently. Brain size is not significantly related to in-telligence, but the neural networks laid down in the process of brain development may be ex-tremely important. One current theory is that differ-ences in brain plasticity may underlie intelligence.

HEREDITY, ENVIRONMENT, AND INTELLIGENCE

To what extent are differences in intelligence due to genetic versus environmental factors? This seemingly simple question has long been a source of controversy and, at times, bitter debate. The answer has important social as well as scientific consequences.

GENES AND INTELLIGENCE

Let's first examine the genetic argument. Suppose that intelligence were totally heritable, that is, suppose that 100 percent of the intellectual varia-tion in the population were determined by genes. (No psychologist today would maintain that this is so, but examining the extreme view can be in-structive.) In that case, any two individuals with exactly the same genes would have identical test scores, so the correlation between test scores of identical (monozygotic) twins would be 1.00. Nonidentical brothers and sisters (including fra-ternal twins, who result from two fertilized eggs) share only half their genes. Therefore the correla-tion between the test scores of fraternal twins and other siblings should be substantially lower. Ex-tending the argument, the correlation between a parent's test scores and his or her children's scores should be about the same as that between sib-lings, because a child inherits only half of his or her genes from each parent.

What do the actual data look like? Table 9.5 summarizes the results from many studies. As you can see, the correlation between the test scores of identical twins is substantially higher than any other correlations in the table (but they are not 1.00). Identical twins separated early in life and reared apart are of special interest because they have identical genes but experienced differ-ent environments. Note that the correlation for identical twins raised apart is nearly as high as that for identical twins reared together. It is also higher than that for fraternal twins raised together. This pattern of findings is a powerful argument for the importance of genetic factors (Bouchard et al., 1990).

Adoption studies are also instructive. As Table 9.5 shows, IQs of adopted children correlate as highly with their biological parents' IQ as with the IQs of the adoptive parents who reared them. Overall, the pattern is quite clear: The more genes people have in common, the more similar their IQs tend to be. This is very strong evidence that genes play a significant role in intelligence, accounting for 50 to 70 percent of group variation in IQ (Petrill, 2003; Plomin & Spinath, 2004).

Although genes are important foundations of the *g* factor (Plomin & Craig, 2002), there clearly is not a single intelligence gene. The diverse abilities measured by intelligence tests are undoubtedly influenced by large numbers of interacting genes, and different combinations seem to underlie specific abilities (Luciano et al., 2001; Plomin & Spinath, 2004).

ENVIRONMENTAL DETERMINANTS

Genes are not the whole story, however. Notice, for example, that the correlation for identical twins raised together is higher than that for identical twins raised apart. The same is true for other types of siblings raised together and raised apart. This rules out an entirely genetic explanation for intelligence. Although one's genotype seems to be an important factor in determining intelligence test scores, it probably accounts for only 50 to 70 percent of the IQ variation among people in the United States (Bouchard et al., 1990; Plomin, 1997). Thus genetics research provides the best possible argument for the contribution of environmental factors to intelligence (Plomin & Spinath, 2004). A good place to look for such factors is in the home and school environments.

TABLE 9.5	Correlations in Intelligence among People Who Differ in Genetic Similarity and Who Live Together or Apart	
Relationship	**Percentage of Shared Genes**	**Correlation of IQ Scores**
Identical twins reared together	100	.86
Identical twins reared apart	100	.75
Nonidentical twins reared together	50	.57
Siblings reared together	50	.45
Siblings reared apart	50	.21
Biological parent–offspring reared by parent	50	.36
Biological parent–offspring not reared by parent	50	.20
Cousins	25	.25
Adopted child–adoptive parent	0	.19
Adopted children reared together	0	.32

SOURCES: Based on Bouchard & McGue, 1981; Bouchard et al., 1990; Scarr, 1992.

Shared Family Environment

How important is the home in which you were reared? **Shared environment** *refers to the environmental conditions that are present to all people living in a given home* (Figure 9.15). If home environment is an important determinant of intelligence, then children who grow up together should be more similar than children who are reared apart. As Table 9.5 shows, siblings who are raised together are more similar to one another than those reared apart, whether identical twins or biological siblings. Note also that there is a correlation of .32 between unrelated adopted children reared in the same home. Overall, it appears that between a quarter and a third of the population variability in intelligence can be attributed to shared environmental factors. To put the importance of these findings in perspective, intelligence is one of the few psychological characteristics that shows

▶ **Focus 26**
How much do family and school environments contribute to intelligence?

FIGURE 9.15

Shared family environment has a significant influence on intelligence, accounting for between a quarter and a third of IQ variation in children.

shared-environment effects. In contrast, personality traits show almost no effects of the shared family environment, so that children who grow up together are as different from one another as those from different families (Harris, 1998).

Environmental Enrichment and Deprivation

Another line of evidence for environmental effects comes from studies of children who are removed from deprived environments and placed in middle- or upper-class adoptive homes. Typically, such children show a gradual increase in IQ on the order of 10 to 12 points (Scarr & Weinberg, 1977; Schiff & Lewontin, 1986). Conversely, when deprived children remain in their impoverished environments, they either show no improvement in IQ or they actually deteriorate intellectually over time (Serpell, 2000). Scores on general intelligence correlate around .40 with the socioeconomic status of the family in which a child is reared (Lubinski, 2004).

Recall also the Flynn effect, the notable IQ increases that have occurred in Western countries over the last century. It's highly unlikely that genetic changes can explain such gains. It is more likely that they are due to better and longer schooling over the past century, more complex and stimulating environments provided by better-educated parents and by technological advances (even television and video games), and better nutrition (Greenfield, 1998). Although the environment we live in may be more complex, fast-paced, and stressful than it was a century ago, it is also more conducive to learning the mental skills that are assessed on measures of intelligence.

Educational Experiences

As we might expect, educational experiences can have a significant positive impact on intelligence.

Many studies have shown that school attendance can raise IQ and that lack of attendance can lower it. A small decrease in IQ occurs over summer vacations, especially among low-income children. IQ scores also drop when children are unable to start school on time due to teacher shortages or strikes, natural disasters, or refusals to integrate schools (Ceci & Williams, 1997). It appears that the opportunity to practice mental skills like those assessed on cognitive tests is important in solidifying those skills.

Research on intelligence has had a strong impact on educational curricula, and much has been learned about what, when, and how to teach. Gains in intelligence are most likely to be observed when the following educational goals are met (Mayer, 2000):

- Rather than "teach to" general mental ability, help students learn the specific cognitive skills and problem-solving approaches that underlie success in particular subjects. This is an outgrowth of education's increasing deemphasis on the *g* factor in favor of specific mental skills.

- Replace the traditional emphasis on repetition and rote learning of facts with instruction in how to learn, critically think about, and apply course content. In this approach, teachers function as "thinking coaches."

- Rather than waiting until low-level skills have been mastered, teach learning tools, such as memory-enhancement strategies, from the very beginning so that the "learning to learn" skills are applied even to the most basic course content.

Many children begin their lives in conditions that are not conducive to developing intellectual skills. An important outgrowth of intelligence research is early intervention in the lives of disadvantaged children. Let's examine several of these programs and what they've accomplished.

▶ **Focus 27**
What effects have been shown in early-intervention programs for disadvantaged children?

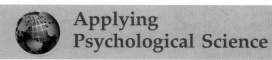

Applying Psychological Science   **Early-Childhood Interventions: A Means of Boosting Intelligence?**

The belief that early-childhood education can influence the life success of poor children can be found in the 18th-century writings of the French social philosopher Jean Jacques Rousseau. In the United States today, that belief translates into the annual expenditure of more than $10 billion on early-intervention programs designed to reverse the downward course of cognitive and social development, school

dropout rate, and joblessness that is so often seen in children from low-income families (Ramey et al., 1998).

In the 1960s, researchers and educators began to design early-childhood intervention programs such as Head Start in an attempt to compensate for the limited learning environments of disadvantaged children. Head Start began as a summer program and gradually increased in scope. But even when it was extended to a full school year, Head Start was only a half-day program that did not begin until age 4. The results were disappointing. Within 2 years, Head Start children were performing in school no better than children who had not attended Head Start (McKey et al., 1985).

What had gone wrong? Was the Head Start program too little, too late? How much might a more intensive program begun earlier in life help disadvantaged children? These questions inspired several notable intervention programs, namely, the Abecedarian Program and the High/Scope Perry Preschool Program.

Participants in the Abecedarian Program were healthy infants born to impoverished families in a southern U.S. community. Many were African American. The children were randomly assigned to an experimental preschool program or to a control group whose families received normal social services. The preschool group was given an intensive early-childhood educational program beginning when they were 6 months old and continuing until they began kindergarten at 5 years of age. Within an educational child care setting, highly trained preschool personnel exposed the children to many stimulating learning experiences designed to foster the growth of cognitive skills (Figure 9.16). At age 5, the preschool program ended, but half of the preschool children and half of the control children were enrolled in a special home-and-school educational program during the first 3 years of school. This experimental design allowed the researchers to test the effects of early versus later intervention.

The long-term effects of the program have now been evaluated. By the time the children had been in the program for 1 year, they tested 18 IQ points higher than the control group. By age 15, the IQ advantage of the children in the preschool condition had decreased to about 5 points, but they also had higher scores on standardized tests of reading and

FIGURE 9.16

The Abecedarian Program provided intensive preschool learning experiences for low-income high-risk children. Here a trainer in an early-intervention program teaches number concepts to preschool children.

mathematics than did the control-group children. Only about half as many had been held back a grade or placed in special education.

A particularly notable IQ effect was found for children in the preschool condition whose mothers were mentally retarded, having IQs below 70. In this sample, every one of the children who had the early intervention attained an IQ at least 20 points higher than their mother's, with an average difference of 32 IQ points. No such effect was found in the control group (Landesman & Ramey, 1989). A difference of this magnitude is truly remarkable for children of mentally retarded parents, one reason being that such parents are unable to provide much in the way of intellectual stimulation for their children. Apparently, the preschool program provided the environmental stimulation needed for normal intellectual development to occur.

What of the control-group children who did not attend the preschool program but were exposed to the special program from 5 to 8 years of age? This delayed training had little effect on any of the outcome measures. Also, the later training had almost no added effects on the children who had been in the preschool program. It thus appears that early intervention has a much stronger effect than does later training. By the time disadvantaged children are in school, it may be too late to influence their future cognitive development to any great degree (Ramey & Ramey, 1998).

The Abecedarian Program showed positive intervention effects that were still apparent in adolescence. What effect does early intervention have on later adult functioning? Here, we turn to another program, the High/Scope Perry Preschool Program, carried out with African American children who lived in an impoverished area of Ypsilanti, Michigan. The participants were considered at high risk for educational and social problems. They were 2 or 3 years old when they were matched on IQ and family variables and randomly assigned to either an intensive preschool program or to a control group that did not receive the program. The intervention continued for 3 years.

The two groups of children have been followed up through age 27, and the results are encouraging. Figure 9.17 compares what happened to the two groups in the 22 years after the program ended. The early-education group had lower crime rates, required less welfare assistance, exhibited better academic performance and progress, and had higher income and home ownership. A cost-benefit analysis showed that the early-intervention program provided taxpayers with a return of $7.16 for every dollar invested in the program (Schweinhart & Weikart, 1998).

Does early intervention work? The Abecedarian and High/Scope Perry programs prove it can provide social, intellectual, educational, and psychological dividends if the program is intensive enough and administered very early in life (Masten & Coatsworth, 1998; Reppucci et al., 1999). A more recent early-intevention program conducted with low-birth-weight children, also considered at risk for later cognitive impairment and academic failure, showed significant IQ gains of 7 to 10 points, but only for those children who had attended the program for at least 400 days

Continued

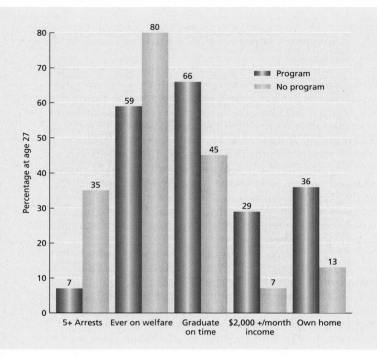

between the ages of 2 and 3 (Hill et al., 2003). We should also note that the positive effects of early-intervention programs seem to occur only for disadvantaged children, for whom quality programs offer learning opportunities and support that the children would not experience at home. Such programs do little for middle- and upper-class children who already have those resources in their homes (Hetherington, 1998).

FIGURE 9.17

Effects of early intervention. This graph shows the differences by age 27 between disadvantaged children who received the High/Scope Perry Preschool Program and matched control children. SOURCE: Schweinhart & Weikart, 1998.

HEREDITY-ENVIRONMENT INTERACTIONS

▶ **Focus 28**
How does the concept of reaction range illustrate the interaction between heredity and environment?

Genes and environment both influence intelligence, but they rarely operate independently. The environment can influence how genes express themselves, as when prenatal factors or malnutrition retard gene-directed brain development. Likewise, genetic factors can influence the effects produced by the environment. For example, genetic factors influence which environments people select for themselves, how they respond to the environment, and how the environment responds to them (Plomin & Spinath, 2004; Scarr & McCartney, 1983). Obviously, then, the question with which this section began—"To what extent are differences in intelligence due to genetic versus environmental factors?"—is too simplistic. The real question should be, "How do heredity and environment *interact* to affect intelligence?"

The concept of *reaction range* provides a useful framework for understanding genetic-environmental interactions. The **reaction range** *for a genetically influenced trait is the range of possibilities— the upper and lower limits—that the genetic code allows.* Thus to say that intelligence is genetically influenced does not mean that intelligence is fixed at birth. Instead, it means that an individual inherits a *range* for potential intelligence that has upper and lower limits. Environmental effects will then determine where the person falls within these genetically determined boundaries.

At present, genetic reaction ranges cannot be measured directly, and we do not know if their sizes differ from one person to another. But studies of IQ gains associated with environmental enrichment and adoption programs suggest that the ranges could be as large as 15 to 20 points on the IQ scale (Dunn & Plomin, 1990). If this is indeed the case, then the influence of environmental factors on intelligence would be highly significant.

Some practical implications of the reaction range concept are illustrated in Figure 9.18. First, consider persons B and H. They have identical reaction ranges, but B develops in a very deprived environment and H in an enriched environment with many cultural and educational advantages. Person H is able to realize her innate potential and has an IQ that is 20 points higher than person B's. Now compare persons C and I. Person C actually has greater intellectual potential than person I but ends up with a lower IQ as a result of living in an environment that does not allow that potential to develop. Finally, note person G, who was born with high genetic endowment and reared in an enriched environment. His IQ of 110 is lower than we would expect, suggesting that he did not take advantage of either his biological capacity or his environmental advantages. This serves to reminds us that intellectual growth depends not only on genetic endowment and environmental advantage but also on interests, motivation, and other personal characteristics that affect how much we apply ourselves or take advantage of our gifts and opportunities.

As noted in Chapter 3, heritability estimates are not universal by any means. They can vary, depending on the sample being studied, and they may be influenced by environmental factors. This fact was brought home forcefully by Eric Turkheimer and colleagues (2003). In a study of 7-year-old identical and fraternal twins, they found that the proportions of IQ variation attributable to genes and environment varied by social class. In impoverished families, fully 60 percent of the IQ variance was accounted for by the shared (family) environment, and the contribution of genes was negligible. In affluent families, the result was almost exactly the reverse, with shared environment accounting for little variance and genes playing an important role. Clearly, genes and social-class environment seem to be interacting in their contribution to IQ.

FIGURE 9.18

Reaction range, environment, and intelligence. Genetic endowment is believed to create a reaction range within which environment exerts its effects. Enriched environments are expected to allow a person's intelligence to develop to the upper region of his or her reaction range, whereas deprived environments may limit intelligence to the lower portion of the range. Where intelligence is concerned, the reaction range may cover as much as 15 to 20 points on the IQ scale.

Beneath the Surface   Does the Environment Become More Important as We Age?

As we have seen, intelligence is influenced by interacting genetic and environmental factors. An interesting question concerning the development of intelligence has been the subject of genetics research: Does the relative contribution of genes and environment change as we age? Heritability estimates of 50 to 70 percent are well established in data from childhood based on comparisons of IQ correlations in identical and fraternal twins. But what happens as identical and fraternal twins leave home and begin to live their separate lives in different environments? Do genetic influences increase or decrease in importance?

What would you predict? Would you expect environmental influences on intelligence to play an increasingly stronger role as differing life experiences accumulate? Since heritability is estimated by doubling the difference in IQ correlations between pairs of identical and fraternal twins, we have a direct way of testing the expectation that heritability decreases with age. Figure 9.19 shows the differences between correlations for identical and fraternal twins tested at different ages. If environmental effects become more important, the difference should narrow with increasing age. Instead, we find that the gap actually widens in adulthood, indicating that the influence of heredity increases rather than decreases in importance.

Other evidence also points to this conclusion. As adopted children age, the modest similarities in IQ they show with their adoptive parents disappear, and they become increasingly more like their biological parents. By age 16, the IQ correlation

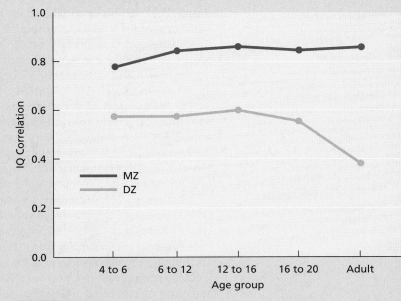

FIGURE 9.19

Genes and intelligence. This graph shows the differences in IQ correlations between monozygotic (MZ) and dizygotic (DZ) twins in childhood, adolescence, and adulthood. The widening gap between the correlations in adulthood indicates an increasing genetic influence as we age. Source: Adapted from Plomin & Spinath, 2004.

Continued

with the adoptive parents decreases to about .07, whereas that with their biological parents increases from .10 to .33 (Plomin & DeFries, 1998).

Why do genetic factors become more important as we age? We can't be sure at this point. One possibility is that completely new genes come on line to affect intelligence as more advanced and sophisticated cognitive processes emerge during development (Plomin & Spinath, 2004). Another possibility is that genetic influences snowball during development, creating larger and larger impacts on intelligence as people create and select environments that are compatible with their genetic characteristics.

GROUP DIFFERENCES IN INTELLIGENCE

Some of the most controversial issues in the study of intelligence revolve around group differences. Ethnic and social-class differences exist, as do differences between men and women. The meaning of these differences—and their political, social, and educational implications—has often sparked bitter debate and, at times, discriminatory policies. It has also inspired stereotypes about certain groups and influenced the self-image of group members.

ETHNIC GROUP DIFFERENCES

Some of the most contentious debates in psychology have concerned the existence and meaning of ethnic and racial group differences in intelligence. Discussions of intellectual differences between ethnic groups and between men and women touch on deeply held notions of social equality. Because the questions under scrutiny are complex and the evidence does not warrant any simple conclusions, the debate is unlikely to be resolved any time soon.

In 1969, in the midst of the civil rights struggle, an article in the *Harvard Educational Review* by Arthur Jensen sparked debate and, in many quarters, outrage. Jensen concluded that because the heritability of intelligence is substantial, genetic differences are "strongly implicated" in ethnic group differences in intelligence. A quarter century later, in a *New York Times* best seller titled *The Bell Curve*, Richard Herrnstein and Charles Murray (1994) painted a pessimistic picture of the future for ethnic groups that lag behind in genetically influenced mental competencies. Like Jensen's article, *The Bell Curve* evoked considerable controversy.

Where ethnic groups are concerned, everyone agrees on certain facts. Today there are consistent differences in the average intelligence test scores of members of different racial and national groups. National comparisons indicate that Japanese children have the highest mean IQ in the world (Hunt, 1995). Their mean score of 111 places 77 percent of Japanese children above the mean scores of U.S. and European children. Within the United States,

significant ethnic differences also exist. Asian Americans test slightly below White American norms on verbal skills but somewhat higher on tests related to spatial and mathematical reasoning. Hispanic people who have become U.S.-acculturated score at about the same level as White Americans. African Americans score, on average, about 12 to 15 IQ points below the White American average (Jencks & Phillips, 1998).

This, of course, does not mean that all White Americans and Hispanic Americans test lower than Asian Americans or that all African Americans test lower than the other ethnic groups. There is great overlap among group IQ distributions, and in all groups, some individuals score at the highest levels. Nonetheless, the average group differences are large enough to have practical consequences, such as ethnic differences in academic achievement. The unanswered question is: Where do these differences come from? Much work is currently underway to separate science from myth (Fish, 2002).

Are the Tests Biased?

Keep in mind that these group differences apply to test scores, which are the standard operational definition of the construct we call *intelligence*. Some have expressed concerns that these tests underestimate the mental competence of minority group members because the tests are based on Euro-American White culture and therefore are culturally biased.

Test bias can actually take two forms (Figure 9.20). **Outcome bias** *refers to the extent that a test underestimates a person's true intellectual ability.* **Predictive bias** *occurs if the test successfully predicts criterion measures, such as school or job performance, for some groups but not for others* (Serpell, 2000).

Defenders of intelligence tests dismiss both types of bias. They point out that ethnic group differences appear throughout intelligence tests, not just on those items that would, at face value, appear to be culturally biased (Jensen, 1980, 1998). They also point out that intelligence test scores predict the performance of minority group members as accurately as they predict White people's performance (Barrett & Depinet, 1991; Kuncel et al., 2004). For example, even though African

▶ **Focus 29**
What explanations have been offered for group differences in IQ between ethnic groups?

Americans as a group score lower than White Americans, the tests predict academic and occupational performance with equal accuracy for both racial groups, indicating that they are measuring relevant mental skills (Hunt, 1995). Test critics remain unconvinced, asserting that current measures can be outcome-biased in underestimating the mental skills of ethnic minorities.

What Factors Underlie the Differences?

The next dispute about racial differences is a rather different one. The nature-nurture discussion tentatively accepts the differences in measures of mental abilities as being real and then asks why they exist. Consider the differences between White Americans and African Americans. On the nurture side, there is no question that a higher proportion of White American than African American children are raised and schooled in enriched environments that optimize the development of cognitive skills. However, social changes over the past 25 years have provided African Americans with greater access to educational and vocational opportunities and have coincided with an increase in African American IQs that has reduced the IQ difference between African Americans and White Americans by about a third (Barnett & Camilli, 2002). These shrinking ethnic differences also extend to reading and mathematics achievement tests in grades 1 through 12, as well as to SAT scores (Block, 2002).

People who are impressed by this decreasing test gap tend to attribute racial differences to environmental differences that could be changed, ranging from nutritional factors to educational opportunities (Grigorenko, 2003; Nisbett, 1998). Meredith Phillips and coworkers (1998) analyzed a wide range of family-environment factors in relation to intellectual differences between 5- and 6-year-old African American and White children. They concluded that family-environment factors alone could account for about two thirds of the test score gap. Figure 9.21 provides an agricultural analogy of how environmental factors (in this case, rich or poor soil) can produce group differences even for a genetically influenced variable.

The key role played by the social environment also may be illustrated by a historical example involving a different minority group. Early in the 20th century, the average Italian American child had an IQ of 87, about the same as the average score of African Americans today. Henry Goddard (1917), a leading hereditarian researcher of the time, concluded that 79 percent of Italian American immigrants were "feebleminded," posed a

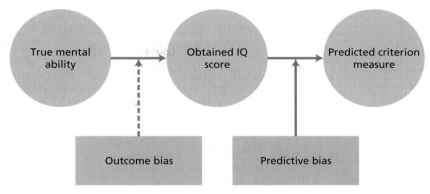

FIGURE 9.20

Test bias can take two forms. Outcome bias would occur if the nature of the test items significantly underestimated true mental ability because of factors such as cultural relevance. Predictive bias would occur if test scores predicted criterion measures accurately for one group, but not for another.

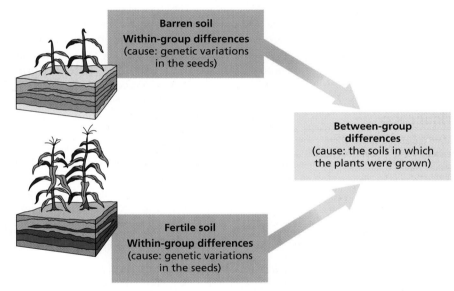

FIGURE 9.21

Heredity and environment. The interaction of heredity and environment is shown in this agricultural analogy. Seeds planted in fertile soil will be, on average, larger than those planted in barren soil. This between-groups variability is attributable to environment. Within each field, however, plants will also differ in size as a result of genetic factors. Applied to intelligence, this analogy indicates how between-group differences could result from environmental factors despite the fact that intelligence has a strong genetic component.

danger to the U.S. gene pool, and should not be allowed to emigrate to the United States. Today, the average Italian American student obtains an above-average IQ (Ceci, 1996). Obviously, genetic changes in Italian Americans could not produce a gain of this size over such a short time. Cultural assimilation and educational and economic opportunity seem much more reasonable explanations for this pronounced increase in test scores.

Another factor worth noting is a tendency, even among some scientists, to overemphasize genetic differences between groups. Indeed, where measured directly, genetic differences, like test scores, tend to be greater *within* any given racial group than they are between racial groups (Block, 2002). For example, both African Americans and White Americans exhibit greater genetic variation among themselves than that which exists between the average African American and the average White American.

SEX DIFFERENCES IN COGNITIVE ABILITIES

Men and women differ in physical attributes and reproductive function. They also differ in their performance on certain types of intellectual tasks. The gender differences lie not in levels of general intelligence but rather in the patterns of cognitive skills that men and women exhibit. Men, on average, tend to outperform women slightly on certain spatial tasks, such as the ones shown in Figure 9.22. Men are more accurate in target-directed skills, such as throwing and catching objects, and they tend to perform slightly better on tests of mathematical reasoning. Women, on average, perform better on tests of perceptual speed, verbal fluency, and mathematical calculation and on precise manual tasks requiring fine motor coordination (Collins & Kimura, 1997; Lippa, 2005). Although typically small, these ability differences have been reported quite consistently by researchers (Halpern, 2004; Hines, 2005). Keep in mind, however, that men and women also vary considerably among themselves

in all of these skills, and the performance distributions of males and females overlap considerably.

Psychologists have proposed explanations for these gender differences, citing both biological and environmental factors. The environmental explanations typically focus on the socialization experiences that males and females have as they grow up, especially the kinds of sex-typed activities that boys and girls are steered into (Crawford & Chaffin, 1997). Prior to the early 1980s, for example, boys were far more likely than girls to play sports that involve throwing and catching balls, which might help account for their general superiority in this ability. Evolutionary theorists have also weighed in on the differences, suggesting that sex-role specialization developed in ancestral environments. Men's roles, such as navigating and hunting, favored the development of the visuospatial abilities that show up in sex-difference research. Women's roles, such as child-rearing and tool-making activities, favored the development of verbal and manual-precision abilities (Joseph, 2000).

Biological explanations have increasingly focused on the effects of hormones on the developing brain (Halpern & Tan, 2001; Hines, 2005). These influences begin during a critical period shortly after conception, when the sex hormones establish sexual differentiation. The hormonal effects go far beyond reproductive characteristics, however. They also alter brain organization and appear to extend to a variety of behavioral differences between men and women, including aggression and problem-solving approaches (Hines, 2005; Lippa, 2005).

Do hormonal factors also influence cognitive performance later in life? Several studies have shown that fluctuations in women's hormonal levels during the menstrual cycle are related to fluctuations in task performance. When women have high levels of the female hormone estrogen, they perform better on some of the "feminine-ability" measures while showing declines in performance on some of the "male-ability" measures (Kimura, 1992; Moody, 1997). However, a more recent study measured a wide range of sex hormones in men and women before they performed a variety of cognitive tasks. Men and women showed the typically reported differences in cognitive skills, but no relations were found between any of the measured hormones and cognitive performance (Halari et al., 2005). Thus the role of sex hormones in adulthood remains unclear.

BELIEFS, EXPECTATIONS, AND COGNITIVE PERFORMANCE

Cognitive abilities are not the only mental determinants of how well people perform on intellectual

---

▶ **Focus 30**
What sex differences exist in cognitive skills? What biological and environmental factors might be involved?

For more on gender differences, see the "Schools and Public Policy" video in Chapter 9 of your CD.

FIGURE 9.22

Male-female cognitive differences. Among the most consistent gender differences in cognitive abilities reported in the scientific literature involve tasks like these.
SOURCE: Adapted from Kimura, 1992.

Problem-solving tasks favoring women

Women tend to perform better than men on tests of perceptual speed, in which people must rapidly identify matching items—for example, pairing the house on the far left with its twin.

On some tests of ideational fluency, for example those in which people must list objects that are the same color, and on tests of verbal fluency, for example those in which participants must list words that begin with the same letter, women also outperform men.

| L _ _ _ | Limp, Livery, Love, Laser, Liquid, Low, Like, Lag, Live, Lug, Light, Lift, Liver, Lime, Leg, Load, Lap, Lucid . . . |

Problem-solving tasks favoring men

Men tend to perform better than women on certain spatial tasks. They do well on tests that involve mentally rotating an object or manipulating it in some fashion such as choosing which of the 3 objects at the right is the same as the one on the left.

Men also are more accurate than women in target-directed motor skills, such as guiding or intercepting projectiles.

and academic measures. Beliefs are also very important. Our beliefs about others' capabilities can affect how we respond to them. For example, many studies have shown that if teachers are told that a particular child has hidden potential or, alternatively, intellectual limitations, they increase or decrease the amount of attention and effort expended on that child, thereby influencing the child's development of cognitive skills (Rosenthal, 1985).

Even more important at times are our own self-beliefs, which tell us who we are and what we can and cannot do. Can self-beliefs and widely held social beliefs about the groups we identify with affect our performance on cognitive tasks? An important line of research, described in the following "Research Close-Up," suggests that stereotypes about the capabilities of minorities and women may indeed affect their performance.

▶ **Focus 31**
How can teachers' expectations and stereotype threat influence academic performance?

Research Close-Up   Stereotype Threat and Cognitive Performance

SOURCE: CLAUDE M. STEELE (1997). A threat in the air: How stereotypes shape intellectual identity and performance. *American Psychologist, 52,* 613–629.

INTRODUCTION

Our self-concept is based on numerous experiences that convey to us who we are, how valued we are, and what we are capable of achieving in our lives. Some of this information comes from observing the consequences of our own behavior. But our self-concept can also be influenced by our membership in racial and gender groups. If certain stereotypes are widely associated with these groups, we may incorporate them into our self-concept. Once accepted, these self-beliefs may push us to behave in a way that is consistent with our self-concept. But even if not incorporated into the self, group members can experience **stereotype threat** *if they believe that certain behaviors on their part would confirm a negative stereotype in the minds of others.* Claude Steele believes that stereotype threat evokes anxiety and undermines performance. To test this hypothesis, Steele and his coworkers assessed the academic-performance effects of evoking two widely held stereotypes: (1) that women have less mathematical ability than men do, and (2) that African Americans have less intellectual ability than do White Americans.

METHOD

Two studies were conducted with students at Stanford University (Spencer et al., 1999; Steele & Aronson, 1995). In the first, men and women who were good in math were given a difficult exam whose items were taken from the advanced mathematics test of the Graduate Record Examination (GRE). Participants were randomly assigned to one of two experimental conditions designed to either activate the gender stereotype or not. Participants in the stereotype-relevant condition were told that the test generally showed sex differences (expected to activate the stereotype of women as being inferior to men in math). In the other condition, the students

were told that scores on the test showed no sex differences. The dependent variable was the students' scores on the math problems.

In the second study, African American and White American students were tested on the most difficult items from the GRE verbal test. Again, there were two experimental conditions, this time varying the racial relevance of the test. In one condition, the students were told that the test was a measure of intelligence (expected to activate the stereotype of African Americans as being less intelligent than White Americans). In the other condition, the students were told that the items were part of a laboratory task that was unrelated to general intellectual ability.

RESULTS

The results of the two experiments, shown in Figure 9.23, were strikingly similar. In the first (Figure 9.23a), women and men performed at an equivalent level on the math problems when they were told there were no sex differences on the test. However, the picture changed dramatically when the task was made relevant to the gender stereotype. Women's performance dropped, and men's performance increased, producing a marked performance difference between the two sexes. In Figure 9.23b, we see a similar pattern of results when the racial stereotype was activated. When the researchers controlled statistically for preexisting ethnic-group differences in verbal ability by using students' college-entrance SAT scores, the Black-White performance difference on the experimental task was far greater if students thought that the task measured intelligence.

DISCUSSION

This research illustrates how stereotype-based aspects of the self-concept can affect behavior, in this case, cognitive performance. Steele (1997) believes that in the stereotype-relevant conditions, the threat of doing poorly on the test and being branded as a "math-deficient woman" or an "intellectually

Continued

(a)

(b)

inferior African American" aroused anxiety that lowered performance. Other studies have supported this interpretation and also suggest that stereotype threat creates distracting thoughts that impair performance (Bosson et al., 2004; Croizet et al., 2004).

The results have broad societal implications and might help explain the fact that, over the course of their academic careers, women exhibit less inclination to pursue mathematics, even though, on average, they are slightly superior to men in mathematical calculation skills (Kimura, 1992; Lee, 1998). Later research has shown that the more strongly women are identified with their female sex role, the more susceptible they are to stereotype threat (Schmader et al., 2004). Perhaps stereotype threat also helps account for the fact that African American children become progressively less identified with and invested in academics as they progress through school and that many drop out altogether (Major et al., 1998). In both cases, the sex and racial ability differences are slight to nonexistent when children first enter school. What happens thereafter as females and minorities confront, and perhaps internalize, the stereotypes about their mental abilities may be an important environmental determinant of their performance.

FIGURE 9.23

Effects of stereotype threat on cognitive performance. (a) The activation of the stereotype that women do less well than men in math was associated with poorer performance by women and enhanced performance by men compared with the control condition, where men and women performed at the same level. (b) Reference to the task as involving intelligence resulted in reduced performance by African American students. SOURCE: Steele, 1997.

EXTREMES OF INTELLIGENCE

Because of the many genetic and environmental influences on intelligence, there are individuals at both ends of the intelligence distribution who have unusual mental abilities. At the upper end are the "intellectually gifted"; at the low end are those labeled "mentally retarded" or "cognitively disabled."

THE INTELLECTUALLY GIFTED

At the top end of the intelligence bell curve are the intellectually gifted, whose IQs of 130 or higher place them in the top 1 percent of the population. Their high IQs do not mean that they are good at everything, however. As we might expect from the theories of multiple intelligences, many are enormously talented in one area of mental competence but quite average in other domains. Even with IQs over 150, large discrepancies are often found between verbal and spatial-mathematical

skills (Achter et al., 1996). Thus a mathematical prodigy who figures out rules of algebra on his own at age 3 may have relatively unexceptional verbal skills.

What distinguishes the thought processes of the gifted? Some theorists believe that gifted children think in the same way as average children but simply do it much more efficiently (Jackson & Butterfield, 1986). Others disagree. When they see a child capable of memorizing an entire musical score after hearing it once, they conclude that this ability is based on a different quality of thinking that involves great intuition and a passion for the specific domain in which the child excels (Winner, 2000).

Only a small percentage of gifted children attain true eminence in later life. Eminence seems to be a special variety of giftedness. Joseph Renzulli (2002) has studied this rare group, and he believes that their success is a product of three interacting factors. The first is highly developed mental abilities—not only

▶ **Focus 32**
What factors allow gifted people to become eminent?

general intelligence but also specific mental abilities related to one's chosen field. Thus Einstein was blessed with unusual mathematical and spatial abilities (but not exceptional verbal skills). The second factor is the ability to engage in creative problem solving, that is, to come up with novel and unconventional ideas, to judge their potential value, and to apply them to challenging problems (Sternberg & Davidson, 2005). The third factor is motivation and dedication. Eminence involves a great deal of elbow grease and a determination to attain the highest levels of performance. Studies of eminent scientists, artists, musicians, writers, and athletes reveal that they tend to work much harder and to dedicate themselves more strongly to excellence than do their less eminent counterparts (Simonton, 2001). Given that the person has the requisite level of intelligence, these nonintellectual factors become especially important. Many eminent figures, including Sigmund Freud and Charles Darwin, showed no signs of being exceptionally gifted as children, but their motivation and dedication helped them achieve greatness in their professions.

Like children at the low end of the competence continuum, intellectually gifted children often need special educational opportunities. They may become bored in regular classrooms and even drop out of school if they are not sufficiently challenged (Fetterman, 1988). Yet many school systems have deemphasized programs for the gifted in the same spirit of egalitarianism that places cognitively challenged children in regular classrooms. Increasingly, parents of gifted children are enrolling their children in special camps and extracurricular programs to provide the needed intellectual stimulation and exposure to peer groups with common interests and abilities (Winner, 2000).

What Do You Think?

ARE GIFTED CHILDREN MALADJUSTED?

The image of the introverted, socially awkward, and unhappy "nerd" is familiar to all of us. Gifted children are often depicted in the media as unathletic, interested in intellectual activities that do not excite most students, and socially inept. Is there truth in this stereotype? What would you expect research on gifted children to show? Think about your answer, then see page 347.

MENTAL RETARDATION

Approximately 3 to 5 percent of the U.S. population, or about 10 million people, are classified as mentally retarded, or cognitively disabled. The American Psychiatric Association has devised a four-level system that classifies mental retardation as mild, moderate, severe, or profound on the basis of IQ scores. Table 9.6 describes these classifications. As you can see, the vast majority are mildly disabled, obtaining IQs between about 50 and 70. Most members of this largest group, given appropriate social and educational support, are capable of functioning adequately in mainstream society, holding jobs and raising families. Progressively greater environmental support is needed as we move toward the profoundly disabled range, where institutional care is usually required.

Mildly disabled children can attend school, but they have difficulties in reading, writing, memory, and mathematical computation. Many of these difficulties result from poorly developed problem-solving strategies. They often have deficiencies in the executive functions discussed in Chapter 3: reasoning, planning, and evaluating feedback from their efforts (Molfese & Molfese, 2002).

Cognitive disability has a variety of causes: some genetic, some due to other biological factors, and some due to environmental causes. Genetic abnormalities account for about 28 percent of all mental retardation cases (Winnepenninckx et al., 2003). More than 100 different genetic causes of retardation have been identified. For example, *Down syndrome* (formerly called *mongolism*), which is characterized by mild to severe mental disability, is caused by an abnormal division of the twenty-first chromosome pair.

Heritability plays a different role in mild retardation than it does in profound retardation (Plomin & Spinath, 2004). Cases of profound retardation are more likely to be caused by genetic accidents instead of an inherited genotype (Zechner et al., 2001). Therefore, profound retardation does not run in families. In one study of 17,000 children, about one half of 1 percent were profoundly retarded. None of these children's siblings had an IQ below 85, and their mean IQ was 103. In contrast, the siblings of the 1.2 percent who were mildly retarded had mean IQs of 85, and a third of the siblings had IQs below 75 (Nichols, 1984).

Mental disability can also be caused by accidents at birth, such as severe oxygen deprivation (anoxia); and by diseases experienced by the

► **Focus 33**
How do causal factors differ in mild and profound mental retardation?

TABLE 9.6   Adaptive Capabilities of Cognitively Challenged People over the Life Span

Category	Percentage of Retarded Population	Characteristics from Birth to Adulthood		
		Birth through Age 5	Age 6 through Age 20	Age 21 and Older
Mild: 50–70 IQ	85	Often not noticed as delayed by casual observer but is slower to walk, feed him- or herself, and talk than most children.	Can acquire practical skills and master reading and arithmetic to a third- to sixth-grade level with special education. Can be guided toward social conformity.	Can usually achieve adequate social, vocational, and self-maintenance skills. May need occasional guidance and support when under unusual social or economic stress.
Moderate: 35–50 IQ	10	Noticeable delays in motor development, especially in speech. Responds to training in various self-help activities.	Can learn simple communication, elementary health and safety habits, and simple manual skills. Does not progress in functional reading or arithmetic.	Can perform simple tasks under sheltered conditions, participate in simple recreation, and travel alone in familiar places. Usually incapable of self-maintenance.
Severe: 20–35 IQ	4	Marked delay in motor development. Little or no communication skill. May respond to training in elementary self-help, such as self-feeding.	Usually walks, barring specific disability. Has some understanding of speech and some response. Can profit from systematic habit training.	Can conform to daily routines and repetitive activities. Needs continuing direction and supervision in protective environment.
Profound: below 20 IQ	1	Gross disability. Minimal capacity for functioning in sensorimotor areas. Needs nursing care.	Obvious delays in all areas of development. Shows basic emotional responses. May respond to skillful training in use of legs, hands, and jaws. Needs close supervision.	May walk, need nursing care, have primitive speech. Usually benefits from regular physical activity. Incapable of self-maintenance.

Reprinted with permission from the *Diagnostic and Statistical Manual of Mental Disorders*, Text Revision. Copyright © 2000, American Psychiatric Association.

mother during pregnancy, such as rubella or syphilis. Likewise, drugs and alcohol taken by the mother—especially in the first weeks of pregnancy when a woman is often unaware she is pregnant—can cause neural damage and mental retardation. Despite this range of potential causes, in a significant majority (75 to 80 percent) of mentally disabled people, no clear biological cause can be found. Experts theorize that these cases may be due to undetectable brain damage, extreme environmental deprivation, or a combination of the two.

In the United States, federal law requires that cognitively disabled children, who were formerly segregated into special education classes, be given individualized instruction in the "least restrictive environment." This has resulted in the practice of *mainstreaming,* or *inclusion programs,* which allows many cognitively challenged children to attend school in regular classrooms and experience a more normal peer environment (Figure 9.24). Many schools also provide for individualized instruction for such children so that they can receive the special attention they may require.

A CONCLUDING THOUGHT

In the preceding chapters, we have seen how humans learn, how they remember what they've learned, and how they think and solve problems.

FIGURE 9.24

To an increasing extent, children of low intelligence have been included in normal classrooms rather than being confined to special education programs.

LEVELS OF ANALYSIS   Factors Related to Intellectual Functioning

Biological

- Genetic factors, which account for significant variation in intelligence
- Biological reaction range, which sets broad limits for potential intellectual development
- Neural efficiency that may underlie intellectual differences
- Possible role of sex hormones in certain types of mental abilities

Psychological

- Contribution of a general mental capacity (*g* factor)
- Specific cognitive and perceptual skills that also underlie intellectual ability
- Adaptive skills that may constitute different types of intelligence
- Beliefs, anxieties, and expectations that affect cognitive performance in specific situations (e.g., stereotype threat)
- Motivation to achieve

Environmental

- Learning environments that interact with biological reaction range
- Cultural factors that influence which behaviors are prized and defined as intelligent
- Sex roles, which may influence the abilities that men and women master
- Intelligence measures, which may place culturally different people at a disadvantage

Intellectual Functioning

FIGURE 9.25

Levels of analysis: Factors related to intellectual functioning.

Language, thinking, and intelligent behavior are intimately related to one another and to the processes of learning and memory. As we have also seen, intelligent behavior has many causal factors. Some of these factors are summarized in Figure 9.25.

In today's world, intellectual skills have become increasingly important for successful adaptation. General intelligence, or the *g* factor, captures the kinds of general mental flexibility needed to cope with novelty, read the environ-ment, draw conclusions, and choose how and when to act (Lubinski, 2004). In addition to the importance of general mental ability, more specific skills, such as those at the first and second levels of Carroll's 3-stratum model, may be needed to cope successfully with more narrowly defined situations and task demands. To an increasing degree, the study of intelligence is focusing on these real-life adaptations and on ways to help people develop and apply their intellectual abilities.

IN REVIEW

- Intelligence is determined by interacting heredi-tary and environmental factors. Genes account for between 50 and 70 percent of population vari-ation in IQ. Shared family environment accounts for perhaps one fourth to one third of the vari-ance during childhood, but its effects seem to dissipate as people age. Educational experi-ences also influence mental skills. Heredity establishes a reaction range with upper and lower limits for intellectual potential. Environ-ment affects the point within that range that will be reached.

- Intervention programs for disadvantaged children have positive effects on later achievement and life outcomes if they begin early in life and are applied intensively. They have little effect when applied after school begins or with middle- or upper-class children.

- Heritability estimates of intelligence can vary, de-pending on sample characteristics. In impover-ished families, shared environment was more important than genes, whereas the opposite was found in affluent families. Twin studies also show that heritability effects on intelligence increase in adulthood.

- Cultural and ethnic differences in intelligence exist (though they may be narrowing), but the relative contributions of genetic and environ-mental factors are still in question. Evidence exists for both genetic and environmental determinants. Whether intelligence tests exhibit outcome bias in underestimating the mental abilities of minorities is a point of contention, but the tests do not appear to have predictive bias.

■ Although the differences are not large, men tend as a group to score higher than women on certain spatial and mathematical reasoning tasks. Women perform slightly better than men on tests of perceptual speed, verbal fluency, mathematical calculation, and fine motor coordination. Both environmental and biological bases of sex differences have been suggested. Stereotype threat is one potential psychological factor for both sex-based and racial performance differences.

■ Even people with IQs in the 150s often show discrepancies in specific skills. Those who achieve eminence tend to have, in addition to high IQs, high levels of interest and motivation in their chosen activities.

■ Cognitive disability can be caused by a number of factors. Biological causes are identified in only about 28 percent of cases. Cognitive disability can range from mild to profound. The vast majority of disabled individuals are able to function in the mainstream of society, given appropriate support. Genetic factors seem relatively unimportant in profound mental retardation, but they seem to play an important role in mild retardation, which is more likely to run in families.

KEY TERMS AND CONCEPTS

Each term has been boldfaced and defined in the chapter on the page indicated in parentheses.

achievement test (p. 325)
aptitude test (p. 325)
cognitive process theories (p. 320)
construct validity (p. 327)
content validity (p. 327)
criterion-related validity (p. 327)
crystallized intelligence (g_c; p. 319)
dynamic testing (p. 329)
emotional intelligence (p. 322)
entity theorists (p. 346)
factor analysis (p. 317)
fluid intelligence (g_f; p. 319)
g factor (p. 318)

incremental theorists (p. 346)
intelligence (p. 313)
intelligence quotient (IQ; p. 315)
interjudge reliability (p. 327)
internal consistency (p. 327)
knowledge-acquisition components (p. 320)
metacomponents (p. 320)
normal distribution (p. 328)
norms (p. 328)
outcome bias (p. 338)
performance components (p. 320)
predictive bias (p. 338)

psychological test (p. 326)
psychometrics (p. 316)
reaction range (p. 336)
reliability (p. 326)
shared environment (p. 333)
standardization (p. 328)
static testing (p. 329)
stereotype threat (p. 341)
test-retest reliability (p. 326)
three-stratum theory of cognitive abilities (p. 319)
triarchic theory of intelligence (p. 320)
validity (p. 327)

? What Do You Think?

IS INTELLIGENCE FIXED OR MALLEABLE? (PAGE 318)

Research has shown that people differ in their lay theories of intelligence. For example, do you see intelligence as a relatively fixed quality of intellectual competence, or do you see it as being malleable or changeable? According to Carol Dweck (1991), **entity theorists** *believe that personal characteristics, including intelligence, are largely fixed and unchangeable,* whereas **incremental theorists** *believe that people are capable of significant change,* including increases in mental skills. Consider where you stand on this distinction: Are you more an entity theorist or an incremental theorist?

Now consider the implications of these two conceptions—fixed versus malleable—on the kinds of achievement orientations people might have. Would they differ in how long and hard they kept trying if they were having trouble succeeding at something? Dweck's research has shown that people who see intelligence as unchangeable (entity theorists) are more likely to decide quickly whether they can succeed in a particular situation. If they think the demands exceed their abilities, they tend to give up. Likewise, their ability self-perceptions are more strongly affected by recent success or failure because they view achievement outcomes as indicative of a stable ability. In a sense, they're only as good as their last success, and their self-concept can be easily shaken by a significant failure. Incremental theorists, on the other hand, view themselves as capable of positive change and are more likely to attribute negative achievement outcomes to insufficient effort or skills, both of which can potentially be remedied. They are therefore more likely to persist in their achievement efforts in the face of setbacks.

Here are some other questions to consider, based on what you've already learned about entity theorists: Would they tend to emphasize relatively more the contributions of genetic or environmental factors in intelligence? How supportive would they be of early-education programs for disadvantaged children? If you thoughtfully consider these questions, we think you'll agree that your (and other people's) conceptions of intelligence can make a difference in how you perceive, think, and behave.

ARE GIFTED CHILDREN MALADJUSTED? (PAGE 343)

Like the cognitively disabled, the gifted are often the victims of stereotypes. Some characterize them as "geeks" and "nerds" who are eccentric and socially maladjusted. As is the case with many stereotypes, there is a grain of truth here. A review of the scientific literature on giftedness by Ellen Winner (2000) revealed that nearly a fourth of children with truly exceptional IQs at the high end of the gifted range (around 180) have social and psychological problems at about twice the rate found in nongifted children. Such children often have different interest patterns and encounter difficulty finding like-minded peers to relate to, resulting in solitude and loneliness. The research also revealed, however, that the vast majority of these highly intelligent children show adequate adjustment, providing evidence against any stereotype that would be applied to gifted children in general.

Consider also a project begun in the 1920s by Lewis Terman, the psychologist who developed the Stanford-Binet test. Terman identified 1,528 California children who had a mean IQ of 150 and began an extensive study of them that has continued for over 70 years. Terman and the researchers who inherited the project found the "Termites," as they were called, to be above average not only in intelligence but also in height, weight, strength, physical health, emotional adjustment, and social maturity. They continued to exhibit high levels of adjustment throughout their adolescent and adult years. By midlife, the 1,528 Termites had authored 92 books, 2,200 scientific articles, and 235 patents. Their marriages tended to be happy and successful, and they seemed well adjusted psychologically (Sears, 1977). Nonetheless, some of the Termites underachieved and experienced social and psychological problems. These individuals tended to come from lower-socioeconomic backgrounds and to have parents who did not emphasize success or convey success expectations. The results were lowered motivation to achieve and a lack of confidence that they could accomplish their goals. Findings such as these show that capitalizing on one's high IQ requires an interest in some domain and the motivation to develop one's gifts.

10 Motivation and Emotion

CHAPTER OUTLINE

One can never consent to creep when one feels an impulse to soar.

—HELEN KELLER

S ampson Davis, Rameck Hunt, and George Jenkins became best friends in high school. They graduated from college and medical school together, established careers as physicians and a dentist, created an educational foundation that sponsors programs for poor inner-city families, and wrote a best-selling book of their experiences to inspire others to achieve. Without doubt, theirs is a record of accomplishment that anyone would be proud of—a record, they note, that beat the odds.

Davis, Hunt, and Jenkins came from broken homes with absentee or drug-addicted fathers. Crime, violence, drugs, and the specter of death pervaded the streets of their impoverished communities in and around Newark, New Jersey—a place, says Hunt, "where the neighborhood either makes you or breaks you." By age 18, Davis and Hunt ran afoul of the law and spent time in juvenile detention.

Throughout his teens, however, Jenkins had cherished the dream of becoming a dentist. In their senior year of high school, Jenkins, Davis, and Hunt made a pact: to attend a special prefreshman remedial program at Seton Hall University, strive academically, and become doctors. For years to come, they studied together, supported each other, and inspired one another. At times the obstacles seemed insurmountable, but the pact kept them going. As Davis notes: "When you've failed repeatedly and think you're done, that last try—the one that requires every ounce of will and strength you have—is often the one to pull you through." (Davis et al., 2002, p. 211)

■ ■ ■ ■ ■

S ara, a former high school valedictorian, gained 15 pounds during her first year of college thanks to late-night pizza-and-beer parties. She dieted and returned to her normal weight of 115 pounds. Proud of her success, Sara (just over 5 feet tall) continued dieting and lost 25 more pounds. Her menstrual period stopped, but she was so afraid of gaining weight that she could not bring herself to eat normally. Finally, weighing a mere 80 pounds, she was hospitalized and began psychotherapy.

Lisa also gained weight during her freshman year and felt like a big fat failure. Then she began to eat lightly during the day but binge at night on pizza and cookies. After bingeing she waited for the laxatives to kick in—the 50 laxatives she usually took, along with 10 diet pills, each morning with breakfast. After a laxative-consuming friend suffered a heart attack at age 20, Lisa became scared. Worried about her own eating patterns, Lisa sought professional help (Hubbard et al., 1999).

Motivation and emotion, two central concepts in psychology, are closely linked. When our motives and goals are gratified, threatened, or thwarted, we often experience emotions. Davis, Hunt, and Jenkins worked hard to become doctors and felt tremendous pride when they succeeded. Sara also took pride in her success at losing weight. Emotions, in turn, can motivate us to act. Lisa's fear upon seeing a friend nearly die from bingeing and purging prompted her to seek treatment. As we will now see, both our motives and our emotions stem from a confluence of biological, psychological, and environmental factors.

MOTIVATION

The term *motivation* often triggers images of people who, like Davis, Hunt, and Jenkins, strive to attain success. But to psychologists, motivational

▶ **Focus 1**
How are motivation and emotion related? How do we define motivation?

issues are broader. What motivates people to eat, have sex, and affiliate? What motivated Sara's self-starvation?

PERSPECTIVES ON MOTIVATION

▶ **Focus 2**
Describe the key motivational concepts introduced by biological, cognitive, psychodynamic, and humanistic perspectives. What are the BAS and the BIS?

Motivation *is a process that influences the direction, persistence, and vigor of goal-directed behavior.* Psychology's diverse theoretical perspectives view motivation through different lenses.

Evolution, Instincts, and Genes

Darwin's theory of evolution inspired early psychological views that instincts motivate much of our behavior. An **instinct** (also called a *fixed action pattern*) *is an inherited characteristic, common to all members of a species, that automatically produces a particular response when the organism is exposed to a particular stimulus.* By the 1920s, researchers had proposed thousands of human instincts (Atkinson, 1964).

Human instinct theories faded because little evidence supported them and they often relied on circular reasoning: Why are people greedy? Because greed is an instinct. How do we know that greed is an instinct? Because people are greedy. As we have seen in earlier discussions of scientific thinking, circular reasoning explains nothing.

Scientists now study genetic contributions to motivation more productively. In gene knockout experiments done with animals (see Chapter 3), they disable specific genes and then examine the resulting effects on motivation. Researchers also conduct twin and adoption studies to examine how strongly heredity accounts for differences among people in many aspects of motivated behavior, such as the tendencies to be outgoing or to behave antisocially. Modern evolutionary psychologists also propose that many human motives have evolutionary underpinnings expressed through the actions of genes (Palmer & Palmer, 2002).

Homeostasis and Drives

Your body's biological systems are delicately balanced to ensure survival. For example, when you are hot, your body automatically tries to cool itself by perspiring. When you are cold, your body generates warmth by shivering. In 1932 Walter Cannon proposed the concept of **homeostasis,** *a state of internal physiological equilibrium that the body strives to maintain.*

Maintaining homeostasis requires a sensory mechanism for detecting changes in the internal environment, a response system that can restore

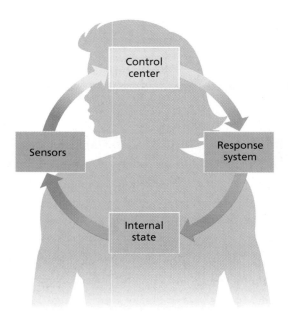

FIGURE 10.1

Homeostatic adaptation. Your body's internal environment is regulated by homeostatic mechanisms. Sensors detect bodily changes and send this information to a control center, which in turn regulates a response system that restores bodily equilibrium.

equilibrium, and a control center that receives information from the sensors and activates the response system (Figure 10.1). The control center functions somewhat like the thermostat in a furnace or air-conditioning unit. Once the thermostat is set at a fixed temperature, or *set point*, sensors detect temperature changes in either direction. The control unit responds by turning on the furnace or air conditioner until the sensor indicates that the set point has been restored, and then turns it off.

According to Clark Hull's (1943) influential *drive theory of motivation*, physiological disruptions to homeostasis produce **drives,** *states of internal tension that motivate an organism to behave in ways that reduce this tension.* Drives such as hunger and thirst arise from tissue deficits (e.g., lack of food and water) and push an organism into action. Hull, a learning theorist, proposed that reducing drives is the ultimate goal of motivated behavior.

Homeostatic models are applied to many aspects of motivation, such as the regulation of hunger and thirst (Woods & Seeley, 2002). But drive concepts are less influential than in the past. For one thing, we often behave in ways that seem to increase rather than reduce states of arousal, as when we skip meals in order to diet or flock to tension-generating horror movies.

Approach and Avoidance Motivation: The BAS and BIS

Motivation impels us toward some things and away from others. We seek to maximize pleasure and minimize pain, gravitate toward rewards and avoid punishment and deprivation. These seemingly universal tendencies reflect the activity of two distinct neural systems in the brain. According to Jeffrey Gray (1991), the **behavioral activation system (BAS)** *is roused to action by signals of potential reward and positive need gratification.* Activity in this neural system causes the person to begin or to increase movement toward positive goals (the things we want) in anticipation of pleasure. The BAS produces emotions of hope, elation, and happiness. Avoidance motivation reflects the activity of the **behavioral inhibition system (BIS),** *which responds to stimuli that signal potential pain, nonreinforcement, and punishment.* The BIS produces fear, inhibition of behavior (as when humans and other animals freeze in terror), as well as escape and avoidance behaviors (Figure 10.2).

Brain researchers are looking for the specific brain mechanisms underlying the pleasure-seeking and pain-minimizing functions of the BAS and the BIS. These mechanisms involve not only different neurotransmitter systems but also different brain regions. EEG and fMRI studies suggest that the prefrontal area in the left hemisphere, a region involved in goal-directed planning and self-regulation, is part of the BAS (Coan & Allen, 2003; Gray & Burgess, 2004). The BIS system is thought to involve several structures of the limbic system and the right frontal lobe (Sutton, 2002). However, there is still much to be learned about the neural underpinnings of the BAS and BIS.

The BAS and BIS are in the forefront of motivational research because they not only address the obviously important distinction between approach and avoidance motivation, but they also help organize the cognitive, physiological, and behavioral process involved in seeking pleasure and avoiding pain. These systems tie motivation and emotion together as well, for the BAS links approach motives and desired incentives with positive emotions, and the BIS links avoidance motives with negative emotions, such as fear, depression, and guilt.

Cognitive Processes: Incentives and Expectancies

Whereas drives are viewed as internal factors that push an organism into action, **incentives** *represent environmental stimuli that pull an organism toward a goal.* To a student, anticipating a good grade can be an incentive for studying, just as food can be an

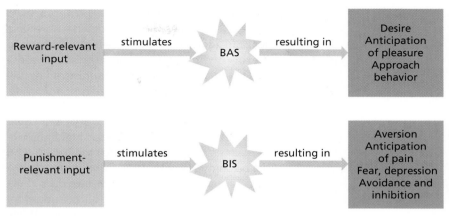

FIGURE 10.2

Approach and avoidance motivation. Two neurological systems, the behavioral activation system (BAS) and the behavioral inhibition system (BIS) underlie the universal tendencies to maximize pleasure and minimize pain. The BAS regulates approach motivation, whereas the BIS regulates avoidance motivation. The systems also link approach and avoidance motivation with positive and aversive emotions.

incentive for someone who is hungry (i.e., someone motivated by the hunger drive).

Why is it, however, that people often respond differently to the same incentive? Consider James, Lenora, and Harrison, students in a calculus class who have similar math aptitudes. James studies hard, but Lenora and Harrison put forth little effort. According to one cognitive approach, the **expectancy × value theory,** *goal-directed behavior is jointly determined by the strength of the person's expectation that particular behaviors will lead to a goal and by the incentive value the individual places on that goal* (Brehm & Self, 1989).

These two factors are multiplied, producing the following equation: Motivation = expectancy × incentive value. James works hard because he believes (expectancy) that the more he studies, the more likely it is he'll get an A (incentive), and he values an A highly. Lenora also believes that studying hard will lead to an A, but an A holds little value for her in this course. In contrast, Harrison values an A but believes that studying hard is unlikely to produce a high grade for him.

Cognitive theorists also distinguish between **extrinsic motivation,** *performing an activity to obtain an external reward or avoid punishment,* and **intrinsic motivation,** *performing an activity for its own sake*—because you find it enjoyable or challenging. In terms of incentives, a student who studies hard solely to get a good grade (rather than learn) is exhibiting extrinsic motivation.

Psychodynamic and Humanistic Views

The psychodynamic and humanistic perspectives view motivation within a broader context of personality development. Freud (1923) proposed that energy from unconscious motives—especially sexual and aggressive instincts—is often disguised and expressed through socially acceptable behaviors. Thus hidden aggressive impulses may fuel one's motivation to be a trial attorney or an athlete.

Research offers little support for Freud's "dual-instinct" model, but his work stimulated other psychodynamic theories that highlight motives such as people's desires for self-esteem and social belonging (Kohut, 1977). Modern psychodynamic theorists continue to emphasize that, along with conscious mental processes, unconscious motives guide how we act and feel (Westen, 1998). Cognitive psychologists hold a different (i.e., information-processing) view of the unconscious mind, but their research—along with studies of human social behavior—indicates that, indeed, people are not always aware of the factors that motivate them to act as they do (Chartrand & Bargh, 2002).

Maslow's Need Hierarchy   Abraham Maslow, a humanistic theorist, proposed a broad motivational model (1954). He believed that psychology's other perspectives ignore a key human motive: our striving for personal growth. He proposed the concept of a *need hierarchy,* a progression containing *deficiency needs* (needs concerned with physical and social survival) at the bottom and uniquely human *growth needs* at the top (Figure 10.3). After

our basic physiological needs are satisfied, we focus on our need for safety and security. Once that is met, we then attend to needs at the next higher level, and so on. If situations change and lower-level needs are no longer met, we refocus our attention on them until they are satisfied.

To Maslow, **self-actualization,** *which represents the need to fulfill our potential,* is the ultimate human motive. It motivates us to perfect ourselves mentally, artistically, emotionally, and socially, to explore activities for their intrinsic satisfaction rather than to gain esteem and belongingness, and to live deep and meaningful lives dedicated to the betterment of all people, not just ourselves. Maslow believed that most people become so focused on attaining satisfaction of the needs lower in the hierarchy that they spend little time focused on becoming all they can be. Those rare people who approach self-actualization, such as Albert Einstein, Abraham Lincoln, Mahatma Gandhi, Mother Teresa, and Martin Luther King, Jr., can make enormous contributions to our world.

Self-Determination Theory   A more recent humanistic theory of motivation has been advanced by Edward Deci and Richard Ryan (1985, 2002). **Self-determination theory** *focuses on three fundamental psychological needs: competence, autonomy, and relatedness.* People are most fulfilled in their lives when they are able to satisfy these fundamental needs. Competence motivation reflects a human need to master new challenges and to perfect skills. This need motivates much exploratory and growth-inducing human behavior. In its purest form, the behavior becomes its own reward, so that it is intrinsically motivated, rather than being done for an extrinsic reward.

The need for autonomy represents an attempt to achieve greater freedom and regulation by the self, rather than by external forces. It leads to greater self-integration, feelings of personal control, and self-actualization. The third basic need, relatedness, refers to the self's desire to form meaningful bonds with others. At first glance, relatedness may seem opposed to autonomy, but the two actually complement one another. When true relatedness is achieved, people often feel freer to be themselves. Adolescents who feel that their autonomy is acknowledged and supported by their parents feel a strong sense of relatedness to their parents (Ryan & Lynch, 1988).

The importance of self-determination theory's three basic needs has been strongly supported by research. They appear to have independent and additive effects on positive outcomes such as

FIGURE 10.3

A motivational hierarchy. Maslow proposed that needs are arranged in a hierarchy. After meeting our more basic needs, we experience need progression and focus on needs at the next level. If a need at a lower level is no longer satisfied, we experience need regression and focus once again on meeting that lower-level need.

psychological well-being, happiness, worker performance and satisfaction, positive social relationships, and a sense of meaningfulness in life (Deci & Ryan, 2002; Sheldon et al., 2003). From a humanistic perspective, self-determination theory represents a new model for the elusive concept of self-actualization.

 What Do You Think?

IS MASLOW'S NEED HIERARCHY VALID?
Does the concept of a need hierarchy, shown in Figure 10.3, make sense to you? How do you feel about the ordering of needs in Maslow's hierarchy? Think about it, then see page 394.

IN REVIEW

- Motivation is a process that influences the direction, vigor, and persistence of goal-directed behavior. On several fronts, scientists are actively exploring how heredity influences motivation.

- Homeostatic models view motivation as an attempt to maintain equilibrium in bodily systems. Drive theories propose that tissue deficits create drives, such as hunger, that push an organism from within to reduce that deficit and restore homeostasis.

- Incentive theories emphasize environmental factors that pull people toward a goal. Expectancy × value theory explains why the same incentive may motivate some people but not others.

- Psychodynamic theories emphasize that unconscious motives guide much of our behavior. Humanist Abraham Maslow proposed that needs exist in a hierarchy, from basic biological needs to the ultimate need for self-actualization. Deci and Ryan's self-determination theory emphasizes the importance of three fundamental needs—competence, autonomy, and relatedness—in maximizing human potential.

HUNGER AND WEIGHT REGULATION

As we have seen in the previous section, psychology's diverse perspectives underscore the complexity of studying motivation. Let's now turn to one of our most basic motives: hunger. If you could give up all food forever and satisfy your nutritional needs with a daily pill, would you? Eating is a necessity, but for many people it also is one of life's delicious pleasures. Numerous biological, psychological, and environmental factors regulate our food intake, and hunger is being studied at all three levels of analysis.

The Physiology of Hunger

Eating and digestion supply the body with the fuel it needs to function and survive. **Metabolism** *is the body's rate of energy (or caloric) utilization*, and several physiological mechanisms keep your body in energy homeostasis by regulating how much you eat. For example, some physiological signals induce hunger and prompt eating, whereas others stop food intake by producing *satiety* (the state in which we no longer feel hungry).

However, it is not the case—as many people believe—that hunger and eating simply occur when we begin to run low on energy and that we feel full when immediate energy supplies are restored (Assanand et al., 1998). Your body monitors its energy supplies, but this information interacts with other factors (e.g., the amount and variety of food) to regulate food intake. Thus hunger and satiety are not necessarily linked to immediate energy needs (Woods & Seeley, 2002). Moreover, homeostatic mechanisms are designed to *prevent* us from running low on energy in the first place. In evolutionary terms, an organism that did not eat until its energy supply started to become low (in any absolute sense) would be at a serious survival disadvantage.

Finally, many researchers believe that there is a **set point,** *a biologically determined standard around which body weight (or, more accurately, fat mass) is regulated* (Powley & Keesey, 1970). This view holds that if we overeat or undereat, homeostatic mechanisms alter our energy utilization and hunger so as to return us close to our original weight. Other researchers argue that set point theory has limitations. They propose that as we overeat or undereat, homeostatic mechanisms make it harder to keep gaining or losing weight but do not necessarily return us to our original weight. Over time we may settle in at a new weight. Stated differently, in this view "biology does not determine a fixed body weight, but rather a range or zone of body weight" (Levitsky, 2002, p. 147).

Signals That Start and Terminate a Meal   Do the muscular contractions (hunger pangs) of an empty stomach produce hunger? In an early experiment, A. L. Washburn swallowed a balloon. When it reached his stomach, the balloon was

▶ **Focus 3**
What physiological factors help regulate hunger, satiety, general appetite, and weight?

FIGURE 10.4

Do stomach sensations regulate hunger? A. L. Washburn swallowed a balloon and inflated it in his stomach. A machine recorded stomach contractions by amplifying changes in the pressure on the balloon, and Washburn pressed a telegraph key every time he felt a hunger pang. Hunger pangs occurred when the stomach contracted. Source: Based on Cannon and Washburn, 1912.

inflated and hooked up to an amplifying device to record his stomach contractions (Figure 10.4). Washburn then pressed a key every time he felt hungry. The results: Washburn's stomach contractions did indeed correspond with his feelings of hunger (Cannon & Washburn, 1912). But did they *cause* the experience of hunger?

Subsequent research found that hunger does not depend on an empty or twitching stomach, or any stomach at all! Animals display hunger and satiety even if all nerves from their stomachs to their brains are cut, and people who have had their stomachs surgically removed for medical reasons continue to feel hungry and satiated (Brown & Wallace, 1980). Thus other signals must help trigger hunger.

When you eat, digestive enzymes break food down into key nutrients, such as **glucose,** *a simple sugar that is the body's (and especially the brain's) major source of immediately usable fuel.* After a meal, some glucose is transported into cells to provide energy, but a large portion is transferred into your liver and fat cells, where it is converted into other nutrients and stored for later use. Sensors in the hypothalamus and liver monitor blood-glucose concentrations. When blood-glucose levels decrease slightly, the liver responds by converting stored nutrients back into glucose, causing blood-glucose levels to rise. Changes in the supply of glucose available to cells provide a signal that helps the brain regulate hunger (Campfield, 1997).

As you eat, several bodily signals cause you to end your meal. Stomach and intestinal distention are satiety signals (French & Cecil, 2001). The walls of these organs stretch as food fills them up, sending nerve signals to the brain. This does not mean, however, that your stomach has to be full for you to feel satiated. As we just noted, patients who have had their stomachs removed continue to experience satiety; this is due not only to intestinal distention but also to chemical signals. For example, **cholecystokinin (CCK)**—*a peptide (a type of hormone) that helps produce satiety*—and other peptides are released into the bloodstream by the small intestine as food arrives from the stomach. These peptides travel to the brain and stimulate receptors in several regions that decrease food intake (Degen et al., 2001).

Signals That Regulate General Appetite and Weight

Leptin *is a hormone secreted by fat cells.* It enters the bloodstream and reaches the brain, where it decreases appetite and increases energy expenditure.

Leptin is a long-term "background" signal. It does not make us feel full like CCK and other short-term satiety signals that respond directly to food intake during a meal. Instead, one way leptin may influence appetite is by increasing the potency of these other signals (Woods & Seeley, 2002). Thus as we gain fat and secrete more leptin, we may tend to eat less because mealtime satiety factors make us feel full sooner. As we lose fat and secrete less leptin, it may take a greater accumulation of satiety signals and thus more food to make us feel full. In essence, lower leptin levels may tell the brain, "There isn't enough fat tissue, so it's time to eat more." Leptin levels, however, seem to fall more quickly when we lose fat (thus increasing appetite) than they rise when we gain fat. Some researchers suggest that this imbalance served a key adaptive function over the course of evolution; it tilted our ancestral scales in favor of maintaining an adequate fat mass when food was plentiful so that the odds of survival would be increased during times when food was scarce (Jéquier, 2002).

Evidence for leptin's important role grew out of research with genetically obese mice (Zhang et al., 1994). A gene called the *ob* gene (*ob* = obesity) normally directs fat cells to produce leptin, but mice with an *ob* gene mutation lack leptin. As they gain weight, the brain does not receive this "curb your appetite" signal, and the mice overeat and become obese (Figure 10.5). Daily leptin injections reduce their appetite, and the mice become thinner. Another strain of obese mice produces ample leptin, but because of a mutation in a different gene (the *db* gene), their brain receptors are insensitive to leptin (Chen et al., 1996). The "curb your appetite" signal is there, but because they can't detect it they become obese. Even injecting these mice with additional leptin does not reduce their food intake and weight.

Are these specific *ob* and *db* gene mutations a major source of human obesity? Probably not, for these genetic conditions seem to be rare among humans. However, when these gene mutations do occur, they are associated with extreme obesity, suggesting the importance of normal leptin functioning in human weight regulation.

Might leptin injections be the magic bullet that helps most obese people lose weight? Unfortunately, probably not, because obese people already have ample leptin in their blood due to their fat mass, but their brain may be resistant to that information (Ravussin & Gautier, 1999).

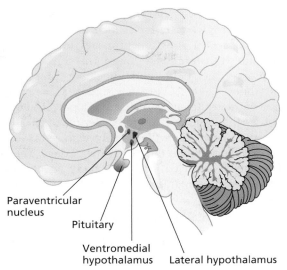

FIGURE 10.6

Motivation and the hypothalamus. Various structures within the hypothalamus play a role in regulating hunger, thirst, sexual arousal, and body temperature. The lateral hypothalamus (LH), ventromedial hypothalamus (VMH), and paraventricular nucleus (PVN) are involved in hunger regulation.

Paraventricular nucleus

Pituitary

Ventromedial hypothalamus   Lateral hypothalamus

Brain Mechanisms Many brain regions—from the primitive brain stem to the lofty cerebral cortex—help regulate hunger and eating (Berthoud, 2002). But is there a master control center? Early experiments pointed to two regions in the hypothalamus. Areas near the side, called the *lateral hypothalamus (LH)*, seemed to comprise a "hunger-on" center (Figure 10.6). Electrically stimulating a rat's LH would cause it to start eating, and lesioning (damaging or destroying) the LH would cause it to refuse to eat, even to the point of starvation (Anand & Brobeck, 1951).

In contrast, structures in the lower-middle area, called the *ventromedial hypothalamus (VMH)*, seemed to comprise a "hunger-off" center. Electrically stimulating the VMH would cause even a hungry rat to stop eating, whereas lesioning the VMH would produce a glutton—like the rat shown in Figure 1.3a—that ate frequently and doubled or tripled its body weight.

As scientists explored further, they learned that although the LH and VMH play a role in hunger regulation, they are not really hunger-on and hunger-off centers. For example, rats with LH damage stop eating and lose weight in part because they develop trouble swallowing and digesting, and they become generally unresponsive to external stimuli, not just to food. Moreover, axons from many brain areas funnel into the hypothalamus and then fan out again upon leaving it. Cutting these nerve tracts anywhere along their paths—not just within the hypothalamus—duplicates some of the effects of the LH and VMH lesions (Schwartz, 1984).

Researchers are examining how specific neural circuits within the hypothalamus regulate food intake. Many pathways involve the **paraventricular**

FIGURE 10.5

The mouse on the left has an *ob* gene mutation. Its fat cells fail to produce leptin, and it becomes obese. Leptin injections help such mice return to normal weight.

nucleus (PVN), *a cluster of neurons packed with receptor sites for various transmitters that stimulate or reduce appetite.* The PVN appears to integrate several short-term and long-term signals that influence metabolic and digestive processes (Berthoud, 2002). One such signal, a chemical transmitter called *neuropeptide Y,* is a powerful appetite stimulant. Rats in one experiment quickly became obese when they received injections of neuropeptide Y into their PVN for 10 days. Their food intake doubled, and their body weight increased sixfold (Stanley et al., 1986).

Psychological Aspects of Hunger

► **Focus 4**
Describe how psychological, environmental, and cultural factors influence hunger and eating.

Eating is positively reinforced by the good taste of food and negatively reinforced by hunger reduction. We develop an expectation that eating will be pleasurable, and this becomes an important motivator to seek and consume food. Indeed, even the mere thought of food can trigger hunger.

Attitudes, habits, and psychological needs also regulate food intake. Have you ever felt stuffed during a meal, yet finished it and even had

dessert? Beliefs such as "don't leave food on your plate" and conditioned habits (autopilot snacking while watching TV) may lead us to eat even when we do not feel hungry. Conversely, countless dieters intentionally restrict their food intake even though they *are* hungry.

Especially for women, such food restriction often stems from social pressures to conform to cultural standards of beauty (Figure 10.7). Studies of *Playboy* centerfolds, Miss America contestants, and fashion models indicate a clear trend toward a thinner and increasingly unrealistic ideal female body shape from the 1950s into the 1990s (Owen & Laurel-Seller, 2000). Given the deluge of "thin = attractive" mass media messages in many parts of the globe, it's no wonder national surveys have revealed that

- although most young Australian women are of average, healthy weight, only a fifth are happy with their weight (Kenardy et al., 2001);
- among 12- to 19-year-old female Chinese students, 80 percent are concerned about their weight and feel fat at least some of the time (Huon et al., 2002);

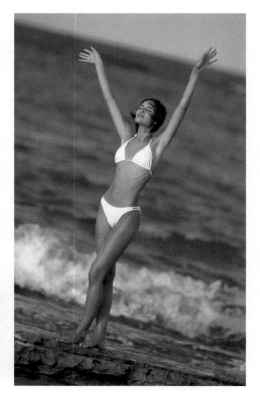

FIGURE 10.7

Throughout much of Western history, a full-bodied woman's figure was esteemed, as illustrated by (*left*) Peter Paul Rubens's 17th-century painting *The Three Graces* and by (*center*) actress Lillian Russell, who represented the American ideal of feminine beauty a century ago. In recent decades, the norm of "thin = beautiful" is illustrated (*right*) by this contemporary swimsuit model.

- compared to male American high school students, female students are less likely to be overweight but much more likely to diet and think of themselves as overweight (Centers for Disease Control and Prevention [CDC], 2002b).

Indeed, relative to men, women became increasingly dissatisfied with their body image throughout the last half of the 20th century (Feingold & Mazzella, 1998).

A classic study by April Fallon and Paul Rozin (1985) suggests an additional reason why this is so. College women overestimated how thin they needed to be to conform to men's preferences, whereas men overestimated how bulky they should be to conform to women's preferences (Figure 10.8). Women also perceived their body shape as heavier than ideal, whereas men viewed their body shape as close to ideal. These results were replicated in a more recent study of American and Spanish college men and women (Carlson & McAndrew, 2004). As Fallon and Rozin noted, "Overall, men's perceptions serve to keep them satisfied with their figures, whereas women's perceptions place pressure on them to lose weight" (1985, p. 102). Whether African American, Hispanic American, or Caucasian American, men seem more likely to have these ego-protective perceptions about their body shape than do women (Demarest & Allen, 2000).

Men too, however, may be influenced by cultural ideals. College men's satisfaction with their bodies decreases when they are exposed to a series of advertisements showing muscular males, but not when the advertisements contain men with average builds (Lorenzen et al., 2004). Male college athletes, who value muscle function, believe that women prefer a more muscular body type than their own, and most would prefer to be more muscular than they are (Raudenbush & Meyer, 2003). In general it appears that women typically want to be thin; males who are overweight also want to be thinner, but those who are thin want to be heavier and more "buff" (Kostanski et al., 2004).

Environmental and Cultural Factors

Food availability is the most obvious environmental regulator of eating. For millions of people who live in poverty or famine-ravaged regions,

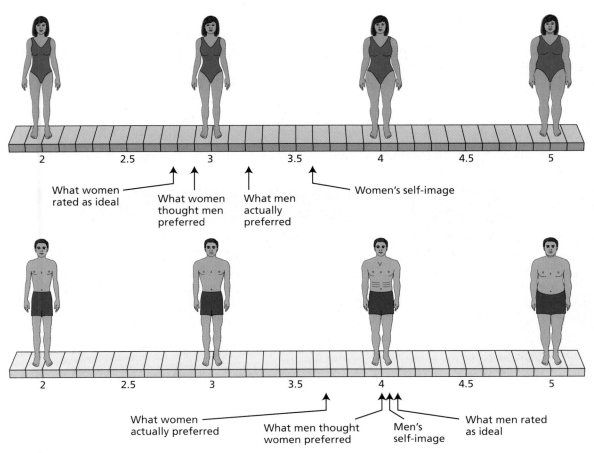

FIGURE 10.8

Preferred body shapes. When making judgments while viewing body-size drawings, college women overestimated how thin they needed to be to conform to men's preferences, and they viewed their own body shape as heavier than ideal. Men overestimated how bulky or "buff" they needed to be to conform to women's preferences, but they viewed their body shape as close to ideal. SOURCE: Based on Fallon & Rozin, 1985.

FIGURE 10.9

Cultural upbringing strongly affects food preferences. Would you like to eat these insect-topped appetizers? Not interested? Perhaps you would prefer some other insects, reptiles, camel eyes, or dog—all delicacies in other cultures.

and these food cues can trigger hunger. Eating may be the last thing on your mind until your nose detects the sensuous aroma wafting from a bakery or popcorn machine. Similarly, rats who have recently eaten and do not appear to be hungry (e.g., they ignore available food) will eat again when presented with classically conditioned sounds and lights that they have learned to associate with food (Weingarten, 1983).

Many other environmental stimuli affect food intake. For example, we typically eat more when dining with other people than when we eat alone (deCastro, 2002). Cultural norms influence when, how, and what we eat. In Mediterranean countries such as Spain and Greece, people often begin dinner in the late evening (say, around 9 P.M.), by which time most North Americans have finished supper. And although we like variety, we usually feel most comfortable selecting familiar foods and often have difficulty overcoming our squeamish thoughts about unfamiliar dishes (Figure 10.9). Figure 10.10 summarizes several factors that help regulate hunger and eating.

food scarcity limits consumption. In contrast, abundant high-fat food in many countries contributes to a high rate of obesity (Wadden et al., 2002).

Food taste and variety also regulate eating. Good-tasting food increases food consumption, but during a meal and from meal to meal we can become tired of eating the same thing, causing us to terminate a meal more quickly (Rolls et al., 1981). In contrast, food variety increases consumption, which you may have observed when you eat at a buffet.

Through classical conditioning, we learn to associate the smell and sight of food with its taste,

FIGURE 10.10

Levels of analysis: Factors related to hunger and eating.

Obesity

The heaviest known man and woman in recorded history, both Americans, weighed 1,400 and 1,200 pounds, respectively (*Guinness Book*, 2000). Few people approach such extreme weight, but as measured by their *body mass index (BMI)*, which takes height and weight into account, a staggering 25 to 30 percent of American adults are obese and another 30 to 35 percent are overweight (Flegal et al., 2002). From Canada to the Palestinian West Bank, adult obesity rates of 20 to 50 percent have been reported in many studies (Abdul-Rahim et al., 2003).

LEVELS OF ANALYSIS   Factors Related to Hunger and Eating

Biological
- Genetic factors that influence energy metabolism
- Bodily sensations, such as stomach distention
- Chemical signals (e.g., glucose utilization, CCK, leptin)
- Neural circuits within and passing through the hypothalamus

Psychological
- Thinking about food; anticipation of tasty food
- Learned food preferences and eating habits
- Memory of when and how much we have recently eaten
- Beliefs and feelings concerning body image

Environmental
- The abundance or scarcity of food
- Food appearance, aroma, taste, and variety
- Other stimuli (e.g., time of day, people) associated with eating
- Norms that affect what, when, where, and how much we eat

Hunger and Eating

Obesity places people at greater risk not only for many medical problems but also for being the target of stereotypes and prejudice (Teachman et al., 2003). Obesity is often blamed on a lack of willpower, a dysfunctional way of coping with stress, heightened sensitivity to external food cues (e.g., the sight and aroma of food), and emotional disturbances. Research, however, does not consistently find such psychological differences between obese and nonobese people (Faith et al., 2002; Leon & Roth, 1977).

Genes and Environment

Do you know people who seem to gain weight easily and others who seem to eat as much as they want without adding pounds? Heredity influences one's basal metabolic rate and the tendency to store energy as either fat or lean tissue. Indeed, identical twins raised apart are about as similar in body mass as identical twins reared together. Overall, genetic factors appear to account for about 40 to 70 percent of the variation in BMI among women and among men (Maes et al., 1997).

Over 200 genes have been identified as possible contributors to human obesity (Comuzzie & Allison, 1998). However, although heredity affects our susceptibility to obesity, so does the environment. Genes have not changed much in recent decades, but obesity rates have increased significantly. According to some experts, the culprits are

- an abundance of inexpensive, tasty foods that are high in fat and/or carbohydrates;

- a cultural emphasis on getting the best value, which contributes to supersizing menu items;

- technological advances that decrease the need for daily physical activity (Wadden et al., 2002).

The Pima Indians of Arizona provide a striking example of how genes and environment interact to produce obesity. The Pimas are genetically predisposed to obesity and diabetes, but both conditions were rare among tribe members before the 20th century. Their native diet and physically active lifestyle prevented their genetic predisposition from expressing itself. But particularly among Pimas born after World War II, obesity rates increased dramatically as they adopted a Westernized diet and sedentary lifestyle. Today Pimas living in Arizona have one of the highest rates of obesity (and diabetes) in the world. In contrast, Pimas living in northwest Mexico eat a more traditional diet and perform more physical labor, and their obesity rate is much lower than that of their Arizonan counterparts (Esparza et al., 2000).

Dieting and Weight Loss

Unfortunately for millions of overweight people, being fat primes them to stay fat, in part by altering body chemistry and energy expenditure (Logue, 1991). For example, obese people generally have higher levels of *insulin* (a hormone secreted by the pancreas that helps convert glucose into fat) than do people of normal weight. Substantial weight gain also makes it harder to exercise vigorously, and dieting slows basal metabolism because the body responds to food deprivation with decreased energy expenditure.

Does this mean that diets are doomed to fail? The common adage that "95 percent of people who lose weight regain it within a few years" evolved from just one study decades ago. According to Albert Stunkard, one of the researchers, 100 obesity patients were "just given a diet and sent on their way. That was state of the art in 1959" (quoted in Fritsch, 1999). In truth, we do not have good long-term estimates of weight-loss success rates, partly because we rarely hear from people who succeed (or fail) on their own without going to clinics or treatment programs.

We do know that about one third of Americans report that they are trying to lose weight, although not all are necessarily the ones who need to lose it. As Figure 10.11 shows, there are significant

▶ **Focus 5**
Describe biological and environmental factors in obesity and how their interaction affects obesity among the Pima.

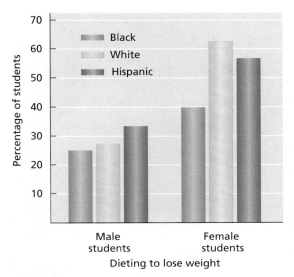

FIGURE 10.11

Ethnicity and dieting. Whether Hispanic, Black, or White, female high school students are less likely than male students to actually be overweight or at risk for overweight, but as this graph shows, they are more likely to be dieting to lose weight. Especially among female students, Hispanics and Whites are most likely to diet. Source: Based on CDC, 2002b.

sex and ethnic differences in dieting that emerge even in adolescence (CDC, 2002b). Health concerns motivate some dieters, but psychological concerns and social pressures to be thin are the primary motivators for many others. Especially among women, what begins as a diet may unfortunately evolve into a health-threatening eating disorder.

Eating Disorders: Anorexia and Bulimia

Sara and Lisa, the college freshmen described at the beginning of the chapter, suffered from eating disorders. Victims of **anorexia nervosa**, like Sara, *have an intense fear of being fat and severely restrict their food intake to the point of self-starvation* (Figure 10.12). Despite looking emaciated and weighing less than 85 percent of what would be expected for their age and height, people with anorexia continue to view themselves as fat. Anorexia causes menstruation to stop, produces bone loss, stresses the heart, and increases the risk of death (Neumäker, 2000; Treasure, 2005).

People like Lisa who suffer from **bulimia nervosa** *are also afraid of becoming fat, and they binge-eat and then purge the food,* usually by inducing vomiting or using laxatives. People with bulimia often consume 2,000 to 4,000 calories during binges, and in some cases may consume 20,000 calories per day (Geracioti et al., 1995). Although most bulimics are of normal body weight, repeated purging

► **Focus 6**
What are the major symptoms, health consequences, and causes of anorexia and bulimia?

What are some of the cultural, psychological, and biological reasons behind eating disorders? Watch the "Eating Disorders" video in Chapter 10 of your CD to find out.

can produce severe physical consequences, including gastric problems and badly eroded teeth. Whereas most anorexics do not see their food restriction as problematic, bulimics typically do. Nonetheless, they find it extremely difficult to alter their binge-purge pattern.

About 90 percent of people with anorexia and bulimia are women. Some surveys indicate that up to 10 percent of college women exhibit symptoms of bulimia, although its general prevalence among North American women is 1 to 3 percent—compared with 0.5 percent for anorexia (Becker et al., 1999).

Causes of Anorexia and Bulimia What motivates such abnormal eating patterns? Researchers obviously can't do experiments to manipulate possible causes and see if people become anorexic or bulimic, but they can examine factors associated with the disorders and changes that occur in people when they are successfully treated. Such research suggests that a combination of environmental, psychological, and biological factors may be involved.

Anorexia and bulimia are more common in industrialized cultures where thinness is equated with beauty. However, cultural norms alone cannot account for eating disorders, because only a small percentage of women within a particular culture are anorexic or bulimic. Personality factors are another piece of the puzzle. People with anorexia often are perfectionists—high achievers like Sara (a high school valedictorian) who strive to live up to lofty self-standards, including strict ideals of an acceptably thin body (Tyrka et al., 2002). For them, losing weight becomes a battle for success and control: "It's me versus food, and I'm going to win." Their perfectionism and need for control may partly stem from their upbringing. They often describe their parents as disapproving and as setting abnormally high achievement standards. For some anorexic children and teens, food refusal may be reinforced by the distress they cause their parents to feel. In essence, self-starvation becomes a way to punish parents and gain some control (Chan & Ma, 2002). As one young anorexic teen said in a therapy session,

> It was, like, a power thing. I was like, look mom, I don't have to eat. I can piss you off. . . . That's the last thing your parents want is for you to die. . . . You can get back at anybody. And I guess . . . I need to find a way to forgive her . . . because . . . I'm killing myself. (*Dying to be Thin*, 2000)

A different pattern emerges for people with bulimia, who tend to be depressed and anxious, exhibit low impulse control, and seem to lack a

FIGURE 10.12

Anorexia nervosa is a potentially life threatening disorder in which people virtually starve themselves to be thin. This anorexic woman returned to normal weight after therapy.

stable sense of personal identity (Strober & Humphrey, 1987). Their food cravings are often triggered by stress and negative mood, and binge-ing temporarily reduces their negative emotional state (Waters et al., 2001). But guilt, self-contempt, and anxiety follow the binge, and purging may be a means of reducing these negative feelings.

On the biological side, genetic factors appear to predispose some people toward eating disorders. Concordance rates for eating disorders are higher among identical twins than fraternal twins and higher among first-degree relatives (parents and siblings) than second- or third-degree relatives (Kortegaard et al., 2001). Researchers are now searching for specific genes and combinations of genes that contribute to eating disorders.

Anorexics and bulimics also exhibit abnormal activity of serotonin, leptin, and other body chemicals (Kaye et al., 2002). Some researchers believe that neurotransmitter and hormonal imbalances help cause eating disorders. Others propose that such chemical changes initially are a *response* to abnormal eating patterns but that once started they *perpetuate* eating and digestive irregularities (Walsh & Devlin, 1998). Other bodily changes also help perpetuate eating disorders. For example, stomach acids expelled into the mouth during vomiting cause bulimics to lose taste sensitivity, making the normally unpleasant taste of vomit more tolerable (Rodin et al., 1990).

Treating eating disorders is difficult and may take years, but with professional help, about half of all anorexic and bulimic patients fully recover (Becker et al., 1999; Westen et al., 2004). Others are able to eat more normally but maintain their pre-occupation with food and weight.

IN REVIEW

- Physiological processes attempt to keep the body in energy homeostasis. Changes in the supply of glucose available to cells provide one signal that helps initiate hunger. During meals, hormones such as CCK are released into the bloodstream and help signal the brain to stop eating. Fat cells release leptin, which acts as a long-term signal that helps regulate appetite. The hypothalamus plays an important role in hunger regulation.

- The expected good taste of food motivates eating, and the thought of food can trigger hunger. Our memory, habits, and psychological needs affect our food intake.

- The availability, taste, and variety of food power-fully regulate eating. Through classical conditioning, neutral stimuli can acquire the capacity to trigger hunger. Cultural norms affect our food preferences and eating habits.

- Heredity and the environment affect our suscepti-bility to becoming obese.

- Anorexia and bulimia occur more often in cultures that value thinness and are associated with some-what different psychological profiles. Heredity predisposes some people toward developing these eating disorders.

SEXUAL MOTIVATION

Why do people have sex? If you're thinking, "Isn't it obvious?" let's take a look. Sex often is described as a biological reproductive motive, yet people usu-ally do not have sex to conceive children. A drive to reproduce does not explain why people masturbate or why couples in their 70s and 80s have sex. Plea-sure, then, must be the key. Evolution shaped our physiology so that sex feels good; periodically, hav-ing sex for pleasure leads to childbirth, through which our genes are passed on. But consider this:

- In a study asking adolescents why they have sex, both genders cited peer pressure more often than sexual gratification (Stark, 1989).

- In the 1920s, British sex researcher Helena Wright found that most women she sur-veyed viewed sex as an unenjoyable marital duty (Kelly, 2001).

- About 10 percent of American men and 20 percent of women report that sex is not pleasurable (Laumann et al., 1994).

In reality, people engage in sex to reproduce, ob-tain and give sensual pleasure, express love, fos-ter intimacy, fulfill one's "duty," conform to peer pressure, and a host of other reasons.

Sexual Behavior: Patterns and Changes

Because most people don't care to let researchers into their bedrooms, scientists typically learn about people's sexual activities by conducting surveys. Alfred Kinsey and his colleagues (1948, 1953) con-ducted the first large-scale American sex surveys in the late 1930s, and many others have been con-ducted since then. One of the most thorough sur-veys, based on a nationally representative sample, found that about 70 percent of 18- to 59-year-old Americans have sex with a partner at least a few

▶ **Focus 7**
How have patterns of sexual behavior changed in recent decades?

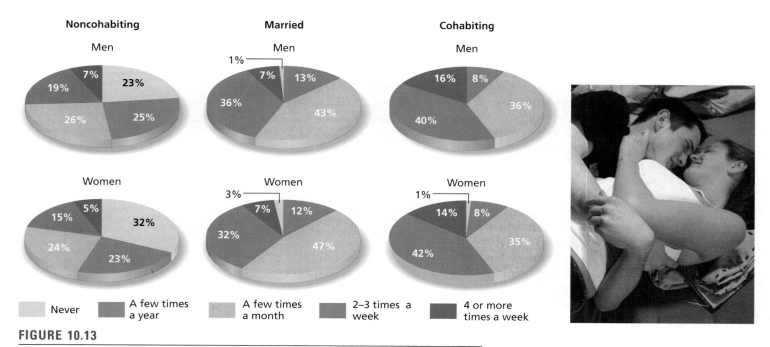

Noncohabiting

Men

7% 23% 19% 26% 25%

Women

5% 32% 15% 24% 23%

Married

Men

1% 7% 13% 36% 43%

Women

3% 7% 12% 32% 47%

Cohabiting

Men

16% 8% 40% 36%

Women

1% 14% 8% 42% 35%

Never | A few times a year | A few times a month | 2–3 times a week | 4 or more times a week

FIGURE 10.13

Sexual behavior patterns. These graphs, based on a nationally representative sample of 18- to 59-year-old Americans, show frequency of sex in the past 12 months by gender and marital status. Source: Adapted from Michael et al., 1994.

▶ **Focus 8**
Describe the sexual response cycle. How do hormones influence sex characteristics and sexual behavior?

times per month (Figure 10.13; Laumann et al., 1994). In general, single adults who cohabit (are not married but live with a sexual partner) are the most sexually active, followed by married adults. Single adults who do not cohabit are the least active.

By their first year in American high school, 41 percent of male students and 29 percent of female students say they have had sexual intercourse (CDC, 2002b). Among unmarried American females in the early 1960s, 27 percent of 19-year-olds had engaged in sexual intercourse. By 1995 the corresponding figure was 72 percent (CDC, 1997). Changing social norms and a tendency to delay marriage have contributed to this rise in premarital sex. Premarital intercourse also became more common in a number of foreign countries during the last half of the 20th century. Findings over the past few years, however, suggest that this trend has leveled off and may be reversing (CDC, 2002b). This could be a response to an increased cultural emphasis on the depth of relationships and to the crisis concerning AIDS and other sexually transmitted diseases.

The Physiology of Sex

In 1953 William Masters and Virginia Johnson began a landmark study in which they examined the sexual responses of 694 men and women under laboratory conditions. In total, they physiologically monitored about 10,000 sexual episodes.

The Sexual Response Cycle   Masters and Johnson (1966) concluded that most people, when sexually aroused, go through a four-stage **sexual response cycle** *of excitement, plateau, orgasm, and resolution* (Figure 10.14). During the *excitement phase*, arousal builds rapidly. Blood flow increases to arteries in and around the genital organs, nipples, and women's breasts, where it pools and causes these body areas to swell. The penis and clitoris begin to become erect, the vagina becomes lubricated, and muscle tension increases throughout the body. In the *plateau phase*, arousal continues to build until there is enough muscle tension to trigger orgasm.

During the *orgasm phase* in males, rhythmic contractions of internal organs and muscle tissue surrounding the urethra project semen out of the penis. In females, orgasm involves rhythmic contractions of the outer third of the vagina, surrounding muscles, and the uterus. In males, orgasm is ordinarily followed by a *resolution phase*, during which physiological arousal decreases rapidly and the genital organs return to their normal condition. During the resolution phase, males enter a *refractory period*, during which they are temporarily incapable of another orgasm. Females may have two or more successive orgasms before the onset of the resolution phase, but Masters and Johnson reported that most women experience only one. Of course, people may experience orgasm on some occasions but not others,

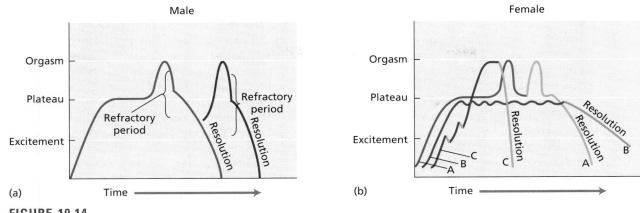

FIGURE 10.14

The human sexual response. Masters and Johnson discovered a four-stage pattern of sexual response. (a) In males, there is a refractory period after orgasm during which no further response is possible. (b) In females, pattern A represents one or more orgasms followed by resolution, pattern B shows a plateau stage with no orgasm, and pattern C shows an orgasm with no preceding plateau stage. Source: Based on Masters & Johnson, 1966.

and orgasm is not the only goal of all human sexual activity.

Hormonal Influences As with hunger, the hypothalamus plays a key role in sexual motivation. It controls the pituitary gland, which regulates the secretion of hormones called *gonadotropins* into the bloodstream. In turn, these hormones affect the rate at which the *gonads* (testes in the male and ovaries in the female) secrete *androgens,* the so-called masculine sex hormones such as *testosterone,* and *estrogens,* the so-called feminine sex hormones such as *estradiol.* Realize that despite these labels, both men and women produce androgens and estrogens.

Sex hormones have *organizational effects* that direct the development of male and female sex characteristics (Byer et al., 2002). In the womb, male and female embryos form a primitive gonad that has the potential to develop into either testes or ovaries. If genetically male, the embryo forms testes about 8 weeks after conception. Then, as the testes release sex hormones during a key period of prenatal development, there typically is sufficient androgen activity to produce a male pattern of genital, reproductive, brain, and other organ development. Years later, as part of this pattern, the hypothalamus stimulates an increased release of sex hormones from the testes when the male reaches puberty. In contrast, a genetically female embryo does not form testes, and in the absence of sufficient androgen activity during this prenatal period, a female pattern of development ensues. As part of this pattern, at puberty the hypothalamus stimulates the release of sex hormones from the ovaries on a cyclical basis that regulates the female menstrual cycle.

Sex hormones also have *activational effects* that stimulate sexual desire and behavior. In nonhuman animals, mature males have a relatively constant secretion of sex hormones, and their readiness for sex is largely governed by the presence of environmental stimuli (e.g., a receptive female). In contrast, hormonal secretions in female animals follow an *estrus* cycle, and they are sexually receptive only during periods of high estrogen secretion (i.e., when they are in heat).

Sex hormones also influence human sexual desire. The natural hormonal surge of puberty increases sexual motivation, as would an artificial boost from receiving doses of testosterone (Tuiten et al., 2000). But in humans, normal short-term hormonal fluctuations have relatively little effect on sexual arousability (Morrell et al., 1984). Desire does not go up and down like a yo-yo as blood levels of sex hormones change, and women may experience high sexual desire at any time during their menstrual cycle. Moreover, in men and women, androgens—rather than estrogens—appear to have the primary influence on sexual desire (Hyde & DeLamater, 2003).

The Psychology of Sex

Sexual arousal involves more than physiological responses. It typically begins with desire and a sexual stimulus that is perceived positively (Walen & Roth, 1987). Such stimuli can even be imaginary.

Sexual fantasy is an important component of many people's lives, although studies in Europe, South America, and North America indicate that men sexually fantasize more often than women

▶ **Focus 9**
Discuss how psychological, cultural, and environmental factors influence sexual behavior.

(Martinez & Raul, 2000). Among American adults, for example, about half of men and a fifth of women fantasize about sex at least once a day (Laumann et al., 1994). Fantasy nicely illustrates how mental processes can affect physiological functioning. Indeed, sexual fantasies alone may trigger genital erection and orgasm in some people and are often used to enhance arousal during masturbation.

Psychological factors can not only trigger sexual arousal but also inhibit it. A person may be engaged in sexual activity and then become turned off by something a partner does. About 1 in 3 American women and 1 in 6 men report that they simply lack an interest in sex (Laumann et al., 1994). Other people desire sex but have difficulty becoming or staying aroused. Stress, fatigue, and anger at one's partner can lead to temporary arousal problems. **Sexual dysfunction** *refers to chronic, impaired sexual functioning that distresses a person.* It may result from injuries, diseases, and drug effects, but some causes are psychological. Arousal difficulties also may stem from performance anxiety or may be a psychological consequence of sexual assault or childhood sexual abuse (Rumstein & Hunsley, 2001).

Cultural and Environmental Influences

Anyone who doubts culture's power to shape human behavior need only examine sexual customs around the globe. During sex, most Westerners probably do not poke a finger into their partner's ear, as do Trukese women of Micronesia, or bite off and then spit out hairs from their partner's eyebrow, as do South American Apinaye women (Hyde & DeLamater, 2003). You may find these practices unusual, but consider how some sexual techniques common in our culture—such as kissing—seem to members of other cultures: "There are a few societies . . . in which kissing is unknown. For example, when the Thonga of Africa first saw Europeans kissing, they laughed and said, 'Look at them; they eat each other's saliva and dirt'" (Hyde & DeLamater, 2003, pp. 10–11).

More important, the psychological meaning of sex itself depends on cultural contexts. Some societies and religions forbid premarital sex and may also prohibit public dress and behavior that arouse sexual desire (Figure 10.15). Many people who view themselves as very religious believe it is important to bring their sexual practices into harmony with their religious beliefs, which may condone sex only within marriage (Janus & Janus, 1993).

In contrast, some societies openly encourage premarital sex. Among Marquesan Islanders of eastern Polynesia, families sleep together in one room, and children have ample opportunity to observe sexual activity. When boys and girls reach adolescence, a middle-aged adult of the opposite sex instructs them in sexual techniques and has intercourse with them. Having other sexual partners prior to marriage is considered normal (Frayser, 1985). Clearly, what is regarded as proper, moral, and desirable varies enormously across cultures.

FIGURE 10.15

Habits of dress that many people take for granted in Western societies, such as wearing tank tops, bare-midriff shirts, and short skirts, are unacceptable in other cultures because they would be considered sexually provocative.

Environmental stimuli are pervasive and dependable elicitors of sexual desire and behavior. Such stimuli are prominently displayed both in everyday life and in the mass media. On a daily basis, TV shows present explicit scenes and sexual themes that would have been unthinkable half a century ago. The envelope is pushed even further by the ready availability of pornography, a multibillion-dollar industry whose primary consumers are men. Social commentators and psychologists have raised the question of whether pornography affects men's sexual attitudes and fosters sexual violence toward women.

Many pornographic materials model *rape myths*, suggesting that men are entitled to sex and that women enjoy being coerced into sex. Correlational studies paint an ambiguous picture of links between pornography and sexual violence against women. Some countries with high rates of rape have little pornography, whereas others have a great deal. Conversely, in some countries pornography is widely available but rates of rape are low (Bauserman, 1996). Similarly, research with sex offenders shows that they do not differ from other men in amount or earliest age of exposure to pornography, and they are actually *less* aroused by nonviolent pornography. Yet they are more aroused by violent pornography and are also more likely to act sexually after viewing violent or even nonviolent pornography (Allen et al., 1995, 2000).

Controlled experiments paint a clearer causal picture. In some studies, male college students were randomly assigned to view material whose content was either neutral (i.e., nonsexual), sexually explicit but nonviolent (e.g., a couple having consensual sex), or sexually aggressive (e.g., a rape-myth depiction showing a woman who initially resists sexual assault but then becomes a willing participant). Later, the students interacted with another person (a female or male accomplice of the experimenter), who made errors on a learning task. Participants were instructed to punish the person with electric shock for each error, but they were free to choose the shock intensity and thus aggress by giving stronger shocks. (The confederate did not really receive any shock.)

The strongest experimental effects emerged when participants viewed violent pornography (Malamuth et al., 2000). At least temporarily, this increased men's tendency to aggress toward women but not toward other men. However, certain types of people, such as those who reported the greatest attraction to sexual violence, were most strongly affected by viewing it. In addition to its connection with aggression, pornography also promotes a belief that sex is impersonal. An un-

welcome side effect is that exposure to pornography decreases viewers' satisfaction with their own sexual partners (Donnerstein & Malamuth, 1997).

Sexual Orientation

Sexual orientation *refers to one's emotional and erotic preference for partners of a particular sex.* Determining one's sexual orientation seems simple: Heterosexuals prefer opposite-sex partners, homosexuals prefer same-sex partners, and bisexuals are sexually attracted to members of both sexes. So how would you classify the sexual orientation of these two 25-year-olds?

- Susan feels sexually attracted to men and women, but she has had sex only with men and thinks of herself as heterosexual.

- Larry has had sex with other men twice since puberty, yet he isn't attracted to men and views himself as heterosexual.

Prevalence of Different Sexual Orientations Some researchers view sexual orientation as a single dimension ranging from "exclusively heterosexual" to "exclusively homosexual," with "equally heterosexual and homosexual" at the midpoint. But others argue that sexual orientation has three dimensions: *self-identity, sexual attraction,* and *actual sexual behavior* (Kelly, 2001).

Figure 10.16 shows that about 2 to 3 percent of American men and 1 percent of American

▶ **Focus 10**
Describe what is known about the effects of watching violent pornography.

▶ **Focus 11**
Describe three dimensions of sexual orientation. Discuss research on the determinants of sexual orientation.

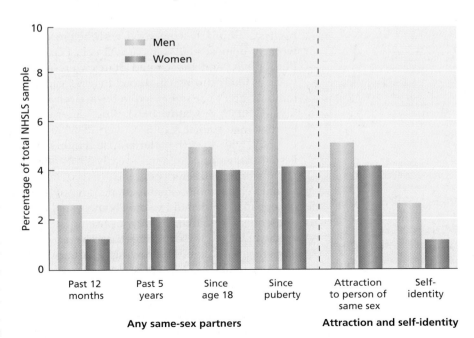

FIGURE 10.16

Behavior and self-perception. More men and women report same-sex attraction and same-sex activity than view themselves as homosexual or bisexual. Source: Adapted from Laumann et al., 1994.

women identify themselves as homosexual or bisexual, but higher percentages report same-sex attraction and at least one same-sex sexual experience (Laumann et al., 1994). Overall, 10 percent of men and 9 percent of women answer affirmatively to at least one of the items in Figure 10.16. Rates of same-sex sexual activity seem to be slightly lower in England and France and slightly higher in Australia (Dunne et al., 2000; Johnson et al., 1992).

Determinants of Sexual Orientation Theories about the origins of sexual orientation abound. An early and unsupported biological view proposed that homosexual and heterosexual males differ in their adult levels of sex hormones. Other early theories hypothesized that male homosexuality develops when boys grow up with a weak, ineffectual father and identify with a domineering mother, or that being sexually seduced by an adult homosexual causes children to divert their sex drive toward members of their own sex.

All of these theories have taken a scientific beating. In one study, Alan Bell and coworkers (1981) interviewed nearly 1,000 homosexual and over 500 heterosexual men and women from the San Francisco area. They searched extensively for childhood or adolescent experiences that might predict adult sexual orientation, but only one consistent pattern emerged: Even in childhood, homosexual men and women felt that they were somehow different from their same-sex peers and were more likely to engage in *gender-nonconforming behaviors*. Similarly, compared with heterosexual women, homosexual women in Brazil, Peru, the Philippines, and the United States were about twice as likely during childhood to be considered tomboys and to be interested in boys' clothes and toys (Whitam & Mathy, 1991). Study after study has obtained similar results (Cohen, 2002).

Still, why do such patterns arise? Highly publicized studies appeared in the early 1990s reporting anatomical differences in the brains of heterosexual versus homosexual men and identifying a genetic marker shared by some homosexual men. Subsequent research, however, has not consistently replicated these findings (Lasco et al., 2002). Nonetheless, there is growing evidence that heredity influences human sexual orientation. In one study, among gay men who had a brother, the concordance rates for sexual orientation (i.e., the brother was gay also) were 52 percent among identical twins, 22 percent among fraternal twins, and 11 percent among adoptive brothers (Bailey & Pillard, 1991). A later study of homosexual

women yielded similar results (Bailey et al., 1993). Thus the closer the genetic relatedness, the higher the concordance rates for sexual orientation (Kirk et al., 2000).

According to another theory, the brain develops a neural pattern that predisposes an individual to prefer either female or male sex partners, depending on whether prenatal-sex-hormone activity follows a masculine or feminine path (Rahman, 2005). Experimentally altering animals' prenatal exposure to sex hormones can influence their sexual orientation. Moreover, in rare cases among humans, some genetically male fetuses are insensitive to their own androgen secretions and some female fetuses experience an atypical buildup of androgens. Studies of these individuals suggest a relation between prenatal-sex-hormone exposure and adulthood sexual orientation (Williams et al., 2000). Of course, the human research is correlational and must be interpreted cautiously. For example, male fetuses who have androgen insensitivity develop the external anatomy of females and are typically raised as girls; socialization could account for their sexual orientation.

What about environmental influences? Even among identical twins, when one is homosexual, often the other is heterosexual. Thus a biological predisposition and socialization experiences may combine to determine sexual orientation. At present, scientists simply do not know what all the factors are. It is also possible, argues Daryl Bem (1996, 2001), that heredity affects sexual orientation only indirectly, by influencing children's basic personality style. He proposes that different personality styles then steer children toward gender-conforming or gender-nonconforming activities, causing them to feel similar to or different from same-sex peers. Ultimately, this affects their attraction to same-sex and opposite-sex peers. Bem's theory has mixed support and needs further testing (Bailey et al., 2000; Peplau et al., 1998).

Finally, there may be multiple paths toward developing a sexual orientation, and the paths for men and women may differ. Consider the intriguing finding shown in Figure 10.17: The greater the number of older brothers (but not older sisters) a newborn boy has, the greater the probability that he will develop a homosexual orientation. In contrast, a woman's sexual orientation is not related to the number of older sisters or brothers in the family. Ray Blanchard (2001), the leading researcher of this *fraternal birth order effect*, has found it in 14 studies, involving over 7,000 total participants.

? What Do You Think?

FRATERNAL BIRTH ORDER AND MALE HOMOSEXUALITY
Why might having older brothers increase the odds that a later-born male will have a homosexual orientation? Think about possible explanations, then see page 394.

IN REVIEW

■ The past half century has witnessed changing patterns of sexual activity, such as an increase in premarital sex, which now appears to have leveled off.

■ During sexual intercourse, people often experience a four-stage physiological response pattern consisting of excitement, plateau, orgasm, and resolution.

■ Sex hormones have organizational effects that guide prenatal organ development along either a male or female pattern. Sex hormones also have activational effects that influence sexual desire.

■ Sexual fantasy can trigger arousal, whereas psychological difficulties can interfere with sexual arousal. Cultural norms help determine the sexual practices and beliefs that are considered proper.

■ Environmental stimuli affect sexual desire. Viewing sexual violence reinforces men's belief in rape myths and generally increases men's aggression toward women, at least temporarily.

■ Sexual orientation involves dimensions of self-identity, sexual attraction, and actual sexual behavior. Scientists still do not know conclusively what determines an individual's sexual orientation.

NEEDS FOR AFFILIATION AND INTIMACY

What makes your life most meaningful? To many people, close relationships are one key. The three doctors Sampson Davis, Rameck Hunt, and George Jenkins surely agree. Their deep friendship and mutual support sustained them through arduous years of college and medical school. Abraham Maslow (1954) viewed belongingness as a basic psychological need, and considerable research indicates that, indeed, "the need to belong is a powerful, fundamental, and extremely pervasive motivation" (Baumeister & Leary, 1995, p. 497).

FIGURE 10.17

Homosexuality: The fraternal birth order effect. The presence of each older brother increases by about one third the relative probability that a later-born male child will be gay. Thus if there is a 2 percent probability that a man with no older brothers is gay, then the probability for a man with one older brother is about 2.6 to 2.7 percent, roughly a one-third relative increase. SOURCE: Adapted from Blanchard and Bogaert, 1996.

Why Do We Affiliate?

Humans are social beings who affiliate in many ways (Figure 10.18). Some theorists propose that over the course of evolution, individuals whose biological makeup predisposed them to affiliate were more likely to survive and reproduce than those who were reclusive. By affording greater access to sexual mates, more protection from predators, an efficient division of labor, and the passing of knowledge across generations, a socially oriented lifestyle had considerable adaptive value (Kottak, 2000).

Craig Hill (1987) suggests that we affiliate for four basic psychological reasons:

- To obtain positive stimulation
- To receive emotional support
- To gain attention
- To permit social comparison

Social comparison *involves comparing our beliefs, feelings, and behaviors with those of other people.* This helps us determine whether our responses are "normal" and enables us to judge the level of our cognitive and physical abilities (Festinger, 1954).

People differ in how strongly they desire to affiliate. In one study, college students who scored high on a personality test of "need for affiliation" made more friends during the semester than students who scored low (Byrne & Greendlinger, 1989). In another study, high school students wore

▶ **Focus 12**
Discuss evolutionary and psychological views of affiliation and factors that influence the desire to affiliate.

FIGURE 10.18

Affiliation brings us companionship, intimacy, love, support, and basic social contact. To satisfy these desires we form friendships, interact with family members, join groups, converse with strangers, and flock together in crowds.

beepers over a 1-week period. They were signaled approximately every 2 hours, at which time they recorded their thoughts and activities. Participants with a high need for affiliation were more likely than their peers to report that they were thinking about friends and wishing that they could be with people (Wong & Csikszentmihalyi, 1991).

Even people with strong affiliation needs, however, usually desire some time alone. Conversely, people with lower affiliation needs still seek periodic social contact. Some theorists, therefore, view affiliation needs within a homeostatic model (O'Connor & Rosenblood, 1996). They propose that each of us has our own optimal range of social contact. After periods when contact exceeds that range, we compensate by temporarily seeking more solitude. After periods when social contact falls below the optimal range, we increase our effort to be with others. Although some human and animal findings are consistent with this model, it needs much more testing.

Many studies have shown, however, that situational factors influence our tendency to affiliate. For example, fear-inducing situations increase our desire to be with others. During emergencies, as in the aftermath of earthquakes, floods, and hurricanes, many people find themselves bonding with strangers. When afraid, we may prefer to be with others who face the same situation we do, which helps us gauge the normalcy of our reactions (Schachter, 1959).

When possible, we seem to desire most strongly to be with others who have already been through the same or similar situations (Kulik & Mahler, 2000). Doing so can provide us with information about what to expect. In one study, hospital patients awaiting open-heart surgery expressed a stronger desire to have roommates who already had been through surgery than preoperative roommates like themselves. In a later study, when patients were actually assigned postoperative rather than preoperative roommates, they became less anxious and later recovered from surgery more quickly (Kulik et al., 1996).

Seeking a Mate

One of the most important and intimate ways that humans affiliate is by seeking a mate. Marriage seems to be universal across the globe, but people also seek mates in other types of relationships (Buss & Schmitt, 1993). Much research has found, however, that on average women and men display different mating strategies and preferences. Compared with women, men typically show more interest in short-term mating, prefer a greater number of short-term sexual mates, have more permissive sexual attitudes, and have more sexual partners over their lifetime (Schmitt et al., 2001). In one study of 266 college undergraduates, two thirds of the women said that they desired only one sexual partner over the next 30 years, but only about half of the men desired only one partner (Pedersen et al., 2002).

TABLE 10.1 What Do You Look for in a Mate?		

Women and men rated each characteristic on a 4-point scale. From top to bottom, the following numbers represent the order (rank) of most highly rated to least highly rated items for Buss's worldwide sample. How would you rate their importance?

Characteristic Desired in a Mate	Rated by	
	Women	Men
Mutual attraction/love	1	1
Dependable character	2	2
Emotional stability/maturity	3	3
Pleasing disposition	4	4
Education/intelligence	5	6
Sociability	6	7
Good health	7	5
Desire for home/children	8	8
Ambitious	9	11
Refinement	10	9
Similar education	11	14
Good financial prospect	12	13
Good looks	13	10
Social status	14	15
Good cook/housekeeper	15	12
Similar religion	16	17
Similar politics	17	18
Chastity	18	16

SOURCE: Based on Buss et al., 1990.

What about the commitment that most men and women make at some point in their lives to a long-term mate? What qualities do women and men seek in such a mate? Once again, we see sex differences. Men typically prefer women somewhat younger than themselves, whereas women prefer somewhat older men. In terms of personal qualities, Table 10.1 shows the overall results of a worldwide study of mate preferences in 37 cultures (Buss et al., 1990). Men and women again show considerable overall agreement, but some differences emerge. Men place greater value on a potential mate's physical attractiveness and domestic skills, whereas women place greater value on a potential mate's earning potential, status, and ambitiousness. The question is, why?

According to an evolutionary viewpoint called **sexual strategies theory** (and a related model called *parental investment theory*), *mating strategies and preferences reflect inherited tendencies, shaped over the ages in response to different types of adaptive problems that*

men and women faced (Buss & Schmitt, 1993; Trivers, 1972). In evolutionary terms, our most successful ancestors were those who survived and passed down the greatest numbers of their genes to future generations. According to this viewpoint, men who had sex with more partners increased the likelihood of fathering more children. Men also may have taken a woman's youth and attractive, healthy appearance as signs that she was fertile and had many years left to bear children (Buss, 1989).

In contrast, ancestral women had little to gain and much to lose by mating with many men. The gender with a greater investment (costs) in producing offspring will be more selective in choosing a mate. In humans and other mammals, females typically make a greater investment than males; females carry the fetus, incur health risks, and nourish the newborn. Engaging in short-term sexual relationships with multiple males creates uncertainty about which one is the father, thereby decreasing a male's willingness to commit resources to helping the mother raise the child. Thus women maximized their reproductive success by being selective and choosing mates who were willing and able to commit time, energy, and other resources (e.g., food, shelter, protection) to the family. Through natural selection, according to evolutionary psychologists, the differing qualities that maximized men's and women's reproductive success eventually became part of their biological nature.

Many scientists challenge this evolutionary explanation for human mating patterns and other social behaviors. Adaptive behavior patterns may have been passed from parents to children not through genes but through learning. In addition, **social structure theory** *proposes that men and women display different mating preferences because society directs them into different social roles* (Eagly & Wood, 1999). Despite the shift over the past several decades toward greater gender equality, women today in general still have less power, lower wages, and less access to resources than men do. In a two-income marriage, the woman is more likely to be the partner who switches to part-time work or becomes a full-time homemaker after childbirth. Thus society's division of labor still tends to socialize men into the breadwinner role and women into the homemaker role.

It makes sense, then, for women to seek men who will be successful wage earners and for men to seek women who can have children and fulfill the domestic worker role. An older male–younger female age gap is favorable because older men are likely to be further along in earning power and younger women more economically dependent, and this conforms to cultural expectations of marital

▶ **Focus 13**
Contrast sexual-strategies and social-structure explanations for mate preferences. Describe cross-cultural evidence.

roles. This division-of-labor hypothesis does not directly address why men emphasize a mate's physical attractiveness more than women do, but Alice Eagly and Wendy Wood (1999) speculate that attractiveness is viewed as part of what women "exchange" in return for a male's earning capacity.

We now have two competing explanations for sex differences in mating behavior: the evolution-based sexual strategies approach and the social structure view. Which view is more valid? Our "Research Close-Up" looks at one attempt to answer this question.

 Research Close-Up   **Sex Differences in the Ideal Mate: Evolution or Social Roles?**

SOURCES: DAVID M. BUSS (1989). Sex differences in human mate preferences: Evolutionary hypotheses tested in 37 cultures. *Behavioral and Brain Sciences, 12,* 1–49; ALICE EAGLY and WENDY WOOD (1999). The origins of sex differences in human behavior: Evolved dispositions versus social roles. *American Psychologist, 54,* 408–423.

INTRODUCTION

How can we possibly test the hypothesis that over the ages, evolution has shaped the psyches of men and women to be inherently different? Evolutionary psychologist David Buss proposes that as a start, we can examine whether gender differences in mating preferences are consistent across cultures. If they are, this would be consistent with the view that men and women follow universal, biologically based mating strategies that transcend culture. Based on principles of evolutionary psychology, Buss hypothesized that *across cultures,* men will prefer to marry younger women, because such women have greater reproductive capacity; men will value a potential mate's attractiveness more than women will, because men use attractiveness as a sign of health and fertility; and women will place greater value than men on a potential mate's earning potential, because this provides survival advantages for the woman and her offspring.

METHOD

A team of 50 scientists administered questionnaires to women and men from 37 cultures around the globe. Although random sampling could not be used, the sample of 10,047 participants was ethnically, religiously, and socioeconomically diverse. Participants reported the ideal ages at which they and a spouse would marry, rank-ordered (from "most desirable" to "least desirable") a list of 13 qualities that a potential mate might have, and rated the importance of 18 mate qualities on a second list (see Table 10.1).

RESULTS

In every culture, men desired to marry younger women. Overall, they believed that the ideal ages for men and women to marry were 27.5 and 24.8 years, respectively. Similarly, women preferred older men, reporting on average an ideal marriage age of 28.8 for husbands and 25.4 for wives.

In every culture, men valued having a physically attractive mate more than women did, and in 36 of 37 cultures, women attached more importance than men did to a mate's earning potential.

EVOLUTIONARY AND SOCIAL ROLES INTERPRETATIONS

David Buss concluded that the findings strongly supported the predictions of evolutionary (sexual strategies) theory. Subsequently, Alice Eagly and Wendy Wood analyzed Buss's data further in order to test the following predictions derived from their social structure theory:

- Men place greater value than women on a mate's having good domestic skills because this is consistent with culturally defined gender roles.
- If economic and power inequalities cause men and women to attach different values to a mate's age, earning potential, and domestic skills, then these gender differences should be smaller in cultures where there is less inequality between men and women.

The potential-mate characteristic "good cook/housekeeper" produced large overall gender differences, with men valuing it more highly. Eagly and Wood then used the United Nations Gender Empowerment Measure to assess the degree of gender equality in each culture. This measure reflects women's percentage share of administrative, managerial, professional, and technical jobs; seats in parliament; and earned income relative to men.

As predicted by the social structure model, in cultures with greater gender equality, men showed less of a preference for younger women, women displayed less of a preference for older men, and the gender gap decreased in mate preferences for a "good cook/housekeeper" and "good financial prospect." Recall that this division-of-labor model does not directly address why men value physical attractiveness more than women; indeed, that gender difference was *not* smaller in cultures with greater gender equality.

DISCUSSION

Buss found remarkably consistent sex differences in worldwide mate preferences. He interpreted this cross-cultural consistency as evidence that men and women follow universal, biologically based mating strategies. Yet the fact that behavior is consistent across cultures does not, by itself, demonstrate *why* those patterns occur (Wood & Eagly, 2000). Eagly and Wood found that a common social condition across cultures, gender inequality, accounts for some—but not all—of the sex differences in mating preferences.

In science, such controversy stimulates opposing camps to find more sophisticated ways to test their hypotheses. Ultimately, everyone's goal is to arrive at the most plausible explanation for behavior. This is why scientists make their data available to one another, regardless of the possibility that their peers may use the data to bolster an opposing point of view.

Although men and women differ in some of their mating preferences and strategies, the similar overall order of mate preferences shown in Table 10.1 indicates that we are talking once again about shades of the same color, not different colors. In fact, Buss and coworkers (1990) found that "there may be more similarity between men and women from the same culture than between men and men or women and women from different cultures" (p. 17).

IN REVIEW

- Humans seek to affiliate in many ways. Affiliation has adaptive advantages and allows people to obtain positive stimulation, receive emotional support, gain attention, and engage in social comparison.

- People differ in how strongly they need to affiliate, and some theorists view affiliative behavior as governed by homeostatic principles.

- Situations that induce fear often increase people's tendency to affiliate. When afraid, people often seek the company of others who have been through or are currently experiencing the same or a similar situation.

- Some reliable sex differences occur in people's mating strategies and preferences, such as men's tendency to seek younger women and women's tendency to seek older men.

- Evolutionary theorists propose that these sex differences in mate preferences reflect inherited biological tendencies, whereas social structure theorists argue that these differences result from sex-role socialization and gender inequities in economic opportunities.

ACHIEVEMENT MOTIVATION

In striving to become doctors, Sampson Davis, Rameck Hunt, and George Jenkins exemplified the desire to achieve. As a college student, you are keenly aware of society's emphasis on achievement, and you know that whether in school, sports, music, or other fields, some people seek out and thrive on challenges and others do not. In the 1950s, David McClelland, John Atkinson, and their coworkers (1953) began to explore individual differences in **need for achievement,** *a positive desire to accomplish tasks and compete successfully with standards of excellence.*

Motive for Success and Fear of Failure

McClelland and Atkinson proposed that achievement behavior can stem from a positively oriented *motive for success* and a negatively oriented motivation to avoid failure, more commonly called *fear of failure.* Need for achievement is the positive orientation toward success. In terms of the behavioral activation and behavioral inhibition systems discussed earlier, motive for success is the part of the BAS that relates to the achievement domain. Fear of failure is a BIS function.

McClelland and Atkinson measured the motive for success with a psychological test that asked participants to write stories in response to a number of pictures, such as the one in Figure 10.19. The stories were then analyzed for achievement-relevant themes using a standardized coding system. The avoidance motive, fear of failure, was measured by psychological tests that asked people to report how much anxiety they experienced in achievement situations. McClelland and Atkinson found that their measures of need for achievement and fear of failure were independent (uncorrelated) dimensions, so that people could be high in both motives, low in both, or high in one and low in the other.

People who have a strong motive for success seek the thrill of victory, whereas those motivated by fear of failure seek to avoid the agony of defeat. Common sense suggests that a strong motive for success combined with a strong fear of failure might lead a person to perform better than someone who is motivated only by a desire for success. But this is not so. The anxiety associated with fear of failure can negate the impact of the need for achievement and can impair performance. In sports, the athlete with a high fear of failure is the one who tends to choke under pressure (Smith, 1996).

People high in achievement and low in fear of failure, called *high-need achievers,* don't necessarily outperform low-need achievers when conditions

FIGURE 10.19

Pictures like this are used to elicit stories that are scored for the motive to succeed. Which of the following two stories, written by different people, reflects a stronger motive to succeed? (1) This young man is sitting in school, but he is dreaming about the day when he will become a doctor. He will study and work harder than anyone else. He goes on to become one of the top medical researchers in the world. (2) The boy is daydreaming about how much he hates being in school. . . . He would like to run away from home and just take it easy on a tropical island. However, he is doomed to be in the rat race the rest of his life.

▶ **Focus 14**
How do the motives and task behaviors of high- versus low-need
achievers differ? Describe the
achievement goal orientations
and motivational climates in
achievement goal theory.

are relaxed and tasks are easy. However, when tasks are challenging or the importance of doing well is stressed, high-need achievers outshine low-need achievers. They perform at a higher level, and they are more persistent when they encounter barriers to achievement (McClelland, 1989). In general, high-need achievers are most likely to strive hard for success when they perceive themselves as personally responsible for the outcome, when they perceive some risk of not succeeding, and when there is an opportunity to receive performance feedback (Koestner & McClelland, 1990).

When given a choice of performing a task that is very easy (a high probability of success), moderately difficult (a 40 to 60 percent probability of success), or very difficult (a low probability of success), which do you predict that high-need achievers will choose? Contrary to what you might expect, they prefer intermediate risks to extremely high or low risks because the outcome—success versus failure—*is most uncertain* (Atkinson & Birch, 1978). In contrast, low-need achievers are more likely to choose tasks that are easy (where success is almost assured) or very difficult (where success is not expected, so that nothing is on the line).

To understand this pattern, realize that it is the individual's *perception* of outcome uncertainty that counts. For most of us, the probability of successfully climbing Mt. Everest is virtually zero. But to highly trained mountaineers, the task is neither impossible nor easy. Decades ago, soci-

ologist and mountain climber Dick Emerson (1966) joined a Mt. Everest expedition. As he predicted, the team members' communications with one another throughout the long climb struck a balance between optimistic and pessimistic comments about the chances of reaching their goal. This kept the climbers' perceived chance of success-failure close to 50-50 and maintained maximum motivation.

Achievement Goal Theory

Another way to understand achievement motivation is to examine the success goals that people seek to attain in task situations. **Achievement goal theory** *focuses on the manner in which success is defined both by the individual and within the achievement situation itself.* At the individual level, achievement goal theorists are interested in the achievement goal orientation that people have (Dweck, 1999). They differentiate between a **mastery orientation**, *in which the focus is on personal improvement, giving maximum effort, and perfecting new skills,* and an **ego orientation**, *in which the goal is to outperform others (hopefully, with as little effort as possible).* At the situational level, the theory focuses on the **motivational climate** *that encourages or rewards either a mastery approach or an ego approach to defining success* (Figure 10.20).

Goal Orientation   Think for a moment about a class you currently are taking. On a scale of 1 ("not at all true of me") to 7 ("very true of me"), rate these statements:

1. I want to learn as much as possible from this class.

2. I am motivated by the thought of outperforming my peers in this class.

3. I just want to avoid doing poorly in this class.

These statements represent three different achievement goals (Elliot & Church, 1997). **Mastery goals** (statement 1) *focus on the desire to master a task and learn new knowledge or skills.* In essence, mastery goals reflect intrinsic motivation. **Ego-approach goals** (statement 2) *reflect a competitive orientation that focuses on being judged favorably relative to other people.* People can be high or low on both orientations or high on one and low on the other. **Ego-avoidance goals** (statement 3) *center on avoiding negative judgments by oneself or others.* They are the achievement goal version of fear of failure.

Do college students' achievement goals for a particular class, measured shortly after classes begin, help predict their psychological responses to

Achievement Goal Theory

FIGURE 10.20

Achievement goal theory. Achievement goal theory focuses on the ways in which success is defined, both by individuals and within achievement environments. Individuals may have mastery or ego goal orientations, and the motivational climate created in achievement situations by significant others may emphasize and support mastery goals, such as effort and skill improvement, or ego definitions of success, such as outperforming others.

upcoming exams and to that course? Do goals predict course grades? Overall, ego avoidance goals are associated with perceiving exams as anxiety-provoking threats, with reporting at the end of the term that the course was less interesting and enjoyable, and with slightly poorer course grades (Harackiewicz et al., 2002; McGregor & Elliot, 2002).

In contrast, mastery goals predict the tendency to perceive exams as a positive challenge and to rate the course as more interesting and enjoyable, even though mastery goals are unrelated to course grades. Ego-approach goals, however, predict grades but not final interest or enjoyment. When it comes to exams, they are weakly associated with feelings of both challenge and threat. Given this pattern of findings, some researchers believe that students who adopt both mastery and ego-approach goals display the optimal pattern of motivation for college courses (Harackiewicz et al., 2002). The mastery goal enhances enjoyment and interest, and the ego-approach goal fosters performance within the competitive college environment, where grades are often determined by one's performance in relation to others.

Not all people are high on both mastery and ego orientations, however. If you are going to be high on one or the other, which would be preferable? Although both goal orientations contribute to success, in achievement contexts ranging from academic to work and sport settings, research indicates that a mastery goal orientation has several psychological advantages over an ego orientation (Dweck, 1999; McArdle & Duda, 2002). When success is defined as "being one's best" rather than "competing with others," people can focus on and enjoy their own improvement and accomplishments. They are more likely to experience intrinsic motivation and enjoyment of the activity, persist in the face of difficulties, select challenging goals, and exert maximum effort. Legendary basketball coach John Wooden captured the mastery orientation in his definition of success: "Success is peace of mind that comes from knowing that you did your best to become the best that you are capable of becoming. No one can do more."

For an ego-oriented person, experiencing personal improvement or knowing that one did her or his best would not in itself occasion feelings of success or competence. Indeed, knowing that one tried hard and failed to outperform others would cause an ego-oriented person to feel especially incompetent. If ego-oriented people begin to question their ability to meet performance demands or to successfully compete with others, they are more likely to reduce persistence and avoid the challenge at hand (Nicholls, 1989). This would be especially likely in those high in the avoidance variant of ego orientation (Elliott & Church, 1997). Former college basketball coach Dean Smith captured one negative consequence of an ego orientation: "If you make winning basketball games a life-or-death situation, you're going to have problems. For one thing, you'll be dead a lot."

Motivational Climate   Besides individual differences in goal orientations, situational factors influence how success is defined. The motivational climate of an achievement setting is influenced by significant others, such as parents, teachers, coaches, and supervisors (Ames, 1992; Chi, 2004). In an ego-involving climate, performers are compared with one another, urged to compete to be the best, and those who perform best get special attention. In a mastery-involving climate, effort, enjoyment of the activity, and personal improvement are emphasized and rewarded. The assumption is that if people work to achieve their potential and give maximum effort, winning will take care of itself. These differing conceptions of success can have strong effects on participants. In children, they help shape the achievement goal orientation(s) that are internalized.

Mastery-involving achievement environments have been linked to a variety of positive effects in school and sport settings. They foster higher intrinsic motivation and enjoyment of the setting, enhance perceptions of learning and mastery, and bolster self-esteem. Performance anxiety is also lower in such settings because the emphasis is on doing one's best (which is personally controllable) rather than on a win outcome that is dependent in part on how others perform. An ego-involving climate fosters the belief that ability, rather than hard work, leads to success, and satisfaction is gained by outperforming others rather than through skill improvement. At the level of task performance, mastery climates result in better skill development and higher performance levels, due in part to increased effort, greater enjoyment, and lowered anxiety (Dweck, 1999; McArdle & Duda, 2002).

Family, Culture, and Achievement Needs

How does achievement motivation develop? Providing a cognitively stimulating home environment fosters children's intrinsic motivation to perform academic tasks (Gottfried et al., 1998). And when parents or other key caregivers encourage and reward achievement but do not punish failure, they foster a strong motive for success

▶ **Focus 15**
How do family and cultural factors influence achievement motivation?

(Koestner & McClelland, 1990). Conversely, fear of failure seems to develop when caregivers take successful achievement for granted but punish failure, thereby teaching the child to dread the possibility of failing (Weiner, 1992). Providing a mastery motivational climate in the home, the school, and the athletic setting also encourages the development of a mastery achievement orientation (Dweck, 1999, McArdle & Duda, 2002).

Cultural norms also shape achievement motivation. Individualistic cultures, such as those in North America and much of Europe, tend to stress personal achievement. In cultures that nurture collectivism, such as those in China and Japan, achievement motivation more strongly reflects a desire to fit into the family and social group, meet its expectations, and work for its goals (Markus & Kitayama, 1991). Chinese high school students, for example, typically care more about meeting their parents' expectations for academic success than do American students (Chen & Lan, 1998). In collectivistic Japan, business organizations have traditionally adopted the concept of *Kaizen* (continuous improvement), encouraging workers to develop skills and increase productivity (Elsey & Fujiwara, 2000). Such companies assume responsibility for their employees' welfare, promote them gradually, and are willing to retain them for life. In turn, the workers are more strongly motivated by loyalty to their managers and to the organization as the company becomes integral to their identities.

At the same time, the human desire to achieve transcends culture and can manifest itself in intriguing ways. Throughout history, some people have left their homelands to seek adventure or better lives elsewhere. Might achievement motivation relate to the desire to emigrate? To answer this question, researchers measured the achievement motivation of college students in Albania, the Czech Republic, and Slovenia and also asked students where they would like to live for most of their adult lives. In each sample, students who expressed a desire to emigrate had higher average achievement motivation scores than students who said they wanted to remain in their homeland (Boneva et al., 1998).

▶ **Focus 16**
Explain and illustrate three types of motivational conflict.

How can more sleep and down time for adolescents influence their motivation to achieve? Watch the video, "Overscheduling Our Adolescents," in Chapter 10 of your CD for one expert's opinion.

IN REVIEW

- High-need achievers have a strong motive for success and relatively low fear of failure. They tend to seek moderately difficult tasks that are challenging but attainable. Low-need achievers are more likely to choose easy tasks, where success is assured, or very difficult tasks where success is not expected.

- Mastery, ego-approach, and ego-avoidance goals are three basic achievement goals. Mastery goals are associated with viewing achievement tasks as a positive challenge, whereas ego-avoidance goals are linked to viewing such tasks as threatening. Ego-approach goals are most strongly linked to eventual course grades for college students, mastery goals to course enjoyment.

- Compared with ego-involving environments, mastery-involving motivational climates foster higher enjoyment and intrinsic motivation, greater feelings of self-determination, lower levels of performance anxiety, and better learning of skills, greater effort, and higher performance.

- Child-rearing and cultural factors influence the nature and expression of achievement motivation.

MOTIVATIONAL CONFLICT

Motivational goals sometimes conflict with one another. Our desires to achieve success and to have fun may clash, for example, when we must choose between studying for an exam and attending a party. When something attracts us, we tend to approach it; when something repels us, we tend to avoid it. Different combinations of these tendencies can produce three basic types of conflict.

Approach-approach conflict *occurs when we face two attractive alternatives and selecting one means losing the other*. Conflict is greatest when both alternatives, such as a choice between two desirable careers, are equally attractive. In contrast, **avoidance-avoidance conflict** *occurs when we must choose between two undesirable alternatives* (Figure 10.21). Do I study boring material for an exam, or do I skip studying and fail? **Approach-avoidance conflict** *involves being attracted to and repelled by the same goal*. A squirrel being offered food by a person on a park bench is motivated by hunger to approach and by fear to keep its distance. A man desires an intimate relationship with a woman but fears the possibility of future rejection.

Approach and avoidance tendencies grow stronger as we get nearer to a desired goal (Miller, 1944). Usually, the avoidance tendency increases in strength faster than the approach tendency

THE FAR SIDE By GARY LARSON

The Far Side® by Gary Larson © 1985 FarWorks, Inc. All Rights Reserved. Used with permission.

© 1985 FarWorks, Inc. All Rights Reserved/Dist. by Creators Syndicate

"C'mon, c'mon—it's either one or the other."

FIGURE 10.21

An unfortunate avoidance-avoidance conflict.

FIGURE 10.22

Approach-avoidance conflict.
According to Neal Miller (1944), the tendency to approach and the tendency to avoid grow stronger as one moves closer to the goal. However, the tendency to avoid increases faster than the tendency to approach. Maximum conflict is experienced where the two gradients cross, because at this point the opposing motives are equal in strength.

(Figure 10.22). Thus at first we may be attracted to a goal and only slightly repelled by its drawbacks, but as we get closer to it the negative aspects become dominant. We may stop, retreat, approach again, and continue to vacillate in a state of conflict. However, the general strength of approach and avoidance tendencies differs across people. BAS-dominated individuals are more attuned to positive stimuli and the possibility of obtaining desired outcomes, whereas those with strong BIS tendencies are more sensitive to actual and anticipated negative outcomes (Elliot & Thrash, 2002; Sutton, 2002).

IN REVIEW

■ Motivational goals may conflict with one another. Approach-approach conflict occurs when a person has to select between two attractive alternatives, whereas avoidance-avoidance conflict involves choosing between two undesirable alternatives.

■ Approach-avoidance conflict occurs when we are attracted to and repelled by the same goal.

EMOTION

Life without emotion would be bland and empty. Our experiences of love, anger, joy, fear, and other emotions energize and add color to our lives. **Emotions** *are feeling (or affect) states that involve a pattern of cognitive, physiological, and behavioral reactions to events.* Emotion theorist Richard Lazarus (2001) believed that motivation and emotions are always linked, because we react emotionally only when our motives and goals are gratified, threatened, or frustrated (Figure 10.23).

Emotions have important adaptive functions. Some emotions, such as fear and alarm, are part of an emergency arousal system that increases our chances of survival, as when we fight or flee when confronted by threat or danger. But positive emotions, such as interest, joy, excitement, contentment, and love, also have important adaptive functions. They help us form intimate relationships and broaden our thinking and behavior so that we explore, consider new ideas, try out new ways to achieve goals, play, and savor what we have (Fredrickson, 1998).

Emotions are also an important form of social communication. By providing clues about our internal states and intentions, emotions influence how other people behave toward us (Isaacs, 1998). Consider, for example, the effects of a baby's crying on adults, who generally respond with caretaking behaviors that have obvious survival value for the infant. Adults' expressions of sadness and distress also evoke concern, empathy, and helping behavior from others.

Positive emotional expressions also pay off. A smiling infant is likely to increase parents' feelings of affection and caring, thereby increasing the likelihood that the child's biological and emotional

▶ **Focus 17**
In what ways are negative and positive emotions adaptive?

FIGURE 10.23

The intimate relations between motivation and emotion are seen in the strong emotional responses that occur when important goals are either attained or lost.

▶ **Focus 18**
Describe the 4 major components of emotion and how they influence one another.

needs will be satisfied. Happy adults also tend to attract others and to have richer and more supportive relationships (Diener & Seligman, 2002).

THE NATURE OF EMOTIONS

Our emotional states share four common features:

1. Emotions are triggered by external or internal *eliciting stimuli*.

2. Emotional responses result from our *appraisals* of these stimuli, which give the situation its perceived meaning and significance.

3. Our *bodies respond physiologically* to our appraisals. We may become physically aroused, as when we feel fear, joy, or anger; or we may experience decreased arousal, as when we feel contentment or depression.

4. Emotions include *behavior tendencies*. Some are *expressive behaviors* (e.g., smiling with

joy, crying). Others are *instrumental behaviors*, ways of doing something about the stimulus that evoked the emotion (e.g., studying for an anxiety-arousing test, fighting back in self-defense).

Figure 10.24 illustrates the general relations among these four emotional components. For example, an insulting remark from another person (eliciting stimulus) may evoke a cognitive appraisal that we have been unfairly demeaned, an increase in physiological arousal, a clenching of jaws and fists (expressive behavior), and a verbal attack on the other person (instrumental behavior). As the two-way arrows indicate, these emotional components can affect one another, so that our thoughts influence our feelings and our feelings influence our appraisals (Frijda et al., 2005). They exist in a larger associative network that also includes links to motives, memories, ideas, and action tendencies. Stimulation of any of the network's components can trigger other elements, depending on

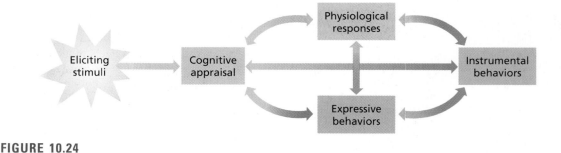

FIGURE 10.24

Components of emotion. Emotion involves relations between eliciting stimuli, cognitive appraisal processes, physiological arousal, expressive behaviors, and instrumental behaviors. Note the reciprocal (two-way) causal relations that exist among the appraisal, physiological arousal, and behavioral components. Appraisal influences arousal and expressive behaviors, and the latter affect ongoing appraisals.

the strengths of the associative links (Berkowitz & Harmon-Jones, 2004). For example, some people can generate strong anger and a tendency toward aggression just by recalling an event in which they were wronged. We'll discuss other linkages as well. Thus emotion is a dynamic, ongoing *process*, and any of its four elements can change rapidly in the course of an emotional episode.

Eliciting Stimuli

Emotions do not occur in a vacuum. They are responses to situations, people, objects, or events. We become angry *at* something or someone; fearful or proud *of* something; in love *with* someone. Moreover, the **eliciting stimuli** *that trigger cognitive appraisals and emotional responses* are not always external; they can be internal stimuli, such as a mental image of an upcoming vacation that makes us feel happy or a memory of an unpleasant encounter that arouses anger in us.

Innate biological factors help determine which stimuli have the greatest potential to arouse emotions (Panksepp, 2005). Newborn infants come equipped with the capacity to respond emotionally with either interest or distress to events in their environment (Galati & Lavelli, 1997). Adults, too, may be biologically primed to experience emotions in response to certain stimuli that have evolutionary significance. As we saw in Chapter 6, this may help explain why the majority of human phobias involve "primal" stimuli such as heights, water, sharks, snakes, or spiders, rather than modern threats such as guns, electrical transformers, and automobiles (Öhman & Wiens, 2005). A wide variety of aversive stimuli—pain, heat and cold, foul odors—can evoke anger and aggressive tendencies toward people who had nothing to do with creating the discomfort (Berkowitz & Harmon-Jones, 2004).

Learning also influences our emotions. Previous experiences can turn certain people or situations into eliciting stimuli. The mere sight of one's lover can evoke feelings of passion; the sight of a disliked person can trigger instantaneous revulsion that seems almost reflexive. On the broadest level, cultures have different standards for defining the good, the bad, and the ugly that affect how we appraise and respond to stimuli. Physical features that provoke sexual arousal and feelings of infatuation in one culture, such as ornamental facial scars or a bone through the nose, may elicit feelings of disgust in another.

The Cognitive Component

Cognitions (thoughts, images, memories, interpretations) are involved in virtually every aspect of emotion. Mental processes can evoke emotional responses. They are part of our inner experience of the emotion, and they influence how we express our emotions and act on them. A situation may evoke pleasure or distress, depending on how we appraise it. For example, a sexual advance may elicit anger, fear, or disgust instead of pleasure if it is unwanted or deemed inappropriate. **Cognitive appraisals** *are the interpretations and meanings that we attach to sensory stimuli.*

Often we are not consciously aware of the appraisals that underlie emotional responses. Some appraisals seem to involve little more than an almost automatic interpretation of sensory input based on previous conditioning (Smith & Kirby, 2004). Indeed, most strong emotions are probably triggered initially in this automatic fashion, after which we may appraise the situation in a more reasoning manner. Even at this more "cognitive" level, however, our habitual ways of thinking can run off in a subconscious shorthand with little or no awareness on our part (Clore & Centebar, 2004; Phelps, 2005). We often fail to appreciate how arbitrarily we interpret "the way things are."

The idea that emotional reactions are triggered by cognitive appraisals rather than external situations helps account for the fact that different people (or even the same person at different times) can have different emotional reactions to the same object, situation, or person (Figure 10.25).

FIGURE 10.25

Differences in appraisal can trigger entirely different emotional reactions, as in this instance. What kinds of appraisals are likely occurring in these people?

Culture and Appraisal   Cross-cultural researchers have asked people in various countries to recall events that triggered certain emotions and to answer questions about how they appraised or interpreted the situations. In one study conducted in 27 different countries, people exhibited strong cross-cultural similarities in the types of appraisals that evoked joy, fear, anger, sadness, disgust, shame, and guilt (Wallbott & Scherer, 1988). Whenever any of these emotions occurred, similar appraisals were involved, regardless of the culture.

Despite these cross-cultural commonalities in appraisal, particular situations can evoke different appraisals and emotional reactions, depending on one's culture (Mesquita & Markus, 2005). Consider, for example, the circumstance of being alone. Tahitians often appraise being alone as an opportunity for bad spirits to bother a person, and fear is the most common emotional response. In the close-knit Utku Inuit, an Eskimo culture, being alone signifies social rejection and isolation, triggering sadness and loneliness. In Western cultures, being alone may at times represent a welcome respite from the frantic pace of daily life, evoking contentment and happiness (Mesquita et al., 1997). Thus, where appraisals are concerned, there seem to be certain universals but also some degree of cultural diversity in the more subtle aspects of interpreting situations.

arousal has been demonstrated clinically and in experimental research. Cross-cultural research indicates considerable agreement across cultures in the appraisals that evoke basic emotions but also some degree of variation in more complex appraisals.

The Physiological Component

When our feelings are stirred up, one of the first things we notice is bodily changes. Many parts of the body are involved in emotional arousal, but certain brain regions, the autonomic nervous system, and the endocrine system play especially significant roles.

Brain Structures and Neurotransmitters   Emotions involve important interactions between several brain areas, including the limbic system and cerebral cortex (Berridge, 2004; Damasio, 2005). If animals are electrically stimulated in specific areas of the limbic system, they will growl at and attack anything that approaches. Destroying the same sites produces an absence of aggression, even if the animal is provoked or attacked. Other limbic areas show the opposite pattern: lack of emotion when they are stimulated and unrestrained emotion when they are removed.

The cerebral cortex has many connections with the hypothalamus, amygdala, and other limbic system structures. Cognitive appraisal processes surely involve the cortex, where the mechanisms for language and complex thought reside. Moreover, the ability to regulate emotion depends heavily on the executive functions of the prefrontal cortex, which lies immediately behind the forehead (LeDoux & Phelps, 2000).

Groundbreaking research by psychologist Joseph LeDoux (2000) has revealed that when the thalamus (the brain's sensory switchboard) receives input from the senses, it can send messages along two independent neural pathways, a "high road" traveling up to the cortex and a "low road" going directly to the nearby amygdala (Figure 10.26). The low road enables the amygdala to receive direct input from the senses and generate emotional reactions before the cerebral cortex has had time to fully interpret what is causing the reaction. LeDoux suggests that this primitive mechanism (which is the only emotional mechanism in species such as birds and reptiles) has survival value because it enables the organism to react with great speed before the cerebral cortex responds with a more carefully processed cognitive interpretation

▶ **Focus 19**
According to LeDoux, which brain structures allow emotional responses to occur at two levels of processing?

IN REVIEW

■ An emotion is a positive or negative feeling (or affective) state consisting of a pattern of cognitive, physiological, and behavioral reactions to events that have relevance to important goals or motives. Emotions further our well-being in several ways: by rousing us to action, by helping us communicate with others, and by eliciting empathy and help.

■ The primary components of emotion are the eliciting stimuli, cognitive appraisals, physiological arousal, and expressive and instrumental behaviors. Innate factors and learning play important roles in determining the arousal properties of stimuli.

■ The cognitive component of emotional experience involves the evaluative and personal appraisal of the eliciting stimuli. Initial appraisals often occur in an automatic fashion that involves little thinking. The ability of thoughts to elicit emotional

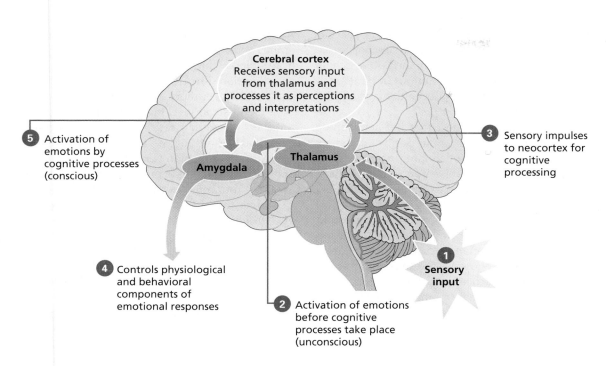

FIGURE 10.26

Dual emotional pathways.
Parallel neural processes may produce conscious and unconscious emotional responses at about the same time. LeDoux's research suggests that sensory input to the thalamus can be routed directly to the amygdala in the limbic system, producing an "unconscious" emotional response before cognitive responses evoked by the other pathway to the cortex can occur.

of the situation. This may be what occurs when a hiker sees what looks like a snake and jumps out of the way, only to realize an instant later that the object is actually a piece of rope.

The amygdala also seems to function as an early-warning system for threatening social stimuli. In one study, participants were asked to rate photos of people on how trustworthy they appeared to be. When the photos were presented later, brain scans using fMRI showed a burst of activity in the amygdala when people viewed those faces they had rated as untrustworthy, but participants showed no such response to faces they judged earlier as trustworthy (Winston et al., 2002). Another fMRI study showed that the amygdala also reacts to stimuli that evoke strong positive emotions (Hamann & Mao, 2002).

The existence of a dual system for emotional processing may help explain some puzzling aspects of our emotional lives. For example, most of us have had the experience of suddenly feeling a strong emotion without understanding why. LeDoux (2000) suggests that not all emotional responses register at the level of the cortex. He also suggests that people can have two simultaneous but different emotional reactions to the same event, a conscious one occurring as a result of cortical activity and an unconscious one triggered by the amygdala. This might help explain instances in which people are puzzled by behavioral reactions that seem to be at odds with the emotion they are consciously experiencing: "I don't know why I came across as being angry. I

felt very warm and friendly." Some psychodynamic theorists are hailing these discoveries as support for the existence of unconscious emotional processes (Westen, 1998). Indeed, there is now little doubt that important aspects of emotional life can occur outside of conscious awareness (Bargh & Chartrand, 1999).

Neuroscientist Candace Pert (1997) argues that because all of the neural structures involved in emotion operate biochemically, it is the ebb and flow of various neurotransmitter substances that activate the emotional programs residing in the brain. For example, dopamine and endorphin activity appears to underlie some pleasurable emotions, whereas serotonin and norepinephrine play a role in anger and in fear (Damasio, 2005; Depue & Collins, 1999). When the final story of the brain and emotion can at last be told, it will undoubtedly involve complex interactions between brain chemicals and neural structures.

Hemispheric Activation and Emotion   Decades ago in Italy, psychiatrists who were treating clinically depressed patients with electroshock treatments to either the right or the left hemisphere observed a striking phenomenon. The electric current temporarily disrupted neural activity in the targeted hemisphere. With the left hemisphere knocked out (forcing the right hemisphere to take charge), patients had what physicians termed a "catastrophic" reaction, wailing and crying until the shock effects wore off. But when they applied shock to the right hemisphere, allowing the left

▶ **Focus 20**
What evidence exists that positive and negative emotions involve different patterns of brain activation?

hemisphere to dominate, the patients reacted much differently; they seemed unconcerned, happy, and sometimes even euphoric. Researchers noted a similar pattern of emotions in patients in whom one hemisphere had been damaged by lesions or strokes (Gainotti, 1972).

These findings suggest that left-hemisphere activation may underlie certain positive emotions and right-hemisphere functioning negative ones (Sutton, 2002). To test this proposition, Richard Davidson and Nathan Fox (1988) obtained EEG measures of frontal lobe activity as people experienced positive and negative emotions. They found that when people felt positive emotions by recalling pleasurable experiences or watching a happy film, the left hemisphere was relatively more active than the right. But when sadness or other negative emotions were evoked by memories or watching a disgusting film, the right hemisphere became relatively more active. Moreover, this hemispheric pattern seems to be innate. Infants as young as 3 to 4 days old showed a similar pattern of hemispheric activation: left-hemisphere activation when given a sweet sucrose solution, which infants like, and right-hemisphere dominance in response to a citric acid solution, which apparently disgusts them.

Davidson and Fox also found individual differences in typical, or *resting,* hemispheric activation when they recorded people's EEG responses under emotionally neutral conditions. These resting differences predicted the tendency to experience positive or negative emotions. For example, human infants with resting right-hemisphere dominance were more likely to become upset and cry if their mothers later left the room than were those with resting left-hemisphere dominance. In adults, a higher resting level of right-hemisphere EEG activity may be a risk factor for the later development of adult depressive disorders (Tomarken & Keener, 1998).

► Focus 21
Are autonomic measures of lie detection scientifically defensible? What factors influence their validity?

Autonomic and Hormonal Processes You are afraid. Your heart starts to beat faster. Your body draws blood from your stomach to your muscles, and digestion slows to a crawl. You breathe harder and faster to get more energy-sustaining oxygen. Your blood-sugar level increases, producing more nutrients for your muscles. The pupils of your eyes dilate, admitting more light to increase your visual acuity. Your skin perspires to keep you cool and to flush out waste products created by extra exertion. Your muscles tense, ready for action.

Some theorists call this state of arousal the *fight-or-flight response.* It is produced by the sympathetic branch of the autonomic nervous system and by hormones from the endocrine system. The sympathetic nervous system produces arousal within a few seconds by directly stimulating the organs and muscles of the body. Meanwhile, the endocrine system pumps epinephrine, cortisol, and other stress hormones into the bloodstream. These hormones produce physiological effects like those triggered by the sympathetic nervous system, but their effects are longer lasting and can keep the body aroused for a considerable length of time.

Do different emotions produce different patterns of arousal? Only subtle autonomic differences occur among basic emotions as different as anger and fear (Cacioppo et al., 2000). Moreover, people differ from one another in their patterns of general arousal, so that we don't all show the same pattern of bodily arousal even when we're experiencing the same emotion. For example, when afraid, some of us might show marked changes in heart rate or blood pressure but only minor changes in muscle tension and respiration. Others would show different patterns. Thus there are no distinctive and universal physiological signatures for the basic emotions.

Beneath the Surface   The Lie Detector Controversy

Given what you have learned so far about the physiology of emotion, do you think emotional arousal can tell us whether someone is telling the truth or lying? A scientific instrument known as a **polygraph** (Figure 10.27) *measures physiological responses, such as respiration, heart rate, and skin conductance (which increases in the presence of emotion due to sweat gland activity).* Because we have less control over physiological responses than over numerous other behaviors, many people regard the polygraph as a nearly infallible means of estab-

lishing whether someone is telling the truth. However, this approach to detecting lying by increases in emotional arousal is highly controversial (Kleiner, 2002).

Figure 10.27 shows a portion of a polygraph record. Polygraph examiners compare physiological responses to critical questions (e.g., "Were you present at the Jesse James National Bank when it was robbed the night of August 4, 2003?") with responses to control questions that make no reference to the crime or crime scene. In this case, note the changes that

Respiration

Event marker

Skin
conductance

Pulse rate
(averaging)

2-second
time marker

FIGURE 10.27

The lie detector. The polygraph records physiological changes that are part of emotional responses. Between points A and B, an emotionally loaded question was asked. Within 2 seconds, the effects of the question were visible in the subject's respiration, skin conductance, and pulse rate. Does this mean he was lying?

occurred on the autonomic measures after an emotionally loaded question was asked (point A to point B in Figure 10.27).

The issue, however, is whether this emotional response to a critical question means that the person was lying. Herein lies one major problem with polygraph tests. Innocent people may appear guilty when doubt, fear, or lack of confidence increases their autonomic activity. Even a thought like, "What if my answer makes me look guilty, even though I'm not?" in response to a critical question could send the polygraph pens into spasms that might suggest a lie. As David Lykken, a leading critic of the lie detector, has noted, "polygraph pens do no special dance when we are lying" (1981, p. 10).

Not only can innocent people appear guilty, but guilty people can also learn to beat the polygraph. For example, by biting their tongue, curling their toes, or contracting their anal sphincter when control questions are asked, people can produce an arousal response to those questions that looks similar to the arousal that occurs when they actually lie on critical questions. William Casey, former director of the U.S. Central Intelligence Agency, used to delight in his ability to fool the lie detector (Carlson & Hatfield, 1992). Fred Fay, a prison convict who had been falsely convicted of murder partly on the basis of a polygraph test, also became an expert at defeating polygraph tests (too late, unfortunately, for his acquittal). On one occasion, Fay coached 27 fellow inmates who were scheduled for polygraph tests. All of the inmates told Fay they were guilty of the relevant crimes. Yet after only 20 minutes of instruction, 23 of the 27 inmates managed

to beat the polygraph (Lykken, 1981). Such results sharply contradict the notion of an infallible lie detector.

Misgivings about the validity of polygraph tests are supported by studies in which experienced polygraph examiners were given the polygraph records of suspects known to be either innocent or guilty on the basis of other evidence. The experts were asked to judge the guilt or innocence of the suspects. They usually did quite well in identifying the guilty, attaining accuracy rates of 80 to 98 percent (Honts & Perry, 1992). However, they were less accurate in identifying the innocent, judging as many as 55 percent of the truly innocent suspects to be guilty in some studies (Kleinmuntz & Szucko, 1984; Lykken, 1984). These error rates call into question the adage that an innocent person has nothing to fear from a polygraph test.

Largely because of an unacceptably high likelihood that an innocent person might be judged guilty, the American Psychological Association has supported legal challenges to polygraph testing. Congressional testimony by psychologists strongly influenced passage of the Employee Polygraph Protection Act of 1988, which prohibits most nongovernmental polygraph testing. Moreover, polygraph results alone cannot be used to convict people of crimes in most jurisdictions (Daniels, 2002). Nonetheless, local and federal governments continue to use polygraph tests in internal criminal investigations and in police officer and national security screening, despite the weight of research evidence against their validity for these purposes (Cochrane et al., 2003; Kleiner, 2002).

The Behavioral Component

Although we can never directly experience another person's feelings, we can often infer that someone is angry, sad, fearful, or happy on the basis of **expressive behaviors,** *the person's observable emotional displays.* Indeed, others' emotional displays can even evoke similar responses in us, a process known as *empathy.* While watching a movie, have you ever experienced the same emotion as the central character? Professional actors sometimes become so immersed in the expressive behaviors of their characters that the boundaries

between self and role begin to fade, as Kirk Douglas reported when he played Vincent Van Gogh, the painter who on one occasion cut off an ear and offered it to a prostitute.

> I was close to getting lost in the character of Van Gogh. . . . I felt myself going over the line, into the skin of Van Gogh. . . . Sometimes I had to stop myself from reaching my hand up and touching my ear to find out if it was actually there. It was a frightening experience. That way lies madness. . . . I could never play him again. (Lehmann-Haupt, 1988, p. 10)

FIGURE 10.28

Similarities among species in the expression of certain basic emotions convinced Darwin and other theorists that certain expressive behaviors have an evolutionary origin.

▶ **Focus 22**
How do evolutionary and cultural factors influence emotionally expressive behavior?

Evolution and Emotional Expression   Where do emotional expressions come from? In his classic work *The Expression of Emotions in Man and Animals* (1872/1965), Charles Darwin argued that emotional displays are products of evolution because they contributed to species survival. Darwin emphasized the basic similarity of emotional expression among animals and humans. For example, both wolves and humans bare their teeth when they are angry (Figure 10.28). As Darwin explained it, this behavior makes the animal look more ferocious and thus decreases its chances of being attacked and perhaps killed in a fight. Darwin did not maintain that all forms of emotional expression are innate, but he believed that many of them are.

Like Darwin, modern evolutionary theorists stress the adaptive value of emotional expression (Izard, 1989; Plutchik, 1994). They believe that a set of **fundamental emotional patterns,** *or innate emotional reactions*, are wired into the nervous system (Panksepp, 2005). Their research shows that certain emotional expressions (e.g., rage and terror) are similar across all cultures, suggesting a universal biological basis for them. The fundamental emotional patterns proposed by three leading evolutionary theorists are shown in Table 10.2. Other emotions are based on some combination of these innate emotions. The evolutionary view does *not* assume

that all emotional expressions are innate, nor does it deny that innate emotional expressions can be modified or inhibited as a result of social learning.

Facial Expression of Emotion   Most of us are fairly confident in our ability to read the emo-

TABLE 10.2	Fundamental or Primary Innate Emotions Proposed by Three Leading Evolutionary Theorists	
Carroll Izard	**Silvan Tomkins**	**Robert Plutchik**
Anger	Anger	Anger
Fear	Fear	Fear
Joy	Joy	Enjoyment
Disgust	Disgust	Disgust
Interest	Interest	Anticipation
Surprise	Surprise	Surprise
Contempt	Contempt	
Shame	Shame	
	Sadness	Sadness
	Distress	
Guilt		
		Acceptance

SOURCES: Based on Izard, 1982; Tomkins, 1991; and Plutchik, 1994.

tions of others. Although many parts of the body can communicate feelings, we tend to concentrate on what the face tells us. Most other species have relatively few facial muscles, so their facial expressions are limited. Only monkeys, apes, and humans have the well-developed facial muscles needed to produce a large number of expressions.

The development of sophisticated measuring procedures, such as Paul Ekman and Wallace Friesen's (1987) Facial Action Coding System (FACS), have permitted the precise study of facial expressions. FACS requires a trained observer to dissect an observed expression in terms of all the muscular actions that produced it. It takes about 100 minutes to score each minute of observed facial expression.

Although facial expressions can be valuable cues for judging emotion, even people within the same culture may learn to express the same emotions differently. For example, some people can appear very calm when they are angry or fearful, whereas others express even mild forms of those same emotions in a highly expressive manner. Fortunately, we usually know something about the situation to which people are reacting, and this often helps us judge their emotions. Researchers have found that people's accuracy and agreement in labeling emotions from pictures are considerably higher when the pictures reveal situational cues (Keltner & Ekman, 2000). If a woman is crying, is she weeping because of sadness or because of happiness? A background showing her being declared the winner of a lottery will result in a different emotional judgment than one showing her standing at a graveside.

Across many different cultures, women have proven to be more accurate judges of emotional expressions than men (Zuckerman et al., 1976). Perhaps the ability to read emotions accurately has greater adaptive significance for women, whose traditional role within many cultures has been to care for others and attend to their needs (Buss, 1991). This ability may also result from cultural encouragement for women to be sensitive to others' emotions and to express their feelings openly (Taylor et al., 2000). However, it is worth noting that men who work in professions that emphasize these skills (such as psychotherapy, drama, and art) are as accurate as women in judging others' emotional expressions (Rosenthal et al., 1974).

What of Darwin's claim that certain facial expressions universally indicate specific emotions? Do people in different cultures agree on the emotions being expressed in facial photographs? Figure 10.29 shows the results of one study. You can see that there is generally high agreement on these photos of basic emotions, but there are also some cultural variations. Other researchers have found levels of agreement ranging from 40 to 70 percent across a variety of cultures, well above chance but still far from perfect (Russell, 1994).

Cultural Display Rules   Cultural display rules *dictate when and how particular emotions are to be expressed* (Yrizarry et al., 2001). Certain gestures,

FIGURE 10.29

Culture and emotional expression. Percentages of people from five different cultures who judged each face as expressing the emotions listed beneath the pictures. SOURCE: Ekman, 1973.

	Happiness	Disgust	Surprise	Sadness	Anger	Fear
United States (N = 99)	97%	92%	95%	84%	67%	85%
Brazil (N = 40)	95%	97%	87%	59%	90%	67%
Chile (N = 119)	95%	92%	93%	88%	94%	68%
Argentina (N = 168)	98%	92%	95%	78%	90%	54%
Japan (N = 29)	100%	90%	100%	62%	90%	66%

body postures, and physical movements can convey vastly different meanings in different cultures. For example, gesturing with an upright thumb while hitchhiking in certain regions of Greece could result in decidedly negative consequences, such as tire tracks on one's body. In those regions, an upright thumb is the equivalent of a raised middle finger in the United States (Morris et al., 1979). In most cultures, spitting on someone is a sign of contempt. Yet in the traditions of the Masai tribe of East Africa, being spat on is considered a great compliment, particularly if the person doing the spitting is a member of the opposite sex (Wierzbicka, 1986). One can only imagine what a Masai singles bar might be like.

More subtle differences exist as well. Nalini Ambady and colleagues have shown that people are generally more accurate at judging emotions when the emotions are expressed by members of their own cultural group rather than by members of a different cultural group (Elfenbein & Ambady, 2003). Just as people exhibit linguistic dialects, they also appear to have culturally based emotional behavior dialects.

An experiment by Paul Ekman, Wallace Friesen, and Phoebe Ellsworth (1972) nicely illustrates cultural commonalities and differences in emotional expression. Japanese and American students viewed a gory, stressful film in private. Unbeknownst to them, their facial expressions were being videotaped by a hidden camera. FACS codings of the students' facial displays showed no differences between the Japanese and American students; they expressed their negative emotions of disgust and anxiety in the same way and with similar intensity as they watched the film. Afterward, the students were individually interviewed by a person of their ethnic group concerning their reactions to the film. The Japanese masked their earlier feelings of anxiety and disgust and presented a happy face throughout the interview, whereas the Americans' negative facial expressions closely mirrored those photographed while they watched the stressful movie. Based on such findings, many emotion theorists conclude that innate biological factors and cultural display rules *combine* to shape emotional expression across different cultures.

▶ Focus 23
How do level of arousal and task complexity interact to affect task performance?

Instrumental Behaviors   Emotional responses are often calls to action, requiring a response to the situation that aroused the emotion. A highly anxious student must find some way to cope with an impending test. A mother angered by her child's behavior must find a nondestructive way to get her point across. A person in love searches for ways to evoke affection from his or her partner. These are **instrumental behaviors,** *directed at achieving some emotion-relevant goal.*

People often assume that high emotional arousal enhances task performance, as when athletes try to psych themselves up for competition. Yet as students who have experienced extreme anxiety during exams could testify, high emotional arousal can also interfere with performance. In many situations, the relation between emotional arousal and performance seems to take the shape of an upside-down, or inverted, U. As physiological arousal increases up to some optimal level, performance improves. But beyond that optimal level, further increases in arousal impair performance. It is thus possible to be either too "flat" or too "high" to perform well.

The relation between arousal and performance depends not only on arousal level but also on how complicated the task is and how much precision it requires (Yerkes & Dodson, 1908). Generally speaking, the more complex the task, the lower the optimal arousal level. Thus even a moderate level of arousal can disrupt performance on a highly complex mental or motor task.

Figure 10.30 illustrates this principle and also shows that performance drops off less at high levels of arousal for the simplest task than for the others. In fact, even extreme arousal can enhance performance of very simple motor tasks, such as running or lifting something. This may account for seemingly superhuman feats we hear about occasionally. When a 110-pound New Hampshire woman was asked how she had managed to lift a 4,000-pound van that had rolled on top of her trapped husband, she answered, "I don't know how I did it. It didn't feel that heavy. I think it was the adrenaline." (*Newsweek*, March 11, 2002, p. 19)

In contrast, high emotionality can interfere with performance on complex mental and physical tasks. People may underachieve on intelligence tests if they are too anxious, and muscle tension can interfere with the skillful execution of complex physical movements (Landers & Arent, 2001). For example, the sport of golf requires precise and complex movements, so the optimal level of arousal is relatively low. Champion golfers often exhibit peak performance in high-pressure competition because they can control their level of arousal and keep it within the optimal range, whereas their opponents choke under the pressure of a putt worth hundreds of thousands of dollars.

FIGURE 10.30

Arousal and performance. The relation between arousal and performance takes the form of an inverted U, with performance declining above and below an optimal arousal level. However, the more complex a task is, the lower the optimal level of arousal for performing it. For which of the tasks above should the optimal level be lower?

THEORIES OF EMOTION

Where do emotional experiences come from? For more than 100 years, scientists have explored this question. Several classic theories have guided their efforts.

The James-Lange Somatic Theory

In 1890, the eminent psychologist William James ignited a controversy when he wrote:

> Common sense says . . . we meet a bear, are frightened, and run; we are insulted by a rival, are angry, and strike. The hypothesis here to be defended says that this order of sequence is incorrect and that the more rational statement is that we feel sorry *because* we cry, angry *because* we strike, afraid *because* we tremble. (James, 1890/1950, p. 451, italics added)

At about the same time, Danish psychologist Carl Lange reached a similar conclusion. According to the **James-Lange theory,** *our bodily reactions determine the subjective emotion we experience.* We know we are afraid or in love because our body's reactions tell us so. Today, this theory lives on as the *somatic theory of emotion* (Papanicolaou, 1989).

The Cannon-Bard Theory

It wasn't long before the James-Lange theory was challenged. In 1927 physiologist Walter Cannon fired back. He pointed out that people's bodies do *not* respond instantaneously to an emotional stimulus; several seconds may pass before signs of

► **Focus 24**
Compare the James-Lange and Cannon-Bard explanations for emotional responses.

physiological arousal appear. Yet people typically experience the emotion immediately. This would be impossible according to the James-Lange theory. Cannon and his colleague L. L. Bard concluded that cognition must be involved as well.

The **Cannon-Bard theory** *proposed that the subjective experience of emotion and physiological arousal do not cause one another but instead are independent responses to an emotion-arousing situation.* When we encounter such a situation, sensory information is sent to the brain's thalamus, which simultaneously sends messages to the cerebral cortex and to the body's internal organs. The message to the cortex produces the experience of emotion, and the message to the internal organs produces physiological arousal. Figure 10.31 compares the James-Lange and Cannon-Bard theories.

The Role of Autonomic Feedback

The James-Lange and Cannon-Bard theories raised intriguing questions about how the various aspects of an emotional experience interact with one another. The theories differ on one crucial point. According to the James-Lange theory, feedback from the body's reactions to a situation tells the brain that we are experiencing an emotion. Without such bodily feedback, there would be no emotional response. In contrast, the Cannon-Bard theory maintains that emotional experiences result from signals sent directly from the thalamus to the cortex, not from bodily feedback. Is there any way to test whether bodily feedback is necessary?

In fact, there is. What if organisms were deprived of sensory feedback from their internal organs? Would they be devoid of emotional reactions? To answer this question, Cannon (1929) carried out experiments with animals in which he severed the nerves that provide feedback from the internal organs to the brain. He found that even after such surgery, the animals exhibited emotional responses, lending support to his theory that direct sensory messages to the brain are the emotional triggers. In like manner, people whose spinal cords have been severed in accidents and who receive no sensory feedback from body areas below the injury continue to feel intense emotions—sometimes more intense than those they experienced before their injuries. Moreover, people with upper and lower spinal cord injuries, who differ in the amount of bodily feedback they receive, do not differ in the intensity of their emotions (Chwalisz et al., 1988).

These results appear to cast doubt on the claim that arousal feedback from the body is absolutely necessary for people to experience intense emotions. But let's take this issue one step further.

▶ **Focus 25**
Evaluate scientific evidence that supports the James-Lange and Cannon-Bard theories.

FIGURE 10.31

Two theories of emotion. Two early theories of emotion continue to influence current-day theorizing. The James-Lange theory holds that the experience of emotion is caused by somatic feedback and physiological arousal. According to the Cannon-Bard theory, the thalamus receives sensory input and simultaneously stimulates physiological responses and cognitive awareness.

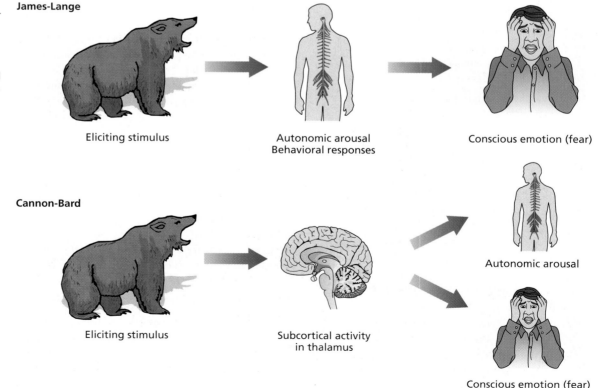

James-Lange

Eliciting stimulus → Autonomic arousal / Behavioral responses → Conscious emotion (fear)

Cannon-Bard

Eliciting stimulus → Subcortical activity in thalamus → Autonomic arousal / Conscious emotion (fear)

The Role of Expressive Behaviors

Arousal feedback is not the only kind of bodily feedback considered important by the James-Lange somatic theory. Facial muscles involved in emotional displays also feed messages to the brain, and these muscles are active even in patients with spinal injuries who receive no sensory input from below the neck. According to the **facial feedback hypothesis,** *feedback from the facial muscles to the brain plays a key role in determining the nature and intensity of emotions that we experience,* as the James-Lange theory would suggest (Adelmann & Zajonc, 1989).

According to the theory, sensory input is first routed to the subcortical areas of the brain that control facial movements. These centers immediately send signals that activate the facial muscles. Sensory feedback from movement of facial muscles is then routed to the cerebral cortex, which produces our conscious experience of the emotion. To return to James's example of the bear, the facial feedback hypothesis says that we are frightened when the bear approaches partly because an automatic expression of terror appears on our face and sends signals from our facial muscles to the cortex, where the subjective feelings of fear are produced.

In support of the facial feedback hypothesis, research shows that feedback from facial muscle patterns can arouse specific emotional reactions (Soussignan, 2002). In one study, Fritz Strack and coworkers (1988) found that when participants held pens in their teeth, activating muscles used in smiling (Figure 10.32a), they rated themselves as feeling more pleasant than when

they held the pens with their lips, activating the muscles involved in frowning (Figure 10.32b). Participants also rated cartoons as funnier while holding pens in their teeth and activating the "happy muscles" than while holding pens with their lips (Figure 10.32c). In another study, researchers compared the subjective experiences of people who pronounced different sounds, such as *eee* and *ooh.* Saying *eee,* which activates muscles used in smiling, was associated with more pleasant feelings than saying *ooh,* which activates muscles involved in negative facial expressions (Zajonc et al., 1989). Perhaps portrait photographers should ask us to say *cheese* not only when they take our picture but also later, when they show us photo proofs that not even our mothers could love.

Cognitive-Affective Theories

Nowhere are mind-body interactions more obvious than in the emotions, where thinking and feeling are intimately connected. *Cognitive-affective theories* examine how cognitions and physiological responses interact (Clore et al., 2004; Smith & Kirby, 2004). Historically, Richard Lazarus and Stanley Schachter have been major figures in this approach.

Lazarus (2001) argued that all emotional responses require some sort of appraisal, whether we are aware of that appraisal or not. Schachter was intrigued with the factors that determine our emotional perceptions. According to Schachter's **two-factor theory of emotion,** *the intensity of physiological arousal tells us* how strongly *we are feeling something, but situational cues give us the information*

▶ **Focus 26**
According to the theories of Lazarus and Schachter, how do appraisal and arousal interact to influence emotions? Describe the two key experiments inspired by these theories.

FIGURE 10.32

Facial feedback and emotional experience. (a) Holding a pencil in the teeth, which activates the muscles used in smiling, evokes more pleasant feelings than (b) holding the pencil in one's lips, which activates muscles associated with negative emotions. (c) The findings shown in this graph provide support for the facial feedback hypothesis.
Source: Based on Strack et al., 1988.

(a)

(b)

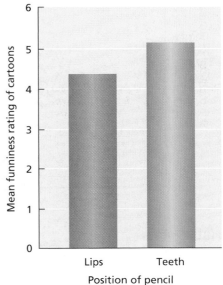

(c)

we need to label the arousal and tell ourselves what *we are feeling*—fear, anger, love, or some other emotion (Schachter, 1966).

If appraisal and arousal affect one another in the ways these theories suggest, then by manipulating appraisals we should be able to influence physiological arousal. Moreover, if we can manipulate arousal, we should be able to influence cognitive appraisals of the situation. Let's examine some research that tests these propositions.

Manipulating Appraisal to Influence Arousal

In one classic study, Lazarus and coworkers showed college students an anthropology film that contained vivid footage of a puberty rite in which the penises of aboriginal boys were cut with a jagged flint knife. The researchers tried to influence the participants' appraisals by experimentally varying the film's sound track (Speisman et al., 1964).

Four different sound tracks were used: A "trauma" sound track emphasized the pain suffered by the boys, the danger of infection, the jaggedness of the flint knife, and other unpleasant aspects of the operation. A "denial" sound track did just the opposite; it denied that the operation was excessively painful or traumatic and emphasized that the boys looked forward to entering adulthood by undergoing the rite and demonstrating their bravery. An "intellectualization" sound track, also designed to produce a less negative appraisal, ignored the emotional elements of the scenes and focused on the traditions and history of the tribe. In a "silent" control condition, the film was shown without any sound track at all.

Physiological arousal was measured through electrodes attached to the participants' palms, recording skin conductance due to sweat gland activity. As shown in Figure 10.33, the sound tracks produced markedly different levels of arousal in response to the same visual stimuli. The trauma sound track resulted in the highest arousal, and the silent condition turned out to be more arousing than either the denial or intellectualization condition, presumably because it left people free to make their own negative appraisals. It seems the denial and intellectualization sound tracks made the subjects' appraisals more benign, resulting in lower levels of arousal. This study, as well as many others, indicate that what we tell ourselves about external situations influences the level of arousal that we experience.

Manipulating Arousal to Influence Appraisal

Is the reverse also true? Can arousal affect our appraisal of situations by giving us feedback about how our bodies are responding or by making us search for situational reasons for the arousal? To study this possibility, we'd have to influence arousal directly in some way, such as with drugs that either increase or decrease arousal. But it would have to be done in a way that left people unaware that their arousal was being caused by the drug. They'd have to believe that their arousal was being caused solely by the external situation they were appraising.

In a key experiment, Schachter and Ladd Wheeler (1962) directly manipulated participants' arousal by injecting them with either epinephrine to increase arousal, a tranquilizer drug to decrease arousal, or a placebo control substance. To hide the fact that participants were being given drugs that would affect their arousal, the researchers told them that they were being injected with a vitamin to study its effects on visual perception and that the vitamin would have no side effects. While presumably waiting for the vitamin to take effect, the participants were shown a short movie "to provide continuous black-and-white stimulation to the eyes." The movie was a comedy featuring a slapstick chase scene.

Schachter and Wheeler hypothesized that if the level of emotional arousal influences appraisals, then the viewers aroused by epinephrine should find the film funnier than the placebo control subjects. Having been told that the vitamin

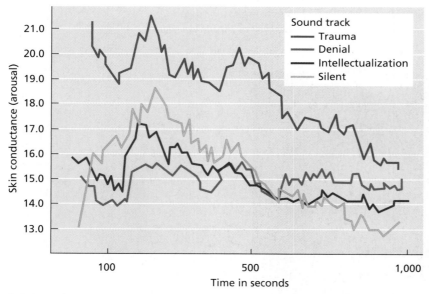

FIGURE 10.33

Does appraisal influence arousal? Participants who viewed a film showing a painful tribal rite in vivid detail exhibited different levels of physiological arousal, depending on the sound track that accompanied the film. SOURCE: Speisman et al., 1964.

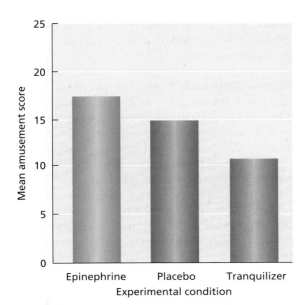

FIGURE 10.34

Does arousal influence appraisal? Participants were injected with either epinephrine, a tranquilizer, or a placebo to affect arousal and then were shown a humorous film. The amount of amusement they displayed varied with their state of arousal. Source: Schachter & Wheeler, 1962.

had no side effects, these viewers were likely to attribute their increased arousal to the slapstick comedy in the film. The researchers also reasoned that those given the tranquilizer should not find the film as funny because the drug would reduce their level of arousal.

While they watched the movie, participants were observed through a one-way mirror by raters who were unaware of which viewers had received which injections. The raters recorded how frequently the participants smiled, grinned, laughed, threw up their hands, slapped their legs, or doubled over with laughter. As Fig-

ure 10.34 shows, the results supported the hypothesis that level of arousal would influence viewers' appraisal of the film. The aroused viewers in the epinephrine group found the film funnier than the tranquilized viewers did, and the placebo control group was in the middle. It appears that as long as one's arousal is attributed to the external situation, arousal cues can affect appraisal.

HAPPINESS

For many years, researchers focused primarily on negative emotions such as anxiety, depression, and anger. More recently, however, attention has turned to the positive emotions (Aspinwall & Staudinger, 2003; Seligman, 2002). Among psychological researchers, there currently is growing interest in the topic of happiness, or its more technical term **subjective well-being (SWB):** *people's emotional responses and their degree of satisfaction with various aspects of their life* (Diener & Seligman, 2002).

SWB is typically assessed by self-report ratings of contentment, happiness, and satisfaction. Before reading on, please see Table 10.3.

How Happy Are People?

Ed and Carol Diener (1996) reviewed findings from nearly 1,000 representative samples in 43 Westernized and developing nations. Across all countries, the mean rating of personal happiness on the 0-to-10 scale was 6.33, indicating mild happiness. In only two economically poor nations, India and the Dominican Republic, did average SWB fall into the unhappy range of the scale. In the United States, all ethnic groups scored well above the neutral point on the happiness scale (Andrews,

TABLE 10.3   How Happy Are You?

Here are two measures of subjective well-being. Answer the following questions, then see the text to compare yourself with others.

First, how would you rate your own general life satisfaction on the following scale?

0	1	2	3	4	5	6	7	8	9	10
Most unhappy									*Most happy*	

Next, answer the following questions:

What percentage of the time are you happy? _____

What percentage of the time are you neutral? _____

What percentage of the time are you unhappy? _____

(Make sure your percentages add up to 100.)

TABLE 10.4 Subjective Well-Being Scores of Various Countries	
Country	**Happiness Ranking**
Iceland	1
Sweden	2
Australia	3
Canada	4
United States	5
Norway	6
Britain	7
Ireland	8
Singapore	9
Philippines	10
Cuba	11
Israel	12
Mexico	13
France	14
Puerto Rico	15
Thailand	16
Jordan	17
Greece	18
Kenya	19
India	20
Dominican Republic	21

NOTE: Most nations (India and the Dominican Republic being exceptions) score in the positive range of the 10-point SWB scale.
SOURCE: Based on Diener et al., 1995.

1991). Nonetheless, as Table 10.4 shows, countries differed in their levels of subjective well-being.

On the second scale in Table 10.3, college students on average reported being happy 65 percent of the time, neutral 15 percent, and unhappy 20 percent of the time (Larsen & Diener, 1985). Thus it appears that across many populations, people report living lives that are more happy than unhappy.

Who's happier, men or women? Research shows that the sexes are about equal in global happiness, but there is an important qualifier: Women on average experience *both* positive and negative emotions more intensely than men do (Wood et al., 1989). The more extreme emotional responses of women balance out, resulting in an average level of happiness similar to that produced by men's less extreme highs and lows.

What Makes People Happy?

To answer this question, some researchers have examined the *resources* that might contribute to happiness, such as attractiveness, intelligence,

▶ Focus 27
What factors predict and fail to predict happiness?

wealth, and health. Others have studied internal *psychological processes* that underlie our experiences of happiness.

Personal Resources   Is health required for happiness? Not necessarily. On average, individuals with severe and disabling medical conditions such as paralyses do report lower levels of life satisfaction than nondisabled people, yet about two thirds of disabled people rate their lives as somewhat or very satisfying (Mehnert et al., 1990).

If you had more money, you'd be happier, correct? Well, perhaps not. Although people in affluent countries are happier on average than people who live in abject poverty, such countries differ in many ways besides wealth (e.g., in terms of social and political turmoil) that could also affect SWB. When wealth and SWB are correlated within the same country, whether the country is poor or affluent, wealth is only weakly related to happiness (Diener et al., 1999). Even extreme changes in wealth, such as a big inheritance or winning a lottery, have only a temporary positive impact on SWB (Brickman et al., 1978). Thus where health and wealth are concerned, not having enough of these resources may create unhappiness because important basic needs can't be met, but once adequate levels are attained, further increases seem to do little to promote lasting happiness.

How about being wise? Overall, intelligence bears little relation to happiness (Seligman, 2002). Educational level does have a weak positive relation to SWB, probably because it helps people avoid poverty and compete for satisfying jobs. Unemployment is one of the strongest predictors of life dissatisfaction, and an adequate educational level can help people avoid this fate (Clark, 1998).

If being healthy, wealthy, and wise won't guarantee happiness, perhaps intimate relationships will. Here researchers consistently find that happy people have more satisfying social relationships (Diener & Seligman, 2002). Additionally, married men and women are significantly happier on average than are single and divorced people. Still, the meaning of these correlational results is not clear. Do social relationships promote greater life satisfaction, or are happier, better-adjusted people more able to establish and sustain good social relationships and stable marriages? Or is there some third variable, such as a personality factor like being more extraverted (i.e., more outgoing), that promotes both happiness and the ability to develop satisfying social relations?

Having a sense of meaning in life also is correlated with happiness. Many people report that their spiritual or religious beliefs contribute to a sense of meaning, and some—though not all—studies find a positive correlation between religiosity and happiness (Diener et al., 1999; Diener & Seligman, 2002). Giving of oneself, such as helping others as a volunteer, contributes to a sense of meaning and life satisfaction (Snyder et al., 2000). But again, causality is difficult to infer. Does a greater sense of meaning promote happiness? Does happiness lead people to feel that their life is more meaningful? Or does some third factor cause both?

Psychological Processes Overall, personal resources and external circumstances account for only about 15 to 20 percent of the total variability among people in happiness ratings (Argyle, 1999). Perhaps psychological processes, rather than resources, are the keys to happiness. For example, research reveals that feelings of life satisfaction are based on how we compare ourselves and our circumstances with other people and their circumstances and with past conditions we have experienced (Bruunk & Gibbons, 1997). When we engage in **downward comparison,** *seeing ourselves as better off than the standard for comparison,* we experience increased satisfaction. In contrast, **upward comparison,** *when we view ourselves as worse off than the standard for comparison,* produces dissatisfaction. In one study, college students kept a written record of every time they compared their appearance, grades, abilities, possessions, or personality with someone else's over a 2-week period. At the same time, they recorded their current mood. Downward comparisons with less fortunate or less talented people were consistently associated with positive moods, and upward comparisons were associated with negative emotional reactions (Wheeler & Miyake, 1992). Thus depending on what or whom you compare yourself with, you can be an eagle among starlings or a moth among butterflies.

Personality factors clearly predispose some people to be happier than others. Individuals who are sociable, optimistic, altruistic, curious, and open to new experiences report higher levels of happiness and are rated by others as happier than are those who have the opposite traits (Larsen & Buss, 2002).

Biological factors may predispose some people to be happier than others. A study of 2,310 identical and fraternal twins revealed that the identical twins were far more similar in SWB, regardless of their life circumstances (Lykken & Tellegen, 1996). Perhaps genetic factors contribute in some way to the individual differences in right- and left-hemisphere activation discussed earlier, or maybe they influence neurotransmitter systems that underlie positive and negative emotions (Hamer & Copeland, 1998).

One's culture may also influence the factors that contribute to happiness. Eunkook Suh and coworkers (1998) found that in the individualistic "me" societies of North America and Europe, successes that people can attribute to their own skill and effort contribute to happiness. In collectivistic cultures of Southeast Asia, however, the well-being of the group seems to be a more important factor in personal happiness than one's own emotional life, and people derive more pleasure from accomplishments achieved as part of a group effort (Kitayama et al., 2000).

Happiness thus turns out to be a rather complex phenomenon having biological, psychological, and environmental determinants (Figure 10.35).

▶ **Focus 28**
Summarize research-based guidelines for increasing your happiness.

FIGURE 10.35

Levels of analysis: Factors related to happiness.

LEVELS OF ANALYSIS   Factors Related to Happiness

Biological	Psychological	Environmental
• Possible genetic predisposition for positive emotions • Relatively greater left-hemisphere activation • Neurotransmitters in positive emotion systems (e.g., dopamine)	• Internalized cultural standards for being happy (e.g., individual vs. group well-being) • Upward and downward comparison processes • Personality traits, such as optimism, extraversion • Meaning-of-life values; spiritual beliefs, desire to be of service to others	• Recent positive life events • Presence of positive relationships • External cultural standards for being happy • Individual or group successes, depending on culture

Happiness

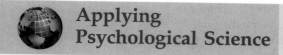

Applying Psychological Science

Being Happy: Guidelines from Psychological Research

As research has accumulated on factors that relate to happiness, psychologists have been able to offer advice based on data rather than intuition (Seligman, 2002). Most psychologists believe that happiness, like a good marriage, is something that one must work at (Seligman & Peterson, 2004). Here, then, are some suggestions that may help you maintain and enhance personal happiness.

- *Spend time with other people, and work to develop close relationships.* Research consistently suggests that good relationships provide the strongest basis for life satisfaction. Even if you tend to be introverted, form at least a few close relationships and nurture them. Make time for social interactions.

- *Look for ways to be helpful to others, and reach out to the less fortunate.* Try to make a positive difference in the lives of others. Doing so will increase your sense of self-worth, add meaning to your life, and deepen relationships with those whose lives you touch. It will also help put your own problems in perspective and direct your energies away from self-absorption. There's a lot to be said for the proposition that we receive by giving.

- *Seek meaning and challenge in work.* Enjoying one's work is a prime ingredient of happiness. If you feel stuck doing something that provides little gratification, be it your job or your major, consider looking for something more satisfying. Everyone has to make a living, but many people spend their lives doing things they don't derive satisfaction or meaning from—hardly a recipe for a happy life. Even if you love your work, strive for balance between work and personal pursuits. People on their death beds rarely, if ever, express the wish that they had spent more time at the office.

- *Set meaningful personal goals for yourself, and make progress toward them.* Whether in work, school, or relationships, engaging in goal-directed activity and seeing yourself moving toward your goals will provide a basis for life satisfaction and foster feelings of being in greater control of your life. Many people find that spiritual development (religiously based or not) confers meaning in their life.

- *Make time for enjoyable activities.* One of the benefits of time-management skills is the ability to schedule everyday activities that provide pleasure around school, work, and other obligations. Make time for a hobby, reading, and recreational activities.

- *Nurture physical well-being.* Many studies show that even moderate physical exercise contributes to emotional well-being (Morgan, 1997). Such activities provide a temporary respite from life stressors. When done in a social context, they add the benefits of social interaction as well. People who exercise, get sufficient sleep, and practice good dietary habits tend to be more stress resistant and satisfied with themselves and their lives (Taylor, 2006).

- *Be open to new experiences.* Some of our most pleasurable experiences can occur when we try new things. It's easy to fall into a rut, so whether it's traveling, developing a new hobby, or taking a college course on a new subject, be open to doing something you haven't done before.

- *Cultivate optimism, and count your blessings.* As we've seen, cognitive appraisals influence emotions, and an upbeat, optimistic approach to life is linked with subjective well-being. Try to look on the positive side of things, to see demanding events as challenges and opportunities rather than threats. Learn to appreciate and be grateful for even the mundane, average day in which nothing bad happens to you. There is a Buddhist saying: "Happiness is a day without a toothache." All of us are gifted in ways that we may take for granted. Perhaps we should focus more often on these typically ignored aspects of good fortune.

IN REVIEW

- There are several theories of emotion. The James-Lange theory maintains that we first become aroused and then judge what we are feeling. The Cannon-Bard theory proposes that arousal and cognition are independent and simultaneously triggered by the thalamus. According to Lazarus's cognitive-affective theory, appraisals trigger emotional arousal; in contrast, according to Schachter's two-factor theory of emotion, arousal tells us how strongly we are feeling while cognitions derived from situational cues help us label the specific emotion.

- As the James-Lange theory maintained, expressive behaviors may trigger other aspects of emotions. The facial feedback hypothesis states that feedback from facial muscle patterns associated with innate emotional displays influences cognitive and physiological processes.

- There is a two-way relation between the cognitive and physiological components. It is possible to manipulate appraisals and thereby influence level of arousal, but arousal changes can also influence appraisal of the eliciting stimuli.

- In most countries, the average person is mildly happy. Psychological processes, such as downward comparison and a sense of personal meaning, are more consistently related to subjective well-being than are resources such as wealth, physical attractiveness, and high intelligence. Cultural differences may exist in the bases for happiness.

A CONCLUDING THOUGHT

As you have seen in this chapter, motivation and emotion lie at the crossroads of cognition, physiology, and behavior. The diversity of human motives, factors that influence their development and strength, and methods for satisfying them help account for important differences both within and across cultures.

Emotion plays a central role in many aspects of normal and abnormal behavior. Emotion also illustrates the many fascinating interfaces between evolutionary processes and social learning. It's little wonder, then, that the study of emotion is a major thrust in contemporary psychological research. We still have much to learn about the basic mechanisms that underlie our emotional experiences and about what we can do to self-regulate them in order to amplify pleasurable emotions and dampen those that create distress.

KEY TERMS AND CONCEPTS

Each term has been boldfaced and defined in the chapter on the page indicated in parentheses.

achievement goal theory (p. 372)
anorexia nervosa (p. 360)
approach-approach conflict (p. 374)
approach-avoidance conflict (p. 374)
avoidance-avoidance conflict (p. 374)
behavioral activation system (BAS; p. 351)
behavioral inhibition system (BIS; p. 351)
bulimia nervosa (p. 360)
Cannon-Bard theory (p. 386)
cholecystokinin (CCK; p. 354)
cognitive appraisal (p. 377)
cultural display rules (p. 383)
downward comparison (p. 391)
drive (p. 350)
ego-approach goals (p. 372)
ego-avoidance goals (p. 372)
ego orientation (p. 372)
eliciting stimuli (p. 377)

emotion (p. 375)
expectancy × value theory (p. 351)
expressive behaviors (p. 381)
extrinsic motivation (p. 351)
facial feedback hypothesis (p. 387)
fundamental emotional patterns (p. 382)
glucose (p. 354)
homeostasis (p. 350)
incentive (p. 351)
instinct (p. 350)
instrumental behaviors (p. 384)
intrinsic motivation (p. 351)
James-Lange theory (p. 385)
leptin (p. 354)
mastery goals (p. 372)
mastery orientation (p. 372)
metabolism (p. 353)
motivation (p. 350)

motivational climate (p. 372)
need for achievement (p. 371)
paraventricular nucleus (PVN; p. 355)
polygraph (p. 380)
self-actualization (p. 352)
self-determination theory (p. 352)
set point (p. 353)
sexual dysfunction (p. 364)
sexual orientation (p. 365)
sexual response cycle (p. 362)
sexual strategies theory (p. 369)
social comparison (p. 367)
social structure theory (p. 369)
subjective well-being (SWB; p. 389)
two-factor theory of emotion (p. 387)
upward comparison (p. 391)

? What Do You Think?

IS MASLOW'S NEED HIERARCHY VALID? (PAGE 353)

More than most psychological theories of motivation, Maslow's model appropriately emphasizes that diverse motives influence human behavior. The concepts of need progression and need regression seem to make intuitive sense. Motives do become stronger and weaker as circumstances change, and it seems logical that when people are starving, finding food becomes more important than contemplating beauty and truth.

Critics, however, have long questioned the validity of the need hierarchy and have argued that the concept of "self-actualization" is vague and hard to measure (Heylighen, 1992). The ordering of needs seems arbitrary, and the concepts of need progression and regression cannot account for important aspects of motivated behavior. How does the hierarchy explain why prisoners of war endure torture rather than betray their comrades? why millions of women choose to live in constant hunger to be thin? why political protestors go on hunger strikes or risk their physical safety to defend principles they believe in? Does a need for knowledge and understanding really become prominent only after needs for social belonging and self-esteem are met? Throughout evolution, was seeking esteem and recognition more important and adaptive to our ancestors than acquiring knowledge to help them survive?

Finally, rather than viewing the journey toward self-actualization as a relatively independent striving to maximize one's potential, some modern humanists view the entire process as more relationship-oriented (Hanley and Abell, 2002). In their view, healthy social relationships not only satisfy deficiency needs for belonging and esteem but also are important for achieving and expressing self-actualization.

Despite these drawbacks, by calling attention to the human desire for growth and incorporating diverse motives, the intuitive appeal of Maslow's model has influenced thinking in fields such as philosophy, education, and business (Zinovieva, 2001).

FRATERNAL BIRTH ORDER AND MALE HOMOSEXUALITY (PAGE 367)

Blanchard (2001) estimates that the presence of each older brother increases by about one third the *relative probability* that a later-born male child will be gay. For example, if there is a 2 percent probability that a man with no older brothers is gay, then the probability for a man with one older brother is about 2.6 to 2.7 percent, roughly a one-third relative increase. As Blanchard (2001) notes, "the probability that a couple's son will be gay rises from 2 to 6 percent for their fifth son. That is a threefold increase. However, 94 percent of fifth sons will still be heterosexual" (p. 108).

So why does this effect occur? Perhaps you thought of one of these explanations: First, it may be that the greater the number of older brothers, the greater the possibility (however small) of having an incestuous sexual encounter with an older male while growing up. However, as Blanchard (2001) notes, evidence does not suggest that such incestuous experiences are linked to adulthood sexual orientation. Second, perhaps if an older brother has a homosexual orientation, awareness of this might influence a younger brother's sexual orientation. A study of gay men with gay brothers, however, found that most were aware of their own homosexual feelings before they became aware of their brother's homosexual orientation (Dawood et al., 2000).

Blanchard (2001) and his coworkers propose a biological explanation, called the *maternal immune hypothesis*. During pregnancy, male (but not female) fetuses contain substances that, as a group, are called *H-Y antigen*, which helps guide the fetal brain toward a male-typical pattern. Sometimes, H-Y antigen passes from the fetus to the mother's bloodstream, in which case it is a foreign substance to the mother. Thus the mother's immune system responds by producing antibodies (proteins) to combat the H-Y antigen. In turn, these antibodies pass from the mother to the fetus and reach the fetal brain. "When that happens, these antibodies partly prevent the fetal brain from developing in the male-typical pattern, so that the individual will later be attracted to men rather than women. The probability—or strength—of maternal immunization increases with each male fetus" (Blanchard, 2001, p. 110). Thus a mother with sons is more likely to carry and pass on these antibodies to any new male fetus, altering H-Y antigen's role in guiding fetal brain development toward a male-typical pattern. Blanchard estimates that for about one quarter of gay men, the development of their sexual orientation proceeded along this path. Of course, like other current theories, the maternal immune hypothesis needs much more testing.

CHAPTER ELEVEN

Development over the Life Span

CHAPTER OUTLINE

> *There are only two lasting bequests we can hope to give our children. One of these is roots; the other, wings.*
>
> —HODDING CARTER

FIGURE 11.1

Victor, the "Wild Boy of Aveyron."

I n 1799 three hunters discovered a remarkable child living in the forests of Aveyron, France. Most likely abandoned at a young age, he grew up isolated from human contact, foraging for food and surviving naked in the wild. About 12 years old, he easily climbed trees, ate nuts and roots, scratched and bit people who interfered with him, and made few sounds. He could walk upright yet ran quickly on all fours. Some regarded him as half-human, half-beast, and they called him the "Wild Boy of Aveyron" (Itard, 1894/1962).

Several medical experts concluded that the boy was incurably "mentally deficient," but others disagreed, noting that it took intelligence to survive in the wild. They argued that special education and care would enable the child to flower into a normal, civilized adult. In Paris, the boy was placed under the care of a prominent young physician, Jean-Marc Itard, who named him Victor and diligently supervised his training (Figure 11.1).

At first, Victor was unresponsive to stimuli that most people find aversive. Unfazed, he would stick his hand into boiling kitchen water to grab food or eagerly roll around half-naked on the cold winter ground. Eventually he learned to sense temperature differences, dress himself, and perform other self-care behaviors. Victor's emotional responses, which at first fluctuated without reason, began to fit the situation: He laughed in playful situations, shed tears over someone's death, and displayed some signs of affection toward Itard. Victor learned to read and write some words, communicate basic needs, and perform simple tasks.

Although Victor changed in important ways, as he grew older his progress slowed considerably. He never learned to speak, and after 5 years of education his cognitive, emotional, and social development remained limited. Pessimism over further progress grew, and Itard's "project" ended. Victor was moved to a nearby home, where a woman cared for him for the rest of his life.

▶ **Focus 1**
Describe four major issues and three special research designs often encountered in developmental research.

In the early 1800s, people expected Victor's case to resolve an intense debate about the role of nature versus nurture in shaping who we are. But it raised more questions than it answered. Was Victor a normal, inherently noble infant who became irreparably harmed by his childhood isolation, or was he born "mentally deficient"?

Some children exposed to extreme adversity are highly resilient and thrive later in life (Ryff & Singer, 2003). We cannot pinpoint why Victor failed to recover, but his famous case begs a fundamental question: Just how does the miracle of human development unfold, and what conditions are required for normal growth?

MAJOR ISSUES AND METHODS

Developmental psychology examines biological, physical, psychological, and behavioral changes that occur as we age. Four broad issues guide much developmental research.

- *Nature and nurture:* To what extent is our development the product of heredity (nature) and the product of environment (nurture)? How do nature and nurture interact?

- *Critical and sensitive periods:* Are some experiences especially important at particular ages?

A **critical period** *is an age range during which certain experiences must occur for development to proceed normally or along a certain path.* A **sensitive period** *is an optimal age range for certain experiences, but if those experiences occur at another time, normal development is still possible.*

- *Continuity versus discontinuity:* Is development continuous and gradual, as when a sapling slowly grows into a tree? Or is it discontinuous, progressing through qualitatively distinct stages, as when a creeping caterpillar emerges from its cocoon as a soaring butterfly?

- *Stability versus change:* Do our characteristics remain consistent as we age?

Psychologists often use special research designs to investigate developmental questions (Figure 11.2). Suppose we wish to study how intellectual abilities change from age 10 to age 60. Using a **cross-sectional design** *we would compare people of different ages at the same point in time.* Thus in the next month we could administer intellectual tasks to 10-, 20-, 30-, 40-, 50-, and 60-year-olds. We would test each person only once and compare how well the different age groups performed. The cross-sectional design is widely used because data from many age groups can be collected relatively quickly, but a key drawback is that the different age groups, called *cohorts,* grew up in different historical periods. Thus if 60-year-olds have poorer intellectual abilities than 20-year-olds, we need to ask whether this is due to aging or possibly to broad environmental differences (e.g., poorer nutrition or medical care) between growing up in the 1940s and 1950s versus the 1980s and 1990s.

To avoid this problem, a **longitudinal design** *repeatedly tests the same cohort as it grows older.* We could test a sample of 10-year-olds this month and then retest them every 10 years, up to age 60, thus ensuring that everyone is exposed to the same historical time frame. Unfortunately, a longitudinal design can be time-consuming, and as years pass, our sample may shrink as people move, drop out of the study, or die. Further, suppose we find that intelligence declines at age 60. Is this really due to aging or to developmental experiences unique to our particular cohort? Researchers can answer this question by using a **sequential design,** *which combines the cross-sectional and longitudinal approaches.* For example, we could test 10- through 60-year-olds now, retest them every 10 years, and then examine whether the various cohorts followed a similar developmental pattern. This design is the most comprehensive but also the costliest and most time-consuming.

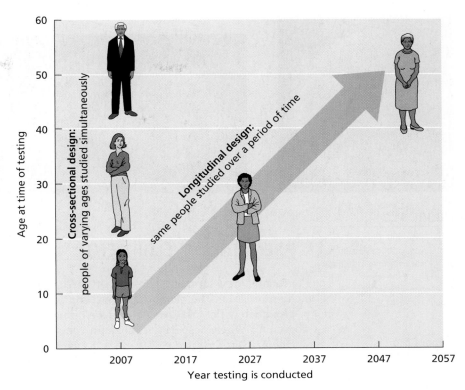

FIGURE 11.2

Developmental research designs. Using a cross-sectional design we would test different age groups in the year 2007 and compare their performance. Using a longitudinal design, we would test individuals of one age group and then retest them every 10 years until age 60. Using a sequential design, we would test 10- through 60-year-olds in the year 2007 and then retest them every 10 years until the youngest cohort reached age 60.

Now let's turn to the process of human development. We begin with the *prenatal period,* approximately 266 days during which each of us developed from a single-celled organism barely larger than a pinhead into a wondrously complex newborn human.

IN REVIEW

- Developmental psychology studies the aging process. Questions about the influence of nature and nurture, critical and sensitive periods, continuity versus discontinuity, and stability versus change have guided much developmental research.

- Cross-sectional designs compare different age groups at one point in time. A longitudinal design repeatedly tests the same age group as it grows older. A sequential design tests several groups at one point in time and then again when they are older.

(a)   (b)   (c)

FIGURE 11.3

These remarkable photos show (a) the moment of conception, as one of many sperm cells fertilizes the ovum, (b) the embryo at 6 to 7 weeks, and (c) the fetus at 3 months of age.

▶ **Focus 2**
Describe the stages of prenatal development, how sex is determined, and the effects of various teratogens.

PRENATAL DEVELOPMENT

Prenatal development consists of three stages (Figure 11.3). The *germinal stage* comprises approximately the first 2 weeks of development, beginning when a sperm fertilizes a female egg (*ovum*). *This fertilized egg is called a* **zygote,** and through repeated cell division it becomes a mass of cells that attaches to the mother's uterus about 10 to 14 days after conception.

The *embryonic stage* is next. The cell mass, now called an **embryo,** *develops from the end of week 2 through week 8 after conception.* Two life-support structures, the placenta and umbilical cord, develop at the start of this stage. Located on the uterine wall, the *placenta* contains membranes that allow nutrients to pass from the mother's blood to the umbilical cord. In turn, the *umbilical cord* contains blood vessels that carry these nutrients and oxygen to the embryo and transport waste products back from the embryo to the mother. Supplied with nutrients, embryonic cells rapidly divide and become specialized. Bodily organs and systems begin to form, and by week 8 the heart of the inch-long embryo is beating, the brain is forming, and facial features such as eyes can be recognized.

Finally, during the *fetal stage,* the **fetus** *develops from week 9 after conception until birth.* Muscles strengthen and other bodily systems develop. At about 24 weeks the eyes open, and by 27 weeks (or several weeks younger, with top medical care) the fetus attains the *age of viability:* it is likely to survive outside the womb in case of premature birth (Subramanian et al., 2002).

GENETICS AND SEX DETERMINATION

Throughout history, many women have been blamed for failing to give birth to a male heir.

Ironically, any father who foolishly feels a need to lay blame should look in the mirror, for it is his genetic contribution that determines the sex of a baby. A female's egg cells and a male's sperm cells each have 23 chromosomes. At conception, an egg and sperm unite to form the zygote, which now contains the full set of 23 *pairs* found in other human cells. The 23rd pair of chromosomes determines the baby's sex. A genetic female's 23rd pair contains two X chromosomes (XX), so called because of their shape (Figure 11.4). Because women carry only X chromosomes, the 23rd chromosome in the egg is always an X. A genetic male's 23rd pair contains an X and a Y chromosome (XY).

FIGURE 11.4

Most human cells contain 23 pairs of chromosomes. Each pair consists of one chromosome from each parent. The 23rd pair determines a person's sex. In males, the 23rd pair, which is shown in the lower right area of the photo, consists of an X chromosome and a Y chromosome. In females, the 23rd pair contains two X chromosomes.

Thus the 23rd chromosome in the sperm is an X in about half of the cases and a Y in the other half. The Y chromosome contains a specific gene, the *TDF (testis determining factor) gene,* that triggers male sexual development. The union of an egg with a sperm cell having a Y chromosome results in an XY combination and therefore a boy. A sperm containing an X chromosome produces an XX combination and therefore a girl.

How does the Y chromosome determine male sex characteristics? At roughly 6 to 8 weeks after conception, the TDF gene initiates the development of testes. Once formed, the testes secrete sex hormones called *androgens* that continue to direct a male pattern of organ development. If the TDF gene is not present, as happens with an XX combination in the 23rd pair, testes do not form and—in the absence of sufficient androgen activity during this *prenatal critical period*—an inherent female pattern of organ development ensues.

ENVIRONMENTAL INFLUENCES

Our genetic blueprint sets forth a path of prenatal development, but nature and nurture become intertwined even before we are born. **Teratogens** *are external agents that cause abnormal prenatal development.* The placenta prevents many dangerous substances from reaching the embryo and fetus, but some harmful chemicals and diseases can pass through. Stress hormones can cross the placenta, and prolonged maternal stress is associated with increased risk of premature birth (Austin & Leader, 2000). If the mother contracts rubella (German measles)—especially when the embryo's eyes, ears, heart, and central nervous system are beginning to form early in pregnancy—it can cause blindness, deafness, heart defects, and mental retardation in the infant (Murdoch, 1984).

Sexually transmitted diseases can pass from mother to fetus and produce brain damage, blindness, and deafness depending on the disease. Among pregnant women with untreated syphilis, about 25 percent of fetuses are born dead. Likewise, without treatment during pregnancy or delivery by cesarean section at birth, about 25 percent of fetuses born to mothers with the human immunodeficiency virus (HIV) also are infected (Meleski & Damato, 2003).

Mercury, lead, radiation, and many other environmental toxins can produce birth defects, as can many drugs. **Fetal alcohol syndrome (FAS)** *is a severe group of abnormalities that results from prenatal exposure to alcohol* (Streissguth, 1977, 2001). FAS

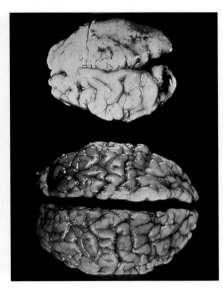

FIGURE 11.5

Children who suffer from fetal alcohol syndrome (FAS) not only look different but also have brains that are underdeveloped and smaller than those of normal children.

children have facial abnormalities and small, malformed brains (Figure 11.5). Psychological symptoms include mental retardation, attentional and perceptual deficits, irritability, and impulsivity. Other children exposed to alcohol in the womb may display milder forms of these deficits.

The threshold level of alcohol exposure needed to produce FAS is not known. About one third to one half of infants born to alcoholic mothers have FAS, but even social drinking or a single episode of binge drinking can increase the risk of prenatal damage and long-term cognitive impairment (Larroque & Kaminski, 1998). Because no amount of prenatal alcohol exposure has been confirmed to be absolutely safe, pregnant women and those trying to become pregnant are best advised to completely avoid drinking alcohol.

Nicotine is also a teratogen. Maternal smoking increases the risk of miscarriage, premature birth, and low birth weight (Kirchengast & Hartmann, 2003). Due to secondhand smoke, regular tobacco use by fathers also has been linked to low infant birth weight and increased risk of respiratory infections (Wakefield et al., 1998). Babies of pregnant mothers who regularly use heroin or cocaine are often born addicted and experience withdrawal symptoms after birth. Their cognitive functioning and ability to regulate their arousal and attention may also be impaired (Lewis et al., 2004).

INFANCY AND CHILDHOOD

Studying infancy poses unique challenges. During research, infants may fuss, cry, soil their diapers, or simply fall asleep! Because infants cannot describe their experiences, psychologists must find clever ways to take advantage of responses that infants can make, such as sucking and moving their eyes, to draw inferences about their capabilities and preferences.

THE AMAZING NEWBORN

After emerging from the womb, does a newborn's world become a "buzzing, blooming confusion," as pioneering psychologist William James (1890/1950) proposed? Contrary to a long-held view of newborns as helpless and passive, research reveals that they are surprisingly sophisticated information processors.

Sensory Capabilities and Perceptual Preferences

Newborns' visual systems are immature. Their eye movements are not well coordinated, and they are very nearsighted (Figure 11.6). Still, infants scan their environment, and although objects look blurry to them, they can perceive some forms only a few days after birth. Newborns can reasonably see objects about 1 foot away, the typical distance between their eyes and their mothers' eyes while nursing.

Robert Fantz (1961) used the *preferential looking procedure* to study infants' visual preferences. He placed infants on their backs, showed them two or more stimuli at the same time, and filmed their eyes to record how long they looked at each stimulus. Infants preferred complex patterns, such as realistic or scrambled drawings of a human face, to simple patterns and solid colors (Figure 11.7). Within hours after birth, newborns can distinguish the familiar face of their mother from that of a female stranger, and they prefer to gaze at the mother's face (Bushnell, 2001).

Just as you would make different facial expressions after tasting sweet, sour, or bitter substances, newborns' facial responses tell us that they have a reasonably well-developed sense of taste. Newborns also respond to touch and distinguish different odors. If exposed to pads taken from inside the bras of several nursing mothers, week-old infants will orient toward the scent of their own mother's pad. Newborns can hear fairly well. They prefer human voices to other sounds and can distinguish their mother's voice from that of a female stranger (DeRegnier et al., 2002). As Figure 11.8 describes, newborns seem to prefer sounds that become familiar to them in their last weeks of fetal development, during

► **Focus 3**
Describe the newborn's sensory capabilities, perceptual preferences, reflexes, and ability to learn.

FIGURE 11.6

Seeing through an Infant's eyes. These three images approximate the visual acuity of an infant at (a) 1 month, (b) 3 months, and (c) 12 months of age.

(a)　　　(b)　　　(c)

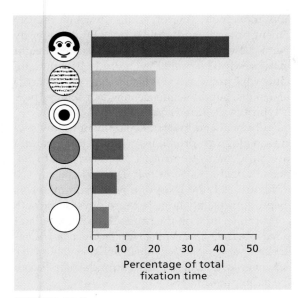

FIGURE 11.7

Infants' visual preferences. Whether 2 days old or 2 to 3 months old (the data shown here), infants prefer to look at complex patterns more than simple patterns or solid colors. Source: Based on Fantz, 1961.

which time they can hear sounds transmitted through the womb (DeCasper & Spence, 1986). Thus, in a rudimentary sense, simple forms of learning can occur inside the womb (Gruest et al., 2004).

Reflexes and Learning

Neonates are equipped with many **reflexes,** *automatic, inborn behaviors that occur in response to specific stimuli.* Some, including breathing, have obvious adaptive significance. Stroke a baby's cheek, and it will turn its head toward the direction it was touched and open its mouth—the *rooting reflex.* When something is placed in the infant's mouth, it will suck on it—the *sucking reflex.* Together, these reflexes increase the infant's ability to feed. In general, healthy reflexes indicate normal neurological maturity at birth.

Newborns learn in several ways. They habituate to repetitive, nonthreatening stimuli and can acquire classically conditioned responses. After a tone (CS) is repeatedly paired with a gentle puff of air to the eye (UCS), they will develop a conditioned eyeblink response to the tone alone (Lipsitt, 1990). Through operant conditioning, newborns learn that they can make things happen. Thus 3-day old infants can learn to suck a plastic nipple with a certain pattern of bursts to activate a tape-recording of their mother's voice (Moon & Fifer, 1990).

As Figure 11.9 shows, within weeks or possibly days after birth, some newborns can reproduce a simple facial expression made by an adult model, providing evidence of a biologically based capacity for imitation (Meltzoff, 2002). By 9 months of age, infants who watch a model act in a novel way (e.g., pushing a button in a box to trigger a sound) can

FIGURE 11.8

Can the fetus learn? (*left*) Twice a day during their last 6 weeks of pregnancy, mothers in one study read out loud the same passage from Dr. Seuss's *The Cat in the Hat.* (*right*) Two or 3 days after birth, their newborns were able to turn on a recording of their mother reading either *The Cat in the Hat* rhyme or an unfamiliar rhyme by sucking on a sensor-equipped nipple at different rates. Compared with infants in a control condition, these newborns more often altered their sucking rate in whichever direction (faster or slower) selected the familiar rhyme. Source: DeCasper & Spence, 1986.

▶ Focus 4
Explain how nature and nurture jointly influence infants' physical growth and motor development.

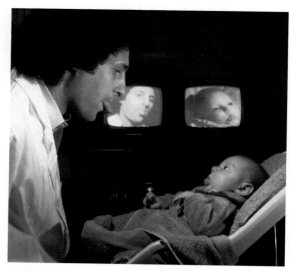

FIGURE 11.9

Young infants have been found to reproduce tongue protrusion after watching an adult model. Here researcher Andrew Meltzoff models the behavior and records an infant's response.

FIGURE 11.10

Infant motor development. Infant motor development occurs in an orderly sequence, but the age at which abilities emerge varies across children. The left end of each bar represents the age by which 25 percent of children exhibit the skill; the right end represents the age by which 90 percent have mastered it.

reproduce that action from memory a day later. In sum, infants are born with an array of mechanisms that help them respond to caretakers and learn other important information.

PHYSICAL DEVELOPMENT

Thanks to **maturation,** *the genetically programmed biological process that governs our growth,* our bodies

and movement (motor) skills develop rapidly during infancy and childhood. On average, by our 1st birthday body weight triples and height increases by 50 percent. As Figure 11.10 shows, infants vary in the age at which they acquire particular skills, but the sequence in which skills appear is typically the same across children.

Physical and motor development follow several biological principles. The **cephalocaudal principle** *reflects the tendency for development to proceed in a head-to-foot direction.* Thus, as you can see in Figure 11.3, the head of a fetus (and infant) is disproportionately large because physical growth concentrates first on the head. The **proximodistal principle** *states that development begins along the innermost parts of the body and continues toward the outermost parts.* Thus a fetus's arms develop before the hands and fingers.

The Young Brain

No organ develops more dramatically than the brain. At birth the newborn's brain is far from mature and has reached only about 25 percent of its eventual adult weight. By age 6 months, however, the brain reaches 50 percent of its adult weight. As Figure 11.11 shows, neural networks that form the basis for cognitive and motor skills develop rapidly. The first brain areas to mature fully lie deep within the brain and regulate basic survival functions such as heartbeat and breathing. Among the last areas to mature is the frontal

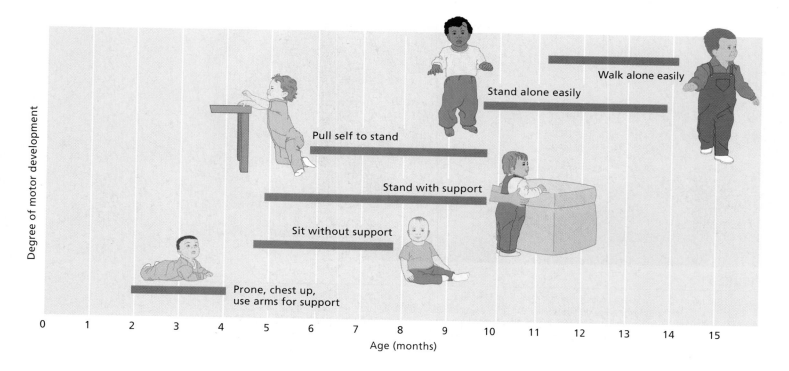

Walk alone easily

Stand alone easily

Pull self to stand

Stand with support

Sit without support

Prone, chest up, use arms for support

Degree of motor development

0   1   2   3   4   5   6   7   8   9   10   11   12   13   14   15

Age (months)

cortex, which is vital to our highest-level cognitive functions.

Rapid brain growth during infancy and early childhood slows in later childhood (Sowell et al., 2001). Yet, although 5-year-olds' brains have reached almost 90 percent of their adult size, brain maturation continues. New synapses form, unnecessary synapses are pruned back and lost, association areas of the cortex mature, and the cerebral hemispheres become more highly specialized.

Environmental and Cultural Influences

Although guided by genetics, physical development is also influenced by experience. Diet is an obvious example. Chronic, severe malnutrition not only stunts general growth and brain development but also is a major source of infant death worldwide (Pelletier & Frongillo, 2003).

Babies thrive in an enriched environment— one in which the infant has the opportunity to interact with others and to manipulate suitable toys and other objects (Needham et al., 2002). Newborn rats (i.e., pups) raised in an enriched environment develop heavier brains, larger neurons, more synaptic connections, and greater amounts of brain neurotransmitters that enhance learning (Rosenzweig & Bennett, 1996).

Physical touch, too, affects growth in infancy. Depriving well-nourished rat pups of normal physical contact with their mothers stunts their development, whereas vigorously stroking the pups with a brush helps restore normal growth (Schanberg et al., 2003). Similarly, massaging premature and full-term human infants accelerates their weight gain and neurological development (Field, 2000).

Experience also can influence basic motor skill development. Infants of the South American Ache tribe typically do not begin to walk until they are almost 2, about a year later than the average Western infant (Kaplan & Dove, 1987). The Ache people roam the dense rain forests of eastern Paraguay foraging for food. For safety, mothers keep their children in direct physical contact almost constantly until the age of 3, providing them little opportunity to move about. Experience also affects various types of complex movement skills that toddlers and children acquire (Figure 11.12).

Our discussion of physical growth reinforces three points that apply across the realm of human development:

- *Biology sets limits on environmental influences.* For example, no infant can be toilet-trained before the nerve fibers that help regulate bladder control have biologically matured.

At birth   1 month   3 months   15 months   24 months

FIGURE 11.11

The brain matures and adapts. Increases in the density of neural networks during early development are apparent in these drawings of tissue from the human cerebral cortex. Source: Reprinted by permission of Harvard University Press from *The postnatal development of the human cerebral cortex, Vols. I–VIII,* by Jesse LeRoy Conel. Copyright © 1939, 1975 by the President and Fellows of Harvard College.

- *Environmental influences can be powerful.* Nurturing environments foster physical and psychological growth, and impoverished environments can stunt growth.
- *Biological and environmental factors interact.* Enriched environments enhance brain development. In turn, brain development facilitates our ability to learn and benefit from environmental experiences.

▶ **Focus 5**
Discuss Piaget's concepts of assimilation and accommodation, his four-stage model, and findings that help us evaluate his theory.

COGNITIVE DEVELOPMENT

How do the thought processes of a child develop? Swiss psychologist Jean Piaget (1926, 1977) spent over 50 years exploring this question.

Piaget's Stage Model

Early in his career, Piaget worked for French psychologist Alfred Binet, a pioneer of intelligence testing. Piaget became intrigued when he noticed that children of the same age often made similar errors on test questions. The key to understanding how children think, Piaget believed, was not whether they got the right answers but *how* they arrived at their answers.

Piaget observed children and listened to them reason as they tried to solve problems. He proposed that children's thinking changes *qualitatively* with age and that it differs from the way adults think. Piaget believed that cognitive development results from an interaction of the brain's biological maturation and personal experiences. He viewed children as natural-born scientists who seek to understand their world.

FIGURE 11.12

At the Parker Ranch in Hawaii, this 2-year-old is learning to ride a horse and use a lasso.

TABLE 11.1		Piaget's Stages of Cognitive Development
Stage	**Age (Years)**	**Major Characteristics**
Sensorimotor	Birth to 2	• Infant understands world through sensory and motor experiences • Achieves object permanence • Exhibits emergence of symbolic thought
Preoperational	2 to 7	• Child uses symbolic thinking in the form of words and images to represent objects and experiences • Symbolic thinking enables child to engage in pretend play • Thinking displays egocentrism, irreversibility, and centration
Concrete operational	7 to 12	• Child can think logically about concrete events • Grasps concepts of conservation and serial ordering
Formal operational	12 on	• Adolescent can think more logically, abstractly, and flexibly • Can form hypotheses and systematically test them

To achieve this understanding, the brain builds **schemas** (or *schemata*), *which are organized patterns of thought and action*. Think of a schema as a mental framework that guides our interaction with the world. For example, infants are born with a sucking reflex that provides a primitive schema for interacting with physical objects. In other words, sucking is a basic way in which the infant "knows" the world. When a child says "doggie" to describe a family pet, this word reflects a schema—a concept that the child is using to understand this particular experience.

Cognitive development occurs as we acquire new schemas and as our existing schemas become more complex. According to Piaget, two key processes are involved. **Assimilation** *is the process by which new experiences are incorporated into existing schemas.* When a young infant encounters a new object—a small plastic toy, a blanket, a doll— she will try to suck it. She tries to fit this new experience into a schema that she already has: Objects are suckable. Similarly, a child who sees a skunk for the first time may exclaim "kitty!" After all, the skunk is about the size of a cat, is furry, and has four legs and a tail, so the child tries to make sense of this new experience by applying his familiar schema: "kitty."

Accommodation *is the process by which new experiences cause existing schemas to change.* As the infant tries to suck different objects, she will eventually encounter ones that are too big or that taste bad. Similarly, the child who calls a skunk a "kitty" may discover that this "kitty" exhibits some smelly behaviors not found in cats. This imbalance, or *disequilibrium*, between existing schemas and new experiences ultimately forces those schemas to change. Thus the infant's "suckability" schema will become more complex: Some objects are suckable, some are not. The child's "kitty" schema also will change, and he will begin to develop new schemas for "doggie," "skunk," and so on. To the infant and child, this is a fundamental change in their understanding of the world.

Cognitive growth thus involves a give-and-take between trying to understand new experiences in terms of what we already know (assimilation) and having to modify our thinking when new experiences don't fit into our current schemas (accommodation). As Table 11.1 shows, Piaget charted four major stages of cognitive growth.

Sensorimotor Stage From birth to about age 2, infants in the **sensorimotor stage** *understand their world primarily through sensory experiences and physical (motor) interactions with objects.* Reflexes are infants' earliest schemas, and as infants mature, they begin to explore their surroundings and realize that they can bang spoons, take objects apart, and make things happen.

For young infants, said Piaget, "out of sight" literally means "out of mind." If you hide 3-month-old Cindy's favorite toy from view, she will not search for it, as if the toy no longer exists (Figure 11.13). But around age 8 months, Cindy will search for and retrieve the hidden toy. She now grasps the concept of **object permanence,** *the understanding that an object continues to exist even when it no longer can be seen.*

FIGURE 11.13

During the early sensorimotor period, a baby will reach for a visible toy (*left*) but not for one that has been hidden from view while the infant watches (*right*). According to Piaget, the child lacks the concept of object permanence; when something is out of sight, it ceases to exist.

Infants begin to acquire language after age 1, and toward the end of the sensorimotor period they increasingly use words to represent objects, needs, and actions. Thus in the space of 2 years, infants grow into planful thinkers who form simple concepts, solve some problems, and communicate their thoughts.

Preoperational Stage At about age 2, children enter a **preoperational stage,** *in which they represent the world symbolically through words and mental images but do not yet understand basic mental operations or rules.* Rapid language development helps children label objects and represent simple concepts, such as that two objects can be the "same" or "different." Children can think about the past ("yesterday") and future ("soon") and can better anticipate the consequences of their actions. Symbolic thinking enables them to engage in make-believe, or pretend play.

Despite these advances, children's cognitive abilities have major limitations. The preoperational child does not understand **conservation,** *the principle that basic properties of objects, such as their volume, mass, or quantity, stay the same (are "conserved") even though their outward appearance may change* (Figure 11.14). For example, 4-year-olds often say that the taller beaker in Figure 10.14c has more liquid than the shorter one. You understand that the liquid can be poured back into the short beaker to return to the original, equal state of affairs, but children's thinking at this age displays *irreversibility:* It is difficult for them to reverse an action mentally. You also pay attention to height and width, recognizing that the liquid is "taller" because the beaker is narrower. But preoperational children exhibit *centration,* focusing (centering) on only one aspect of the situation, such as the height of the liquid.

Preoperational children often display *animism,* attributing lifelike qualities to physical objects and natural events. When it rains, "the sky is crying," and stars twinkle at night "because they're winking at you." Their thinking also reflects **egocentrism,** *difficulty in viewing the world from someone else's perspective.* By *egocentrism* Piaget did not mean "selfishness" but rather that children at this stage believe that other people perceive things in the same way they do (Figure 11.15).

Concrete Operational Stage From about ages 7 to 12, said Piaget, children in the **concrete operational stage** *can perform basic mental operations*

(a)   Initial equality

(b)   Transformation

(c)   Which glass has more juice?

(d)

(e)

FIGURE 11.14

Conservation tasks. (*a, b, c*) Conservation of volume: At the end of this sequence (*from left to right*), when the preoperational child is asked which beaker contains more liquid, he points to the taller one. (d) Conservation of number: Two rows with an equal number of objects are aligned. After one row is spread out, preoperational children will say that it has more objects than the other row. (e) Conservation of mass: Preoperational children watch as one of two identically sized clay balls is rolled into a new shape. They typically will say that the new shape now has more clay.

FIGURE 11.15

The three-mountain problem. Piaget used the three-mountain problem to illustrate the egocentrism of young children. Suppose that a preoperational child named Ted is looking at the mountains just as you are. Another child, Beth, is standing at the opposite (far) side of the table. Ted is asked what Beth sees. Because Ted is able to see the road, he will mistakenly say that Beth also can see it, indicating that he has failed to recognize Beth's perspective as different from his own.

concerning problems that involve tangible (i.e., "concrete") objects and situations. They now grasp the concept of reversibility, display less centration, and easily solve conservation problems that baffled them as preschoolers.

When concrete operational children confront problems that are hypothetical or require abstract reasoning, however, they often have difficulty or show rigid types of thinking. To demonstrate this, ask a few 9-year-olds, "If you could have a third eye, where on your body would you put it? Draw a picture." Then ask them to explain their reasons. David Shaffer (1989) reports that 9-year-olds typically draw a face with a row of three eyes across it. Their thinking is concrete, bound by the reality that eyes appear on the face, and their justifications often are unsophisticated (e.g., "so I could see you better"). Many find the task silly because "Nobody has three eyes" (Shaffer, 1989, p. 324).

Formal Operational Stage Piaget's model ends with the **formal operational stage,** *in which individuals are able to think logically and systematically about both concrete and abstract problems, form hypotheses, and test them in a thoughtful way.* Formal thinking begins around ages 11 to 12 and increases through adolescence (Ward & Overton, 1990).

Children entering this stage begin to think more flexibly when tackling hypothetical problems, such as brainteasers, and typically enjoy the challenge. Shaffer (1989) reports that $11\frac{1}{2}$- to 12-year-olds provide more creative answers and justifications to the third-eye problem than do 9-year-old concrete thinkers. One child placed the eye on the palm of his hands so that he could use it to "see around corners." Another placed it on top of his head, so that he could "revolve the eye to look in all directions." Formal operational children enjoy these hypothetical tasks and often beg for more.

Assessing Piaget's Theory: Stages, Ages, and Culture

Tests of Piaget's theory conducted around the world yield several general findings. First, it appears that *the general cognitive abilities associated with Piaget's four stages occur in the same order across cultures* (Berry et al., 1992). For example, children understand object permanence before symbolic thinking blooms, and concrete reasoning emerges before abstract reasoning.

Second, *children acquire many cognitive skills and concepts at an earlier age than Piaget believed* (Wang et al., 2005). Even $3\frac{1}{2}$- to $4\frac{1}{2}$-month-olds display a basic grasp of objective permanence when they are tested on special tasks that only require them to look at events rather than physically search for a hidden object.

Third, *cognitive development within each stage seems to proceed inconsistently.* A child may perform at the preoperational level on most tasks yet solve some tasks at a concrete operational level (Siegler, 1986). This challenges the idea that development proceeds in distinct stages: A child at a given stage should not show large inconsistencies in solving conceptually similar tasks.

Fourth, *culture influences cognitive development.* Piaget's Western perspective equated cognitive development with scientific-logical thinking, but "Many cultures . . . consider cognitive development to be more relational, involving the thinking skills and processes to engage in successful interpersonal contexts" (Matsumoto & Hull, 1994, p. 105). In Africa's Ivory Coast, the Baoulé people most strongly value a type of social intelligence that reflects the skills to get along with others and to be respectful, helpful, and responsible (Dasen et al., 1985).

Fifth, and most broadly, *cognitive development is more complex and variable than Piaget proposed* (Larivée et al., 2000). Although all children progress from simpler to more sophisticated thinking, they don't necessarily follow the same developmental path.

In sum, newer research challenges many of Piaget's ideas. Nevertheless, he revolutionized thinking about children's cognitive development, and his work still guides many researchers, called *neo-Piagetians,* who have modified his theory to account for the issues discussed above (Becker, 2004).

The Social Context of Cognitive Development

Piaget acknowledged that social factors influence children's thinking, but he focused mainly on children's independent exploration of the physical world. In contrast, Russian psychologist Lev Vygotsky (1935/1978) highlighted how the sociocultural context of cognitive development interacts with the brain's biological maturation.

To illustrate, suppose that 5-year-olds Joshua and Juanita cannot solve Piaget's conservation problems. However, with guidance from a parent, teacher, or older sibling, Juanita can now solve these problems. Joshua, even with assistance, just doesn't understand. Are these two children really at the same cognitive level? Vygotsky says no, introducing a concept called the **zone of proximal development:** *the difference between what a child can do independently and what the child can do with assistance from adults or more advanced peers.*

Why is the zone of proximal development important? For one thing, it helps us recognize what children may soon be able to do on their own. Second, it emphasizes that we can help move a child's cognitive development forward within limits (the "zone") dictated by the child's biological maturation. Parents who assist a child on scientific tasks may push the child's understanding further along by using age-appropriate but cognitively demanding speech (e.g., introducing scientific concepts) than by using only simpler speech (Tenenbaum & Leaper, 2003).

Having older siblings around the house also may stimulate a younger child's cognitive development, as long as the child is biologically ready for the input. In one study of 2- to 6-year-old English and Japanese children, those over age 3 who grew up with older brothers and sisters performed better on a cognitive task than children who grew up alone or with younger brothers and sisters (Ruffman et al., 1998). But children under age 3 performed poorly regardless of how many older siblings they had: The task was simply beyond their cognitive capacity.

Information-Processing Approaches

In contrast to Piaget's stage approach, many researchers view cognitive development as a continuous, gradual process in which the same set of information-processing abilities become more efficient over time. For example, perhaps young children fail to solve conservation problems because they don't search for key information or are unable to hold enough pieces of information in memory simultaneously (Siegler, 1996).

Information-Search Strategies   Look at the two houses in Figure 11.16. Are they identical? This task is easy for you but not for young children. Elaine Vurpillot (1968) recorded the eye movements of 3- to 10-year-olds during tasks like this one. Preschoolers often failed to compare each window in the house on the left to the corresponding window in the house on the right, but older children methodically scanned the houses. In short, older children are better able to search systematically for relevant information (Merrill & Lookadoo, 2004).

Processing Speed, Attention, and Response Inhibition
As Robert Kail's (1991) review of 72 studies shows in Figure 11.17, the speed with which children process information becomes faster with age. Notice that processing speed improves continuously and that the relatively rapid rate of change between ages 8 and about 12 slows during adolescence. Children's attention span and ability to inhibit impulsive responses to distracting stimuli also improve with age. When performing tasks, older children are better able to focus their attention on relevant details and ignore irrelevant information (Luna et al., 2004).

Working Memory and Long-Term Memory   Children's working memory improves with age (Gathercole et al., 2004). If you read older children a list of words or numbers or sentences of increasing length, they will be able to store more of that

▶ **Focus 6**
Explain how Vygotsky's approach and information-processing models challenge Piaget's views.

FIGURE 11.16

A visual-search task. Elaine Vurpillot used stimuli like these to assess visual inspection through filmed eye movements. Preschoolers fail to scan the pictures systematically, which often leads them to claim that the two houses are identical. SOURCE: Adapted from Vurpillot, 1968.

FIGURE 11.17

Information-processing speed quickens during childhood. These two graphs show how information-processing speed for visual-search and mental-addition tasks becomes faster with age. The relatively rapid rate of change between ages 8 and about 12 slows during adolescence. A similar nonlinear pattern also occurs on name-retrieval, mental-rotation, and other cognitive tasks. SOURCE: Adapted from Kail, 1991.

Visual search

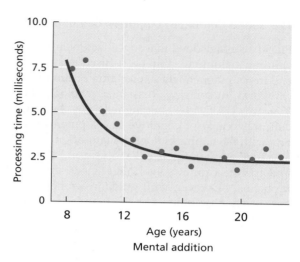

Mental addition

▶ **Focus 7**
Explain violation-of-expectation and theory-of-mind research. How do these challenge Piaget's views?

information in working memory and repeat it to you than will younger children. Older children also can retain and manipulate visuospatial information in working memory more effectively than younger children. For example, they can perform mental-rotation tasks (see Figure 8.30) more easily, and if you asked them to draw you a map to a friend's house several blocks and a few turns away, they would likely have little difficulty. A younger child might be able to lead you to the friend's house but would have difficulty drawing the route.

Older children are also more likely than younger children to use strategies to improve memory (Schneider et al., 2004). In one study, when given lists of words or numbers to remember, preschoolers rarely used rehearsal spontaneously, whereas 8- to 10-year-olds could often be heard rehearsing words or numbers under their breath (Flavell, 1970). More effective rehearsal helps older children to temporarily hold information in working memory for a greater period of time and to process information into long-term memory. Given their more advanced brain maturation, years of additional schooling, and other life experiences, older children also can call upon a larger library of information stored in long-term memory when they need to solve problems or perform tasks.

Metacognition As we discussed in Chapter 8, metacognition refers to your awareness of your own cognitive processes. Compared to younger children, older children can better judge how well they understand material for a test. In turn, this helps them decide whether they need to study more or ask for help.

Despite the rise of information-processing approaches to cognitive development, the *discon-*tinuity versus continuity debate (gradual development versus the emergence of distinct stages) is still far from resolved. Some psychologists propose that cognitive development involves both processes. For example, Susan Gathercole (1998) suggests that memory capabilities change qualitatively (i.e., new abilities emerge) between infancy and age 7 but then undergo only gradual quantitative improvements through adolescence. Robbie Case (1987; Case et al., 2001) offered another integrative view, proposing that gradual increases in information-processing capabilities within stages enable children to move qualitatively from one stage of cognitive development to the next.

Understanding the Physical World

We noted above that infants and children acquire many concepts at an earlier age than Piaget proposed. Because infants cannot express their knowledge in words, developmental psychologists have created some ingenious approaches—such as the *violation-of-expectation experiment*—to examine infants' understanding of basic concepts (Baillargeon, 2004). This approach measures a basic aspect of infants' information processing: attention (i.e., time spent looking at a stimulus).

In these experiments, researchers begin with the hypothesis that young infants possess a certain concept—an expectation—about how the world works. For example, let's make the radical assumption that young infants have an expectation about the addition of very small numbers of objects, such as "one of a thing" plus "another one of the thing" equals "two of the things." Then researchers expose the infants to an "impossible event" that violates this expectation and a "possible event" that does not violate this expectation, as shown in Figure 11.18. If the infants stare longer at the impossible event, then the researchers take this as evidence that the infants understand the concept being tested. In other words, just as you would stare longer at a dropped pencil that suddenly stopped in mid-air than you would at one that fell to the ground, infants pay more attention to events that violate their understanding of the world.

These experiments suggest that young infants possess basic concepts about the physical properties of objects, such as that two solid objects cannot occupy the same space at the same time, and about the addition and subtraction of small numbers of objects, such as $1 + 1 = 2$, $2 + 1 = 3$, and $2 - 1 = 1$ (Spelke, 1994; Wynn, 1998). This approach is not without controversy, because as critics note, researchers are making large inferences about what must be going on inside the infant's head. Even so, as new research accumulates, it suggests that even $2\frac{1}{2}$-month-olds (younger infants have not yet been tested) understand more about how the physical world operates than was thought possible just two decades ago (Wang et al., 2005).

FIGURE 11.18

A violation-of-expectancy experiment. Five-month-old infants watch the sequence of events shown in steps 1 through 4. Then in step 5 they witness a "possible" or "impossible" event. Infants stare longer at the impossible event, suggesting that they were expecting only 1 object and are surprised to see 2 objects still there. In other words, they understand that $2 - 1$ should equal 1. In another experiment, in steps 1 to 4, infants watch 1 object being added to another object. Then the screen is raised and lowered, revealing either 2 objects ("possible event") or just 1 object ("impossible event"). Once again, infants stare longer at the impossible event, suggesting that they understand that $1 + 1$ should equal 2. SOURCE: Wynn, 1992.

Theory of Mind: Understanding Mental States

The term **theory of mind** *refers to a person's beliefs about the "mind" and the ability to understand other people's mental states.* Piaget believed that children younger than 6 or 7 have trouble recognizing what other people are thinking. But consider the following story:

> Angela puts a candy bar inside a green box on the table, and then she goes away. Then her mother takes the candy bar out of the box and puts it inside a red bag on the bed. Angela doesn't see her mother do this. Later, Angela comes back and wants to get her candy because she is hungry. Where will Angela look for her candy bar?

On problems like this, most 2- and 3-year-olds indicate that Angela will look in the red bag, as if she had the same knowledge that they have. Piaget would not have been surprised. But many 4-year-olds say she will choose the green box, recognizing that Angela does not have the information they do. Thus, at some level, they comprehend that Angela's mental state—her "mind"—is different from theirs (Ruffman et al., 1998). Studies of young children from African tribal societies, Canada, China, Japan, the United Kingdom, and the United States yield similar findings (Vinden, 2002).

Lying and deception also provide evidence of theory of mind. They imply an ability to recognize that one person can have information that another does not and therefore that we can influence what other people think by withholding the truth. Researchers find that most 3-year-olds are capable of trying to deceive someone else and recognize the difference between providing someone with false information in the form of a lie and providing false information due to an innocent mistake (Carlson et al., 1998). Overall, it appears that children begin to understand some aspects of other people's thinking by age 3 to 4, well before Piaget proposed they could (Flavell, 2004).

SOCIAL-EMOTIONAL AND PERSONALITY DEVELOPMENT

Children grow not only physically and mentally but also emotionally and socially. They form attachments and relationships, and each child displays a unique personality—a distinctive yet somewhat consistent pattern of thinking, feeling, and behaving.

Early Emotions and Emotion Regulation

Emotional responses communicate our inner states to other people and influence how others

▶ **Focus 8**
Discuss children's emotional development, including emotional expressiveness, emotion regulation, and temperament.

FIGURE 11.19

(*left*) Emotional responses communicate our internal states, and they can influence how others respond to us, providing us with the aid and comfort we need. (*right*) Young infants display a variety of basic emotions.

(joy)　　(sadness)　　(disgust)

(anger)　　(interest)　　(fear)

respond to us (Figure 11.19). Although infants can't describe their feelings, Figure 11.19 illustrates that their facial expressions, vocalizations, and other behaviors provide a window into their emotional life (Izard, 1982). If you've heard a newborn cry (and cry and cry) or watched a newborn's face after it has been fed, then you know that they can experience distress and contentment. By focusing their gaze and staring at objects and people, they also express interest. Around the world, within about 6 months after birth, infants begin to express joy and surprise ("peekaboo . . . I see you!"), and distress branches out into the separate emotions of disgust, anger, fear, and sadness (Lewis, 2000).

Around 18 months of age, infants begin to develop a sense of self, as illustrated by their ability to recognize themselves in a mirror. This growing self-awareness sets the stage for envy, embarrassment, and empathy to emerge. After age 2, as toddlers learn about performance standards and rules that they are supposed to follow, they begin to display pride and shame. Around the same age, they also display guilt—as evidenced by avoiding eye contact, shrugging shoulders, and making facial expressions (Kochanska et al., 1995).

Just as emotional reactions become more diverse with age, so does **emotion regulation,** *the processes by which we evaluate and modify our emotional reactions.* Young infants may suck their thumb or pacifier, turn their head away from something unpleasant, or cling to a caretaker to soothe themselves. To reduce distress, toddlers may seek out a caretaker, cling to a doll or teddy bear, fling unpleasant objects away, and learn to smile, pout, or throw a tantrum to get what they want. Once they acquire language, children can reduce distress by talking to themselves and other people.

As children age, their emotional expressiveness and ability to regulate their emotions become part of their overall *emotional competence,* which in turn influences their social behavior and how well their peers and other people like them. Children who frequently display sadness or who can't control their anger are less likely to be popular, and emotional competence remains important for well-being as children develop (Eisenberg, 2002).

Socialization influences children's emotional development, as parents, teachers, and peers serve as models and reinforce children for some types of emotional responses but not others (Ahn, 2005). But as we will now explore, heredity also contributes to children's basic emotional-behavioral style.

Temperament

From the moment of birth, infants differ from one another in **temperament,** *a biologically based general style of reacting emotionally and behaviorally to the environment.* Some infants are calm and happy; others are irritable and fussy. Some are outgoing and active; others are shy and inactive. Indeed, within any age group—children, adolescents, or adults—people differ in temperament (Fox et al., 2005; McCrae & Costa, 1990).

In a pioneering study, Alexander Thomas and Stella Chess (1977) had parents describe their babies' behavior. They found that most infants could be classified into three groups. "Easy infants" ate and slept on schedule, were playful, and accepted new situations with little fuss. "Difficult infants" were irritable, were fussy eaters and sleepers, and reacted negatively to new situations. "Slow-to-warm-up infants" were the least active, had mildly negative responses to new situations, but slowly adapted over time. Subsequently, the difficult infants were most likely to develop emotional and behavior problems during childhood.

This study was admired but also criticized for relying on parents' reports of their infants' behavior. Other researchers directly observed infants and identified temperamental styles that differed from those described by Thomas and Chess (1977). Moreover, researchers often found that temperament is only weakly to moderately stable during infancy (Carnicero et al., 2000). Some infants maintain a consistent temperament during their first 2 years of life, whereas others change.

Consider shyness, which forms part of a more general temperament style called *behavioral inhibition*. Inhibited infants are quiet and timid; they cry and withdraw when exposed to unfamiliar people, places, objects, and sounds. Uninhibited infants are more sociable, verbal, and spontaneous. Research by Jerome Kagan and coworkers (1988) found that about 20 to 25 percent of infants displayed this inhibited pattern, which remained moderately stable during infancy. They also studied these infants until age $7\frac{1}{2}$. For the vast majority—those who were only mildly to moderately inhibited or uninhibited between the ages of 1 and 2 years—their temperament did not predict how shy or outgoing they would be as children. But for infants who were *highly* uninhibited or inhibited, the findings were different. Highly uninhibited infants tended to become sociable and talkative 7-year-olds, whereas highly inhibited infants developed into quiet, cautious, and shy 7-year-olds (Kagan, 1989).

? What Do You Think?

SHY CHILD, SHY ADULT?

We have just seen that very shy or very outgoing infants tend to retain these traits into early childhood. Do you think that the very shy or outgoing child grows into a shy or outgoing adult? In general, does childhood temperament predict adult behavior? Think about it, then see page 439.

Erikson's Psychosocial Theory

Psychoanalytic psychologist Erik Erikson (1968) believed that personality develops through confronting a series of eight major **psychosocial**

TABLE 11.2 Erikson's Psychosocial Stages

Age (Approximate Years)	Major Psychosocial Crisis
Infancy (first year)	Basic trust vs. basic mistrust
Toddlerhood (1–2)	Autonomy vs. shame and doubt
Early childhood (3–5)	Initiative vs. guilt
Middle childhood (6–12)	Industry vs. inferiority
Adolescence (12–20)	Identity vs. role confusion
Early adulthood (20–40)	Intimacy vs. isolation
Middle adulthood (40–65)	Generativity vs. stagnation
Late adulthood (65+)	Integrity vs. despair

stages, *each of which involves a different "crisis" (i.e., conflict) over how we view ourselves in relation to other people and the world* (Table 11.2). Each crisis is present throughout life but takes on special importance during a particular age period. Four of these crises occur in infancy and childhood:

1. *Basic trust versus basic mistrust:* Depending on how well our needs are met and how much love and attention we receive during the first year of life, we develop a basic trust or basic mistrust of the world.

2. *Autonomy versus shame and doubt:* During the next 2 years, children become ready to exercise their individuality. If parents unduly restrict children or make harsh demands during toilet training, children develop shame and doubt about their abilities and later lack the courage to be independent.

3. *Initiative versus guilt:* From age 3 through age 5, children display great curiosity about the world. If they are allowed freedom to explore and receive answers to their questions, they develop a sense of initiative. If they are held back or punished, they develop guilt about their desires and suppress their curiosity.

4. *Industry versus inferiority:* From age 6 until puberty, the child's life expands into school and peer activities. Children who experience pride and encouragement in mastering tasks develop *industry*—a striving to achieve. Repeated failure and lack of praise for trying leads to a sense of inferiority.

▶ **Focus 9**
Describe Erikson's psychosocial theory.

Although critics argue that Erikson's model lacks detail and question its stage approach, the model captures several major issues that developing children confront. As Erikson proposed and as some research supports, successfully resolving each crisis helps prepare us to meet the next (McAdams & de St. Aubin, 1998). Because each stage of life creates new opportunities, possibilities for change are ever present. Yet like the early chapters of a novel, themes that emerge in childhood help set the stage for the unfolding story of our lives.

Attachment

▶ **Focus 10**
Discuss imprinting, Harlow's attachment research, and attachment in humans.

Imagine a single-file procession of ducklings following you around campus and everywhere you went, as if you were their mother. For this to happen, we would only need to isolate the ducklings after they hatched and then expose them to you at a certain time. If they later encountered their real parents, the ducklings would ignore them and continue to follow you (Hess, 1959).

German ethologist Konrad Lorenz (1937) called this behavior **imprinting,** *a sudden, biologically primed form of attachment* (Figure 11.20). It occurs in some bird species, including ducks and geese, and in a few mammals, such as shrews. Imprinting involves a critical period. In mallard ducklings, the strongest imprinting occurs within 1 day after hatching, and by $2\frac{1}{2}$ days the capacity to imprint is lost (Hess, 1959). Thus, in some species, offspring must be exposed to parents within hours or days after entering the world to attach to them.

Attachment *refers to the strong emotional bond that develops between children and their primary caregivers* (see Figure 11.20). Human infants do not automatically imprint on a caregiver, and there is not an immediate postbirth critical period during which contact is required for infant-caregiver bonding. Instead, the first few years of life seem to be a sensitive period when we can most easily form a secure bond with caregivers that enhances our adjustment later in life (Sroufe, 2002). Although it may be more difficult to form strong first attachments to caregivers later in childhood, it is still possible.

The Attachment Process   For decades, people assumed that infant-caregiver bonding resulted primarily from the mother's role in satisfying the infant's need for nourishment. Harry Harlow (1958) tested this notion by separating infant rhesus monkeys from their biological mothers shortly after birth. Each infant was raised in a cage with two artificial "surrogate mothers." One was a bare-wire cylinder with a feeding bottle attached to its "chest." The other was a wire cylinder covered with soft terry cloth without a feeding bottle.

Faced with this choice, the infant monkeys became attached to the cloth mother. When exposed to frightening situations, the infants ran to the cloth figure and clung tightly to it. They even maintained contact with the cloth mother while feeding from the wire mother's bottle (Figure 11.21). Thus Harlow showed that *contact comfort—*body contact with a comforting object—is more important in fostering attachment than the provision of nourishment.

Around this time, other researchers studied human attachment in African, European, and North American societies. Based on this work, British psychoanalyst John Bowlby (1969) proposed that attachment in infancy develops in three phases:

1. *Indiscriminate attachment behavior:* Newborns cry, vocalize, and smile toward everyone, and these behaviors evoke caregiving from adults.

FIGURE 11.20

(*bottom*) Canadian wildlife sculptor Bill Lishman imprinted Canada geese hatchlings to the sight of his ultralight airplane. Although they have now matured, the ultralight still represents "mother" to the geese, and they follow it in flight. (*right*) In humans, infant-caretaker attachment is more complex and forms over a much longer period.

FIGURE 11.21

Infant monkeys, reared with a cloth-covered surrogate and a bare-wire surrogate from birth, preferred contact with the cloth "mother" even though the wire "mother" satisfied nutritional needs. SOURCE: From Harlow, 1958.

2. *Discriminate attachment behavior:* Around 3 months of age, infants direct their attachment behaviors more toward familiar caregivers than toward strangers.

3. *Specific attachment behavior:* By 7 or 8 months of age, infants develop a meaningful attachment to specific caregivers. The caregiver becomes a secure base from which the infant can crawl about and explore the environment.

As an infant's attachment becomes more focused, two types of anxiety occur. **Stranger anxiety,** *distress over contact with unfamiliar people,* often emerges around age 6 or 7 months and ends by age 18 months. When approached by, touched by, or handed over to a stranger, the infant becomes afraid, cries, and reaches for the caregiver. **Separation anxiety,** *distress over being separated from a primary caregiver,* typically begins a little later, peaks around age 12 to 16 months, and disappears between 2 and 3 years of age. Here the infant becomes anxious and cries when the caregiver is out of sight. Both forms of anxiety show a similar pattern across many cultures (Figure 11.22).

These responses, which coincide with infants' increasing cognitive and physical abilities, may be adaptive reactions shaped through evolution (Bowlby, 1973). At an age when infants master crawling and then learn to walk, fear of strangers and of separation may help prevent them from wandering beyond the sight of caretakers, especially in unfamiliar situations.

Around age 3 to 4, as children's cognitive and verbal skills grow, they develop a better understanding of their attachment relationships. According to Bowlby (1969), a stage of *goal-corrected partnership* emerges, in which children and caregivers can describe their feelings to each other and maintain their relationship whether they are together or apart.

Types of Attachment Infants develop different types of attachments with their caretakers. Psychologist Mary Ainsworth and coworkers (1978) developed the **strange situation,** *a standardized procedure for examining infant attachment.* The infant, typically a 12- to 18-month-old, first plays with toys in the mother's presence. Then a stranger enters the room and interacts with the child. Soon the mother departs, leaving the child with the stranger. Later the stranger departs, and the child is alone. Finally, the mother returns. The infant's behavior is observed throughout this procedure.

In the mother's presence, "securely attached" infants explore the playroom and react positively to the stranger (Ainsworth et al., 1978). They are distressed when the mother leaves and happily greet her when she returns. In contrast, there are two types of "insecurely attached" infants. "Anxious-resistant" infants are fearful when the mother is present, demand her attention, and are distressed when she leaves. They are not soothed when she returns and may angrily resist her attempts at contact.

▶ **Focus 11**
Describe types of attachment, how they are measured, and how attachment deprivation affects development.

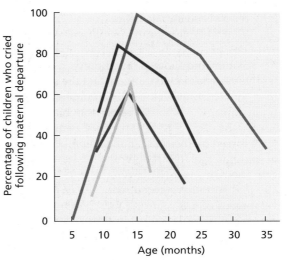

FIGURE 11.22

Separation anxiety across cultures. The rise and fall of separation anxiety in infancy shows a similar pattern across cultures. SOURCE: Based on Kagan et al., 1978.

"Anxious-avoidant" infants show few signs of attachment, seldom cry when the mother leaves, and don't seek contact when she returns.

Across most cultures studied, about one half to three quarters of infants are securely attached. Mothers who are more sensitive to their babies' needs at home tend to have infants who are more securely attached in the strange situation (Posada et al., 2002). Moreover, whether raised by their biological parents or by adoptive parents, securely attached infants seem to be better adjusted socially during childhood. Establishing a secure attachment early in life also may help foster a capacity for compassion and altruism that carries forward into adulthood (Mikulincer & Shaver, 2005). This lends credence to Erikson's view that entering a stable, trusting relationship with a caregiver is an important component of early social development.

Attachment Deprivation

If infants and young children are deprived of a stable attachment with a caregiver, how do they fare in the long run? Harry Harlow studied this issue under controlled conditions. After rearing "isolate" monkeys either alone or with artificial surrogate mothers, Harlow returned them to the monkey colony at 6 months of age. Exposed to other monkeys, the isolates were indifferent, terrified, or aggressive. When they became adults, some female isolates were artificially inseminated and gave birth, and they were highly abusive toward their firstborns (Harlow & Suomi, 1970). The conclusion: Being raised without a secure attachment to a real, interactive caregiver produced long-term social impairment.

What of isolate human children? Victor, the Wild Boy of Aveyron, was severely impaired after his isolation and showed only limited recovery after intensive remedial training. Did the lack of human contact stunt Victor's development, or was it brain damage, possibly present from birth?

In the 1960s, twin boys in Czechoslovakia were forced by their father and stepmother to live in extreme isolation beginning at 18 months of age. The twins were discovered at age 7, emotionally and socially retarded, with the cognitive development of a 3-year-old and speech skills of a 2-year-old. Jarmila Koluchova (1972, 1991) studied the boys for over 20 years and found that they went on to become happy, sociable, and firmly attached to their foster family. Their IQs increased to normal levels, and they became well-adjusted adolescents and young adults.

Why the difference? Unlike Victor, the twins had each other's company, but in other cases even

Find out more about infant attachment by watching the "Attachment Theory" video in Chapter 11 of your CD.

FIGURE 11.23

In the 1980s, about 100,000 Romanian infants and children were warehoused in filthy, disease-ridden orphanages where they were often left unattended for days and had no opportunity to bond with caretakers. Studies of Romanian infants who were adopted into American homes before age 2 showed that about a third formed secure attachments, in contrast to the more typical 60 percent figure found in attachment studies. Still, that so many formed secure attachments is a testament to their resilience in bouncing back from extreme adversity.

"lone" isolate children have recovered. Perhaps most important, the twins' isolation ended and their rehabilitation began at a younger age, when the brain's neural plasticity is greater. They were 7; Victor was about 12.

In the 1980s, 100,000 Romanian infants and children were warehoused in orphanages under the most neglectful and squalid conditions imaginable (Figure 11.23). Despite this horrific neglect, after being adopted about a third of the Romanian infants studied had become securely attached to their adoptive parents (Wilson, 2003). Examining less extreme circumstances, Barbara Tizard and Jill Hodges (1978) studied children raised in orphanages where the nurses were attentive but high staff turnover prevented the children from forming a stable bond with any caretaker. Those adopted between ages 2 and 8 years typically formed healthy attachments with their adoptive parents, though in adolescence many had difficulty forming peer relationships because they were viewed as needing "too much attention" (Hodges & Tizard, 1989). Still, the vast majority of adopted children are normally adjusted and differ little from children raised by their biological parents (Miller et al., 2000).

In sum, infancy appears to be a sensitive, though not critical, period during which an initial attachment to caregivers forms most easily and facilitates subsequent development. Prolonged attachment deprivation creates developmental risks, but when deprived children are placed into a nurturing environment at a young enough age, many if not most become attached to their caretakers and grow into well-adjusted adults.

The Day-Care Controversy

When you were a young child, did someone other than a parent regularly care for you during the day? Over half of American preschoolers fall into this category (Brooks-Gunn et al., 2002). High-quality day care provides a stimulating environment with well-trained caretakers who are responsive to children's needs, few children per caretaker, and low staff turnover, whereas poor day care does not (Marshall, 2004). In either case, many parents worry about how day care will affect their child's development. In the most comprehensive research project to date, psychologists working with the National Institute of Child Health and Human Development (NICHD) Early Child Care Research Network have studied approximately 1,400 American children from birth through third grade. Here are some major findings:

- *Attachment:* Overall, as measured by the strange-situation procedure, high-quality day care did not seem to disrupt infants' or very young children's attachment to their parents, even when they attended for many hours a week. When several negative factors combined—the day care was poor, the child spent many hours there, and parents were not sensitive to the child at home—the risk of insecure attachment increased (NICHD, 2001b).

- *Social behavior:* Compared to children with less day-care experience, by age 3, children with more experience exhibited better social skills when interacting with peers at day care, although this did not generalize to play situations with friends outside of day care (NICHD, 2001a). By age $4\frac{1}{2}$, however, children who averaged 30 or more hours a week in day care displayed more behavior problems (e.g., arguing) than children who spent less than 10 hours a week in child care (NICHD, 2002). Fortunately, this seems to have dissipated by the end of the third grade; children's social behavior problems were no longer associated with how much time they had spent in day care (Vandell et al., 2005).

- *Cognitive performance:* Regardless of their sex or ethnicity or their parents' socioeconomic status or parenting quality, $4\frac{1}{2}$-year-olds who spent a lot of time in day-care centers performed better on several cognitive and linguistic tasks than did peers who spent less time in day-care centers (NICHD, 2002). Exposure to high quality day care was associated with even better cognitive performance. These benefits seemed to persist at least through third grade (Vandell, 2005).

Concerns about disrupted parent-child relations also surface when parents divorce. Our "Applying Psychological Science" feature examines this societally important issue.

▶ **Focus 12**
How do day care, divorce, and remarriage affect children's development?

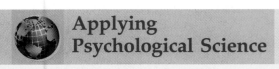
Applying Psychological Science — Understanding How Divorce and Remarriage Affect Children

Divorce creates a stressful life transition for parents and their children. Because most divorced parents remarry, they and their children also experience a second major transition: becoming part of a stepfamily.

Decades ago, there was little scientific information on children of divorce and remarriage, but research now provides us with a better understanding of how these major transitions affect children. With this knowledge, local governments in over 35 American states require soon-to-be-divorced parents to take classes on helping children cope with divorce.

HOW DOES DIVORCE AFFECT CHILDREN?

Many children report that parental divorce is one of the most painful experiences of their lives. In the short term, they may experience anxiety, fear, anger, confusion, depression, and behavior problems at school.

In the long term, children of divorce remain at greater risk for various difficulties, including academic problems, troubled relationships with family members and peers, low self-esteem, and depression (Dawson-McClure et al., 2004). When they become adolescents, children of divorced parents are more likely to drop out of school, be unemployed, use drugs, and become unmarried teen parents. In adulthood, they experience more marital conflict and have a higher divorce rate (Teachman, 2002).

Most of these problems, however, tend to cluster together into an overall pattern of maladjustment. Leading divorce researcher E. Mavis Hetherington and coworkers (1998) estimate that about 20 to 25 percent of children in divorced families, versus 10 percent of children in nondivorced families,

Continued

experience this cluster of problems. This is a significantly elevated risk for maladjustment, but still, most children of divorced parents grow up to be normally adjusted adults.

SHOULD WE STAY TOGETHER FOR THE SAKE OF THE CHILD?

Many parents considering divorce wonder whether they should stay together for the child's sake. Reviewing 92 studies, Paul Amato and Bruce Keith (1991) found that when divorce ends a highly conflicted marriage, children's psychological adjustment typically benefits in the long run. Children living with married but contentious parents have poorer school achievement, lower self-esteem, and more behavior problems than children from divorced families. But many unhappy marriages do not involve extensive conflict, and in those cases divorce usually puts children at greater risk for maladjustment (Booth & Amato, 2001).

HOW CAN DIVORCED PARENTS HELP THEIR CHILDREN?

The major factor affecting a child's adjustment to divorce is the quality of life within the postdivorce family. The period during and after divorce can intensify parents' anger and conflicts. By fighting over their children or trying to enlist them in loyalty battles, parents can damage their children's well-being. In contrast, cooperative and amicable parental behaviors can cushion the negative effects of divorce during this rocky transition (Hetherington & Stanley-Hagan, 2002). By remaining emotionally close to his or her children, the parent who does not have custody (usually the father) can help them adjust to living with the custodial parent (Marsiglio et al., 2000). For children, the lasting problems of divorce often lie in lingering parental conflicts, economic hardships that parents (especially mothers) often experience after divorce, and other factors that destabilize the parents' own lives.

HOW DO CHILDREN RESPOND TO REMARRIAGE AND STEPFAMILIES?

Forming a stepfamily temporarily disrupts children's relationships with the remarried custodial parent and typically increases children's short-term problem behaviors. In turn, such behavior can increase the risk of marital conflict between the stepparents (Jenkins et al., 2005). It can take several years for parents and children to adjust to their new roles within the stepfamily. In general, young adolescents seem to have the most difficulty coping with the transition into a stepfamily.

In remarriages, children may be hostile and reject the stepparent, especially when the stepparent attempts to be a strong disciplinarian. Children usually adjust better to living in a stepfamily when the custodial parent is warm but firm and has primary responsibility for discipline, and when the stepparent is warm but supports the custodial parent's authority (Bray & Berger, 1993).

▶ **Focus 13**
Identify parenting styles and their associated child outcomes. How do parenting and children's heredity interact?

Styles of Parenting

Beyond divorce and remarriage, how do different child-rearing practices affect children's development? After studying how parents interacted with their preschool children, Diana Baumrind (1967) identified two key dimensions of parental behavior. The first is *warmth versus hostility.* Warm parents communicate love and caring for the child. Hostile parents express rejection and behave as if they do not care about the child. The second dimension is *restrictiveness versus permissiveness.* Parents differ in the extent to which they make and enforce rules. As Figure 11.24 shows, combining these dimensions yields four parenting styles that are associated with different patterns of child development (Linver et al., 2002).

Authoritative parents *are controlling but warm.* They establish clear rules, consistently enforce them, and reward children's compliance with warmth and affection. They communicate high expectations, caring, and support. This style is associated with the most positive childhood outcomes. Children with authoritative parents tend to have higher self-esteem, are higher achievers in school, and have fewer conduct problems.

Authoritarian parents *also exert control but do so within a cold, unresponsive, or rejecting relationship.* Their children tend to have lower self-esteem, be less popular with peers, and perform more poorly in school than children with authoritative parents.

Indulgent parents *have warm, caring relationships with their children but do not provide the guidance and discipline that help children learn responsibility*

	Warmth/acceptance	Hostility/rejection
Restrictive	**Authoritative** — Demanding, but caring; good child-parent communication	**Authoritarian** — Assertion of parental power without warmth
Permissive	**Indulgent** — Warm toward child, but lax in setting limits	**Neglecting** — Indifferent and uninvolved with child

FIGURE 11.24

Four styles of child rearing. Combining two basic dimensions of parental behavior (warmth-hostility and restrictiveness-permissiveness) yields four different styles of child rearing. Source: Adapted from Maccoby & Martin, 1983.

and concern for others. Their children tend to be more immature and self-centered.

Neglectful parents *provide neither warmth nor rules nor guidance.* Their children are most likely to be insecurely attached, to have low achievement motivation and disturbed peer relationships, and to be impulsive and aggressive. Neglectful parenting is associated with the most negative developmental outcomes.

Do these findings extend to adolescence? Laurence Steinberg and coworkers (1994) studied several thousand California and Wisconsin high school students. They found that overall, authoritative parenting and neglectful parenting were, respectively, associated with the most positive and negative developmental outcomes. Many of the findings held true across African American, Asian American, Caucasian American, and Hispanic American students (Lamborn et al., 1991).

Parenting-Heredity Interactions

Keep in mind that parent-child influences are bidirectional, illustrating once again the interaction of biology and environment in shaping behavior. For example, children whose biologically based temperament is irritable tend to elicit harsher and less warm parenting behaviors, which in turn can further promote the child's difficult behavior. Also realize that parents do not mold their children's personality and behavior like lumps of clay. Parenting makes a difference, but the way children turn out also depends on their heredity, peer and community influences, other experiences, and interactions among these factors (Rose et al., 2003).

Antisocial behavior provides another example of how the family environment and heredity interact. Children of a highly antisocial parent (i.e., a parent with high aggression, irritability, and a history of illegal activities) are at increased genetic risk for displaying antisocial behavior (e.g., lying, fighting, having a hot temper). This genetic risk is present, of course, even if the highly antisocial parent (usually the father) is completely absent from the home and the child is raised by the other parent. However, as Sara Jaffee and coworkers (2003) found, when high-antisocial fathers live at home and are involved in caretaking, this further increases children's antisocial behavior and risk of developing a conduct disorder (Figure 11.25). In contrast, when low-antisocial fathers live at home and participate in caretaking, this tends to decrease children's antisocial behavior. Jaffee and coworkers concluded that children of high-antisocial fathers who are involved in caretaking receive "a 'double

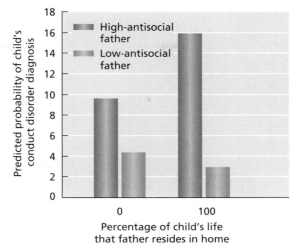

FIGURE 11.25

Father's presence and children's risk for conduct disorder. In one study, among children who had a high-antisocial father, the risk of developing a conduct disorder (e.g., aggression toward people and animals, property destruction, deceit, or theft) increased if the father lived at home with the mother and child. If the father was low-antisocial, living at home slightly reduced the risk of developing a conduct disorder. SOURCE: Adapted from Jaffee et al., 2003.

whammy' of genetic and environmental risk for conduct problems" (p. 109).

Gender Identity and Socialization

Parenting also influences children's development in other ways, such as helping children develop a **gender identity,** *a sense of "femaleness" or "maleness" that becomes a central aspect of one's personal identity.* Most children develop a basic gender identity between the ages of 2 and 3 and can label themselves (and others) as being either a boy or a girl, but their understanding of gender is still fragile. They may believe that a boy wearing a dress is a girl and that a girl can grow up to become a man. **Gender constancy,** *which is the understanding that being male or female is a permanent part of a person,* develops around age 6 to 7 (Szkrybalo & Ruble, 1999).

As gender identity develops, children also acquire *sex-role stereotypes,* which are beliefs about the characteristics and behaviors that are appropriate for boys and girls to possess. Every group, including family and cultural groups, has norms for expected and accepted gender behavior. Parents, siblings, friends, the mass media, and other socializing agents convey these norms to us as we grow up. Ultimately, as we internalize these norms, they become part of our identity (Martin & Ruble, 2004).

Sex-typing *involves treating others differently based on whether they are female or male.* From infancy onward, girls and boys are viewed and treated differently. Fathers use more physical and verbal

▶ **Focus 14**
How does socialization influence children's beliefs about gender?

 For an example of how children grasp that being male or female is a constant, unchanging state, watch the "Gender Identity Development" video in Chapter 11 of your CD.

FIGURE 11.26

Do parents provide more scientific explanations to sons than daughters? Fathers and mothers provided more explanations to their 1- to 8-year-old sons than to their daughters while engaged with science exhibits at a children's museum. Similar results were obtained regardless of the children's age. SOURCE: Adapted from Crowley et al., 2001.

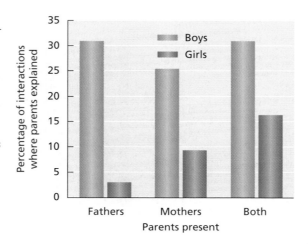

and television and movie characters (Bandura, 1965). In ways obvious and subtle, others approve of us and reinforce our behavior when we meet their expectations and disapprove of us when we don't. In turn, this influences the way children think about gender. Some children as young as 2 to 3 years of age display sex-role stereotypes in their ability to identify objects (such as hammers and brooms) and behaviors as "belonging with" one gender or the other (Campbell et al., 2004). By age 7 or 8, stereotyped thinking is firmly in place; children believe that boys and girls possess different personality traits and should hold different occupations as adults.

As children enter junior high school, they often display more flexible thinking about gender. Some come to believe that traditionally masculine and feminine traits can be blended within a single person—what is called an *androgynous gender identity*—as when a person is both assertive and compassionate. During junior high and high school, some adolescents maintain this view, but overall, gender stereotypes seem to become a little more rigid at this age, so that by early adulthood most people continue to adhere to relatively traditional beliefs (Alfieri et al., 1996).

prohibition with their 12-month-old sons than with their daughters, and they steer their sons away from activities that are considered stereotypically feminine (Snow et al., 1983). Even when their sons and daughters display equal interest and aptitude in science, fathers and mothers are more likely to believe that sons have the greater interest and will find science easier (Tenenbaum & Leaper, 2003). Indeed, as Figure 11.26 shows, when parents interact with their 1- to 8-year-olds at science exhibits in a children's museum, they are much more likely to explain the exhibits to their sons than to their daughters—even though the children rarely ask for such explanations (Crowley et al., 2001).

Sex-role stereotypes are also transmitted through observational learning and operant conditioning (Figure 11.27). Children observe and often attempt to emulate parents, other adults, peers,

MORAL DEVELOPMENT

All societies attempt to teach their members right from wrong. How does children's moral thinking change as they grow older?

Moral Thinking

Drawing on Piaget's cognitive stage model, Lawrence Kohlberg (1963, 1984) developed an influential theory of moral reasoning. He presented children, adolescents, and adults with hypothetical moral dilemmas such as the following:

> Heinz's wife was dying from cancer. There was a rare drug that might save her, but the druggist who made the drug for $200 would not sell it for less than $2,000. Heinz tried hard, but he could only raise $1,000. The druggist refused to give Heinz the drug for that price even though Heinz promised to pay the rest later. So Heinz broke into the store to steal the drug. What do you think? Should Heinz have stolen the drug? Why or why not?

Kohlberg was interested not in whether people agreed or disagreed with Heinz's behavior but rather in the *reasons for their judgment*. He analyzed responses to various moral dilemmas and identified three main levels of moral reasoning, with two substages within each level (Table 11.3).

▶ **Focus 15**
Describe Kohlberg's model of moral thinking and factors that influence the development of moral behavior.

FIGURE 11.27

In subtle and not so subtle ways, cultures socialize most female and male children in gender-stereotypic ways.

TABLE 11.3   Kohlberg's Stages of Moral Reasoning

Level of Moral Reasoning	Basis for Judging What Is Moral
Level 1: Preconventional Morality	**Actual or anticipated punishments or rewards, rather than internalized values**
Stage 1: Punishment-obedience orientation	Obeying rules and avoiding punishment
Stage 2: Instrumental-hedonistic orientation	Self-interest and gaining rewards
Level 2: Conventional Morality	**Conformity to the expectations of social groups; person adopts other people's values**
Stage 3: Good-child orientation	Gaining approval and maintaining good relationships with others
Stage 4: Law-and-order orientation	Doing one's duty, showing respect for authority, and maintaining social order
Level 3: Postconventional Morality	**Moral principles that have been internalized as part of one's belief and value system**
Stage 5: Social-contract orientation	General principles agreed on by society that foster community welfare and individual rights; recognition that society can decide to modify laws that lose their social utility
Stage 6: Universal ethical principles	Abstract ethical principles based on justice and equality; following one's conscience

Source: Adapted from Kohlberg, 1984.

Preconventional moral reasoning *is based on anticipated punishments or rewards.* Consider reasons given for stealing the drug. In stage 1, children focus on punishment: "Heinz should steal the drug because if he lets his wife die he'll get into trouble." In stage 2, morality is judged by anticipated rewards and doing what is in the person's own interest: "Heinz should steal the drug because that way he'll still have his wife with him."

Conventional moral reasoning *is based on conformity to social expectations, laws, and duties.* In stage 3, conformity stems from the desire to gain people's approval: "People will think that Heinz is bad if he doesn't steal the drug to save his wife." In stage 4, children believe that laws and duties must be obeyed simply because rules are meant to be followed. Thus: "Heinz should steal the drug because it's his duty to take care of his wife."

Postconventional moral reasoning *is based on well-thought-out, general moral principles.* Stage 5 involves recognizing the importance of societal laws but also taking individual rights into account: "Stealing breaks the law, but what Heinz did was reasonable because he saved a life." In stage 6, morality is based on abstract, ethical principles of justice that are viewed as universal: "Saving life comes before financial gain, even if the person is a stranger."

Kohlberg believed that progress in moral reasoning depends on cognitive maturation and the opportunity to confront moral issues, particularly when such issues can be discussed with someone who is at a higher stage of development.

Culture, Gender, and Moral Reasoning

From North, Central, and South America to Africa, Asia, Europe, and India, studies of moral reasoning indicate that, overall:

- from childhood through adolescence, moral reasoning changes from preconventional to conventional levels;

- in adolescence and even in adulthood, postconventional reasoning is relatively uncommon;

- a person's moral judgments do not always reflect the same level or stage within levels (Eckensberger & Zimba, 1997).

Critics claim that Kohlberg's theory has a Western cultural bias. Fairness and justice are Kohlberg's postconventional ideals, but in many cultures the highest moral values focus on principles that do not fit easily into Kohlberg's model, such as respect for all animal life, collective harmony, and respect for the elderly (Iwasa, 2001).

Carol Gilligan (1982) argues that Kohlberg's emphasis on justice also reflects a male bias. She claims that highly moral women place greater value than men do on caring and responsibility for others' welfare. Overall, however, evidence of gender bias is mixed. Women use justice reasoning when the situation calls for it, and men use reasoning based on caring and relationships when appropriate. Nevertheless, Gilligan's analysis reinforces the key point that high-level moral reasoning can be based on values other than justice (Gump et al., 2000).

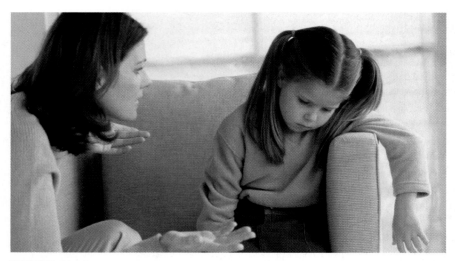

FIGURE 11.28

By firmly but not harshly signaling that this child's behavior was wrong and by explaining why it was wrong, this parent can help her child internalize moral values. The fact that the child experiences a negative emotion may be important to the internalization process.

Moral Behavior and Conscience

Moral reasoning doesn't necessarily translate into moral behavior. B. F. Skinner (1971) proposed that we learn which behaviors are "good" and "bad" through their association with reinforcement and punishment. Other researchers propose that for children to conform to their culture's moral standards, they must understand that there are moral rules, be able to control their impulses to engage in forbidden behavior, and experience some negative emotion when they violate these rules (Figure 11.28).

By the age of 2, children come to understand that there are rules for behavior, and their emotional expressions suggest that they experience guilt when they break a known rule. Children's ability to stop themselves from engaging in forbidden behavior develops slowly, but even toddlers can do so at times. This internal regulatory mechanism, often referred to as *conscience,* tends to restrain individuals from acting in destructive or antisocial ways when they are not being monitored by parents or other adults (Kochanska et al., 2005).

Sigmund Freud (1935) believed that children develop a conscience by identifying with their parents. Few developmentalists believe in Freud's theory of how identification occurs (which we will discuss in Chapter 12), but they acknowledge that internalizing the societal values transmitted by parents or other caretakers provides the basis of a moral conscience. Children are most likely to internalize parents' values when they have a positive relationship with them, when parents establish clear rules and provide explanations that facilitate children's awareness of parental values, and when discipline is firm but not harsh (Laible & Thompson, 2000).

Children's temperament also enters into the picture. Fearful, inhibited children tend to internalize parental values more easily and at an earlier age than less fearful children, particularly when their parents provide gentle discipline. For relatively fearless, uninhibited children, however, whether discipline is gentle or harsh is less important. A secure attachment with warm parents, rather than fear of punishment, appears to motivate fearless children to internalize their parents' standards. Thus the development of moral behavior is linked not only to children's moral thinking but also to their emotional development, attachment, and temperament (Kochanska et al., 2004).

IN REVIEW

- Newborns distinguish between different visual patterns, sounds, odors, and tastes. They display perceptual preferences, learn through classical and operant conditioning, and have a primitive capacity for imitation.

- Biology (e.g., the cephalocaudal and proximodistal principles) and environment (e.g., deprivation and enrichment) jointly steer children's physical and psychological development.

- According to Piaget, cognitive development depends on processes of assimilation and accommodation and occurs in four stages: sensorimotor, preoperational, concrete operational, and formal operational.

- Cognitive development is more complex and variable than Piaget believed. Vygotsky emphasized the sociocultural context of cognitive development. Each child has a zone of proximal development, reflecting the difference between what a child can do independently and what the child can do with assistance from others.

- Information-processing capacities improve with age. Older children search for information more systematically, process it more quickly, and display better memory.

- Children display more types and greater complexity of emotions as they age. The strategies they use to regulate their emotions also become more varied.

- Temperament reflects a biologically based pattern of reacting emotionally and behaviorally to the environment. Extreme temperamental styles in infancy and childhood can predict some aspects of functioning years later.

- Erikson believed that personality development proceeds through eight major psychosocial stages. Each stage involves a major crisis, and how we resolve it affects our ability to meet the challenges of the next stage.

- Infant-caretaker attachment develops in three phases, and infants experience periods of stranger and separation anxiety. Secure attachment is associated with better developmental outcomes than is insecure attachment. For most children, day care does not disrupt attachment. Divorce typically disrupts children's short-term psychological adjustment; for some, it is associated with a long-term pattern of maladjustment.

- Parenting styles vary along dimensions of warmth-hostility and restrictiveness-permissiveness. The children of authoritative parents generally display the best developmental outcomes. Gender identity begins to form early in childhood, and socialization influences children's acquisition of sex-role stereotypes.

- Kohlberg proposed that moral reasoning proceeds through preconventional, conventional, and postconventional levels. The development of moral behavior is linked to children's cognitive, emotional, and social development.

ADOLESCENCE

We call it Sunrise Dance. It's the biggest ceremony of the White Mountain Apache—when a girl passes from childhood to womanhood. . . . On Friday evening Godmother dressed me . . . Saturday is like an endurance test. Men begin prayer chants at dawn. Godmother tells me to dance. . . . When the time comes for running, I go fast around a sacred cane. . . . Next, my father pours candies and corn kernels over me to protect me from famine. My Godfather directs my dancing on Sunday. . . . Godfather paints me. . . . On Monday there is more visiting and blessing. (Quintero, 1980, pp. 262–271)

In some cultures, ceremonies like the Sunrise Dance represent *rites of passage* that mark a transition from childhood into adulthood status (Figure 11.29). But what of **adolescence,** *the period of development and gradual transition between childhood and adulthood?* Alice Schlegel and Herbert Barry (1991) found that among almost 200 nonindustrial societies worldwide, nearly all recognize some type of transition period between childhood and adulthood. Yet in many societies this period is brief and is not marked by a special term analogous to *adolescence.*

As we know it, the lengthy period called *adolescence* is largely an invention of 18th- to 20th-century Western culture (Valsiner & Lawrence, 1997). In preindustrial times, biological maturity was a major criterion for adult status. In many cultures, for example, girls were expected to marry once they became capable of bearing children. But as the Industrial Revolution brought new technology and a need for more schooling, recognition of adult status was delayed and the long transition period of adolescence evolved.

Adolescence differs from **puberty,** *a period of rapid maturation in which the person becomes capable of sexual reproduction.* These developmental periods

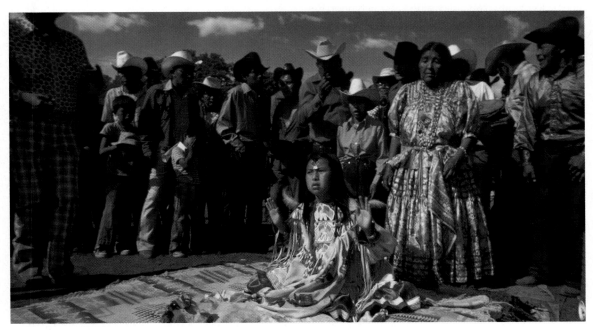

FIGURE 11.29

A White Mountain Apache girl participates in the Sunrise Dance, a four-day ceremony that initiates her into womanhood.

▶ Focus 16
How does adolescence differ
from puberty? Describe psychological consequences of early
maturation, and adolescents'
brain development.

overlap, but puberty is a biologically defined period, whereas adolescence is a broader social construction (Spear, 2000). Puberty is an important
aspect of adolescence, but adolescence is also ushered in and out by changes in thinking, interests,
social circumstances, and parental and societal
expectations. In research studies, 12- to 18-year-
olds—give or take a year at each end—are typically
considered to be adolescents, but it's essential to
keep in mind that the transition into, through, and
out of adolescence is gradual (Arnett, 2001).

PHYSICAL DEVELOPMENT

During puberty, marked bodily changes occur
when the brain's hypothalamus signals the pituitary gland to increase its hormonal secretions.
Pituitary hormones stimulate other glands, speeding up maturation of the *primary sex characteristics*
(the sex organs involved in reproduction). Hormonal changes also produce *secondary sex characteristics* (nonreproductive physical features, such
as breasts in girls and facial hair in boys).

The pubertal landmark in girls is *menarche,*
the first menstrual flow. For boys, it is the production of sperm and the first ejaculation. In North
America and Europe, these events occur most often around age 11 to 13 for girls and 12 to 14 for
boys (Kaltiala-Heino et al., 2003). Considerable
variation, however, occurs among people and
across cultures. In parts of New Guinea, for example, 50 percent of girls have their first menstrual
period after they turn 17 (Roche, 1979).

The physical changes of puberty have psychological consequences. For one thing, hormones that
steer puberty also can affect mood and behavior. Reactions to puberty are also influenced by whether it
occurs early or late. Overall, early maturation tends
to be associated with fewer negative outcomes for
boys than for girls. Early-maturing boys are at somewhat heightened risk for engaging in delinquent behavior and using drugs (Kaltiala-Heino et al., 2003).
However, the physical strength and size that they
acquire often contribute to a positive body image,
success in athletics, and popularity among peers.

In contrast, although some early-maturing
girls welcome their changed appearance, the
weight gain that comes with puberty results in a
negative body image for others. Moreover, early
maturation often exposes girls to greater social
and sexual pressures from boys. Thus, compared
to girls who mature later, early-maturing girls
typically feel more self-conscious about their
bodies and are more likely to eventually develop
eating disorders, problems in school, major
depression, and anxiety (Graber et al., 2004).

▶ Focus 17
Discuss the major cognitive
changes that occur during
adolescence.

The Adolescent Brain

Compared to infancy and early childhood, overall
brain growth slows from late childhood to adolescence (Sowell et al., 2001). Still, "the adolescent
brain is a brain in flux," establishing new neural
connections while at the same time pruning away
and losing a massive number of the overabundant
synaptic connections formed during earlier years
of explosive brain growth (Spear, 2000, p. 438).
This streamlining of neural networks permits
more efficient communication between brain regions and may help explain why, when adolescents perform tasks, neural activity within brain
regions is more highly focused than it was during
childhood.

Neural restructuring is especially prominent
in the prefrontal cortex and the limbic system, regions that play a key role in planning and coordinating behaviors that satisfy motivational goals
and emotional urges. Moreover, restructuring
within the prefrontal cortex includes an upsurge
in activity of dopamine, a neurotransmitter involved in regulating emotional arousal, pleasure
and reward, and learning (Spear, 2000). Psychologists are actively exploring how these brain
changes provide a biological basis for the increase
in drug use, risk taking, sensation seeking, and
aggression displayed by many adolescents.

COGNITIVE DEVELOPMENT

Supported by continuing brain maturation and
learning experiences, cognitive changes during adolescence can be as dramatic as physical ones. Compared to children, teens can think more abstractly,
process information more effectively, and reflect
more deeply on their own and others' thoughts.

Abstract Reasoning and Information Processing

Abstract reasoning abilities increase substantially
during adolescence. Adolescents can more easily
contemplate hypothetical issues, ranging from
scientific problems to questions about social justice and the meaning of life (Figure 11.30a). They
reason more flexibly than children and use both
the deductive and inductive problem-solving
methods described in Chapter 8. Recall that in
Piaget's (1970) view, this signifies that adolescents
have moved beyond concrete operational thinking and entered a new stage of cognitive development: formal operational thinking.

Consider the pendulum problem in Figure
11.30b. Which variable(s)—length of string, weight
of object, how hard it is pushed, and release point

(a)

Adjustable string

Variable release point

Pendulum arc

Weights

(b)

FIGURE 11.30

Adolescent thinking and the pendulum problem. (a) When adolescents attain formal operational thought, they can use deductive reasoning to solve scientific problems systematically. (b) The materials for the pendulum problem used by Inhelder and Piaget include an adjustable string and a set of weights. The problem is to determine which factors influence how long it takes the pendulum to move through its arc. String length is the only relevant factor: The shorter the string, the less time it takes the pendulum to swing back and forth. SOURCE: Adapted from Inhelder & Piaget, 1958.

(height in the arc)—influence(s) how quickly the pendulum oscillates? This problem is best solved by forming and testing an organized set of deductive hypotheses (e.g., "*If* string length is a factor, *then* the swing time with a short versus long string should differ"). Concrete operational children struggle with this task (Inhelder & Piaget, 1958). For example, when they adjust the string length they often adjust the weight as well, making it impossible to draw a conclusion about either variable. In contrast, adolescents think more systematically and manipulate one variable at a time while holding the others constant.

From an information-processing view, continued improvements in working memory and other basic mental capacities help abstract thinking to develop and foster better performance across a wide range of tasks. Although advancing at a slower rate than during childhood, the speed with which adolescents process information quickens, their working memory becomes more efficient, and they become better able to ignore distracting information, suppress irrelevant responses, and keep their focus on the task at hand. In one recent study, information-processing speed and visuospatial working-memory abilities began to approach adultlike levels by middle adolescence, and the ability to suppress task-irrelevant responses did so by late adolescence (Luna et al., 2004).

Social Thinking

Does Figure 11.31 strike a familiar chord? Teenagers can spend a lot of time thinking about themselves and their social circumstances. Such thinking, argues David Elkind (1967), often reflects **adolescent egocentrism,** *a self-absorbed and distorted*

FIGURE 11.31

According to David Elkind (1967), this type of thinking reflects adolescent egocentrism. SOURCE: Copyright © Zits Partnership. Reprinted with special permission of King Features Syndicate.

ZITS By Jerry Scott and Jim Borgman

view of one's uniqueness and importance. Elkind proposes that adolescent egocentrism has two main parts. First, adolescents often overestimate the uniqueness of their feelings and experiences, which Elkind calls the *personal fable.* Examples would be, "My parents can't possibly understand how I really feel" and "Nobody's ever felt love as deeply as ours." Second, many adolescents feel that they are always "on stage" and that "everybody's going to notice" how they look and what they do. Elkind calls this oversensitivity to social evaluation the *imaginary audience.*

Adolescents who think more egocentrically are somewhat more likely to engage in risky behaviors, due perhaps in part to a sense of invulnerability (Greene et al., 2000). At the same time, it's not clear that this self-consciousness truly reflects a thinking bias. Some theorists view teens' greater self-reflection as a natural outgrowth of the search for individuality and of realistic social consequences that teens face (Bell & Bromnick, 2003). They also suggest that young adults, overall, can be just as self-absorbed as adolescents.

SOCIAL-EMOTIONAL AND PERSONALITY DEVELOPMENT

G. Stanley Hall (1904), the first psychologist to study adolescence, viewed it as a time of "storm and stress." Indeed, as they cross the bridge between childhood and adulthood, adolescents may grapple with many difficult issues. Yet, although some experience adolescence as a period of conflict, others find it to be a positive period of life. Thus, Jeffrey Arnett proposes a modified view of storm and stress, noting that "not all adolescents experience storm and stress, but storm and stress is more likely during adolescence than at other ages" (1999, p. 317).

The Search for Identity

▶ Focus 18
Discuss adolescents' search for identity and the general nature of their relationships with parents and peers.

"Who am I?" "What do I believe in?" Erik Erikson (1968) proposed that such questions reflect the pivotal crisis of adolescent personality development: *identity versus role confusion* (see Table 11.2). Erikson believed that an adolescent's "identity crisis" (a term he coined) can be resolved positively, leading to a stable sense of identity, or it can end negatively, leading to confusion over one's identity and values.

Building on Erikson's work, James Marcia (1966, 2002) studied adolescents' and young adults' search for identity. Marcia classified the "identity status" of each person as follows:

- *Identity diffusion:* These teens and adults had not yet gone through an identity crisis. They seemed unconcerned or even cynical about identity issues and were not committed to a coherent set of values.

- *Foreclosure:* These individuals had not yet gone through an identity crisis either but for a different reason: They committed to an identity and set of values before experiencing a crisis. For example, some automatically adopted peer-group or parental values without giving these values much thought.

- *Moratorium:* These people wanted to establish a clear identity, were currently experiencing a crisis, but had not yet resolved it.

- *Identity achievement:* These individuals had gone through an identity crisis, successfully resolved it, and emerged with a coherent set of values.

Marcia found that most young adolescents are in identity diffusion or foreclosure; they have not experienced an identity crisis. But during the teen years, people typically begin to think more deeply about who they are, or they reconsider values they have adopted previously. This often leads to an identity crisis, and over half successfully resolve it by early adulthood.

Identity, of course, is not a simple concept, and our sense of identity has multiple components (Camilleri & Malewska-Peyre, 1997). These include (1) our gender, ethnicity, and other attributes by which we define ourselves as members of social groups ("daughter," "student," "athlete"); (2) how we view our personal characteristics ("shy," "friendly"); and (3) our goals and values pertaining to areas we view as important, such as family and peer relations, career, and so forth. Typically, we achieve a stable identity regarding some components before others, and changing situations may trigger new crises and cause us to reevaluate prior goals and values.

Culture plays a key role in identity formation, one that goes beyond the simple idea that we view ourselves as belonging to certain cultural groups. Our cultural upbringing influences the very way we view concepts such as "self" and "identity." Having grown up in an individualistic culture, my sense of identity assumes that I am an autonomous individual with clear boundaries separating me from other people. But in collectivistic cultures, the concept of "self" is traditionally based more strongly on the connectedness between people (Kagitçibasi, 1997). Thus the question "Who am I?" is more likely to be answered in ways that reflect a person's relationships with family members, friends, and others. Still, keep in mind that we are talking about relative differences. Across cultures, people's sense of identity incorporates elements that involve autonomy from—and interdependence with—other people (Mascolo & Li, 2004).

Relationships with Parents

When it comes to teenagers' relationships with parents, is "storm and stress" the rule or the exception? In a national survey conducted during the socially turbulent 1970s, 56 percent of American teens reported getting along "very well" with their parents and 41 percent reported getting along "fairly well" (Gallup Organization, 1988). Other studies of American, Chinese, Dutch, and other families also suggest that storm and stress is less prevalent than commonly assumed (Chen et al., 1998). Even when conflict is moderately frequent, its intensity is usually mild.

Consider a study by Andrew Fuligni (1998) involving 1,341 female and male American students in 6th, 8th, and 10th grades. They came from immigrant and native-born families of Mexican, Chinese, Filipino, and European ancestry. Fuligni found that among all four ethnic groups,

- adolescents agreed with their parents' right to "make the rules" more strongly on some issues than others (Figure 11.32); and

- older adolescents felt it was less appropriate for parents to make the rules.

So what about actual conflicts with parents? Fuligni found that overall,

- there was somewhat more conflict with mothers than with fathers; but

- regardless of adolescents' gender, ethnic group, or age, conflict was low with *both* mothers and fathers.

Of course, some parents and teenagers do struggle a lot, and parent-teen conflict is correlated with other signs of distress. Chuansheng Chen and coworkers (1998) studied 7th- and 8th-graders from America, Taiwan, and China. Among the 600 participants, parent-teen conflict was generally low in each cultural group, but young teens who reported more conflict had higher levels of school misconduct (e.g., cheating, skipping school) and more antisocial behavior (e.g., getting into fistfights, damaging property). Teens who report having more conflict with parents also experience greater hopelessness, lower self-esteem, more drug use, and less life satisfaction (Caughlin & Malis, 2004; Shek, 1998). Recalling the principle that correlation does not equal causation, we must consider that although parent-teen conflict may be a cause of teens' psychological problems, it also is likely to be caused *by* such problems.

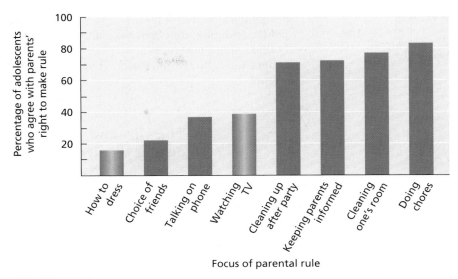

FIGURE 11.32

Do parents have the right to set rules? Using a questionnaire developed by Judy Smetana (1988), Andrew Fuligni found that the percentage of teenagers who agree that their parents have the right to make the rules depends on the particular issue. SOURCE: Based on Fuligni, 1998.

Peer Relationships

Peer relationships increase in importance during adolescence. From Alabama to the Arctic, teens like to spend time hanging out with friends. According to some studies, adolescents spend more time with peers than doing almost anything else and tend to identify more with peers than with adults. But this pattern may be stronger in North America than in Europe or Asia, where people of all ages, teens included, generally place a relatively strong emphasis on family relationships (Chen et al., 1998).

Adolescent friendships are typically more intimate than those at previous ages and involve a greater sharing of problems. Perhaps one reason intimacy increases is that in choosing friends, adolescents (like adults) tend to select peers who are similar to themselves (Iervolino et al., 2002). In turn, peer relationships facilitate the process of separating from parents and establishing one's own identity.

Peers can strongly influence a teenager's values and behaviors, and for some adolescents peer pressure increases the risk of misconduct, such as skipping school, damaging property, or disobeying parental rules. Fortunately, peer pressure *against* misconduct typically has an even stronger effect, and closeness to parents is an added buffer that helps many teenagers resist peer pressure to do misdeeds (Chen et al., 1998). Despite increased peer influence on dress, hairstyles, and attitudes toward other people,

► **Focus 19**

How do emotions change during the teenage years? Why is this important?

parental influence remains high on issues of politics, religion, morality, and career decisions. In these and other important areas, the so-called generation gap is narrower than we might assume.

Given the many life changes that occur during adolescence, how do children fare emotionally as they make the transition into and through the teenage years? Our "Research Close-Up" takes a look at this question.

Research Close-Up

The Ups and Downs of Adolescence: Does Emotion Change during the Teen Years?

SOURCE: REED W. LARSON, GIOVANNI MONETA, MARYSE H. RICHARDS, and SUZANNE WILSON (2002). Continuity, stability, and change in daily emotional experience across adolescence. *Child Development, 73,* 1151–1165.

INTRODUCTION

How happy were you in late childhood? As a teenager progressing through high school, did you generally become more or less happy? The question of "stability versus change" is a central developmental issue, and this study by Reed Larson and coworkers used a powerful method to examine whether boys' and girls' typical daily emotions change during the teenage years.

METHOD

At Time 1, participants were 328 randomly selected 5th- through 8th-graders (ages 10 to 14) from working- and middle-class suburban families living near Chicago. Students carried electronic pagers and paper booklets with them for 1 week, and the time of year that each student did this was randomly determined. From morning through evening, each student was beeped at a random time once during each 2-hour period. The students rated how happy or unhappy, cheerful or irritable, and friendly or angry they felt at that moment, using a +3 to −3 scale (with 0 = neutral) for each emotion. At the end of the week, students completed psychological tests that measured their general self-esteem and level of depression and the number of major stressful events they had experienced over the last 6 months.

At Time 2 (4 years later), this procedure was repeated. The participants were now 9th- through 12th-graders (ages 13 to 18), and 220 were still living in the area and able to complete the study.

RESULTS

On average, students' emotions became less positive with age, with this downward trend leveling off in later adolescence (Figure 11.33). Girls of all ages generally reported slightly more positive emotions than boys, but both sexes showed a similar downward trend between early and late adolescence.

Although emotions became less positive overall, students' average ratings remained on the positive side of the scale. Comparing students' emotions at Time 1 versus Time 2 revealed that as they became older,

FIGURE 11.33

Emotionality changes in the teenage years. In this graph, the zero point on the Y-axis represents a neutral level of overall emotion. In general, students' emotions become less positive during early to middle adolescence and then level off in later adolescence. SOURCE: Adapted from Larson et al., 2002.

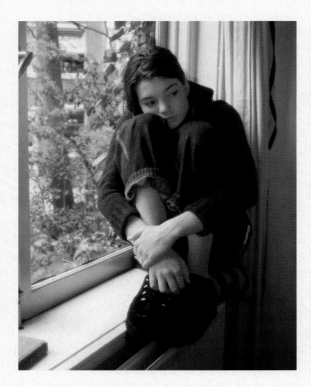

- 34 percent showed a major downward change (more negative emotion), and 16 percent showed a major upward change (more positive emotion);
- the remaining half of students showed a smaller amount of change in emotion, although once again, downward changes were twice as common as upward changes.

Finally, at both Time 1 and Time 2, students who reported less positive emotion tended to have lower self-esteem, higher depression scores, and a greater frequency of major stressful events over the preceding 6 months.

DISCUSSION

Girls' and boys' daily emotional experience became less positive as they moved into and through early adolescence, with changes leveling off and emotion becoming more stable during late adolescence. These findings fit the modified storm-and-stress view of adolescence. Although emotions became less positive overall during the teen years, the typical amount of change was not great. One half of the teens studied showed a relatively small change in their general day-to-day emotionality, and one sixth even shifted substantially toward greater happiness. Still, we must remember that one third of the students reported substantially more negative emotion as they aged, and negative emotionality was related to more stressful life events, lower self-esteem, and greater depression.

Because emotions became more stable in later adolescence, a downward emotional shift during the early teen years may be especially significant. As the researchers note, "This suggests that individuals' baseline emotional states may be less easily changed after they pass early adolescence [and that] future efforts . . . need to focus on what factors account for the largest downturns in early adolescence and what can be done to avert them" (p. 1162). Perhaps averting emotional downturns early would help alleviate a growing problem of teen depression: The largest increase in the incidence of clinical depression occurs between 15 and 19 years of age (Hankin et al., 1998).

Finally, this study nicely illustrates a sequential research design. It combined a cross-sectional component (at each time period, four school grades were studied) with a longitudinal component (each participant was tested twice, 4 years apart). This allowed the researchers to compare different age groups with one another and to examine changes over time for each student. Moreover, rather than relying on students' memory by using general questions (e.g., "How happy or unhappy were you over the past week?"), the beeper procedure provided a powerful way to gather immediate, real-time ratings of students' emotions.

IN REVIEW

- Adolescence is a socially constructed transition period between childhood and adulthood. Puberty is a major component of adolescence. Generally, early maturation is a more positive experience for boys than it is for girls.

- Abstract thinking blossoms and information-processing abilities improve during adolescence, but adolescents may show egocentrism in their social thinking.

- The search for identity is a key task of adolescence. With age, teens who have not yet experi-enced an identity crisis become more likely to do so, and most resolve it successfully.

- During adolescence, peer relationships become more important. Most teens maintain good rela-tionships with their parents.

- Overall, girls' and boys' daily emotional experi-ence becomes less positive as they move into and through early adolescence, with changes leveling off and emotion becoming more stable during late adolescence.

ADULTHOOD

It was a grand birthday party. Jeanne Louise Calment was born in France 10 years after the American Civil War, and as a girl she met Vincent Van Gogh in her father's shop. By age 60, she had lived through a world war and the invention of the radio, telephone, motion picture, automobile, and airplane. Still to come was another world war, television, space flight, computers, the Internet, and riding a bicycle until age 100. Yes, her 120th birthday was grand indeed. When a reporter asked how her future looked, Jeanne replied with a wry sense of humor, "Very brief" (Figure 11.34).

Older adults are the fastest-growing segment of the population in many countries. By 2025, almost 1 in 5 Americans will be over 65 years of age (Bureau of the Census, 2002). Here, we examine the transition to adulthood and explore some physical, cognitive, and social changes that occur

FIGURE 11.34

Jeanne Louise Calment of Arles, France, was born in 1875 and died in 1997 at the age of 122. Calment's life is the longest that has been verified.

among adolescents (average age 16 years), less than a fifth said that they had reached adulthood, whereas among people in their 20s (average age 24 years), almost half said that they had. Still, in both of these age groups, the transitional "yes and no" response was most common. Only among people in midlife (average age 42 years) did most view themselves as having fully attained adulthood.

If so many people in their 20s feel that they have not yet become adults, then psychologically, the transition to adulthood must involve more than just reaching a certain age (say, 18 or 21 years) or legal status in which you can officially drive, drink, vote, and make decisions without parental consent. Perhaps becoming an adult rests on certain role transitions, such a getting married, finishing school, getting a full-time job, and so forth. Arnett (2001) notes that according to anthropologists, in traditional cultures marriage typically is the key transitional event into adulthood. Through socialization, males develop skills that will enable them to protect and provide for a family of their own, and females learn skills needed to eventually care for children and run a household. Marriage signifies that in the eyes of the culture, each partner has acquired these skills and is deemed capable of raising a family.

Studies across the United States, however, reveal that on the psychological road to adulthood, marriage, other role transitions, age, and legal status take a backseat. Arnett (2001) asked his participants to rate ("yes" or "no") whether each of 38 characteristics "must be achieved before a person can be considered an adult." Items such as "reaching age 18," "employed full-time," and "marriage," were endorsed by only 47, 32, and 13 percent of participants, respectively. In contrast, regardless of the age group, about 90 percent of people endorsed "accept responsibility for the consequences of your actions." Establishing one's own values and beliefs, seeing oneself as an equal with one's parents, and attaining financial independence were the next most frequently chosen qualities among all age groups. Thus *individualism*—becoming a responsible, independent person—was the single most important general criterion. Still, in making the transition from adolescence to adulthood, many of the factors listed in Table 11.4 are likely to come into play over time.

during early adulthood (roughly 20 to 40 years of age), middle adulthood (ages 40 to 65), and late adulthood (ages 65 and older).

THE TRANSITION TO ADULTHOOD

▶ **Focus 20**
Is adulthood simply a matter of age or legal status? Explain.

Have you reached adulthood? Would you say, "yes," "no," or "in some respects yes, and in some respects no"? And in your view, just what does it take to be considered an adult?

Jeffrey Arnett (2001) posed these questions to 519 Midwestern Americans. As Figure 11.35 shows,

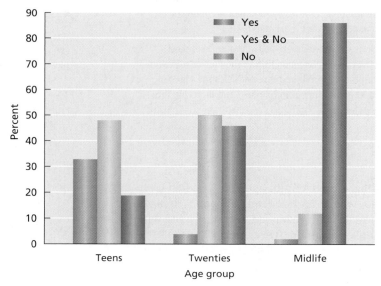

Have You Reached Adulthood?

FIGURE 11.35

Have you reached adulthood? This graph shows the percentage of people in their teens, 20s, and 30s to 40s who felt that they had not, partially had, or fully had reached adulthood. Source: Arnett, 2001.

PHYSICAL DEVELOPMENT

Young adults are at the peak of their physical, sexual, and perceptual functioning. The legs, arms, and other body parts typically reach maximum muscle strength at age 25 to 30. Vision, hearing, reaction time, and coordination peak in the early

TABLE 11.4   What Does It Take to Become an Adult?

The 6 main categories and about half of the 38 specific qualities studied by Arnett are shown below. The numbers represent the percentage of people who, on average, endorsed the items within each category.

Individualism	74%	Be responsible for one's actions; determine own values/beliefs; see oneself as an "equal" in relationship with parents; attain financial independence
Family Capacities	58%	Capable of caring, protecting, and financially supporting a family
Norm Compliance	47%	Refrain from crime, irresponsible sex, drunk driving, and illegal drug use
Biological Transitions	42%	Capable of fathering/bearing children
Legal/Chronological Transitions	42%	Reach age 18; reach age 21; obtain driver's license
Role Transitions	22%	Get full-time employment; establish career; finish education; get married

SOURCE: Based on Arnett, 2001.

to mid-20s (Hayslip & Panek, 1989). Yet although many physical capacities decline in the mid-30s, the changes aren't noticeable until years later.

After age 40, muscles become weaker and less flexible, particularly in people with sedentary habits. *Basal metabolism*, the rate at which the resting body converts food into energy, also slows, resulting in a tendency to gain weight. Middle age is also the time when many people find their visual acuity declining, especially for close viewing. Women's fertility, which begins to decrease in early adulthood, now drops dramatically as the ovaries produce less estrogen; this process culminates in *menopause*, the cessation of menstruation, which occurs on average around age 50. Male fertility often persists throughout the life span, although it tends to decline after middle age.

Despite these declines, many middle-aged adults remain in excellent health and are vigorously active. From climbing mountains to running marathons, they may achieve physical goals well beyond those attained by many younger adults. By late adulthood, physical changes become more pronounced. By age 70, bones become more brittle and hardened ligaments make movements stiffer and slower. But with regular exercise and good nutrition and barring major disease, many adults maintain physical vigor and an active lifestyle well into old age (Figure 11.36).

The Adult Brain

During the earliest years of adulthood the brain's neural networks generally become more efficiently

FIGURE 11.36

Many older adults maintain a physically active lifestyle.

FIGURE 11.37

These photographs portray the average amount of brain tissue loss that 92 men and women, ages 59 to 85 (who did not have brain disease), experienced over a 4-year period. Areas in red had the greatest loss. SOURCE: Resnick et al., 2003.

▶ **Focus 21**
Describe how physical abilities and the brain change in adulthood.

integrated (Luna et al., 2004). But like other parts of the body, the brain declines later in adulthood. In a longitudinal study, psychologist Susan Resnick and her coworkers (2003) used magnetic resonance imaging to measure the loss of brain tissue among 92 men and women over a 4-year period. The participants were 59 to 85 years old at the start of the study, and none of them exhibited abnormal cognitive impairments. On average, over the next 4 years, they lost tissue at a rate of 5.4 percent per year in the brain regions studied, with the frontal and parietal lobes showing the greatest loss (Figure 11.37). Participants who were very healthy experienced less tissue loss than those who experienced medical problems (3.7 versus 6.1 percent per year), but still, even among physically and mentally healthy older adults, tissue loss is normal as the brain ages.

COGNITIVE DEVELOPMENT

Many people assume that cognitive and intellectual functioning decline throughout much of adulthood. Research shows that this is true in some ways but not in others.

Changes in Processing Speed and Memory

▶ **Focus 22**
How do cognitive and intellectual abilities change in adulthood? Describe characteristics of senile dementia.

Perceptual speed (reaction time) begins to decline steadily in early adulthood, by some estimates as soon as one's early 20s (Salthouse, 2004). As

they grow older, it takes adults longer to visually identify and evaluate stimuli, such as when looking at two patterns of lines and deciding whether they are the same.

Memory for new factual information also declines. With increasing age, adults generally find it harder to remember new series of numbers, names and faces of new people, new map directions, and directions for using new prescription drugs. On some tasks, such as recalling lists of unrelated words, performance worsens somewhat by the late 30s and then steadily declines after age 50 (Salthouse, 2004). Certain types of verbal memory, however, show less decline with aging. Thus the ability to immediately repeat meaningful sentences decreases more slowly than the ability to repeat single, unrelated words. Even in late adulthood, healthy adults do well in recognizing familiar stimuli from long ago, such as the faces of high school classmates (Bahrick et al., 1975).

The effects of aging on prospective memory—the ability to remember to perform some action in the future—are less clear (McDaniel et al., 2003). By late adulthood, people generally display poorer prospective memory than young adults in time-based laboratory tasks (e.g., remembering to push a button every 15 minutes). On event-based tasks (e.g., remembering to push a button whenever a light comes on), age differences are less consistent. Moreover, when tested outside the laboratory, older adults may perform as well as young adults, even when the tasks (e.g., simulated pill taking) are time-based. However, when older people recall that they are supposed to execute a task ("Ah, I'm supposed to call Sylvia") and something temporarily delays them from performing it, they will be less likely to remember to perform the task immediately after the delay ends (McDaniel et al., 2003).

Intellectual Changes

How do intellectual abilities change in adulthood? The conclusion from early research seemed clear: After 30, adults are over the hill. When IQ scores of different age groups were compared in cross-sectional studies, a noticeable decline began between ages 30 and 40 (Doppelt & Wallace, 1955).

Researchers made a breakthrough by examining separate intellectual abilities rather than overall IQ. They studied *fluid intelligence,* which reflects the ability to perform mental operations (e.g., abstract and logical reasoning, solving spatial problems), and *crystallized intelligence,* which reflects the accumulation of verbal skills and factual knowledge (Horn & Cattell, 1966). Cross-sectional

(a)

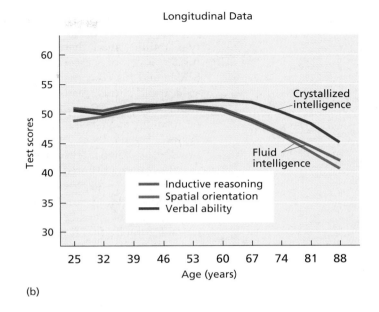

(b)

FIGURE 11.38

Intellectual abilities change during adulthood. (a) Cross-sectional data (ages 25–81) indicate that fluid abilities (reasoning and spatial task performance) begin to decline in young adulthood, whereas crystallized intelligence (verbal ability) begins to decline in late adulthood. (b) However, longitudinal data (ages 25–88) from the same study indicate that both fluid and crystallized intelligence remain fairly stable through young and middle adulthood and do not decline significantly until late adulthood. The longitudinal and cross-sectional data are consistent in showing that crystallized abilities decline at a later age than fluid abilities. Source: Adapted from Schaie, 2005.

research typically found that fluid intelligence began to decline steadily in early adulthood, whereas crystallized intelligence peaked during middle adulthood and then began to decline in late adulthood (Figure 11.38a).

Was this early decline in fluid abilities really a function of aging or instead the result of different experiences encountered by the various generations? The older adults may have had less exposure to scientific problem solving in school or jobs that required less use of abstract intellectual skills. Such factors could have artificially depressed their scores.

To answer this question, K. Warner Schaie of Pennsylvania State University and coworkers (Schaie, 1994, 2005) began a study in 1956 that has now involved several thousand adults. This study uses a sequential design, incorporating longitudinal and cross-sectional components. The longitudinal data do not support an early decline in either fluid or crystallized intelligence. Rather, most abilities are relatively stable throughout early and middle adulthood and do not reliably decline until late adulthood (Figure 11.38b). But both the cross-sectional and longitudinal data, along with findings from other studies, indicate that fluid intellectual abilities typically begin to decline at an earlier age than crystallized intelligence (Singer et al., 2003).

Use It or Lose It?

As we progress through adulthood, is the declining trajectory painted in Figure 11.38b inevitable? Schaie (1994, 2005) notes that the average intellectual decline in old age shown in Figure 11.38b is a bit deceiving, disproportionately influenced by a minority of older participants who declined markedly. For each intellectual ability, he found that between 67 and 74 years of age about 70 percent of participants *maintained* their level of functioning and that 65 percent maintained it between ages 74 and 81.

Age-related intellectual declines are partly due to poorer perceptual speed, memory, vision, and hearing. Thus we find a bigger intellectual decline during old age when test questions call for quick responses (i.e., timed tests) than when they involve unlimited or ample time (untimed tests). This decrease in intellectual speed shows up in various real-world tasks, such as learning to use a computer. But although 75- to 89-year-olds may take longer to acquire computer skills than their 60- to 74-year-old counterparts, the key is that many retain the intellectual capacity to learn (Echt et al., 1998).

Can we predict who will maintain intellectual functioning the longest? According to Schaie (1994, 2005), it appears to be people who have above-average education, engage in cognitively stimulating jobs and personal activities (e.g., reading, travel), marry a spouse with greater intellectual abilities than their own, and maintain a higher level of perceptual processing speed. Schaie and his coworkers also found that 65- to 95-year-old adults' spatial and reasoning abilities could be improved by teaching them strategies for performing such tasks (Saczynski et al., 2002; Willis & Schaie, 1986). For many adults who had previously shown intellectual declines in these areas, the training restored their performance to the level it had been 14 years earlier, and these gains often persisted for years.

Still, as in the case of physical fitness, the moral for intellectual fitness appears to be "use it or lose it." In fact, regular physical exercise and perceptual-motor activities—even playing video games that require fast reaction times—may help preserve 70- and 80-year-olds' cognitive abilities (Goldstein et al., 1997). At the same time, it's important not to sugarcoat the fact that the risk of cognitive impairment increases significantly throughout late adulthood.

Cognitive Impairment in Old Age

As we noted in Chapter 7, *dementia* is a gradual loss of cognitive abilities that accompanies abnormal brain deterioration and interferes with daily functioning. In people with dementia, an abnormal progressive degeneration of brain tissue occurs as a result of disease or injury.

Dementia is most common in late adulthood, and the term **senile dementia** *refers to dementia that begins after age 65.* Alzheimer's disease, which we previously discussed in relation to memory loss, is the most common cause of senile dementia, but Parkinson's disease, Huntington's disease, and Creutzfeldt-Jakob disease are other common causes. Complications from high blood pressure and stroke may also be causes.

A large Canadian study found an overall rate of senile dementia of about 8 percent, and a female-to-male ratio of about 2 to 1. Whereas 2 percent of 65- to 74-year-olds are estimated to have dementia, that rate increases to 11 percent for 75- to 84-year-olds and 34 percent for people 85 and older (Costa, 1996).

Impaired memory, particularly for very recent events, typically is one of the first symptoms of dementia to appear (Figure 11.39). Poor judgment, language problems, and disorientation may appear gradually or sporadically, and people who develop dementia typically have episodes of distress because they feel confused. Their behavior may become uninhibited, they may lose the ability to perform familiar tasks, and they may experience significant physical decline in addition to cognitive impairments.

Compared to other adults aged 65 years and older, those who more frequently engage in stimulating cognitive activity show a lower risk for subsequently developing Alzheimer's disease, but whether this truly reflects a causal relation remains to be seen (Wilson & Bennett, 2003). One thing is certain: As people live longer lives, finding a cure for Alzheimer's disease and other forms of senile dementia becomes more urgent. Until then, many of us can expect our own family members to become Alzheimer's patients.

Unfortunately, being a caregiver for a spouse or for one's elderly parent who has developed dementia often is a stressful and psychologically painful experience (Pinquart & Sörensen, 2003). Over half of the people diagnosed with senile dementia show combinations of depression, anxiety, agitation, paranoid reactions, and disordered thinking that may resemble schizophrenia. Ultimately, they may not even be able to walk, talk, or recognize close friends or family members.

In-depth studies in Finland, Germany, and the United States find that among adults over the age of 65 who do not suffer from dementia, 20 to 25 percent do have mild cognitive impairment

FIGURE 11.39

Impaired memory on a word-recall task. Participants in this nationally representative sample of Americans were read a list of 20 words and asked to recall as many as they could. Most healthy adults were able to recall between 5 and 9 words. This graph shows that the percentage of people who recalled 4 or fewer words increased steadily during late adulthood. Source: Federal Interagency Forum on Aging-Related Statistics, 2000.

(Unverzagt et al., 2001). Combining cases of mild impairment and dementia, some experts estimate that 79 percent of 65- to 74-year-olds and 45 percent of people age 85 and older remain "cognitively normal" (Unverzagt et al., 2001). Surely, these are not pleasant statistics, but they also make clear that even well into old age, cognitive impairment is not inevitable. Moreover, even when some mental abilities decrease with age, people can still accumulate knowledge that leads to greater wisdom. Let's take a closer look "Beneath the Surface."

▶ **Focus 23**
Identify aspects of wisdom, and discuss whether we become "older but wiser" during adulthood.

Beneath the Surface   Older but Wiser?

In many traditional cultures around the world, elderly adults are esteemed for their wisdom. Common sense says that as we progress through adulthood, we become "older but wiser," but is this true?

THE NATURE OF WISDOM

Wisdom represents a system of knowledge about the meaning and conduct of life. To quickly refresh your memory, in Chapter 8 we described several major components of wisdom identified by psychologist Paul Baltes and his coworkers (2002, 2004), which included:

- Rich factual knowledge about life (e.g., about human nature and social relationships)
- Rich procedural knowledge about life (e.g., strategies for making decisions, handling conflict, giving advice)
- An understanding of life-span contexts (e.g., family, friends, work; past, present, future)
- An awareness that values and priorities differ across people and societies
- An ability to recognize and manage uncertainty (e.g., "the future cannot be fully known")

AGING AND WISDOM

Does age bring greater wisdom? To find out, Baltes and other researchers presented participants of different ages with various life problems (e.g., a 15-year-old girl wants to get married right away; an adult realizes that she hasn't achieved major goals) and asked them what the hypothetical person should do. Experts blind to the participants' ages then scored their solutions, using the five criteria of wisdom described above.

What did they find? Older teens gave wiser solutions than younger teens, adults in their early 20s gave still wiser solutions, and older adults—on average—showed no greater or lesser wisdom. As these findings suggest, wisdom seems to rise steadily from age 13 to 25 and then remain relatively stable through age 75 (Baltes & Staudinger, 2000; Pasupathi et al., 2001). Beyond that, wisdom may decline, but the researchers were able to study relatively few people older than 75.

Let's turn, however, to a different type of task. Read the story below, then answer the question that follows.

> A burglar who has just robbed a shop is making his getaway. As he is running home, a policeman on his beat sees him drop his glove. He doesn't know the man is a burglar, he just wants to tell him he dropped his glove. But when the policeman shouts out to the burglar, "Hey, you! Stop!" the burglar turns round, sees the policeman, and gives himself up. *Question:* Why did the burglar do that? (Happé et al., 1998, p. 362)

Did you find this task easy? A good answer would be that the burglar mistakenly assumed that the officer knew he had robbed the shop and didn't realize that the officer was only trying to return the dropped glove. This task measures how well you understand "what someone else is thinking" based on their behavior. This type of social wisdom comes into play when we need to infer what people must have been thinking to have acted as they did or need to predict how others will behave based on what is "going on in their head." Francesca Happé and coworkers (1998) found that on such tasks, younger adults (average age 21 years) generally gave good responses, but older adults (average age 73 years), on average, displayed superior social reasoning. Several other researchers also have found superior performance among older adults on various reasoning tasks.

As a critical thinker, you should recognize that all of the studies just mentioned are cross-sectional; that is, they compare people from different age groups. Asking whether 75-year-olds are wiser than 25-year-olds is not quite the same as asking whether the same young adults will become wiser as they age. Only longitudinal and sequential studies can answer that question.

At present, then, research suggests that "older but wiser" may apply only up to a point, beyond which "older but at least as wise" is more appropriate. Of course, these are averages. Some older adults—even into their 80s—display greater wisdom than many young adults. To stereotype elderly adults as "wise," however, is just as inappropriate as to stereotype them as "senile." Erik Erikson (Erikson et al., 1986) emphasized that old age brings with it only the *potential* for wisdom. And even in traditional cultures where elders are revered, such as among the Inuit of the Canadian Arctic, members readily acknowledge that not everyone ages successfully.

SOCIAL-EMOTIONAL AND PERSONALITY DEVELOPMENT

Adults display a great diversity of life paths. As Bernice Neugarten notes, "If you look at people's lives, they're like the spreading of a fan. The longer they live, the greater the differences between them" (Neugarten & Hall, 1980, p. 78). Yet all adults confront biological realities of aging, and most are also influenced by a **social clock,** *a set of cultural norms concerning the optimal age range for work, marriage, parenthood, and other life experiences.*

Stages and Critical Events

> ▶ **Focus 24**
> According to Erikson, what are three major developmental challenges of adulthood?

Many researchers view adult social development as a progression through age-related stages (Levinson, 1990). According to Erik Erikson (1959/1980; see Table 11.2), *intimacy versus isolation* is the major developmental challenge of early adulthood (ages 20 to 40). Intimacy is the ability to open oneself to another person and to form close relationships. This is the period of adulthood when many people form close adult friendships, fall in love, and marry.

> ▶ **Focus 25**
> Describe research findings on family structure, cohabitation and divorce, and the course of marital satisfaction.

Middle adulthood (ages 40 to 65) brings with it the issue of *generativity versus stagnation.* Through their careers, raising children, or involvement in other activities, people achieve generativity by doing things for others and making the world a better place. Certainly, many young adults make such contributions, but generativity typically becomes a more central issue later in adulthood (Slater, 2003).

Late adulthood (age 65 and older) accentuates the final crisis, *integrity versus despair.* Older adults review their life and evaluate its meaning. If the major crises of earlier stages have been successfully resolved, the person experiences integrity: a sense of completeness and fulfillment. Older adults who have not achieved positive outcomes at earlier stages may experience despair, regretting that they had not lived their lives in a more fulfilling way.

Consistent with Erikson's model, many goals increase in importance as people age, and successfully resolving certain life tasks contributes to mastering others (McAdams & de St. Aubin, 1998). But critics caution that we should avoid viewing early, middle, and late adulthood as strict stages in which one life task takes over while others fade away. Although older adults are more concerned about generativity and integrity than are younger adults, they remain highly concerned about intimacy (Sheldon & Kasser, 2001).

Another way to view adult social development is through the major life events that people experience. Sigmund Freud (1935) once defined psychological adjustment as "the ability to love and work," and many key life events revolve around these two themes.

Marriage and Family

Around the world, most people marry or form another type of family union at some point in their lives, and family structures can vary widely both across and within different cultures (Figure 11.40). The "average" family in America and some other countries has changed in several ways over recent generations. For example, Baby Boomers were born a few years after the end of World War II, and their children (born in the 1960s through the early 1980s) became known as Generation X. As Figure 11.41 shows, compared to the families that Baby Boomers grew up in, members of Generation X are more likely to have experienced parental divorce, had two working parents, had a smaller number of siblings, and yet maintained a similar level of closeness to their parents (Bengtson, 2001).

Like their parents, today's adults typically expect much from marriage, including satisfaction of social, emotional, and sexual needs. Many

FIGURE 11.40

These children, from a family of herders in the Republic of Mongolia, are living in an extended family unit that includes parents, grandparents, great-grandparents, and other relatives. In the United States in 2001, one-third of all children lived in a single-parent household. SOURCE: Bureau of the Census, 2002.

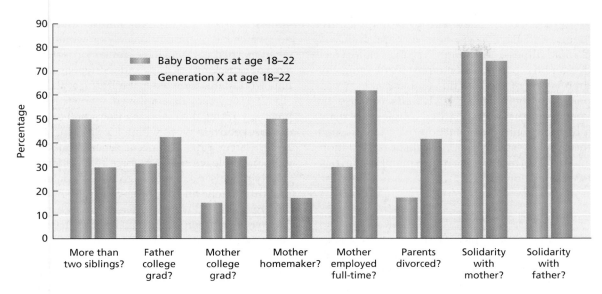

FIGURE 11.41

Growing up in different generations. Baby Boomers were surveyed when they were 18 to 22 years old and asked to identify various characteristics of the families in which they had grown up. A generation later, when the Baby Boomers' children (Generation X) had turned 18 to 22 years old, they answered the same survey questions as their parents had. SOURCE: Bengtson, 2001.

couples realize these goals, but a high divorce rate—not just in the United States but also in many foreign countries—indicates that marital happiness is by no means automatic. Successful marriages are characterized by emotional closeness, positive communication and problem solving, agreement on basic values and expectations, and a willingness to accept and support changes in the partner (Cordova et al., 2005).

Some couples in committed relationships *cohabit*—that is, live together without being married. In 1960 the ratio of married to cohabiting households in the United States was about 95 to 1. By 2000 that ratio had shrunk to 10 to 1, representing almost 5.5 million cohabiting households (Bureau of the Census, 2003). Some couples cohabit as a permanent alternative to marriage, but many do so as a "trial marriage" to determine if they are compatible before tying the knot. In Sweden, premarital cohabitation appears to be the norm (Duvander, 1999).

? What Do You Think?

COHABITATION AS A "TRIAL MARRIAGE"
What would you predict? Do couples who live together before getting married have a lower, higher, or similar rate of divorce compared to couples who do not live together before they get married? Why? Think about it, then see page 439.

Marital Satisfaction, Parenthood, and the Empty Nest On average, marital satisfaction declines over the first few years after the knot is tied (McNulty & Karney, 2004). This does not mean,

however, that most couples are unhappy. They are still satisfied, just less so than they were. In a sense, the honeymoon is over.

The birth of a first baby dramatically alters the way couples spend their time. For many couples, marital satisfaction decreases in the year or two after their first child is born (Cowan & Cowan, 2000). Compared with husbands, wives are more likely to leave their outside job, spend more time parenting, and feel that their spouse is not helping enough. Disagreements over the division of labor and parenting are a major contributor to the drop in marital satisfaction (Frisco & Williams, 2003).

Over a broader age period, cross-sectional studies suggest a U-shaped relation between marital satisfaction and progression through major life events. The percentage of couples reporting that they are "very satisfied" in their marriage typically is highest before or just as the first child is born, drops during child-rearing years, and increases after all the children have left home (Orbuch et al., 1996). Although some longitudinal research does not find this late-adulthood rebound in marital satisfaction, overall these findings challenge a myth about the so-called empty nest. Contrary to this popular stereotype, most middle-aged couples do not become significantly depressed or suffer a crisis when their children leave home (Chiriboga, 1989). Couples maintain meaningful relationships with their children but have more time to spend with each other and pursue leisure activities.

Despite the stresses that accompany marriage and parenthood, studies around the globe find that married people experience greater subjective well-being than unmarried adults (Keyes &

Waterman, 2003). They tend to be happier, live longer, and have lower rates of depression and chronic illness. Although raising children is demanding, parents often report that having children is one of the best things that has ever happened in their lives. Newlyweds can use the knowledge that many married couples experience a drop in marital satisfaction over time to help themselves establish more realistic expectations and to take a more active role in maintaining a satisfying relationship.

Establishing a Career

▶ **Focus 26**
Identify common stages of establishing a career, and describe sex differences in career paths.

In the adult world, one of the first questions a new acquaintance typically asks is "What do you do?" A child might answer "About what?" but adults know the question is short for "What do you do for a living?" A career helps us earn a living and defines part of our identity. Work provides an outlet for achievement, gives us structure, and is a significant source of social interactions. Having satisfying relationships at work is especially important in collectivistic countries (Siu, 2003).

▶ **Focus 27**
Evaluate the concept of midlife crisis and the view that dying people experience a sequence of psychological stages.

According to Donald Super (1957), a pioneer in the field of vocational psychology, from childhood through our mid-20s we first enter a *growth stage* of career interests, in which we form initial impressions about the types of jobs we like or dislike, followed by a more earnest *exploration stage,* in which we form tentative ideas about a preferred career and pursue the necessary education or training.

From the mid-20s to mid-40s, people often enter an *establishment phase,* during which they begin to make their mark. Initially, they may experience some job instability. After college, for example, many people are likely to change careers at least once. Eventually, careers tend to become more stable, and people enter a *maintenance stage* that continues into late adulthood. Finally, during the *decline stage,* people's investment in work tends to decrease, and they eventually retire.

Although this general model is useful, people's career paths vary quite a bit, and this is especially true for women. Joy Schneer and Frieda Reitman (1997) found, for example, that, among college students who obtained an MBA (master of business administration) degree and then pursued managerial careers, women were more likely than men to experience work gaps by mid-career. Such work gaps tended to retard professional advancement and salary level.

Overall, compared to their parents' generation at the same age, today's young women hold higher career aspirations than those of their mothers and fathers (Bengtson, 2001). Still, family responsibilities, which fall disproportionately on women even when married partners have similar job status, are a major cause of work gaps and reductions to part-time work status for women (Smithson et al., 2004). About 75 percent of employed women become pregnant during their working years, and over half of those return to work within a year (Muchinsky, 2000). Career gaps also occur when adults must temporarily leave the workforce to care for their elderly parents. As in raising children, women disproportionately fill this elder-care role. Not surprisingly, married women often experience greater *interrole conflict* than married men as they try to juggle the demands of career and family (Berry, 1998). But as children grow up and leave home, this conflict decreases. After raising a family, many women enter the workforce for the first time, reinvigorate an earlier career, or return to college to prepare for a new one.

Midlife Crisis: Fact or Fiction?

Popular wisdom holds that along the developmental path of career and family, people hit a massive pothole called the *midlife crisis.* Is it a reality? Daniel Levinson and his coworkers (1978, 1986) studied 85 men and women longitudinally and found that many experienced a turbulent midlife transition between the ages of 40 and 45. They began to focus on their mortality and realize that some of their life's dreams pertaining to career, family, and relationships would not come true.

Critics note that Levinson's sample was small and nonrepresentative. In fact, there is considerable evidence that the notion of an inevitable, full-blown midlife crisis is a myth (Lachman, 2004). Research conducted around the world shows that happiness and life satisfaction generally do not decrease throughout adulthood (Diener et al., 1999). In one study of adolescents and people in early, middle, and late adulthood from eight Western European countries, about 80 percent of each age group reported they were "satisfied" or "very satisfied" with their lives (Ingelhart & Rabier, 1986). Moreover, people in their 40s do *not* have the highest rates of divorce, suicide, depression, feelings of meaninglessness, or emotional instability (Kessler et al., 2004; McCrae & Costa, 1990).

In sum, middle-aged adults surely experience important conflicts, disappointments, and worries—and some indeed experience major crises—but so do people of all ages (Wethington, 2000). As Erikson emphasized, there are major goals to achieve, crises to resolve, and rewards to experience in every phase of life.

Retirement and the "Golden Years"

Retirement is an important milestone. Some adults view it as a reminder that they are growing older, but many look forward to leisure and other opportunities they were unable to pursue during their careers. Most retired people do not become anxious, depressed, or dissatisfied with life due to retirement itself, although those who have strong work values are most apt to miss their jobs (Hyde et al., 2004).

The decision to retire or keep working typically involves many factors, such as one's feelings about the job, leisure interests, physical health, and family relationships. Family income, leisure time, and family roles change with retirement, and married couples often experience increased marital stress after a spouse retires, especially if the other spouse is still working. Over time, however, they typically adjust to their new circumstances and marital quality is enhanced (Moen et al., 2001).

Some people, of course, do not have the luxury to choose their work status. They may be forced into retirement or feel compelled to keep working for economic reasons, and these circumstances can have a significant impact on well-being. Whether in their 50s, 60s, or 70s, adults who are working or retired because this is what *they* prefer report higher life satisfaction and better physical and mental health than adults who are involuntarily working or retired (Shultz et al., 1998).

Death and Dying

Part of being human is the fact that we are mortal. Like other aspects of life-span development summarized in Figure 11.42, death can be viewed at several levels. It is an inevitable biological process, but one with important psychological and environmental components.

In her pioneering work on dying, Elisabeth Kübler-Ross (1969) found that terminally ill patients often experienced five stages as they coped with impending death. *Denial* typically came first, as the person refused to accept that the illness was terminal. Next, denial often gave way to *anger* and then to *bargaining,* such as "Lord, please let me live long enough to see my grandchild." *Depression* ushered in the fourth stage, as patients began to grieve. Finally, many experienced *acceptance* and a resigned sense of peacefulness.

It is essential to keep in mind that these stages do not represent a "normal" or "correct" way to face death and that terminally ill patients' reactions may not typify those of people facing death under other circumstances (Doka, 1995). Even among terminally ill patients, some move back and forth between stages, do not experience all the stages, or look forward to death. Indeed, some scientists question whether people's psychological responses to their impending death are stage-like at all (Kastenbaum, 2000). Nevertheless, Kübler-Ross's work spurred great interest in understanding and helping people cope with death.

As Figure 11.43 illustrates, beliefs and customs concerning death vary across cultures and among individuals (Werth et al., 2002). To some, death means the complete end of one's existence. Others believe in reincarnation or an afterlife. Death also means different things to people of different ages. By late and even middle adulthood, people typically have lost more friends and loved

FIGURE 11.42

Levels of analysis: Factors related to life-span development.

LEVELS OF ANALYSIS	Factors Related to Life-Span Development	
Biological	**Psychological**	**Environmental**
• Sex determination and genetic contribution to temperament	• Changes in schemas, information processing, and intellectual capacities	• Teratogens that affect prenatal development
• Brain maturation underlying cognitive growth in childhood	• Secure or insecure attachment to caregiver; peer relations	• Parenting styles and childhood socialization experiences
• Pubertal changes, including early and late maturation	• Development of gender-identity and sex-role stereotypes	• Major life events (marriage, parenthood, career)
• Biologically-based physical and cognitive changes in adulthood	• Personality formation and resolution of psychosocial stages	• Exercise and lifestyle norms that affect biological functions at all ages

Life-Span Development

FIGURE 11.43

Many cultures honor a person's death with a ceremony that involves family, friends, and the wider community. In some cultures, this traditionally is a somber occasion; in others, it is a more joyous celebration.

IN REVIEW

■ The age at which people feel that they have become adults varies widely. Among Americans, it may depend most strongly on viewing oneself as a responsible, independent person.

■ Young adults are at the peak of their physical capabilities, but brain functioning undergoes a general decline later in adulthood.

■ Information-processing speed slows beginning in early adulthood, but many intellectual abilities do not begin to decline reliably until late adulthood. Wisdom appears to increase steadily from early adolescence through the mid-20s and then level off through the mid-70s.

■ Erikson proposed that intimacy versus isolation, generativity versus stagnation, and integrity versus despair are the main crises of early, middle, and late adulthood.

■ For many couples, marital satisfaction tends to decline in the years following the birth of children but increases later in adulthood.

■ Work serves important psychological and social functions. Overall, women experience more career gaps, and their career paths are more variable than men's. Most adults do not experience a full-blown midlife crisis. Similarly, most retired people do not become more anxious, depressed, or lonely due to retirement.

■ Many terminally ill patients experience similar psychological reactions as they cope with their impending death, but beliefs and feelings about death vary with culture and age, and there is no "normal" way to approach death.

ones and have thought more about their own eventual death than have younger people. As one 80-year-old put it, "More of the people I know are in heaven now than on earth."

Understandably, the elderly are more accepting of their own death than any other age group. In the midst of a fatal heart attack, an 81-year-old man we know reassuringly told his family, "It's my time. It's been a good life." We should all wish for this blessing of a fulfilled life's journey.

KEY TERMS AND CONCEPTS

Each term has been boldfaced and defined in the chapter on the page indicated in parentheses.

❓ What Do You Think?

SHY CHILD, SHY ADULT? (PAGE 411)

To answer this question, psychologists must patiently conduct longitudinal research, measuring people's temperament in childhood and then examining whether it correlates with people's traits or behaviors in adulthood. For example, studies find that in America and Sweden, shy, behaviorally inhibited 8- to 12-year-old boys are more likely than nonshy peers to delay marriage and fatherhood when they grow up, possibly reflecting their reluctance to enter new social relationships (Caspi et al., 1988; Kerr et al., 1996). Shy American girls are more likely as adults to quit work after marriage and become homemakers, whereas shy Swedish girls are less likely to complete college than nonshy girls.

Other childhood traits also are associated with adulthood outcomes. Longitudinal studies in Finland find that children who are more aggressive at age 8 are more likely to experience long-term unemployment 20 to 30 years later, and that 8-year-olds with a highly agreeable (e.g., compliant and self-controlled) or disagreeable temperament are, respectively, more likely to become generally pleasant or unpleasant adults (Kokko & Pulkkinen, 2000).

But what about temperament in early childhood? Denise Newman and coworkers (1997) measured the temperament of 961 New Zealanders at age 3, based on a 90-minute observation of each child. At age 21, participants were studied again. Compared with 3-year-olds with a "well-adjusted temperament," those who were "undercontrolled" (i.e., irritable, impulsive, inattentive) reported more antisocial behavior in adulthood and greater conflict in family and romantic relationships, and they were more likely to have been fired from a job. Other adults rated them as being less reliable. In contrast, children with an "inhibited temperament" (i.e., socially shy and fearful) reported having less overall companionship in adulthood, and other adults rated them as less affiliative.

What shall we conclude? Most young children are well adjusted and display only mild to moderately strong temperamental traits; differences in temperament among these children predict only weakly how they will function as adults. But for the remaining children, their strong temperamental traits can provide a better insight into adulthood functioning. Still, predicting how any individual child will turn out as an adult is difficult. Many factors influence development, and even during childhood, strong temperaments often mellow (Pfeifer et al., 2002). Finally, temperament usually predicts overall *patterns* of adult functioning better than any single adult behavior. But as Newman and coworkers (1997) note, it is remarkable that a mere 90-minute observation of children at age 3 can modestly predict different patterns of adjustment 18 years later.

COHABITATION AS A "TRIAL MARRIAGE" (PAGE 435)

Scientists began to examine the relation between cohabitation and divorce rates in the 1980s. Since then, large national surveys in several countries, including Canada, Germany, Sweden, and the United States, have found that premarital cohabitation is associated with a *higher* risk of subsequent divorce (Heaton, 2002). Conducting experiments to find out why this relation exists would, of course, be impractical, not to mention unethical. We cannot randomly assign engaged couples, for example, to cohabitation and no-cohabitation conditions and then try to explore factors that increase or decrease their divorce rate!

Many researchers feel that the cohabitation-divorce relation does not reflect cause and effect. Rather, couples who choose to cohabit before marriage appear to differ psychologically from couples who don't cohabit first. They tend to be less religious and less committed to their partners and to marriage as an institution (Stanley et al., 2004). Taken together, these preexisting factors would increase the risk of divorce even if these couples had not cohabited before tying the knot. In some studies, when researchers focus on cohabiting couples who start out with a strong orientation toward marriage, they find that the risk of divorce is no higher and the quality of marital relations is no poorer than among couples who did not cohabit prior to marriage (Bruederl et al., 1997). Still, research does *not* support the view that, overall, cohabitation reduces the risk of subsequent divorce.

Personality

CHAPTER OUTLINE

Much of our lives is spent in trying to understand others and in wishing others understood us better than they do.

—GORDON ALLPORT

O n a hot summer evening in 1966, a University of Texas student wrote the following letter:

> I don't really understand myself these days. I am supposed to be an average, reasonable, and intelligent young man. However, lately (I can't recall when it started) I have been the victim of many unusual and irrational thoughts. These thoughts constantly recur, and it requires a tremendous mental effort to concentrate on useful and progressive tasks. In March when my parents made a physical break I noticed a great deal of stress. I consulted a Dr. Cochrum at the University Health Center and asked him to recommend someone that I could consult with about some psychiatric disorders I felt I had. I talked with a doctor once for about two hours and tried to convey to him my fears that I felt overcome by overwhelming violent impulses. After one session I never saw the doctor again, and since then I have been fighting my mental turmoil alone, and seemingly to no avail. After my death I wish that an autopsy would be performed on me to see if there is any visible physical disorder. I have had some tremendous headaches in the past and have consumed two large bottles of Excedrin in the past three months. (Lavergne, 1997, p. 8)

Later that night, Charles Whitman killed his wife and mother, both of whom were lovingly supportive of him. The next morning he carried a high-powered hunting rifle to the top of a 307-foot tower on the busy University of Texas campus in Austin and opened fire on all those passing by below. Within 90 horrifying minutes, he killed 16 people and wounded 30 others before he himself was killed by police.

On the surface, Charles Whitman (Figure 12.1) seemed as solid and upstanding as the University of Texas tower from which he rained death on unsuspecting strangers. He came from a wealthy, prominent Florida family and was an outstanding student, an accomplished pianist, one of the youngest Eagle Scouts in state history, and a former U.S. Marine who had been awarded a Good Conduct Medal and the Marine Corps Expeditionary Medal. He married the woman of his dreams, and the two were seen as an ideal couple. Whitman became a University of Texas student when he was selected by the Marines for a prestigious engineering scholarship. In his spare time, he served as a scoutmaster in Austin.

What could have caused this exemplary citizen to commit such extraordinary acts of violence? On December 18, 2001, the Austin History Center opened its records on Charles Whitman to public scrutiny. These records provide important insights into the complexities of Whitman's personality and the turmoil that existed within him. Although the Whitman incident occurred decades

(a)

(b)

FIGURE 12.1

(a) Charles Whitman with his wife, whom he later murdered. Few thought this exemplary citizen capable of the heinous acts of violence he committed. (b) Whitman (arrow) fires from the University of Texas tower onto the campus below.

ago, it is sadly reminiscent of more recent acts of violence in schools, communities, and workplaces across the United States. In this chapter, we will consider the factors that triggered Whitman's violence through the lenses of the major personality perspectives. Doing so can help us paint a more complete portrait of Whitman and may further our understanding not only of him but also of others who commit acts of violence and terrorism.

WHAT IS PERSONALITY?

► **Focus 1**
Which behavioral observations give rise to the concept of personality? Identify three characteristics of "personality behaviors."

The concept of personality arises from the fascinating spectrum of human individuality. We observe that people differ meaningfully in the ways they customarily think, feel, and act. These distinctive behavior patterns help define one's identity as a person. As one group of theorists noted, each of us is in certain respects like *all other* people, like *some other* people, and like *no other* person who has lived in the past or will exist in the future (Kluckhohn & Murray, 1953).

The concept of personality also rests on the observation that a given person seems to behave somewhat consistently over time and across different situations. From this perceived consistency comes the notion of *personality traits* that characterize an individual's customary ways of responding to his or her world. Although only modest consistency is found from childhood personality to adult personality, consistency becomes greater as we enter adulthood (Caspi & Roberts, 1999). Nonetheless, even in adulthood, a capacity for meaningful personality change remains (Lewis, 1999; Roberts et al., 2002). Combining these notions of individuality and consistency, we

► **Focus 2**
What three standards determine the scientific usefulness of a personality theory?

can define **personality** *as the distinctive and relatively enduring ways of thinking, feeling, and acting that characterize a person's responses to life situations.*

The thoughts, feelings, and actions that are seen as reflecting an individual's personality typically have three characteristics. First, they are seen as *behavioral components of identity* that distinguish that person from other people. Second, the behaviors are viewed as being caused primarily by *internal rather than environmental factors.* Third, the person's behaviors seem to have *organization and structure;* they seem to fit together in a meaningful fashion, suggesting an inner personality that guides and directs behavior (Figure 12.2).

The study of personality has been guided by the psychodynamic, humanistic, biological, behavioral, cognitive, and sociocultural perspectives. These perspectives provide different conceptions of what personality is and how it functions. As one pair of observers noted,

> It seems hard to believe that all the theorists are talking about the same creature, who is now angelic and now depraved, now a black-box robot shaped by reinforcers and now a shaper of its own destiny, now devious . . . and now hardheadedly oriented to solid reality. (Stone & Church, 1968, p. 4)

Yet this very diversity of viewpoints arises from the fact that the theorists have their own personalities that influence how they perceive and understand themselves and their world. No doubt, you will find some of their theories more in accord with your own life views than you will find others.

For personality psychologists, the subjective truth of a theory is less important than its *usefulness.* As discussed in Chapter 2, a scientific theory is useful to the extent that it (1) provides a comprehensive framework within which known facts can be incorporated, (2) allows us to predict future events with some precision, and (3) stimulates the discovery of new knowledge. We will evaluate each of the theories we describe in terms of these scientific standards. We will consider a number of approaches to the study of personality, beginning with the seminal work of Sigmund Freud, whose psychodynamic theory set the stage for a century of progress in the study of personality.

Behaviors

FIGURE 12.2

The behaviors of personality. Certain perceived characteristics of behavior are seen as reflecting an individual's personality.

IN REVIEW

■ The concept of personality arises from observations of individual differences and consistencies in behavior. Personality refers to the distinctive and relatively enduring ways of thinking, feeling, and acting that characterize a person's responses to life situations. Behaviors attributed to personality are viewed as establishing an individual's personal identity, having an internal cause, and having a meaningful organization and structure.

■ Personality theories differ considerably in their conceptions of what personality is and how it functions. Scientifically useful personality theories organize existing knowledge, allow the prediction of future events, and stimulate the discovery of new knowledge.

THE PSYCHODYNAMIC PERSPECTIVE

The first formal theory of personality was advanced by Sigmund Freud in the early years of the 20th century, and it is the prototype of the psychodynamic approach. Psychodynamic theorists look for the causes of behavior in a dynamic interplay of inner forces that often conflict with one another. They also focus on unconscious determinants of behavior. Sigmund Freud's psychoanalytic theory is one of the great intellectual contributions of modern times, and it continues to influence Western thought today. Opposition to Freud's ideas was a stimulus for most of the other theories discussed in this chapter.

FREUD'S PSYCHOANALYTIC THEORY

Freud (1856–1939) spent most of his life in Vienna, where he attended medical school with the intention of becoming a medical researcher (Figure 12.3). He was particularly interested in brain functioning. A pivotal event in his life occurred when he was awarded a fellowship to study in Paris with the famous French neurologist Jean Charcot. Charcot was treating patients who suffered from a disorder called *conversion hysteria*, in which physical symptoms such as paralysis and blindness appear suddenly and with no apparent physical cause. Freud's experiences in treating these patients convinced him that their symptoms were related to painful memories and feelings that seemed to have been *repressed*, or pushed out of awareness. When his patients were able to reexperience these traumatic memories and unacceptable feelings, which were often sexual or aggressive in nature, their physical symptoms often disappeared or improved markedly.

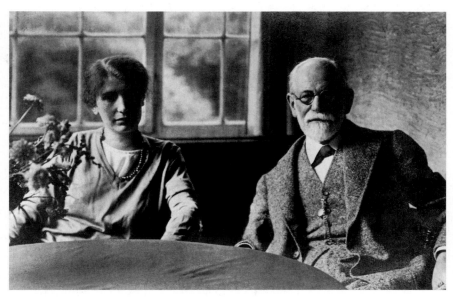

FIGURE 12.3

Sigmund Freud is shown here with his daughter Anna, who herself became an influential psychoanalytic theorist.

These observations convinced Freud that an unconscious part of the mind exerts great influence on behavior. He began to experiment with various techniques to unearth the buried contents of the unconscious mind, including hypnosis, *free association* (saying whatever comes to mind, no matter how trivial or embarrassing), and dream analysis. In an attempt to relieve his own painful bouts of depression, Freud also conducted an extensive self-analysis based on his own dreams.

In 1900 Freud published *The Interpretation of Dreams*. The book sold only 600 copies in the first six years after its publication, but his revolutionary ideas began to attract followers. His theory also evoked scathing criticism from a Victorian society that was not ready to regard the human being as a seething cauldron of sexual and aggressive impulses. In the words of one commentator,

> It is a shattering experience for anyone seriously committed to the Western tradition of morality and rationality to take a steadfast, unflinching look at what Freud has to say. It is humiliating to be compelled to admit the grossly seamy side of so many grand ideals. . . . To experience Freud is to partake a second time of the forbidden fruit. (Brown, 1959, p. xi)

Freud based his theory on careful clinical observation and constantly sought to expand it. Over time, psychoanalysis became (1) a theory of personality, (2) an approach to studying the mind, and (3) a method for treating psychological disorders.

Psychic Energy and Mental Events

Inspired by the hydraulic models of 19th-century physics, which emphasized exchanges and releases of physical energy, Freud considered personality to be an energy system, somewhat like the steam engines of his day. According to Freud, instinctual drives generate *psychic energy*, which powers the mind and constantly presses for either direct or indirect release. For example, a buildup of energy from sexual drives might be discharged directly in the form of sexual activity or indirectly through such diverse behaviors as sexual fantasies, farming, or painting.

Mental events may be conscious, preconscious, or unconscious. The *conscious mind* consists of mental events in current awareness. The *preconscious mind* contains memories, feelings, thoughts, and images that we are unaware of at the moment but that can be recalled, such as a friend's telephone number or memories of your 16th birthday.

Because we can be aware of their contents, we are likely to see the conscious and preconscious areas of the mind as the most prominent ones. But Freud believed that these areas are dwarfed in both size and importance by the *unconscious mind*, a dynamic realm of wishes, feelings, and impulses that lies beyond our awareness. He wrote, "The (conscious) mind is an iceberg—it floats with only one-seventh of its bulk above water." Only when impulses from the unconscious are discharged in one way or another, such as in dreams, slips of the tongue, or some disguised behavior, does the unconscious reveal itself, sometimes with unfortunate consequences. In the throes of passion, a young man proclaimed his love for his fiancée by gasping, "I love you, Marcia." The only problem was that his fiancée's name was Amy. Marcia was a former girlfriend. Freud would probably have concluded (as did Amy) that the slip of the tongue was a sign that erotic feelings for Marcia, which the man vehemently denied, were still bubbling within his subconscious mind. Psychoanalysts believe that such verbal slips are holes in our armor of conscious control and expressions of our true feelings.

▶ **Focus 3**
Describe Freud's structures of personality, their operating principles, and how they interact with one another.

The Structure of Personality

Freud divided personality into three separate but interacting structures: *id, ego,* and *superego.* The **id** *is the innermost core of the personality, the only structure present at birth, and the source of all psychic energy.* It exists totally within the unconscious mind (Figure 12.4). Freud described the id as "a chaos, a cauldron of seething excitations" (Freud, 1900/1965, p. 73). The id has no direct contact with reality and functions in a totally irrational manner. Operating according to the **pleasure principle,** *it seeks immediate gratification or release, regardless of rational considerations and environmental realities.* Its dictum: "Want . . . take!"

The id cannot directly satisfy itself by obtaining what it needs from the environment because it has no contact with the outer world. In the course of development, a new structure therefore develops. The **ego** *has direct contact with reality and functions primarily at a conscious level.* It operates according to the **reality principle,** *testing reality to decide when and under what conditions the id can safely discharge its impulses and satisfy its needs.* For example, the ego would seek sexual gratification within a consenting relationship rather than allowing the pleasure principle to dictate an impulsive sexual assault on the first person who happened by. Freud wrote, "In popular language, we may say that the ego stands for reason and sanity, in contrast to the id which contains untamed passions" (Freud, 1900/1965, p. 238).

FIGURE 12.4

Freud's model of personality.
Freud's own representation of his three-part conception of personality shows the relation of the id, ego, and superego to the unconscious, preconscious, and conscious areas of the mind. Note how relatively small the conscious portion of the mind is compared with the unconscious. SOURCE: Adapted from Smith, 1998.

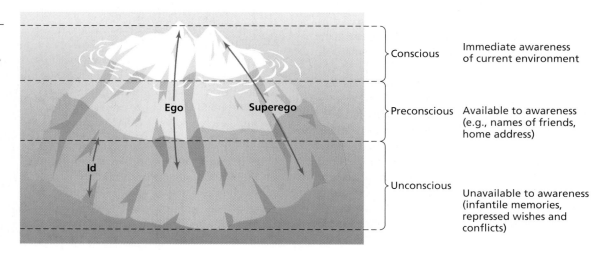

Conscious — Immediate awareness of current environment

Preconscious — Available to awareness (e.g., names of friends, home address)

Unconscious — Unavailable to awareness (infantile memories, repressed wishes and conflicts)

The last personality structure to develop is the **superego,** *the moral arm of the personality.* Developing by the age of 4 or 5, the superego contains the traditional values and ideals of family and society. These ideals are internalized by the child through identification with his or her parents, who also use reinforcement and punishment to teach the child what is "right," what is "wrong," and how the child "should" be. With the development of the superego, self-control is substituted for external control. Like the ego, the superego strives to control the instincts of the id, particularly the sexual and aggressive impulses that are condemned by society. In a sense the id says "I want!" and the superego replies "Don't you dare! That would be evil!" Whereas the ego simply tries to postpone instinctual gratification until conditions are safe and appropriate, the superego, in its blind quest for perfection, tries to block gratification permanently. For the superego, moralistic goals take precedence over realistic ones, regardless of the potential cost to the individual. Thus the superego might cause a person to experience intense guilt over sexual activity even within marriage because it has internalized the idea that "sex is dirty."

With the development of the superego, the ego is squarely in the eye of a psychic storm. It must achieve compromises between the demands of the id, the constraints of the superego, and the demands of reality. This balancing act has earned the ego the title "executive of the personality."

Conflict, Anxiety, and Defense

The dynamics of personality involve a never-ending struggle between instincts and drives in the id striving for release and counterforces generated by the ego and superego to contain them. Observable behavior often represents compromises between motives, needs, impulses, and defenses. When the ego confronts impulses that threaten to get out of control or is faced with dangers from the environment, anxiety results. Like physical pain, anxiety serves as a danger signal and motivates the ego to deal with the problem at hand. In many instances, the anxiety can be reduced through realistic coping behaviors, as when a person who is extremely angry at someone works out the problem through rational discussion instead of murderous assault. However, when realistic strategies are ineffective in reducing anxiety, the ego may resort to **defense mechanisms,** *unconscious mental operations that deny or distort reality.* Some of the defense mechanisms permit the release of impulses from the id in disguised forms that will not conflict with forces in the external world or with the prohibitions of the superego. The major defense mechanisms are described in Table 12.1.

▶ **Focus 4**
What roles do (1) conflict and defense and (2) psychosexual development play in Freud's theory?

TABLE 12.1 Psychoanalytic Ego Defense Mechanisms

Defense Mechanism	Description	Example
Repression	An active defensive process pushes anxiety-arousing impulses or memories into the unconscious mind.	A person who was sexually abused in childhood develops amnesia for the event.
Denial	A person refuses to acknowledge anxiety-arousing aspects of the environment. The denial may involve either the emotions connected with the event or the event itself.	A man who is told he has terminal cancer refuses to consider the possibility that he will not recover.
Displacement	An unacceptable or dangerous impulse is repressed, then directed at a safer substitute target.	A man who is harassed by his boss experiences no anger at work but then goes home and abuses his wife and children.
Intellectualization	The emotion connected with an upsetting event is repressed, and the situation is dealt with as an intellectually interesting event.	A person who has been rejected in an important relationship talks in a highly rational manner about the "interesting unpredictability of love relationships."
Projection	An unacceptable impulse is repressed, then attributed to (projected onto) other people.	A woman with strong repressed desires to have an affair continually accuses her husband of being unfaithful to her.
Rationalization	A person constructs a false but plausible explanation or excuse for an anxiety-arousing behavior or event that has already occurred.	A student caught cheating on an exam justifies the act by pointing out that the professor's tests are unfair and, besides, everybody else was cheating, too.
Reaction formation	An anxiety-arousing impulse is repressed, and its psychic energy finds release in an exaggerated expression of the opposite behavior.	A mother who harbors feelings of resentment toward her child represses them and becomes overprotective of the child.
Sublimation	A repressed impulse is released in the form of a socially acceptable or even admired behavior.	A man with strong hostile impulses becomes an investigative reporter who ruins political careers with his stories.

Psychoanalysts believe that repression is the primary means by which the ego keeps the lid on the id. In **repression,** *the ego uses some of its energy to prevent anxiety-arousing memories, feelings, and impulses from entering consciousness.* Repressed thoughts and wishes remain in the unconscious, striving for release, but they may be expressed indirectly, as in slips of the tongue or in dreams. Through the defense mechanism of **sublimation,** *taboo impulses may even be channeled into socially desirable and admirable behaviors, completely masking the sinister underlying impulses.* For example, hostile impulses may find expression in becoming a bounty hunter or a trial lawyer. Although Freud described several defense mechanisms, his primary interest was in repression. His daughter Anna Freud, also a psychoanalyst, extended his ideas and described many of the defense mechanisms shown in Table 12.1.

Defense mechanisms operate unconsciously, so people are usually unaware that they are using self-deception to ward off anxiety. Almost everyone uses defense mechanisms at times, but maladjusted people use them excessively in place of more realistic approaches to dealing with problems.

Psychosexual Development

Freud's clinical experiences convinced him that adult personality traits are powerfully influenced by experiences in the first years of life. He proposed that children pass through a series of **psychosexual stages** *during which the id's pleasure-seeking tendencies are focused on specific pleasure-sensitive areas of the body—the erogenous zones.* Potential deprivations or overindulgences can arise during any of these stages, resulting in **fixation,** *a state of arrested psychosexual development in which instincts are focused on a particular psychic theme.* **Regression,** *a psychological retreat to an earlier psychosexual stage,* can occur in the face of stressful demands that exceed one's coping capabilities.

The first of these stages is the *oral stage,* which occurs during infancy. Infants gain primary satisfaction from taking in food and from sucking on a breast, a thumb, or some other object. Freud proposed that either excessive gratification or frustration of oral needs can result in fixation on oral themes of self-indulgence or dependency as an adult.

In the second and third years of life, children enter the *anal stage,* and pleasure becomes focused on the process of elimination. During toilet training, the child is faced with society's first attempt to control a biological urge. According to Freud,

harsh toilet training can produce compulsions, overemphasis on cleanliness, obsessive concerns with orderliness, and insistence on rigid rules and rituals. In contrast, Freud speculated that extremely lax toilet training results in a messy, negative, and dominant adult personality.

The most controversial of Freud's stages is the *phallic stage,* which begins at 4 to 5 years of age. This is the time when children begin to derive pleasure from their sexual organs. Freud believed that during this stage of early sexual awakenings, the male child experiences erotic feelings toward his mother, desires to possess her sexually, and views his father as a rival. At the same time, however, these feelings arouse strong guilt and a fear that the father might find out and castrate him, hence the term *castration anxiety. This conflictual situation involving love for the mother and hostility toward the father is the* **Oedipus complex,** named for the Greek character Oedipus, who unknowingly killed his father and married his mother. Girls, meanwhile, discover that they lack a penis, blame the mother for their lack of what Freud considered the more desirable sex organ, and wish to bear their father's child as a substitute for the penis they lack. *The female counterpart of the Oedipus complex was termed the* **Electra complex.**

Freud believed that the phallic stage is a major milestone in the development of gender identity, for children normally resolve these conflicts by repressing their sexual impulses and moving from a sexual attachment to the opposite-sex parent to *identification* with the same-sex parent. Boys take on the traits of their fathers and girls those of their mothers. Identification allows the child to possess the opposite-sex parent indirectly, or vicariously, and also helps form the superego as the child internalizes the parent's values and moral beliefs.

As the phallic stage draws to a close at about 6 years of age, children enter the *latency stage,* during which sexuality becomes dormant for about 6 years. Sexuality normally reemerges in adolescence as the beginning of a lifelong *genital stage,* in which erotic impulses find direct expression in sexual relationships.

NEOANALYTIC AND OBJECT RELATIONS APPROACHES

Freud's ideas were so revolutionary that they generated disagreement even within his circle of disciples. **Neoanalytic theorists** *were psychoanalysts who disagreed with certain aspects of Freud's thinking and developed their own theories.* Among them were Alfred Adler, Karen Horney, Erik Erikson, and

▶ **Focus 5**
How do neoanalytic and object relations theories depart from and build on Freudian theory?

Carl Jung. The neoanalysts believed that Freud did not give social and cultural factors a sufficiently important role in the development and dynamics of personality. In particular, they believed that he stressed infantile sexuality too much (Kurzweil, 1989). The second major criticism was that Freud laid too much emphasis on the events of childhood as determinants of adult personality. Neoanalytic theorists agreed that childhood experiences are important, but some theorists, such as Erikson, believed that personality development continues throughout the life span as individuals confront challenges that are specific to particular phases in their lives.

In contrast to Freud's assertion that behavior is motivated by inborn sexual and aggressive instincts and drives, Alfred Adler (1870–1937) insisted that humans are inherently social beings who are motivated by *social interest*, the desire to advance the welfare of others. They care about others, cooperate with them, and place general social welfare above selfish personal interests (Figure 12.5). In contrast, Freud seemed to view people as savage animals caged by the bars of civilization. Perhaps influenced by his own struggles to overcome childhood illnesses and accidents, Adler also postulated a general motive of *striving for superiority*, which drives people to compensate for real or imagined defects in themselves (the *inferiority complex*) and to strive to be ever more competent in life.

Like Adler, Carl Jung (1875–1961) was Freud's friend and associate before he broke away and developed his own theory. Jung expanded Freud's notion of the unconscious in unique directions. For example, he believed that humans possess not only a **personal unconscious** *based on their life experiences* but also a **collective unconscious** *that consists of memories accumulated throughout the entire history of the human race*. These memories are represented by **archetypes,** *inherited tendencies to interpret experiences in certain ways*. Archetypes find expression in symbols, myths, and beliefs that appear across many cultures, such as the image of a god, an evil force, the hero, the good mother, and the quest for self-unity and completeness (Figure 12.6). Jung's ideas bear some similarities to those of contemporary evolutionary theorists who emphasize innate cognitive processes.

Following Freud's death in 1939, Melanie Klein (1975), Otto Kernberg (1984), Margaret Mahler (1968), and Heinz Kohut (1971) developed a new psychodynamic emphasis. **Object relations theories** *focus on the images or mental representations that people form of themselves and other*

FIGURE 12.5

In Alfred Adler's theory, people have an inborn social interest that can cause them to put society's welfare above their interests. Mother Teresa's selfless service to others is one striking example.

people as a result of early experiences with caregivers. Whether realistic or distorted, these internal representations of important adults—for example, of the mother as kind or malevolent, the father as protective or abusive—become lenses, or working models, through which later social interactions are viewed, and these relational themes exert an unconscious influence on a person's relationships throughout life (Westen, 1998). People who have difficulties forming and maintaining intimate relationships tend to mentally represent themselves and others in negative ways, expecting painful interactions and attributing malevolence or rejection to others (Kernberg, 1984; Nigg et al., 1992). These working models often create self-fulfilling prophesies, influencing the recurring relationships people form with others.

John Bowlby's (1969) attachment theory, discussed in Chapter 11, is an outgrowth of the object relations approach. Correlational research relating early attachment experiences to later adult relationships is yielding provocative results. For example, college students with a history of positive early attachments tend to have longer and more satisfying romances (Shaver & Clark, 1996). In contrast, child-abusing parents often have mental representations of their own parents as punitive, rejecting,

▶ **Focus 6**
What is meant by object relations? Describe three adult attachment styles.

FIGURE 12.6

Shown here is the famous neoanalyst Carl Jung. Behind him is a *mandala* (Sanskrit for "circle"), which symbolizes wholeness and completion. The mandala symbol occurs within numerous cultures and religions of the world, suggesting to Jung that it is a reflection of the collective unconscious.

TABLE 12.2   Attachment Styles in Adult Relationships

Question: Which of the following best describes your feelings?*

1. I find it relatively easy to get close to others and am comfortable depending on them and having them depend on me. I don't often worry about being abandoned or about someone getting too close to me. (secure)

2. I am somewhat uncomfortable being close to others; I find it difficult to trust them completely, difficult to allow myself to depend on them. I am nervous when anyone gets too close, and often, love partners want me to be more intimate than I feel comfortable being. (avoidant)

3. I find that others are reluctant to get as close as I would like. I often worry that my partner doesn't really love me or won't want to stay with me. I want to merge completely with another person, and this desire sometimes scares people away. (anxious-ambivalent)

*The first type of attachment style is described as "secure," the second as "avoidant," and the third as "anxious-ambivalent."
SOURCE: Based on Shaver et al., 1988.

---

and abusive (van Ijzendoorn, 1995). Table 12.2 shows descriptive statements that characterize people who manifest "secure," "avoidant," and "anxious-ambivalent" adult attachment styles. These attachment styles are associated with adjustment and well-being. Three studies by Benjamin Hankin and coworkers (2005) examined the relation between adult attachment dimensions and symptoms of emotional distress (anxiety and depression). Across all three studies, avoidant and anxious-ambivalent attachment predicted depressive symptoms, and anxious attachment was associated with anxiety symptoms. Today, many psychodynamic therapists say that they rely more heavily on object relations concepts than on classical psychoanalytic theory (Aron, 1996; Westen, 1998). The concepts in object relations theories are also easier to operationally define and measure, making them more amenable to research.

EVALUATING THE PSYCHODYNAMIC APPROACH

Freud was committed to testing his ideas through case studies and clinical observations. He believed that careful observations of everyday behavior and clinical phenomena were the best source of evidence. He opposed experimental research, believing that the complex phenomena he had identified could not be studied under controlled conditions (Rosenzweig, 1992). Most modern psychologists do not believe that clinical observations are sufficient proof, but they do acknowledge the difficulty of studying psychoanalytic concepts under controlled laboratory conditions (Carver & Scheier, 2003; Mischel et al., 2004). Indeed, a major shortcoming of psychoanalytic theory is that many of its concepts are ambiguous and difficult to measure or even to define operationally. How, for example, can we measure the strength of an individual's id impulses and unconscious ego defenses or study processes that are by definition unconscious and inaccessible to the person?

Although psychoanalytic theory has profoundly influenced psychology, psychiatry, and other fields, it has often been criticized on scientific grounds. One reason is that many of its specific propositions have not held up under the scrutiny of research (Fisher & Greenberg, 1996). To some critics, psychoanalytic theory seems to be more science fiction than science. A great drawback of the theory is that it is hard to test, not because it doesn't explain enough but because it often explains too much to allow clear-cut behavioral predictions (Meehl, 1995). For example, suppose we predict on the basis of psychoanalytic theory that participants in an experimental condition will behave aggressively but they behave instead in a loving manner. Is the theory wrong, or is the aggression being masked by the operation of a defense mechanism such as reaction formation (which produces exaggerated behaviors that are the opposite of the impulse)? The difficulties in making clear-cut behavioral predictions mean that some psychoanalytic hypotheses cannot be disproved, and this detracts greatly from the theory's scientific usefulness.

Freud's emphasis on the unconscious was scorned by a Victorian society that emphasized rationality, and later generations of personality psychologists with a behaviorist orientation condemned it as unscientific. However, research over the past 20 years has vindicated Freud's belief in unconscious psychic events by showing that nonconscious mental and emotional phenomena do indeed occur and can affect our behavior (Chartrand & Bargh, 2002; Erdelyi, 2001). On the other hand, the unconscious processes that have been demonstrated experimentally are by no means as exotic as the seething cauldron of forbidden wishes and desires described by Freud (Kihlstrom, 1999). Rather, current research is unearthing what one theorist describes as "a kinder, gentler unconscious" (Greenwald, 1992).

Freud's ideas about psychosexual development are the most controversial feature of his theory. Although many theorists reject Freud's assertions about childhood sexuality and the notion of specific psychosexual stages, there is strong evidence that childhood experiences do indeed influence the development of personality (Lewis, 1999). The previously wide gulf between psychodynamic theories and other psychological perspectives is starting to narrow, due largely to the development of new methods for studying unconscious mental processes.

Can the psychodynamic perspective offer possible insights into Charles Whitman's personality and his eventual eruption into violence? Although born into a family of means and showered with material goods, Whitman grew up within a chaotic home environment. His father was a self-made but brutal man who ruled his house with an iron fist and frequently beat his wife. He tolerated no weakness from his sons and viciously belittled them for any perceived failures. Whitman was very close to his mother and deeply resented his father's treatment of her, which, according to

Freud, would only enhance any unresolved Oedipal hostility toward the father. In his suicide note, he wrote, "The intense hatred I feel for my father is beyond description" (Lavergne, 1997, p. 168). Lacking a good paternal model with whom to identify, Whitman seemed to have a poorly developed superego and constantly wrote himself notes about how to behave appropriately, using the notes as a substitute for his tenuous inner controls. A friend describing Whitman said he was "like a computer. He would install his values into the machine, then program the things he had to do, and out would come the results" (Lavergne, 1997, p. 79).

Object relations theories also have applicability to Whitman. Despite his hatred for his father, his own family experiences caused him to enter his marriage with an internal working model of "abusive husband" and "submissive wife." To his later regret, he beat his own wife on two occasions in the early years of his marriage. He was determined not to repeat this behavior and kept a journal in which he constantly wrote self-instructions about how to be a good husband. For the most part, these external constraints were effective in keeping his intense hostility under control—until the accumulation of severe life stressors caused his controls to disintegrate. "Unusual and irrational thoughts" began to intrude into consciousness as his defenses were strained to the breaking point, and he eventually exploded into violence. The psychiatrist at the student health center who interviewed him several months before the tower incident (referred to in Whitman's letter at the opening of this chapter as "the doctor") found that he "had something about him that expressed the all-American boy," but "seemed to be oozing with hostility." Whitman told the psychiatrist that he had frequent fantasies about "going up on the tower with a deer rifle and shooting people," but the psychiatrist did not take them seriously because of his nonviolent history (Lavergne, 1997, p. 137).

? What Do You Think?

HOW SERIOUSLY SHOULD WE TAKE PEOPLE'S VIOLENT FANTASIES?

What are we to make of people's reports of violent fantasies? Should Whitman's report of his violent fantasies have alerted the psychiatrist about his penchant for violence and caused the psychiatrist to contact authorities? What would you have done? Think about it, then read the discussion on page 484.

► **Focus 7**
What are personal constructs, and how do they account for personality differences?

IN REVIEW

■ Freud's psychoanalytic theory views personality as an energy system. Personality dynamics involve modifications and exchanges of energy within this system. Mental events may be conscious, preconscious, or unconscious.

■ Freud divided the personality into three structures: id, ego, and superego. The id is irrational and seeks immediate instinctual gratification on the basis of the pleasure principle. The ego operates on the reality principle, which requires it to test reality and to mediate between the demands of the id, the superego, and reality. The superego is the moral arm of the personality.

■ The dynamics of personality involve continuous conflict between impulses of the id and counterforces of the ego and superego. When dangerous id impulses threaten to get out of control or when the environment poses dangers, the result is anxiety. To deal with threat, the ego may develop defense mechanisms to ward off anxiety and permit instinctual gratification in disguised forms.

■ Freud's psychosexual theory of personality development held that adult personality traits are molded by how children deal with instinctual urges and social reality during the oral, anal, and phallic stages.

■ Neoanalytic theorists modified and extended Freud's ideas in important ways, stressing social and cultural factors in personality development. Today, object relations theorists focus on the mental representations that people form of themselves, others, and relationships.

THE PHENOMENOLOGICAL-HUMANISTIC PERSPECTIVE

The approaches we will describe next were in part a reaction to Freud's conception of people as driven by "those half-tamed demons that inhabit the human beast" (Freud, 1900/1965, p. 202). In contrast to Freud, these theorists believed that our behavior is not a reaction to unconscious drives and conflicts but rather a response to our immediate conscious experience of self and environment (Kelly, 1955; Rogers, 1951). This *emphasis on the primacy of immediate experience is known as* **phenomenology,** and it focuses our attention on the present instead of the past. These theorists also regarded themselves as humanists. They embraced a positive

view that affirms the inherent dignity and goodness of the human spirit, as well as the individual's creative potential and inborn striving toward personal growth (Figure 12.7).

GEORGE KELLY'S PERSONAL CONSTRUCT THEORY

> To the humanist every man is a scientist by disposition as well as by right, every subject is an incipient experimenter, and every person is by daily necessity a fellow psychologist. (Kelly, 1966, quoted in Maher, 1979, p. 205)

A theory developed by George Kelly (1905–1967) in the 1950s has had a strong and pervasive influence on many other theorists. According to Kelly, people's primary goal is to make sense out of the world, to find personal meaning in it. When they are unable to do so, they experience uncertainty and anxiety. To achieve understanding, they try to explain and understand the events of their lives, and they test this understanding in the same way scientists do: by attempting to anticipate, to predict.

Kelly's primary interest was how people construct reality. They do so by their individual system of **personal constructs,** *cognitive categories into which they sort the persons and events in their lives.* In Kelly's theory, the personal construct system was the primary basis for individual differences in personality.

As noted in our discussion of concept formation in Chapter 8, all perception involves categorizing. From birth onward, Kelly maintained, stimuli are categorized, given meaning, and reacted to in terms of the categories, or personal constructs, into which they are placed. Every person has her or his own pattern of preferred personal constructs (such as "good," "bad," "successful," "powerful," and so on), which vary in personal importance. By understanding these constructs, the rules an individual uses to assign events to categories, and her or his hypotheses about how the categories relate to one another, Kelly believed that we can understand the person's psychological world. If we can understand the individual's internal world, then we can understand and predict that person's behavior.

The same event can be categorized, or perceived, in entirely different ways by different people. For example, suppose that two lovers break up. One observer may construe the event as "simple incompatibility"; another may think that one person was "jilted" by the other; another might describe the breakup as the "result of parental meddling";

another might call it "a terrible development"; and a fifth might see it as "a blessing in disguise."

Rather than evaluating alternative constructions according to whether or not they are true (which we cannot know), Kelly examined the consequences of construing in particular ways. For example, if one of the people in the broken relationship interpreted what happened as "being rejected," Kelly would try to discover the consequences for the person of construing the situation in that way. If the construction led to bad outcomes, such as feelings of worthlessness or the conclusion that "No one will ever love me, and I'll never get involved again," then the task would be to find a more useful alternative (for example, "I am someone who hasn't found the right person yet but who will if I keep trying."). Kelly, a clinical psychologist, saw psychotherapy as a way of demonstrating to clients that their constructions are *hypotheses* rather than facts. Once clients realize this, they can be encouraged to test the hypotheses that govern their lives, just as scientists do, and to replace maladaptive ones with more useful ones.

As people seek to understand events within the world, they develop habitual tendencies related to categorization of people and events. Such tendencies can be measured by tasks that determine the extent to which particular categories are used in making such distinctions (Robinson, 2004). Kelly developed a measure called the **Role Construct Repertory Test,** or **Rep Test,** *to assess individuals' personal construct systems.* In taking the Rep Test, you are asked to consider people or events in your life that are important to you. You then consider them in groups of three (for example, father, best friend, romantic partner) and indicate how any two of them are similar to one another and different from the third. In this way, the basic dimensions of similarity and difference that you use to categorize people and events—your personal constructs—will begin to emerge. The Rep Test can also assess other aspects of your construct system, such as the number of different constructs that you use.

In order to help clients experiment with new viewpoints and behaviors, Kelly developed a therapeutic technique called *fixed-role therapy.* He wrote role descriptions and behavioral scripts for his clients that differed from their typical views of themselves. For example, a shy person might be asked to play the role of a more confident and assertive person for two or three days, to think and act like a confident person. Kelly and the client would practice the role within the therapy setting to be certain that the client had a command of the

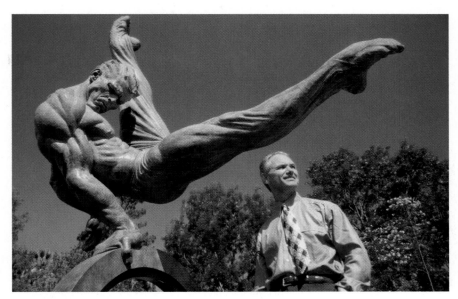

FIGURE 12.7

The motivations underlying behavior are much different for humanistic theorists than they are for Freudians. In the view of humanistic theorists like Abraham Maslow and Carl Rogers, creative and artistic accomplishments are a product not of intrapsychiatric conflict and sublimation but rather an expression of an innate tendency toward self-actualization.

required behaviors and the view of the world that a confident individual would have. Kelly hoped that by trying out the new role, the client might gain a firsthand appreciation for the ways in which different constructions and behaviors could lead to more satisfying life outcomes. Kelly suggested that the willingness to experiment with new roles and ways of thinking can help all of us develop in ways that enhance our lives.

CARL ROGERS'S THEORY OF THE SELF

Carl Rogers (1902–1987), a colleague of George Kelly's on the Ohio State University faculty in the 1950s, was one of the most influential humanistic theorists. As a humanist, Rogers believed that the forces that direct behavior are within us and that when they are not distorted or blocked by our environment, they can be trusted to direct us toward **self-actualization,** *the highest realization of human potential.*

The Self

The central concept in Rogers's theory is the **self,** *an organized, consistent set of perceptions of and beliefs about oneself* (Rogers, 1959). Once formed, the self plays a powerful role in guiding our perceptions and directing our behavior. The self thus has two facets: It is an object of perception (the self-concept) and an internal entity that directs behavior.

▶ **Focus 8**
Describe the roles of self-consistency, congruence, threat, and conditions of worth in Rogers's self theory.

"I can't say I like the looks of that bunch."

FIGURE 12.8

Tendencies to behave in accordance with one's self-concept can at times have ominous implications. Source: Copyright © The New Yorker Collection 1971 Dana Fradon. All rights reserved. Used with permission from cartoonbank.com.

Rogers theorized that at the beginning of their lives, children cannot distinguish between themselves and their environment. As they interact with their world, children begin to distinguish between the "me" and the "not-me." The self-concept continues to develop in response to our life experiences, though many aspects of it remain quite stable over time.

Once the self-concept is established, there is a tendency to maintain it, for it helps us understand our relationship to the world around us. We therefore have needs for **self-consistency,** *an absence of conflict among self-perceptions,* and **congruence,** *consistency between self-perceptions and experience.* Any experience we have that is inconsistent, or incongruous, with our self-concept, including our perceptions of our own behavior, evokes **threat,** *or anxiety.* Well-adjusted individuals can respond to threat adaptively by modifying the self-concept so that the experiences are congruent with the self. But other people choose to deny or distort their experiences to remove the incongruence, a strategy that can lead to what Rogers termed "problems in living." Thus a person who always attributes interpersonal difficulties to shortcomings in another person will be unlikely to consider the possibility that he or she may have some self-defeating behavior patterns that deserve attention.

To preserve their self-concepts, people not only interpret situations in self-congruent ways, but they also behave in ways that will lead others

to respond to them in a self-confirming fashion (Brown, 1998). If Camille has an image of herself as unlovable and certain to be rejected if she lets people get close enough to hurt her, she may behave in ways that distance others. When her behavior is successful, others pull away from her, confirming in her mind that she is indeed unlovable. As Rogers frequently noted, people are pushed by self-consistency needs to behave in accord with their self-concept (Figure 12.8).

According to Rogers, the degree of congruence between self-concept and experience helps define one's level of adjustment. The more rigid and inflexible people's self-concepts are, the less open they will be to their experiences and the more maladjusted they will become (Figure 12.9a). If there is a significant degree of incongruence between self and experience and if the experiences are forceful enough, the defenses used to deny and distort reality may collapse, resulting in

(a)

(b)

FIGURE 12.9

Degree of congruence between self-concept and experience.
(a) Maladjustment occurs when a person faced with incongruities between self and experience distorts or denies reality to make it consistent with the self-concept. (b) In contrast, extremely well-adjusted, or fully functioning, people integrate experiences into the self with minimal distortion, so that they are able to profit fully from their experiences.

extreme anxiety and a temporary disorganization of the self-concept.

The Need for Positive Regard

Rogers believed that we are born with an innate **need for positive regard**—*for acceptance, sympathy, and love from others.* Rogers viewed positive regard as essential for healthy development. Ideally, positive regard received from the parents is unconditional—that is, independent of how the child behaves. **Unconditional positive regard** *communicates that the person is inherently worthy of love, regardless of accomplishments or behavior.* In contrast, *conditional positive regard* is dependent on how the child behaves; in the extreme case, love and acceptance are given to the child *only* when the child behaves as the parents want. A study by Avi Assor and coworkers (2004) suggests long-term negative consequences of this child-rearing approach. College students who reported that their mothers and fathers used conditional regard in four domains (emotion control, prosocial behavior, academics, and sports performance) also experienced up-and-down fluctuations in their self-esteem and perceived parental disapproval, and resented their parents as young adults.

People need positive regard not only from others but also from themselves. Thus a **need for positive self-regard,** *the desire to feel good about ourselves,* also develops. Lack of unconditional positive regard from parents and other significant people in the past teaches people that they are worthy of approval and love only when they meet certain standards. This fosters the development of **conditions of worth** *that dictate the circumstances under which we approve or disapprove of ourselves.* A child who experiences parental approval when behaving in a friendly fashion but disapproval whenever she becomes angry or aggressive may come to disapprove of her own angry feelings, even when they are justified. As an adult, she may deny in herself all feelings of anger and struggle to preserve a self-image of being totally loving. Rogers believed that conditions of worth can tyrannize people and cause major incongruence between self and experience, as well as a need to deny or distort important aspects of experience. Conditions of worth are similar to the "shoulds" and "musts" that populate the Freudian superego.

Fully Functioning Persons

Toward the end of his career, Rogers became particularly interested in **fully functioning persons,** *individuals who were close to achieving self-actualization.* As Rogers viewed them, such people do not hide behind masks or adopt artificial roles. They feel a sense of inner freedom, self-determination, and choice in the direction of their growth. They have no fear of behaving spontaneously, freely, and creatively. Because they are fairly free of conditions of worth, they can accept inner and outer experiences as they are, without modifying them defensively to suit a rigid self-concept or the expectations of others. Thus a fully functioning unmarried woman would be able to (1) state quite frankly that her career is more important to her than a role as wife and mother (*if* she truly felt that way), even if others did not approve of her choice, and (2) act comfortably on those feelings. In this sense, she could be true to herself (see Figure 12.9b).

What Do You Think?

IS SELF-ACTUALIZATION A USEFUL SCIENTIFIC CONSTRUCT?

Self-actualization is a central concept for humanistic theorists such as Maslow and Rogers. Consider what you have learned about formulating a psychological construct and evaluating a theory according to scientific principles. Can you see any problems with establishing the existence of this core motivation from a scientific perspective? Think about it, then see page 484 for a discussion.

RESEARCH ON THE SELF

By giving the self a central place in his theory, Rogers helped stimulate a great deal of research on the self-concept. Two topics at the forefront are (1) the development of self-esteem and its effects on behavior, and (2) the roles played by self-verification and self-enhancement motives.

Self-Esteem

Self-esteem, *how positively or negatively we feel about ourselves,* is a very important aspect of personal well-being, happiness, and adjustment (Brown, 1998; Diener, 2000). Table 12.3 shows the types of test items that are used to measure differences in self-esteem. Men and women do not differ in overall level of self-esteem on such measures (Brown, 1998; Maccoby & Jacklin, 1974).

Level of self-esteem is quite stable over the life span, with correlations of .50 to .70 from childhood to old age (Trzesniewski et al., 2003). High self-esteem is related to many positive behaviors and life outcomes. People with high self-esteem are happier with their lives, have fewer

Examine the video, "Adolescent Self-Concept at Age 16," in Chapter 12 of your CD for a discussion among three 16-year-old girls concerning how the views of friends, boys, and parents influence their self-esteem.

TABLE 12.3	Items Similar to Those Found on Self-Esteem Scales*

1. I believe I am a worthwhile person.

2. There are many things I would change about myself if I could. (reverse scored)

3. I approve of myself as a person.

4. I have many positive traits.

5. I like who I am.

6. There are many things I don't like about myself. (reverse scored)

*Items are scored on a scale ranging from –3 ("strongly disagree") to +3 ("strongly agree").

▶ **Focus 9**
How does self-esteem develop? Describe the roles of self-verification and self-enhancement as motivational forces.

 Does adolescent's self-esteem vary according to the particular setting in which an adolescent finds himself or herself? View the video, "Adolescent Self-Esteem," in Chapter 12 of your CD for one researcher's viewpoint.

interpersonal problems, achieve at a higher and more consistent level, are less susceptible to social pressure, and are more capable of forming satisfying love relationships (Brown, 1998). In contrast, people with poor self-images are less likely to try to make themselves feel better when they experience negative moods in response to perceived failures in their lives (Heimpel et al., 2002). This may be one reason why they are more prone to psychological problems such as anxiety and depression, to physical illness, and to poor social relationships and underachievement (Brown, 1998).

What conditions foster the development of high self-esteem? Children develop higher self-esteem when their parents communicate unconditional acceptance and love, establish clear guidelines for behavior, and reinforce compliance while giving the child freedom to make decisions and express opinions within those guidelines (Brown, 1998; Coopersmith, 1967). Beginning in early childhood, success in achieving positive outcomes builds a sense that one is an effective person (Hawley & Little, 2002). Feedback received from other people also has an impact on the child's sense of self. One study showed that when low-self-esteem children were exposed to highly supportive youth sport coaches who gave them large amounts of positive reinforcement and encouragement, the children's self-esteem increased significantly over the course of the sports season (Smoll et al., 1993). Apparently, the positive feedback caused the children to revise their self-concepts in a positive direction.

Self-Verification and Self-Enhancement Motives

Rogers proposed that people are motivated to preserve their self-concepts by maintaining self-consistency and congruence. **Self-verification** *refers to this need to confirm the self-concept.* In one study, researchers asked college students to describe themselves in order to measure their self-concepts. In a later and supposedly unrelated experiment, the students interacted with other participants and received fake feedback from them in the form of adjectives that were either consistent or inconsistent with their self-concepts. Later, when the students were asked to recall and identify the adjectives that had been attributed to them, they showed greater recall for the consistent adjectives, suggesting that people selectively attend to and recall self-consistent information (Suinn et al., 1962).

Self-verification needs are also expressed in people's tendency to seek out self-confirming relationships. One study found that if people with firmly held negative self-views marry spouses who appraise them favorably, they tend to eventually withdraw from the marriage. Such people are more likely to remain with spouses who agree with the negative image they have of themselves. In contrast, people with positive self-concepts prefer spouses who share their positive views of themselves (Swann et al., 1992).

Rogers (1959) also suggested that people have a need to regard themselves positively, and research confirms the existence of **self-enhancement,** *a strong and pervasive tendency to gain and preserve a positive self-image.* Self-enhancement needs have been demonstrated across many cultures (Sedikides et al., 2003), and several self-enhancement strategies have been identified. For example, people show a marked tendency to attribute their successes to their own abilities and effort but to attribute their failures to environmental factors. Furthermore, most people rate themselves as better than average on virtually any socially desirable characteristic that is subjective in nature (Leary, 2004). The vast majority of businesspeople and politicians rate themselves as more ethical than the average. In defiance of mathematical possibility, about 80 percent of high school students rate themselves in the top 10 percent in their ability to get along with others. Even people who have been hospitalized after causing auto accidents rate themselves as more skillful than the average driver (Greenberg et al., 1997). People generally view themselves as improving over time, relative to their peers (Ross & Wilson, 2003). Indeed, as evidence on self-serving biases in self-perception continues to accumulate, researchers are concluding that positive illusions of this sort are the rule rather than the exception in well-adjusted people and that these self-enhancement tendencies contribute to people's psychological well-being (Taylor & Brown, 1988; Taylor et al., 2003).

For people low in self-esteem, self-enhancement needs sometimes override self-verification tendencies (Tesser, 2004). In a series of experimental studies, Tiffiny Bernichon and coworkers (2003) found that low-self-esteem individuals have a strong tendency to seek out positive feedback about themselves even when it is not self-verifying. The pervasiveness of self-enhancement tendencies makes one wonder why so many people have low self-esteem. The following "Research Close-Up" may provide a partial answer to this question.

▶ **Focus 10**
What does the "Research Close-Up" study tell us about the maintenance of low self-esteem?

Research Close-Up   If We're Self-Enhancing, What Maintains Low Self-Esteem?

SOURCE: ROBERT A. JOSEPHS, JENNIFER K. BOSSON, and CHRISTOPHER G. JACOBS (2003). Self-esteem maintenance processes: Why self-esteem may be resistant to change. *Personality and Social Psychology Bulletin, 29,* 920–933.

INTRODUCTION

Once established, self-esteem tends to remain stable over time (Baumeister, 1993). Although research shows that people have a pronounced tendency toward self-enhancement, we all know people who have low self-esteem that persists even in the face of social reassurance and positive experiences that should make them feel better about themselves. If people strive to maximize feelings of self-worth, what accounts for the persistence of low self-esteem in some people? The authors of this article tested the hypothesis that low self-esteem is maintained because such people have difficulty accepting positive feedback not so much from others but from *themselves*.

METHOD

To test their hypothesis, the researchers needed to create an experimental situation in which they could examine the relative effects of external and self-generated feedback on feelings of accomplishment and self-worth. They chose an anagrams task consisting of sets of 5 scrambled letters that could be rearranged into words (e.g., OTLHE).

Students who had scored in the top or bottom 25 percent on a self-esteem scale were told that the purpose of the study was to test their anagram-solving ability, believed to be related to "an important indicator of overall intellectual ability." They were told that because the task was unfamiliar to them, the degree of improvement over trials was the most important indicator of ability. The participants were then seated at a computer screen, where 15 anagrams appeared one at a time. They were to unscramble the letters mentally and then type in the correct word as quickly as they could. The computer timed their performance.

The experiment had four experimental conditions. The researchers either made the 15 anagrams easier over time so performance would improve, or they arranged them in random order so that performance would remain relatively constant. This manipulation was designed to affect participants' *self-generated feedback* to themselves (positive or neutral) based on their perceptions of how well they had done. Half of the participants in these improvement versus no-improvement conditions were then given either positive or neutral *external feedback* from the experimenter. About 2 minutes into the study, the experimenter entered the room and said that he wanted to check the participant's previous responses to make sure the computer was recording things correctly. He examined the previous responses and gave the positive ("Looks good. It looks like you did really well on a couple near the end.") or neutral ("This is about what I expected.") external feedback. Of interest was how the high- and low-self-esteem participants responded in these four experimental conditions, particularly the improvement condition. How would they be affected by their feedback to themselves based on their perceived performance and by the external feedback from the experimenter?

Two dependent variables were measured after the anagrams task. The first was perceived performance: "Do you think your performance got better or worse over the series of anagrams?" (answered on a scale that ranged from 1, "got much worse," to 9, "got much better"). The second was a measure of how positively they felt about themselves at that moment.

RESULTS

The time taken to solve all 15 anagrams did not differ according to whether they were presented in decreasing order of difficulty or in random order, and the high- and low-self-esteem groups did not differ in their performance levels, either. This was important, so that the results on the two dependent variables could be attributed to the internal and external feedback effects.

Figure 12.10 shows the results for perceived performance and feelings of self-esteem for the condition in which the anagrams occurred in decreasing order of difficulty (i.e., the improvement condition). As shown in Figure 12.10a, students low in self-esteem rated their degree of improvement much lower than those high in self-esteem when they received only

Continued

(a)

(b)

FIGURE 12.10

Maintaining Low Self-Esteem. (a) This graph shows the perceived improvement during the anagrams task for low- and high-self-esteem participants who were in the improvement condition. Low-self-esteem participants gave themselves less positive feedback in both experimenter conditions, but especially when the experimenter gave neutral feedback. (b) This graph shows current feelings of self-esteem in response to success among low- and high-self-esteem participants in the improvement condition and whose feedback came from their own observations or from the experimenter's positive comment on their performance. Low-self-esteem participants felt less positively about themselves even when the experimenter told them they had done well.

neutral feedback from the experimenter. Despite what should have been obvious improvement, they did not give themselves positive performance feedback, whereas the high-self-esteem people did. In contrast, the low-self-esteem students given positive external feedback by the experimenter rated their performance nearly as highly as did students high in self-esteem.

Figure 12.10b shows the impact of improvement on the anagrams (in the improvement condition only) task and the two kinds of experimenter feedback on participants' current feelings about themselves. Here, we see that the participants low in self-esteem felt much less positively about themselves than did those high in self-esteem, even those who received positive feedback from the experimenter after their improvement on the anagrams. This result shows how difficult it is to convince people low in self-esteem that they should feel good about themselves, even when they are told that they have done something very well.

DISCUSSION

This study sheds light on an important process in low-self-esteem maintenance. Consistent with the investigators' hypothesis, people low in self-esteem seem resistant to giving themselves credit when they do something well. And although they do accept positive feedback from others, such feedback doesn't have the same positive effects on feelings of self-worth as it does for those high in self-esteem.

Another experiment in this series of studies showed that when the anagrams were ordered in increasing order of difficulty, so that performance declined over the series of anagrams, low-self-esteem participants viewed themselves as performing far more poorly than did students high in self-esteem. Although low-self-esteem individuals are reluctant to give themselves positive feedback, they are very ready to give themselves negative feedback. This pattern of self-produced feedback, considered in light of other research showing that people low in self-esteem are far less likely to get positive feedback from others (Swann et al., 2002), helps us understand why low self-esteem can be so resistant to change. If one cannot say nice things to oneself, the kind of positive input that builds self-worth may be hard to come by.

EVALUATING THE PHENOMENOLOGICAL-HUMANISTIC APPROACH

What matters most in phenomenological-humanistic approaches is how people view themselves and the world. Some critics believe that the humanistic view relies too heavily on individuals' reports of their personal experiences. For example, psychoanalytic critics maintain that accepting what a person says at face value can easily lead to erroneous conclusions because

of the always-present influence of unconscious defenses.

Although humanism may indeed seem non-scientific to some, Rogers (1959) dedicated himself to developing a theory whose concepts could be measured and its laws tested. One of his most notable contributions was a series of groundbreaking studies on the process of self-growth that can occur in psychotherapy. To assess the effectiveness of psychotherapy, Rogers and his coworkers measured the discrepancy between clients' *ideal selves* (how they would like to be) and their *perceived selves* (their perceptions of what they were actually like). The studies revealed that when clients first entered therapy, the discrepancy was typically large but that it got smaller as therapy proceeded, suggesting that therapy may help the client become more self-accepting and perhaps also more realistic. Rogers and his coworkers also discovered important therapist characteristics that either aid or impede the process of self-actualization in therapy. We will describe this research in Chapter 15.

Several recent developments have put humanistic concepts back into the scientific spotlight. Deci and Ryan's self-determination theory, described in Chapter 10, has focused new scientific attention on humanistic concepts such as autonomy, competence, and relatedness. New methods for measuring brain activation are enabling psychologists to study self-processes as they occur at a biological level (Heatherton et al., 2004). Additionally, the positive psychology movement, described in Chapter 1, has redirected many psychologists to the study of human strengths, happiness, virtue, and other humanistic concerns. As part of a major research project known as the Values in Action Classification Project, Christopher Peterson and Martin Seligman (2004) have proposed a set of universal character strengths and virtues, as well as methods for measuring individual differences in them (Table 12.4).

What kinds of insights can the phenomenological-humanistic perspective contribute to the Charles Whitman case? The obvious starting point is Whitman's self-concept. Despite the successful facade of achievement and exemplary behavior erected during his childhood and adolescent years, the abuse and denigration Whitman received from his father took a heavy toll on his self-concept. After years of being belittled, he was anxious to prove himself as a man when he enlisted in the Marines. He worked hard and successfully at being a good soldier, but things began to deteriorate after he enrolled at the University of Texas on the Marine Corps scholarship. In the absence of the disciplinary structure provided first by his father and then by the Marines, he began to get into trouble, and his grades suffered to the point that his scholarship was withdrawn. He was ordered to return to his former Marine unit, where he now found military life oppressive. His conduct deteriorated, and he was court-martialed for gambling and for threatening the life of a fellow Marine with a pistol. This proved to be an early indication of his potential for violence.

Eventually, thanks to his father's political influence, Whitman was honorably discharged and returned to the University of Texas. Academic difficulties there left him riddled with self-doubt, and

TABLE 12.4   Universal Human Strengths and Virtues Identified in the Values in Action Classification Project

Strengths of Wisdom and Knowledge

- Creativity (originality, ingenuity)
- Curiosity (interest, novelty-seeking, openness to experience)
- Open-mindedness (judgment, critical thinking)
- Love-of-learning perspective (wisdom)

Strengths of Courage

- Bravery (valor)
- Persistence (perseverance, industriousness)
- Integrity (authenticity, honesty)
- Vitality (zest, enthusiasm, vigor, energy)

Strengths of Humanity

- Love
- Kindness (generosity, nurturance, care, compassion, altruistic love, "niceness")
- Social intelligence (emotional intelligence, personal intelligence)

Strengths of Justice

- Citizenship (social responsibility, loyalty, teamwork)
- Fairness
- Leadership

Strengths of Temperance

- Forgiveness and mercy
- Modesty and humility
- Prudence
- Self-regulation (self-control)

Strengths of Transcendence

- Appreciation of beauty and excellence (awe, wonder, elevation)
- Gratitude and hope (optimism, future-mindedness, future orientation)
- Humor (playfulness)
- Spirituality (religiousness, faith, purpose)

SOURCE: Peterson & Seligman, 2004

he struggled desperately to reduce the discrepancy between his ideal self and his perceived self. He wrote numerous self-improvement journals filled with instructions designed to program himself into behaving as a good husband, scholar, and citizen. He frequently studied all night and took amphetamines to stay awake, but the drugs made him even less efficient. Soon he began to despair of ever being the person he wanted to be, and failure to live up to his conditions of worth undermined his self-esteem even further. After he killed his wife while she slept, Whitman left a letter on her body in which he professed his love for her and his desire to relieve her of the shame she would surely experience as his wife.

IN REVIEW

- Humanistic theories emphasize the subjective experiences of the individual and thus deal with perceptual and cognitive processes. Self-actualization is viewed as an innate positive force that leads people to realize their positive potential if not thwarted by the environment.

- Kelly's theory addressed the manner in which people differ in their constructions of reality by the personal constructs they use to categorize their experiences.

- Rogers's theory attaches central importance to the role of the self. Experiences that are incongruous with the established self-concept produce threat and may result in a denial or distortion of reality. Conditional positive regard may result in unrealistic conditions of worth that can conflict with self-actualization. Rogers described a number of characteristics of the fully functioning person.

- Rogers's theory helped stimulate a great deal of research on the self-concept, including studies on the origins and effects of differences in self-esteem, self-enhancement and self-verification motives, and self-concept change. Recent humanistic developments include self-determination theory and the character strengths and virtues identified by Peterson and Seligman.

▶ **Focus 11**
Describe and compare two models of personality derived from factor analysis.

THE TRAIT PERSPECTIVE: MAPPING THE STRUCTURE OF PERSONALITY

What are the ways in which people differ in personality? People have described others' traits from time immemorial. So have personality psychologists known as *trait theorists*. The goals of trait theorists are to describe the basic classes of behavior that define personality, to devise ways of measuring individual differences in personality traits, and to use these measures to understand and predict a person's behavior.

Personality traits *are relatively stable cognitive, emotional, and behavioral characteristics of people that help establish their individual identities and distinguish them from others.* The starting point for the trait researcher is identifying the behaviors that define a particular trait. But here we have an embarrassment of riches. Years ago, the trait theorist Gordon Allport went through the English dictionary and painstakingly recorded all of the words that could be used to describe personal traits. The result: a gigantic list of 17,953 words (Allport & Odbert, 1936). Obviously, it would be impractical, if not impossible, to describe people in terms of where they fall on roughly 18,000 dimensions. The trait theorist's goal is to condense all of these behavioral descriptors into a manageable number of basic traits that can capture personal individuality.

FACTOR ANALYTIC APPROACHES

Psychologists have taken two major approaches to discover and define personality traits. One approach is to propose traits (e.g., "dominance," "friendliness," "self-esteem") on the basis of words or concepts from everyday discourse or from concepts in existing personality theories. This is referred to as the *lexical approach*. A more systematic approach uses the statistical tool of *factor analysis*, the approach described in Chapter 9 that has been used to identify distinct mental abilities. In personality research, **factor analysis** *is used to identify clusters of behaviors that are highly correlated (positively or negatively) with one another, but not with behaviors in other clusters.* Such behavior clusters can be viewed as reflecting a basic dimension, or trait, on which people vary. For example, you might find that most people who are socially reserved also avoid parties, enjoy quiet activities, and like being alone. At the other end of the spectrum are people who are very talkative and sociable, like parties and excitement, dislike solitary activities such as reading, and constantly seek out new acquaintances. These behavioral patterns define a general factor, or dimension, that we might label *introversion-extraversion* (or simply *extraversion*). At one end of the dimension are highly introverted behaviors, and at the other end are highly extraverted behaviors (Figure 12.11). Presumably, each of us could be placed at some point along this dimension in terms of our customary behavior patterns. In fact, as we will see, factor analytic studies have shown introversion-extraversion to be a major dimension of personality.

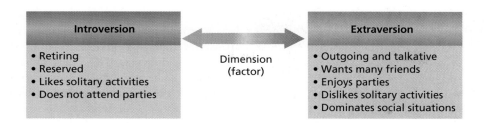

FIGURE 12.11

Describing personality through factor analysis. Factor analysis allows researchers to reduce many behaviors to a smaller number of basic dimensions, or factors, that are relatively independent of one another. A factor comprises behaviors that are highly correlated with one another (either positively or negatively) and are therefore assumed to have common psychological meaning. Here we see the kinds of behaviors that might fall on the two ends of an introversion-extraversion dimension.

Cattell's Sixteen Personality Factors

If you were asked to describe and compare every person you know, how many different traits would it take to do the job? This is where trait theorists begin to part company. Because factor analysis can be used and interpreted in different ways, trait theorists have cut up the personality pie into smaller or larger pieces. For example, the pioneering trait theorist Raymond B. Cattell (1965) asked thousands of participants to rate themselves on numerous behavioral characteristics; he also obtained ratings from people who knew the participants well. When he subjected this mass of data to factor analysis, he identified 16 basic behavior clusters, or factors (Figure 12.12). Using this information, Cattell developed a widely used personality test called the *16 Personality Factor Questionnaire (16PF)* to measure individual differences on each of the dimensions and provide a comprehensive personality description. He was able to develop personality profiles not only for individuals but also for groups of people. For example, Figure 12.12 compares average scores obtained by creative artists and Olympic athletes.

The Five Factor Model

Other trait researchers believe that Cattell's 16 dimensions are more than we need. Their factor analytic studies suggest that five higher-order factors, each including several of Cattell's more specific factors, are all that we need to capture the basic structure of personality (McCrae & Costa, 2003). These theorists also propose that these "Big Five" factors may be universal to the human species, for the same five factors have been found consistently in trait ratings within diverse North American, Asian, Hispanic, and European cultures (John & Srivastava, 1999; Trull & Geary, 1997).

The Big Five factors are shown in Table 12.5. (The acronym OCEAN—for Openness, Conscientiousness, Extraversion, Agreeableness, and Neuroticism—may help you remember them.) Proponents of the *Five Factor Model* believe that when a person is placed at a specific point on each of these five dimensions by means of a psychological test, behavior ratings, or direct observations

of behavior, the essence of her or his personality has been captured (McCrae & Costa, 2003).

What do you think about that conclusion? Your reaction may be one of skepticism, since it seems that there *must* be more to individuality than can be captured by only five dimensions. However, we should remember that, as discussed in Chapter 4, the incredible number of colors that the human visual system can distinguish is based on the activity patterns of only *three* types of cones. Thus the many variations that can occur from the blending of five personality dimensions could account for enormous variation in personality patterns.

Trait theorists not only try to describe the basic structure of personality but also attempt to predict real-life behavior on the basis of a person's traits. Even if a few general traits such as the Big Five seem adequate to describe important features of personality, it is entirely possible that a larger number of specific traits such as Cattell's would capture nuances of behavior within particular situations and would therefore be better for

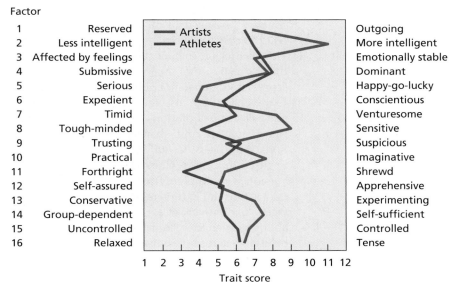

FIGURE 12.12

Cattell's 16 personality factors. Raymond B. Cattell identified 16 basic personality traits through factor analysis. Here we see personality profiles (mean scores) for Olympic athletes and creative artists on the 16PF, the test developed by Cattell to measure the traits. SOURCE: Cattell, 1965.

TABLE 12.5	The Big Five Personality Factors and Underlying Behavior Dimensions

Big Five Factors	Behavioral Traits
Openness	Artistically sensitive vs. artistically insensitive
	Intellectual vs. unreflective, narrow
	Polished, refined vs. crude, boorish
	Imaginative vs. simple, direct
Conscientiousness	Fussy, tidy vs. careless
	Responsible vs. undependable
	Scrupulous vs. unscrupulous
	Persevering vs. quitting, fickle
Extraversion	Talkative vs. silent
	Cheerful vs. dour
	Adventurous vs. cautious
	Sociable vs. reclusive
Agreeableness	Good-natured vs. irritable
	Not jealous vs. jealous
	Mild, gentle vs. headstrong
	Cooperative vs. negativistic
Neuroticism	Nervous, tense vs. poised
	Anxious vs. calm
	Excitable vs. composed
	Moody, unstable vs. emotionally stable

predictive purposes. Measures of the global Big Five factors seldom correlate above .20 to .30 with real-life behavioral outcomes (e.g., Paunonen, 2003). In recognition of this fact, the Big Five Model now includes six subcategories, or *facets*, under each of the five major factors, and the personality test used to measure the Big Five (the *NEO Personality Inventory*, or *NEO-PI*) now provides scores on each of these facets as well as on the corresponding major factor. For example, scores are obtained not only for the main factor of Extraversion, but also for facets such as Activity and Positive Emotions. These more specific dimensions permit sharper behavioral predictions (McCrae & Costa, 2003). For example, the Positive Emotions/Cheerfulness facet of Extraversion is more highly related to life satisfaction than is the total Extraversion score based on all six facets (Schimmack et al., 2004). Nonetheless, the ability of even these more specific traits to predict behavior across varying situations is limited (Cervone, 1999).

Stability of Personality Traits over Time

Because traits are viewed as enduring behavioral predispositions, they should show some degree of stability over time. Yet they should not be un-

changeable. As we might expect, the research literature shows evidence for both stability and change (Caspi & Roberts, 1999; Helson et al., 2002). Some personality dimensions tend to be more stable than others. On the one hand, introversion/extraversion, as well as more basic traits such as emotionality and activity level, tend to be quite stable from childhood into adulthood and across the adult years (Eysenck, 1990; Zuckerman, 1991). Self-esteem also shows strong stability (Trzesniewski et al., 2003). On the other hand, both cross-sectional and longitudinal studies indicate that among the Big Five, Neuroticism, Openness, and Extraversion exhibit average declines from the late teens to the early 30s, whereas Agreeableness and Conscientiousness tend to increase (Costa & McCrae, 2002). Likewise, individuals can show developmental changes in many aspects of personality given influential life experiences, including involvement in counseling and psychotherapy.

Certain habits of thought may also be fairly stable. One is our tendency to think optimistically or pessimistically. Melanie Burns and Martin Seligman (1991) coded diaries and letters that elderly people had written approximately 50 years earlier for the tendency to respond either optimistically or pessimistically to life events. The elderly people also completed a personality test that measured their current optimistic-pessimistic tendencies. Although little consistency over time was shown for dealing optimistically or pessimistically with positive events, Burns and Seligman found a stable tendency to respond with optimism or pessimism to negative life events. The authors suggested that the tendency to be pessimistic might constitute an enduring risk factor for depression, low achievement, and physical illness, and they are now studying such linkages. Table 12.6 contains items from the *Life Orientation Test* (Scheier & Carver, 1985), used by personality researchers to measure the trait of optimism-pessimism.

TABLE 12.6	Sample Items from a Trait Measure of Optimism-Pessimism*

1. In uncertain times, I usually expect the best.
2. Overall, I expect more good things to happen to me than bad.
3. If something can go wrong for me, it will.
4. I rarely count on good things happening to me.

*Items on the Life Orientation Test are answered on a 5-point scale ranging from "strongly disagree" to "strongly agree."
SOURCE: Adapted from Scheier et al., 1994.

▶ Focus 12
How stable are personality traits across time and situations? What factors decrease consistency across situations?

Beneath the Surface | How Consistent Is Our Behavior Across Situations?

As noted at the beginning of the chapter, one of the reasons we have a concept of personality is because we view people as behaving consistently across situations. Is that assumption of consistency warranted by the data? When Walter Mischel reviewed the evidence in 1968, he came to a surprising conclusion: There was more evidence for inconsistency than for consistency. Even on a trait so central as honesty, people can show considerable behavioral variability across situations. In a classic study done 60 years earlier, Hugh Hartshorne and Mark May (1928) tested the honesty of thousands of children. The children were given opportunities to lie, steal, and cheat in a number of different settings: at home, in school, at a party, and in an athletic contest. The rather surprising finding was that "lying, cheating and stealing as measured by the test situations in this study are only very loosely related. . . . Most children will deceive in certain situations but not in others" (p. 411). More than a half century later, Mischel (1984) reported similar findings for college students on the trait of conscientiousness. A student might be highly conscientious in one situation (e.g., coming to work on time) without being conscientious in another (e.g., turning in class assignments on time). Many other studies revealed similar behavioral inconsistency across situations.

To some, this called the very concept of personality into question. They reasoned that if behavior is so inconsistent, maybe only the situation is important and we don't need an internal concept called "personality" to account for behavior. This conclusion triggered a lively debate that continued for nearly two decades. Let's consider some of the insights that have arisen from the consistency debate.

FACTORS THAT REDUCE SITUATIONAL CONSISTENCY

Three factors make it difficult to predict on the basis of personality traits how people will behave in particular situations. First, personality traits interact with other traits, as well as with characteristics of different situations. This melding accounts for the incredible richness we see in personality, but it also poses a challenge to psychologists who want to predict behavior. When two or more traits, such as honesty, dominance, and agreeableness, influence a behavior in a particular situation, our ability to predict on the basis of only one of the traits is bound to be quite limited (Ahadi & Diener, 1989).

Second, the degree of consistency across situations is influenced by how important a given trait is for the person.

TABLE 12.7 Sample Items from the Self-Monitoring Scale*

1. In different situations and with different people, I often act like very different persons.
2. I am not always the person I appear to be.
3. I have trouble changing my behavior to suit different people and different situations.
4. I would not change my opinion (or the way I do things) in order to please someone or win their favor.

*Items 1 and 2 are keyed "true" and items 3 and 4 "false" for self-monitoring.
SOURCE: Based on Snyder, 1987.

A person for whom honesty is a cornerstone of the self-concept may show considerable stability in honest behaviors across situations because her or his feelings of self-worth may be linked to living up to moral standards regardless of the circumstances (Kenrick & Funder, 1988).

Third, people differ in their tendency to tailor their behavior to what is called for by the situation. This personality trait is called *self-monitoring* (Table 12.7). People who are high in **self-monitoring** *are very attentive to situational cues and adapt their behavior to what they think would be most appropriate.* Extreme self-monitors are behavioral chameleons, who act very differently in various situations. Low self-monitors, on the other hand, tend to act primarily in terms of their internal beliefs and attitudes rather than the demands of the situation. The saying "What you see is what you get" applies well to low self-monitors, and such people show greater consistency across situations than do high self-monitors (Snyder, 1987).

According to some trait theorists, the stability and distinctiveness that we see in personality does not come from the fact that we behave the same way in every situation. Rather, people exhibit different *average* amounts of extraversion, emotional stability, agreeableness, honesty, and other traits across many different situations (Epstein, 1983; Kenrick & Funder, 1988). Nonetheless, if they wish to understand more about these interactions between personality traits, situations, and behavior, personality researchers need to define the relevant characteristics of both the person and the situation (Shoda & Mischel, 2000).

EVALUATING THE TRAIT APPROACH

Despite differences of opinion concerning the nature and number of basic personality dimensions, trait theorists have made an important contribution by focusing attention on the value of identifying, classifying, and measuring stable, enduring personality dispositions. Several challenges confront trait theorists, however. If we are to capture the true complexities of personality, we must pay more attention to how traits combine with one another to affect various behaviors (Ahadi & Diener, 1989; Smith et al., 1990). All too often, researchers try to make specific predictions on the basis of a single measured personality trait without taking into account other personality factors that might also influence the behavior in question. This approach sells short the complexity of personality.

In evaluating the trait perspective, we must remember the distinction between description and explanation. To say that someone is outgoing and fun-loving *because* she is high in extraversion is merely to describe the behavior with a trait name, not to explain the inner disposition and how it operates. Traditionally, the trait perspective has been more concerned with describing the structure of personality, measuring individual differences in personality traits, and predicting behavior than with understanding the psychological processes that underlie the traits. For example, a shortcoming of the Five Factor Model is its lack of explanatory power; it tells us nothing about the causal factors that produce extraverted, neurotic, or agreeable people's experiences and actions (Cervone, 1999).

What can the trait perspective tell us about Charles Whitman? Personality psychologists with a trait orientation would be interested in where he falls on a number of relevant personality dimensions. On the Big Five, he likely would have scored high on Extraversion and Agreeableness (with some notable departures from agreeableness when frustrated), inconsistent on Conscientiousness, and high on Neuroticism. If Whitman had been given a battery of personality tests shortly before the incident, would he have exhibited a profile showing a low level of self-esteem, poor stress-management skills, high hostility, and poor impulse control? How would his scores have changed from the period when he was functioning well in adolescence to the period after he was in the Marines? Unfortunately, we will never be able to answer these questions because, to our knowledge, Whitman never took a personality test. It's quite possible that had Whitman been tested in the days preceding his murderous acts, his test results might have served to warn professionals about his potential for violent behavior.

▶ **Focus 13**
How does evolutionary theory account for personality similarities and differences?

IN REVIEW

■ Trait theorists try to identify and measure the basic dimensions of personality. Factor analysis identifies clusters of behavior that are highly cor-

related with one another and thus constitute a dimension along which people may vary. Theorists disagree on the number of traits needed to describe personality adequately. Cattell suggested 16 basic traits; other theorists insist that 5 (or even fewer) may be adequate. Prediction studies indicate that a larger number of more specific traits may be superior for predicting behavior in specific situations.

■ Traits have not proved to be highly consistent across situations, and they also vary in stability over time. Individuals differ in their self-monitoring tendencies, and this variable influences the amount of cross-situational consistency they exhibit in social situations. Traits produce inconsistency by interacting not only with situations but also with one another.

BIOLOGICAL FOUNDATIONS OF PERSONALITY

Both nature and nurture influence the development of personality traits, but their contributions differ according to the trait in question (Plomin & Caspi, 1999). Biological explanations for personality differences focus on three levels. One group of theorists apply evolutionary principles to explain why particular traits exist in the human species (e.g., Buss, 1999). Others seek the genetic bases for trait inheritance (Plomin, 1997). And still others search for differences in the functioning of the nervous system (Heatherton et al., 2004; Pickering & Gray, 1999).

EVOLUTIONARY APPROACHES TO PERSONALITY

An approach called **evolutionary personality theory** *looks for the origin of personality traits in the adaptive demands of our species' evolutionary history.* It asks the basic question, "Where did the personality traits exhibited by humans come from in the first place?"

Consider the Big Five personality factors. Why should these traits be found so consistently in the languages and behaviors of cultures around the world? According to David Buss, an evolutionary personality theorist, they exist in humans because they have helped us achieve two overriding goals: physical survival and reproductive success (Buss, 1999). Traits such as extraversion and emotional stability would have been helpful in attaining positions of dominance and mate selection. Conscientiousness and agreeableness are important in group survival, as well as in reproduction and the care of children. Finally, because openness to experience may be the basis for problem solving and creative activities that could affect the ultimate survival of the species, there has always been a need for intelligent and creative people. Thus evolutionary theorists regard the behaviors underlying the Big Five as sculpted by natural-selection pressures until they ultimately became part of human nature.

The Big Five may also reflect the ways in which we are biologically prepared to think about and discriminate among people. Lewis Goldberg (1981) suggests that over the course of evolution, people have had to ask five basic questions when interacting with another person, questions that have survival and reproductive implications:

1. Is person X active and dominant or passive and submissive? Can I dominate X, or will I have to submit to X?

2. Is X agreeable and friendly or hostile and uncooperative?

3. Can I count on X? Is X conscientious and dependable?

4. Is X sane (stable, rational, predictable) or crazy (unstable, unpredictable, possibly dangerous)?

5. How smart is X, and how quickly can X learn and adapt?

Not surprisingly, according to Goldberg, these questions relate directly to the Big Five factors. He believes that this is the reason factor analyses of trait ratings reveal Big Five consistency across very diverse cultures.

Goldberg's analysis shows how an evolutionary approach can be applied to understanding human nature (i.e., the traits humans have in common). Evolutionary theorists account for individual differences in those personality traits by focusing on gene-environment interactions. Evolutionary development may provide humans with species-typical behavior patterns, but environmental inputs influence how they are manifested. For example, dominance may be the behavior pattern encouraged by innate mechanisms in males, but an individual male who has many early experiences of being subdued or dominated may develop a submissive personality. For evolutionists who assume that the innate female behavior pattern is submissiveness, an individual female who has the resources of high intelligence and physical strength may be quite willing and able to behave in a competitive and dominant fashion.

Another important evolutionary concept is **strategic pluralism,** *the idea that multiple—even contradictory—behavioral strategies* (for example, introversion and extraversion) *might be adaptive in certain environments and would therefore be maintained through natural selection.* This would help account for genes favoring individual differences on personality dimensions.

GENETICS AND PERSONALITY

The comedian Rodney Dangerfield recounted the day his son came home from kindergarten looking very troubled. When asked why he seemed so depressed, the little boy replied that they had learned a new saying in school that day: "Like father, like son."

Have you ever been told that you share a personality trait with a parent or relative? Perhaps you wondered where the presumed similarity originated. Could it possibly have been inherited? Twin studies are particularly informative for studying the role of genetic factors because they compare the degree of personality resemblance between monozygotic twins, who have identical genetic makeup, and dizygotic twins, who do not (Rowe, 1999). On a great many psychological characteristics, identical twins are more similar to each other than are fraternal twins, suggesting a role for genetics. However, the issue is clouded by the possibility that identical twins may also have more similar environments than fraternal twins because others are inclined to treat them more similarly.

The ideal solution to this problem would be to compare personality traits in identical and fraternal twins who were raised together and those who were raised apart. If the identical twins who were reared in different families were as similar as those reared together, a more powerful argument could be made for the role of genetic factors. Moreover, this research design would allow us to divide the total variation among individuals on each personality trait into three components: (1) variation attributable to genetic factors; (2) variation due to a shared family environment in those raised together; and (3) variation attributable to other factors, including unique individual life experiences. The relative influence of these sources of variation can be estimated by comparing personality test correlations in twins raised together and apart.

The most comprehensive study (which included the Jim twins described at the beginning of Chapter 3) was conducted by Auke Tellegen and his colleagues at the University of Minnesota. The

▶ **Focus 14**
What do twin studies reveal about the roles of heredity and environment in personality development?

▶ **Focus 15**
What biological factors underlie (1) Eysenck's dimensions of Extraversion and Stability and (2) the behaviors of inhibited children and adults?

four groups of twin pairs were administered measures of 14 different personality traits, and the personality variation attributable to genetic, familial environment, and unique environment was calculated for each personality characteristic. As shown in Table 12.8, genetic factors accounted for approximately 40 to 50 percent of the variance among people in trait scores. In contrast, the degree of resemblance did not differ much whether the twin pairs were reared together or apart, showing that general features of the family environment, such as its emotional climate and degree of affluence, accounted for little variance in any of the traits. However, this does not mean that experience is not important. Rather than the family environment, it was the individual's unique environmental experiences, such as his or her school experiences and interactions with peers, that accounted for considerable personality variance. Even within the same family, therefore, individual children have different experiences while growing up, and it is these unique experiences that help shape personality development.

PERSONALITY AND THE NERVOUS SYSTEM

One logical place to look for biological underpinnings of personality is in individual differences in brain functioning. Two examples are Hans

Eysenck's research and theorizing on extraversion and emotional stability and more recent work on temperament.

Eysenck's Extraversion-Stability Model

We've now seen that among trait theorists, there are "splitters," such as Cattell, who posit a large number of basic traits, and "lumpers," such as the Big Five theorists, who favor a smaller number. Hans J. Eysenck (1916–1997), one of Britain's leading psychologists, was the ultimate lumper (Figure 12.13a). He maintained that normal personality can be understood in terms of only *two* basic dimensions. These dimensions of Introversion-Extraversion and Stability-Instability (sometimes called Neuroticism) blend together to form all of the more specific traits. Eysenck's two "supertraits" are comparable to the Big Five traits of Extraversion and Neuroticism.

Eysenck's Extraversion-Stability model is shown in Figure 12.13b. Note that the two basic dimensions intersect at right angles, meaning that they are statistically independent, or uncorrelated. The secondary traits shown in the circle reflect varying combinations, or mixtures, of the two primary dimensions. Thus we can see that the emotionally stable extravert is a carefree, lively person who tends to be well adjusted and to seek out leadership roles. In contrast, unstable extraverts tend to be touchy, aggressive, and restless. The stable introvert is calm, reliable, and even-tempered, but the unstable introvert tends to be rigid, anxious, and moody. Different combinations of the two basic personality dimensions can thus produce very diverse personality patterns.

Eysenck (1967) was one of the first modern theorists to suggest a biological basis for major personality traits. He linked Introversion-Extraversion and Stability-Instability to differences in individuals' normal patterns of arousal within the brain. He started with the notion that there is an optimal, or preferred, level of biological arousal in the brain. Eysenck believed that extreme introverts are chronically *overaroused*; their brains are too electrically active, so they try to minimize stimulation and reduce arousal to get down to their optimal arousal level, or comfort zone. In contrast, the brains of extreme extraverts are chronically *underaroused*, so they need powerful or frequent stimulation to achieve an optimal level of cortical arousal and excitation. The extravert thus seeks social contact and physical arousal, likes parties, takes chances, is assertive, and suffers boredom easily.

TABLE 12.8   Estimates of the Percentages of Group Variance in 14 Personality Traits Attributable to Genetic and Environmental Factors

Trait	Genetic	Familial Environment	Unique Environment
Well-being	.48	.13	.39
Social potency	.54	.10	.36
Achievement	.39	.11	.50
Social closeness	.40	.19	.41
Stress reaction	.53	.00	.47
Alienation	.45	.11	.54
Aggression	.44	.00	.56
Control	.44	.00	.56
Harm avoidance	.55	.00	.45
Traditionalism	.45	.12	.43
Absorption	.50	.03	.47
Positive emotionality	.40	.22	.38
Negative emotionality	.55	.02	.43
Constraint	.58	.00	.42

NOTE: The variance estimates are based on a comparison of the degree of personality similarity in identical and fraternal twins who were reared together or apart.

SOURCE: Adapted from Tellegen et al., 1988.

(a)

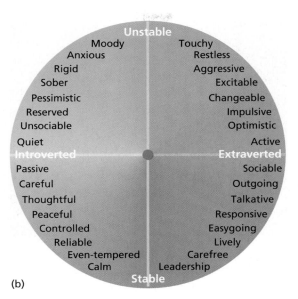

(b)

Unstable

Moody   Touchy
Anxious   Restless
Rigid   Aggressive
Sober   Excitable
Pessimistic   Changeable
Reserved   Impulsive
Unsociable   Optimistic
Quiet   Active

Introverted ————————— **Extraverted**

Passive   Sociable
Careful   Outgoing
Thoughtful   Talkative
Peaceful   Responsive
Controlled   Easygoing
Reliable   Lively
Even-tempered   Carefree
Calm   Leadership

Stable

FIGURE 12.13

A two-factor model. According to Hans Eysenck (a), various combinations of two major dimensions of personality, Introversion-Extraversion and Stability-Instability (or Neuroticism), combine to form more specific traits (b). Source: Eysenck, 1967.

Whereas Introversion-Extraversion reflects a person's *customary* level of arousal, Stability-Instability represents the suddenness with which *shifts* in arousal occur. Unstable people have hair-trigger nervous systems that show large and sudden shifts in arousal, whereas stable people show smaller and more gradual shifts (Pickering & Gray, 1999). Eysenck also called this stability dimension *Neuroticism* because he found that people with extremely unstable nervous systems are more likely to experience emotional problems that require clinical attention.

Eysenck proposed that the arousal patterns that underlie Introversion-Extraversion and Stability-Instability have genetic bases. A growing body of evidence from twin studies supports his view. Identical twins are much more alike on these traits than are fraternal twins, and about half of the variance among people can be attributed to hereditary factors (Loehlin et al., 1988; Plomin, 1997). Eysenck believed that although personality is strongly influenced by life experiences, the ways people respond to those experiences may be at least partly programmed by biological factors. Contemporary research using brain imaging continues to find brain activation patterns related to Extraversion and Stability. These studies show that the neural bases of these factors go beyond general arousal, involving specific brain structures (Canli, 2004).

Temperament: Building Blocks of Personality

Temperament *refers to individual differences in emotional and behavioral styles that appear so early in life that they are assumed to have a biological basis.* Such temperamental factors as emotionality, activity level, sociability, and impulsivity are visible even in infancy (Buss & Plomin, 1975, 1984). Temperamental factors are not assumed to be personality traits in their own right, but they are viewed as biological building blocks that influence the subsequent development of personality. The fact that these temperamental factors are more highly correlated in identical than in fraternal twins suggests a genetic link (Buss & Plomin, 1984).

Recent research has focused on biological differences in inhibited and uninhibited people. First identified by Jerome Kagan (1999) on the basis of behavioral observations and biological functioning, inhibited infants and children are shy, restrained in their behavior, and react to unfamiliar people and situations with distress and avoidance (Figure 12.14a). In contrast, uninhibited children respond positively to new situations and people and seem to enjoy novelty. About 20 percent of infants are inhibited, and about 40 percent are uninhibited. Kagan (1999) found that these temperamental patterns can be identified in the first 4 months of life and that they persist into later childhood in many (but not all) children. These two groups of children also differ physiologically, with the inhibited children showing higher levels of physiological arousal and stress-hormone secretion in response to unfamiliar situations and people.

Recent research sheds light on brain regions that contribute to inhibited and uninhibited tendencies. One important region is the amygdala, the structure in the limbic system that organizes fear responses. Kagan suggested that the amygdala was involved in the physiological overreactivity he measured in inhibited children. In a more recent

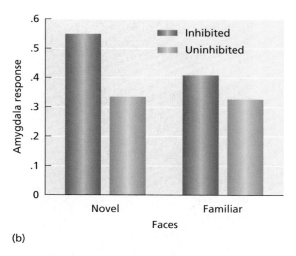

(a)   (b)

FIGURE 12.14

Does childhood temperament predict adult personality? (a) Inhibited temperament expresses itself as shyness and negative reactions to novel situations and people (even Santa) early in life and is assumed to have a biological basis. (b) Adults who were identified as inhibited in childhood showed elevated reactions in the amygdala (a brain region known to initiate and organize fear responses) when exposed to faces they had not seen before, suggesting stability of this temperamental factor into adulthood. SOURCE: Data from Schwartz et al., 2003.

study, fMRI brain recordings were taken in young adults who had been categorized as either highly inhibited or as uninhibited when they were 2 years old (Schwartz et al., 2003). Of interest was how their amygdala would react to pictures of familiar and unfamiliar human faces. As shown in Figure 12.14b, those adults who had been uninhibited as children showed relatively low amygdala reactivity to both familiar and novel faces, whereas the formerly inhibited participants showed particularly high reactivity to the novel faces. This study thereby demonstrated a negative response to novel stimuli in inhibited people that extended from childhood to adulthood, as well as a possible biological basis for this tendency.

We should note that temperament is not destiny. Although biological factors are clearly involved, the environment also can bring about some degree of change in temperamental characteristics. We should remember that temperamentally based behavior patterns help create environments that can perpetuate the behavior patterns. For example, people are unlikely to gravitate toward shy, inhibited individuals, thereby depriving them of positive experiences that might counteract their shyness. Likewise, temperamental traits may need particular kinds of environments to express themselves. Elaine Aron and coworkers (2005) found that adult shyness occurred most predictably when the underlying temperamental characteristic was paired with an adverse childhood environment. Although the link between child temperament and adult personality is far from perfect, there is little doubt that temperament is one building block in personality development.

EVALUATING THE BIOLOGICAL APPROACH

Biological research, spurred by technical advances in measuring nervous system activity and in evaluating genetic influences, is forging new frontiers in personality science. As we learn more about how biological functions are affected by developmental experiences and how they interact with situational factors, new insights about personality development will be achieved.

Can the biological perspective offer clues to Charles Whitman's behavior? In Whitman's letter, we find references to "tremendous headaches" for which he had been medicating himself and a request that an autopsy be done after his death to see if a "visible physical disorder" existed. In fact, a postmortem examination of his brain detected a fast-growing tumor in the hypothalamus, an area that includes some of the aggression circuitry in the brain (Raine et al., 2000). Medical authorities evaluating Whitman's case differed on the importance of the tumor. If the tumor played a role in his violent acts, it seems unlikely that it was the primary causal factor. However, it could have been a predisposing factor that lowered his inhibitions against violent behavior.

Another possibility arises from information that Whitman's father had a penchant for violent behavior and frequently beat his wife and children. Thus a second potential biological factor could be the genes Whitman inherited from his father. Aggression can have a genetic basis (Wasserman & Wachbroit, 2001), and it is possible that a genetic predisposition interacted with environmental factors to increase the potential for violent behavior.

IN REVIEW

- Biological perspectives on personality traits focus on differences in the functioning of the nervous system, the contribution of genetic factors, and the possible role of evolution in the development of universal human traits and ways of perceiving behavior.

- Studies comparing identical and fraternal twins reared together and apart indicate that genetic factors may account for as much as half of the variance in personality test scores, with individual experiences accounting for most of the remainder. Evolutionary theories of personality attribute some personality dispositions to genetically controlled mechanisms based on natural selection.

- Eysenck suggested that normal personality differences can be accounted for by variations on the dimensions of Introversion-Extraversion and Stability-Instability, both of which are assumed to have a biological basis. In Eysenck's theory, Introversion-Extraversion reflects a person's customary level of arousal, whereas Stability-Instability represents the suddenness with which shifts in arousal occur.

- Differences in temperament appear early in life and are assumed to have a biological basis. Temperament is assumed to contribute to the development of personality, and there is evidence for stability of temperamental behavior tendencies during childhood and into adulthood. Inhibited children and adults appear to have a highly reactive amygdala that triggers fear responses to unfamiliar people and situations.

BEHAVIORAL AND SOCIAL-COGNITIVE THEORIES

To understand behavior, psychodynamic, humanistic, and trait theorists emphasize internal personal causes of behavior, such as unconscious conflicts, self-actualization tendencies, and personality traits. In a sense, they account for behavior from the inside out. In contrast, behaviorists emphasize environmental causes and view humans as reactors to external events (Parker et al., 1998). To them, behavior is to be explained from the outside in. Behaviorists such as Ivan Pavlov, John Watson, and B. F. Skinner were more interested in discovering universal laws of learning than in identifying individual differences in behavior, and they rejected the notion of an "internal personality" that directs behavior. Nonetheless, the laws of learning that they discovered have great

relevance for understanding personality. Many behaviors ascribed to personality are acquired through classical and operant conditioning, and the role of life experiences is undeniable.

Despite the power of the environment, however, some behaviorists believed that a purely behavioral account could not fully capture the workings of human personality. They believed that the learner is not simply a passive reactor to environmental forces and that internal processes could not be excluded from an understanding of personality. They viewed the human as perceiver, a thinker, and a planner who mentally interprets events, thinks about the past, anticipates the future, and decides how to behave. Environmental effects are filtered through these cognitive processes and are influenced—even changed—by them. **Social-cognitive theories** *combine the behavioral and cognitive perspectives into an approach to personality that stresses the interaction of a thinking human with a social environment that provides learning experiences.* Social-cognitive theorists believe that the debate on whether behavior is more strongly influenced by personal factors or by the person's environment is basically a meaningless one (Fleeson, 2004). Instead, according to the social-cognitive principle of **reciprocal determinism,** *the person, the person's behavior, and the environment all influence one another in a pattern of two-way causal links* (Bandura, 1986; Figure 12.15).

As an example, let us consider how these interactions or linkages might operate in the case of a hostile and disagreeable man we'll call Tom. Tom's disagreeableness trait manifests itself in an irritable, cynical, and uncooperative behavior pattern (his personality influences his behavior).

▶ **Focus 16**
Describe the major features of social-cognitive theories and the importance of reciprocal determinism.

FIGURE 12.15

Reciprocal determinism. A key concept in social-cognitive theory is reciprocal determinism, in which characteristics of the person, the person's behavior, and the environment all affect one another in reciprocal, or two-way, causal relations.

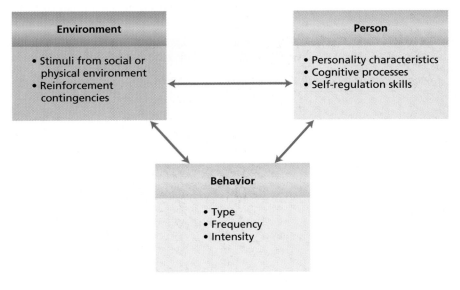

Reciprocal Determinism

Tom's disagreeable behaviors tend to evoke negative responses from others (his behavior causes his social environment to respond to him in kind). These negative social consequences reinforce and strengthen still further his personality trait (including his expectations that others will eventually reject him), and they also strengthen his disagreeable behavior tendencies (his environment influences both his personality trait and his social behavior). Thus Tom's personality, his behavior, and his environment all influence one another.

JULIAN ROTTER: EXPECTANCY, REINFORCEMENT VALUE, AND LOCUS OF CONTROL

In 1954 Julian Rotter (whose name rhymes with *motor*) laid the foundation for today's social-cognitive approaches. According to Rotter, the likelihood that we will engage in a particular behavior in a given situation is influenced by two factors: *expectancy* and *reinforcement value*. Expectancy is our perception of how likely it is that certain consequences will occur if we engage in a particular behavior within a specific situation. Reinforcement value is basically how much we desire or dread the outcome that we expect the behavior to produce. Thus a student who strongly values academic success and also expects that studying will result in high grades is likely to study (Rotter, 1954). Note that this approach makes use of reinforcement, a central behaviorist concept, but views its effects within a cognitive framework that emphasizes how we think about our behavior and its expected outcomes.

Locus of Control

One of Rotter's most influential expectancy concepts is **internal-external locus of control,** *an*

▶ **Focus 17**
Describe Rotter's concepts of expectancy, reinforcement value, and locus of control.

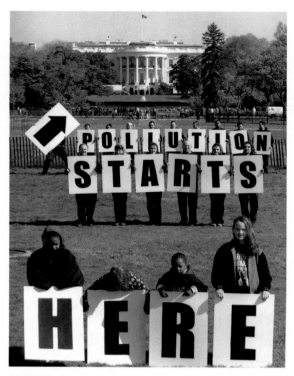

FIGURE 12.16

Research shows that people with an internal locus of control are more likely to take an active role in social-change movements.

expectancy concerning the degree of personal control we have in our lives. People with an *internal* locus of control believe that life outcomes are largely under personal control and depend on their own behavior (Figure 12.16). In contrast, people with an *external* locus of control believe that their fate has less to do with their own efforts than with the influence of external factors, such as luck, chance, and powerful others. Table 12.9 contains items from Rotter's (1966) *Internal-External (I-E) Scale*, used to measure individual differences in locus of control. Locus of control is called a *generalized expectancy* because it applies across many life domains as a general worldview.

Locus of control is a highly researched personality variable. Quite consistently, people with an internal locus of control behave in a more self-determined fashion (Pervin et al., 2005). In the 1960s, African Americans who actively participated in the civil rights movement were more internal on the I-E Scale than were those who did not (Rotter, 1966). "Internal" college students achieve better grades than do "external" students of equal academic ability, probably because they link their studying to degree of success and work harder. Internals are more likely to actively seek out the information needed to succeed in a given situation

---

TABLE 12.9   Sample Items from Rotter's Internal-External Scale

Choose statement (a) or (b) from each numbered choice.

1. (a) Many times I feel that I have little influence over the things that happen to me.
   (b) It is impossible for me to believe that chance or luck plays an important part in my life.

2. (a) The average citizen can have an influence in government decisions.
   (b) The world is run by the few people in power, and there isn't much the little guy can do about it.

3. (a) In the long run, people get the respect they deserve in this world.
   (b) Unfortunately, an individual's worth often passes unrecognized no matter how hard one tries.

NOTE: 1b, 2a, and 3a are the internal alternatives.
SOURCE: Adapted from Rotter, 1966.

(Ingold, 1989). Interpersonally, internals are more resistant to social influence, whereas externals tend to give in to high-status people they see as powerful.

Internal locus of control is positively related to self-esteem and feelings of personal effectiveness, and internals tend to cope with stress in a more active and problem-focused manner than do externals (Jennings, 1990). They are also less likely to experience psychological maladjustment in the form of depression or anxiety (Hoffart & Martinson, 1991).

ALBERT BANDURA: SOCIAL LEARNING AND SELF-EFFICACY

Albert Bandura has made major contributions to the development of the social-cognitive approach. His early studies of modeling, described in Chapter 6, helped combine the psychology of learning with the cognitive perspective. Bandura's social learning analyses of aggression, moral behavior, and behavioral self-control demonstrated the wide applicability of the social-cognitive approach (Bandura, 1986). Perhaps his most influential contribution, however, is his theory and research on self-efficacy.

Self-Efficacy

According to Bandura (1997), a key factor in how people regulate their lives is their sense of **self-efficacy,** *their beliefs concerning their ability to perform the behaviors needed to achieve desired outcomes.* People whose self-efficacy is high have confidence in their ability to do what it takes to overcome obstacles and achieve their goals.

A good deal of research has been done on the factors that create differences in self-efficacy (Figure 12.17). Four important determinants have been identified (Bandura, 1997). First and most important is our previous *performance experiences* in similar situations. Such experiences shape our beliefs about our capabilities. For example, as shown in Figure 12.18, college women who felt that they had mastered the martial arts and emotional-control skills taught in a physical self-defense training program showed dramatic increases in their belief that they could escape from or disable a potential assailant or rapist (Weitlauf et al., 2000).

Bandura stresses that self-efficacy beliefs are always specific to particular situations. Thus we may have high self-efficacy in some situations and low self-efficacy in others. For example, the women who mastered the physical self-defense skills did not feel more capable in all areas of their lives, despite their enhanced self-defense efficacy.

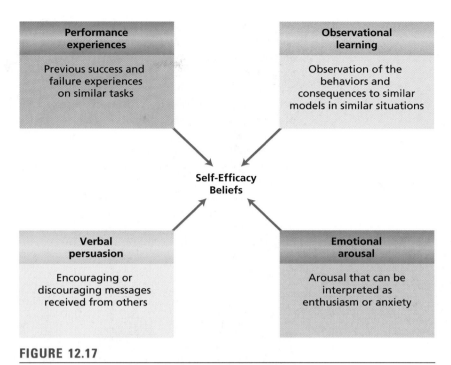

Performance experiences	Observational learning
Previous success and failure experiences on similar tasks	Observation of the behaviors and consequences to similar models in similar situations

Self-Efficacy Beliefs

Verbal persuasion	Emotional arousal
Encouraging or discouraging messages received from others	Arousal that can be interpreted as enthusiasm or anxiety

FIGURE 12.17

Self-efficacy beliefs. Four classes of information affect self-efficacy beliefs. Source: Based on Bandura, 1997.

(a)

▶ **Focus 18**
Describe four determinants of self-efficacy.

(b)

FIGURE 12.18

Effects of self-defense training. (a) Physical self-defense training has dramatic effects on women's self-efficacy to perform the behaviors needed to defend themselves. (b). The physical defense self-efficacy scores in this study could extend from 6 to 60. Source: Based on Weitlauf et al., 2000.

A second determinant of self-efficacy is *observational learning*—that is, observing others' behaviors and their outcomes. If you observe a person similar to yourself accomplish a particular goal, then you are likely to believe that if you perform those same behaviors you will also succeed. A striking example of how powerful such expectations can be comes from the world of sports. At one time, physiologists insisted that it was physically impossible for a human being to run a mile in less than 4 minutes, and no one in the history of track and field had ever done it. When the Englishman Roger Bannister broke the 4-minute barrier in 1954, that limiting belief was shattered. The impact on other runners' performance was immediate and dramatic. In

the year following Bannister's accomplishment, 37 other runners broke the barrier, and in the year after that, nearly 300 runners did the "impossible." Apparently, a great many people came to believe that "if he can do it, so can I," and their new sense of self-efficacy enhanced their performance.

Third, self-efficacy can be increased or decreased by *verbal persuasion*. The messages we get from other people who affirm our abilities or downgrade them affect our efficacy beliefs. Thus inspirational teachers who convey high standards and a "you can do it" conviction can inspire their students to great accomplishments, as exemplified in the true-life story of Jaime Escalante, the mathematics teacher featured in the movie *Stand and Deliver* (Figure 12.19). By convincing inner-city minority students who had trouble doing simple arithmetic that they were capable of much more, and by helping them prove their hidden competencies to themselves, Escalante helped them achieve award-winning success in calculus.

Fourth, high *emotional arousal* that is interpreted as anxiety or fatigue tends to decrease self-efficacy. However, if we find ourselves able to control such arousal, it may enhance efficacy beliefs and subsequent performance. For example, test-anxious college students who were given training in stress-management relaxation techniques showed increases in their belief that they could remain relaxed and focused during tests, and their test performance and grade point average improved significantly as they controlled anxious arousal (Smith, 1989).

Efficacy beliefs are strong predictors of future performance and accomplishment (Bandura, 1997). They become a kind of self-fulfilling prophecy. In the words of Henry Ford, "Whether you believe you can do something or you believe you can't, you're probably right."

FIGURE 12.19

The film *Stand and Deliver* depicted the extraordinary accomplishments of math teacher Jaime Escalante, who inspired his inner-city students to exceptional achievement in calculus. His stated faith in their potential and their own performance accomplishments enhanced their sense of self-efficacy.

▶ **Focus 19**
Summarize the procedures for successful goal setting.

 Applying Psychological Science   **Increasing Self-Efficacy through Systematic Goal Setting**

In Chapter 10, we described motivation as the impetus for goal-directed behavior. Because positive self-efficacy beliefs are consistently related to success in behaving effectively and achieving goals, Bandura and other social-cognitive theorists have been strongly interested in practical measures for enhancing self-efficacy. When people are successful and when they attribute their success to their own competencies (internal locus of control), their self-efficacy increases and assists them in subsequent goal-directed

efforts. Moreover, successful people have usually mastered the skills involved in setting challenging and realistic goals, figuring out what they need to do on a day-to-day basis to achieve them, and making the commitment to do what is required. As they achieve each goal they have set, they become more skillful and increase their sense of personal efficacy (Bandura, 1997).

Not all goal-setting procedures are created equal, and it is important to apply the principles that make goal-setting programs most effective (Locke & Latham, 2002). Here are some research-derived guidelines for effective goal setting.

- *Set specific, behavioral, and measurable goals.* The first step in changing some aspect of your life is to set a goal. The kind of goal you set is very important, because certain kinds of goals encourage us to work harder, enjoy success, and increase self-efficacy. Studies show that specific and fairly narrow goals are far more effective than general "do your best" goals (Locke & Latham, 2002). A general goal like "improve my tennis game" is less helpful than "increase the number of serves I put in play by 20 percent." The latter goal refers to a specific behavior that you can focus on and measure.

One of the most important aspects of goal setting is systematically measuring progress toward the goal. This was shown in a study by Bandura and Daniel Cervone (1983) in which participants worked on a strenuous bicycle-pedaling task over a number of sessions. Two independent variables were manipulated: (1) whether the participants were given specific improvement goals before each session after the first one and (2) whether the participants were given feedback about their performance during the previous session. A control condition got neither goals nor feedback and provided a basis for evaluating the effects of goals and feedback, alone or in combination. The dependent variable was the speed and power with which the participants pedaled.

As shown in Figure 12.20, simply having goals was not enough, nor was feedback effective by itself. But having both goals and feedback was a powerful combination. This shows how important it is to measure your progress toward the goal so that you get performance feedback and can see your improvement. Visible movement toward realistic goals builds self-efficacy.

FIGURE 12.20

Goals are not enough. This graph shows the effects of improvement goals and performance feedback on performance improvement on a grueling bicycling task. Clearly, the combination of explicit goals *and* performance feedback resulted in greater improvement in performance than did either element by itself. Source: Based on Bandura & Cervone, 1983.

- *Set behavioral, not outcome, goals.* Many of our goals relate to outcomes in the future, such as getting an A in this course. You are more likely to achieve such goals if you use the means-ends heuristic discussed in Chapter 8 and think about the specific things you must *do* to achieve that outcome goal. Behavioral goals (what one has to do) work better than outcome goals because they keep the focus on the necessary behaviors. A behavioral goal might be "read and outline the textbook and outline the lecture notes for 1 hour each day." Achieving this behavioral goal can also be measured quickly and repeatedly, giving you constant feedback. Many people focus on outcome goals and forget what has to be done day-to-day to achieve them. It has been said that there are three kinds of people in this world: those who make things happen, those who wait for things to happen, and those who wonder what happened. Make sure you're someone who makes things happen.

- *Set difficult but realistic goals.* Moderately difficult goals challenge and motivate us and give us a sense of hope. When reached, they increase self-efficacy. Easy goals do not provide a sense of accomplishment, and extremely difficult or unattainable goals do not provide the success experiences you need to increase your self-efficacy.

- *Set positive, not negative, goals.* In Chapter 6 we discussed the advantages of positive reinforcement over punishment. Working toward positive goals, such as "study for 1 hour before dinner" is better than avoiding a negative consequence, as in "don't waste time." Again, positive goals keep you focused on the positive steps that you need to take to achieve them.

- *Set short-range and long-range goals.* Short-range goals are important because they provide the opportunity for immediate mastery experiences, and they keep you working positively. A long-range goal like "take all the courses for a double major" can easily be divided into a series of subgoals that you can be working toward right now. Short-range goals are like the steps on a staircase leading to the long-range goal. As each step is accomplished, you enjoy mastery experiences that also lead you toward your ultimate goal. In reaching any goal, "divide and conquer" is a cliché that works.

- *Set definite time spans for achievement.* To keep your goal-setting program on track, it is important to specify the dates by which you will meet specific performance goals or subgoals, as well as the behaviors needed to attain them in that time span.

Most of the preceding guidelines can be summarized in the acronym SMART: specific, measurable, action-oriented, realistic, and time-based. And it is true that systematic goal setting is one of the smartest ways to work toward goals.

Goal setting is a motivational technique that has resulted in remarkable improvements in productivity in many work, social, and academic settings (Locke & Latham, 2002). Moreover, for purposes of increasing self-efficacy, it has the added advantage of providing the repeated mastery experiences that are the most powerful sources of efficacy information.

WALTER MISCHEL AND YUICHI SHODA: THE COGNITIVE-AFFECTIVE PERSONALITY SYSTEM

Walter Mischel, who studied under George Kelly and Julian Rotter at Ohio State and was a colleague of Albert Bandura's at Stanford, is a third key figure in social-cognitive theory. Bandura and Mischel became part of the "cognitive revolution" that occurred among behaviorists during the 1960s. They believed that a more cognitive approach to personality was required, one that takes into account not only the power of situational learning factors but also how people characteristically deal mentally and emotionally with experiences. Mischel set out to identify the important "person variables" that could help account for individual differences in personality.

In the most recent formulation of social-cognitive theory, Mischel and his former student Yuichi Shoda describe a **cognitive-affective personality system (CAPS),** *an organized system of five variables that interact continuously with one another and with the environment, generating the distinctive patterns of behavior that characterize the person* (Mischel, 1999). The dynamic interplay among these five factors, together with the characteristics of the situation, accounts for individual differences between people, as well as differences in people's behavior across different situations. The processes represented within the CAPS are summarized in Table 12.10.

Encodings and Personal Constructs

We respond to the world as perceived. As Kelly proposed in his theory of personal constructs, dis-

▶ **Focus 20**
Describe the five "person variables" in Mischel and Shoda's Cognitive-Affective Personality System (CAPS).

cussed earlier in this chapter, people differ greatly in how they customarily *encode* (mentally represent, categorize, interpret) situations. An unkempt man dressed in a caveman-style loincloth who steps onto an elevator carrying a large snake might be sorted into the personal construct category "dangerous" by one fellow passenger and as "an intriguing person I'd like to get to know" by another. These different encodings, or appraisals, will affect the other elements of the CAPS, including emotions, expectancies, and motivation to exit the elevator.

Our encodings determine how we respond emotionally and behaviorally to situations. For example, studies of highly aggressive youth reveal that they have a strong tendency to perceive others as having disrespect and hostile intent toward them. Thus they are primed to interpret ambiguous acts by others, such as being unintentionally brushed against on a stairway at school, as an aggressive act and to react with a violent response (Dodge, 1986). Other individuals tend to encode ambiguous interpersonal events, such as not being greeted by a fellow student, as instances of personal rejection and to become depressed as a result (Downey & Feldman, 1996). As object relations theorists have suggested, the mental representations or working models we have of relationships influence how we perceive (encode) and respond to others in our later relationships. This is an example of how the social-cognitive approach can incorporate concepts and insights from other theories, including psychodynamic ones.

Expectancies and Beliefs

As Rotter emphasized, what we expect will happen if we behave in a particular way is a strong determinant of our behavioral choices. **Behavior-outcome expectancies** *represent the "if-then" links between alternative behaviors and possible outcomes.* If I take that course in organic chemistry, *then* what will happen to my grade point average? How likely is it that I'll be forgiven *if* I apologize? Will I make enough money to support myself *if* I become a teacher? Different people may have very different answers to such questions and therefore vary in their responses to the same situation.

In addition to behavior-outcome expectancies, beliefs about our competencies and about the degree of personal control we have influence our actions. Thus the CAPS model also includes Bandura's self-efficacy and Rotter's locus of control as important expectancy variables.

TABLE 12.10   Psychological Components of the Cognitive-Affective Personality System

1. What is my perception of the situation? ***Encoding strategies*** help us categorize and understand events.

2. How likely is it that certain outcomes will occur if I behave in manner X? in manner Y? How likely am I to succeed/how much personal control do I have? These are the person's ***expectancies and beliefs.***

3. How much do I want to experience, or to avoid, those outcomes? This relates to the person's ***goals and values,*** or the person's motivational structure.

4. How do I feel about this? These emotional responses constitute the person's ***affects,*** or feelings.

5. Do I have the behavioral skills needed to deal with this situation? What should I do? ***Personal competencies and self-regulatory processes*** affect behavior as well.

SOURCE: Based on Mischel, 1999.

Goals and Values

Motivation plays a central role in attempts to understand behavior, and it is represented in the CAPS system as goals and values that guide our behavior, cause us to persist in the face of barriers, and determine the outcomes and situations we seek and our reactions to them (Higgins, 1996). People differ in the goals that are important to them and the values that guide their lives. These differences can cause people to behave very differently in situations that are relevant to these important personality factors.

Affects (Emotions)

Anything that implies important consequences for us, whether beneficial or harmful, can trigger an emotional response (Lazarus, 2001). Once aroused, emotions color our perceptions and influence our behavior. For example, if you are already feeling bad due to an argument with a friend and you then get negative feedback in the form of a poor grade on a test, you may feel demoralized for a time. Emotions also affect other CAPS components. Anxiety, for example, can significantly lower outcome expectancies in performance situations (Shepperd et al., 2005).

Research shows that people exhibit stable individual differences in emotionality. For example, people who are high on Eysenck's trait of Instability (Neuroticism) have a tendency to experience negative *affect*, or emotion, in an intense fashion, a factor that influences many of their perceptions and behaviors. Other people seem predisposed to experience mainly positive affect in their lives (Watson & Clark, 1992).

Competencies and Self-Regulatory Processes

Social-cognitive theorists stress that people extensively control, or regulate, their own behavior. People's ability to control their own behavior is a distinguishing aspect of personality, as are the competencies they develop that allow them to adapt to life successfully and pursue important goals. Some of these competencies are cognitive problem-solving methods (such as systematic goal setting) that allow them to plan successful strategies, whereas others involve the ability to exert personal control over thoughts, emotions, and behaviors. People who score high on measures of self-esteem tend to have better self-regulation abilities and to enjoy more positive outcomes (Di Paula & Campbell, 2002). These successes undoubtedly contribute to their positive feelings about themselves.

One important way people regulate their own behavior is through self-administered consequences. **Self-reinforcement processes** *refer to internal, self-administered rewards and punishments* (Bandura, 1999; Mischel, 1999). In response to our own behaviors, we generate positive evaluations and emotions such as pride, self-approval, and the conviction that we did "the right thing." In contrast, we may respond with negative responses such as self-reproach, shame, and guilt when we violate our personal standards. Self-reinforcement processes often override external consequences, making us more autonomous and self-directed.

RECONCILING PERSONALITY COHERENCE WITH BEHAVIORAL INCONSISTENCY

As noted in our earlier discussion of the trait perspective, people's behavior often shows a notable lack of consistency across situations, a fact that has caused some to question the traditional concept of personality. How can we have a coherent and stable personality yet show such inconsistency across different situations? Does personality really matter? Recent social-cognitive research and theoretical advances may provide the answer to this paradox of personality coherence and inconsistent behavior.

In CAPS theory, personality is defined in terms of the cognitive-affective person variables and the interactions among them. The CAPS system is assumed to be stable and consistent, although it can surely be modified by significant experiences. Behavior, however, need not be consistent. How a person behaves depends on many factors, including the features of the situation, how these features are encoded, the expectancies and beliefs that are activated, the goals that are relevant, the emotions that might occur, and the plans and self-regulatory processes that help determine the behavior. Thus it is entirely possible for people to behave inconsistently across situations that seem very similar to an outside observer. People will behave similarly in situations that, *to them*, have important characteristics in common, but they may behave inconsistently in situations that differ in ways that evoke different responses from the CAPS (Shoda & Mischel, 2000).

As a result of interactions between situations and the personality system, people exhibit distinctive **behavioral signatures,** *consistent ways of responding in particular classes of situations.* These behavioral signatures are the outward manifestation

▶ **Focus 21**
How does the concept of behavioral signatures help reconcile the seeming paradox of personality coherence and behavioral inconsistency?

FIGURE 12.21

Stable situation-behavior patterns. This chart shows the aggressive responses of two children, A and B, in five different summer camp situations. These data show the children's distinctive behavioral signatures for aggressive responding, even though their aggression scores averaged across the five settings were quite similar. The zero point on the vertical axis represents the average amount of verbal aggression shown in each situation by all the children in the study. SOURCE: Adapted from Shoda et al., 1994.

of personality that establish a person's unique identity (Mischel et al., 2002). Research shows that people can have very distinctive behavioral signatures. For example, Figure 12.21 shows the behavioral patterns of two verbally aggressive children in a residential summer camp (Shoda et al., 1994). The children's behaviors were systematically observed and coded for more than 150 hours per child. Overall, these two children were quite similar in the overall number of verbally aggressive responses they made. However, inspection of the *situational patterns* of aggression reveals that child A reacted very aggressively toward adults, whether they were behaving toward the child in a warm or a punitive fashion. In contrast, this child consistently showed relatively little aggression toward peers. Child B showed quite a different pattern, consistently reacting with low levels of aggression toward adults or when being teased by peers but showing a consistently high level of aggression when peers approached him in a friendly manner.

The important lesson here is that if we simply averaged the aggressive behavior counts across the five situations, the two children would look equally aggressive. But in so doing, we would mask the distinctive and consistent behavioral signatures that define each child's individuality. Thus the coherence of personality is shown not at the level of individual behaviors but at the level of behavioral signatures.

EVALUATING SOCIAL-COGNITIVE THEORIES

A strength of the social-cognitive approach is its strong scientific base. It brings together two perspectives that have strong research traditions: the behavioral and the cognitive. The constructs of social-cognitive theory can be defined, measured,

and researched with considerable precision. As a result, the social-cognitive approach has advanced our understanding of how processes within the person and characteristics of the situation interact with one another to influence behavior. Another strength is its ability to translate insights derived from other perspectives into cognitive-behavioral concepts (Mischel et al., 2004).

Social-cognitive theory also helps resolve an apparent contradiction between the central assumption that personality produces stability in behavior and research findings that people's behavior is not very consistent across different situations. Mischel and Shoda's CAPS theory suggests that the inconsistency of a person's behavior across situations is actually a manifestation of a stable underlying cognitive-affective personality structure that reacts to certain features of situations. However, the ability of the CAPS to predict specific behavior needs further examination, and it will be challenging to measure the numerous interactions among the CAPS components. Much more needs to be learned about how the CAPS operates, but this question is being explored by many current researchers (Cervone & Shoda, 1999a; Mischel et al., 2004). Another major challenge will be to find out what active ingredients of situations cause people to encode them in similar ways, thereby producing the consistencies in behavior that constitute behavioral signatures (Ten-Berge et al., 2002).

To conclude our analysis of Charles Whitman, let's view him from a social-cognitive perspective. The behavioral aspect of the social-cognitive perspective would focus on past learning experiences that predisposed him to violence. These are not hard to find in his history. First, his father provided an aggressive model during his formative years, controlling his wife and children with physical abuse. His father was also a gun enthusiast, and there were guns hanging in virtually every room of the Whitman home. Family photos show young Charles holding guns when he was only 2 years old, and his father made sure he received plenty of training in using them. Long before he enlisted in the Marines, Whitman was an expert marksman, and the Marines built on this expertise with sniper training that earned him a sharpshooter's badge. As other aspects of his life were crumbling, Whitman's marksmanship was a continuing and positive part of his personal self-identity, and he told several University of Texas acquaintances how easy it would be to pick off people from the tower. His expertise made him a deadly killer as he fired from the tower with stunning accuracy, killing people up to a half mile away.

How might Charles Whitman be represented within the CAPS model? At the level of encoding processes, Mischel and Shoda would focus on how he viewed himself and his world. Aggression is fueled by perceptions that we have been wronged and that the provocation was intentional (Lazarus, 2001). Clearly, Whitman felt victimized both by his father and by the Marines, and he saw the world as so malevolent that he regarded killing his wife and mother as an act of mercy. Moreover, his view of himself became increasingly negative as his life's fortunes declined. His outcome and self-efficacy expectancies became increasingly negative. One source of self-efficacy that remained unchanged was his exceptional marksmanship, and this competency became the medium for the expression of his rage, as well as his entrée to the death he desired.

Whitman's values involved success in his career, in academics, and as a husband. Success was nowhere in sight, producing feelings of frustration and creating unbearable stress (negative affect) in his life. He felt unworthy of his wife and deeply regretted the two incidents early in their marriage when he had beaten her.

At the level of affect, what also stands out is Whitman's internal rage. In the words of the psychiatrist who saw him shortly before his outburst, he was "fairly oozing" with generalized hostility. Whitman tried to achieve his goals and exercise self-control with elaborate manuals filled with specific self-instructions about how to act, what to say, and how to inhibit his hostility. Eventually, though, in the absence of adequate self-regulation skills, these external controls failed, with tragic consequences.

Applying the concept of behavioral signatures to Charles Whitman, it is clear that Whitman's behavior differed dramatically across situations. Most of the time, he was an all-American boy, charming, witty, agreeable, and a loving husband. However, when under stress, his defenses against his inner rage began to crumble and he became hostile and aggressive, capable of abusing his wife and threatening to shoot a fellow Marine. When stress reached a sufficiently severe level, his controls broke down completely and he committed the murderous acts. In the if-then language of behavioral signatures, we might summarize this aspect of his personality as: *if* not under stress, *then* friendly and well controlled; but *if* under stress and facing severe failure, *then* hostile and impulsive.

Having now described the various perspectives on personality, we have seen that each presents us with a different picture of human nature and that each focuses on particular determinants of human individuality. Moreover, each perspective provides us with different pieces of the puzzle that was Charles Whitman.

Figure 12.22 summarizes the determinants emphasized by the various theories at the biological, psychological, and environmental levels of analysis.

FIGURE 12.22

Levels of analysis: Factors related to personality differences.

LEVELS OF ANALYSIS   Factors Related to Personality Differences

Biological
- Personality differences shaped by evolutionary factors (evolutionary personality theory)
- Genetic bases for individual differences and temperament (behavior genetics)
- Individual differences in customary level of cortical arousal and suddenness with which autonomic shifts occur (Eysenck)
- Individual differences in biological bases for temperament

Psychological
- Psychodynamic processes involving impulse, defense, unconscious conflicts, and psychosexual factors (Freud)
- Differences in object relations and attachment styles
- Differences in personal construct systems (Kelly)
- Processes involving the self-concept and striving for self-actualization (Rogers)
- Personality dispositions to act, think, and feel in particular ways (trait theorists)
- Cognitive social learning variables that interact with situational factors (Bandura, Rotter, Mischel)

Environmental
- Early relationship experiences (psychodynamic theories)
- Environmental factors that support or stifle self-actualization (humanistic theorists)
- Past social learning experiences and current environmental factors that interact with social cognitive person variables (social-cognitive theorists)

Personality Differences

► Focus 22
In what three ways can cultures differ, thereby influencing personality? What personality and gender differences occur within individualistic and collectivistic cultures?

FIGURE 12.23

Culture and personality. This model shows how cultural elements are transmitted to the individual through the medium of social environment and family influences. SOURCE: Based on factors cited by Locke, 1992, and Sue & Sue, 1990.

IN REVIEW

■ Social-cognitive theories are concerned with how social relationships, learning experiences, and cognitive processes jointly contribute to behavior. A key concept is reciprocal determinism, relating to two-way causal relations between people, their behavior, and the environment.

■ Rotter's theory viewed behavior as influenced by expectancies and the reinforcement value of potential outcomes. His concept of locus of control is a generalized belief in the extent to which we can control the outcomes in our life.

■ Bandura's concept of self-efficacy relates to our self-perceived ability to carry out the behaviors necessary to achieve goals in a particular situation. It is influenced by past performance attainments, verbal persuasion, observation of others' attainments, and perceived emotional arousal. Self-efficacy can be enhanced through the application of systematic goal-setting procedures.

■ According to Mischel and Shoda, situational features activate the person's cognitive-affective personality system (CAPS). The CAPS involves individual differences in encoding strategies, expectancies and beliefs, goals and values, affects, and competencies and self-regulatory processes. The CAPS interacts with features of the environment, helping to explain why people have specific behavioral signatures and do not necessarily behave consistently across situations.

CULTURE, GENDER, AND PERSONALITY

As we have seen, personality is a product of interacting biological and environmental influences. Environment exists at many different levels, ranging from the physical surroundings in which we develop to the increasingly global social contexts shown in Figure 12.23. Among the most important, yet unappreciated, environmental influences is the culture in which we develop. We are often unaware of these influences because they serve as an amorphous background against which the specific events of our lives unfold. Culture encompasses unstated assumptions (including assumptions about the very nature of reality), norms, values, sex roles, and habitual ways of behaving that are shared by members of a social group. It influences what we perceive, how we perceive, how we relate to ourselves and others, and how we behave.

Cultures differ along a number of dimensions that can affect personality development (Triandis & Suh, 2002). One is *complexity*. Consider how much more complex a Western information-age culture is than a hunter-gatherer culture in a remote region of an undeveloped country. Consider also how much more potential for diversity and conflict of values and behavioral norms exists in a highly complex culture.

A second cultural dimension is *tightness*. In tight cultures, there are many rules about behavior, and those who deviate from the cultural norms, even in minor ways, are likely to be punished. In Singapore, for example, adolescents are expected to adhere strictly to social norms that forbid experimenting with alcohol, tobacco, or sexual intercourse (Ball & Mosselle, 1995). As a result of explicit norms, people tend to differ less from one another in tight cultures than they do in loose cultures, where diversity in beliefs, values, and "doing your own thing" is permitted or even encouraged. Loose cultures are most likely to occur where people within a social group are not

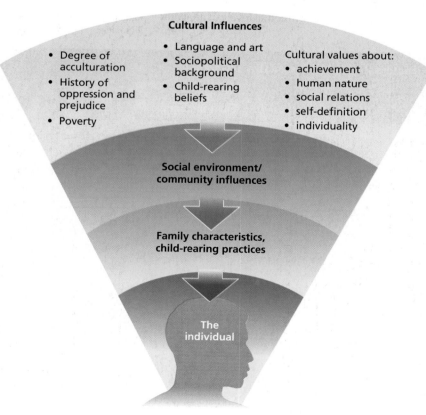

Cultural Influences

- Degree of acculturation
- History of oppression and prejudice
- Poverty

- Language and art
- Sociopolitical background
- Child-rearing beliefs

Cultural values about:
- achievement
- human nature
- social relations
- self-definition
- individuality

Social environment/ community influences

Family characteristics, child-rearing practices

The individual

highly dependent on one another and where diversity is tolerated or even encouraged. Thus we would expect American adolescents to show greater diversity and feelings of individuality than those in Singapore. They might also experience more conflicts in deciding which values to embrace and what type of person they want to be.

Important personality differences have been found between people in *individualistic* and *collectivistic* cultures, although we should emphasize that significant variation can be found within any given culture because, on average, only about 40 percent of people within a particular culture strongly embrace individualistic or collectivistic goals (Triandis & Suh, 2002). In one study, American and Japanese college students were given a self-concept questionnaire on which they listed their five most important attributes. The researchers then classified each statement according to whether it referred to a personal attribute (e.g., "I am honest," "I am smart"), a social identity (e.g., "I am an oldest son," "I am a student"), or something else, such as a physical trait. As Figure 12.24 shows, the Americans were far more likely than the Japanese to list personal traits, abilities, or dispositions, whereas the Japanese more frequently described themselves in social identity terms. Thus the social embeddedness of the col-

lectivistic Japanese culture was reflected in their self-perceptions, as was cultural individualism in the Americans' self-concepts (Cousins, 1989). Interestingly, personality trait measures do not predict behavior as well in collectivistic cultures as they do in individualistic cultures, possibly because environmental factors play a stronger role in the behavior of collectivistic individuals (Church & Katigbak, 2000).

Self-enhancement needs are equally strong in individualistic and collectivistic cultures, but they are satisfied in different ways. Individualists enhance the self through personal successes, whereas collectivists feel better about themselves when their group succeeds (Sedikides et al., 2003). In individualistic cultures, personal success also serves to increase people's motivation, whereas in collectivistic cultures, motivation increases after failure, as the person attempts to change the self and conform to the demands of the situation (Heine et al., 2000). Even emotional lives differ. In a study of cultural differences in experienced emotions, Americans reported more self-oriented positive emotions, such as self-pride and personal happiness, whereas Japanese reported more interpersonally oriented positive emotions, such as closeness, friendliness, and respect (Kitayama et al., 2000). On self-esteem measures, Japanese score lower than Americans. Shinobu Kitayama and Hazel Markus (1999) explain that in Japanese culture, self-criticism is not bad, for it serves the valuable function of encouraging self-improvement that can benefit the individual and society. In Western cultures, self-criticism is predictive of depression, but this is not the case in Japan.

Gender-role socialization provides us with **gender schemas,** *organized mental structures that contain our understanding of the attributes and behaviors that are appropriate and expected for males and females* (Bem, 1981). Within a given culture, gender schemas tell us what the typical man or woman should be like. In Western cultures, men tend to prize attributes related to achievement, emotional strength, athleticism, and self-sufficiency, whereas women prize interpersonal competencies, kindness, and helpfulness to others (Beyer, 1990; Marsh, 1990). In this sense, men in Western cultures tend to develop more of an individualistic self-concept, emphasizing achievement and separateness from others, whereas women's self-concepts tend to be more collectivistic, emphasizing their social connectedness with others (Kashima et al., 1995). Nonetheless, we should keep in mind that significant individual differences exist within each gender group, with many women being individualists and many men collectivists (Triandis

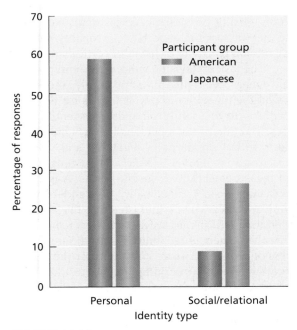

FIGURE 12.24

Cultural differences in the self-concept. This graph shows the percentages of personal identity and social/relational self-attributes given by Japanese and American college students as key aspects of their self-concepts. Source: Adapted from Cousins, 1989.

& Suh, 2002). As noted earlier, men and women do not differ significantly in self-esteem in United States samples, suggesting that there are numerous behavioral routes to feeling good about oneself.

IN REVIEW

- Cultures differ along several important dimensions, including complexity, tightness, and individualism-collectivism, all of which can affect personality development.

- People in collectivistic cultures tend to see the environment as fixed (i.e., having rigid rules and expectations) and themselves as changeable, with a capacity to fit in. In contrast, members of individualistic cultures are more likely to see themselves and their personalities as relatively stable and the environment as malleable.

- Culture influences self-concept development. People from individualistic cultures tend to describe themselves in terms of personal traits, abilities, or dispositions, whereas those from collectivistic cultures are more likely to describe themselves in social identity terms.

- Gender schemas are organized mental structures that contain our understanding of the attributes and behaviors that are appropriate and expected for males and females. In Western cultures, men tend to value achievement, emotional strength, and self-sufficiency, whereas women prize interpersonal skills, kindness, and helpfulness to others.

PERSONALITY ASSESSMENT

If you were to be introduced to Jennifer, a woman you had never met before, and given one week to provide a complete personality description of her, what would you do? Chances are, you would seek information in a variety of ways. You might start by interviewing Jennifer and finding out as much as you could about her. Based on your knowledge of the theories we have discussed, what questions would you ask? Would you ask about early-childhood experiences and dreams? about how she sees herself and others? Would you be interested in the kinds of traits embodied in the Big Five Model or in Eysenck's dimension of Introversion-Extraversion? Would you want to know how Jennifer customarily feels and responds in various situations? Your answers to these

▶ **Focus 23**
Describe two characteristics that personality measures must have in order to be scientifically and practically useful.

questions and your other assessment decisions would in some sense reflect your own theory of what is important in describing personality.

You probably would not be content simply to interview Jennifer. You might also decide to interview other people who know her well and get their views of what she is like. You might even ask them to rate her on a variety of traits, and you could ask Jennifer to rate herself on the same measures to see if her self-concept agrees with how others see her.

Finally, you might decide that it would be useful to actually observe how Jennifer behaves in a variety of situations. You would want to observe her in a way that would allow you to get as natural and characteristic a sample of her behavior as possible. This information, together with that obtained from Jennifer and from those who know her best, might provide a reasonable basis for a personality description.

Figure 12.25 shows the major methods that psychologists use to assess personality characteristics. As you can see, they use some of the same methods you might have chosen: the interview, trait ratings, and behavior reports, as well as behavioral assessment, or direct observation and measurement of the subject's behavior. In addition, psychologists have developed several types of tests, including objective self-report measures and projective tests that ask respondents to interpret ambiguous stimuli, such as inkblots or pictures. Finally, physiological measures can be used to measure various aspects of personality, such as emotional reactivity or levels of cortical arousal.

The task of devising valid and useful personality measures is anything but simple, and it has taxed the ingenuity of psychologists for nearly a century. To be useful from either a scientific or a practical perspective, personality tests must conform to the standards of reliability and validity discussed in Chapter 9. *Reliability*, or consistency of measurement, takes several forms. A test that measures a stable personality trait should yield similar scores when administered to the same individuals at different times (test-retest reliability). Another aspect of reliability is that different professionals should score and interpret the test in the same way (interjudge reliability). *Validity* refers to the most important question of all: Is the test actually measuring the personality variable that it is intended to measure? A valid test allows us to predict behavior that is influenced by the personality variable being measured. Research on test reliability and validity is an important activity of personality psychologists, and good measures of personality are an absolute must for scientific research on personality and for ethical clinical application (Domino, 2000).

INTERVIEWS

Interviews are one of the oldest methods of assessment. Long before the invention of writing, people undoubtedly made judgments about others by observing them and talking with them. Interviewers can obtain information about a person's thoughts, feelings, and other internal states, as well as information about current and past relationships, experiences, and behavior. This assessment method is particularly popular among psychodynamic and phenomenological-humanistic workers.

Structured interviews *contain a set of specific questions that are administered to every participant.* An attempt is made to create a standardized situation so that interviewees' responses to more-or-less identical stimuli can be interpreted and compared. Such interviews are frequently used to collect research data or to make a psychiatric diagnosis. Other interviews are unstructured, with interviewers tailoring their questions to the particular individual and situation.

Good interviewers do not limit their attention to what an interviewee says; they also look at how she or he says it. They note interviewees' general appearance and grooming, their voice and speech patterns, the content of their statements, and their facial expressions and posture. Sometimes, attitudes that are not expressed verbally can be inferred from behavior, as in this instance:

> During the interview she held her small son on her lap. The child began to play with his genitals. The mother, without looking directly at the child, moved his hand away and held it securely for a while. . . . Later in the interview the mother was asked what she ordinarily did when the child masturbated. She replied that he never did this—he was a very "good" boy. She was evidently entirely unconscious of what had transpired in the very presence of the interviewer. (Maccoby & Maccoby, 1954, p. 484)

The interview is valuable for the direct personal contact it provides, but it has some limitations. First, characteristics of the interviewer may influence how the interviewee responds and thus affect the validity of the information. In addition, the validity of information obtained depends on the interviewee's desire to cooperate, to respond honestly, and to report accurately what the interviewer is trying to assess.

Despite its limitations, the face-to-face interview is essential for certain purposes. For example,

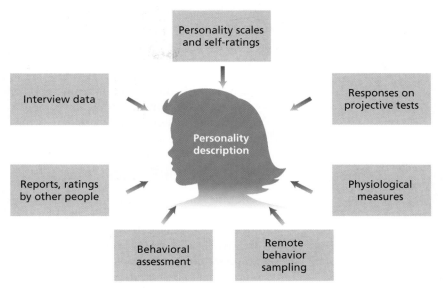

FIGURE 12.25

Measurement approaches used to assess personality.

a clinical psychologist needs to observe and converse with a person who is being considered for admission to a mental hospital. Interviews are often used in research as well. The challenge is to design and conduct interviews in ways that maximize the validity of the data obtained from the respondent.

BEHAVIORAL ASSESSMENT

Personality psychologists can sometimes observe the behaviors they are interested in rather than asking people about them. In **behavioral assessment,** *psychologists devise an explicit coding system that contains the behavioral categories of interest.* Then they train observers until they show high levels of agreement (interjudge reliability) in using the coding categories to record behavior. Assessors may code the behavior in live settings, or they made code videotaped behavior sequences. A staple of behaviorists, behavioral assessment can provide valuable information about how frequently and under what conditions certain classes of behavior occur (Haynes, 2000). Social-cognitive researchers used this method to measure the behavioral signatures of the verbally aggressive children in the summer camp environment discussed earlier.

Behavioral assessment requires precision in defining the behaviors of interest and the conditions under which they occur. For example, observers studying a young child who is having problems in school do not simply say, "Jerry is disruptive." Instead, they try to answer the question, "What, specifically, does Jerry *do* that causes disruption?" Once they have identified Jerry's

▶ **Focus 24**
How are interviews, behavioral assessment, and remote behavioral sampling used to assess personality?

specific behaviors, the next questions are, "How often and under what conditions does the disruptive behavior occur?" and "What kinds of outcomes do the behaviors produce?" Answers to these questions can be particularly important not only in measuring differences in people's personality characteristics but also in identifying potential situational causes of their behavior (Greene & Ollendick, 2000).

REMOTE BEHAVIOR SAMPLING

It is not practical or possible for behavioral assessors to follow people around from situation to situation on a daily basis. In addition, assessors are frequently interested in unobservable events, such as emotional reactions and thinking patterns, that may shed considerable light on personality functioning. Through **remote behavior sampling,** *researchers and clinicians can collect self-reported samples of behavior from respondents as they live their daily lives.* A tiny computerized device resembling a cell phone is used. The device pages respondents at randomly determined times of the day (Figure 12.26). When the beeper sounds, respondents rate or record their current thoughts,

▶ **Focus 25**
Compare the rational-theoretical and empirical approaches to developing personality scales.

FIGURE 12.26

In remote behavior sampling, a computerized device resembling a cell phone is used to collect responses from participants—such as ratings of their mood at a certain time—as they live their daily lives.

feelings, or behaviors, depending on what the researcher or therapist is assessing (Stone et al., 2000). Respondents may also report on aspects of the situation they are in so that situation-behavior interactions can be examined. Remote sampling procedures can be used over weeks or even months to collect a large behavior sample across many situations. This approach to personality assessment holds great promise, for it enables researchers and clinicians to detect patterns of personal functioning that might not be revealed by other methods.

PERSONALITY SCALES

Personality scales, or inventories, are widely used for assessing personality in both research and clinical work. They are considered *objective* measures because they include standard sets of questions, usually in a true-false or rating-scale format, that are scored using an agreed-on scoring key (Nezami & Butcher, 2000). Their advantages include (1) the ability to collect data from many people at the same time, (2) the fact that all people respond to the same items, and (3) ease of scoring. Their major disadvantage is the possibility that some people will choose not to answer the items truthfully, in which case their scores will not be valid reflections of the trait being measured. To combat this threat to validity, some widely used tests have special *validity scales* that detect tendencies to respond in a socially desirable manner or to present an overly negative image of oneself.

The items on personality scales are developed in two major ways. In the **rational-theoretical approach,** *items are based on the theorist's conception of the personality trait to be measured.* For example, to develop a measure of introversion-extraversion, we would ask ourselves what introverts and extraverts often say about themselves, and then we would write items that captured those kinds of self-descriptions (e.g., "I love to be at large social gatherings" or "I'm very content to spend time by myself"). One frequently used measure of this kind is the **NEO Personality Inventory (NEO-PI),** *which measures the Big Five personality traits of Openness, Conscientiousness, Extraversion, Agreeableness, and Neuroticism* (Costa & McCrae, 1992). Other scales developed according to the rational approach are the measures of optimism-pessimism, self-monitoring, and locus of control shown in Tables 12.6, 12.7, and 12.9.

A different approach to developing personality scales is the **empirical approach,** *in which items are chosen not because their content seems relevant to the trait on rational grounds, but because each item has* been answered differently by groups of people (for example, introverts and extraverts) *known to differ in the personality characteristic of interest.* The **Minnesota Multiphasic Personality Inventory-2 (MMPI-2)** *is a widely used personality test developed according to the empirical approach.* The MMPI was originally designed to provide an objective basis for psychiatric diagnosis. Its 567 true-false items consist of statements that were answered by groups of patients diagnosed with specific psychiatric disorders (e.g., hysteria, paranoia, and schizophrenia) in ways different from the answers given by respondents in a nonpsychiatric comparison sample. The items vary widely in content; some are concerned with attitudes and emotions, others relate to overt behavior and symptoms, and still others refer to the person's life history.

The MMPI-2 has 3 validity scales and 10 clinical scales (Table 12.11). The validity scales are used to detect tendencies to present either an overly positive picture or to exaggerate the degree of psychological disturbance. Though the scales were originally intended to measure severe personality deviations such as schizophrenia, depression, and psychopathic personality, the *profile* of scores obtained on the various scales also reveals important aspects of personality functioning even in people who do not display such disorders (Graham, 2006). Thus the MMPI-2 is used not only as an aid to psychiatric diagnosis but also for personality description and as a screening device in industrial and military settings.

PROJECTIVE TESTS

Freud and other psychodynamic theorists emphasized the importance of unconscious factors in understanding behavior. By definition, however, people are unaware of unconscious dynamics, so they cannot report them to interviewers or on self-report tests like the NEO-PI or the MMPI-2. Other methods were therefore needed to assess them.

Projective tests *present subjects with ambiguous stimuli and ask for some interpretation of them.* The assumption is that because the meaning of the stimulus is unclear, the subject's interpretation will have to come from within, reflecting the projection of inner needs, feelings, and ways of viewing the world onto the stimulus. The following fictional story helps illustrate the rationale for projective techniques:

> During the administration of a set of Rorschach inkblots, the man being tested saw every one of the inkblots as either sex organs or people engaging in sexual acts. After the last inkblot, the psy-

TABLE 12.11	The Validity and Clinical Scales of the Minnesota Multiphasic Personality Inventory-2 (MMPI-2) and the Behavioral Characteristics Associated with High Scores on the Scales	
Scale	**Abbreviation**	**Behavioral Correlates**
Validity Scales		
Lie	L	Lies or is highly conventional
Frequency	F	Exaggerates complaints, answers haphazardly
Correction	K	Denies problems
Clinical Scales		
Hypochondriasis	Hs	Expresses bodily concerns and complaints
Depression	D	Is depressed, pessimistic, guilty
Hysteria	Hy	Reacts to stress with physical symptoms, lacks insight into negative feelings
Psychopathic deviate	Pd	Is impulsive, in conflict with the law, involved in stormy relationships
Masculinity, femininity	Mf	Has interests characteristic of the opposite sex
Paranoia	Pa	Is suspicious, resentful
Psychasthenia	Pt	Is anxious, worried, high-strung
Schizophrenia	Sc	Is confused, disorganized, disoriented, and withdrawn from others
Hypomania	Ma	Is energetic, active, restless
Social introversion	Si	Is introverted, with little social contact

chologist declared, "I've never in my entire career seen anyone as obsessed with sex as you seem to be." The man responded indignantly, "What do you mean, *I'm* obsessed with sex? *You're* the one with all the dirty pictures!"

The stimuli that people are asked to respond to include inkblots and pictures. The **Rorschach test** *consists of 10 inkblots.* The person being tested is shown each one in succession and asked, "What does this look like? What might it be?" (Figure 12.27). After responding, the person is asked to explain what specific feature of the inkblot (e.g., its shape or its color) makes it seem that way. Examiners categorize and score responses in terms of the kinds of objects reported, the features attended to (e.g., the whole blot, colored portions, tiny details), and the emotional tone of particular types of responses (Erdberg, 2000).

Interpretations made by Rorschach examiners are often based on what the responses seem to symbolize. For example, people who see peering eyes and threatening figures in the inkblots are likely to be viewed as projecting their own paranoid fears and suspicions onto the stimuli. One drawback of the Rorschach is that different examiners may interpret the same response very differently, producing unreliability among examiners.

▶ **Focus 26**
How do projective tests differ from objective measures? Describe and compare two projective tests.

FIGURE 12.27

During a Rorschach test administration, the person being tested is shown a series of inkblots similar to this one and is asked to indicate what each resembles and what feature of the stimulus (for example, its shape or its color) makes it appear that way.

In an attempt to minimize clinician subjectivity in interpreting Rorschach responses, John Exner (1991) developed a scoring system with specific coding categories and scoring criteria. Although this system created greater uniformity in scoring, many of the personality interpretations derived from the Rorschach lack research support (Lilienfeld et al., 2000). Nonetheless, many psychodynamic clinicians maintain their faith in the Rorschach, insisting that they find it useful for gaining insight into unconscious processes.

The **Thematic Apperception Test (TAT)** *consists of a series of pictures derived from paintings, drawings, and magazine illustrations.* In general, the pictures are less ambiguous than the Rorschach inkblots, but they still require an interpretation. To illustrate, look at the picture in Figure 12.28, and then write a story that addresses the following questions:

- What is happening? Who are the people involved?

- What has led up to this situation?

- What is being thought, felt, and wanted, and by whom?

- What will happen? How will the story turn out?

The stories told in response to a set of 10 to 20 pictures are analyzed for recurrent themes that are assumed to reflect important aspects of the respondent's personality. These might include the kinds of personal relationships depicted in the stories, the types of motives and feelings that are attributed to the characters, whether positive or negative outcomes occur, and factors that produce these outcomes such as personal weaknesses or forces in the environment.

The TAT, like the Rorschach, typically relies on the subjective interpretation of test responses, which can result in different interpretations of the same stories. Since not everyone can be right, the possibility of erroneous interpretations is obvious. Where specific systems have been developed to score stories, however, the TAT has proven to be a useful and valid test (Atkinson, 1958). As discussed in Chapter 10, scoring of stories told to TAT pictures is used by researchers to measure achievement motivation. The TAT appears to provide a more valid measure of this and other motives, such as power, than do objective self-report measures of the same motives, showing stronger relations with motivated behavior (Ferguson, 2000). Despite such exceptions, however, objective measures of personality have generally been found to have better reliability and validity than projective measures (Lilienfeld et al., 2000; Nezami & Butcher, 2000).

FIGURE 12.28

A picture from the Thematic Apperception Test. Subjects are asked to make up a story about the picture, covering specific points, such as those listed in the text. The stories are analyzed for recurrent themes that are assumed to reflect significant aspects of personality. SOURCE: Reprinted by permission of the publisher from Henry A. Murray, *Thematic Apperception Test,* Plate 12F. Cambridge, MA: Harvard University Press. Copyright © 1943 by the president and fellows of Harvard College; Copyright © 1971 by Henry A. Murray.

IN REVIEW

■ Methods used by psychologists to assess personality include the interview, behavioral assessment, remote behavior sampling, objective personality scales, and projective tests.

■ The major approaches to constructing personality scales are the rational approach, in which items are written on an intuitive basis, and the empirical approach, in which items discriminate between groups known to differ on the trait of interest. The NEO-PI, reflecting the rational approach, measures individual differences in the Big Five factors. The MMPI-2 is the best-known test developed with the empirical approach.

■ Projective tests present ambiguous stimuli to people. It is assumed that interpretations of such stimuli give clues to important internal processes. The Rorschach inkblot test and the Thematic Apperception Test are the most commonly used projective tests.

A CLOSING THOUGHT

The topic of personality has captured the imagination of humans throughout history. The first systematic theory of personality was formulated by the Greek physician Hippocrates in the 5th century B.C. Personality dynamics and individuality have been celebrated and explored in the great literatures of many cultures, including the Bible and the Quran. In psychology, the study of personality has contributed to the development of all of our diverse perspectives on behavior. Yet in its second century as a formal subject of scientific study, it remains one of the most vibrant areas in psychology. The fascinating topic of human diversity continues to attract theorists and researchers, who forge new understandings each day. Moreover, the field of personality is seeing increased collaboration among experts from diverse areas of psychology, including social, developmental, physiological, cognitive, and evolutionary psychology.

In the following chapters, we will build on what we have learned about personality. We will see that personality factors influence health and people's responses to life stress. As we explore the behavior disorders, we will see what happens when personality development goes awry, resulting in deviant and maladaptive behavior patterns. We will explore the various disorders from the perspectives and theories you have read about in this chapter. Then we will see how our knowledge of personality development and personality change is being applied to the treatment of psychological disorders and how personality both influences and is shaped by our social behavior.

KEY TERMS AND CONCEPTS

Each term has been boldfaced and defined in the chapter on the page indicated in parentheses.

archetypes (p. 447)
behavioral assessment (p. 479)
behavioral signatures (p. 473)
behavior-outcome expectancy (p. 472)
cognitive-affective personality system (CAPS; p. 472)
collective unconscious (p. 447)
conditions of worth (p. 453)
congruence (p. 452)
defense mechanisms (p. 445)
ego (p. 444)
Electra complex (p. 446)
empirical approach (p. 480)
evolutionary personality theory (p. 462)
factor analysis (p. 458)
fixation (p. 446)
fully functioning persons (p. 453)
gender schemas (p. 477)

id (p. 444)
internal-external locus of control (p. 468)
Minnesota Multiphasic Personality Inventory-2 (MMPI-2; p. 481)
need for positive regard (p. 453)
need for positive self-regard (p. 453)
neoanalytic theorists (p. 446)
NEO Personality Inventory (NEO-PI; p. 480)
object relations theories (p. 447)
Oedipus complex (p. 446)
personal constructs (p. 456)
personality (p. 442)
personality traits (p. 458)
personal unconscious (p. 447)
phenomenology (p. 450)
pleasure principle (p. 444)
projective tests (p. 481)
psychosexual stages (p. 446)

rational-theoretical approach (p. 480)
reality principle (p. 444)
reciprocal determinism (p. 467)
regression (p. 446)
remote behavior sampling (p. 480)
repression (p. 446)
Role Construct Repertory (Rep) Test (p. 451)
Rorschach test (p. 481)
self (p. 451)
self-actualization (p. 451)
self-consistency (p. 452)
self-efficacy (p. 469)
self-enhancement (p. 454)
self-esteem (p. 453)
self-monitoring (p. 461)
self-reinforcement processes (p. 473)
self-verification (p. 454)

? What Do You Think?

HOW SERIOUSLY SHOULD WE TAKE PEOPLE'S VIOLENT FANTASIES? (PAGE 449)

In some cases, critical thinking requires the balancing of competing demands. In the case of Charles Whitman, the psychiatrist who interviewed him needed to balance the competing demands of traditional patient confidentiality and public safety. In hindsight, we might conclude that the therapist should have sacrificed confidentiality and warned university security personnel. But the issue is clouded by the fact that, in general, mental health professionals have a very poor record of success in predicting violent behavior (Monahan, 1992).

In 1966 when the Whitman incident occurred, it was solely up to the therapist to decide whether a breach of confidentiality was warranted. Following the Whitman tragedy, a formal inquiry was held, and although many professionals questioned his judgment in not alerting authorities, the psychiatrist who saw Whitman was exonerated of professional misconduct. But three years later, at the University of California, a college student murdered his estranged girlfriend after telling his therapist he intended to do so. Although the therapist notified campus police, who released the assailant after questioning him, the victim's family sued the university and the therapist, claiming that he should also have warned the victim and her family. The family won the case. Thereafter, most jurisdictions passed laws requiring mental health professionals to violate confidentiality and report threats of violence in order to protect potential victims. The "duty to protect" is granted precedence over the seal of confidentiality. Had today's standards existed in 1966, the tragedy in Texas might have been averted. Still, legal mandates call for the therapist to exercise professional judgment as to whether a given client and a given set of circumstances constitute a clear and present danger. Therapists are hesitant to break the seal of confidentiality unless they are confident in their judgment of imminent danger to the community. In Whitman's case, a professional who didn't know about Whitman's earlier aggressive acts may well have concluded that his stated fantasies were not a compelling danger signal. Thus it is part of a psychologist's professional responsibility to have the training and expertise to make such judgments.

IS SELF-ACTUALIZATION A USEFUL SCIENTIFIC CONSTRUCT? (PAGE 453)

Self-actualization is a centerpiece of some humanistic theories, but it is troublesome from a scientific perspective. Some critics believe that it is impossible to define an individual's actualizing tendency except in terms of the behavior that it supposedly produces. This would be an example of circular reasoning: Why did the person achieve such success? Because of self-actualization. How do we know self-actualization was at work? Because the person achieved great success.

Unless a construct can be operationally defined in a manner independent of the phenomena it is supposed to cause, it is not scientifically useful. A construct must also be measurable. While it is true that concepts related to the self-actualization motive (such as people's beliefs that they are fulfilling their potential) could potentially be measured, most psychologists suggest that rather than being a scientific construct, self-actualization is better considered a philosophical concept.

CHAPTER THIRTEEN

Adjusting to Life:
Stress, Coping, and Health

CHAPTER OUTLINE

Life is largely a process of adaptation to the circumstances in which we exist.

—HANS SELYE

P riscilla, now 18, had anything but an idyllic childhood. She grew up in an impoverished inner-city home with an alcoholic father who physically and sexually abused her and her younger sister. Priscilla's mother, too helpless and fearful to protect her children, was hospitalized twice for "nervous breakdowns." When Priscilla was 8 years old, a neighbor who suspected the sexual abuse reported the father to Child Protective Services. Upon being notified of the impending investigation, Priscilla's father called his family together in the living room and told them, "You drove me to this." He then put a gun to his head and committed suicide as his wife and children watched in horror. From that point on, Priscilla had to work after school to help support her family. For a time, the family was homeless and lived in a shelter. Her mother became increasingly disturbed and sometimes beat her.

Given her life circumstances, how could Priscilla become anything except an unhappy, maladjusted person, her emotional life dominated by anxiety, anger, and depression? Instead, she grew into a delightful and popular young woman who was emotionally well adjusted, president of her high school class, a talented singer, and an honor student who was awarded a scholarship to an Ivy League university.

■■■■■

I n his book *Persuasion and Healing*, psychiatrist Jerome Frank (1961) describes a treatment performed by the German physician Hans Rheder on three bedridden patients. One patient had an inflamed gall bladder and chronic gallstones. The second was having difficulty recovering from pancreatic surgery and had experienced such severe weight loss that Rheder described her as "skeletal." The third patient was dying from a painful uterine cancer that had spread throughout her body.

Since conventional medicine had done all that was possible for the women, Rheder decided to try the unconventional: He told the women that he had discovered a powerful faith healer who could cure with remarkable success simply by directing his healing power to a particular place. Rheder told each woman that he had arranged for this healing power to be projected to her room on a specific day and hour. In truth, he had already tried the healer without telling the women, and there had been no change in their conditions.

Within a few days after the appointed healing date, the patient with gallstones lost all of her symptoms, returned home, and remained symptom-free for a year. The woman who had been wasting away began to eat and subsequently gained 30 pounds. The patient with cancer was already a terminal case, but her bloated body soon excreted excess fluids, she gained strength, and her blood count improved. She was able to return home and lived for 3 months in relative comfort.

These cases illustrate some of the intriguing phenomena studied in an area known as *health psychology*. Children like Priscilla have been termed "invulnerable" or "resilient" youngsters because they somehow develop normally or even exceptionally in the face of great adversity (Garmezy, 1983; Masten, 2001). What allows resilient people to rise above extraordinarily stressful environments while other individuals, blessed with more benign life histories, collapse under the weight of relatively minor stresses? And what are we to think of the dramatic physical changes that followed Rheder's invocation of the faith healer's curative powers? How can mind triumph over matter to such a degree? Can a simple belief that one will be healed stop illness in its tracks? The answers to these questions will show us that adapting to the demands and challenges in our lives involves complex interactions between the person, the environment, and behavior. Figure 13.1 previews some of the biological, psychological, and environmental factors that influence our health and well-being.

Health psychology *addresses factors that influence well-being and illness, as well as measures that can be taken to promote health and prevent illness.* It therefore confronts many of the leading problems of our times. For example, because stress has negative effects on both physical and psychological well-being, the study of stress and coping is a central focus of health psychology. Pain is another important topic because it is a central feature of many illnesses and a major stressor. Health psychologists explore factors that influence pain perceptions and develop psychological interventions to reduce people's suffering. As we shall see, they also develop and evaluate health-promotion and disease-prevention programs.

STRESS AND WELL-BEING

The term *stress* appears regularly in our everyday discourse. It is also a leading topic of study in psychology. What, exactly, is stress?

Psychologists have viewed stress in three different ways: as a stimulus, as a response, and as an ongoing interaction between an organism and its environment. Some scientists define stress as events that place strong demands on us. These *demanding or threatening situations are* **stressors.** We refer to stress as a *stimulus* when we make statements such as, "I've got a lot of stress in my life right now. I have three exams next week, I lost my class notes, my fiancé just announced a vow of eternal celibacy, and my car broke down."

Stress can also be a *response* that has cognitive, physiological, and behavioral components. Thus a person might say, "I'm feeling all stressed out. I'm tensed up, I'm having trouble concentrating on things, and I've been flying off the handle all week." The presence of negative emotions is an important feature of the stress response and links the study of stress with the field of emotion (Zautra, 2003).

A third way of thinking about stress combines the stimulus and response definitions into a

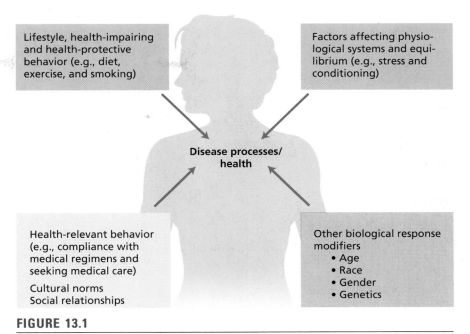

FIGURE 13.1

Biological, psychological, and environmental factors that contribute to disease processes and health.
SOURCE: Adapted from Baum, 1994.

more inclusive model. Here stress is viewed as a *person-situation interaction,* or, more formally, as an ongoing transaction between the organism and the environment (Lazarus, 1991, 1998). This conception of stress is the basis for the model shown in Figure 13.2, and it will guide our discussion of stress. From this perspective, **stress** can be defined as *a pattern of cognitive appraisals, physiological responses, and behavioral tendencies that occurs in response to a perceived imbalance between situational demands and the resources needed to cope with them.*

To explore the topic of stress, we will begin by describing different types of stressors, as well as the methods that scientists have developed to measure life stress. Then we will explore the mind-body interaction that constitutes our response to stressors and the manner in which stress affects our psychological and physical health. Next we will examine factors that influence the relations between stress and health. Finally, we will describe the process of coping with stress.

STRESSORS

Let us begin with the situational component of stress. Stressors are specific kinds of stimuli. Whether physical or psychological, they place demands on us that endanger our well-being and require us to adapt in some manner. The more the demands of a situation outweigh the resources we

▶ **Focus 1**
Describe three ways that theorists have defined the term stress.

Stressor characteristics

- Intensity/severity
- Duration
- Predictability
- Controllability
- Chronicity

Situation demands/resources (stressor)

Internal processes

Cognitive appraisal
- of demands (primary)
- of resources (secondary)
- of consequences
- of meaning of consequences

Physiological responses
- sympathetic arousal
- stress hormones

Coping and task behaviors

Effects

- Worry
- Racing thoughts
- Low self-confidence
- Expecting the worst
- Feeling hopeless

- Muscle tension
- Elevated heart rate
- Shortness of breath
- Increased susceptibility to illness

- Task-irrelevant responses
- Behavioral rigidity or disorganization
- Self-destructive behaviors (e.g., substance abuse, alcoholism)

FIGURE 13.2

The nature of stress. Stress involves complex interactions among situational (stressor) characteristics, cognitive appraisal processes, physiological responses, and behavioral attempts to cope with the situational demands. Stressor characteristics that influence stress responses are shown. The lower panels show potential cognitive, physiological, and behavioral stress responses that can interfere with well-being.

FIGURE 13.3

Stressful life events can vary from catastrophic ones, such as 2005's Hurricane Katrina, to microstressors, or daily hassles. Both classes of stressor take their toll on physical and psychological well-being.

have to deal with them, the more stressful a situation is likely to be.

Stressors differ in their severity (Figure 13.3). They can range from *microstressors*—the daily hassles and minor annoyances, such as difficult coworkers, traffic jams, and academic deadlines—to more severe stressors. *Major negative events*, such as the death or loss of a loved one, an academic or career failure, a serious illness, or being the victim of a serious crime, place strong demands on us and require major efforts to cope. *Catastrophic events* tend to occur unexpectedly and typically affect large numbers of people (Resick, 2005). They include traumatic natural disasters such as the Indian Ocean tsunami of 2004, acts of war or terrorism, and physical or psychological torture. As we shall see, all three classes of stressors can have significant negative effects on

TABLE 13.1 Sample Items from a Self-Report Measure of Positive and Negative Life Events for Adolescents						
Experience	Happened in Last 6 Months?		Good or Bad?		"Minor" or "Major"?	
Parents discover something you didn't want them to know	No	Yes	Good	Bad	Minor	Major
Pressures or expectation by parents	No	Yes	Good	Bad	Minor	Major
Receiving a gift	No	Yes	Good	Bad	Minor	Major
Having plans fall through (not going on a trip, etc.)	No	Yes	Good	Bad	Minor	Major
Losing job (quitting, getting fired, laid off, etc.)	No	Yes	Good	Bad	Minor	Major
Making honor roll or other school achievement	No	Yes	Good	Bad	Minor	Major
Making love or sexual intercourse	No	Yes	Good	Bad	Minor	Major
Something good happens to a friend	No	Yes	Good	Bad	Minor	Major
Work hassles (rude customers, unpleasant jobs, etc.)	No	Yes	Good	Bad	Minor	Major
Death of a friend or family member	No	Yes	Good	Bad	Minor	Major

SOURCE: Adapted from Smith et al., 1990.

psychological and physical well-being (van Praag, 2004; Zautra, 2003).

In addition to intensity or severity, other characteristics that make situations more or less stressful are listed at the far left of Figure 13.2. In general, events over which a person has little or no control, which occur suddenly and unpredictably, and which impact a person over a long period of time seem to take the greatest toll on physical and psychological well-being (Lazarus & Folkman, 1984; Taylor, 2006).

Measuring Stressful Life Events

Researchers have attempted to study the relation between life events and well-being. Sometimes we may know that a person has lived through a natural disaster or lost a loved one to death. In other cases, researchers may have to rely on people's self-reports, using *life event scales* to quantify the amount of life stress that a person has experienced over a given period of time (e.g., the past 3 months or the past year). The life event scale shown in Table 13.1 asks people to indicate not only whether a particular event occurred but also whether the event was positive or negative and whether it was a major event (defined as having a significant and long-term impact on the person's life) or a minor event (Smith et al., 1990). We can thus score the scale for the number of specific kinds of events that occurred (for example, "minor negative," "major negative," "major positive"). We could obtain additional information by asking respondents to rate the predictability, controllability, and duration of each event they experienced, permitting an analysis of these factors as well. Life event scales have been widely used in life stress research. Like

other self-report measures, however, we know that they are subject to possible distortion and failures of memory (R. E. Smith et al., 1999).

Some early theorists considered a stressor to be any life event that requires significant life adjustments, whether a negative event such as those described above or a positive one such as a job promotion (Holmes & Rahe, 1967; Selye, 1976). Because later research showed that only negative life changes consistently predicted adverse health and behavioral outcomes, most modern researchers now define stress in terms of negative life changes only (Cohen et al., 1995; Lazarus, 1998). Indeed, positive life events sometimes counter or even cancel out the impact of negative events (Thoits, 1983).

THE STRESS RESPONSE: A MIND-BODY LINK

Let's now consider how people respond to stressors. Like the emotional responses discussed in Chapter 10, the **stress response** *has cognitive, physiological, and behavioral components.*

Cognitive Appraisal

We respond to situations as we perceive them. The starting point for the stress response is therefore our cognitive appraisal of the situation and its implications for us. As Figure 13.2 indicates, four aspects of the appraisal process are particularly significant:

- appraisal of the *nature and demands* of the situation *(primary appraisal)*
- appraisal of the *resources* available to cope with it *(secondary appraisal)*

▶ **Focus 2**
What four types of appraisals occur in response to a potential stressor? Contrast primary and secondary appraisal.

- judgments of what the *consequences* of the situation could be

- appraisal of the *personal meaning*, that is, what the outcome might imply about us

Let us apply these appraisal steps to a real-life situation. You are about to have an important job interview. According to Richard Lazarus (1991), a leading stress researcher, you will first engage in a **primary appraisal,** *interpreting the situation as either benign, neutral/irrelevant, or threatening in terms of its demands* (how difficult the interview will be) *and its significance for your well-being* (how badly you want or need the job). At the same time, through the process of **secondary appraisal,** *you will be appraising your perceived ability to cope with the situation, that is, the resources you have to deal with it.* Coping resources include your knowledge and abilities, your verbal skills, and your social resources, such as people who will give you emotional support and encouragement. If you believe that the demands of the interview greatly exceed your resources, you will likely experience stress.

You will also take into account *potential consequences* of failing to cope successfully with the situation, including both the seriousness of the consequences and the likelihood that they will occur. Will you be able to pay your tuition if you perform poorly in the interview and don't get the job? How likely is it that you will fail? Appraising the consequences of failing as very costly and very likely to occur increases the perceived stressfulness of the situation.

Finally, the *psychological meaning of the consequences* may be related to your basic beliefs about yourself or the world. Certain beliefs or personal standards can make people vulnerable to particular types of situational demands. For example, if your feelings of self-worth depend on how successful you are in situations like this one, you may regard doing poorly during the interview as evidence that you are a worthless failure.

Distortions and mistaken appraisals can occur at any of the four points in the appraisal process, causing inappropriate stress responses. People may overestimate the difficulty of the demands, they may underestimate their own resources, they may exaggerate the seriousness of the consequences and the likelihood that they will occur, or they may have irrational self-beliefs that confer inappropriate meaning on the consequences (e.g., "If I don't succeed at this, it means I am a total loser and always will be"). The fact that appraisal patterns can differ so greatly from person to person helps us understand why people

respond differently to the same event or situation and why some people are particularly vulnerable to certain types of demands.

Physiological Responses

As soon as we make appraisals, the body responds to them (Kemeny, 2004; Steckler et al., 2005). Although appraisals begin the process, appraisals and physiological responses affect one another (Sun, 2005). Sensory feedback from our body's response can cause us to reappraise how stressful a situation is and whether our resources are sufficient to cope with it. Thus if you find yourself trembling and your heart pounding as you enter the interview room, you may appraise the situation as even more threatening than you did initially. The two-way arrows between the cognitive and physiological elements in Figure 13.2 illustrate this.

Endocrinologist Hans Selye (1976) was a pioneer in studying the body's response to stress. He described a physiological response pattern to strong and prolonged stressors. The **general adaptation syndrome (GAS)** *consists of three phases: alarm, resistance, and exhaustion* (Figure 13.4).

In response to a physical or psychological stressor, organisms exhibit an immediate increase in physiological arousal as the body mobilizes itself to respond to the threat. This *alarm reaction* occurs because of the sudden activation of the sympathetic nervous system and the release of stress hormones by the endocrine system. The alarm stage cannot last indefinitely, however, and the body's natural tendency to maintain the balanced internal state of homeostasis causes activity in the parasympathetic nervous system, which reduces arousal. The body continues to remain on red alert, however, responding with the second stage, resistance.

During *resistance,* the body's resources are mobilized by the continued outpouring of stress hormones by the endocrine system, particularly the adrenal glands. Resistance can last for a relatively long time, but the body's resources are being depleted and immune system functioning is being partially suppressed by the stress hormones (Chiappelli, 2000). If the stressor is intense and persists too long, the body will eventually reach a stage of *exhaustion,* in which there is increased vulnerability to disease and, in some extreme cases, collapse and death. Selye theorized that whichever body system is weakest (e.g., cardiovascular, respiratory, gastrointestinal) will be the one most affected.

▶ **Focus 3**
Describe the three stages of Selye's GAS and their effects on health.

EFFECTS OF STRESS ON WELL-BEING

From a biological perspective, it seems that a high-arousal fight-or-flight biological mechanism sculpted by evolution to help us survive life-threatening *physical* stressors may be maladaptive for dealing with the *psychological* stressors of modern life. In terms of survival, taking a final exam or sitting in rush-hour traffic is not equivalent to an attack by a hungry saber-toothed tiger, where high arousal could facilitate fighting or fleeing. In Selye's view, our physiological responses may thereby take an unnecessary toll on our physical and psychological well-being. Selye's work inspired a generation of psychological and medical researchers to explore the effects of stress on psychological and physical well-being.

Stress and Psychological Well-Being

Effects of stress on psychological well-being are clearest and most dramatic among people who have experienced catastrophic life events. Anthony Rubonis and Leonard Bickman (1991) surveyed the results of 52 studies of victims of catastrophic floods, hurricanes, and fires. In the wake of natural disasters, they found an average increase of 17 percent in rates of psychological disorders such as anxiety and depression.

Some stressors are so traumatic that they can have a strong and long-lasting psychological impact (Resick, 2005). More than 50 years after the horrors of the Holocaust, psychological scars remain for Jewish survivors of Nazi concentration camps (Nadler & Ben-Slushan, 1989; Valent, 2000). Many survivors are still troubled by high levels of anxiety and recurrent nightmares about their traumatic experiences. Those who were children and lost their families continue to experience sudden fears that something terrible will happen to their spouses or children whenever they are out of sight. Depression and crying spells are also common, as are feelings of insecurity and difficulties in forming close relationships. As one researcher reported, "child survivors (now in their 50s and 60s) . . . despite their outward normalcy, remain entrapped in this survival mode" (Valent, 1998, p. 751).

Long-lasting psychological symptoms have also been found among American soldiers who experienced the trauma of combat during the Vietnam War. Paula Schnurr and her coworkers (1998) found a significantly greater number of stress symptoms in Vietnam veterans who experienced combat than in veterans from the same era who did not experience combat. As we will see in Chapter 14, some women who experience the

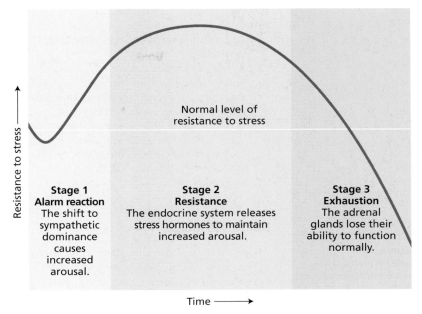

FIGURE 13.4

Hans Selye's general adaptation syndrome. When a person is exposed to a stressor, the body's resistance is temporarily reduced by a state of shock until the alarm reaction mobilizes the body's resources. During the stage of resistance, stress hormones maintain the body's defensive changes, and the body reactions characteristic of the alarm reaction virtually disappear. But if the stress persists over a long time, the body's resources become depleted, and exhaustion occurs; the organism can no longer cope and is highly vulnerable to breakdown. SOURCE: Selye, 1976.

trauma of rape have psychological scars that are intense and long-lasting. In one long-term study of female rape victims, one fourth of the women felt that they had not recovered psychologically 6 years after the rape (Meyer & Taylor, 1986). Even more common stressors such as unemployment leave scars. In a 15-year longitudinal study of German workers, unemployment led to significant declines in subjective well-being, and even after regaining employment, the workers never returned to their previous level of life satisfaction (Lucas et al., 2004).

Many researchers have examined relations between self-reported negative life events and measures of psychological well-being. Findings consistently show that the more negative life events people report on measures such as the one shown in Table 13.1, the more likely they are to also report symptoms of psychological distress, which include anxiety, depression, and unhappiness (Holahan & Moos, 1990; Monroe & Peterman, 1988). Many medical and psychological researchers have therefore concluded that stress causes distress, and this conclusion has been widely accepted among the general public and in the mass media.

► **Focus 4**
What links exist between stress and psychological well-being?

▶ Focus 5
Describe physiological and
behavioral mechanisms through
which stress can contribute to
illness.

What Do You Think?

DO STRESSFUL EVENTS CAUSE PSYCHOLOGICAL DISTRESS?
A consistent statistical relation has been shown between stressful life events and psychological distress; the greater the number of stressful events people have experienced, the more distress they are likely to report. Based on these results, are you willing to accept the conclusion that life stress causes distress, or can you think of other possible reasons for this relation? Think about it, then see page 526 for a commentary.

Stress and Illness

There are indications that stress can combine with other physical and psychological factors to influence the entire spectrum of physical illnesses, from the common cold to cancer, heart disease, diabetes, and sudden death (Lovallo, 2005; Suls & Wallston, 2003). Sometimes the effects are immediate. On the day of the 1994 Northridge, California earthquake, the number of sudden deaths due to heart attacks in the greater Los Angeles area nearly tripled from an average of 35.7 per day during the previous seven days to 101 (Leor et al., 1996).

Other effects of major stressors on physical well-being are less immediate but no less severe. Within 1 month following the death of a spouse, bereaved widowers and widows begin to show a higher mortality rate than married people of the same age who have not lost a spouse (Kaprio et al., 1987), and within 1 year after spousal death, about two thirds of bereaved people decline in health (Irwin et al., 1987). A notably increased rate of mortality is found in men, who tend to respond to the death of their spouse with relatively greater distress and health declines than do women (Stroebe et al., 2001). Stressful life events have also been linked to a higher risk of developing cancer (Sklar & Anisman, 1981). People who experience the chronic stress that attends caring for a spouse with Alzheimer's disease have significantly increased risk for health problems (Vitaliano et al., 2004).

A traumatic life event can worsen an already existing medical condition, as in this case of a 7-year-old African American girl with sickle-cell anemia:

> This little girl was bused to a new elementary school in a white neighborhood. . . . She and other black children were met with cries by angry whites to "go back to where you belong!" The little girl was quite upset by the incident. After some time at the school she went to the principal's office crying and complaining of chest pains. She died

later that day in the hospital, apparently from a sickle-cell crisis brought on by stress. As she died, she kept repeating "go back where you belong." (Friedman & DiMatteo, 1989, p. 169)

Linkages between long-term stress and illness are not surprising, for physiological responses to stressors can directly harm other body systems. For example, the secretion of stress hormones, such as epinephrine, norepinephrine, and cortisol, is a major part of the stress response. These hormones affect the activity of the heart, and excessive secretions can damage the lining of the arteries. By reducing fat metabolism, the stress hormones can also contribute to the fatty blockages in arteries that cause heart attacks and strokes (Lovallo & Gerin, 2003; Willenberg et al., 2000).

Stress can also contribute to health breakdowns by causing people to behave in ways that increase the risk of illness. For example, people with diabetes can frequently control their disease through medication, exercise, and diet. When under stress, however, diabetics are less likely to regulate their diets and take their medication, resulting in an increased risk of serious medical consequences (Brantley & Garrett, 1993). People are also more likely to quit exercising when under stress, even if the primary reason they began exercising in the first place was to reduce stress (Stetson et al., 1997). Stress may also lead to smoking, alcohol and drug use, sleep loss, undereating or overeating, and other health-compromising behaviors. Poor dietary and sleep patterns in students studying for final exams may increase risk of illness and help ruin the semester break.

Stress and Aging

Sometimes, people who are under intense, chronic stress seem to age before our eyes. Scientists have long suspected that stress can accelerate the aging process, but only recently has a physiological mechanism been identified. Elissa Epel and her coworkers (2004) studied 39 mothers who experienced the constant stress of caring for a child who suffered from a serious chronic illness, such as infantile paralysis or autism, and 19 similar women who had healthy children. The researchers examined structures called *telomeres* that are found at the tips of chromosomes. Every time a cell divides, telomeres become shorter. When the telomeres become too short, the cell can no longer divide and it dies. Cell death produces the effects of aging as muscles weaken, skin becomes wrinkled, hearing and eyesight fade, organs fail, and cognitive abilities decline. Fortunately, the body has an enzyme called *telomerase* that helps counter telomere shortening. This enzyme can slow the aging process.

When Epel and coworkers examined the white blood cells of the two groups of women, they made a startling discovery. The mothers with the disordered children had significantly shorter telomeres and lower levels of the enzyme telomerase, and the more stressful the women rated their lives as being, the more pronounced these effects were. Women with the highest levels of perceived stress had telomeres equivalent to women 10 years older. Although the mechanisms whereby stress produces these effects are currently unknown, it is possible that chronically elevated levels of stress hormones such as cortisol damage the telomeres and lower telomerase levels, thereby speeding the aging process.

Stress and the Immune System

Considerable evidence suggests that life stress can weaken immune functioning (Suls & Wallston, 2003; Taylor, 2006). Research by Ronald Glaser, Janet Kiecolt-Glaser, and their coworkers at Ohio State University has shown that reduced immune system effectiveness is one possible reason for increased risk of illness (Kiecolt-Glaser et al., 2002; Marsland et al., 2001). In one study, researchers closely followed medical students over a 1-year period. They collected blood samples from the students during three stressful academic examination periods in order to measure immune cell activity. The researchers found that immune system effectiveness was reduced during the stressful exam periods and that this reduction was linked to the likelihood of becoming ill. Other studies have shown that stress hormones released into the bloodstream by the adrenal glands can suppress the activity of specific immune system cells, increasing the likelihood of illness (Cohen & Herbert, 1996; Maier & Watkins, 1999).

Within the broader field of health psychology, a field called *psychoneuroimmunology* studies relations between psychological and immune system processes (Ader, 2001). One of the major topics of research in this area involves relations between stress and immune functions. Research has shown that external stressors can "get into" the immune system in several ways. Fibers extending from the brain into lymph tissues can release a wide variety of chemicals that bind to receptors on white blood cells, thus influencing immune functions. As noted earlier, stress hormones such as cortisol and epinephrine also bind to cells in the immune system and influence their functions. Third, people's attempts to cope with stressors sometimes lead them to behave in ways (e.g., substance use or not sleeping enough) that impair immunity (Taylor, 2006).

Although stress can affect immune functions, this chapter's "Research Close-Up" shows us that the relations are far from simple, depending on the nature of the stressor, specific immune functions, and characteristics of the person.

▶ **Focus 6**
How do various kinds of stressors affect immune functioning?

Research Close-Up   How Does Stress Affect the Immune System?

SOURCE: SUZANNE C. SEGERSTROM and GREGORY E. MILLER (2004). Psychological stress and the human immune system: A meta-analytic study of 30 years of inquiry. *Psychological Bulletin, 130,* 601–630.

INTRODUCTION

More than three decades ago, Hans Selye (1975), a pioneer in the study of stress and its effects on well-being, concluded that stress exerts some of its negative effects on health by suppressing the immune system, making organisms more susceptible to disease and organic breakdowns. In the 30 years since, literally hundreds of studies have tested relations between stress and immunity. These studies have shown that both stress and the immune system are more complex than Selye's notion of a general suppressive effect might suggest.

Stressors differ in their characteristics, and the immune system is incredibly complex and carries out its functions in a variety of ways.

In their article in *Psychological Bulletin,* the American Psychological Association's journal devoted to reviews of the scientific literature, Suzanne Segerstrom and Gregory Miller used the statistical approach of meta-analysis (see Chapter 2) to summarize the results of more than 300 scientific studies on stress and immune function. Meta-analysis allows scientists to combine the results of many studies and derive a statistic called *effect size* to indicate how strongly variables are related to one another. In addition, separate effect sizes can be computed for subgroups of studies that used different methods or measures, helping to provide a clearer picture of a body of scientific results.

Continued

METHOD

As noted earlier, stressors differ from one another in important ways, and it seemed reasonable to assume that these differences might influence their impact on immune functioning. Accordingly, Segerstrom and Miller divided stressors into five categories:

1. *Acute time-limited stressors,* typically used in laboratory studies, include challenging cognitive tasks, such as counting backwards by sevens from 13,206 under time pressure. (Try this yourself if you want to get stressed out.)
2. *Brief naturalistic stressors* include real-world challenges such as academic examinations.
3. *Stressful event sequences* occur when stressful events, such as the loss of a spouse or a major natural disaster, give rise to a series of related challenges over a period of time.
4. *Chronic stressors* usually do not have an end in sight, and they tend to pervade a person's life. Examples include caring for a spouse with Alzheimer's disease, long-term unemployment, or being a refugee forced from one's home by war.
5. *Distant stressors* are traumatic experiences, such as childhood sexual abuse, death of one's parents, or previous combat experience, that occurred in the past but continue to affect the person emotionally.

The immune system also functions in a number of ways that could be affected differently by various forms of stress. Immunologists make two important distinctions in immune responses:

1. *Natural immunity* occurs quickly, often within minutes of an immune challenge, and is relatively nonspecific in nature. The immune cells involved attack and kill invading antigens (pathogens that trigger immune responses). One type of natural immunity is inflammation, in which certain immune cells congregate at the site of an infection and release toxic substances that kill invaders. One class of molecules released by immune cells are **cytokines,** *which help produce fever and inflammation, promote the healing of injured tissue, and activate and direct other immune cells.* Natural killer (NK) cells also attack invaders, as well as tumors, and help keep invaders at bay during the early stages of infection. NK cells are among those ravaged by the HIV virus.
2. *Specific immunity* is a much more targeted process than is natural immunity, and it takes longer to occur, sometimes up to several days. One common specific immunity response is the identification of the specific properties of an antigen and the development of specific antibodies that can neutralize bacteria, kill cancerous cells, or bind to viruses to prevent their entry into healthy cells. There are two kinds of specific immunity: cellular and humoral. Cellular immunity works within the body's cells, particularly against invading viruses. Humoral responses attack extracellular pathogens, such as bacteria and parasites.

With these distinctions between types of stressors and natural versus specific immune responses in mind,

Segerstrom and Miller carefully analyzed the results of studies reported in 319 separate articles involving 18,941 participants that were published over the past 30 years, most in the 1990s and early 2000s. They examined relations between the 5 kinds of stressors and the many immune functions (nearly 40 of them) involved in natural and specific immunity. Effect sizes were calculated for each study and averaged within the 10 cells (5 stressors × 2 immune system responses), providing a comprehensive overall picture of how different kinds of stressors affect immunity.

RESULTS

The meta-analysis of stressor-immune interactions provided a fairly clear pattern of results. In contrast to Selye's original notion of a broad suppression of immunity by stressors, a far more complex picture emerged.

- Rather than suppressing the immune system, acute time-limited stressors actually enhanced immunity, especially natural immunity. The number of NK cells in the blood increased, ready to be quickly transported to wherever they might be needed in the body. Other changes suggested a readying of the immune system for possible infection. Specific immunity was not increased, however, probably because the stressor was short-lived.
- Brief naturalistic stressors, such as school examinations, were associated with a different pattern of immune response, created largely by different types of cytokines. Some cytokines suppress cellular immune responses against viruses, whereas others enhance humoral immune responses against bacteria and parasites. Thus brief naturalistic stressors might make people more susceptible to viral infections but not to bacterial ones.
- Stressful event sequences did not have universal effects on immune functions. Death of a spouse was associated with declines in the fast-acting natural immune response against invading pathogens. In contrast, natural disasters did not have this effect.
- Chronic stressors, such as caring for a spouse with Alzheimer's disease, severe marital conflict, and unemployment, had a clear negative impact on both natural and specific immunity (Figure 13.5). This suppressive effect occurred equally for men and women and across all age groups.
- Finally, stressors from the distant past (5 years or more) bore no relation to current immune function.

CRITICAL DISCUSSION

This study illustrates the value of meta-analysis for discerning patterns in the combined results of a large mass of studies. We find that stress's effects on immunity are variable, depending on the nature of the stressor and the particular kind of immunity. The results support a *biphasic model* in which acute stress enhances the immune response whereas chronic stress suppresses it (Dhabhar & McEwen, 2001). From an evolutionary perspective, enhanced immunity would be an adaptive feature of the fight-or-flight

(a)

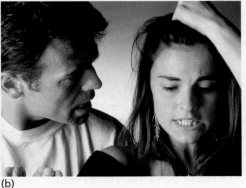
(b)

FIGURE 13.5

The meta-analysis of results from more than 300 studies showed that acute stress (a), such as that caused by physical attack, increases natural immunity as the immune system prepares to cope with possible wounds. In contrast, chronic stress (b), such as that produced by conflicted marriages, suppresses both natural and specific immunity.

response to an acute physical stressor that increases the risk of injury and the entry of pathogens into the body through wounds. Natural immunity fights such invaders and promotes wound repair. In contrast, chronic stress taxes the body over an extended period of time, eventually resulting in impaired immunity and increasing vulnerability to illness.

We should note that the stress-immunity patterns identified in this meta-analysis represent broad trends across many individuals. Most studies do not take account of individual differences in psychological or behavioral characteristics. When this is done, however, we often find that such characteristics make a difference. It is clear, for example, that older people's immune systems are more vulnerable to stress than are younger people's. Likewise, Segerstrom and Miller found that cognitive appraisal differences sometimes determined whether stress impaired immunity. Greater suppression of immune functions occurred in people who appraised their lives in a negative fashion. In contrast, optimistic people showed less immune suppression even in response to severe stressors. As this meta-analysis clearly shows, therefore, links between stress and immune system functioning are complex, and a transactional model that takes both stressor and individual characteristics into account is likely to lead to new insights in relations between stress, immune functioning, and illness.

IN REVIEW

- Various theorists view stress as a stimulus; as a response having cognitive, physiological, and behavioral components; or as an interaction (i.e., transaction) between the person and the environment. The latter view incorporates the stimulus and response conceptions into a more dynamic model.

- Stressors are events that place physical or psychological demands on organisms. The stressfulness of a situation is defined by the balance between demands and resources. Life events vary in terms of how positive or negative they are and how intense they are. Other dimensions that affect their impact include duration, predictability, controllability, and chronicity.

- Cognitive appraisal processes play an essential role in people's responses to stressors. People appraise the nature of the demands, the resources available to deal with them, the possible consequences of the situation, and the personal meaning of these consequences. Distortions at any of these levels can result in inappropriate stress responses.

- The physiological response to stressors is mediated by the autonomic and endocrine systems and involves a pattern of arousal that mobilizes the body to deal with the stressor. Selye described a general adaptation syndrome (GAS), which involves the stages of alarm, resistance, and exhaustion.

- Measures of both major negative life events and microstressors are associated with negative psychological outcomes, such as anxiety and depression. Life stress also is related to negative health changes. It can worsen preexisting medical conditions and increase the risk of illness and death. Reduced immune system functioning may underlie some negative health effects caused by stress.

FACTORS THAT INFLUENCE STRESS-HEALTH RELATIONS

As we saw with Priscilla at the opening of the chapter, some highly resilient individuals seem to tolerate extremely demanding stressors over a long period of time without negative effects. Others appear to quickly fall prey to relatively minor stressors. The fact that people differ so dramatically in their responses to stressful events has prompted many health psychologists to search for personal and environmental factors that make people more or less reactive to stressful events. **Vulnerability factors** *increase people's susceptibility to stressful events.* They include low social support, poor coping skills, tendencies to become anxious or pessimistic, excessive bottling-up of feelings, and other factors that reduce stress resistance. In contrast, **protective factors** *are environmental or personal resources that help people cope more effectively with stressful events.* They include physiological reactivity, social support, effective coping skills, and personality factors such as hardiness, coping self-efficacy, optimism, and an ability to find meaning in stressful events.

Social Support

▶ **Focus 7**
In what ways can social support protect against stressful events?

Social support is one of the most important environmental resources (Suls & Wallston, 2003). The knowledge that we can rely on others for help and support in a time of crisis helps blunt the impact of stress (Figure 13.6). In contrast, lack of social support is a significant vulnerability factor. Studies carried out in the United States, Finland, and

Sweden carefully tracked the well-being of some 37,000 people for up to 12 years. Even after taking into account medical risk factors such as age, smoking, high blood pressure, high cholesterol levels, obesity, and lack of physical exercise, the researchers found that people with weak social ties were twice as likely to die during the period of the study as those with strong ties to others (House et al., 1988). The relation between social isolation and poor health was stronger for men than for women.

One way that social support protects against stress is by enhancing immune system functioning. Robert Baron and his coworkers (1990) studied people whose spouses were being treated for cancer and who were experiencing psychological distress. When they were exposed to an antigen, spouses who rated themselves as high in social support produced more immune cells, particularly at high levels of the allergen, than did those who indicated lower social support in their lives. These results may help explain why people who have high levels of social support are more disease-resistant when they are under stress (House et al., 1988).

Many other studies show that social support decreases psychological distress in people who are dealing with stressful life events of all kinds (Holahan & Moos, 1986, 1990; Schwarzer, 1998). In one such study, 86 women undergoing breast cancer treatment at Stanford Medical School were randomly assigned either to a weekly psychotherapy group designed to increase social support and strengthen their coping skills or to a control condition that received just the medical center's regular cancer treatment. As shown in Figure 13.7, those in the therapy groups survived nearly twice as long as did the controls (Spiegel et al., 1989). A later study using a similar intervention failed to find greater longevity among breast cancer patients, but it did find significant quality-of-life benefits, such as lowered depression, feelings of closeness with other group members, and a positive reordering of life priorities (Goodwin et al., 2001). Peer support groups appear especially helpful to breast cancer victims who lack support from their spouses and physicians (Helgeson et al., 2000).

Besides enhancing immune system functioning, social support has a number of other stress-buffering benefits. People who feel that they are part of a social system experience a greater sense of identity and meaning in their lives, which in turn results in greater psychological well-being (Cohen, 1988; Rodin & Salovey, 1989). Social networks also reduce exposure to other risk factors, such as loneliness. Third, having the backing of others can increase one's sense of control over stressors. Finally, true friends can apply social pressure to prevent

FIGURE 13.6

Social support is one of the strongest protective factors against stress.

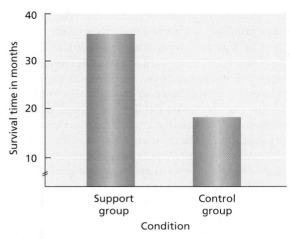

FIGURE 13.7

The effect of coping and social support. This graph shows the mean survival time for breast cancer patients who received a coping-skills and social-support intervention compared with control patients who received normal cancer treatment. SOURCE: Based on Spiegel et al., 1989.

people from coping with stressors in maladaptive ways (e.g., through alcohol or drug use).

Social support benefits the giver as well as the recipient. In one 5-year longitudinal study of elderly people, Stephanie Brown and coworkers (2003) found that those who gave help and support to friends, relatives, and family members had lower mortality rates than those who did not, even when health and other quality-of-life variables were statistically controlled. Likewise, highly sociable people are more resistant to infectious diseases, despite their greater exposure to other people who might be contagious (Cohen et al., 2003).

Physiological Reactivity

Responses of the autonomic and endocrine systems appear to underlie many of the negative psychological and health consequences of stress (McEwen, 2001). The fact that people differ widely in the pattern and intensity of their physiological responses makes people more or less vulnerable to stressors. As we saw in Chapter 12, people high in neuroticism, who tend to have intense and prolonged autonomic responses, seem more vulnerable to stress than are people low in this personality factor (Eysenck, 1990; Snyder, 2001). People whose autonomic and endocrine systems are wired for high reactivity have increased risk for a wide range of diseases, including hypertension and coronary disease (Lovallo & Gerin, 2003; Taylor, 2006).

Two types of stress hormones, catecholamines and cortisol, are important links between physiological reactivity and health. Both mobilize the body's fight-or-flight response in the face of stressors, but they have somewhat different effects on the body. Cortisol's arousal effects last much longer and seem to be more damaging than those produced by the catecholamines (unless the catecholamines are secreted at high levels over a long period of time). Cortisol reduces immune system functioning and helps create fatty deposits in the arteries that lead to heart disease. In contrast, catecholamine secretion increases immune system functioning (Taylor, 2006). Increased vulnerability to bodily breakdowns occurs when the person responds to stress with high levels of cortisol instead of catecholamines. The fact that physical exercise creates catecholamine-produced arousal may help account for its health-enhancing effects and its ability to promote stress resistance (Ehrman, 2003; Morgan, 1997).

Type A Behavior Pattern

The Type A behavior pattern was discovered by an upholsterer working on the chairs in the office of a physician who specialized in treating heart attack victims. The upholsterer noticed an unusual wear pattern at the front of the seats, not the back, indicating that the patients were constantly sitting on the edges of their seats and moving about.

This edge-of-the-seat pattern typifies the behaviors seen in people with the **Type A behavior pattern,** *who tend to live under great pressure and demand much of themselves and others.* Many Type A people are workaholics, continually striving to get more done in less time. Type A people are also characterized by high levels of competitiveness and ambition, which can foster aggressiveness and hostility when things get in their way (Figure 13.8).

▶ **Focus 8**
Describe the role of stress hormones in well-being.

▶ **Focus 9**
Describe the Type A behavior pattern and how it can contribute to coronary heart disease.

FIGURE 13.8

Studies of the hard-driving Type A behavior pattern have shown that the most damaging aspect is the negative emotions, particularly anger and hostility, that these people experience.

Does your personality type more closely reflect a Type A or a Type B behavior pattern? Try the interactive video exercise, "Type A Behavior," in Chapter 13 of your CD to find out.

In contrast, people labeled Type B show the opposite pattern of patience, serenity, and lack of time urgency.

Several large-scale studies suggest that even when other physical risk factors, such as obesity and smoking, are taken into account, Type A men and women have about double the risk for coronary heart disease (CHD) compared with less driven people (Rosenman et al., 1975). However, research indicates that not all components of the Type A pattern increase vulnerability to CHD. The Type A person's fast-paced, time-conscious lifestyle and high ambition apparently are not the culprits. Rather, the crucial component seems to be negative emotions, particularly anger. The Type A behavior pattern virtually guarantees that these people will encounter many stressful situations, such as time pressures of their own making and frustrations that anger them. A cynical hostility marked by suspiciousness, resentment, frequent anger, distrust, and antagonism is likely to alienate others, produce interpersonal stress and conflict, and reduce the amount of social support the person receives. In addition, Type A people tend to overreact physiologically to stressful events and take longer to recover, a biological factor that may contribute to their tendency to develop heart disease (Taylor, 2006). John Hunter, an 18th-century pioneer in cardiovascular medicine, recognized his own vulnerability when he said, "My life is in the hands of any rascal who chooses to put me in a passion." Hunter's statement was all too prophetic; he died of a heart attack during an angry debate at a hospital board meeting.

Mind as Healer or Slayer

The mind as well as the body can make people more or less vulnerable to stressors. Considering the important role that appraisal processes play in emotions and stress, we should not be surprised that our beliefs about situations and ourselves are significant protective and vulnerability factors.

Hardiness In the 1970s, Suzanne Kobasa of the University of Chicago began an intensive study of 200 executives who worked in highly stressful jobs. She found that some of them responded to their circumstances with psychological distress and physical illness, whereas others continued to function well both physically and psychologically. How did the two groups differ? The answer came in the form of *three beliefs, comprising a stress-protective factor that she termed* **hardiness.** The three Cs of hardiness are *commitment, control,* and *challenge.*

▶ **Focus 10**
How do hardiness, coping self-efficacy, optimism-pessimism, and spiritual beliefs affect stress outcomes?

Hardy people are committed to their work, their families, and their other involvements, and they believe that what they are doing is important. Second, they view themselves as having control over their outcomes, as opposed to feeling powerless to influence events. Finally, they appraise the demands of the situations as challenges, or opportunities, rather than as threats. As a result, demanding situations not only become less stressful, but they can actually stimulate higher levels of performance (Kobasa et al., 1985).

Of these three hardiness components, perceived control is apparently the strongest in buffering stress (Funk, 1992; Steptoe, 2000). A 5-year longitudinal study showed that women who felt in control of their lives did not show increases in future illness when stress increased, whereas those low in perceived control did (Lawler & Schmied, 1992).

Coping Self-Efficacy When confronted by a stressor, one of the most significant appraisals we make is whether we have sufficient resources to cope with the demands (Bandura, 1997). Small wonder, then, that **coping self-efficacy**—*the belief that we can perform the behaviors necessary to cope successfully*—is an important protective factor (Bandura, 1989). As hardiness research shows, even events that are appraised as extremely demanding may generate little stress if we believe that we have the skills to deal with them.

Self-efficacy is always specific to the particular situation: "Can I handle *these* demands?" As noted in Chapter 12, previous successes in similar situations increase efficacy; failures undermine it (Bandura, 1997). People can also increase efficacy expectancies by observing others cope successfully and through social persuasion and encouragement from others. The teacher who befriended Priscilla constantly gave her the message "I believe in you. You can do it!" Finally, experiencing a low level of physiological arousal in the face of a stressor can convey a sense of strength and ability to cope, demonstrating another way in which arousal can affect appraisal.

Feelings of self-efficacy may fortify our bodies as well as our minds against stressful events. An intriguing finding came from a laboratory study in which people with phobias confronted a feared object. When participants reported high self-efficacy while confronting the stressful situation, their immune systems actually began to function more effectively. In contrast, those who reported low coping efficacy showed a drop in immune system functioning (Wiedenfeld et al., 1990).

Optimistic Expectations and Positive Attitudes

Our beliefs about how things are likely to turn out also play an important role in dealing with stressors. Recent research indicates that optimistic people are at lowered risk for anxiety and depression when they confront stressful events. Edward Chang (1998) found that people with optimistic beliefs felt less helpless in the face of stress and adjusted better to negative life events than did pessimists. In one year-long study, optimists had about half as many infectious illnesses and visits to doctors as did pessimists (Peterson & Seligman, 1987). In another study, researchers followed women who came to the National Cancer Institute for breast cancer treatment for 5 years. On average, women who were optimistic about their recovery lived longer than pessimists, even when the physical severity of the disease was the same at the beginning of the 5-year period (Levy et al., 1988).

The process of aging is a background stressor in many people's lives. People's reactions differ considerably as their hair thins, wrinkles deepen, physical and sexual capacity diminish, health declines, acquaintances begin to die, and a sense of mortality becomes more salient. Some dread the aging process, whereas others accept or even find value in it. In one study (Levy et al., 2002), researchers assessed attitudes toward aging in a large community sample of men and women who were over 50 years of age and then followed them up over a 23-year period. Statistically controlling for age, physical health, and loneliness, the researchers found that attitudes toward aging predicted how long people lived even better than their physical health did (Figure 13.9). On average, people with positive attitudes toward their aging lived an average of 7.6 years longer than did their counterparts with negative attitudes. This survival advantage existed whether the positive-attitude people were in their 50s, 60s, 70s, or 80s when the study began. Clearly, attitude makes a difference, and perhaps a life-or-death difference.

Finding Meaning in Stressful Life Events

Humanistic theorists emphasize the human need to find meaning in one's life and the psychological benefits of doing so (May, 1961; Watson & Greenberg, 1998). Some people find personal meaning through spiritual beliefs, which can be a great comfort in the face of crises. Daniel McIntosh and coworkers (1993) studied 124 parents who had lost their babies to sudden infant death syndrome. They found that grieving parents whose religious beliefs provided some higher meaning to their loss experienced greater well-being and less distress 18 months later. In another study, researchers

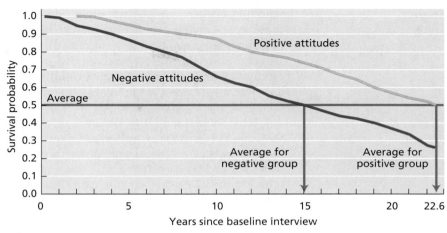

FIGURE 13.9

Aging attitudes and longevity. Research has shown a relation between positive or negative self-perceptions of one's aging and subsequent longevity. These survival curves show the likelihood that a randomly selected group member will still be alive in a given year after the beginning of the study. The median number of years until death was 15 in the group with negative self-attitudes and 22.6 among positive-attitude participants. Source: Adapted from Levy et al., 2002.

found that people who were able to find meaning in the death of a family member experienced less distress during the year following the loss. Finding a sense of meaning from their own process of coping with the loss (e.g., the sense that the event helped them grow spiritually) had even longer-term positive effects (Davis et al., 1998).

Religious beliefs can be a two-edged sword, however: They can either decrease or increase stress, depending on their nature and the type of stressor to which they are applied. In one study of elderly people with medical problems, poorer physical and psychological adjustment occurred in patients who viewed God as punishing them; saw themselves as the victims of demonic forces; expressed anger toward God, clergy, or church members; or questioned their faith (Koenig et al., 1998). Religious beliefs may have positive effects in dealing with some types of stressors but not with others. Such beliefs seem to help people cope more effectively with losses, illnesses, and personal setbacks. In contrast, they can increase the negative impact of other stressors such as marital problems and abuse, perhaps by inducing guilt or placing internal pressures on individuals to remain in the stressful relationship (Strawbridge et al., 1998).

Resilient Children: Superkids or Ordinary Magic?

At the beginning of this chapter we described Priscilla, a child who grew up in a terrible home environment with a psychotic mother and a father

► **Focus 11**
What factors create stress-resilience in children?

who abused her and committed suicide in her presence. Somehow, despite these experiences, Priscilla grew into a highly successful young woman. Since the 1970s, psychologists such as Emmy Werner have been studying children who are somehow resilient to highly stressful environments (Werner & Smith, 1982).

What factors matter in the lives of resilient children like Priscilla, who rise far above what their environments would predict for them? Are they "superkids," as a *New York Times* writer referred to them? After reviewing many studies of unusually resilient children and adolescents, Ann Masten (2001) concluded that such children are a monument to the ordinary adaptive processes that occur in the lives of most children, factors she termed "ordinary magic." Masten and J. Douglas Coatsworth (1998) found that these children have certain characteristics that contribute to a positive outcome even in the face of stressful life events (Table 13.2). These characteristics include adequate intellectual functioning, social skills, self-efficacy, and faith (optimism and hope), as well as environmental factors such as a relationship with at least one caring, prosocial adult.

To be resilient, a child need not have all of the characteristics listed in Table 13.2, but he or she must have some of them. Good intellectual functioning and a supportive relationship with a caring adult seem to be the most important (Masten & Coatsworth, 1998). In Priscilla's case, this positive adult relationship did not exist with either parent. Instead, the critical relationship was provided by a loving elementary school teacher who befriended, encouraged, and guided her during the critical formative period of middle childhood. This key relationship, combined with Priscilla's obvious intelligence, allowed her to develop self-esteem, a belief in her own capabilities, and the will to nurture her talents.

In Priscilla, then, we have an example of what can happen even in the face of great adversity when certain critical protective factors are present. As Masten (2001) concluded,

> What began as a quest for the extraordinary has revealed the power of the ordinary. Resilience does not come from rare and special qualities, but from the everyday magic of ordinary, normative human resources in the minds, brains, and bodies of children, in their families and relationships, and in their communities. (p. 235)

As we have now seen, a variety of biological, cognitive, and environmental factors influence stress and its effects on us. Figure 13.10 summarizes these important influences.

TABLE 13.2 Personal and Environmental Factors That Contribute to Stress-Resilience in Children

Source	Characteristic
Individual	Good intellectual functioning
	Appealing, sociable, easygoing disposition
	Self-efficacy, self-confidence, high self-esteem
	Talents
	Faith
Family	Close relationship to caring parent figure
	Authoritative parenting: warmth, structure, high expectations
	Socioeconomic advantages
	Connections to extended supportive family networks
Extrafamilial context	Bonds to prosocial adults outside the family
	Connections to prosocial organizations
	Attending effective schools

Source: Masten & Coatsworth, 1998.

IN REVIEW

■ Vulnerability and protective factors make people more or less susceptible to stressors. Social support is an important protective factor, having both direct and buffering effects that help people cope with stress.

■ Individual differences in physiological reactivity also affect well-being. People who exhibit strong and prolonged arousal responses are more susceptible to negative psychological and health effects. Physiological reactivity can predispose people to health problems, particularly if they respond with high levels of cortisol. The Type A behavior pattern increases vulnerability to coronary heart disease.

■ Hardiness is a protective factor against stress. Hardy individuals are committed, have feelings of personal control, and tend to perceive stressful situations as challenges. Other cognitive protective factors are self-efficacy and optimism. Spiritual beliefs often help people cope more

LEVELS OF ANALYSIS   **Factors Related to the Stress Response**

Biological

- Evolutionary mechanisms for responding to stressors
- Physiological responses of autonomic and endocrine systems to situational stressors
- Stress effects on immune system
- Individual differences in physiological reactivity to stressors (e.g., physiological toughness)

Psychological

- Cognitive appraisal of environmental demands, resources, potential consequences, and personal meaning of consequences
- Personality factors, such as optimism and hardiness, that affect responses to stressors
- Coping strategies and the skill with which they are applied
- Self-efficacy and expectations of available social support

Environmental

- Number, intensity, and duration of the stressful events
- Predictability, controllability, and chronicity of stressors
- Availability of social support
- Cultural factors that teach one how to respond to stressors

Stress Response

FIGURE 13.10

Levels of analysis: Factors related to the stress response.

▶ **Focus 12**
Describe the three major classes of coping strategies. How does stressor controllability influence their outcomes?

effectively with stressful life events, but certain religious beliefs seem capable of increasing stress.

- Studies of highly resilient children reveal important characteristics that contribute to positive outcomes as children mature, such as good intellectual functioning, social skills, self-efficacy, and hope, usually nurtured by social support from at least one caring adult in the child's life.

COPING WITH STRESS

My courage sank, and with each succeeding minute it became less possible to resist this horror. My cue came, and on I went to that stage where I knew with grim certainty I would not be capable of remaining more than a few minutes. . . . I took one pace forward and stopped abruptly. My voice had started to fade, my throat closed up and the audience was beginning to go giddily round. (Aaron, 1986, p. 24)

This account of stage fright was given not by a novice actor in his first play but by Sir Laurence Olivier, considered by many the greatest actor of his generation. Few people were aware that for most of his career, Olivier experienced a private hell before every performance. His audiences saw only what happened once he stepped onto the stage: another flawless performance. Olivier had a remarkable ability to purge the terror from his mind, relax his body, and concentrate fully on his role once showtime arrived (Aaron, 1986).

Although there are countless ways people might respond to a stressor, coping strategies can be divided into the three broad classes shown in Figure 13.11. **Problem-focused coping** *strategies attempt to confront and directly deal with the demands of the situation or to change the situation so that it is no longer stressful.* Examples of problem-focused strategies might include studying for a test, going directly to another person to work out a misunderstanding, or signing up for a course to improve one's time-management skills.

Rather than dealing directly with the stressful situation, **emotion-focused coping** *strategies attempt to manage the emotional responses that result from it.* Olivier was obviously able to control his paralyzing fear once he stepped on stage. Some forms of emotion-focused coping involve appraising the situation in a manner that minimizes its emotional impact. A person might deal with the stress from an interpersonal conflict by denying that any problem exists. Other forms involve avoidance or acceptance of the stressful situation. Thus a student might decide to deal with anxiety about an upcoming test by going to a party and forgetting about it. Informed that he has a terminal illness, a man might decide that nothing can be done about the situation and simply accept this unwelcome reality—or he might use the avoidance strategy of discontinuing medical treatment and keeping the illness a secret, even from close family members.

A third class of coping strategies involves **seeking social support,** *that is, turning to others for assistance and emotional support in times of stress.* Thus the student might seek the help of a classmate

FIGURE 13.11

Ways of coping. Coping strategies fall into three general categories: (1) problem-focused coping, actively attempting to respond to situational demands; (2) emotion-focused coping, directed at minimizing emotional distress; and (3) seeking or accepting social support.

in preparing for the test, and the man with the terminal illness might choose to join a support group for the terminally ill. Priscilla accepted and benefited from the social support provided by the teacher who befriended her.

EFFECTIVENESS OF COPING STRATEGIES

Which of the three general classes of coping strategies would you expect to be most generally effective? Whenever we ask this question in our classes, the majority of our students vote for problem-focused coping. This response is understandable, for many people, particularly in Western cultures, approach problems with the attitude that if something needs fixing, we should fix it.

What does the research literature say? Charles Holahan and Rudolf Moos (1990) studied coping patterns and psychological outcomes in more than 400 California adults over a 1-year period. Although people often used several coping methods in dealing with a stressor, problem-focused coping methods and seeking social support were most often associated with favorable adjustment to stressors. In contrast, emotion-focused strategies that involved avoiding feelings or taking things out on other people predicted depression and poorer adjustment. Other studies have yielded similar results. In children and adults and across many different types of stressors, emotion-focused strategies that involve avoidance, denial, and wishful thinking seem to be related to less effective adaptation (Snyder, 2001). On the other hand, there are adaptive emotion-focused strategies, such as identifying and chang-

ing irrational negative thinking and learning relaxation skills to control arousal. These are effective methods for reducing stress responses without avoiding or distorting reality (DeLongis, 2000; Meichenbaum, 1985).

CONTROLLABILITY AND COPING EFFICACY

Despite the evidence generally favoring problem-focused coping, attempting to change the situation is not always the most adaptive way to cope with a stressor. Problem-focused coping works best in situations where there is some prospect of controlling the stressor (Park et al., 2004). However, there are situations that we cannot influence or modify, and in those cases problem-focused coping may do more harm than good. Instead, emotion-focused coping may be the most adaptive approach we can take, for while we cannot master the situation, we may be able to prevent or control maladaptive emotional responses to it (Auerbach, 1989). Of course, reliance on emotion-focused coping is likely to be maladaptive if it prevents us from acting to change situations in which we actually *do* have control.

Thomas Strentz and Stephen Auerbach (1988) demonstrated the effectiveness of emotion-focused coping in adapting to a stressful situation with limited personal control. As part of a Federal Bureau of Investigation (FBI) program to deal with potential airline hijackings, airline employees volunteered to participate in a training exercise. The employees were randomly assigned to one of two experimental conditions or to a control condition. In one experimental condition, employees were trained in problem-focused techniques that hostages can use to actively deal with their situation. They were shown how to interact with captors and maintain a facade of dignity and composure through appearance and behavior. They also learned ways of supporting one another nonverbally and communicating with one another by using a prisoner-of-war tap code.

Training for the second experimental group focused on the emotional reactions the hostages would likely experience and techniques they could use to minimize their stress responses. These emotion-focused techniques included deep breathing, muscle relaxation, stopping unwanted thoughts, and generating pleasant fantasies. Employees in the control condition were given no coping skills training.

Weeks later, the employees were unexpectedly abducted by FBI agents posing as terrorists and held hostage for 4 days under very realistic

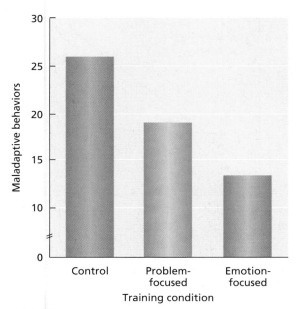

FIGURE 13.12

Coping with captivity. These data show the behavioral ratings of participants in a mock airline-hostage crisis. Participants who received instruction in emotion-focused coping fared better than did those in the problem-focused and control conditions. SOURCE: Based on Strentz & Auerbach, 1988.

and stressful conditions. During their captivity, the hostages completed self-report measures of emotional distress and psychiatric symptoms. In addition, trained observers rated the adaptiveness of their behavior. Results indicated that the hostage groups trained in either problem-focused or emotion-focused strategies fared better than did the untrained employees on both the self-report and the behavioral measures. However, employees who had received emotion-focused training adapted better to the largely uncontrollable conditions of captivity than did those who had received problem-focused coping instruction (Figure 13.12).

The important conclusion from this and many other studies is that no coping strategy or technique is equally effective in all situations. Instead, effectiveness depends on the characteristics of the situation, the appropriateness of the technique, and the skill with which it is carried out. People are likely to adapt well to the stresses of life if they have mastered a variety of coping techniques and know how and when to apply them most effectively. The importance of controllability in the choice of techniques recalls the wisdom in theologian Reinhold Niebuhr's famous prayer that asks for the courage to change those things that can be changed, the forbearance to accept those that cannot be changed, and the wisdom to discern the difference.

TRAUMA DISCLOSURE AND EMOTIONAL RELEASE

Is there any truth to the popular wisdom that when we are stressed out and upset, it's good to talk with someone about it? James Pennebaker (1995, 1997) conducted several studies in which college students talked about past traumas to an experimenter in an adjoining room or they tape-recorded or wrote about the experiences. Many tearfully recounted incidents of personal failure, family tragedies, shattered relationships, sexual or physical abuse, and traumatic accidents. Participants in a control group were asked to talk or write about trivial everyday matters. A comparison of blood samples taken from the students before and after their sessions indicated enhanced immune system functioning in those who had purged themselves of negative emotions but not in those who had not. Moreover, the students who had disclosed the traumatic incidents had 50 percent fewer visits to the campus health center over the next 6 months compared with the control group.

In another study, Denise Sloan and Brian Marx (2004) used the written-disclosure procedure with college students who had reported experiencing a traumatic event in their lives. The students completed measures of stress symptoms, depression, and number of days they had been sick since the beginning of the school term. In an experimental condition, participants were then asked to write about the traumatic event, whereas the control condition did an unrelated task. Physiological arousal was recorded as the participants performed the tasks. One month later, the students again completed the measures of psychological symptoms and sick days. The students had not differed on any of these measures at baseline, but they differed strongly afterwards (Figure 13.13). Those who had written about their traumas showed lowered stress and depression scores. They also reported fewer sick days at the follow-up. The more physiologically aroused the participants in the written-disclosure group became while they wrote about their traumatic events, the healthier they looked physically and psychologically a month later. The researchers concluded that writing or talking about traumatic events affords exposure to the situational cues that accompanied the trauma and now function as conditioned stimuli that trigger distress. Exposure allows extinction to occur, thus reducing the stimuli's emotional impact.

▶ **Focus 13**
How do trauma disclosure and emotional constraint affect well-being?

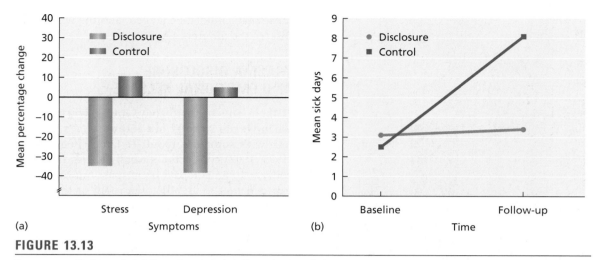

FIGURE 13.13

Does trauma disclosure help? These data show the effects of written disclosure concerning a previous traumatic life event on (a) subsequent stress symptoms, depression, and (b) number of self-reported sick days. Source: Based on Sloan and Marx, 2004.

BOTTLING UP FEELINGS: THE HIDDEN COSTS OF EMOTIONAL CONSTRAINT

You can probably think of several people in your life who differ greatly in how they express their negative emotions in response to stress. While constantly venting strong negative feelings may not be a good way to make friends and influence people, an inability to express negative feelings can also have its costs. Some studies have reported relations between cancer development and the use of denial or repressive coping strategies, but others have not (McKenna et al., 1999).

In one long-term European study, people who were experiencing high stress levels but were too emotionally restrained to express negative feelings, even when appropriate, had a significantly higher likelihood of developing cancer than did highly stressed people who were not so emotionally restrained. Seeking to reduce this potential vulnerability factor, the researchers designed a treatment program to help stress-ridden but emotionally constrained people who had not yet developed cancer. The program focused on teaching participants how to express their emotions in an adaptive fashion and to build stress-coping skills to manage their feelings without bottling them up. A control group of similar people did not receive the training. Thirteen years later, a follow-up study revealed that 90 percent of the trained participants were still alive, whereas 62 percent of the control group participants had died from cancer and other ailments (Eysenck, 1994; Eysenck & Grossarth-Maticek, 1991).

The question of whether there is indeed a "cancer-prone personality" remains a topic of scientific study and debate (Suls & Wallston, 2003; Taylor, 2006). Nonetheless, in the eyes of many researchers, there is enough evidence to suggest that a rigid pattern of emotional constraint can have negative effects on health.

So, is it better to purge one's feelings or bottle them up? As in the earlier discussion of coping strategies, the best outcomes may occur if we have the flexibility to do either, depending on the situation. George Bonnano and coworkers (2004) studied New York City college students shortly after the September 11th terrorist attacks. In a series of laboratory tasks, participants were required to either openly express emotional responses or suppress them. The researchers found that the students who were most able to engage in either expression or suppression reported less distress about the terrorist attacks and less general life distress 2 years later than did participants who were less flexible in their emotional responses.

GENDER, CULTURE, AND COPING

Many factors, including gender roles and culture, influence our tendency to favor one coping strategy over another. Although men and women both use problem-focused coping, men are more likely to use it as the first strategy when they confront a stressor (Ptacek et al., 1992). Women, who tend to have larger support networks and higher needs for affiliation than men, are more likely than men to seek social support (Billings & Moos, 1984; Schwarzer, 1998). Women also are somewhat more likely than men to use emotion-focused coping (Carver et al., 1989; Pearlin & Schooler, 1978).

▶ **Focus 14**
How do gender and cultural factors affect the tendency to use particular coping strategies?

This general pattern of coping preferences is consistent with the socialization that boys and girls traditionally experience. In most cultures, boys are pushed to be more independent, assertive, and self-sufficient, whereas girls are expected to be more emotionally expressive, supportive, and dependent (Eccles, 1991; Lytton & Romney, 1991). In the words of stress researcher Shelley Taylor (2006), the common male response is "fight or flight," whereas women are more likely than men to "tend and befriend." *Tending* involves nurturant activities designed to protect the self, offspring, and significant others. These behaviors promote safety and reduce distress. *Befriending* is the creation and maintenance of social networks that may aid in this process.

Taylor and coworkers (2000) speculate that the tend-and-befriend pattern is a product of biological mechanisms that underlie attachment and caregiving behavioral tendencies in women. The female hormone oxytocin, acting in conjunction with female reproductive hormones and endorphin mechanisms, may be a key player in this biological system.

Researchers have also found cultural differences in coping. North Americans and Europeans show a tendency to use problem-focused coping more than do Asian and Hispanic people, who tend to favor emotion-focused coping and social support (Essau & Trommsdorff, 1996; Jung, 1995). Asians also show a greater tendency to avoid stressful situations involving interpersonal conflict, perhaps reflecting their culture's emphasis on interpersonal harmony (Chang, 1996). In a study of how American married couples deal with marital stress, African Americans reported a greater tendency than Caucasian Americans to seek social support (Sistler & Moore, 1996). The manner in which particular coping strategies affect well-being under differing cultural conditions is an important topic for future research.

What Do You Think?

WHY DO WOMEN OUTLIVE MEN?
In the United States, women live an average of about 5.2 years longer than men do (National Center for Health Statistics, 2004). A leading news magazine suggested that this difference is probably caused by the fact that men live more stressful lives. Given what you've learned so far, can you think of alternative explanations for the longevity difference? What would you need to know in order to rule out the life-stress explanation? Think about it, then see the discussion on page 526.

STRESS-MANAGEMENT TRAINING

Because stress takes a toll on people's physical and psychological well-being, much effort has gone into developing methods for reducing stress. The model shown in Figure 13.2 suggests that we can reduce stress by modifying any of its major components (Linden, 2005). Thus we can change the situation that constitutes the stressor, modify cognitive appraisals that trigger the rest of the stress response, or learn ways to control the physiological arousal. Finally, we can adopt more effective behaviors for meeting the demands of the situation.

In many coping-skills programs, people learn to modify habits of thought that trigger inappropriate emotional responses and to control physiological arousal responses through relaxation skills (Barlow et al., 2001; Greenberg, 2005). Figure 13.14 previews the most common stress-management techniques taught by psychologists.

Cognitive Coping Skills

Because cognitive appraisal processes play a central role in generating stress, Richard Lazarus, Albert Ellis, and other cognitive theorists maintain that the

► **Focus 15**
Which stress-management/ coping-skills training procedures are used to control cognitive and physiological stress responses?

FIGURE 13.14

Stress-management training. Many stress-management/coping-skills programs teach self-modification techniques, such as cognitive restructuring and self-instructional training to alter stress-producing cognitive appraisals. Relaxation techniques such as progressive relaxation and meditation help counter physiological arousal.

most powerful means of regulating feelings is by controlling how we think about stressful situations and about ourselves. Ellis (1962) suggests that a relatively small number of irrational core beliefs lie at the root of most maladaptive negative feelings. For example, we tell ourselves that we *must* achieve and be approved of in virtually every respect if we are to consider ourselves worthwhile people; that it is terrible, awful, and *catastrophic* when life or other people are not the way that we demand they be; that people who do not behave as we wish are bad and therefore deserving of punishment. In Ellis's terms, these "*must*urbation" and "catastrophizing" tendencies, together with other irrational ideas, generate unnecessary anxiety, despair, and anger. When people use the technique of **cognitive restructuring** *to systematically detect, challenge, and replace these irrational ideas,* their feelings can change dramatically, as in the following case:

> Whenever I find myself getting guilty or upset, I immediately tell myself that there must be some silly sentence that I am saying to myself to cause this upset; and almost immediately . . . I find this sentence. . . . [It] invariably takes the form of "Isn't it terrible that . . ." or "Wouldn't it be awful if . . ."

And when I look at and question these sentences and ask myself, "How is it really terrible that . . . ?" or "Why would it actually be awful if . . . ?" I always find that it isn't terrible or wouldn't be awful, and I get over being upset very quickly. . . . I can hardly believe it, but I seem to be getting to the point, after so many years of worrying over practically everything and thinking I was a slob no matter what I did, of now finding that nothing is so terrible or awful, and I now seem to be recognizing this in advance rather than after I have seriously upset myself (Ellis, 1962, pp. 31–32).

Another approach to changing cognitions does not involve attacking irrational ideas that cause disturbance. In **self-instructional training,** *people learn to talk to themselves and guide their behavior in ways that help them cope more effectively* (Meichenbaum, 1985). They prepare different self-instructions to use at four critical stages of the stressful episode: preparing for the stressor, confronting the stressor, dealing with the feeling of being overwhelmed, and appraising coping efforts after the stressful situation. Table 13.3 provides examples of self-instructions that can be used at these stages of the coping process.

Relaxation Techniques

Coping-skills training can also help people control their physiological responses in stressful situations. Because relaxation is incompatible with arousal, **somatic relaxation training** *provides a means of voluntarily reducing or preventing high levels of arousal.* To learn this skill, people typically tense the various muscle groups of their body and pair tension release with a trigger word (e.g., "Relax") and the exhalation (relaxing) phase of the breathing cycle. The goal is to condition relaxation to the trigger word and to exhalation so that a state of relaxation can be immediately produced in stressful situations by exhaling and mentally saying the trigger word. Most people can learn this technique with about a week of practice. Somatic relaxation training is a cornerstone of most stress-management training programs.

Another type of relaxation can be produced through meditation. Meditation not only relaxes the body but also produces **cognitive relaxation,** *a peaceful, mind-clearing state.* In one approach, the person sits quietly in a comfortable position with eyes closed and mentally concentrates on the word *one* with each exhalation. This procedure is continued for about 20 minutes and, when mastered, quickly relaxes both body and mind (Benson & Klipper, 1976). One key difference between meditation and somatic relaxation is that

TABLE 13.3   Self-Instructional Training: Examples of Adaptive Self-Statements That Can Be Applied at Various Stages of the Coping Process

Phase of Coping Process	Self-Statements
Preparing for the stressor	• What do I have to do? • I can work out a plan to deal with it. • Remember, stick to the issues and don't take it personally. • Stop worrying. Worrying won't help anything.
Confronting and handling the stressor	• As long as I keep my cool, I'm in control of the situation. • I can meet this challenge. This tenseness is just a cue to use my coping techniques. • Don't think about stress, just about what I have to do. • Take a deep breath and relax. Ah, good.
Coping with the feeling of being overwhelmed	• Keep my focus on the present. What is it I have to do? • Relax and slow things down. • Don't try to eliminate stress totally; just keep it manageable. • Let's take the issue point by point.
Evaluation and self-reinforcement	• OK, what worked and what didn't? • I handled it pretty well. • It didn't work, but that's OK. I'll do better next time. • Way to go! You did it!

Source: Adapted from Meichenbaum, 1985.

the latter can be applied at any time during the stressful situation, whereas meditation is best done in a quiet, private space. Many people who meditate practice their technique daily as a means of counteracting ongoing stressors in their lives and preventing short-term stressors from taking a toll.

IN REVIEW

■ Three major ways of coping with stressors are problem-focused coping, emotion-focused coping, and seeking social support. Problem-focused coping and seeking social support generally relate to better adjustment than emotion-focused coping. However, in situations involving low personal control, emotion-focused coping may be the most appropriate and effective strategy.

■ Trauma disclosure has shown positive effects on physical and psychological well-being. Severe emotional constraint may be a risk factor for cancer and perhaps other disorders. Flexibility in emotional expression and suppression seems desirable.

■ Stress-management training teaches people adaptive coping skills for handling stressful situations. Cognitive restructuring and self-instructional training can be used to develop adaptive cognitive coping responses; somatic relaxation training and meditation can be used to develop greater control of physiological arousal.

PAIN AND PAIN MANAGEMENT

Physical pain surely is one of the most unpleasant realities of life, and most of us do our best to avoid it. Hundreds of thousands seek relief from unbearable pain, and one third of all people experience pain that requires medical attention at some time in their lives. Half of all adult Americans suffer from back pain and 10 percent from severe headaches. Pain is a significant feature of many illnesses, and some form of pain is responsible for 80 percent of all medical complaints in North America and Europe (National Center for Health Statistics, 2004; Salovey et al., 2000).

Pain, however, is a two-edged sword. Despite its unpleasantness, pain also has important survival functions. It serves as a warning signal when the body is being threatened or damaged, and it can trigger a variety of behavioral reactions that help us cope with the threat, such as jerking back from a hot skillet or going to see a doctor (Figure 13.15).

FIGURE 13.15

Although pain is an aversive state, it also is adaptive. Pain signals that something is wrong in the body, and it motivates behaviors, such as seeking medical aid, that promote healing and survival.

On the surface, we might think that pain is a purely sensory phenomenon and wonder why it is of interest to psychologists. When we examine it more carefully, however, we see that pain is a complex perceptual phenomenon that involves the operation of numerous psychological processes. For example, it is possible for people to experience excruciating pain in the absence of tissue damage (Melzack, 1998). Conversely, people may suffer severe physical damage and experience no pain, as has occurred in soldiers engaged in combat who were unaware for several hours that they had been wounded (Fordyce, 1988).

BIOLOGICAL MECHANISMS OF PAIN

Pain receptors are found in all body tissues with the exception of the brain, bones, hair, nails, and nonliving parts of the teeth. Free nerve endings in the skin and internal organs respond to intense mechanical, thermal, or chemical stimulation and then send nerve impulses into the spinal cord, where sensory tracts carry pain information to the brain. Once in the brain, the sensory information about pain intensity and location is relayed by the thalamus to the somatosensory and frontal areas of the cerebral cortex (Fields, 2005). Other tracts from the thalamus direct nerve impulses to the limbic system, which is involved in motivation and emotion. These tracts seem to control the emotional component of pain (Melzack, 1998). Thus pain has both a sensory and an emotional component. *Suffering* occurs when both painful sensations and a negative emotional response are present (Fordyce, 1988; Turk, 2001).

▶ **Focus 16**
How does gate control theory explain pain perception and control? How are glial cells and cytokines involved?

Spinal and Brain Mechanisms

Gate control theory, developed by Canadian psychologist Ronald Melzack and physiologist Patrick Wall (1982), was a major advance in the study of pain. **Gate control theory** *proposes that the experience of pain results from the opening and closing of gating mechanisms in the nervous system.* Events in the spinal cord can open a system of spinal cord "gates" and allow the nerve impulses to travel toward the brain. However, other sensory input can partially or completely close the gates and blunt our experiencing of pain. For example, rubbing a bruise or scratching an itch can produce relief. Gate control theorists also suggest that acupuncture achieves its pain-relieving effects because the acupuncture needles stimulate mostly tactile receptors that close the pain gates.

From a psychological perspective, perhaps the most intriguing feature of gate control theory is that nerve impulses in fibers descending from the brain can also influence the spinal gates, thereby increasing or decreasing the flow of pain stimulation to the brain. This *central control mechanism* allows thoughts, emotions, and beliefs to influence the experience of pain and helps explain why pain is a psychological phenomenon as well as a physical one. Gate control theory has been valuable in suggesting techniques for pain control and in stimulating research on psychological factors in pain (Turk & Melzack, 2001).

Gate control and other theorists have traditionally viewed pain as reflecting solely the action of neurons. However, the immune system also plays a role in pain. Recent research has shown that glial cells, which structurally support and service neurons within the spinal cord, are involved in the creation and maintenance of pathological pain (Watkins & Maier, 2003). These glial cells become activated by immune challenges (viral or bacterial infection) and by substances released by neurons within the pain pathway. They then amplify pain by releasing cytokines (messenger molecules) that promote inflammation. This may help account for that "ache all over" sensation that many of us experience when we are ill.

The Endorphins

▶ **Focus 17**
How do endorphins influence pain perception and physical well-being?

In 1680 an English physician wrote, "Among the remedies which it has pleased Almighty God to give man to relieve his suffering, none is so universal and so efficacious as opium" (quoted in Snyder, 1977). Opiates (such as opium, morphine, and heroin) have been used for centuries to relieve pain, and they strongly affect the brain's pain and pleasure systems. In the 1970s, scientists discovered that opiates produce their effects by locking into specific receptor sites in brain regions associated with pain perception.

But why would the brain have built-in receptors for opiates unless there was some natural chemical in the brain for the receptor to receive? Later research disclosed what had to be true: The nervous system has its own built-in analgesics (painkillers) with opiate-like properties. These natural opiates were named **endorphins** (meaning *endogenous, or internally produced, morphines*). Endorphins exert some of their pain-killing effects by inhibiting the release of neurotransmitters involved in the synaptic transmission of pain impulses from the spinal cord to the brain (Fields, 2005). Some endorphins are enormously potent. One of the brain endorphins isolated by scientists is more than 200 times more powerful than morphine (Franklin, 1987). Endorphins are of great interest to psychologists because they may help explain how psychological factors "in the head" can have such strong effects on pain and suffering.

In 2001 John-Kar Zubieta and coworkers published a landmark study that showed the endorphins in action within the brain. They injected a radioactive form of an endorphin into volunteer participants, then stimulated them with painful injections of saltwater into the jaw muscles. Brain scans allowed the researchers to see which areas of the brain lit up from endorphin activity and to relate this activity to pain reports given by the participants every 15 seconds. The scans revealed a surge of endorphin activity within several brain regions, including the thalamus (the sensory switchboard), the amygdala (an emotion center), and a sensory area of the cortex. As the endorphin surge continued over 20 minutes of pain stimulation, participants reported decreased sensory and emotional ratings of pain.

Two other findings were noteworthy. First, people differed in their pain experiences despite identical pain stimulation. Second, these differences were linked to variations in (1) the number of opioid receptors the participants had for the endorphins to bind to and (2) their own ability to release endorphins. Thus biological as well as psychological factors seem to underlie differences in people's ability to tolerate pain (Zubieta et al., 2001).

Acupuncture is a pain-reduction technique that may ultimately be understood in terms of endorphin mechanisms. Injections of naloxone, a drug that counteracts the effects of endorphins, greatly decrease the pain-reducing effects of acupuncture (Oleson, 2002). This suggests that acupuncture normally releases endorphins (Figure 13.16).

Another phenomenon attributable to endorphins is **stress-induced analgesia,** *a reduction in—or absence of—perceived pain that occurs under stressful conditions.* For example, research has shown that about 65 percent of soldiers wounded during combat report having felt no pain at the time of their injury (Warga, 1987). Likewise, people involved in accidents are sometimes unaware of serious injuries until the crisis is over. This analgesic response could be highly adaptive. In a life-threatening situation, fight-or-flight defensive behavior must be given immediate priority over normal responses to pain, which typically involve immobility. By reducing or preventing pain sensations through the mechanism of endorphin release, stress-induced analgesia helps suppress these pain-related behaviors so that the person or animal can perform the actions needed for immediate survival, such as fleeing, fighting, or getting help (Fanselow, 1991). As an example, consider the report of a man who was so severely bitten during an attack by a grizzly bear that he required more than 200 stitches:

> I had read the week before about someone who was killed and eaten by a grizzly bear. So I was thinking that this bear was going to eat me unless I got away. I did not have time for pain. I was fighting for my life. It was not until the next day that I started feeling pain and fear. (Kolb & Whishaw, 2001, p. 386)

The release of endorphins seems to be part of the body's natural response to stress, but we may pay a price for this temporary relief from pain. It appears that chronically high levels of endorphin release help block the activity of immune system cells that recognize and selectively kill tumor cells. This may be one way in which stress makes us more susceptible to serious illnesses such as cancer (Shavit, 1990).

CULTURAL AND PSYCHOLOGICAL INFLUENCES ON PAIN

As a complex perception, pain is influenced by numerous factors. Cultural learning, meanings attributed to pain, beliefs, and personality factors all affect our experiences of pain.

Cultural Factors

Our interpretation of pain impulses sent to the brain depends in part on our experiences and beliefs, and both of these factors are influenced by

the culture in which we develop (Rollman, 1998). Consider, for example, the experience of childbirth. This event is widely perceived as a painful ordeal in Western cultures, and many women express considerable anxiety about going through it (Blechman & Brownell, 1998). Yet in some cultures, women show virtually no distress during childbirth. Indeed, in one culture studied by anthropologists, it was customary for the woman's husband to get into bed and groan as if he were in great pain while the woman calmly gave birth to the child. The husband stayed in bed with the baby to recover from his terrible ordeal while the mother returned to work in the fields almost immediately (Kroeber, 1948).

Certain societies in India practice an unusual hook-hanging ritual. A holy person, chosen to bless children and crops, travels from village to village on a special ceremonial cart. Large steel hooks, attached by ropes to the top of the cart, are shoved under the skin and muscles on each side of the holy person's back. At the climax of the ceremony, he leaps from the cart and swings free, hanging only by the hooks embedded in his back (Figure 13.17). Incredibly, though hanging from the hooks with his entire body weight, the celebrant shows no evidence of pain during the ritual; on the contrary, he appears to be in a state of ecstasy. When the hooks are removed, the wounds

FIGURE 13.16

Acupuncture is a proven pain-reduction procedure. Gate control theory attributes its effects to the stimulation of sensory fibers that close sensory gates in the pain system. In addition, there is evidence that acupuncture stimulates endorphin release.

FIGURE 13.17

Cultural beliefs and pain tolerance. Illustrated here is a hook-swinging ceremony practiced in remote villages in India. After blessing all the children and farm fields in a village, the celebrant leaps from the cart and hangs suspended by the hooks embedded in his back in a state of ecstasy, showing no sign of pain. SOURCE: Adapted from Kosambi, 1967.

► Focus 18
How do cultural factors influence
pain experience and behavior?

heal rapidly and are scarcely visible within two weeks (Kosambi, 1967).

Although ethnic groups do not appear to differ in their ability to discriminate among pain stimuli, members of different cultural groups may differ greatly in their interpretation of pain and the amount of suffering they experience (Rollman, 1998; Zatzick & Dimsdale, 1990). In the Indian hook-hanging ceremony, for example, the religious meanings attached to the act seem to transform the interpretations and meaning of the sensory input from the hooks. Likewise, childbearing mothers in cultures where the pain of childbirth is not feared do not attach strong negative emotions to the associated sensations, and they therefore suffer far less.

The role of cultural factors in pain perception is found even within modern Western subcultures. In Massachusetts, researchers studied pain perception in 372 medical patients who represented six different ethnic groups: "Old Americans" (at least third-generation U.S.-born Caucasians who identified with no ethnic group except "Americans"), Hispanic Americans, Italian Americans, Irish Americans, French Canadians, and Polish Americans. All of the patients suffered from chronic pain conditions that had persisted for at least 3 months and were beyond the point of healing. The patients completed self-report measures about their pain experiences.

► Focus 19
How do cognitive and personality
factors affect people's responses
to pain stimuli?

The ethnic groups did not differ overall in type of physical affliction, how long they had had it, or the kinds of treatments and medications they were receiving. They did differ, however, in the pain levels they reported, and these differences were associated with different attitudes and beliefs about their pain. The Hispanic American and Italian American patients believed most strongly that they had no control over their pain, reported feeling worried and angry about it, and believed that they would be unhappy as long as they experienced it. They also believed that it is appropriate to express one's pain openly. These two ethnic groups reported the highest levels of pain and suffering. In contrast, the Old American and Polish American patients felt it best to suppress the outward expression of pain, reported feeling less upset about their pain sensations, and believed that they had greater personal control over their lives. These attitudinal differences were associated with much lower levels of reported suffering (Bates et al., 1993).

Meanings and Beliefs

Differences exist not only between cultural groups but also within them, as physician Henry Beecher (1959) observed while working at Anzio Beachhead in World War II and later at Massachusetts General Hospital. At Anzio, Beecher found that only about 25 percent of the severely wounded soldiers he observed required pain medication, compared with 80 percent of civilian men who had received similarly serious "wounds" from surgeons at Massachusetts General. Why the difference? Beecher concluded that for the soldiers, the wounds had a fundamentally positive meaning: They spelled evacuation from the war zone and a socially acceptable ticket back home to their loved ones. For the civilian surgical patients, on the other hand, the operations meant a major life disruption and possible complications. The different meanings attributed to the pain stimuli resulted in very different levels of suffering and, consequently, different needs for pain relief (Figure 13.18).

Perhaps nowhere is the influence of belief on pain perception more evident than in the effects of **placebos,** *physiologically inert substances that have no medicinal value but are thought by the patient to be helpful* (Shapiro & Shapiro, 1997). At the beginning of this chapter we described the observations made by German physician Hans Rheder, whose female patients responded with startling improvements in their symptoms to the news

FIGURE 13.18

The amount of pain a wounded soldier experiences may be influenced by the meaning it has for him. Does the wound represent a ticket home to his loved ones, or does it herald a lifetime of pain and disability?

that he had invoked the healing powers of a faith healer. Similar observations have been made in pain research. In one classic study by Henry Beecher (1959), either a placebo or a morphine injection was given to 122 surgical patients who were suffering postoperative pain. All were told they were receiving pain medication. Of those who received morphine, 67 percent reported relief, but 42 percent of those given placebos reported equal relief. More recent medical studies of placebo effects have yielded even higher rates of pain relief, as high as 100 percent in some studies (Turner et al., 1994). However, it is also clear that placebos work only if people *believe* they are going to work. Research using PET-scan technology at the Karolinska Institute in Sweden indicates that given a positive belief in the placebo's effectiveness, the brain sends messages that result in the release of endorphins to reduce pain (Petrovic et al., 2002).

Where pain is concerned, the statement "I can control it" may be more than an idle boast or an empty reassurance. In one experiment, patients suffering from the prolonged pain of a bone-marrow transplant were randomly assigned to one of two conditions. One group was allowed to directly control the amount of pain medication that they received intravenously. The other patients were given prescribed amounts of the same medication by the hospital staff (and told they could request additional medication if needed). The patients who had direct control over their medication not only rated their pain as less intense but also gave themselves less pain medication (Zucker et al., 1998). As in the case of placebo effects, beliefs about personal control apparently exert their effects by increasing endorphin release. Naloxone injections, which counteract endorphin activity, sharply reduce the ability of people to endure intensely painful stimuli, no matter how high their confidence in their pain tolerance (Bandura et al., 1987).

Personality Factors and Social Support

Beginning with Sigmund Freud, personality theorists have suggested that emotional and personality factors can play a role in experiencing and responding to pain. Pain and suffering can be a way of attaining certain goals. For some bitter and deprived people, pain can be a way of dramatizing their unhappiness; eliciting caring, sympathy, or guilt from others; or gaining favors. Pain may also be a way of escaping from or avoiding threatening situations. For example, an athlete who dreads the possibility of failing may avoid the feared competition by experiencing severe pain that prevents participation. This coping process, different from consciously faking being hurt, occurs at an unconscious level (May & Sieb, 1987).

People who have the personality trait of neuroticism, the tendency to experience negative emotions such as anxiety and depression, report higher levels of physical pain, both in relation to medical conditions and in controlled laboratory administrations of painful stimuli such as heat, cold, electrical shock, or pressure (Turner & Aaron, 2001). In contrast, personality styles that include optimism and a sense of personal control over one's life are associated with lower pain perception and less suffering (Pellino & Ward, 1998). Moreover, patients with chronic pain conditions who are able to simply accept the pain rather than bemoaning their fate and responding emotionally to it have less disability, better social adjustment, and higher work performance (McCracken, 1998). Thus it seems clear that psychological factors play important roles in pain perception and adaptation.

Further evidence that one's emotional state and social support network are associated with one's experience of pain comes from a study by Carmen Alonso and Christopher Coe (2001). In a sample of 184 college women, the researchers found that self-reported depression and anxiety were strongly associated with ratings of menstrual pain. More significantly, perhaps, the greatest pain and distress occurred in women who had recently lost a significant source of social support.

Does life stress increase pain experiences? Many studies with medical patients have suggested that it does (Fields, 2005/06). Linda Watkins and Steven Maier (2003) explain how this might occur. Normally, sensory nerves cannot respond to stress hormones because they have no receptors for them. After nerve damage resulting from injury, however, receptors for stress hormones begin to appear on the surface of sensory nerves. These new receptors increase the excitability of damaged nerves when stress hormones are present, therefore allowing life stress to increase pain.

The fact that psychological processes are so central to the experience of pain has stimulated many health psychologists to research methods that can be used to control or reduce pain and suffering. The following "Applying Psychological Science" feature highlights this important area of application.

▶ **Focus 20**
Describe cognitive, informational, and behavioral interventions for pain reduction.

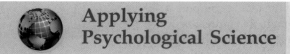

Applying Psychological Science   Psychological Techniques for Controlling Pain and Suffering

We all occasionally experience physical pain, and for some people, pain is a never-ending nightmare. In recent years, psychological pain-control strategies have received increasing attention from health psychologists (Gatchel, 2005; Turk, 2001).

COGNITIVE STRATEGIES

Recent attention has focused on two classes of cognitive strategies known as *dissociation* and *association*. A *dissociative strategy* involves dissociating, or distracting, oneself from the painful sensory input. This can be done in a variety of ways: by directing your attention to some other feature of the external situation, by vividly imagining a pleasurable experience, or by repeating a word or thought to yourself. Research has shown that dissociative strategies are most effective when they require a great deal of concentration or mental activity, thereby directing attention away from the painful stimuli.

If you are a recreational jogger or a long-distance runner, you may be familiar with the discomfort of extending yourself. Endurance running seems an ideal real-life task to use in the study of cognitive strategies. William Morgan and coworkers (1983) gave this simple dissociative strategy to participants who were running on a treadmill to exhaustion: "Focus your attention on a spot in front of you on the treadmill and say 'Down' each time your right foot comes down on the treadmill." A control group also ran the treadmill but did not receive the strategy. Although the two groups did not differ physiologically while running the treadmill, the mental-strategy group was able to tolerate the discomfort of treadmill running 32 percent longer than the control group.

A more dramatic, high-tech dissociative strategy is being tested in the burn center at the Harborview Medical Center in Seattle, Washington. There children and adults with burns covering up to 60 percent of their bodies are donning virtual-reality goggles during the often agonizing processes of wound cleansing and physical therapy. The goggles take patients into a visually compelling world of shapes and colors. Pain ratings are significantly lower when these patients are immersed in virtual reality than when they are in a nondistracted condition (Hoffman et al., 2001).

Associative strategies are just the opposite of dissociative ones. Here you focus your attention on the physical sensations and study them in a detached and unemotional fashion, taking care not to label them as painful or difficult to tolerate. It appears that when pain is intense, associative strategies become more effective than dissociative ones (McCaul & Malott, 1984). There seems to be a point at which pain stimuli become too intense to ignore and dissociative strategies become ineffective. Thus one strategy is to use dissociation as long as possible and then shift to an associative mode.

FIGURE 13.19

Coping strategies and pain tolerance. These data show the increases in pain tolerance in an ice-water/hand-immersion task exhibited by a cognitive-skills training group, a placebo condition, and a control group that repeated the task with no intervention. SOURCE: Based on Bandura et al., 1987.

Combined dissociative and associative strategies can be quite effective in dealing with acute pain. In one study, participants' pain tolerance was tested by measuring how long they could keep their hand immersed in ice water. One group of participants was then trained and practiced a number of dissociative coping strategies (such as attention diversion and the use of distracting imagery) and associative strategies (such as imagining that the hand immersed in the ice water was detached from the body and focusing nonemotionally on the pain sensations). Two control groups equated in initial pain tolerance were given either no strategies or a placebo pain reducer. Then their ice-water pain tolerance was tested a second time. As shown in Figure 13.19, the cognitive-skills training resulted in a large increase in pain tolerance (Bandura et al., 1987).

HOSPITAL INTERVENTIONS: GIVING PATIENTS INFORMATIONAL CONTROL

Having relevant information about a challenging environment and event is also a kind of cognitive control, since it tells us what to expect. In the medical setting of the past, doctors typically gave patients no more information than needed about a specific medical procedure and its aftermath. However, psychological research on how certain types of information reduce anxiety and contribute to positive medical outcomes has ushered in a new era in many medical settings. Imagine that you're in the hospital for major surgery. You know that this surgical procedure entails risk and that your recovery will be painful. What kinds of information would help you cope and recuperate more easily?

FIGURE 13.20

A key to preventing chronic pain and disability is to begin physical activity again as soon as possible.

You might profit from *sensory information* about what you will feel after the operation. Knowing, for example, that patients often have shooting pains in their stomach after the surgery could prevent surprise or fear if it occurred to you. You would see the pain as a normal consequence of the surgery and the recovery process rather than as a sign of danger.

Second, *procedural information* on the surgery itself would help you understand what exactly is going to be done and why. You might be shown a model of the body part to demonstrate what will be done in the surgery, or you may see a video describing the procedure. This kind of information would give you a sense of predictability and control and reassure you that precautions were being taken to anticipate and reduce possible hazards.

Third, you could profit from *coping guidance* about handling the pain or other complications from the surgery. For example, you might learn breathing exercises designed to reduce pain by helping you relax (Tollison et al., 2002). You might also be taught some of the cognitive strategies previously described to get through sieges of acute pain during the recovery process.

Informational interventions have proved helpful in many medical settings. Surgical patients show a better course of recovery and require less pain medication than those treated in a traditional fashion (Faust, 1991). Such interventions have proven remarkably successful in decreasing distress in hospitalized children, who are likely to find major medical procedures particularly frightening (Christopherson & Mortweet, 2001).

A KEY BEHAVIORAL STRATEGY: BECOMING ACTIVE AGAIN

Recovering patients who avoid activity and become overly protective of an injured body part are at risk for developing a chronic pain condition (Turk, 2001). It is important to return to activity after an injury as soon as the healing process will allow (Figure 13.20). A key to successfully treating chronic pain patients who have "shut themselves down" is to decrease their guarding and resting behaviors and to modify their belief that their pain signals body damage. Such interventions produce significant decreases in patient disability (Jensen et al., 2001). Wilbert Fordyce (1988), a leader in the behavioral treatment of pain, emphasizes the negative effects that unnecessary rest and disuse of a body part can have on recovery:

> The lavish prescription of rest virtually ensures adverse disuse effects. With disuse in the musculoskeletal system, movement then becomes painful. But pain from disuse risks being interpreted by patient and professional as an indication of lack of healing. The result may become more prescribed rest or practical disuse and yet more pain with movement. . . . Pain problems originating in tissue injury but in which healing has occurred are made better by use. Patients must be helped to understand the dictum "To make it better, use it.". . . People who have something better to do don't suffer as much. (p. 282)

LEVELS OF ANALYSIS **Factors Related to Pain Perception**

Biological
- Stimulation of nerve endings and pressure receptors within the body activates pain centers in brain
- Action of endorphins reduces pain perception
- Opening, closing of spinal "gates"
- Downward neural impulses from brain

Psychological
- Cognitive factors, such as beliefs about meaning of pain and personal control
- Placebo effects produced by positive expectations of pain relief
- Cultural beliefs and expectations influence pain perception

Environmental
- Environmental stressors can decrease pain perception through endorphin release
- Cultural learning experiences produce beliefs and expectations regarding pain and its expression
- Painful physical stimuli

Pain Perception

FIGURE 13.21

Levels of analysis: Factors related to pain perception.

Pain is an intriguing and complex biological, psychological, and social phenomenon. Figure 13.21 provides a levels-of-analysis summary of the factors we've discussed.

IN REVIEW

■ Pain is a complex perception influenced by biological, psychological, and sociocultural factors. At the biological level, the major pain receptors appear to be free nerve endings. Gate control theory attributes pain to the opening and closing of gates in the spinal cord and to influences from the brain. Glial cells and cytokines are also involved in pain. The nervous system contains endorphins, which play a major role in pain reduction.

■ Expectations of relief produced by placebos can markedly reduce medical symptoms and pain. Cultural factors also influence the appraisal and response to painful stimuli, as do control beliefs. Negative emotional states increase suffering and decrease pain tolerance.

■ Psychological techniques for pain control include (1) cognitive strategies, such as dissociative and associative techniques; (2) providing medical patients with sensory and procedural information to increase cognitive control and support; and (3) increasing activity level to counter chronic pain.

HEALTH PROMOTION AND ILLNESS PREVENTION

In 1979 the Surgeon General of the United States issued a landmark report entitled *Healthy People* (U.S. Public Health Service, 1979). The report concluded that improvements in the health of Americans are more likely to result from efforts to prevent disease and promote health than from new drugs and medical technologies. Two recent U.S. government reports, *Healthy People 2010* (2005) and *Health, United States 2004* (2004) provide strong evidence for that assertion.

Consider the leading causes of death in the United States and Europe in comparison with the leading killers in 1900. As Figure 13.22 shows, the leading culprits have changed from influenza, pneumonia, tuberculosis, and gastroenteritis to heart disease, cancer, and stroke. The major killers of the early 1900s have been largely controlled by medical advances. In contrast, the death rate has almost doubled for heart disease and tripled for cancer since 1900. As shown in Table 13.4, these diseases and today's other killers are strongly influenced by behavioral factors. Health authorities estimate that half of all cases of early mortality (deaths occurring prior to the life-expectancy age within a culture) from the 10 leading causes of death can be traced to risky behaviors, such as cigarette smoking, excessive alcohol consumption, insufficient exercise, poor dietary habits, use of illicit drugs, failure to adhere to doctors' instructions, unsafe sex practices, and failure to wear automobile seat belts (Mokdad et al., 2004).

Recognition of the crucial role that behavior plays in health maintenance has prompted much research in the field of health psychology. Psychologists have helped identify many of the psychological and social causes for risky health behaviors, and the clear need for lifestyle interventions has spurred attempts around the world to promote positive changes in such behaviors (Suls & Wallston, 2003; Taylor, 2006). Modifying people's health behaviors as a form of illness prevention can reduce medical costs and avert the physical and psychological distress that illness produces.

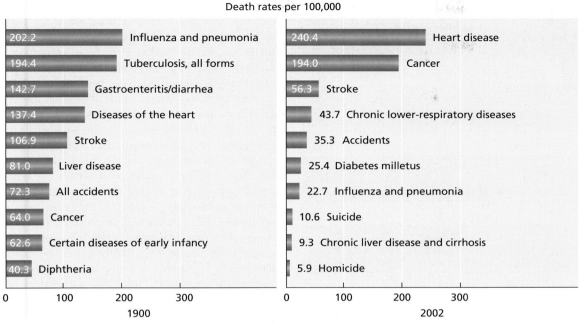

Death rates per 100,000

1900

202.2	Influenza and pneumonia
194.4	Tuberculosis, all forms
142.7	Gastroenteritis/diarrhea
137.4	Diseases of the heart
106.9	Stroke
81.0	Liver disease
72.3	All accidents
64.0	Cancer
62.6	Certain diseases of early infancy
40.3	Diphtheria

2002

240.4	Heart disease
194.0	Cancer
56.3	Stroke
43.7	Chronic lower-respiratory diseases
35.3	Accidents
25.4	Diabetes milletus
22.7	Influenza and pneumonia
10.6	Suicide
9.3	Chronic liver disease and cirrhosis
5.9	Homicide

FIGURE 13.22

Causes of death, 1900 versus 2002. Modern causes of death are far more attributable to health-endangering behaviors. SOURCES: Based on Murphy, 2000; Sexton, 1979; U.S. Centers for Disease Control, 2002a; and National Center for Health Statistics, 2004.

Health-related behaviors fall into two main categories. *Health-enhancing behaviors* serve to maintain or increase health. Such behaviors include exercise, healthy dietary habits, safe sexual practices, regular medical checkups, and breast and testicular self-examination. *Health-impairing behaviors* promote the development of illness. They include tobacco use, fatty diets, a sedentary lifestyle, and unprotected sexual activity. Psychologists have developed programs that focus on both classes of behavior (Schneiderman, 2004).

HOW PEOPLE CHANGE: THE TRANSTHEORETICAL MODEL

In order to increase health-enhancing behaviors and reduce health-impairing ones, we need to understand the processes that underlie behavior change in general. In the 1980s, psychologists James Prochaska and Carlo DiClemente began to study the process that occurs as people modify their thoughts, feelings, and behaviors in positive ways, either on their own or with professional help. Their research resulted in a **transtheoretical model** *that identified six major stages in the change process* (DiClemente, 2003; Prochaska & DiClemente, 1984).

1. *Precontemplation:* The person does not perceive a health-related problem, denies that it is something that endangers well-being, or feels powerless to change.

2. *Contemplation:* The person perceives a problem or the desirability of a behavior change but has not yet decided to take action.

Thus some smokers are well aware of the health risks of their habit, yet they are not ready to make a decision to quit. Until the perceived benefits of changing outweigh the costs or effort involved, contemplators will not take action.

3. *Preparation:* The person has decided to change the behavior, is making preliminary plans to do so, and may be taking preliminary steps, such as cutting down on the number of cigarettes per day.

4. *Action:* The person actively begins to engage in behavior change, perhaps stopping smoking altogether. Success at this stage hinges on the behavior-control skills

▶ **Focus 21**
Describe the transtheoretical model and the rationale for stage-matched interventions.

TABLE 13.4	Behavioral Risk Factors for the Leading Causes of Death in the United States
Disease	**Risk Factors**
Heart disease	Tobacco, obesity, elevated blood pressure, cholesterol, sedentary lifestyle
Cancer	Tobacco, improper diet, alcohol, environmental exposure
Cerebrovascular disease (stroke)	Tobacco, elevated blood pressure, cholesterol, sedentary lifestyle
Accidental injuries	Safety belt nonuse, alcohol, home hazards
Chronic lung disease	Tobacco, environmental exposure

SOURCE: Based on McGinnis, 1994.

FIGURE 13.23

Stages of change. The transtheoretical model identifies a series of stages through which people pass as they modify their behavior. People may move up and down through the stages several times before they reach the final stage of termination. SOURCE: Prochaska et al., 1998.

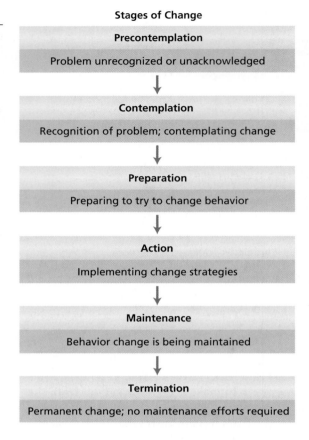

Stages of Change

Precontemplation

Problem unrecognized or unacknowledged

↓

Contemplation

Recognition of problem; contemplating change

↓

Preparation

Preparing to try to change behavior

↓

Action

Implementing change strategies

↓

Maintenance

Behavior change is being maintained

↓

Termination

Permanent change; no maintenance efforts required

necessary to carry out the plan of action. The action stage requires the greatest commitment of effort and energy.

5. *Maintenance:* The person has been successful in avoiding relapse and has controlled the target behavior for at least 6 months. This does not mean that the struggle is over. Many people lapse back into their former behavior pattern at various times, but they reinstate their change efforts, as would be expected when one is trying to change deeply ingrained habits. It typically takes smokers three to five cycles through the action stage before they finally beat the habit, and New Year's resolutions are typically made for 5 or more consecutive years before they are finally carried out successfully (Prochaska et al., 1994; Schachter, 1982).

6. *Termination:* The change in behavior is so ingrained and under personal control that the original problem behavior will never return.

The transtheoretical model, shown in Figure 13.23, does not assume that people go through the stages in a smooth sequence. Longitudinal studies have shown that many people move for-

ward and backward through the stages as they try to change their behavior over time, and many people make repeated efforts to change before they finally succeed (Davidson, 1998; Evers et al., 1998). However, failure at a given stage is likely to occur if the previous stages have not been mastered.

The transtheoretical model helps us understand how people change, and it has important applied implications. For example, we know that different intervention procedures are needed for people at various stages. Psychologists have therefore developed ways of determining what stage people are in so that they can apply *stage-matched interventions* designed to move the person toward the action, maintenance, and termination stages. Precontemplators need consciousness-raising information that finally convinces them that there is a problem, as well as social support to change (De Vries et al., 1998). Contemplators often need a wake-up emotional experience that increases their motivation to change or causes them to reevaluate themselves in relation to the behavior. For example, a serious auto accident while intoxicated may finally convince a problem drinker that her or his behavior has to change. In the preparation stage, the person needs to develop a specific plan (ideally based on the goal-setting procedures described in Chapter 12) and have the skills to carry it out before action is likely to be successful. Only when the person is ready for the action stage are change techniques, however powerful, likely to have their intended effect.

INCREASING BEHAVIORS THAT ENHANCE HEALTH

During the 1970s, the role of behavior in maintaining health and living longer became evident as researchers began to study the effects of lifestyle. Figure 13.24 shows the results of one longitudinal study of nearly 7,000 adults. The researchers studied the relation of seven good-health practices to life expectancy. These included sleeping 7 to 8 hours per day, eating breakfast, not smoking, rarely eating between meals, being at or near one's prescribed body weight, engaging in regular physical activity, and drinking only small to moderate amounts of alcohol. For men and women alike, these behaviors predicted a longer life. A higher mortality rate among those with poor health practices began to appear in men between the ages of 45 and 64 and in women between 55 and 64 (Belloc, 1973). Let's examine some of these health-enhancing behaviors and what can be done to encourage them.

Exercise

The couch potato lives! (But apparently not as long.) A sedentary lifestyle is a significant risk factor for health problems, including coronary heart disease and obesity (Rodin & Salovey, 1989; Taylor, 2006). Despite this widely publicized fact, about 70 percent of Americans are inactive (Baum et al., 1997; Ehrman, 2003). As fewer people now engage in vigorous manual labor, inactivity has helped double the rate of obesity since 1900, despite a 10 percent decrease in daily caloric intake over the same period (Friedman & DiMatteo, 1989).

Aerobic exercise *is sustained activity,* such as jogging, swimming, and bicycling, *that elevates the heart rate and increases the body's need for oxygen.* This kind of exercise has many physical benefits. In a body that is well conditioned by regular aerobic exercise, the heart beats more slowly and efficiently, oxygen is better utilized, slow-wave sleep increases, cholesterol levels may be reduced, faster physiological adaptation to stressors occurs, and more calories are burned (Baum & Posluszny, 1999; deGeus, 2000).

Exercise is associated with physical health and longevity (Figure 13.25). A study that followed 17,000 Harvard undergraduates into middle age revealed that death rates were one quarter to one third lower among moderate exercisers than among those in a less active group of the same age. Surprisingly, perhaps, extremely high levels of exercise were not associated with enhanced health; instead, moderate exercise (burning 2,000 to 3,500 calories per week) on a regular basis produced the best health benefits (Paffenbarger et al., 1986). Performing at 70 to 85 percent of maximal heart rate nonstop for 15 minutes three times a week significantly reduces risk for coronary heart disease (Dishman, 1982). Such exercise also has positive psychological effects, reducing depression and anxiety (Morgan, 1997).

Findings such as these have inspired behavioral interventions designed to promote regular exercise. Typically, these programs have an educational component that addresses the benefits of regular exercise and the best ways to exercise. They may also include other components of behavior change, such as setting goals, writing explicit contracts that specify an exercise regimen, monitoring one's exercise behavior on a daily basis, and increasing social support by choosing an exercise partner or group.

Despite the demonstrated benefits of regular exercise, people in developed countries have a strong tendency either to avoid or discontinue it after a short period. In the United States, for example, only one fourth of the adult population exercises at levels high enough to maintain cardiorespiratory fitness and reduce the risk of premature death (Ehrman, 2003). When employers offer exercise programs to their employees, it is uncommon for more than 30 percent to participate, and dropout rates of 50 percent within 6 months are found in virtually all exercise programs that have been studied (Chenoweth, 2002; Dishman, 1994). On the other hand, people who are able to persist for 3 to 6 months are likely to continue as exercise becomes a healthy habit (McAuley, 1992).

What factors predict dropout? This is an important research question, for if we can identify the risk factors, we can take measures to counteract

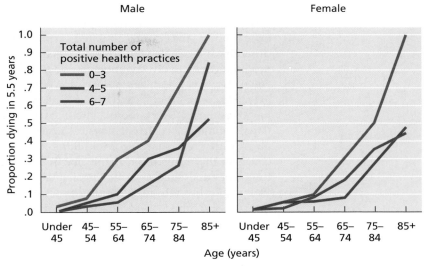

FIGURE 13.24

Healthy habits and longevity. These data show the relation between the number of positive health practices and longevity in men and women. Those who adhered to few of the health practices experienced earlier mortality, with the pattern appearing earlier in men than in women. SOURCE: Adapted from Belloc, 1973.

▶ **Focus 22**
What is aerobic exercise? What evidence exists that it promotes health and longevity?

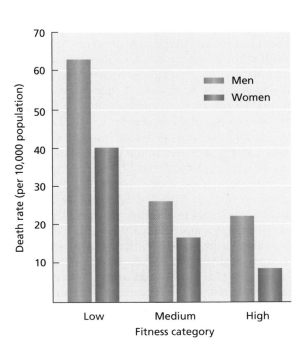

FIGURE 13.25

Aerobic exercise and health. Aerobic exercise is an important health-enhancing behavior, contributing to physical well-being. Significantly higher death rates occur for both men and women who are low in physical fitness. SOURCE: Data from Blair et al., 1989.

▶ **Focus 23**
How large are exercise dropout rates? What factors do and do not predict dropout?

them. Research has shown that general attitudes toward physical fitness do *not* predict adherence or dropout; the exercise-related attitudes of dropouts and people who adhere to their exercise programs are equally favorable (Suls & Wallston, 2003). However, low self-efficacy for success in exercising regularly ("I can't do this"), Type A behavior pattern ("Sorry, too busy to exercise"), inflated estimates of current physical fitness ("I'm already in great shape from walking from my couch to the refrigerator"), and inactive leisure-time pursuits (such as watching television and walking to the refrigerator) all predict dropout (Martin & Dubbert, 1985; Wilcox & Storandt, 1996). The strongest social-environmental factor related to dropout is lack of social support from friends, family, or other exercisers (Ehrman, 2003).

Psychologists have been able to increase compliance by helping exercisers identify these impediments and prepare specific strategies to deal with them before they occur (Rosen, 2000; Simkin & Gross, 1994). For example, a person who anticipates feeling too tired to work out at the end of the day might prepare a set of self-statements about how much better she will feel after exercising. If she is not receiving social support and encouragement from others, she could also arrange for a pleasurable activity after her workout to positively reinforce her exercising (Courneya, 1995).

Weight Control

Health statistics indicate that nearly 30 percent of the adult American population is obese, defined as being more than 20 percent overweight (Figure 13.26). Since 1980 the average American adult's body weight has increased by about 8 pounds, and the upward trend continues (Suls & Wallston, 2003). A significant proportion of children (13.7 percent) and adolescents (11.5 percent) are also obese (Buet & Harris, 1994). If current trends continue, obesity's death toll will soon exceed 500,000 each year in the United States alone (Mokdad et al., 2004).

Obesity is a risk factor for a variety of chronic diseases, such as cardiovascular disease, kidney disease, and diabetes. Women who are 30 percent overweight are more than 3 times more likely to develop heart disease than normal-weight women (Manson et al., 1990). For reasons yet unknown, fat that is localized in the abdomen is a far greater risk factor for cardiovascular disease, diabetes, and cancer than is excessive fat in the hips, thighs, or buttocks (Taylor, 2006). Accumulation of abdominal fat is increased by yo-yo dieting that results in big weight fluctuations. Such dieting markedly increases the risk of dying from cardiovascular disease, an excellent reason to avoid this practice (Hafen & Hoeger, 1998; Rodin et al., 1990).

Were you to enroll in a behavioral intervention program for weight loss, here is what would happen: The program would begin with a period of self-monitoring, during which you would keep careful records of what, how much, and under what circumstances you eat. This is designed to make you more aware of your eating habits and to identify situational factors (antecedents) that affect your food intake. You would then learn to take control over those antecedents. For example, you would learn to make low-calorie foods such as raw vegetables freely available and to limit high-calorie foods in the house. You would then learn stimulus-control techniques, such as confining your eating to one location in the house and eating only at certain times of the day. Because overeaters tend to wolf down their food and overload their stomachs, you would also learn to slow down your eating by putting down eating utensils until each bite is chewed and swallowed, and you would learn to pause between mouthfuls. These behaviors reduce food intake and help you learn to pay attention to how full you are. You would also be told to savor each mouthful of food. The goal is to eat less but enjoy it more. Finally, you would learn to chart the amount of food you eat to provide constant feedback, and you would arrange to positively reinforce yourself for successful performance. These behavioral practices would be combined with nutritional guidelines to help you eat a healthier diet. Table 13.5 shows specific guidelines from a highly successful weight-reduction program developed by Yale psychologist Kelly Brownell (1994).

Research shows that the addition of an exercise program increases the positive effects of behavioral eating-control programs (Avenell et al., 2004; Wadden et al., 1997). High levels of physical activity are associated with initial weight loss and its maintenance, and exercise adds to the effectiveness of other weight-loss methods, such as dietary change. Research indicates that many overweight people are able to attain gradual weight loss of about 2 pounds per week for up to 20 weeks and to keep the weight off for 2 years and beyond (Jackson et al., 1999; Taylor, 2003).

Lifestyle Changes and Medical Recovery

Teaching people how to control their health-related programs can have dramatic benefits even

▶ **Focus 24**
What are the behavior-change techniques used in behavioral weight-control programs?

FIGURE 13.26

An alarmingly large percentage of adults and children are overweight, increasing health risks. Obesity contributes annually to nearly 500,000 deaths in the United States.

for those who are already afflicted with serious illnesses. William Haskell and coworkers (1994) randomly divided a sample of patients suffering from coronary artery disease into two groups. Both groups received the usual high-quality medical care from their physicians at Stanford University Medical School. In addition, the experimental group received a behavioral self-regulation program that targeted health factors such as smoking, exercise, weight, nutrition, and medication adherence.

A 4-year follow-up revealed dramatic results. Those receiving the usual medical care showed either no improvement or a worsening of their condition, and their health habits had not improved. In contrast, those who also received the behavioral self-regulation program showed significant positive changes in their health habits. They reduced their intake of dietary fat, lowered their bad (LDL) cholesterol and raised their good (HDL) cholesterol, increased their exercise, and raised their cardiovascular capacity. The program also influenced the progression of the disease, as the self-management group had 47 percent less buildup of blockage material on artery walls. During the 4-year follow-up period, 45 percent of the control patients either died or had nonfatal heart attacks or other cardiac emergencies, compared with only 24 percent in the behavior self-regulation group. This study, like the others we've discussed, demonstrates the value of psychologically based health-promotion efforts.

REDUCING BEHAVIORS THAT IMPAIR HEALTH

We now turn our attention to several types of health-impairing behaviors. We begin with a class of behaviors that two decades ago was not considered a major health threat. Although a number of serious diseases can be transmitted through sexual contact, the majority of them can be successfully treated. In the early 1980s, however, a mysterious and lethal sexually transmitted disease emerged.

Psychology and the AIDS Crisis

On June 5, 1981, the Centers for Disease Control reported the first case of *acquired immune deficiency syndrome (AIDS).* In the decades that followed, AIDS grew from an unknown disease into a devastating worldwide epidemic for which no medical cure has been found. According to the World Health Organization (2004), about 16,000 new infections occur each day. Worldwide, 1 in every

TABLE 13.5 A Sample of Effective Behavioral Weight-Control Techniques	
Keep an eating diary	Keep problem foods out of sight
Examine your eating patterns	Serve and eat one portion at a time
Prevent automatic eating	Use gradual shaping for behavior change
Examine triggers for eating	Distinguish hunger from cravings
Do nothing else while eating	Focus on behavior, not weight loss
Eat in one place	Cope positively with slips, lapses
Put fork down between bites	Keep an exercise diary
Pause during the meal	Understand benefits of exercise
Shop on a full stomach	Know calorie values of various exercise activities
Buy foods that require preparation	Program exercise activity

SOURCE: Based on Brownell, 1994.

100 adults between the ages of 15 and 49 is infected with the HIV virus that causes AIDS, and the disease has so far claimed the lives of nearly 20 million people. Forty-five percent of the HIV-positive are women. Of the 3.1 million people who died from AIDS in 2004, 37 percent were women and 20 percent were children. In some countries of southern Africa, 25 to 40 percent of the population is infected, including a third of all pregnant women. Globally, only 5 to 10 percent of the cases now occur in homosexual men (the population typically identified with the affliction), and women now make up half of all HIV cases (United Nations, 2002). In the early 2000s, the rates of infection began to rise again among homosexual men in North America, Europe, and Australia due to increases in risky sexual behavior (CDC, 2003). The AIDS epidemic threatens to overwhelm the world's health-care financing and delivery systems.

AIDS is caused by the *human immunodeficiency virus (HIV),* which cripples the immune system. The patient then becomes vulnerable to invading viruses, bacteria, and tumors, which are the actual killers. Because the HIV virus evolves rapidly, vaccines are at present ineffective in preventing its spread. Moreover, the incubation period between initial HIV infection and the appearance of AIDS symptoms may be as long as 10 years, meaning that an infected person may unknowingly pass the virus on to many other people. The major modes of transmission are direct exposure to infected semen, vaginal fluids, and blood through either heterosexual or homosexual contact; the sharing of infected needles in intravenous drug use; and exposure to infected blood through transfusion or in the womb. Breast milk is also a major means of transmission through

▶ **Focus 25**
Describe the nature and effectiveness of behavior-change techniques used in AIDS prevention projects.

which many women have unknowingly transmitted the HIV virus to their children.

In the absence of a vaccine or cure, the only existing means of controlling the AIDS epidemic is by changing the high-risk behaviors that transmit the virus. In this respect, AIDS is as much a psychological problem as a medical one. Prevention programs are typically designed to (1) educate people concerning the risks that attend certain behaviors, such as unprotected sex; (2) motivate people to change their behavior and convince them that they can do so; (3) provide specific guidelines for changing the risky behaviors and teach the skills needed for change; and (4) give support and encouragement for the desired changes (O'Leary et al., 2001).

Early AIDS interventions were directed at homosexual men, who were originally the major at-risk group. In this population, a primary mechanism of HIV transmission is anal intercourse without the use of a condom. In one successful prevention study (Kelly et al., 1989), 42 homosexual men went through a program that instructed them on the risks accompanying unprotected intercourse, helped them develop and rehearse strategies for avoiding high-risk situations (such as sexual relations with strangers), and taught them how to be more assertive in refusing to engage in high-risk behaviors. Another group of 43 homosexual men also completed the program after initially serving as an untreated control group.

Both groups were assessed before and after the first group went through the program and then were followed for 8 months after completing the program to assess long-term behavior changes. As Figure 13.27 shows, the intervention program resulted in a substantial and lasting increase in the use of condoms during sexual activity. Similar programs are now being conducted with adolescent populations, where unprotected heterosexual intercourse is resulting in a surge of new infections (Jemmott et al., 1998). Another target for interventions is heterosexual women, who not only are the fastest-growing segment of the HIV population but also have the potential to infect their babies if they become pregnant.

Even when something as urgent as AIDS prevention is involved, research has shown that the success of prevention programs depends on the extent to which the individual's social system supports the desired changes. When sexual abstinence or the use of condoms runs contrary to the values of an individual or cultural group, people may continue to engage in high-risk behaviors even though they have been informed of the dangers involved (Herdt & Lindenbaum, 1992; Huff & Kline, 1999). Likewise, within both homosexual and heterosexual populations, and particularly among adolescents and young adults, many individuals continue to have an irrational sense of invulnerability to infection, and this belief contributes to a failure to abstain from sex or to engage in protected sexual practices (Kelly, 2001). Counteracting these barriers to safe sexual behavior is a major challenge for health psychologists. One successful approach to this problem was a program described in the Chapter 6 "Research Close-Up," in which modeling procedures were transmitted through an engaging radio drama to promote safe sex in Tanzania (Bandura, 2000).

Combating Substance Abuse

Substance abuse exacts a fearsome toll on society. Tobacco use harms smokers and those who breathe their secondhand smoke. Smoking ranks as the single largest cause of preventable death, killing nearly half a million Americans each year (Mokdad et al., 2004). Although tobacco use has leveled off in the United States since 1985, tobacco products have been aggressively marketed in other countries, and sales have nearly doubled over the past 15 years. The coming decades will therefore witness an appalling increase in the diseases caused by smoking, particularly in developing countries that are ill equipped to provide good medical treatment.

Alcohol abuse also contributes enormously to human suffering. In the United States alone, alcohol abuse costs over $100 billion a year in decreased work productivity and treatment costs and $13.8 billion in alcohol-related automobile accidents (National Center for Health Statistics,

FIGURE 13.27

Effects of an AIDS prevention program. An AIDS prevention program for homosexual men increased their use of condoms during sexual activity. The program educated the men on the risks involved in sexual behaviors (especially unprotected sex), promoted the use of condoms, and taught them coping skills to deal with high-risk situations. SOURCE: Based on Kelly et al.,1989.

2004). Alcohol is implicated in half of all fatal automobile accidents and is a leading factor in industrial and farm accidents (Figure 13.28). Alcohol abuse is also highly damaging to one's health. Death rates among those who abuse alcohol are 2 to 4 times higher for men and 3 to 7 times higher for women, depending on the disease in question. Life expectancy is 10 to 12 years less (CDC, 2002a). Alcohol affects the welfare of others as well. Some children are born with fetal alcohol syndrome, and others are subjected to disrupted family relationships, including domestic violence. For every person who has a problem with alcohol, an average of four other people's lives are adversely affected on a daily basis (Levinthal, 1996).

Other varieties of substance abuse also have adverse effects. Many crimes are committed by users of illicit drugs in order to support their habits (Kendall, 1998). Moreover, substance abuse is highly associated with psychological disorders, often being part of a larger pattern of maladjustment in both adolescents and adults (Miller & Brown, 1997).

Psychological principles discussed in earlier chapters have been successfully applied to the treatment of smoking, problem drinking, and drug use (Taylor, 2006). As the transtheoretical model has shown, however, even the best programs are unlikely to be utilized effectively by people until they are ready to change. In recent years, there has been an emphasis on bringing precontemplators and contemplators to the point where they are ready to engage themselves in a change process.

Motivational Interviewing If smokers, problem drinkers, drug abusers, and others who practice self-defeating behaviors are to change, they must increase their awareness of their problems, have a desire to take action, and believe that they can change (Miller & Rollnick, 2002; Miller, 1996). Rather than confronting the person with his or her problem (which often drives away people who need help), the technique of **motivational interviewing** *leads the person to his or her own conclusion by asking questions that focus on discrepancies between the current state of affairs and the individual's ideal self-image, desired behaviors, and desired outcomes.* Focusing on these discrepancies may help motivate change. Consider the following exchange:

Client: I really don't believe I have a drinking problem.

Counselor: You're the best judge of that. May I ask how many drinks you have a day?

Client: Oh, it varies. Probably 5 or 6.

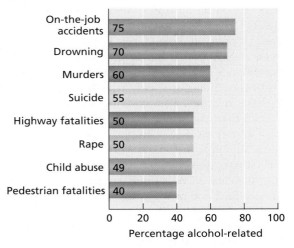

FIGURE 13.28

Societal costs of alcohol abuse. This graph shows the percentage of common negative events that are alcohol-related. Source: Based on Carroll, 1993.

Counselor: Is that about what you'd like to be drinking?

Client: Well, I'd probably be better off if I cut down a little—maybe to 3 or 4.

Counselor: How would that be helpful to you?

Client: Well, I could study better and reduce the arguments with my roommate. I can get pretty nasty when I'm buzzed. I hate being nasty. I'm not that kind of person. Our relationship is going downhill, and I'd hate to lose a friend.

Counselor: Well, you know, you don't have to have a big problem in order to want to make a change. I'm sure you could do so if you really want to.

Client: I can see that I'd be more the person I want to be if I worked on this.

Counselor: And I'd be happy to help you make your change.

Following a client's decision to pursue behavior change, the counselor helps the client set specific goals and select from a menu of behavior-change strategies the ones he or she would like to employ. Thereafter, the counselor provides feedback and support for the client's efforts. Motivational interviewing has proven to be an effective and low-cost treatment approach for substance abusers (Miller & Rollnick, 2002). In one large-scale study of alcohol-abuse patients, a 4-session motivational interviewing intervention proved to be as effective as a 12-session program modeled on Alcoholics Anonymous (Project MATCH Research Group, 1997).

Multimodal Treatment Approaches All substance-abuse behaviors are resistant to change, and for good reason. Some people may be more vulnerable

Why do some people become addicted to alcohol while others do not? Watch the video, "Neurochemical Basis of Addiction," in Chapter 13 of your CD to learn some compelling answers.

▶ **Focus 26**
What are the major goals and techniques in motivational interviewing?

▶ **Focus 27**
What kinds of behavior-change procedures are employed in multimodal treatments for substance abuse?

than others because of genetic factors (Crabbe, 2002). Craving, caused by either psychological need or physical dependence, is a huge barrier to overcome. Negative emotions, such as anxiety, irritability, or depression, are temporary results of abstinence that cause many who quit successfully to have relapses. Past conditioning may create stimuli that trigger the behavior in certain common situations. For example, coffee drinking or social situations are linked with smoking for many individuals, thus encouraging lapses in behavioral control when those stimuli are present. The numerous factors that encourage smoking, drinking, or drug abuse make these behaviors very hard to change. Psychologists are therefore willing to combine anything that has proven effective into what they hope will be a more powerful behavior-change package to apply when people are ready to make a change. These **multimodal treatments** *often include biological measures* (for example, the use of nicotine patches to help smokers quit), *together with psychological measures* such as the following:

- Aversion therapy, in which the undesired behavior is associated with an aversive stimulus, such as electric shock or a nausea-producing drug, in an attempt to create a negative emotional response to the currently pleasurable substance

- Relaxation and stress-management training, which help the person adapt to and deal with stressful situations

▶ Focus 28
How serious are the consequences of heavy drinking among college students?

- Self-monitoring procedures that help the person identify the antecedents and consequences of the abuse behaviors

- Coping and social-skills training for dealing with high-risk situations that trigger abuse

- Marital and family counseling to reduce conflicts and increase social support for change

- Positive-reinforcement procedures to strengthen change

This broad-based multimodal approach appears to produce favorable outcomes for many people who have substance addictions. For example, in one of the more successful multimodal treatment outcome studies, 427 alcoholic patients were followed for 12 to 20 months after completing an inpatient program that included aversion therapy (using a drug that produces nausea when alcohol is consumed), personal counseling, and coping-skills training. Follow-up assessments revealed that 65 percent were totally abstinent for 1 year after treatment. The best outcome occurred in cases where the urge to drink had been eliminated (presumably by aversion therapy) and alternate coping skills were increased through the use of cognitive-behavioral techniques such as those just described (Smith & Frawley, 1993). Despite these encouraging results, typical treatment results are less favorable: Long-term maintenance of behavior changes often occurs in fewer than 30 percent of treated individuals, whether the target behavior is smoking, drinking, or some other substance abuse (Ockene et al., 2001). The goal of many researchers is therefore to develop more effective treatment packages.

Beneath the Surface   College-Age Drinking: Harmless Fun or Russian Roulette?

The harmful problems that result from the behaviors of alcoholics and drug addicts are self-evident. But because college students view themselves as different from these populations, many fail to realize the extent to which they place themselves in harm's way through their use of alcohol. Many students view heavy-drinking parties as a natural part of college life, like going to classes or athletic events. Studies have found that many heavy-drinking students, who average 40 to 50 drinks per week, do not view their behavior as either abnormal or problematic (Marlatt, 1998).

Beneath this surface of complacency lies evidence that heavy-drinking students are placing themselves at considerable risk. In one national study carried out by the Harvard School of Public Health, binge drinking was defined as having more than 4 (for women) or 5 (for men) drinks at a time on at least three occasions during the previous 2 weeks (Wechsler et al., 1994). Data from 18,000 students at 140 U.S. colleges revealed that 50 percent of the males and 40 percent of the women met this bingeing criterion, yet fewer than 1 percent saw themselves as having an alcohol problem. However, the dangerous consequences of their drinking became clear when binge drinkers were asked about alcohol-related problems (Table 13.6).

Frequent binge drinkers were 7 to 10 times more likely than moderate drinkers to engage in unplanned and unprotected sexual intercourse, to suffer injuries, to drive under the influence of alcohol, to damage property, and to get in to trouble with the law. At schools with the highest alcohol consumption rates, nondrinkers and moderate drinkers were 2 to 3 times more likely to report physical assault, sexual harassment, destruction of their property, and interruption of their sleep and studying by heavy drinkers. Some college women (sound sleepers, apparently) complained that they woke up Sunday after Sunday to find a strange man in bed with their roommate (and all too frequently the heavy-drinking roommate didn't know him either). So, while common belief may have it that heavy drinking is harmless fun, scientific findings suggest otherwise.

TABLE 13.6 Percentage of Binge-Drinking College Students Who Reported Drinking-Related Problems	
Missed a class	61%
Forgot where they were or what they did	54%
Had 5 or more alcohol-related problems in school year	47%
Engaged in unplanned sex	41%
Got hurt	23%
Had unprotected sex	22%
Damaged property	22%
Got into trouble with campus or local police	11%

SOURCE: Based on Wechsler et al., 1994.

Harm-Reduction Approaches to Prevention

Substance abuse not only has negative effects on physical well-being but often results in other severe consequences, such as self-defeating sexual and aggressive behaviors. **Harm reduction** *is a prevention strategy that is designed not to eliminate a problem behavior but rather to reduce the harmful effects of that behavior when it occurs* (MacCoun, 1998; Weingardt & Marlatt, 1998). In the area of drug abuse, harm-reduction approaches include needle and syringe exchange programs to reduce the spread of HIV infections. Another example is methadone maintenance programs for heroin addicts, which are targeted at reducing addicts' need to engage in criminal activity to feed their heroin habit. The reasoning is that even if an addictive behavior cannot be eliminated, it is possible to modify how often and under what conditions it occurs and thereby minimize its harmful effects on the person and society.

The harm that can befall college students who abuse alcohol has inspired a new generation of intervention programs focused on helping problem drinkers control how much and under what circumstances they drink. The goal is to reduce harmful consequences to the problem drinkers and others (Marlatt et al., 2001). In one harm-reduction project carried out at a large western-U.S. university, incoming freshmen were screened for alcohol problems before they arrived on campus (Marlatt et al., 1998). Once on campus, those identified as problem drinkers were randomly assigned to either an intervention condition or to a no-treatment control condition. Over the next 2 years, the students in both conditions regularly reported on their alcohol consumption and alcohol-

related problems. People who knew them well also furnished reports, and high agreement between the two sources of data indicated that the students were being truthful and accurate.

The intervention, occurring in the winter of the freshman year, was a brief one based on the motivational-interviewing approach described earlier. The goal was to prevent or reduce harmful consequences of drinking by increasing motivation to make constructive changes, rather than to stop students' drinking. Clinical psychologists met with each student individually for one session. The interviewer reviewed the drinking data submitted by the student over the previous academic term and gave individualized feedback in graphic form. The graph compared his or her drinking rate with college student averages, which were invariably much lower. The interviewers listed the potential risks for heavy college drinkers (such as those shown in Table 13.6) and discussed environmental risk factors, such as being in a fraternity or sorority or having heavy-drinking friends, if relevant. The interviewers were never confrontational but instead helped students evaluate their situation ("What do you make of this? Are you surprised?"), to think about present and possible future problems ("Would you be worried about something like this happening to you? What impact would it have on your life?"), and to consider the possibility of change. Specific goals of behavior change were left to the student and not imposed by the interviewer.

At the end of 2 years, the students in the intervention group were still drinking more than the average college student, and although they continued to have more alcohol-related problems than the

► **Focus 29**

What is a harm-reduction approach, and how does it differ from an abstinence-based one?

▶ **Focus 30**
Which factors increase or decrease relapse? How does relapse-prevention training address these factors?

FIGURE 13.29

Effects of a brief intervention on alcohol-related problems. At 1 year and 2 years after the intervention, high-risk drinkers who underwent the harm-reduction program still reported more alcohol-related problems than the average college student but fewer than the high-risk drinkers in the control group. SOURCE: Adapted from Marlatt et al., 1998.

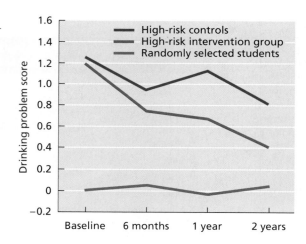

FIGURE 13.30

Relapse and relapse prevention. Relapse is most likely to occur as a result of inadequate coping skills for dealing with high-risk situations, a focus on anticipated positive effects of engaging in the behavior, and a resulting abstinence violation effect that causes the person to feel incapable of successful change and to abandon attempts at behavior control. SOURCE: Marlatt & Gordon, 1985.

average student, they had far fewer alcohol-related problems than did students in the untreated high-risk group (Figure 13.29). Thus despite the lack of an explicit focus on reducing drinking, the brief one-session intervention had significant positive effects. In particular, students learned to moderate their drinking in potentially hazardous situations, thereby reducing harmful consequences.

RELAPSE PREVENTION: MAINTAINING POSITIVE BEHAVIOR CHANGE

Despite the availability of effective methods for changing behavior, high dropout rates and failure to maintain positive behavior changes are a major problem in every health-relevant behavior we've discussed, from exercise maintenance to weight control to ending substance abuse. Why do people relapse into their problem behaviors, and what can be done to prevent this? Research on

these questions has led to a better understanding of the relapse process and an intervention known as **relapse prevention** *that is designed to reduce the risk of relapse* (Marlatt & Gordon, 1985). Research with substance abusers shows that most *relapses* (a full-fledged return to the undesirable behavior pattern) tend to occur after the person has suffered one or more *lapses* (occasional "slips") in response to high-risk situations. High-risk situations include stressful events, interpersonal conflicts, social pressure to perform the undesirable behavior, being in the company of other individuals using the substance, and experiencing negative emotions (Marlatt, 1996).

The path to relapse is shown in the bottom portion of Figure 13.30. Increased likelihood of relapse occurs when people have not developed strong enough coping skills to deal successfully with the high-risk situations. As a result, they experience low self-efficacy, believing that they are not strong enough to resist the temptation, or they allow expected positive benefits (such as enjoyment of the substance or anticipated stress reduction) to influence their decision to perform the undesirable behavior. A lapse then occurs, followed by a critically important reaction called the **abstinence violation effect,** *in which the person becomes upset and self-blaming over the lapse and views it as proof that he or she will never be strong enough to resist temptation.* This sense of hopelessness places people at great risk to abandon all attempts to change, and in many cases a total relapse will occur. In one study of relapses in dieting, the abstinence violation effect was more strongly associated with relapse episodes than were temptations (Carels et al., 2004).

Relapse resistance is shown in the upper portion of Figure 13.30. When confronting high-risk

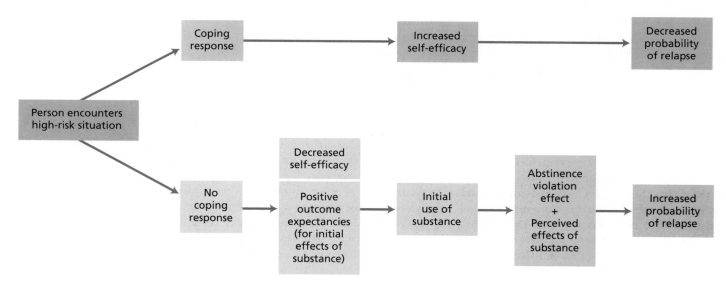

situations, people who have effective coping skills feel confident in their ability to handle them and are far less likely to relapse, even if they slip once in a while. To develop this adaptive process, relapse prevention specialists tell people that a lapse means only that they've encountered a situation that exceeded their current coping skills. Moreover, the lapse has given them valuable information about the specific situational, cognitive, and emotional antecedents that they must learn to handle more effectively. When they master the needed skills, they will be better able to resist high-risk situations. Attention is then directed at learning and practicing the required skills so that self-efficacy improves. The continuing focus is on "progress, not perfection."

Relapse prevention training is increasingly being incorporated into many behavior change programs. It has proven effective in changing many problematic behaviors, including overeating, smoking, cocaine and marijuana abuse, and sexual offending (Witkiewicz & Marlatt, 2004). Relapse prevention is also an important complement to the transtheoretical model, which tells us that many people regress from the action and even maintenance stages back into a previous stage because they are not prepared to deal with the lapses that almost inevitably occur as they try to alter ingrained behavior patterns. Being prepared for occasional lapses helps people move more smoothly from the preparation stage to the action and maintenance stages (DiClemente, 2003).

IN REVIEW

■ The transtheoretical model identifies six stages through which people may move during the process of successful long-term behavioral change: precontemplation, contemplation, preparation, action, maintenance, and termination. The model has inspired stage-matched interventions focused on the individual's current stage, with the intent of moving the person to the action, maintenance, and termination stages.

■ Exercise is an important health-enhancing behavior that affects both physical and psychological well-being. Numerous behavioral interventions have been developed to promote exercise, but many people fail to adhere to exercise programs. One factor that influences adherence is social support. People who are able to stick with an exercise program for 3 to 6 months have a better chance of adhering to it thereafter.

■ About a third of the American population is obese, as are 1 in 6 children and adolescents. Behavioral weight-control programs feature self-monitoring, stimulus-control procedures, and eating procedures designed to help people eat less but enjoy it more. The addition of an exercise program to weight-control procedures enhances weight loss.

■ Because HIV infection is caused by high-risk sexual and drug-abuse behaviors (e.g., sharing needles), a prevention approach is essential. Behavioral changes have been accomplished in homosexual populations, and efforts are centering on high-risk heterosexual populations, such as teenagers. Cultural factors sometimes conflict with safe-sex practices, increasing the challenges of reducing health-endangering behaviors.

■ Substance abuse is highly associated with other disorders and is often part of a larger pattern of maladjustment. Multimodal treatments combine a number of techniques, including aversion training, stress-management and coping-skills training, and positive reinforcement for change. A promising new approach is motivational interviewing, a nonconfrontational procedure designed to engage the person's own motivation to change self-defeating behaviors.

■ Harm-reduction approaches attempt to reduce the negative consequences that a behavior produces rather than to focus on stopping the behavior itself. Examples include needle exchange programs for drug addicts and programs designed to reduce the destructive consequences of binge drinking in college students.

■ Relapse prevention is designed to keep lapses from becoming relapses by building effective coping skills to deal with high-risk situations and countering the abstinence violation effect when lapses occur. This approach enhances the effects of many behavior-change programs.

A CONCLUDING THOUGHT

The enterprise of living involves a constant process of adjusting to environmental demands. When those demands exceed our personal and social resources, we experience stress and may attempt to reduce it by changing our environment or our own behavior. Thus stress can be a catalyst for growth and change, or it can drag us down physically and psychologically, depending on how effectively we respond to it. Psychologists have been at the forefront of stress research and have developed interventions to help people cope more effectively.

We have also seen that people's behavior contributes strongly to both illness and physical well-being. The field of health psychology focuses on psychological and behavioral processes that affect physical well-being. Health psychologists have made important contributions to helping people reduce health-impairing behaviors and acquire healthier lifestyles, but many challenges remain.

Unfortunately, people do not always have the resources to cope with life's demands. As a result, they may engage in thought processes, emotional responses, and behaviors that are hurtful to themselves or to society. In the next chapter, we will consider the behavior disorders that can result from failures to adapt successfully.

KEY TERMS AND CONCEPTS

Each term has been boldfaced and defined in the chapter on the page indicated in parentheses.

abstinence violation effect (p. 524)
aerobic exercise (p. 517)
cognitive relaxation (p. 506)
cognitive restructuring (p. 506)
coping self-efficacy (p. 498)
cytokines (p. 494)
emotion-focused coping (p. 501)
endorphins (p. 508)
gate control theory (p. 508)
general adaptation syndrome (GAS; p. 490)
hardiness (p. 498)

harm reduction (p. 523)
health psychology (p. 487)
motivational interviewing (p. 521)
multimodal treatments (p. 522)
placebo (p. 510)
primary appraisal (p. 490)
problem-focused coping (p. 501)
protective factors (p. 496)
relapse prevention (p. 524)
secondary appraisal (p. 490)
seeking social support (p. 501)

self-instructional training (p. 506)
somatic relaxation training (p. 506)
stress (p. 487)
stress-induced analgesia (p. 509)
stressors (p. 487)
stress response (p. 489)
transtheoretical model (p. 515)
Type A behavior pattern (p. 497)
vulnerability factors (p. 496)

? What Do You Think?

DO STRESSFUL EVENTS CAUSE PSYCHOLOGICAL DISTRESS? (PAGE 492)

As we noted, the relation between stress and distress is correlational. Now let's think critically and challenge the causal interpretation. Certainly, it's possible that life stress causes psychological distress—and there are other kinds of evidence to suggest that it does. But it is also possible that distress may be the causal factor instead of the effect. That is, distressed people may be more likely than nondistressed people to remember and report negative things that have happened to them. Or they may tend to view more events as negative, resulting in higher negative life-change scores. Moreover, psychological distress could actually cause people to behave in ways that produce more negative events. For example, research has shown that anxious and depressed people often evoke negative reactions from others because of their gloomy outlook and their tendency to frustrate others' attempts to help them feel better.

And that's not all: A third causal possibility is that some other variable causes both negative life events *and* psychological distress to go up or down, thus creating the relation between them. The Big Five personality trait of neuroticism, discussed in Chapter 12, might be such a third variable. We know that people who are high in neuroticism have a tendency to experience lots of negative emotions *and* to get themselves into stressful situations through their self-defeating behaviors. Differences in neuroticism could thus cause the relation between stress and distress. These different causal possibilities remind us that stressful life events are part of a network of causal relations and that stressful life events can function as either a cause or an effect.

WHY DO WOMEN OUTLIVE MEN? (PAGE 505)

According to the World Health Organization, women live an average of 5 to 8 years longer than men in most industrialized countries. Only in underdeveloped countries, where many women die in childbirth, do men live longer. Is stress the reason? This popular media interpretation is contradicted by research results showing that women report as many stressful events as men do and are, in fact, more susceptible to a variety of stress-related psychological disorders. So, what other factors could be at work?

One possibility is that women are simply more biologically fit than men are. Although more males than females are conceived, more male children are miscarried or stillborn, and more males die in infancy and at every age thereafter. Some biological survival factors may be genetic, some hormonal. One possibility is that females' XX chromosomal structure may protect them against certain diseases that afflict males. Another suggestion is that the female hormones estrogen and prolactin may help protect them against some major diseases, including heart disease.

Other explanations focus on behavioral and social differences between the sexes. Men engage in more risky and health-impairing behaviors. They are more likely to die in accidents and to smoke and drink heavily. In fact, smoking differences may account for as much as 40 percent of the mortality difference between adult men and women. Finally, men are more likely to have physically hazardous occupations than are women.

At the environmental level, explanations focus on the important protective functions of social support on health and well-being. On average, women have larger and more active social support networks and more intimate relationships than do men. Whether this difference contributes to women's greater longevity is not known. Once again, however, we see the usefulness of considering potential causal factors at biological, psychological, and environmental levels of analysis.

Which of these sex differences do you think might be particularly important? Can you think of other differences that might matter? Finally, do you think that the diminishing differences in sex roles, which place increasingly more women into traditionally male work settings and lifestyles, might reduce the longevity difference in coming decades?

Psychological Disorders

Mark has been depressed for several years, but things are even worse now. He feels totally inadequate and inferior. The future looks hopeless, and he cannot sleep at night. During the day, he can barely function, and his moods alternate between deadening depression and intense anxiety. A friend has suggested that he seek professional counseling, but Mark is convinced that he has slipped too deeply into the black hole of despair to ever feel good again. He wonders how long he wants to go on living in his private hell.

■ ■ ■ ■ ■

Naomi was walking across campus the first time it happened. Suddenly, her heart began pounding and skipping beats. She grew weak and shaky, began sweating profusely, and felt an indescribable sense of impending doom. She was sure she was either going insane or was about to die on the spot. Gathering all her strength, she made it to her dormitory room and began to feel better. Now, after several such incidents while on campus, she is afraid to leave her dorm.

■ ■ ■ ■ ■

Unwashed, unshaven, and wearing tattered clothes, Eddie lives in the downtown area of the city. He often sits in a park mumbling to himself. Occasionally, he covers his ears and yells, "Shut up!" to try to still the voices in his head. Some nights he eats and sleeps at a shelter, but more often he rolls himself in a filthy blanket and sleeps under a freeway overpass. Eddie has been committed to a state mental hospital more than 10 times. In the hospital, he responds quickly to antipsychotic drugs and begins to behave more normally. But soon after being released back into the community, he stops taking his medication and gradually slides once again into a deteriorated mental state. Today a social service caseworker notices him and asks how he's doing. Staring vacantly into space, he replies, "Life is trouble, bubble, double, zubble."

These three people could very well live in your city or town. Mark or Naomi could be students at your college. Many people are unaware of how common psychological disorders are. According to U.S. government statistics:

- At any given time, 22 percent of the U.S. population suffers from a diagnosable mental disorder.

- Nearly half of all Americans between the ages of 15 and 54 will experience a psychological disorder at some point in their lives.

- Psychological disorders are the second leading cause of disability, after heart disease.

- Medications used to treat anxiety and depression are among the most frequently prescribed drugs in the United States.

- One adolescent commits suicide every 90 seconds.

- Each year, more than a million students withdraw from college because of emotional problems.

- One in four Americans will have a substance-abuse disorder during his or her lifetime. Alcohol abuse alone costs the U.S. economy about $117 billion a year (National Center for Health Statistics, 2004; Satcher, 1999).

These cold statistics, startling though they may be, cannot possibly capture the intense suffering that they reflect. They cannot communicate the confusion and alienation felt by the schizophrenic patient whose psychological world is disintegrating, the intense personal misery of a depressed person who is sinking into a quagmire of hopelessness, the terror experienced by someone with a panic disorder, or the frustration endured by the families and friends of those who have psychological disorders.

This chapter is therefore not just about the problems of "someone else." Even if you are fortunate enough never to experience a psychological disorder in your lifetime, statistics suggest that you'll almost surely have a family member, friend, or acquaintance who will.

HISTORICAL PERSPECTIVES ON DEVIANT BEHAVIOR

Psychological disorders are not just a modern problem. The pages of history are filled with accounts of prominent people who suffered from psychological disorders. The Bible describes King Saul's mad rages and terrors. The 18th-century French philosopher Jean-Jacques Rousseau developed marked paranoid symptoms in the latter part of his life and was plagued by fears of secret enemies. Mozart was convinced he was being poisoned during the time he was composing his *Requiem*. Abraham Lincoln suffered recurrent bouts of depression throughout his life and was, on one occasion, so depressed that he failed to show up for his own wedding. Winston Churchill also periodically suffered from severe depression, referring to it as his "black dog." The billionaire aviator Howard Hughes became so terrified of being infected with germs that he became a bedridden recluse for the last decade of his life (Figure 14.1).

Dysfunctional behaviors such as these do not go unnoticed. Throughout history, human societies have explained and responded to abnormal

▶ **Focus 1**
Describe the demonological, behavioral, cognitive, humanistic, and sociocultural perspectives on abnormal behavior.

FIGURE 14.1

Abraham Lincoln and Winston Churchill suffered from severe depression during their lifetimes. Billionaire Howard Hughes had a debilitating obsessive-compulsive disorder involving fears of contamination that kept him isolated and bedridden for many years.

FIGURE 14.2

An early treatment for disordered behavior was trephination, in which a hole was chiseled through the skull to release the evil spirit thought to be causing the abnormal behavior. Some people survived the operation, but many died from it.

behavior in different ways at different times, based on their values and assumptions about human life and behavior. The belief that abnormal behavior is caused by supernatural forces goes back to the ancient Chinese, Egyptians, and Hebrews, all of whom attributed deviance to the work of the devil. One ancient treatment was based on the notion that bizarre behavior reflected an evil spirit's attempt to escape from a person's body. In order to release the spirit, a procedure called *trephination* was carried out. A sharp tool was used to chisel a hole in the skull about 2 centimeters in diameter (Figure 14.2). It seems likely that in many cases trephination successfully

FIGURE 14.3

This painting by Francisco de Goya reflects the widespread belief that disordered people were possessed by the devil. *Sabbath* portrays the weekly gathering of Satan and the witches he possessed.

eliminated abnormal behavior by putting an end to the patient's life.

In medieval Europe, the demonological model of abnormality held that disturbed people either were possessed involuntarily by the devil or had voluntarily made a pact with the forces of darkness (Figure 14.3). The killing of witches was justified on theological grounds, and various "diagnostic" tests were devised. One was to bind a woman's hands and feet and throw her into a lake or pond. Based on the notion that impurities float to the surface, a woman who sank and drowned could be posthumously declared pure. Of course, a woman who floated was in *real* trouble. During the 16th and 17th centuries, more than 100,000 people with psychological disorders were identified as witches, hunted down, and executed.

Centuries earlier, about the 5th century B.C., the Greek physician Hippocrates suggested that mental illnesses are diseases just like physical disorders. Anticipating the modern viewpoint, Hippocrates believed that the site of mental illness was the brain. By the 1800s, Western medicine had returned to viewing mental disorders as biologically based and was attempting to extend medical diagnoses to them. The biological emphasis was given impetus by the discovery that *general*

paresis, a disorder characterized in its advanced stages by mental deterioration and bizarre behavior, resulted from massive brain deterioration caused by the sexually transmitted disease syphilis. This was a breakthrough—the first demonstration that a psychological disorder was caused by an underlying physical malady.

In the early 1900s, Sigmund Freud's theory of psychoanalysis ushered in psychological interpretations of disordered behavior. As we shall see, psychodynamic theories of abnormal behavior were soon joined by other models based on behavioral, cognitive, and humanistic conceptions. These various conceptions focus on different classes of causal factors and help capture the complex determinants of abnormal behavior. The importance of cultural factors has also received increasing attention. Although many questions remain, these perspectives have given us a deeper understanding of how biological, psychological, and environmental factors can combine to cause psychological disorders.

Today, many psychologists find it useful to incorporate these factors into a more general framework. According to the **vulnerability-stress model** (Figure 14.4), *each of us has some degree of vulnerability (ranging from very low to very high) for developing a psychological disorder, given sufficient stress.* The *vulnerability,* or predisposition, can have a biological basis, such as our genotype, over- or underactivity of a neurotransmitter system in the brain, a hair-trigger autonomic nervous system, or a hormonal factor. It could also be due to a personality factor, such as low self-esteem or extreme pessimism, or to previous environmental factors, such as poverty or a severe trauma or loss

▶ **Focus 2**
How does the vulnerability-stress model illustrate person-situation interactions?

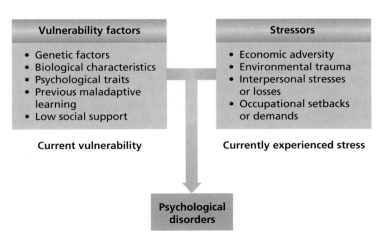

FIGURE 14.4

The vulnerability-stress model. This popular conception attributes behavior disorders to interactions between personal vulnerability factors and life stressors. Personal vulnerability factors contribute to maladaptive efforts to cope with life's challenges.

earlier in life. Likewise, cultural factors can create vulnerability to certain kinds of disorders (Ingram & Price, 2001).

But vulnerability is only part of the equation. In most instances, a predisposition creates a disorder only when a *stressor*—some recent or current event that requires a person to cope—combines with a vulnerability to trigger the disorder (van Praag, 2004). Thus a person who has a genetic predisposition to depression or who suffered a traumatic loss of a parent early in life may be primed to develop a depressive disorder *if* faced with the stress of a loss later in life. As we shall see, the biological, psychological, and environmental levels of analysis have all contributed to the vulnerability-stress model and to our understanding of behavior disorders and how they develop.

DEFINING AND CLASSIFYING PSYCHOLOGICAL DISORDERS

So far, we have discussed historical and contemporary accounts of abnormal behavior without actually defining what we mean by *abnormal*. Doing so is not as easy as it might at first appear.

WHAT IS "ABNORMAL"?

Defining what is normal and what is abnormal is problematic. Judgments about where the line between normal and abnormal should be drawn differ depending on the time and the culture. For example, cannibalism has been practiced in many cultures around the world (Walker, 2001). In contemporary Western culture, however, such behavior would be viewed as extraordinarily pathological. Until December 15, 1973, homosexuality was officially considered to be a form of mental illness. On that day, the trustees of the American Psychiatric Association voted unanimously to remove homosexuality from the psychiatric classification system—surely the quickest and most widespread cure in the history of psychiatry. Despite this formal change in the psychiatric status of this sexual orientation, some people in our society continue to view homosexuality as an indicator of psychological disturbance, illustrating to some the arbitrary nature of abnormality judgments (Herek, 2002).

Despite the arbitrariness of time, place, and value judgments, three criteria—distress, dysfunction, and deviance—seem to govern decisions about abnormality, and one or more of them seem to apply to virtually any behavior regarded

▶ Focus 3
Cite the three Ds that typically underlie judgments that behavior is abnormal.

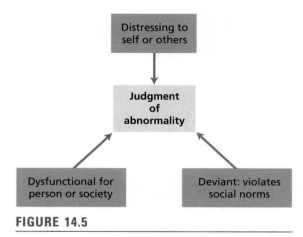

FIGURE 14.5

Deviance as a social construct. Whether a behavior is considered abnormal involves a social judgment made on the basis of the three Ds: distress, dysfunction, and deviance.

as abnormal (Figure 14.5). First, we are likely to label behaviors as abnormal if they are intensely *distressing* to the individual. People who are excessively anxious, depressed, dissatisfied, or otherwise seriously upset about themselves or about life circumstances may be viewed as disturbed, particularly if they seem to have little control over these reactions. On the other hand, personal distress is neither necessary nor sufficient to define abnormality. Some seriously disturbed mental patients are so out of touch with reality that they seem to experience little distress, and yet their bizarre behaviors are considered very abnormal. And although all of us experience suffering as a part of our lives, our distress is not likely to be judged abnormal unless it is disproportionately intense or long-lasting relative to the situation.

Second, most behaviors judged abnormal are *dysfunctional* either for the individual or for society. Behaviors that interfere with a person's ability to work or to experience satisfying relationships with other people are likely to be seen as maladaptive and self-defeating, especially if the person seems unable to control such behaviors. Some behaviors are labeled as abnormal because they interfere with the well-being of society. But even here, the standards are not cut-and-dried. For example, is a suicide bomber who detonates a bomb in a public market psychologically disturbed, a criminal, or a patriot?

The third criterion for abnormality is society's judgments concerning the *deviance* of a given behavior. Conduct within every society is regulated by *norms*, behavioral rules that specify how people are expected to think, feel, and behave. Some norms are explicitly codified as laws, and violation of these norms defines criminal behavior.

Other norms, however, are far less explicit. For example, it is generally expected in our culture that one should not carry on animated conversations with people who are not present, nor should one face the rear of an elevator and stare intently into the eyes of a fellow passenger (don't try this unless you want to see an elevator empty out quickly). People are likely to be viewed as psychologically disturbed if they violate these unstated norms, especially if the violations make others uncomfortable and cannot be attributed to environmental causes.

To summarize, both personal and social judgments of behavior enter into considerations of what is abnormal. Thus we may define **abnormal behavior** *as behavior that is personally distressing, personally dysfunctional, and/or so culturally deviant that other people judge it to be inappropriate or maladaptive.*

DIAGNOSING PSYCHOLOGICAL DISORDERS

Classification is a necessary first step toward introducing order into discussions of the nature, causes, and treatment of psychological disorders. To be scientifically and practically useful, a classification system must meet standards of diagnostic reliability and validity. **Reliability** *means that clinicians using the system should show high levels of agreement in their diagnostic decisions.* Because professionals with different types and amounts of training—including psychologists, psychiatrists, social workers, and physicians—make diagnostic decisions, the system should be couched in terms of observable behaviors that can be reliably detected in order to minimize subjective judgments (American Psychiatric Association, 2000). **Validity** *means that the diagnostic categories should accurately capture the essential features of the various disorders.* Thus if research and clinical observations show that a given disorder has four behavioral characteristics, the diagnostic category for that disorder should also have those four features. Moreover, the diagnostic categories should allow us to differentiate one psychological disorder from another.

The Diagnostic and Statistical Manual of Mental Disorders, Fourth Edition, Text Revision (DSM-IV-TR; American Psychiatric Association, 2000), is the most widely used diagnostic classification system in the United States. For each of its more than 350 diagnostic categories, the manual contains detailed lists of observable behaviors that must be present in order for a diagnosis to be made. Table 14.1 samples the range of DSM-IV-TR categories.

TABLE 14.1 A Sample of Major Diagnostic Categories in the DSM-IV-TR

1. *Anxiety disorders:* Intense, frequent, or inappropriate anxiety, but no loss of reality contact; includes phobias, generalized anxiety reactions, panic disorders, obsessive-compulsive disorders, and posttraumatic stress disorders

2. *Mood (affective) disorders:* Marked disturbances of mood, including depression and mania (extreme elation and excitement)

3. *Somatoform disorders:* Physical symptoms, such as blindness, paralysis, or pain, that have no physical basis and are assumed to be caused by psychological factors; also, excessive preoccupations and worry about health (hypochondriasis)

4. *Dissociative disorders:* Psychologically-caused problems of consciousness and self-identification, including amnesia and multiple personalities (dissociative identity disorder)

5. *Schizophrenic and other psychotic disorders:* Severe disorders of thinking, perception, and emotion that involve loss of contact with reality and disordered behavior

6. *Substance-abuse disorders:* Personal and social problems associated with the use of psychoactive substances, such as alcohol, heroin, or other drugs

7. *Sexual and gender identity disorders:* Inability to function sexually or enjoy sexuality (sexual dysfunctions); deviant sexual behaviors, such as child molestation and arousal by inappropriate objects (fetishes); strong discomfort with one's gender accompanied by the desire to be a member of the other sex

8. *Eating disorders:* Includes anorexia nervosa (self-starvation) and bulimia nervosa (patterns of bingeing and purging)

9. *Personality disorders:* Rigid, stable, and maladaptive personality patterns, such as antisocial, dependent, paranoid, and narcissistic disorders

SOURCE: Based on American Psychiatric Association, 2000.

Reflecting an awareness of interacting personal and environmental factors, the DSM allows diagnostic information to be represented along five dimensions, or *axes*, that take both the person and her or his life situation into account. Axis I, the primary diagnosis, represents the person's primary clinical symptoms, that is, the deviant behaviors or thought processes that are occurring at the present time. Axis II reflects longstanding personality disorders or mental retardation, both of which can influence the person's behavior and response to treatment. Axis III notes any medical conditions that might be relevant, such as high blood pressure or a recent concussion. Reflecting the vulnerability-stress model discussed earlier, the clinician also rates the intensity of psychosocial or environmental problems in the person's recent life on Axis IV and the person's coping resources, as reflected in recent adaptive functioning, on Axis V. Figure 14.6 shows how the axes are represented in a sample DSM-IV diagnosis.

Although the reliability and validity of DSM-IV-TR are still being evaluated, the highly specific behavioral criteria in the diagnostic categories clearly have improved Axis I reliability over earlier versions (Brown et al., 2001; Nathan &

► **Focus 4**
What is meant by diagnostic reliability and validity?

► **Focus 5**
Describe the five axes of the DSM-IV-TR.

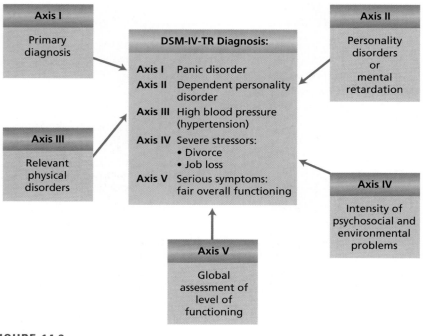

FIGURE 14.6

The DSM classification system. The DSM-IV-TR uses a five-axis system to arrive at a comprehensive diagnosis that takes into account not only deviant behaviors but also other relevant personal and environmental factors. SOURCE: Based on American Psychiatric Association, 2000.

Lagenbucher, 1999). One trade-off, however, is that the criteria are so detailed and specific that many people don't fit neatly into the categories. Moreover, debate continues over the reliability and validity of certain categories, particularly some of the Axis II personality disorders, whose characteristics overlap extensively with one another and with some Axis I disorders (Beutler & Malik, 2002). Such overlap leads to diagnostic disagreements and validity concerns about how different these disorders really are from one another (Widiger & Sankis, 2000). An important goal in the development of the next version of the DSM is to develop categories with less overlap (Helzer & Hudziak, 2002).

CONSEQUENCES OF DIAGNOSTIC LABELING

Beyond their clinical and scientific utility, diagnostic labels can have important personal, social, and legal consequences for people who receive them.

Social and Personal Consequences

Once a diagnostic label is attached to a person, it becomes all too easy to accept the label as an accurate description of the *individual* rather than of the *behavior*. It then becomes difficult to look at the

person's behavior objectively, without preconceptions about how he or she will act. It is also likely to affect how we will interact with that person. Consider how you might react if you were told that your new next-door neighbor had been diagnosed as a pedophile. It would be surprising indeed if this label did not influence your perceptions and interactions with that person, whether or not the label was accurate.

In one famous study, eight normal individuals, including psychologist David Rosenhan (1973), got themselves admitted to psychiatric hospitals in five different states by telling mental health workers that they were hearing strange voices. Not surprisingly, they received diagnoses of schizophrenia upon admission. Once in the hospitals, however, they acted completely normal for the duration of their stay. When they were discharged after intervals ranging from 7 to 52 days, they typically received the diagnosis "schizophrenia, in remission." This label means that even in the absence of deviant behavior, the disorder was still presumed to be present, though not currently active. Once attached (understandably in this case, given their reports of hearing strange voices), diagnostic labels are not easily shed even when the disordered behaviors are no longer present.

Psychiatrist Thomas Szasz (1963, 2004) has long been an outspoken critic of psychiatric diagnosis. Indeed, he argues that the concept of mental illness is itself a myth, a poor analogy to physical illness. In contrast to physical illness diagnoses, there are no clear physical criteria for mental illness. According to Szasz, the deviations that psychiatry calls *mental illness* are better viewed as "problems in living" rather than "inner disorders." He suggests that society invented the concept of mental illness to make it easier to control or change people whose behavior upsets or threatens the existing social order. Although many mental health experts disagree with Szasz's extreme argument, they readily acknowledge the arbitrary elements in judgments of deviance.

Diagnostic labels may also play a role in creating or worsening psychological disorders (Corrigan, 2005). When people become aware that a psychiatric label has been applied to them, they may accept the new identity implied by the label and develop the expected role and outlook. Because psychiatric labels often carry degrading and stigmatizing implications, the effects on morale and self-esteem can be devastating. Moreover, a person may despair of ever changing and therefore give up trying to deal with life circumstances that may be responsible for the problems. In this

▶ **Focus 6**

How can psychiatric labels affect social and self-perceptions?

way, the expectations that accompany a label may result in a self-fulfilling prophecy, in which expectation becomes reality. Many people with psychological disorders do not seek treatment because of the stigma attached to "mental illness."

Legal Consequences

Psychiatric diagnoses also have important legal consequences. Individuals judged to be dangerous to themselves or others may be involuntarily committed to mental institutions under certain circumstances. When so committed, they lose some of their civil rights and may be detained indefinitely if their behavior does not improve.

The law tries to take into account the mental status of individuals accused of crimes. Two particularly important legal concepts are *competency* and *insanity*. **Competency** *refers to a defendant's state of mind at the time of a judicial hearing* (not at the time the crime was committed). A defendant judged to be too disturbed to understand the nature of the legal proceedings may be labeled "not competent to stand trial" and institutionalized until judged competent.

Insanity *relates to the presumed state of mind of the defendant at the time the crime was committed*. Defendants may be declared "not guilty by reason of insanity" if they are judged to have been so severely impaired during the commission of a crime that they lacked the capacity either to appreciate the wrongfulness of their acts or to control their conduct. It is important to understand that insanity is a legal term, not a psychological one.

Despite the fact that the insanity plea is entered in only 1 of every 500 felony cases and that in 85 percent of those cases the prosecution agrees that the person was indeed insane, the insanity defense has long been hotly debated. There was an uproar upon the acquittal of John Hinckley, who attempted to assassinate President Ronald Reagan in 1981 (Figure 14.7). Instead of going to prison, Hinckley was committed to a mental hospital. Twelve years later, Jeffrey Dahmer, accused of the grisly murders and mutilations of 17 men, also entered a plea of not guilty by reason of insanity. The defense contended that no sane person could have committed the shocking acts that Dahmer freely admitted to doing, which included cutting up his victims and eating their body parts. Diagnostic interview and psychological test results also indicated severe psychological disturbance. Yet the insanity plea was rejected, and Dahmer was found guilty.

Both defendants clearly had serious mental disorders. Why the different verdicts? At the time

Hinckley was tried, the law required that the prosecution prove that Hinckley was *sane*. They could not do so beyond a reasonable doubt, and Hinckley was acquitted and sent to a mental hospital. Partly in response to Hinckley's acquittal, the law was changed, and the burden of proof was shifted from the prosecution to the defense, who now had to convince the jury that their client was *insane* when he committed his crimes. Dahmer's attorneys were not able to prove insanity, so Dahmer was convicted of murder.

To balance punishment for crimes with concerns about a defendant's mental status and possible need for treatment, Canada and an increasing number of U.S. jurisdictions have adopted a verdict of "guilty but mentally ill." This verdict imposes a normal sentence for a crime but sends the defendant to a mental hospital for treatment. Defendants who are considered to have recovered before serving out their time are sent to prison for the remainder of the sentence.

> ► **Focus 7**
> Contrast the legal concepts of competency and insanity. What is the current burden of proof in insanity hearings?

? What Do You Think?

"DO I HAVE THAT DISORDER?"
When people read descriptions of disorders, whether physical or psychological, they often see some of those symptoms or characteristics in themselves. In medical education, this is sometimes termed "medical students' disease." If you experience such concerns as you read about the various psychological disorders in this chapter, how should you decide whether you have a problem worthy of professional attention? After thinking about this, compare your standards with those discussed on page 571.

IN REVIEW

■ Abnormality is largely a social judgment. Behavior that is judged to reflect a psychological disorder typically is (1) distressing to the person or to other people; (2) dysfunctional, maladaptive, or self-defeating; and/or (3) socially deviant in a way that arouses discomfort in others and cannot be attributed to environmental causes.

■ The major psychiatric classification system in the United States is the DSM-IV-TR, which describes the current status of the individual using five different dimensions, or axes, that capture personal and environmental factors. Reliability (diagnostic agreement) and validity are important issues in diagnostic classification systems.

FIGURE 14.7

Both John Hinckley (*top*), who shot Ronald Reagan and his press secretary, James Brady, and the mass murderer Jeffrey Dahmer (*bottom*) pleaded not guilty by reason of insanity. Hinckley won his plea, whereas Dahmer's was rejected. These cases focused considerable attention on the insanity defense.

■ Among the important issues in psychiatric diagnosis are the potential negative effects of labeling on social perceptions and self-perceptions. Legal implications of competency and insanity judgments are also receiving attention. Competency to stand trial means that the individual is in sufficient contact with reality to understand the legal proceedings. Insanity refers to an inability to appreciate the wrongfulness of one's act or to control one's behavior at the time the crime was committed.

ANXIETY DISORDERS

We have all experienced **anxiety,** *the state of tension and apprehension that is a natural response to perceived threat.* In **anxiety disorders,** *the frequency and intensity of anxiety responses are out of proportion to the situations that trigger them, and the anxiety interferes with daily life.*

Anxiety responses have four components: (1) a *subjective-emotional* component, including feelings of tension and apprehension; (2) a *cognitive* component, including worrisome thoughts and a sense of inability to cope; (3) *physiological* responses, including increased heart rate and blood pressure, muscle tension, rapid breathing, nausea, dry mouth, diarrhea, and frequent urination; and (4) *behavioral* responses, such as avoidance of certain situations and impaired task performance (Barlow, 2002; Figure 14.8). Anxiety disorders take a number of different forms, including phobic disorder, generalized anxiety disorder, panic disorder, obsessive-compulsive disorder, and posttraumatic stress disorder.

▶ **Focus 8**
Describe the four components of anxiety.

FIGURE 14.8

Components of anxiety. Anxiety consists of subjective-emotional, cognitive, physiological, and behavioral components.

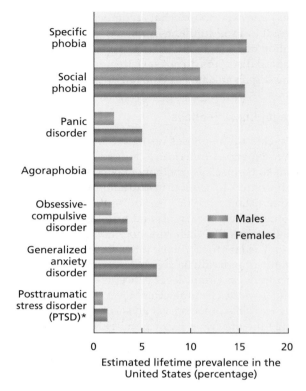

FIGURE 14.9

Prevalence rates for anxiety disorders. This graph shows the lifetime prevalence rates for anxiety disorders in men and women. All of the anxiety disorders occur more frequently in women. SOURCES: Based on Kessler et al., 1994; Robins & Regier, 1991.

Prevalence refers to the number of people who have a disorder during a specified period of time. Large-scale population studies indicate that anxiety disorders are the most prevalent psychological disorders in the United States, affecting 17.6 percent of Americans during their lifetimes (Kessler et al., 1994; Robins & Regier, 1991). Figure 14.9 shows lifetime prevalence rates for the various anxiety disorders, each of which occurs more frequently in females than in males. In more than 70 percent of cases, anxiety disorders are considered *clinically significant,* meaning that they interfere significantly with life functions or cause the person to seek medical or psychological treatment (Narrow et al., 2002).

PHOBIC DISORDER

Laura's fear of the water dates back to her childhood. She recalls that on several occasions her mother, who had a similar fear, vividly described seeing a schoolmate drown at a school picnic.

Laura's fear of water intensified after she inhaled some water and panicked when a playmate dunked her at a swimming pool. She floundered and was sure she was going to drown until a lifeguard pulled her to safety. Although she took swimming lessons as a child, she now dreads the thought of swimming or even wading. For the past 15 years, Laura has avoided outings that would take her near the ocean, a lake, or even a pool. She once turned down a free trip to Hawaii because of the anxiety she knew she would experience flying over the ocean.

Phobias *are strong and irrational fears of certain objects or situations.* The word is derived from *Phobos,* the Greek god of fear, whose likeness was painted on masks and shields to frighten enemies in battle. Today's phobic individual fights a different kind of battle, with fears of a less realistic but no less intense nature.

People with phobias realize that their fears are out of proportion to the danger involved, but they feel helpless to deal with these fears. Instead, they make strenuous efforts to avoid the phobic situation or object. Among the most common phobias in Western society are **agoraphobia**, *a fear of open or public places from which escape would be difficult;* **social phobias,** *excessive fear of situations in which the person might be evaluated and possibly embarrassed;* and **specific phobias,** *such as a fear of dogs, snakes, spiders, airplanes, elevators, enclosed spaces, water, injections, or germs.* Animal fears are common among women; fear of heights, among men (Curtis et al., 1998). Phobias can develop at any point in life, but many of them arise during childhood, adolescence, and early adulthood. Once phobias develop, they seldom go away on their own, and they may broaden and intensify over time (Stein & Hollander, 2002).

The degree of impairment produced by a phobia depends in part on how often the phobic stimulus is encountered in the individual's normal activities. For example, fear of flying is a common phobia that occurs in some 25 million Americans (Bruce & Sanderson, 1998). An airplane phobia may be a relatively minor inconvenience for a person who never needs to fly, but it would be a serious handicap for a sales representative whose job requires extensive travel. Some people, such as TV sports announcer John Madden, simply refuse to fly despite great personal inconvenience (Figure 14.10).

GENERALIZED ANXIETY DISORDER

As its name implies, **generalized anxiety disorder** *is a chronic (ongoing) state of diffuse, or free-floating, anxiety that is not attached to specific situations or objects.* The anxiety may last for months, with the signs almost continually present.

▶ **Focus 9**
Describe the features of phobic, generalized anxiety, panic, and obsessive-compulsive disorders.

FIGURE 14.10

People who suffer from phobic disorders cope in different ways. TV sports announcer John Madden (*left*) has such an intense fear of flying that he travels to his weekly assignments, sometimes separated by thousands of miles, in this specially equipped motor home. In contrast, Jenny Dibley's (*right*) acrophobia (fear of heights) has not prevented her from operating the glass-walled elevator to the top of Seattle's 600-foot Space Needle for more than 20 years. She never looks out the window or through the narrow crack between her elevator door and the observation deck. Away from her job, Ms. Dibley is afraid to climb a ladder or stand on a chair.

Emotionally, John feels jittery, tense, and constantly on edge. Cognitively, he expects something awful to happen but doesn't know what. Physically, John sweats constantly under his arms, his stomach is usually upset, he has diarrhea, and he is unable to attain a refreshing level of sleep.

As we might expect, this disorder can markedly interfere with daily functioning, even if the symptoms are not continually present for the 6 months required for a formal diagnosis (Kessler & Wittchen, 2002). The person may find it hard to concentrate, to make decisions, and to remember commitments. One large-scale study found that 5 percent of people between the ages of 15 and 45 reported having experienced the symptoms of generalized anxiety disorder. Onset tends to occur in childhood and adolescence (Wittchen et al., 1994).

PANIC DISORDER

In contrast to generalized anxiety disorder, which involves chronic tension and anxiety, **panic disorders** *occur suddenly and unpredictably, and they are much more intense.* The symptoms of panic attacks can be terrifying. As in the case of Naomi, the college student described at the beginning of the chapter, it is not unusual for victims to believe that they are dying (Ballenger, 2000).

> Ms. Watson reported that until the onset of her current problems two years ago, she had led a normal and happy life. She was returning from work one night when suddenly she felt that she couldn't catch her breath. Her heart began to pound, and she broke out into a cold sweat. Things began to seem unreal, her legs felt leaden, and she became sure she would die or faint before she reached home. She asked a passerby to help her get a taxi and went to a nearby hospital emergency room. (Spitzer et al., 1983, pp. 7–8)

As in Naomi's and Ms. Watson's cases, panic attacks usually occur out of the blue and in the absence of any identifiable stimulus. It is this unpredictable quality that makes panic attacks so mysterious and terrifying to their victims. About 60 percent of people with daytime panic disorders also experience attacks during their sleep. Their symptoms awaken them, and they fear that they are dying (Craske & Rowe, 1997).

Many people who suffer recurrent panic attacks develop agoraphobia, an aversion to public places, because they fear that they will have an attack in public. In extreme cases, they may fear leaving the familiar setting of the home, and some have been known to remain housebound for years

at a time because of their "fear of fear" (Milrod et al., 1997). Ms. Watson developed an agoraphobic pattern:

> As the attacks continued, Ms. Watson began to dread going out of the house alone. She feared that while out she would have an attack and would be stranded and helpless. She stopped riding the subway to work out of fear she might be trapped in a car between stops when an attack struck, preferring instead to walk the 20 blocks between her home and work. Social and recreational activities, previously frequent and enjoyed, were severely curtailed because an attack might occur. (Spitzer et al., 1983, p. 8)

Formal diagnosis of a panic disorder requires recurrent attacks that do not seem tied to environmental stimuli, followed by psychological or behavioral problems. These typically involve persistent fear of future attacks or agoraphobic responses. Panic disorders with or without agoraphobia tend to appear in late adolescence or early adulthood and affect about 3.5 percent of the population (Kessler et al., 1994). Even more common are occasional panic attacks. In one survey of Canadian students, 34 percent reported having had at least one unexpected panic attack within the previous year, usually during periods of extreme stress (Norton et al., 1985). Under DSM-IV-TR criteria, these students would *not* be diagnosed as having a panic disorder unless they developed an inordinate fear of having future attacks or other maladaptive behaviors such as agoraphobia.

OBSESSIVE-COMPULSIVE DISORDER

> A 38-year-old mother of one child had been obsessed by fears of contamination during her entire adult life. Literally hundreds of times a day, thoughts of being infected by germs would occur to her. Once she began to think that either she or her child might become infected, she could not dismiss the thought. The constant concern about infection resulted in a series of washing and cleaning rituals that took up most of her day. Her child was confined to one room only, which the woman tried to keep entirely free of germs by scrubbing it—floor to ceiling—several times a day. Moreover, she opened and closed all doors with her feet, in order to avoid contaminating her own hands. (Rachman & Hodgson, 1980)

This woman was diagnosed as having an *obsessive-compulsive disorder.* Such disorders usually consist of two components, one cognitive, the other behavioral, although either can occur alone.

Obsessions *are repetitive and unwelcome thoughts, images, or impulses that invade consciousness, are often abhorrent to the person, and are very difficult to dismiss or control.* This mother was tyrannized by thoughts and images of contamination. **Compulsions** *are repetitive behavioral responses*—like the woman's cleaning rituals—*that can be resisted only with great difficulty.* Compulsions are often responses that function to reduce the anxiety associated with the intrusive thoughts (Clark & O'Connor, 2005; De Silva & Rachman, 1998). Once the mother performed her compulsive cleaning acts, she was relatively free from anxiety, at least until the thoughts of contamination intruded once more.

In this case, the woman's germ obsession clearly interfered with her life, as well as her daughter's. One man's obsession resulted in a far more favorable outcome: Louis Pasteur's discovery of a process for eliminating destructive microorganisms and limiting fermentation in milk, beer, and other liquids. His tireless work on this invention was fueled in part by his own obsession about contamination and infection. Pasteur refused to shake hands with others and had a ritual of vigorously wiping his plate and glass before dining (Asimov, 1997).

Behavioral compulsions are extremely difficult to control. They often involve checking things repeatedly (for example, whether the door was locked or the gas burners on the stove were turned off), cleaning or hand washing, and repeating tasks endlessly. If the person does not perform the compulsive act, he or she may experience tremendous anxiety, perhaps even a panic attack. Like phobic avoidance responses, compulsions are strengthened through a process of negative reinforcement because they allow the person to avoid anxiety (Jenike, 1998).

Recent studies have found the lifetime prevalence of obsessive-compulsive disorder in the United States and Canada to be about 2.5 per 100 people. Onset typically occurs in the 20s (Robins & Regier, 1991; Weissman et al., 1994).

POSTTRAUMATIC STRESS DISORDER

Posttraumatic stress disorder (PTSD) *is a severe anxiety disorder that can occur in people who have been exposed to traumatic life events* (Figure 14.11). Four major symptoms commonly occur in this anxiety disorder (Falsetti et al., 2005; Wilson & Keane, 2004):

1. The person experiences severe symptoms of anxiety, arousal, and distress that were not present before the trauma.

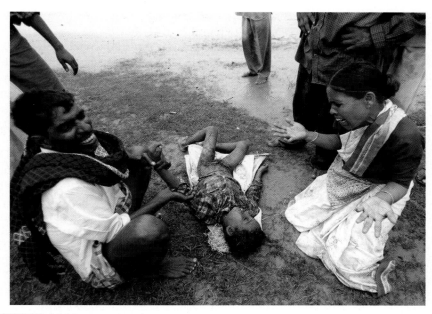

FIGURE 14.11

The devastation and loss of life caused by the 2004 Indian Ocean tsunami traumatized millions of people in 11 countries. One effect of the trauma was the development of posttraumatic stress disorder in many people, particularly those who were personally affected by the destruction.

2. The victim relives the trauma recurrently in flashbacks, in dreams, and in fantasy.

3. The person becomes numb to the world and avoids stimuli that serve as reminders of the trauma.

4. The individual experiences intense survivor guilt in instances where others were killed and the individual was somehow spared.

The PTSD category arose in part from studies of soldiers who had been subjected to the horrors of war. One study found the incidence of PTSD to be 7 times more likely for Vietnam veterans who spent significant time in combat and were wounded than for other Vietnam-era veterans (Centers for Disease Control [CDC], 1988). Another study reported a 12-month PTSD rate of 27.8 percent following combat exposure (Prigerson et al., 2002). Civilian war victims may be even more vulnerable than soldiers. Amy Ai and coworkers (2002) found a PTSD rate of 60.5 percent in a sample of refugees from the bloody civil war in Kosovo. On average, the refugees reported having experienced 15 war-related traumatic events. Traumas caused by human actions, such as war, rape, and torture, tend to precipitate more severe PTSD reactions than do natural disasters, such as hurricanes or earthquakes (Corales, 2005; O'Donohue & Elliot, 1992). Compared with men, women exhibit twice the

▶ **Focus 10**
Describe the four major features of PTSD.

rate of PTSD following exposure to traumatic events (Kimerling et al., 2003).

Terrorist acts can exact a heavy toll in PTSD. Interviews with 1,008 adult residents of Manhattan revealed that 7.5 percent experienced symptoms consistent with a PTSD diagnosis in the 5 to 8 weeks following the September 11, 2001 attacks. In those living closest to the World Trade Center, the PTSD rate was 20 percent (Galea et al., 2002).

The psychological wreckage caused by PTSD may increase vulnerability to the later development of other disorders. One study found that women who experienced PTSD had double the risk of developing a depressive disorder and 3 times the risk of developing alcohol-related problems in the future (Bresalau et al., 1997). Such findings highlight the importance of prompt post-trauma intervention aimed at preventing the development of PTSD (Litz, 2004).

CAUSAL FACTORS IN ANXIETY DISORDERS

Anxiety is a complex phenomenon having biological, psychological, and environmental causes. Within the vulnerability-stress model presented earlier, any of these factors can create predispositions to respond to stressors with an anxiety disorder.

Biological Factors

▶ **Focus 11**
What biological factors seem involved in anxiety disorders?

▶ **Focus 12**
Compare psychoanalytic and cognitive explanations of anxiety disorders.

Genetic factors may create a vulnerability to anxiety disorders (Jang, 2005). Where clinical levels of anxiety are concerned, identical twins have a concordance rate (i.e., if one twin has it, so does the other) of about 40 percent for anxiety disorders, compared with a 4 percent concordance rate in fraternal twins (Carey & Gottesman, 1981). Although such findings indicate a genetic predisposition, the concordance rate even in identical twins is far from 100 percent, indicating the significance of psychological and environmental factors.

Psychologist David Barlow (2002), a leading expert on anxiety disorders, suggests that genetically caused vulnerability may take the form of an autonomic nervous system that overreacts to perceived threat, creating high levels of physiological arousal. Hereditary factors may also cause overreactivity of neurotransmitter systems involved in emotional responses (Mineka et al., 1998). One such transmitter is GABA (gamma-aminobutyric acid), an inhibitory transmitter that reduces neural activity in the amygdala and other brain structures that trigger emotional arousal. Some researchers believe that abnormally low levels of inhibitory

GABA activity in these arousal areas may cause some people to have highly reactive nervous systems that quickly produce anxiety responses to stressors (Bremner, 2000). In support of this hypothesis, brain scans show that patients with a history of panic attacks have a 22 percent lower concentration of GABA in the occipital cortex than age-matched controls without panic disorder (Goddard et al., 2001). Such people could also be more susceptible to classically conditioned phobias because they already have a strong unconditioned arousal response in place, ready to be conditioned to new stimuli. Other transmitter systems may also be involved in the anxiety disorders.

As noted earlier, women exhibit anxiety disorders more often than men do. In a large-scale study of adolescents, Peter Lewinsohn and coworkers (1998) found that this sex difference emerges as early as 7 years of age. Even when the researchers applied statistical methods to control for sex differences in 11 psychosocial factors (including negative life events, self-esteem, and social support), a large sex difference in anxiety disorders remained. Such findings suggest a sex-linked biological predisposition for anxiety disorders, but social conditions that give women less power and personal control may also contribute (Craske, 2003). As in other instances of sex differences, it seems likely that biological, psychological, and environmental factors combine in complex ways.

Psychological Factors

Psychodynamic Theories Anxiety is a central concept in psychoanalytic conceptions of abnormal behavior. Freud referred to anxiety-based disorders as *neuroses*. According to Freud, **neurotic anxiety** *occurs when unacceptable impulses threaten to overwhelm the ego's defenses and explode into consciousness or action.* How the ego's defense mechanisms deal with neurotic anxiety determines the form of the anxiety disorder. Freud believed that in phobic disorders, neurotic anxiety is displaced onto some external stimulus that has symbolic significance in relation to the underlying conflict. For example, in one of Freud's most celebrated cases, a 5-year-old boy named Hans suddenly developed a fear of horses and the possibility of being bitten. Seeing a horse fall down near his home worsened his fear, and little Hans began to dread leaving his home. To Freud, the phobia resulted from the boy's unresolved Oedipus complex. The powerful horse represented Hans's father, and the fear of being bitten symbolized Hans's unconscious fear of being castrated by his father if he acted on his sexual desire for his mother; the falling horse symbolized Hans's forbidden triumph over his father.

Psychoanalysts believe that obsessions and compulsions are also ways of handling anxiety. According to Freud, the obsession is symbolically related to, but less terrifying than, the underlying impulse. A compulsion is a way of taking back, or undoing, one's unacceptable urges, as when obsessive thoughts about dirt and compulsive hand washing are used to deal with one's "dirty" sexual impulses. Finally, generalized anxiety and panic attacks are thought to occur when one's defenses are not strong enough to control or contain neurotic anxiety but are strong enough to hide the underlying conflict.

Cognitive Factors Cognitive theorists stress the role of maladaptive thought patterns and beliefs in anxiety disorders. People with anxiety disorders catastrophize about demands and magnify them into threats. They anticipate that the worst will happen and feel powerless to cope effectively (Clark, 1988; Mineka et al., 1998). Intrusive thoughts about the previous traumatic event are a central feature of posttraumatic stress disorder, and the presence of such thoughts after the trauma predicts the later development of PTSD (Falsetti et al., 2005).

Cognitive processes also play an important role in panic disorders. According to David Barlow (2002), panic attacks are triggered by exaggerated misinterpretations of normal anxiety symptoms, such as heart palpitations, dizziness, and breathlessness. The person appraises these as signs that a heart attack or a psychological loss of control is about to occur, and these catastrophic appraisals create even more anxiety until the process spirals out of control, producing a full-blown state of panic (Figure 14.12). Helping panic patients replace such mortal-danger appraisals with more benign interpretations of their bodily symptoms (e.g., "It's only a bit of anxiety, not a heart attack") results in a marked reduction in panic attacks (Barlow, 1997; Craske, 1999).

The Role of Learning From the behavioral perspective, classical conditioning, observational learning, or operant conditioning can contribute to the development of an anxiety disorder. Some fears are acquired as a result of traumatic experiences that produce a classically conditioned fear response (Rachman, 1998). For example, a person who has suffered a traumatic fall from a high place may develop a fear of heights (CR) because the high place (CS) was associated with the pain and trauma of the fall (UCS).

Classical conditioning cannot be the whole story, however, because many phobic people have

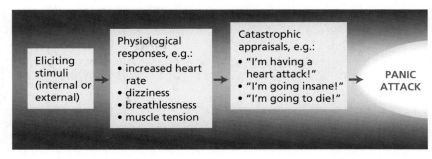

FIGURE 14.12

What causes panic attacks? Cognitive explanations of panic attacks describe a process in which normal manifestations of anxiety are appraised catastrophically, increasing anxiety to a level that ultimately results in a full-blown panic attack.

never had a traumatic experience with the phobic object or situation that they now fear (Bruce & Sanderson, 1998; Menzies & Clarke, 1995). Most people who are afraid to fly have never been in an airplane crash. So how did they learn their fear? Clearly, phobias can also be acquired through observational learning. For example, televised images of airplane crashes evoke high levels of fear in some people. Yet most people do not develop phobias under these conditions, so there must be still more going on. It may be that biological dispositions and cognitive factors help determine whether a person develops a phobia from observing or even hearing about a traumatic event. Recall, for example, how Laura's fear of the water began with her mother's description of her classmate's drowning. Thus if a person has a biological disposition toward intense fear, experiences traumatic scenes vicariously, and comes to believe that "the same thing could happen to me," the likelihood of developing a phobia on the basis of observational learning may increase.

Once anxiety is learned, either classically or vicariously, it may be triggered either by cues from the environment or by internal cues, such as thoughts and images (Pitman et al., 2000). In phobic reactions, the cues tend to be external ones relating to the feared object or situation. In panic disorders, the anxiety-arousing cues tend to be internal ones, such as bodily sensations (e.g., one's heart rate) or mental images (such as the image of collapsing and having a seizure in a public place; Craske, 1999).

In addition to classical conditioning and observational learning, operant conditioning also plays a role. People are highly motivated to avoid or escape anxiety because it is such an unpleasant emotional state. Behaviors that are successful in reducing anxiety, such as compulsions or phobic avoidance responses, become stronger through negative reinforcement. Thus the obsessive-compulsive

▶ **Focus 13**
Explain anxiety disorders in terms of classical conditioning, observational learning, and operant conditioning.

FIGURE 14.13

Panic and agoraphobia. This diagram illustrates how panic disorders contribute to the development of agoraphobia. Negative reinforcement through anxiety reduction fosters avoidance of feared situations (a), as well as an attraction to safety signals, such as one's own home (b), where panic does not occur.

FIGURE 14.14

Levels of analysis: Factors related to anxiety disorders.

mother's scrubbing ritual reduces anxiety about contamination, and Laura's avoidance of swimming prevents her from experiencing anxiety. In the case of agoraphobia, remaining at home also serves as a *safety signal,* a place where the person is unlikely to experience a panic attack (Seligman & Binik, 1977). Again, anxiety reduction reinforces the response of staying at home (Figure 14.13). Unfortunately, successful avoidance prolongs the problem because it prevents the learned anxiety response from being extinguished, which would occur eventually if these people exposed themselves to the feared stimuli enough times without experiencing the feared consequence.

Sociocultural Factors

Social and cultural factors also play a role in the development of anxiety disorders (Lopez & Guarnaccia, 2000). The role of culture is most dramatically shown in **culture-bound disorders** *that occur only in certain locales.* One such disorder found in Japan is a social phobia called *Taijin Kyofushu* (Tanaka-Matsumi, 1979). People with this disorder are pathologically fearful of offending others by emitting offensive odors, blushing, staring inappropriately, or having a blemish or improper facial expression. Taijin Kyofushu has been attributed to the Japanese cultural value of extreme interpersonal sensitivity and to cultural prohibitions against expressing negative emotions or causing discomfort in others (Kleinknecht et al., 1997). Another culture-bound disorder is *koro,* a Southeast Asian anxiety disorder in which a man fears that his penis is going to retract into his abdomen and kill him.

Western culture also spawns culture-specific anxiety reactions. Although formally classified as an eating disorder, anorexia nervosa has a strong phobic component, namely the fear of getting fat. It also has obsessive-compulsive elements. This eating disorder is found almost exclusively in developed countries, where being thin has become a cultural obsession (Becker et al., 1999).

As we have seen, the causes of anxiety disorders are complex. They often interact with one another and can be viewed at biological, psychological, and environmental levels of analysis (Figure 14.14).

LEVELS OF ANALYSIS Factors Related to Anxiety Disorders

Biological
- Evolutionary preparedness to fear certain stimuli
- Genetic predisposition
- Overreactive autonomic nervous system
- Low levels of inhibitory transmitter GABA
- Other possible neurotransmitter dysfunctions
- Possible sex-linked biological factors

Psychological
- Displacement of neurotic anxiety (e.g., phobia, obsessions)
- "Catastrophizing" appraisals of threatening events
- Exaggerated appraisals of anxiety symptoms (panic disorder)
- Classically conditioned fear responses
- Observationally learned fear responses
- Negatively reinforced avoidance responses

Environmental
- Previous exposure to aversive unconditioned stimuli
- Traumatic experiences (PTSD)
- Avoidable fear-inducing conditioned stimuli
- Exposure to fearful models or to others' traumatic experiences
- Fear-inducing media exposure
- Cultural learning experiences (culture-bound disorders)

Anxiety Disorders

IN REVIEW

- Anxiety involves four components: (1) subjective-emotional feelings of tension and discomfort; (2) cognitive processes involving worry, perceptions of threat, and lack of control; (3) excessive physiological arousal; and (4) behaviors that reflect the anxious state and others that are designed to escape or avoid the feared object or situation.

- Anxiety disorders include phobic disorder (an irrational fear of a specific object or situation), generalized anxiety disorder (recurrent anxiety reactions that are difficult to link to specific environmental stimuli), panic disorder, obsessive-compulsive disorder (which involves uncontrollable and unwelcome thoughts and repetitive behaviors), and posttraumatic stress disorder.

- Biological factors in anxiety disorders include both genetic and biochemical processes, possibly involving the action of neurotransmitters, such as GABA, within parts of the brain that control emotional arousal. The greater prevalence of anxiety disorders in women has been explained in both biological and sociocultural terms.

- Psychoanalytic theorists believe that neurotic anxiety results from the inability of the ego's defenses to deal with internal psychological conflicts. The cognitive perspective stresses the role of cognitive distortions, including the tendencies to magnify the degree of threat and danger and, in the case of panic disorder, to misinterpret normal anxiety symptoms in ways that can evoke panic.

- The behavioral perspective views anxiety as a learned response established through classical conditioning or vicarious learning. The avoidance responses in phobias and compulsive disorders are seen as operant responses that are negatively reinforced through anxiety reduction.

- Sociocultural factors are also involved in anxiety disorders, as illustrated by certain culture-bound anxiety disorders.

SOMATOFORM AND DISSOCIATIVE DISORDERS: ANXIETY INFERRED

The anxiety disorders just considered involve anxiety and stress reactions that are vividly experienced by the sufferer and, often, are externally observable. In some other disorders, however, underlying anxiety is largely inferred, or assumed to be present, rather than outwardly expressed. In somatoform and dissociative disorders, for example, the person may not consciously feel any anxiety because the function of the disorders is to protect the person from strong psychological conflict (Rosenhan & Seligman, 1989). Psychodynamic theorists believe that whatever distress the person may experience in such disorders is less stressful than the underlying anxiety that is being defended against.

SOMATOFORM DISORDERS

Somatoform disorders *involve physical complaints or disabilities that suggest a medical problem but that have no known biological cause and are not produced voluntarily by the person* (Finell, 1997). In **hypochondriasis,** *people become unduly alarmed about any physical symptom they detect and are convinced that they have or are about to have a serious illness.* People with **pain disorder** *experience intense pain that either is out of proportion to whatever medical condition they might have or for which no physical basis can be found.*

Somatoform disorders differ from *psychophysiological disorders*, in which psychological factors cause or contribute to a real medical condition, such as migraine headaches, asthma, hypertension (chronic high blood pressure), or cardiac problems. In peptic ulcers, for example, stress-produced outpouring of peptic acid into the stomach produces an actual lesion in the stomach wall. The resulting pain is therefore caused by the actual physical damage. In a somatoform disorder, no physical basis for the pain would be found.

Perhaps the most fascinating of the somatoform disorders is **conversion disorder,** *in which serious neurological symptoms, such as paralysis, loss of sensation, or blindness, suddenly occur.* In such cases, electrophysiological recordings and brain imaging indicate that sensory and motor pathways in the brain are intact (Black et al., 2004). People with conversion disorders often exhibit *la belle indifference,* a strange lack of concern about their symptom and its implications (Pajer, 2000). In some cases, the complaint itself is physiologically impossible. An example is *glove anesthesia*, in which a person loses all sensation below the wrist. As Figure 14.15 shows, the hand is served by nerves that also provide sensory input to the wrist and arm, making glove anesthesia anatomically impossible.

Although *psychogenic blindness* is rare in the general population, researchers discovered the

▶ **Focus 14**
Describe three kinds of somatoform disorders. What causal factors might be involved?

Glove   Actual nerve
anesthesia   innervation

FIGURE 14.15

An impossible conversion symptom. Glove anesthesia is a conversion disorder in which all feeling is lost below the wrist. The skin areas served by nerves in the arm make this symptom physiologically impossible.

FIGURE 14.16

A physician examines a Cambodian refugee who appears to be suffering from psychologically induced blindness. There is nothing wrong with his eyes, but he cannot see.

▶ **Focus 15**
What is the central feature of dissociative disorders? Describe the three major dissociative disorders.

largest known civilian group of people in the world with trauma-induced blindness. They were Cambodian refugees who escaped from their country and settled in southern California. These survivors of the "killing fields" of Cambodia were subjected to unspeakable horror at the hands of the Khmer Rouge in the years following the Vietnam War (Cooke, 1991). More than 150 of them became functionally blind, even though their eyes appeared intact and electrophysiological monitoring showed that visual stimuli registered in their visual cortex (Figure 14.16). Many of the victims reported that their blindness came on suddenly after they witnessed traumatic scenes of murder. Were the sights from the outer world so painful that the visual system involuntarily shut down? An intriguing but as yet unanswered question is how cultural factors might have affected the development of this response to trauma.

To Freud, conversion symptoms were a symbolic expression of an underlying conflict that aroused so much anxiety that the ego kept the conflict in the unconscious by converting the anxiety into a physical symptom. In one of Freud's cases, a young woman who was forced to take care of her hostile, verbally abusive, and unappreciative father suddenly developed paralysis in her arm. According to Freud, this occurred when her repressed hostile impulses threatened to break through and cause her to strike him using that arm (Freud, 1935). Contemporary psychodynamic theorists continue to accept explanations consistent with Freud's beliefs (Phillips, 2001).

A predisposition to somatoform disorders may involve a combination of biological and psychological vulnerabilities. Somatoform disorders tend to run in families, though it is not clear whether this reflects the role of genetic factors, environmental learning and social reinforcement for

bodily symptoms, or both (Trimble, 2003). Additionally, some people may experience internal sensations more vividly than others, or they may focus more attention on them. Somatoform patients are also very suggestible. One study found them to be far more responsive to hypnotic suggestions than were matched controls, and conversion patients' hypnotic susceptibility scores were significantly correlated with the number of conversion symptoms they reported (Roelofs et al., 2002).

The incidence of somatoform disorders tends to be much higher in cultures that discourage open discussion of emotions or that stigmatize psychological disorders (Tanaka-Matsumi & Draguns, 1997). Within western culture, there are subgroups, such as the police and military, where open discussion of feelings and self-disclosure of psychological problems are frowned on. In such settings, somatic symptoms may be the only acceptable outlet for emotional distress. The same may occur in people who are so emotionally constricted that they cannot acknowledge their emotions or verbally communicate them to others (Trae & Deighton, 2000).

DISSOCIATIVE DISORDERS

Ordinarily, personality has unity and coherence, and the many facets of the self are integrated so that people act, think, and feel with some degree of consistency. Memory plays a critical role in this integration, for it connects past with present and provides a sense of personal identity that extends over time. **Dissociative disorders** *involve a breakdown of normal personality integration, resulting in significant alterations in memory or identity.* Three forms that such disorders can take are *psychogenic amnesia, psychogenic fugue,* and *dissociative identity disorder.*

In **psychogenic amnesia,** *a person responds to a stressful event with extensive but selective memory loss.* Some people can remember nothing about their past. Others can no longer recall specific events, people, or places, although other contents of memory, such as cognitive, language, and motor skills remain intact.

Psychogenic fugue *is a more profound dissociative disorder in which a person loses all sense of personal identity, gives up her or his customary life, wanders to a new faraway location, and establishes a new identity.* Usually the fugue (derived from the Latin word *fugere,* "to flee") is triggered by a highly stressful event or trauma, and it may last from a few hours or days to several years. Some adolescent runaways have been found to be in a fugue state, and married fugue victims may wed someone else and start a new career (Loewenstein, 1991). Typically the fugue ends when the person suddenly recovers his or her original identity and "wakes up," mystified and distressed at being in a strange place under strange circumstances.

Dissociative Identity (Multiple Personality) Disorder

In **dissociative identity disorder (DID)** (formerly called *multiple personality disorder*), *two or more separate personalities coexist in the same person.* DID is the most striking and widely publicized of the dissociative disorders, and several celebrated cases have been the topic of books and movies, such as *Sybil, The Three Faces of Eve,* and *Psycho* (Figure 14.17). In DID, a primary personality, or *host personality,* appears more often than the others (called *alters*), but each personality has its own integrated set of memories and behaviors. The personalities may or may not know about the existence of the others. They can differ in age and gender. The personalities can differ not only mentally and behaviorally but also physiologically, as in the following case.

> A 38-year-old woman named Margaret was admitted to a hospital with paralysis of her legs following a minor car accident. During the course of her interview the woman, a member of an ultra-religious sect, reported that she sometimes heard a strange voice inside her threatening to "take over

FIGURE 14.17

In one celebrated depiction of dissociative identity disorder, motel clerk Norman Bates is shocked to discover the body of a woman murdered in her shower by his mother (actually his alter personality) in the movie *Psycho.*

completely." The physician suggested that she let the voice "take over." Here is his report of what happened:

> The woman closed her eyes, clenched her fists, and grimaced for a few moments during which she was out of contact with those in the room. Suddenly she opened her eyes and one was in the presence of another person. Her name, she said, was "Harriet." Whereas Margaret had been paralyzed, and complained of fatigue, headache, and backache, Harriet felt well and she at once proceeded to walk around the room unaided. She spoke scornfully of Margaret's religiousness, her invalidism, and her puritanical life, professing that she herself liked to drink and "go partying" but that Margaret was always going to church and reading the Bible. . . . At length, at the interviewer's suggestion, Harriet reluctantly agreed to "bring Margaret back" and after more grimacing and fist clenching, Margaret reappeared paralyzed, complaining of her headache and backache, and completely amnesic for the brief period of Harriet's release from her prison. (Nemiah, 1978, pp. 179–180)

Mental health workers and researchers have reported dramatic differences among the alternate personalities of DID patients, including physical health differences, voice changes, and even changes in right- and left-handedness. Some patients have severe allergies when one personality is present but no allergies when the others are active. One patient nearly died of a violent allergic reaction to a bee sting; a week later, when an alternate personality was active, another sting produced no reaction. Female patients frequently have different menstrual cycles for each female personality; one patient had three periods per month. Other patients need eyeglasses with different prescriptions for different personalities; one may be farsighted, another nearsighted (Miller et al., 1991). Epileptic patients with DID often have their seizures in one personality but not another (Drake et al., 1988).

What Causes DID?

According to Frank Putnam's **trauma-dissociation theory,** *the development of new personalities occurs in response to severe stress.* For the vast majority of patients, this begins in early childhood, frequently in response to physical or sexual abuse. Putnam (1989) studied the life histories of 100 diagnosed DID cases and found that 97 of them reported severe abuse and trauma in early and middle childhood, a time when children's identities are not well established and it is quite easy for them to dissociate. Putnam believes that in response to the

▶ **Focus 16**
Summarize the trauma-dissociation theory of DID. On what grounds do critics challenge and explain DID?

trauma and their helplessness to resist it, children may engage in something akin to self-hypnosis and dissociate from reality. They create an alternate identity to detach themselves from the trauma, to transfer what is happening to someone else who can handle it, and to blunt the pain. Over time, it is theorized, the protective functions served by the new personality remain separate in the form of an alternate personality rather than being integrated into the host personality (Meyer & Osborne, 1987; Putnam, 2000).

DID has become a controversial diagnosis. Some critics question how often it actually occurs, and others question its very existence (Beahrs, 1994; Spanos, 1994). Prior to 1970, only about 100 cases had been reported worldwide, and even today DID is virtually unknown in many cultures, including Japan (Takahashi, 1990). But after the disorder was highly publicized in popular books and movies, many additional cases appeared, numbering in the tens of thousands by the mid-1990s. The number of alternate personalities also had increased from 2 or 3 to an average of about 15 (Spanos, 1994). Could this dramatic increase in the prevalence of DID and number of alters be the result of publicity and patient or therapist expectations? As we noted in our discussion of hypnosis in Chapter 5, people can become so immersed in an imagined role (such as an alter personality) that it becomes quite real to them, and they act accordingly (Spanos, 1996). The controversy that swirls around DID is inspiring research that may advance our understanding of factors that can produce alterations in memory, physiological responses, and behavior.

 What Do You Think?

DID: DISSOCIATION OR ROLE-PLAYING?
Suppose you knew of several experimental studies that convincingly demonstrated that average people could, by means of role-playing, produce all of the DID phenomena described in this section. What would this tell you about the validity of the DID cases described by mental health workers? Think about it, then see the discussion on page 571.

IN REVIEW

- Somatoform disorders involve physical complaints that do not have a physiological explanation. They include hypochondriasis, pain disorders, and conversion disorders.

- Familial similarities in somatoform disorders may have a biological basis, or they may be the result of environmental shaping through attention and sympathy. Somatoform patients may be highly vigilant and reactive to somatic symptoms. Such disorders tend to occur with greater frequency in cultures that discourage open expression of negative emotions.

- Dissociative disorders involve losses of memory and personal identity. The major dissociative disorders are psychogenic amnesia, psychogenic fugue, and dissociative identity disorder (DID).

- The trauma-dissociation theory holds that DID emerges when children dissociate to defend themselves from severe trauma or sexual abuse. This model has been challenged by other theorists who believe that multiple personalities result from role immersion and therapist expectations.

MOOD DISORDERS

Another set of emotion-based disorders are **mood disorders,** *which include depression and mania (excessive excitement).* Together with anxiety disorders, mood disorders are the most frequently experienced psychological disorders. There is high *comorbidity* (co-occurrence) involving anxiety and mood disorders. About half of all depressed people also experience an anxiety disorder.

DEPRESSION

Almost everyone has experienced depression, at least in its milder and more temporary forms. Loss and pain are inevitable parts of life, and when they occur, most of us feel blue, sad, discouraged, apathetic, and passive. The future looks bleak, and some of the zest goes out of living. Such reactions are normal; at any point in time, 25 to 30 percent of college undergraduates experience mild depression (Seligman, 1991). These feelings usually fade after the event has passed or as the person becomes accustomed to the new situation.

In clinical depression, however, the frequency, intensity, and duration of depressive symptoms are out of proportion to the person's life situation. Some people may respond to a minor setback or loss with **major depression,** *an intense depressed state that leaves them unable to function effectively in their lives.* Mark, the young man described at the beginning of the chapter, suffers from a major depression. Other people exhibit **dysthymia,** *a less*

► **Focus 17**
Describe the four classes of symptoms that characterize depression. What is bipolar disorder?

intense form of depression that has less dramatic effects on personal and occupational functioning. Dysthymia, though less intense, is a more chronic and longer-lasting form of misery, occurring for years on end with some intervals of normal mood that never last more than a few weeks or months.

The *negative mood state* is the core feature of depression. When depressed people are asked how they feel, they most commonly report sadness, misery, and loneliness. Whereas people with anxiety disorders retain their capacity to experience pleasure, depressed people lose it (Mineka et al., 1998). Activities that used to bring satisfaction and happiness feel dull and flat. Even biological pleasures, such as eating and sex, lose their appeal.

Although depression is primarily a disorder of emotion or mood, there are three other types of symptoms: cognitive, motivational, and somatic (physical) (Figure 14.18). *Cognitive symptoms* are a central part of depression. Depressed people have difficulty concentrating and making decisions. They usually have low self-esteem, believing that they are inferior, inadequate, and incompetent. When setbacks occur in their lives, depressed people tend to blame themselves; when failure has not yet occurred, they expect that it will and that it will be caused by their own inadequacies. Depressed people almost always view the future with great pessimism and hopelessness (Clark et al., 1999).

Motivational symptoms in depression involve an inability to get started and to perform behaviors that might produce pleasure or accomplishment. A depressed student may be unable to get out of bed in the morning, let alone go to class or study. Everything seems too much of an effort. In extreme depressive reactions, the person may have to be prodded out of bed, clothed, and fed. In some cases of severe depression, the person's movements slow down and she or he walks or talks slowly and with excruciating effort.

Somatic (bodily) *symptoms* often include loss of appetite and weight loss in moderate and severe depression, whereas in mild depression, weight gain sometimes occurs as a person eats compulsively. Sleep disturbances, particularly insomnia, are common. Sleep disturbance and weight loss lead to fatigue and weakness, which tend to add to the depressed feelings. Depressed people also may lose sexual desire and responsiveness.

BIPOLAR DISORDER

When a person experiences only depression, the disorder is called *unipolar depression.* In a **bipolar disorder,** *depression (which is usually the dominant state) alternates with periods of* **mania,** *a state of*

Emotional symptoms
- Sadness
- Hopelessness
- Anxiety
- Misery
- Inability to enjoy

Cognitive symptoms
- Negative cognitions about self, world, and future

DEPRESSION

Motivational symptoms
- Loss of interest
- Lack of drive
- Difficulty starting anything

Somatic symptoms
- Loss of appetite
- Lack of energy
- Sleep difficulties
- Weight loss/gain

FIGURE 14.18

Facets of depression. Depression includes emotional, cognitive, motivational, and somatic features.

Watch the video, "Bipolar Disorder," in Chapter 14 of your CD for insights into one man's lifelong struggle to overcome bipolar disorder.

highly excited mood and behavior that is quite the opposite of depression. In a manic state, mood is euphoric and cognitions are grandiose. The person sees no limits to what he or she can accomplish and fails to consider negative consequences that may ensue if grandiose plans are acted on. At a motivational level, manic behavior is hyperactive. The manic person engages in frenetic activity, be it in work, in sexual relationships, or in other areas of life. The 19th-century composer Robert Schumann produced 27 works during a one-year manic phase, but his productivity ground to a halt when he sank back into the depressive phase of his bipolar disorder (Jamison, 1995). Manic people can become very irritable and aggressive when their momentary goals are frustrated in any way.

In a manic state, speech is often rapid or pressured, as if the person must say as many words as possible in the time allotted. With this flurry of activity comes a greatly lessened need for sleep. A person may go for several days without sleeping, until exhaustion inevitably sets in and the mania slows down. The following case illustrates a severe manic episode:

Robert B, a 56-year-old dentist, awoke one morning with the idea that he was the most gifted dental surgeon in his tri-state area; his mission then was to provide service for as many persons as possible so that they could benefit from his talents. Consequently, he decided to enlarge his 2-chair practice to a 20-chair one, and his plan was to reconstruct his two dental offices into 20 booths so that he could simultaneously attend to as many patients. That very day he drew up the plans for this arrangement and telephoned a number of remodelers and invited them to submit bids for the work.

Toward the end of that day he became irritated with the "interminable delays" and, after he attended to his last patient, rolled up his sleeves and began to knock down the walls of his dental offices. When he discovered that he couldn't manage this chore with the sledge hammer he had purchased for this purpose earlier, he became frustrated and proceeded to smash his more destructible tools, washbasins, and X-ray equipment. He justified this behavior in his own mind by saying, "This junk is not suitable for the likes of me; it'll have to be replaced anyway."

He was in perpetual motion and his speech was "overexcited." When Robert was later admitted to a hospital, he could not sit in his chair; instead he paced the office floor like a caged animal. (Kleinmuntz, 1980, pp. 309–310)

PREVALENCE AND COURSE OF MOOD DISORDERS

Epidemiological studies in the United States suggest that at this moment, about 1 in 20 Americans is severely depressed (Narrow et al., 2002). Statistically, the chances are that nearly 1 in 5 Americans will have a depressive episode of clinical proportions at least once in her or his lifetime. No age group is exempt from depression. It appears in infants as young as 6 months who have been separated from their mothers for prolonged periods. The rate of depressive symptoms in children and adolescents is as high as the adult rate (Essau & Petermann, 1999).

Data from numerous studies indicate that depression is on the rise among young people, with the onset of depression increasing dramatically in 15- to 19-year-olds (Burke et al., 1991). Figure 14.19

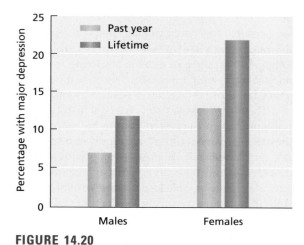

FIGURE 14.20

Sex differences in depression. This graph shows the prevalence rates for major depression in men and women. Source: Based on Kessler et al., 1994.

shows that the lifetime prevalence of major depression in the United States has increased in every decade since the 1930s, and the steepness of the curve indicates an earlier onset in those born after 1966.

Prevalence of depressive disorders is similar across socioeconomic and ethnic groups, but there is a major sex difference in our culture. Although men and women do not differ in prevalence of bipolar disorder, women appear to be about twice as likely as men to suffer unipolar depression (Figure 14.20). Women are most likely to suffer their first episode of depression in their 20s, men in their 40s (Keyes & Goldman, 2006).

Many people who suffer depressive episodes never seek treatment. What is likely to happen to such people? Perhaps the one positive thing that can be said about depression is that it usually dissipates over time. After the initial episode, which typically comes on suddenly after a stressful experience, depression typically lasts an average of 5 to 10 months when untreated (Tollefson, 1993).

Once a depressive episode has occurred, one of three patterns may follow. In perhaps 40 percent of all cases, clinical depression will not recur following recovery. Many other cases show a second pattern: recovery with recurrence. On average, these people will remain symptom-free for perhaps 3 years before experiencing another depressive episode of about the same severity and duration. The interval between subsequent episodes of depression tends to become shorter over the years (Rubin, 2000). Finally, about 10 percent of people who have a major depressive

FIGURE 14.19

The rising incidence of depression. Depression rates in the United States have increased every decade from the 1930s to the 1990s. Some theorists think that the "me" generation, with its emphasis on individual attainment and reduced commitment to traditional values of family, religion, and the common good, has sowed the seeds of its own depression. Source: U.S. Department of Health and Human Services, 2002.

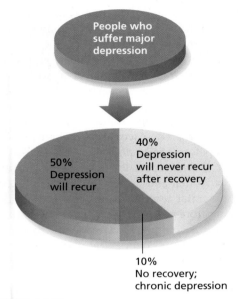

FIGURE 14.21

What follows major depression? One of three outcomes may follow a major depressive episode. About 40 percent never have a recurrence, perhaps 50 percent have a recurrence, and about 10 percent suffer chronic (ever present) depression.

episode will not recover and will remain chronically depressed (Figure 14.21).

Manic episodes, though less common than depressive reactions, are far more likely to recur. Fewer than 1 percent of the population experiences mania, but more than 90 percent of those who do have a recurrence (American Psychiatric Association, 2000; Kessler et al., 1994).

CAUSAL FACTORS IN MOOD DISORDERS

As in the case of anxiety disorders, the mood disorders are a product of interacting biological, psychological, and environmental factors.

Biological Factors

Both genetic and neurochemical factors have been linked to depression (Donaldson, 1998). Genetic factors surface in both twin and adoption studies (McGuffin et al., 2005). Identical twins have a concordance rate of about 67 percent for experiencing clinical depression, compared with a rate of only 15 percent for fraternal twins (Gershon et al., 1989). Among adopted people who develop depression, biological relatives are about 8 times more likely than adoptive relatives to also suffer from depression (Wender et al., 1986). What is likely to be inherited is a predisposition to develop a depressive disorder, given certain kinds of

environmental factors such as significant losses and low social support (Barondes, 1999; Jang, 2005).

Increasingly, biological research has focused on the possible role of brain chemistry in depression. One influential theory holds that depression is a disorder of motivation caused by underactivity in a family of neurotransmitters that include norepinephrine, dopamine, and serotonin (Davidson, 1998). These transmitters play important roles in several brain regions involved in experiencing reward and pleasure. When neural transmission decreases in these brain regions, the result is the lack of pleasure and loss of motivation that characterize depression (Donaldson, 1998; White & Milner, 1992). Also in support of this theory, several highly effective antidepressant drugs operate by increasing the activity of these neurotransmitters, thereby further stimulating the neural systems that underlie positive mood and goal-directed behavior. A study by Lescia Tremblay and coworkers (2002) tested the amount of reward experienced by depressed patients when these centers were activated by a stimulant drug. As shown in Figure 14.22, severely depressed individuals showed a much stronger pleasure response to the drug, supporting the hypothesis of a "pleasure deficit" in the brain. Later research by Ian Gotlib and coworkers (2004a) using fMRI readings of emotion areas of the brain showed low levels of neuron responsiveness to both happy and sad scenes, as if the emotion response systems had shut down. This may account for the lack of positive emotionality and the "emptiness" of the depressive emotional experience.

Bipolar disorder, in which depression alternates with less frequent periods of mania, has been studied primarily at the biological level because it appears to have a stronger genetic basis than does unipolar depression (Young & Joffe,

▶ **Focus 18**
What evidence exists for genetic and biochemical factors in depression and mania?

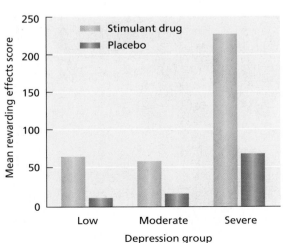

FIGURE 14.22

An underactive reward system? This graph shows an increase in pleasure ratings produced by a stimulant drug or a placebo in nondepressed, moderately depressed, and severely depressed males and females. The magnitude of the increase in pleasure reported by severely depressed people suggests a normally underactive reward system in the brain. SOURCE: Adapted from Tremblay et al., 2002.

1997). Among both men and women, the lifetime risk of developing a bipolar disorder is just below 1 percent. Yet about 50 percent of patients with bipolar disorder have a parent, grandparent, or child with the disorder (Barondes, 1999; Rubin, 2000). The concordance rate for bipolar disorder is 5 times higher in identical twins than in fraternal twins, suggesting a genetic link.

Manic disorders may stem from an overproduction of the same neurotransmitters that are underactive in depression. This might explain the symptom picture that is quite the opposite of that seen in depression. Significantly, lithium chloride, the drug most frequently used to calm manic disorders, works by decreasing the activity of these transmitters in the brain's motivational/pleasure activation system (LeMoal, 1999; Robinson, 1997).

Psychological Factors

Biological factors seem to increase vulnerability to certain types of psychological and environmental events that can then trigger the disorders. Other perspectives specify what those events might be.

Personality-Based Vulnerability Psychoanalysts Karl Abraham (1911) and Sigmund Freud (1917/1957) believed that early traumatic losses or rejections create vulnerability for later depression by triggering a grieving and rage process that becomes part of the individual's personality (Figure 14.23). Subsequent losses and rejection

► **Focus 19**
Describe the cognitive triad, the depressive attributional pattern, and learned helplessness in relation to depression.

FIGURE 14.23

Psychoanalysts believe that early catastrophic losses increase vulnerability to later depressive disorders.

reactivate the original loss and cause a reaction not only to the current event but also to the unresolved loss from the past.

Were he alive today, Freud would surely point to research by the British sociologists George Brown and Terrill Harris (1978) to support his theory of early loss. Brown and Harris interviewed women in London and found that the rate of depression among women who had lost their mothers before age 11 and who had also experienced a severe recent loss was almost 3 times higher than that among women who had experienced a similar recent loss but had not lost their mothers before age 11. Experiencing the death of a father during childhood is also associated with increased risk of later depression (Barnes & Prosen, 1985; Bowlby, 2000).

Cognitive Processes According to Aaron Beck (1976), depressed people victimize themselves through their own beliefs that they are defective, worthless, and inadequate. They also believe that whatever happens to them is bad and that negative things will continue happening because of their personal defects (Clark et al., 1989). This **depressive cognitive triad** *of negative thoughts concerning (1) the world, (2) oneself, and (3) the future* seems to pop into consciousness automatically, and many depressed people report that they cannot control or suppress the negative thoughts (Wenzlaff et al., 1988). Depressed people also tend to recall most of their failures and few of their successes, and they tend to focus much of their attention on their perceived inadequacies (Clark et al., 1999; Haaga et al., 1991). Depressed people also detect pictures of sad faces at lower exposure times and remember them better than do nondepressed people (Gotlib et al., 2004b), indicating a perceptual and memory sensitivity to the negative.

As noted in the discussion of self-enhancement tendencies in Chapter 12, most people tend to take personal credit for the good outcomes in their lives and to blame their misfortunes on factors outside themselves, thereby maintaining and enhancing their self-esteem. According to Beck, depressed people do exactly the opposite: They exhibit a **depressive attributional pattern,** *attributing successes or other positive events to factors outside the self while attributing negative outcomes to personal factors* (Figure 14.24). Beck believes that taking no credit for successes but blaming themselves for failures helps depressed people maintain low self-esteem and their belief that they are worthless failures. Quite literally, they can't win, even when they do!

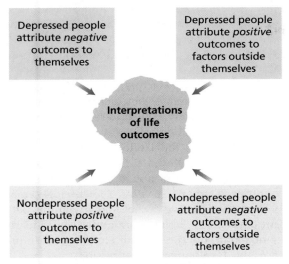

Depressive attributional pattern

Depressed people attribute *negative* outcomes to themselves

Depressed people attribute *positive* outcomes to factors outside themselves

Interpretations of life outcomes

Nondepressed people attribute *positive* outcomes to themselves

Nondepressed people attribute *negative* outcomes to factors outside themselves

Self-enhancement attributional pattern (nondepressed people)

FIGURE 14.24

The depressive attributional pattern. Cognitive theorists believe that the attributional patterns of depressed people are the opposite of the self-enhancing patterns that characterize nondepressed people. In the depressive attributional pattern, people attribute negative outcomes to themselves and positive outcomes to factors outside themselves.

Another prominent cognitive account of depression, **learned helplessness theory,** *holds that depression occurs when people expect that bad events will occur and that there is nothing they can do to prevent them or cope with them* (Abramson et al., 1978; Seligman & Isaacowitz, 2000). The depressive attributional pattern plays a central role in the learned helplessness model, but learned helplessness theorists take it a step further by specifying what the negative attributions for failures are like. They suggest that chronic and intense depression occurs as the result of negative attributions for failures that are personal ("It's all *my* fault"), stable ("I'll *always* be this way"), and global ("I'm a *total* loser"). Thus people who attribute negative events in their lives to factors such as low intelligence, physical repulsiveness, or an unlovable personality tend to believe that their personal defects will render them helpless to avoid negative events in the future, and their sense of hopelessness places them at significantly greater risk for depression.

Learning and Environmental Factors   The behavioral perspective also has important things to say about depression. Peter Lewinsohn and his colleagues (1985) believe that depression is usually triggered by a loss, by some other punishing event, or by a drastic decrease in the amount of positive

reinforcement that the person receives from her or his environment. As the depression begins to take hold, people stop performing behaviors that previously provided reinforcement, such as hobbies and socializing. Moreover, depressed people tend to make others feel anxious, depressed, and hostile (Joiner & Coyne, 1999). Eventually, these other people begin to lose patience, failing to understand why the person doesn't snap out of it. This diminishes social support still further and may eventually cause depressed people to be abandoned by those who are most important to them (Nezlek et al., 2000). Longitudinal studies show that reductions in social support are a good predictor of subsequent depression (Burton, 2004). Figure 14.25 shows the cyclical course of depression.

Behavioral theorists believe that to begin feeling better, depressed people must break this vicious cycle by initially forcing themselves to engage in behaviors that are likely to produce some degree of pleasure. Eventually, positive reinforcement produced by this process of *behavioral activation* will begin to counteract the depressive affect, undermine the sense of hopelessness that characterizes depression, and increase feelings of personal control over the environment (Martell et al., 2004).

Environmental factors may also help explain why depression tends to run in families. Constance Hammen (1991) studied the family histories of depressed people and concluded that children of depressed parents often experience poor parenting and many stressful experiences as they grow up.

▶ **Focus 20**
How does Lewinsohn's learning theory explain the spiraling-downward course that occurs in depression?

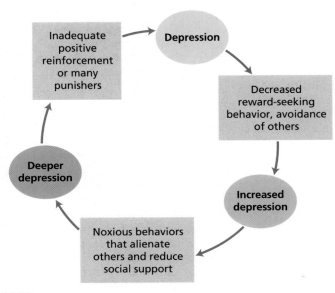

FIGURE 14.25

Lewinsohn's behavioral model of depression. Behaviorists focus on the environmental causes and effects of depression. Depression results from loss of positive reinforcement and produces further declines in reinforcement and social support in a vicious-cycle fashion.

As a result, they may fail to develop good coping skills and a positive self-concept, making them more vulnerable later in life to stressful events that can trigger depressive reactions. This conclusion is supported by findings that children of depressed parents exhibit a significantly higher incidence of depression and other disorders as adolescents and young adults (Lieb et al., 2002).

Sociocultural Factors

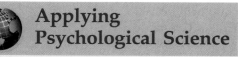

▶ Focus 21
How are sociocultural factors related to prevalence, manifestations, and sex differences in depression?

▶ Focus 22
What are the major motives and risk factors for suicide? Describe four guidelines for helping a suicidal person.

Although depression exists in virtually all cultures, its prevalence, symptom pattern, and causes reflect cultural variation (Lopez & Guarnaccia, 2000). For example, the prevalence of depressive disorders is far lower in Hong Kong and Taiwan than in Western nations. People in these societies tend to have strong social support from family and other groups, which helps reduce the negative impact of loss and disappointments when they occur (Tseng et al., 1990).

Cultural factors also can affect the ways in which depression is manifested. Feelings of guilt and personal inadequacy seem to predominate in North American and western European countries, whereas somatic symptoms of fatigue, loss of appetite, and sleep difficulties are more often reported in Latin, Chinese, and African cultures (Manson, 1994).

Finally, cultural factors may influence who develops depression. As noted earlier, women are about twice as likely as men to report feeling depressed in technologically advanced countries such as Canada, the United States, and other Western nations (Keyes & Goodman, 2006). Yet this sex difference is not found in developing countries (Culbertson, 1997; Nolen-Hoeksema, 1990). At present, we do not know why this pattern occurs, but attempts are underway to learn more about how the cultural environment influences the development of depression.

At one time or another, many depressed people consider suicide as a way to escape from the unhappiness of their lives. We now examine suicide, its causes, and what can be done to prevent this tragic event.

Applying Psychological Science   Understanding and Preventing Suicide

Suicide *is the willful taking of one's own life.* The World Health Organization estimates that worldwide, nearly 500,000 people commit suicide each year—almost 1 per minute. Ten times that number engage in nonfatal suicide attempts. In the United States, suicide is the second most frequent cause of death (after accidents) among high school and college students, and suicide rates among 15- to 24-year-olds tripled between 1957 and 1992 (Figure 14.26; National Center for Health Statistics, 1995). More suicides (31,000) than homicides (23,000) occur in the United States each year (CDC, 2002a).

Women attempt suicide about 3 times more often than men, but men are 3 times more likely to actually kill themselves. These differences may be due to (1) a higher incidence of depression in women and (2) men's choice of more lethal methods, such as shooting themselves or jumping off buildings. The suicide rate for both men and women is higher among those who have been divorced or widowed. Women's suicides are more likely to be triggered by failures in love relationships, whereas career failure more often prompts men's suicides (Shneidman, 1976). A history of sexual or physical abuse significantly increases the likelihood of later suicide attempts (Garnefski & Arends, 1998).

Depression is one of the strongest predictors of suicide. About 15 percent of clinically depressed individuals will

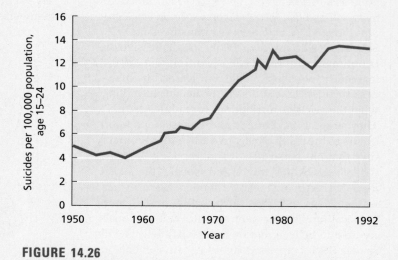

FIGURE 14.26

The rising suicide rate in young people. This graph illustrates the suicide rate per 100,000 persons ages 15 to 24, from 1950 to 1992. Source: Based on National Center for Health Statistics, 1995.

eventually kill themselves, a rate that is 22 to 36 times higher than the suicide rate for the general population. An estimated 80 percent of suicidal people are significantly depressed

(Yen et al., 2003). It is noteworthy, however, that suicides do not usually occur when depression is deepest. Instead, suicide often occurs unexpectedly as a depressed person seems to be emerging from depression and feeling better. The lifting of depression may provide the energy needed to complete the suicidal act but not reduce the person's underlying sense of hopelessness and despair.

MOTIVES FOR SUICIDE

There appear to be two fundamental motivations for suicide: the desire to end one's life and the desire to manipulate and coerce other people into doing what the suicidal person wants (Beck et al., 1979; Shneidman, 1998). Those who wish to end their lives have basically given up. They see no other way to deal with intolerable emotional distress, and in death they see an end to their problems. In one study, 56 percent of suicide attempts were classified as having been motivated by the desire to die (Beck, 1976). These attempts were accompanied by high levels of depression and hopelessness, and they tended to be more lethal than other suicide attempts. In some instances, a suicide decision is based on a desire to stop being a burden to others.

The second primary motivation for suicide is manipulation of others. Many *parasuicides* (suicide attempts that do not end in death) are cries for help or attempts to coerce people to meet one's needs. Trying to prevent a lover from ending a relationship, induce guilt in others, or dramatize one's suffering are manipulative motives. Manipulative suicide attempters tend to use less lethal means (such as drug overdose or wrist slashing) and to make sure help is available. In the study cited earlier (Beck, 1976), 13 percent of the suicide attempts were classified as manipulative. The remaining 31 percent combined the two types of motivation. A small minority of suicides result from altruistic decisions to sacrifice one's life for the survival of others; examples include the soldier who dives on a hand grenade to save his comrades' lives or the mother who elects to give birth rather than aborting her baby, knowing that she will die in the process.

WARNING SIGNS FOR SUICIDE

The best predictor of suicide attempts in both men and women is a verbal or behavioral threat to commit suicide, and such threats should always be taken seriously. One of the most destructive myths about suicide is that people who talk openly about suicide are just seeking attention and don't actually intend to carry out the act. Yet research shows that a high proportion of suicide attempts—perhaps 80 percent—are preceded by some kind of warning (Bagley & Ramsay, 1997). Sometimes the warning is an explicit statement of intent, such as "I don't want to go on living" or "I won't be a burden much longer." Other times, the warnings are more subtle, as when a person expresses hopelessness about the future, withdraws from others or from favorite activities, gives away treasured possessions, or takes unusual risks. Other important risk factors are a history of previous suicide attempts and a detailed plan that involves a lethal method (Chiles & Strossahl, 1995; Shneidman, 1998). Substance use and abuse also increase suicide risk (Yen et al., 2003).

SUICIDE PREVENTION: WHAT YOU CAN DO

Scientific research has taught us much about the dynamics and prevention of suicide. These findings provide the following guidelines for preventing this tragic answer to life's problems and for helping potentially suicidal people:

1. Another myth about suicide is that broaching the topic with a potentially suicidal person may prompt the person to carry out the act. In truth, the best first step if you suspect that someone may be suicidal is to ask the person directly whether he or she is considering suicide: "Have you thought about hurting yourself or ending your life?" If the person responds affirmatively, try to find out if he or she has a plan or a timeframe in mind. Do not be hesitant to approach the person. *Diffusion of responsibility* (discussed in Chapters 2 and 16) could result in your assuming that someone else is helping the person when in fact no one is (Goldsmith, 2003). Your ultimate goal should be to help the person receive assistance from a qualified professional as soon as possible, not to treat the person yourself. Nonetheless, you can take some immediate steps that may be helpful.

2. Many suicidal people feel alone in their misery. It is important to provide social support and empathy at this critical juncture. An expression of genuine concern can pave the way for other potentially helpful interventions (Barnett & Porter, 1998). For example, a frank discussion of the problem that is foremost in the person's life can be helpful. Suicidal people often feel totally overwhelmed by life, and focusing on a specific problem may help the person realize that it is not unsolvable and need not cloud his or her total perception of life.

3. When people are distressed and hopeless, their time orientation tends to narrow, and they have difficulty seeing beyond their current distress. Try to help the person see his or her present situation within a wider time perspective and to consider positive possibilities that might exist in the future. In particular, discuss reasons for continuing to live, and focus on any doubts the person might have about electing suicide. For example, if the person indicates that his or her family will suffer greatly from the suicide, adopt this as one of your arguments for finding a different solution to the problem. Many suicidal people would like to feel that they do not have to commit suicide. Capitalize on such feelings.

4. If a person is suicidal, stay with him or her and seek professional assistance. Most cities have suicide-prevention centers that offer 24-hour services, including telephone and direct counseling. These centers are usually listed under *suicide* or *crisis* in the phone book.

IN REVIEW

■ Mood disorders include several depressive disorders and bipolar disorder, in which intermittent periods of mania (intense mood and behavior activation) occur. Depression has four sets of symptoms: emotional, cognitive, motivational, and somatic. The symptoms of negative emotions and thoughts, loss of motivation, and behavioral slowness are reversed in mania.

■ Both genetic and neurochemical factors have been linked to depression. One prominent biochemical theory links depression to an underactivity of neurotransmitters (norepinephrine, dopamine, and serotonin) that activate brain areas involved in pleasure and positive motivation. Drugs that relieve depression increase the activity of these transmitters. Bipolar disorder seems to have an even stronger genetic component than unipolar depression does.

■ Psychoanalytic theorists view depression as a long-term consequence of traumatic losses and rejections early in life that create a personality vulnerability pattern.

■ Cognitive theorists emphasize the role of negative beliefs about the self, the world, and the future (the depressive cognitive triad) and describe a depressive attributional pattern, in which negative outcomes are attributed to personal causes and successes to situational causes. Seligman's theory of learned helplessness suggests that attributing negative outcomes to personal, stable, and global causes fosters depression.

■ The behavioral approach focuses on the vicious cycle in which depression-induced inactivity and aversive behaviors reduce reinforcement from the environment and thereby increase depression still further.

■ Manipulation and a desire to escape distress are the two major motives for suicide. The risk for suicide increases if the person is depressed and has a lethal plan and a past history of parasuicide.

SCHIZOPHRENIA

▶ **Focus 23**
What is meant by the term schizophrenia? What are its major cognitive, behavioral, emotional, and perceptual features?

Of all the psychological disorders, schizophrenia is the most bizarre and, in many ways, the most puzzling. It is also one of the most challenging disorders to treat effectively (Hogarty, 2003). Despite many theories of schizophrenia and thousands of research studies, a complete understanding of this disorder continues to elude us. **Schizophrenia** *includes severe disturbances in thinking, speech, perception, emotion, and behavior* (Herz & Marder, 2002). Schizophrenia is one of a family of *psychotic* disorders, all of which involve some loss of contact with reality, as well as bizarre behaviors and experiences.

The term *schizophrenia* was introduced by the Swiss psychiatrist Eugen Bleuler in 1911. Literally, the term means "split mind," which has often led people to confuse schizophrenia with dissociative identity disorder ("split personality") or with a Dr. Jekyll–Mr. Hyde phenomenon. But multiple personalities are not what Bleuler had in mind when he coined the term. Instead, he intended to suggest that certain psychological functions, such as thought, language, and emotion, which are normally integrated with one another, are somehow split apart or disconnected in schizophrenia.

CHARACTERISTICS OF SCHIZOPHRENIA

A diagnosis of schizophrenia requires evidence that a person misinterprets reality and exhibits disordered attention, thought, or perception. In addition, she or he typically withdraws from social interactions, communicates in strange or inappropriate ways, neglects personal grooming, and behaves in a disorganized fashion (American Psychiatric Association, 1994, 2000).

The schizophrenic thought disorder sometimes entails **delusions,** *false beliefs that are sustained in the face of evidence that normally would be sufficient to destroy them.* A schizophrenic person may believe that his brain is being turned to glass by ray guns operated by his enemies from outer space (a *delusion of persecution*) or that Jesus Christ is one of his special agents (a *delusion of grandeur*). Several aspects of thought disorder were described by a schizophrenic patient during a period of recovery:

> The most wearing aspect of schizophrenia is the fierce battle that goes on inside my head in which conflicts become unresolvable. I am so ambivalent that my mind can divide on a subject, and those two parts subdivide over and over until my mind feels like it is in pieces, and I am totally disorganized. At other times, I feel like I am trapped inside my head, banging against its walls, trying desperately to escape while my lips can utter only nonsense. (*New York Times,* March 18, 1986, p. C12)

Perceptual disorganization and disordered thought become more pronounced as people progress into a schizophrenic condition (McKenna & Oh, 2003). Unwanted thoughts constantly intrude into consciousness (Morrison, 2005). What the world might come to look like from inside the schizophrenic mind is illustrated in art created by schizophrenic patients during periods of disturbance (Figure 14.27b). Some experience **hallucinations,** *false perceptions that have a compelling sense of reality.* Auditory hallucinations (typically voices speaking to the patient) are most common, although visual and tactile hallucinations may also occur. This person describes his hallucinations:

> Recently, my mind has played tricks on me, creating The People inside my head who sometimes come out to haunt me and torment me. They surround me in rooms, hide behind trees and under the snow outside. They taunt me and scream at me and devise plans to break my spirit. The voices come and go, but The People are always there, always real. (*New York Times,* March 18, 1986, p. C12)

The language of people with schizophrenia is often disorganized, and it may contain strange words.

> I am here from a foreign university . . . and you have to have a "plausity" of all acts of amendment to go through for the children's code . . . and it is no mental disturbance or "putenance" . . . it is an "amorition" law . . . it is like their "privatilinia." (Vetter, 1969, p. 189)

Patients' language sometimes contains word associations that are based on rhymes or other associations rather than meaning. Consider the following conversation between a psychologist and a hospitalized schizophrenic:

> After two weeks, the psychologist said to him: "As you say, you are wired precisely wrong. But why won't you let me see the diagram?" Carl answered: "Never, ever will you find the lever, the eternalever that will sever me forever with my real, seal, deal, heel. It is not on my shoe, not even on the sole. It walks away." (Rosenhan & Seligman, 1989, p. 369)

Schizophrenia can affect emotions in a number of ways. Many people with schizophrenia have *blunted affect,* manifesting less sadness, joy, and anger than most people. Others have *flat affect,* showing almost no emotions at all. Their voices are monotonous, their faces impassive. *Inappropriate affect* can also occur, as in the following case:

> The psychologist noted that Carl "smiles when he is uncomfortable, and smiles more when in pain. He cries during television comedies. He seems angry when justice is done, frightened when someone compliments him, and roars with laughter on

(a)   (b)

FIGURE 14.27

(a) Patients diagnosed with schizophrenia are tormented by bizarre and intrusive thoughts and images.
(b) This picture, drawn by a patient diagnosed with schizophrenia, may offer insights into his subjective world.

reading that a young child was burned in a tragic fire." (Rosenhan & Seligman, 1989, p. 369)

SUBTYPES OF SCHIZOPHRENIA

Schizophrenia has cognitive, emotional, and behavioral facets that can vary widely from case to case. The DSM-IV-TR differentiates among four major subtypes of schizophrenia:

- **Paranoid schizophrenia,** *whose most prominent features are delusions of persecution, in which people believe that others mean to harm them, and delusions of grandeur, in which they believe they are enormously important.* Suspicion, anxiety, or anger may accompany the delusions, and hallucinations may also occur in this subtype.

- **Disorganized schizophrenia,** *whose central features are confusion and incoherence, together with severe deterioration of adaptive behavior, such as personal hygiene, social skills, and self-care.* Thought disorganization is often so extreme that it is difficult to communicate with these individuals. Their behavior often appears silly and childlike, and their emotional responses are highly inappropriate. People with disorganized schizophrenia are usually unable to function on their own.

- **Catatonic schizophrenia,** *characterized by striking motor disturbances ranging from*

▶ **Focus 24**
Describe the four major subtypes of schizophrenic disorders. What are positive and negative symptoms and their significance?

 What is it like for a mathematical genius and his similarly talented son to live with schizophrenia? View the video, "Beautiful Minds: An Interview with John Nash and Son," in Chapter 14 of your CD to find out.

FIGURE 14.28

The woman pictured here exhibits catatonic rigidity. She might hold this position for several hours. If someone were to move her limbs into another position, she would maintain that position, a phenomenon known as *waxy flexibility*.

▶ **Focus 25**
Describe the evidence for genetic, neurological, and biochemical factors in schizophrenia.

muscular rigidity to random or repetitive movements. People with catatonic schizophrenia sometimes alternate between stuporous states, in which they seem oblivious to reality, and agitated excitement, during which they can be dangerous to others. While in a stuporous state, they may exhibit *waxy flexibility,* in which their limbs can be molded by another person into grotesque positions that they will then maintain for hours (Figure 14.28).

• **Undifferentiated schizophrenia,** *a category assigned to people who exhibit some of the symptoms and thought disorders of the above categories but who do not have enough of the specific criteria to be diagnosed in those categories.*

In addition to these formal DSM-IV-TR categories, many mental health workers and researchers divide schizophrenic reactions into two main categories on the basis of two classes of symptoms. One type is characterized by a predominance of **positive symptoms,** *bizarre behaviors such as delusions, hallucinations, and disordered speech and thinking.* These symptoms are called *positive* because they represent pathological extremes of normal processes. The second type features **negative symptoms**—*an absence of normal reactions, such as lack of emotional expression, loss of motivation, and an absence of speech* (Herz & Marder, 2002).

The distinction between positive- and negative-symptom subtypes seems to be an important one. Researchers have found differences in brain function between schizophrenics having positive symptoms and those with primarily negative symptoms (Gur et al., 1998; Zakzanis, 1998). The subtypes also show differences in life history and prognosis. Negative symptoms are likely to be associated with a long history of poor functioning prior to diagnosis and with a poor outcome following treatment (McGlashan & Fenton, 1992). In contrast, positive symptoms, especially those associated with a diagnosis of paranoid schizophrenia, are associated with good functioning prior to breakdown and a better prognosis for eventual recovery, particularly if the symptoms came on suddenly and were preceded by a history of relatively good adjustment (Fenton & McGlashan, 1991a, 1991b).

Schizophrenia afflicts only 1 to 2 percent of the population, yet schizophrenic patients occupy about half of all psychiatric hospital beds in the United States. Many who are not hospitalized, such as Eddie, the man described at the beginning of the chapter, barely function as homeless street people in large cities (Herman et al., 1998). About 10 percent of people with schizophrenia remain permanently impaired, and 65 percent show intermittent periods of normal functioning. The other 25 percent recover from the disorder (American Psychiatric Association, 2000).

CAUSAL FACTORS IN SCHIZOPHRENIA

Because of the seriousness of the disorder and the many years of anguish and incapacitation that its victims are likely to experience, schizophrenia has long been a focus of research. There is a growing consensus that schizophrenia results from a biologically based vulnerability factor that is set into motion by psychological and environmental events (Herz & Marder, 2002; McGuffin et al., 2005).

Biological Factors

Genetic Predisposition Strong evidence exists for a genetic predisposition to schizophrenia, though the specific genes involved and their roles in creating the disposition are still unknown (Jang, 2005; McGuffin et al., 2005). As Figure 14.29 shows, the more closely one is related to a person diagnosed with schizophrenia, the greater is the likelihood of developing the disorder during one's lifetime. Twin studies show that identical twins have higher concordance rates than fraternal twins, and adoption studies show much higher concordance with biological parents than with adoptive parents (Kety, 1988; Wahlberg et al., 1997). But, again, genetics do not by themselves account for the development of schizophrenia. If they did, the concordance rate in identical twins would be 100 percent, not 48 percent.

Brain Abnormalities   Brain scans have indicated a number of structural abnormalities in the brains of schizophrenic patients. According to the *neurodegenerative hypothesis,* destruction of neural tissue can cause schizophrenia (Weinberger & McClure, 2002). MRI studies have shown mild to moderate *brain atrophy,* a general loss or deterioration of neurons in the cerebral cortex and limbic system, together with enlarged ventricles (cavities that contain cerebrospinal fluid; Figure 14.30). The atrophy is centered in brain regions that influence cognitive processes and emotion, which may help explain the thought disorders and inappropriate emotions that are seen in such patients. Likewise, MRI images of the thalamus, which collects and routes sensory input to various parts of the brain, reveal abnormalities (Williamson, 2006). This may help account for the disordered attention and perception reported by schizophrenic patients whose cerebral cortex may be getting garbled or unfiltered information from the thalamus (Andreason et al., 1994). All of these structural differences are more common in patients who exhibit the negative-symptom pattern (Herz & Marder, 2002). As we have seen, these patients have a poorer chance of recovery than those with the positive-symptom pattern.

Biochemical Factors   Dopamine, a major excitatory neurotransmitter, may play a key role in schizophrenia. According to the **dopamine hypothesis,** *the symptoms of schizophrenia—particularly positive symptoms—are produced by overactivity of the dopamine system in areas of the brain that regulate emotional expression, motivated behavior, and cognitive functioning* (Heinrichs, 2001). People diagnosed with schizophrenia have more dopamine receptors on neuron membranes than do nonschizophrenics, and these receptors seem to be overreactive to dopamine stimulation (Black et al., 1988; Wong et al., 1986). Additional support comes from the finding that the effectiveness of antipsychotic drugs used to treat schizophrenia is positively related to their ability to reduce dopamine-produced synaptic activity (Creese et al., 1976; Green, 1997). Other neurotransmitter systems are probably involved in this complex disorder as well.

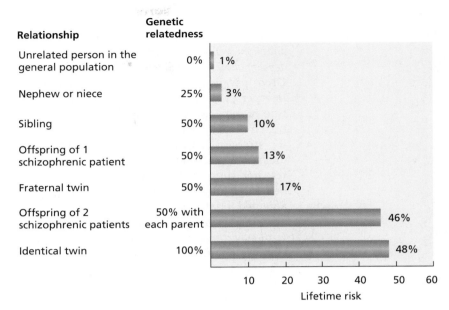

FIGURE 14.29

Genes and schizophrenia. The degree of risk for developing schizophrenia in one's lifetime correlates highly with the degree of genetic relationship with someone who has that disorder. These data summarize the results of 40 concordance studies conducted in many countries. SOURCE: Based on Gottesman, 1991.

The biochemical and brain findings concerning schizophrenia are intriguing. What is not clear is whether they cause the disorder or are caused by it. Future research is almost certain to reveal other biological bases for the complex disorders of schizophrenia.

Psychological Factors

Freud and other psychoanalytic thinkers viewed schizophrenia as a retreat from unbearable stress and conflict. For Freud, schizophrenia represented

▶ **Focus 26**
How do psychoanalytic and cognitive theorists explain the symptoms of schizophrenia?

FIGURE 14.30

Schizophrenia and the brain. One difference between the brains of schizophrenics and nonschizophrenics is enlarged ventricles (the butterfly-shaped spaces seen in the middle of the MRIs) in the schizophrenic brain (right). Findings like these support the position that brain abnormalities play a role in schizophrenia.

an extreme example of the defense mechanism of **regression,** *in which a person retreats to an earlier and more secure (even infantile) stage of psychosocial development in the face of overwhelming anxiety.* Other psychodynamic thinkers, focusing on the interpersonal withdrawal that is an important feature of schizophrenia, view the disorder as a retreat from an interpersonal world that has become too stressful to deal with. Although Freud's regression explanation has not received much direct research support (Fisher & Greenberg, 1996), the belief that life stress is a causal factor is generally accepted today (Crook & Copolov, 2000).

Some cognitive theorists believe that people with schizophrenias have a defect in the attentional mechanism that filters out irrelevant stimuli, so that they are overwhelmed by both internal and external stimuli. Sensory input thus becomes a chaotic flood, and irrelevant thoughts and images flash into consciousness. The stimulus overload produces distractability, thought disorganization, and the sense of being overwhelmed by disconnected thoughts and ideas. As one schizophrenic noted, "Everything seems to come pouring in at once . . . I can't seem to keep anything out" (Carson et al., 1988, p. 329). The recent MRI findings of thalamic abnormalities described earlier may help explain how this stimulus overload could occur through a malfunction of the brain's switchboard.

Environmental Factors

Stressful life events seem to play an important role in the emergence of schizophrenic behavior. These events tend to cluster in the 2 or 3 weeks preceding the "psychotic break," when the acute signs of the disorder appear (Day et al., 1987). Stressful life events seem to interact with biological or personality vulnerability factors. A highly vulnerable person may require little in the way of life stress to reach the breaking point (van Praag, 2004). In one study, psychotic and nonpsychotic people rated their emotional responses as they encountered stressful events in their daily lives. Psychotic individuals reacted to their stressors with more intense negative emotions, suggesting that emotional overreactivity may be a vulnerability factor (Myin-Germeys et al., 2001).

Family dynamics have long been a prime suspect in the origins of schizophrenia, but the search for parent or family characteristics that might cause the disorder has been largely unsuccessful. Significantly, children of biologically normal parents who are raised by schizophrenic adoptive parents do *not* show an increased risk of developing schizophrenia (Kety, 1988). Although persons with schizophrenia often come from families with problems, the nature and seriousness of those problems are not different from those of families in which nonschizophrenics are raised.

This does not mean that family dynamics are not important; rather, it may mean that an individual must have a biological vulnerability factor in order to be damaged by stressful family events to such a degree. Indeed, there is evidence that this vulnerability factor may appear early in life. In one study, researchers analyzed home movies showing preschizophrenic children (those who were later to develop schizophrenic behaviors) and their nonschizophrenic brothers and sisters. Even at these early ages—sometimes as young as 2 years of age—preschizophrenic children tended to show more odd and uncoordinated movements and less emotional expressiveness, especially for positive emotions (Grimes & Walker, 1994). These behavioral oddities may not only reflect a vulnerability factor, but they may also help create environmental stress by evoking negative reactions from others.

Although researchers have had difficulty pinpointing family factors that contribute to the *initial* appearance of schizophrenia, one consistent finding is that previously hospitalized schizophrenics are more likely to relapse if they return to a home environment that is high in a factor called *expressed emotion* (Vaughn & Leff, 1976). **Expressed emotion** *involves high levels of criticism* ("All you do is sit in front of that TV"), *hostility* ("We're getting sick and tired of your craziness"), *and overinvolvement* ("You're not going out unless I go with you"). One review of 26 studies showed that within 9 to 12 months of their return home, an average relapse rate of 48 percent occurred in patients whose families were high in expressed emotion, compared with a relapse rate of 21 percent when families were low in this factor (Kavanagh, 1992).

Before we conclude that high expressed emotion causes patients to relapse, however, we should note a finding from another study in which researchers videotaped actual interactions involving patients and their families (Rosenfarb et al., 1995). Analyses of the videotapes revealed that families high in expressed emotion did indeed make more negative comments to patients when they engaged in strange behaviors, but they also showed that the patients in these families engaged in about 4 times as many strange and disruptive behaviors, clouding the issue of what causes what. Thus high expressed emotion may be either a cause of or a response to patients'

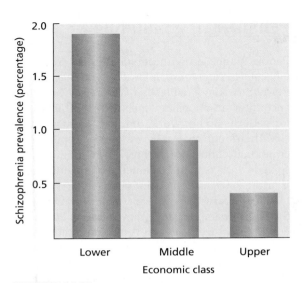

FIGURE 14.31

Social class and schizophrenia. This graph shows the relation between economic status and prevalence of schizophrenia. Is economic status a cause or an effect of schizophrenia? Or does some other factor cause both? SOURCE: Based on Keith et al., 1991.

disordered behaviors. Because individuals with schizophrenia may be overly sensitive to stress, even mildly negative family reactions may trigger underlying biological vulnerabilities that could result in relapse (Hooley, 2004).

Sociocultural Factors

Sociocultural factors are undoubtedly linked to schizophrenia (Murray et al., 2003). Many studies have found that the prevalence of schizophrenia is highest in lower-socioeconomic populations (Figure 14.31). Why is this? Is poverty a cause of schizophrenia, or is it an effect of the disorder? Two views give opposite answers. The **social causation hypothesis** *attributes the higher prevalence of schizophrenia to the higher levels of stress that low-income people experience*, particularly within urban environments. In contrast, the **social drift hypothesis** *proposes that as people develop schizophrenia, their personal and occupational functioning deteriorates, so that they drift down the socioeconomic ladder* into poverty and migrate to economically depressed urban environments. Perhaps social causation and social drift are both at work, for the factors that link poverty, social and environmental stressors, and schizophrenia are undoubtedly complex.

In contrast to most of the disorders we have described so far, schizophrenia may be a culture-free disorder. A worldwide epidemiological study sponsored by the World Health Organization indicated that the prevalence of schizophrenia is not dramatically different throughout the world (Jablensky et al., 1992). However, researchers have found that the likelihood of recovery is greater in developing countries than in the developed nations of North America and Western Europe. This may reflect a stronger community orientation and greater social support extended to disturbed people in developing countries (Tanaka-Matsumi & Draguns, 1997).

Schizophrenia reflects complex interactions among biological, psychological, and environmental factors. Figure 14.32 presents prominent causal factors identified at these levels of analysis.

FIGURE 14.32

Levels of analysis: Factors related to schizophrenia.

LEVELS OF ANALYSIS Factors Related to Schizophrenia

Biological
- Clear genetic predisposition
- Degenerative brain atrophy
- Abnormalities in thalamus may produce disordered sensory input
- Overactivity of excitatory neurotransmitters, particularly dopamine
- Frontal lobe dysfunction impairs executive functions

Psychological
- Regression to early developmental stage under severe stress (psychoanalysis)
- Attentional filtering problem; overwhelmed by stimulation
- Disordered language processes that impair comprehension, communication
- Executive function deficits, resulting in poor self-management
- Deficits in emotional responding
- Thought disorder, including possible delusions

Environmental
- Stressful life events typically precede breakdown
- Possible but as yet unidentified family dynamics
- Negative responses from others evoked by individual's odd behaviors
- Expressed emotion by family related to relapses
- Low socioeconomic settings (may be cause or effect)
- Similar incidence across cultures, but better recovery in developing countries

Schizophrenia

► **Focus 27**
Describe the major characteristics of the antisocial personality disorder.

IN REVIEW

■ Schizophrenia is a psychotic disorder featuring disordered thinking and language; poor contact with reality; flat, blunted, or inappropriate emotion; and disordered behavior. The cognitive portion of the disorder can involve delusions (false beliefs) or hallucinations (false perceptions).

■ Schizophrenias have been categorized in a number of ways. The DSM-IV-TR lists four subtypes: paranoid, disorganized, catatonic, and undifferentiated. Another categorization is based on the nature of the symptoms: positive versus negative. Positive symptoms, such as delusions or hallucinations, predict a better outcome than negative symptoms, such as lack of emotional expression.

■ There is strong evidence for a genetic predisposition to schizophrenia that makes some people particularly vulnerable to stressful life events. The dopamine hypothesis states that schizophrenia involves overactivity of the dopamine system, resulting in too much stimulation.

■ Psychoanalytic theorists regard schizophrenia as a profound regression to a primitive stage of psychosocial development in response to unbearable stress, particularly within the family. Stressful life events do often precede a schizophrenic episode, but researchers have not been successful in identifying a family pattern related to the onset of schizophrenia. However, expressed emotion is a family variable related to relapse among formerly hospitalized schizophrenic individuals.

■ Cognitive theorists focus on the thought disorder that is central to schizophrenia. One idea is that people with schizophrenia have a defect in their attentional filters, so that they are overwhelmed by internal and external stimuli and become disorganized. Deficiencies may also exist in the executive functions needed to organize behavior.

■ Sociocultural accounts of the higher incidence of schizophrenia at lower socioeconomic levels include the social causation hypothesis, which attributes schizophrenia to the higher levels of life stress that poor people experience, and the competing social drift hypothesis, which attributes the relation to the downward drift into poverty as the disorder progresses. Schizophrenia does not appear to differ in prevalence across cultures.

PERSONALITY DISORDERS

People diagnosed with **personality disorders** *exhibit stable, ingrained, inflexible, and maladaptive ways of thinking, feeling, and behaving.* When they encounter situations in which their typical behavior patterns do not work, they are likely to intensify their inappropriate ways of coping, their emotional controls may break down, and unresolved conflicts tend to reemerge (Lenzenweger & Clarkin, 2005; Millon et al., 2004).

Personality disorders are an important part of the DSM system because they increase the likelihood of acquiring several Axis I (symptom) disorders, particularly anxiety, depression, and substance-abuse problems. They are also associated with a poorer course of recovery from these disorders. Ann Massion and coworkers (2002) followed people suffering from anxiety disorders for 5 years and found that those also diagnosed with personality disorders were 30 to 40 percent less likely to recover from their anxiety disorders.

Table 14.2 briefly describes the 10 personality disorders in Axis II of DSM-IV-TR. The disorders are divided into three clusters that capture important commonalities: dramatic and impulsive behaviors, anxious and fearful behaviors, and odd and eccentric behaviors.

As many as 10 to 15 percent of adults in the United States and European countries may have personality disorders. A study in Norway found a rate of 13.4 percent, equally distributed among men and women. The most frequently encountered were avoidant, paranoid, histrionic, and obsessive-compulsive personality disorders (Torgerson et al., 2001).

Among the personality disorders, the most destructive to society is the *antisocial personality disorder* (Livesley, 2003). This personality disorder has received by far the greatest attention from clinicians and researchers over the years (Reich, 2006). A second personality disorder that is attracting a great deal of current attention is the *borderline personality disorder.* We will focus on these two disorders.

ANTISOCIAL PERSONALITY DISORDER

In the past, individuals with antisocial personality disorder were referred to as *psychopaths* or *sociopaths;* those terms are still in use today, though not for formal diagnostic purposes. In the 19th century, such people were sometimes referred to as "moral imbeciles." People with antisocial personality disorder are among the most interpersonally destructive and emotionally harmful individuals. Males outnumber females 3 to 1 in this diagnostic group (American Psychiatric Association, 2000).

People with **antisocial personality disorder** *seem to lack a conscience; they exhibit little anxiety or guilt and tend to be impulsive and unable to delay gratification of their needs.* They also exhibit a lack of emotional attachment to other people, as suggested in this report by a man diagnosed as having an antisocial personality disorder:

> When I was in high school my best friend got leukemia and died and I went to his funeral. Everybody else was crying . . . (but) . . . I suddenly realized I wasn't feeling anything at all. . . . That night I thought about it some more and found I wouldn't miss my mother and father if they died and that I wasn't too nuts about my brothers and sisters for that matter. I figured there wasn't anybody I really cared for but, then, I didn't need any of them anyway so I rolled over and went to sleep. (McNeil, 1967, p. 87)

A lack of capacity to care about others can make antisocial individuals a danger to society (Black, 1999). For example, murderers Charles Manson, Ted Bundy, and Jeffrey Dahmer failed to show any remorse for their crimes or sympathy for their victims. Although antisocial individuals often verbalize feelings and commitments with great sincerity, their behaviors indicate otherwise. They often appear very intelligent and charming, and they have the ability to rationalize their inappropriate behavior so that it appears reasonable and justifiable. Consequently, they are often virtuosos at manipulating others and talking their way out of trouble.

The characteristics we've discussed can be reflected in psychological test responses as well as in social behavior. Figure 14.33 shows the Minnesota Multiphasic Personality Inventory (MMPI) profile of Milwaukee serial killer Jeffrey Dahmer. Over a 3-year period, he killed and dismembered at least 17 male victims. He slept with the dead bodies, engaged in sex acts with them, stored body parts in jars, and cannibalized many of them. He was convicted of the serial murders and sentenced to 1,070 years in prison.

According to MMPI expert Alex B. Caldwell (1994), several aspects of this profile help explain Dahmer's bizarre and destructive behavior. The extraordinarily high score on the Psychopathic Deviate scale reflects an extreme antisocial impulsiveness coupled with a total lack of capacity for compassion and empathy. His victims were in all likelihood regarded as little more than objects to satisfy his perverse needs. Caldwell viewed the marked discrepancy between the Depression and

---

TABLE 14.2   DSM-IV-TR Personality Disorders and Their Major Features

Dramatic/Impulsive Cluster

Antisocial personality disorder: Severe irresponsible and antisocial behavior beginning in childhood and continuing past age 18; impulsive need gratification and lack of empathy for others; often highly manipulative and seem to lack conscience

Histrionic personality disorder: Excessive, dramatic emotional reactions and attention seeking; often sexually provocative; highly impressionable and suggestible; out of touch with negative feelings

Narcissistic personality disorder: Grandiose fantasies or behavior, lack of empathy, and oversensitivity to evaluation; constant need for admiration from others; proud self-display

Borderline personality disorder: Pattern of severe instability of self-image, interpersonal relationships, and emotions, often expressing alternating extremes of love and hatred toward the same person; high frequency of manipulative suicidal behavior

Anxious/Fearful Cluster

Avoidant personality disorder: Extreme social discomfort and timidity; feelings of inadequacy and fearfulness of being negatively evaluated

Dependent personality disorder: Extreme submissive and dependent behavior; fears of separation from those who satisfy dependency needs

Obsessive-compulsive personality disorder: Extreme perfectionism, orderliness, and inflexibility; preoccupied with mental and interpersonal control

Odd/Eccentric Cluster

Schizoid personality disorder: Indifference to social relationships and a restricted range of experiencing and expressing emotions

Schizotypal personality disorder: Odd thoughts, appearance, and behavior, and extreme discomfort in social situations

Paranoid personality disorder: An unwarranted tendency to interpret the behavior of other people as threatening, exploiting, or harmful

SOURCE: Based on DSM-IV-TR, American Psychiatric Association, 2000.

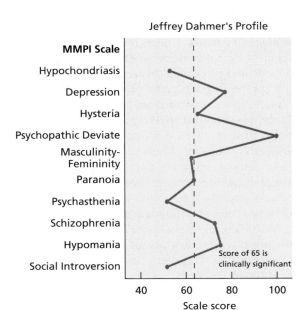

Jeffrey Dahmer's Profile

FIGURE 14.33

A serial killer's MMPI. The Minnesota Multiphasic Personality Inventory (MMPI) profile of serial killer Jeffrey Dahmer reveals severe antisocial tendencies. Scores beyond the dotted line are assumed to reflect pathological tendencies. Dahmer's extraordinarily elevated score on the Psychopathic Deviate scale reflects a callous disregard for other people and is consistent with his pattern of unrestrained and vicious victimization of others. SOURCE: Caldwell, 1994.

Psychasthenia (anxiety) scales—rarely seen on the MMPI—as reflecting Dahmer's sense of being fated or doomed to repeat his acts until he would be caught (the high Depression score), together with an absence of fear that, in normal people, might inhibit murderous behavior (the low Psychasthenia score). Although the profile clearly indicates Dahmer's high level of psychological disturbance, it also reflects an ability to mask his pathology under the normal facade that for years fooled law enforcement officials. Indeed, Dahmer's general demeanor looked so normal that despite the horror of his acts and the level of psychopathology shown in his test results, his plea of not guilty by reason of insanity was rejected by the jury. Instead, he went to prison, where he was murdered by another inmate.

People with antisocial personalities also display a perplexing failure to respond to punishment. Because of their lack of anxiety (seen, for example, in Dahmer's MMPI profile), the threat of punishment does not deter them from engaging in self-defeating or illegal acts again and again. As a result, some of them develop imposing prison records.

To be diagnosed with antisocial personality disorder, a person must be at least 18 years of age. However, the diagnostic criteria also require substantial evidence of antisocial behavior before the age of 15, including such acts as habitual lying, early and aggressive sexual behavior, excessive drinking, theft, vandalism, and chronic rule violations at home and school. Thus antisocial personality disorder is the culmination of a deviant behavior pattern that typically begins in childhood (Kernberg, 2000).

Causal Factors

▶ Focus 28
How do biological, psychoanalytic, and behavioral theorists account for antisocial personality disorder?

Biological Factors   Biological research on antisocial personality disorder has focused on both genetic and physiological factors. Evidence for a genetic predisposition is shown in consistently higher rates of concordance for antisocial behavior among identical twins than among fraternal twins (Rutter, 1997). Adoption studies suggest a similar conclusion. When researchers compared the criminal records of men who had been adopted early in life with those of their biological fathers and their adoptive fathers, they found that the criminality rate was nearly twice as high if the biological father had a criminal record and the adoptive father did not, clearly suggesting the operation of genetic factors (Cloninger & Gottesman, 1989).

How might genetic factors predispose individuals to engage in antisocial behavior? One clue might lie in the relative absence of anxiety and guilt that seems to characterize antisocial personality disorder. Many researchers have suggested that the physiological basis for the disorder might be some dysfunction in brain structures that govern emotional arousal and behavioral self-control (Blair, 2005). This results in behavioral impulsiveness and a chronically underaroused state that impairs avoidance learning, causes boredom, and encourages a search for excitement (Arnett, 1997; Ishikawa et al., 2001). In support of a physiological basis, both children and adults with antisocial behavior patterns have lower heart rates, particularly when under stress (Ortiz & Raine, 2004). MRIs also reveal that antisocial individuals have subtle neurological deficits in the prefrontal lobes—the seat of executive functions such as planning, reasoning, and behavioral inhibition; these neurological deficits are associated with reduced autonomic activity (Raine et al., 2000). It thus appears, as long suspected, that severely antisocial individuals may indeed be wired differently at a neurological level, responding with less arousal and greater impulsiveness to both pleasurable and unpleasant stimuli (Verona et al., 2004).

Psychological and Environmental Factors   Psychodynamic theorists regard antisocial personalities as people without a conscience. Psychoanalytic theorists suggest that such people lack anxiety and guilt because they did not develop an adequate superego (Gabbard, 1990). In the absence of a well-developed superego, the restraints on the id are reduced, resulting in impulsive and hedonistic behavior. The failure to develop a strong superego is thought to result from inadequate identification with appropriate adult figures because these figures were either physically or psychologically unavailable to the child (Kernberg, 2000). In support of this position, the absence of the father from the home is related to a higher incidence of antisocial symptoms in children, even when socioeconomic status is equated (Pfiffner et al., 2001).

Cognitive theorists believe that an important feature in antisocial individuals is their consistent failure to think about or anticipate the long-term negative consequences of their acts. As a result, they behave impulsively, thinking only of what they want at that moment (Bandura, 1997). From this perspective, a key to preventing these individuals from getting into trouble is to help them develop the cognitive controls (i.e., the executive functions) needed to think before acting.

Learning through modeling may also play an important role. Many antisocial individuals come from homes where parents exhibit a good deal of aggression and are inattentive to their children's needs (Rutter, 1997). Such parents provide role models for both aggressive behavior and disregard for the needs of others. Another important environmental factor is exposure to deviant peers. Children who become antisocial often learn some of their deviant behaviors from peer groups that both model antisocial behavior and reinforce it with social approval (Bandura, 1997). It is easy to see how such environmental factors, combined with a possible genetic predisposition for antisocial behavior, would encourage the development of deviant behavior patterns.

Like some biological theories, learning explanations suggest that persons with antisocial personality disorder lack impulse control. Learning theorists believe that poor impulse control occurs in these individuals because of an impaired ability to develop conditioned fear responses when punished. This results in a deficit in avoidance learning. Hans Eysenck (1964) maintained that developing a conscience depends on the ability to learn fear and inhibitory avoidance responses, and people who fail to do so will be less able to inhibit their behavior.

In accord with this hypothesis, Adrian Raine and coworkers (1996) did a 14-year follow-up of males who had been subjected at age 15 to a classical conditioning procedure in which a soft tone was used as the CS and a loud, aversive tone as the UCS. Conditioned fear was measured by the participant's skin conductance response when the CS occurred after a number of pairings with the loud UCS. The researchers found that men who accumulated a criminal record by age 29 had shown much poorer fear conditioning at age 15 than had those with no criminal record.

▶ **Focus 29**
How does the Schachter-Latané study support the arousal-deficit theory of antisocial personality disorder.

Research Close-Up   Fear, Avoidance Learning, and Psychopathy

SOURCE: STANLEY SCHACHTER and BIBB LATANÉ (1964). Crime, cognition, and the autonomic nervous system. In D. Levine (Ed.), *Nebraska symposium on motivation—1964*. Lincoln, NE: University of Nebraska Press.

INTRODUCTION

In antisocial personality disorder, punishment seems to have little effect on future destructive behavior. As we have seen, one explanation for this is a deficit in fear arousal, which serves to inhibit antisocial behavior in normal people (Blair, 2005). This lack of fear arousal contributes to poor avoidance learning, so that such people get into trouble repeatedly.

What would happen if it were possible to make people with antisocial personality disorder more physiologically reactive, or fearful? Would their avoidance-learning deficit disappear? Stanley Schachter and Bibb Latané set out to answer this important question.

METHOD

Schachter and Latané selected two groups of inmates at state prisons on the basis of psychologists' diagnoses and life-history data. One group consisted of psychopaths (the still-popular term that preceded the DSM category of antisocial behavior disorder). These prisoners were described by prison psychologists as being free from any symptoms of anxiety, lacking a sense of responsibility or shame, being habitual liars and manipulators, able to commit antisocial acts without guilt or remorse, lacking insight, and unable to profit from negative experiences. Most, if not all, of these prisoners would meet current diagnostic criteria for antisocial personality disorder. A normal (nonpsychopathic) group consisted of prisoners matched in age and intelligence who did not exhibit this behavioral pattern. Life-history data showed that the psychopaths had been arrested more often (8.3 versus 3.3 arrests) and had spent more of their adult lives in prison (36.2 percent versus 18.1 percent).

The two groups of prisoners were recruited as paid participants in an investigation of "a newly developed hormone thought to enhance learning." The researchers used an experimental apparatus that required participants to learn a complicated mental maze. It consisted of a metal cabinet on which was mounted a counter, two pilot lights, and four switches. The maze consisted of 20 choice points. At each choice point, the participant selected one of the four switches. If it was the correct one, a green light flashed and the learner advanced to the next choice point. If one of the three incorrect switches was selected, a red light flashed and an error was recorded on the counter visible to the participant. When the 20th choice point was reached, the procedure began again from the start. The learner repeated the maze 21 times, the objective being to learn the correct response at each choice point so as to minimize the total number of errors.

To study avoidance learning, one of the three incorrect switches at each choice point not only activated the red light and recorded an error, but it also resulted in a moderately painful electric shock to the learner. Thus the learner would do well to learn not only the correct switch at each point but also to avoid the one that delivered a shock (i.e., to do good *and* avoid evil).

To manipulate emotional arousal, the prisoners were given an injection of the "experimental hormone, Suproxin," being

Continued

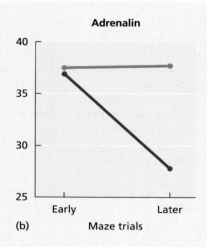

tested to see if it enhanced learning ability. They were told that this hormone would have no side effects. The injection was used to manipulate autonomic arousal. It contained either adrenalin, which would increase arousal, or a placebo, which would not. Each participant worked until he learned two different mental mazes, one while under the influence of adrenalin and the other while under the placebo. Half received adrenalin on the first maze and then received the placebo for the second maze; the other half received injections in the reverse order.

RESULTS

The two groups of prisoners did not differ in their overall learning of the two mazes; they made similar numbers of correct responses and errors. Thus the psychopaths did not differ in their ability to learn the positively reinforced "correct" responses. Of major interest, then, was the avoidance-learning measure, that is, the ability to learn to avoid choosing the switch at each choice point that would result in electric shock. The dependent variable here was the percentage of incorrect responses made by each participant that resulted in electric shock. The lower the percentage of shocked incorrect responses, the better the avoidance learning over trials through each maze.

Figure 14.34a shows avoidance learning under the placebo condition, in which the psychopathic and normal prisoners experienced their normal levels of arousal. As you can see, the normal prisoners made a lower percentage of shocked responses during their later trips through the maze, indicating avoidance learning. In contrast, the psychopaths showed almost no evidence of learning. On their later trials through the maze, they were still as likely to select the shocked switch as they were in their early trials.

If lack of fear underlies the psychopaths' lack of conditioning, what would happen if one artificially increased their level of arousal? In Figure 14.34b, we see the effect of doing so. When injected with adrenalin, the psychopaths showed dramatic evidence of avoidance learning. Indeed, they actually performed better than the normal prisoners, whose performance on this complex task may have been somewhat impaired by increasing their already-existing fear responses.

CRITICAL DISCUSSION

This study, done nearly a half-century ago, is still considered a classic. Schachter and Latané cleverly tested a clinical explanation for a behavior disorder under controlled laboratory conditions. They not only demonstrated the avoidance-learning deficit presumed to underlie antisocial behavior, but they also showed that this deficit could be reversed if it were possible to experimentally create the physiological arousal that psychopaths lack. Indeed, the increase in arousal produced by the adrenalin injection had an especially notable effect on the psychopaths, who learned to avoid even better than the normal prisoners did in the placebo condition. This may be because the psychopaths' arousal in this fear-inducing situation was so different from their normal experience.

It is important to rule out other possible explanations for the results. For example, what if the pain experiences of the prisoner groups were affected differently by the injections, thereby affecting motivation to avoid the shock? The researchers were able to rule this out by showing that the two groups of prisoners rated the pain as equally unpleasant under both injection conditions. Therefore, the psychopathic and normal prisoners apparently experienced equal pain when shocked. As in this case, it is important to anticipate factors that could affect results and make sure that they are measured.

This study exemplifies a research area known as *experimental psychopathology*. Researchers bring clinical populations into the laboratory to study processes assumed to underlie a particular disorder under controlled conditions, using state-of-the-science techniques from other areas of psychology, such as cognitive psychology, social psychology, and behavioral neuroscience. This kind of research helps identify the mechanisms that contribute to behavior disorders. It also allows researchers to test hypotheses derived from existing theories of psychopathology and, sometimes, to directly pit competing theories against one another. In this manner, clinical observation informs science, and science helps inform clinical understanding and, it is hoped, the treatment of behavior disorders.

BORDERLINE PERSONALITY DISORDER

The borderline personality disorder (BPD) has become the focus of intense interest among clinical researchers because of its chaotic effects on those who suffer from the disorder, their families, and their therapists. The disorder may occur in 3 to 5 percent of the general population (Clarkin et al., 1992; Frances & Widiger, 1986). About two thirds of those diagnosed are women.

Before 1980 the term *borderline* referred to an intermediate level of disturbance between neurotic and psychotic. Now, however, **borderline personality disorder** *refers to a collection of symptoms characterized primarily by serious instability in behavior, emotion, identity, and interpersonal relationships.* Borderline individuals have intense and unstable personal relationships and experience chronic feelings of extreme anger, loneliness, and emptiness, as well as momentary losses of personal identity. They are inclined to engage in impulsive behavior such as running away, promiscuity, binge eating, and drug abuse, and their lives are often marked by repetitive self-destructive behaviors, such as self-mutilation and suicide attempts that seem designed to call forth a "saving" response from other people in their lives. The complex nature of the borderline disorder is shown in the following case:

> A 27-year-old woman was married and had two small children. She had had a stormy adolescence, having been forced into sexual relations with a brother 6 years her senior whom she at first idolized and later feared. Their relationship continued until just before she left home for college, when she told her parents of it. In the ensuing emotional turmoil, she made a gesture of suicide (overdose of aspirin) but was not hospitalized. . . . Outwardly flirtatious, although inwardly shy and ill at ease, she felt intensely lonely and went through a period of mild alcohol abuse and brief sexual affairs in an effort to cope with her anxiety and sense of inner emptiness. At age 19, she married a classmate and dropped out of school.
>
> Fairly at ease in the first years of her marriage, she became anxious, bored, and given to fits of sadness and tearfulness after the birth of her second child. Her mood fluctuated widely from hour to hour and day to day, but negative feelings were greatly intensified on the 3 or 4 days before her period. Her husband had grown less attentive as the family expanded, in response to which she became increasingly irritable, provocative, and at times abusive (smashing plates, hurling insults). Her husband began to carry on an extramarital relationship, which she eventually discovered. At that

point, she became seriously depressed, lost sleep and appetite, began to abuse alcohol and sedatives, and made several gestures of suicide, including one instance of cutting her wrist. On two occasions she hid for several nights in motels without informing anyone where she was. (Stone, 1986, p. 210)

BPD is highly associated with a number of other disorders, including mood disorders, PTSD, and substance abuse disorders. In one study, the BPD symptoms of emotional instability and impulsivity predicted recurrent problems in academic achievement and social relationships 2 years later (Bagge et al., 2004). One intensive study of 57 people diagnosed with BPD revealed a total of 42 suicide threats, 40 drug overdoses, 36 instances of self-mutilation and cutting, 38 episodes of drug abuse, 36 instances of promiscuity with near-strangers, and 14 accidents, mainly caused by reckless driving.

The chaos that marks the lives of borderline patients extends to their relationships with their psychotherapists. They are considered to be among the most difficult clients to treat because of their clinging dependency, their irrational anger, and their tendency to engage in manipulative suicide threats and gestures as efforts to control the therapist (Linehan, 1993). Many borderline individuals, perhaps 6 to 9 percent, eventually do kill themselves, either by miscalculation or by design (Davis et al., 1999).

Causal Factors

Borderlines tend to have chaotic personal histories marked by interpersonal strife, abuse, and inconsistent parenting. This history is sometimes reflected in their earliest memories. In one study, borderline and normal participants were asked to describe their earliest memories in life. When the researchers analyzed the content of the memory reports, they found that the borderlines reported six times more events in which someone had treated them in a malevolent manner or had injured them emotionally or physically. Borderline individuals also viewed potential helpers as far less helpful to them (Nigg et al., 1992). Parents of many borderline individuals are described as abusive, rejecting, and nonaffirming, and some theorists suggest that an early lack of acceptance by parents may cripple self-esteem and lead to clinging dependency and an inability to cope with separation (Cardasis et al., 1997). As they mature, the behaviors of borderlines tend to evoke negative reactions and rejection from others, affirming their sense of worthlessness and their view of the world as malevolent.

▶ **Focus 30**
Describe the major features of BPD and the hypothesized causes of the disorder.

FIGURE 14.35

Actress Glenn Close's portrayal of Alex in the movie *Fatal Attraction* illustrated the tendency of people with borderline personality disorder to show dramatic shifts in their relationships. During her affair with the man played by Michael Douglas, Alex went from consuming love to a homicidal rage in which she tried to murder her lover with a butcher knife when he tried to end the relationship.

Psychoanalyst Otto Kernberg has focused on the dramatic changes that borderlines exhibit in their relationships with others (Kernberg, 1984; Kernberg & Caligor, 2005). Their sudden and vitriolic shifts from extreme love and clinging dependence to intense hatred or feelings of abandonment reflect a cognitive process that he calls **splitting,** *the failure to integrate positive and negative aspects of another's behavior* (for example, a parent who is usually accepting but sometimes voices disapproval) *into a coherent whole.* As a result, the borderline may react as if the other person has two separate identities, one deserving of love and the other of hatred. Whichever of these seemingly independent images the borderline individual is reacting to at the moment totally determines how she or he relates or feels (Figure 14.35). Together with severe problems in emotional control, splitting makes for chaotic and unpredictable relationships.

Biological factors also seem to be at work (Depue & Lenzenweger, 2005). Close relatives of those with BPD are five times more likely than those in the general population to also have the disorder (Torgerson, 2000). The emotional explosiveness and impulsivity of borderlines may also reflect some biological abnormality in neurotransmitter systems or areas of the brain that contribute to emotional self-regulation (Gurvitz et al., 2000). It seems entirely possible that BPD reflects an interaction between biological factors and an early history of trauma, rejection, and psychological if not physical abandonment. Finally, sociocultural factors may also contribute. Cases of BPD seem to increase in societies that are unstable and rapidly changing, leaving some of its members with a sense of emptiness, problems of identity, and fears of abandonment (Paris, 1993).

Beneath the Surface   How Dangerous Are People with Psychological Disorders?

When they occur, violent acts committed by mentally ill people or former mental patients often are sensationalized in the media. Fictional depictions of psychologically disturbed individuals often involve violent behavior. One analysis of prime-time TV programs revealed that 73 percent of mentally ill characters committed violent acts, compared with 40 percent of normal characters (Gerbner et al., 1981). In the climactic scene of the movie *Fatal Attraction,* a woman resembling a borderline individual attempts to murder her former lover when he abandons her. Part of the stigma attached to psychological disorders is the widespread belief that such people are especially prone to

commit violent acts (Monahan, 1992). How valid are such concerns?

The preceding discussion of antisocial personality disorder notes characteristics that can make such people prone to violence. Individuals such as Ted Bundy, Jeffrey Dahmer, and Charles Manson represent extreme examples of how destructive a mentally ill individual can be. Other subgroups with elevated violence potential are people with paranoid and catatonic schizophrenia who have stopped taking their medications (Torrey & Zdanowicz, 2001). The fact is, however, that the vast majority of people with psychological disorders do not fall into these categories. The two largest diagnostic groups, people with anxiety disorders and depression, are likely to be no more dangerous than the average person, and severely depressed people in particular are of greater danger to themselves than they are to others.

As we've seen, severe disorders such as schizophrenia are more common in lower socioeconomic groups, and violent behavior is also more common at lower socioeconomic levels. In a study designed to control for this factor, people with mental disorders were followed for 1 year following their discharge from psychiatric hospitals (Steadman et al., 1998). The frequency with which they, family members, or police records revealed violent acts was compared with the frequency of similar acts in "normal" people from the same lower-socioeconomic neighborhoods where the former patients lived.

As shown in Figure 14.36, former inpatients without substance-abuse problems differed little in violence rates from nonpatients without substance-abuse problems during the year-long period. However, substance abuse (which occurred more often among the former patients) was associated with a significant increase in the mean number of violent acts in both the patient and nonpatient groups. The researchers also found that violent acts by the former mental patients were most frequently directed toward family members and acquaintances. Nonpatients were actually more likely than former patients to commit the kinds of violent acts outside of the home that most frighten the public.

Based on this and other research, the following conclusion by two prominent mental health researchers appears reasonable:

> To date, nearly every modern study indicates that public fears are way out of proportion to the empirical reality. The magnitude of the violence risk associated with mental illness is comparable to

FIGURE 14.36

Challenging a popular stereotype. This graph shows the mean number of violent acts committed by former psychiatric inpatients during the year following their discharge, as compared with similar acts committed by nonpatients living in their lower-socioeconomic neighborhoods. No difference was found between former patients and other community members when neither group engaged in substance abuse; however, when substance abuse was a factor, it was associated with more violence in both patient and nonpatient samples. SOURCE: Based on Steadman et al., 1998.

that associated with age, educational attainment, and gender and is limited to only some disorders and symptom constellations. Furthermore, because serious mental illness is relatively rare and the excess risk modest, the contribution of mental illness to overall levels of violence in our society is miniscule. (Link & Steuve, 1998, p. 403)

IN REVIEW

- Personality disorders are rigid, maladaptive patterns of behavior that persist over a long time. They fall on Axis II of DSM-IV-TR. Personality disorders can contribute to the development of Axis I disorders and reduce the chances of recovery from those disorders.

- Antisocial personality disorder is the most studied of the Axis II disorders. It is characterized by an egocentric and manipulative tendency toward immediate self-gratification, a lack of empathy for others, a tendency to act out impulsively, and a failure to profit from punishment.

- Research on antisocial personality disorder suggests that genetic and physiological factors that result in underarousal may contribute to the disor-

der's causes. Psychoanalysts view the disorder as a failure to develop the superego, which might otherwise restrain the individual's impulsive self-gratification. Learning explanations focus on the failure of punishment to inhibit maladaptive behaviors and exposure to aggressive, uncaring models.

- Borderline personality disorder is characterized by serious instability in behavior, emotions, interpersonal relationships, and personal identity, as well as impulsive and self-destructive behaviors.

- It appears that the majority of people with psychological disorders are not a danger to others. Research is identifying the subgroups that are more dangerous, and substance abuse is an important risk factor.

CHILDHOOD DISORDERS

▶ **Focus 31**
Describe the major features and causal factors in ADHD and autistic disorder, as well as implications for adult functioning.

Psychological disorders can occur at any point in the life span. Mental health professionals have observed symptoms resembling clinical depression in infants, and older children exhibit a wide range of problem behaviors (Mash & Barkley, 2003). In one study of several thousand children between the ages of 2 and 5, researchers diagnosed over 20 percent of the children with a DSM-IV disorder and considered half of these to be significantly impaired by their symptoms (Lavigne et al., 1996). Similar levels of incidence and impairment exist in children between the ages of 9 and 17 (Satcher, 1999).

Other studies show that only about 40 percent of children with psychological disorders receive professional attention, and only half of this group is seen by qualified mental health professionals (Satcher, 1999). In contrast, 74 percent of children with physical handicaps receive professional treatment (U.S. Office of Behavior Technology, 1990). Failure to treat childhood behavior disorders not only results in needless distress for children and families, but such disorders tend to continue into adulthood as psychological problems. In one New Zealand study, 4 in 5 adults with diagnosed DSM disorders had histories of childhood or adolescent problems that also met DSM criteria (Newman et al., 1996).

Although many childhood disorders are the subject of current research, two are receiving particular attention. *Attention deficit/hyperactivity disorder* is of interest because it is the most frequently diagnosed childhood disorder. *Autism* is being scrutinized because it is becoming more common and is one of the most baffling disorders.

ATTENTION DEFICIT/HYPERACTIVITY DISORDER

In **attention deficit/hyperactivity disorder (ADHD)**, *problems may take the form of inattention, hyperactivity/ impulsivity, or a combination of the two.* Ratings by teachers and parents indicate that 7 to 10 percent of American children meet DSM-IV-TR criteria for the disorder, making ADHD the most common childhood disorder. The disorder occurs at least 4 times more frequently in boys than in girls. Boys are more likely to exhibit aggressive and impulsive behaviors, whereas girls are more likely to be primarily inattentive. Some professionals believe that the ADHD diagnosis is applied too liberally, since normal children also exhibit the behaviors in question. They worry that some children

may be inappropriately labeled and medicated (Carlson, 2000).

It may be tempting to assume that children routinely outgrow ADHD, but follow-up studies of individuals diagnosed with the disorder suggest that for 50 to 80 percent, the problems persist into adolescence and, for 30 to 50 percent, into adulthood (Biederman, 1998). Overall, adults with ADHD have more occupational, family, emotional, and interpersonal problems.

Despite many years of research, the precise causes of ADHD are unknown. Genetic factors are probably involved, as concordance rates are higher in identical than fraternal twins. In adoption studies of ADHD children, the children's biological parents are more likely to have ADHD than the adoptive parents (Smalley et al., 2000). Experts have long suspected that the disorder has a biological basis, but EEG studies of electrical brain activity and imaging studies of brain structures and neurotransmitters have failed to reveal consistent differences between people with ADHD and control groups (Green, 1999). This may be due to the fact that ADHD is a multi-faceted disorder with several subcategories of biological patterns. Environmental factors, such as inconsistent parenting, are also involved, perhaps in complex combinations with biological factors.

AUTISTIC DISORDER

One of the most mysterious and perplexing of all disorders is autism. First identified by the American psychiatrist Leo Kanner in 1943, **autistic disorder** *is a long-term disorder characterized by extreme unresponsiveness to others, poor communication skills, and highly repetitive and rigid behavior patterns.* Autism affects about 5 in every 10,000 children, about 80 percent of them boys (American Psychiatric Association, 2000). Typically appearing in the first three years of life in the form of unresponsiveness and lack of interest in others, autism tends to be a life-long disorder. Approximately 70 percent remain severely disabled into adulthood and cannot lead independent lives. More than two thirds are mentally retarded, having IQs below 70 and frequently below 35. The rest have normal to above-average intelligence. But even the highest-functioning adults with autism have problems in communication, restricted interests and activities, and difficulty relating to others (American Psychiatric Association, 2000).

Lack of social responsiveness to others is a central feature of autism. Autistic infants typically do not reach out to or even make eye contact with their parents. They seem not to recognize or care who is around them. Autistic children do not engage in normal play with either adults or peers. They do not include others in their play and often do not even acknowledge their presence.

Language and communication difficulties are also common, with half of autistic people not developing language. The language that does develop is often strange, involving repetition of words or phrases with little recognition of meaning. Many engage in *echolalia*, the exact echoing of phrases spoken by others.

Sameness and routine are very important, and autistic children become extremely upset at even minute changes. The movement of a piece of furniture even slightly or the change of one word in a song may evoke a tantrum. Some theorists believe that sameness is an attempt to avoid overstimulation, but nobody knows for sure.

Autistic individuals have repetitive and stereotyped behavior patterns and interests (Figure 14.37). They may spend their time spinning objects, playing with objects like jar tops, flicking their fingers, or rocking their bodies. Some engage in self-injurious behaviors, such as banging their heads against sharp objects or biting chunks of flesh out of their bodies, and these children may have to be physically restrained.

Some autistic people, such as the man portrayed by Dustin Hoffman in *Rain Man*, exhibit extraordinary *savant* (from the French word for "wise," or "learned") abilities. A common savant skill is calendar calculation. An autistic person with this ability could tell you in an instant what day of the week your birthday will fall on in 2039. Others can perfectly reproduce any song or commercial after hearing it once. Sometimes, these skills give the impression of superior intelligence, even in people who are mentally retarded.

Causal Factors

Leo Kanner (1943), who first described childhood autism, offered a psychodynamic explanation. He speculated that these children had been driven into their own worlds by a cold and ungiving family environment during infancy. Parents (particularly the mother) were described as "refrigerator parents" who had thawed out just long enough to conceive a child. These were purely theoretical statements, and no evidence for such a family pattern has ever existed, but generations of parents who were exposed to this hypothesis suffered the agony of thinking they had caused their child's autistic disorder.

Today, it is widely accepted that autism has a biological basis (Kabot et al., 2003). What that

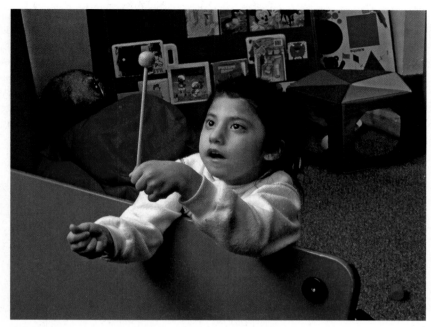

FIGURE 14.37

People with autism often engage in odd and repetitive stereotyped behaviors. For example, an autistic child may manipulate an object for hours at a time, showing no interest in playing with other children or relating to adults.

might be remains undetermined, however. Widespread anomalies in the structures and functioning of the brain have been found in autistic children. For example, brain-imaging studies show that the brains of autistic children are larger than average, reflecting abnormal brain growth during the first year of life, and they also reveal abnormal development in the cerebellum, which coordinates movement and is involved in shifting attention (Courchesne et al., 2003).

Genetic factors have been linked to autism. Siblings of autistic children are 200 times more likely to have the disorder than are children in the general population, and concordance is highest in identical twins (Piven et al., 1997). No single gene seems involved; instead, there may be multiple interacting genes. One notable finding is that many relatives of autistic children, though not manifesting the disorder themselves, have unusual personality characteristics that parallel autism, including aloofness and very narrow and specialized interests (Rutter, 2000).

Another line of research is examining autism from the *theory of mind* perspective. As discussed in Chapter 11, theory of mind refers to an awareness of what others are thinking and how they may be reacting internally. Normal children become aware of some characteristics of other people's thinking by age 3 or 4 (Ritblatt, 2000). Autistic people seem to have poorly developed skills in this area, making it difficult for them to communicate with others or understand how other people might be internally reacting to them (Heerey et al., 2003). Autistic children also show poor comprehension of others' emotional responses, such as expressions of distress (Dawson et al., 2004). Theory of mind deficits could severely impair language and social development, and they are a strong focus of current research on autism.

> ■ Autistic disorder is a severe disorder that involves extreme unresponsiveness to others, poor communication skills, and highly repetitive and rigid behavior. Both disorders appear to have biological underpinnings, but the nature of these causal factors is not fully understood.

IN REVIEW

- ■ Psychological disorders can occur at any point in the life span, and epidemiological data show that both children and adolescents exhibit a variety of disorders. Moreover, many childhood disorders are precursors for psychological disorders in adulthood.

- ■ Attention deficit/hyperactive disorder (ADHD) and autistic disorder originate in childhood and often persist into adulthood. ADHD can involve inattention, hyperactivity, or a combination of the two.

A CLOSING THOUGHT

All of us do the best we can to adapt to the many demands we face during the course of our lives. In this chapter, we have seen the intense personal and societal suffering that occurs when biologically and experientially produced vulnerabilities combine with stressful demands to create psychological disorders. It is our hope that this discussion has increased your understanding and compassion for those who suffer from these disorders. No one wants to be dysfunctional and miserable, and everyone deserves the opportunity to live a meaningful and fulfilling life. In the next chapter, we will focus on what can be done through psychological and biological treatments to ease the suffering that results from psychological disorders.

KEY TERMS AND CONCEPTS

Each term has been boldfaced and defined in the chapter on the page indicated in parentheses.

abnormal behavior (p. 533)
agoraphobia (p. 537)
antisocial personality disorder (p. 561)
anxiety (p. 536)
anxiety disorders (p. 536)
attention deficit/hyperactivity disorder (ADHD; p. 568)
autistic disorder (p. 568)
bipolar disorder (p. 547)
borderline personality disorder (BPD; p. 565)
catatonic schizophrenia (p. 555)
competency (p. 535)
compulsion (p. 539)
conversion disorder (p. 543)
culture-bound disorders (p. 542)
delusions (p. 554)
depressive attributional pattern (p. 550)
depressive cognitive triad (p. 550)
disorganized schizophrenia (p. 555)

dissociative disorders (p. 544)
dissociative identity disorder (DID; p. 545)
dopamine hypothesis (p. 557)
dysthymia (p. 546)
expressed emotion (p. 558)
generalized anxiety disorder (p. 537)
hallucinations (p. 555)
hypochondriasis (p. 543)
insanity (p. 535)
learned helplessness theory (p. 551)
major depression (p. 546)
mania (p. 547)
mood disorders (p. 546)
negative symptoms (p. 556)
neurotic anxiety (p. 540)
obsession (p. 539)
pain disorder (p. 543)
panic disorder (p. 538)
paranoid schizophrenia (p. 555)
personality disorder (p. 560)

phobia (p. 537)
positive symptoms (p. 556)
posttraumatic stress disorder (PTSD; p. 539)
psychogenic amnesia (p. 544)
psychogenic fugue (p. 544)
regression (p. 558)
reliability (p. 533)
schizophrenia (p. 554)
social causation hypothesis (p. 559)
social drift hypothesis (p. 559)
social phobia (p. 537)
somatoform disorder (p. 543)
specific phobia (p. 537)
splitting (p. 566)
suicide (p. 552)
trauma-dissociation theory (p. 545)
undifferentiated schizophrenia (p. 556)
validity (p. 533)
vulnerability-stress model (p. 531)

❓ What Do You Think?

"DO I HAVE THAT DISORDER?" (PAGE 535)

Wondering if you have a psychological disorder when reading about their features is quite understandable. We all experience problems in living at various times, and we may react in ways that bear similarities to the disorders described in this chapter. Logically, seeing such a similarity does not necessarily mean that you have the disorder at a clinically significant level. On the other hand, if you find that maladaptive behaviors such as those described in this chapter are interfering with your happiness or personal effectiveness, then you should not hesitate to seek professional assistance in changing these behaviors. In addition to the three Ds discussed earlier (distress, dysfunction, and deviance), you will want to consider the frequency with which the particular behaviors or experiences occur, as well as their intensity and their duration. When problem behaviors occur frequently, are intense, and/or last for a long time, they are more likely to be clinically significant. In such a case, it is important not to let any stigma you might attach to having a psychological problem keep you from acting in your best interest and discussing your problem with a mental health professional.

DID: DISSOCIATION OR ROLE-PLAYING? (PAGE 546)

If a person asked to role-play different people could exhibit radically different behavioral and physiological features, could we conclude that the trauma-dissociation model of DID is disproven or that DID does not exist? A critical thinker will reframe this as follows: Does the fact that one explanation of a given phenomenon is supported prove that all other potential explanations are impossible? Not at all, as supporters of the trauma-dissociation theory would correctly maintain. Indeed, a compelling depiction of an autistic adult by a skilled actor such as Dustin Hoffman in *Rain Man* does not imply that autistic disorder involves nothing more than acting. However, from a scientific perspective, the principle of parsimony dictates that if two different theories can each account for *all* the phenomena, then we should choose the simpler of the two theories. Although intriguing, our view is that the role theory explanation has not yet achieved the scientific support needed to displace other DID theories.

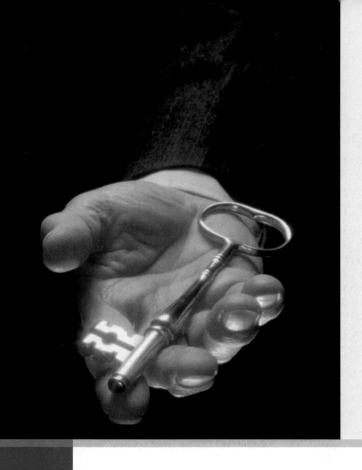

Treatment of Psychological Disorders

CHAPTER OUTLINE

*It is a process, a thing-in-itself, an experience,
a relationship, a dynamic.*

—CARL ROGERS

I fought my way through Harvard in the midst of psychosis and "spaciness." . . . There is no doubt in my mind that therapy helped me get through school. . . . For so long I wondered why my therapist insisted on talking about my relationship with him. He was not my problem; the problem was my life—my past, my fears, what I was going to do tomorrow, how I would handle things, sometimes just how to survive. . . . It took a long time, but finally I saw why it was important to explore my relationship with my therapist—it was the first real relationship I had ever had: that is, the first I felt safe enough to invest myself in. I rationalized that it was all right because I would learn from this relationship how to relate to other people and maybe even one day leave behind the isolation of my own world. . . . I often felt at odds with my therapist until I could see that he was a real person and he related to me and I to him, not only as patient and therapist, but as human beings. Eventually I began to feel that I too was a person, not just an outsider looking in on the world.

Medication or superficial support is not a substitute for the feeling that one is understood by another human being. For me, the greatest gift came the day I realized that my therapist really had stood by me for years and that he would continue to stand by me and help me achieve what I wanted to achieve. With that realization, my viability as a person began to grow. ("A Recovering Patient," 1986, pp. 68–70)

In this poignant account, written by a person who had suffered from schizophrenia for much of her life, we see that even in this most serious of behavior disorders, humans can reach out and help one another. This chapter explores the many approaches that are being taken to treat psychological disorders, as well as the critical issue of their effectiveness. Although first-person reports, like the one above, suggest that many people derive considerable benefit from psychotherapy, psychologists demand much more in the way of evidence. Nearly 60 years of research on psychological treatments has taught us that the question of efficacy, or treatment outcome, is a tremendously complex one that has no simple answers. Yet as we shall see, much has been learned about the effectiveness of these various therapeutic approaches and about the factors that influence treatment outcome.

PSYCHOLOGICAL TREATMENTS

The basic goal of all psychotherapy, whatever the approach, is to help people change maladaptive thoughts, feelings, and behavior patterns so that

they can live happier and more productive lives. As the remarks of the "recovering patient" suggest, the relationship between the client and the person providing help is a prime ingredient of psychotherapeutic success (Binder & Strupp, 1997; Gabbard et al., 2005). Within that helping relationship, therapists use a variety of treatment techniques to promote positive changes in the client. These techniques vary widely, depending on the therapists' own theories of cause and change, and they may range from biomedical approaches (such as administering psychoactive drugs) to a wide variety of psychological treatments. Both of these elements—relationship and techniques—are important to the success of the treatment enterprise (Figure 15.1).

A number of professional groups provide psychological treatments. *Clinical and counseling psychologists* make up one group. These psychologists, who typically hold a PhD (Doctor of Philosophy) or PsyD (Doctor of Psychology), have received 5 or more years of intensive training and supervision in a variety of psychotherapeutic techniques, as well as training in research and psychological assessment techniques. The PhD, typically conferred by university psychology departments, is a more

► **Focus 1**
How do client, therapist, and treatment techniques combine in the process of therapy?

573

FIGURE 15.1

FIGURE 15.1

The process of therapy involves a relationship between a client and a therapist, who applies the techniques dictated by his or her approach to treatment.

science-oriented degree. The PsyD degree, usually conferred by professional schools, is more professionally than scientifically oriented. Another major group of psychotherapists, *psychiatrists,* are medical doctors who specialize in psychotherapy and in biomedical treatments, such as drug therapy.

In addition to psychologists and psychiatrists, a number of other professionals provide treatment. These professionals typically receive a master's degree based on 2 years of highly focused and practical training. They include *psychiatric social workers,* who often work in community agencies; *marriage and family counselors,* who specialize in problems arising from family relationships; *pastoral*

counselors, who tend to focus on spiritual issues; and *substance-abuse counselors,* who work with substance and sexual abusers and their victims.

Having previewed the nature of therapy and those who provide it, we will now consider the therapeutic approaches that have developed within the major perspectives on human behavior (Figure 15.2).

PSYCHODYNAMIC THERAPIES

Of the many psychotherapeutic approaches, psychodynamic treatments have the longest tradition. Their historical roots lie in Sigmund

FIGURE 15.2

Major approaches to treatment.
This diagram gives an overview of the major treatment approaches to behavior disorders.

Freud's psychoanalytic theory. Although both the theory and the techniques of therapy were later modified by his followers and by those who defected to pursue rival approaches, the psychodynamic principles underlying Freud's approach continue to exert a major influence today (Alexander, 2004). Psychodynamic approaches have in common a focus on internal conflicts and unconscious factors that underlie maladaptive behavior.

PSYCHOANALYSIS

The term *psychoanalysis* refers not only to Freud's theory of personality but also to the specific approach to treatment that he developed. The goal of psychoanalysis is to help clients achieve **insight,** *the conscious awareness of the psychodynamics that underlie their problems.* Such awareness permits clients to adjust their behavior to their current life situations, rather than repeating the maladaptive routines learned in childhood. Analysts believe that as the client repeatedly encounters and deals with long-buried emotions, motives, and conflicts within and outside of therapy, the psychic energy that was previously devoted to keeping unconscious conflicts under control can be released and redirected to more adaptive ways of living (Gabbard, 2004). We now consider the methods and concepts that Freud developed to achieve the end product of successful therapy: "Where there was id, there shall ego be" (Freud, 1923, p. 148).

Free Association

Freud believed that mental events are meaningfully associated with one another, so that clues to the contents of the unconscious can be found in the ongoing stream of thoughts, memories, images, and feelings that we experience. In the technique of **free association,** *clients verbally report without censorship any thoughts, feelings, or images that enter their awareness.* Analysts sit out of sight behind the client so that the client's thought processes will be determined primarily by internal factors (Figure 15.3).

The analyst does not expect that free association will necessarily lead directly to unconscious material but rather that it will provide clues concerning important themes or issues (Hoffer & Youngren, 2004). For example, a client's stream of thoughts may suddenly stop after she mentions her father, suggesting that she was approaching a loaded topic that activated repressive defenses.

FIGURE 15.3

In classical Freudian psychoanalysis, the client reclines on a couch while the analyst sits out of view to minimize external stimuli that might influence the client's thought processes.

▶ **Focus 2**
What is the major therapeutic goal in psychoanalysis?

Dream Interpretation

Psychoanalysts believe that dreams express impulses, fantasies, and wishes that the client's defenses keep bottled up in the unconscious during waking hours (Glucksman, 2001). Even in dreams, which Freud termed "the royal road to the unconscious," defensive processes usually disguise the threatening material to protect the dreamer from the anxiety that the material might evoke. In dream interpretation, the analyst helps the client search for the unconscious material contained in the dreams. One means of doing so is to ask the client to free-associate to each element of the dream. The analyst then helps the client arrive at an understanding of what the symbols in the dream might really represent (Figure 15.4).

"HAVE A COUPLE OF DREAMS, AND CALL ME IN THE MORNING."

FIGURE 15.4

Dream analysis is a central technique in psychoanalysis. SOURCE: Copyright © 2003 by Sidney Harris: ScienceCartoonsPlus.com. Reprinted with permission.

▶ **Focus 3**
Describe the roles of free association, dream analysis, resistance, transference, and interpretation in psychoanalysis.

Resistance

Although clients come to therapists for help, they also have an unconscious investment in maintaining the status quo. After all, underlying their problems are unconscious conflicts so threatening and painful that the ego has resorted to maladaptive defensive patterns to deal with them. These avoidance patterns emerge in the course of therapy as **resistance,** *defensive maneuvers that hinder the process of therapy.* Resistance can appear in many different forms. A client may suddenly experience difficulty in free-associating, arrive late to a therapy session or "forget" about it altogether, or avoid talking about certain topics. Resistance is a sign that anxiety-arousing material is being approached. An important task of analysis is to explore the reasons for resistance, both to promote insight and to guard against the ultimate resistance: the client's decision to drop out of therapy prematurely.

Transference

As noted earlier, the analyst sits out of view of the client and reveals nothing to the client about herself or himself. Eventually, Freud discovered, clients begin to project onto the "blank screen" of the therapist important perceptions and feelings related to their underlying conflicts. **Transference** *occurs when the client responds irrationally to the analyst as if she or he were an important figure from the client's past.* Transference is considered a most important process in psychoanalysis, for it brings into the open repressed feelings and maladaptive behavior patterns that both the therapist and client can discover and explore.

Transference takes two basic forms. *Positive transference* occurs when a client transfers feelings of intense affection, dependency, or love to the analyst, whereas *negative transference* involves irrational expressions of anger, hatred, or disappointment. Analysts believe that until transference reactions are analyzed and resolved, there can be no full resolution of the client's problems. In the following excerpt from a psychoanalytic session, a client traces her transference reaction to its source and then recognizes the operation of similar reactions in other relationships.

> *Client:* I have conflicting emotions about you. Sometimes I like you too much and sometimes I get mad at you for no reason. I often can't think of you, even picture you. . . . Yes, I don't want to like

you. If I do, I won't be able to help myself. I'll get hurt. But why do I feel or insist that I'm in love with you?

> *Therapist:* Are you?

> *Client:* Yes. And I feel so guilty and upset about it. At night I think of you and get sexual feelings and it frightens me.

> *Therapist:* Do I remind you of anyone?

> *Client:* Yes. (Pause) There are things about you that remind me of my brother. (Laughs) I realize this is silly.

> *Therapist:* Mmhmm.

> *Client:* My brother Harry, the one I had the sex experiences with when I was little. He made me do things I didn't want to. . . . I'm afraid of you taking advantage of me. If I tell you I like you, that means you'll make me do what you want.

> *Therapist:* Just like Harry made you do what he wanted.

> *Client:* Yes. I didn't want to let him do what he did, but I couldn't help myself. I hated myself. That's why. I know it now because there is no reason why I should feel you are the same way. That's why I act that way with other people too. . . . I don't like to have people get too close to me. The whole thing is the same as happens with you. It's all so silly and wrong. You aren't my brother and the other people aren't my brother. I never saw the connection until now. (Wolberg, 1967, pp. 660–661)

In this interchange, we see both positive and negative transference reactions based on an important past relationship. The client's feelings about her brother continue to play out in her fear of getting close to others and being exploited once again.

Interpretation

How can analysts help clients detect and understand resistances, the meaning of dream symbols, and transference reactions? The analyst's chief therapeutic technique for these purposes is **interpretation,** *any statement by the therapist that is intended to provide the client with insight into his or her behavior or dynamics.* An interpretative statement confronts clients with something that they have not previously admitted into consciousness, for example, "It's almost as if you're angry with me without realizing it."

A general rule in psychoanalytic treatment is to interpret what is already near the surface and just beyond the client's current awareness (McWilliams, 2004). Offering "deep" interpretations of strongly defended unconscious dynamics is considered poor technique because, even if they are correct, such interpretations are so far removed from the client's current awareness that they cannot be informative or helpful. This is one reason that even after the analyst fully understands the causes of the client's problems, psychoanalysis may require several more years of treatment. It is the client who must eventually arrive at the insights, then translate them into behavior changes within important life domains and relationships.

BRIEF PSYCHODYNAMIC AND INTERPERSONAL THERAPIES

Classical psychoanalysis as practiced by Freud (and by a declining number of contemporary analysts) is an expensive and time-consuming process, for the goal is no less than rebuilding the client's personality. In classical psychoanalysis, it is not uncommon for a client to be seen 5 times a week for 5 years or more. Today, however, many therapists consider this level of client-therapist commitment both impractical and unnecessary. Their conclusion is supported by psychotherapy studies in which researchers and clients rated the degree of improvement that occurred by the end of therapy. Figure 15.5 plots the amount of improvement in relation to the number of sessions the clients were seen for treatment (Howard et al., 1986). As you can see, about half of the clients improved markedly within 8 sessions, and most therapeutic effects as rated by researchers occurred within 26 sessions. Other studies have also shown sudden gains early in treatment (Stiles et al., 2003).

To an increasing extent, psychodynamic therapists are adopting briefer and more economical approaches. Like psychoanalysis, brief psychodynamic psychotherapies focus on understanding the maladaptive influences of the past and relating them to current patterns of self-defeating behavior. Many of these brief therapies utilize basic concepts from psychoanalysis, such as the importance of insight and the use of interpretation, but they employ them in a more focused and active fashion (Binder, 2004). The therapist and client are likely to sit facing each other and conversation typically replaces free association. Clients are seen 1 or 2 times a week rather than daily, and the goal is typically limited to helping the client deal with specific life problems rather than attempting a complete rebuilding of the client's personality. Therapy is therefore more likely to focus on the client's current life situations than on past childhood experiences and may involve teaching the client specific interpersonal and emotion-control skills (Benjamin, 2003).

One recently developed brief therapy, **interpersonal therapy,** *focuses almost exclusively on clients' current relationships with important people in their lives* (Weissman & Markowitz, 1994). This therapy, designed in part for research on the treatment of depression, is highly structured and seldom takes longer than 15 to 20 sessions. Therapeutic goals include resolving role disputes such as marital conflict, adjusting to the loss of a relationship or to a changed relationship, and identifying and correcting deficits in social skills that make it difficult for the client to initiate or maintain satisfying relationships. The therapist collaborates very actively with the client in finding solutions to these problems and may invite the client to link issues in current relationships with those in important past relationships, thereby showing that what happened in the past need not be carried into the present. In controlled outcome studies, interpersonal therapy has proven effective for several disorders, particularly depression (Chambless & Hollon, 1998; DeRubeis & Crits-Christoph, 1998). Its relative brevity appeals not only to clinicians but also to insurance companies and health maintenance organizations that are interested in reducing therapy costs.

▶ **Focus 4**
How do brief psychodynamic and interpersonal therapies differ from classical psychoanalysis? Which research results support their use?

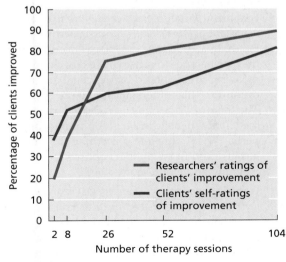

FIGURE 15.5

How quickly does improvement occur? These data, based on researchers' and clients' ratings, suggest that many psychotherapy clients improve within 8 months and that most improvement occurs within the first 26 sessions. SOURCE: Adapted from Howard et al., 1986.

HUMANISTIC PSYCHOTHERAPIES

▶ **Focus 5**
How does the goal of humanistic therapies differ from that of psychodynamic therapies?

▶ **Focus 6**
What three therapist attributes did Rogers find to be crucial to therapeutic success?

In contrast to psychodynamic theorists, who view behavior as a product of unconscious processes, humanistic theorists view humans as capable of consciously controlling their actions and taking responsibility for their choices and behavior. These theorists also believe that everyone possesses inner resources for self-healing and personal growth and that disordered behavior reflects a blocking of the natural growth process. This blocking is brought about by distorted perceptions, lack of awareness about feelings, or a negative self-image.

When these assumptions about human nature are applied to psychotherapy, they inspire treatments that are radically different from psychoanalysis. Humanistic psychotherapy is seen as a human encounter between equals. The therapist's goal is to create an environment in which clients can engage in self-exploration and remove the barriers that block their natural tendencies toward personal growth (Greenberg & Rice, 1997). These barriers often result from childhood experiences that fostered unrealistic or maladaptive standards for self-worth. When people try to live their lives according to the expectations of others rather than their own desires

and feelings, they often feel unfulfilled and empty and unsure about who they really are.

In contrast to classical psychoanalytic therapy, humanistic approaches focus primarily on the present and future instead of the past. Therapy is directed at helping clients to become aware of feelings as they occur rather than to achieve insights into the childhood origins of those feelings.

CLIENT-CENTERED THERAPY

The best-known and most widely used humanistic therapy is the *client-centered* (now sometimes called *person-centered*) *approach* developed by Carl Rogers (1959, 1980; Figure 15.6). In the 1940s, Rogers began to depart from psychoanalytic methods. He became convinced that the important active ingredient in therapy is the relationship that develops between client and therapist, and he began to focus his attention on the kind of therapeutic environment that seemed most effective in fostering self-exploration and personal growth (Bozarth et al., 2002). Rogers's research and experiences as a therapist identified three important and interrelated therapist attributes:

- **Unconditional positive regard** *is communicated when the therapist shows that he or she genuinely cares about and accepts the client, without judgment or evaluation.* The therapist also communicates a sense of trust in the client's ability to work through her or his problems. In part, this sense of trust is communicated in the therapist's refusal to offer advice or guidance.

- **Empathy,** *the willingness and ability to view the world through the client's eyes,* is a second vital factor. In a good therapeutic relationship, the therapist comes to sense the feelings and meanings experienced by the client and communicates this understanding to the client. The therapist does this by *reflecting* back to the client what she or he is communicating— perhaps by rephrasing something the client has just said in a way that captures the meaning and emotion involved.

- **Genuineness** *refers to consistency between the way the therapist feels and the way he or she behaves.* The therapist must be open enough to express his or her own feelings honestly, whether positive or negative. In the case of negative feelings, this may seem to be contradictory to the attribute of unconditional positive regard, but that is not necessarily the case. Indeed, the most striking demonstrations of both attributes occur when a therapist can express displeasure with a client's behavior and at the same time communicate acceptance of the client as a person. For example, a therapist might say, "I feel frustrated with the way you handled that situation because I want things to work out better than that for you."

Rogers believed that when therapists can express these three key therapeutic attributes, they create a climate in which the client feels accepted, understood, and free to explore basic attitudes and feelings without fear of being judged or rejected. Within such a climate, the client experiences the courage and freedom to grow. These therapeutic attitudes are exhibited in the following excerpt from one of Rogers's therapy sessions:

> *Client:* I cannot be the kind of person I want to be. I guess maybe I haven't the guts or the strength to kill myself, and if someone else would relieve me of the responsibility or I would be in an accident, I—just don't want to live.
>
> *Rogers:* At the present time things look so black that you can't see much point in living. (Note the use of empathic reflection and the absence of any criticism.)
>
> *Client:* Yes, I wish I'd never started this therapy. I was happy when I was living in my dream world. There I could be the kind of person I wanted to be. But now there is such a wide, wide gap between my ideal and what I am. . . . (Notice how the client responds to reflection with more information.)
>
> *Rogers:* It's really tough digging into this like you are and at times the shelter of your dream world looks more attractive and comfortable. (Reflection.)
>
> *Client:* My dream world or suicide. . . . So I don't see why I should waste your time coming in twice a week—I'm not worth it—what do you think?
>
> *Rogers:* It's up to you. . . . It isn't wasting my time. I'd be glad to see you whenever you come, but it's how you feel about it. . . . (Note the genuineness in stating an honest desire to see the client and the unconditional positive regard in trusting her capacity and responsibility for choice.)
>
> *Client:* You're not going to suggest that I come in oftener? You're not alarmed and think I ought to come in every day until I get out of this?

> *Rogers:* I believe you're able to make your own decision. I'll see you whenever you want to come. (Trust and positive regard.)
>
> *Client:* (Note of awe in her voice.) I don't believe you are alarmed about—I see—I may be afraid of myself but you aren't afraid for me. (She experiences the therapist's confidence in her.)
>
> *Rogers:* You say you may be afraid of yourself and are wondering why I don't seem to be afraid for you. (Reflection.)
>
> *Client:* You have more confidence in me than I have. I'll see you next week, maybe. (Based on Rogers, 1951, p. 49) [The client did not attempt suicide.]

Rogers believed that as clients experience a constructive therapeutic relationship, they exhibit increased self-acceptance, greater self-awareness, enhanced self-reliance, increased comfort with other relationships, and improved life functioning (Rogers, 1959). Research does indicate that therapists' characteristics have a strong effect on the outcome of psychotherapy. Therapy is most likely to be successful when the therapist is perceived as genuine, warm, and empathic (Sachse & Elliott, 2002).

GESTALT THERAPY

Frederick S. (Fritz) Perls, a European psychoanalyst who was trained in Gestalt psychology, developed another humanistic approach to treatment. As noted in Chapter 4, the term *gestalt* ("organized whole") refers to perceptual principles through which people actively organize stimulus elements into meaningful "whole" patterns. Ordinarily, whatever we perceive, whether external stimuli, ideas, or emotions, we concentrate on only part of our whole experience—the figure—while largely ignoring the background against which the figure appears. For people who have psychological difficulties, that background includes important feelings, wishes, and thoughts that are blocked from ordinary awareness because they would evoke anxiety. Gestalt therapy's goal is to bring them into immediate awareness so that the client can be whole once again.

Gestalt therapy, often carried out in groups, entails a variety of imaginative techniques to help clients "get in touch with their inner selves." These methods are much more active and dramatic than client-centered approaches and sometimes even confrontational. Therapists often ask clients to role-play different aspects of themselves so that they may directly experience their inner dynamics. In the *empty-chair technique,* a client may be asked

FIGURE 15.6

"Psychotherapy is the releasing of an already existing capacity in a potentially competent individual, not the expert manipulation of a more or less passive personality."—Carl Rogers

▶ **Focus 7**
What is the goal of gestalt therapy?

to imagine his mother sitting in the chair, then carry on a conversation in which he alternatively role-plays his mother and himself, changing chairs for each role and honestly telling her how he feels about important issues in their relationship. These techniques can evoke powerful feelings and make clients aware of unresolved issues that affect other relationships in their lives as well. Recent research on the empty-chair technique indicates that it does indeed help clients resolve "unfinished business" with significant others from their pasts (Greenberg & Malcolm, 2002). Although Perls died in 1970, Gestalt therapy remains a vital force, and its principles and techniques are being incorporated into nonhumanistic therapies as well (Burley & Freier, 2004; Cain & Seeman, 2002).

IN REVIEW

■ Humanistic psychotherapies attempt to liberate the client's natural tendency toward self-actualization by establishing a growth-inducing therapeutic relationship.

■ Rogers's client-centered therapy emphasizes the importance of three therapist characteristics: unconditional positive regard, empathy, and genuineness.

■ The goal of Gestalt therapy is to remove blockages to clients' awareness of the wholeness of immediate experience by making them more aware of their feelings and the ways in which they interact with others.

COGNITIVE THERAPIES

As we saw in the previous chapter, many behavior disorders, including anxiety, mood, and schizophrenic disorders, involve maladaptive ways of thinking about oneself and the world. Cognitive approaches to psychotherapy focus on the role of irrational and self-defeating thought patterns, and therapists who employ this approach try to help clients discover and change the cognitions that underlie their problems.

In contrast to psychoanalysts, cognitive therapists do not emphasize the importance of unconscious psychodynamic processes. They do, however, point out that because our habitual thought patterns are so well-practiced and ingrained, they tend to "run off" almost automatically, so that we may be only minimally aware of them and may

▶ **Focus 8**
How is the ABCD model used in rational-emotive therapy? Which disorders respond well to Beck's cognitive therapy?

simply accept them as reflecting reality (Clark et al., 1999). Consequently, clients often need help in identifying the beliefs, ideas, and self-statements that trigger maladaptive emotions and behaviors. Once identified, these cognitions can be challenged and, with practice and effort, changed. Albert Ellis and Aaron Beck are the most influential figures in the cognitive approach to therapy.

ELLIS'S RATIONAL-EMOTIVE THERAPY

Albert Ellis originally trained as a psychoanalytic therapist, became convinced that irrational thoughts, rather than unconscious dynamics, were the most immediate cause of self-defeating emotions. In the 1960s, his new approach of rational-emotive therapy helped launch the cognitive revolution in clinical psychology.

Ellis's theory of emotional disturbance and his rational-emotive therapy are embodied in his ABCD model (Figure 15.7).

- *A* stands for the *activating event* that seems to trigger the emotion.
- *B* stands for the *belief system* that underlies the way in which a person appraises the event.

FIGURE 15.7

Ellis's ABCD model. Albert Ellis's ABCD model describes his theory of the cause—and remediation—of maladaptive emotional responses and behaviors. In rational-emotive therapy, the goal is to discover, dispute, and change the client's maladaptive beliefs.

- C stands for the emotional and behavioral *consequences* of that appraisal.
- D is the key to changing maladaptive emotions and behaviors: *disputing*, or challenging, an erroneous belief system.

Ellis points out that people are accustomed to viewing their emotions (C) as being caused directly by events (A). Thus a young man who is turned down for a date may feel rejected and depressed. However, Ellis would insist that the woman's refusal is *not* the true reason for the emotional reaction. Rather, the young man's depression is caused by his irrational belief that "Because she doesn't want to be with me, I'm worthless, and no one will ever want me." If the young man does not want to feel depressed and rejected, this belief must be countered and replaced by a more rational interpretation (e.g., "It would have been nice if she had accepted my invitation, but I don't need to turn it into a catastrophe. It doesn't mean other women will never care about me.").

Rational-emotive therapists introduce clients to commonly held irrational beliefs (Table 15.1) and then train them to ferret out the particular

ideas that underlie their maladaptive emotional responses (Figure 15.8). Clients are given homework assignments to help them analyze and change self-statements. They may be asked to place themselves in challenging situations and practice control over their emotions by using new self-statements. For example, a shy person might be required to go to a party and practice rational thoughts that counteract social anxiety. Ellis reports that he overcame his own fears of women's rejection by going to Central Park in New York, practicing anxiety-reducing self-statements and striking up conversations with more than 100 different women. He reports that he got only one date, but he overcame his anxiety without being either assaulted or arrested. By learning and practicing cognitive coping responses, clients can eventually modify underlying belief systems in ways that enhance well-being (Dryden, 2002).

BECK'S COGNITIVE THERAPY

Like Ellis, Aaron Beck's goal is to point out errors of thinking and logic that underlie emotional disturbance and to help clients identify and reprogram

FIGURE 15.8

"The essence of effective therapy according to rational-emotive therapy is full tolerance of people as individuals combined with a ruthless campaign against their self-defeating ideas. . . . These can be easily elicited and demolished by any scientist worth his or her salt; and the rational-emotive therapist is exactly that: an exposing and nonsense-annihilating scientist."—Albert Ellis

TABLE 15.1 Irrational Ideas That Cause Disturbance and Alternatives That Might Be Offered by a Rational-Emotive Therapist	
Irrational Belief	**Rational Alternative**
It is a dire necessity that I be loved and approved of by virtually everyone for everything I do.	Although we might prefer approval to disapproval, our self-worth need not depend on the love and approval of others. Self-respect is more important than giving up one's individuality to buy the approval of others.
I must be thoroughly competent and achieving to be worthwhile. To fail is to be a *failure*.	As imperfect and fallible human beings, we are bound to fail from time to time. We can control only effort; we have incomplete control over outcome. We are better off focusing on the process of doing rather than on demands that we do well.
It is terrible, awful, and catastrophic when things are not the way I demand that they be.	Stop catastrophizing and turning an annoyance or irritation into a major crisis. Who are we to demand that things be different from what they are? When we turn our preferences into dire necessities, we set ourselves up for needless distress. We had best learn to change those things we can control and accept those that we can't control (and be wise enough to know the difference).
Human misery is externally caused and forced on us by other people and events.	Human misery is produced not by external factors but rather by what we tell ourselves about those events. We feel as we think, and most of our misery is needlessly self-inflicted by irrational habits of thinking.
Because something deeply affected me in the past, it must continue to do so.	We hold ourselves prisoner to the past because we continue to believe philosophies and ideas learned in the past. If they are still troubling us today, it is because we are still propagandizing ourselves with irrational nonsense. We *can* control how we think in the present and thereby liberate ourselves from the "scars" of the past.

FIGURE 15.9

"The formula for treatment may be stated in simple terms: The therapist helps the patient to identify his warped thinking and to learn more realistic ways to formulate his experience."—Aaron Beck

▶ **Focus 9**
Which classical and operant conditioning principles underlie exposure therapy? What problems is it applied to?

their overlearned automatic thought patterns (Figure 15.9). In treating depressed clients, a first step is to help clients realize that their thoughts, and not the situation, cause their maladaptive emotional reactions. This sets the stage for identifying and changing the self-defeating thoughts:

> *Client:* I get depressed when things go wrong. Like when I fail a test.
>
> *Beck:* How can failing a test make you depressed?
>
> *Client:* Well, if I fail, I'll never get into law school.
>
> *Beck:* So failing a test means a lot to you. But if failing a test could drive people into clinical depression, wouldn't you expect everyone who failed a test to have a depression? Did everyone who failed get depressed enough to require treatment?
>
> *Client:* No, but it depends on how important the test was to the person.
>
> *Beck:* Right, and who decides the importance?
>
> *Client:* I do.
>
> *Beck:* Now what did failing mean?
>
> *Client:* (Tearful) That I couldn't get into law school.
>
> *Beck:* And what does that mean to you?
>
> *Client:* That I'm just not smart enough.
>
> *Beck:* Anything else?
>
> *Client:* That I can never be happy.
>
> *Beck:* And how do those thoughts make you feel?
>
> *Client:* Very unhappy.
>
> *Beck:* So it is the *meaning* of failing a test that makes you very unhappy. In fact, believing that you can never be happy is a powerful factor in producing unhappiness. So you get yourself into a trap—by definition, failure to get into law school equals "I can never be happy." (Beck et al., 1979, pp. 145–146, italics added)

Beck's contributions to understanding and treating depression have made his cognitive therapy a psychological treatment of choice for that disorder (Moorey, 2003). Cognitive therapy has also been applied to the treatment of anxiety and personality disorders (Beck et al., 2004; Clark, 2004). As we shall see, cognitive therapy is also

being combined with other therapeutic techniques to form highly effective treatment packages for certain disorders.

BEHAVIOR THERAPIES

In the 1960s, behavioral approaches emerged as a dramatic departure from the assumptions and methods that characterized psychoanalytic and humanistic therapies. The new practitioners of behavior therapy denied the importance of inner dynamics. Instead, they insisted that (1) maladaptive behaviors are not merely symptoms of underlying problems but rather *are* the problem; (2) problem behaviors are learned in the same ways normal behaviors are; and (3) maladaptive behaviors can be unlearned by applying principles derived from research on classical conditioning, operant conditioning, and modeling. Behaviorists demonstrated that these learning procedures could be applied effectively to change the behaviors of schizophrenia, to treat anxiety disorders, and to modify many child and adult behavior problems that seemed resistant to traditional therapy approaches (Hersen, 2002).

Classical conditioning procedures have been used in two major ways. First, they have been used to reduce, or decondition, anxiety responses. Second, they have been used in attempts to condition aversive emotional responses to a particular class of stimuli, such as alcohol or inappropriate sexual objects. The most commonly used classical conditioning procedures are *exposure therapies, systematic desensitization,* and *aversion therapy.*

EXPOSURE: AN EXTINCTION APPROACH

From a behavioral point of view, phobias and other fears result from classically conditioned emotional responses. The conditioning experience is assumed to involve a pairing of the phobic object (the neutral stimulus) with an aversive unconditioned stimulus (UCS). As a result, the phobic stimulus becomes a conditioned stimulus (CS) that elicits the conditioned response (CR) of anxiety. According to the two-factor learning theory discussed in Chapters 6 and 14, avoidance responses to the phobic situation are then reinforced by anxiety reduction (operant conditioning based on negative reinforcement). Thus a person who is bitten by a dog may subsequently be afraid of dogs. Moreover, each time he avoids a dog, his avoidance response is strengthened through anxiety reduction.

According to this formulation, the most direct way to reduce the fear is through a process of classical extinction of the anxiety response. This requires **exposure** *to the feared CS in the absence of the UCS* while using **response prevention** *to keep the operant avoidance response from occurring.* This is the theoretical basis for the exposure approach (Marks, 1991; Zinbarg et al., 1992). The client may be exposed to real-life stimuli (Figure 15.10) or asked to imagine scenes involving the stimuli. These stimuli will, of course, evoke considerable anxiety, but the anxiety will extinguish in time if the person remains in the presence of the CS and the UCS does not occur (Rosqvist & Hersen, 2006).

Some critics of exposure treatment are concerned that the intense anxiety created by the treatment may worsen the problem or cause clients to flee from treatment (Bruce & Sanderson, 1998). In a study of women being treated for post-traumatic stress disorder with exposure created by imaging the traumatic event, 15.4 percent of the women did indeed show a temporary increase in PTSD symptom intensity when exposure began. However, this increase did not impair treatment effectiveness or increase the likelihood of withdrawal from treatment (Foa et al., 2002).

Exposure has proved to be a highly effective technique for extinguishing anxiety responses in both animals and humans (Roth & Fonagy, 2005; Spiegler & Guevremont, 2003). Both real-life (*in vivo*) and imaginal exposure are effective. An additional advantage is that clients can administer exposure treatment to themselves under a therapist's direction with high success rates (Marks, 1991).

Computer technology has provided a new method for delivering exposure treatments by bringing the external environment into the therapy room. **Virtual reality (VR)** *involves the use of computer technology to create highly realistic virtual environments that simulate actual experience so vividly that they evoke many of the same reactions that a comparable real-world environment would.* Observers typically wear helmets containing two small video monitors (one for each eye) attached to a high-speed computer. The image to each eye is slightly different, producing binocular depth-perception cues that result in a 3-D image. With the aid of position-tracking devices, the computer monitors the person's physical movements and adjusts the images and sounds accordingly (Figure 15.11). Observers thus have a vivid sense of

FIGURE 15.10

A behavior therapist guides and supports a client with a dog phobia during an *in vivo* exposure therapy session. As a result of exposure, the man's anxiety will extinguish and he will be able to interact more comfortably with this animal and with other dogs.

being "present" in a different place when navigating through the virtual world. VR is increasingly being applied to the treatment of anxiety disorders, particularly phobias (Wiederhold & Wiederhold, 2005). The following "Research Close-Up" describes the use of VR in treating patients with a fear of flying.

FIGURE 15.11

This woman with a spider phobia views a virtual "spider world" inside the helmet. She also handles a realistic toy spider whose movements inside the virtual environment are linked to her manipulation of the toy. The monitor shows the scene being experienced by the client.

Research Close-Up   Exposure Treatment for Fear of Flying Using Virtual Reality

SOURCE: BARBARA O. ROTHBAUM, LARRY HODGES, PAGE L. ANDERSON, LARRY PRICE, and SAMANTHA SMITH (2002). Twelve-month follow-up of virtual reality and standard exposure therapies for the fear of flying. *Journal of Consulting and Clinical Psychology, 70,* 428–432.

INTRODUCTION

Approximately 25 million Americans suffer from a fear of flying in airplanes. They cope with their fear by flying under the influence of drugs or alcohol or by avoiding flying altogether. These coping methods can have negative medical, social, and occupational consequences.

Exposure therapy based on classical extinction principles offers a proven anxiety-reduction approach. In this study, exposure therapy using VR was compared with a standard exposure approach having in vivo and imaginal components and with a waiting-list control condition that did not immediately receive treatment. If effective, VR can be an economical method for treating people with a variety of fear-based conditions, for the stimuli can be easily tailored to the specific problem and client.

METHOD

Forty-nine people who replied to an advertisement offering treatment for severe fear of flying were randomly assigned to three conditions: VR exposure therapy, a standard exposure therapy, and a waiting-list control group that was offered its choice of the two exposure therapies after the exposure groups were treated. Forty-five completed the study.

The VR and standard exposure treatments consisted of 8 individual sessions over a 6-week period. In the first 4 sessions, clients were oriented to the program and learned to reduce anxiety using deep breathing and to counter irrational thoughts, such as "This plane is going to crash. I'm doomed." Exposure therapy was carried out in the final 4 sessions. In the VR condition, clients donned a head-mounted display like that shown in Figure 15.11 and sat in specially equipped airplane seats. Stereo earphones piped in realistic recorded sounds of takeoffs and landings and flying in both clear and stormy weather. Woofers under the seats provided realistic sounds and vibrations to simulate flight stimuli and turbulence. The therapist encouraged the clients to continue their exposure to the stimuli until their anxiety diminished.

In the standard exposure condition, clients were taken to the Atlanta airport and went through ticketing and security checks, rode a train to a remote gate, sat in the gate area with passengers, and then boarded an empty airliner, where they were seated and asked to imagine scenes like those experienced by the VR clients.

After the clients in the two exposure conditions completed their treatment, all clients in the three groups were offered the opportunity to take a round-trip commercial flight from Atlanta to Houston. Later, clients in the waiting-list control condition were offered their choice of the two exposure treatments. All but one of the 15 control clients chose the VR treatment.

RESULTS

After randomly assigning participants to experimental and control conditions, the researchers assessed the clients before treatment began, at the end of the exposure treatments, and 12 months after the completion of treatment. Outcome measures included both a self-report measure of fear of flying and a behavioral measure of actually flying in an airliner.

Figure 15.12 shows the intensity of clients' fear of flying at the three assessment periods. At the end of treatment, both exposure groups showed significant fear reduction as

FIGURE 15.12

Effects of exposure treatment on self-reported fear of flying. Exposure was carried out in two ways. Standard exposure involved in vivo and imaginal exposure, whereas virtual reality presented airline-related stimuli. Both exposure methods resulted in significant fear reduction that was maintained over a 12-month period. The waiting-list control group showed similar improvement when given the treatment. SOURCE: Based on Rothbaum et al., 2002.

compared to the waiting-list clients, who had not yet received treatment. Treatment gains in the exposure clients were maintained over the next 12 months, indicating that the treatment provides long-term benefits. After the control clients received treatment, they exhibited similar improvement on the fear measure.

On the behavioral measure of flying, 8 of 15 VR clients, 10 of 15 standard exposure clients, and only 1 of 15 waiting-list clients accepted the invitation to take the posttreatment flight to Houston. By the 12-month follow-up, however, over 90 percent of the clients in the two exposure conditions had taken at least one commercial airline flight. No differences were found between the exposure groups on overall self-ratings of improvement or on satisfaction with the treatments they received.

DISCUSSION

This study affirms the usefulness of short-term exposure treatments for anxiety-based problems, an effect shown in many previous studies (Rosqvist & Hersen, 2006). More significantly, results indicate that VR was similar in effectiveness to the traditional in vivo and imaginal exposure treatment, both in its initial effects at posttreatment and in the maintenance of therapy gains over the following 12 months. This was the first VR outcome study to conduct a follow-up assessment of treatment gains over such an extended period of time.

Conducting exposure treatment using VR may have some practical advantages. If the VR program is standardized for a particular fear, as in this study, then once the software has been developed, many therapists can apply the treatment to clients in their offices. Standard exposure treatments may require the therapist to leave the office and accompany the client to remote sites, an added treatment expense. With VR, a client may be able to experience many takeoffs and landings per hour, whereas repeated experiences on real airplanes would be prohibitively expensive. Another advantage of VR is the degree of stimuli control; in the real world, specific stimuli are not always available on demand. On the other hand, customizing stimuli for a client may require extensive VR programming that could be very expensive. It thus appears that standardized VR presentations for specific fears (e.g., driving, heights, exposure to various animals) may be most feasible at this time. Future research is certain to provide more information about the effectiveness, advantages, and possible limitations of VR for a variety of other disorders.

SYSTEMATIC DESENSITIZATION: A COUNTERCONDITIONING APPROACH

In 1958 Joseph Wolpe introduced **systematic desensitization,** *a learning-based treatment for anxiety disorders.* Wolpe also presented impressive outcome data for 100 phobic patients he had treated with the technique. Systematic desensitization remains a widely used treatment today. In many controlled studies, its success rate in treating a wide range of phobic disorders has been 80 percent or better (Rachman, 1998; Spiegler & Guevremont, 2003).

Wolpe viewed anxiety as a classically conditioned emotional response. His goal was to eliminate the anxiety by using a procedure called **counterconditioning,** *in which a new response that is incompatible with anxiety is conditioned to the anxiety-arousing CS.* The difference between extinction and counterconditioning is that extinction requires only exposure to the CS; it does not require a substitute response to counter the anxiety response.

The first step in systematic desensitization is to train the client in the skill of voluntary muscle relaxation, using an approach similar to that described in Chapter 10. Next the client is helped to construct a **stimulus hierarchy** *of 10 to 20 scenes arranged in roughly equal steps from low-anxiety scenes to high-anxiety ones.* Table 15.2 shows a stimulus hierarchy that was used in treating a college student with high test anxiety.

In the desensitization sessions, the therapist deeply relaxes the client and then asks the client to vividly imagine the first scene in the hierarchy (the least anxiety-arousing one) for several seconds. The client can't be both relaxed and anxious at the

▶ **Focus 10**
How does systematic desensitization differ from exposure in terms of its underlying principle and techniques?

TABLE 15.2	A Stimulus Hierarchy Used in the Systematic Desensitization Treatment of a Test-Anxious College Student
Scene	**Hierarchy of Anxiety-Arousing Scenes**
1	Hearing about someone else who has a test
2	Instructor announcing that a test will be given in 3 weeks
3	Instructor reminding class that there will be a test in 2 weeks
4	Overhearing classmates talk about studying for the test, which will occur in 1 week
5	Instructor reminding class of what it will be tested on in 2 days
6	Leaving class the day before the exam
7	Studying the night before the exam
8	Getting up the morning of the exam
9	Walking toward the building where the exam will be given
10	Walking into the testing room
11	Instructor walking into the room with the tests
12	Tests being passed out
13	Reading the test questions
14	Watching others finish the test
15	Seeing a question I can't answer
16	Instructor waiting for me to finish the test

same time, so if the relaxation is strong enough, it replaces anxiety as the CR to that stimulus—the counterconditioning process. When the client can imagine that scene for increasingly longer periods without experiencing anxiety, the therapist proceeds to the next scene. When low-arousal scenes have been deconditioned, some of the total anxiety has been reduced and the person is now ready to imagine more anxiety-arousing scenes without becoming anxious. Therapists can also accomplish desensitization through carefully controlled exposure to a hierarchy of real-life situations (e.g., having a person with a phobia of heights actually stand on a step stool and, eventually, walk across a suspension bridge while voluntarily relaxing). Both imaginal and real-life desensitization approaches are highly effective in reducing anxiety (Hersen, 2003).

Although both exposure therapy based on extinction and systematic desensitization are very effective in reducing fear responses, there are practical tradeoffs. Systematic desensitization is sometimes preferred over exposure therapy because it produces far less anxiety for the client during the treatment. Exposure, however, often achieves the desired reduction in anxiety with a briefer course of therapy than does systematic desensitization (Bruce & Sanderson, 1998).

? What Do You Think?

ARE CONDITIONING TECHNIQUES COMPATIBLE WITH PSYCHOANALYTIC THEORY?
Conditioning techniques such as exposure and systematic desensitization are highly effective in treating fears and phobias. Assume, however, that you are a psychoanalyst who believes that the phobia is the result of an underlying unconscious conflict. From your theoretical perspective, what concerns would you have about using these behavioral techniques? Think about it, then see the discussion on page 611.

AVERSION THERAPY

▶ **Focus 11**
Which learning principles underlie aversion therapy? What are its limitations, and how can its effects be enhanced?

For some clients, the therapeutic goal is not to reduce anxiety but actually to condition anxiety to a particular stimulus that triggers deviant behavior. In **aversion therapy**, *the therapist pairs a stimulus that is attractive to the client (the CS) with a noxious UCS in an attempt to condition an aversion to the CS.* For example, aversion treatment for alcoholics may involve injecting the client with a nausea-producing drug and then having him or her drink alcohol (the CS) as nausea (the UCS) develops.

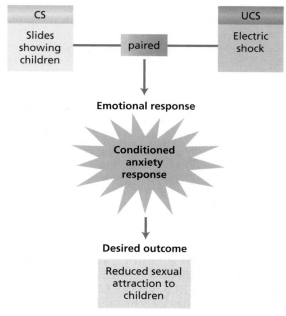

FIGURE 15.13

Aversion therapy. The classical conditioning that occurs in aversion therapy is illustrated in the treatment of pedophiles who receive electric shocks as they view pictures of children. The goal of the treatment is the development of a conditioned aversion in order to reduce sexual attraction to children.

Electric shock may also be paired with alcohol ingestion. Similarly, pedophiles (child molesters) have undergone treatment in which strong electric shocks are paired with slides showing children similar to those the offenders sexually abused (Figure 15.13). To measure the effects of the treatment for males, therapists can use a physiological recording device that measures penile blood-volume responses to the slides; the therapists can then compare the readings before and after treatment (Sandler, 1986).

Aversion therapies have been applied to a range of disorders, with variable results. In one study of 278 alcoholics who underwent aversion therapy, 190 (63 percent) were still abstinent a year after treatment had ended. Three years later, a third of the patients were still abstinent, an impressive result given the traditionally high relapse rate in chronic alcoholic individuals (Wiens & Menustik, 1983). Unfortunately, treatment gains from aversion therapies often fail to generalize from the treatment setting to the real world. A recovering alcoholic or drug addict who goes to a party where friends abuse the substance is likely to have difficulty resisting the temptation to relapse. Some experts believe that aversion therapy is most likely to succeed if it is part of a more comprehensive treatment program in which the client also learns specific coping skills for avoiding relapses (Marlatt & Gordon, 1985).

OPERANT CONDITIONING TREATMENTS

The term **behavior modification** *refers to treatment techniques that apply operant conditioning procedures in an attempt to increase or decrease a specific behavior.* These techniques may use any of the operant procedures for manipulating the environment that we discussed in Chapter 6: positive reinforcement, extinction, negative reinforcement, or punishment.

The focus in behavior modification is on externally observable behaviors. The behaviors targeted for change are measured throughout the treatment program, allowing the therapist to track the progress of the treatment program and to make modifications if behavior change begins to lag.

Behavior modification techniques have been successfully applied to many different behavior disorders. They have yielded particularly impressive results when used in populations that are difficult to treat with more traditional therapies, such as hospitalized schizophrenic patients, profoundly disturbed children, and mentally retarded individuals (Ayllon & Azrin, 1968; DeRubeis & Crits-Christoph, 1998; Lovaas, 1977). We now consider the use of positive reinforcement and punishment in two of these populations.

Positive-Reinforcement Techniques

One of the dangers of long-term psychiatric hospitalization is the gradual loss of social, personal-care, and occupational skills needed to survive outside the hospital. Such deterioration is common among chronic schizophrenic patients who have been hospitalized for an extended period. Verbal psychotherapies have very limited success in rebuilding such skills.

In the 1960s, Teodoro Ayllon and Nathan Azrin (1968) introduced a revolutionary approach to the treatment of hospitalized schizophrenic patients. The **token economy** *is a system for strengthening desired behaviors*—such as personal grooming, appropriate social responses, housekeeping behaviors, working on assigned jobs, and participation in vocational training programs—*through the systematic application of positive reinforcement.* Rather than being given reinforcers such as food or grounds privileges directly, patients earn a specified number of plastic tokens for the performance of each desired behavior listed on a kind of menu. Patients can then redeem the tokens for a wide range of tangible reinforcers,

such as a private room, exclusive rental of a radio or TV set, selection of personal furniture, freedom to leave the ward and walk around the grounds, recreational activities, and items from the hospital commissary. The long-term goal of token-economy programs is to jump-start the behaviors that the patient will need to get along in the world outside the hospital. The tangible reinforcers used in these programs eventually come under the control of social reinforcers and self-reinforcement processes (such as self-pride). When this begins to occur, the tokens can be phased out and the desired behaviors will continue (Kazdin, 2003). Using this technique, Ayllon and Azrin reported remarkable increases in adaptive behavior in patients for whom change seemed hopeless.

Token-economy programs have proven highly effective with some of the most challenging populations. In one study, a token-economy program was carried out over a 4-year period with severely disturbed schizophrenic patients who had been hospitalized an average of more than 17 years. During the course of the program, 98 percent of the patients from the behavioral treatment program were able to be released from the hospital (most to shelter-care facilities in the community), compared with only 45 percent of a control group that received the normal hospital treatments (Paul & Lentz, 1977). Token economies have also been applied successfully within business, school, prison, and home environments to increase desirable behaviors (Sullivan & O'Leary, 1990).

In one recent study, researchers used a positive-reinforcement program to reduce cocaine and opium use among drug addicts receiving methadone treatment. Patients received weekly urine tests for drug detection. Those who had negative tests were eligible to draw a piece of paper from a bowl. Half of the papers earned them prizes ranging in value from $1 to $100. Bonus draws were given for extended periods of abstinence (for example, 2 consecutive weeks of negative urine tests earned six bonus draws). The patients randomly assigned to the positive-reinforcement program had a significantly higher percentage of negative urine tests over the 12-week period. By abstaining from drugs, the patients had a greater opportunity to build coping responses to avoid relapse following treatment (Petry & Martin, 2002).

Therapeutic Application of Punishment

As we saw in Chapter 6, punishment is the quickest way to stop a behavior from occurring, but most psychologists regard it as the least preferred way to control behavior because of its aversive

Watch the "Alcohol Addiction" video in Chapter 15 of your CD for a personal perspective on treatment for alcoholism.

▶ **Focus 12**
How are positive reinforcement and punishment used therapeutically? What evidence exists for their effectiveness?

qualities and potential negative side effects. Therefore, before deciding to use punishment as a therapy technique, therapists ask themselves two important questions: (1) Are there alternative, less painful approaches that might be effective? (2) Is the behavior to be eliminated sufficiently injurious to the individual or to society to justify the severity of the punishment?

Sometimes the answers to these questions lead to a decision to use punishment. For example, some of the most startling self-destructive behaviors occur in certain severely disturbed autistic children. Such children may strike themselves repeatedly, bang their heads on sharp objects, bite or tear pieces of flesh from their bodies, or engage in other self-mutilating behaviors. O. Ivar Lovaas (1977), a UCLA psychologist who pioneered the use of operant conditioning techniques in the treatment of such children, successfully eliminated such behaviors with a limited number of contingent electric shocks. One 7-year-old boy had been self-injurious for 5 years and had to be kept in physical restraints. During one 90-minute period when his restraints were removed, he struck himself more than 3,000 times. With the consent of his parents, shock electrodes were attached to the boy, and he was given a painful electric shock each time he struck himself. Only 12 shocks were needed to virtually eliminate the self-destructive behavior. In another case, 15 shocks eliminated self-destructive behavior in a severely disturbed girl with a history of banging her head against objects. Punishment is never employed without the consent of the client or the client's legal guardian in cases when the client is a minor or is mentally incompetent to give consent.

MODELING AND SOCIAL SKILLS TRAINING

▶ Focus 13
How is modeling used in social skills training? How is self-efficacy involved in its effectiveness?

Modeling is one of the most important and effective learning processes in humans, and modeling procedures have been used to treat a variety of behavioral problems. One of the most widely used applications is designed to teach clients social skills that they lack.

In **social skills training,** *clients learn new skills by observing and then imitating a model who performs a socially skillful behavior.* In the following example, a therapist served as a model for his client, a socially anxious college student who had great difficulty asking women for dates. The client began by pretending to ask for a date over the telephone:

Client: By the way (pause), I don't suppose you want to go out Saturday night?

Therapist: Up to actually asking for the date you were very good. However, if I were the girl, I might have been offended when you said, "By the way." It's like asking her out is pretty casual. Also, the way you posed the question, you are kind of suggesting to her that she doesn't want to go out with you. Pretend for the moment I'm you. Now, how does this sound: "There's a movie at the Varsity Theater that I want to see. If you don't have other plans, I'd very much like to take you."

Client: That sounded good. Like you were sure of yourself and like the girl, too.

Therapist: Why don't you try it? (Rimm & Masters, 1979, p. 74).

Social skills training has been used with many populations, including individuals who have minor deficits in social skills, delinquents who need to learn how to resist negative peer pressures, and even hospitalized schizophrenic patients who need to learn social skills in order to function adaptively outside the hospital (Bellack et al., 2004). It is often used in conjunction with other psychological or biological treatments to jump-start new adaptive behaviors that can then be strengthened by natural reinforcers in the client's everyday environment.

Research demonstrates that increased self-efficacy is a key factor in the effectiveness of social skills training. When clients come to believe that they are capable of performing the desired behaviors, they are more likely to be successful in doing so (Bandura, 1997; Maddux, 1999). Observing successful models also increases self-efficacy by encouraging the view, "If she can do that, so can I."

INTEGRATING AND COMBINING THERAPIES

▶ Focus 14
What is eclecticism? Give two examples of new treatment approaches.

We have now surveyed a variety of therapeutic orientations. To an increasing extent, clinicians are embracing **eclecticism,** *a willingness to combine treatments and use whatever orientations and therapeutic techniques seem appropriate for the particular client they are treating* (Lazarus, 1995; Snyder & Ingram, 2000). In a recent survey of practicing clinical psychologists, 45 percent reported using concepts and methods from multiple therapeutic orientations (Holloway, 2003). Many therapists now label themselves *cognitive-behavioral therapists* because their techniques include elements of both perspectives. In recent years, Albert Ellis and other rational-emotive therapists have renamed their technique *rational-emotive behavior therapy* (Dryden, 2002).

In part, this tendency toward eclecticism reflects a responsiveness to research findings that certain approaches to therapy are well suited for some problems and ill suited for others. For example, Gestalt techniques are highly effective for helping people discover underlying feelings, but a behavioral approach would be the treatment of choice for treating a phobia. Cognitive therapy is highly effective for depression, but so are interpersonal therapy and a behavioral approach called **behavioral activation treatment,** *designed to counter depression by helping clients develop action plans that increase the amount of positive reinforcement they experience in their lives* (Jacobson et al., 2001). A broadly trained therapist could choose to use any combination of techniques for a client who has depression or multiple problems. One national survey of eclectic therapists revealed that 72 percent included psychodynamic principles within their version of treatment, 54 percent included cognitive approaches, 45 percent used behavioral techniques, and a smaller percentage used various humanistic techniques (Jensen et al., 1990).

The move toward eclecticism has resulted in some integrations that are tailored to address particular disorders. An example is **dialectical behavior therapy (DBT),** *developed by Marsha Linehan* (Figure 15.14) *for the treatment of borderline personality disorder.* As described in Chapter 14, this complex disorder is characterized by chaotic interpersonal relationships, poor emotional control, self-destructive behaviors, and low self-esteem. The word *dialectic* describes the contradictions in emotional and interpersonal behavior, thinking, and self-concept that characterize the borderline client's life (Linehan, 1993). DBT includes elements from cognitive, behavioral, humanistic, and psychodynamic therapies to address the many aspects of this disorder. It is intensive in nature, with clients seen in both individual and group sessions by multiple therapists. Behavioral techniques are used to help clients learn interpersonal, problem-solving, and emotion-control skills. Cognitive approaches are employed to help clients learn more adaptive thinking about the world, relationships, and themselves. A psychodynamic element traces the history of early deprivation and rejection that created many of the problems. Recently, a humanistic emphasis on acceptance of thoughts and feelings has been added to help clients better tolerate unhappiness and negative emotions as they occur. A major goal early in

FIGURE 15.14

Marsha Linehan's dialectical behavior therapy approach is an eclectic blend of principles and techniques from cognitive, behavioral, humanistic, and short-term psychodynamic treatments.

treatment is to bring self-destructive behaviors, such as suicide attempts and self-mutilation, under control, and this is approached in a very direct manner throughout treatment. Linehan describes other goals of DBT:

> Many borderline patients react to themselves with extreme loathing, bordering on self-hate. All but a few feel enormous shame in general, and shame about their own abuse history, the troubles they have caused, and their present emotional activity in particular. Cherishing oneself is the opposite of these emotional reactions. Thus, the therapist must target the self-hate, the self-blame, and the sense of shame. . . . The therapist must ultimately pull back and relentlessly reinforce within the therapeutic relationship self-validation, self-care, self-soothing, and problem-solving. (Linehan, 1993, p. 160)

IN REVIEW

■ Cognitive and behavior therapies are among the most popular and effective approaches to psychological treatment.

■ Ellis's rational-emotive therapy and Beck's cognitive therapy focus on discovering and changing maladaptive beliefs and logical errors of thinking that underlie maladaptive emotional responses and behaviors.

- Behavioral treatments based on classical conditioning are directed at modifying emotional responses. Exposure to a CS and prevention of avoidance responses promote extinction. Exposure may be provided in vivo (real life), through imagination, or through virtual reality (VR) technology.

- Systematic desensitization is designed to counter-condition a response to anxiety-arousing stimuli that is incompatible with anxiety, such as relaxation. Aversion therapy is used to establish a conditioned aversion response to a stimulus that triggers deviant behavior.

- Operant procedures have been applied successfully in many behavior modification programs. The token economy is a positive reinforcement program designed to strengthen adaptive behaviors. Punishment has been used to reduce self-destructive behaviors in disturbed children.

- Modeling is an important component of social skills training programs, which help clients learn and rehearse more effective social behaviors.

- Psychotherapy today shows a growing trend toward eclecticism—the combination of various theoretical perspectives and the development of new, more effective therapeutic techniques.

FIGURE 15.15

Family therapists focus on the total pattern of family interactions, and they include the entire family in treatment.

GROUP, FAMILY, AND MARITAL THERAPIES

Most of the therapeutic approaches we have discussed so far can be carried out with groups of clients as well as with individuals (Brabender et al., 2004). Therapy groups typically include 6 to 8 clients and a single therapist. Within a group, clients can experience acceptance, support, and a sense of belonging. They soon see that other people also struggle with problems, a realization that helps counter feelings of isolation and deviance. Clients can also observe how others approach problems, and the interpersonal relations that develop within the group can be a training ground for learning new interpersonal skills. Furthermore, clients can gain insight into how they are perceived by others.

FAMILY THERAPY

▶ **Focus 15**
What principles underlie family and marital therapy? What is the importance of acceptance in marital therapy?

Sometimes the group being treated is a family. Family therapy arose from the clinical observation that many clients who had shown marked improvement in individual therapy—often in institutional settings—suffered relapses when they

returned home and began interacting with their families. This observation led to an important concept in the field of psychotherapy, namely, that the disorder shown by the "identified patient" may reflect dysfunctional relationships within the family system and that permanent change in the client may require that the entire family system be the focus of therapy (Minuchin, 1974). Family therapists therefore help the family understand how it functions and how its unique patterns of interaction contribute to conflicts and to the problems of one or more members (Figure 15.15):

In one family, Jessica, an anorexic 14-year-old girl, was the identified patient. However, as the therapist worked with the family, he saw a competitive struggle for the father's attention and observed that the girl was able to compete and get "cuddly" affection from her father only when she presented herself to him as a "sick" person. To bring the hidden dynamics out into the open, the therapist worked at getting the family members to express their desires more directly—in words instead of through hidden behavioral messages. In time, Jessica became capable of expressing her need for affection directly to her father, and her anorexia disappeared. (Based on Aponte & Hoffman, 1973)

MARITAL THERAPY

Today's soaring divorce rate is a stark reflection of the difficulties that exist in many marriages. Nearly half of all first marriages end in divorce, and the divorce rate is even higher among people who remarry (Hetherington, 1998). Couples frequently seek marital therapy because they are troubled by their relationship or because they are contemplating separation or divorce. Typically, the therapist works with both partners together, and therapy focuses on clarifying and improving the interactions between them (Harway, 2005). Research has shown that happily married couples differ from distressed couples in that they talk more to one another, keep channels of communication open, show more sensitivity to each other's feelings and needs, and are more skilled at solving problems (Gottman & Levinson, 1992). Marital therapy targets improvement in these areas.

Distressed couples frequently have faulty communication patterns, as demonstrated in the following case:

> *Husband:* She never comes up to me and kisses me. I am always the one to make the overtures.
>
> *Therapist:* Is this the way you see yourself behaving with your husband?
>
> *Wife:* Yes, I would say he is the demonstrative one. I didn't know he wanted me to make the overtures.
>
> *Therapist:* Have you told your wife you would like this from her—more demonstration of affection?
>
> *Husband:* Well, no. You'd think she'd know.
>
> *Wife:* No, how would I know? You always said you didn't like aggressive women.
>
> *Husband:* I don't, I don't like dominating women.
>
> *Wife:* Well, I thought you meant women who make the overtures. How am I to know what you want?
>
> *Therapist:* You'd have a better idea if he had been able to tell you. (Satir, 1967, pp. 72–73)

An important recent addition to marital therapy is a focus on *acceptance* (Jacobson & Christensen, 1996). This addition was based on findings that in well-functioning couples, as well as in those who profit from treatment, partners make a deci-

sion to accept those aspects of the partner's behavior that probably are too ingrained to change. For example, it makes little sense to demand that a person with a highly introverted personality style suddenly become a social gadfly and life of the party. The therapeutic emphasis is on helping couples work toward change in those areas where change is possible and helping them learn to accept aspects of the partner and the relationship that seem unlikely to change. Doing so reduces frustration, lessens demands on the other spouse, and allows the couple to focus on and enjoy the positive aspects of their relationship. The addition of acceptance training to the other elements of marital therapy has improved treatment outcomes (Jacobson et al., 2000).

CULTURAL AND GENDER ISSUES IN PSYCHOTHERAPY

Psychological treatments reflect the cultural context in which they develop. Within the dominant cultures of western Europe and North America, personal problems are seen as originating within people in the form of dysfunctional thinking, conflict, and stress responses. People are assumed to be capable of expressing their feelings and taking personal responsibility for improving themselves. We can easily see these values and assumptions reflected in the therapies we have discussed. Psychodynamic, humanistic, and cognitive treatments all focus on changing these internal factors.

These values are not shared by all cultures and ethnic groups, however. For example, people from some Asian cultures might view the "therapeutic" expression of hostility toward one's parents as unthinkable (Hall & Okazaki, 2003). Likewise, the suggestion that assertiveness training would be helpful in competing more successfully with others and standing up for one's rights might be appalling to a person from a collectivistic culture (Cooper & Denner, 1998). Given diverse cultural norms and values, we should not be surprised that some individuals from non-Western cultures view psychotherapy as a totally inappropriate, and even shameful, option for the solution of their problems in living (Foulks et al., 1995).

CULTURAL FACTORS IN TREATMENT UTILIZATION

Recent large-scale epidemiological studies suggest that rates of mental illness differ among

▶ **Focus 16**
What barriers to therapy exist for ethnic minorities? What characteristics are found in culturally competent and gender-sensitive therapists?

ethnic groups. Summarizing the results, Stanley Sue and June Chu (2003) concluded that African Americans appear to have low rates despite a history of prejudice, discrimination, and the resulting stress. American Indians and Alaska Natives have high rates, and Mexican Americans and Asian American and Pacific Islanders show slightly lower or very similar rates compared to non-Hispanic Whites. Even more clear, however, is the fact that members of minority groups use mental health services far less than the majority White population does (Wang et al., 2002). Even when minority group members seek out mental health services, they often fail to stay in treatment. As a result, many problems that could benefit from psychological treatment go untreated (Sue, 1998; Wang et al., 2002).

Psychologists Derald Sue and David Sue (1990) have identified several barriers to treatment among minority groups. One of them is a cultural norm against turning to professionals outside one's own culture for help. Instead these individuals turn to family, clergy, acupuncturists, herbalists, and folk healers for assistance. Moreover, for many minority group members, a history of frustrating experiences with White bureaucracies makes them unwilling to approach a hospital or mental health center. There may also be language barriers.

Sometimes access to treatment is a major problem. Because many minority groups suffer high rates of unemployment and poverty, they may lack health insurance and be unable to afford therapy. Likewise, many community mental health agencies and professional therapists are located outside the areas where the underserved populations live. But even within health systems like Medicare, minorities do not receive equal treatment. In one study of individuals 65 years or older in Medicare+ Choice plans, researchers assessed the percentage of members receiving mental health services, rates of follow-up after hospitalization for mental illness, the number of practitioner contacts for antidepressant medication management, and the number of referrals to effective treatments. On all of these measures, elderly members of minority groups received poorer treatment than did Whites (Virnig et al., 2004).

But according to Stanley Sue and Nolan Zane (1987), the biggest problem of all is the shortage of skilled counselors who can provide culturally responsive forms of treatment. Therapists often have little familiarity with the cultural backgrounds and personal characteristics of ethnic groups other than their own. For example, a therapeutic goal that emphasizes the direct and assertive expression of negative feelings may conflict with the cultural norms of a client from an Asian culture. Sometimes, as well, therapists operate on the basis of inaccurate stereotypes that result in unrealistic and possibly inappropriate goals and expectations, as well as great difficulty in establishing the positive client-therapist relationship that has been shown to be a powerful factor in therapeutic success.

What can be done to increase access of culturally diverse groups to psychological treatment? One answer is to take therapy to the people. Studies have shown that establishing mental health service agencies in minority population areas increases utilization of mental health services, particularly if agencies are staffed by culturally skilled counselors (Sue, 1998). Another solution might be to train more therapists from these ethnic groups. Stanley Sue and his coworkers (1991) found that dropout rates fell and the number of therapy sessions increased when clients saw ethnically similar therapists. However, for clients who elect to remain in therapy, it has *not* been demonstrated that treatment outcomes are better for clients who work with therapists from their own ethnic group. What seems more important than an ethnic match is for the therapist and client to form a good relationship and to share similar viewpoints regarding goals for treatment and preferred means for resolving problems (Figure 15.16).

Stanley Sue (1998) suggests that **culturally competent therapists** *are able to use knowledge*

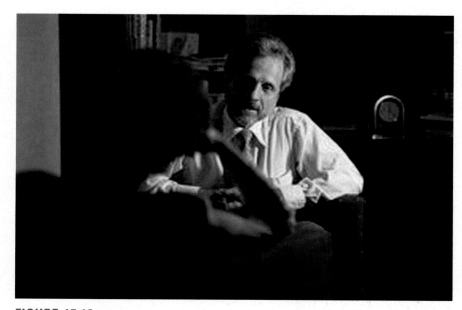

FIGURE 15.16

Research suggests that the outcome of therapy with minority populations is affected more by the cultural sensitivity and competency of the therapist than it is by the ethnic similarity of therapist and client.

about the client's culture to achieve a broad understanding of the client. At the same time, they are attentive to how the client may differ from the cultural stereotype, thereby balancing cultural understanding with the individual characteristics and needs of the client. They are also able to introduce *culture-specific elements* into the therapy. Thus a therapist might draw on some of the techniques used by folk healers within that culture (e.g., prayer or a specific ritual) to effect changes in the client. Obviously, this would require a good working knowledge of the client's culture, plus a willingness to take advantage of what is therapeutically effective for promoting positive changes in that culture (Mishne, 2002). When therapists receive cultural competence training, they are able to work more effectively with members of other cultures, and clients are more likely to remain in treatment (Wade & Bernstein, 1991).

GENDER ISSUES IN THERAPY

Even within the same culture, the lives of men and women can differ in many ways, as can the life demands they must cope with. As we saw in Chapter 14, psychological disorders, particularly those involving anxiety and depression, occur more frequently among women in Western cultures. This may reflect the impact of specific stressors that women face, such as poverty (women are overrepresented at the poverty level); lack of opportunity fostered by sexism; strains created by the demanding multiple roles of mother, worker, and spouse among married women; and the violence and histories of abuse that many women experience. In many instances, psychological problems arise not so much from internal problems and conflicts but from oppressive elements in the family, social, and political worlds. As women strive for more egalitarian relationships with men and for equal opportunity to develop their potential, they often meet external barriers that are deeply embedded in their culture's traditional sex roles and, in some cultures, religious traditions.

Feminist therapy *focuses on women's issues and strives to help women achieve greater personal freedom and self-determination* (Brown, 1994; Worell & Remer, 2003). It is not a specific therapeutic technique but rather an orientation that takes into account issues that affect women's lives. In the eyes of many therapists, it may be more important to focus on what can be done to change women's life circumstances than to help them adapt to sex-role expectations that constrain them (Brown, 1994).

It is important for therapists to support people in making choices that meet their needs, whether it be a man who wishes to stay at home and care for children or a woman who wants a career in the military. Whether the therapist is a man or a woman, what seems most important is the therapist's sensitivity to gender issues.

IN REVIEW

- Group approaches offer clients a number of advantages, including opportunities to form close relationships with others, to gain insights into how they interact with others and are perceived by them, and to observe how others approach problems.

- Family therapy is based on the notion that individuals' problems are often reflections of dysfunctional family systems. Such systems should be treated as a unit.

- Marital therapies help couples improve their communication patterns and resolve difficulties in their relationships. The recent addition of acceptance training has improved outcomes.

- Research has shown that members of minority groups underutilize mental health services. Barriers include lack of access to therapists who can provide culturally responsive forms of treatment. More important to outcome than an ethnic match is a therapist who can understand the client's cultural background and has a similar viewpoint on therapy goals and the means to achieve them. Culturally competent therapists take into account both cultural and individual factors to understand and treat the client.

- For female clients, the most helpful therapist is one who is aware of oppressive environmental conditions and is willing to support life goals that do not necessarily conform to gender expectations. Whether the therapist is a man or a woman seems less important to outcome than gender sensitivity.

EVALUATING PSYCHOTHERAPIES

Given the human suffering created by psychological disorders, the effects of psychotherapy have both personal and societal implications. Practicing clinicians and clinical researchers want to know which approaches are most effective against which kinds of problems and what the effective active ingredients of each treatment are.

► Focus 17
What is the specificity question in psychotherapy research? How did Eysenck challenge beliefs about therapeutic effectiveness?

Today the basic question "Does psychotherapy work?" is viewed as a gross oversimplification of a much more involved question known as the **specificity question**: *"Which types of therapy administered by which kinds of therapists to which kinds of clients having which kinds of problems produce which kinds of effects?* After nearly a half century of psychotherapy research involving many hundreds of studies, this complex question is still not fully answered (Roth & Fonagy, 2005). Nonetheless, for many reasons, this question demands answers. Selecting and administering the most appropriate kind of intervention is vital in human terms. It is also important for economic reasons. Billions of dollars are spent each year on psychological treatments, with an increasing share of these costs paid by so-called third parties such as insurance companies, health maintenance organizations, and government agencies. As the costs rise, those who bear the financial burden increase their demands for accountability and for demonstrations that the treatments are useful.

EYSENCK'S GREAT CHALLENGE

In the 1930s and 1940s, individual case studies provided most of the psychotherapy outcome data. Indeed, Freud and other psychoanalysts opposed the use of experimental methods to evaluate psychoanalysis, insisting that case studies left no doubt regarding its effectiveness (Fisher & Greenberg, 1996). They assumed that without therapy, patients would not improve, and they saw plenty of people who did improve in treatment.

In 1952 British psychologist Hans Eysenck mounted a frontal assault on this assumption. Using recovery data from insurance companies on people who applied for disability because of psychological problems, Eysenck (1952) concluded that the rate of **spontaneous remission**—*symptom reduction in the absence of any treatment*—was as high as the success rates reported by psychotherapists. He therefore concluded that troubled people who receive psychotherapy are no more likely to improve than are those who go untreated. He also pointed out, quite correctly, that virtually all of the existing outcome data were based on therapists' evaluations of their clients' improvement, and he suggested that these evaluations could be biased by therapists' needs to see themselves as competent and successful.

Eysenck's conclusions sparked intense debate—even outrage—among clinicians, but they provided an important wake-up call that could not be ignored. Eysenck's challenge triggered a vigorous increase in psychotherapy research and stimulated the development of more sophisticated methods for evaluating treatment outcomes.

PSYCHOTHERAPY RESEARCH METHODS

Conducting good psychotherapy research is one of the most challenging tasks in all of psychology because there are so many variables that cannot be completely controlled. In contrast to laboratory studies, in which the experimental conditions can be highly standardized, therapist-client interactions are by their nature infinitely varied. Another difficulty involves measuring the effects of psychotherapy. Figure 15.17 shows some of the typical ways of measuring change. These measures differ in the outcome variable assessed (thoughts, emotions, or behaviors) and in the source of the data (the therapist, the client, or other informants). Which measures of change are most important or valid? What if one set of measures indicates improvement, another indicates no change, and a third suggests that the client is worse off than before treatment? How should we evaluate the effects of the therapy? These are just a few of the vexing issues that can arise in psychotherapy research.

A variety of methods have been used to assess the effects of psychotherapy. The individual case study can provide useful information, particularly if objective data are collected throughout and following therapy. However, it can be difficult to generalize conclusions from the individual case. One remedy to this problem is to present multiple case studies of people who have received similar treatment (Kazdin, 2003).

FIGURE 15.17

Psychotherapy outcome measures. The measures used to assess the outcome of psychotherapy may come from a variety of data sources, and they may measure different aspects of the client's functioning.

A second approach is to survey large numbers of people who have been in therapy and measure their reactions to their experience. This provides us with information about what is happening in the world of clinical practice. A third method is the experimental approach as embodied in the **randomized clinical trial**, *in which clients are randomly assigned to treatment or control conditions, and the treatment and control groups are compared on outcome measures.*

Survey Research

A good example of the survey approach is a study carried out by the periodical *Consumer Reports (CR;* Seligman, 1995). One form of *CR*'s 1994 annual survey, mailed to 184,000 randomly selected subscribers, contained a section on stress and mental health. Readers were asked to complete the mental health section if they had sought help for emotional problems in the past 3 years. A total of 22,000 readers responded to the questionnaire—a 13 percent response rate that is typical of *CR* surveys. Of these, 35 percent reported that they had a mental health problem, and 40 percent (approximately 2,900 respondents) of this group reported that they had sought professional help from a psychologist, psychiatrist, social worker, or marriage counselor. The respondents were asked to indicate how much they improved as a result of treatment and how satisfied they were with the treatment they received.

As shown in Figure 15.18, the majority of clients said that they had improved as a result of treatment and that they were satisfied with their therapy. No overall outcome differences were found among mental health professionals, but clients were less satisfied with marriage counselors than with psychologists, psychiatrists, and social workers. The *CR* survey found no effectiveness differences between the various types of psychotherapy the clients said they had received. Seligman concluded that "*CR* has provided empirical validation of the effectiveness of therapy" (1995, p. 974). Further, he concluded that the survey method used in this study might actually have provided data that are more representative of real-life outcomes than data yielded by highly controlled clinical trials.

What Do You Think?

DO SURVEY RESULTS PROVIDE AN ACCURATE PICTURE OF TREATMENT EFFECTIVENESS?

Based on what you've already learned about research methods, do you agree with Seligman's conclusion that

Problem improvement

42% "Helped a lot"

14% "Not helped"

44% "Helped somewhat"

(a)

Therapy satisfaction

27% "Fairly satisfied"

11% "Not satisfied"

62% "Very/completely satisfied"

(b)

FIGURE 15.18

The *Consumer Report* study. These graphs show the ratings of (a) self-perceived improvement and (b) satisfaction with therapy outcome made by 2,900 subscribers of *Consumer Reports* who had been in psychotherapy for the treatment of psychological disorders. SOURCE: Based on Seligman, 1995.

▶ **Focus 18**
What were the major findings of the *CR* survey? On what bases can Seligman's conclusions be challenged?

the *CR* data may be a more valid reflection of therapy success than data from randomized clinical trials? Can you think of any aspects of the *CR* methods that might limit your ability to conclude how effective psychotherapy is? Compare your thoughts with the issues discussed on page 612.

Randomized Clinical Trials

For many of the reasons mentioned in Chapter 2, where we discussed the value of experimental methods for drawing conclusions about causality, most psychotherapy researchers favor randomized clinical trials in which participants who have well-defined psychological disorders and are similar on other variables that might affect response to treatment (e.g., age and ethnic status) are randomly assigned to either an experimental condition that gets treatment or to a control condition (Kazdin, 2003). The control group may be either a no-treatment condition (typically, a waiting-list condition) or a **placebo control group** *that gets an intervention that is not expected to work.* The placebo condition is designed to control for client expectations of improvement and for being seen by a therapist. (For ethical

▶ **Focus 19**
Describe randomized clinical trials with regard to design, treatment standardization, measures of improvement, and follow-up.

reasons, clients in the control group, whether it be a no-treatment or placebo condition, are given the option of receiving the real treatment later.)

Another research design, which avoids the ethical dilemma of withholding or delaying treatment for some participants, involves randomly assigning participants to either the treatment being studied or to another kind of treatment that has proven effective for that disorder. If the new treatment being tested in the experimental condition is found to be at least as effective as the established treatment, then its value is supported. Sometimes, the design of a study involves a group in which the treatment is combined with another intervention such as a drug treatment. It is then possible to see if the group that received the drug *plus* psychotherapy does better than the groups that got only the drug or only the therapy (Hollon, 1996).

To standardize a research treatment, much as one would do in a laboratory experiment, one American Psychological Association (APA) treatment-evaluation committee recommended issuing a manual containing procedures that therapists have to follow exactly and evaluating therapists' compliance with these procedures by observing them or taping their sessions (Chambless & Hollon, 1998). These recommendations aim to ensure that participants in a particular treatment condition are truly receiving the same kind of therapy. The committee also recommended that at least some of the measures of improvement be behavioral in nature. Further, to minimize experimenter bias in evaluating change during interviews or behavioral observations following treatment, interviewers and observers should not know whether a given client was in the control group or the experimental group.

Finally, the committee recommended that therapists collect follow-up data. This is extremely important, for we want to know not only how the treatment conditions differ at the end of the clinical trial but also how long-lasting the effects are. For example, in some studies comparing psychotherapy for depression with the effects of antidepressant drugs, the drug treatment effects occurred more quickly and were stronger at the end of the treatment period, suggesting a superiority for drug therapy. But follow-up data showed psychotherapy to be more effective in the long term. Because clients had learned specific psychological skills that they could apply after therapy ended, there were fewer relapses into depression (Hollon & Beck, 1994; Weissman & Markowitz, 1994).

Empirically Supported Treatments   In the late 1990s, an APA task force surveyed the results of randomized clinical trials that met the rigorous criteria described above. The goal was to identify **empirically supported treatments (ESTs),** *treatments that had been demonstrated in several independent studies to be efficacious for treating specific disorders.* Most of the therapies identified by the task force were cognitive or behavioral in nature. As examples, cognitive therapy and interpersonal therapies were deemed efficacious for depression. Exposure procedures and systematic desensitization were treatments of choice for anxiety disorders, and dialectical behavior therapy was the most effective treatment for borderline personality disorder. Efficacious treatments for other disorders were also identified.

Although the EST approach can provide useful guidelines for both clinical practice and for the training of therapists, concerns have been raised by critics of this approach. They point out that only cognitive and behavioral treatments are "manualized," so that longer-term, more flexible psychodynamic and humanistic treatments are being left out. Critics also point out that in real-world clinical practice, therapists do not rigorously follow a treatment manual, preferring to structure the treatment approach to the individual client. Another problem is the requirement that the patients in the clinical trials have only one DSM-diagnosed clinical disorder. Unfortunately, however, 30 to 50 percent of clinical cases do not fit into a DSM category, and many have more than one disorder. In some randomized clinical trials with certain disorders, up to 70 percent of the potential clients had to be excluded because they had additional disorders (Westen et al., 2004). Finally, critics fear that a premature adherence to today's empirically supported treatments will stifle the development of new therapies that could be even more effective (Goldfried & Eubanks-Carter, 2004; Levant, 2004).

The Search for Therapeutic Principles   The EST approach focuses on the efficacy of particular treatment packages. A suggested alternative is to broaden the inquiry to identify *empirically supported principles* that predict therapeutic outcomes (Castonguay & Beutler, 2005; Goldfried & Eubanks-Carter, 2004). Another APA task force has been formed to explore empirically supported treatment *principles* (Castonguay & Beutler, 2005). Principles are general statements of strategies or variables that promote change (for example, "The therapist helps the patient appraise and increase the accuracy of self- and other perceptions" or "The therapist focuses on and builds upon the patient's strengths"). These principles could be about patient variables, therapist variables, diagnostic type, or treatment strategies. Although priority would be given to results derived from randomized clinical trials, other types of research, including data-oriented case studies and survey studies, would also be surveyed.

Meta-Analysis: A Look at the Big Picture

As discussed in Chapter 2, the technique of **meta-analysis** *allows researchers to combine the statistical results of many studies to arrive at an overall conclusion.* In the psychotherapy research literature they can compute an effect size statistic that represents a common measure of treatment effectiveness. The **effect size** *tells researchers what percentage of clients who received therapy had a more favorable outcome than that of the average control client who did not receive the treatment.*

In 1977 Mary Ann Smith and Gene Glass used meta-analysis to combine the effects of 375 studies of psychotherapy involving 25,000 clients and 25,000 control participants. These studies differed in many ways, but they all compared a treatment condition with a control condition. The results indicated that the average therapy client had a more favorable outcome than 75 percent of the untreated cases. These results prompted Smith and Glass to dispute Eysenck's earlier conclusion, maintaining that therapy does indeed have positive effects beyond spontaneous remission. More recent therapy meta-analyses support this conclusion. Glass and Smith also concluded that psychodynamic, client-centered, and behavioral approaches were quite similar in their effectiveness. *This finding of similar efficacy for widely differing therapies has been termed the* **dodo bird verdict,** after the dodo bird's statement in *Alice in Wonderland* that "Everybody has won and all must have prizes" (Luborsky et al., 2002). Other researchers challenge this conclusion, maintaining that lumping together studies involving different kinds of clinical problems may mask *differential effectiveness,* i.e., the fact that specific therapies might be highly effective for treating some clinical disorders but not others (Beutler, 2002; Westen & Morrison, 2001). Later meta-analyses have tended to focus on specific disorders and the treatments that are most effective for them. Table 15.3 shows the results of recent meta-analyses of EST studies for the treatment of several disorders (Westen et al., 2004).

In evaluating the results of meta-analyses, we should remember that the studies lumped together in a meta-analysis can differ in many ways, including the nature and severity of the problems that were treated, the outcome measures that were used, and the quality of the methodology. Psychotherapy

TABLE 15.3   Meta-Analyses of Improvement and Recovery Rates for Empirically Supported Treatments Applied to Various Adult Disorders

Disorder	Percentage Improved or Recovered*
Obsessive-compulsive disorder	66.7
Panic disorder	63.3
Generalized anxiety disorder	52.1
Major depression	50.8
Bulimia	50.0

*NOTE: *Improvement* typically means at least a 30 to 50 percent reduction in symptoms; *recovery* means total symptom reduction. The data for bulimia are for recovery only. The number of randomized clinical trials summarized range from 7 to 26 for the various disorders.

SOURCES: Adapted from Thompson-Brenner et al., 2003; Westen et al., 2004; Westen & Morrison, 2001.

researchers point out that combining good studies with less adequate ones can produce misleading results (Kazdin, 2003). When studies that meet rigorous research standards are compared in meta-analyses with less rigorous studies, the rigorous studies tend to yield more favorable outcomes for therapy conditions (Matt & Navarro, 1997). Apparently, the rigorous methods used in such studies allow effective therapies to show their true effects.

▶ **Focus 20**
What have meta-analyses shown about the effectiveness of therapies?

FACTORS AFFECTING THE OUTCOME OF THERAPY

Clearly, not everyone who enters therapy profits from it. There is even evidence that some clients—perhaps 10 percent—may get worse as a result of treatment (Binder & Strupp, 1997; Lambert et al., 1986). What, then, are the factors that influence treatment outcome? Research to answer this question has focused on three sets of variables: client variables, therapist variables, and technique variables (Figure 15.19). The APA task force on

▶ **Focus 21**
What client, therapist, technique, and common factors influence treatment outcome?

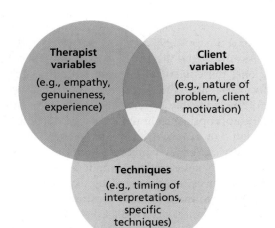

FIGURE 15.19

Determinants of therapy outcome. Research on factors that influence therapy outcome has focused on three sets of interacting variables: client variables, therapist variables, and technique variables.

empirically supported principles has identified variables that make a difference within each of these categories (Castonguay & Beutler, 2005).

Where client variables are concerned, three important factors are the client's openness to therapy, self-relatedness, and the nature of the problem (Castonguay & Beutler, 2005). **Openness** *involves clients' general willingness to invest themselves in therapy and take the risks required to change themselves.* **Self-relatedness** *refers to their ability to experience and understand internal states such as thoughts and emotions, to be attuned to the processes that go on in their relationship with their therapist, and to apply what they learn in therapy to their lives outside of treatment* (Howard et al., 1993). The third important client factor is the nature of the problem and its degree of fit with the therapy being used, i.e., the EST for that disorder. For example, specific problems such as phobias may respond best to a behavioral anxiety-reduction treatment such as systematic desensitization or exposure, whereas a more global problem, such as a search for self-discovery and greater meaning in life, may respond better to a psychodynamic, cognitive, or humanistic approach. Patient age, gender, ethnicity, and intelligence do not seem to affect outcome (Castonguay & Beutler, 2005).

Among therapist variables, perhaps the most important is the quality of the relationship that the therapist is able to establish with the client (Castonguay & Beutler, 2005). Carl Rogers's emphasis on the importance of therapist qualities such as empathy, unconditional acceptance of the client as a person, and genuineness has been borne out in a great many studies. An empathic, trusting, and caring relationship forms the foundation on which the specific techniques employed by the therapist can have their most beneficial effects.

When therapists do not manifest these behaviors, the effects of therapy are not simply null; clients can actually get worse. For example, hostile interchanges between therapist and client can contribute to a *deterioration effect* in therapy (Binder & Strupp, 1997).

Assuming the therapy relationship is a positive one, there is still the consideration of technique variables. A therapist needs to be skilled and knowledgeable in selecting and implementing the appropriate techniques for each client and situation. For example, a large-scale study at the University of Pennsylvania revealed that the correctness of the interpretations made by psychoanalytic therapists, as measured by expert ratings, was related to more positive treatment outcome (Crits-Christoph et al., 1988). Likewise, in a detailed analysis of the audiotaped therapy sessions of 21 psychotherapists, Enrico Jones and coworkers (1988) found that the most effective therapists adjusted their techniques to the specific needs of their clients. They concluded that "general relationship factors, such as therapeutic alliance, are closely bound with the skillful selection and application of psychotherapeutic techniques" (p. 55).

Despite dramatic differences in the techniques they employ, various therapies tend to enjoy similar success rates, perhaps because people who differ on the client variables are lumped together within studies. This finding has led many experts to search for **common factors,** *characteristics shared by these diverse forms of therapy that might contribute to their success.* These common factors include:

- clients' faith in the therapist and a belief that they are receiving help;
- a plausible explanation for clients' problems and an alternative way of helping them look at themselves and their problems;
- a protective setting where clients can experience and express their deepest feelings within a supportive relationship;
- an opportunity for clients to practice new behaviors;
- clients' achieving increased optimism and self-efficacy.

How important these common factors are in comparison with specific therapeutic techniques is currently unknown, and the dodo bird verdict described earlier may reflect a failure to identify specific factors that underlie therapeutic success (Beutler, 2002). The complexities of psychotherapy pose a formidable challenge for clinical researchers. Despite decades of research on the efficacy of psychotherapy techniques, there is still much to learn. We know that some techniques are very effective for certain problems. Yet in the words of the eminent British psychotherapy researcher Isaac Marks, "Little is known about which treatment components produce improvement, how they do so, and why they do not help all sufferers" (Marks, 2002, p. 200).

IN REVIEW

■ The *Consumer Reports* survey of therapy clients suggested high levels of improvement and client satisfaction with their treatment. Randomized clinical trials are considered the most powerful approach to researching the effects of therapy, and a number of standards have been established for conducting psychotherapy research. Meta-analyses of treatment outcome studies found more improvement in therapy clients than in 75 percent of control clients and little difference in effectiveness among various therapies (the so-called dodo bird verdict).

- Three sets of interacting factors affect the outcome of treatment: client characteristics (including the nature of the problem), therapist characteristics, and therapy techniques.

- Client variables that contribute to therapy success include openness, self-relatedness, and a good match between the nature of the problem and the kind of therapy being received.

- A crucial factor in the success of various therapies is the quality of the relationship that the therapist establishes with the client. The three therapist characteristics suggested by Rogers—empathy, unconditional positive regard, and genuineness—are particularly important.

- Factors common to many therapies, such as faith in the therapist, a protected environment for self-exploration, and the ability to try out new behaviors, contribute to therapeutic outcome.

BIOLOGICAL APPROACHES TO TREATMENT

In the previous chapter, we found that biological factors play an important role in many psychological disorders. Thus a medical approach designed to alter the brain's functioning is an alternative (or an addition) to psychological treatment.

DRUG THERAPIES

Drug therapies are the most commonly used biological interventions. Discoveries in the field of *psychopharmacology* (the study of how drugs affect cognitions, emotions, and behavior) have revolutionized the treatment of the entire range of behavior disorders. Each year in the United States alone, doctors ranging from primary care physicians to psychiatrists to psychopharmacologists write more than 200 million prescriptions for drugs that affect mood, thought, and behavior (Lieberman, 1998). The most commonly prescribed drugs fall into three major categories: antipsychotic drugs, antianxiety drugs, and antidepressant drugs. Effective drugs (e.g., lithium) also exist for the treatment of mania. Many experts recommend using such drugs in conjunction with psychotherapy to achieve a higher level of long-term success (Hollon, 1996; Thase et al., 1997).

Antipsychotic Drugs

Perhaps the most dramatic effects of drug therapy have occurred in the treatment of severely disordered people, permitting many of them to function outside of the hospital setting (Shorter, 1998). As shown in Figure 15.20, a sharp decline in the number of inpatients in public mental hospitals has occurred since 1955, when antipsychotic drugs were first introduced on a wide scale.

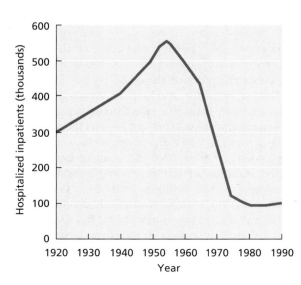

FIGURE 15.20

Effects of antipsychotic drugs. Antipsychotic drugs have revolutionized the treatment of severely disturbed individuals, allowing many of them to leave mental hospitals. Note the decline that occurred following the introduction of antipsychotic drugs in the mid-1950s. SOURCE: National Institute of Mental Health, 1992.

▶ **Focus 22**
What is tardive dyskinesia, and what causes it?

▶ **Focus 23**
How do antianxiety drugs work, and how effective are they? Do they have any drawbacks?

The revolution in drug therapy for severe psychological disorders began in the early 1950s, when it was accidentally discovered that *reserpine,* a drug derived from the root of the snakeroot plant, calmed psychotic patients. This discovery resulted in the development of synthetic *antipsychotic drugs* (also called *major tranquilizers*), used today to treat schizophrenic disorders. The primary effect of the major tranquilizers is to decrease the action of dopamine, the neurotransmitter whose overactivity is thought to be involved in schizophrenia (Schatzberg et al., 2002). These drugs dramatically reduce positive symptoms, such as hallucinations and delusions. However, they have little effect on negative symptoms, such as apathy and withdrawal, and 20 to 40 percent of people with schizophrenia get little or no relief from them (Tamminga, 1997). Antipsychotic drugs are now so widely used that nearly all schizophrenic patients living in the United States, Canada, and western Europe have received them at one time or another. Because patients often relapse very quickly if they stop taking the drugs, it is common practice to continue the medication indefinitely once the individual has returned to the community.

Antipsychotic drugs have reduced the need for padded cells, straitjackets, and other restraints that were formerly used to control the disordered behavior of hospitalized patients. Although they allow many patients to be released from hospitals, these drugs can produce **tardive dyskinesia,** *a severe movement disorder* (Kane, 1992). Uncontrollable and grotesque movements of the face and tongue are especially prominent in this disorder, and sometimes the patient's arms and legs flail uncontrollably. Tardive dyskinesia can be more debilitating than the psychotic symptoms that prompted the drug treatment, and it appears to be irreversible once it develops. One study found that within 4 years of beginning antipsychotic medications, 18.5 percent of young adults and 31 percent of those over 55 developed tardive dyskinesia symptoms (Saltz et al., 1991).

Researchers are working to develop new drugs that can control schizophrenic symptoms without producing side effects, such as the devastating symptoms of tardive dyskinesia. A newer drug called *clozapine* (Clozaril) reduces not only positive symptoms but negative ones as well, and it appears not to produce tardive dyskinesia (Marangell, 2002). Unfortunately, it produces a fatal blood disease (agranulocytosis) in 1 to 2 percent of people who take it, requiring expensive weekly blood tests for patients who use the medication.

Antipsychotic drugs can often be used effectively in conjunction with psychotherapy. For example, drugs may be used to bring psychotic symptoms under control so that the patient can benefit from other approaches such as social skills training, family therapy, and group therapy.

Antianxiety Drugs

Surveys have shown that more than 15 percent of Americans between the ages of 18 and 74 use antianxiety or tranquilizing drugs such as the brandnames Valium, Xanax, and BuSpar. These drugs are designed to reduce anxiety as much as possible without affecting alertness or concentration. Sometimes antianxiety drugs are used in combination with psychotherapy to help clients cope successfully with problematic situations (Stahl, 1998). A temporary reduction in anxiety from the use of a drug may allow a client to enter anxiety-arousing situations and learn to cope more effectively with them.

Antianxiety drugs work by slowing down excitatory synaptic activity in the nervous system. For example, *buspirone* (BuSpar) functions by blocking receptors of the excitatory transmitter serotonin and by enhancing the postsynaptic activity of GABA, an inhibitory transmitter that reduces neural activity in areas of the brain associated with emotional arousal (Gorman, 2002; Pies, 1998).

Antianxiety drugs can have a variety of undesirable side effects, such as drowsiness, lethargy, and concentration difficulties. A more serious drawback is psychological and physical dependence that can result from their long-term use. People who have developed physiological dependence can experience characteristic withdrawal symptoms, such as intense anxiety, nausea, and restlessness when they stop taking the drug (Lieberman, 1998). In addition, anxiety symptoms often return when people stop taking the drugs.

Antidepressant Drugs

▶ **Focus 24**
How do antidepressant drugs achieve their effects? What concerns have been raised about them?

Antidepressant drugs fall into three major categories: *tricyclics* (e.g., Elavil, Tofranil), *monoamine oxidase (MAO) inhibitors* (e.g., Nardil, Parnate), and *selective serotonin reuptake inhibitors,* or *SSRIs* (e.g., Prozac, Zoloft, Paxil). The first two classes increase the activity of the excitatory neurotransmitters norepinephrine and serotonin, whose lowered level of activity in brain regions involved in positive emotion and motivation is related to depression. The tricyclics work by preventing reuptake of the excitatory transmitters into the presynaptic neurons, allowing them to continue stimulating postsynaptic neurons. The MAO inhibitors reduce the activity of monoamine oxidase, an enzyme that breaks down the neurotransmitters in the synapse.

MAO inhibitors have more severe side effects than the tricyclics. They can cause dangerous elevations in blood pressure when taken with certain foods, such as cheeses and some types of wine. Many patients have abandoned their antidepressant medications because of severe side effects. The SSRIs were designed to decrease side effects by increasing the activity of just one transmitter, serotonin (Marangell, 2002). Like the other antidepressants, however, SSRIs do have side effects. For example, about 30 percent of patients on Prozac report nervousness, insomnia, sweating, joint pain, or sexual dysfunction (Hellerstein et al., 1993). Nonetheless, the SSRIs are gradually replacing the tricyclics because, in addition to milder side effects, they reduce depressive symptoms more rapidly and also reduce anxiety symptoms that often accompany depression (Lieberman, 1998). Figure 15.21 shows how the SSRIs produce their effects.

Increasingly, depression researchers are studying the effects of combining drugs and psychother-

FIGURE 15.21

SSRI mechanisms. (a) When a presynaptic neuron releases serotonin into the synaptic space, a reuptake mechanism begins to pull neurotransmitter molecules back into the "sending" neuron, limiting the stimulation of the postsynaptic neuron. (b) Selective serotonin reuptake inhibitors (SSRIs) allow serotonin, whose activity is reduced in depressed clients, to continue its stimulation of postsynaptic neurons by inhibiting the reuptake of serotonin into the presynaptic neuron.

apy. A meta-analysis of such studies revealed that recovery rates for psychotherapy and the combined treatments did not differ for less severely depressed people. However, the combination of psychotherapy and drug treatment yielded the best recovery rates in more severe cases of depression (Thase et al., 1997).

 Are antidepressants over prescribed? Watch the video on "Depression Theories and Treatments" in Chapter 15 of your CD for some thoughts.

Beneath the Surface   Some Depressing Facts about Antidepressant Drugs

Antidepressant drugs have become a treatment of choice for depression in both adults and children. As a less expensive form of treatment than psychotherapy, they are especially attractive to insurers and managed-care providers, and with good reason. Clinicians often observe dramatic improvements in people given SSRIs and other antidepressants. In recent years, however, increasing concerns have been raised about their efficacy and about potential side effects.

PLACEBO EFFECTS

When compared with no-treatment control conditions, antidepressant medication (ADM) effects are quite impressive. But when placebo controls are introduced in randomized clinical trials, the picture can change dramatically. If placebo patients simply believe they are receiving an antidepressant, they frequently show improvement that rivals drug effects. By dividing the amount of change shown in the placebo group by the magnitude of change shown by the drug group, one can estimate how much of the drug effect is truly attributable to the pharmacological effects of the drug. For example, in

two clinical trials of the SSRI Zoloft in depressed children and adolescents, placebo patients showed 85 percent as much improvement as those who received Zoloft. Both groups showed notable decreases in self-reported depression, but the difference between Zoloft and placebo groups was so small as to be of no practical significance (Wagner et al., 2003).

Typical placebo results for adults are shown in a reanalysis of data from 38 clinical trials submitted to the U.S. Food and Drug Administration (FDA). The outcome measure in these studies was based on ratings of depression symptoms by clinicians who were blind to the experimental condition. As shown in Figure 15.22, improvement rates in the placebo conditions ranged from 68 to 89 percent of those shown in the antidepressant medication conditions, suggesting that expectancies and beliefs account for much of the drugs' effects and that the actual pharmacological effects of the drugs are quite small. Indeed, the data on Paxil, Zoloft, and Celexa actually underestimate placebo effects because in 9 other trials where no significant differences were found between the drugs and placebos, the investigators did not provide depression change scores

Continued

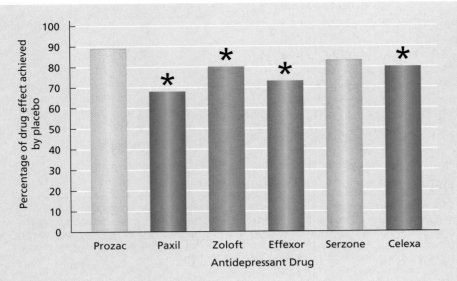

FIGURE 15.22

Placebo effects and antidepressant (SSRI) drugs. These data were derived by dividing the magnitude of improvement shown by placebo controls by the magnitude of change shown by the drug group. They suggest that, on average, around 79 percent of the drug effects may be attributable to patient expectations that they will be helped by the drug, rather than to pharmacological effects. The asterisks indicate drugs for which depression improvement scores were not submitted because the drug and placebo groups did not differ significantly, suggesting even stronger placebo effects for those drugs. SOURCE: Adapted from Kirsch et al., 2002.

(Kirsch et al., 2002). In such studies, the placebo effect could account for as much as 100 percent of patient improvement, so that the placebo effect means for those drugs would be even higher than the ones shown in Figure 15.22. Even where statistically significant differences were found between drug and placebo conditions on depression ratings, the actual differences were typically too small to be of any clinical significance.

The strength of placebo effects may also be underestimated in many studies because of the practice of dropping from clinical trials any patient in the placebo condition who shows 20 percent or more improvement in the first week or two of the trial. Such patients are called *placebo washouts*. In contrast, patients in the drug condition who show similar levels of improvement are retained in the study. Obviously, this practice loads the dice in favor of the drug condition. Another factor favoring drug effects is the selective publication of results. Although the drug companies (who conduct or sponsor much of the research on their drugs) are required to submit the raw data from all trials to the FDA, studies that do not show significant drug effects may not find their way into the published literature (Antonuccio et al., 2003).

DO THE BENEFITS OUTWEIGH THE DANGERS?

Given the small treatment effects that can be attributed to pharmacological factors, some are questioning whether the benefits achieved through antidepressant drug treatment outweigh possible costs. Despite the fact that SSRIs have less severe side effects than older antidepressants, such side effects do exist. Even when patients have shown improvement on the drugs, they sometimes abandon them because of these effects. In a study of 161 SSRI quitters conducted by Madelon Bolling and Robert Kohlenberg (2004), 46 percent complained of having experienced a narrowed range of emotions, 32.9 percent of "not feeling like myself," 24 per-

cent of a loss of creativity, 18 percent of apathy, 17 percent of concentration difficulties, and 13 percent of increased anger. When people stop taking SSRIs, about 25 percent experience a *discontinuation syndrome*, which can include severe sensory, somatic, gastrointestinal, and sleep problems, as well as irritability and anxiety. Some patients report that these discontinuation symptoms are worse than the original depression. Finally, reports of suicidal thoughts and behaviors in patients on SSRIs have raised concerns. One study compared suicide attempts and suicides of adults in randomized clinical trials comparing SSRIs with placebos (Healy, 2004). Overall, 1 in 80 of all SSRI recipients attempted or committed suicide, compared with 1 in 200 of all placebo patients. In children, the risk may be even greater (Jureidini et al., 2004). At the urging of the British Medical Society, the United Kingdom Committee on Safety in Medicines has banned the use of all SSRIs with the exception of Prozac for patients under 18 years of age. In the United States, new clinical guidelines recommend the use of psychological interventions, such as cognitive-behavioral and interpersonal therapy, over antidepressants for treating children except in the most extreme cases of danger to the patient and nonresponsiveness to other forms of treatment, and then only with the informed consent of parents (Wong et al., 2004). The link between SSRIs and suicide risk is still a subject of debate, but in October, 2004 the FDA announced that it would reanalyze its database and examine whether antidepressants pose a risk of increased suicidal thoughts among adults, as they do in children. This followed an earlier FDA Public Health Advisory suggesting caution in using antidepressants in treating both adults and children.

Clearly, the results of ongoing studies of the efficacy, side effects, and cost/benefit aspects of antidepressants have enormous clinical and economic implications. Meanwhile, research continues on the development of new drugs that are more effective and have fewer side effects.

ELECTROCONVULSIVE THERAPY

Another biologically based treatment, *electroconvulsive therapy (ECT)*, was based on the observation by a Hungarian physician that schizophrenia and epilepsy rarely occur in the same person. (Apparently, he didn't stop to consider the fact that the probability of epilepsy and *any* other disorder occurring together is very low.) The physician therefore suggested that seizure induction might be useful in the treatment of schizophrenia. In 1938 two Italian physicians, Ugo Cerletti and Lucio Bini, began to treat schizophrenic patients by attaching electrodes to their skulls and inducing a seizure by means of an electric current administered to the brain. In early applications of ECT, a wide-awake patient was strapped to a table, electrodes were attached to the patient's scalp, and a current of roughly 100 volts was applied to the brain, producing violent convulsions and loss of consciousness. Sometimes the seizures were so violent that patients fractured their arms or legs.

Today the procedure is quite different (Figure 15.23). A patient is first given a sedative and a muscle relaxant to prevent injuries from the convulsions. The patient is then placed on a well-padded mattress, and electrodes are attached to his or her scalp. A modified procedure in which electrodes are placed on only one side of the head is often used. The duration of the shock is less than a second, causing a seizure of the central nervous system. There is little observable movement in the patient, other than a twitching of the toes and a slight facial grimace. The patient wakes up 10 to 20 minutes after ECT, possibly with a headache, sore muscles, and some confusion. Recently, scientists have been able to calibrate the amount of electric current a patient needs so that treatments can be individualized, and research is being carried out to determine whether certain drugs can further reduce seizure-induced confusion and amnesia.

When ECT was first introduced in the 1930s, it was applied to a wide range of disorders, but later research revealed that it cannot relieve anxiety disorders and is of questionable value for schizophrenic patients (Herrington & Lader, 1996). However, ECT can be useful in treating severe depression, particularly if there is a high risk of suicide. In such cases, the use of antidepressant drugs may be impractical because they will likely take several weeks to begin reducing the depression. In contrast, the effects of ECT can be immediate. Controlled studies indicate that 60 to 70 percent of severely depressed people given

FIGURE 15.23

A severely depressed and possibly suicidal patient is prepared for an ECT session. The patient has been sedated and given a muscle relaxant to minimize limb movements during the brief electrical stimulation of the brain. The rubber object in her mouth prevents her from biting her tongue or damaging her teeth during the convulsion.

ECT improve, but no one knows why ECT works (Rey & Walter, 1997).

ECT has many critics. Some note that even when the effects are dramatically positive, the possibility of a depressive relapse is high, perhaps 85 percent (Swartz, 1995). Concerns have been raised about the safety of ECT because in some instances permanent memory loss has been reported, and there are also concerns about the possibility of permanent brain damage when ECT is used repeatedly. Today the number of ECT treatments is limited to fewer than 10, and scientific evidence suggests that today's ECT is a safer treatment than previous forms were. For example, MRI studies of patients who received brief pulse treatment to both sides of the brain revealed no evidence of brain damage (Coffey et al., 1991). After reviewing both sides of the issue, the American Psychiatric Association (1990) concluded that this therapy should be regarded as a useful procedure for major depression in patients who cannot take or do not respond to medication.

PSYCHOSURGERY

Psychosurgery *refers to surgical procedures that remove or destroy brain tissue in an attempt to change disordered behavior.* It is the least used of the biomedical procedures, but such was not always the case. In the 1930s, before the advent of antipsychotic drugs, Portuguese surgeon Egas Moniz

▶ **Focus 25**
Which disorders do and do not respond favorably to ECT and psychosurgery? What are their drawbacks?

reported that cutting the nerve tracts that connect the frontal lobes with subcortical areas of the brain involved in emotion resulted in a calming of psychotic and uncontrollably violent patients. The operation eliminated emotional input from the limbic system into the areas of the brain connected with executive functions of planning and reasoning. Walter Freeman developed a 10-minute *lobotomy* operation performed by inserting an ice pick–like instrument with sharp edges through the eye socket into the brain, then wiggling it back and forth to sever the targeted nerve tracts. During the 1930s and 1940s, tens of thousands of patients—50,000 in the United States alone—underwent the operation. Moniz received a Nobel Prize for his discovery.

Initial enthusiasm for lobotomy was soon replaced by a sober recognition that the massive neural damage it caused had severe side effects on mental and emotional functioning. Seizures, stupor, memory and reasoning impairments, and listlessness occurred frequently. With the development of antipsychotic drugs in the 1950s, the frequency of lobotomies decreased, and they are hardly ever used today. However, more precise and limited psychosurgery procedures are sometimes used in the most extreme cases and when every other avenue has been tried. One procedure called *cingulotomy* involves cutting a small fiber bundle near the corpus callosum that connects the frontal lobes with the limbic system. Cingulotomy has been used successfully in treating severe depressive and obsessive-compulsive disorders that have failed to improve with drug treatment or psychotherapy. However, this more limited procedure can also produce side effects, including seizures (Pressman, 1998). Appropriately, cingulotomy and other forms of psychosurgery are considered to be last-resort procedures.

MIND, BODY, AND THERAPEUTIC INTERVENTIONS

The impact of drug and electroconvulsive therapies on psychological disorders illustrates once again the important interactions between biological and psychological phenomena. In the final analysis, both psychological and biological treatments affect brain functioning in ways that can change disordered thoughts, emotions, and behavior. Moreover, they may constitute different routes to the same changes, as illustrated in a study by Tomas Furmark and coworkers (2002) at Uppsala University in Sweden. The researchers randomly assigned patients with social phobia to 9-week treatments that involved

either drug therapy with an SSRI or a course of cognitive and behavioral psychotherapy involving exposure to feared social situations and cognitive modification of anxiety-arousing thoughts. Before and after treatment, the participants received PET scans while they gave a hastily prepared speech to a group of 6 to 8 persons standing around the scanner bed. They also provided subjective ratings of their anxiety during the procedure. Uniformly high anxiety scores were reported by all participants prior to treatment.

In general, both treatments were effective, although overall, the psychological treatment produced a stronger reduction in fear and social phobia symptoms than did the drug treatment. Nonetheless, when the researchers compared the pre- and posttreatment PET scans of those participants who responded to the two treatments with reduced social anxiety, the psychotherapy and drug groups showed basically the same changes in cerebral blood flow from the first speech situation to the second. These changes involved reduced neural activity in an "anxiety circuit" involving the amygdala, the hippocampus, and areas of the temporal cerebral cortex (Figure 15.24). Treatment nonresponders did not show these brain changes. Thus different forms of therapy, whether psychological or biological, may

FIGURE 15.24

Drug and therapy effects on the brain. Clients treated for social phobia received either psychotherapy or drug therapy. Those clients who responded to their respective treatments with reduced anxiety showed nearly identical changes in PET-scan recordings of neural activity in three areas of the brain whose activation is thought to underline anxiety. Source: Based on Furmark et al., 2002.

LEVELS OF ANALYSIS Factors Related to Therapeutic Behavior Change

Biological	Psychological	Environmental
• Changes in neurotransmitter, autonomic, or hormonal activity brought about by drug treatment, psychotherapy, or surgical procedures • Structural changes in brain circuitry and synaptic networks produced by cognitive, emotional, and behavioral changes	• Cognitive and emotional changes brought about by cognitive therapies • Modification of conditioned emotional responses by deconditioning procedures such as exposure, desensitization, and aversion therapy • Behavioral changes produced by operant procedures • Self-concept changes brought about by psychotherapy (e.g., client-centered, Gestalt therapy) • Insight into unconscious dynamics and development of more mature defenses brought about by short- and long-term psychodynamic therapies	• Life-situation changes resulting from constructive behavior changes learned in therapy or produced by biological means • Exposure to specific therapeutic techniques administered by a mental health expert • A positive therapeutic relationship that helps promote change and allows therapy techniques to be effective • Cultural factors that affect access to therapy, type of therapy, and exposure to a culturally competent therapist

Therapeutic Behavior Change

FIGURE 15.25

Levels of analysis: Factors related to therapeutic behavior change.

result in similar changes at a neurological level and, ultimately, at a behavioral level.

An important factor to keep in mind is that drug treatments, however effective they may be in modifying some disordered behaviors in the short term, do not cure the disorder. They suppress symptoms but do not teach the client coping and problem-solving skills to deal with stressful life situations (DeLongis, 2000; Nezu et al., 2000). They may even prevent people from taking steps to confront the real causes of their problems. Many therapists believe that one of the major benefits of psychological treatments is their potential not only to help clients deal with current problems but also to increase their personal resources so that they might enjoy a higher level of adjustment and life satisfaction in the future (Hollon, 1996).

We have now considered a wide spectrum of approaches to treating abnormal behavior. Figure 15.25 summarizes biological, psychological, and environmental mechanisms for therapeutic change.

IN REVIEW

■ Drugs have revolutionized the treatment of many behavior disorders and have permitted many hospitalized patients to function outside of institutions. Drugs and psychotherapy may be combined to hasten the relief of symptoms while establishing more effective coping responses to deal with the sources of a disorder. Drug treatments exist for anxiety, depression, schizophrenia, and mania. Some of these drugs have undesirable side effects and can be addictive. All of them affect neurotransmission within the brain, and they work on specific classes of neurotransmitters.

■ Electroconvulsive therapy is used less frequently than in the past, and its safety has been increased. It is used primarily to treat severe depression, particularly when a strong threat of suicide exists.

■ Psychosurgery techniques have become more precise, but they are still generally used only after all other treatment options have failed.

■ Studies have shown that successful therapeutic treatments, whether involving drugs or psychotherapy, are associated with similar alterations of brain functioning.

PSYCHOLOGICAL DISORDERS AND SOCIETY

Since the days of insane asylums, first established in the 16th century to segregate the mentally ill from society, severe behavior disorders have been treated in institutional settings. In the United States, a national network of nearly 300 state-funded mental hospitals was built between 1845 and 1945. Many private facilities were also built. The number of patients being treated in public mental hospitals increased steadily from about 250,000 in 1920 to more than 500,000 in 1950. By 1955 psychiatric patients occupied half of all hospital beds in the United States. However, it was readily apparent to mental health experts that although there were some high-quality institutions, many public mental hospitals were not fulfilling their intended role as treatment facilities. They were overcrowded, understaffed, and underfinanced. Many of them could provide little more than minimal custodial care and a haven from the stresses and demands of the outside world. Moreover, people who were admitted to such hospitals often sank into a chronic "sick" role in which passive dependence and "crazy" behavior were not only tolerated but expected (Goffman, 1961; Scheff, 1966). They lost the self-confidence, motivation, and skills needed to return and adapt to the outside world and had little chance of surviving outside the hospital.

DEINSTITUTIONALIZATION

▶ **Focus 26**
What is the rationale for deinstitutionalization? What prevents the achievement of its goals?

By the 1960s, the stage was set for a new approach to the treatment of behavior disorders. Concerns about the inadequacies of mental hospitals, together with the ability of antipsychotic drugs to normalize patients' behavior, resulted in a **deinstitutionalization movement** *to transfer the primary focus of treatment from the hospital to the community.*

In 1963 Congress passed the Community Mental Health Centers Act, which provided for the establishment of one mental health center for every 50,000 people. Community mental health centers are designed to provide outpatient psychotherapy and drug treatment so that clients can remain in their normal social and work environments. The centers can also arrange for short-term inpatient care, usually at a local general hospital, when clients are acutely disturbed, and many have crisis centers and telephone hotlines to respond to emergency situations. Finally, community mental health centers provide education and consultation. For example, staff members may provide drug education programs to local schools or educate police officers on how to deal with seriously disturbed people they might encounter in the line of duty.

Combined with the development of effective drug treatments, the impact of deinstitutionalization on the treatment of behavior disorders has been dramatic. According to the National Institute

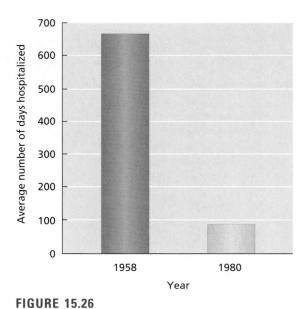

FIGURE 15.26

Hospital stays. The average length of psychiatric hospitalization at Veterans Administration Hospitals dropped dramatically between 1958 and 1980, and it has remained low. Source: Based on National Institute of Mental Health, 1992.

of Mental Health, 77.4 percent of all patients were being treated as inpatients in public and private hospitals in 1955. By 1990 the inpatient figure had shrunk to 27.1 percent. As Figure 15.26 indicates, the average length of hospitalization for patients having severe (typically schizophrenic) disorders has also decreased markedly.

The concept of community treatment is a good one, for it allows people to remain in their social and work environments and to be treated with minimal disruption of their lives. However, it requires the availability of high-quality mental health care in community clinics, halfway houses, sheltered workshops, and other community facilities. When these facilities are available, deinstitutionalization can work. Unfortunately, many communities have never been able to fund the needed facilities, and the 1980s saw sharp cutbacks in federal funding of community mental health centers. As a result, many patients are being released into communities that are ill prepared to care for their needs. The result is a *revolving door phenomenon* involving repeated rehospitalizations. Nearly three-fourths of all hospital admissions involve formerly hospitalized patients. Eddie, the homeless man described at the beginning of Chapter 14, is one such person. While in the hospital, he responds well to antipsychotic medications and is soon released back into a community that cannot offer him the care he requires. Following his release, he stops taking his medication, his

FIGURE 15.27

The revolving door phenomenon created by inadequate funding of community-based treatment facilities has produced a large population of severely disturbed homeless people who live on our nation's streets.

condition deteriorates to the point where he must be rehospitalized, and the cycle begins again.

This revolving door has produced a growing population of disturbed and homeless people who have nowhere to go for help (Figure 15.27). In some states with large urban populations, the largest mental wards exist not in hospitals but on city streets. There are as many as 1 million homeless people in the United States, and approximately one-third have a severe mental disorder, typically schizophrenia (Torrey, 1997). One large-scale public health survey study revealed that only 15.3 percent of people with serious mental disorders had received minimally adequate treatment during the previous year (Wang et al., 2002).

MENTAL HEALTH TREATMENT IN A MANAGED-CARE ENVIRONMENT

Rising medical and insurance costs have swelled the rolls of health maintenance organizations (HMOs), and managed care has altered the mental health treatment landscape dramatically. The desire of HMOs and insurance providers to contain health costs translates into a strong preference for drug treatments and short-term versus more costly long-term forms of psychotherapy, as well as the use of masters-level counselors who charge lower fees. Third-party providers are also demanding evidence that the treatments they are paying for are effective. These pressures have had

some positive results, including the stimulation of research on treatment outcomes and the development of some effective short-term therapies.

There are, however, some negative effects as well. To many psychologists, the most serious is that many decisions about the type and duration of therapy are being made by untrained representatives of insurers or HMOs rather than by the client or a mental health professional. In some instances, the number of sessions permitted may be woefully inadequate to treat a serious disorder (Figure 15.28). Although many psychologists concede that some of the more effective treatments are short-term cognitive-behavioral and interpersonal therapies, they do not believe that these treatments are best for every problem and client. Current data suggest that about 12 to 18 sessions are required to achieve a 50 percent recovery rate for most disorders (Hansen et al., 2002). Managed-care plans frequently limit payment to fewer sessions than this, so that many managed-care subscribers do not receive the level of care that they need. Likewise, the preference for drug treatments that require minimal contact between the patient and a professional may provide short-term improvement at the cost of a more satisfactory long-term result that could occur with psychological treatments that allow the development of better coping skills. Moreover, as we have seen in this chapter's "Beneath the Surface" feature, drug therapy has its own negative consequences.

"IT'S YOUR INSURANCE COMPANY, THEY SAY YOU'RE CURED."

► **Focus 27**
What therapeutic issues exist in managed-care environments?

FIGURE 15.28

In today's managed-care environment, treatment decisions may be made by untrained representatives of an insurance company instead of a health-care professional. SOURCE: Cartoon by Ron Delgado, *The Wall Street Journal*, 1997. By permission of Cartoon Features Syndicate.

PREVENTIVE MENTAL HEALTH

Describe two major approaches to prevention, and provide an example of each.

Up to now, we have focused entirely on what can be done to help people once they have developed a behavior disorder. Successful treatment is one way to reduce the toll of human suffering produced by failures to adapt. Another way is to try to *prevent* the development of disorders through psychological intervention. In terms of economic, personal, and societal costs, it may indeed be the case that "an ounce of prevention is worth a pound of cure." If current efforts to enhance personal well-being and to slow the rise of health-care costs are to be successful, the prevention of behavior disorders must be a focal point of social policy. In some cases, this may involve treating psychological disorders during childhood in an attempt to prevent their continuation into adult life. School-based intervention programs have proven effective in preventing and reducing aggressive behaviors in children (Wilson et al., 2003). In addition, anxiety, depression, conduct disorders, and attention-deficit/hyperactivity disorder have responded positively to interventions applied in childhood (Compton et al., 2002; Farmer et al., 2002), but additional research is needed to see if the positive treatment effects persist into adulthood.

People may become vulnerable to psychological disorders as the result of situational factors, personal factors, or both. Thus prevention can be approached from two perspectives (Figure 15.29). **Situation-focused prevention** *is directed at either reducing or eliminating the environmental causes of behavior disorders or enhancing situational factors that help prevent the development of disorders.* Programs designed to enhance the functioning of

families, reduce stress within organizations, provide better educational opportunities for children, and develop a sense of connection to other people and the community at large all have the potential to help prevent the development of behavior disorders (Albee, 1997; Taylor & Wang, 2000). One community intervention program was designed to prevent the development of antisocial personality disorder in a high-risk inner-city environment. Between the ages of 3 and 5 years, children randomly assigned to the experimental group participated in an intensive nutritional, physical-exercise, and educational program. Children exposed to this program had lower scores on measures of antisocial personality disorder at age 17 and lower criminal records at age 23 compared with a control group (Raine et al., 2003).

The personal side of the equation is addressed by **competency-focused prevention,** *designed to increase personal resources and coping skills.* Such programs may focus on strengthening resistance to stress, improving social and vocational competencies, enhancing self-esteem, and helping people gain the skills needed to build stronger social support systems. One illustrative program, developed by Edna Foa and her coworkers (1995), focused on preventing posttraumatic stress disorder (PTSD) in women who had recently been raped or assaulted.

The victims were randomly assigned to either a treatment condition or to an untreated control condition. In hourly sessions over a 4-week period, the women in the treatment group learned about the common psychological reactions to being raped, helping them to realize that their responses were understandable, given what they had experienced. They relived their trauma through guided imagery to help defuse their lingering fears through exposure. The women also learned stress-management coping skills such as relaxation, and they went through a cognitive therapy procedure to replace stress-producing cognitions with more realistic appraisals.

The results of the prevention program are shown in Figure 15.30. The women exposed to the prevention treatment had less severe symptoms at both the 2-month and 5.5-month assessments. Moreover, 2 months after their trauma, diagnostic interviews with the women in the two groups revealed that 70 percent of the women in the control condition met the DSM-IV criteria for PTSD compared with only 10 percent of the women who had received the prevention program. Thus for many of the women, an efficient 4-week program prevented what might have been a PTSD disorder that would have created tremendous personal

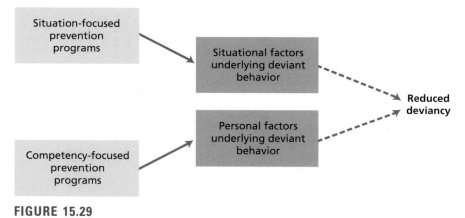

FIGURE 15.29

Preventive mental health. Two approaches to the prevention of psychological disorders are based on the principle that deviant behavior represents the interaction of personal and situational factors. Situation-focused approaches increase situational protective factors or reduce vulnerability factors in the environment. Competency-focused approaches reduce personal vulnerability factors or strengthen personal competencies and coping skills.

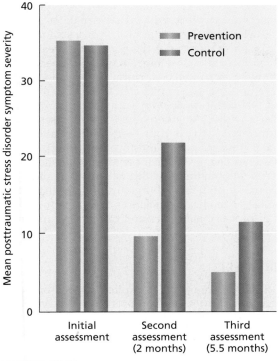

FIGURE 15.30

Preventing PTSD. A competency-based prevention project was designed to prevent PTSD in women who were victims of rape and assault. The program, which combined a number of behavioral and cognitive therapy techniques to increase stress-management coping skills, sharply reduced the likelihood of developing PTSD. SOURCE: Foa et al., 1995.

misery and required a far more expensive and time-consuming course of therapy.

Although many mental health experts believe that more resources need to be focused on the prevention of maladaptive behavior, they also recognize that prevention presents its own challenges. For one, we cannot develop an intervention program until we understand the causes of the disorder we want to reduce. Even when causal factors are known, we also need to understand what kinds of interventions will be successful in modifying them. This requires careful research into which types of programs are most effective in preventing which types of problems in which types of people—our old specificity question.

Another practical problem is that the effects of prevention are usually not immediately obvious. It may take years for their effects to become evident. Moreover, their effects (which usually involve the *absence* of a disorder) can be hard to measure. For these reasons, prevention programs can be difficult to justify when funding priorities are being set, even though the programs may, in the long run, have greater positive impact than programs that focus on treating disorders that have already developed.

Having described the nature and benefits of treatments, we end this chapter with some research-derived guidelines for seeking and profiting from therapy.

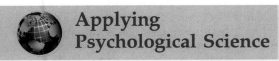

Applying Psychological Science   When and Where to Seek Therapy

No one is immune to the problems of living. Every day, each of us does the best we can to balance our personal and social resources against the demands created by our life circumstances. We all have certain vulnerabilities, and if environmental demands and our vulnerabilities combine to exceed our resources, we may experience psychological problems for which professional assistance would be helpful. Here are some general guidelines for seeking such help and profiting from it.

WHEN TO SEEK HELP

First is the issue of when to seek help. In general terms, you should consider seeking professional assistance if any of the following apply:

- You are experiencing serious emotional discomfort, such as feelings of depression or anxiety, that are adversely affecting your personal, work, or family life.

- You are encountering a serious problem or life transition that you feel unable to handle on your own.
- A problem that has interfered with your life or personal happiness in the past is worsening or has suddenly resurfaced.
- You have experienced some traumatic event, either in the past or recently, that you find yourself frequently thinking about, dreaming about, or responding to with negative emotions.
- You are preoccupied with your weight or body image and are taking extreme steps, such as not eating or purging yourself by vomiting or taking laxatives.
- You have severe and recurring conflicts with other people.
- You hear voices telling you what to do, or you feel that others are controlling your thoughts.

Continued

WHERE TO SEEK HELP

How does one go about getting help in dealing with psychological problems? Help may be sought at a college counseling center, at a community agency, at an HMO, or from a professional in private practice. The campus counseling center is often a good place for a college student to start, for it can provide direct help or an appropriate referral to a reputable mental health professional. If you are at a larger university that has a graduate program in clinical or counseling psychology, there may also be an on-campus psychology training clinic administered by that program. There you would typically work with a graduate student who is being closely supervised by a licensed clinician.

How expensive is treatment? For students it is often offered free or at a nominal fee at a campus facility or HMO. Community agencies typically have a sliding-fee scale based on the client's income, so financial considerations need not be a barrier to seeking professional assistance. A private practitioner may charge as much as medical doctors, dentists, and attorneys do, often exceeding $100 per 50-minute session. As a prospective client, you should always ask beforehand about the fee. You should also check into the mental health benefits provided by your health insurance policy, including what kinds of treatments and the number of sessions it covers and whether it will reimburse your chosen treatment provider. Student insurance plans usually cover on-campus treatment.

WHAT TO LOOK FOR IN A THERAPIST

In choosing a therapist, what should you look for? It is important that your therapist be well trained and competent. Ask the therapist about her or his degree, license, training, therapeutic orientation, and the problems in which she or he specializes. This chapter has provided an overview of the major theoretical orientations, and one or more of them may seem especially attractive to you or suited to the problems you wish to address.

As we've seen, the relationship between client and therapist is of the utmost importance. You will want a therapist who can create a good working relationship with you. The degree of "value similarity" between you and the therapist can be important. Timothy Kelly and Hans Strupp (1992) found that the most positive therapeutic outcomes were achieved when the client and therapist were neither very similar nor very dissimilar in values. High similarity may result in a failure to explore value-related issues, whereas too much dissimilarity may interfere with building a good therapeutic relationship. One exception to this general rule may occur in the area of religious values. Clients who have strong and committed religious values may profit most from a therapy that supports those values and uses them to help change problem behaviors (Probst et al., 1992).

Some clients prefer to work with either a male or female therapist, or one who is heterosexual or gay or lesbian, depending in part on the nature of the personal issues that have caused them to seek counseling. As we have seen, research has shown that personal warmth, sincere concern, and empathy are important therapist characteristics. You should like and feel comfortable with your therapist, and you should feel at ease with the methods the therapist uses. Under no circumstances should your therapeutic relationship involve physical intimacy of any kind (even hugging). If a therapist should ever engage in such behavior, you should immediately terminate treatment with that therapist and notify the appropriate professional organization, such as the state psychological or medical association. Such conduct is a serious breach of professional ethics and cannot be condoned under any circumstances.

WHAT CAN YOU EXPECT?

You and your therapist should have explicit, agreed-on goals for the treatment program. If therapy proceeds well, you will experience beneficial changes that indicate movement toward your goals. It may take some time for these changes to occur, however, since long-standing personal vulnerabilities are not easily changed, and significant change seldom occurs overnight. If you do not see any progress after several months or if you seem to be functioning less well than before, you should discuss your progress with the therapist. The therapist may be more satisfied with your progress than you are. However, if you continue to be dissatisfied with your progress or with the therapeutic relationship, you may at some point decide to terminate it. This should not prevent you from seeking help from another therapist.

Entering a helping relationship is a courageous step, and resolving problems in living may involve taking risks and experiencing pain. However, many clients look back on the pain and risks and feel that the process was a valuable one that enabled them to live happier lives than they otherwise could have. Here is a reflection by Dr. Sandra L. Harris, a prominent clinical psychologist, on the course of therapy she undertook as a college student:

> When I think about the girl I was in my freshman year at the University of Maryland and the young woman I was when I graduated four years later, it is clear that it was not only the issues Jim and I discussed, but how we talked that made the difference. The intangibles of trust, respect, and caring were at least as important as the active problem solving that transpired in our weekly meetings. It was not a dramatic transformation, rather it was a slight shifting of a path by a few degrees on the compass. Over the years that shift has had a cumulative effect and I walk a very different road than I would have without him. (Harris, 1981, p. 3)

IN REVIEW

- The introduction of drug therapies that normalize disturbed behavior, as well as concerns about the deterioration of life skills during hospitalization, has helped stimulate a move toward deinstitutionalization—the treatment of people in their communities.

- Research has shown that deinstitutionalization can work when adequate community treatment is provided. Unfortunately, many communities have been unable to fund the needed facilities, resulting in a revolving door of release and rehospitalization, as well as a new generation of homeless people who

live on the streets and do not receive needed treatment.

- Managed care is requiring therapists to demonstrate the efficacy of their techniques and to develop shorter, more economical treatments. An issue of concern is that decisions about the type and duration of treatment are increasingly being taken out of the hands of trained professionals.

- Prevention programs may be either situation-focused or competency-focused, depending on whether they are directed at changing environmental conditions or personal factors.

KEY TERMS AND CONCEPTS

Each term has been boldfaced and defined in the chapter on the page indicated in parentheses.

aversion therapy (p. 586)
behavioral activation treatment (p. 589)
behavior modification (p. 587)
common factors (p. 598)
competency-focused prevention (p. 608)
counterconditioning (p. 585)
culturally competent therapist (p. 592)
deinstitutionalization movement (p. 606)
dialectical behavior therapy
  (DBT; p. 589)
dodo bird verdict (p. 597)
eclecticism (p. 588)
effect size (p. 597)
empathy (p. 578)

empirically supported treatments
  (ESTs; p. 596)
exposure (p. 583)
feminist therapy (p. 593)
free association (p. 575)
genuineness (p. 578)
insight (p. 575)
interpersonal therapy (p. 577)
interpretation (p. 576)
meta-analysis (p. 597)
openness (p. 598)
placebo control group (p. 595)
psychosurgery (p. 603)
randomized clinical trial (p. 595)

resistance (p. 576)
response prevention (p. 583)
self-relatedness (p. 598)
situation-focused prevention (p. 608)
social skills training (p. 588)
specificity question (p. 594)
spontaneous remission (p. 594)
stimulus hierarchy (p. 585)
systematic desensitization (p. 585)
tardive dyskinesia (p. 600)
token economy (p. 587)
transference (p. 576)
unconditional positive regard (p. 578)
virtual reality (VR; p. 583)

? What Do You Think?

ARE CONDITIONING TECHNIQUES COMPATIBLE WITH PSYCHOANALYTIC THEORY? (PAGE 586)

Behaviorists and psychoanalytic theorists have very different viewpoints about psychological symptoms, such as a phobia. For the behaviorist, the phobia *is* the problem, period. Decondition it and the problem is resolved. In contrast, the psychodynamic view is based on a "medical model" analogy that distinguishes between symptoms and underlying causes. As noted in Chapter 14, a psychoanalyst would view a phobia as a behavioral manifestation of some underlying, probably unconscious conflict. Simply treating the observed symptom does nothing to resolve the psychodynamic issues assumed to cause it, in much the same way that reducing a malaria

victim's fever with aspirin does nothing to cure the underlying disease. The analyst would therefore maintain that the goal of therapy should be to treat the underlying dynamics, after which the phobia should disappear on its own. Even if the phobia were successfully treated with behavioral conditioning therapies, the underlying problem would remain unresolved, and some new symptom might well appear in place of the phobia. This prediction of *symptom substitution* was frequently raised by psychodynamic critics of behavior therapies, but no indisputable evidence of new symptoms popping up after behavior therapy treatment has ever materialized (Paul, 2001). In instances when new symptoms appeared, they could be attributed to new posttreatment learning experiences.

Continued

DO SURVEY RESULTS PROVIDE AN ACCURATE PICTURE OF TREATMENT EFFECTIVENESS? (PAGE 595)

Seligman's conclusion that the *CR* survey provides a realistic appraisal of treatment effects is thought-provoking, but before you accept this conclusion, you should consider some of the survey's shortcomings. First, consider the nature of the *CR* sample. Only 1.6 percent of the original 184,000 people contacted described their therapy experience. Is it possible that among the other 98.4 percent are a significant number of people who had been in therapy with unfavorable results and chose not to share their experiences? If so, the effectiveness of therapy could be exaggerated in this self-selected sample.

Second, what about the nature and quality of the data? We have only global, after-the-fact reports from clients. There is no way to corroborate respondents' reports with other sources of data. How do we know that they are not biased by memory distortions or by rationalizing their investment ("If I spent that much time and money, I must have gotten better")? Rationalization could also account for the apparent superiority of long-term therapy, where more time and money were expended, as well as the tendency to return the questionnaire and share the success story.

Third, what has the *CR* study told us about the more important specificity question? We don't know if some matches of clinical problems with specific forms of therapy yielded better outcomes than others. In fact, we can't even

be sure what kinds of therapy were administered because respondents didn't describe their treatments in detail.

Fourth, how about the absence of a control group? Can we rule out spontaneous remission of symptoms? As we saw in Chapter 14, many mental health problems (e.g., depression and anxiety) fluctuate or improve with time. People who are assessed at their low points, when they are most likely to seek therapy, are almost certain to improve, with or without therapy (Mintz et al., 1996). Could this factor alone explain the respondents' perceptions that they had improved? As Seligman himself conceded, "Because there are no control groups, the *CR* . . . study cannot tell us directly whether talking to sympathetic friends or merely letting time pass would have produced just as much improvement as treatment by a mental-health professional" (1995, p. 972).

Despite the interpretive challenges that attend community studies like this, psychotherapy researchers agree that it is critically important to see how well the treatment principles and techniques identified in controlled studies work in the real world (Westen et al., 2004). One way to accomplish this is by systematically measuring the variables of interest within individual cases being seen by practicing therapists in the community. A large number of single-client case studies containing such measurement can provide important data on the effectiveness of specific therapies and the factors that influence those outcomes (Goldfried & Eubanks-Carter, 2004).

CHAPTER SIXTEEN

Social Thinking and Behavior

CHAPTER OUTLINE

> *Without the human community, one single human being cannot survive.*
>
> —THE DALAI LAMA

The prison had become a living hell. Hidden behind their mirrored sunglasses, the guards asserted their total authority over the prisoners. They made the prisoners ask permission to do virtually anything, including going to the toilet. The guards conducted roll calls in the middle of the night to assert their power and disrupt the prisoners' sleep, and they forced prisoners to do push-ups, sometimes with their foot pushing down on the prisoner's back. For their part, the prisoners became increasingly passive and depressed. They hated the guards but were powerless against them. After a few days, one prisoner cracked emotionally. Soon another broke down. Before long, the demoralized prisoners became nothing more than what the guards expected them to be: piteous objects of scorn and abuse.

This prison was not in some brutal dictatorship, the prisoners were not hardened criminals, nor were the guards sadistic psychopaths. Instead, this prison was in the basement of the psychology building at Stanford University, and the guards and prisoners were college students who had volunteered for a study of "prison life." Before the study, screening questionnaires, interviews, and psychological tests showed the participants to be well adjusted.

Philip Zimbardo, the social psychologist who designed the study, watched in disbelief as scenes of callous inhumanity unfolded before him. What began as a 2-week simulation of prison life had to be halted after only 6 days. Afterward, Zimbardo and his associates held several sessions with the participants to help them work through their powerful emotional reactions, and they maintained contact over the following year to minimize the risk that participants would experience lasting negative effects.

What transformed normal college students into people they would not have recognized a week earlier? As one guard recalled, "I was surprised at myself. I made them . . . clean out the toilets with their bare hands. I practically considered the prisoners cattle. . . ." (Zimbardo et al., 1973, p. 42). Decades later, the Stanford prison study remains a landmark for dramatically illustrating a basic concept: Behavior is determined not only by our biological endowment and past learning experiences but also by the power of the immediate social situation (Haney & Zimbardo, 1998).

As social creatures, we spend our days in an ever changing series of social environments that profoundly shape how we behave, think, and feel. This chapter explores the field of social psychology, which studies how we think about our social world (*social thinking*), how other people influence our behavior (*social influence*), and how we relate toward other people (*social relations*).

SOCIAL THINKING

In your judgment, why did some guards in the Stanford prison study act so brutally? Did you form any impressions of the guards or prisoners as you read about the study? Do you feel that the study was worthwhile? These questions focus on three key aspects of social thinking: *attributions*, *impressions*, and *attitudes*.

ATTRIBUTION: PERCEIVING THE CAUSES OF BEHAVIOR

In everyday life we often make **attributions,** *judgments about the causes of our own and other people's behavior and outcomes* (Figure 16.1). Was my A on the midterm due to hard work and ability, or was it just an easy test? Did Bill criticize Linda because he is a rude person, or was he provoked? Did the guards' brutal behavior reflect their personalities or some aspect of the situation? In the courtroom, jurors' attributions about a defendant's behavior influence their decisions about guilt versus innocence.

Personal versus Situational Attributions

Our attempts to understand why people behave as they do typically involve either personal attributions or situational attributions (Heider, 1958). *Personal (internal) attributions* infer that people's characteristics cause their behavior: "Bill insulted Linda because he is rude." "My A on the midterm exam reflects my high ability." *Situational (external) attributions* infer that aspects of the situation cause a behavior: "Bill was provoked into insulting Linda." "I received an A because the test was easy."

How do we decide whether a behavior is caused by personal or situational factors? Suppose you ask Kim for advice on whether to take a particular course, Art 391, and she tells you that the course is terrible. Is Art 391 really poor (a situational attribution), or is it something about Kim (a personal attribution) that led to this response? According to Harold Kelley (1973), three types of information determine the attribution we make: *consistency, distinctiveness,* and *consensus.* First, is Kim's response consistent over time? If you ask Kim again two weeks later and she still says that Art 391 is terrible, then consistency is high. Second, is her response distinctive? If Kim dislikes only Art 391, then distinctiveness is high; if she thinks that most of her courses are terrible, then distinctiveness is low. Finally, how do other people respond? If other students agree with Kim that Art 391 is poor, then consensus is high, but if they disagree with her, then consensus is low.

FIGURE 16.1

"He's been under a lot of stress lately." "He only thinks about himself. What a jerk!" Depending on which attribution she makes for her husband's outburst, this woman may respond with understanding or anger.

▶ **Focus 1**
What types of information lead us to make situational rather than personal attributions?

As Figure 16.2 illustrates, when consistency, distinctiveness, and consensus are all high, we are likely to make a situational attribution: "The course is bad." But when consistency is high and the other two factors are low, we make a personal attribution: "Perhaps Kim is overly critical." Humans, however, are often not so logical. We often take mental shortcuts and make snap judgments that bias our attributions.

Attributional Biases

Social psychology teaches us that the immediate social environment profoundly influences behavior, yet at times we ignore this when making attributions. Instead, we commit a bias called the **fundamental attribution error:** *We underestimate*

Behavior	Attributional factors			Attribution
	Consistency	Distinctiveness	Consensus	
	High	**Low**	**Low**	**Personal attribution**
Kim says that Art 391 is boring	When asked, Kim always says that Art 391 is boring	Kim says that all her classes are boring	Other students say that Art 391 is great	Kim is overly critical
	High	**High**	**High**	**Situational attribution**
	When asked, Kim always says that Art 391 is boring	Kim says that only Art 391 is boring	Other students say that Art 391 is boring	Art 391 is boring

FIGURE 16.2

Forming personal and situational attributions. Consistency, distinctiveness, and consensus information help us determine whether to make personal or situational attributions for someone else's behavior. Note that in both examples consistency is high. If Kim's behavior has low consistency (sometimes she says Art 391 is boring, and other times she says it's interesting), we typically attribute the behavior to transient conditions (e.g., changes in Kim's mood) rather than to stable personal or situational factors. SOURCE: Based on Kelley, 1973.

▶ **Focus 2**
Describe the fundamental attribution error and the self-serving bias, and discuss how they are affected by culture.

the impact of the situation and overestimate the role of personal factors when explaining other people's behavior (Ross, 2001).

Imagine that as part of a course assignment you write an essay on whether physicians should be allowed to help terminally ill patients commit suicide. The professor gives you the choice of writing in favor of or against physician-assisted suicide. Your classmates read the essay, and because they know you had a choice, they logically assume that the essay's content reflects your personal views. Thus if the essay opposes physician-assisted suicide, your classmates will conclude that you are against this practice.

But suppose instead that the professor assigns you to write a supportive essay or assigns you to write an opposing essay. Your classmates know that you were not given a choice. Logically, the content of the essay reflects the situation to which you were assigned. After all, perhaps you are against physician-assisted suicide but were told to write an essay in favor of it, or vice versa. Yet experiments indicate that the content of the essay will still influence your classmates' perception of whether you support or oppose the issue (Jones & Harris, 1967). Similarly, you would be making the fundamental attribution error if—solely on the basis of their professional roles—you expected TV and movie stars to have the same personal traits as the characters they played.

Psychologists debate what causes the fundamental attribution error, but they agree that it's not inevitable (Sabini et al., 2001). When people have time to reflect on their judgments or are highly motivated to be careful, the fundamental attribution error is reduced. Moreover, keep in mind that the fundamental attribution error

applies to how we perceive other people's behavior rather than our own. As comedian George Carlin noted, the slow driver ahead of us is a "moron," and the fast driver trying to pass us is a "maniac." Yet we don't think of ourselves as a moron or a maniac when we do these things, perhaps because we are more aware of situational factors (e.g., an unfamiliar road) impinging on us. After the Stanford prison study ended, guards who had treated prisoners cruelly were quick to attribute their behavior to the role that they had been in rather than to their personal qualities.

Indeed, when it comes to explaining our own behavior, we often make attributions that protect or enhance our self-esteem by displaying a **self-serving bias,** *the tendency to make personal attributions for successes and situational attributions for failures* (Ross & Nisbett, 1991). The strength of this bias, however, depends on many factors. For example, a meta-analysis of 266 studies by Amy Mezulis and her coworkers (2004) found that depressed individuals are much less likely than most people to display a self-serving bias. Indeed, depressed people often display the opposite pattern—taking too little credit for successes and too much credit for failures—which helps keep them depressed.

Culture and Attribution

Culture influences how we perceive our social world. Consider the fundamental attribution error. Many studies suggest that the tendency to attribute other people's behavior to personal factors reflects a Westernized emphasis on individualism (Triandis, 2001). In one study, participants of varying ages from India and the United States attributed causality for other people's behavior (Miller, 1984). As Figure 16.3 shows, with increasing age, Indians made more situational attributions, whereas Americans made more personal attributions. Culture also influences attributions for our own behavior. Asians living in their homelands are less likely to display a self-serving attributional bias than are Americans or other Westerners (Mezulis et al., 2004). Modesty, for example, is highly valued in China's collectivistic culture, and Chinese college students take less personal credit for successful social interactions and accept more responsibility for their failures than do American students.

Beyond influencing the types of attributions that we make, our cultural background also affects how we go about making attributions.

FIGURE 16.3

Culture influences attributions.
With increasing age from childhood to adulthood, Americans show a greater tendency to make personal attributions for other people's behaviors. In contrast, participants from India show an increased tendency to make situational attributions. SOURCE: Adapted from Miller, 1984.

Consider that East Asians tend to hold a more holistic view of the universe than Westerners (Nisbett, 2003). This view, reflected in the belief that all events are interconnected, leads East Asians to develop more complex views about the causes of behavior. Accordingly, Incheol Choi and coworkers (2003) predicted and found that compared to European American college students, Korean college students scored higher on measures of holistic thinking and also took more information into account when making causal attributions for other people's behavior.

FORMING AND MAINTAINING IMPRESSIONS

As social beings, we constantly form impressions of other people, just as they form impressions of us. Attributions play a key role: Do you attribute the guards' behavior in the Stanford prison study to the role they were placed in or to their personal characteristics? Other factors, however, also affect how we form and maintain impressions.

How Important Are First Impressions?

Try this exercise. Tell a few people that you know someone who is "intelligent, industrious, impulsive, critical, stubborn, and envious," and ask them how much they "like" this person. Repeat the process with a few others, only describe the person as "envious, stubborn, critical, impulsive, industrious, and intelligent." Solomon Asch (1946) found that the person in the first description is perceived more positively—as more sociable and happier—than the person in the second description, even though both groups received identical information but in reverse order.

When forming impressions, the **primacy effect** *refers to our tendency to attach more importance to the initial information that we learn about a person.* New information can change our opinion, but it has to "work harder" for two reasons. First, we tend to be most alert to information we receive first. Second, initial information may shape how we perceive subsequent information. Imagine an athlete who gets off to a great start in training camp. The coach attributes high ability to the athlete. But as time goes on, the athlete's performance declines. To maintain this positive initial impression, the coach may attribute the performance decline to fatigue or a string of bad breaks. First impressions also carry extra weight because they influence our desire to make further contact with a person (Sunnafrank et al., 2004).

It's difficult to overcome someone's negative first impression of you if that person subsequently avoids or ignores you.

Primacy is the rule of thumb in impression formation, especially for people who dislike ambiguity and uncertainty (Kruglanski, 2004). We seem to have a remarkable capacity for forming snap judgments based on small amounts of initial information, and some evolutionary psychologists propose that evaluating stimuli quickly (such as rapidly distinguishing friend from foe) was adaptive for our survival (Krebs & Denton, 1997). But we are not slaves to primacy. Primacy effects decrease—and *recency effects* (giving greater weight to the most recent information) may occur—when we are asked to avoid making snap judgments, reminded to consider the evidence carefully, and made to feel accountable for our judgments (Webster et al., 1996).

Seeing What We Expect to See

Imagine that we are going to a party and I tell you that the host, George, is a distant, aloof, cold person. You meet him and try to make conversation, but George doesn't say much and avoids eye contact. A bit later, you say to me, "You were right, he's really a cold fish." Now let's roll back this scene. Suppose I describe George as nice but extremely shy. Later when you try to make conversation, he doesn't say much and avoids eye contact. You say to me, "You were right, he's really shy." Same behavior, different impression. This example reminds us of a basic perceptual principle highlighted in Chapter 4. Whether perceiving objects or people, our *mental set,* which is a readiness to perceive the world in a particular way, powerfully shapes how we interpret a stimulus.

What creates our mental sets? One factor that we have discussed throughout the book is *schemas,* mental frameworks that help us organize and interpret information. By telling you that our host is "cold" or "shy," I activate a set of concepts and expectations (your schema) for how such a person is likely to behave. The host's behavior can be interpreted in many ways, but you fit his behavior into the schema that is already activated.

A **stereotype,** *which is a generalized belief about a group or category of people,* represents a powerful type of schema. In one study, participants watched a videotape of a 9-year-old girl named Hannah and then judged her academic potential (Darley & Gross, 1983). They were told either that Hannah came from an upper-middle-class

To learn more about attribution, watch the "Fundamental Attribution Error" video in Chapter 16 of your CD.

▶ **Focus 3**
Discuss how the primacy effect, stereotypes, and self-fulfilling prophecies influence impression formation.

environment and had parents with white-collar careers or that she came from a poor neighborhood and had parents who were blue-collar workers. On the videotape, Hannah displayed average performance, answering some questions correctly and missing others. All participants saw the same performance, but those who thought Hannah came from a poor background rated her as having less ability. This study illustrates how our stereotypes (e.g., about social class) can bias the way we perceive other people's behavior.

▶ **Focus 4**
What is an attitude? Describe three conditions under which people's attitudes best predict their behavior.

Creating What We Expect to See

Seeing what we expect to see is only one way we confirm our initial impressions. Usually without conscious awareness, a **self-fulfilling prophecy** *occurs when people's erroneous expectations lead them to act toward others in a way that brings about the expected behaviors, thereby confirming their original impression.* Returning to our party example, if you expect George to be cold and aloof, then perhaps when you meet him you smile less and stand farther away than you would have if I had told you that George was a great guy. Perhaps when he looks at you, you avert your gaze, leading him to perceive you as less likable (Mason et al., 2005). In any case, his reserved response, in part, could be a reaction to *your* behavior (Figure 16.4a).

Self-fulfilling prophecies have been demonstrated in hundreds of studies across different settings, including schools, businesses, sports, close relationships, and interactions with strangers (Eden, 2003; Snyder, 2001). When we interact with other people, our initially unfounded expectations can influence how we behave toward them, shaping their behavior in a way that confirms our expectations (Figure 16.4b).

ATTITUDES AND ATTITUDE CHANGE

Beyond attributions and impressions, much of our social thinking involves the attitudes that we hold. Indeed, from political elections and war to the latest fashion craze, attitudes help steer the course of world events. An **attitude** *is a positive or negative evaluative reaction toward a stimulus, such as a person, action, object, or concept* (Tesser & Shaffer, 1990). Whether agreeing or disagreeing with a political policy or a friend's opinion of a movie, you are displaying an evaluative reaction (Figure 16.5). Our attitudes help define our identity, guide our actions, and influence how we judge people (Fazio & Roskos-Ewoldsen, 2005).

Do Our Attitudes Influence Our Behavior?

If we tell you that, according to research, people's attitudes strongly guide their behavior, you

(a)

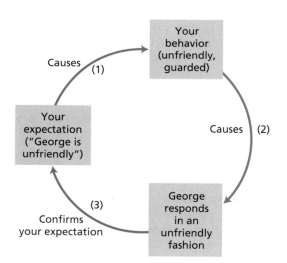

FIGURE 16.4

A self-fulfilling prophecy. (a) Your expectation concerning George may influence your behavior, and his response to you. (b) What first impressions will these people form of each other? How might these impressions influence their behavior and possibly create a self-fulfilling prophecy?

(b)

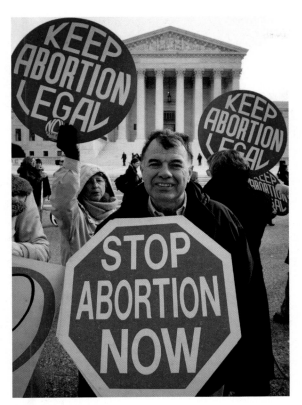

FIGURE 16.5

Attitudes represent an important form of social thinking. They help define who we are, and they affect the way people judge one another. Do the attitudes expressed by these protestors influence your impression of them?

might reply "So what? That's just common sense." But consider a classic study by Richard LaPiere (1934). In the 1930s, he toured the United States with a young Chinese couple, stopping at 251 restaurants, hotels, and other establishments. At the time, prejudice against Asians was widespread, yet the couple—who often entered the establishment before LaPiere did—were refused service only once. Later LaPiere wrote to all of these establishments, asking if they would provide service to Chinese patrons. More than 90 percent of those who responded stated that they would not.

We cannot be sure that the people who expressed negative attitudes in the survey were the same ones who, months earlier, had served the Chinese couple. Yet the discrepancy between prejudicial attitudes and nondiscriminatory behavior seemed overwhelming and called the "commonsense" assumption of attitude-behavior consistency into question. Decades of better-controlled research, however, indicate that attitudes do predict behavior (Fazio & Roskos-Ewoldsen, 2005). Three factors help explain why the attitude-

behavior relationship is strong in some cases but weak in others.

First, *attitudes influence behavior more strongly when situational factors that contradict our attitudes are weak.* For example, conformity pressures may lead us to behave in ways that are at odds with our inner convictions. According to the **theory of planned behavior** and similar models (Ajzen, 1991), *our intention to engage in a behavior is strongest when we have a positive attitude toward that behavior, when subjective norms (our perceptions of what other people think we should do) support our attitudes, and when we believe that the behavior is under our control.* Researchers have used this theory to predict successfully whether people will become smokers, exercise regularly, drive safely, donate blood, and perform many other behaviors (Victoir et al., 2005).

Second, *attitudes have a greater influence on behavior when we are aware of them and when they are strongly held.* Sometimes we seem to act without thinking, out of impulse or habit. Attitude-behavior consistency increases when people consciously think about or are reminded of their attitudes before acting (White et al., 2002).

Third, *general attitudes best predict general classes of behavior, and specific attitudes best predict specific behaviors.* For example, Martin Fishbein and Icek Ajzen (1974) found almost no relation between people's general attitudes toward religion and 70 specific religious behaviors (such as the frequency of attending services). But when they combined the 70 specific behaviors into a single global index of religious behavior, the relation between general religious attitudes and overall religious behavior was substantial.

Does Our Behavior Influence Our Attitudes?

Under the proper conditions, our attitudes guide our behavior. But attitude-behavior consistency is not a one-way street: We also come to develop attitudes that are consistent with how we behave (Cooper et al., 2005). In the Stanford prison study, as the guards slipped into their roles and began mistreating the prisoners, they began to view the prisoners as little more than animals. Why should this be?

Cognitive Dissonance Imagine that you volunteer for an experiment, arrive at the laboratory, and repeatedly perform two extremely boring tasks: emptying and filling a tray with spools and turning 48 pegs stuck into holes. After you endure 60 minutes of sheer boredom, the experimenter enters, thanks you for participating, and asks for

▶ **Focus 5**
Explain the causes of cognitive dissonance and how it produces attitude change.

your help: It is important for the next student to begin the study with a positive attitude about the tasks, and all you have to do is tell the student that the boring tasks are interesting. Depending on the condition to which you have been randomly assigned, the experimenter offers to pay you either $1 or $20 for, essentially, lying to the next participant. You agree to do so. Afterward, you go to the psychology department's main office to collect your money and fill out a "routine form" that asks how much you enjoyed the tasks in the experiment.

Make a prediction: Comparing participants who lied for $1 and who lied for $20 with a control group that simply rated the boring tasks without telling any lie beforehand, which of the three groups rated the task most positively? Why?

Common sense might suggest that participants paid $20 would feel happiest about the experiment and rate the tasks most highly. However, as Leon Festinger and J. Merrill Carlsmith (1959) predicted in a classic experiment, participants who were paid $1 gave the most positive ratings. Indeed, they actually rated the boring tasks as "somewhat enjoyable" (Figure 16.6)!

According to Festinger's (1957) **theory of cognitive dissonance,** *people strive for consistency in their cognitions.* When two or more cognitions contradict one another (such as "I am a truthful person" and "I just told another student that those boring tasks were interesting"), the person experiences an uncomfortable state of tension, which Festinger calls *cognitive dissonance,* and becomes motivated to reduce this dissonance. The theory predicts that to reduce dissonance and restore a state of cognitive consistency, people will change one of their cognitions or add new cognitions. Participants who received $20 could justify their behavior by adding a new cognition—"Who wouldn't tell a little lie for $20?"—and there was little reason for them to change their attitude toward the boring tasks. Those who had lied for only $1 could not use this trivial monetary gain to justify their behavior. But if they could convince themselves that the tasks actually were enjoyable, then they wouldn't have been lying after all. Thus they changed their attitude about the task to bring it more in line with how they had behaved.

Behavior that is inconsistent with one's attitude is called *counterattitudinal behavior,* and it produces dissonance only if we perceive that our actions were freely chosen rather than coerced. Freely chosen behaviors that produce foreseeable negative consequences or that threaten our sense of self-worth are especially likely to arouse disso-

▶ **Focus 6**
Evaluate dissonance versus self-perception theory views of why counterattitudinal behavior produces attitude change.

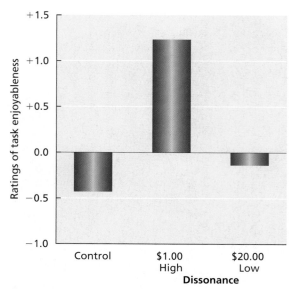

FIGURE 16.6

Cognitive dissonance and external justification. Participants lied to a fellow student by saying that a boring task was interesting. Those offered $1 to lie later rated the task most positively. Presumably, they reduced their cognitive dissonance about lying by convincing themselves that the task was interesting after all. Participants offered $20 had an external justification to lie, experienced little dissonance, and therefore did not need to convince themselves that the task was enjoyable. They and control participants who had not lied rated the boring task less favorably than the $1 group. SOURCE: Based on Festinger & Carlsmith, 1959.

nance. Once the behavior occurs, people start to consider the meaning of what they have done, and this produces dissonance (Cooper et al., 2005). Recall the statement by one of the guards in the Stanford prison study regarding his treatment of the prisoners: "I was surprised at myself." If the guard thought of himself as a good, moral person, then his callous behavior toward the prisoners should have created dissonance. Changing his attitude toward the prisoners—essentially coming to see them as "cattle" who did not have the same rights as humans—would have reduced dissonance.

Dissonance, however, does not always lead to attitude change. People can reduce dissonance by finding external justifications or by making other excuses (Cooper et al., 2005). In Scandinavian surveys, among people who drank alcohol despite having negative attitudes toward drinking, one rationalization seemed to be "I may not be perfect, but other people are still worse" (Mäkelä, 1997). Despite the many ways to reduce dissonance, the theory helps explain many interesting aspects of human behavior (Figure 16.7).

Self-Perception If we see someone campaigning for a political candidate, we will likely assume that this person has a positive attitude toward the candidate. If we see someone exerting great effort to achieve a goal, we will logically judge that the goal is important to that person. In short, we infer what other people's attitudes must be by watching how they behave. According to Daryl Bem's (1972) **self-perception theory,** *we make inferences about our own attitudes in much the same way: by observing how we behave.* Knowing that for very little external justification ($1) you have told a fellow student that the boring experimental tasks are enjoyable, you logically conclude that deep down you must feel that the tasks were at least somewhat enjoyable. In Bem's view, your attitude is not produced by a mysterious concept called *cognitive dissonance;* rather you simply observe how you have acted and infer how you must have felt to have behaved in this fashion.

Self-perception theory and cognitive dissonance theory both predict that counterattitudinal behavior produces attitude change. How, then, can we determine which theory more accurately explains the reason behind such attitude change? One key difference is that only dissonance theory assumes that we experience heightened physiological arousal (tension produced by dissonance) when we engage in counterattitudinal behavior. Do we? At least in some instances it appears so. In one study, college students consumed an unpleasant-tasting drink and were then asked to write a sentence stating that they liked the taste. Students who were given a high degree of choice whether to write this counterattitudinal statement showed higher arousal (measured by sweat gland activity) and greater attitude change than participants who were simply told to write the statement (Harmon-Jones et al., 1996).

These and other findings indicate that dissonance theory best explains why people change their views after behaving in ways that openly contradict their clearly defined attitudes, especially when such behaviors threaten their self-image (Stone & Cooper, 2003). Lying to someone for a measly dollar threatens our self-image of honesty, and acting inhumanely toward prisoners threatens our self-image of being a good, decent person—unless we can somehow justify those actions to ourselves. However, when counterattitudinal behavior does not threaten self-worth and we have weak attitudes to begin with, such behavior is less likely to create significant arousal—yet people may still alter their attitudes to be more consistent with how they have behaved. In this case, self-perception theory may provide the better explanation. Thus both dissonance theory and self-perception theory appear to be correct, but

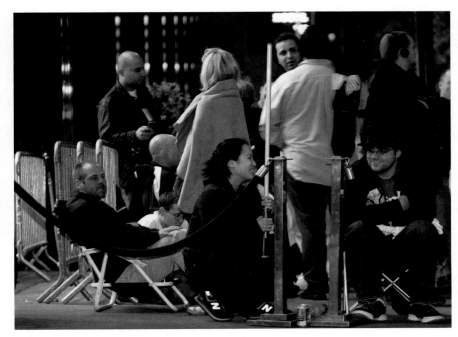

FIGURE 16.7

Effort justification: "May the force (of dissonance) be with you!" In 1999, fans began camping out days in advance to see *Star Wars: Episode I—The Phantom Menace.* In contrast to 2005's well-regarded *Episode III,* most critics and many moviegoers found *Episode I* disappointing. But fans who waited in line for days said the movie was "awesome." No doubt, a major reason for their positive attitude was that they were hard-core fans. But might cognitive dissonance have played a role? Experiments show that when people invest a lot of time and energy toward a goal, finding out that the goal wasn't all it was cracked up to be creates cognitive dissonance. To justify their effort and thus reduce dissonance, people may convince themselves that the goal (e.g., the movie) is more attractive or worthwhile than it really is.

under different circumstances (Tesser & Shaffer, 1990). Both theories, however, agree that *our behaviors can influence our attitudes.*

Persuasion

Persuasion is a fact of everyday life, and it represents the intersection of social thinking and our next topic: social influence. Persuaders try to influence our beliefs and attitudes so that we will vote for them, buy their products, do them favors, or otherwise behave as they want us to. Here we examine three aspects of the persuasion process.

The Communicator Communicator credibility— *how believable we perceive the communicator to be*—is often a key to effective persuasion. In fact, audience members who do not enjoy thinking deeply about issues may pay little attention to the content of a message and simply go along with the opinions of a highly credible source. Credibility has two major components: *expertise* and *trustworthiness* (Hovland et al., 1953). The most effective persuader is one who appears to be an expert and to be presenting the truth in an unbiased manner.

▶ **Focus 7**
Describe how communicator, message, and audience characteristics affect the persuasion process.

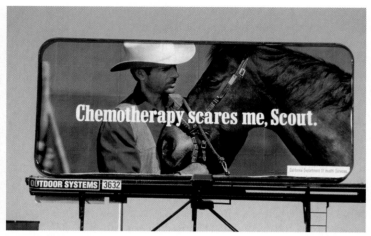

FIGURE 16.8

Fear appeals are a common approach to persuasion. They are most effective when people believe that a feared event could occur ("Driving after drinking can increase my risk of an accident"), that the consequences would be aversive ("I could lose my license or be killed"), that there is an effective way to reduce the risk ("If I drink, I won't drive"), and that they can carry out this behavior without great cost ("Have a designated driver; call a friend").

We are especially likely to perceive communicators as trustworthy when they advocate a point of view that is contrary to their own self-interest (Petty et al., 2001). Communicators who are physically attractive, likable, and similar to us (such as in interests or goals) may also gain a persuasive edge, which is why advertisers spend millions of dollars hiring attractive, likable stars to promote their products.

The Message   In trying to persuade someone, is it more effective to present only your side of the issue or to also present the opposition's arguments and then refute them? Overall, research indicates that the *two-sided refutational approach* is most effective (Allen, 1991). Especially if an audience initially disagrees with the communicator's viewpoint or is aware that there are two sides to the issue, a two-sided message will be perceived as less biased.

Many messages, such as those in Figure 16.8, attempt to persuade by arousing fear. Does it work? Or do people reduce their fear simply by denying the credibility of the message or the communicator? Overall, fear arousal seems to work best when the message evokes moderate to strong fear and also provides people with effective, feasible (i.e., low-cost) ways to reduce the threat (Dillard & Anderson, 2004). High-fear messages accompanied by inadequate information about "what to do" typically lead to denial.

The Audience   A message loaded with logical arguments and facts may prove highly persuasive to some people yet fall flat on its face with others.

One reason is that people differ in their *need for cognition*. Some enjoy analyzing issues; others prefer not to spend much mental effort.

According to Richard Petty and John Cacioppo, there are two basic routes to persuasion (Petty & Cacioppo 1986; Petty et al., 2005). The **central route to persuasion** *occurs when people think carefully about the message and are influenced because they find the arguments compelling*. The **peripheral route to persuasion** *occurs when people do not scrutinize the message but are influenced mostly by other factors such as a speaker's attractiveness or a message's emotional appeal*. Attitude change that results from the central route tends to last longer and to predict future behavior more successfully.

People who have a high need for cognition tend to follow the central route to persuasion. In forming attitudes about consumer services and products, for example, they pay attention to information about the service and product (Wood & Swait, 2002). In contrast, people with a low need for cognition are more strongly influenced by peripheral cues, such as the attractiveness of the person who endorses the product.

IN REVIEW

■ Consistency, distinctiveness, and consensus information jointly influence whether we make a personal or situational attribution for a particular act.

- The fundamental attribution error is the tendency to attribute other people's behavior to personal factors while underestimating the role of situational factors. The self-serving bias is the tendency to attribute one's successes to personal factors and one's failures to situational factors.

- Impressions may change over time, but our first impression generally carries extra weight. Stereotypes and schemas create mental sets that shape our impressions.

- Through self-fulfilling prophecies, our initially false expectations shape the way we act toward someone. In turn, this person responds to our behavior in a way that confirms our initially false belief.

- Attitudes predict behavior best when situational influences are weak, when the attitude is strong, and when we consciously think about our attitude.

- Behavior also influences attitudes. Counterattitudinal behavior is most likely to create cognitive dissonance when the behavior is freely chosen and threatens our self-worth or produces foreseeable negative consequences.

- To reduce dissonance, we may change our attitude to become more consistent with how we have acted. When our attitudes are weak and counterattitudinal behavior doesn't threaten our self-worth, we may change our attitudes through self-perception.

- Communicator, message, and audience characteristics influence the effectiveness of persuasion. Communicator credibility is highest when the communicator is perceived as expert and trustworthy. Fear-arousing communications may be effective if they arouse moderate to strong fear and suggest how to avoid the feared result. The central route to persuasion works best with listeners who have a high need for cognition; for those with a low cognition need, the peripheral route works better.

SOCIAL INFLUENCE

Patricia, a novice piano player, makes more mistakes after her parents enter the room to listen to her practice. Brad, a guard in the Stanford prison study, starts treating prisoners harshly after witnessing several of his fellow guards do the same. These diverse situations share a basic ingredient: They involve social influence.

THE MERE PRESENCE OF OTHERS

Norman Triplett (1898) helped launch the field of social psychology by testing a deceptively simple hypothesis: The presence of others energizes performance. Triplett analyzed the records from numerous bicycle races. In some races, cyclists performed individually against the clock; in other races of similar distance, they performed together in a pack. As Triplett predicted, cyclists' average speed was much faster in group races than in individual races, but from experience he knew that other factors (e.g., racers riding behind one another to cut wind resistance) could also explain this finding. So in a laboratory experiment, Triplett had children perform a simple physical task, either alone or in the presence of another child (called a *coactor*) who independently performed the same task. Indeed, the children's performance improved when in each other's presence.

Many early studies revealed that the *mere presence* of coactors or of a silent audience enhanced performance. Even ants carried more dirt with other ants present (Chen, 1937). Yet some research found that the mere presence of others impaired performance on certain tasks.

In 1965 Robert Zajonc proposed a theory to explain this seeming paradox. First, the mere physical presence of another person (or member of the same species) increases our arousal. Second, as arousal increases, we become more likely to perform whatever behaviors happen to be our *dominant responses* (i.e., most typical responses) to that specific situation. When a task is complex and we are first trying to learn it, our dominant responses are likely to be incorrect ones, so we make errors. Therefore, performing in front of other people will impair performance. But when a task is either simple or complex but well learned, our dominant responses usually are correct ones. In these situations, performing in the presence of others will enhance performance (Figure 16.9).

This phenomenon is called **social facilitation,** *an increased tendency to perform one's dominant responses in the mere presence of others.* It may be the most basic form of social influence, occurring in species ranging from fruit flies to hens and humans (Thomas et al., 2002), and it has an important practical implication: When learning complex tasks, minimize the presence of other people.

NORMS, CONFORMITY, AND OBEDIENCE

Years ago, a professor on our campus gave his class an unusual assignment: Without doing

▶ **Focus 8**
When does the mere presence of others enhance performance or impair performance? Why?

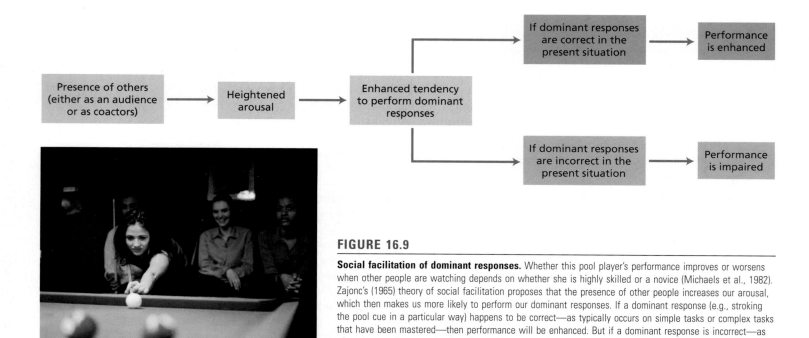

FIGURE 16.9

Social facilitation of dominant responses. Whether this pool player's performance improves or worsens when other people are watching depends on whether she is highly skilled or a novice (Michaels et al., 1982). Zajonc's (1965) theory of social facilitation proposes that the presence of other people increases our arousal, which then makes us more likely to perform our dominant responses. If a dominant response (e.g., stroking the pool cue in a particular way) happens to be correct—as typically occurs on simple tasks or complex tasks that have been mastered—then performance will be enhanced. But if a dominant response is incorrect—as often occurs when a novice is trying to learn a complex task—then the presence of other people most likely will impair performance.

anything illegal, each student was to violate some unspoken rule of social behavior and observe how others reacted. One student licked her plate clean at a formal dinner, receiving cold stares from the other guests. Another boarded a nearly empty city bus, sat down next to the only other passenger, and said "Hi!" The passenger sat up stiffly and stared out the window.

Social norms *are shared expectations about how people should think, feel, and behave,* and they are the glue that binds social systems together (Schaller & Crandall, 2004). Some norms are formal laws, but many—as illustrated by the preceding examples—are implicit and unspoken. Such norms regulate daily behavior without our conscious awareness; we take them for granted until they are violated.

A **social role** *consists of a set of norms that characterizes how people in a given social position ought to behave.* The social roles of "college student," "professor," "police officer," and "spouse" carry different sets of behavior expectations. Because we may wear many hats in our daily life, *role conflict* can occur when the norms accompanying different roles clash. College students who hold jobs and have children often experience role conflict as they try to juggle the competing demands of school, work, and parenthood.

Norms and roles can influence behavior so strongly that they compel a person to act uncharacteristically. The guards in the Stanford prison

study were well-adjusted students, yet norms related to the role of "guard" seemed to override their values, leading to their dehumanizing treatment of the prisoners.

Norm Formation and Culture

Social norms lose invisibility not only when they are violated but also when we examine behavior across cultures and historical periods. In doing so, we see that many social customs we take for granted as "normal"—from gender roles and child rearing to views about love and marriage—are arbitrary. Norms even regulate such subtle aspects of social behavior as the amount of *personal space* that we prefer when interacting with people (Li, 2001). For example, Japanese sit farther apart when conversing than Venezuelans do, and Americans prefer an intermediate distance (Sussman & Rosenfeld, 1982).

It is difficult to imagine any society, organization, or social group functioning well without norms. In a classic experiment, Muzafer Sherif (1935) found that even randomly created groups develop norms. The task involved an optical illusion called the *autokinetic effect:* When people stare at a dot of light projected on a screen in a dark room, they begin to perceive the dot as moving, even though it really is stationary. When Sherif tested college students individually over several trials, each student perceived the light to

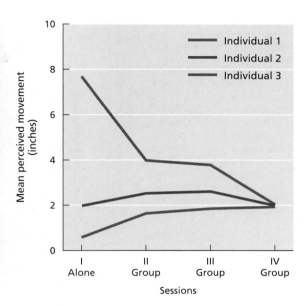

FIGURE 16.10

The evolution of norms across time and cultures. (*left*) The Academy Award–winning movie *Million Dollar Baby* portrayed an aspiring American professional female boxer—an activity that women would be barred from in many countries, and that women were barred from decades ago in America. (*right*) Even randomly created groups spontaneously form norms. In Sherif's experiments, individuals' autokinetic judgments made alone (session I) began to converge when they were made in the presence of two other participants (sessions II, III, and IV). Each mean is based on 100 judgments per session. These data are from one of the three-person groups. Notice that the final norm is not simply the average of the original judgments that the group members made while alone. SOURCE: Based on Sherif, 1935.

move a different amount, from an inch or two to almost a foot.

Later the students were randomly placed into groups of 3 and made further judgments. As group members heard one another's judgments over several sessions, their judgments converged and a group norm evolved. The participants did not say "Hey, let's develop a group norm." It just happened. And, just as norms vary across cultures, the evolved norm for the autokinetic effect varied from group to group (Figure 16.10).

Sherif's finding has been replicated in other countries and with different tasks. Whether at a cultural level or in small random groups, humans develop common standards for behavior and judgment (Arrow & Burns, 2004).

Why Do People Conform?

Norms can influence behavior only if people conform to them. Without *conformity*—the adjustment of individual behaviors, attitudes, and beliefs to a group standard—we would have social chaos. As Figure 16.11 illustrates, at times we conform due to **informational social influence,** *following the opinions or behavior of other people because we believe that they have accurate knowledge and*

that what they are doing is right. We also may succumb to **normative social influence,** *conforming to obtain the rewards that come from being accepted by other people while at the same time avoiding their rejection* (Cialdini & Goldstein, 2004; Deutsch & Gerard, 1955).

Solomon Asch's (1951, 1956) landmark conformity experiments illustrated both types of influence. In the experimental condition, groups of college students performed several trials of a

▶ **Focus 9**
Use the concepts of informational and normative social influence to explain how social norms and roles guide behavior.

"Well, heck! If all you smart cookies agree, who am I to dissent?"

FIGURE 16.11

Often we conform to a majority because we believe that their opinion "must be right." SOURCE: Copyright © The New Yorker Collection 1972 J. B. Handelsman. All rights reserved. Used with permission from cartoonbank.com.

FIGURE 16.12

Asch's classic conformity experiment. (a) In Asch's (1956) conformity experiments, students were asked to judge which of three comparison lines was the same length as the standard line. They performed this task for multiple trials, using a different set of standard and comparison lines each time. (b) Upon hearing other group members unanimously say that line 1 was the correct match, this participant wondered whether his own judgment (line 2) was correct.

(a)

(b)

simple visual task (Figure 16.12a) in which they were asked—for various sets of lines—which of 3 comparison lines was the same length as a standard line (line A). Only one member of the group, however, actually was a participant. The rest were accomplices of the experimenter. Group members sat around a table and were called on in order. The real participant sat next to last. According to plan, every accomplice intentionally gave the same wrong answer on some trials. Imagine yourself hearing the first group member choose line 1. (You think to yourself, "Huh?") Then the next four members also choose line 1. (You're wondering, "Can this really be?") Now it is your turn.

Would anybody conform to the group's incorrect judgments? Asch found that overall, participants conformed 37 percent of the time, compared with a mere 1 percent error rate in a control condition where people judged the lines by themselves. This finding stunned many scientists because the task was so easy and the confederates did not overtly pressure participants to conform.

After the task was over, some participants told the experimenter that they felt the group was wrong but went along to avoid making waves and suffering possible rejection. This reflects normative social influence. After several trials, other participants yielded to informational social influence and began to doubt their eyesight and judgment (Figure 16.12b).

Factors That Affect Conformity

Asch showed that complex social behavior could be studied under controlled conditions. In other experiments, he manipulated different variables

and measured their effects on conformity. Consider two examples:

- *Group size:* Conformity increased from about 5 to 35 percent as group size increased from 1 to about 4 or 5 confederates, but contrary to what we might expect, further increases in group size did not increase conformity.

- *Presence of a dissenter:* According to plan, one confederate disagreed with the others (e.g., the majority said "line 3"; the dissenter said "line 2" or even "line 1"). This greatly reduced participants' conformity. When someone dissents, this serves as a model for remaining independent from the group.

Reviewing 97 conformity experiments conducted in the United States from 1951 to 1990, Rod Bond and Peter Smith (1996) found that the overall level of conformity decreased slightly over this time period. Around the globe, conformity tends to be greater among research participants from collectivistic cultures, where group harmony is valued more highly than in individualistic cultures.

Minority Influence

Although majority influence is powerful, in political, business, and other real-world contexts, dissenting information presented by the minority may cause majority members to change their view (Nemeth & Goncalo, 2005). Dissenting opinions are more likely to sway the majority when they come from several minority members rather than just one (Clark, 2001). Serge Moscovici (1985) proposes that to maximize its influence, the minority must be highly committed to its point of view, remain

▶ **Focus 10**
Describe situational factors that influence conformity to the group. When will minority influence be strongest?

independent in the face of majority pressure, yet appear to keep an open mind. Indeed, reviewing almost 100 studies, Wendy Wood and coworkers (1994) found that minority influence is strongest when the minority maintains a highly consistent position over time. However, if the minority appears too unreasonable, deviant, or negative, it may cause the majority to become entrenched.

Obedience to Authority

Like conformity to a group, obedience to an authority figure is inherently neither good nor bad. As an airplane passenger, you would not be amused if the copilot disregarded the pilot's commands simply because he or she didn't feel like obeying, putting the flight and your life at risk. Without obedience, society would face chaos. But obedience can also produce tragic results. After

World War II, the famous Nuremberg trials were held to judge Nazi war criminals who had slaughtered millions of innocent people in concentration camps. In many instances, the defendants argued that they had only followed orders. In the massacre of men, women, and children at My Lai during the Vietnam War, American soldiers accused of atrocities gave the same explanation. No doubt we will continue to hear the cry "I was just following orders" as accountability is judged for more recent mass atrocities around the globe.

Just as the Nuremberg court did, many of us reject justifications based on obedience to authority as mere rationalizations, secure in our conviction that we would behave more humanely in such situations. But would we? Our "Research Close-Up"—part of the most famous series of studies ever conducted in social psychology— suggests some provocative answers.

► **Focus 11**
Describe Milgram's research, factors that increase and decrease obedience, and implications for society.

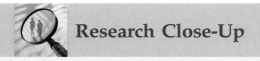

Research Close-Up | **The Dilemma of Obedience: When Conscience Confronts Malevolent Authority**

SOURCE: Stanley Milgram, 1974. *Obedience to Authority.* New York: Harper & Row.

INTRODUCTION

Fueled by a scientific interest in social influence and a desire to understand the horrors of the Holocaust, psychologist Stanley Milgram (1974) asked a disturbing question: Would ordinary citizens obey the orders of an authority figure if those orders meant physically harming an innocent person? He conducted 18 studies between 1960 and 1963 to answer this question and to identify factors that increased or decreased obedience to authority. Let's examine one study.

METHOD

Forty men, ranging in age from 20 to 50 and representing a cross section of occupations and educational backgrounds, participated in the study. At the laboratory, each participant met a middle-aged man who was introduced as another participant but who was actually a confederate. Participants were told that the experiment examined the effects of punishment on memory. Then through a supposedly random draw (it was rigged), the real participant became the "teacher" and the confederate became the "learner." The teacher presented a series of memory problems to the learner through a two-way intercom system. Each time the learner made an error, the teacher was instructed to administer an electric shock using a machine that had 30 switches, beginning with

15 volts and increasing step-by-step to 450 volts (Figure 16.13a). As the teacher watched, the experimenter strapped the learner into a chair in an adjoining room and hooked him up to wires from the shock generator (Figure 16.13b). The learner expressed concern about the shocks and mentioned that he had a slight heart problem.

Returning to the main room, the experimenter gave the teacher a sample shock (45 volts) and then ordered the experiment to begin. Unbeknownst to the teacher, the learner intentionally committed many errors, and he did *not* actually receive any shock. The learner made verbal protests that were standardized on a tape recorder, so that they were the same for all participants.

As the learner's errors mounted, the teacher increased the shock. If the teacher balked at continuing, the experimenter issued one or more escalating commands, such as "Please continue," "You must continue," and "You have no other choice." At 75 volts, the learner moaned when the teacher threw the switch. At 150 volts, he moaned again and said, "Experimenter! That's all. Get me out of here. I told you I had heart trouble. My heart's starting to bother me now. Get me out of here, please. . . . I refuse to go on. Let me out." Beyond 200 volts, he emitted agonized screams every time a shock was delivered, yelling "Let me out! Let me out!" At 300 volts, the learner refused to answer and continued screaming to be let out. At 345 volts and beyond, there was only silence. Full obedience was operationally defined as continuing to the maximum shock level of 450 volts.

Continued

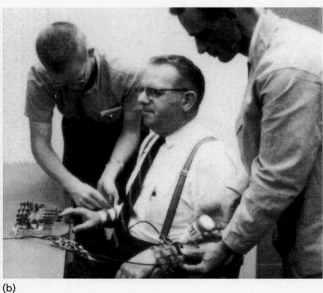

(a)   (b)

FIGURE 16.13

(a) Switches on the shock generator ranged from 15 volts ("slight shock") to 450 volts ("XXX"). (b) The participant (teacher) saw the learner being strapped into the chair.

RESULTS

Participants wrestled with a dilemma. Should they continue to hurt this innocent person, as the experimenter commanded, or should they stop the learner's pain by openly disobeying? Most participants became distressed. Some trembled, sweated, laughed nervously, or, in a few cases, experienced convulsions. But would they obey? Make a prediction: What percentage of people obeyed to 450 volts?

Before the study, Milgram had asked psychiatrists, professors, university students, and middle-class adults to predict the outcome. They said that virtually no one (1 percent) would obey fully. Indeed, most participants balked or protested at one time or another and said they would not continue. But ultimately, 26 of the 40 men (65 percent) obeyed all the way to the end (Figure 16.14).

DISCUSSION

Milgram's research has generated controversy for decades (Blass, 2002; Miller, 2004). Its ethics were harshly criticized because participants were deceived, were exposed to substantial stress, and risked long-lasting negative effects to their self-image (Baumrind, 1964). Milgram countered that the research was so socially significant as to warrant the deception, that participants were carefully debriefed afterward, and that psychiatric follow-ups of a sample of obedient participants suggested no long-term ill effects. Weighing the costs and benefits, do you believe that this research was justified?

Researchers also debate why obedience was high, but many agree with Milgram's view that participants psychologically transferred much of the "responsibility" for the

FIGURE 16.14

You must obey. This graph shows the percentage of male participants who continued to shock the learner through various voltage levels. SOURCE: Based on Milgram, 1974.

learner's fate to the experimenter. Participants viewed the experimenter as an expert, legitimate authority figure (Blass & Schmitt, 2001). While administering the shock, some participants stated that they "were not responsible" for what happened. Others asked, "Who is responsible if something happens to the learner?" When the experimenter replied,

"I am responsible," participants felt greater freedom to continue. Yet they were the ones flipping the switch.

Would similar results occur today? We suspect so. For 25 years after Milgram's research, experiments in different countries, in "real-world" settings, and with children, adolescents, and adults, yielded consistent results. In the 1980s, Dutch researchers Wim Meeus and Quinten Raaijmakers (1986, 1995) conducted 19 obedience studies. In one, 92 percent of participants completely obeyed an experimenter's orders to repeatedly disrupt the performance of a job applicant (actually a confederate) taking an important job-screening test. The applicant pleaded with participants to stop, to no avail.

How would you have responded in Milgram's experiment? Almost all of our students say that they would have disobeyed either before or when the victim began protesting at the 150-volt level. Indeed, in one study, students in psychology classes—whether familiar with Milgram's results or not—said that they would stop at around 150 volts (Geher et al., 2002). So suppose we conduct an obedience study today but with real electric shocks and with you as the learner. The teacher will be a randomly selected student from your class. Are you confident that this student will disobey the experimenter and stop giving you shocks when you start yelling in protest? Few of our students or other students express such confidence (Geher et al., 2002). In short, virtually all of us are confident that *we* would disobey early on, but we are less sure about *other* people—and they in turn are not so sure about *us*.

Factors That Influence Obedience

By manipulating the following aspects of the laboratory situation, Milgram and other researchers obtained obedience rates ranging from 0 to over 90 percent:

- *Remoteness of the victim:* Obedience was greatest when the learner was out of sight. When the teacher and learner were placed in the same room, obedience dropped to 40 percent. Further, when the teacher had to make physical contact and force the learner's hand onto a "shock plate," obedience dropped to 30 percent (Figure 16.15).

- *Closeness and legitimacy of the authority figure:* Obedience was highest when the authority figure was close by and perceived as legitimate. When the experimenter left the scene and gave orders by phone or when an "ordinary person" (a confederate) took over and gave the orders, obedience dropped to about 20 percent.

- *Diffusion of responsibility:* When another "participant" (actually a confederate) flipped the shock switch and the real participants only had to perform another aspect of the task, 93 percent obeyed. In short, *obedience increases when someone else does the dirty work.* In contrast, when Harvey Tilker (1970) made participants feel fully responsible for the learner's welfare, not a single person obeyed to the end.

- *Personal characteristics:* Milgram compared the political orientations, religious affiliations, occupations, education, length of military service, and psychological characteristics of obedient versus disobedient participants. Differences were weak or nonexistent.

 ## What Do You Think?

DO WOMEN DIFFER FROM MEN IN OBEDIENCE?
Suppose that the participants in Milgram's featured study had been women. Keeping everything else constant (i.e., the same male experimenter and male learner), would you expect women to be more or less obedient than the men or equally obedient? Why? Think about it, then see page 654.

FIGURE 16.15

In one of Milgram's studies (touch proximity), the teacher was ordered to physically force the learner's hand onto a "shock plate" after the learner refused to continue. Here, 30 percent of participants obeyed fully to 450 volts. Although touch proximity strongly reduced obedience, that a significant minority still obeyed raises considerable concern.

Lessons Learned

What lessons shall we draw from this research? Certainly, it is *not* that people are apathetic or evil. Participants became stressed precisely because they did care about the learner's welfare. Neither is the lesson that we are sheep. If we were, obedience would be high across all situations, which is not the case. Rather, Milgram sums up a key lesson as follows:

> It would be a mistake . . . to make the simpleminded statement that kindly and good persons disobey while those who are cruel do not . . . often, it is not so much the kind of person a man is as the kind of situation in which he finds himself that determines how he will act. (Milgram, 1974, p. 205)

Thus by arranging the situation appropriately, most people—ordinary, decent citizens—can be induced to follow orders from an authority figure they perceive as legitimate, even when doing so contributes to harming an innocent person. The applicability of this principle to the Holocaust and other atrocities seems clear (Blass, 2002). During the Holocaust, obedience was made easier because most of the personnel working at the concentration camps were cogs in a horrendous wheel: They didn't pull the switch to flood the chambers with gas but instead performed other tasks. Their victims also were "remote" at the moment of their murder. Further, to lessen concentration camp workers' feelings of responsibility, Hitler's subordinate Heinrich Himmler told them in manipulative speeches that only he and Hitler were personally responsible for what took place (Dawidowicz, 1975).

Does obedience research suggest that we are not responsible for following orders? This is a moral and legal question, not a scientific one. But if anything, this research should heighten our responsibility for being aware of the pitfalls of blind obedience and prevent us from being so smug or naive as to feel that such events "could never happen here." Beyond obedience, Milgram's research provides yet another powerful example of how social contexts can induce people to behave in ways that they never would have imagined possible (Figure 16.16).

DETECTING AND RESISTING COMPLIANCE TECHNIQUES

From telemarketers and salespeople to TV and Internet advertisements, would-be persuaders often come armed with special *compliance techniques:* strategies that may manipulate you into saying yes when you really want to say no. By learning to identify these techniques, you will be in a better position to resist them.

The powerful **norm of reciprocity** *involves the expectation that when others treat us well, we should respond in kind.* Thus to get you to comply with a request, I can do something nice for you now—such as an unsolicited favor—in hopes that you will feel pressure to reciprocate later when I present you with my request (Cialdini & Sagarin, 2005). As Figure 16.17 illustrates, the Hare Krishna Society (a religious group) cleverly used flower power to manipulate the norm of reciprocity and raise millions of dollars in donations.

Now consider the **door-in-the-face technique:** *A persuader makes a large request, expecting you to reject it* (you "slam the door" in the persuader's face), *and then presents a smaller request.* Telemarketers feast on this technique. Rather than ask you directly for a modest monetary contribution to some organization or cause, they first ask for a much larger contribution, knowing that you will say no. After you politely refuse, they ask for the smaller contribution. In one experiment, after people declined an initial request to donate $25 to a charity, they were more likely to donate $2 than were participants who were directly asked for $2 (Wang et al., 1989). To be effective, the same persuader must make both requests. The persuader "compromises" by making the second, smaller request, so we feel pressure to reciprocate by complying. Refusing the first request also may produce guilt, and complying with the smaller request may help us reduce guilt or feel socially responsible (Tusing & Dillard, 2000).

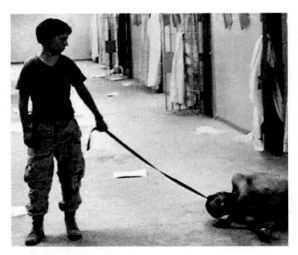

FIGURE 16.16

Do you remember how this photograph shocked the world? In 2005, U.S. Army reservist Lynndie England faced a court martial for assaulting prisoners in the 2003 Abu Ghraib Iraqi prisoner scandal. Was this the real Lynndie England? Her family said it couldn't be the same loving person that they knew. Army reservist Charles Graner, the presumed ringleader of the guards involved in the scandal, claimed in his own court martial that they were following orders. The military jury rejected the claim. In editorials and news reports, the media turned to the lessons of Milgram's research and the Stanford prison study to try to make sense of the guards' behavior.

▶ **Focus 12**
Identify four common compliance techniques and explain how they work.

Using the **foot-in-the-door technique,** *a persuader gets you to comply with a small request first (getting the "foot in the door") and later presents a larger request.* Imagine receiving an e-mail from a stranger who asks for simple advice about a word processing program. It takes less than 1 minute to reply, and you do—as did all the participants in an actual experiment (Guéguen, 2002). After you comply, the person sends a second e-mail asking you to help with a class project by filling out a 20-minute online questionnaire. In the experiment, 76 percent of college students complied, compared to only 44 percent in a control group that received only the class-project request. Although hypotheses abound, researchers are not sure why the foot-in-the-door technique is effective.

With a final technique, **lowballing,** *a persuader gets you to commit to some action and then—before you actually perform the behavior—he or she increases the "cost" of that same behavior.* Imagine negotiating to buy a used car for $8,000, a "great price." The salesperson says, "I need to confirm this with my manager," comes back shortly, and states, "I'm afraid my manager says the price is too low. But you can have the car for only $400 more. It's still a great price." At this point, you are more likely to go through with the deal than you would have been, had the "real" $8,400 price been set at the outset.

Both lowballing and the foot-in-the-door technique involve moving from a smaller request to a larger, more costly one. But with lowballing, the stakes for the *same behavior* are raised after you commit to it but *before* you consummate the behavior. Having made a commitment, you may find it easier to rationalize the added costs or may feel obligated to the person to whom you made the commitment (Cialdini & Sagarin, 2005).

By recognizing when compliance techniques are being used to manipulate your behavior, you are in a better position to resist them. Consider the norm of reciprocity. Robert Cialdini (2001), an expert on influence techniques, suggests that the key is not to resist the initial gift or favor; instead, accept the unsolicited "favor," but if the person then asks you for a favor in return, recognize this as a manipulative trick. Similarly, if a telemarketer makes a large initial request and then, after you decline, immediately asks for a smaller commitment, respond by thinking or saying, "I see. It's the door-in-the-face technique." Of course, you can still choose to comply if you believe it's the right thing to do. The goal is not to automatically reject every social influence attempt but to avoid feeling coerced into doing something you don't want to do.

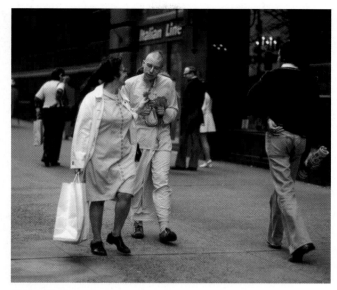

FIGURE 16.17

In the 1970s, members of the Hare Krishna Society approached passersby and gave them a small flower. If a passerby refused, the member said "Please. It is a gift for you." Reluctantly, people often accepted. Then the member asked for a donation. People felt pressure to reciprocate, donated money, and often threw the flower away.

BEHAVIOR IN GROUPS

Much of human behavior occurs in groups. People often form groups to share interests and activities and to perform tasks and achieve goals that are too complex or demanding to be accomplished by one person.

Social Loafing

In 1913 Max Ringelmann, a French agricultural engineer, measured the force that men exerted while pulling on a rope as hard as they could. Individually, the men averaged 63 kilograms (kg) of pull. Thus you might expect that 8 men pulling in unison would exert a combined force of about 504 kg (i.e., 8 × 63 kg). Surprisingly, group performance was 51 percent below expectations, and one contributing factor was **social loafing,** *the tendency for people to expend less individual effort when working in a group than when working alone.* In contrast to social facilitation experiments, in which a person performs a task individually (in front of an audience or with a coactor) and does not pool her or his effort with anyone, social loafing involves collective performance. Social loafing also occurs on cognitive tasks, as when groups have to evaluate written materials or make decisions. Why does social loafing occur? Steven Karau and Kipling Williams (1993, 2001) propose a *collective effort model:* On a collective task, people will put forth only as much effort as they expect is needed to attain a valued

▶ **Focus 13**
Describe social loafing, social compensation, and the causes and consequences of group polarization and groupthink.

goal. In support of this model, studies reveal that social loafing is *more* likely to occur when

- the person believes that individual performance within the group is not being monitored;
- the task (goal) or the group has less value or meaning to the person;
- the person generally displays low motivation to strive for success and expects that coworkers will display high effort (Hart et al., 2004).

Social loafing also depends on gender and culture. It occurs more strongly in all-male groups than in all-female or mixed-sex groups, possibly because women may be more concerned about group outcomes than are men. Participants from individualistic cultures (e.g., Canada and the United States) exhibit more social loafing than people from collectivistic cultures (e.g., China, Japan, Taiwan), in which group goals are especially valued.

Social loafing suggests that in terms of group performance, the whole is less than the sum of its parts. But this is not always the case. Social loafing may disappear when individual performance is monitored or when members highly value their group or the task goal. In fact, to achieve a highly desired goal, some people may engage in **social compensation,** *working harder in a group than when alone to compensate for other members' lower output* (Hart et al., 2001).

Group Polarization

Key decisions are often entrusted to groups, such as committees, because groups are assumed to be more conservative than individuals and less likely to go off the deep end. Is this assumption correct? It is, as long as the group is generally conservative to begin with. In such cases, the group's final opinion or attitude will likely be even *more conservative.* But if the group members lean toward a liberal or risky viewpoint to begin with, the group's decision will tend to become *more liberal or riskier.* This principle is called **group polarization:** *When a group of like-minded people discusses an issue, the "average" opinion of group members tends to become more extreme* (Moscovici & Zavalloni, 1969).

Why does group polarization occur? One reason, reflecting normative social influence, is that individuals who are attracted to a group may be motivated to adopt a more extreme position to gain the group's approval. A second reason, reflecting informational social influence, is that during group discussions people hear arguments supporting their positions that they had not previously considered (Sia et al., 2002).

Groupthink

After the U.S. military ignored warning signs of imminent attack by Japan in 1941, the fleet at Pearl Harbor was destroyed in a "surprise" attack. In 1961 President Kennedy and his advisors launched the hopelessly doomed Bay of Pigs invasion of Cuba. After analyzing these and other historical accounts of disastrous group decisions, Irving Janis (1982) concluded that in each case the decision makers fell victim to a process that he named **groupthink,** *the tendency of group members to suspend critical thinking because they are striving to seek agreement.*

As shown in Figure 16.18, Janis proposed that groupthink is most likely to occur when a group

- is under *high stress* to reach a decision;
- is *insulated* from outside input;
- has a *directive leader* who promotes a personal agenda;
- has *high cohesiveness,* reflecting a spirit of closeness and ability to work well together.

Under these conditions, the group is so committed to reaching consensus, and remaining loyal

Antecedent conditions

1. High stress to reach a decision
2. Insulation of the group
3. Directive leadership
4. High cohesiveness

↓

Some symptoms of groupthink

1. Illusion of invulnerability (group overestimates itself)
2. Direct pressure on dissenters
3. Self-censorship
4. Illusion of unanimity
5. Self-appointed mind guards

↓

Groupthink increases risk of defective decision making

1. Incomplete survey of alternatives
2. Incomplete survey of objectives
3. Failure to examine risks of preferred choice
4. Poor information search
5. Failure to reappraise alternatives

FIGURE 16.18

Groupthink. This diagram illustrates the antecedents, symptoms, and negative effects of groupthink on decision making. Source: Adapted from Janis, 1982.

"All those in favor say 'aye'."
"Aye." "Aye." "Aye." "Aye." "Aye."

and agreeable, that members suspend their critical judgment. In the business world, groupthink can contribute to poor management decisions that adversely affect the financial value and public reputation of the company (Eaton, 2001).

Various symptoms signal that groupthink is at work. Group members who express doubt get *direct pressure* to stop rocking the boat. Some members serve as *mind guards* and prevent negative information from reaching the group. Ultimately, members display *self-censorship* and withhold their doubts, creating an *illusion of unanimity* in which each member comes to believe that everyone else seems to agree with the decision (Figure 16.19).

Many aspects of groupthink were present during the decision-making process leading up to the fatal launch of the space shuttle *Challenger* in 1986 (Esser & Lindoerfer, 1989). The engineers who designed the rocket boosters opposed the launch, fearing that freezing weather would make the rocket's rubber seals too brittle to contain hot gasses. But NASA was under high stress, and leadership was directive. This mission was carrying America's first civilian into space, there had been several delays, and NASA didn't want another. To foster an illusion of unanimity, a key NASA executive excluded the engineers from the final decision-making process (Magnuson, 1986). Thanks to mind guarding, the NASA official who gave the final go-ahead never knew of the engineers' concerns.

In 2003, in the days leading up to the fiery disintegration of the space shuttle *Columbia* as it reentered earth's atmosphere, engineers, supervisors, and some NASA officials debated whether *Columbia*'s left wing had been damaged during launch. But as the Columbia Accident Investigation

Board found, tragically, "dangerous aspects of NASA's 1986 culture . . . remained unchanged," such as a "need to produce consensus at each level" that filtered out dissenting information on safety risks (2003, p. 198).

Can groupthink be prevented? Janis suggested that it might, if the leader remains impartial during discussions, encourages critical thinking, brings in outsiders to offer their opinions, and divides the larger group into subgroups—to see if each subgroup independently reaches the same decision. Of course, while critical debate may enhance the odds of making a good decision, it does not guarantee a positive outcome and in some cases may cause the group to become deadlocked (Kowert, 2002).

Deindividuation

Years ago in New York City, a man sat perched on the ledge of an upper-story window for an hour while a crowd of nearly 500 people on the street below shouted at him to jump. Fortunately, police rescued the man. Yet New York is hardly alone. When Leon Mann (1981) analyzed newspaper reports of incidents in which crowds were present when a person threatened to jump off a building, in 10 of 21 cases the crowd had encouraged the person to jump. Why would people in crowds act this way?

In crowds, people may experience **deindividuation,** *a loss of individuality that leads to disinhibited behavior* (Festinger et al., 1952; Zimbardo, 2004). But what is the primary aspect of deindividuation that disinhibits behavior? Tom Postmes and Russell Spears (1998) meta-analyzed 60 deindividuation studies and determined that *anonymity to outsiders* was the key. Conditions that make an individual less identifiable to people *outside* the group reduce feelings of accountability and,

▶ **Focus 14**
Describe deindividuation, its main cause, and how conditions in the Stanford prison study may have fostered it.

FIGURE 16.20

Deindividuation can lead to a loss of restraint that causes people to engage in uncharacteristic behaviors.

slightly but consistently, increase the risk of anti-social actions (Figure 16.20). Postmes and Spears suggest that being anonymous to outsiders enhances the individual's tendency to focus on her or his identity with the group and makes the person more responsive to emerging group norms.

During the Stanford prison study, no names were used and prisoners had to address guards as "Mr. Correctional Officer." All guards wore identical uniforms and reflecting sunglasses that prevented the prisoners from making direct eye contact. The guards were unaware that their behavior was being monitored by the experimenters, and antisocial norms evolved from the role of "tough prison guard" adopted by participants who spontaneously took over leadership roles (Zimbardo et al., 1973). These factors led Zimbardo to conclude that deindividuation was a key factor in the cruelty exhibited by the guards. Reducing anonymity—and thereby increasing public accountability—may be the most basic approach to counteracting deindividuation.

IN REVIEW

- A social norm is a shared rule or expectation about how group members should think, feel, and behave. A social role is a set of norms that defines a particular position in a social system.

- People conform to a group because of informational social influence and normative social influence. The size of the majority and the presence or absence of dissenters influence the degree of conformity. Minority influence is strongest when the minority maintains a consistent position over time but does not appear too deviant.

- Milgram's obedience research raised strong ethical concerns and found unexpectedly high percentages of people willing to obey destructive orders. Such obedience is stronger when the victim is remote and when the authority figure is close by, legitimate, and assumes responsibility for what happens.

- People often use special techniques to get us to comply with their requests, such as the norm of reciprocity, the door-in-the-face technique, the foot-in-the-door technique, and lowballing.

- Social loafing occurs when people exert less individual effort when working as a group than when working alone. Loafing decreases when the goal is valued highly and when performance within the group is individually monitored.

- When the members of a decision-making group share the same conservative or liberal viewpoint, the group's final decision often becomes more extreme than the average initial opinion of the individual members.

- Cohesive decision-making groups that have directive leaders, are under high stress, and are insulated from outside input may display groupthink, a suspension of critical thinking to maintain cohesion and loyalty to the leader's viewpoint.

- Deindividuation is a temporary lowering of restraints that can occur when a person is immersed in a group. Anonymity to outsiders appears to be the key factor in producing deindividuation.

SOCIAL RELATIONS

People like and love, and dislike and hate. They help one another and harm one another. As we now explore, social relations take many forms.

ATTRACTION: LIKING AND LOVING OTHERS

Commenting on friendship and love, humorist Mason Cooley once quipped, "Friendship is love minus sex and plus reason. Love is friendship plus sex and minus reason" (Columbia, 1996). Alas, the difference between *liking* and *loving* may not be so simple, but attraction is indeed the first phase of most friendships and romantic relationships.

What causes us to connect with some people but not others?

Initial Attraction: Proximity, Mere Exposure, and Similarity

People cannot develop a relationship unless they first meet, and proximity (nearness) is the best predictor of who will cross paths with whom. In today's increasingly wired world, friendships and romances sometimes develop after strangers make initial contact through Internet chat rooms or e-mail. Still, *physical proximity* matters. We tend to interact most with people who are physically closer. Residents in married-student apartments are most likely to form friendships with other residents who live close by, and students assigned specific classroom seats are most likely to become friends with students seated nearby.

Proximity increases the chance of frequent encounters, and over 200 experiments in different countries provide evidence of a **mere exposure effect:** *Repeated exposure to a stimulus typically increases our liking for it.* No matter the stimuli—college classmates, photographs of faces, random geometric shapes, and so on—as long as they are not unpleasant and we are not oversaturated, exposure generally enhances liking (Peskin & Newell, 2004).

After two people meet, then what? When it comes to attraction, folk wisdom covers all the bases. On the one hand, "opposites attract." On the other hand, "birds of a feather flock together." So which is it? Cross-cultural evidence overwhelmingly supports the role of *similarity:* People most often are attracted to others who are similar to themselves. For psychological attributes, similarity of attitudes and values seems to matter the most (Buss, 1985).

In the laboratory, college students' degree of liking for a stranger can be predicted very accurately simply by knowing the proportion of similar attitudes that they share (Byrne, 1997). Outside the laboratory, researchers matched college students on a brief 30-minute date, pairing people with partners who had either highly similar or dissimilar attitudes (Byrne et al., 1970). Students were more attracted to similar partners and had a stronger desire to date them. One reason we like people with similar attitudes is that they validate our view of the world. Yet even trivial or chance similarities between people also boost attraction (J. Jones et al., 2004).

Like mismatched roommates Felix Unger (an uptight neatnik) and Oscar Madison (a carefree slob) in the classic movie *The Odd Couple,* do opposites ever attract? At times, of course. But more often, opposites repel. When choosing potential friends or mates, we typically screen out people who are dissimilar to us. And when dissimilar people do form relationships, they tend not to last as long. Often, when we initially find a dissimilar characteristic of another person appealing, we come to dislike it over time (Felmlee, 1998).

Spellbound by Beauty

It may be shallow and unfair, but most people seem drawn to beauty like moths to a flame. In many studies, when men and women rate the desirability of short-term dating partners, their judgments are influenced most strongly by how good-looking the person is. Indeed, throughout the animal kingdom, species have evolved distinct physical features to attract mates (Figure 16.21)

In a classic study, Elaine Walster and coworkers (1966) randomly paired over 700 first-year University of Minnesota students on blind dates for a Welcome Week dance. Earlier, the researchers had given all the participants a battery of personality, intelligence, and social skills tests and had other students rate each participant's physical attractiveness. During an intermission at the dance, students rated how desirable they found their partner. Did any of the psychological characteristics predict who would like whom? No. Only one factor did. Women and men with physically attractive partners liked them more and had a stronger desire to date them again. Similarly, among 100 gay men whom researchers paired together for a date, men's liking for their partner and desire to date him again were most strongly influenced by the partner's physical attractiveness (Sergios & Cody, 1985–1986).

Facial Attractiveness: Is "Average" Beautiful?
Given beauty's power, what makes a face physically attractive? Beauty may be in the eye of the beholder, but within and across cultures, people are seeing through similar eyes; their ratings of facial attractiveness agree strongly (Langlois et al., 2000).

Look at face 3 and face 5 in Figure 16.22. The first thing you need to know is that these people don't exist. These photos are composites, "averaged" male and female faces created digitally by blending 16 photographs of young men and 16 photographs of young women (Johnston et al., 2001). Using different sets of photographs, studies in North America, Europe, and Asia consistently find that people typically rate "averaged" male and female faces as more attractive than almost all of the individual faces used to create the composites

▶ **Focus 15**
Discuss how proximity, mere exposure, similarity, and beauty influence initial attraction.

FIGURE 16.21

Hey good lookin'! Many species, such as these frigate birds (male on the left), have evolved distinct features and ritualized mating displays to attract a potential mate's attention.

Watch the "Attraction and Mate Selection" video in Chapter 16 of your CD to see a lively debate between two prominent researchers in this field.

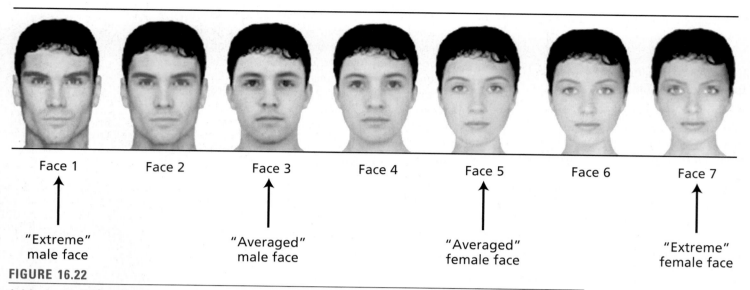

Face 1   Face 2   Face 3   Face 4   Face 5   Face 6   Face 7

"Extreme"
male face

"Averaged"
male face

"Averaged"
female face

"Extreme"
female face

FIGURE 16.22

Judging beauty. Which male face do you find most attractive? Which female face? Face 3 and face 5 are "averaged" composite photographs digitally created by blending photos of 16 men and 16 women, respectively. These averaged composites were then digitally altered to accentuate either masculine or feminine features. Faces 1 and 7 are extremely masculinized and feminized, respectively; faces 2 and 6, moderately so. Face 4 blends the masculine and feminine features. In actual experiments, masculinization-feminization changes typically are done very gradually, creating many more choices than you see here. Source: From Johnston et al., 2001, Figure 1. Adapted with permission.

(Langlois & Roggman, 1990). Moreover, people perceive individual faces as more attractive when those faces are digitally modified to look more like the "averaged" face (Rhodes et al., 2001). One reason that averaged faces seem more attractive is that they are more symmetrical, and people prefer facial symmetry (B. Jones et al., 2004). However, even when viewing faces from the side, where symmetry is not an issue, averaged faces are still rated as more attractive.

As Gestalt psychologists noted, in visual perception, the whole is more than the sum of its parts. As individual facial features—noses, eyes, lips, and so on—conform more to an "averaged" norm, we perceive the "whole face" as more attractive. But keep in mind that some individual faces, which deviate from their composite, are rated the most attractive of all. Moreover, as Figure 16.22 shows, some researchers have taken composite faces and digitally altered them to progressively appear more masculine (e.g., larger jaw and brow ridges) or more feminine (e.g., fuller lips, a narrower jaw). Consistently, people perceive moderately feminized composite faces as the most attractive (Johnston et al., 2001; Perret et al., 1998). In contrast, depending on the study, male faces that have been somewhat masculinized or feminized are rated as the most attractive.

Affiliating with Beautiful People   What motivates the desire to affiliate with attractive people? One factor may be the widespread stereotype that "what

is beautiful is good"; we often assume that attractive people have more positive personality characteristics than unattractive people. The popular media reinforce this stereotype. Analyzing 5 decades of top-grossing U.S. movies, Stephen Smith and coworkers (1999) found that good-looking male and female characters were portrayed as more intelligent, moral, and sociable than less attractive characters. Because we are often judged by the company we keep, we also may prefer to associate with attractive people to buttress our self-esteem (Richardson, 1991). Evolutionary psychologists propose that we are biologically predisposed to be drawn to attractive people. They point to research showing that newborns prefer to look at attractive faces and that 6-month-olds can categorize faces as attractive or unattractive (Ramsey et al., 2004).

Lest you conclude that beauty is the key to happiness, we should note that physical attractiveness during the college years is unrelated to life satisfaction in middle age (Kaner, 1995). And physically attractive people do not necessarily have the highest levels of self-esteem. Beauty is sometimes linked with self-doubt, because highly attractive individuals may attribute the positive responses of others solely to their surface beauty rather than to their inner personal qualities.

Although we are attracted to "beautiful people," romantic relationships typically reveal a **matching effect:** *We are most likely to have a partner whose level of physical attractiveness is similar to our own* (Feingold, 1988). In this case, "birds of equally attractive feathers flock together." One reason for this is that the most attractive people may match up first and are "taken," then the next most attractive people match up, and so on. Another factor is that people may refrain from approaching potential dating partners who are more attractive than they are to lessen the risk of rejection.

As Attraction Deepens: Close Relationships

Budding relationships grow closer as people share more diverse and meaningful experiences (Altman & Taylor, 1973). *Self-disclosure*—the sharing of innermost thoughts and feelings—plays a key role (Dindia, 2002). In friendships, dating relationships, and marriages, more extensive and intimate self-disclosure is associated with greater emotional involvement and relationship satisfaction. This relation is reciprocal. Self-disclosure fosters intimacy and trust, and intimacy and trust encourage self-disclosure.

Social exchange theory *proposes that the course of a relationship is governed by rewards and costs that the partners experience* (Thibaut and Kelley, 1959). Rewards include companionship, emotional support, and the satisfaction of other needs. Costs may include the effort spent to maintain the relationship, arguments, conflicting goals, and so forth. The overall *outcome* (rewards minus costs) in a relationship can be positive or negative.

Outcomes are evaluated against two standards (Figure 16.23). The first, called the *comparison level*, is the outcome that a person has grown to expect in relationships, and it influences the person's *satisfaction* with the present relationship. Outcomes that meet or exceed the comparison level are satisfying; those that fall below this standard are dissatisfying. The second standard, called the *comparison level for alternatives*, focuses on potential alternatives to the relationship, and it influences the person's degree of *commitment*. Even when a relationship is satisfying, partners may feel low commitment if they perceive that something better is available. In turn, the partners' sense of commitment helps predict whether they will remain together or end their relationship in the future (Sprecher, 2001).

Sociocultural and Evolutionary Views

According to social exchange theory, a partner's desirable characteristics can be viewed as rewards, whereas undesirable characteristics represent costs. But what specific characteristics do people desire in a partner? In a massive study involving 10,000 men and women from 37 cultures around the world, evolutionary psychologist David Buss and coworkers asked people to iden-

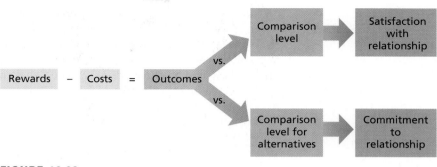

FIGURE 16.23

Social relationships: Are you satisfied and committed? According to Thibaut and Kelley's (1959) social exchange theory, rewards minus costs equal the outcome of a relationship. Comparing our outcomes with two standards, the comparison level and the comparison level for alternatives, determines our satisfaction and commitment to the relationship, respectively.

tify the qualities they sought in an ideal long-term mate (Buss, 1989; Buss et al., 1990). Overall, for both sexes, mutual attraction/love, dependable character, emotional stability, and a pleasing disposition emerged (in that order) as the most highly rated of the 18 characteristics evaluated.

The importance attached to many qualities, however, varied considerably across cultures. For example, whereas American men and women viewed refinement/neatness as having only modest importance, Iranian men and women viewed it as the most important quality they desired in a mate. In many cultures, a mate's chastity (no previous experience in sexual intercourse) was viewed as last or near-last in importance, but in China and India, men and women viewed chastity as an important quality in a mate.

There also are remarkably consistent sex differences in mate preferences across cultures. Men tend to place greater value on a potential mate's physical attractiveness and domestic skills, whereas women place greater value on a potential mate's earning potential, status, and ambitiousness. Men tend to desire a mate who is a few years younger, whereas women desire a mate who is a few years older. Men also are more likely to desire and pursue a greater number of short-term romantic encounters than are women (Schmitt et al., 2001).

As we discussed in detail in Chapter 10, some evolutionary psychologists argue that these sex differences reflect inherited predispositions, shaped by natural selection in response to different adaptive problems that men and women have faced over the ages (Buss & Schmitt, 1993; Schmitt et al., 2001). According to the *sexual strategies theory*, ancestral men who were predisposed to have sex with more partners increased the likelihood of fathering more children and passing on their genes. Such men may have perceived a woman's youth and attractive appearance as signs that she

▶ **Focus 16**
Based on social exchange theory, what factors determine whether a relationship will be satisfying and will continue?

▶ **Focus 17**
Contrast evolutionary and sociocultural explanations for sex differences in mate preferences.

was fertile and had many years left to bear children (Buss, 1989). Ancestral women, however, maximized their reproductive success by selecting mates who were willing and able to commit time, energy, and other resources (e.g., food, shelter, protection) to the family (Buss, 1989).

Do men and women have different biological wiring when it comes to romantic attraction and relationships? *Social structure theory* proposes that most of these sex differences in mating strategies and preferences occur because society directs men into more advantaged social and economic roles (Eagly & Wood, 1999; Johannesen-Schmidt & Eagly, 2002). As this theory predicts, in cultures with more gender equality, many of the sex differences in mate preferences shrink. Women place less emphasis, for example, on a mate's earning power and status, and men and women seek mates more similar in age. Men's tendency to place more emphasis on a mate's physical attractiveness, however, does not decrease in such cultures. But it is still a leap, say critics, to conclude that sex differences in mating preferences reflect a hereditary predisposition rather than some other aspect of gender socialization that may be consistent across cultures.

This issue is far from settled, but perhaps the most important point for you to realize is that the notion that men and women come from "different planets" when it comes to attraction, romance, and close relationships is more pop psychology than reliable science. Sex differences exist, but cross-cultural differences tend to be stronger. That is, men and women within the same culture are typically more similar to one another than are

men from different cultures or women from different cultures (Buss et al., 1990).

Indeed, even some evolutionary theorists disagree with the sexual strategies model. Cindy Hazan and Lisa Diamond (2000) argue that evolution has shaped the human psyche toward seeking **attachment,** *a deep bond between two individuals.* In their view, the same biological hardwiring that predisposes infants to bond with a caregiver also steers adult humans toward becoming attached to a mate. As they note:

> The (over)emphasis on sex differences has distracted us from the reality that men and women are basically similar in what they seek in a mate, the processes by which they become attached to a mate, and the benefits that accrue to them as a result of being in a stable pair bond (2000, p. 194).

Love

Love must be powerful, for as a common adage says, "it makes the world go round." Indeed, Buss and coworkers (1990) found that mutual attraction/love was highly valued in a mate across cultures. But what is love?

When it comes to romantic relationships, many psychologists identify two basic types of love: *passionate* and *companionate* (Hatfield, 1988). **Passionate love** *involves intense emotion, arousal, and yearning for the partner.* We may ride an emotional roller coaster that ranges from ecstasy when the partner is present to heartsickness when the person is absent. **Companionate love** *involves affection and deep caring about the partner's well-being.* At least when studied in Westernized countries, both types of love contribute to satisfaction in long-term romantic relationships (Sprecher & Regan, 1998). In general, passionate love is less stable and declines more quickly over time than companionate love, but this does not mean that the flames of passionate love inevitably extinguish.

Psychologist Robert Sternberg (1988, 1997), however, views love as more complex. His **triangular theory of love** *proposes that love involves three major components: passion, intimacy, and commitment.* Passion refers to feelings of physical attraction and sexual desire; *intimacy* involves closeness, sharing, and valuing one's partner; and *commitment* represents a decision to remain in the relationship. Research suggests that these three components do a good job of capturing the way people commonly think about love (Aron & Westbay, 1996).

Figure 16.24 shows that different combinations of these components characterize seven

▶ **Focus 18**
Describe types of love, and discuss research-based principles that may help enhance relationship quality.

FIGURE 16.24

The complexity of love According to Sternberg, different types of love involve varying combinations of intimacy, commitment, and passion. Consummate love involves the presence of all three factors, whereas nonlove represents the absence of all three.

types of love (plus *nonlove,* which is the absence of all three). Sternberg proposes that the ultimate form of love between people—*consummate love*—occurs when intimacy, passion, and commitment are all present. Clearly, for close relationships to develop and endure, they need more than passion alone. Intimacy and commitment provide a basis for the friendship and trust that sustain and increase love. As our "Applying Psychological Science" feature highlights, other behaviors also help make close relationships successful.

Applying Psychological Science

Making Close Relationships Work: Lessons from Psychological Research

Close relationships go through good times and bad, persisting or dissolving over time. Consider marriage. Although highly intimate, this union is often fragile, and many marriages end in divorce. How can people make their close relationships more satisfying and stable? Research on marriage suggests several answers that also can be applied to dating relationships and friendships.

For decades, most marital research simply asked people about their marriages. But as Figure 16.25 shows, researchers are now bringing couples into laboratories to videotape their interactions and chart their facial reactions, stress hormones, and other physiological responses as they discuss emotionally charged issues (Kiecolt-Glaser et al., 2003). Rather than focusing only on unhappy couples to find out what is going wrong in their relationships, researchers are also studying happy couples to discover the secrets of their success.

Using these methods, psychologists have predicted with impressive accuracy whether marriages will last or dissolve. In one laboratory study, John Gottman and coworkers (1998) collected behavioral and physiological data from 130 newly-wed couples as they discussed areas of marital conflict (e.g., in-laws, finances, sex) during the first 6 months of their marriage. Six years later, participants reported whether they were happily married, unhappily married, or divorced. Using data collected while the couples were newlyweds, the researchers predicted martial happiness/unhappiness and divorce with 80 percent accuracy.

Surprisingly, the amount of anger expressed by husbands and wives in their laboratory interactions was not the predictor. Instead, the crucial factor was the manner in which couples dealt with their anger. Four behaviors were particularly important: *criticism, contempt, defensiveness,* and *stonewalling* (listener withdrawal and nonresponsiveness).

Couples headed for unhappiness or divorce often exhibit these behaviors while discussing conflict, thereby escalating their conflict and negative emotions. When the wife criticizes the husband, he often responds defensively or stonewalls and withdraws from her attempts to reach some resolution. Her resulting frustration leads to stronger emotional displays and criticism, and the interaction degenerates into exchanges of

Rolled eyes

Dimpled cheeks

Contempt: If prolonged, this expression is a red alert. Especially when accompanied by sarcasm and insults, it suggests a marriage in serious trouble.

FIGURE 16.25

The "love lab." In Gottman's "love lab," married couples (husband shown in rear) are filmed while interacting. Researchers record facial expressions, actions, heart rate, breathing rate, perspiration, fidgeting, and other responses.

Continued

contempt in which the partners tear each other down. Once this negative cycle develops, even positive overtures by one spouse are likely to evoke a negative response from the other.

Happily married couples also experience conflict and anger but keep the spiral of negativity from getting out of control. Instead, they make frequent "repair attempts" to resolve their differences in a spirit of mutual respect and support. In happy marriages, the wife often introduces the conflict topic gently, rather than with criticism and strong emotion. Next a key factor occurs: The husband responds to the wife's issues with concern and respect, which de-escalates negative emotion. A husband who turns off the TV and listens to his wife or who says, "I can see you're upset, so let's work this out," demonstrates that her concerns are important to him. In happy marriages, after the husbands' responsiveness de-escalates the conflict, couples soothe one another with positive comments and humor, resulting in more emotionally positive interchanges and lowered physiological arousal.

Happily married couples maintain a much higher ratio of positive to negative interactions than couples headed for divorce, and this history provides a positive "emotional bank account" that helps them repair and recover from their immediate anger and conflict (Wilson & Gottman, 2002). They also strive to get to know each other deeply—their fears, dreams, attitudes, and values—and they continually update their knowledge. This allows each partner to be more responsive to the other's needs and to navigate around relationship roadblocks (Gottman & DeClaire, 2002). Such behavior contributes to an essential aspect of happy marriages: an intimate friendship between the partners. The lessons of happy marriages can be applied to other types of close relationships, and affirmative answers to the questions in Table 16.1 suggest that such relationships are on solid psychological ground.

TABLE 16.1 How Strong Is Your Relationship?		
Answer each question True (T) or False (F):		
I can tell you about some of my partner's dreams.	T	F
We just love talking to each other.	T	F
My partner is one of my best friends.	T	F
My partner listens respectfully, even when we disagree.	T	F
We generally mesh well on basic values and goals in life.	T	F
I feel that my partner knows me pretty well.	T	F

The greater the number of "True" answers, the stronger your relationship.
SOURCE: Courtesy of John Gottman.

Ostracism: Rejection Hurts

▶ **Focus 19**
Discuss the psychological effects of ostracism.

We've been focusing on close relationships, but obviously, many relationships never get off the ground. All of us shoulder the risk of rejection when we try to initiate a new friendship or romantic relationship, join an established group (e.g., a social club), or simply participate with people in some temporary activity. Even after initial acceptance, social tides may change and people may reject or ignore us out of newfound disinterest, dislike, or anger.

Research on *ostracism* (ignoring or excluding someone) suggests that there is more truth to the phrase "rejection hurts" than you might think. Psychologist Naomi Eisenberger and coworkers (2003) measured the brain activity of research participants who played an interactive computer game with, presumably, two other unseen players. In reality, there were no other players and the game was computer-controlled. The game, *Cyberball*, involved tossing a virtual ball back and forth among the three players. After a period during which all three players interacted online, the other two players suddenly ignored the participant by tossing the ball back and forth only to each other. The real participants felt excluded and distressed, and neural activity patterns in their cerebral cortex were "very similar to those found in studies of physical pain . . . providing evidence that the experience . . . of social and physical pain share a common neuroanatomical basis" (p. 291).

Ostracism, whether it occurs while playing online video games, participating in online chat rooms, or participating in face-to-face interactions, exerts a psychological cost (Williams et al., 2003). In experiments, being ignored and excluded dampens people's moods, decreases their sense of belonging, and—perhaps by heightening their fear of further rejection—makes them more likely to conform to the clearly incorrect judgments of a group. Especially when it occurs face-to-face, social exclusion reduces people's self-esteem and feelings of control.

If ostracism can produce these effects in the laboratory, then it's no wonder that it is used so frequently and powerfully to influence people in everyday life. One common example: the infamous silent treatment. According to one survey, two thirds of Americans say that they have even used the silent treatment on someone they love (Faulkner et al., as cited in Williams et al., 2000). And keeping in mind that most people, when ostracized, don't retaliate physically, it's worth noting that social rejection has repeatedly cropped up as a potential contributing factor in cases of extreme school violence. Mark Leary and coworkers (2003) examined 15 highly publicized cases (e.g., Littleton, Colorado; Jonesboro, Arkansas) in which students had shot other students during school hours. In all but two cases, the shooters had experienced either prolonged social rejection (e.g., ostracism, teasing) or more immediate romantic rejection. Combined with other factors, such as existing psychological problems (e.g., depression, sadistic tendencies), painful social rejection may have created a deadly mix.

PREJUDICE: BIAS AGAINST OTHERS

Walk into a party, classroom, job interview—any social situation—and just by looking at your body build and facial attractiveness, people will start to form an impression of you (Crandall et al., 2001). Children and adults tend to form less favorable impressions of people who are less attractive. They expect them to have less desirable personality traits and to achieve less success and happiness in life, even though these factors actually are unrelated or only weakly related to attractiveness and other facial features (Zebrowitz et al., 1996).

Perhaps above all characteristics, ethnicity and gender matter the most in impression formation. They are likely to be the first characteristics someone notices about you and, like so many other personal qualities, can be the basis for prejudice and discrimination (Fiske, 2002). **Prejudice** *refers to a negative attitude toward people based on their membership in a group.* Thus we *prejudge* people—dislike them or hold negative beliefs about them—simply because they are female or male, belong to one ethnic group or religion rather than to another, are gay or straight, and so on. **Discrimination** *refers to overt behavior that involves treating people unfairly based on the group to which they belong.*

Explicit and Implicit Prejudice

Even in this day and age, overt prejudice and discrimination are in abundant supply. Armed conflicts based on ethnic or religious divisions continue across the globe; hate crimes persist; and people's race, gender, religion, and sexual orientation spark unfair treatment (Herek, 2000). In some ways, however, the most blatant forms of prejudice and discrimination have decreased in many countries. Racial segregation is no longer sanctioned by government policy in the United States or South Africa, and opinion polls indicate that fewer people express prejudiced attitudes toward other ethnic groups than was the case decades ago.

Although prejudiced attitudes may have faded a bit, in many ways modern racism, sexism, and other forms of prejudice have gone underground and are more difficult to detect. In contrast to **explicit prejudice**, *which people express publicly,* **implicit prejudice** *is hidden from public view.* Many people intentionally hide their prejudices, expressing them only when they feel it is safe or socially appropriate. In other cases, people may honestly believe that they are not prejudiced but still show unconscious biases when tested in sophisticated ways (Fazio et al., 1995).

We can use questionnaires to measure explicit prejudice, but how can we measure implicit prejudice? Some researchers have found that subtle movements of facial muscles involved in smiling (and in some studies, in frowning) can be used to predict people's biases toward members of another ethnic group (Vanman et al., 2004). But most often, measures of implicit prejudice assess people's reaction times at special cognitive tasks (Greenwald et al., 1998; Olson & Fazio, 2003).

To give you a general idea of how an implicit prejudice test might work (they're actually more complicated than this), suppose that a series of word pairs, such as "black-pleasant" and "white-pleasant" are flashed on a computer screen. As soon as you see each pair, your task is to press a computer key as quickly as you can, and this represents your reaction time. The principle underlying this task is that people react more quickly when they perceive that the concepts (i.e., the two words in each pair) "fit" together than when the concepts don't. Thus *without conscious control,* a person prejudiced against Blacks will react more slowly to the "black-pleasant" pair than to the "white-pleasant" pair. Again, this example is simplified. The actual tests measure how quickly people make judgments about concepts and groups.

Psychologists have found that implicit measures, such as the *Implicit Association Test (IAT)* can reveal many types of unconscious prejudice (Greenwald et al., 2002). These tests also can predict other types of biased responses that explicit measures—which can be easily distorted by people unaware of or trying to hide their prejudice—fail to predict. For example, Kurt Hugenberg and Galen Bodenhausen (2003) used the IAT to measure White college students' implicit prejudice toward Blacks; they also used a self-report rating scale to measure explicit prejudice. Finally, they showed the students short, computer generated movie clips that portrayed the faces of either White or Black males making a range of angry,

▶ **Focus 20**
How is implicit prejudice measured? Describe cognitive and motivational roots of prejudice.

ambiguous, and happy expressions. Compared to students who had lower implicit prejudice, those who had higher implicit prejudice were more likely to perceive the ambiguous facial expressions of Black males as expressing anger. In contrast, students' reactions to the facial expressions were not related to their explicit prejudice scores.

Cognitive Roots of Prejudice

Whether overt or subtle, prejudice and discrimination are caused by a constellation of factors. These include historical and cultural norms that legitimize differential treatment of various groups and socialization processes through which parents and other adults transmit values and beliefs to their children. Let's examine several cognitive and motivational causes of prejudice.

Categorization and "Us-Them" Thinking   To organize and simplify our world, we have a tendency to categorize people and objects. At times, this helps us predict other people's behavior and react quickly to environmental stimuli (Ito & Cacioppo, 2000). But our tendency to categorize people also helps lay a foundation for prejudice.

Categorization leads to the perception of in-groups and out-groups, groups to which we do and do not belong, respectively. In turn, in-group versus out-group distinctions spawn several common biases. *In-group favoritism* represents the tendency to favor in-group members and attribute more positive qualities to "us" than to "them," whereas *out-group derogation* reflects a tendency to attribute more negative qualities to "them" than to "us." Although people may display both biases, especially when they feel threatened, in-group favoritism is usually the stronger of the two (Hewstone et al., 2002).

People also display an *out-group homogeneity bias*. They generally view members of out-groups as being more similar to one another than are members of in-groups (Brauer, 2001). In other words, we perceive that "they are all alike" but recognize that "we are diverse." The mere fact that we identify people as "Asian," "Hispanic," "Black," and "White" reflects such a bias, because each of these ethnic categories contains many subgroups. In one study, Anglo-American college students were less likely to distinguish among "Hispanic" subgroups than were Cuban American, Mexican American, and Puerto Rican American college students (Huddy & Virtanen, 1995). But just like the Anglo-American students, the Cuban American, Mexican American, and Puerto Rican American students also engaged in us-them

thinking: They saw their own subgroup as distinct from the others but did not differentiate between the other two Hispanic subgroups.

Stereotypes and Attributional Distortions   Categorization and in-group biases enhance the tendency to judge other people based on their perceived group membership rather than their individual characteristics. Whether at a conscious or unconscious level, category labels pertaining to people's race, gender, and other attributes seem to activate stereotypes about them (Wheeler & Fiske, 2005). Figure 16.26 illustrates two ways in which racial categorization and gender categorization activate stereotypes and affect our perceptions.

What happens when we encounter individual members of out-groups whose behavior clearly contradicts our stereotypes? One possibility is that we may change our stereotype; but if we are motivated to hold on to our prejudiced belief, we may explain away discrepant behavior in several ways. For example, the out-group member may be seen as an exceptional case or as having succeeded at a task not because of high ability but because of tremendous effort, good luck, or special advantage (Pettigrew, 1979).

Motivational Roots of Prejudice

People's ingrained ways of perceiving the world—categorizing, forming in-groups and out-groups, and so forth—prepare the wheels of prejudice to go into motion, but motivational factors affect how fast those wheels spin. For example, prejudice and stereotyping increase when social motives squarely focus our attention on the fact that people belong to in-groups or out-groups (Wheeler & Fiske, 2005).

Competition and Conflict   According to **realistic conflict theory,** *competition for limited resources fosters prejudice.* In the United States and Europe, hostility toward minority groups increases when economic conditions worsen (Pettigrew & Meertens, 1995). Originally, it was believed that a threat to one's personal welfare (as in the fear of losing one's job to a minority worker) was the prime motivator of prejudice, but research suggests that prejudice is triggered more strongly by a *perceived threat to one's in-group.* Among Whites, prejudice against Blacks is not related to personal resource gains and losses but to the belief that White people as a group are in danger of being "overtaken" (Bobo, 1988). Likewise, as the Robber's Cave summer camp experiment illustrated in Chapter 1, competition between groups can breed

(a)

(b)

FIGURE 16.26

Classic experiments on prejudice. (a) Who is holding the razor knife? Allport and Postman (1947) showed this picture to one person, who then described it while looking at it. A second person listened to this description and was asked to repeat it "as exactly as possible" to another person, who repeated this description to another person, and so on (up to six or seven tellings). In over half of the trials following this procedure, at some point the Black man was erroneously described as holding the knife. (b) Which person contributes most strongly to this research team? When the drawing shows an all-male group, an all-female group, or a mixed-gender group with a man at the head of the table (seat 3), participants say that the person in seat 3 is the strongest member. But in this mixed-gender drawing with a woman in seat 3, most male and female participants pick one of the two men. SOURCE: Based on Porter & Geis, 1981.

intense hostility toward an out-group (Sherif et al., 1961). Indeed, even when people are angry and know that an out-group did not cause that anger, their implicit prejudice still increases toward the out-group. David DeSteno and coworkers (2004) suggest that the emotion of anger is so closely linked to conflict and competition between groups that it automatically activates feelings of prejudice toward out-groups.

Enhancing Self-Esteem   According to **social identity theory,** *prejudice stems from a need to enhance our self-esteem.* Some experiments find that people express more prejudice after their self-esteem is threatened (e.g., receiving negative feedback about their abilities) and that the opportunity to derogate others helps restore self-esteem (Fein & Spencer, 1997). Self-esteem, however, is based on two components: a personal identity and a group identity (Tajfel & Turner, 1986). We can raise self-esteem not only by acknowledging our own virtues but also by associating ourselves with our in-group's accomplishments. Conversely, threats to our in-group threaten our self-esteem and may

prompt us to derogate the out-group that constitutes the threat (Perdue et al., 1990).

How Prejudice Confirms Itself

Self-fulfilling prophecies are one of the most invisible yet damaging ways of maintaining prejudiced beliefs. An experiment by Carl Word and his colleagues (1974) illustrates this point. The researchers began with the premise—supported by research at the time—that Whites held several negative stereotypes of Blacks. In the experiment, White male college students interviewed White and Black high school students who were seeking admission into a special group. The college students used a fixed set of interview questions provided by the experimenter, and unknown to them, each applicant was an accomplice who had been trained to respond in a standard way to the questions. The findings indicated that these White participants sat farther away, conducted shorter interviews, and made more speech errors when the applicants were Black. In short, their behavior was discriminatory.

▶ **Focus 21**
How do self-fulfilling prophecies and stereotype threat perpetuate prejudice? How can prejudice be reduced?

But this is only half the picture. In a second experiment—a job interview simulation—White male undergraduates served as *job applicants*. Through random assignment, they were treated either as the White applicants had been treated in the first experiment or as the Black applicants had been treated. Thus for half the participants, the interviewer sat farther away, held a shorter interview, and made more speech errors. The findings revealed that White participants who were treated more negatively performed worse during the job interview, were less composed, made more speech errors, and rated the interviewer as less friendly. In short, these experiments suggest that an interviewer's negative stereotypes can lead to discriminatory treatment during a job interview, and this discriminatory behavior can cause the applicant to perform more poorly—ultimately confirming the interviewer's initial stereotype.

Stanford psychologist Claude Steele (1997) has demonstrated another debilitating way that prejudice ends up confirming itself. As described in Chapter 9, his concept of **stereotype threat** *proposes that stereotypes create self-consciousness among stereotyped group members and a fear that they will live up to other people's stereotypes.* For example, in a study comparing female and male college students who major in various fields, women majoring in the traditionally "male" fields of math, science, and engineering reported the highest level of stereotype threat (Steele et al., 2002). They were more likely to feel that they (as well as other women in their major) had been targets of sex discrimination and that because of their gender, other people (including their professors) expected them to have less ability and do more poorly.

Stereotype threat can occur even if group members do not accept the stereotype themselves, and experiments reveal its debilitating consequences. Given the stereotype that "Blacks are not as intelligent as Whites," Black college students who take a difficult verbal ability test perform more poorly when it is described as an "intelligence test" than when it is described merely as a "laboratory task." In contrast, the intelligence-test description does not decrease White students' performance. Similar results were found for other stereotypes relating to mathematical ability, namely, "Whites are inferior to Asians," "Latinos are inferior to Whites," and "women are inferior to men." When a difficult standardized math test is given in situations that activate these stereotypes, Whites, Latinos, and women perform more poorly than when the test is presented in a more neutral way (Aronson et al., 1999; Gonzales et al., 2002).

Reducing Prejudice

Psychologists do more than just study the causes of prejudice; they also develop and examine ways to reduce prejudice and its harmful effects. For example, stereotype threat's negative effects on women's math performance can be reduced by allowing them to take math tests without men present and by exposing them to female role models who succeed at such tasks (McIntyre et al., 2003). Might a direct educational approach also work?

An Educational Approach to Reducing Stereotype Threat
Michael Johns and his coworkers (2005) asked male and female college students to take a difficult math test. To minimize stereotype threat, one group of randomly assigned students was told that the test was merely an exercise in problem solving. To maximize stereotype threat, a second group and a third group were told that the test assessed mathematical aptitude and that women's and men's scores would be compared. The third group, however, also received educational information about stereotype threat, and the women in this group were told that if they felt anxious during the test, stereotype threat might be the cause.

Would teaching women about stereotype threat make them even more anxious and further impair their math performance, or would it improve their performance by letting them know what to expect and allowing them to make an external attribution (i.e., to the societal stereotype) for their anxiety? As Figure 16.27 shows, compared to the "math test" condition, the teaching intervention boosted women's performance.

Promoting Equal Status Contact to Reduce Prejudice
What about reducing people's prejudice toward one another? The best-known approaches to prejudice reduction are based on a principle called **equal status contact:** *Prejudice between people is most likely to be reduced when they (1) engage in sustained close contact, (2) have equal status, (3) work to achieve a common goal that requires cooperation, and (4) are supported by broader social norms* (Allport, 1954; Figure 16.28).

In 1954 the United States Supreme Court handed down a momentous decision in the case of *Brown v. Board of Education,* ruling that school segregation based solely on race violates the constitutional rights of racial minorities. Providing key testimony, several psychologists stated that segregation contributed to racial prejudice and hostility. Unfortunately, decades later, when Walter Stephan (1990) reviewed more than 80 evaluation studies of desegregation programs, he concluded that desegregation did not consistently reduce racial prejudice.

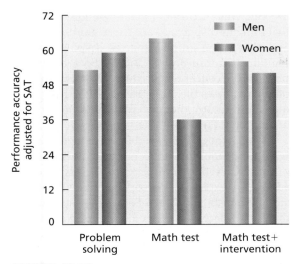

FIGURE 16.27

Reducing stereotype threat. This graph shows the results of Johns and coworkers' (2005) study of stereotype threat. In the "math test + intervention" condition, women were told that the task was a math test, but they were also given educational information about stereotype threat. Thus armed, they ended up performing significantly better than the women who were told only that the task was a math test. Moreover, their performance was not significantly poorer than that of the women who were told that the task was merely a problem-solving exercise.

Why weren't the results more positive? First, the condition of equal-status contact was often not met, and contact when status is unequal serves only to perpetuate both groups' negative stereotypes of one another. Second, in many integrated school situations, close and personal contact between group members did not occur. Black and White students were sometimes placed in different learning tracks that minimized in-class contact, and they tended to associate only with members of their own ethnic group outside of class. Third, classroom experiences focused on individual rather than cooperative learning. And finally, intergroup contact was often not supported by broader social norms; in the early years of desegregation, many White politicians, parents, teachers, and school officials militantly opposed school integration.

When intergroup contact takes place under proper conditions, however, prejudice often decreases (Pettigrew & Tropp, 2000). In school settings, *cooperative learning programs* (such as the "jigsaw classroom" described in Chapter 1) place children into multiracial learning groups. Contact is close and sustained, each child is accorded equal status, and each has responsibility for learning and then teaching other group members one piece of the information that is needed for the group to succeed in its assignment (Aronson et al., 1978). The children also can forge a common group identity, much as athletes on a team or members of a military unit form a group identity. Overall, such programs reduce prejudice and promote appreciation of ethnic group differences (Johnson, 2000).

Using Simulations to Reduce "Shooter Bias"

Finally, let's examine another type of racial bias. In several highly publicized cases over the past decade, police officers investigating a crime have shot and killed unarmed Black men. The officers, faced with a split-second decision about whether to shoot, mistakenly perceived that these men were either reaching for or holding a weapon. Was the victims' race a factor in these shootings? Social psychologists devised experiments in which college students and other adults had to quickly decide whether to shoot armed and unarmed White and Black suspects who appeared on a computer screen during a video simulation. The results revealed a "shooter bias" in which participants—both White and Black participants in some studies—were more likely to shoot unarmed suspects who were Black (Correll et al., 2002).

Subsequently, in separate computer simulation experiments with college students and police officers, E. Ashby Plant and coworkers have been able to reduce this shooter bias (Plant & Peruche, 2005; Plant et al., 2005). The shooting simulation program, like those used in other experiments, was designed so that White and Black criminal suspects were equally likely to be armed or unarmed. Over time, with repeated exposure to the simulation program, the shooter bias that students and police officers displayed on the earlier trials disappeared. As the researchers note, these findings are only a promising first step that await further testing in more rigorous police academy training programs.

FIGURE 16.28

Reducing prejudice: Equal status contact. Prejudice between two people or groups is most likely to decrease when contact between them occurs under these four conditions.

FIGURE 16.29

Like this rescue worker, many people seek careers or join volunteer organizations that allow them to help other people.

PROSOCIAL BEHAVIOR: HELPING OTHERS

Helping, or *prosocial behavior,* comes in many forms, from performing heroic acts of bravery to tutoring a classmate. Acts of violence often dominate the headlines, but we should not lose sight of the mountains of good deeds performed around the world each day (Figure 16.29).

Why Do People Help?

▶ **Focus 22**
Discuss evolutionary, social learning, and empathy-altruism explanations for helping behavior.

What motivates prosocial behavior? The debate over this question has practical consequences and profound implications for our conception of human nature.

Evolution and Prosocial Behavior   Prosocial behavior occurs throughout the animal kingdom. Evolutionary psychologists and sociobiologists (biologists who study species' social behavior) propose that helping has a genetic basis, shaped by evolution (Hamilton, 1964). According to the principle of **kin selection,** *organisms are most likely to help others with whom they share the most genes, namely, their offspring and genetic relatives* (Figure 16.30). By protecting their kin, prosocial individuals increase the odds that their genes will survive across successive generations, and the gene pool of the species increasingly represents the genes of its prosocial members (West et al., 2002). In this manner, over the course of evolution, helping became a biologically predisposed response to certain situations. Sociobiologists note that identical twins are more similar in the trait of helpfulness than are fraternal twins or nontwin siblings (Rushton, 1989).

But what accounts for the abundant helping that humans display toward friends and strangers, and that some animal species display toward nonkin (Clutton-Brock, 2002)? Sociobiologists propose the concept of *reciprocal altruism:* Helping others increases the odds that they will help us or our kin in return, thereby enhancing the survival of our genes (Trivers, 1971).

Critics question sociobiologists' generalizations from nonhumans to humans, and in some cases kin selection and reciprocal altruism do not adequately explain why people or animals cooperate (Clutton-Brock, 2002). Sociobiologists counter that genetic factors only predispose us to act in certain ways. Experience also shapes helping behavior.

Social Learning and Cultural Influences   Beginning in childhood, we are exposed to helpful models and taught prosocial norms. The *norm of reciprocity* states that we should reciprocate when others treat us kindly, and the *norm of social responsibility* states that people should help others and contribute to the welfare of society (De Cremer & van Lange, 2001). We receive approval for adhering to these norms, receive disapproval for violating them, and observe other people receiving praise for following these norms. Eventually, we internalize prosocial norms and values as our own.

FIGURE 16.30

Spotting a predator, this female ground squirrel may sound an alarm call that warns other squirrels. Is the call truly a prosocial act, much like a human yelling "Look out!"? Perhaps it simply indicates the squirrel's own sense of alarm, much as we might scream out of fear for our own safety. But if this is the case, why is she more likely to sound this call when her own kin—rather than other squirrels—are nearby?

Studies in Europe, Asia, and North America confirm that socialization matters (Eisenberg, 2004). Children are more likely to act prosocially when they have been raised by parents who have high moral standards, who are warm and supportive, and who encourage their children to develop empathy and "put themselves in other people's shoes" (Krevans & Gibbs, 1996). However, there also are cross-cultural differences in beliefs about when and why we should help. For example, Joan Miller and coworkers (1990) found that Hindu children and adults in India believe that one has a moral obligation to help friends and strangers, whether their need is serious or mild. In contrast, when a person's need for assistance is mild, American children and adults view helping as more of a choice than an obligation.

Empathy and Altruism   C. Daniel Batson (Batson et al., 2004) proposes that prosocial behavior can be motivated by altruistic as well as egoistic goals. *Altruism* refers to unselfishness, or helping another for the ultimate purpose of enhancing that person's welfare. In contrast, *egoistic goals* involve helping others to improve our own welfare, such as to increase our self-esteem, avoid feeling guilty for not helping, obtain praise, or alleviate the distress we feel when seeing someone suffer. Do humans truly have a capacity to help others without any concern for themselves? Batson believes that true altruism exists, and according to his **empathy-altruism hypothesis,** *altruism is produced by empathy—the ability to put oneself in the place of another and to share what that person is experiencing* (Batson, 1991).

 What Do You Think?

DOES PURE ALTRUISM REALLY EXIST?
Do you believe that people ever help one another for purely altruistic reasons? Or is even a small degree of egoism always involved? Think about it, then see page 654.

When Do People Help?

Ordinary citizens often go to great lengths to help strangers yet at times fail to assist people who are clearly in distress (Figure 16.31). Recall the infamous Kitty Genovese murder discussed in Chapter 2. Genovese was stabbed and raped by an assailant outside her New York City apartment. It was about 3 A.M., the attack lasted for half an hour, and 38 of her neighbors heard her

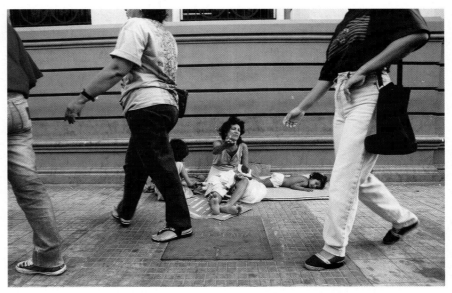

FIGURE 16.31

Why do bystanders sometimes fail to assist a person in need?

screams and pleas for help. Yet no one even called the police until it was too late, and Genovese died.

What, then, influences whether a bystander will intervene? Many situational and personal factors, such as not being in a hurry, recently observing a prosocial role model, and being in a good mood, increase the odds that we will help someone in need (Eisenberg, 2000).

Bibb Latané and John Darley (1970) view bystander intervention as a 5-step process (Figure 16.32). First, a bystander will not help unless

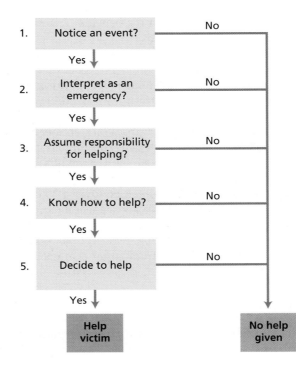

FIGURE 16.32

When will a bystander intervene? Bystander intervention in an emergency situation can be viewed as a 5-step process. If the answer at each step is yes, help is given.
SOURCE: Based on Latané & Darley, 1970.

▶ Focus 23
When and whom are people most likely to help? How can prosocial behavior be increased?

she or he notices the situation. So imagine that as you walk along a street, you hear two people yelling and then hear a scream coming from inside a house. Now what? Many social situations are ambiguous, and step 2 involves deciding whether this really is an emergency. To answer this question, we often engage in *social comparison*: We look around to see how other people are responding. You might say to yourself, "No one else seems concerned, so it mustn't be serious." In Kitty Genovese's murder, some bystanders mistakenly thought that because nobody else intervened they were merely witnessing a "lovers' quarrel" (Darley & Latané, 1968).

If you conclude that the situation is an emergency, then you move to step 3: assuming responsibility to intervene. If you are the only person to hear someone screaming, then responsibility for helping falls squarely on you. But if others are present, there may be a *diffusion of responsibility*— "If I don't help, someone else will"—and if each bystander has this thought, the victim won't receive help. In the Kitty Genovese murder, many bystanders who *did* interpret the incident as an emergency failed to intervene because they were certain that someone must already have called the police (Darley & Latané, 1968).

If you do take responsibility, then in step 4 your self-efficacy (confidence in dealing with the situation) comes into play. Sometimes, we fail to help because we don't know how to or believe our help will be ineffective. But even if self-efficacy is high, in step 5 you still may decide not to intervene. For example, you may perceive that the costs of helping outweigh the benefits (Fritzsche et al., 2000).

As this model indicates, the commonsense adage "there is safety in numbers" is not always true when it comes to receiving help. Many experiments find a **bystander effect**: *The presence of multiple bystanders inhibits each person's tendency to help, largely due to social comparison* (at step 2) *or diffusion of responsibility* (at step 3). This inhibition is more likely to occur when the bystanders are strangers rather than friends; it even occurs when communicating over the Internet. Over a 30-day period, P. M. Markey (2000) sent a general request for help ("Can anyone tell me how to look at someone's profile?") to 200 chat groups. Assistance came more slowly from larger chat groups than from smaller ones.

Whom Do People Help?

Some people are more likely to receive help than others, for the following reasons:

- *Similarity:* Whether in attitudes, nationality, or other characteristics, perceiving that a person is similar to us increases our willingness to provide help (Dovidio, 1984).
- *Gender:* Male bystanders are more likely to help a woman than a man in need, whereas female bystanders are equally likely to help women and men (Eagly & Crowley, 1986).
- *Perceived fairness and responsibility:* Beliefs about fairness influence people's willingness to help others (Blader & Tyler, 2002). For example, people are more likely to help someone if they perceive that the person is not responsible for causing his or her own misfortune.

Increasing Prosocial Behavior

Can prosocial behavior be increased? One approach, consistent with social learning theory, is to expose people to prosocial models. Psychologists have used prosocial modeling as part of a nationwide program to increase blood donations (Sarason et al., 1991). Students in 66 high schools watched an audiovisual program showing high school donors giving blood. Compared with a control condition presented with a standard appeal from the local blood bank, the prosocial video increased blood donations by 17 percent.

Research suggests that developing feelings of empathy and connectedness with others also may make people more likely to help (Eisenberg, 2000), and simply learning about factors that hinder bystander intervention may increase the tendency to help someone in distress. Arthur Beaman and coworkers (1978) exposed some college students to information about the bystander effect. Control participants did not receive this information. Two weeks later, more than half of the students who had learned about the bystander effect provided aid to the victim of an accident (staged by the researchers), compared with only about one fourth of the control group participants.

AGGRESSION: HARMING OTHERS

We love. We nurture. We help. But as current events and the history of humankind attest, we also harm. In humans, *aggression* represents any form of behavior that is intended to harm another person. What causes people to aggress?

Biological Factors in Aggression

From barnyard bulls to laboratory rats, animals can be selectively bred to be more or less aggressive

▶ Focus 24
Describe how biological factors, environmental stimuli, learning, and psychological factors influence aggression.

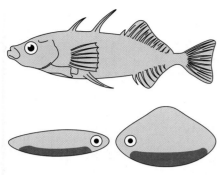

FIGURE 16.33

Sex and the stickleback: Triggers for aggression. During the mating season, the male stickleback fish develops a red belly. The sight of another red-bellied male—a potential rival for a mate—reflexively triggers an attack by the first male. The key releaser stimulus for this fixed action pattern is the red marking. A male stickleback will not attack a realistic-looking male model that has no red belly, but it will attack unrealistic fish models that have this red marking. SOURCE: Based on Tinbergen, 1951.

(Lagerspetz et al., 1968). In some species, certain aggressive behaviors are reflexively triggered by specific environmental stimuli (Figure 16.33). Humans don't display such rigid, inborn aggressive responses, but heredity influences why some people are more aggressive than others. Even when raised in different homes, identical twins display more similar patterns of aggression than do fraternal twins (Beatty et al., 2002).

Some theorists propose that, as in other species, a genetic predisposition toward aggression can be traced to evolutionary adaptation. Aggression at the proper time, they argue, helped our ancestors to compete successfully for mates, food, and shelter and to survive against attack. This increased the odds that individuals who were predisposed to such aggression would pass their genes on to the next generation (Rushton, 1989).

There is no single brain center for aggression, nor one "aggression chemical." Electrically stimulate certain neural pathways in a cat's hypothalamus, and it will arch its back and attack. Surgically destroy areas of the amygdala—an approach that has been used with some violent human criminals—and in many species, defensive aggression will decrease (Aggleton, 1993). Especially in humans, aggression also involves activity in the frontal lobes—the seat of reasoning and impulse control. Deficient frontal-lobe activity makes it more difficult to regulate aggressive impulses generated by deeper brain regions (Raine, 2002).

Atypically low levels of serotonin activity appear to play a role in impulsive aggression, as when people lash out from emotional rage (Moore et al.,

2002). In many species of mammals, higher levels of the sex hormone testosterone (found in males and females) contribute to greater *social aggression*, acts that establish a dominance hierarchy among members of a species. But in humans and other primates, the association between testosterone and aggression is weaker (O'Connor et al., 2002).

Environmental Stimuli and Learning

Our present environment and past learning experiences also influence aggression. *Frustration*, which occurs when some event interferes with our progress toward a goal, increases the risk of verbal and physical aggression, as do aversive events such as extreme heat, provocation, painful stimuli, and crowding. But we do not always respond to frustration by acting aggressively. Inhibited by our internal moral standards, we may simply control ourselves and find nonaggressive ways of dealing with conflict (Anderson & Bushman, 2002).

Aggression, like other behaviors, is influenced by learning. Nonaggressive animals can be trained to become vicious aggressors if reinforcement is arranged so that they are consistently victorious in fights with weaker animals. Such operant conditioning also affects human aggression. Preschool children become increasingly aggressive when their aggressive behavior produces positive outcomes for them, such as when they successfully force another child to give up a desired toy (Patterson et al., 1967).

As Albert Bandura's (1965) classic "Bobo doll" experiments (see Chapter 6) clearly demonstrated, aggression also can be learned by observing others. Children learn how to aggress even when they witness an aggressive model being punished. Later, if the punishing agent is not present or if rewards are available for aggressing, children are likely to reproduce the model's actions. Correlational studies, while not establishing cause and effect, find that aggressive and delinquent children tend to have parents who often behave aggressively (Stormshak et al., 2000).

Psychological Factors in Aggression

Many psychological factors affect whether we behave aggressively in specific situations. From gang violence to rape and war, people may employ several types of *self-justification* to make it psychologically easier to harm other people (Lanier, 2001). Aggressors may blame the victim for imagined wrongs or otherwise convince themselves that the victim "deserves it." They may also dehumanize their victims, as the guard in the

Stanford prison study did when he began to view the prisoners as "cattle."

Our *attribution of intentionality* and degree of empathy also affect how we respond to provocation. When we believe that someone's negative behavior toward us was intentional, we are more likely to become angry and retaliate (Graham et al., 1992). And when someone offends us and then apologizes, whether we forgive the person partly depends on how well we empathize with his or her viewpoint (McCullough et al., 1997).

Sigmund Freud believed that impulses from aggressive instincts build up inside us over time, have to be released, and then build up again in a never-ending cycle. His principle of **catharsis** *stated that performing an act of aggression discharges aggressive energy and temporarily reduces our impulse to aggress.* But how does one do this in a world where violence is punished? Freud proposed that we can channel aggressive impulses into socially acceptable behaviors (such as sports) and discharge aggressive impulses *vicariously* by watching and identifying with other people who behave aggressively.

If people can't express their aggressive impulses, will the pressures build up and explode? Sometimes, meek or unassertive people do commit shocking and brutal crimes. These people, whom Edwin Megargee (1966) describes as having *overcontrolled hostility,* show little immediate reaction to provocations. Instead, they bottle up their anger and, after provocations accumulate, suddenly erupt into violence. The final provocation that triggers their outburst is often trivial. One 10-year-old boy with no prior history of aggression stabbed his sister more than 80 times with an ice pick after she changed the channel during his favorite TV show. After the aggressive outburst, such people typically revert to their former passive, unassertive state. Female prison inmates who score high on tests measuring overcontrolled hostility are more likely to have committed a one-time violent crime than repeated violent crimes or a nonviolent crime (Verona & Carbonell, 2000; Figure 16.34).

Cases of overcontrolled hostility seem to be consistent with the concept of catharsis, but much research is not. For example, hitting a punching bag while thinking about someone who has just angered them increases—not decreases—people's subsequent aggressive behavior toward that person (Bushman, 2002). And what about watching violent movies and TV programs? Do these activities help people blow off steam, as some stars in the entertainment industry claim?

▶ **Focus 25**
Discuss catharsis and social learning views on effects of media violence. Do violent video games promote aggression?

FIGURE 16.34

Overcontrolled hostility: Behind prison bars. Female inmates at a state prison completed psychological tests that identified whether they had high overcontrolled hostility (High O-H) or low overcontrolled hostility (Low O-H). Inmates with high overcontrolled hostility—but not inmates with low overcontrolled hostility—were much more likely to have committed a one-time violent crime than a nonviolent crime or multiple violent crimes. SOURCE: Adapted from Verona & Carbonell, 2000.

Media (and Video Game) Violence: Catharsis versus Social Learning

Many movies and TV programs are saturated with violence. To psychodynamic theorists, media violence should be a cathartic pot of gold. But social learning theorists argue that by providing numerous aggressive models—including many that are reinforced—media violence is more likely to increase viewers' aggressive behavior than to reduce it.

Headline-making "copycat" acts of violence clearly illustrate social learning effects. Still, hundreds of millions of people are entertained by media violence, and few commit copycat crimes. What, then, are the more general effects of media violence on aggression? Over the past 30 years, hundreds of experiments and correlational studies have shed light on the "catharsis versus social learning" debate.

To most experts, the verdict is clear: The evidence favors the social learning view (Johnson et al., 2002). For example, American children who watch greater amounts of TV violence are more likely than their peers to display physical aggression when they become young adults (Eron, 1987; Huesmann et al., 2003). This association is not simply due to the fact that children who watch the most TV violence are already more aggressive to begin with. Moreover, boys and girls who perceive TV violence to be highly realistic and identify strongly with same-sex aggressive TV characters are most likely to act aggressively as adults (Huesmann et al., 2003). Experiments in laboratory and field settings reveal a clearer causal link between watching media violence and behaving more aggressively (Leyens et al., 1975).

Media violence appears to exert its effects through multiple avenues (Huesmann, 1997):

- Viewers learn new aggressive behaviors through modeling.
- Viewers come to believe that aggression usually is rewarded, or at least rarely punished.
- Viewers become desensitized to the sight and thought of violence and to the suffering of victims.

Beyond movies and TV, the question of whether violent video games promote aggression also has raised much public and scientific concern (Figure 16.35). In 2005 some Washington State legislators drafted a bill to make it easier for parents to sue violent video game manufacturers in cases where playing those games could be

FIGURE 16.35

Do children who play graphically violent video games become desensitized to violence and more likely to behave aggressively toward other people?

linked to the commission of violent crimes (KING Broadcasting Company, 2005). Political reaction or overreaction? What does science have to say?

 ## Beneath the Surface   Do Violent Video Games Promote Aggression?

American children and teens love violent video games. In one study of Midwestern junior high students, boys reported playing video games for 13 hours a week; girls, for 5 hours a week. Respectively, 70 percent and 50 percent of their favorite games had violent content (Gentile et al., 2004).

Do violent video games breed aggression? Psychologist and retired military officer David Grossman (1996) argues that humans have a natural inhibition against killing. In World War II, for example, only 15 percent of soldiers fired at the enemy when they had a clear shot. This forced modern armies to develop behavioral training programs that gradually overcome soldiers' reluctance to kill. Violent video games, say Grossman, have a similar effect: They weaken players' inhibition against aggressing toward others.

What does research say? Correlational studies find that compared to their peers, youngsters who have more exposure to violent video games get into more physical fights with other people (Gentile et al., 2004). But as a critical thinker—drawing on what you have learned about correlational evidence—you should be able to come up with several explanations for this finding. (If you're having trouble, see pages 42–43.)

First, violent video games may cause youngsters to get into more fights. Second (the bidirectionality problem), perhaps getting into fights produces consequences (e.g., stress, anger, frustration) that prompt youngsters to play violent video games. Lastly (the third-variable problem), perhaps these youngsters have a more hostile, aggressive personality to begin with, which causes them to play more violent video games and also to get into more fights. Indeed, Douglas Gentile and coworkers (2004) found that among young adolescents, those exposed to more violent video games also

Continued

scored higher on psychological tests of hostility. So, to take this possible confounding factor into account, the researchers conducted special analyses that statistically adjusted for the hostility differences among adolescents. These analyses indicated that violent video game exposure was still correlated—albeit weakly—with a tendency to get into more physical fights.

Experiments in which researchers directly manipulate people's exposure to violent video games provide a clearer causal picture. Roland Irwin and Alan Gross (1995) randomly assigned sixty 7- and 8-year-old boys to play either a violent or nonviolent video game for 20 minutes. In the violent game, *Double Dragon,* the player assumed the role of a martial arts hero who kicks, punches, and uses a rope or chain to whip and defeat ruthless street gang members. In the nonviolent game, *Excitebike,* the player raced a motorcycle against the clock.

After playing one of the games, each child engaged in a 10-minute "free-play" period with another boy (an accomplice). Next, as each participant competed against this boy on a task for a prize, the boy (according to plan) cheated. Compared with participants who had played *Excitebike,* those who had played *Double Dragon* displayed more physical and verbal aggression toward inanimate objects (e.g., toys), more verbal aggression toward the other boy during the free-play period, and more physical aggression toward the other boy during the frustrating competition.

Let's think critically about this result too, because even in experiments there may be confounding variables that provide alternative explanations for the results. For example, did *Double Dragon*'s violent content increase participants' aggression, or was it simply a more exciting game? If so, perhaps it was only greater arousal that led to more aggression? If you were the experimenter, what could you do to rule out this possible confounding factor? Irwin and Gross measured participants' heart rate both before and during the video game play. The result: no heart rate differences between the two video game conditions, strengthening the conclusion that the content of the violent game was the key factor.

To date, most studies employing this procedure have found that children's aggression toward peers increases after playing violent video games. Even among college students, briefly playing a violent video game (*Mortal Kombat*) increased women's and especially men's aggressive behavior toward a female student (actually a confederate) who had earlier aggressed against them (Bartholow & Anderson, 2002).

THE BIG PICTURE

A recent meta-analysis of over 30 experiments and real-world correlational studies on violent video games indicates that:

- the evidence clearly does *not* support the catharsis hypothesis that playing violent video games decreases people's aggression by letting them blow off steam; and, to the contrary,
- playing violent video games is linked to increased aggressive behavior, thoughts, and emotions (Anderson, 2004).

Certainly, the overwhelming majority of children, teens, and adults who play violent video games do not go out and assault or kill people. But aggression comes in many forms, physical and verbal, obvious and subtle. Still, continued research focusing on long-term effects is needed to pinpoint how strongly children and adults are affected by a world full of *Mortal Kombat* and *Doom.*

FIGURE 16.36

Levels of analysis: Factors related to aggression.

As we close this section on social relations, Figure 16.36 highlights some of the biological, psychological, and environmental factors that contribute to human aggression.

IN REVIEW

- Proximity, mere exposure, similarity of attitudes, and physical attractiveness typically enhance our attraction toward someone. Social exchange theory analyzes relationships in terms of the rewards and costs experienced by each partner.

- Evolutionary theorists propose that gender difference in mate preferences reflect inherited biological tendencies, whereas sociocultural theorists believe that these differences result from socialization and gender inequities in economic opportunities.

- Partners are more likely to remain happily married when they understand each other and deal with conflicts by de-escalating their emotions and providing mutual support.

- Ostracism produces negative psychological consequences and activates many of the same brain regions that underlie physical pain.

- People display explicit prejudice publicly. When people conceal or are not consciously aware of their prejudice, they are exhibiting implicit prejudice.

- Prejudice stems partly from our tendency to perceive in-groups and out-groups. People typically display in-group favoritism and an out-group homogeneity bias. Perceived threats to one's in-group and a need to enhance one's self-esteem can motivate prejudice.

- Prejudice often is reduced when in-group and out-group members work closely together, with equal status, on tasks involving common goals, and under conditions of broader institutional support.

- Some theorists propose that through kin selection and reciprocal altruism, evolution has shaped a genetic predisposition toward prosocial behavior among humans. Social learning theorists emphasize how norms, modeling, and reinforcement shape prosocial behavior.

- The presence of multiple bystanders may decrease bystander intervention through social comparison processes and a diffusion of responsibility for helping. We are most likely to help others whom we perceive as similar to us and as not responsible for their plight.

- Prosocial behavior can be increased by enhancing people's feelings of empathy for victims and providing prosocial models.

- Heredity influences an organism's tendency to aggress. The hypothalamus, amygdala, and frontal lobes play central roles in aggression.

- Provocation, heat, crowding, and stimuli that cause frustration or pain increase the risk of aggression. Learning experiences help shape a tendency to behave more or less aggressively. People are more likely to aggress when they find ways to justify and rationalize their aggressive behavior, perceive provocation as intentional, and have little empathy for others.

- Most research supports the social learning theory prediction that watching movie and TV violence and playing violent video games increase the risk that children and adults will act aggressively.

A FINAL WORD

In Chapter 1, we began a shared journey through the sprawling domain of modern-day psychology. That journey has taken us from the inner recesses of the mind to our social world. We have examined how the brain's intricate workings underlie our thoughts, feelings, and behaviors. We have also explored the learning mechanisms that enable us to profit from our experiences and adapt to our environment. We have seen how the environment in which we live, including our culture, exerts powerful influences over who we become and how we behave. We have achieved greater understanding of the cognitive processes that help define our humanity. We have also gained insights into the processes by which we develop from a single cell into the most psychologically complex creature on our planet, and we have explored the personality processes that help make each of us unique. We have learned about the many ways in which people cope, both adaptively and maladaptively, with the demands of living, as well as the many interventions that help people live happier and more fulfilling lives. As we have found in every area of psychological study, the brain, mind, and environment interact in complex ways to influence our behavior.

We are privileged to have been your guides in this psychological journey. We hope that your introductory psychology course has influenced your conception of human nature, your understanding of yourself and others, your capacity to think critically about your world, and your ability to utilize psychological principles to enrich your life.

KEY TERMS AND CONCEPTS

Each term has been boldfaced and defined in the chapter on the page indicated in parentheses.

attachment (p. 638)
attitude (p. 618)
attribution (p. 614)
bystander effect (p. 648)
catharsis (p. 650)
central route to persuasion (p. 622)
communicator credibility (p. 621)
companionate love (p. 638)
deindividuation (p. 633)
discrimination (p. 641)
door-in-the-face technique (p. 630)
empathy-altruism hypothesis (p. 647)
equal status contact (p. 644)
explicit prejudice (p. 641)
foot-in-the-door technique (p. 631)
fundamental attribution error (p. 615)

group polarization (p. 632)
groupthink (p. 632)
implicit prejudice (p. 641)
informational social influence (p. 625)
kin selection (p. 646)
lowballing (p. 631)
matching effect (p. 636)
mere exposure effect (p. 635)
normative social influence (p. 625)
norm of reciprocity (p. 630)
passionate love (p. 638)
peripheral route to persuasion (p. 622)
prejudice (p. 641)
primacy effect (p. 617)
realistic conflict theory (p. 642)
self-fulfilling prophecy (p. 618)

self-perception theory (p. 621)
self-serving bias (p. 616)
social compensation (p. 632)
social exchange theory (p. 637)
social facilitation (p. 623)
social identity theory (p. 643)
social loafing (p. 631)
social norms (p. 624)
social role (p. 624)
stereotype (p. 617)
stereotype threat (p. 644)
theory of cognitive dissonance (p. 620)
theory of planned behavior (p. 619)
triangular theory of love (p. 638)

? What Do You Think?

DO WOMEN DIFFER FROM MEN IN OBEDIENCE? (PAGE 629)

After we describe Milgram's research to our own students, one of the first questions they usually ask is, "Did Milgram study women?" The answer is yes. After conducting the study described in the "Research Close-Up," Milgram repeated the identical procedure with 40 women who, like the prior male participants, varied in age and occupation.

What was your hypothesis about sex differences in obedience? A few of our students predict no sex differences, but almost all expect women to differ from men. About half of them predict that women would be more likely to obey the experimenter's orders and keep shocking the learner all the way to the 450-volt level. Their rationale: Given the traditional sex-role expectation that men are more dominant than women, and especially given how strong this expectation was at the time of Milgram's research (the early 1960s), women would be less likely to defy the authority of a male experimenter.

The other half of our class usually disagrees, predicting that women would be less obedient because they have more empathy than men for people who are suffering. Thus the learner's screams and pleas to stop would affect women more, and they would stop giving the shocks.

Are either of these hypotheses similar to yours? They both sound plausible, highlighting once again that different people have different "common sense," leading to opposite predictions that cover all the bases. And what did Milgram find? In the study with men, 26 of 40 (65 percent) obeyed fully. Among the women, the results were identical: 26 of 40 (65 percent) obeyed fully.

Using procedures similar to Milgram's, other researchers also failed to find consistent sex differences in obedience rates. Occasionally, a particular study would find that women were more obedient than men, another would show that men were more obedient, while others—including Milgram's—found no sex differences in obedience rates.

One study, conducted in Jordan, examined three age groups of boys and girls (6- to 8-year-olds, 10- to 12-year-olds, and 14- to 16-year-olds) who were placed in the role of "teacher" (Shanab & Yahya, 1977). The experimenter was female, and the "learner" was a confederate matched in age and sex to each participant (e.g., 10- to 12-year-old girls administered shocks to a similarly aged girl). Overall, 73 percent of the participants were fully obedient, and neither their sex nor age significantly influenced the results. In sum, the most reasonable conclusion is that there are no consistent sex differences in obedience rates in studies like those conducted by Milgram.

DOES PURE ALTRUISM REALLY EXIST? (PAGE 647)

Do you believe that people ever help others for purely altruistic reasons? Perhaps your response is, "Sure. Some Good Samaritans care only about the victim's welfare and even help people at a cost to themselves." Certainly, people make anonymous donations to charity and help strangers when no one (including the recipient) finds out. In such cases we can seemingly rule out motives for helping based on gaining recognition or others' approval. But still, doesn't helping someone make us feel good about ourselves?

Moreover, by helping someone, don't we feel better knowing that the person's plight has been reduced? According to the *negative state relief model*, high empathy causes us to feel distress when we learn of others' suffering, so by helping them we reduce our own personal distress—a self-focused, egoistic goal, not an altruistic one (Cialdini et al., 1987).

Batson and many psychologists believe that while egoistic motives account for some prosocial behavior, at times people do help others for purely altruistic reasons (Batson et al., 2002). Yet other psychologists remain unconvinced, arguing that some negative state relief is always involved (Cialdini et al., 1997).

Recent brain-imaging findings add some provocative fuel to this debate. Empathizing with someone else's pain does not produce the same sensations (i.e., somatosensory cortex activation) that we experience when we are in pain, but it does activate many of the brain areas (e.g., other parts of the cortex, brain stem, thalamus, and cerebellum) that process emotional aspects of our own pain (Singer et al., 2004). Moreover, people who feel greater empathy for another's pain experience greater activation in these brain areas. So what do you think? Does this suggest that when helping behavior stems from empathy, it does indeed involve negative state relief and therefore is not purely altruistic?

Appendix: Statistics in Psychology

At various points throughout the text we have briefly described statistical procedures to help you understand the information being presented. This appendix discusses statistics in greater detail and focuses on the concepts underlying these procedures. Our goal is to help you understand how psychologists use statistics in their research.

For some students, the prospect of studying statistics evokes visions of complex higher mathematics. You will find, however, that if you can add, subtract, multiply, and divide, you can easily perform basic statistical operations.

DESCRIPTIVE STATISTICS

Psychological research often involves a large number of measurements. Typically, it is difficult to make sense of the data merely by examining the individual scores of each participant. **Descriptive statistics** *summarize and describe the characteristics of a set* (also called a *distribution*) *of scores*.

To summarize a set of scores, we might first construct a **frequency distribution,** *which shows how many participants received each score*. For example, suppose that 50 college students took a 32-item psychological test that measured their level of self-esteem. The frequency distribution in Table A.1 tells us that two participants had scores of 30, 31, or 32; one had a score of 27, 28, or 29; eleven had scores of 15, 16, or 17, and so on. Note that the researcher chose to use *intervals* of three points (e.g., 30–32) rather than to show the number (frequency) of participants who

obtained each of the 33 possible (0–32) scores. She could have done the latter if she had wished to break down the scores even further. The number of intervals chosen is somewhat arbitrary, but frequency distributions often contain 10 to 12 categories.

This frequency distribution tells us at a glance about certain characteristics of the data, such as whether scores tend to cluster in one region of the distribution or are scattered throughout. We can easily convert these data into a **histogram,** *which is a graph of a frequency distribution*. Typically, the scores (or in this case, score intervals) are plotted along the horizontal axis (i.e., *X-axis,* or *abscissa*), and the frequencies are plotted on the vertical axis (i.e., *Y-axis,* or *ordinate*). This produces a column or bar above each score or score interval that shows how frequently the score occurred. Figure A.1 represents a histogram of the self-esteem scores for our sample of 50 college students.

MEASURES OF CENTRAL TENDENCY

Frequency distributions and histograms give us a general picture of how scores are distributed. As we briefly discussed in Chapter 2, **measures of central tendency** *describe a distribution in terms of a single statistic that is in some way "typical" of the sample as a whole*. There are three commonly used measures of central tendency: the *mode,* the *mean,* and the *median*. For example, Table A.2 shows how 10 hypothetical college seniors performed on the midterm exam in an advanced psychology class. In this class, the instructor assigns grades such that a score of 90 equals an A; 80, a B; and 70, a C. Our task is to arrive at a single number that somehow typifies the exam scores of the group as a whole.

The **mode** *is the most frequently occurring score in a distribution*. In this class, 88 is the mode because it is the only score obtained by more than one person (Rowe and Miyamoto). Although the mode is easy to identify in a distribution, it is not always the most representative score, particularly if it falls far from the center of the distribution. For example, suppose that Rowe's exam grade had been 94, rather than 88. In this case, the most frequent score—the mode—would now be 94 (Wilson and Rowe). But if we told you that on this exam the typical score was 94, it would provide you with an overly optimistic view of how the class performed.

The most commonly used measure of central tendency, the **mean,** *represents the arithmetic average of a set of scores*. The mean is calculated by adding up all the scores and dividing by the number of scores. The statistical formula for computing the mean is:

$$M = \frac{\Sigma X}{N}$$

TABLE A.1 Frequency Distribution of Self-Esteem Scores

Self-Esteem Scores	Frequency
30–32	2
27–29	1
24–26	4
21–23	6
18–20	9
15–17	11
12–14	8
9–11	3
6–8	4
3–5	1
0–2	1

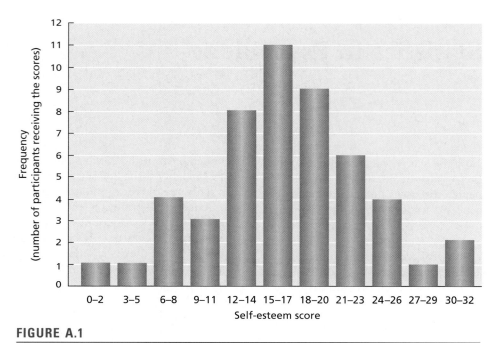

FIGURE A.1

A histogram of the self-esteem distribution shown in Table A.1.

X is the symbol for an individual score, N denotes the number of scores, and M is the symbol for the mean of the individual scores. The Greek letter Σ (sigma) means "the sum." Thus to compute the mean score on this exam, we simply add the individual scores and divide the total by 10, the number of scores. As Table A.2 shows, the mean score is 83.

As we noted in Chapter 2, one shortcoming of the mean is that it can be strongly affected by one or more extremely high or low scores that are not representative of the group as a whole. Suppose, for example, that Kruger and Thompson, rather than getting scores of 73 and 70, hadn't studied for this test at all and completely bombed it, getting scores of 30 and 23, respectively. This would change the mean from 83 to 74, giving you the impression that the typical score was a C+ when in fact the other 8 students all had scores ranging between A and B.

Our third measure of central tendency, the **median,** is the *point that divides the distribution in half when the individual scores are arranged in order from lowest to highest.* In other words, half of the scores lie above the median and half below it. If there is an odd number of scores, there will be one score that is exactly in the middle. If there were 11 exam scores in Table A.2, the sixth-ranked score would be the median, because 5 scores would fall above and 5 below. In a distribution having an even number of scores, such as in Table A.2, the median is halfway between the 2 middle scores. In our exam score distribution, the median is the point halfway between student 5 (83 points) and student 6 (82 points), or 82.5 points.

The median has an important property that the mean does not have: It is unaffected by extreme scores. Whether Kruger and Thompson respectively have scores of 73 and 70 or scores of 30 and 23, the median remains the same. Therefore the median is

TABLE A.2 Midterm Exam Scores of 10 College Seniors	
Student	**Score**
1. Wilson	94
2. Ibanez	91
3. Rowe	88
4. Miyamoto	88
5. Stein	83
6. Diaz	82
7. Anderson	81
8. Bradford	80
9. Kruger	73
10. Thompson	70
$N = 10$	$\Sigma X = 830$

Mode = The score that occurs most often—in this case, 88.

Mean = The arithmetic average, computed by the following formula:

$$M = \frac{\Sigma X}{N} = \frac{830}{10} = 83$$

Median = The point above and below which there is an equal number of scores. In this case, because there is an even number of scores, the median is midway between the 5th and 6th scores—that is, 82.5.

more representative of the group as a whole in instances when there are very extreme scores. The median, however, can fail to capture important information. For example, suppose that the top four students on this test had achieved perfect scores of 100.

TABLE A.3   Computation of the Variance and Standard Deviation for Two Distributions of Scores with Identical Means ($M = 10$)

Distribution A			Distribution B		
X (score)	X − M = x	x^2	X (score)	X − M = x	x^2
12	+2	4	18	+8	64
12	+2	4	18	+8	64
11	+1	1	15	+5	25
11	+1	1	15	+5	25
10	0	0	10	0	0
10	0	0	10	0	0
9	−1	1	5	−5	25
9	−1	1	5	−5	25
8	−2	4	2	−8	64
8	−2	4	2	−8	64
$\Sigma X = 100$	$\Sigma x = 0$	$\Sigma x^2 = 20$	$\Sigma X = 100$	$\Sigma x = 0$	$\Sigma x^2 = 356$

$N = 10$

$M = 10.00$

x (deviation) $= X - M$

$$\text{variance} = \frac{\Sigma x^2}{N} = \frac{20}{10} = 2.00$$

SD (standard deviation) $= \sqrt{2.00} = 1.414$

$N = 10$

$M = 10.00$

$$\text{variance} = \frac{\Sigma x^2}{N} = \frac{356}{10} = 35.60$$

$SD = \sqrt{35.60} = 5.967$

In this case the median would not change, because the "middle score" would still be the midpoint between student 5 and student 6. The mean, however, would increase from 83 to almost 87 (869 points/10 = 86.9 points) and reflect the higher scores obtained by these four students.

MEASURES OF VARIABILITY

Measures of central tendency provide us with a single score that typifies the distribution. But to describe a distribution adequately, we need to know more. One key question concerns the amount of variability, or spread, that exists among scores. Do they tend to cluster closely about the mean, or do they vary widely? **Measures of variability** *provide information about the spread of scores in a distribution.*

The **range,** *which is the difference between the highest and the lowest score in a distribution,* is the simplest but least informative measure of variability. On the midterm exam in Table A.2, the range is 94 − 70 = 24 points. But suppose that, in Table A.2, all the other students (student 2 through student 9) had scores of 85. If we knew only the range of scores, we might be led to believe that the scores in this distribution varied far more from one another than they actually do. Thus it would be more useful to know how much, on average, each score varies or deviates from the mean of the distribution.

To do this we first create a *deviation score* (represented by a lowercase x) that measures the distance between each score (X) and the mean (M). To provide a simple example, suppose we

have two distributions, A and B, each composed of 10 scores. Looking at the "X (score)" column in Table A.3 for each distribution, you can see that although each distribution has a mean of 10, the scores in distribution B are more spread out than in distribution A. Now for each score we compute how much it differs from the mean (i.e., $x = X - M$). At this stage, you might think that to measure the variability of each distribution we need only add up its deviation scores and then compute the average deviation. But we have a problem. Even though distribution B is more spread out than distribution A, adding up the deviation scores for each distribution yields a sum of zero ($\Sigma x = 0$). In fact, the sum of deviation scores for any distribution will always add up to zero.

To avoid this problem we must get rid of the plus and minus signs that end up canceling each other out. As the rightmost column (i.e., the "x^2" column) under each distribution in Table A.3 shows, we achieve this goal by taking each deviation score, squaring it, and then adding up these squared deviation scores. This produces a sum of 20 for distribution A and 356 for distribution B. Now we divide by 10 (i.e., the number of scores in each distribution) to find the average squared deviation. This statistic, called the **variance,** *is the average of the squared deviation scores about the mean.* You can see that the variance for distribution B (35.60) is considerably greater than the variance for distribution A (2.00), reflecting the greater spread of the scores in B.

The most popular measure of variability, the **standard deviation (SD),** *is the square root of the variance.* Because we had to square the deviation scores to compute the variance, we now

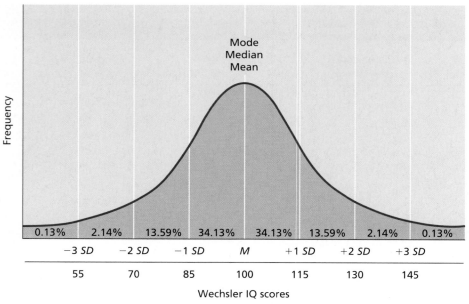

FIGURE A.2

The normal curve, showing the percentage of cases falling within each area of the normal distribution and also showing Wechsler IQ scores that correspond to standard deviation (SD) units.

return to the original scale of measurement by taking the square root of the variance. Thus the standard deviation describes variability in the same units of measurement as the original data. You can see in Table A.3 that the standard deviation from the mean of distribution B (5.967) is more than four times greater than the standard deviation from the mean of distribution A (1.414).

THE NORMAL CURVE

The **normal curve** *is a symmetrical bell-shaped curve that represents a theoretical distribution of scores in the population.* In the normal curve, 50 percent of the cases fall on each side of the mean, and the median and mode have the same value as the mean. Figure A.2 shows that in a normal curve, as we move away from the mean the frequency of each score steadily decreases. The normal curve is important because many variables in the population—weight, height, IQ, and anxiety, to name a few—are distributed in a way that approximates the normal curve. Thus a few people are extremely tall or short, a greater number of people are moderately tall or short, and most are close to average in height.

The normal curve has several key properties. The most important of these is that the standard deviation can be used to divide the normal curve into areas containing known percentages of the population. In a normal curve, about two thirds of the scores fall within plus or minus 1 standard deviation of the mean; about 95 percent of cases fall within plus or minus 2 standard deviations; and nearly all of the cases fall between 3 standard deviations above and 3 standard devia-

tions below the mean. Therefore if we know that a psychological characteristic or any other variable is normally distributed, then we can deduce more information about it. For example, IQ scores as measured by the Wechsler intelligence tests (see Chapter 9) are normally distributed with a mean of 100 and a standard deviation of 15. Knowing this, we can use our knowledge of the normal curve to answer questions like these:

1. What percentage of people have IQs between 70 and 130? (Approximately 95 percent. These scores are +2 SD and −2 SD from the mean, respectively. As Figure A.2 shows, this area below the curve includes 13.59 + 34.13 + 34.13 + 13.59 percent of the cases, or 95.44 percent.)

2. My IQ is 115, so where does that place me? (115 is +1 SD above the mean, so as Figure A.2 shows, about 16 percent of the population will have a higher IQ, and 84 percent will have a lower IQ. That is, the area to the right of +1 SD represents 13.59 + 2.14 + 0.13 percent of the cases, or 15.86 percent.)

3. What is the probability that a person selected at random from the population will have an IQ of 145 or more? (About one eighth of 1 percent. This probability corresponds to the area under the curve beyond +3 SD, or 0.13 percent.)

These examples point to a major use of the normal curve: It allows us to estimate the probability that a given event will occur. Indeed, the statistical tests we describe next are methods for arriving at probability statements based on the assumption that the variables being investigated are normally distributed.

STATISTICAL METHODS FOR DATA ANALYSIS

Given a set of data for any single variable, such as the scores of a sample of people on a self-esteem test, we use descriptive statistics to summarize the characteristics of those data. But psychologists do more than describe variables individually. They seek to explain and predict behavior by examining how variables are *related* to one another. The following statistical methods are used to analyze relations among variables and draw inferences about the meaning of those relations.

ACCOUNTING FOR VARIANCE IN BEHAVIOR

Behavior varies. It varies between individuals (e.g., some people are more aggressive or helpful than others), and it varies for the same individual across time and situations (a person may perform a task well under some conditions but more poorly under other circumstances). Explaining why variations in behavior occur (i.e., accounting for variance) is a central goal of psychological science.

As an example, suppose we want to examine how the number of bystanders present during an emergency influences the speed with which they assist a person in distress. In this instance, the number of bystanders is the independent variable, and the speed of helping is the dependent variable. We conduct an experiment, randomly assign participants to different conditions (one, two, or four bystanders present), and find that, overall, bystanders who were alone responded most quickly and groups of four responded most slowly. We also find that the speed of response varied even within each condition; for example, among those bystanders who were alone, some simply responded more quickly than others. Maybe they were in a better mood, had more altruistic personalities, and so on.

In any experiment, the total amount of variation in people's behavior (e.g., speed of helping) may be divided into two components: the amount of *variance accounted for* by the differences in the independent variable(s) being manipulated (e.g., being placed alone or with other bystanders) and the amount of variance that is left over and therefore must be due to other factors (e.g., participants' mood, personality). Thus

Total variance	=	Variance accounted for (due to independent variables)	+	Variance not accounted for (due to random, unmeasured, or uncontrolled factors)

In our experiment, suppose a statistical analysis reveals that 20 percent of the total variance in the speed with which participants helped a person in distress can be accounted for by our independent variable—the number of other bystanders present. Figure A.3 shows this schematically. The other 80 percent of the variance in speed of helping is due to other factors that were not controlled in the experiment. Some of these other factors, which are random and beyond the control of the experimenter, produce what is called *error variance*. For example,

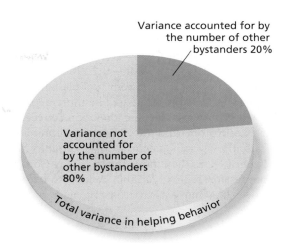

FIGURE A.3

The total amount of variation in the dependent variable (speed of responding to another person in distress) is represented within the circle. The total variance may be divided into one portion accounted for by the independent variable (number of bystanders) and another portion not accounted for by the independent variable.

some participants may have been momentarily preoccupied with personal problems and thus responded more slowly than they otherwise would have. The rest of the unexplained variance results from factors that systematically affect the speed of helping but which the researcher either does not know about or were not examined in the experiment. Such variables may include the participants' personality characteristics or mood, the victim's gender, the nature of the emergency, and so forth. In future research, we might introduce additional independent variables, such as manipulating (i.e., creating) an environment that puts bystanders in a good or bad mood just prior to the emergency. By studying other independent variables, we attempt to increase the amount of variance accounted for, thereby increasing the size of the "accounted for" area in Figure A.3. Perhaps we will find that by knowing both the number of bystanders present and the participants' mood, we can now account for 35 percent of the variance in people's speed of helping.

From this perspective, understanding and/or predicting behavior involves isolating factors that account for behavioral variance. The more important a particular variable is, the more variance it helps us account for. To be sure, we can never completely eliminate the random factors that produce error variance. But as scientific research proceeds, the goal is to discover new variables that account for additional portions of the total variance in people's behavior.

CORRELATIONAL METHODS

The concept of "variance accounted for" applies not only to experiments but also to correlational studies. As discussed in Chapter 2, correlational research does not involve manipulating independent variables. Rather it involves measuring two or more variables and determining whether changes in one variable are associated with changes in the other. Suppose that we administer two psychological tests—one measuring self-esteem and the other measuring depression—to 200 adults. On each test we will find that the scores vary: Some people will have higher self-esteem than others, and some will be more depressed than others. The question is this: Is there a relation between the variance in self-esteem scores and the variance in depression scores? Stated differently, as self-esteem scores (variable X) become higher or lower (i.e., as they move further away from the mean of X), do depression scores (variable Y) tend to become either higher or lower (i.e., move away from the mean of Y) in a systematic manner?

The Correlation Coefficient

Relations between variables can differ in *direction* (positive or negative) and in *strength*. To illustrate, imagine that we have a sample of six people, with scores on two variables (X and Y) for each person. Table A.4 shows five hypothetical sets of X and Y scores for these six people. In set A the relation between variables X and Y is positive in direction. That is, higher scores on variable X are associated with higher scores on Y, and lower scores on X are associated with lower scores on Y. In contrast, set E reveals a negative relation. Here, higher scores on X are associated with lower Y scores, and vice versa. In set C the pairs of X and Y scores bear no clear relation to each other: They are not correlated. As scores on X change, scores on Y do not change in any consistent manner. Thus in sets A, C, and E, we see three different types of relations—positive, none, and negative.

To illustrate how relations between variables differ in strength, let us compare set A with set B. In set A, there is a perfect positive relation between X and Y: As each X score increases by a constant amount (in this case, by 1), each Y score also increases by a constant amount (in this case, by 2). In set B, individuals having higher X scores also tend to have higher Y scores, but this positive relation is not as consistent as in Set A. For example, in set B participant 3 has a higher X score than participant 2 yet a lower Y score. Likewise, compare set E with set D. Set E displays a perfect negative relation: As each X score increases by a constant amount, each Y score decreases by a constant amount. In set D, the negative relation between X and Y is not as consistent and thus is not as strong.

The **Pearson product-moment correlation coefficient** *is a statistic that reflects the direction and strength of the relation between two variables.* The correlation coefficient (designated r) can range in magnitude from -1.00 to $+1.00$. If $r = +1.00$, this reflects a perfect positive relation between X and Y scores, as in set A of Table A.4. A correlation coefficient of -1.00 signifies a perfect negative relation, as in set E. Correlations close to 0.00 indicate no systematic relation between the variables, as in set C.

In actual research, a correlation of -1.00 or $+1.00$ is rare; psychological variables tend to be imperfectly correlated with one another. More typically, correlation coefficients might resemble those in sets B ($r = +.58$) and D ($r = -.75$). Remember that it is the magnitude of the correlation coefficient and not its sign (direction) that indicates the degree to which two variables are related to one another. Thus X and Y are more strongly related in set D ($r = -.75$) than in set B ($r = +.58$), even though the correlation in set D is negative.

How shall we interpret a correlation coefficient? A correlation of $+.50$, for example, does *not* mean that X and Y are 50 percent related. Rather, squaring the correlation coefficient (r^2) indicates the amount of variance that the two variables share or have in common. Stated another way, r^2 tells us how much of the variance in

TABLE A.4   Five Data Sets Illustrating Various Relations That May Exist between Two Variables

Participant	Set A X	Set A Y	Set B X	Set B Y	Set C X	Set C Y	Set D X	Set D Y	Set E X	Set E Y
1	1	2	1	4	1	5	1	6	1	12
2	2	4	2	5	2	8	2	8	2	10
3	3	6	3	2	3	6	3	10	3	8
4	4	8	4	10	4	2	4	4	4	6
5	5	10	5	6	5	6	5	2	5	4
6	6	12	6	8	6	7	6	1	6	2
$N = 6$	$r = +1.00$		$r = +.58$		$r = .00$		$r = -.75$		$r = -1.00$	

Each set consists of the scores of 6 people on two variables, X and Y. The Pearson product–moment correlation coefficient (r) has been computed for each set. The computational formula for r is as follows:

$$r = \frac{N(\Sigma X_i Y_i) - (\Sigma X_i)(\Sigma Y_i)}{\sqrt{[N(\Sigma X_i^2) - (\Sigma X_i)^2][N(\Sigma Y_i^2) - (\Sigma Y_i)^2]}}$$

Where X_i = Each person's score on variable X; ΣX_i = sum of Xs

Y_i = Each person's score on variable Y; ΣY_i = sum of Ys

N = Total number of people

$$r = +.50$$

FIGURE A.4

Squaring the correlation coefficient provides an estimate of the amount of variance shared by two variables. In this instance, $r = +.50$, indicating that 25 percent of the variance in engineering grades in this sample can be accounted for by individual differences in mechanical aptitude.

one measure can be accounted for by differences in the other measure. For example, suppose we obtain a correlation of $+.50$ between scores on a mechanical aptitude test and grades in a college engineering course. As illustrated in Figure A.4, squaring the correlation coefficient ($+.50^2 = .25$) tells us that 25 percent of the total variance in course grades can be accounted for by differences in mechanical aptitude scores. Obviously, the more highly two variables are correlated, the more common variance they share. If the two variables in Figure A.4 correlated .70, the area of overlap would include about half of each circle, because $(+.70)^2 = .49$. Finally, if two variables are perfectly correlated, the two circles in Figure A.4 would overlap completely.

Recall from Chapter 2 that a correlation between two variables does not allow us to conclude that one caused the other. We know only that they are statistically related to one another. If variables X and Y are correlated, it is possible that X causes Y or that Y causes X—or that both X and Y are caused by some third variable, Z (for example, spatial reasoning ability).

Correlation and Prediction

If two variables are correlated and we know an individual's score on one variable, then this information will help us estimate his or her score on the other variable. *The more highly two variables are correlated, the more accurate our predictions will be.* In fact, if two variables are perfectly correlated—if their variance overlaps completely—we can make precise predictions. For example, in set A of Table A.4, once we know a person's score on X, we can accurately predict that $Y = 2X$. (Conversely, if we know Y, we can predict that $X = .5Y$.) In statistical prediction based on correlation, we are thus taking advantage of lawful relations among variables to predict to the individual case.

There are many practical applications for predictions based on correlational analysis. Industrial-organizational psychologists, for example, often help organizations develop aptitude tests that correlate with on-the-job performance.

Personnel managers can therefore use job applicants' test scores to predict which applicants are most likely to perform well, just as colleges use high school students' scores on standardized tests (e.g. the SAT) to help estimate potential college performance. The more highly a *predictor variable* (e.g., aptitude test scores) is correlated with the *criterion variable* (e.g., job performance or college grades), the more accurate the selection decisions will be.

Factor Analysis

Researchers often measure many variables and examine the correlations among them. For example, suppose we want to develop a psychological test to measure individual differences in anxiety. Let us assume that we write 40 items that we think would be answered differently by people who are high and low in anxiety. We then administer these items to a large sample of people. For each item, the person responds on the following scale: 0 ("not at all like me"); 1 ("a little like me"); 2 ("somewhat like me"); and 3 ("very much like me"). We then correlate scores on each of the 40 items with one another. We reason that if test items are correlated highly with one another—if scores on these items "cluster," or "hang together"—then these items are probably measuring the same underlying aspect of anxiety. Further, if the items within one cluster correlate highly with one another but are not correlated highly with items in other clusters, then these various item clusters probably reflect different aspects of people's experiences of anxiety. Thus we also hope to determine the number of item clusters and to use this information to infer the nature of anxiety.

When the sets of scores for the 40 items are correlated with one another ($N =$ the number of items, we will end up with 780 correlations—that is, $[N \times (N - 1)]/2$, or $[40 \times 39]/2$ correlations—to examine. Obviously, with so many correlations, trying to determine visually which items cluster together (while not clustering with other items) is a hopeless task. Fortunately, a statistical technique called **factor analysis** *reduces a large number of correlations among many measures to a smaller number of clusters, with each cluster containing variables that correlate highly with one another.* Today, computers can analyze the patterns of correlations and perform a factor analysis in a few seconds. The term *factor* refers to the underlying characteristic that presumably accounts for why the measures within each cluster are linked.

Factor analysis is complex, and for purposes of this discussion, we need not be concerned with its mathematical basis. Our interest is in how psychologists use it as a research tool, so consider a simple example. Let us assume that the factor analysis indicates that there are two distinct clusters of items that include 38 of the 40 items. Table A.5 shows the correlations among only 6 of those 38 items. Such a table is called a *correlation matrix*. The correlation coefficients of 1.00 along the diagonal of the matrix reflect the obvious fact that each variable correlates perfectly with itself. Because the bottom half of the matrix contains the same correlations as the top, we need concern ourselves with only the upper half.

TABLE A.5   Intercorrelations among Six Items from an Anxiety Scale

Test	1	2	3	4	5	6
1	1.00	.84	.76	.47	.53	.42
2		1.00	.79	.44	.39	.51
3			1.00	.50	.38	.46
4				1.00	.82	.74
5					1.00	.92
6						1.00

Table A.5 shows that items 1, 2, and 3 correlate highly with one another. Likewise, items 4, 5, and 6 correlate strongly with one another. Notice also that items 1, 2, and 3 have much lower correlations with items 4, 5, and 6, indicating that the two clusters are measuring different things. But just what do these two clusters of items measure? Factor analysis cannot answer this question directly; it can only identify the clusters for us. Now it is up to us to examine the nature of the items in each cluster and decide what the underlying factors might be.

Suppose that item 1 says "My body feels tense much of the time," item 2 reads "My heart often pounds in my chest," and item 3 says "My underarms are often wet with perspiration." Because all three items relate to bodily arousal responses, we might decide to call this first factor *physiological arousal* or *somatic anxiety*. Now, let's take a look at items 4, 5, and 6 and see if we can figure out what they're measuring. Item 4 reads "I worry that something bad is going to happen," item 5 says "I have great difficulty concentrating because of worrisome thoughts," and item 6 says "I worry that I will not be able to handle important situations." These items seem to capture mental aspects of anxiety rather than physiological responses, so we might decide to call our second factor *worry* or *cognitive anxiety*. And, in fact, this factor structure is what typically is found when anxiety items are subjected to factor analysis. Indeed, consistent findings that the somatic and cognitive components are distinct aspects of anxiety (and other emotions) have stimulated and supported the models of emotion and stress described in Chapters 10 and 13 of this book. From a practical perspective, we now have a scientific basis for constructing two subscales from our anxiety measure so that, in addition to a total score, we can also measure differences between people in both somatic and cognitive anxiety. We can see, therefore, why factor analysis is a valuable tool within psychology, where researchers often attempt to identify basic dimensions of behavior and experience.

INFERENTIAL STATISTICS AND HYPOTHESIS TESTING

Regardless of the type of research, psychologists rarely have access to the entire population of people they are interested in. Instead, they must be satisfied with studying relatively small samples of participants. Thus 80 introductory psychology students might participate in an experiment on bystander helping, and 400 adults recruited through newspaper advertisements might participate in a correlational study examining the relation between self-esteem and depression. On the basis of the results obtained from such samples, researchers seek to generalize their conclusions to the population as a whole.

In experiments, we are typically interested in overall differences between the various conditions. Suppose we find that participants randomly assigned to be alone help a victim more quickly than participants assigned to groups of two or four bystanders. Before concluding that the independent variable (number of bystanders) truly influenced the dependent variable (speed of helping), we must first ask whether this difference is "real" or is merely a "chance" finding. In other words, because our data are based only on a particular sample of people in each condition, how do we know that similar results would have occurred if we had tested other samples? Perhaps for one reason or another the participants we tested were not truly representative of the populations from which they were drawn. Perhaps, despite random assignment, participants assigned to be alone happened by chance to have more highly altruistic personalities than participants in the other conditions, and this (rather than being alone) is the reason they helped more quickly.

Inferential statistics *tell us how confident we can be in drawing conclusions or inferences about a population based on findings obtained from a sample.* Thus if we observe differences in an experiment between experimental and control groups or find that there is a correlation between two variables, we use inferential statistics to determine the likelihood that these results occurred by chance alone and thus do not reflect a genuine difference in the population from which the sample was drawn. When researchers analyze their data and conclude that a correlation or a difference in behavior between groups in an experiment is "statistically significant," the term **statistical significance** *means that it is unlikely that the particular finding occurred by chance alone.* Psychologists typically consider a result to be statistically significant only if it could have occurred by chance alone less than 5 times in 100.

The logic underlying tests of statistical significance is related to our previous discussion of the normal curve and its statistical properties. Determining statistical significance is in many ways similar to the IQ problem presented earlier in the Appendix: If IQ is normally distributed with a mean of 100 and a standard deviation of 15, what is the likelihood of randomly selecting a person with an IQ of 145? To answer that question, all we had to do was to determine what proportion of cases are 3 standard deviations above the mean in a normal distribution. We found that proportion to be about one eighth of 1 percent. Thus we would expect to randomly select a person with an IQ that high about 1 in 1,000 times—pretty small odds. With this example in mind, let us consider the logic of statistical inference in greater detail.

Suppose we are interested in the effects of a stress-management program on the academic performance of freshmen college students who are high in test anxiety. We hypothesize that learning to control anxiety during tests will result in better performance.

We randomly assign 40 students who have received high scores on a self-report measure of test anxiety to either an experimental group (20 participants) that participates in a stress-management program for test anxiety, or to a control group (20 participants) that receives no guidance or treatment. All of the students take the same required courses, and at the end of the academic year we compare the mean grade point averages of the two groups. On a 0.0 (F) to 4.0 (A) scale, we find that the experimental group (training program condition) obtains a mean grade point of 3.17 and the control group has a mean grade point of 2.61. Thus the difference between the two groups is 3.17 − 2.61 = +0.56 grade points. How can we decide whether this difference between the two samples reflects a difference in the respective populations (i.e., all high-test-anxious students who might participate in a stress-management program and all who do not)?

If we repeated our experiment several times with different high-anxiety participants, we would find that the means for the two samples would vary in each experiment. For example, the next three times we performed the study the means might be 2.94 (experimental) versus 2.77 (control), 3.34 versus 2.31, and 2.89 versus 2.83, yielding differences between the groups of 0.17, 1.03, and 0.06, respectively. By repeating the experiment a great many times, we could create a distribution of experimental versus control difference scores, and mathematical theory tells us that this distribution would be a *normal* distribution. This gives us the key. Because we have a normal distribution, just as we previously assessed the exact likelihood of randomly selecting a person with an IQ of 145, we can now determine the likelihood of randomly obtaining a difference of any particular size between our sample means. But to do this, we must first know what the mean and standard deviation of our distribution of differences are. As we've seen, one way to determine these values would be to perform our experiment a large number of times. But, fortunately, we can estimate these values on the basis of a single experiment and thereby avoid the need for many replications.

To do this, we use an approach to statistical analysis that involves testing the **null hypothesis,** *which states that any observed differences between the samples are due to chance.* We begin by assuming that the null hypothesis is true—that there is no real difference, for example, in grade point average between the populations of trained and untrained test-anxious students. If the null hypothesis is true, then if we repeated our experiment a great many times, we would expect the mean of our distribution of difference scores to be zero. Therefore, the normal distribution of difference scores would cluster around this mean of zero. The standard deviation of this normal distribution can be estimated from the standard deviations of the two samples, although the mathematics need not concern us here.

In our hypothetical experiment, we obtained grade point means of 3.17 for the experimental group and 2.61 for the control group, a difference of +0.56. Let us now suppose that the standard deviation of our distribution of differences between means was estimated on the basis of our samples to be .25. Thus our obtained difference of +0.56 is slightly more than 2 SD above the mean (0) of the null hypothesis distribution. From the properties of the normal curve, we know that more than 95 percent of the cases fall in the area of the curve between −2 SD and +2 SD. Thus, *if the null hypothesis were true,* we would expect a difference in means as large as .56 (either above or below zero) less than 5 percent of the time on the basis of chance factors. This probability level meets the criterion for statistical significance described earlier. In view of this fact, we would reject the null hypothesis and conclude that there is a real difference in grade point average in the two populations. Thus our experimental hypothesis that the stress-management program resulted in a higher level of academic performance would be supported.

Note that we used the term *supported,* not *proven,* because we are making an inference based on a probability statement. There is, after all, some possibility (though less than 5 percent) that the null hypothesis is true and this really was a chance finding. Note also that this statistical analysis does not tell us why the stress-management group performed better (e.g., Did they perform better due to the program's content or the mere attention they received?). This is one reason why repeating or replicating research studies is so valuable. If another study—particularly one with more control groups—also yields statistically significant results, we can have more confidence that the difference we obtained reflects a real relation between the independent and dependent variables. But no matter how many times we repeat the experiment, we shall never move from the world of probability into the world of absolute truth.

IN REVIEW

- Descriptive statistics summarize the characteristics of a set of data. A frequency distribution shows how many participants received each score. Histograms are graphs of frequency distributions.

- The mean, median, and mode are measures of central tendency, and each describes a distribution in terms of a single "typical" score. The range, variance, and standard deviation are measures of variability, and each describes how much variation there is within a set of scores.

- A normal curve is a theoretical, symmetrical bell-shaped curve. Fifty percent of the cases fall on each side of the mean, and the mean, median, and mode all have the same value. The standard deviation can be used to make probability estimates by dividing the normal distribution into areas containing known percentages of a population.

- Researchers seek to determine how much behavioral variance can be accounted for by relations between variables, including experimental manipulations, and how much is due to random, unmeasured, or uncontrolled factors.

■ Two variables are correlated when changes in the scores of one variable correspond reliably with changes in the scores of the other variable. Correlations may be positive, negative, or zero, as well as weak or strong. Squaring the correlation coefficient tells us how much of the variance in one measure can be accounted for by differences in the other measure. Correlation does not allow us to assume causality, but it often gives us the basis for predictions.

■ Factor analysis reduces a large number of measures to a smaller number of clusters. The measures within each cluster are highly inter-correlated and reflect the same underlying psychological dimension.

■ Inferential statistics tell us how likely it is that differences between groups or correlations among variables are the result of chance alone. We need inferential statistics because most research is done with samples, and such statistics allow us to generalize conclusions to the population from which the sample was drawn.

■ Typically, a result is considered statistically significant only if it could have occurred by chance alone less than 5 times in 100. Statistical analysis often involves testing the null hypothesis, which assumes that any observed difference between group means or correlation among variables is due to chance. Inferential statistics yield probability statements, not absolute proof.

KEY TERMS AND CONCEPTS

descriptive statistics (A-1)
factor analysis (A-7)
frequency distribution (A-1)
histogram (A-1)
inferential statistics (A-8)
mean (A-1)

measures of central tendency (A-1)
measures of variability (A-3)
median (A-2)
mode (A-1)
normal curve (A-4)
null hypothesis (A-9)

Pearson product-moment correlation
  coefficient (A-6)
range (A-3)
standard deviation (SD; A-3)
statistical significance (A-8)
variance (A-3)

Credits

11.14a-c © Tony Freeman/PhotoEdit; **11.19a** © Bob Daemm-rich/Stock, Boston LLC; **11.19b** © Carroll E. Izard; **11.20a** Courtesy of Operation Migration, www.operationmigra-tion.org; **11.20b** © Myrleen Ferguson Cate/PhotoEdit; **11.21** © Harlow Primate Laboratory; **11.23** © Josef Pelleross/The Image Works; **11.27a** © SuperStock, Inc.; **11.27b** © LWA-JDC/CORBIS; **11.28** © Darama/CORBIS; **11.29** © Bill Gillette/Stock Boston; **11.30** © Bob Daemm-rich/Stock, Boston LLC; **11.33** © age fotostock/SuperStock; **11.34** © FONLUPT GILLES/GAMMA; **11.36a** © George Shelley/Masterfile; **11.36b** © Ken Fisher/Getty Images; **11.37a-b** From: Resnick et al., Longitudinal Magnetic Resonance Imaging Studies of Older Adults, The Journal of Neuroscience, April 15, 2003. Fig 6, p. 3300, Vol 23, Issue 8.; **11.40** National Geographic Society/James L. Stanfield.; **11.43** © Reuters/CORBIS

Chapter 12

Opener © Mehau Kulyk/Photo Researchers; **12.1a** © Bettmann/CORBIS; **12.1b** © Bettmann/CORBIS; **12.3** © CORBIS; **12.5** © Photoedit; **12.6** © Dmitri Kessel/Time Life Pictures/Getty Images; **12.7** © Gregg Mancuso/Stock Boston; **12.13** © Randy J. Larsen, 1987; **12.14a** © Sean Cayton/The Image Works; **12.16** © AFP/CORBIS; **12.18** © Spencer Grant/Stock Boston; **12.19** The Kobal Collection; **12.26** © Wei Yan/Masterfile; **12.27** This image is not coming from the original series of the Rorschach®-Test. Printed with the permission of Verlag Hans Huber, Hogrefe AG, Bern. Rorschach is a worldwide registered trademark.; **12.28** Reprinted by permission from Henry A. Murray, *Thematic Apperception Test*, Plate 12 F. Cambridge, MN: Harvard University Press. © 1943 by the President and Fellows of Harvard College; © 1971 by Henry A. Murray

Chapter 13

Opener © Steve Prezant/CORBIS; **13.3a** © Ben Sklar, Stringer/Associated Press; **13.3b** © PhotoDisc Blue/Getty; **13.5a** © BUU-TURPIN/GAMMA; **13.5b** © Oscar Burriel/Latin Stock/SPL/Photo Researchers; **13.6** © Jennie Woodcock; Reflections Photolibrary/CORBIS; **13.8** © Jeff Smith; **13.15** © Ed Kashi/CORBIS; **13.16** © J.P. Laffont/Corbis-Sygma; **13.18** © LAFARGUE FREDERIC/GAMMA; **13.20** © Ronnie Kaufman/CORBIS; **13.26** © Bruce Ayers/Stone/Getty

Chapter 14

Opener © Tom & Dee Ann McCarthy/CORBIS; **14.1a** © CORBIS; **14.1b** © Bettmann/CORBIS; **14.1c** © Bettmann/CORBIS; **14.2** © Kjell Sandved/Visuals Unlimited, Inc.; **14.3** Witches' Sabbath: The He-Goat. 1798 Museo Lazaro Galdiano, Madrid Spain. Giraudon/Art Resource, NY; **14.7a** © Bettmann/Corbis; **14.7b** © AP/Wide World Photos; **14.10a** © AP Photo/G. Paul Burnette; **14.10b** © JIMI LOTT/THE SEATTLE TIMES; **14.11** © ARKO DATTA/ Reuters/Corbis; **14.16** © Steve Smith; **14.17a** © Paramount Pictures/Courtesy of Getty Images; **14.23** © Alan Oddie/ Photo Edit, Inc; **14.27a** © Tom & Dee Ann McCarthy/CORBIS; **14.27b** © Bettmann/CORBIS; **14.28** © Grunnitus/Photo Researchers; **14.30a-b** © Nancy C. Andreason/The National Institute of Mental Health; **14.35a** © SUNSET BOULEVARD/ CORBIS SYGMA; **14.35b** Paramount Pictures/Photofest; **14.37** © Robin Sachs/Photo Edit

Chapter 15

Opener © James L. Amos/CORBIS; **15.1** © David Buffington/Photodisc/Getty; **15.3** © Bruce Ayres/Stone/Getty; **15.6** Courtesy of Natalie Rogers; **15.7** Courtesy of Dr. Albert Ellis; **15.9** Courtesy of Dr. Aaron T. Beck; **15.10** © Geri Engberg/The Image Works; **15.11** Courtesy of Hunter Hoffman; photo by Mary Levin, University of Washington.; **15.14** Courtesy of Marsha Linehan, University of Washington; **15.15** © David Kelly Crow/PhotoEdit; **15.16** © Ed Lallo/Index Stock; **15.20** © Stephen Frisch/McGraw-Hill; **15.23** © Will & Deni McIntyre/Photo Researchers; **15.27** © David Young-Wolff/Photo Edit

Chapter 16

Opener © Randy Faris/Corbis; **16.1** © Bruce Ayres/Getty; **16.4** © Spencer Grant/PhotoEdit; **16.5** © Mark Wilson/Getty Images; **16.7** © DIMA GAVRYSH/GAMMA.; **16.8a** © Tony Freeman/Photoedit; **16.8b** © A. Ramey/Photoedit; **16.9** © PhotoAlto/SuperStock; **16.10** © Merie W. Wallace/Warner Bros/Bureau L.A.Collections/Corbis; **16.12** William Vandivert, Scientific American, November 1955, Vol. 193, Issue 5, pp. 31–35.; **16.13a** © 1965 by Stanley Milgram. From the film OBEDIENCE, distributed by Penn State, Media Sales; **16.13b** © 1965 by Stanley Milgram. From the film OBEDIENCE, distributed by Penn State, Media Sales; **16.15** © 1965 by Stanley Milgram. From the film OBEDIENCE, distributed by Penn State, Media Sales; **16.16** © Gamma; **16.17** © Owen Franken/Stock, Boston LLC; **16.19** © NASA; **16.20** © Reuters NewMedia Inc./CORBIS; **16.21** © Sid Bahrt/Photo Researchers; **16.22a-g** Johnston, V.S. et al. Male Facial Attractiveness: Evidence for Hormone-Mediated Adaptive Design. Fig 1, p 255, Evaluation and Behavior, Vol 22, pp. 251–267. Elsevier Publishing; **16.25a** © Andrew Brusso; **16.25b** © Andrew Brusso; **16.29** © Das Fotoarchiv GmbH/Peter Arnold, Inc; **16.30a** © Richard R. Hansen/Photo Researchers; **16.31** © Viviane Moos/CORBIS; **16.35** © Johathan Nourok/PhotoEdit

TEXT AND LINE ART CREDITS

Chapter 1

Fig. **1.24** Adapted with permission from data in Table 4, Employment characteristics of APA members by membership status, 2000 in *2000 APA Directory Survey*. Copyright © 2000 by the American Psychological Association. Note: The data in this graph have been derived from the APA membership and as such may not accurately represent the distribution of employment settings in which the larger population of doctoral-level psychologists is found in the United States.

Table 1.2 Levine, R., Sato, S., Hashimoto, T., & Verma, J. (1995). Love and marriage in eleven cultures. *Journal of Cross-Cultural Psychology, 26*, 554–571. Copyright © 1995 by Western Washington University. Reprinted by permission of Sage Publications, Inc.

Chapter 2

Fig. **2.3** Latane, Bibb & Darley, John M., *The Unresponsive Bystander: Why Doesn't He Help?*, 1st Edition. Copyright © 1970. Adapted by permission of Pearson Education, Inc., Upper Saddle River, NJ.

Fig. **2.17b** Wilson, G.T. & Lawson, D.M. (1976). Expectancies, alcohol, and sexual arousal in male social drinkers. *Journal of Abnormal Psychology, 85*, 591, Table 1. Copyright © 1976 by the American Psychological Association. Adapted with permission.

Table 2.1 Courtesy of National Sleep Foundation, 2002.

Chapter 3

Fig. **3.7a & c** Smith, B.D, (1998) *Psychology: Science and understanding*, Fig. 10.4. Copyright © 1998 by The McGraw-Hill Companies, Inc. Reprinted with permission from The McGraw-Hill Companies.

Fig. **3.21** Adapted from *The Cerebral Cortex of Man* by Penfield and Rasmussen, Macmillan, 1950. Copyright © 1950 Macmillan. Reprinted by permission from The Gale Group.

Chapter 4

Fig. **4.5** Pritchard, R.M. (June, 1961). Stabilized images on the retina. *Scientific American*, p. 75. Illustration adapted with permission of Eric Mose, Jr.

Fig. **4.17** Koch, K. (2004). *The Quest for Consciousness: A Neurobiological Approach*, Fig. **2.2**, p. 30. Reprinted by permission of Roberts & Company Publishers.

Fig. **4.23** Adapted from Smith, B.D, (1998) *Psychology: Science and Understanding*, Fig. **4.33**. Copyright © 1998 by The McGraw-Hill Companies, Inc. Reprinted with permission from The McGraw-Hill Companies.

Fig. **4.43** Smith, B.D, (1998) *Psychology: Science and understanding*, Fig. **4.21**. Copyright © 1998 by The McGraw-Hill Companies, Inc. Reprinted with permission from The McGraw-Hill Companies.

Fig. **4.51a** Gregory, R.L. & Gombrich, E.H. (1973). *Illusion in nature and art*. Adapted by permission of Gerald Duckworth & Co. Ltd.

Fig. **4.51b** Hudson, W. (1960). Pictorial depth perception in sub-cultural groups in Africa. *Journal of Social Psychology, 52*, 183–208. Copyright © 1960. Published by Heldref Publications, 1319 Eighteenth Street, NW, Washington, DC 20036-1802. Adapted with the permission of the Helen Dwight Reid Educational Foundation.

Fig. **4.53** Blakemore, C. & Cooper, G.F. (1970). Development of the brain depends on visual environment. *Nature, 228*, 477–478. Copyright © 1970 Macmillan Publishers Ltd. Adapted with permission.

Chapter 5

Table 5.1 Smith, C.S., Folkard, S., Schmieder, R.A., Parra, L.F., Spelten, E., & Almiral, H. (2002). Investigation of morning-evening orientation in six countries using the preference scale. *Personality and Individual Differences, 32*, 949–968. Copyright © 2002 International Society for the Study of Individual Differences. Reprinted with permission from Elsevier.

Fig. **5.6** Monk, T.H., Folkard, S. & Wedderburn, A.I. (1996). Maintaining safety and high performance on shift work. *Applied Ergonomics, 27*, 18, Fig. 1. Copyright © 1996 Elsevier. Adapted with permission from Elsevier.

Fig. **5.9** Data adapted with permission from Mersch, P.P.A., Middendorp, H.M., Bouhuys, A.L., Beersma, D.G.M. & van den Hoofdakker, R.H. (1999). Seasonal affective disorder and latitude: A review of the literature. *Journal of Affective Disorders, 53*, 35–48. Copyright © 1999 Elsevier. Map graphic of U.S. reproduced with permission from *The New York Times*, December 29, 1993, p. B7. Copyright © 1993 The New York Times Co.

Fig. **5.16** Adapted with permission from Roffwarg, H.P., Muzio, J.N., & Dement, W.C. Ontogentic development of human dream-sleep cycle. *Science, 152*, 604, Fig. 1. Copyright © 1966 AAAS.

Fig. **5.18** Adapted with permission of the authors and the publisher from Agnew, H.W., Jr., Webb, W.B. & Williams, R.L. Comparison of Stage Four and 1-REM sleep deprivation. *Perceptual and Motor Skills*, 1967, 24, 851–858. Copyright © 1967 Southern Universities Press.

Fig. **5.20** Fosse, R., Stickgold, R. & Hobson, J.A. (2001). Brain-mind states: Reciprocal variation in thoughts and hallucinations. *Psychological Science, 12, No. 1*, 33, Fig. 3. Copyright © 2001 American Psychological Society. Adapted with permission of Blackwell Publishing.

Fig. **5.27** MacDonald, T.K., Zanna, M.P., & Fong, G.T. (1995). Decision making in altered states: Effects on alcohol on attitudes toward drinking and driving. *Journal of Personality and Social Psychology, 68* (6), 979, Fig. 1. Copyright © 1995 by the American Psychological Association. Reprinted with permission.

Fig. **5.36** Kosslyn, S.M., Thompson, W.L., Costantini-Ferrando, M.F., Alpert, N.M., & Spiegel, D. (2000). Hypnotic visual illusion alters color processing in the brain. *American Journal of Psychiatry, 157*, 1279–1284, Fig. 1. Copyright © 2000 American Psychiatric Association. Adapted with permission.

Chapter 6

Fig. **6.1** Hailman, J.P. (1969). How an instinct is learned. *Scientific American, 221*, 98–106. Illustration adapted with permission of Eric Mose, Jr.

Fig. **6.26** Garcia, J. & Koelling, R.A. (1966). Relation of cue to consequence in avoidance learning. *Psychonomic Science, 4*, 123–124. Adapted with permission of Psychonomic Society Inc.

Chapter 7

Fig. **7.1(b)** Milner, B. (1965). Memory disturbances after bilateral hippocampal lesions. In Peter Milner and S.G. Glickman, eds., *Cognitive processes and the brain*, p. 108, Fig. 6. Princeton, NJ: Van Nostrand Co., Inc. Adapted with permission of Brenda Milner.

Fig. **7.2** Atkinson, R.C. & Shriffrin, R.M. (1968). Human memory: A proposed system and its control processes. In K.W. Spence & J.T. Spence, eds., *Advances in the psychology of learning and motivation: Research and theory, Vol. 2.* Copyright © 1968 Academic Press. Adapted with permission from Elsevier.

Fig. **7.6** Baddeley, A. (2000). The episodic buffer. *Trends in Cognitive Sciences, 4* (11): Fig. 1, p. 421. Copyright © 2000 Elsevier Ltd. Adapted with permission from Elsevier.

Fig. **7.7** Glanzer, M., & Cunitz, A. (1966). Two storage mechanisms in free recall. *Journal of Verbal Learning and Verbal Behavior (now Journal of Memory and Language), 5,* 358, fig. 2. Copyright © 1966 Academic Press. Adapted with permission from Elsevier.

Fig. **7.12** Collins, A.M. & Loftus, E.F. (1975). A spreading activation theory of semantic processing. *Psychological Review, 82,* 412, Fig. 1. Copyright © 1975 by the American Psychological Association. Adapted with permission.

Fig. **7.15 (a-b)** Adapted from Jennifer M. Talarico & David C. Rubin. Confidence, not consistency, characterizes flashbulb memories. *Psychological Science,* 14, No. 5. Copyright © 2003 American Psychological Society. Reprinted by permission of Blackwell Publishing.

Fig. **7.16** Godden, D.R. & Baddeley, A.D. (1975). Context-dependent memory in two natural environments: On land and under water. *British Journal of Psychology, 66,* 325–331. Copyright © 1975 British Psychological Society. Adapted with permission of Alan Baddeley.

Fig. **7.21** Nickerson, R.S. & Adams, M.J. (1979). Long-term memory for a common object. *Cognitive Psychology, 11,* 287–307. Copyright © 1979 Academic Press. Adapted with permission from Elsevier.

Fig. **7.24** Alzheimer's Disease: Unraveling the Mystery. NIH Publication #02-3782, October 2002, p. 29. U.S. Department of Health & Human Services, National Institute of Health.

Fig. **7.25** Bahrick, H.P., Hall, L.K., & Berger, S.A. (1996). Accuracy and distortion in memory for high school grades. *Psychological Science, 7,* 265–271. Copyright © 1996 American Psychological Society. Adapted with permission of Blackwell Publishing.

Fig. **7.26** Courtesy of Helen Intraub.

Chapter 8

Fig. **8.11b** Savage-Rumbaugh, E.S., McDonald, K., Sevik, R.A., Hopkins, W.D. & Rupert, E. (1986). Spontaneous symbol acquisition and communicative use by pygmy chimpanzees *(Pan paniscus). Journal of Experimental Psychology: General, 115,* 220, Fig. 1. Copyright © 1986 by the American Psychological Association. Adapted with permission for the American Psychological Association and Dr. Sue Savage-Rumbaugh, Language Research Center, Georgia State University.

Fig. **8.14** Bialystok, E. & Martin, M. Attention inhibition in bilingual children: Evidence from the dimensional change card sort tasks. *Developmental Science 7* (3): 325–339. Copyright © 2004. Adapted with permission of Blackwell Publishing.

Fig. **8.30a-d** Adapted with permission from Shepard, R.N. & Metzler, J. (February, 1971). Mental rotation of three-dimensional objects. *Science, 171,* Figs. 1 & 2. Copyright © 1971 AAAS.

Fig. **8.31** Kosslyn, S.M., Ball, T.M., Reiser, B.J. (1978). Human Perception and Performance. *Journal of Experimental Psychology, 4,* 51, Fig. 2. Copyright © 1978 by the American Psychological Association. Adapted with permission.

Fig. **8.33** Thiede, K.W. & Anderson, M. (2003). Summarizing can improve metacomprehension accuracy. *Contemporary Education Psychology, 28,* 147, Fig. 3. Copyright © 2003 Academic Press. Adapted with permission of Blackwell Publishing.

Chapter 9

Fig. **9.6** *Human Cognitive Abilities: A Survey of Factor-Analytic Studies,* Appendix B: Hierarchical factor matrix files by J.B. Carroll. Copyright © 1993 Cambridge University Press. Adapted with the permission of Cambridge University Press.

Fig. **9.14** Carpenter, P.A., Just, M.A., and Shell, P. (1990). What one intelligence test measures. *Psychological Review, 97,* 404–431, Fig. 2. Copyright © 1990 by the American Psychological Association. Adapted with permission.

Fig. **9.17** Schweinhart, Lawrence J. & Weikart, David P. Figure 5.1, "Major Findings at Age Twenty-Seven." In *Social Programs that Work,* edited by Jonathan Crane. Copyright © 1998 Russell Sage Foundation, 112 East 64th Street, New York, NY 10021. Reprinted with permission.

Fig. **9.19** McGue, M., Bouchard Jr., T.J., Iacono, W.G., and Lykken, D.T. (1993). Behavioral Genetics of Cognitive Ability: A Life-Span Perspective, Fig. 1, p. 63, *Nature, Nuture, and Psychology* by R. Plomin and G.E. McClearn (Eds.). Copyright © 1993 by the American Psychological Association. Adapted with permission.

Fig. **9.22** Kimura, D. (1992). Sex differences in the brain. *Scientific American, 267* (3), 121–122, Fig. 1. Adapted by permission of Jared Schneidman Design.

Fig. **9.23** Steele, C.M. (1997). A threat in the air: How stereotypes shape intellectual identity and performance. *American Psychologist, 52,* 620–621, Figs. 1 & 2. Copyright © 1997 by the American Psychological Association. Reprinted with permission.

Table 9.1 Copyright © 1972 by The Riverside Publishing Company. All rights reserved. Reproduced from the Stanford-Binet Intelligence Scales, Form L-M, by L.M. Terman and M.A. Merrill, with permission of the publisher. Note: these items are not from the current edition of Stanford-Binet.

Table 9.3 Thurston, L.L. (1938). *Primary mental abilities.* Reprinted by permission of the University of Chicago Press.

Table 9.6 From the *Diagnostic and Statistical Manual of Mental Disorders,* 4th Edition. Copyright © 2000 American Psychiatric Association. Reprinted with permission.

Chapter 10

Fig. **10.13** Michael, R.T., Gagnon, J.H., Laumann, E.O., & Kolata, G., *Sex in America.* Copyright © 1994 by C.S.G. Enterprises, Inc., Edward O. Laumann, Robert T. Michael, and Gina Kolata. Adapted with permission of Little Brown and Co., Inc. and Time Warner Book Group UK.

Fig. **10.16** Michael, R.T., Gagnon, J.H., Laumann, E.O., & Kolata, G., *Sex in America.* Copyright © 1994 by C.S.G. Enterprises, Inc., Edward O. Laumann, Robert T. Michael, and Gina Kolata. Adapted with permission of Little Brown and Co., Inc. and Time Warner Book Group UK.

Fig. **10.17** Blanchard, R. & Bogaert, A.F. (1996). Homosexuality in men and number of older brothers. *American Journal of Psychiatry, 153,* 27–31. Copyright © 1996 American Psychiatric Association. Adapted with permission.

Fig. **10.33** Speisman, J., Lazarus, R.S., Mordkoff, A., & Davidson, L. (1964). Experimental reduction of stress based on ego-defense theory. *Journal of Abnormal and Social Psychology, 68,* 373, Fig. 1. Copyright © 1964 by the American Psychological Association. Reprinted with permission.

Chapter 11

Fig. **11.11** Reprinted by permission of the publisher from *The postnatal development of the human cerebral cortex, Vols. I–VIII* by Jesse LeRoy Conel. Cambridge, MA: Harvard University Press. Copyright © 1939, 1975 by the President and Fellows of Harvard College.

Fig. **11.16** Vurpillot, E. (1968). The development of scanning strategies and their relation to visual differences. *Journal of Experimental Child Psychology, 6,* 632–650. Copyright © 1968 Elsevier Inc. Adapted with permission from Elsevier.

Fig. **11.17** Kail, R. (1988). Development functions for speeds of cognitive processes. *Journal of Child Psychology, 45,* 339–364. Copyright © 1988 Elsevier Inc. Adapted with permission from Elsevier.

Fig. **11.18** From Wynn, Karen (August, 1992). Addition and subtraction by human infants. *Nature, 358:* 749. Used with permission.

Fig. **11.24** Maccoby, E.E. & Martin, J.A. (1983). Socialization in the context of the family: Parent-child interaction. In E.M.

Hetherington, ed., *Handbook of Child Psychology,* 4th ed. Adapted with permission of John Wiley & Sons, Inc.

Fig. **11.25** Jaffee, S.R., Moffitt, T.E., Caspi, A. & Taylor, A. (2003). Life with (or without) father: The benefits of living with two biological parents depend on the father's antisocial behavior. *Child Development, 74,* 118, Fig. 2. Copyright © 2003 The Society for Research in Child Development, Inc. Adapted with permission of Blackwell Publishing.

Fig. **11.26** Crowley, K., Callanan, M.A., Tenenbaum, H.R. & Allen, E. (2001). Parents explain more often to boys than to girls during shared scientific thinking. *Psychological Science, 12,* 258–261. Copyright © 2001 The American Psychological Society. Adapted with permission of Blackwell Publishing.

Fig. **11.30b** Inhelder, B. & Piaget, J. (1958). *The growth of logical thinking from childhood to adolescence.* Copyright © 1958 by Basic Books, Inc. Adapted with permission of Basic Books, a member of Perseus Books, L.L.C., and by permission of Thomson Publishing Services for Routledge & Kegan Paul Ltd.

Fig. **11.33** Larson, R.W., Moneta, G., Richards, M.H., & Wilson, S. (2002). Continuity, stability., and change in daily emotional experience across adolescence. *Child Development, 73,* 1158, Fig. 1. Copyright © 2002 The Society for Research in Child Development, Inc. Adapted with permission of Blackwell Publishing.

Fig. **11.35** Arnett, J. (2001). Conceptions of the Transition to Adulthood. *Journal of Adult Development, 8* (2), Fig. 2, p. 140. Adapted with kind permission of Springer Science and Business Media.

Fig. **11.38** *Developmental Influences on Adult Intelligence: The Seattle Longitudinal Study* by Schaie, K.W. Copyright © 2005 by Oxford University Press, Inc. Adapted with permission of Oxford University Press, Inc.

Fig. **11.41** Bengston, V.L. (2001, Feb.) Beyond the nuclear family: The increasing importance of multigenerational bonds. *Journal of Marriage and Family, 63* (1), 1–16, Fig. 2. Copyright © 2001 by the National Council on Family Relations, 3989 Central Ave., NE, Suite 550, Minneapolis, MN 55421. Reprinted by permission.

Table 11.3 Kohlberg, L. (1984). *The psychology of moral development: Essays on moral development, Vol. 2,* 176–177, Table 2. Copyright © 1984 Harper & Row. Reprinted by Adapted with Pearson Education.

Chapter 12

P. 441 Excerpt from *A Sniper in the Tower: The Charles Whitman Murders* by G.M. Lavergne. Copyright © 1997 University of North Texas Press. Used with permission.

Fig. **12.4** Adapted from Smith, B.D. (1998). *Psychology: Science and Understanding,* Fig. 14.2. Copyright © 1998 by The McGraw-Hill Companies, Inc.

Fig. **12.13** From Eysenck, H.J. (1967). *The biological basis of personality,* Fig. 13. Courtesy of Charles C. Thomas Publisher, Ltd., Springfield, IL.

Fig. **12.24** Cousins, S.D. (1989). Culture and self-perception in the United States and Japan. *Journal of Personality and Social Psychology, 56,* 124–131, Table 2. Copyright © 1989 by the American Psychological Association. Adapted with permission.

Table 12.6 Scheier, M.F., Carver, C.S., & Bridges, M.W. (1994). Distinguishing optimism from neuroticism (and trait anxiety, self-mastery, and self-esteem): A reevaluation of the Life Orientation Test. *Journal of Personality and Social Psychology, 67,* 1073, Table 6. Copyright © 1994 by the American Psychological Association. Adapted with permission.

Table 12.8 Tellegen, A., Lykken, D.T., Bouchard, T.J., Wilcox, K.L., Segal, N.L. & Rich, S. (1988). Personality similarity in twins reared apart and together. *Journal of Personality and Social Psychology, 54,* 1036, Table 5. Copyright © 1988 by the American Psychological Association. Adapted with permission.

Table 12.9 Rotter, J.B. (1966). Generalized expectancies for internal versus external control of reinforcement. *Psychological Monographs, 80 (Whole No. 609),* 11–12, Table 1. Copyright © 1966 by the American Psychological Association. Adapted with permission.

Chapter 13

Fig. **13.4** Selye, H., *The Stress of Life*, Second Edition, p. 476. Copyright © 1976 by the McGraw-Hill Companies, Inc. Reprinted with permission from The McGraw-Hill Companies.

Fig. **13.9** Levy, B.R., Slade, M.D., Kinkel, S.R., & Kasl, S.V. (2002). Longevity increased by positive self-perceptions of aging. *Journal of Personality and Social Psychology, 83,* 264, Fig. 1. Copyright © 2002 by the American Psychological Association. Adapted with permission.

Fig. **13.17** Drawings based on photographs by Kosambi, D.D. (February, 1967). Living in prehistory India. *Scientific American, 216,* 110–111.

Fig. **13.23** Prochaska, J.O., Johnson, S. & Lee, P. (1988). The transtheoretical model of behavior change. In S.A. Shumaker & E.B. Schron, eds., *The Handbook of Health Behavior Change,* 2nd ed. Copyright © 1988 Springer Publishing Company, Inc., New York, NY 10036. Used by permission.

Fig. **13.24** Belloc, N.B. (1973). Relationship of health practices and mortality. *Preventive Medicine, 2,* 67–81. Copyright © 1973 by Academic Press. Adapted with permission from Elsevier.

Fig. **13.29** Marlatt, G.A., Baer, J.S., Kivlahan, D.R., et al. (1998). Screening and brief intervention for high-risk college student drinkers: Results from a 2-year follow-up assessment. *Journal of Consulting and Clinical Psychology, 66,* 611, Fig. 2. Copyright © 1998 by the American Psychological Association. Adapted with permission.

Fig. **13.30** Marlatt, G.A. & Gordon, J.R. (1985). *Relapse prevention: Maintenance strategies in the treatment of addiction,* p. 38, Fig. 1-4. Copyright © 1985 by Guilford Publications, Inc. Reprinted with permission.

Table 13.1 Smith, R.E., Smoll, F.L. & Schultz, R.W. (1990). Measurement and correlates of sport-specific cognitive and somatic trait anxiety: The Sports Anxiety Scale. *Anxiety, Stress & Coping (formerly, Anxiety Research), 2,* 263–280. Copyright © 1990 Brunner-Routledge. Adapted by permission of the publisher: http://www.tandf.co.uk.

Table 13.2 Masten, A.S. & Coatsworth, J.D. (1998). The development of competence in favorable and unfavorable environments: Lessons from research on successful children.

American Psychologist, 53, 212, Table 2. Copyright © 1998 by the American Psychological Association. Reprinted with permission.

Chapter 14

P. 545 Excerpt from Nemiah reprinted by permission of the publisher from *Harvard Guide to Modern Psychiatry,* edited by Armand, M. Nicholi, Jr., pp. 179–180. Cambridge, MA: The Belknap Press of Harvard University Press. Copyright © 1978 by the President and Fellows of Harvard College.

Pp. 547–548 Excerpt from Kleinmuntz, B. (1980). *Essentials of Abnormal Psychology,* 2nd ed. Copyright © 1980 Harper & Row. Reprinted by permission of Benjamin Kleinmuntz.

Fig. **14.22** Tremblay, L.K., Naranjo, C.A., Cardenas, L., Hermann, N. & Busto, U.E. (2002). Probing brain reward system function in major depressive disorder. *Archives of General Psychiatry, 59,* 412, Fig. 2. Adapted with permission of the American Medical Association.

P. 554 Excerpt from "I Feel Like I'm Trapped," *The New York Times,* March 18, 1986, p. C12. Copyright © 1986 by The New York Times Co. Reprinted with permission.

Fig. **14.33** Caldwell, A.B. (1994). The profile of Jeffrey Dahmer (videotape). Published by Caldwell Report, Inc. Used by permission of Caldwell Report.

P. 565 Excerpts from Stone, M.H., Borderline Disorder. *Psychiatry, Vol. I,* edited by R. Michels and J.O. Cavenar. Copyright © 1986 by Basic Books, Inc. Reprinted with permission.

Chapter 15

P. 573 Excerpt from "A Recovering Patient (1986). "Can We Talk?" The schizophrenic patient in psychotherapy. *American Journal of Psychiatry, 143,* 68–70. Copyright © 1986 by the American Psychiatric Association. Reprinted with permission.

P. 576 Excerpt from Wolberg, L.R. (1967). *The technique of psychotherapy,* 2nd ed., pp. 660–661. Copyright © 1967 Grune and Stratton. Reprinted with permission from Elsevier.

Fig. **15.5** Howard, K.L., Kopta, S.M., Krause, M.S. & Orlinsky, D.E. (1986). The dose-effect relationship in psychotherapy. *American Psychologist, 41,* 160, Fig. 1. Copyright © 1986 by the American Psychological Association. Adapted with permission.

P. 579 Excerpt from Rogers, Carl R., *Client-centered therapy,* p. 49. Copyright © 1951 by Houghton Mifflin Company. Used with permission.

P. 582 Excerpt from Beck, A.T., Rush, A.J., Shaw, B.F. & Emery, G. (1979). *Cognitive Therapy of Depression,* pp. 145–146. Copyright © 1979 by Guilford Publications, Inc. Reprinted with permission.

Fig. **15.30** Foa, E.B., Hearst-Ikeda, D. & Perry, K.J. (1995). Evaluation of a brief cognitive-behavioral program for the prevention of PTSD in recent assault victims. *Journal of Consulting and Clinical Psychology, 63,* 952, Fig. 1. Copyright © 1995 by the American Psychological Association. Reprinted with permission.

Chapter 16

Fig. **16.3** Miller, J.G. (1984). Culture and the development of everyday social explanation. *Journal of Personality and Social Psychology, 46,* 961–978, Table 2. Copyright © 1984 by the American Psychological Association. Reprinted with permission.

Fig. **16.18** Janis, Irving L. *Groupthink: Psychological Studies of Policy Decisions and Fiascos,* 2nd ed. Copyright © 1982 by Houghton Mifflin Company. Adapted with permission.

Fig. **16.26a** Allport, G.W. & Postman, L. (1947). *The Psychology of Rumor.* Copyright © 1947 Henry Holt & Company. Copyright © Graphic Presentation Services.

Fig. **16.27** Johns, M. et al., Knowing is Half the Battle. *Psychological Science, 16* (3): 175–179, Fig. 1. Copyright © 2005 American Psychological Society. Adapted with permission of Blackwell Publishing.

Fig. **16.34** Verona, E. & Carbonell, J.L. (April, 2000). Female violence and personality: Evidence for a pattern of overcontrolled hostility among one time violent female offenders. *Criminal Justice and Behavior, 27* (2), 187, Fig. 1. Copyright © 2000 by American Association for Correctional Psychologists. Adapted with permission of Sage Publications.

Glossary

A

abnormal behavior Behavior that is personally distressful, personally dysfunctional, and/or so culturally deviant that other people judge it to be inappropriate or maladaptive.

absolute refractory period The brief time interval following an action potential when a neuron is incapable of being stimulated to fire another impulse.

absolute threshold The lowest intensity at which a stimulus can be detected 50 percent of the time.

abstinence violation effect A response to a lapse in which a person blames himself or herself and concludes that he or she is incapable of resisting high-risk situations.

accommodation In cognitive development, the process by which new experiences cause existing schemas to change.

acetylcholine (ACh) An excitatory neurotransmitter that operates at synapses with muscles and is also the transmitter in some neural networks involved in memory.

achievement goal theory A theory of achievement motivation that stresses the goals (ego versus mastery) and motivational climates that influence achievement strivings.

achievement test A measure of an individual's degree of accomplishment in a particular subject or task based on a relatively standardized set of experiences.

action potential A nerve impulse resulting from the depolarization of an axon's cell membrane.

activation-synthesis theory Maintains that dreams represent the brain's attempt to interpret random patterns of neural activation triggered by the brain stem during sleep.

adaptations Biological and behavioral changes that allow organisms to meet recurring environmental challenges to their survival, thereby increasing their reproductive ability.

adaptive significance The manner in which a particular behavior enhances an organism's chances of survival and reproduction in its natural environment.

adolescence The period of development that involves a gradual transition between childhood and adulthood.

adolescent egocentrism Highly self-focused thinking, particularly in the early teenage years.

adoption study A research method in behavior genetics in which adopted people are compared on some characteristic with both their biological and adoptive parents in an attempt to determine the strength of the characteristic's genetic component.

adrenal glands Endocrine glands that release stress hormones, including catecholamines and corticosteroids.

aerobic exercise Sustained activity that elevates the heart rate and increases the body's need for oxygen.

agonist A drug that increases or mimics the activity of a neurotransmitter.

agoraphobia A fear of being in places or situations (e.g., on a bridge or a bus, in crowds or wide open spaces) from which escape might be difficult in the event of sudden incapacitation.

alcohol myopia When intoxicated, a "shortsightedness" in thinking (a failure to consider consequences) caused by an inability to pay attention to as much information as when sober.

algorithms Procedures, such as mathematical formulas, that automatically generate correct solutions to problems.

all-or-none law States that an action potential is not proportional to the intensity of stimulation; a neuron either fires with maximum intensity or it does not fire (compare with *graded potential*).

alpha waves A brain-wave pattern of 8 to 12 cycles per second that is characteristic of humans in a relaxed, drowsy state.

Alzheimer's disease (AD) A brain disorder, typically but not always occurring in old age, whose prominent features are memory loss and confused thinking.

amplitude The vertical size of the sound wave, which gives rise to the perception of loudness and is measured in terms of decibels.

amygdala A limbic system structure that helps organize emotional response patterns.

anorexia nervosa An eating disorder involving a severe and sometimes fatal restriction of food intake.

antagonist A drug that inhibits or decreases the action of a neurotransmitter.

anterograde amnesia Memory loss for events that occur after the initial onset of amnesia.

anticipatory nausea and vomiting (ANV) Classically conditioned nausea and vomiting that occur when cancer patients are exposed to stimuli associated with their treatment.

antigens Literally, antibody generators, or foreign substances that activate the cells of the immune system.

antisocial personality disorder A long-term stable disorder characterized by a lack of conscience, defects in empathy, and a tendency to act out in an impulsive manner that disregards future consequences.

anxiety An emotional state characterized by apprehension accompanied by physiological arousal and fearful behavior.

anxiety disorders A group of behavior disorders in which anxiety and associated maladaptive behaviors are the core of the disturbance.

aphasia The partial or total loss of ability to understand speech (receptive aphasia) or to produce it (productive aphasia).

applied behavior analysis A process in which operant conditioning is combined with scientific data collection to solve individual and societal problems.

applied research   Research that is designed to solve or examine specific, practical problems.

approach-approach conflict   A conflict in which an individual is simultaneously attracted to two incompatible positive goals.

approach-avoidance conflict   A conflict in which an individual is simultaneously attracted to and repelled by the same goal.

aptitude test   A measure of a person's ability to profit from further training or experience in an occupation or skill; usually based on a measure of skills gained over a person's lifetime rather than during a specific course of study.

archetypes   In Jung's theory, innate concepts and memories (e.g., God, the hero, the good mother); memories that reside in the collective unconscious.

archival measures   Records or past documents that contain information about some type of behavior.

assimilation   In cognitive development, the process by which new experiences are incorporated into existing schemas.

association cortex   The areas of the cerebral cortex that do not have sensory or motor functions but are involved in the integration of neural activity that underlies perception, language, and other higher-order mental processes.

associative network   The view that long-term memory is organized as a massive network of associated ideas and concepts.

attachment   The strong emotional bond that develops between two people; developmentally, the bond between children and their primary caregivers.

attention deficit/hyperactivity disorder (ADHD)   A disorder, usually originating in childhood, that may take the form of attentional difficulties, hyperactivity/impulsivity, or a combination of the two that results in impaired functioning.

attitude   A positive or negative evaluative reaction toward a stimulus (e.g., toward a person, action, object, or concept).

attribution   A judgment about the causes of our own and other people's behavior.

authoritarian parents   Caregivers who exert control over their children within a cold, unresponsive, or rejecting relationship.

authoritative parents   Caregivers who are controlling but warm; they establish and enforce clear rules within a caring, supportive atmosphere.

autistic disorder   A severe developmental disorder characterized by extreme unresponsiveness to others, poor communication skills, and highly repetitive and rigid behavior patterns.

autobiographical memories   Recollections of personally experienced events that make up the "story of our life."

automatic (unconscious) processing   Mental activities that occur with minimal or no conscious control or awareness.

autonomic nervous system   The branch of the peripheral nervous system that stimulates the body's involuntary muscles (e.g., heart) and internal organs.

availability heuristic   A rule of thumb used to make likelihood judgments based on how easily examples of that category of events come to mind or are "available" in memory.

aversion therapy   A form of therapy in which a conditioned stimulus that currently evokes a positive but maladaptive response is paired with a noxious, unpleasant unconditioned stimulus, in an attempt to condition a repulsion toward the conditioned stimulus.

aversive punishment (positive punishment, punishment by application)   A type of punishment in which an operant response is weakened by the subsequent presentation of a noxious stimulus.

avoidance-avoidance conflict   A conflict in which an individual must choose between two undesirable alternatives.

avoidance conditioning   A form of learning in which an organism learns a response to avoid an undesirable consequence.

axon   An extension from one side of the neuron cell body that conducts nerve impulses to other neurons, muscles, or glands.

B

basic research   Research designed to obtain knowledge for its own sake.

basilar membrane   A membrane that runs the length of the cochlea and contains the organ of Corti and its sound receptor hair cells.

behavioral activation system (BAS)   A neural system that is activated by cues indicating potential reward and positive need gratification. Activity in this neural system causes the person to begin or to increase movement toward positive goals in anticipation of pleasure.

behavioral activation treatment   A treatment for depression that engages clients in life activities designed to increase positive reinforcement in their lives.

behavioral assessment   The measurement of behavior through direct observation and application of a coding system.

behavioral inhibition system (BIS)   A neural system that is activated by cues indicating potential pain, nonreinforcement, and punishment. Activity in this neural system produces fear, inhibition of behavior, as well as escape and avoidance behaviors.

behavioral neuroscience   A subfield of psychology that examines brain processes and other physiological functions that underlie our behavior, sensory experiences, emotions, and thoughts.

behavioral perspective   A view that emphasizes how the environment and learning experiences shape and control behavior.

behavioral signatures   Consistent ways of responding in particular classes of situations.

behavior genetics   The scientific study of the role of genetic inheritance in behavior.

behaviorism   A school of psychology that emphasizes the effects of learning and environmental control on behavior and maintains that the proper subject matter of psychology is observable behavior.

behavior modification   Therapeutic procedures based on operant conditioning principles, such as positive reinforcement, operant extinction, and punishment.

behavior-outcome expectancy   The subjective likelihood that a particular consequence will follow a particular behavior in a given situation.

belief bias   The tendency to abandon logical rules and to form a conclusion based on one's existing beliefs.

beta waves   A brain-wave pattern of 15 to 30 cycles per second that is characteristic of humans who are in an alert waking state.

bilingualism   The use of two languages in daily life.

binocular depth cues   Depth cues that require the use of both eyes.

binocular disparity   The binocular depth cue produced by the projection of slightly different images of an object on the retinas of the two eyes.

biologically based mechanisms   Evolved biological structures that receive input from the environment, process the information, and respond to it.

biological perspective   A view that focuses on the role of biological factors in behavior, including biochemical and brain processes, as well as genetic and evolutionary factors.

bipolar disorder   A mood disorder in which intermittent mania appears against a background of depression.

blindsight   A disorder in which people are blind in part of their visual field yet, in special tests, respond to stimuli in that field despite reporting that they cannot see those stimuli.

blood-brain barrier   A specialized lining of cells in the brain's blood vessels that screens out foreign substances while letting nutrients pass through to neurons.

bottom-up processing   Perceptual processes that begin with the analysis of individual elements of the stimulus and work up to the brain's integration of them into a unified perception.

borderline personality disorder (BPD)   A serious personality disorder characterized by severe instability in behavior, emotion, identity, and interpersonal relationships.

brain stem   The portion of the brain formed by the swelling of the spinal cord as it enters the skull; its structures regulate basic survival functions of the body, such as heart rate and respiration.

British empiricism   A 17th-century school of philosophy championed by Locke, according to which all the contents of the mind are gained experientially through the senses.

Broca's area   A region of the left frontal lobe involved in speech production.

bulimia nervosa   An eating disorder that involves a repeated cycle of binge eating followed by purging of the food.

bystander effect   The principle that the presence of multiple bystanders inhibits each person's tendency to help, largely due to social comparison or diffusion of responsibility.

C

Cannon-Bard theory   A theory of emotion that proposed that the thalamus sends simultaneous messages to the cortex (producing our experience of emotion) and to the viscera and skeletal muscles, producing actions and physiological responses.

case study   An in-depth analysis of an individual, group, or event.

catatonic schizophrenia   A schizophrenic reaction characterized by alternating stuporous states and agitated excitement, during which the person can be quite dangerous.

catharsis   The idea that performing an act of aggression discharges aggressive energy and temporarily reduces our impulse to aggress.

central nervous system   The portion of the nervous system that includes the brain and the spinal cord.

central route to persuasion   Occurs when people think carefully about a message and are influenced because they find the arguments compelling.

cephalocaudal principle   The tendency for physical development to proceed in a head-to-foot direction.

cerebellum   A convoluted hindbrain structure involved in motor coordination and some aspects of learning and memory.

cerebral cortex   The gray, convoluted outer covering of the brain that is the seat of higher-order sensory, motor, perceptual, and mental processes.

cerebrum   The most advanced portion of the brain, containing the cerebral cortex and underlying structures.

chaining   An operant conditioning procedure used to develop a sequence (chain) of responses by reinforcing each response with the opportunity to perform the next response.

cholecystokinin (CCK)   A peptide (hormone) that helps produce satiety and cessation of eating.

chromosomes   Tightly coiled strands of deoxyribonucleic acid (DNA) and protein that contain the genes.

chunking   Combining individual items into larger units of meaning.

circadian rhythms   Biological cycles within the body that occur on an approximately 24-hour cycle.

classical conditioning   A procedure in which a formerly neutral stimulus (the conditioned stimulus) comes to elicit a conditioned response by virtue of being paired with an unconditioned stimulus that naturally elicits a similar response (the unconditioned response).

cochlea   A small coil-shaped structure of the inner ear that contains the receptors for sound.

cognitive-affective personality system (CAPS)   A model that organizes five "person variables" that account for how a person might respond to a particular situation; the dynamic interplay among these five factors, together with the characteristics of the situation, accounts for individual differences between people, as well as differences in people's behavior across different situations.

cognitive appraisal   The process of making judgments about situations, personal capabilities, likely consequences, and personal meaning of consequences.

cognitive behaviorism   A behavioral approach that incorporates cognitive concepts, suggesting that the environment influences our behavior by affecting our thoughts and giving us information.

cognitive map   A mental representation of the spatial layout of an area.

cognitive neuroscience   An area of psychology that intersects the subfields of cognitive psychology and physiological psychology and examines brain processes that underlie mental activity.

cognitive perspective   A view that emphasizes humans as rational information processors and problem solvers, and that focuses on the mental processes that influence behavior.

cognitive-process dream theories   Approaches that focus on how (rather than why) we dream, and propose that dreaming and waking thought are produced by the same mental systems in the brain.

cognitive process theories   Approaches to intelligence that analyze the mental processes that underlie intelligent thinking.

cognitive psychology   An area of psychology that specializes in studying mental processes such as thinking, memory, planning, reasoning, attention, and perception.

cognitive relaxation   A state of mental quiescence produced by meditation and other methods.

cognitive restructuring   A cognitive stress-reduction approach that involves attempts to detect, dispute, and change maladaptive or irrational ideas that trigger negative emotions.

collective unconscious   Jung's notion of an unconscious that consists of innate ancestral memories.

collectivism   A cultural orientation that emphasizes the achievement of group rather than individual goals and in which personal identity is largely defined by ties to the larger social group (compare with *individualism*).

common factors   Therapeutic elements that are possessed by virtually any type of therapy and that may contribute to the similar positive effects shown by many different treatment approaches.

communicator credibility   The degree to which an audience views a communicator as believable, largely based on the communicator's expertise and trustworthiness.

companionate love   An affectionate relationship characterized by commitment and caring about the partner's well-being; sometimes contrasted with passionate love, which is more intensely emotional.

compensatory response   A bodily response that opposes a drug's effects and occurs in an attempt to restore homeostasis.

competency   A legal decision that a defendant is mentally capable of understanding the nature of the charges, participating meaningfully in the trial, and consulting with his or her attorney.

competency-focused intervention   Prevention programs that are designed to enhance personal resources needed to cope with situations that might otherwise cause psychological disorders.

compulsion   A repetitive act that the person feels compelled to carry out, often in response to an obsessive thought or image.

computerized axial tomography (CT, or CAT) scan   A method of scanning the brain with narrow beams of X rays that are then analyzed and combined by a computer to provide pictures of brain structures from many different angles.

concept   A mental category containing similiar objects, people, and events.

concordance   The likelihood that two people share a particular characteristic.

concrete operational stage   In Piaget's theory, the stage of cognitive development during which children can perform basic mental operations concerning problems that involve tangible (i.e., "concrete") objects and situations.

conditioned response (CR)   In classical conditioning, a response to a conditioned stimulus; the conditioned response is established by pairing a conditioned stimulus with an unconditioned stimulus that evokes a similar response.

conditioned stimulus (CS)   A stimulus that comes to evoke a conditioned response after being paired with an unconditioned stimulus.

conditioned taste aversion   A learned repulsion to a food that formerly was neutral or desired, by virtue of pairing the food with an aversive unconditioned stimulus.

conditions of worth   Internalized standards for self-worth fostered by conditional positive regard from others.

conduct disorder   A pattern of abnormal behavior in which children violate important social norms and show disregard for the rights of others.

conduction deafness   Hearing loss caused by damage to the mechanical system that conducts sound waves to the cochlea.

cones   Photoreceptors in the retina that function best in bright light and are differentially sensitive to red, green, or blue wavelengths.

confirmation bias   The tendency to seek and favor information that reinforces our beliefs rather than to be open to disconfirming information.

confounding of variables   In experiments, a situation in which the independent variable is intertwined or mixed up with another, uncontrolled variable; thus we cannot tell which variable is responsible for changes in the behavior of interest (i.e., in the dependent variable).

congruence   Consistency between self-perceptions and experience.

consciousness   Our moment-to-moment awareness of ourselves and our environment; consciousness involves selective attention to ongoing thoughts, perceptions, and feelings.

conservation   The principle that basic properties of objects, such as their mass or quantity, stay the same (are "conserved") even though their outward appearance may change.

construct validity   The extent to which a test measures the psychological construct (e.g., intelligence, anxiety) that it is purported to measure.

content validity   The extent to which test items adequately sample the domain that the test is supposed to measure (e.g., intelligence, mathematical reasoning).

context-dependent memory   The phenomenon that it is typically easier to remember something in the same environment in which it was originally learned or experienced.

continuous reinforcement   A reinforcement schedule in which each response of a particular type is followed by reinforcement.

control group   In an experiment, the group that either is not exposed to the treatment or receives a zero level of the independent variable.

controlled (conscious) processing   Mental processing that requires volitional control and attentiveness.

conventional moral reasoning   According to Kohlberg, the stage at which moral judgments are based on conformity to social expectations, laws, and duties.

convergence   A binocular depth cue produced by the muscles that rotate the eyes as they focus on nearby objects.

conversion disorder   A disorder in which serious neurological symptoms, such as paralysis, loss of sensation, or blindness suddenly occur without physical cause.

coping self-efficacy   Beliefs relating to our ability to deal effectively with a stressful stimulus or situation, including pain.

corpus callosum   A broad band of white, myelinated fibers that connects the left and right cerebral hemispheres and allows the two hemispheres to communicate with one another.

correlational research   Research that measures two or more naturally occurring variables and examines whether they are statistically related.

correlation coefficient   A statistic that indicates the direction and strength of a relation between two variables; values can range from +1.00 to −1.00.

counterbalancing   In experiments, a procedure in which each participant engages in all of the conditions. The order of the conditions is altered for different participants so that, overall, no condition has an order advantage relative to the other conditions.

counterconditioning   The process of conditioning an incompatible response to a particular stimulus to eliminate a maladaptive response (e.g., anxiety), as occurs in systematic desensitization.

creativity   The ability to produce something that is both new and valuable.

criterion-related validity   The ability of psychological test scores to correlate with some present or future behavior assumed to be influenced by the construct measured by the test.

critical periods   Limited time periods during which plasticity can occur as a result of experience or in response to injury; in development, a time period in which exposure to particular kinds of stimulation is required for normal growth to occur.

cross-sectional design   A research design that simultaneously compares people of different ages at a particular point in time.

crystallized intelligence (g_c)   Intellectual abilities that depend on a store of information and the acquisition of particular skills (compare with *fluid intelligence*).

cultural display rules   Cultural norms that regulate when and how emotions are expressed.

culturally competent therapists   Practitioners who have a set of therapeutic skills, including scientific mindedness, the ability to consider both cultural and individual factors, and the capacity to introduce culture-specific elements into therapy with people from minority cultures.

cultural psychology   An area of psychology, sometimes called *cross-cultural psychology,* that explores how culture is transmitted to its members and examines psychological similarities and differences that occur between people from diverse cultures.

culture   The enduring values, beliefs, behaviors, and traditions that are shared by a large group of people and passed from one generation to the next.

culture-bound disorders   Behavior disorders whose specific forms are restricted to one particular cultural context.

cytokines   Chemical molecules released by immune cells that produce fever and inflammation, promote the healing of injured tissue, and activate and direct other immune cells.

D

dark adaptation   The progressive increase in brightness sensitivity that occurs over time as photopigments regenerate themselves during exposure to low levels of illumination.

decay theory   Maintains that with time and disuse, the physical memory trace in the nervous system fades away.

decibel   A logarithmic measure of sound intensity.

decision criterion   In signal detection theory, the potentially changing standard of how certain a person must be that a stimulus is present in order to report its presence.

declarative memory   Our memory for factual knowledge, which comprises two subcategories: knowledge pertaining to personal experiences (episodic memory) and knowledge of general facts and language (semantic memory).

deductive reasoning   Reasoning from a general principle to a specific case.

deep structure   A linguistic term that refers to the underlying meaning of a spoken or written sentence; the meanings that make up deep structure are stored as concepts and rules in long-term memory.

defense mechanisms   Unconscious processes that help us cope with anxiety and the pain of traumatic experiences. Defense mechanisms prevent the expression of anxiety-arousing impulses or allow them to appear in disguised forms.

deindividuation   A state of increased anonymity in which a person, often as part of a group or crowd, engages in disinhibited behavior.

deinstitutionalization movement   The attempt to move the primary locus of treatment from mental hospitals to the community.

delta waves   Low-frequency, high-amplitude brain waves that occur in stage 3 sleep and predominate in stage 4 sleep.

delusions   False beliefs, often involving themes of persecution or grandeur, that are sustained in the face of evidence that normally would be sufficient to destroy them.

demand characteristics   Cues picked up by research participants to guess the purpose or hypothesis of a study, thereby causing them to alter their behavior.

dementia   The gradual loss of cognitive abilities that accompanies brain deterioration and interferes with normal functioning.

dendrites   Small branching fibers that extend from the soma of a neuron and receive messages from adjacent neurons.

dependent variable   In an experiment, the factor measured by the researcher that presumably is influenced by the independent variable.

depressants   Drugs—including alcohol, barbiturates, and tranquilizers—that reduce neural activity and can decrease feelings of tension and anxiety.

depressive attributional pattern   The tendency of depressed people to attribute negative outcomes to their own inadequacies and positive outcomes to factors outside of themselves.

depressive cognitive triad   A pattern of negative evaluations of the self, the world, and the future often found in depressed people.

descriptive research   Research in which the main goal is to carefully describe how organisms behave, particularly in natural settings.

descriptive statistics   Statistics that summarize and describe the characteristics of a set of scores.

dialectical behavior therapy (DBT)   A recently developed cognitive-behavioral treatment for borderline personality disorder.

difference threshold   The smallest difference between two similar stimuli that people can detect; also called the *just noticeable difference (jnd).*

discourse   The combining of sentences into larger language units, such as paragraphs, articles, novels, and so on.

discrimination (classical conditioning) The occurrence of a conditioned response to one stimulus but not to another stimulus.

discrimination (social behavior) Treating people unfairly based on the group to which they belong.

discriminative stimulus An antecedent stimulus that signals the likelihood of certain consequences if a response is made.

disorganized schizophrenia A schizophrenic disorder marked by verbal incoherence, disordered thought processes, disorganized behavior, and inappropriate emotional responses.

displacement The capacity of language to represent objects and conditions that are not physically present.

dissociation theories (of hypnosis) Views that focus on hypnosis as an altered state involving a division ("dissociation") of consciousness; one theory proposes that the hypnotized person simultaneously experiences two streams of consciousness that are cut off from one another.

dissociative disorders Disorders that involve a major dissociation of personal identity or memory.

dissociative identity disorder (DID) A dissociative disorder in which two or more separate identities or personalities coexist within an individual.

divergent thinking A creative form of thinking that involves generating novel ideas that diverge from the normal ways of thinking about something.

divided attention The ability to perform more than one activity at the same time.

dodo bird verdict The conclusion reached by some psychotherapy researchers that virtually all treatment approaches have similar success rates.

door-in-the-face technique A manipulation technique in which a persuader makes a large request, expecting you to reject it, and then presents a smaller request.

dopamine hypothesis States that the symptoms of schizophrenia are produced by overactivity of the dopamine system in areas of the brain that regulate emotional expression, motivated behavior, and cognitive functioning.

double-blind procedure A procedure in which both the participant and the experimenter are kept unaware of the research condition to which the participant has been assigned.

downward comparison Seeing oneself as better off than the standard for comparison.

drive A state of internal tension that motivates an organism to behave in ways that reduce this tension.

dual coding theory Maintains that if we encode information using both verbal and imagery codes, the chances improve that at least one of the two codes will be available later to support recall.

dual-process theory A modern theory of color vision that combines the trichromatic and opponent-process theories. Light waves are coded by red-, blue-, and green-sensitive cones in the retina and by opponent processes thereafter in the visual system.

dynamic testing A procedure in which static (standardized testing) is followed up with an interaction in which the examiner gives the subject guided feedback on how to improve performance and observes how the subject utilizes the information.

dysthymia A depressive mood disorder of moderate intensity that occurs over a long period of time but does not disrupt functioning as a major depression does.

E

eclecticism An approach to therapy that incorporates principles and procedures from multiple therapies to provide the most suitable treatment to a client.

effect size In meta-analysis, a measure of treatment effectiveness that indicates what percentage of treated clients improve more than the average untreated client.

ego The "executive" of the personality that is partly conscious and that mediates between the impulses of the id, the prohibitions of the superego, and the dictates of reality.

ego-approach goals An achievement orientation that focuses on being judged successful as a result of outperforming others.

ego-avoidance goals An achievement orientation that focuses on avoiding negative judgments by self or others due to failing to outperform others.

egocentrism Difficulty in viewing the world from someone else's perspective.

ego orientation In achievement goal theory, an orientation that defines success in terms of performing at a higher level than others.

elaborative rehearsal Focusing on the meaning of information or relating it to other things we already know.

Electra complex The female version of the Oedipus complex in which the female child experiences erotic feelings toward her father, desires to possess him sexually, and views her mother as a rival.

electroencephalograph (EEG) A device used to record the simultaneous activity of many thousands of neurons through electrodes attached to the scalp.

eliciting stimuli Internal or external cues that evoke an emotional response.

embryo A scientific term for the prenatal organism during the 2nd week through the 8th week after conception.

emotion A pattern of cognitive, physiological, and behavioral responses to situations and events that have relevance to important goals or motives.

emotional intelligence The ability to respond adaptively in the emotional realm by reading and responding appropriately to others' emotions, to be aware of and have the ability to control one's own emotions.

emotion-focused coping Coping strategies directed at minimizing or reducing emotional responses to a stressor.

emotion regulation The processes by which we evaluate and modify our emotional reactions.

empathy The capacity for experiencing the same emotional response being exhibited by another person; in therapy, the ability of a therapist to view the world through the client's eyes and to understand the client's emotions.

empathy-altruism hypothesis The view that pure altruism does exist and that it is produced by the capacity to empathize with the person in need of aid.

empirical approach An approach to test construction in which items (regardless of their content) are chosen that differentiate between two groups that are known to differ on a particular personality variable.

empirically supported therapies (ESTs) Psychotherapy and behavior-change techniques that have been shown to be efficacious in controlled clinical trials.

encoding Getting information into the memory system by translating it into a neural code that the brain processes and stores.

encoding specificity principle States that memory is enhanced when conditions present during retrieval match those that were present during encoding.

endocrine system The body's system of glands that secrete hormones into the bloodstream and thereby affect many bodily functions.

endorphins Natural opiate-like substances that are involved in pain reduction.

entity theorist An individual who believes that people's characteristics are fixed and relatively unchangeable.

episodic memory Our store of factual knowledge concerning personal experiences—when, where, and what happened in the episodes of our lives.

equal status contact The principle that prejudice between people is most likely to be reduced when they engage in sustained close contact, have equal status within the context of their interaction, work to achieve a common goal that requires cooperation, and are supported by broader social norms that encourage prejudice reduction.

escape conditioning A form of learning in which the organism learns to perform a behavior to terminate an aversive stimulus.

evolution A change over time in the frequency with which particular genes, and the characteristics they produce, occur within an interbreeding population.

evolutionary/circadian sleep models The view that in the course of evolution, each species developed an adaptive circadian sleep-wake pattern that increased its chances of survival in relation to its environmental demands.

evolutionary personality theory A recently developed attempt to account for personality traits such as the Big Five in terms of the evolutionary history of the human species; these traits are thought to develop from processes of natural selection.

evolutionary psychology A field of study that focuses on the role of evolutionary processes (especially natural selection) in the development of adaptive psychological mechanisms and social behavior in humans.

expectancy × value theory A cognitive theory stating that goal-directed behavior is jointly influenced by (1) the person's expectancy that a particular behavior will contribute to reaching the goal and (2) how positively or negatively the person values the goal.

experiment A research method in which the researcher manipulates an independent variable under controlled conditions and measures whether this produces changes in a dependent variable.

experimental group In an experiment, the group that receives a treatment or is exposed to an active level of the independent variable.

experimenter expectancy effects Subtle and unintentional ways in which an experimenter influences participants to behave in a way that will confirm the experimenter's hypothesis.

explicit memory Conscious or intentional memory retrieval.

explicit prejudice Prejudice that is expressed publicly, as when talking with someone or responding to a questionnaire.

exposure therapies Therapeutic techniques designed to extinguish anxiety responses by exposing clients to anxiety-arousing stimuli or situations while preventing escape or avoidance.

expressed emotion A family interaction pattern, involving criticism, hostility, and overinvolvement, that is associated with relapse in formerly hospitalized schizophrenic patients who return home.

expressive behaviors Observable behavior that accompanies subjectively experienced emotions.

external validity The degree to which the results of a study can be generalized to other people, settings, and conditions.

extinction (classical conditioning) Occurs when a conditioned stimulus is presented without the unconditioned stimulus, causing the conditioned response to weaken and eventually stop occurring.

extinction (operant conditioning) See *operant extinction*.

extrinsic motivation Motivation to perform a behavior to obtain external rewards and reinforcers, such as money, status, attention, and praise.

F

facial feedback hypothesis States that somatic feedback from facial muscles to the brain influences emotional experience.

factor analysis A statistical technique that permits a researcher to reduce a large number of measures to a small number of clusters or factors; it identifies the clusters of behavior or test scores that are highly correlated with one another.

fantasy-prone personality The tendency of some people to spend much of their waking time living in a vivid, rich fantasy world that they control.

feature detectors Sensory neurons that respond to particular features of a stimulus, such as its shape, angle, or color.

feminist therapy An orientation that focuses on women's issues and strives to help female clients achieve greater self-determination.

fetal alcohol syndrome (FAS) A severe group of abnormalities that results from prenatal exposure to alcohol.

fetus A scientific term for the prenatal organism from the 9th week after conception until birth.

figure-ground relations Perceptual organization in which a focal stimulus is perceived as a figure against a background of other stimuli.

fixation A state of arrested development due to unresolved conflicts at a particular earlier psychosexual stage.

fixed action pattern An unlearned response that is automatically triggered by a simple (releaser) stimulus.

fixed-interval (FI) schedule A reinforcement schedule in which the first response of a particular type is reinforced after a constant time interval.

fixed-ratio (FR) schedule A reinforcement schedule in which reinforcement is given after a constant number of responses of a particular type.

flashbulb memories Recollections that seem so vivid and clear that we can picture them as if they were snapshots of moments in time.

fluid intelligence (g_f)   The ability to deal with novel problem-solving situations for which personal experience does not supply a solution (compare with *crystallized intelligence*).

foot-in-the-door technique   A manipulation technique in which the persuader gets you to comply with a small request first and later presents a larger request.

forebrain   Brain structures above the midbrain, including the thalamus, hypothalamus, limbic system, and the cerebral hemispheres; involved in higher-order sensory, motor, and cognitive functions.

formal operational stage   In Piaget's theory, the period in which individuals are able to think logically and systematically about both concrete and abstract problems, form hypotheses, and test them in a thoughtful way.

fovea   A small area in the center of the retina that contains only cones and where visual acuity is greatest.

free association   In psychoanalysis, the procedure of verbalizing all thoughts that enter consciousness without censorship.

frequency   In audition, the number of cycles per second in a sound wave that is responsible for the pitch of the sound; the measure of frequency is the hertz (Hz), which equals one cycle per second.

frequency distribution   For a set of data, a table that shows how frequently each score value has occurred for a particular variable.

frequency theory of pitch perception   Maintains that the number of nerve impulses sent to the brain by the hair cells of the cochlea corresponds to the frequency of the sound wave; this theory is accurate at low frequencies.

fully functioning persons   Rogers's term for self-actualized people who are free from unrealistic conditions of worth and who exhibit congruence, spontaneity, creativity, and a desire to develop still further.

functional fixedness   A phenomenon often found in problem-solving tasks in which the customary use of an object interferes with its use in a novel situation.

functionalism   An early school of American psychology that focused on the functions of consciousness and behavior in helping organisms adapt to their environment and satisfy their needs.

functional MRI (fMRI)   A brain scanning procedure that produces pictures of blood flow in the brain taken less than a second apart.

fundamental attribution error   The tendency to underestimate the impact of the situation and overestimate the role of personal factors when explaining other people's behavior.

fundamental emotional patterns   Basic emotional response patterns that are believed to be innate.

G

gate control theory   A theory of pain that postulates the existence of gating mechanisms in the spinal cord and brain that can increase or decrease the experience of pain by regulating the flow of pain impulses to the brain.

gender constancy   The understanding that being male or female is a permanent part of a person.

gender identity   The sense of "femaleness" or "maleness" that is an integral part of our identity.

gender schemas   Organized mental structures that contain our understanding of the attributes and behaviors that are appropriate and expected for males and females.

general adaptation syndrome (GAS)   Selye's description of the body's responses to a stressor, which includes successive phases of alarm, resistance, and exhaustion.

generalized anxiety disorder   A chronic state of diffuse, or "free-floating," anxiety that is not attached to specific situations or objects.

generativity   The principle that, in any given language, symbols can be combined to generate an infinite number of messages that have novel meaning.

genes   The biological units of heredity, located on the chromosomes.

genotype   The specific genetic makeup of the individual, which may or may not be expressed in the observable phenotype.

genuineness   The ability of a therapist to honestly express her or his feelings to a client.

Gestalt laws of perceptual organization   The notion that people group and interpret stimuli in accordance with similarity, proximity, closure, and continuity.

Gestalt psychology   A German school of psychology that emphasized the natural organization of perceptual elements into wholes, or patterns, as well as the role of insight in problem solving.

***g* factor**   A general intellectual capacity that underlies more specific intellectual abilities.

glucose   A simple sugar that is the body's (and especially the brain's) major source of immediately usable fuel.

graded potential   A change in the electrical potential of a neuron that is proportional to the intensity of the incoming stimulation but not sufficient to produce an action potential.

grammar   In any given language, the set of rules that dictates how symbols can be combined to create meaningful units of communication.

group polarization   When a group of like-minded people discusses an issue, the "average" opinion of group members tends to become more extreme.

groupthink   The tendency of group members to suspend critical thinking because they are motivated to seek agreement.

gustation   The sense of taste.

H

habituation   A decrease in the strength of a response to a repeated stimulus.

hallucinations   False perceptions that have a compelling sense of reality.

hallucinogens   Drugs, such as LSD and PCP, that distort or intensify sensory experiences and evoke hallucinations and disordered thought processes.

hardiness   A stress-resistant personality pattern that involves the factors of commitment, control, and challenge.

harm reduction   A prevention strategy that is designed not to eliminate a problem behavior but to reduce its harmful consequences.

health psychology   The study of psychological and behavioral factors in the prevention and treatment of illness and in enhancement of health.

Hering's opponent-process theory   The color vision theory stating that the retina contains three sets of color receptors that respond differentially to red-green, blue-yellow, and black-white; the opponent processes that result can produce a perception of any hue.

heritability coefficient   A numerical estimate of the percentage of group variability in a particular characteristic that can be attributed to genetic factors.

hertz (Hz)   The measure of sound wave frequency as cycles per second.

heuristics   A method of problem solving characterized by quick and easy search procedures similar to rules of thumb.

higher-order conditioning   In classical conditioning, a neutral stimulus becomes a conditioned stimulus after it is paired with another conditioned stimulus (rather than with the original unconditioned stimulus).

hindbrain   The part of the brain situated immediately above the spinal cord that contains the brain stem and cerebellum.

hippocampus   A structure of the limbic system that plays a key role in the formation and storage of memories.

histogram   A graph of a frequency distribution.

homeostasis   The maintenance of biological equilibrium, or balance, within the body.

hormones   Chemical substances secreted by the glands of the endocrine system that travel in the bloodstream and affect bodily organs, psychological functions, and development.

humanistic perspective (humanism)   A psychological view that emphasizes personal freedom, choice, and self-actualization.

hypnosis   A condition of enhanced suggestibility in which some people are able to experience imagined situations as if they were real.

hypnotic susceptibility scale   A set of induction procedures and test questions that enable researchers to measure a person's responsiveness to hypnotic suggestions.

hypochondriasis   A somatoform disorder characterized by an overreaction to physical symptoms and a conviction that one has or is on the verge of a serious illness.

hypothalamus   A forebrain structure located below the thalamus and above the pituitary gland that controls autonomic and hormonal processes and plays a major role in many aspects of motivation and emotional behavior.

hypothesis   A tentative explanation or a prediction about some phenomenon.

I

id   The primitive and unconscious part of the personality that contains the instincts.

illusions   Incorrect perceptions based on false perceptual hypotheses that often result from constancies that do not apply to the stimuli in question.

imaginal thought   A form of thinking that uses images that can be from any sense modality.

implicit memory   Occurs when memory influences our behavior without conscious awareness.

implicit prejudice   Prejudice that is hidden from public view, either intentionally or because the person is not aware that he or she is prejudiced.

imprinting   In some species, a sudden, biologically primed form of attachment.

inattentional blindness   The failure of unattended stimuli to register in consciousness.

incentive   An environmental stimulus or condition that motivates behavior.

incremental theorist   An individual who believes that people's characteristics are changeable, not fixed.

incubation   A phenomenon in which the solution to a problem suddenly appears in consciousness after a problem solver has stopped thinking about it for a while.

independent variable   In an experiment, the factor that is manipulated by the researcher.

individualism   A cultural orientation, characteristic of many Western nations, that favors the achievement of individual over group goals; self-identity is based primarily on one's own attributes and achievements (compare with *collectivism*).

inductive reasoning   Reasoning that proceeds from a set of specific facts to a general conclusion or principle.

indulgent parents   Caregivers who have warm and caring relationships with their children but do not provide much guidance and discipline.

infantile amnesia   An inability to remember personal experiences from the first few years of our lives.

inferential statistics   Statistics that tell us how confident we can be in drawing conclusions or inferences about a population based on findings obtained from a sample.

informational social influence   Following the opinions or behavior of other people because we believe that they have accurate knowledge and that what they are doing is "right."

informed consent   The principle that prior to agreeing to participate in research, a person should be fully informed about the procedures, the benefits, the risks involved, the right to withdraw at any time without penalty, and matters of confidentiality and privacy.

insanity   A legal decision that a defendant was so severely impaired at the time a crime was committed that he or she was incapable of appreciating the wrongfulness of the act or controlling his or her behavior.

insight   In Gestalt psychology, the sudden perception of a useful relation or solution to a problem; in psychoanalysis, the conscious awareness of unconscious dynamics that underlie psychological problems.

insomnia   A sleep disorder involving chronic difficulty in falling asleep, staying asleep, or experiencing restful sleep.

instinct   An inherited characteristic, common to all members of a species, that automatically produces a particular response when the organism is exposed to a particular stimulus.

instinctive drift   The tendency for instinctive behaviors to override a conditioning procedure, thus making it difficult to create or maintain a conditioned response.

instrumental behaviors   In emotion, coping behaviors that are directed at achieving the goal or performing the task that is relevant to the emotion.

intelligence   The ability to acquire knowledge, to think and reason effectively, and to deal adaptively with the environment.

intelligence quotient (IQ)   Originally defined as mental age (MA) divided by chronological age (CA) multiplied by 100 (IQ = [MA/CA] × 100); an IQ of 100 indicates that an individual is average for his or her age group. IQ scores today are based on norms derived from people of various ages.

interaction   In analyzing causal factors, an interaction occurs when the way in which one factor influences behavior depends on the presence of another factor.

interjudge reliability   The extent to which different observers or scorers agree in their scoring of a particular test or observed behavior.

internal consistency   The extent to which items within a psychological test correlate with one another, indicating that they are measuring a common characteristic.

internal-external locus of control   In Rotter's theory, a generalized expectancy that one's outcomes are under personal versus external control.

internal validity   The degree to which an experiment produces clear causal conclusions; internal validity is high when there is no confounding of variables.

interneurons   Neurons that are neither sensory nor motor neurons but that perform associative or integrative functions within the nervous system.

interpersonal therapy   A form of brief therapy that focuses on the client's interpersonal problems and seeks to develop new interpersonal skills.

interpretation   In psychoanalysis, a statement made by the analyst that is intended to promote insight in the client.

intrinsic motivation   The motivation to perform a task simply because one finds it interesting or enjoyable for its own sake.

J

James-Lange theory   A theory of emotion that proposed that emotional experience is based on a person's perception of her or his bodily responses.

K

kin selection   The view that organisms are most likely to help others with whom they share the most genes—namely, their offspring and genetic relatives.

kinesthesis   The body sense that provides feedback on the position and movements of our body parts.

knowledge-acquisition components   In Sternberg's triarchic model of intelligence, the mental capabilities that allow us to learn from our experiences, store information in memory, and combine new insights with previously acquired information.

L

language   A system of symbols and rules for combining them that can produce an infinite number of possible messages and meanings.

language acquisition device (LAD)   In Chomsky's theory, an innate, biologically based mechanism that facilitates the learning of language.

language acquisition support system (LASS)   The social learning opportunities involved in learning a language.

latent learning   Learning that occurs in the absence of reinforcement but is not displayed until reinforcement is later introduced into the situation.

lateralization   The degree of localization of a function in either the right or the left cerebral hemisphere.

law of effect   Thorndike's concept that a response followed by satisfying consequences will become more likely to occur, whereas a response followed by unsatisfying consequences will become less likely to occur.

learned helplessness theory   A theory of depression maintaining that if people are unable to control life events, they develop a state of helplessness that leads to depressive symptoms.

learning   A relatively enduring change in an organism's behavior or performance capabilities that occurs as a result of experience.

lens   The transparent structure behind the pupil that changes its shape to focus images on the retina.

leptin   A hormone secreted by fat cells that decreases general appetite.

levels of processing   The concept that the more deeply we process information, the better it will be remembered.

limbic system   A group of subcortical structures, including the hippocampus and amygdala, that are involved in organizing many goal-directed and emotional behaviors.

linguistic relativity hypothesis   The idea, suggested by Whorf, that people's language determines the ways in which they perceive and think about their world.

longitudinal design   A research approach in which the same people are repeatedly tested as they grow older.

long-term memory   Our vast library of more durable stored memories.

long-term potentiation   An enduring increase in synaptic strength that occurs after a neural circuit is rapidly stimulated.

lowballing   A manipulation technique in which a persuader gets you to commit to some action and then—before you actually perform the behavior—she or he increases the "cost" of that same behavior.

M

magnetic resonance imaging (MRI)   A brain-scanning procedure that produces a highly detailed image of living tissue based on the tissue's response to a magnetic field; can be used to study both structure and, in the case of functional MRI (fMRI), brain functions as they occur.

maintenance rehearsal   The simple rote repetition of information.

major depression   A mood disorder characterized by intense depression that interferes markedly with functioning.

mania   A state of intense emotional and behavioral excitement in which a person feels very optimistic and energized.

mastery goals   Achievement goals that focus on the desire to master a task and learn new knowledge or skills.

mastery orientation   In achievement goal theory, an orientation that defines success in terms of task mastery and achieving one's potential through effort and commitment.

matching effect   In romantic relationships, the tendency for partners to have a similar level of physical attractiveness.

maturation   A genetically programmed biological process that governs our growth.

mean   A statistic that represents the arithmetic average of a set of scores.

means-ends analysis   A heuristic problem-solving device in which people first define a subgoal that they hope to achieve (an "end"), compare that subgoal with their present state of knowledge, and, if there is a discrepancy between them, try to find the means to reduce the difference.

measures of central tendency   Statistics that describe a distribution (a set of data) in terms of a single number that is in some way "typical" of the distribution as a whole.

measures of variability   Statistics that provide information about the spread of scores in a distribution.

median   In a set of data, the point that divides the distribution in half when the individual scores are arranged in order from lowest to highest.

medulla   A brain stem structure that controls vital functions, including heartbeat and respiration.

melatonin   A hormone, secreted by the pineal gland, that has a relaxing effect on the body and promotes a readiness for sleep.

memory   The processes that allow us to record, store, and later retrieve experiences and information.

memory codes   Mental representations of some type of information or stimulus.

memory consolidation   The creation and binding together of neural codes that allow information to be transferred from working memory into long-term memory.

menstrual synchrony   The tendency for some women who live together or are close friends to become more similar to one another in the timing of their menstrual cycles over time.

mental image   A representation of a stimulus that originates inside your brain, rather than from external sensory input.

mental representations   Cognitive representations of the world, including images, ideas, concepts, and principles, that are the foundations of thinking and problem solving.

mental set   The tendency to stick to problem-solving strategies or solutions that have worked in the past.

mere exposure effect   The tendency to evaluate a stimulus more favorably after repeated exposure to it.

meta-analysis   A statistical procedure for combining the results of different studies that examine the same topic.

metabolism   The rate of energy expenditure by the body.

metacognition   Your awareness and understanding of your own cognitive abilities.

metacomponents   In Sternberg's triarchic model of intelligence, the higher-level intellectual abilities used to plan and regulate task performance.

method of loci   A memory aid in which pieces of information (e.g., items in a list) are each associated with a mental image of a different physical location.

midbrain   Brain structures above the hindbrain that are involved in sensory and motor functions and in attention and states of consciousness.

mind-body dualism   The philosophical position that the mind is a nonphysical entity that is not subject to physical laws and therefore cannot be reduced to physical processes; body and mind are separate entities.

Minnesota Multiphasic Personality Inventory-2 (MMPI-2)   A widely used personality test whose items were developed using the empirical approach of comparing various kinds of psychiatric patients with a nonpsychiatric sample.

misinformation effect   The distortion of a memory by misleading postevent information.

mnemonic device   A strategy or technique that aids memory.

mnemonist (memorist)   A person who displays extraordinary memory skills.

mode   A statistic that represents the most frequently occurring score in a distribution of data.

monism   The philosophical position that mental events are reducible to physical events in the brain, so that mind and body are one and the same.

monocular depth cues   Depth cues that require only one eye; include linear perspective, decreasing size, height in the horizontal plane, texture, clarity, light and shadow, motion parallax, and interposition.

mood disorders   Psychological disorders whose core conditions involve maladaptive mood states, such as depression or mania.

mood-congruent recall   The tendency to recall information or events that are congruent with our current mood.

morpheme   The smallest unit of meaning in a given language; English morphemes include whole words, prefixes, and suffixes. There are over 100,000 English morphemes.

motivation   A process that influences the direction, persistence, and vigor of goal-directed behavior.

motivational climate   The achievement context created by adults. In an ego-involving climate, performers are compared with one another and urged to compete to be the best; those who perform best get special attention. In a mastery-involving climate, effort, enjoyment of the activity, and personal improvement are emphasized and rewarded.

motivational interviewing   A treatment approach that avoids confrontation and leads clients to their own realization of a problem and increases their motivation to change.

motor cortex   The cortical area in the rear portion of the frontal lobes that controls voluntary movements on the opposite sides of the body.

motoric thought   Mental representations of motor movements, such as throwing an object.

motor neurons   Specialized neurons that carry neural messages from the brain and spinal cord to the muscles and glands.

multimodal treatments   Substance-abuse interventions that combine a number of treatments, such as aversion therapy and coping skills training.

myelin sheath   A fatty insulating substance on the axon of some neurons that increases the speed of neural transmission.

N

narcolepsy   A sleep disorder that involves extreme daytime sleepiness and sudden, uncontrollable sleep attacks during waking hours.

naturalistic observation   A method in which the researcher observes behavior in a natural setting and tries to avoid influencing the participants being observed.

natural selection   The evolutionary process through which characteristics that increase the likelihood of survival and reproduction are preserved in the gene pool and thereby become more common in a species over time.

need for achievement   The desire to accomplish tasks and attain standards of excellence.

need for positive regard   In Rogers's personality theory, an innate need to be positively evaluated by significant others, which enhances survival potential and need satisfaction.

need for positive self-regard   In Rogers's personality theory, the psychological need to feel positively about oneself that underlies self-enhancement behaviors.

negative correlation   A relation between two variables in which higher scores on one variable are associated with lower scores on the other variable.

negative reinforcement   A response is strengthened by the subsequent removal of an aversive stimulus.

negative symptoms   Schizophrenic symptoms that reflect a lack of normal reactions, such as emotions, speech, or social behaviors.

neglectful parents   Caregivers who provide neither warmth nor rules or guidance.

neoanalytic theorists   Former followers of Freud, such as Adler and Jung, who developed their own psychodynamic theories that generally deemphasized psychosexual factors in favor of social ones and gave increased emphasis to ego functioning.

NEO-PI   An objective personality test that measures the Big Five personality factors.

nerve deafness   Hearing loss caused by damage to the cochlear receptor cells or to the auditory nerve.

neural network (connectionist) model   States that each concept stored in memory is represented by a unique pattern of distributed and simultaneously activated nodes that process information in parallel; also known as a *parallel distributed processing model.*

neural plasticity   The ability of neurons to modify their structure and function in response to experiential factors or injury.

neural stem cells   Immature "uncommitted" cells that can mature into any type of neuron or glial cell needed by the brain.

neurogenesis   The production of new neurons in the nervous system, sometimes to replace neurons that have died or been damaged.

neuromodulators   Neurotransmitter substances that are released by neurons and circulate within the nervous system to affect the sensitivity of many neurons to their natural transmitter substances.

neurons   Nerve cells that constitute the basic building blocks of the nervous system.

neurotic anxiety   In psychoanalytic theory, a state of anxiety that arises when impulses from the id threaten to break through into awareness or behavior.

neurotransmitters   Chemical substances that are released from the axons of one neuron, travel across the synaptic space, and bind to specially keyed receptors in another neuron, where they produce a chemical reaction that is either excitatory or inhibitory.

night terrors   A disorder in which a sleeper—often feeling a strong sense of dread or danger—becomes aroused to a near panic state.

normal curve   A symmetrical bell-shaped curve that represents a theoretical distribution of scores in the population.

normal distribution   A frequency distribution in the shape of a symmetrical or bell-shaped curve that satisfies certain mathematical conditions deduced from the theory of probability.

normative social influence   Conformity motivated by gaining social acceptance and avoiding social rejection.

norm of reciprocity   The tendency to respond in kind when other people treat us well or poorly.

norms (cultural or group)   Rules (often unwritten) that specify what behavior is acceptable and expected for members of a particular culture or group.

norms (test)   Test scores derived from a relevant sample used to evaluate individuals' scores.

null hypothesis   The hypothesis that any observed differences between samples on the variable(s) of interest are due to chance (i.e., in an experiment, the hypothesis that the independent variable had no effect on the dependent variable).

O

object permanence   The recognition that an object continues to exist even when it no longer can be seen.

object relations theories   The view that people form images or mental representations of themselves and other people as a result of early experiences with caregivers.

observational learning   Learning through observing the behavior of a model.

obsession   An unwanted and disturbing thought or image that invades consciousness and is very difficult to control.

Oedipus complex   The male child experiences erotic feelings toward his mother, desires to possess her sexually, and views his father as a rival.

olfaction   The sense of smell.

olfactory bulb   A forebrain structure that receives input from the receptors for the sense of smell.

openness   The client's willingness to become personally invested in the process of therapy that predicts favorable therapeutic outcomes.

operant conditioning   A type of learning in which behavior is modified by its consequences, such as by reinforcement and punishment.

operant discrimination   An operant response occurs when a particular antecedent stimulus is present but not when another antecedent stimulus is present.

operant extinction   Occurs when the absence of reinforcement for a previously reinforced response causes that response to weaken and eventually stop.

operant generalization   An operant response occurs to a new antecedent stimulus that is similar to the original antecedent stimulus.

operational definition   Defining a concept or variable in terms of the specific procedures used to produce or measure it.

opiates   A category of drugs consisting of opium and drugs derived from it, such as morphine, codeine, and heroin.

optic nerve   The bundle of ganglion cell axons that carries information from the visual receptors to the visual area of the thalamus.

organ of Corti   Structures embedded in the basilar membrane that contain the hair cell receptors for sound.

outcome bias   Occurs when an intelligence test score underestimates a person's true intellectual ability.

overconfidence   The pervasive tendency to overestimate one's degree of knowledge and predictive ability.

overlearning   Continued rehearsal past the point of initial learning that significantly improves performance on memory tasks.

P

pain disorder   A somatoform disorder in which the person's complaints of pain cannot be accounted for in terms of degree of physical damage.

panic disorder   An anxiety disorder characterized by unpredictable panic attacks and a pervasive fear that another will occur; may also result in agoraphobia.

parallel distributed processing (PDP) model   A computer model in which each item in memory is represented by a particular pattern of distributed yet interconnected nodes that are activated simultaneously (i.e., that operate in parallel); also known as a *neural network model*.

paranoid schizophrenia   A schizophrenic disorder marked by delusional thinking and suspiciousness.

parasympathetic nervous system   The branch of the autonomic nervous system that slows down bodily processes to conserve energy and reduce arousal.

paraventricular nucleus (PVN)   A cluster of neurons in the hypothalamus packed with receptor sites for transmitters that stimulate or reduce appetite.

partial (intermittent) reinforcement   A reinforcement schedule in which only a portion of the responses of a particular type are followed by a reinforcer.

passionate love   A form of love that involves intense emotional arousal and yearning for one's partner.

Pearson product-moment correlation coefficient   A statistic that reflects the direction and strength of the relation between two variables; can range in magnitude from −1.00 to +1.00.

perception   The process of organizing stimulus input and giving it meaning.

perceptual constancies   The ability to recognize stimulus characteristics— size, color, and so on—under varying conditions.

perceptual schemas   Internal representations that contain the essential features of an object of perception.

perceptual set   A readiness to perceive a stimulus in a particular way based on expectations, motives, emotions, or beliefs.

performance components   In Sternberg's triarchic model of intelligence, the specific mental processes used to perform a task.

peripheral nervous system   All of the neurons that connect the central nervous system with the sensory receptors, the muscles, and the glands.

peripheral route to persuasion   Occurs when people do not scrutinize a message but are influenced mostly by other factors such as a speaker's attractiveness or a message's emotional appeal.

personal constructs   In George Kelly's personality theory, the cognitive categories used to sort events and make comparisons among people and events.

personality   Those biologically and environmentally determined characteristics within the person that account for distinctive and relatively enduring patterns of thinking, feeling, and acting.

personality disorders   Stable, inflexible, and maladaptive ways of thinking, feeling, and acting.

personality traits   Relatively stable cognitive, emotional, and behavioral characteristics that help establish people's individual identities.

personal unconscious   According to Jung, those aspects of the unconscious that arise from the individual's life experiences.

phenomenology   A philosophical approach that focuses on immediate subjective experience.

phenotype   The observable characteristics produced by one's genetic endowment.

pheromones   Chemical signals found in natural body scents.

phobias   Strong and irrational fears of particular objects or circumstances.

phoneme   The smallest unit of sound in a language; the vowel and consonant sounds that are recognized in any given language. English has 40 phonemes.

photopigments   Protein molecules within the rods and cones whose chemical reactions when absorbing light result in the generation of nerve impulses.

placebo   An inactive or inert substance.

placebo control group   A control group that receives an intervention that is assumed to have no therapeutic value.

placebo effect   A change in behavior that occurs because of the expectation or belief that one is receiving a treatment.

place theory of pitch perception   States that sound frequencies are coded in terms of the portion of the basilar membrane where the fluid wave in the cochlea peaks; this theory accounts for perception of frequencies above 4,000 hertz.

pleasure principle   The drive for instant need gratification that is characteristic of the id.

polygenic transmission   A number of genes working together to create a particular phenotypic characteristic.

polygraph   A research and clinical instrument that measures a wide array of physiological responses.

pons   A brain stem structure having sensory and motor tracts whose functions are involved in sleep and dreaming.

population   In a survey, the entire set of individuals about whom we wish to draw a conclusion.

positive correlation   A relation between two variables in which higher scores on one variable are associated with higher scores on the other variable.

positive psychology movement   A view that emphasizes the study of human strengths, fulfillment, and optimal living.

positive reinforcement   A response is strengthened by the subsequent presentation of a stimulus.

positive symptoms   Schizophrenic symptoms such as delusions, hallucinations, and disordered speech and thinking.

positron emission tomography (PET) scan   A procedure that provides a visual display of the absorption of a radioactive substance by neurons, indicating how actively they are involved as the brain performs a task.

postconventional moral reasoning   According to Kohlberg, the stage at which moral judgments are based on a system of internalized, well-thought-out moral principles.

posttraumatic stress disorder (PTSD)   A pattern of distressing symptoms, such as flashbacks, nightmares, avoidance, and anxiety responses that recur after a traumatic experience.

pragmatics   A knowledge of the practical aspects of using language, such as how our choice of words depends on the social context.

preconventional moral reasoning   According to Kohlberg, the stage at which moral judgments are based on anticipated punishments or rewards.

predictive bias   Occurs when an intelligence test successfully predicts criterion measures, such as school or job performance, for some groups but not for others.

prefrontal cortex   The area of the frontal lobe just behind the eyes and forehead that is involved in the executive functions of planning, self-awareness, and responsibility.

prejudice   A negative attitude toward people based on their membership in a group.

preoperational stage   In Piaget's theory, the stage of cognitive development in which children represent the world symbolically through words and mental images but do not yet understand basic mental operations or rules.

preparedness   The notion that, through evolution, animals have become biologically predisposed to learn some associations more readily than other associations.

primacy effect   In impression formation, our tendency to attach more importance to the initial information that we learn about a person.

primary appraisal   The initial appraisal of a situation as benign, irrelevant, or threatening; a perception of the severity of demands.

primary reinforcer   A positive reinforcer that satisfies a biological need, such as food or water.

priming   Occurs when exposure to a stimulus influences how you subsequently respond to that same or another stimulus; in long-term memory, refers to the activation of one concept by another.

proactive interference   Occurs when material learned in the past interferes with the recall of newer material.

problem-focused coping   Coping strategies that involve direct attempts to confront and master a stressful situation.

problem-solving dream models   The view that dreams can help us find creative solutions to our problems and conflicts because they are not constrained by reality.

problem-solving schemas   Step-by-step scripts for selecting information and solving specialized classes of problems.

procedural (nondeclarative) memory   Memory that is reflected in learned skills and actions.

projective tests   Tests, such as the Rorschach and the Thematic Apperception Test, that present ambiguous stimuli to the subject; the responses are assumed to be based on a projection of internal characteristics of the person onto the stimuli.

proposition   A statement that expresses an idea.

propositional thought   A thought that expresses an idea in linguistic form, as when we seem to hear or say a sentence in our mind.

prospective memory   Remembering to perform an activity in the future.

protective factors   Environmental or personal resources that help people fare better in the face of stress.

prototype   The most typical and familiar member of a class that defines a concept.

proximodistal principle   The tendency for physical development to begin along the innermost parts of the body and continue toward the outermost parts.

psychoactive drugs   Chemicals that produce alterations in consciousness, emotion, and behavior.

psychoanalysis   A psychological theory, developed by Freud, that emphasizes internal and primarily unconscious causes of behavior.

psychodynamic behavior therapy   An integration of psychoanalysis and behavior therapy.

psychodynamic perspective   A psychological perspective that focuses on how personality processes—including unconscious impulses, defenses, and conflicts—influence behavior.

psychogenic amnesia   An extensive but selective memory loss that occurs after a traumatic event.

psychogenic fugue   A dissociative phenomenon in which a person loses all sense of personal identity and wanders to another place and establishes a new identity.

psycholinguistics   The scientific field that studies psychological aspects of language.

psychological test   A method for measuring individual differences related to some psychological construct, based on a sample of relevant behavior obtained under standardized conditions.

psychology   The scientific study of behavior and the mind.

psychometrics   The statistical study of psychological tests; the psychometric approach to intelligence focuses on the number and nature of abilities that define intelligence.

psychophysics   The study of relations between the physical characteristics of stimuli and the sensory experiences they evoke.

psychosexual stages   Stages of development in which psychic energy is focused on certain body parts. The major childhood stages are the oral, anal, and phallic stages; experiences during these stages are assumed to shape personality development.

psychosocial stages   A sequence of eight developmental stages proposed by Erikson, each of which involves a different "crisis" (i.e., conflict) over how we view ourselves in relation to other people and the world.

psychosurgery   Surgical procedures, such as lobotomy or cingulotomy, in which brain tissue involved in a behavior disorder is removed or destroyed.

puberty   A period of rapid biological maturation in which the person becomes capable of sexual reproduction.

punishment   A response is weakened by an outcome that follows it.

R

random assignment   A procedure in which each participant has an equal likelihood of being assigned to any one group within an experiment.

randomized clinical trial   A research design that involves the random assignment of clients having specific problems to an experimental (therapy) group or to a control condition so as to draw sound causal conclusions about the therapy's efficacy.

random sampling   In survey research, a method of choosing a sample in which each member of the population has an equal probability of being included in the sample.

range   A statistic that represents the difference between the highest and the lowest scores in a distribution.

rational-theoretical approach   An approach to test construction in which test items are made up on the basis of a theorist's conception of a construct.

reaction range   The genetically influenced limits within which environmental factors can exert their effects on an organism.

realistic conflict theory   Maintains that competition for limited resources fosters prejudice.

reality principle   The ego's tendency to take reality factors into account and to act in a rational fashion in need satisfaction.

receptor sites   Protein molecules on neurons' dendrites or soma that are specially shaped to accommodate a specific neurotransmitter molecule.

reciprocal determinism   Bandura's model of two-way causal relations between the person, behavior, and the environment.

reflexes   Automatic, inborn behaviors triggered by specific stimuli.

regression   A psychoanalytic defense mechanism in which a person retreats to an earlier stage of development in response to stress.

reinforcement   A response is strengthened by an outcome that follows it.

relapse prevention   A treatment approach designed to teach coping skills, increase self-efficacy, and counter the abstinence violation effect, thus reducing the likelihood of relapse.

reliability   In psychological testing, the consistency with which a measure assesses a given characteristic or different observers agree on a given score. Diagnostic reliability refers to agreement among clinicians making diagnostic judgments.

remote behavior sampling   A method of collecting samples of behavior from respondents as they live their daily lives.

REM sleep   A recurring sleep stage characterized by rapid eye movements, increased physiological arousal, paralysis of the voluntary muscles, and a high rate of dreaming.

REM-sleep behavior disorder (RBD)   A sleep disorder in which the loss of muscle tone that causes normal REM-sleep paralysis is absent, thereby enabling sleepers to move about—sometimes violently—and seemingly act out their dreams.

replication   The process of repeating a study to determine whether the original findings can be duplicated.

representativeness heuristic   A rule of thumb in estimating the probability that an object or event belongs to a certain category based on the extent to which it represents a prototype of that category.

representative sample   A sample that accurately reflects the important characteristics of the population.

repression   The basic defense mechanism that actively keeps anxiety-arousing material in the unconscious.

resistance   Largely unconscious maneuvers that protect clients from dealing with anxiety-arousing material in therapy.

response cost (negative punishment, punishment by removal)   A type of punishment in which an operant response is weakened by the subsequent removal of a stimulus that was not the cause of the original response (e.g., TV privileges are taken away from a child who is misbehaving in order to gain attention).

response prevention   The prevention of escape or avoidance responses during exposure to an anxiety-arousing conditioned stimulus so that extinction can occur.

resting potential   The voltage differential between the inside and outside of a neuron (about −70 mv) caused by the unequal distribution of ions inside the neuron's membrane and outside in the fluid surrounding the neuron when the neuron is at rest.

restoration model   The theory that sleep recharges our run-down bodies and

allows us to recover from physical and mental fatigue.

reticular formation   A structure extending from the hindbrain into the lower forebrain that plays a central role in consciousness, sleep, and attention, in part by alerting and activating higher brain centers (ascending portion) and by selectively blocking some inputs to higher regions in the brain (descending portion).

retina   The light-sensitive tissue at the back of the eye that contains the visual receptors.

retrieval   The process of accessing information in long-term memory.

retrieval cue   Any stimulus, whether internal or external, that triggers the activation of information stored in long-term memory.

retroactive interference   Occurs when newly acquired information interferes with the ability to recall information learned at an earlier time.

retrograde amnesia   Memory loss for events that occurred prior to the onset of amnesia.

reuptake   The process whereby transmitter substances are taken back into the presynaptic neuron so that they do not continue to stimulate postsynaptic neurons.

rods   Photoreceptors in the retina that function under low levels of illumination and do not give rise to color sensations.

Role Construct Repertory (Rep) Test   The technique developed by personality psychologist Kelly to assess people's personal constructs by asking them to describe the ways in which people resemble and differ from one another.

Rorschach test   A projective technique involving the interpretation of inkblots that is used by psychodynamic psychologists to assess perceptual and psychodynamic aspects of personality.

S

sample   In a survey, a subset of individuals drawn from the population.

scatterplot   A graph commonly used to examine correlational data; each pair of scores on variable X and variable Y is plotted as a single point.

schema   A mental framework; an organized pattern of thought about some aspect of the world, such as a class of people, events, situations, or objects.

schizophrenia   A psychotic disorder involving serious impairments of attention, thought, language, emotion, and behavior.

script   A specialized schema that represents a sequence of events (e.g., "going to the movies") that unfolds in a regular, almost standardized order.

seasonal affective disorder (SAD)   A disorder in which depressive symptoms appear or worsen during certain seasons of the year (most typically, fall and winter) and then improve during the other seasons.

secondary appraisal   One's judgment of the adequacy of personal resources needed to cope with a stressor.

secondary (conditioned) reinforcer   A stimulus that acquires reinforcing qualities by being associated with a primary reinforcer.

seeking social support   Turning to others for assistance or emotional support in times of stress.

selective attention   A cognitive process that focuses awareness on some stimuli to the exclusion of others.

self   In Rogers's theory, an organized, consistent set of perceptions and beliefs about oneself.

self-actualization   In humanistic theories, an inborn tendency to strive toward the realization of one's full potential.

self-consistency   An absence of conflict among self-perceptions.

self-determination theory   A humanistic theory formulated by Deci and Ryan that focuses on three fundamental psychological needs: competence, autonomy, and relatedness.

self-efficacy   The conviction that we can perform the behaviors necessary to produce a desired outcome.

self-enhancement   Processes whereby one enhances positive self-regard.

self-esteem   How positively or negatively we feel about ourselves.

self-fulfilling prophecy   Occurs when people's erroneous expectations lead them to act toward others in a way that brings about the expected behaviors, thereby confirming the original impression.

self-instructional training   A cognitive coping approach of giving adaptive self-instructions to oneself at crucial phases of the coping process.

self-monitoring   A personality trait that reflects people's tendencies to regulate their social behavior in accord with situational cues, as opposed to internal values, attitudes, and needs.

self-perception theory   Maintains that we make inferences about our own attitudes by observing how we behave.

self-reinforcement processes   Self-administered rewards and punishments that are contingent on meeting certain standards for behavior that are an important basis for self-regulation of behavior.

self-relatedness   A client's ability to be flexible to change, to listen carefully to the therapist, and to constructively use what is learned in therapy.

self-serving bias   The tendency to make relatively more personal attributions for success and situational attributions for failures.

self-verification   The tendency to try to verify or validate one's existing self-concept (i.e., to satisfy congruence needs).

semantic memory   General factual knowledge about the world and language, including memory for words and concepts.

semantics   The linguistic rules for connecting symbols in language to what they represent.

senile dementia   Dementia (a gradual loss of cognitive abilities due to normal brain deterioration) that begins after age 65.

sensation   The process by which stimuli are detected, transduced into nerve impulses, and sent to the brain.

sensitive period   An optimal age range for certain experiences, but if those experiences occur at another time, normal development will still be possible.

sensorimotor stage   In Piaget's theory, the stage of cognitive development in which children understand their world primarily through sensory experiences and physical (motor) interactions with objects.

sensory adaptation   Diminishing sensitivity to an unchanging stimulus with the passage of time as sensory neurons habituate to the stimulation.

sensory memory   Memory processes that retain incoming sensory information just long enough for it to be recognized.

sensory neurons   Specialized neurons that carry messages from the sense organs to the spinal cord and brain.

sensory prosthetic device   A device for providing sensory input that can, to some extent, substitute for what cannot be supplied by the person's own sensory receptors.

separation anxiety   Distress experienced by infants when they are separated from a primary caregiver, peaking between ages 12 and 16 months and disappearing between ages 2 and 3 years.

sequential design   A research approach that involves repeatedly testing several age cohorts as they grow older.

serial position effect   The finding that recall is influenced by an item's position in a series.

set point   A biologically determined standard around which body weight (or more specifically, our fat mass) is regulated.

sex-typing   Treating other people differently based on whether they are female or male.

sexual dysfunction   Chronic, impaired sexual functioning that distresses a person.

sexual orientation   A person's emotional and erotic preference for partners of a particular sex.

sexual response cycle   A physiological response to sexual stimulation that involves stages of excitement, plateau, orgasm, and resolution.

sexual strategies theory   Maintains that sex differences in mating strategies and mating preferences reflect inherited biological predispositions that have been shaped in women and men over the course of evolution.

shaping   An operant conditioning procedure in which reinforcement begins with a behavior that the organism can already perform and then is made contingent on behaviors that increasingly approximate the final desired behavior.

shared environment   The environmental conditions shared by a family or other social group over a period of time.

short-term memory   A memory store that temporarily holds a limited amount of information.

signal detection theory   A theory that assumes that stimulus detection is not based on a fixed absolute threshold but rather is affected by rewards, punishments, expectations, and motivational factors.

situation-focused intervention   Prevention efforts that focus on altering environmental conditions that are known to promote the development of psychological disorders.

Skinner box   An experimental chamber in which animals learn to perform operant responses, such as pressing a bar or pecking, so that the learning process can be studied.

sleep apnea   A disorder characterized by a repeated cycle in which the sleeper stops breathing, momentarily awakens gasping for air, and then returns to sleep.

slow-wave sleep   Stages 3 and 4 of sleep, in which the EEG pattern shows large, slow brain waves called delta waves.

social causation hypothesis   The proposition that attributes the higher prevalence of schizophrenia in low-income people to the greater stress they experience.

social clock   A set of cultural norms concerning the optimal age range during which work, marriage, parenthood, and other major life experiences should occur.

social-cognitive theories (of hypnosis)   The view that hypnotic experiences occur because people are highly motivated to assume the role of being hypnotized; the person develops a readiness to perceive hypnotic experiences as real and involuntary.

social-cognitive theory   A cognitive behavioral approach to personality developed by Bandura and Mischel that emphasizes the role of social learning, cognitive processes, and self-regulation.

social comparison   The act of comparing one's personal attributes, abilities, and opinions with those of other people.

social compensation   Working harder when in a group than when alone to compensate for other members' lower output.

social constructivism   The view that people construct their reality and beliefs through their cognitions.

social drift hypothesis   The notion that as people develop schizophrenia, their personal and occupational functioning deteriorates, so that they drift down the socioeconomic ladder.

social exchange theory   A theory proposing that a social relationship can best be described in terms of exchanges of rewards and costs between the two partners.

social facilitation   An increased tendency to perform one's dominant response in the mere presence of others.

social identity theory   Maintains that prejudice stems from a need to enhance our self-esteem.

socialization   The process by which culture is transmitted to new members and internalized by them.

social learning theory   Bandura's former name for *social-cognitive theory.*

social loafing   The tendency for people to expend less individual effort when working collectively in a group than when working alone.

social norms   Shared expectations about how people should think, feel, and behave.

social phobia   An excessive and inappropriate fear of social situations in which a person might be evaluated and possibly embarrassed.

social role   A set of norms that characterizes how people in a given social position (e.g., "the college student," "the police officer") ought to behave.

social skills training   A technique in which a client learns more effective social behaviors by observing and imitating a skillful model.

social structure theory   Maintains that men and women behave differently, such as expressing different mate preferences, because society directs them into different social and economic roles.

sociocultural perspective   A view that emphasizes the role of culture and the social environment in understanding commonalities and differences in human behavior.

somatic nervous system   The branch of the peripheral nervous system that provides input from the sensory receptors and output to the voluntary muscles of the body.

somatic relaxation training   A means of voluntarily reducing or preventing high arousal using muscle relaxation.

somatic sensory cortex   Cortical strips in the front portions of the parietal lobes that receive sensory input from the opposite side of the body.

somatoform disorder   A disorder in which a person complains of bodily symptoms that cannot be accounted for in terms of actual physical damage or dysfunction.

source confusion   The tendency to recall something or recognize it as familiar but to forget where it was encountered. *Also called source monitoring error.*

specificity question   The ultimate question of psychotherapy research: "Which types of therapy administered by which kinds of therapists to which kinds of clients having which kinds of problems produce which kinds of effects?"

specific phobia   An irrational and excessive fear of specific objects or situations that pose little or no actual threat.

speech segmentation   The task of perceiving where each word within a spoken sentence begins and ends.

splitting   A tendency, often found in people with borderline personality disorder, to not integrate the positive and negative aspects of another's behavior into a coherent cognitive representation of the person.

spontaneous recovery   In classical conditioning, the reappearance of a previously extinguished conditioned response after a period of time has passed following extinction.

spontaneous remission   Improvements in symptoms in the absence of any therapy.

standard deviation (SD)   A measure of variability that takes into account how much each score in a distribution deviates from the average score. Statistically, the square root of the variance of a set of scores.

standardization   In psychological testing, refers to (1) creating a standard set of procedures for administering a test or making observations and (2) deriving norms with which an individual's performance can be compared.

state-dependent memory   The enhanced ability to retrieve information when our internal state at the time of retrieval matches our original state during learning.

static testing   The traditional approach to testing, in which the test is administered under highly standardized conditions.

statistical significance   In research, a term that means it is unlikely that a particular finding occurred by chance alone. Psychologists typically consider a result to be statistically significant only if it could have occurred by chance less than 5 times in 100.

stereotype   A generalized belief about a group or category of people.

stereotype threat   The anxiety created by the perceived possibility that one's behavior or performance will confirm a negative stereotype about one's group.

stimulants   Drugs that stimulate neural activity, resulting in a state of excitement or aroused euphoria.

stimulus control   The occurrence of an operant behavior in response to a discriminative stimulus.

stimulus generalization   A conditioned response occurs to stimuli other than the original conditioned stimulus, based on the similarity of these stimuli to the conditioned stimulus.

stimulus hierarchy   In systematic desensitization, the creation of a series of anxiety-arousing stimuli that are ranked in terms of the amount of anxiety they evoke.

storage   The retention of information in memory over time.

stranger anxiety   Distress over contact with strangers that typically develops in the first year of infancy and dissipates in the second year.

strange situation   A standardized procedure used to determine the type of emotional attachment between an infant and a caregiver.

strategic pluralism   The notion that multiple—even contradictory—behavioral strategies (for example, introversion and extraversion) might be adaptive in certain environments and would therefore be maintained through natural selection.

stress   A term variously used to refer to (1) situations that place strong demands on an organism, (2) the cognitive, physiological, and behavioral responses to such situations, and (3) the ongoing transaction between individuals and demanding situations.

stress-induced analgesia   A reduction in pain sensitivity that occurs when endorphins are released under stressful conditions.

stressors   Situations that place demands on organisms that tax or exceed their resources.

stress response   The pattern of cognitive, physiological, and behavioral reactions to demands that exceed a person's resources.

stroboscopic movement   The illusory movement produced when adjacent lights are illuminated and extinguished at specific time intervals.

structuralism   An early German school of psychology established by Wundt that attempted to study the structure of the mind by breaking it down into its basic components, which were believed to be sensations.

structured interview   A standardized interview protocol in which specific questions are asked.

subgoal analysis   A problem-solving heuristic in which people attack a large problem by formulating subgoals, or intermediate steps toward a solution.

subjective well-being   Happiness; the overall degree of satisfaction with one's life.

sublimation   The channeling of unacceptable impulses into socially accepted behaviors, as when aggressive drives are expressed in violent sports.

subliminal stimuli   Weak stimuli below the perceptual threshold that are not consciously perceived.

substance dependence   A maladaptive pattern of substance use that causes a person significant distress or substantially impairs that person's life; substance dependence is diagnosed as occurring "with physiological dependence" if drug tolerance or withdrawal symptoms have developed.

suicide   The willful taking of one's own life.

superego   In psychonalysis, the moral arm of the personality that internalizes the standards and values of society and serves as the person's conscience.

suprachiasmatic nuclei (SCN)   The brain's master "biological clock," located in the hypothalamus, that regulates most circadian rhythms.

surface structure   A linguistic term for the words and organization of a spoken or written sentence. Two sentences may have quite different surface structure but still mean the same thing.

survey research   A method using questionnaires or interviews to obtain information about many people.

sympathetic nervous system   The branch of the autonomic nervous system that has an arousal function on the body's internal organs, speeding up bodily processes and mobilizing the body.

synaptic space   The microscopic space between the axons of one neuron and the dendrites or cell body of another over which the nerve impulse is transmitted.

synaptic vesicles   Chambers within the axon that contains the neurotransmitter substance.

synesthesia   A condition in which stimuli are experienced not only in the normal sensory modality but in others as well.

syntax   The rules for the combination of symbols within a given language.

systematic desensitization   A procedure used to eliminate anxiety using counter-conditioning, in which a new response that is incompatible with anxiety is conditioned to the anxiety-arousing conditioned stimulus.

T

tardive dyskinesia   An irreversible motor disorder that can occur as a side effect of certain antipsychotic drugs.

taste buds   Chemical receptors for taste in the tongue and in the roof and back of the mouth that are sensitive to the qualities of sweet, sour, salty, and bitter.

temperament   A biologically based general style of reacting emotionally and behaviorally to the environment.

teratogens   Environmental (nongenetic) agents that cause abnormal prenatal development.

test-retest reliability   The extent to which scores on a presumably stable characteristic are consistent over time.

thalamus   A major sensory integration and relay center in the forebrain, sometimes referred to as the brain's sensory switchboard.

THC (tetrahydrocannabinol)   The major active ingredient in marijuana.

theory   A set of formal statements that explains how and why certain events or phenomena are related to one another.

theory of cognitive dissonance   States that people strive to maintain consistency in their beliefs and actions and that inconsistency creates dissonance (i.e., unpleasant arousal) that motivates people to restore balance by changing their cognitions or behavior.

theory of mind   A person's beliefs about the "mind" and the ability to understand other people's mental states.

theory of planned behavior   Maintains that our intention to engage in a behavior is strongest when we have a positive attitude toward that behavior, when subjective norms (our perceptions of what other people think we should do) support our attitudes, and when we believe that the behavior is under our control.

threat   In Rogers's theory, any experience we have that is inconsistent with our self-concept, including our perceptions of our own behavior. Threat evokes anxiety.

three-stratum theory of cognitive abilities   A model of intelligence based on factor analysis that contains three hierarchical levels of ability, from specific skills to a general intellectual (*g*) factor.

tip-of-the-tongue (TOT) state   The experience of being unable to recall something but feeling that you are on the verge of remembering it.

token economy   A procedure in which desirable behaviors are reinforced with tokens or points that can later be redeemed for other reinforcers.

tolerance   A condition in which increasingly larger doses of a drug are required to produce the same level of bodily responses; caused by the body's compensatory responses, which counter the effects of the drug.

top-down processing   Perceptual processing in which existing knowledge, concepts, ideas, or expectations are applied in order to make sense of incoming stimulation.

transduction   The conversion of one form of energy into another; in sensation, the process whereby physical stimuli are translated into nerve impulses.

transference   The psychoanalytic phenomenon in which a client responds irrationally to the analyst as if the latter were an important person from the client's past who plays a significant role in the client's dynamics.

transtheoretical model   A model of behavior change that includes the phases of precontemplation, contemplation, preparation, action, maintenance, and termination.

trauma-dissociation theory   Accounts for the development of dissociative identity disorder as a defense against severe childhood abuse or trauma.

triangular theory of love   Maintains that various types of love result from different combinations of three core factors: intimacy, commitment, and passion.

triarchic theory of intelligence   Sternberg's theory of intelligence that distinguishes between analytical, practical, and creative forms of mental ability.

twin study   A research method in behavior genetics in which identical (monozygotic) and fraternal (dizygotic) twins are compared on some characteristic; this method is particularly informative if the twins have been raised in different environments.

two-factor theory of avoidance learning   Maintains that avoidance learning first involves the classical conditioning of fear, followed by learning operant responses that avoid an anticipated aversive stimulus and thus are reinforced by anxiety reduction.

two-factor theory of emotion   Schachter's theory stating that intensity of physiological arousal determines perceived intensity of emotion, whereas appraisal of environmental cues tells us which emotion we are experiencing.

Type A behavior pattern   A sense of time urgency, pressured behavior, and hostility that appears to be a risk factor in coronary heart disease.

U

unconditional positive regard   A communicated attitude of total and unconditional acceptance of another person that conveys the person's intrinsic worth.

unconditioned response (UCR)   A response (usually reflexive or innate) that is elicited by a specific stimulus (the unconditioned stimulus) without prior learning.

unconditioned stimulus (UCS)   A stimulus that elicits a particular reflexive or innate response (the unconditioned response) without prior learning.

undifferentiated schizophrenia   A residual category of schizophrenia for people who show some of the symptoms of paranoid, disorganized, and catatonic types but not enough to be placed in one of those diagnostic categories.

unobtrusive measures   Techniques for measuring behavior in which participants are kept unaware that their behavior is being recorded or observed.

upward comparison   Seeing oneself as worse off than the standard for comparison.

V

validity   The extent to which a test actually measures what it is supposed to measure; the degree to which a diagnostic system's categories contain the core features of the behavior disorders and permit differentiation among the disorders.

variable   Any characteristic of an organism or situation that can vary.

variable-interval (VI) schedule   A reinforcement schedule in which reinforcement follows the first response of a particular type that occurs after an average but variable time interval following the last reinforced response.

variable-ratio (VR) schedule   A reinforcement schedule in which reinforcement is based on an average but variable number of responses of a particular type.

variance   A statistic that measures the average of the squared deviation scores about the mean of a distribution.

vestibular sense   The sense of body orientation, or equilibrium.

virtual reality (VR)   Computer-produced virtual environments that immerse an individual and produce experiences similar to those of a corresponding real environment.

visual acuity   The ability to see fine detail.

visual agnosia   A disorder in which an individual is unable to visually recognize objects.

vulnerability factors   Situational or physical factors that increase susceptibility to the negative impact of stressful events.

vulnerability-stress model   Explains behavior disorders as resulting from predisposing biological or psychological vulnerability factors that are triggered by a stressor.

W

Weber's law   States that to perceive a difference between two stimuli, the stimuli must differ by a constant percentage or ratio.

Wernicke's area   An area of the left temporal lobe that is involved in speech comprehension.

wisdom   A system of knowledge about the meaning and conduct of life.

wish fulfillment   In Freudian theory, the partial or complete satisfaction of a psychological need through dreaming or waking fantasy.

withdrawal   The occurrence of compensatory responses after drug use is discontinued, causing the person to experience physiological reactions opposite to those that had been produced by the drug.

working memory   A mental workspace that temporarily stores information, actively processes it, and supports other cognitive functions.

Y

Young-Helmholtz trichromatic theory   The color vision theory stating that there are three types of color receptors in the retina—one for red, one for blue, and one for green—and that combinations of activation of these receptors can produce perception of any hue in the visible spectrum.

Z

zone of proximal development   The difference between what a child can do independently and what the child can do with assistance from adults or more advanced peers.

zygote   The fertilized egg.

References

Aaron, S. (1986). *Stage fright*. Chicago: University of Chicago Press.

Abdul-Rahim, H. F., Holmboe-Ottesen, G., Stene, L. C. M., Husseini, A., Giacaman, R., Jervell, J., & Bjertness, E. (2003). Obesity in a rural and an urban Palestinian West Bank population. *International Journal of Obesity, 27*, 140–146.

Abel, T., & Kandel, E. (1998). Positive and negative regulatory mechanisms that mediate long-term memory storage. *Brain Research Reviews, 26*, 360–378.

Abraham, K. (1911). Notes on the psycho-analytic investigation and treatment of manic-depressive insanity and allied conditions. In *Selected papers of Karl Abraham*. New York: Basic Books, 1968.

Abramov, I., & Gordon, J. (1994). Color appearance: On seeing red—or yellow, or green, or blue. *Annual Review of Psychology, 45*, 451–485.

Abramson, L. Y., Seligman, M. E. P., & Teasdale, J. D. (1978). Learned helplessness in humans: Critique and reformulation. *Journal of Abnormal Psychology, 87*, 49–74.

Achter, J., Lubinski, D., & Benbow, C. P. (1996). Multipotentiality among the intellectually gifted: "It was never there and already it's vanishing." *Journal of Counseling Psychology, 43*, 65–76.

Adair, R. K. (1990). *The physics of baseball*. New York: Harper & Row.

Adams, P. R., & Cox, K. J. A. (2002). Synaptic Darwinism and neocortical function. *Neurocomputing, 42*, 197–214.

Adelmann, P. K., & Zajonc, R. B. (1989). Facial efference and the experience of emotion. *Annual Review of Psychology, 40*, 249–280.

Ader, R. (2001). Psychoneuroimmunology. *Current Directions in Psychological Science, 10*, 94–98.

Ader, R., & Cohen, N. (1975). Behaviorally conditioned immunosuppression. *Psychosomatic Medicine, 37*, 333–340.

Ader, R., & Cohen, N. (1982). Behaviorally conditioned immunosuppression and murine systemic lupus erythematosus. *Science, 215*(4539), 1534–1536.

Adrés, P. (2003). Frontal cortex as the central executive of working memory: Time to revise our view. *Cortex, 39*, 871–895.

Aggleton, J. P. (1993). The contribution of the amygdala to normal and abnormal emotional states. *Trends in Neurosciences, 16*, 328–333.

Agnew, H. W., Jr., Webb, W. B., & Williams, R. L. (1967). Comparison of stage four and 1-REM sleep deprivation. *Perceptual and Motor Skills, 24*, 851–858.

Ahadi, S. & Diener, E. (1989). Multiple determinants and effect size. *Journal of Personality and Social Psychology, 56*, 398–406.

Ahn, H. J. (2005). Child care teachers' strategies in children's socialization of emotion. *Early Child Development & Care, 175*, 49–61.

Ai, A. K., Peterson, C., & Ubelhor, D. (2002). War-related trauma and symptoms of posttraumatic stress disorder among adult Kosovar refugees. *Journal of Traumatic Stress, 15*, 157–160.

Aiello, R. (Ed.). (1994). *Musical perceptions*. London: Oxford University Press.

Ainsworth, M., Blehar, M. C., Waters, E., & Wall, S. (1978). *Patterns of attachment: A psychological study of the strange situation*. Hillsdale, NJ: Erlbaum.

Aitchison, J. (1998). *The articulate mammal: An introduction to psycholinguistics*. Florence, KY: Taylor & Francis/Routledge.

Aitken, S., & Bower T. G. (1982). Intersensory substitution in the blind. *Journal of Experimental Child Psychology, 33*, 309–323.

Ajzen, I. (1991). The theory of planned behavior. *Organizational Behavior and Human Decision Processes, 50*, 179–211.

Akerstedt, T., Kecklund, G., & Hoerte, L. G. (2001). Night driving, season and the risk of highway accidents. *Sleep: Journal of Sleep and Sleep Disorders Research, 24*, 401–406.

Alanko, L. O., Laitinen, J. T., Stenberg, D., & Porkka-Heiskanen, T. (2004). Adenosine Al receptor-dependent G-protein activity in the rat brain during prolonged wakefulness. *Neuroreport: For Rapid Communication of Neuroscience Research, 15*, 2133–2137.

Albee, G. W. (1997). Speak no evil? *American Psychologist, 52*, 1143–1144.

Alcock, J. (2002). *Animal behavior: An evolutionary approach*. New York: Sinauer.

Alcock, J. E. (2003). Give the null hypothesis a chance: Reasons to remain doubtful about the existence of psi. In J. E. Alcock, J. E. Burns, & A. Freeman (Eds.), *Psi wars: Getting to grips with the paranormal*. Charlottesville, VA: Imprint Academic.

Aldridge, S. (1998). *The thread of life: The story of genes and genetic engineering*. New York: Cambridge University Press.

Alexander, F. (2004). A classic in psychotherapy integration revisited: The dynamics of psychotherapy in the light of learning theory. *Journal of Psychotherapy Integration, 14*, 347–359.

Alfieri, T., Ruble, D. N., & Higgins, E. T. (1996). Gender stereotypes during adolescence: Developmental changes and the transition to junior high school. *Developmental Psychology, 32*, 1129–1137.

Allen, M. (1991). Meta-analysis comparing the persuasiveness of one-sided and two-sided messages. *Western Journal of Speech Communication, 55*, 390–404.

Allen, M., D'Alessio, D., & Brezgel, K. (1995). A meta-analysis summarizing the effects of pornography: II. Aggression after exposure. *Human Communication Research, 22*, 258–283.

Allen, M., D'Alessio, D., & Emmers-Sommer, T. M. (2000). Reactions of criminal sexual offenders to pornography: A meta-analytic summary. In M. Roloff (Ed.), *Communication Yearbook 22*. Thousand Oaks, CA: Sage.

Allport, G. W. (1954). *The nature of prejudice*. Reading, MA: Addison-Wesley.

Allport, G. W., & Odbert, H. S. (1936). Trait names: A psycho-lexical study. *Psychological Monographs, 47*(Whole No. 211).

Alonso, C., & Coe, C. J. (2001). Disruptions of social relationships accentuate the association between emotional distress and menstrual pain in young women. *Health Psychology, 20*, 411–416.

Altman, I., & Taylor, D. A. (1973). *Social penetration: The development of interpersonal relationships*. New York: Holt, Rinehart & Winston.

Altman, J., & Bayer, S. A. (1996). *Development of the cerebellar system: In relation to its evolution, structure and functions*. Boca Raton, FL: CRC Press.

Amato, P. R., & Keith, B. (1991). Parental divorce and the well-being of children: A meta-analysis. *Psychological Bulletin, 110*, 26–46.

American Psychiatric Association. (1990). *The practice of ECT: Recommendations for treatment, training, and privileging*. Washington, DC: American Psychiatric Press.

American Psychiatric Association. (1994). *The diagnostic and statistical manual of mental disorders* (4th ed.). Washington, DC: Author.

American Psychiatric Association. (2000). *The diagnostic and statistical manual of mental disorders, fourth edition, text revision (DSMIV)*. Washington, DC: Author.

American Psychological Association. (2002). Ethical principles of psychologists and code of conduct. *American Psychologist, 57*, 1060–1073.

American Psychological Association. (2005). About APA. Retrieved March 13, 2005, from http://www.apa.org/about/

American Psychological Association Research Office. (2001). Employment characteristics of APA members by membership status, 2000 (Table 4). In *2000 APA Directory Survey.* Washington, DC: American Psychological Association.

American Psychological Society. (2005). History of APS. Retrieved March 13, 2005, from http://www.psychologicalscience.org/about/history.cfm

Ames, C. (1992). Achievement goals and adaptive motivation patterns: The role of the environment. In G. Roberts (Ed.), *Motivation in sport and exercise.* Champaign, IL: Human Kinetics.

Anand, B. K., & Brobeck, J. R. (1951). Hypothalamic control of food intake in rats and cats. *Yale Journal of Biology and Medicine, 24,* 123–140.

Anderson, C. A. (2004). An update on the effects of playing violent video games. *Journal of Adolescence, 27,* 113–122.

Anderson, C. A., & Bushman, B. J. (2002). Human aggression. *Annual Review of Psychology, 53,* 27–51.

Anderson, J. R. (1985). *Cognitive psychology and its implications* (2nd ed.). New York: Freeman.

Anderson, J. R. (1991). The adaptive nature of human categorization. *Psychological Review, 98,* 409–429.

Anderson, M. C., & Neely, J. H. (1996). Interference and inhibition in memory retrieval. In E. L. Bjork & R. A. Bjork (Eds.), *Memory: Handbook of perception and cognition* (2nd ed.). San Diego: Academic Press.

Anderson, N. D., & Craik, F. I. M. (2000). Memory in the aging brain. In E. Tulving & F. I. M. Craik (Eds.), *The Oxford handbook of memory.* New York: Oxford University Press.

Andreason, N. C., Arndt, S., Swayze, V., Cizadlo, T., et al. (1994). Thalamic abnormalities in schizophrenia visualized through magnetic resonance image averaging. *Science, 266,* 294–298.

Andrews, F. M. (1991). Stability and change in levels and structure of subjective well-being: USA 1972 and 1988. *Social Indicators Research, 25,* 1–30.

Ankney, C. D. (1992). Sex differences in relative brain size: The mismeasure of women, too? *Intelligence, 16,* 329–336.

Anthony, J. C., Warner, L. A., & Kessler, R. C. (1997). Comparative epidemiology of dependence on tobacco, alcohol, controlled substances, and inhalants: Basic findings from the National Comorbidity Survey. In G. A. Marlatt & G. R. VandenBos (Eds.), *Addictive behaviors: Readings on etiology, prevention and treatment.* Washington, DC: American Psychological Association.

Anton, R. F. (2001). Pharmacologic approaches to the management of alcoholism. *Journal of Clinical Psychiatry, 62,* 11–17.

Antonuccio, D. O., Danton, W. G., et al. (2003). Psychology in the prescription era: Building a firewall between marketing and science. *American Psychologist 58,* 1028–1043.

Antrobus, J. (1991). Dreaming: Cognitive processes during cortical activation and high afferent thresholds. *Psychological Review, 98,* 96–121.

APA Monitor (1997, December). *Author, 28*(12).

Aponte, H., & Hoffman, L. (1973). The open door. A structural approach to a family with an anorectic child. *Family Process, 12,* 1–44.

Arendt, J., Skene, D. J., Middleton, B., Lockley, S. W., & Deacon, S. (1997). Efficacy of melatonin treatment in jet lag, shift work, and blindness. *Journal of Biological Rhythms, 12,* 604–617.

Argyle, M. (1999). Causes and correlates of happiness. In D. Kahneman, E. Diener, & N. Schwarz (Eds.), *Well-being: The foundations of hedonic psychology.* New York: Russell Sage Foundation.

Ariznavarreta, C., Cardinali, D. P., Villanua, M. A., Granados, B., Martin, M., Chiesa, J. J., et al. (2002). Circadian rhythms in airline pilots submitted to long-haul transmeridian flights. *Aviation, Space, and Environmental Medicine, 73,* 445–455.

Arnett, J. J. (1999). Adolescent storm and stress, reconsidered. *American Psychologist, 54,* 317–326.

Arnett, J. J. (2001). Conceptions of the transition to adulthood: Perspectives from adolescence through midlife. *Journal of Adult Development, 8,* 133–143.

Arnett, P. A. (1997). Autonomic responsivity in psychopaths: A critical review and theoretical proposal. *Clinical Psychology Review, 17,* 903–936.

Aron, A., & Westbay, L. (1996). Dimensions of the prototype of love. *Journal of Personality and Social Psychology, 70,* 535–551.

Aron, E., Aron, A., & Davies, K. M. (2005). Adult shyness: The interaction of temperamental sensitivity and an adverse childhood environment. *Personality and Social Psychology Bulletin, 31,* 181–197.

Aron, L. (1996). *A meeting of minds: Mutuality in psychoanalysis.* Hillsdale, NJ: Analytic Press.

Aronson, E., Stephan, C., Sikes, J., Blaney, N., & Snopp, M. (1978). *The jigsaw classroom.* Beverly Hills, CA: Sage.

Aronson, J., Lustina, M. J., Good, C., Keough, K., Steele, C. M., & Brown, J. (1999). When White men can't do math: Necessary and sufficient factors in stereotype threat. *Journal of Experimental Social Psychology, 35,* 29–46.

Arrow, H., & Burns, K. L. (2004). Self-organizing culture: How norms emerge in small groups. In M. Schaller, & C. S. Crandall (Eds.), *The psychological foundations of culture.* Mahwah, NJ: Erlbaum.

Asch, S. E. (1946). Forming impressions of personality. *Journal of Abnormal and Social Psychology, 41,* 258–290.

Asch, S. E. (1951). Effects of group pressure upon the modification and distortion of judgment. In H. Guetzkow (Ed.), *Groups, leadership, and men.* Pittsburgh: Carnegie Press.

Asch, S. E. (1956). Studies of independence and conformity: A minority of one against a unanimous majority. *Psychological Monographs, 70,* 416.

Asimov, I. (1997). *Isaac Asimov's book of facts.* New York: Random House/Wings Books.

Aspinwall, L. G., & Staudinger, U. M. (Eds.). (2003). *A psychology of human strengths: Fundamental questions and future directions for a positive psychology.* Washington, DC: American Psychological Association.

Assanand, S. P., John, P. J., & Lehman, D. R. (1998). Teaching theories of hunger and eating: Overcoming students' misconceptions. *Teaching of Psychology, 25,* 44–46.

Assor, A., Roth, G., & Deci, E. L. (2004). The emotional costs of parents' conditional regard: A self-determination theory analysis. *Journal of Personality, 72,* 47–88.

Atkinson, J. W. (Ed.). (1958). *Motives in fantasy, action, and society.* Princeton, NJ: Van Nostrand.

Atkinson, J. W. (1964). *An introduction to motivation.* Princeton, NJ: Van Nostrand.

Atkinson, J. W., & Birch, D. (1978). *An introduction to motivation.* New York: Van Nostrand.

Atkinson, R. C., & Shiffrin, R. M. (1968). Human memory: A proposed system and its control processes. In K. W. Spence & J. T. Spence (Eds.), *Advances in the psychology of learning and motivation: Research and theory* (Vol. 2). New York: Academic Press.

Auerbach, S. M. (1989). Stress management and coping research in the health care setting: An overview and methodological commentary. *Journal of Consulting and Clinical Psychology, 57,* 388–395.

Auld, F., Hyman, M., & Rudzinski, D. (2005). *Resolution of inner conflict: An introduction to psychoanalytic therapy.* Washington, DC: American Psychological Association.

Austin, M., & Leader, L. (2000). Maternal stress and obstetric and infant outcomes: Epidemiological findings and neuroendocrine mechanisms. *Australian and New Zealand Journal of Obstetrics and Gynaecology, 40,* 331–337.

Avenell, A., Brown, T. J., McGee, M. A., Campbell, M. K. et al. (2004). What interventions should we add to weight reducing diets in adults with obesity? A systematic review of randomized controlled trials of adding drug therapy, exercise, behaviour therapy or a combination of these interventions. *Journal of Human Nutrition and Dietetics, 17,* 293–316.

Ayllon, T., & Azrin, N. H. (1968). *The token economy: A motivational system for therapy and rehabilitation.* New York: Appleton-Century-Crofts.

Ayres, J. J. B. (1998). Fear conditioning and avoidance. In W. T. O'Donohue (Ed.), *Learning and behavior therapy.* Boston: Allyn & Bacon.

Baars, B. J. (1997). In the theatre of consciousness: Global workspace theory, a rigorous scientific theory of consciousness. *Journal of Consciousness Studies, 4,* 292–309.

Baars, B. J. (2002). The conscious access hypothesis: Origins and recent evidence. *Trends in Cognitive Sciences, 6,* 47–52.

Backhaus, W. G., Kliegl, R., & Werner, J. S. (Eds.). (1998). *Color vision: Perspectives from different disciplines.* New York: Walter de Gruyter.

Baddeley, A. D. (1990). *Human memory: Theory and practice.* Boston: Allyn & Bacon.

Baddeley, A. D. (2002). Is working memory still working? *European Psychologist, 7,* 85–97.

Baddeley, A. D., & Hitch, G. J. (1974). Working memory. In G. H. Bower (Ed.), *The psychology of learning and motivation* (Vol. 8). New York: Academic Press.

Baehr, E. K. (2001). Circadian phase-delaying effects of nocturnal exercise in older and young adults. *Dissertation Abstracts International: Section B: The Sciences and Engineering, 62*(4-B), 2105.

Bagge, C., Nickell, A., Stepp, S., Durrett, C., Jackson, K., & Trull, T. J. (2004). Borderline personality disorder features predict negative outcomes 2 years later. *Journal of Abnormal Psychology, 113,* 279–288.

Bagley, C., & Ramsay, R. (1997). *Suicidal behaviour in adolescents and adults: Research, taxonomy and prevention.* Ashgate, England: Ashgate Publishing.

Bahrick, H. P. (1984). Semantic memory content in permastore: Fifty years of memory for Spanish learned in school. *Journal of Experimental Psychology: General, 113,* 1–29.

Bahrick, H. P. (2005). The long-term neglect of long-term memory: Reasons and remedies. In A. F. Healy (Ed.), *Experimental cognitive psychology and its applications: Decade of behavior.* Washington, DC: American Psychological Association.

Bahrick, H. P., Bahrick, P. O., & Wittlinger, R. P. (1975). Fifty years of memory for names and faces: A cross-sectional approach. *Journal of Experimental Psychology: General, 104,* 54–75.

Bahrick, H. P., Hall, L. K., & Berger, S. A. (1996). Accuracy and distortion in memory for high school grades. *Psychological Science, 7,* 265–271.

Bailey, J. M., Dunne, M. P., & Martin, N. G. (2000). Genetic and environmental influences on sexual orientation and its correlates in an Australian twin sample. *Journal of Personality and Social Psychology, 78,* 524–536.

Bailey, J. M., & Pillard, R. C. (1991). A genetic study of male sexual orientation. *Archives of General Psychiatry, 48,* 1089–1096.

Bailey, J. M., Pillard, R. C., Neale, M. C., & Agyei, Y. (1993). Heritable factors influence sexual orientation in women. *Archives of General Psychiatry, 50,* 217–223.

Baillargeon, R. (2004). Infants' physical world. *Current Directions in Psychological Science, 13,* 89–94.

Ball, J., & Mosselle, K. (1995). Health risk behaviors of adolescents in Singapore. *Asian Journal of Psychology, 1,* 54–62.

Ballenger, J. C. (2000). Panic disorder and agoraphobia. In G. Fink (Ed.), *Encyclopedia of stress.* San Diego, CA: Academic Press.

Baltes, P. B., Glück, J., & Kunzmann, U. (2002). Wisdom: Its structure and function in successful lifespan development. In C. R. Snyder & S. J. Lopez (Eds.), *Handbook of positive psychology* (pp. 327–350). New York: Oxford University Press.

Baltes, P. B., & Kunzmann, U. (2004). The two faces of wisdom: Wisdom as a general theory of knowledge and judgment about excellence in mind and virtue vs. wisdom as everyday realization in people and products. *Human Development, 47,* 290–299.

Baltes, P., & Staudinger, U. M. (2000). Wisdom: A metaheuristic (pragmatic) to orchestrate mind and virtue toward excellence. *American Psychologist, 55,* 122–136.

Bandura, A. (1965). Influence of models' reinforcement contingencies on the acquisition of imitated responses. *Journal of Personality and Social Psychology, 1,* 589–595.

Bandura, A. (1969). *Principles of behavior modification.* New York: Holt, Rinehart & Winston.

Bandura, A. (1986). *Social foundations of thought and action: A social-cognitive theory.* Englewood Cliffs, NJ: Prentice Hall.

Bandura, A. (1989). Social cognitive theory. *Annals of Child Development, 6,* 3–58.

Bandura, A. (1997). *Self-efficacy: The exercise of control.* New York: W. H. Freeman.

Bandura, A. (1999). Social cognitive theory of personality. In D. Cervone & Y. Shoda (Eds.), *The coherence of personality.* New York: Guilford Press.

Bandura, A. (2000). Health promotion from the perspective of social cognitive theory. In P. Norman, C. Abraham, & M. Conner (Eds.), *Understanding and changing health and behaviour.* Reading, England: Harwood.

Bandura, A. (2002a). Environmental sustainability by sociocognitive deceleration of population growth. In P. Schmuck & W. P. Schultz (Eds.), *Psychology of sustainable development.* Dordrecht, Netherlands: Kluwer.

Bandura, A. (2002b). Growing primacy of human agency in adaptation and change in the electronic era. *European Psychologist, 7,* 2–16.

Bandura, A. (2004). Social cognitive theory for personal and social change by enabling media. In A. Singhal, M. J. Cody, E. M. Rogers, & M. Sabido (Eds.), *Entertainment-education and social change: History, research, and practice.* Mahwah, NJ: Erlbaum.

Bandura, A., & Cervone, D. (1983). Self-evaluative and self-efficacy mechanisms governing the motivational effects of goal systems. *Journal of Personality and Social Psychology, 45,* 1017–1028.

Bandura, A., O'Leary, A., Taylor, C., et al. (1987). Perceived self-efficacy and pain control: Opioid and nonopioid mechanisms. *Journal of Personality and Social Psychology, 53,* 563–571.

Barber, J. (1998). The mysterious persistence of hypnotic analgesia. *International Journal of Clinical and Experimental Hypnosis, 46,* 28–43.

Barber, T. X. (1961). Death by suggestion. *Psychosomatic Medicine, 23,* 153–155.

Bardo, M. T. (1998). Neuropharmacological mechanisms of drug reward: Beyond dopamine in the nucleus accumbens. *Critical Reviews in Neurobiology, 12,* 37–67.

Barefoot, J. C., Peterson, B. L., Harrell, F. E., Hlatky, M. A., Pryor, D. B., Haney, T. L., et al. (1989). Type A behavior and survival: A follow-up study of 1,467 patients with coronary artery disease. *The American Journal of Cardiology, 64,* 427–432.

Bargh, J. A., & Chartrand, T. L. (1999). The unbearable automaticity of being. *American Psychologist, 54,* 462–479.

Barlow, D. H. (1997). Cognitive-behavioral therapy for panic disorder: Current status. *Journal of Clinical Psychiatry, 58*(Suppl. 2), 32–36.

Barlow, D. H. (2002). *Anxiety and its disorders.* New York: Guilford Press.

Barlow, D. H., Rapee, R. M., & Reisner, L. C. (2001). *Mastering stress 2001: A lifestyle approach.* Dallas, TX: American Health.

Barnes, G. E., & Prosen, H. (1985). Parental death and depression. *Journal of Abnormal Psychology, 94,* 64–69.

Barnett, J. E., & Porter, J. E. (1998). The suicidal patient: Clinical and risk management strategies. In L. VandeCreek & S. Knapp (Eds.), *Innovations in clinical practice: A source book* (Vol. 16). Sarasota, FL: Professional Resource Press.

Barnett, W. S., & Camilli, G. (2002). Compensatory preschool education, cognitive development, and "race." In J. Fish (Ed.), *Race and intelligence: Separating science from myth.* Mahwah, NJ: Erlbaum.

Baron, A., & Perone, M. (2001). Explaining avoidance: Two factors are still better than one. *Journal of the Experimental Analysis of Behavior, 75,* 357–361.

Baron, R. S., Cutrona, C. E., Hicklin, D., Russell, D. W., & Lubaroff, D. M. (1990). Social support and immune responses among spouses of cancer patients. *Journal of Personality and Social Psychology, 59,* 344–352.

Barondes, S. H. (1999). *Mood genes: Hunting for origins of mania and depression.* New York: Oxford University Press.

Barrett, G. V., & Depinet, R. L. (1991). A reconsideration of testing for competence rather than intelligence. *American Psychologist, 46,* 1012–1024.

Barrow, C. J. (2003). *Environmental change and human development: The place of environmental change in human evolution.* New York: Oxford University Press.

Bartholomew, D. L. (2005). *Measuring intelligence: Facts and fallacies.* New York: Cambridge University Press.

Bartholow, B. D., & Anderson, C. A. (2002). Effects of violent video games on aggressive behavior: Potential sex differences. *Journal of Experimental Social Psychology, 38,* 283–290.

Bartlett, F. C. (1932). *Remembering: A study in experimental and social psychology.* New York: Cambridge University Press.

Basedow, H. (1925). *The Australian aboriginal.* Adelaide, Australia: F. W. Preece.

Bastik, T. (1982). *Intuition: How we think and act.* New York: Wiley.

Bates, M. S., Edwards, W. T., & Anderson, K. O. (1993). Ethnocultural influences on variation in chronic pain perception. *Pain, 52,* 101–112.

Batson, C. D. (1991). *The altruism question: Toward a social-psychological answer.* Hillsdale, NJ: Erlbaum.

Batson, C. D., Ahmad, N., Lishner, D. A., & Tsang, J. A. (2002). Empathy and altruism. In C. R. Snyder & S. J. Lopez (Eds.), *Handbook of positive psychology.* London: Oxford University Press.

Batson, C. D., Ahmad, N., & Stocks, E. L. (2004). Benefits and liabilities of empathy-induced altruism. In A. G. Miller (Ed.), *The social psychology of good and evil.* New York: Guilford Press.

Bauer, R. M., & Verfaellie, M. (1988). Electrodermal discrimination of familiar but not unfamiliar faces in prosopagnosia. *Brain and Cognition, 8,* 240–252.

Baum, A. (1994). Disease processes: Behavioral, biological, and environmental interactions in disease processes. In S. J. Blumenthal, K. Matthews, & S. M. Weiss (Eds.), *New research frontiers in behavioral medicine: Proceedings of the national conference.* Washington, DC: NIH Publications.

Baum, A., Krantz, D. S., & Gatchel, R. J. (1997). *An introduction to health psychology* (3rd ed.). Boston: McGraw-Hill.

Baum, A., & Posluszny, D. M. (1999). Health psychology: Mapping biobehavioral contributions to health and illness. *Annual Review of Psychology, 50,* 137–164.

Baumeister, R. (Ed.). (1993). *Self-esteem: The puzzle of low self regard.* New York: Plenum.

Baumeister, R. F., & Leary, M. R. (1995). The need to belong: Desire for interpersonal attachments as a fundamental human motivation. *Psychological Bulletin, 117,* 497–529.

Baumeister, R. F., & Tice, D. M. (1990). Anxiety and social exclusion. *Journal of Social and Clinical Psychology, 9,* 165–195.

Baumrind, D. (1964). Some thoughts on ethics of research: After reading Milgram's behavioral study of "obedience." *American Psychologist, 19,* 421–423.

Baumrind, D. (1967). Child care practices anteceding three patterns of preschool behavior. *Genetic Psychology Monographs, 75,* 43–88.

Baumrind, D., Larzelere, R. E., & Cowan, P. A. (2002). Ordinary physical punishment: Is it harmful? Comment on Gershoff (2002). *Psychological Bulletin, 128,* 580–589.

Bauserman, R. (1996). Sexual aggression and pornography: A review of correlational research. *Basic and Applied Social Psychology, 18,* 405–427.

Bayley, T. M., Dye, L., Jones, S., DeBono, M., & Hill, A. J. (2002). Food cravings and aversions during pregnancy: Relationships with nausea and vomiting. *Appetite, 38,* 45–51.

Beahrs, J. O. (1994). Dissociative identity disorder: Adaptive deception of self and others. *Bulletin of the American Academy of Psychiatric Law, 22,* 223–237.

Beaman, A. L., Barnes, P. J., Klentz, B., & McQuirk, B. (1978). Increasing helping rates through information dissemination: Teaching pays. *Personality and Social Psychology Bulletin, 4,* 406–411.

Beatty, M. J., Heisel, A. D., Hall, A. E., Levine, T. R., & La France, B. H. (2002). What can we learn from the study of twins about genetic and environmental influences on interpersonal affiliation, aggressiveness, and social anxiety? A meta-analytic study. *Communication Monographs, 69,* 1–18.

Beauchamp, G. K., & Bartoshuk L. (Eds.). (1997). *Tasting and smelling.* Philadelphia: Academic Press.

Beck, A. T. (1976). *Cognitive therapy and the emotional disorders.* New York: International Universities Press.

Beck, A. T. (2002). Cognitive patterns in dreams and daydreams. *Journal of Cognitive Psychotherapy, 16,* 23–28.

Beck, A. T., Freeman, A., & Davis, D. D. (2004). *Cognitive therapy of personality disorders* (2nd ed.). New York: Guilford.

Beck, A. T., Rush, A. J., Shaw, B. F., & Emery, G. (1979). *Cognitive therapy of depression.* New York: Guilford Press.

Becker, A. E., Grinspoon, S. K., Klibanski, A., & Herzog, D. B. (1999). Current concepts: Eating disorders. *New England Journal of Medicine, 340,* 1092–1098.

Becker, J. (2004). Reconsidering the role of overcoming perturbations in cognitive development: Constructivism and consciousness. *Human Development, 47,* 77–93.

Beecher, H. K. (1959). Generalization from pain of various types and diverse origins. *Science, 130,* 267–268.

Beilcock, S. L., & Carr, T. H. (2001). On the fragility of skilled performance: What governs choking under pressure? *Journal of Experimental Psychology: General, 130,* 701–725.

Bekesy, G. von. (1957). The ear. *Scientific American, 230,* 66–78.

Bell, A. P., Weinberg, M. S., & Hammersmith, S. K. (1981). *Sexual preference: Its development in men and women.* Bloomington: Indiana University Press.

Bell, J. H., & Bromnick, R. D. (2003). The social reality of the imaginary audience: A ground theory approach. *Adolescence, 38,* 205–219.

Bellack, A. S., Mueser, K. T., Gingerich, S., & Agresta, J. (2004). *Social skills training for schizophrenia* (2nd ed.). New York: Guilford Press.

Belloc, N. B. (1973). Relationship of health practices and mortality. *Preventive Medicine, 2,* 67–81.

Bem, D. J. (1972). Self-perception theory. In L. Berkowitz (Ed.), *Advances in experimental social psychology* (Vol. 6). New York: Academic Press.

Bem, D. J. (1996). Exotic becomes erotic: A developmental theory of sexual orientation. *Psychological Review, 103,* 320–335.

Bem, D. J. (2001). Exotic becomes erotic: Integrating biological and experiential antecedents of sexual orientation. In A. R. D'Augelli & C. J. Patterson (Eds.), *Lesbian, gay, and bisexual identities and youth: Psychological perspectives.* London: Oxford University Press.

Bem, D. J., & Honorton, C. (1994). Does psi exist? Replicable evidence for an anomalous process of information transfer. *Psychological Bulletin, 115,* 4–18.

Bem, S. L. (1981). Gender schema theory: A cognitive account of sex typing. *Psychological Review, 88,* 354–364.

Benedito-Silva, A. A., Menna-Barreto, I. S., Cipolla-Neto, J., Marques, N., & Tenreiro, S. (1989). A self-evaluation questionnaire for the determination of morningness-eveningness types in Brazil. *Chronobiologia, 16,* 311.

Bengtson, V. L. (2001). Beyond the nuclear family: The increasing importance of multigenerational bonds. *Journal of Marriage and the Family, 63,* 1–16.

Benjamin, A. S., & Bjork, R. A. (2000). On the relationship between recognition speed and accuracy for words rehearsed via rote versus elaborative rehearsal. *Journal of Experimental Psychology: Learning, Memory, and Cognition, 26,* 638–648.

Benjamin, L. S. (2003). *Interpersonal reconstructive therapy: Promoting change in nonresponders.* New York: Guilford Press.

Bennett, H. L. (1983). Remembering drink orders: The memory skills of cocktail waitresses. *Human Learning, 2,* 157–169.

Benson, H., & Klipper, M. Z. (1976). *The relaxation response.* New York: Morrow.

Berg, C. A. (2000). Intellectual development in adulthood. In R. J. Sternberg (Ed.), *Handbook of intelligence.* New York: Cambridge University Press.

Berkowitz, L., & Harmon-Jones, E. (2004). Toward an understanding of the determinants of anger. *Emotion, 4,* 107–130.

Bernichon, T., Cook, K. E., & Brown, J. D. (2003). Seeking self-evaluative feedback: The interactive role of global self-esteem and specific self-views. *Journal of Personality and Social Psychology, 84,* 194–204.

Bernstein, S. E., & Carr, T. H. (1996). Dual-route theories of pronouncing printed words: What can be learned from concurrent task performance? *Journal of Experimental Psychology: Learning, Memory, and Cognition, 22,* 86–116.

Berntsen, D. (2001). Involuntary memories of emotional events: Do memories of traumas and extremely happy events differ? *Applied Cognitive Psychology, 5*, S135–S158.

Berridge, K. C. (2004). Motivation concepts in behavioral neuroscience. *Physiology and Behavior, 81*, 179–209.

Berry, J. W., Poortinga, Y. H., Segall, M. H., & Dasen, P. (1992). *Cross-cultural psychology: Research and application.* New York: Cambridge University Press.

Berry, L. M. (1998). *Psychology at work* (2nd ed.). Boston: McGraw-Hill.

Berthoud, H. R. (2002). Multiple neural systems controlling food intake and body weight. *Neuroscience and Biobehavioral Reviews, 26*, 393–428.

Best, S. J., Krueger, B., Hubbard, C., & Smith, A. (2001). An assessment of the generalizability of Internet surveys. *Social Science Computer Review, 19*, 131–145.

Beutler, L. E. (2002). The dodo bird is extinct. *Clinical Psychology: Science and Practice, 9*, 30–34.

Beutler, L. E., & Malik, M. L. (2002). *Rethinking the DSM: A psychological perspective.* Washington, DC: American Psychological Association.

Beyer, S. (1990). Gender differences in the accuracy of self-evaluations of performance. *Journal of Personality and Social Psychology, 59*, 960–970.

Bialystok, E. (2001). *Bilingualism in development: Language, literacy, and cognition.* New York: Cambridge University Press.

Bialystok, E., & Martin, M. M. (2004). Attention and inhibition in bilingual children: Evidence from the dimensional change card sort task. *Developmental Science, 7*, 325–339.

Biederman, J. (1998). Attention-deficit/hyper-active disorder: A life-span perspective. *Journal of Clinical Psychology, 59*, 1–13.

Bieling, P. J., Israeli, A. L., & Antony, M. M. (2004). Is perfectionism good, bad, or both? Examining models of the perfectionism construct. *Personality and Individual Differences, 36*, 1373–1385.

Billings, A. G., & Moos, R. H. (1984). Coping, stress, and social resources among adults with unipolar depression. *Journal of Personality and Social Psychology, 46*, 877–891.

Binder, J. L. (2004). *Key competencies in brief dynamic psychotherapy.* New York: Guilford Press.

Binder, J. L., & Strupp, H. H. (1997). "Negative process": A recurrently discovered and underestimated facet of therapeutic process and outcome in the individual psychotherapy of adults. *Clinical Psychology: Science and Practice, 4*, 121–139.

Birdsong, D., & Molis, M. (2001). On the evidence for maturational constraints in second-language acquisition. *Journal of Memory and Language, 44*, 235–249.

Bjorklund, D. F., & Pellegrini, A. D. (2002). Evolutionary perspectives on social development. In P. K. Smith & C. H. Hart (Eds.), *Blackwell handbook of childhood social development.* Malden, MA: Blackwell.

Black, D. N., Seritan, A. L., Taber, K. H., & Hurley, R. A. (2004). Conversion hysteria: Lessons from functional imaging. *Journal of Neuropsychiatry & Clinical Neurosciences, 16*, 245–251.

Black, D. W. (1999). *Bad boys, bad men: Confronting antisocial personality disorder.* New York: Oxford University Press.

Black, D. W., Yates, W. R., & Andreason, N. C. (1988). Schizophrenia, schizophreniform disorder, and delusional paranoid disorders. In J. A. Talbott, R. E. Hales, & S. C. Yudofsky (Eds.), *Textbook of psychiatry.* Washington, DC: American Psychiatric Press.

Blader, S. L., & Tyler, T. R. (2002). Justice and empathy: What motivates people to help others? In M. Ross & D. T. Miller (Eds.), *The justice motive in everyday life.* New York: Cambridge University Press.

Blair, J. (2005). *Development of the psychopath: Emotion and the brain.* St. Louis, MO: Blackwell.

Blair, S. N., Kohl, H. W., III, Paffenbarger, R. S., et al. (1989). Physical fitness and all-cause mortality: A prospective study of healthy men and women. *Journal of the American Medical Association, 262*, 2395–2401.

Blakemore, C., & Cooper, G. G. (1970). Development of the brain depends on visual environment. *Nature, 228*, 477–478.

Blanchard, R. (2001). Fraternal birth order and the maternal immune hypothesis of male homosexuality. *Hormones and Behavior, 40*, 105–114.

Blanchard, R., & Bogaert, A. F. (1996). Homosexuality in men and number of older brothers. *American Journal of Psychiatry, 153*, 27–31.

Blanke, O., Ortigue, S., Landis, T., & Seeck, M. (2002). Stimulating illusory own-body perceptions. *Nature, 419* (6904), 269–270.

Blanton, H., Pelham, B., DeHart, T., & Carvallo, M. (2001). Overconfidence as dissonance reduction. *Journal of Experimental Social Psychology, 37*, 373–385.

Blass, T. (2002). Perpetrator behavior as destructive obedience: An evaluation of Stanley Milgram's perspective, the most influential social-psychological approach to the Holocaust. In L. S. Newman & R. Erber (Eds.), *Understanding genocide: The social psychology of the Holocaust.* London: Oxford University Press.

Blass, T., & Schmitt, C. (2001). The nature of perceived authority in the Milgram paradigm: Two replications. *Current Psychology: Developmental, Learning, Personality, Social, 20*, 115–121.

Blechman, E., & Brownell, K. D. (1998). *Behavioral medicine and women: A comprehensive handbook.* New York: Guilford Press.

Blessing, W. W. (1997). *The lower brainstem and bodily homeostasis.* New York: Oxford University Press.

Block, N. (2002). How heritability misleads about race. In J. M. Fish (Ed.), *Race and intelligence: Separating science from myth.* Mahwah, NJ: Erlbaum.

Blodgett, H. C. (1929). The effect of the introduction of reward on the maze performance of rats. *University of California Publications in Psychology, 4*(8), 114–126.

Blodgett, R. (1986, May). Lost in the stars: Psychics strike out (again). *People Expression, 32*–35.

Bloomfield, K., Greenfield, T. K., Kraus, L., & Augustin, R. (2002). A comparison of drinking patterns and alcohol-related problems in the United States and Germany, 1995. *Substance Use and Misuse, 37*, 399–428.

Bobo, L. (1988). Attitudes toward the black political movement: Trends, meaning, and effects of racial policy preferences. *Social Psychology Quarterly, 51*, 287–302.

Boehm, S. L., Reed, C. L., McKinnon, C. S., & Phillips, T. J. (2002). Shared genes influence sensitivity to the effects of ethanol on locomotor and anxiety-like behaviors, and the stress axis. *Psychopharmacology, 161*, 54–63.

Boesch, C. (1991). Teaching among wild chimpanzees. *Animal Behaviour, 41*, 530–532.

Bolles, R. C., & Beecher, M. D. (Eds.). (1988). *Evolution and learning.* Hillsdale, NJ: Erlbaum.

Bolling, M. Y., & Kohlenberg, R. J. (2004). Reasons for quitting serotonin reuptake inhibitor therapy: Paradoxical psychological side effects and patient satisfaction. *Psychotherapy and Psychosomatics, 73*(6), 380–385.

Bonanno, G. A, Papa, A., Lalande, K., Westphal, M., & Coifman, K. (2004). The importance of being flexible. *Psychological Science, 15*, 482–487.

Bond, R., & Smith, P. B. (1996). Culture and conformity: A meta-analysis of studies using Asch's (1952b, 1956) line judgment task. *Psychological Bulletin, 119*, 111–137.

Boneva, B., Frieze, I. H., Ferligoj, A., Pauknerova, D., & Orgocka, A. (1998). Achievement, power, and affiliation motives as clues to (e)migration desires: A four-countries comparison. *European Psychologist, 3*, 247–254.

Bonnel, A. M., & Hafter, E. R. (1998). Divided attention between simultaneous auditory and visual signals. *Perception & Pychophysics, 60*, 179–190.

Bonvillian, J. D., & Patterson, F. G. P. (1997). Sign language acquisition and the development of meaning in a lowland gorilla. In C. Mandell & A. McCabe (Eds.), *The problem of meaning: Behavioral and cognitive perspectives.* Amsterdam: North-Holland/Elsevier Science.

Booth, A., & Amato, P. R. (2001). Parental pre-divorce relations and offspring postdivorce well-being. *Journal of Marriage and the Family, 63*, 197–212.

Bootzin, R. R. (2002). Cognitive-behavioral treatment of insomnia: Knitting up the ravell'd sleeve of care. In D. T. Kenny, J. G. Carlson, F. J. McGuigan, & J. L. Sheppard (Eds.), *Stress and health: Research and clinical applications*. Amsterdam: Harwood.

Borod, J. C. (2000). *The neuropsychology of emotion*. New York: Oxford University Press.

Boschker, M. S., Baker, F. C., & Michaels, C. F. (2002). Memory for the functional characteristics of climbing walls: Perceiving affordances. *Journal of Motor Behavior, 34,* 25–36.

Bosson, J. K., Haymovitz, E. L., & Pinel, E. C. (2004). When saying and doing diverge: The effects of stereotype threat on self-reported versus non-verbal anxiety. *Journal of Experimental Social Psychology, 40,* 247–255.

Bouchard, T. J. (2004). Genetic influence on human psychological traits. *Current Directions in Psychological Science 13,* 148–151.

Bouchard, T. J., Lykken, D. T., McGue, M., Segal, N. L., & Tellegen, A. (1990). Sources of human psychological differences: The Minnesota study of twins reared apart. *Science, 250,* 223–228.

Bouchard, T. J., & McGue, M. (1981). Familial studies of intelligence: A review. *Science, 212,* 1055–1059.

Boulos, Z. (1998). Bright light treatment for jet lag and shift work. In R. Lam & W. Raymond (Eds.), *Seasonal affective disorder and beyond: Light treatment for SAD and non-SAD conditions*. Washington, DC: American Psychiatric Press.

Boutros, N. N., Gelernter, J., Gooding, D. C., Cubells, J., Young, A., Krystal, J. H., & Kosten, T. (2002). Sensory gating and psychosis vulnerability in cocaine-dependent individuals: Preliminary data. *Biological Psychiatry, 51,* 683–686.

Bower, G. H., Clark, M. C., Lesgold, M. A., & Winzenz, D. (1969). Hierarchical retrieval schemes in recall of categorized word lists. *Journal of Verbal Learning & Verbal Behavior, 8,* 323–343.

Bowlby, J. (1969). *Attachment and loss: Vol. 1. Attachment*. New York: Basic Books.

Bowlby, J. (1973). *Attachment and loss: Vol. 2. Separation: Anxiety and anger*. London: Hogarth.

Bowlby, J. (2000). *Loss: Sadness and depression*. New York: Basic Books.

Boyd, R., & Richerson, P. J. (2005). *The origin and evolution of cultures*. New York: Oxford University Press.

Bozarth, J. D., Zimring, F. M., & Tausch, R. (2002). Client-centered therapy: The evolution of a revolution. In D. J. Cain (Ed.), *Humanistic psychotherapies: Handbook of research and practice*. Washington, DC: American Psychological Association.

Brabender, V., Fallon, A. E., & Smolar, A. I. (2004). *Essentials of group therapy*. New York: Wiley.

Brandon, S., Boakes, J., Glaser, D., & Green, R. (1998). Recovered memories of childhood sexual abuse: Implications for clinical practice. *British Journal of Psychiatry, 172,* 296–307.

Bransford, J. D., & Johnson, M. K. (1972). Contextual prerequisites for understanding: Some investigations of comprehension and recall. *Journal of Verbal Learning & Verbal Behavior, 11,* 717–726.

Brantley, P., & Garrett, V. D. (1993). Psychobiological approaches to health and disease. In B. Sutker & H. E. Adams (Eds.), *Comprehensive handbook of psychopathology* (2nd ed.). New York: Plenum.

Brauer, M. (2001). Intergroup perception in the social context: The effects of social status and group membership on perceived out-group homogeneity and ethnocentrism. *Journal of Experimental Social Psychology, 37,* 15–31.

Bray, J. H., & Berger, S. H. (1993). Developmental issues in Step Families Research Project: Family relationships and parent-child interactions. *Journal of Family Psychology, 7,* 76–90.

Brazel, C. Y., & Rao, M. S. (2004). Aging and neuronal replacement. *Ageing Research Reviews, 3,* 465–483.

Brehm, J. W., & Self, E. A. (1989). The intensity of motivation. *Annual Review of Psychology, 40,* 109–131.

Breland, K., & Breland, M. (1961). The misbehavior of organisms. *American Psychologist, 16,* 681–684.

Breland, K., & Breland, M. (1966). *Animal behavior*. New York: Macmillan.

Bremner, J. D. (2000). Neurobiology of post-traumatic stress disorder. In G. Fink (Ed.), *Encyclopedia of stress*. San Diego, CA: Academic Press.

Bremner, J. D. (2005). *Brain imaging handbook*. New York: Norton.

Breslau, N. S., Davis, G. C., Andreski, P., Peterson, E. L., & Schultz, L. R. (1997). Sex differences in post-traumatic stress disorder. *Archives of General Psychiatry, 54,* 1044–1048.

Brewin, C. R. (2004). Commentary on McNally "Is traumatic amnesia nothing but psychiatric folklore?" *Cognitive Behaviour Therapy, 33,* 102–104.

Brickman, P., Coates, D., & Janoff-Bulman, R. (1978). Lottery winners and accident victims: Is happiness relative? *Journal of Personality and Social Psychology, 36,* 917–927.

Briere, J., & Lanktree, C. (1983). Sex role-related effects of sex bias in language. *Sex Roles, 9,* 625–632.

Broadbent, D. E. (1958). *Perception and communication*. London: Pergamon Press.

Broberg, D. J., & Bernstein, I. L. (1987). Candy as a scapegoat in the prevention of food aversions in children receiving chemotherapy. *Cancer, 60,* 2344–2347.

Bronzaft, A. L., Ahern, K. D., McGinn, R., O'Connor, J., & Savino, B. (1998). Aircraft noise: A potential health hazard. *Environment & Behavior, 30,* 101–113.

Brooks-Gunn, J., Han, W. J., & Waldfogel, J. (2002). Maternal employment and child cognitive outcomes in the first three years of life: The NICHD study of early child care. *Child Development, 73,* 1052–1072.

Brown, E., Deffenbacher, K., & Sturgill, W. (1977). Memory for faces and the circumstances of encounter. *Journal of Applied Psychology, 62,* 311–318.

Brown, G. W., & Harris, T. O. (1978). *Social origins of depression*. London: Tavistock Press.

Brown, J. A. (1958). Some tests of the decay theory of immediate memory. *Quarterly Journal of Experimental Psychology, 10,* 12–21.

Brown, J. D. (1998). *The self*. Boston: McGraw-Hill.

Brown, L. S. (1994). *Subversive dialogues: Theory in feminist therapy*. New York: Basic Books.

Brown, N. O. (1959). *Life against death*. New York: Random House.

Brown, R. (1973). *A first language: The early stages*. Cambridge, MA: Harvard University Press.

Brown, R., & Kulik, J. (1977). Flashbulb memories. *Cognition, 5,* 73–99.

Brown, S. L., Nesse, R. M., Vinokur, A. D. & Smith, D. M. (2003). Providing social support may be more beneficial than receiving it: Results from a prospective study of mortality. *Psychological Science, 14,* 320–327.

Brown, T. A., Di-Nardo, P. A., Lehman, C. L., & Campbell, L. A. (2001). Reliability of DSM-IV anxiety and mood disorders: Implications for the classification of emotional disorders. *Journal of Abnormal Psychology, 110,* 49–58.

Brown, T. S., & Wallace, P. (1980). *Physiological psychology*. New York: Academic Press.

Brownell, K. D. (1994). *The LEARN program for weight control*. Dallas, TX: American Health.

Bruce, T. J., & Sanderson, W. C. (1998). *Specific phobias: Clinical applications of evidence-based psychotherapy*. Northvale, NJ: Aronson.

Bruck, M., Ceci, S. J., & Hembrooke, H. (1998). Reliability and credibility of young children's reports: From research to policy and practice. *American Psychologist, 53,* 136–151.

Bruederl, J., Diekmann, A., & Engelhardt, H. (1997). Erhoeht eine Probeehe das Scheidungsrisiko? Eine empirische Untersuchung mit dem Familiensurvey [Does a trial marriage increase divorce risk? Empirical study of the Families Survey]. *Koelner Zeitschrift fuer Soziologie und Sozialpsychologie, 49,* 205–222.

Bruner, J. (1983). *Child's talk*. New York: Norton.

Bruunk, B., & Gibbons, F. X. (Eds.). (1997). *Health, coping, and well-being: Perspectives from social comparison theory*. Mahwah, NJ: Erlbaum.

Bryan, J., III. (1986). *Hodgepodge: A commonplace book*. New York: Ballantine.

Buck, L., & Axel, R. (1991). A novel multigene family may encode odorant receptors: A molecular basis for odor recognition. *Cell, 65,* 175–187.

Buet, V. I., & Harris, T. (1994). The third national health and nutrition examination survey: Contributing data. *Gerontologist, 34,* 486–490.

Bullier, J. (2002). Neural basis of vision. In H. Pashler & S. Yantis (Eds.), *Steven's handbook of experimental psychology: Vol. 1. Sensation and perception* (3rd ed.). New York: Wiley.

Bureau of the Census. (2002). *Demographic Trends in the 20th Century: Census 2000 Special*

Reports, CENSR-4, November. Available online: http://www.census.gov/population/www/cen2000/briefs.html

Bureau of the Census. (2003). *Married-couple and unmarried-partner households: 2000. Census 2000 Special Reports, CENSR-5.* Available online: http://www.census.gov/population/www/cen2000/briefs.html

Burgess, C. A., & Kirsch, I. (1999). Expectancy information as a moderator of the effects of hypnosis on memory. *Contemporary Hypnosis, 16,* 22–31.

Burgwyn-Bailes, E., Baker-Ward, L., Gordon, B. N., & Ornstein, P. A. (2001). Children's memory for emergency medical treatment after one year: The impact of individual difference variables on recall and suggestibility. *Applied Cognitive Psychology, 15,* S25–S48.

Burke, K. C., Burke, J. D., Rae, D. S., & Regier, D. A. (1991). Comparing age at onset of major depression and other psychiatric disorders by birth cohorts in five U.S. community populations. *Archives of General Psychiatry, 48,* 789–795.

Burley, T., & Freier, M. C. (2004). Character structure: A gestalt-cognitive theory. *Psychotherapy: Theory, Research, Practice, Training, 41,* 321–331.

Burns, M. O., & Seligman, M. E. P. (1991). Explanatory style, helplessness, and depression. In C. R. Snyder & D. R. Forsyth (Eds.), *Handbook of social and clinical psychology: The health perspective.* New York: Pergamon Press.

Burnstein, E., Crandall, C., & Kitayama, S. (1994). Some neo-Darwinian decision rules for altruism: Weighing cues for inclusive fitness as a function of the biological importance of the decision. *Journal of Personality and Social Psychology, 67,* 773–789.

Burton, E., Stice, E., & Seeley, J. R (2004). A prospective test of the stress-buffering model of depression in adolescent girls: No support once again. *Journal of Consulting and Clinical Psychology, 72,* 689–697.

Busey, T. A., Tunnicliff, J. J., Loftus, G. R., & Loftus, E. F. (2000). Accounts of the confidence-accuracy relation in recognition memory. *Psychonomic Bulletin and Review, 7,* 26–48.

Bushman, B. J. (2002). Does venting anger feed or extinguish the flame? Catharsis, rumination, distraction, anger and aggressive responding. *Personality and Social Psychology, 28,* 724–731.

Bushman, B. J., & Bonacci, A. M. (2002). Violence and sex impair memory for television ads. *Journal of Applied Psychology, 87,* 557–564.

Bushnell, I. W. R. (2001). Mother's face recognition in newborn infants: Learning and memory. *Infant and Child Development, 10,* 67–74.

Buske-Kirschbaum, A., Kirschbaum, C., & Hellhammer, D. H. (1994). Conditioned modulation of NK cells in humans: Alteration of cell activity and cell number by

conditioning protocols. *Psychologische Beitraege, 36,* 100–111.

Buske-Kirschbaum, A., Kirschbaum, C., Stierle, H., & Lehnert, H. (1992). Conditioned increase of natural killer cell activity (NKCA) in humans. *Psychosomatic Medicine, 54,* 123–132.

Buss, A., & Plomin, R. (1975). *A temperament theory of personality development.* New York: Wiley.

Buss, A., & Plomin, R. (1984). *Temperament: Early developing personality traits.* Hillsdale, NJ: Erlbaum.

Buss, D. M. (1985). Human mate selection. *American Scientist, 73,* 47–51.

Buss, D. M. (1989). Sex differences in human mate preferences: Evolutionary hypotheses tested in 37 cultures. *Behavioral and Brain Sciences, 12,* 1–49.

Buss, D. M. (1991). Evolutionary personality theory. *Annual Review of Psychology, 42,* 459–491.

Buss, D. M. (1995). Evolutionary psychology: A new paradigm for psychological science. *Psychological Inquiry, 6,* 1–30.

Buss, D. M. (1999). Human nature and individual differences: The evolution of human personality. In L. A. Pervin & O. P. John (Eds.), *Handbook of personality: Theory and research.* New York: Guilford Press.

Buss, D. M. (2005). *The handbook of evolutionary psychology.* New York: Wiley.

Buss, D. M., Abbott, M., Angleitner, A., Asherian, A., Biaggio, A., Blanco-Villasenor, A., et al. (1990). International preferences in selecting mates: A study of 37 cultures. *Journal of Cross-Cultural Psychology, 21,* 5–47.

Buss, D. M., & Schmitt, D. P. (1993). Sexual Strategies Theory: An evolutionary perspective on human mating. *Psychological Review, 100,* 204–232.

Byer, C. O., Shainberg, L. W., & Galliano, G. (2002). *Dimensions of human sexuality* (6th ed.). Boston: McGraw-Hill.

Byrd, M. R., Richards, D. F., Hove, G., & Frima, P. C. (2002). Treatment of early onset hair pulling as a simple habit. *Behavior Modification, 26,* 400–411.

Byrne, D. (1997). An overview (and underview) of research and theory within the attraction paradigm. *Journal of Social and Personal Relationships, 14,* 417–431.

Byrne, D., Ervin, C. R., & Lamberth, J. (1970). Continuity between the experimental study of attraction and real-life computer dating. *Journal of Personality and Social Psychology, 16,* 157–165.

Byrne, D., & Greendlinger, V. (1989). *Need for affiliation as a predictor of classroom friendships.* Unpublished manuscript, State University of New York at Albany.

Cabeza, R., Nyberg, L., & Park, D. C. (2005). *Cognitive neuroscience of aging: Linking cognitive and cerebral aging.* New York: Oxford University Press.

Cacioppo, J. T., Berntson, J. T., Poehlmann, K. M., & Ito, T. A. (2000). The psychophysiology

of emotion. In M. Lewis & J. M. Haviland-Jones (Eds.), *Handbook of emotions* (2nd ed.). New York: Guilford Press.

Cain, D. J., & Seeman, J. (Eds.). (2002). *Humanistic psychotherapies: Handbook of research and practice.* Washington, DC: American Psychological Association.

Cairns, H. (1952). Disturbances of consciousness in lesions of the mid-brain and diencephalon. *Brain, 75,* 107–114.

Caldwell, A. B. (1994). *The profile of Jeffrey Dahmer* [Videotape]. Los Angeles: Caldwell Report.

Camilleri, C., & Malewska-Peyre, H. (1997). Socialization and identity strategies. In J. W. Berry, P. R. Dasen, & T. S. Saraswathi (Eds.), *Handbook of cross-cultural psychology: Basic processes and human development: Vol. 2. Handbook of cross-cultural psychology* (2nd ed.). Boston: Allyn & Bacon.

Campbell, A., Shirley, L., & Candy, J. (2004). A longitudinal study of gender-related cognition and behaviour. *Developmental Science, 7,* 1–9.

Campfield, L. A. (1997). Metabolic and hormonal controls of food intake: Highlights of the last 25 years: 1972–1997. *Appetite, 29,* 135–152.

Canivez, G. L., & Watkins, M. W. (1998). Long-term stability of the Wechsler Intelligence Scale for Children—Third Edition. *Psychological Assessment, 10,* 285–291.

Canli, T. (2004). Functional brain mapping of extraversion and neuroticism: Learning from individual differences in emotion processing. *Journal of Personality, 72,* 1105–1132.

Cannon, W. B. (1929). *Bodily changes in pain, hunger, fear, and rage.* New York: Appleton-Century.

Cannon, W. B. (1942). "Voodoo" death. *American Anthropologist, 44,* 169–181.

Cannon, W. B., & Washburn, A. L. (1912). An explanation of hunger. *American Journal of Physiology, 29,* 441–454.

Cardasis, W., Hochman, J. A., & Silk, K. R. (1997). Transitional objects and borderline personality disorder. *American Journal of Psychiatry, 154,* 250–255.

Cardeña, E., Lynn, S. J., & Krippner, S. (2000). Introduction: Anomalous experiences in perspective. In E. Cardeña, S. J. Lynn, & S. Krippner (Eds.), *Varieties of anomalous experience: Examining the scientific evidence.* Washington, DC: American Psychological Association.

Carels, R. A., Douglass, O. M., & Cacciapaglia, H. M. (2004). An ecological momentary assessment of relapse crises in dieting. *Journal of Consulting and Clinical Psychology, 72,* 341–348.

Carey, F. (1977). The child as a word learner. In M. Halle, J. Bresnan, & G. Miller (Eds.), *Linguistic theory and psychological reality.* Cambridge, MA: MIT Press.

Carey, G., & Gottesman, I. I. (1981). Twin and family studies of anxiety, phobic, and obsession disorders. In D. F. Klein &

J. Rabkin (Eds.), *Anxiety: New research and changing concepts*. New York: Raven Press.

Carlson, C. (2000). ADHD is overdiagnosed. In R. L. Atkinson, R. C. Atkinson, E. E. Smith, D. J. Bem, & S. Nolen-Hoeksema, *Hilgard's introduction to psychology* (13th ed.). Ft. Worth, TX: Harcourt Brace.

Carlson, E. A., & McAndrew, F. T. (2004). Body shape ideals and perceptions of body shape in Spanish and American college students. *Perceptual and Motor Skills, 99*, 1071–1074.

Carlson, J. G., & Hatfield, E. (1992). *Psychology of emotion*. Ft. Worth, TX: Harcourt Brace Jovanovich.

Carlson, S. M., Moses, L. J., & Hix, H. R. (1998). The role of inhibitory processes in young children's difficulties with deception and false belief. *Child Development, 69*, 672–691.

Carney, L. H. (2002). Neural basis of audition. In H. Pashler & S. Yantis (Eds.), *Steven's handbook of experimental psychology: Vol. 1. Sensation and perception* (3rd ed.). New York: Wiley.

Carnicero, J. A. C., Perez-Lopez, J., Salinas, M. D. C. G., & Martinez-Fuentes, M. T. (2000). A longitudinal study of temperament in infancy: Stability and convergence of measures. *European Journal of Personality, 14*, 21–37.

Carpenter, P. A., Just, M. A., & Shell, P. (1990). What one intelligence test measures: A theoretical account of the processing in the Raven Progressive Matrices Test. *Psychological Review, 97*, 404–431.

Carpenter, R., & Robson, J. (Eds.). (1999). *Vision research: A practical guide to laboratory methods*. New York: Oxford University Press.

Carroll, C. R. (1993). *Drugs in modern society*. Madison, WI: Brown & Benchmark.

Carroll, J. B. (1993). *Human cognitive abilities: A survey of factor-analytic studies*. New York: Cambridge University Press.

Carson, R. C., Butcher, J. N., & Coleman, J. C. (1988). *Abnormal psychology and modern life* (8th ed.). Glenview, IL: Scott, Foresman.

Carter, S. J., & Cassaday, H. J. (1998). State dependent retrieval and chlorpheniramine. *Human Psychopharmacology: Clinical and Experimental, 13*, 513–523.

Cartwright, R. D. (1977). *Night life: Explorations in dreaming*. Englewood Cliffs, NJ: Prentice Hall.

Carver, C. S., & Scheier, M. F. (2003). *Perspectives on personality* (5th ed.). Boston: Allyn & Bacon.

Carver, C. S., Scheier, M. F., & Weintraub, J. K. (1989). Assessing coping strategies: A theoretically based approach. *Journal of Personality and Social Psychology, 56*, 267–283.

Case, R. (1987). The structure and process of intellectual development. *International Journal of Psychology, 22*, 571–607.

Case, R., Demetriou, A., Platsidou, M., & Kazi, S. (2001). Integrating concepts and tests of intelligence from the differential and developmental traditions. *Intelligence, 29*, 307–336.

Caspi, A., Elder, G. H., & Bem, D. J. (1988). Moving away from the world: Life course patterns of shy children. *Developmental Psychology, 24*, 824–831.

Caspi, A., & Roberts, B. W. (1999). Personality continuity and change across the life course. In L. A. Pervin & O. P. John (Eds.), *Handbook of personality: Theory and research*. New York: Guilford Press.

Castonguay, L. G., & Beutler, L. E. (in press). *Principles of therapeutic change that work*. New York: Oxford University Press.

Catania, A. C. (2001). Positive psychology and positive reinforcement. *American Psychologist, 56*, 86–87.

Catania, C. A. (1998). *Learning* (4th ed.). Upper Saddle River, NJ: Prentice Hall.

Catchpole, C. K., & Rowell, A. (1993). Song sharing and local dialects in a population of the European wren *Troglodytes troglodytes*. *Behaviour, 125*, 67–78.

Catrambone, R. (1998). The subgoal learning model: Creating better examples so that students can solve novel problems. *Journal of Experimental Psychology: General, 127*, 355–376.

Cattabeni, F., Colciaghi, F., & Di Luca, M. (2004). Platelets provide human tissue to unravel pathogenic mechanisms of Alzheimer disease. *Progress in Neuro-Psychopharmacology & Biological Psychiatry, 28*, 763–770.

Cattell, R. B. (1965). *The scientific analysis of personality*. Chicago: Aldine.

Cattell, R. B. (1971). *Abilities: Their growth, structure, and action*. Boston: Houghton Mifflin.

Cattell, R. B. (1998). Where is intelligence? Some answers from the triarchic theory. In J. J. McArdler et al. (Eds.), *Human cognitive abilities in theory and practice*. Mahwah, NJ: Erlbaum.

Caughlin, J. P., & Malis, R. S. (2004). Demand/withdraw communication between parents and adolescents: Connections with self-esteem and substance use. *Journal of Social and Personal Relationships, 21*, 125–148.

Ceci, S. J. (1996). *On intelligence: A bioecological treatise on intellectual development*. Cambridge, MA: Harvard University Press.

Ceci, S. J., Bruck, M., & Battin, D. B. (2000). The suggestibility of children's testimony. In D. F. Bjorklund (Ed.), *False-memory creation in children and adults: Theory, research, and implications*. Mahwah, NJ: Erlbaum.

Ceci, S. J., & Williams, W. M. (1997). Schooling, intelligence, and income. *American Psychologist, 52*, 1051–1058.

Centers for Disease Control and Prevention. (1988). *Posttraumatic stress disorders*. Atlanta, GA: Author.

Centers for Disease Control and Prevention. (1997). *Fertility, family planning, and women's health: New data from the 1995 National Survey on Family Growth* (Series 23, No. 19). Washington, DC: Author.

Centers for Disease Control and Prevention. (2002a). *Causes of death in the United States*. Atlanta, GA: Author.

Centers for Disease Control and Prevention. (2002b). Youth risk behavior surveillance—United States, 2001. *Morbidity and Mortality Weekly Report, 51*(SS04), 1–64. Washington, DC: Author.

Centers for Disease Control and Prevention. (2003). *HIV/AIDS statistics*. Atlanta, GA: Author.

Cervone, D. (1999). Bottom-up explanation in personality psychology: The case of cross-situational consistency. In D. Cervone & Y. Shoda (Eds.), *The coherence of personality*. New York: Guilford Press.

Cervone, D., & Shoda, Y. (1999). *The coherence of personality: Social-cognitive bases of consistency, variability, and organization*. New York: Guilford Press.

Chalmers, D. J. (1995). The puzzle of conscious experience. *Scientific American, 273*(6), 80–86.

Chambless, D. L., & Hollon, S. D. (1998). Defining empirically supported therapies. *Journal of Consulting and Clinical Psychology, 66*, 7–18.

Chan, Z. C. Y., & Ma, J. L. C. (2002). Family themes of food refusal: Disciplining the body and punishing the family. *Health Care for Women International, 23*, 49–58.

Chandler, M. J., Lacritz, L. H., Cicerello, A. R., Chapman, S. B., Honig, L. S., Weiner, M. F., & Cullum, C. M. (2004). Three-word recall in normal aging. *Journal of Clinical and Experimental Neuropsychology, 26*, 1128–1133.

Chang, E. C. (1996). Cultural differences in optimism, pessimism, and coping: Predictors of subsequent adjustment in American and Caucasian American college students. *Journal of Counseling Psychology, 43*, 113–123.

Chang, E. C. (1998). Dispositional optimism and primary and secondary appraisal of a stressor: Controlling for confounding influences and relations to coping and psychological and physical adjustment. *Journal of Personality and Social Psychology, 74*, 1109–1120.

Chappell, M., & Humphreys, M. S. (1994). An auto-associative neural network for sparse representations: Analysis and application to models of recognition and cued recall. *Psychological Review, 101*, 103–128.

Chartrand, T. L., & Bargh, J. A. (2002). Nonconscious motivations: Their activation, operation, and consequences. In A. Tesser, D. A. Stapel, & J. V. Wood (Eds.), *Self and motivation: Emerging psychological perspectives*. Washington, DC: American Psychological Association.

Chartrand, T. L., Bargh, J. A., & van Baaren, R. (2002). *Consequences of automatic evaluation for mood*. Manuscript submitted for publication.

Chase, W. G., & Simon, H. A. (1973). Perception in chess. *Cognitive Psychology, 4*, 55–81.

Chen, C., Greenberger, E., Lester, J., Dong, Q., & Guo, M. S. (1998). A cross-cultural study of family and peer correlates of adolescent misconduct. *Developmental Psychology, 34*, 770–781.

Chen, H., Charlat, O., Tartaglia, L. A., Woolf, E. A., Weng, X., & Ellis, S. J. (1996). Evidence that the diabetes gene encodes the leptin receptor: Identification of a mutation in the leptin receptor gene in db/db mice. *Cell, 84,* 491–495.

Chen, H., & Lan, W. (1998). Adolescents' perceptions of their parents' academic expectations: Comparison of American, Chinese-American, and Chinese high school students. *Adolescence, 33,* 385–390.

Chen, S. C. (1937). Social modification of the activity of ants in nest-building. *Physiological Zoology, 10,* 420–436.

Chenoweth, D. (2002). *Evaluating worksite health promotion.* Champaign, IL: Human Kinetics.

Chi, L. (2004). Achievement goal theory. In T. Morris & J. Summers (Eds.), *Sport psychology: Theories, applications, and issues* (2nd ed.). Sydney, Australia: Wiley.

Chi, M. T. H. (1997). Creativity: Shifting across ontological categories flexibly. In T. B. Ward et al. (Eds.), *Creative thought: An investigation of conceptual structures and processes.* Washington, DC: American Psychological Association.

Chiappe, D., & MacDonald, K. (2005). The evolution of domain-general mechanisms in intelligence and learning. *Journal of General Psychology, 132,* 5–40.

Chiappelli, F. (2000). Immune suppression. In G. Fink (Ed.), *Encyclopedia of stress.* San Diego, CA: Academic Press.

Chiles, J. A., & Strossahl, K. D. (1995). *The suicidal patient: Principles of assessment, treatment, and case management.* Washington, DC: American Psychiatric Press.

Chiriboga, D. A. (1989). Mental health at the midpoint: Crisis, challenge, or relief? In S. Hunter & M. Sundel (Eds.), *Midlife myths: Issues, findings, and practice implications.* Newbury Park, CA: Sage.

Choi, I., Dalal, R., Kim Prieto, C., & Park, H. (2003). Culture and judgement of causal relevance. *Journal of Personality and Social Psychology, 84,* 46–59.

Chomsky, N. (1965). *Aspects of a theory of syntax.* Cambridge, MA: MIT Press.

Chomsky, N. (1972). *Language and mind.* New York: Harcourt.

Chomsky, N. (1987). Language in a psychological setting. *Sophia Linguistic Working Papers in Linguistics, 22,* Sophia University, Tokyo.

Christianson, S. A., & Nilsson, L. G. (1989). Hysterical amnesia: A case of aversively motivated isolation of memory. In T. Archer & L. G. Nilsson (Eds.), *Aversion, avoidance, and anxiety: Perspectives on aversively motivated behavior.* Hillsdale, NJ: Erlbaum.

Christopherson, E. R., & Mortweet, S. L. (2001). *Treatments that work with children: Empirically supported strategies for managing childhood problems.* Washington, DC: American Psychological Association.

Church, A. T., & Katigbak, M. S. (2000). Trait psychology in the Philippines. *American Behavioral Scientist, 44,* 73–94.

Chwalisz, K., Diener, E., & Gallagher, D. (1988). Autonomic arousal feedback and emotional experience: Evidence from the spinal cord injured. *Journal of Personality and Social Psychology, 54,* 820–828.

Chwilla, D. J., & Kolk, H. H. J. (2002). Three step priming in lexical decision. *Memory and Cognition, 30,* 217–225.

Cialdini, R. B. (2001). *Influence: Science and practice* (4th ed.). Boston: Allyn & Bacon.

Cialdini, R. B., Brown, S. L., Lewis, B. P., & Luce, C. (1997). Reinterpreting the empathy-altruism relationship: When one into one equals oneness. *Journal of Personality and Social Psychology, 73,* 481–494.

Cialdini, R. B., & Goldstein, N. J. (2004). Social influence: Compliance and conformity. *Annual Review of Psychology, 55,* 591–621.

Cialdini, R. B., & Sagarin, B. J. (2005). Principles of interpersonal influence. In T. C. Brock & M. C. Green (Eds.), *Persuasion: Psychological insights and perspectives* (2nd ed.). Thousand Oaks, CA: Sage.

Cialdini, R. B., Schaller, M., Hoolihan, D., Arps, K., Fultz, J., & Beaman, A. L. (1987). Empathy-based helping: Is it selflessly or selfishly motivated? *Journal of Personality and Social Psychology, 52,* 749–758.

Cianelli, S. N., & Fouts, R. S. (1998). Chimpanzee to chimpanzee American Sign Language. *Human Evolution, 13,* 147–159.

Cigales, M., Field, T., Lundy, B., Cuadra, A., & Hart, S. (1997). Massage enhances recovery from habituation in normal infants. *Infant Behavior and Development, 20,* 29–34.

Clancy, S. A., McNally, R. J., Schacter, D. L., Lenzeweger, M. F., & Pitman, R. K. (2002). Memory distortion in people reporting abduction by aliens. *Journal of Abnormal Psychology, 111,* 455–461.

Claparède, E. (1911). Recognition et moïté. *Archives de Psychologies, 11,* 79–90.

Clark, A. E. (1998). *The positive externalities of higher unemployment: Evidence from household data.* Working paper, Universite d'Orleans, Orleans, France.

Clark, D. A. (2004). *Cognitive-behavioral therapy for OCD.* New York: Guilford Press.

Clark, D. A., Beck, A. T., & Alford, B. A. (1999). *Scientific foundations of cognitive theory and therapy of depression.* New York: Wiley.

Clark, D. A., Beck, A. T., & Brown, G. (1989). Cognitive mediation in general psychiatric outpatients: A test of the content-specificity hypothesis. *Journal of Personality and Social Psychology, 56,* 958–964.

Clark, D. A., & O'Connor, K. (2005). Thinking is believing: Ego-dystonic intrusive thoughts in obsessive-compulsive disorder. In D. A. Clark (Ed.), *Intrusive thoughts in clinical disorders: Theory, research, and treatment.* New York: Guilford Press.

Clark, D. M. (1988). A cognitive model of panic attacks. In S. Rachman & J. D. Maser (Eds.), *Panic: Psychological perspectives.* Hillsdale, NJ: Erlbaum.

Clark, K. B., & Clark, M. P. (1947). Racial identification and preference in Negro children. In T. N. Newcomb & E. L. Hartley (Eds.), *Readings in Social Psychology.* New York: Holt.

Clark, R. D., III. (2001). Effects of majority defection and multiple minority sources on minority influence. *Group Dynamics, 5,* 57–62.

Clark, W. R., & Grunstein, M. (2005). *Are we hardwired?: The role of genes in human behavior.* New York: Oxford University Press.

Clarke, A. M., & Clarke, A. D. B. (2000). *Early experience and the life path.* London: Kingsley.

Clarkin, J. F., Marziali, E., & Munroe-Blum, H. (1992). *Borderline personality disorder: Clinical and empirical perspectives.* New York: Guilford Press.

Clay, R. A. (2002). Advertising as science. *Monitor on Psychology, 33*(9), 38–41.

Clifford, B. R. (2004). Levels of processing 30 years on: A special issue of memory: Book review. *Applied Cognitive Psychology, 18,* 486–489.

Cloninger, C. R., & Gottesman, I. I. (1989). Genetic and environmental factors in antisocial behavior disorders. In S. Mednick, T. Moffitt, & S. Strack (Eds.), *The causes of crime: New biological approaches.* Cambridge, England: Cambridge University Press.

Clore, G. L., & Centerbar, D. (2004). Analyzing anger: How to make people mad. *Emotion, 4,* 139–144.

Clutton-Brock, T. (2002). Breeding together: Kin selection and mutualism in cooperative vertebrates. *Science, 296,* 69–72.

Coan, J. A., & Allen, J. (2003). Frontal EEG asymmetry and the behavioral activation and inhibition systems. *Psychophysiology, 40,* 106–114.

Cochrane, R. E., Tett, R. P., & Vandecreek, L. (2003). Psychological testing and the selection of police officers: A national survey. *Criminal Justice and Behavior, 30,* 115–120.

Coffey, C., Carlin, J. B., Degenhardt, L., Lynskey, M., Sanci, L., & Patton, G. C. (2002). Cannabis dependence in young adults: An Australian population study. *Addiction, 97,* 187–194.

Coffey, C. E., Weiner, R. D., Djang, W. T., et al. (1991). Brain anatomic effects of electro-convulsive therapy: A prospective magnetic resonance imaging study. *Archives of General Psychiatry, 48,* 1013–1020.

Cohen, K. M. (2002). Relationships among childhood sex-atypical behavior, spatial ability, handedness, and sexual orientation in men. *Archives of Sexual Behavior, 31,* 129–143.

Cohen, S. (1988). Psychosocial models of the role of social support in the etiology of physical disease. *Health Psychology, 7,* 269–297.

Cohen, S., Doyle, W. J., Turner, R., Alper, C. M. & Skoner, D. P. (2003). Sociability and susceptibility to the common cold. *Psychological Science, 14,* 389–395.

Cohen, S., & Herbert, T. B. (1996). Health psychology: Psychological factors and physical disease from the perspective of human psychoneuroimmunology. *Annual Review of Psychology, 47,* 113–142.

Cohen, S., Kessler, R. C., & Gordon, L. U. (1995). *Measuring stress.* New York: Oxford University Press.

Cohen, S. I. (1985). Psychosomatic death: Voodoo death in a modern perspective. *Integrative Psychiatry, 3,* 46–51.

Collings, P. (2001). If you got everything, it's good enough: Perspectives on successful aging in a Canadian Inuit community. *Journal of Cross-Cultural Gerontology, 16,* 127–155.

Collins, A. M., & Loftus, E. F. (1975). A spreading activation theory of semantic processing. *Psychological Review, 82,* 407–428.

Collins, D. W., & Kimura, D. (1997). A large sex difference on a two-dimensional mental rotation task. *Behavioral Neuroscience, 111,* 845–849.

Columbia. (1996). *The Columbia world of quotations.* Retrieved March 21, 2003, from http://www.bartleby.com

Columbia Accident Investigation Board. (2003). *Report* (Vol. 1). Retrieved October 2, 2003 from http://www.nasa.gov/columbia/home/index.html

Committee on Animal Research and Ethics (CARE). (2005). Research with animals in psychology. American Psychological Association. Retrieved March 14, 2005, from http://www.apa.org/science/animal2.html

Compton, S., Burns, B. J., Egger, H. L., & Robertson, E. (2002). Review of the evidence base for treatment of childhood psychopathology: Internalizing disorders. *Journal of Consulting and Clinical Psychology, 71,* 1240–1266.

Comuzzie, A. G., & Allison, D. B. (1998). The search for human obesity genes. *Science, 280,* 1374–1377.

Conrad, R. (1964). Acoustic confusions in immediate memory. *British Journal of Psychology, 55,* 75–84.

Cooke, P. (1991, June 23). They cried until they couldn't see. *New York Times Magazine, 25,* 43.

Cooper, C. R., & Denner, J. (1998). Theories linking culture and psychology: Universal and community-specific processes. *Annual Review of Psychology, 49,* 559–584.

Cooper, J., Mirabile, R., & Scher, S. J. (2005). Actions and attitudes: The theory of cognitive dissonance. In T. C. Brock & M. C. Green (Eds.), *Persuasion: Psychological insights and perspectives* (2nd ed.). Thousand Oaks, CA: Sage.

Coopersmith, S. (1967). *The antecedents of self-esteem.* San Francisco: Freeman.

Corales, T. A. (Ed.). (2005). *Focus on posttraumatic stress disorder research.* Hauppauge, NY: Nova Science.

Cordova, J. V., Gee, C. B., & Warren, L. Z. (2005). Emotional skillfulness in marriage: Intimacy as a mediator of the relationship between emotional skillfulness and marital satisfaction. *Journal of Social and Clinical Psychology, 24,* 218–235.

Core Institute. (2002). *Statistics on substance use by college students.* Carbondale, IL: Author.

Correll, J., Park, B., Judd, C. M., & Wittenbrink, B. (2002). The police officer's dilemma: Using ethnicity to disambiguate potentially threatening individuals. *Journal of Personality and Social Psychology, 83,* 1314–1329.

Corrigan, P. W. (2005). *On the stigma of mental illness: Practical strategies for research and social change.* Washington, DC: American Psychological Association.

Cosmides, L., & Tooby, J. (2002). Unraveling the enigma of human intelligence: Evolutionary psychology and the multimodular mind. In R. J. Sternberg & J. C. Kaufman (Eds.), *The evolution of intelligence.* Mahwah, NJ: Erlbaum.

Costa, L. (1996). Lifespan neuropsychology. *Clinical Neuropsychologist, 10,* 365–374.

Costa, P. T., & McCrae, R. R. (1992). The five-factor model of personality and its relevance to personality disorders. *Journal of Personality Disorders, 6,* 343–359.

Costa, P. T., & McCrae, R. R. (2002). Looking backward: Changes in the mean levels of personality traits from 80 to 12. In D. Cervone & W. Mischel (Eds.), *Advances in personality science.* New York: Guilford Press.

Courchesne, E., Carper, R., & Aksboomoff, N. (2003). Evidence of brain overgrowth in the first year of life. *Journal of the American Medical Association, 290,* 337–344.

Courneya, K. S. (1995). Understanding readiness for regular physical activity in older individuals: An application of the theory of planned behavior. *Health Psychology, 14,* 80–87.

Cousins, S. D. (1989). Culture and self-perception in the United States and Japan. *Journal of Personality and Social Psychology, 56,* 124–131.

Cowan, C. P., & Cowan, P. A. (2000). *When partners become parents: The big life change for couples.* Mahwah, NJ: Erlbaum.

Crabbe, J. C. (2002). Genetic contributions to addiction. *Annual Review of Psychology, 53,* 435–462.

Craik, F. I. M., & Lockhart, R. S. (1972). Levels of processing: A framework for memory research. *Journal of Verbal Learning and Verbal Behavior, 11,* 671–684.

Craik, F. I. M., & Tulving, E. (1975). Depth of processing and the retention of words in episodic memory. *Journal of Experimental Psychology: General, 104,* 268–294.

Crandall, C. S., D'Anello, S., Sakalli, N., Lazarus, E., Wieczorkowska, G., & Feather, N. T. (2001). An Attribution-Value model of prejudice: Anti-fat attitudes in six nations. *Personality and Social Psychology Bulletin, 27,* 30–37.

Craske, M. (1999). *Anxiety disorders: psychological approaches to theory and treatment.* Boulder, CO: Westview Press.

Craske, M. (2003). *Origins of phobias and anxiety disorders: Why more women than men?* New York: Elsevier Science.

Craske, M. G., & Rowe, M. K. (1997). Nocturnal panic. *Clinical Psychology: Science and Practice, 4,* 153–174.

Crawford, M., & Chaffin, R. (1997). The meanings of difference: Cognition in social and cultural context. In P. J. Caplan & M. Crawford (Eds.), *Gender differences in human cognition. Counterpoints: Cognition, memory, and language.* New York: Oxford University Press.

Creese, I., Burd, D. R., & Snyder, S. H. (1976). Dopamine receptor binding predicts clinical and pharmacological potencies of antischizophrenic drugs. *Science, 192,* 481–483.

Crits-Christoph, P., Cooper, A., & Luborsky, L. (1988). The accuracy of therapists' interpretations and the outcome of dynamic psychotherapy. *Journal of Consulting and Clinical Psychology, 56,* 490–495.

Croizet, J.-C., Despres, G., Gauzins, M.-E., Huguet, P., Leyens, J.-P., & Meot, A. (2004). Stereotype threat undermines intellectual performance by triggering a disruptive mental load. *Personality and Social Psychology Bulletin, 30,* 721–731.

Crook, J. M., & Copolov, D. L. (2000). Schizophrenia. In G. Fink (Ed.), *Encyclopedia of stress.* San Diego, CA: Academic Press.

Crowe, L. C., & George, W. H. (1989). Alcohol and human sexuality: Review and integration. *Psychological Bulletin, 105,* 374–386.

Crowley, K., Callanan, M. A., Tenenbaum, H. R., & Allen, E. (2001). Parents explain more often to boys than to girls during shared scientific thinking. *Psychological Science, 12,* 258–261.

Culbertson, F. M. (1997). Depression and gender: An international review. *American Psychologist, 52,* 25–31.

Cull, W. L. (2000). Untangling the benefits of multiple study opportunities and repeated testing for cued recall. *Applied Cognitive Psychology, 14,* 215–235.

Cummings, L. (2005). *Pragmatics: A multidisciplinary perspective.* Mahwah, NJ: Erlbaum.

Curtis, G. C., Magee, W. J., Eaton, W. W., Wittchen, H.-U., & Kessler, R. C. (1998). Specific fears and phobias: Epidemiology and classification. *British Journal of Psychiatry, 173,* 112–117.

Curtiss, S. (1977). *Genie: A psychological study of a modern day "wild child."* New York: Academic Press.

Cytowic, R. E. (2002). *Synesthesia: A union of the senses* (2nd ed.). Boston: MIT Press.

Dalton, P. (2002). Olfaction. In H. Pashler & S. Yantis (Eds.), *Steven's handbook of experimental psychology: Vol. 1. Sensation and perception* (3rd ed.). New York: Wiley.

Daly, M., & Wilson, M. (1988). *Homicide.* New York: Aldine de Gruyter.

Damasio, A. R. (2005). Emotions and feelings: a neurobiological perspective. In A. S. R. Manstead, N. H. Frijda, A. H. Fischer, &

K. Oatley (Eds.), *Feelings and Emotions: The Amsterdam Symposium.* New York: Cambridge University Press.

Daniels, C. W. (2002). Legal aspects of polygraph admissibility in the United States. In M. Kleiner (Ed.), *Handbook of polygraph testing.* San Diego, CA: Academic Press.

Darley, J. M., & Gross, P. H. (1983). A hypothesis-confirming bias in labeling effects. *Journal of Personality and Social Psychology, 44,* 20–33.

Darley, J. M., & Latané, B. (1968). Bystander intervention in emergencies: Diffusion of responsibility. *Journal of Personality and Social Psychology, 8,* 377–383.

Darwin, C. (1859). *On the origin of species by means of natural selection.* London: Murray.

Darwin, C. (1965). *The expression of emotion in man and animals.* Chicago: University of Chicago Press. (Original work published 1872)

Dasen, P. R., Barthélémy, D., Kan, E., Kouamé, K., Daouda, K., Adjéi, K. K., & Assandé, N. (1985). N'glouele, l'intelligence chez les Baoulé [N'glouele, intelligence according to the Baoulé]. *Archives de Psychologie, 53,* 293–324.

Davidoff, J. (2004). Coloured thinking. *Psychologist, 17,* 570–572.

Davidson, R. J. (1998). *Neuropsychological perspectives on affective and anxiety disorders.* Chicago: Psychology Press.

Davidson, R. J., & Fox, N. A. (1988). Cerebral asymmetry and emotion: Developmental and individual differences. In D. L. Molfese & S. J. Segalowitz (Eds.), *Brain lateralization in children: Developmental implications.* New York: Guilford Press.

Davis, C. G., Nolen, H. S., & Larson, J. (1998). Making sense of loss and benefiting from the experience: Two construals of meaning. *Journal of Personality and Social Psychology, 75,* 561–574.

Davis, S., Jenkins, G., & Hunt, R. (Eds.). (2002). *The pact: Three young men make a promise and fulfill a dream.* New York: Riverhead.

Davis, T., Gunderson, J. G., & Myers, M. (1999). Borderline personality disorder. In D. G. Jacobs (Ed.), *The Harvard Medical School Guide to suicide assessment and intervention.* San Francisco: Jossey-Bass.

Dawidowicz, L. S. (1975). *The war against the Jews, 1933–1945.* New York: Holt, Rinehart & Winston.

Dawood, K., Pillar, R. C., Horvath, C., Revelle, W., & Bailey, J. M. (2000). Familial aspects of male homosexuality. *Archives of Sexual Behavior, 29,* 155–163.

Dawson, G., Toth, K., Abbott, R., Osterling, J., Munson, J., Estes, A., & Liaw, J. (2004). Early social attention impairments in autism: Social orienting, joint attention, and attention to distress. *Developmental Psychology, 40,* 271–283.

Dawson-McClure, S. R., Sandler, I. N., Wolchik, S. A., & Millsap, R E. (2004). Risk as a moderator of the effects of prevention programs for children from divorced families: A six-year longitudinal study. *Journal of Abnormal Child Psychology, 32,* 175–190.

Day, R., Nielsen, J. A., Korten, A., et al. (1987). Stressful life events preceding the acute onset of schizophrenia. *Culture, Medicine, and Psychiatry, 11,* 123–205.

Deary, I. J., Whiteman, M. C., Starr, J. M., Whalley, L. J., & Fox, H. (2004). The impact of childhood intelligence on later life: Following up the Scottish Medical Surveys of 1932 and 1947. *Journal of Personality and Social Psychology, 86,* 130–147.

DeCasper, A. J., & Spence, M. J. (1986). Prenatal maternal speech influences newborns' perceptions of speech sounds. *Infant Behavior and Development, 9,* 133–150.

deCastro, J. M. (2002). Age-related changes in the social, psychological, and temporal influences on food intake in free-living, healthy, adult humans. *Journals of Gerontology: Series A. Biological Sciences and Medical Sciences, 57A,* 368–377.

Deci, E. L., & Ryan, R. M. (1985). *Intrinsic motivation and self-determination in human behavior.* New York: Plenum Press.

Deci, E. L., & Ryan, R. M. (2002). *Handbook of self-determination theory research.* Rochester, NY: University of Rochester Press.

De Cremer, D., & van Lange, P. A. M. (2001). Why prosocials exhibit greater cooperation than proselfs: The roles of social responsibility and reciprocity. *European Journal of Personality, 15,* 5–18.

Deese, J. (1959). Influence of inter-item associative strength upon immediate free recall. *Psychological Reports, 5,* 305–312.

Degen, L., Matzinger, D., Drewe, J., & Beglinger, C. (2001). The effect of cholecystokinin in controlling appetite and food intake in humans. *Peptides, 22,* 1265–1269.

deGeus, E. J. C. (2000). Aerobics in stress reduction. In G. Fink (Ed.), *Encyclopedia of stress.* San Diego, CA: Academic Press.

Dehaene, S., & Naccache, L. (2001). Towards a cognitive neuroscience of consciousness: Basic evidence and a workspace framework. *Cognition, 79,* 1–37.

Dekker, E., & Groen, J. (1956). Reproducible psychogenic attacks of asthma. *Journal of Psychosomatic Research, 1,* 56–67.

DeLongis, A. (2000). Coping skills. In G. Fink (Ed.), *Encyclopedia of stress.* San Diego, CA: Academic Press.

Demarest, J., & Allen, R. (2000). Body image: Gender, ethnic, and age differences. *Journal of Social Psychology, 140,* 465–472.

Dement, W. C. (1974). *Some must watch while some must sleep.* San Francisco: Freeman.

Démonet, J. F., Thierry, G., & Cardebat, D. (2005). Renewal of the neurophysiology of language: Functional neuroimaging. *Physiological Reviews, 85,* 49–95.

DeMoranville, B. M., Jackson, I., Ader, R., Madden, K. S., Felten, D. L., & Bellinger, D. L. (2000). Endocrine and immune systems. In B. S. Fogel, R. B. Schiffer, & S. M. Rao (Eds.), *Synopsis of neuropsychiatry.* Philadelphia: Lippincott-Raven.

Depue, R. A., & Collins, P. F. (1999). Neurobiology of the structure of personality: Dopamine, facilitation of incentive motivation, and extraversion. *Behavioral and Brain Sciences, 22,* 491–569.

Depue, R. A., & Lenzenweger, M. F. (2005). A neurobehavioral dimensional model of personality disorders. In M. F. Lenzenweger & J. F. Clarkin (Eds.), *Major theories of personality disorder.* New York: Guilford Press.

DeRegnier, R. A., Wewerka, S., Georgieff, M. K., Mattia, F., & Nelson, C. A. (2002). Influences of postconceptional age and postnatal experience on the development of auditory recognition memory in the newborn infant. *Developmental Psychobiology, 41,* 216–225.

Deregowski, J. B. (1989). Real space and represented space: Cross-cultural perspectives. *Behavior and Brain Sciences, 12,* 51–119.

Derogatis, L. R. (1986). *Clinical psychopharmacology.* Menlo Park, CA: Addison-Wesley.

DeRubeis, R. J., & Crits-Christoph, P. (1998). Empirically supported individual and group psychological treatments for adult mental disorders. *Journal of Consulting and Clinical Psychology, 66,* 37–52.

De Silva, P., & Rachman, J. (1998). *Obsessive-compulsive disorders.* New York: Oxford University Press.

DeSteno, D., Dasgupta, N., Bartlett, M. Y., & Cajdric, A. (2004). Prejudice from thin air: The effect of emotion on automatic intergroup attitudes. *Psychological Science, 15,* 319–324.

DeStefano, D., & LeFevre, J. (2004). The role of working memory in mental arithmetic. *European Journal of Cognitive Psychology, 16,* 353–386.

Deutsch, M., & Gerard, H. B. (1955). A study of normative and informational social influence upon individual judgment. *Journal of Abnormal and Social Psychology, 51,* 629–636.

Devane, W. A., Hanus, L., Breuer, A., Pertwee, R. G., Stevenson, L. A., & Griffin, G. (1992). Isolation and structure of a brain constituent that binds to the cannabinoid receptor. *Science, 18,* 1946–1949.

DeVries, H., Mudde, A. N., Dijkstra, A., & Willemsen, M. C. (1998). Differential beliefs, perceived social influences, and self-efficacy expectations among smokers in various motivational phases. *Preventive Medicine, 27,* 681–689.

Dhabhar, F. S., & McEwen, B. S. (2001). Bidirectional effects of stress and glucocorticoid hormones on immune function: Possible explanations for paradoxical observations. In R. Ader, D. L. Feiten, & N. Cohen (Eds.), *Psychoneuroimmunology* (Vol. 1). San Diego, CA: Academic Press.

Diaz, J. (1997). *How drugs influence behavior: A neuro-behavioral approach.* Upper Saddle River, NJ: Prentice Hall.

DiClemente, C. C. (2003). *Addiction and change: How addictions develop and addicted people recover.* New York: Guilford Press.

Diener, E. (2000). Subjective well-being: The science of happiness and a proposal for a national index. *American Psychologist, 55,* 34–43.

Diener, E., & Diener, C. (1996). Most people are happy. *Psychological Science 7,* 181–185.

Diener, E., Diener, M., & Diener, C. (1996). Factors predicting the well-being of nations. *Journal of Personality and Social Psychology, 69,* 851–864.

Diener, E., & Seligman, M. (2004). Beyond money: Toward an economy of well-being. *Psychological Science in the Public Interest, 5,* 1–31.

Diener, E., & Seligman, M. E. P. (2002). Very happy people. *Psychological Science, 13,* 81–84.

Diener, E., Suh, E., Lucas, R. E., & Smith, H. L. (1999). Subjective well-being: Three decades of progress. *Psychological Bulletin, 125,* 276–302.

DiLalla, L. F. (Ed.). (2004). *Behavior genetics principles: Perspectives in development, personality, and psychopathology.* Washington, DC: American Psychological Association.

Dillard, J. P., & Anderson, J. W. (2004). The role of fear in persuasion. *Psychology & Marketing, 21,* 909–926.

Dimberg, U. (1997). Psychophysiological reactions to facial expressions. In U. C. Segerstrale et al. (Eds.), *Nonverbal communication: Where nature meets culture.* Mahwah, NJ: Erlbaum.

Dindia, K. (2002). Self-disclosure research: Knowledge through meta-analysis. In M. Allen, R. W. Preiss, B. M. Gayle, & N. A. Burrell (Eds.), *Interpersonal communication research: Advances through meta-analysis.* Mahwah, NJ: Erlbaum.

Di Paula, A., & Campbell, J. D. (2002). Self-esteem and persistence in the face of failure. *Journal of Personality and Social Psychology, 83,* 711–724.

Dishman, R. K. (1982). Compliance/adherence in health-related exercise. *Health Psychology, 1,* 237–267.

Dishman, R. K. (1994). *Advances in exercise adherence.* Champaign, IL: Human Kinetics.

Dixon, N. F. (1981). *Preconscious processing.* New York: Wiley.

Dodge, K. A. (1986). A social information processing model of social competence in children. *Cognitive perspectives on children's social behavioral development. The Minnesota symposium on child psychology, 18,* 77–125.

Doka, K. J. (1995). Coping with life-threatening illness: A task model. *Omega: Journal of Death and Dying, 32,* 111–122.

Dolezal, H. (1982). *Living in a world transformed: Perceptual and performatory adaptation to a visual distortion.* New York: Academic Press.

Domhoff, G. W. (1999). Drawing theoretical implications from descriptive empirical findings on dream content. *Dreaming: Journal of the Association for the Study of Dreams, 9,* 201–210.

Domhoff, G. W. (2001). A new neurocognitive theory of dreams. *Dreaming: Journal of the Association for the Study of Dreams, 11,* 13–33.

Domino, G. (2000). *Psychological testing.* Upper Saddle River, NJ: Prentice Hall.

Domjan, M. (2000a). *The essentials of conditioning and learning* (2nd ed.). Belmont, CA: Wadsworth/Thomson.

Domjan, M. (2000b). General process learning theory: Challenges from response and stimulus factors. *International Journal of Comparative Psychology, 13,* 101–118.

Donaldson, D. (1998). *Psychiatric disorders with a biochemical basis.* New York: Parthenon.

Donnerstein, E., & Malamuth, N. (1997). Pornography: Its consequences on the observer. In L. B. Schlesinger & E. Revitch (Eds.), *Sexual dynamics of anti-social behavior* (2nd ed.). Springfield, IL: Charles C Thomas.

Doppelt, J. E., & Wallace, W. L. (1955). Standardization of the Wechsler Adult Intelligence Scale for older persons. *Journal of Abnormal and Social Psychology, 51,* 312–330.

Dossenbach, M., & Dossenbach H. D. (1998). *All about animal vision.* Chicago: Blackbirch Press.

Dovidio, J. F. (1984). Helping behavior and altruism: An empirical and conceptual overview. In L. Berkowitz (Ed.), *Advances in experimental social psychology* (Vol. 17). New York: Academic Press.

Downey, G., & Feldman, S. L. (1996). Implications of rejection sensitivity for intimate relationships. *Journal of Personality and Social Psychology, 70,* 1327–1343.

Drake, M. E., Pakalnis, A., & Denio, L. C. (1988). Differential diagnosis of epilepsy and multiple personality: Clinical and EEG findings in 15 cases. *Neuropsychiatry, Neuropsychology, and Behavioral Neurology, 1,* 131–140.

Driscoll, I., McDaniel, M. A., & Guynn, M. J. (2005). Apolipoprotein E and prospective memory in normally aging adults. *Neuropsychology, 19,* 28–34.

Driskell, J. E., Willis, R. P., & Copper, C. (1992). Effect of overlearning on retention. *Journal of Applied Psychology, 77,* 615–622.

Drukin, K. (1998). Implicit content and implicit processes in mass media use. In K. Kirsner et al. (Eds.), *Implicit and explicit mental processes.* Mahwah, NJ: Erlbaum.

Dryden, W. (Ed.). (2002). *Handbook of individual therapy.* Thousand Oaks, CA: Sage.

Duffy, J. F., Rimmer, D. W., Czeisler, C. A. (2001). Association of intrinsic circadian period with morningness-eveningness, usual wake time, and circadian phase. *Behavioral Neuroscience, 115,* 895–899.

Duncan, P. M., Alici, T., & Woodward, J. D. (2000). Conditioned compensatory response to ethanol as indicated by locomotor activity in rats. *Behavioural Pharmacology, 11,* 395–402.

Dunn, J., & Plomin, R. (1990). *Separate lives: Why siblings are so different.* New York: Basic Books.

Dunne, M. P., Bailey, J. M., Kirk, K. M., & Martin, N. G. (2000). The subtlety of sex-atypicality. *Archives of Sexual Behavior, 29,* 549–565.

Durrant, J. E. (2000). Trends in youth crime and well-being since the abolition of corporal punishment in Sweden. *Youth and Society, 31,* 437–455.

Duvander, A. Z. E. (1999). The transition from cohabitation to marriage: A longitudinal study of the propensity to marry in Sweden in the early 1990s. *Journal of Family Issues, 20,* 698–717.

Dweck, C. (1991). Self-theories and goals: Their role in motivation, personality, and development. In R. Dienstbier (Ed.), *Perspectives on motivation.* Lincoln: University of Nebraska Press.

Dweck, C. (1999). *Self theories: Their role in motivation, personality, and development.* Philadelphia: Psychology Press/Taylor and Francis.

Dying to be thin. (2000). *Nova* [Television series]. Boston: WGBH.

Eacott, M. J., & Crawley, R. A. (1998). The offset of childhood amnesia: Memory for events that occurred before age 3. *Journal of Experimental Psychology: General, 127,* 22–33.

Eagly, A. H., & Crowley, M. (1986). Gender and helping behavior: A meta-analytic review of the social psychological literature. *Psychological Bulletin, 100,* 283–308.

Eagly, A. H., & Wood, W. (1999). The origins of sex differences in human behavior: Evolved dispositions versus social roles. *American Psychologist, 54,* 408–423.

Eaton, J. (2001). Management communication: The threat of groupthink. *Corporate Communications, 6,* 183–192.

Ebbinghaus, H. (1964). *Über das Gedächtnis: Untersuchungen Zur Experimentellen Psychologie [Memory: A contribution to experimental psychology]* (H. A. Ruger & C. E. Bussenius, Trans.). New York: Dover. (Original work published 1885)

Eccles, J. (1991). Gender-role socialization. In R. M. Baron, W. G. Graziano, & C. Stangor (Eds.), *Social psychology.* Ft. Worth, TX: Holt, Rinehart & Winston.

Echt, K. V., Morrell, R. W., & Park, D. C. (1998). Effects of age and training formats on basic computer skill acquisition in older adults. *Educational Gerontology, 24,* 3–25.

Eckensberger, L. H., & Zimba, R. F. (1997). The development of moral judgment. In J. W. Berry, P. R. Dasen, & T. S. Saraswathi (Eds.), *Handbook of cross-cultural psychology* (2nd ed., Vol. 2). Boston: Allyn & Bacon.

Eden, D. (2003). Self-fulfilling prophecies in organizations. In J. Greenberg (Ed.), *Organizational behavior: The state of the science* (2nd ed.). Mahwah, NJ: Erlbaum.

Edser, S. J. (2002). Hypnotically facilitated counter conditioning of anticipatory nausea and vomiting associated with chemotherapy: A case study. *Australian Journal of Clinical Hypnotherapy and Hypnosis, 23,* 18–30.

Edwards, A. E. (1962). A demonstration of the long-term retention of a conditioned galvanic skin response. *Psychosomatic Medicine, 24,* 459–463.

Ehrman, J. (2003). *Clinical exercise psychology.* Champaign, IL: Human Kinetics.

Eisenberg, N. (2000). Emotion, regulation, and moral development. *Annual Review of Psychology, 51,* 665–697.

Eisenberg, N. (2002). Emotion related regulation and its relation to quality of social functioning. In W. Hartup & R. A. Weinberg (Eds.), *Child psychology in retrospect and prospect: In celebration of the 75th anniversary of the Institute of Child Development. The Minnesota symposia on child psychology* (Vol. 32). Mahwah, NJ: Erlbaum.

Eisenberg, N. (2004). Prosocial and moral development in the family. In T. A. Thorkildsen & H. J. Walberg (Eds.), *Nurturing morality. Issues in children's and families' lives.* New York: Kluwer Academic/Plenum Press.

Eisenberger, N. I., Lieberman, M. D., & Williams, K. D. (2003). Does rejection hurt? An fMRI study of social exclusion. *Science, 302,* 290–292.

Ekman, P. (1973). Cross-cultural studies of facial expression. In P. Ekman (Ed.), *Darwin and facial expression.* San Diego, CA: Academic Press.

Ekman, P., & Friesen, W. V. (1987). *Facial Action Coding System.* Palo Alto, CA: Consulting Psychologists Press.

Ekman, P., Friesen, W. V., & Ellsworth, P. (1972). *Emotion in the human face: Guidelines for research and an integration of findings.* Oxford, England: Pergamon Press.

Elbert, T., Pantev, C., Wienbruch, C., Rockstroh, B., & Taub, E. (1995). Increased cortical representation of the fingers of the left hand in string players. *Science, 270,* 305–307.

Elfenbein, H. A., & Ambady, N. (2003). Universals and cultural differences in recognizing emotions. *Current Directions in Psychological Science, 12,* 159–164.

Eliassen, J. C., Souza, T., Sanes, J. N. (2003). Experience-dependent activation patterns in human brain during visual-motor associative learning. *Journal of Neuroscience, 23,* 10540–10547.

Elkind, D. (1967). Egocentrism in adolescence. *Child Development, 38,* 1025–1034.

Elliot, A. J., & Church, M. A. (1997). A hierarchical model of approach and avoidance achievement motivation. *Journal of Personality and Social Psychology, 72,* 218–232.

Elliot, A. J., & Thrash, T. M. (2002). Approach-avoidance motivation in personality: Approach and avoidance temperaments and goals. *Journal of Personality and Social Psychology, 82,* 804–818.

Ellis, A. (1962). *Reason and emotion in psychotherapy.* New York: Lyle Stuart.

Elsey, B., & Fujiwara, A. (2000). Kaizen and technology transfer instructors as work-based learning facilitators in overseas transplants: A case study. *Journal of Workplace Learning, 12,* 333–342.

Emerson, R. M. (1966). Mount Everest: A case study of communication feedback and sustained group goalstriving. *Sociometry, 29,* 213–227.

Emery, C. E., Jr. (2001, January/February). Cracked crystal balls? Psychics' predictions for past year a litany of prognostive failures. *The Skeptical Inquirer, 25*(1), 7–8.

Emlen, S. T. (1975, August). The stellar-orientation system of a migratory bird. *Scientific American,* 102–111.

Epel, E. S., Blackburn, E. H., Lin, J., Dhabhar, F. S., Adler, N. E., et al. (2004). Accelerated telomere shortening in response to life stress. *Proceedings of the National Academy of Sciences, 101*(49), 17312–17315.

Epstein, M. A., & Bottoms, B. L. (2002). Explaining the forgetting and recovery of abuse and trauma memories: Possible mechanisms. *Child Maltreatment: Journal of the American Professional Society on the Abuse of Children, 7,* 210–225.

Epstein, R., Kirshnit, C. E., Lanza, R. P., & Rubin, L. C. (1984). "Insight" in the pigeon: Antecedents and determinants of an intelligent performance. *Nature, 308,* 61–62.

Epstein, S. (1983). Aggregation and beyond: Some basic issues on the production of behavior. *Journal of Personality, 51,* 360–392.

Erdberg, P. (2000). Rorschach assessment. In G. Goldstein & M. Hersen (Eds.), *Handbook of psychological assessment* (3rd ed.). New York: Elsevier.

Erdelyi, M. H. (2001). Defense processes can be conscious or unconscious. *American Psychologist, 56,* 761–762.

Ericsson, K. A., & Chase, W. G. (1982). Exceptional memory. *American Scientist, 70,* 607–615.

Ericsson, K. A., Chase, W. G., & Faloon, S. (1980). Acquisition of a memory skill. *Science, 208,* 1181–1182.

Ericsson, K. A., Delaney, P. F., Weaver, G., & Mahadevan, R. (2004). Uncovering the structure of a memorist's superior "basic" memory capacity. *Cognitive Psychology, 49,* 191–237.

Ericsson, K. A., Krampe, R. T., & Tesch R. C. (1993). The role of deliberate practice in the acquisition of expert performance. *Psychological Review, 100,* 363–406.

Ericsson, K. A., & Polson, P. G. (1988). An experimental analysis of the mechanisms of a memory skill. *Journal of Experimental Psychology: Learning, Memory, and Cognition, 14,* 305–316.

Erikson, E. H. (1968). *Identity, youth and crisis.* New York: Norton.

Erikson, E. H. (1980). *Identity and the life cycle.* New York: Norton. (Original work published 1959)

Erikson, E. H., Erikson, J. M., & Kivnick, H. Q. (1986). *Vital involvement in old age.* New York: Norton.

Eron, L. D. (1987). The development of aggressive behavior from the perspective of a developing behaviorism. *American Psychologist, 42,* 435–442.

Eron, L. D. (2000). A psychological perspective. In V. B. Van Hasselt & M. Hersen (Eds.), *Aggression and violence: An introductory text.* Boston: Allyn & Bacon.

Esparza, J., Fox, C., Harper, I. T., Bennett, P. H., Schulz, L. O., Valencia, M. E., & Ravussin, E. (2000). Daily energy expenditure in Mexican and USA Pima Indians: Low physical activity as a possible cause of obesity. *International Journal of Obesity and Related Metabolic Disorders, 24,* 55–59.

Essau, C., & Petermann, F. (1999). *Depressive disorders in children and adolescents: Epidemiology, risk factors, and treatment.* Northvale, NJ: Aronson.

Essau, C., & Trommsdorff, G. (1996). Coping with university-related problems: A cross-cultural comparison. *Journal of Cross-Cultural Psychology, 27,* 315–328.

Esser, J. K., & Lindoerfer, J. S. (1989). Groupthink and the space shuttle Challenger accident: Toward a quantitative case analysis. *Journal of Behavioral Decision Making, 2,* 167–177.

Estes, T. H., & Vaughn, J. L. (1985). *Reading and learning in the content classroom: Diagrams and instructional strategies* (3rd ed.). Boston: Allyn & Bacon.

Evers, K. E., Harlow, H. L., Redding, C. A., & LaForge, R. G. (1998). Longitudinal changes in stages of change for condom use in women. *American Journal of Health Promotion, 13,* 19–25.

Exner, J. E. (1991). *The Rorschach—A comprehensive system: Assessment of personality and psychopathology* (Vol. 2). New York: Wiley.

Eysenck, H. J. (1952). The effects of psychotherapy: An evaluation. *Journal of Consulting Psychology, 16,* 319–324.

Eysenck, H. J. (1964). *Crime and personality.* Boston: Houghton Mifflin.

Eysenck, H. J. (1967). *The biological basis of personality.* Springfield, IL: Charles C. Thomas.

Eysenck, H. J. (1990). Biological dimensions of personality. In L. A. Pervin (Ed.), *Handbook of personality: Theory and research.* New York: Guilford Press.

Eysenck, H. J. (1994). Cancer, personality, and stress: Prediction and prevention. *Advances in Behaviour Research and Therapy, 16,* 167–215.

Eysenck, H. J., & Grossarth-Marticek, R. (1991). Creative novation behavior therapy as a prophylactic treatment for cancer and coronary heart disease: II. Effects of treatment. *Behavior Research and Therapy, 29,* 17–31.

Fabbro, F. (2001). The bilingual brain: Bilingual aphasia. *Brain & Language, 79,* 201–210.

Fagley, N. S. (1987). Positional response bias in multiple-choice tests of learning: Its relation to testwiseness and guessing strategy. *Journal of Educational Psychology, 79,* 95–97.

Fain, G. L. (1999). *Molecular and cellular physiology of neurons.* Cambridge, MA: Harvard University Press.

Faith, M. S., Matz, P. E., Jorge, M.A. (2002). Obesity depression associations in the population. *Journal of Psychosomatic Research, 53*, 935–942.

Fallon, A. E., & Rozin, P. (1985). Sex differences in perceptions of desirable body shape. *Journal of Abnormal Psychology, 94*, 102–105.

Falsetti, S. A., Monnier, J., & Resnick, H. S. (2005). Intrusive thoughts in posttraumatic stress disorder. In D. A. Clark (Ed.), *Intrusive thoughts in clinical disorders: Theory, research, and treatment.* New York: Guilford Press.

Fanselow, M. S. (1991). Analgesia as a response to aversive Pavlovian conditional stimuli: Cognitive and emotional mediators. In M. R. Denny (Ed.), *Fear, avoidance, and phobias: A fundamental analysis.* Hillsdale, NJ: Erlbaum.

Fanselow, M. S., & Poulos, A. M. (2005). The neuroscience of mammalian associative learning. *Annual Review of Psychology, 56*, 207–234.

Fantz, R. L. (1961, May). The origin of form perception. *Scientific American, 204*, 66–72.

Farberman, R. (2002). Antiviolence campaign ads air more than 168,000 times nationwide. *Monitor on Psychology, 33*, 10.

Farmer, E. M. Z., Compton, S. N., Burns, B. J., & Robertson, E. (2002). Review of the evidence base for treatment of childhood psychopathology: Externalizing disorders. *Journal of Consulting and Clinical Psychology, 71*, 1267–1302.

Faulkner, S., Williams, K., Sherman, B., & Williams, E. (1997, May). *The "silent treatment": Its incidence and impact.* Paper presented at the 69th Annual Meeting of the Midwestern Psychological Association, Chicago. Cited in Williams, K. D., Cheung, C. K. T., & Choi, W. (2000). Cyberostracism: Effects of being ignored over the Internet. *Journal of Personality & Social Psychology, 79*, 748–762.

Faust, J. (1991). Same-day surgery preparation: Reduction of pediatric patient arousal and distress through participant modeling. *Journal of Consulting and Clinical Psychology, 59*, 473–478.

Fazio, R. H., Jackson, J. R., Dunton, B. C., & Williams, C. J. (1995). Variability in automatic activation as an unobstrusive measure of racial attitudes: A bona fide pipeline? *Journal of Personality and Social Psychology, 69*, 1013–1027.

Fazio, R. H., & Roskos-Ewoldsen, D. R. (2005). Acting as we feel: When and how attitudes guide behavior. In T. C. Brock & M. C. Green (Eds.), *Persuasion: Psychological insights and perspectives* (2nd ed., pp. 41–62). Thousand Oaks, CA: Sage.

Federal Interagency Forum on Aging-Related Statistics. (2000). Older Americans 2000: *Key indicators of well-being.* Available online: http://www.agingstats.gov/chartbook2000

Fein, S., & Spencer, S. J. (1997). Prejudice as self-image maintenance: Affirming the self through derogating others. *Journal of Personality and Social Psychology, 73*, 31–44.

Feingold, A. (1988). Matching for attractiveness in romantic partners and same-sex friends: A meta-analysis and theoretical critique. *Psychological Bulletin, 104*, 226–235.

Feingold, A., & Mazzella, R. (1998). Gender differences in body image are increasing. *Psychological Science, 9*, 190–195.

Felmlee, D. H. (1998). "Be careful what you wish for . . .": A quantitative and qualitative investigation of "fatal attractions." *Personal Relationships, 5*, 235–253.

Felton, D. L., & Maida, M. E. (2000). Neuroimmunomodulation. In G. Fink (Ed.), *Encyclopedia of stress.* San Diego, CA: Academic Press.

Fenton, W. S., & McGlashan, T. H. (1991a). Natural history of schizophrenia subtypes: I. Longitudinal study of paranoid, hebe-phonic, and undifferentiated schizophrenia. *Archives of General Psychiatry, 48*, 969–977.

Fenton, W. S., & McGlashan, T. H. (1991b). Natural history of schizophrenia subtypes: II. Positive and negative symptoms and long-term course. *Archives of General Psychiatry, 48*, 978–986.

Ferguson, E. D. (2000). *Motivation: A biosocial and cognitive integration of motivation and emotion.* New York: Oxford University Press.

Fernald, A., Taeschner, T., Dunn, J., Papousek, M., De Boysson-Bardies, B., & Fukui, I. (1989). A cross-cultural study of prosodic modification in mothers' and fathers' speech to preverbal infants. *Journal of Child Language, 16*, 477–501.

Ferster, C. B., & Skinner, B. F. (1957). *Schedules of reinforcement.* Englewood Cliffs, NJ: Prentice Hall.

Festinger, L. (1954). A theory of social comparison processes. *Human Relations, 2*, 117–140.

Festinger, L. (1957). *A theory of cognitive dissonance.* Stanford, CA: Stanford University Press.

Festinger, L., & Carlsmith, J. M. (1959). Cognitive consequences of forced compliance. *Journal of Abnormal and Social Psychology, 58*, 203–210.

Festinger, L., Pepitone, A., & Newcomb, T. (1952). Some consequences of deindividuation in a group. *Journal of Abnormal Psychology, 47*, 382–389.

Fetterman, D. M. (1988). *Excellence and equality: A qualitatively different perspective on gifted and talented education.* Albany: State University of New York Press.

Fiedler, K., Nickel, S., Muehlfriedel, T., & Unkelbach, C. (2001). Is mood congruency an effect of genuine memory or response bias? *Journal of Experimental Social Psychology, 37*, 201–214.

Field, T. (2000). Infant massage therapy. In C. H. Zeanah, Jr. (Ed.), *Handbook of infant mental health* (2nd ed.). New York: Guilford Press.

Field, T. (2001). Massage therapy facilitates weight gain in preterm infants. *Current Directions in Psychological Science, 10*, 51–54.

Field, T. M., Schanberg, S. M., Scafidi, F., Bauer, C. R., Vega-Lahr, N., Garcia, R., Nystrom, J., & Kuhn, C. M. (1986). Tactile/kinesthetic stimulation effects on preterm neonates. *Pediatrics, 77*, 654–658.

Fields, H. L. (2005). *Pain: Mechanisms and management.* New York: McGraw-Hill.

Filogamo, G. (1998). *Brain plasticity: development and aging: Advances in neurobiology: plasticity and regeneration.* New York: Plenum.

Finell, J. S. (1997). *Mind-body problems: Psychotherapy with psychosomatic disorders.* Northvale, NJ: Aronson.

Fish, J. M. (2002). The myth of race. In J. M. Fish (Ed.), *Race and intelligence: Separating science from myth.* Mahwah, NJ: Erlbaum.

Fishbein, M., & Ajzen, I. (1974). Attitudes toward objects as predictors of single and multiple behavioral criteria. *Psychological Review, 81*, 59–74.

Fisher, C., Kahn E., Edwards, A., Davis, D. M., & Fine, J. (1974). A psychophysiological study of nightmares and night terrors: III. Mental content and recall of stage 4 night terrors. *Journal of Nervous and Mental Disease, 158*, 174–188.

Fisher, S., & Greenberg, R. P. (1996). *Freud scientifically reappraised: Testing the theories and therapy.* New York: Wiley.

Fiske, S. T. (2002). What we know about bias and intergroup conflict, the problem of the century. *Current Directions in Psychological Science, 11*, 123–128.

Flavell, J. H. (1970). Developmental studies of mediated behavior. In H. W. Reese and L. P. Lipsett (Eds.), *Advances in child development and behavior* (Vol. 5). New York: Academic Press.

Flavell, J. H. (2004). Theory-of-mind development: Retrospect and prospect. *Merrill-Palmer Quarterly, 50*, 274–290.

Fleeson, W. (2004). Moving personality beyond the person-situation debate. *Current Directions in Psychological Science, 13*, 83–87.

Flegal K. M., Carroll, M. D., Ogden, C. L., & Johnson, C. L. (2002). Prevalence and trends in obesity among U.S. adults, 1999–2000. *Journal of the American Medical Association, 288*, 1723–1727.

Flege, J. E., Yeni-Komshian, G. H., & Liu, S. (1999). Age constraints on second-language acquisition. *Journal of Memory & Language, 41*, 78–104.

Flinn, M. V. (1997). Culture and the evolution of social learning. *Evolution and Human Behavior, 18*, 23–67.

Flohr, H. (2000). NMDA receptor-mediated computational processes and phenomenal consciousness. In T. Metzinger (Ed.), *Neural correlates of consciousness: Empirical and conceptual questions.* Cambridge, MA: The MIT Press.

Flynn, J. R. (1987). Massive IQ gains in 14 nations: What IQ tests really measure. *Psychological Bulletin, 101*, 171–191.

Flynn, J. R. (1998). IQ gains over time: Toward finding the causes. In U. Neisser et al. (Eds.),

The rising curve: Long-term gains in IQ and related measures. Washington, DC: American Psychological Association.

Foa, E. B., Riggs, D. S., & Gershuny, B. S. (1995). Arousal, numbing, and intrusion: Symptom structure of posttraumatic stress disorder following assault. *American Journal of Psychology, 152,* 116–120.

Foa, E. B., Zoellner, L. A., Feeny, N. C., Hembree, E. A., & Alvarez-Conrad, J. (2002). Does imaginal exposure exacerbate PTSD symptoms? *Journal of Consulting and Clinical Psychology, 70,* 1022–1028.

Fordyce, W. E. (1988). Pain and suffering: A reappraisal. *American Psychologist, 43,* 276–283.

Fosse, R., Stickgold, R., & Hobson, J. A. (2001). Brain-mind states: Reciprocal variation in thoughts and hallucinations. *Psychological Science, 2001, 12,* 30–36.

Foulkes, D. (1982). REM-dream perspectives on the development of affect and cognition. *Psychiatric Journal of the University of Ottawa, 7,* 48–55.

Foulks, F. F., Bland, I. J., & Shervington, D. (1995). Psychotherapy across cultures. *Review of Psychiatry, 14,* 511.

Fouts, R. S., Fouts, D. H., & Van Cantfort, T. E. (1989). The infant Loulis learns signs from other cross-fostered chimpanzees. In R. A. Gardner, B. T. Gardner, & T. E. Van Cantfort (Eds.), *Teaching sign language to chimpanzees.* Albany: State University of New York Press.

Fox, D. K., Hopkins, B. L., & Anger, W. K. (1987). The long-term effects of a token economy on safety performance in open-pit mining. *Journal of Applied Behavior Analysis, 20,* 215–224.

Fox, N. A., Henderson, H. A., Marshall, P. J., Nichols, K. E., & Ghera, M. M. (2005). Behavioral inhibition: Linking biology and behavior within a developmental framework. *Annual Review of Psychology, 56,* 235–262.

Frances, A., & Widiger, T. A. (1986). Methodological issues in personality disorder diagnosis. In T. Millon & G. L. Klerman (Eds.), *Contemporary directions in psychopathology: Toward the DSM-IV.* New York: Guilford Press.

Frank, J. (1961). *Persuasion & healing: A comparative study of psychotherapy.* Baltimore: John Hopkins University Press.

Frank, N. C., Spirito, A., Stark, L., & Owens-Stively, J. (1997). The use of scheduled awakenings to eliminate childhood sleepwalking. *Journal of Pediatric Psychology, 22,* 345–353.

Franklin, B. *Remarks Concerning the Savage of North America.* (1784).

Franklin, J. (1987). *Molecules of the mind: The brave new science of molecular psychology.* New York: Atheneum.

Franklin, T. R., Acton, P. D., Maldjian, J. A., Gray, J. D., Croft, J. R., Dackis, C. A., O'Brien, C. P., & Childress, A. R. (2002). Decreased gray matter concentration in the insular, orbitofrontal, cingulate, and temporal cortices of cocaine patients. *Biological Psychiatry, 51,* 134–142.

Frayser, S. G. (1985). *Varieties of sexual experience: An anthropological perspective on human sexuality.* New Haven, CT: HRAF.

Fredrickson, B. L. (1998). What good are positive emotions? *Review of General Psychology, 2,* 300–319.

French, S. J., & Cecil, J. E. (2001). Oral, gastric and intestinal influences on human feeding. *Physiology and Behavior, 74,* 729–734.

Freud, S. (1957). Mourning and melancholia. In J. Strachey (Ed.), *The standard edition of the complete psychological works of Sigmund Freud,* (Vol. 14). London: Hogarth. (Original work published 1917)

Freud, S. (1923). *The ego and the id.* New York: Norton.

Freud, S. (1935). *A general introduction to psychoanalysis.* New York: Washington Square Press.

Freud, S. (1953). The interpretation of dreams. In J. Strachey (Ed.), *The standard edition of the complete psychological works of Sigmund Freud* (Vols. 4 and 5). London: Hogarth. (Original work published 1900)

Freud, S. (1965). *The interpretation of dreams.* New York: Avon. (Original work published 1900)

Friedman, H., & DiMatteo, M. R. (1989). *Health psychology.* New York: Prentice Hall.

Frijda, N. H., Manstead, A. S. R., & Bem, S. (Eds.). (2005). *Emotions and beliefs: How feelings influence thoughts.* New York: Cambridge University Press.

Frisby, J. P. (1980). *Seeing: Illusion, brain and mind.* Oxford, England: Oxford University Press.

Frisco, M. L., & Williams, K. (2003). Perceived housework equity, marital happiness, and divorce in dual earner households. *Journal of Family Issues, 24,* 51–73.

Fritsch, J. (1999, May 25). 95% Regain Lost Weight. Or Do They? *New York Times,* p. F7.

Fritzsche, B. A., Finkelstein, M. A., & Penner, L. A. (2000). To help or not to help: Capturing individuals' decision policies. *Social Behavior and Personality, 28,* 561–578.

Fuligni, A. J. (1998). Authority, autonomy, and parent-adolescent conflict and cohesion: A study of adolescents from Mexican, Chinese, Filipino, and European backgrounds. *Developmental Psychology, 34,* 782–792.

Funk, S. C. (1992). Hardiness: A review of theory and research. *Health Psychology 11,* 335–345.

Furmark, T., Tillfors, M., Marteinsdottir, I., Fischer, H., Pissiota, A., Langstroem, B., Fredrikson, M. (2002). Common changes in cerebral blood flow in patients with social phobia treated with citalopram or cognitive-behavioral therapy. *Archives of General Psychiatry, 59,* 425–433.

Gabbard, G. O. (1990). *Psychodynamic psychiatry in clinical practice.* Washington, DC: American Psychiatric Press.

Gabbard, G. O. (2004*). Long-term psychodynamic psychotherapy.* Washington, DC: American Psychiatric Publishing.

Gabbard, G. O., Beck, J., & Holmes, J. (2005). *Oxford textbook of psychotherapy.* New York: Oxford University Press.

Gabrieli, J. D. E. (1998). Cognitive neuroscience of human memory. *Annual Review of Psychology, 49,* 87–115.

Gabrieli, J. D. E., Desmond, J. E., Demb, J. B., & Wagner, A. D. (1996). Functional magnetic resonance imaging of semantic memory processes in the frontal lobes. *Psychological Science, 7,* 278–283.

Gainotti, G. (1972). Emotional behavior and hemispheric side of lesion. *Cortex, 8,* 41–55.

Galanter, E. (1962). Contemporary psychophysics. In R. Brown (Ed.), *New directions in psychology.* New York: Holt, Rinehart & Winston.

Galati, D., & Lavelli, M. (1997). Neonate and infant emotion expression perceived by adults. *Journal of Nonverbal Behavior, 21,* 57–83.

Galea, S., Ahern, J., Resnick, H., Kilpatrick, D., Bucuvalas, M., Gold, J., & Vlahov, D. (2002). Psychological sequelae of the September 11 terrorist attacks in New York City. *New England Journal of Medicine, 346,* 982–987.

Gallup, G. G. (1970). Chimpanzees: Self-recognition. *Science, 167*(3914), 86–87.

Gallup Organization (1988). *America's youth 1977–1988.* Princeton, NJ: Author.

Galton, F. (1869). *Hereditary genius.* London: Macmillan.

Ganis, G., Thompson, W. L., & Kosslyn, S. M. (2004). Brain areas underlying visual mental imagery and visual perception: An fMRI study. *Cognitive Brain Research, 20,* 226–241.

Garbarino, S., Beelke, M., Costa, G., Violani, C., Lucidi, F., Ferrillo, F., et al. (2002). Brain function and effects of shift work: Implications for clinical neuropharmacology. *Neuropsychobiology, 45,* 50–56.

Garcia, J., & Koelling, R. A. (1966). The relation of cue to consequence in avoidance learning. *Psychonomic Science, 4,* 123–124.

Garcia, J., Lasiter, P. S., Bermudez, R. F., & Deems, D. A. (1985). A general theory of aversion learning. *Annals of the New York Academy of Sciences, 443,* 8–21.

Gardner, H. (2000). *Multiple intelligences: The theory in practice.* New York: Basic Books.

Gardner, H. (2003). Three distinct meanings of intelligence. In R. J. Sternberg, J. Lautrey, & T. I. Lubart (Eds.), *Models of intelligence: International perspectives.* Washington, DC: American Psychological Association.

Gardner, R. A., & Gardner, B. T. (1969). Teaching language to a chimpanzee. *Science, 165,* 664–672.

Garland, D. J., & Barry, J. R. (1991). Cognitive advantage in sport: The nature of perceptual structures. *American Journal of Psychology, 104,* 211–228.

Garlick, D. (2002). Understanding the nature of the general factor of intelligence: The role of individual differences in neural plasticity as an explanatory mechanism. *Psychological Review, 109,* 116–136.

Garmezy, N. (1983). *Stress, coping and development in children*. New York: McGraw-Hill.

Garnefski, N., & Arends, E. (1998). Sexual abuse and adolescent maladjustment: Differences between male and female victims. *Journal of Adolescence, 21,* 99–107.

Gatchel, R. J. (2005). *Clinical essentials of pain management*. Washington, DC: American Psychological Association.

Gathercole, S. E. (1998). The development of memory. *Journal of Child Psychology and Psychiatry and Allied Disciplines, 39,* 3–27.

Gathercole, S. E., Pickering, S. J., Knight, C., & Stegmann, Z. (2004). Working memory skills and educational attainment: Evidence from national curriculum assessments at 7 and 14 years of age. *Applied Cognitive Psychology, 18,* 1–16.

Gazzaniga, M. S., & Smylie, C. S. (1983). Facial recognition and brain asymmetries: Clues to underlying mechanisms. *Annals of Neurology, 13,* 536–540.

Geary, D. (1995). Reflections of evolution and culture in children's cognition: Implications for mathematical instruction and development. *American Psychologist, 50,* 24–37.

Geher, G., Bauman, K. P., Hubbard, S. E. K., & Legare, J. R. (2002). Self and other obedience estimates: Biases and moderators. *Journal of Social Psychology, 142,* 677–689.

Gentile, D. A., Lynch, P. J., Linder, J. R., & Walsh, D. A. (2004). The effects of violent video game habits on adolescent hostility, aggressive behaviors, and school performance. *Journal of Adolescence, 27,* 5–22.

George, W. H., Stoner, S. A., Norris, J., Lopez, P. A., & Lehman, G. L. (2000). Alcohol expectancies and sexuality: A self-fulfilling prophecy analysis of dyadic perceptions and behavior. *Journal of Studies on Alcohol, 61,* 168–176.

Geracioti, T. D., Loosen, P. T., Ebert, M. H., & Schmidt, D. (1995). Fasting and postprandial cerebrospinal fluid glucose concentrations in healthy women and in an obese binge eater. *International Journal of Eating Disorders, 18,* 365–369.

Gerbner, G., Gross, L., Morgan, M., & Signiorelli, N. (1981). Health and medicine on television. *New England Journal of Medicine, 305,* 901–904.

Gergen, K. (2000). *An invitation to social constructivism*. Thousand Oaks, CA: Sage.

Gershoff, E. T. (2002a). Corporal punishment by parents and associated child behaviors and experiences: A meta-analytic and theoretical review. *Psychological Bulletin, 128,* 539–579.

Gershoff, E. T. (2002b). Corporal punishment, physical abuse, and the burden of proof: Reply to Baumrind, Larzelere, and Cowan (2002), Holden (2002), and Parke (2002). *Psychological Bulletin, 128,* 602–611.

Gershon, E. S., Berrettini, W. H., & Golden, L. E. (1989). Mood disorders: Genetic aspects. In H. I. Kaplan & B. J. Sadock (Eds.), *Comprehensive textbook of psychiatry/V.* Baltimore: Williams & Wilkins.

Gerwirtz, J. C., & Davis, M. (2000). Using Pavlovian higher-order conditioning paradigms to investigate the neural substrates of emotional learning and memory. *Learning & Memory, 7,* 257–266.

Ghetti, S., Qin, J., & Goodman, G. S. (2002). False memories in children and adults: Age, distinctiveness, and subjective experience. *Developmental Psychology, 38,* 705–718.

Gibson, E., & Walk, R. D. (1960). The visual cliff. *Scientific American, 202,* 80–92.

Gibson, J. J. (1979). *The ecological approach to visual perception*. Boston: Houghton Mifflin.

Gilbert, P. (2001). Evolutionary approaches to psychopathology: The role of natural defences. *Australian and New Zealand Journal of Psychiatry, 35,* 17–29.

Gilligan, C. (1982). *In a different voice: Psychological theory and women's development*. Cambridge, MA: Harvard University Press.

Glanzer, M. (1972). Storage mechanisms in recall. In G. H. Bower (Ed.), *The psychology of learning and motivation: Advances in research and theory* (Vol. 5). New York: Academic Press.

Glanzer, M., & Cunitz, A. R. (1966). Two storage mechanisms in free recall. *Journal of Verbal Learning and Verbal Behavior, 5,* 351–360.

Glaser, R., & Bassok, M. (1989). Learning theory and the study of instruction. *Annual Review of Psychology, 40,* 631–666.

Glucksman, M. L. (2001). The dream: A psychodynamically informative instrument. *Journal of Psychotherapy Practice and Research, 10,* 223–230.

Gobet, F., & Simon, H. A. (2000). Five seconds or sixty? Presentation time in expert memory. *Cognitive Science, 24,* 651–682.

Goddard, A. W., Mason, G. F., Almai, A., et al. (2001). Reductions in occipital cortex GABA levels in panic disorder detected with sup-1H-magnetic resonance spectroscopy. *Archives of General Psychiatry, 58,* 556–561.

Goddard, H. H. (1917). Mental tests and immigrants. *Journal of Delinquency, 2,* 243–277.

Godden, D. R., & Baddeley, A. D. (1975). Context-dependent memory in two natural environments: On land and under water. *British Journal of Psychology, 66,* 325–332.

Goffman, E. (1961). *Asylums: Essays on the social situation of mental patients and other inmates*. New York: Doubleday.

Goldberg, L. R. (1981). Unconfounding situational attributions from uncertain, neutral, and ambiguous ones: A psychometric analysis of descriptions of oneself and various types of others. *Journal of Personality and Social Psychology, 41,* 517–552.

Golden, C., Golden, C. J., & Schneider, B. (2003). Cell phone use and visual attention. *Perceptual and Motor Skills, 97,* 385–389.

Goldfried, M. R., & Eubanks-Carter, C. (2004). On the need for a new psychotherapy research paradigm: Comment on Westen, Novotny, & Thompson-Brenner. *Psychological Bulletin, 139,* 669–673.

Goldsmith, S. K. (2003). *Reducing suicide: A national imperative*. Washington, DC: National Academy Press.

Goldstein, B. (2002). *Sensation and perception* (6th ed.). Belmont, CA: Wadsworth.

Goldstein, E. B. (2005). *Blackwell handbook of sensation and perception*. Malden, MA: Blackwell.

Goldstein, G. (2000). Comprehensive neuropsychological assessment batteries. In G. Goldstein & M. Hersen (Eds.), *Handbook of psychological assessment* (3rd ed.). New York: Elsevier.

Goldstein, J. H., Cajko, L., Oosterbroek, M., Michielsen, M., Houten, O., & Salverda, F. (1997). Video games and the elderly. *Social Behavior and Personality, 25,* 345–352.

Gonzales, P. M., Blanton, H., & Williams, K. J. (2002). The effects of stereotype threat and double minority status on the test performance of Latino women. *Personality and Social Psychology Bulletin, 28,* 659–670.

Gonzalez, R. A., & Jaworski, J. N. (1997). Alcohol and glutamate. *Alcohol Health and Research World, 21,* 120–127.

Goodale, M. A. (1995). The cortical organization of visual perception and visuomotor control. In S. Kosslyn & D. N. Osheron (Eds.), *Visual cognition: An invitation to cognitive science* (2nd ed.). Cambridge, MA: MIT Press.

Goodale, M. A. (2000). Perception and action in the human visual system. In M. S. Gazzaniga (Ed.), *The new cognitive neurosciences* (2nd ed.). Cambridge, MA: MIT Press.

Goodall, J. (1986). *The chimpanzees of Gombe: Patterns of behavior*. Cambridge, MA: Harvard University Press.

Goode, W. J. (1959). The theoretical importance of love. *American Sociological Review, 24,* 38–47.

Goodman, W. (1982, August 9). Of mice, monkeys and men. *Newsweek,* 61.

Goodwin, P. J., Leszcz, M., Ennis, M., et al. (2001). The effect of group psychosocial support on survival in metastatic breast cancer. *New England Journal of Medicine, 34,* 1719–1726.

Gorman, J. M. (2002). Treatment of generalized anxiety disorder. *Journal of Clinical Psychiatry, 63*(Suppl. 8), 17–23.

Gosling, S. D., Vazire, S., Srivastava, S., & John, O. P. (2004). Should we trust web-based studies? A comparative analysis of six preconceptions about Internet questionnaires. *American Psychologist, 59,* 93–104.

Gotlib, I. H., Kasch, K. L, Traill, S., Joormann, J., Arnow, B. A., & Johnson, S. L. (2004). Coherence and specificity of information-processing biases in depression and social phobia. *Journal of Abnormal Psychology, 113,* 386–398.

Gotlib, I. H., Krasnoperova, E., Yue, D. N., & Joormann, J. (2004). Attentional biases for negative interpersonal stimuli in clinical depression. *Journal of Abnormal Psychology, 113*, 127–135.

Gottesman, I. I. (1991). *Schizophrenia genesis: The origins of madness.* New York: Freeman.

Gottfried, A. E., Fleming, J. S., & Gottfried, A. W. (1998). Role of cognitively stimulating home environment in children's academic intrinsic motivation: A longitudinal study. *Child Development, 69,* 1448–1460.

Gottman, J. M., Coan, J., Carrere, S., & Swanson, C. (1998). Predicting marital happiness and stability from newlywed interactions. *Journal of Marriage and the Family, 60,* 5–22.

Gottman, J. M., & DeClaire, J. (2002). *The relationship cure: A five-step guide to strengthening your marriage, family, and friendships.* New York: Three Rivers Press.

Gottman, J. M., & Levenson, R. (1992). Marital processes predictive of later dissolution: Behavior, psychology and health. *Journal of Personality and Social Psychology, 63,* 221–233.

Graber, J. A., Seeley, J. R., Brooks-Gunn, J., & Lewinsohn, P. M. (2004). Is pubertal timing associated with psychopathology in young adulthood? *Journal of the American Academy of Child & Adolescent Psychiatry, 43,* 718–726.

Gracely, R. H., Farrell, M. J., & Grant, M. A. B. (2002). Temperature and pain perception. In H. Pashler & S. Yantis, (Eds.), *Steven's handbook of experimental psychology: Vol. 1. Sensation and perception* (3rd ed.). New York: Wiley.

Graham, J. R. (2006). *MMPI-2: Assessing personality and psychopathology.* New York: Oxford University Press.

Graham, S., Hudley, C., & Williams, E. (1992). Attributional and emotional determinants of aggression among African-American and Latino young adolescents. *Developmental Psychology, 28,* 731–740.

Grant, H. M., Bredahl, L. C., Clay, J., Ferrie, J., Groves, J. E., McDorman, T. A., & Dark, V. J. (1998). Context-dependent memory for meaningful material: Information for students. *Applied Cognitive Psychology, 12,* 617–623.

Graw, P., Werth, E., Kraeuchi, K., Gutzwiller, F., Cajochen, C., & Wirz-Justice, A. (2001). Early morning melatonin administration impairs psychomotor vigilance. *Behavioural Brain Research, 121,* 167–172.

Gray, J. A. (1991). Neural systems, emotions, and personality. In J. Madden IV (Ed.), *Neurobiology of learning, emotion, and affect.* New York: Raven Press.

Gray, J. R., & Burgess, G. C. (2004). Personality differences in cognitive control? BAS, processing efficiency, and the prefrontal cortex. *Journal of Research in Personality, 38,* 35–36.

Green, J. T., & Woodruff-Pak, D. S. (2000). Eyeblink classical conditioning: Hippocampal formation is for neutral stimulus associations as cerebellum is for association-response. *Psychological Bulletin, 126,* 138–158.

Green, M. (1999). Diagnosis of attention-deficit/hyperactivity disorder. *Technical Review Number 3, Publication No. 99–0050.* Rockville,

MD: Agency for Health Care Policy and Research.

Green, M. F. (1997). *Schizophrenia from a neuro-cognitive perspective: Probing the impenetrable darkness.* Boston: Allyn & Bacon.

Greenberg, J., Solomon, S., & Pyszynski, T. (1997). Terror management theory of self-esteem and cultural worldviews: Empirical assessments and conceptual refinements. In M. P. Zanna (Ed.), *Advances in experimental social psychology* (Vol. 29). San Diego, CA: Academic Press.

Greenberg, J. S. (2005). *Comprehensive stress management.* New York: McGraw-Hill.

Greenberg, L. S., & Malcolm, W. (2002). Resolving unfinished business: Relating process to outcome. *Journal of Consulting and Clinical Psychology, 70,* 406–416.

Greenberg, L. S., & Rice, L. N. (1997). Humanistic approaches to psychotherapy. In P. L. Wachtel & S. B. Messer (Eds.), *Theories of psychotherapy: Origins and evolution.* Washington, DC: American Psychological Association.

Greene, K., Krcmar, M., Walters, L. H, Rubin, D. L. & Hale, J. L. (2000). Targeting adolescent risk-taking behaviors: The contribution of egocentrism and sensation seeking. *Journal of Adolescence, 23,* 439–461.

Greene, R. L. (1992). *Human memory: Paradigms and paradoxes.* Hillsdale, NJ: Erlbaum.

Greene, R. W., & Ollendick, T. H. (2000). Behavioral assessment of children. In G. Goldstein & M. Hersen (Eds.), *Handbook of psychological assessment* (3rd ed.). New York: Elsevier.

Greenfield, P. M. (1998). The cultural evolution of IQ. In U. Neisser (Ed.), *The rising curve: Long-term gains in IQ and related measures.* Washington, DC: American Psychological Association.

Greenleaf, E. (1973). "Senoi" dream groups. *Psychotherapy: Theory, Research and Practice, 10,* 218–222.

Greenwald, A. G. (1992). New look 3: Unconscious cognition reclaimed. *American Psychologist, 47,* 766–779.

Greenwald, A. G., & Banaji, M. R. (1995). Implicit social cognition: Attitudes, self-esteem, and stereotypes. *Psychological Review, 102,* 4–27.

Greenwald, A. G., Banaji, M. R., Rudman, L. A., Farnham, S. D., Nosek, B. A., & Mellott, D. S. (2002). A unified theory of implicit attitudes, stereotypes, self-esteem, and self-concept. *Psychological Review, 109,* 3–25.

Greenwald, A. G., McGhee, D. E., & Schwartz, J. (1998). Measuring individual differences in implicit cognition: The implicit association test. *Journal of Personality and Social Psychology, 74,* 1464–1480.

Greenwald, A. G., Spangenberg, E. R., Pratkanis, A. R., & Eskenazi, J. (1991). Double-blind tests of subliminal self-help tapes. *Psychological Science, 2,* 119–122.

Gregory, R. J. (1998). *Foundations of intellectual assessment: The WAIS-III and other tests in clinical practice.* Boston: Allyn & Bacon.

Gregory, R. L. (1966). *Eye and brain.* New York: McGraw-Hill.

Gregory, R. L. (2005). *Illusion: The phenomenal brain.* New York: Oxford University Press.

Gregory, R. L., & Gombrich, E. H. (1973). *Illusion in nature and art.* London: Duckworth.

Grice, H. P. (1975). Logic and conversation. In P. Cole & J. L. Morgan (Eds.), *Syntax and semantics: Vol. 3. Speech acts.* New York: Seminar.

Grigorenko, E. L. (2003). Selected links between nutrition and the mind. In R. J. Sternberg, J. Lautrey, & T. I. Lubart (Eds.), *Models of intelligence: International perspectives.* Washington, DC: American Psychological Association.

Grimes, K., & Walker, E. F. (1994). Childhood emotional expressions, educational attainment, and age at onset of illness in schizophrenia. *Journal of Abnormal Psychology, 103,* 784–790.

Gross, A. M., Bennett, T., Sloan, L., Marx, B. P., & Juergens, J. (2001). The impact of alcohol and alcohol expectancies on male perception of female sexual arousal in a date rape analog. *Experimental and Clinical Psychopharmacology, 9,* 380–388.

Grossberg, S., Finkel, L., & Field, D. (Eds.). (2005). *Vision and brain: How the brain sees: New approaches to computer vision.* St. Louis: Elsevier.

Grossman, D. (1996). *On killing: The psychological cost of learning to kill in war and society.* Boston: Little, Brown.

Groth-Marnat, G. (1999). *Handbook of psychological assessment.* New York: Wiley.

Gruest, N., Richer, P., & Hars, B. (2004). Emergence of long-term memory for conditioned aversion in the rat fetus. *Developmental Psychobiology, 44,* 189–198.

Guéguen, N. (2002). Foot in the door technique and computer mediated communication. *Computers in Human Behavior, 18,* 11–15.

Guilford, J. P. (1959). Three faces of intellect. *American Psychologist, 14,* 469–479.

Guilford, J. P. (1967). *The nature of human intelligence.* New York: McGraw-Hill.

Guilleminault, C., Poyares, D., Abat, F., & Palombini, L. (2001). Sleep and wakefulness in somnambulism: A spectral analysis study. *Journal of Psychosomatic Research, 51,* 411–416.

Guinness book of records. (2000). Stamford, CT: Guinness Media.

Gulevich, G., Dement, W., & Johnson, L. (1966). Psychiatric and EEG observations on a case of prolonged (264 hours) wakefulness. *Archives of General Psychiatry, 15,* 29–35.

Gump, L. S., Baker, R. C., & Roll, S. (2000). Cultural and gender differences in moral judgment: A study of Mexican Americans and Anglo-Americans. *Hispanic Journal of Behavioral Sciences, 22,* 78–93.

Gupta, P., & Cohen, N. J. (2002). Theoretical and computational analysis of skill learning, repetition priming, and procedural memory. *Psychological Review, 109,* 401–448.

Gur, R. E., Cowell, P., Turetsky, B. I., Gallacher, F., Cannon, T., Bilker, W., & Gur, R. B. (1998). A follow-up magnetic resonance imaging study of schizophrenia: Relationship of neuroanatomical changes to clinical and neurobehavioral measures. *Archives of General Psychiatry, 55,* 145–152.

Gurvitz, I. G., Koenigsberg, H. W., & Siever, L. J. (2000). Neurotransmitter dysfunction in patients with borderline personality disorder. *Psychiatric Clinics of North America, 23,* 27–40.

Gustavson, C. R., Garcia, J., Hankins, W. G., & Rusiniak, K. W. (1974). Coyote predation control by aversive conditioning. *Science, 184,* 581–583.

Gustavson, C. R., & Gustavson, J. C. (1985, June). Predation control using conditioned food aversion methodology: Theory, practice, and implications. *Annals of the New York Academy of Sciences, 443,* 348–356.

Guthrie, J. P., Ash, R. A., & Bendapudi, V. (1995). Additional validity evidence for a measure of morningness. *Journal of Applied Psychology, 80,* 186–190.

Guthrie, R. V. (1976). *Even the rat was white: A historical view of psychology.* New York: Harper & Row.

Haaga, D. A. F., Dyck, M. J., & Ernst, D. (1991). Empirical status of cognitive theory of depression. *Psychological Bulletin, 110,* 215–236.

Hafen, B. Q., & Hoeger, W. W. K. (1998). *Wellness: Guidelines for a healthy lifestyle.* Englewood, CO: Morton.

Haier, R. J., Siegel, B. V., Crinella, F. M., & Buchsbaum, M. S. (1993). Biological and psychometric intelligence: Testing an animal model in humans with positron emission tomography. In D. K. Detterman (Ed.), *Individual differences and cognition: Current topics in human intelligence* (Vol. 3). Norwood, NJ: Ablex.

Hailman, J. P. (1967). The ontogeny of an instinct. *Behaviour Supplements, 15,* 1–159.

Hailman, J. P. (1969). How an instinct is learned. *Scientific American, 221,* 98–106.

Haines, R. F. (1991). A breakdown in simultaneous information processing. In G. Obrecht & L. W. Stark (Eds.), *Presbyopia research.* New York: Plenum Press.

Halari, R., Hines, M., Kumari, V., Mehrotra, R., Wheeler, M., Ng, V., & Sharma, T. (2005). Sex differences and individual differences in cognitive performance and their relationship to endogenous gonadal hormones and gonadotropins. *Behavioral Neuroscience, 119,* 104–117.

Hall, C. S., & Van de Castle, R. (1966). *The content analysis of dreams.* New York: Appleton-Century-Crofts.

Hall, G. C. N., & Okazaki, S. (2003). *Asian American psychology: The science of lives in context.* Washington, DC: American Psychological Association.

Hall, G. S. (1904). *Adolescence* (Vols. 1 and 2). New York: Appleton-Century-Crofts.

Halligan, P. W., Fink, G. R., Marshall, J. C., & Vallar, G. (2003). Spatial cognition: Evidence from visual neglect. *Trends in Cognitive Sciences, 7,* 125–133.

Halpern, B. (2002). Taste. In H. Pashler & S. Yantis (Eds.). *Steven's handbook of experimental psychology: Vol. 1. Sensation and perception* (3rd ed.). New York: Wiley.

Halpern, D. F. (2000). *Sex differences in cognitive abilities* (3rd ed.). Mahwah, NJ: Erlbaum.

Halpern, D. F., & Tan, U. (2001). Stereotypes and steroids: Using a psychobiosocial model to understand cognitive sex differences. *Brain and Cognition, 45,* 392–414.

Hamann S., & Mao, H. (2002). Positive and negative emotional verbal stimuli elicit activity in the left amygdala. *Neuroreport, 13*(1), 15–19.

Hamer, D. H., & Copeland, P. (1998). *Living with our genes: Why they matter more than you think.* New York: Doubleday.

Hamilton, R. J. (1985). A framework for the evaluation of the effectiveness of adjunct questions and objectives. *Review of Educational Research, 55,* 47–85.

Hamilton, W. D. (1964). The genetical theory of social behaviour, I, II. *Journal of Theoretical Biology, 12,* 12–45.

Hammen, C. (1991). *Depression runs in families: The social context of risk and resilience in children of depressed mothers.* New York: Springer-Verlag.

Haney, C., & Zimbardo, P. (1998). The past and future of U.S. prison policy: Twenty-five years after the Stanford Prison Experiment. *American Psychologist, 53,* 709–727.

Hankin, B. L., Abramson, L. Y., Moffit, T. E., Silva, P. A., McGee, R., & Angell, K. E. (1998). Development of depression from preadolescence to young adulthood: Emerging gender differences in a 10-year longitudinal study. *Journal of Abnormal Psychology, 107,* 128–140.

Hankin, B. L., Kassel, J. D., & Abela, R. Z. (2005). Adult attachment dimensions and specificity of emotional distress symptoms: Prospective investigations of cognitive risk and interpersonal stress generation as mediating mechanisms. *Personality and Social Psychology Bulletin, 31,* 136–151.

Hanley, S. J., & Abell, S. C. (2002). Maslow and relatedness: Creating an interpersonal model of self-actualization. *Journal of Humanistic Psychology, 42,* 37–56.

Hansen, C. H., & Hansen, R. D. (1988). Finding the face in the crowd: An anger superiority effect. *Journal of Personality and Social Psychology, 54,* 917–924.

Hansen, N. B., Lambert, M. J., & Forman, E. M. (2002). The psychotherapy dose-response effect and its implications for treatment delivery services. *Clinical Psychology: Science and Practice, 9,* 329–343.

Happé, F. G. E., Winner, E., & Brownell, H. (1998). The getting of wisdom: Theory of mind in old age. *Developmental Psychology, 34,* 358–362.

Harackiewicz, J. M., Barron, K. E., Tauer, J. M., & Elliot, A. J. (2002). Predicting success in college: A longitudinal study of achievement goals and ability measures as predictors of interest and performance from freshman year through graduation. *Journal of Educational Psychology, 94,* 562–575.

Harley, K., & Reese, E. (1999). Origins of autobiographical memory. *Developmental Psychology, 35,* 1338–1348.

Harlow, H. F. (1958). The nature of love. *The American Psychologist, 13,* 673–685.

Harlow, H. F., & Suomi, S. J. (1970). The nature of love-simplified. *American Psychologist, 25,* 161–168.

Harlow, J., & Roll, S. (1992). Frequency of day residue in dreams of young adults. *Perceptual and Motor Skills, 74,* 832–834.

Harlow, J. M. (1868). Recovery from the passage of an iron bar through the head. *Massachusetts Medical Society, 2,* 327.

Harmon-Jones, E., Brehm, J. W., Greenberg, J., Simon, L., & Nelson, D. E. (1996). Evidence that the production of aversive consequences is not necessary to create cognitive dissonance. *Journal of Personality and Social Psychology, 70,* 5–16.

Harris, C. (2002, August 27). Amazing memory for digits still loses track of car keys. *Naples Daily News.*

Harris, J. R. (1998). *The nurture assumption: Why children turn out the way they do.* New York: Free Press.

Harris, S. L. (1981). A letter from the editor on loss and trust. *Clinical Psychologist, 34*(3), 3.

Harrison, J. E., & Baron-Cohen, S. C. (1997). Synaesthesia: A review of psychological theories. In S. C. Baron et al. (Eds.), *Synaesthesia: Classic and contemporary readings.* Oxford, England: Blackwell.

Hart, J. W., Bridgett, D. J., & Karau, S. J. (2001). Coworker ability and effort as determinants of individual effort on a collective task. *Group Dynamics, 5,* 181–190.

Hart, J. W., Karau, S. J., Stasson, M. F., & Kerr, N. A. (2004). Achievement motivation, expected coworker performance, and collective task motivation: Working hard or hardly working? *Journal of Applied Social Psychology, 34,* 984–1000.

Hartmann, E., Kunzendorf, R., Rosen, R., & Grace, N. G. (2001). Contextualizing images in dreams and daydreams. *Dreaming: Journal of the Association for the Study of Dreams, 11,* 97–104.

Hartshorne, H., & May, A. (1928). *Studies in the nature of character: Vol. 1. Studies in deceit.* New York: Macmillan.

Harway, M. (2005). *Handbook of couples therapy.* New York: Wiley.

Hasegawa, I., & Myashita, Y. (2002). Categorizing the world: Expert neurons look into key features. *Nature: Neuroscience, 5,* 90–91.

Hasher, L., & Zacks, R. T. (1979). Automatic and effortful processes in memory. *Journal of Experimental Psychology: General, 108,* 356–388.

Haskell, W. L., Alderman, E. L., Fair, J. M., et al. (1994). Effects of intensive multiple risk factor reduction on coronary atherosclerosis and clinical cardiac events in men and women with coronary artery disease. *Circulation, 89,* 975–990.

Hatfield, E. (1988). Passionate and companionate love. In R. J. Sternberg & M. L. Barnes (Eds.), *The psychology of love.* New Haven, CT: Yale University Press.

Hauri, P. (1982). *The sleep disorders* (2nd ed.). Kalamazoo, MI: Upjohn.

Hawley, P., & Little, T. D. (2002). Evolutionary and developmental perspectives on the agentic self. In D. Cervone & W. Mischel (Eds.), *Advances in personality science.* New York: Guilford Press.

Haynes, S. N. (2000). Behavioral assessment of adults. In G. Goldstein & M. Hersen (Eds.), *Handbook of psychological assessment* (3rd ed.). New York: Elsevier.

Hayslip, B., & Panek, P. E. (1989). *Adult development and aging.* New York: Harper & Row.

Hazan, C., & Diamond, L. M. (2000). The place of attachment in human mating. *Review of General Psychology, 4,* 186–204.

Health, United States 2004. (2004). Hyattsville, MD: National Center for Health Statistics.

Healthy People 2010. (2005). Retrieved April 17, 2005, from http://www.healthypeople.gov

Healy, D. (2004). *Let them eat Prozac: The unhealthy relationship between the pharmaceutical industry and depression.* New York: New York University Press.

Hearold, S. (1986). A synthesis of 1043 effects of television on social behavior. In G. Comstock (Ed.), *Public communications and behavior* (Vol. 1). New York: Academic Press.

Heath, A. C., Bucholz, K. K., Madden, P. A. F., Dinwiddie, S. H., Slutske, W. S., & Bierut, L. J. (1997). Genetic and environmental contributions to alcohol dependence risk in a national twin sample: Consistency of findings in women and men. *Psychological Medicine, 27,* 1381–1396.

Heath, A. C., Kendler, K. S., Eaves, L. J., & Martin, N. G. (1990). Evidence for genetic influences on sleep disturbance and sleep pattern in twins. *Sleep, 13,* 318–335.

Heath, R. G. (1972). Pleasure and brain activity in man. *Journal of Nervous and Mental Disease, 154,* 3–18.

Heatherton, T. F., Macrae, C. N. & Kelley, W. M. (2004). What the social brain sciences can tell us about the self. *Current Directions in Psychological Science 13,* 190–193.

Heaton, T. B. (2002). Factors contributing to increasing marital stability in the U.S. *Journal of Family Issues, 23,* 392–409.

Hebb, D. O. (1949). *The organization of behavior.* New York: Wiley.

Heerey, E. A., Keltner, D., & Capps, L. M. (2003). Making sense of self-conscious emotion: Linking theory of mind and emotion in children with autism. *Emotion, 3,* 394–400.

Heider, F. (1958). *The psychology of interpersonal relations.* New York: Wiley.

Heimpel, S. A., Wood, J. V., Marshall, M. A., & Brown, J. D. (2002). Do people with low self-esteem really want to feel better? Self-esteem differences in motivation to repair negative moods. *Journal of Personality and Social Psychology, 82,* 128–147.

Heine, S. J., Kitayama, S., Lehman, D. R., Takata, T., Ide, E., et al. (2000). *Divergent consequences of success and failure in Japan and North America: An investigation of self-improving motivations and malleable selves.* Vancouver: University of British Columbia.

Heinrichs, R. W. (2001). *In search of madness: Schizophrenia and neuroscience.* New York: Oxford University Press.

Helgeson, V. S., Cohen, S., Schultz, R., & Yasko, J. (2000). Group support interventions for women with breast cancer: Who benefits from what? *Health Psychology, 19,* 107–114.

Heller, M. A., & Schiff, W. (Eds.). (1991). *The psychology of touch.* Hillsdale, NJ: Erlbaum.

Hellerstein, D., Yankowitch, P., Rosenthal, J., et al. (1993). A randomized double-blind study of fluoxetine versus placebo in the treatment of dysthymia. *American Journal of Psychiatry, 150,* 1169–1175.

Helson, R., Jones, C., & Kwan, V. S. Y. (2002). Personality change over 40 years of adulthood: Hierarchical linear modeling analyses of two longitudinal samples. *Journal of Personality and Social Psychology, 83,* 752–766.

Helzer, J. E., & Hudziak, J. J. (Eds). (2002). *Defining psychopathology in the 21st century: DSM-V and beyond.* Washington, DC: American Psychiatric Publishing.

Herdt, G., & Lindenbaum, S. (Eds.). (1992). *Social analysis in the time of AIDS.* Newbury Park, CA: Sage.

Herek, G. M. (2000). The psychology of sexual prejudice. *Current Directions in Psychological Science, 9,* 19–22.

Herek, G. M. (2002). Gender gaps in public opinion about lesbians and gay men. *Public Opinion Quarterly, 66,* 40–66.

Herman, D. B., Susser, E. S., Jandorf, L., Lavelle, J., & Bromet, E. J. (1998). Homelessness among individuals with psychotic disorders hospitalized for the first time: Findings from the Suffolk County Mental Health Project. *American Journal of Psychiatry, 155,* 109–113.

Hernnstein, R. J., & Murray, C. (1994). *The bell curve: Intelligence and class structure in American life.* New York: Free Press.

Herrington, R., & Lader, M. H. (1996). *Biological treatments in psychiatry* (2nd ed.). New York: Oxford University Press.

Hersen, M. (2002). *Clinical behavior therapy: Adults and children.* New York: Wiley.

Hersen, M. (2003). *Effective brief therapies.* New York: Academic Press.

Herz, M., & Marder, S. (2002). *Schizophrenia: A comprehensive text.* New York: Williams & Wilkins.

Herzog, H. A. (2005). Dealing with the animal research controversy. In C. K. Akins, S. Panicker, & C. L. Cunningham (Eds.), *Laboratory animals in research and teaching: Ethics, care, and methods.* Washington, DC: American Psychological Association.

Hess, E. H. (1959). Imprinting. *Science, 130,* 133–141.

Hess, W. R. (1965). Sleep as phenomenon of the integral organism. In K. Akert, C. Bally, & J. P. Schade (Eds.), *Sleep mechanisms.* New York: Elsevier.

Hetherington, E. M. (1998). Relevant issues in developmental science: Introduction to the special issue. *American Psychologist, 53,* 93–94.

Hetherington, E. M., Bridges, M., & Insabella, G. M. (1998). What matters? What does not? Five perspectives on the association between marital transitions and children's adjustment. *American Psychologist, 53,* 167–184.

Hetherington, E. M., & Stanley-Hagan, M. (2002). Parenting in divorced and remarried families. In M. H. Bornstein (Ed.), *Handbook of parenting: Being and becoming a parent* (2nd ed., Vol. 3). Mahwah, NJ: Erlbaum.

Hewstone, M., Rubin, M., & Willis, H. (2002). Intergroup bias. *Annual Review of Psychology, 53,* 575–604.

Heylighen, F. (1992). A cognitive-systemic reconstruction of Maslow's theory of self-actualization. *Behavioral Science, 37,* 39–58.

Higgins, E. T. (1996). The "self digest": Self-knowledge serving self-regulatory functions. *Journal of Personality and Social Psychology, 71,* 1062–1083.

Hilgard, E. R. (1977). *Divided consciousness: Multiple controls in human thought and action.* New York: Wiley.

Hilgard, E. R. (1991). A neodissociation interpretation of hypnosis. In S. J. Lynn & J. W. Rhue (Eds.), *Theories of hypnosis: Current models and perspectives.* New York: Guilford Press.

Hill, C. A. (1987). Affiliation motivation: People who need people but in different ways. *Journal of Personality and Social Psychology, 52,* 1008–1018.

Hill, J. L., Brooks-Gunn, J., & Waldfogel, J. (2003). Sustained effects of high participation in an early intervention for low-birth-weight premature infants. *Developmental Psychology, 2003,* 730–744.

Hill, M. M., Dodson, B. B., Hill, E. W., & Fox, J. (1995). An infant sonicguide intervention program for a child with a visual disability. *Journal of Visual Impairment and Blindness, 89,* 329–336.

Hill, W. F. (1963). *Learning: A survey of psychological interpretations.* San Francisco: Chandler.

Hillman, D. C., Siffre, M., Milano, G., & Halberg, F. (1994). Free-running psycho-physiologic circadians and three-month pattern in a woman isolated in a cave. *New Trends in Experimental and Clinical Psychiatry, 10,* 127–133.

Himle, M. B., Miltenberger, R. G., Flessner, C., & Gatheridge, B. (2004). Teaching safety skills to children to prevent gun play. *Journal of Applied Behavior Analysis, 37*, 1–9.

Hines, M. (2005). *Brain gender*. New York: Oxford University Press.

Hobson, J. A. (1996). *Chemistry of conscious states: How the brain changes its mind.* Boston: Little, Brown.

Hobson, J. A., Pace-Schott, E. F., & Stickgold, R. (2000). Dreaming and the brain: Toward a cognitive neuroscience of conscious states. *Behavioral and Brain Sciences, 23*, 793–842.

Hodges, J., & Tizard, B. (1989). Social and family relationships of ex-institutional adolescents. *Journal of Child Psychology and Psychiatry, 30*, 77–97.

Hoffart, A., & Martinson, E. W. (1991). Mental health locus of control in agoraphobia and depression: A longitudinal study of inpatients. *Psychological Reports, 68*, 1011–1018.

Hoffer, A., & Youngren, V. R. (2004). Is free association still at the core of psychoanalysis? *International Journal of Psychoanalysis, 85*, 1489–1492.

Hoffman, H. G., Patterson, D. R., Canougher, G. J., & Sharar, S. R. (2001). Effectiveness of virtual reality-based pain control with multiple treatments. *Clinical Journal of Pain, 17*, 229–235.

Hofmann, S. G., Moscovitch, D. A., & Heinrichs, N. (2004). Evolutionary mechanisms of fear and anxiety. In P. Gilbert (Ed.), *Evolutionary theory and cognitive therapy* (pp. 119–136). New York: Springer.

Hogan, R. (1983). A socioanalytic theory of personality. In M. Page & R. Dienstbier (Eds.), *Nebraska Symposium on Motivation, 1982.* Lincoln: University of Nebraska Press.

Hogarty, G. E. (2003). *Personal therapy for schizophrenia and related disorders.* New York: Guilford Press.

Hogue, M. E., Beaugrand, J. P., & Lauguee, P. C. (1996). Coherent use of information by hens observing their former dominant defeating or being defeated by a stranger. *Behavioural Processes, 38*, 241–252.

Holahan, C. J., & Moos, R. H. (1986). Personality, coping, and family resources in stress resistance: A longitudinal analysis. *Journal of Personality and Social Psychology 51*, 389–395.

Holahan, C. J., & Moos, R. H. (1990). Life stressors, resistance factors, and improved psychological functioning: An extension of the stress resistance paradigm. *Journal of Personality and Social Psychology, 58*, 909–917.

Holden, G. W. (2002). Perspectives on the effects of corporal punishment: Comment on Gershoff (2002). *Psychological Bulletin, 128*, 590–595.

Hollis, K. L. (1997). Contemporary research on Pavlovian conditioning: A "new" functional analysis. *American Psychologist, 52*, 956–965.

Hollon, S. D. (1996). The efficacy and effectiveness of psychotherapy relative to medications. *American Psychologist, 51*, 1025–1030.

Hollon, S. D., & Beck, A. T. (1994). Cognitive and cognitive-behavioral therapies. In A. E. Bergin & S. L. Garfield (Eds.), *Handbook of psychotherapy and behavior change.* New York: Wiley.

Holloway, J. D. (2003). Snapshot from the therapy room: In session strategies are not limited by overall theoretical orientation, finds Practice-Net survey. *APA Monitor, 34*(11), 23.

Holmes, D. S. (1990). The evidence for repression: An examination of sixty years of research. In J. L. Singer (Ed.), *Repression and dissociation.* Chicago: University of Chicago Press.

Holmes, T. H., & Rahe, R. H. (1967). The Social Readjustment Rating Scale. *Journal of Psychosomatic Research, 11*, 213–218.

Holtzer, R., Stern, Y., & Rakitin, B. C. (2005). Predicting age-related dual-task effects with individual differences on neuropsychological tests. *Neuropsychology, 19*, 18–27.

Honts, C. R., & Perry, M. V. (1992). Polygraph admissibility: Changes and challenges. *Law and Human Behavior, 16*, 357–379.

Hooley, J. M. (2004). Do psychiatric patients do better clinically if they live with certain kinds of families? *Current Directions in Psychological Science, 13*(5), 202–205.

Hooper, J., & Teresi, M. (1986). *The three-pound universe.* New York: Macmillan.

Horn, J. (1985). Remodeling old models of intelligence. In B. B. Wolman (Ed.), *Handbook of intelligence: Theory, measurement, and application.* New York: Wiley.

Horn, J. L., & Cattell, R. C. (1966). Refinement and test of the theory of fluid and crystallized general intelligences. *Journal of Educational Psychology, 57*, 253–270.

Horn, J. L., & Masunaga, H. (2000). On the emergence of wisdom: Expertise development. *Understanding wisdom: Sources, science, & society.* Philadelphia: Templeton Foundation Press.

Horn, J. L., & Noll, J. (1997). Human cognitive capabilities: Gf-Gc theory. In D. P. Flanagan, J. L. Genshaft, & P. L. Harrison (Eds.), *Contemporary intellectual assessment: Theories, tests, and issues.* New York: Guilford Press.

Houpt, T. A., Boulos, Z., Moore, E., & Martin, C. (1996). MidnightSun: Software for determining light exposure and phase-shifting schedules during global travel. *Physiology and Behavior, 59*, 561–568.

House, J. S., Landis, K. R., & Umberson, D. (1988). Social relationships and health. *Science, 241*, 540–545.

Hovland, C. I., Janis, I., & Kelley, H. H. (1953). *Communication and persuasion.* New Haven, CT: Yale University Press.

Howard, I. P. (2002). Depth perception. In H. Pashler & S.Yantis (Eds.), *Steven's handbook of experimental psychology: Vol. 1. Sensation and perception* (3rd ed.). New York: Wiley.

Howard, K. I., Kopta, S. M., Krause, M. S., & Orlinsky, D. E. (1986). The dose-effect relationship in psychotherapy. *American Psychologist, 41*, 159–164.

Howard, K. I., Lueger, R. J., Maling, M. S., & Martinovich, Z. (1993). A phase model of psychotherapy outcome: Causal mediation of change. *Journal of Consulting and Clinical Psychology, 61*, 678–685.

Hubbard, K., O'Neill, A. M., & Cheakalos, C. (1999, April 12). Out of control. *People, 52*–72.

Hubel, D. H., & Wiesel, T. N. (1979). Brain mechanisms of vision. *Scientific American, 241*, 150–162.

Hubel, D. H., & Wiesel, T. N. (2005). *Brain and visual perception: The story of a 25-year collaboration.* New York: Oxford University Press.

Hublin, C., Kaprio, J., Partinen, M., Heikkila, K., & Koskenvuo, M. (1997). Prevalence and genetics of sleepwalking: A population-based twin study. *Neurology, 48*, 177–181.

Hublin, C., Kaprio, J., Partinen, M., & Koskenvuo, M. (2001). Parasomnias: Co-occurrence and genetics. *Psychiatric Genetics, 11*, 65–70.

Huddy, L., & Virtanen, S. (1995). Subgroup differentiation and subgroup bias among Latinos as a function of familiarity and positive distinctiveness. *Journal of Personality and Social Psychology, 68*, 97–108.

Hudson, W. (1960). Pictorial depth perception in sub-cultural groups in Africa. *Journal of Social Psychology, 52*, 183–208.

Huesmann, L. R. (1997). Observational learning of violent behavior: Social and biosocial processes. In A. Raine, P. A. Brennan, D. P. Farrington, & S. A. Mednick (Eds.), *Biosocial bases of violence.* New York: Plenum Press.

Huesmann, L. R., Moise-Titus, J., Podolski, C. L., & Eron, L. D. (2003). Longitudinal relations between children's exposure to TV violence and their aggressive and violent behavior in young adulthood: 1977–1992. *Developmental Psychology, 39*, 201–221.

Huettel, S. A., Song, A. W., & McCarthy, G. (2005). *Functional magnetic resonance imaging.* New York: Sinauer.

Huff, R. M., & Kline, M. V. (Eds.). (1999). *Promoting health in multicultural populations: A handbook for practitioners.* Thousand Oaks, CA: Sage.

Hugdahl, K., & Davidson, R. A. (Eds.). (2005). *The asymmetrical brain.* Boston: MIT Press.

Hugenberg, K., & Bodenhausen, G. V. (2003). Facing prejudice: Implicit prejudice and the perception of facial threat. *Psychological Science, 14*, 640–643.

Hull, C. L. (1943). *Principles of behavior: An introduction to behavior theory.* New York: Appleton-Century.

Human Genome Project. (2004). Retrieved October 21, 2004, from http://www.genome.gov/

Human Genome Project. (2005). Retrieved January 12, 2005, from http://www.genome.gov/

Hunt, E. (1995). The role of intelligence in modern society. *American Scientist, 83*, 356–368.

Hunt, E. (1997). The status of the concept of intelligence. *Japanese Psychological Research, 39*, 1–11.

Hunt, E., & Agnoli, F. (1991). The Whorfian hypothesis: A cognitive psychology perspective. *Psychological Review, 98*, 377–389.

Hunter, J. E., & Hunter, R. F. (1984). Validity and utility of alternative predictors of job performance. *Psychological Bulletin, 96*, 72–98.

Huon, G. F., Mingyi, Q., Oliver, K., & Xiao, G. (2002). A large-scale survey of eating disorder symptomatology among female adolescents in the people's Republic of China. *International Journal of Eating Disorders, 32*, 192–205.

Huttenlocher, P. R. (1979). Synaptic density in human frontal cortex: Developmental changes and effects of aging. *Brain Research, 163*, 195–205.

Huttenlocher, P. R. (2002). *Neural plasticity.* Cambridge, MA: Harvard University Press.

Hyde, J. S. (Ed.). (2005). *Biological substrates of human sexuality.* Washington, DC: American Psychological Association.

Hyde, J. S., & DeLamater, J. (2003). *Understanding human sexuality* (8th ed.). Boston: McGraw-Hill.

Hyde, M., Ferrie, J., Higgs, P., Mein, G., & Nazroo, J. (2004). The effects of pre-retirement factors and retirement route on circumstances in retirement: Findings from the Whitehall II study. *Ageing & Society, 24*, 279–296.

Hyman, R. (1994). Anomaly or artifact? Comments on Bem and Honorton. *Psychological Bulletin, 115*, 19–24.

Iervolino, A. C., Pike, A., Manke, B., Reiss, D., Hetherington, E. M., & Plomin, R. (2002). Genetic and environmental influences in adolescent peer socialization: Evidence from two genetically sensitive designs. *Child Development, 73*, 162–174.

Ikemi, Y., & Nakagawa, A. (1962). A psychosomatic study of contagious dermatitis. *Kyushu Journal of Medical Science, 13*, 335–350.

Ingelhart, R., & Rabier, J. R. (1986). Aspirations adapt to situations—but why are the Belgians so much happier than the French? A cross-cultural study of the quality of life. In F. M. Andrews (Ed.), *Research on the quality of life.* Ann Arbor, MI: Institute for Social Research, University of Michigan.

Ingold, C. H. (1989). Locus of control and use of public information. *Psychological Reports, 64*, 603–607.

Ingram, R. E., & Price, J. M. (2001). *Vulnerability to psychopathology: Risk across the lifespan.* New York: Guilford Press.

Inhelder, B., & Piaget, J. (1958). *The growth of logical thinking from childhood to adolescence.* New York: Basic Books.

Institute of Education Sciences. (2005). About the Institute of Education Sciences. Retrieved March 13, 2005, from http://www.ed.gov/about/offices/list/ies/index.html?src=mr

International Union of Psychological Sciences. (2005). Members in IUPsyS. Retrieved March 13, 2005, from http://www.am.org/iupsys/members.html

Intraub, H. (2002). Anticipatory spatial representation of natural scenes: Momentum without movement? *Visual Cognition, 9*, 93–119.

Intraub, H., Gottesman, C. V., Willey, E. V., & Zuk, I. J. (1996). Boundary extension for briefly glimpsed photographs: Do common perceptual processes result in unexpected memory distortions? *Journal of Memory and Language, 35*, 118–134.

Ip, M. S. M., Tsang, W. T., Lam, W. K., & Lam, B. (1998). Obstructive sleep apnea syndrome: An experience in Chinese adults in Hong Kong. *Chinese Medical Journal, 111*, 257–260.

Irie, M., Maeda, M., & Nagata, S. (2001). Can conditioned histamine release occur under urethane anesthesia in guinea pigs? *Physiology and Behavior, 72*, 567–573.

Irwin, A. R., & Gross, A. M. (1995). Cognitive tempo, violent video games, and aggressive behavior in young boys. *Journal of Family Violence, 10*, 337–350.

Irwin, J. R., & McCarthy, D. (1998). Psychophysics: Methods and analyses of signal detection. In K. A. Lattal & M. Perone (Eds.), *Handbook of research methods in human operant behavior: Applied clinical psychology.* New York: Plenum Press.

Irwin, M., Daniels, M., & Weiner, H. (1987). Immune and neuroendocrine changes during bereavement. *Psychiatric Clinics of North America, 10*, 449–465.

Isaacs, K. S. (1998). *Uses of emotion: Nature's vital gift.* New York: Praeger.

Isaacson, R. L. (2002). Unsolved mysteries: The hippocampus. *Behavioral and Cognitive Neuroscience Reviews, 1*, 87–107.

Ishikawa, S. L., Raine, A., Lencz, T., Bihrle, S., & Lacasse, L. (2001). Autonomic stress reactivity and executive functions in successful and unsuccessful criminal psychopaths from the community. *Journal of Abnormal Psychology, 110*, 423–432.

Itard, J. M. G. (1962). *The wild boy of Aveyron* (G. Humphrey & M. Humphrey, Trans.). New York: Appleton-Century-Crofts. (Original work published 1894)

Ito, K., Momose, T., Oku, S., Ishimoto, S.-I., Yamasoba, T., Sugasawa, M., & Kaga, K. (2004). Cortical activation shortly after cochlear implantation. *Audiology & Neurotology, 9*, 282–293.

Ito, T. A., & Cacioppo, J. T. (2000). Electrophysiological evidence of implicit and explicit categorization processes. *Journal of Experimental Social Psychology, 36*, 660–676.

Itti, L., & Rees, G. (2005). *Neurobiology of attention.* St. Louis: Elsevier.

Iwasa, N. (2001). Moral reasoning among adults: Japan U.S. comparison. In H. Shimizu & R. A. LeVine (Eds.), *Japanese frames of mind: Cultural perspectives on human development.* New York: Cambridge University Press.

Iwawaki, S., & Sarmany-Schuller, I. (2001). Cross-cultural (Japan-Slovakia) comparison of some aspects of sleeping patterns and anxiety. *Studia Psychologica, 43*, 215–224.

Izard, C. (Ed.). (1982). *Measuring emotions in infants and children.* Cambridge, England: Cambridge University Press.

Izard, C. E. (1989). The structure and functions of emotions: Implications for cognition, motivation, and personality. In I. S. Cohen (Ed.), *The G. Stanley Hall Lecture Series* (Vol. 9). Washington, DC: American Psychological Association.

Jablensky, A., Sartorius, N., Enberg, C., Anker, M., Korten, A., et al. (1992). Schizophrenia: Manifestation, incidence, and course in different cultures: A World Health Organization ten country study. *Psychological Medicine Monograph Supplement 20.* Cambridge, England: Cambridge University Press.

Jackson, A., Morrow, J., Hill, D., & Dishman, R. (1999). *Physical activity for health and fitness.* Champaign, IL: Human Kinetics.

Jackson, N., & Butterfield, E. (1986). A conception of giftedness designed to promote research. In R. J. Sternberg & J. E. Davidson (Eds.), *Conceptions of giftedness.* New York: Cambridge University Press.

Jacobs, B. L (2004). Depression: The brain finally gets into the act. *Current Directions in Psychological Science, 13*, 103–106.

Jacobson, N. S., & Christensen, A. (1996). *Integrative couple therapy: Promoting acceptance and change.* New York: Norton.

Jacobson, N. S., Christensen, A., Prince, S. E., Cordova, J., & Eldridge, K. (2000). Integrative couple behavior therapy: An acceptance-based, promising new treatment for couple discord. *Journal of Consulting and Clinical Psychology, 68*, 351–355.

Jacobson, N. S., Martell, C. R., & Dimidjian, S. (2001). Behavioral activation therapy for depression: Returning to contextual roots. *Clinical Psychology: Science and Practice, 8*, 255–270.

Jaffee, S. R., Moffitt, T. E., Caspi, A., & Taylor, A. (2003). Life with (or without) father: The benefits of living with two biological parents depend on the father's antisocial behavior. *Child Development, 74*, 109–126.

James, W. (1879). Are we automata? *Mind, 4*, 1–22.

James, W. (1950). *Principles of psychology* (Vol. 2). New York: Dover. (Original work published 1890)

Jamison, K. (1995, February). Manic-depressive illness and creativity. *Scientific American*, 63–67.

Jang, C.-G., Lee, S.-Y., Yoo, J.-H., Yan, J.-J., Song, D.-K., Loh, H. H., & Ho, I. K. (2003). Impaired water maze learning performance in mu-opioid receptor knockout mice. *Molecular Brain Research, 117*, 68–72.

Jang, K. (2005). *The behavioral genetics of psychopathology: A clinical guide.* Hillsdale, NJ: Erlbaum.

Janis, I. L. (1982). *Groupthink: Psychological studies of policy decisions and fiascos* (2nd ed.). Boston: Houghton Mifflin.

Jansma, J. M., Ramsey, N. F., Slagter, H. A., & Kahn, R. S. (2001). Functional anatomical correlates of controlled and automatic processing. *Journal of Cognitive Neuroscience, 13,* 730–743.

Janus, S. S., & Janus, C. L. (1993). *The Janus report on sexual behavior.* New York: Wiley.

Jemmott, J. B., Jemmott, L. S., & Fong, G. T. (1998). Abstinence and safer sex HIV risk-reduction interventions for African American adolescents. *Journal of the American Medical Association, 279,* 1529–1536.

Jencks, C., & Phillips, M. (Eds). (1998). *The Black-White test score gap.* Washington, DC: Brookings Institution.

Jenike, M. A. (1998). *Obsessive-compulsive disorders.* St. Louis, MO: Mosby.

Jenkin, M., & Harris., L. (2005). *Seeing spatial form.* New York: Oxford University Press.

Jenkins, J., Simpson, A., Dunn, J., Rasbash, J., & O'Connor, T. G. (2005). Mutual influence of marital conflict and children's behavior problems: Shared and nonshared family risks. *Child Development, 76,* 24–39.

Jennings, B. M. (1990). Stress, locus of control, social support, and psychological symptoms among head nurses. *Research in Nursing & Health, 13,* 393–401.

Jensen, A. (1969). How much can we boost IQ and scholastic achievement? *Harvard Educational Review, 39,* 2.

Jensen, A. (1980). *Bias in mental testing.* New York: Free Press.

Jensen, A. R. (1998). The g factor and the design of education. In R. J. Sternberg & W. M. Williams (Eds.), *Intelligence, instruction, and assessment: Theory into practice.* Mahwah, NJ: Erlbaum.

Jensen, J. P., Bergin, A. E., & Greaves, D. W. (1990). The meaning of eclecticism: New survey and analysis of components. *Professional Psychology: Research and Practice, 21,* 124–130.

Jensen, M. P., Turner, J. A., & Romano, J. M. (2001). Changes in beliefs, catastrophizing, and coping are associated with improvement in multidisciplinary pain treatment. *Journal of Consulting and Clinical Psychology, 69,* 655–662.

Jéquier, E. (2002). Pathways to obesity. *International Journal of Obesity and Related Metabolic Disorders, 26,* 12–17.

Jimenez, L., & Mendez, C. (2001). Implicit sequence learning with competing explicit cues. *Quarterly Journal of Experimental Psychology: Comparative and Physiological Psychology, 54,* 345–369.

Johannesen-Schmidt, M. C., & Eagly, A. H. (2002). Another look at sex differences in preferred mate characteristics: The effects of endorsing the traditional female gender role. *Psychology of Women Quarterly, 26,* 322–328.

John, O. P., & Srivastava, S. (1999). The Big Five trait taxonomy: History, measurement, and theoretical perspectives. In L. A. Pervin & O. P. John (Eds.), *Handbook of personality: Theory and research.* New York: Guilford Press.

Johns, M., Schmader, T., & Martens, A. (2005). Knowing is half the battle: Teaching stereotype threat as a means of improving women's math performance. *Psychological Science, 16,* 175–179.

Johnson, A. M., Wadsworth, J., Wellings, K., & Bradshaw, S. (1992). Sexual lifestyles and HIV risk. *Nature, 360,* 410–412.

Johnson, D. W. (2000). Cooperative learning processes reduce prejudice. In S. Oskamp (Ed.), *Reducing prejudice and discrimination.* Mahwah, NJ: Erlbaum.

Johnson, J. G., Cohen, P., Smailes, E. M., Kasen, S., & Brook, J. S. (2002). Television viewing and aggressive behavior during adolescence and adulthood. *Science, 295,* 2468–2471.

Johnson, J. L., & Newport, E. L. (1989). Critical period effects in second language learning: The influence of maturational state on the acquisition of English as a second language. *Cognitive Psychology, 21,* 60–99.

Johnston, L. D., O'Malley, P. M., Bachman, J. G., & Schulenberg, J. E. (2004). *Monitoring the Future national survey results on drug use, 1975–2003: Vol. 2. College students and adults ages 19–45* (NIH Publication No. 04-5508). Bethesda, MD: National Institute on Drug Abuse.

Johnston, M. S., Kelley, C. S., Harris, F. F., & Wolf, M. M. (1966). An application of reinforcement principles to development of motor skills of a young child. *Child Development, 37,* 379–387.

Johnston, V. S., Hagel, R., Franklin, M., Fink, B., & Grammer, K. (2001). Male facial attractiveness: Evidence for hormone-mediated adaptive design. *Evolution and Human Behavior, 22,* 251–267.

Joiner, T. E., & Coyne, J. C. (Eds.). (1999). *The interactional nature of depression: Advances in interpersonal approaches.* Washington, DC: American Psychological Association.

Jones, B. C., Little, A. C., Feinberg, D. R., Penton-Voak, I. S., Tiddeman, B. P., & Perrett, D. I. (2004). The relationship between shape symmetry and perceived skin condition in male facial attractiveness. *Evolution and Human Behavior, 25,* 24–30.

Jones, E., Cumming, J. D., & Horowitz, M. J. (1988). Another look at the nonspecific hypothesis of therapeutic effectiveness. *Journal of Consulting and Clinical Psychology, 56,* 48–55.

Jones, E. E., & Harris, V. A. (1967). The attribution of attitudes. *Journal of Experimental Social Psychology, 3,* 2–24.

Jones, J. T., Pelham, B. W., Carvallo, M., & Mirenberg, M. C. (2004). How do I love thee? Let me count the Js: Implicit egotism and interpersonal attraction. *Journal of Personality and Social Psychology, 87,* 665–683.

Jones, M. C. (1924). A laboratory study of fear: The case of Peter. *Pedagogical Seminary, 31,* 308–315.

Joseph, R. (2000). The evolution of sex differences in language, sexuality, and visual-spatial skills. *Archives of Sexual Behavior, 29,* 35–66.

Josephs, R. A., Bosson, J. K., & Jacobs, C. G. (2003). Self-esteem maintenance processes: Why self-esteem may be resistant to change. *Personality and Social Psychology Bulletin, 29,* 920–933.

Julien, R. M. (2005). *A primer of drug action: A comprehensive guide to the actions, uses, and side effects of psychoactive drugs* (10th ed.). New York: Worth.

Jung, J. (1995). Ethnic group and gender differences in the relationship between personality and coping. *Anxiety, Stress & Coping: An International Journal, 8,* 113–126.

Jureidini, J. N., Doecke, C. J., Mansfield, P. R., Haby, M. M., Menkes, D. B., & Tonkin, A. L. (2004). Efficacy and safety of antidepressants for children and adolescents. *British Medical Journal, 328*(7444), 879–883.

Kabot, S., Masi, W., & Segal, M. (2003). Advances in the diagnosis and treatment of autism spectrum disorders. *Professional Psychology: Research and Practice, 34,* 26–33.

Kagan, J. (1989). Temperamental contributions to social behavior. *American Psychologist, 44,* 668–674.

Kagan, J. (1999). The concept of behavioral inhibition. In L. A. Schmidt & J. Schulkin (Eds.), *Extreme fear, shyness, and social phobia: Origins, biological mechanisms, and clinical outcomes.* New York: Oxford University Press.

Kagan, J., Kearsley, R. B., & Zelazo, P. (1978). *Infancy: Its place in human development.* Cambridge, MA: Harvard University Press.

Kagan, J., Reznick, S., & Snidman, N. (1988). Biological bases of childhood shyness. *Science, 240,* 167–171.

Kagitçibasi, C. (1997). Individualism and collectivism. In J. W. Berry, M. H. Segall, & C. Kagitçibasi (Eds.), *Handbook of cross-cultural psychology* (Vol. 3). Boston: Allyn & Bacon.

Kahneman, D., & Tversky, A. (1979). Prospect theory: An analysis of decisions under risk. *Econometrica, 47,* 263–291.

Kahneman, D., & Tversky, A. (1982). On the study of statistical intuitions. *Cognition, 11,* 123–141.

Kail, R. (1991). Developmental change in speed of processing during childhood and adolescence. *Psychological Bulletin, 109,* 490–501.

Kaku, M. (2004). *Einstein's cosmos: How Albert Einstein's vision transformed our understanding of space and time.* New York: Norton.

Kaltiala-Heino, R., Marttunen, M., Rantanen, P., & Rimpela, M. (2003). Early puberty is associated with mental health problems in middle adolescence. *Social Science & Medicine, 57,* 1055–1064.

Kampmann, K. M., Volpicelli, J. R., Mulvaney, F., Rukstalis, M., Alterman, A. I., Pettinati, H., et al. (2002). Cocaine withdrawal severity and urine toxicology results from treatment entry predict outcome in medication trials for cocaine dependence. *Addictive Behaviors, 27,* 251–260.

Kandel, E. R. (2001). The molecular biology of memory storage: A dialogue between genes and synapses. *Science, 294,* 1030–1038.

Kane, J. M. (Ed.). (1992). *Tardive dyskinesia: A task force report of the American Psychiatric Association.* Washington, DC: American Psychiatric Press.

Kaner, A. (1995). Physical attractiveness and women's lives: Findings from a longitudinal study. *Dissertation Abstracts International: Section B. The Sciences and Engineering, 56,* 2942.

Kanfer, F. H., & Goldstein, A. P. (Eds.). (1991). *Helping people change: A textbook of methods* (4th ed.). New York: Pergamon Press.

Kanner, L. (1943) Autistic disturbance of affective contact. *Nervous Child, 12,* 17–50.

Kanwisher, N. (1998). The modular structure of human visual recognition: Evidence from functional imaging. In M. Sabourin et al. (Eds.), *Advances in psychological science: Vol. 2. Biological and cognitive aspects.* Hove, England: Psychology Press/Erlbaum (UK) Taylor & Francis.

Kaplan, H., & Dove, H. (1987). Infant development among the Ache of eastern Paraguay. *Developmental Psychology, 23,* 190–198.

Kaprio, J., Koskenvu, M., & Rita, H. (1987). Mortality after bereavement: A prospective study of 95,647 widowed persons. *American Journal of Public Health, 77,* 283–287.

Karau, S. J., & Williams, K. D. (1993). Social loafing: A meta-analytic review and theoretical integration. *Journal of Personality and Social Psychology, 65,* 681–706.

Karau, S. J., & Williams, K. D. (2001). Understanding individual motivation in groups: The collective effort model. In M. E. Turner (Ed.), *Groups at work: Theory and research: Applied social research.* Mahwah, NJ: Erlbaum.

Karon, B. P. (2002). Psychoanalysis: Legitimate and illegitimate concerns. *Psychoanalytic Psychology 19,* 564–571.

Kashima, Y., Yamaguchi, S., Kim, U., Choi, S., Gelfand, M., & Yuki, M. (1995). Culture, gender, and self: A perspective from individualism-collectivism research. *Journal of Personality and Social Psychology, 69,* 925–937.

Kastenbaum, R. (2000). *The psychology of death* (3rd ed.). New York: Springer.

Katapodi, M. C., Facione, N. C., Humphreys, J. C., & Dodd, M. J. (2005). Perceived breast cancer risk: Heuristic reasoning and search for a dominance structure. *Social Science & Medicine, 60,* 421–432.

Katz, J., & Melzack, R. (1990). Pain "memories" in phantom limbs: Review and clinical observations. *Pain, 43,* 319–336.

Kaufman, A. S., & Kaufman, N. (1997). The Kaufman Adolescent and Adult Intelligence Test. In D. P. Flanagan, J. L. Genshaft, &

P. L. Harrison (Eds.), *Contemporary intellectual assessment: Theories, tests, and issues.* New York: Guilford Press.

Kavanagh, D. (1992). Schizophrenia. In P. H. Wilson (Ed.), *Principles and practice of relapse prevention.* New York: Guilford Press.

Kay, L. (1982). *Spatial perception through an acoustic sensor.* Christchurch, New Zealand: University of Canterbury Press.

Kaye, W. H., Strober, M., & Klump, K. L. (2002). Serotonin neuronal function in anorexia nervosa and bulimia nervosa. In F. Lewis Hall et al. (Eds.), *Psychiatric illness in women: Emerging treatments and research.* Washington, DC: American Psychiatric Publishing.

Kazdin, A. E. (1975). The impact of applied behavior analysis on diverse areas of research. *Journal of Applied Behavior Analysis, 8,* 213–229.

Kazdin, A. E. (Ed.). (2003). *Methodological issues and strategies in clinical research* (3rd ed.). Washington, DC: American Psychological Association.

Keinan, G. (2002). The effects of stress and desire for control on superstitious behavior. *Personality and Social Psychology Bulletin, 28,* 102–108.

Keith, S. J., Regier, D. A., & Rae, D. S. (1991). Schizophrenic disorders. In L. N. Robins & D. A. Regier (Eds.), *Psychiatric disorders in America: The Epidemiological Catchment Area Study.* New York: Free Press.

Keller, H. (1955). *The story of my life.* New York: Doubleday.

Kelley, H. H. (1973). The process of causal attribution. *American Psychologist, 28,* 107–128.

Kelly, G. (1955). *The psychology of personal constructs.* New York: Norton.

Kelly, G. F. (2001). *Sexuality today: The human perspective* (6th ed.). Boston: McGraw-Hill.

Kelly, G. F. (2004). *Sexuality today: The human perspective* (7th ed.). Boston: McGraw-Hill.

Kelly, J. A., St. Lawrence, J. S., Hood, H. V., & Brasfield, T. L. (1989). Behavioral intervention to reduce AIDS risk activities. *Journal of Consulting and Clinical Psychology, 57,* 60–67.

Kelly, T. A., & Strupp, H. H. (1992). Patient and therapist values in psychotherapy: Perceived changes, assimilation, similarity, and outcome. *Journal of Consulting and Clinical Psychology, 60,* 34–40.

Keltner, D., & Ekman, P. (2000). Facial expression of emotion. In M. Lewis & J. M. Haviland-Jones (Eds.), *Handbook of emotions* (2nd ed.). New York: Guilford Press.

Kemeny, M. E., (2004). The psychobiology of stress. *Current Directions in Psychological Science, 12,* 124–129.

Kenardy, J., Brown, W. J., & Vogt, E. (2001). Dieting and health in young Australian women. *European Eating Disorders Review, 9,* 242–254.

Kendall, D. (1998). *Social problems in a diverse society.* Boston: Allyn & Bacon.

Kenrick, D. T., & Funder, D. C. (1988). Profiting from controversy: Lessons from the person-situation debate. *American Psychologist, 43,* 23–34.

Kensinger, E. A., Ullman, M. T., & Corkin, S. (2001). Bilateral medial temporal lobe damage does not affect lexical or grammatical processing: Evidence from amnesic patient H. M. *Hippocampus, 11,* 347–360.

Kentridge, R. W., Heywood, C. A., & Weiskrantz, L. (2004). Spatial attention speeds discrimination without awareness in blindsight. *Neuropsychologia, 42,* 831–835.

Kernberg, O. F. (1984). *Severe personality disorders: Psychotherapeutic strategies.* New Haven, CT: Yale University Press.

Kernberg, O. F. (2000). *Personality disorders in children and adolescents.* Poulsbo, WA: H-R Press.

Kernberg, O. F., & Caligor, E. (2005). A psychoanalytic theory of personality disorders. In M. F. Lenzenweger & J. F. Clarkin (Eds.), *Major theories of personality disorder.* New York: Guilford Press.

Kerr, M., Lambert, W. W., & Bem, D. J. (1996). Life course sequelae of childhood shyness in Sweden: Comparison with the United States. *Developmental Psychology, 32,* 1100–1105.

Kessler, R. C., Gilman, S. E., Thornton, L. M., & Kendler, K. S. (2004). Health, well-being, and social responsibility in the MIDUS twin and sibling subsamples. In O. G. Brim, C. D. Ryff, & R. C. Kessler (Eds.), *How healthy are we? A national study of well-being in midlife.* Chicago: University of Chicago Press.

Kessler, R. C., McGonagle, K. A., Zhao, S., Nelson, C., et al. (1994). Lifetime and 12-month prevalence of DSM-III-R psychiatric disorder in the United States. *Archives of General Psychiatry, 51,* 8–19.

Kessler, R. C., & Wittchen, H. U. (2002). Patterns and correlates of generalized anxiety disorder in community samples. *Journal of Clinical Psychiatry, 63*(Suppl. 8), 4–10.

Ketellar, T. (1995). *Emotion as mental representations of fitness affordances: I. Evidence supporting the claim that the negative and positive emotions map onto fitness costs and benefits.* Paper presented at the annual meeting of the Human Behavior and Evolution Society, Santa Barbara, CA.

Kety, S. S. (1988). Schizophrenic illness in the families of schizophrenic adoptees: Findings from the Danish national sample. *Schizophrenia Bulletin, 14,* 217–222.

Kety, S. S., Rosenthal, D., Wender, P. H., Schulsinger, F., & Jacobson, B. (1978). The biological and adoptive families of adopted individuals who become schizophrenic: Prevalence of mental illness and other characteristics. In L. C. Wynne, R. L. Cromwell, & S. Matthysse (Eds.), *The nature of schizophrenia: New approaches to research and treatment.* New York: Wiley.

Keyes, C. L. M., & Waterman, M. B. (2003). Dimensions of well-being and mental health in adulthood. In M. H. Bornstein, L. Davidson, C. L. M. Keyes, & K. A. Moore (Eds.), *Well-being: Positive development across the life course: Crosscurrents in contemporary psychology.* Mahwah, NJ: Erlbaum.

Keyes, L. M., & Goodman, S. H. (2006). *Women and depression: A handbook for social, behavioral, and biomedical sciences.* New York: Cambridge University Press.

Kiecolt-Glaser, J., Bane, C., Glaser, R., & Malarkey, W. B. (2003). Love, marriage, and divorce: Newlyweds' stress hormones foreshadow relationship changes. *Journal of Consulting and Clinical Psychology, 71,* 176–188.

Kiecolt-Glaser, J., McGuire, L., Robles, T. F., & Glaser, R. (2002). Emotions, morbidity, and mortality: New perspectives from psycho-neuroimmunology. *Annual Review of Psychology, 53,* 83–107.

Kihlstrom, J. F. (1998). Dissociations and dissociation theory in hypnosis: Comment on Kirsch and Lynn. *Psychological Bulletin, 123,* 186–191.

Kihlstrom, J. F. (1999). The psychological unconscious. In L. A. Pervin & O. P. John (Eds.), *Handbook of personality: Theory and research.* New York: Guilford Press.

Kimble, D. P. (1992). *Biological psychology* (2nd ed.). Ft. Worth, TX: Harcourt Brace Jovanovich.

Kimerling, R., Ouimette, P., & Wolfe, J. (2003). *Gender and PTSD.* New York: Guilford Press.

Kimura, D. (1992). Sex differences in the brain. *Scientific American, 267*(3), 119–195.

Kimura, K., Tachibana, N., Aso, T., Kimura, J., & Shibasaki, H. (1997). Subclinical REM sleep behavior disorder in a patient with corticobasal degeneration. *Sleep, 20,* 891–894.

KING Broadcasting Company. (2005, March 2). 5 P.M. Evening News. Seattle, WA.

King, N. J., Dudley, A., Melvin, G., Pallant, J., & Morawetz, D. (2001). Empirically supported treatments for insomnia. *Scandinavian Journal of Behaviour Therapy, 30,* 23–32.

Kinsey, A. C., Pomeroy, W. B., & Martin, C. E. (1948). *Sexual behavior in the human male.* Philadelphia: Saunders.

Kinsey, A. C., Pomeroy, W. B., Martin, C. E., & Gebhard, P. H. (1953). *Sexual behavior in the human female.* Philadelphia: Saunders.

Kirchengast, S., & Hartmann, B. (2003). Nicotine consumption before and during pregnancy affects not only newborn size but also birth modus. *Journal of Biosocial Science, 35,* 175–188.

Kirk, K. M., Bailey, J. M., & Martin, N. G. (2000). Etiology of male sexual orientation in an Australian twin sample. *Psychology, Evolution, and Gender, 2,* 301–311.

Kirsch, I. (2001). The response set theory of hypnosis: Expectancy and physiology. *American Journal of Clinical Hypnosis, 44,* 69–73.

Kirsch, I., & Braffman, W. (2001). Imaginative suggestibility and hypnotizability. *Current Directions in Psychological Science, 10,* 57–61.

Kirsch, I., Moore, T. J., Scoboria, A., & Nicholls, S. S. (2002). The emperor's new drugs: An analysis of antidepressant medication data submitted to the U.S. Food and Drug Administration. *Prevention & Treatment, 5.*

Kitayama, S., & Markus, H. (1999). The yin and yang of the Japanese self. In D. Cervone & Y. Shoda (Eds.), *The coherence of personality.* New York: Guilford Press.

Kitayama, S., Markus, H. R., & Kurokawa, M. (2000). Culture, emotion, and well-being: Good feelings in Japan and the United States. *Cognition and Emotion, 14,* 93–124.

Kleim, J. A., Barbay, S., Cooper, N. R., Hogg, T. M., Reidel, C. N., Remple, M. S., & Nudo, R. J. (2002). Motor learning-dependent synaptogenesis is localized to functionally reorganized motor cortex. *Neurobiology of Learning & Memory, 77,* 63–77.

Klein, M. (1975). *The writings of Melanie Klein.* London: Hogarth Press.

Klein, S. B., & Mowrer, R. R. (1989). *Contemporary learning theories: Vol I. Pavlovian conditioning and the status of tradition.* Hillsdale, NJ: Erlbaum.

Kleiner, M. (Ed). (2002). *Handbook of polygraph testing.* San Diego, CA: Academic Press.

Kleinknecht, R. A., Dinnel, D. L., Kleinknecht, E. E., Hiruma, N., et al. (Eds.). (1997). Cultural factors in social anxiety: A comparison of social phobia symptoms and Taijin Kyofusho. *Journal of Anxiety Disorders, 2,* 157–177.

Kleinman, A. (2004). Culture and depression. *New England Journal of Medicine, 351,* 951–953.

Kleinmuntz, B. (1980). *Essentials of abnormal psychology* (2nd ed.). New York: Harper & Row.

Kleinmuntz, B., & Szucko, J. J. (1984). Lie detection in ancient and modern times: A call for contemporary scientific study. *American Psychologist, 39,* 766–776.

Kleitman, N. (1963). *Sleep and wakefulness* (2nd ed.). Chicago: University of Chicago Press.

Kluckhohn, C., & Murray, H. A. (1953). Personality formation: The determinants. In C. Kluckhohn, H. A. Murray, & D. M. Schneider (Eds.), *Personality in nature, society, and culture.* New York: Knopf.

Kluft, R. P. (1999). True lies, false truths, and naturalistic raw data: Applying clinical research findings to the false memory debate. In L. M. Williams & V. L. Banyard (Eds.), *Trauma and memory.* Thousand Oaks, CA: Sage.

Knauth, P. (1996). Designing better shift systems. *Applied Ergonomics, 27,* 39–44.

Knoblauch, K. (2002). Color vision. In H. Pashler & S. Yantis (Eds.), *Steven's handbook of experimental psychology: Vol. 1. Sensation and perception* (3rd ed.). New York: Wiley.

Knopik, V. S., Heath, A. C., Madden, P., Bucholz, K. K., Slutske, W. S., Nelson, E. C., Statham, D., Whitfield, J. B., & Martin, N. G. (2004). Genetic effects on alcohol dependence risk: Re-evaluating the importance of psychiatric and other heritable risk factors. *Psychological Medicine, 34,* 1519–1530.

Kobasa, S. C., Maddi, S. R., Puccetti, M. C., & Zola, M. A. (1985). Effectiveness of hardiness, exercise and social support as resources against illness. *Journal of Psychosomatic Research, 29,* 525–533.

Koch, K. (2004). *The quest for consciousness: A neurobiological approach.* Denver, CO: Roberts.

Kochanska, G., Aksan, N., Knaack, A., & Rhines, H. M. (2004). Maternal parenting and children's conscience: Early security as moderator. *Child Development, 75,* 1229–1242.

Kochanska, G., Casey, R. J., & Fukumoto, A. (1995). Toddlers' sensitivity to standard violations. *Child Development, 66,* 643–656.

Kochanska, G., Forman, D. R., Aksan, N., & Dunbar, S. B. (2005). Pathways to conscience: Early mother-child mutually responsive orientation and children's moral emotion, conduct, and cognition. *Journal of Child Psychology and Psychiatry, 46,* 19–34.

Koenig, H. G., Pargament, K. L., & Nielsen, J. (1998). Religious coping and health status in medically ill hospitalized older adults. *Journal of Nervous and Mental Disease, 186,* 513–521.

Koestner, R., & McClelland, D. C. (1990). Perspectives on competence motivation. In L. A. Pervin (Ed.), *Handbook of personality theory and research.* New York: Guilford Press.

Kogi, K. (1985). Introduction to the problems of shift work. In S. Folkard & T. H. Monk (Eds.), *Hours of work.* West Sussex: Wiley.

Kohlberg, L. (1963). The development of children's orientations toward a moral order: I. Sequence in the development of moral thought. *Human Development, 6,* 11–33.

Kohlberg, L. (1984). *The psychology of moral development: Essays on moral development* (Vol. 2). New York: Harper & Row.

Köhler, W. (1925). *The mentality of apes* (Trans. from the 2nd rev. ed. by Ella Winter). New York: Harcourt.

Kohut, H. (1971). *Analysis of the self.* New York: International Universities Press.

Kohut, H. (1977). *The restoration of self.* New York: International Universities Press.

Kokko, K., & Pulkkinen, L. (2000). Aggression in childhood and long-term unemployment in adulthood: A cycle of maladaptation and some protective factors. *Developmental Psychology, 36,* 463–472.

Kolb, B., & Whishaw, I. Q. (2001). *An introduction to brain and behavior.* New York: Worth.

Kolb, B., & Whishaw, I. Q. (2003). *Fundamentals of human neuropsychology* (5th ed.). New York: Worth.

Kollar, E. J., & Fisher, C. (1980). Tooth induction in chick epithelium: Expression of quiescent genes for enamel synthesis. *Science, 207,* 993–995.

Koluchova, J. (1972). Severe deprivation in twins: A case study. *Journal of Child Psychology and Psychiatry, 13,* 107–114.

Koluchova, J. (1991). Severely deprived twins after 22 years of observation. *Studia Psychologica, 33,* 23–28.

Koriat, A., & Bjork, R. A. (2005). Illusions of competence in monitoring one's knowledge during study. *Journal of Experimental Psychology: Learning, Memory, and Cognition, 31,* 187–194.

Koriat, A., Goldsmith, M., & Pansky, A. (2000). Toward a psychology of memory accuracy. *Annual Review of Psychology, 51,* 481–537.

Kortegaard, L., Hoerder, K., Joergensen, J., Gillberg, C., & Kyvik, K. O. (2001). A preliminary population-based twin study of self-reported eating disorder. *Psychological Medicine, 31,* 361–365.

Kosambi, D. D. (1967). Living prehistory in India. *Scientific American, 216,* 105.

Kosslyn, S. M. (1978). Measuring the visual angle of the mind's eye. *Cognitive Psychology, 10,* 356–389.

Kosslyn, S. M., Ball, T. M., & Reiser, B. J. (1978). Visual images preserve metric spatial information: Evidence from studies of image scanning. *Journal of Experimental Psychology: Human Perception and Performance, 4,* 47–60.

Kosslyn, S. M., Thompson, W. L., Costantini-Ferrando, M. F., Alpert, N. M., & Spiegel, D. (2000). Hypnotic visual illusion alters color processing in the brain. *American Journal of Psychiatry, 157,* 1279–1284.

Kostanski, M., Fisher, A., & Gullone, E. (2004). Current conceptualisation of body image dissatisfaction: Have we got it wrong? *Journal of Child Psychology and Psychiatry, 45,* 1317–1325.

Kottak, C. P. (2000). *Cultural anthropology* (8th ed.). Boston: McGraw-Hill.

Kowert, P. A. (Ed.). (2002). *Groupthink or deadlock: When do leaders learn from their advisors? SUNY series on the presidency.* New York: State University of New York Press.

Kraft, C. L. (1978). A psychophysical contribution to air safety: Simulator studies of illusions in night visual approaches. In H. L. Pick, Jr., H. W. Leibowitz, J. E. Singer, A. Steinschneider, & H. W. Stevenson (Eds.), *Psychology: From research to practice.* New York: Plenum Press.

Kramsch, C. J. (2003). *Language acquisition and language socialization: Ecological perspectives.* New York: Continuum International.

Krasnegor, N. A., Lyon, G. R., & Goldman, R. P. S. (1997). *Development of the prefrontal cortex: Evolution, neurobiology, and behavior.* Baltimore, MD: Paul H. Brookes.

Krebs, D. L., & Denton, K. (1997). Social illusions and self-deception: The evolution of biases in person perception. In J. A. Simpson & D. T. Kenrick (Eds.), *Evolutionary social psychology.* Mahwah, NJ: Erlbaum.

Kreiman, G., Koch, C., & Fried, I. (2000). Imagery neurons in the human brain. *Nature, 408,* 357–361.

Krevans, J., & Gibbs, J. C. (1996). Parents' use of inductive discipline: Relations to children's empathy and prosocial behavior. *Child Development, 67,* 3263–3277.

Kribbs, N. B. (1993). Siesta. In M. A. Carskadon (Ed.), *Encyclopedia of sleep and dreaming.* New York: Macmillan.

Kroeber, A. L. (1948). *Anthropology.* New York: Harcourt Brace Jovanovich.

Krosnick, J. A., Betz, A. L., Jussim, L. J., & Lynn, A. R. (1992). Subliminal conditioning of attitudes. *Personality and Social Psychology Bulletin, 18,* 152–162.

Kruger, J., Wirtz, D., & Miller, D. T. (2005). Counterfactual thinking and the first instinct fallacy. *Journal of Personality and Social Psychology, 88,* 725–735.

Kruglanski, A. W. (2004). *The psychology of closed mindedness.* New York: Psychology Press.

Kryger, M. H., Walid, R., & Manfreda, J. (2002). Diagnoses received by narcolepsy patients in the year prior to diagnosis by a sleep specialist. *Sleep: Journal of Sleep and Sleep Disorders Research, 25,* 36–41.

Kübler-Ross, E. (1969). *On death and dying.* New York: Macmillan.

Kulik, J. A., & Mahler, H. I. M. (2000). Social comparison, affiliation, and emotional contagion under threat. In J. Suls & L. Wheeler (Eds.), *Handbook of social comparison: Theory and research.* Dordrecht, Netherlands: Kluwer.

Kulik, J. A., Mahler, H. I. M., & Moore, P. J. (1996). Social comparison and affiliation under threat: Effects of recovery from major surgery. *Journal of Personality and Social Psychology, 66,* 301–309.

Kuncel, N. P., Hezlett, S. A., & Ones, D. S. (2004). Academic performance, career potential, and job performance: Can one construct predict them all? *Journal of Personality and Social Psychology, 86,* 148–161.

Kunzendorf, R. G., Hartmann, E., Cohen, R., & Cutler, J. (1997). Bizarreness of the dreams and daydreams reported by individuals with thin and thick boundaries. *Dreaming: Journal of the Association for the Study of Dreams, 7,* 265–271.

Kunzman, U., & Baltes, P. B. (2003). Beyond the traditional scope of intelligence: Wisdom in action. In R. J. Sternberg, J. Lautrey, & T. I. Lubart (Eds.), *Models of intelligence: International perspectives.* Washington, DC: American Psychological Association.

Kurzweil, E. (1989). *The Freudians: A comparative perspective.* New Haven, CT: Yale University Press.

LaBar, K. S., & Phelps, E. A. (1998). Arousal-mediated memory consolidation: Role of the medial temporal lobe in humans. *Psychological Science, 9,* 490–493.

Lachman, M. E. (2004). Development in midlife. *Annual Review of Psychology, 55,* 305–331.

Lagerspetz, K. Y., Tirri, R., & Lagerspetz, K. M. (1968). Neurochemical and endocrinological studies of mice selectively bred for aggressiveness. *Scandinavian Journal of Psychology, 9,* 157–160.

Laible, D., & Thompson, R. A. (2000). Mother-child discourse, attachment security, shared positive affect, and early conscience development. *Child Development, 71,* 1424–1440.

Lakein, A. (1973). *How to get control of your time and your life.* New York: Peter H. Wyden.

Lambert, M. J., Shapiro, D. A., & Bergin, A. E. (1986). The effectiveness of psychotherapy. In L. Garfield & A. E. Bergin (Eds.), *Handbook of psychotherapy and behavior change* (3rd ed.). New York: Wiley.

Lambert, W. E., Genesee, F., Holobow, N., & Chartrand, L. (1993). Bilingual education for majority English-speaking children. *European Journal of Psychology of Education, 8,* 3–22.

Lamborn, S. D., Mounts, N. S., Steinberg, L., & Dornbusch, S. M. (1991). Patterns of competence and adjustment among adolescents from authoritative, authoritarian, indulgent, and neglectful families. *Child Development, 62,* 1049–1065.

Land, B. B., & Seeley, T. D. (2004). The grooming invitation dance of the honey bee. *Ethology, 110,* 1–10.

Landers, D. M., & Arent, S. (2001). Arousal-performance relations. In J. M. Williams (Ed.), *Applied sport psychology: Personal growth to peak performance* (4th ed.). Boston: McGraw-Hill.

Landesman, S., & Ramey, C. T. (1989). Developmental psychology and mental retardation: Integrating scientific principles with treatment practices. *American Psychologist, 44,* 409–415.

Lane, R. D., Reiman, E. M., Ahern, G. L., & Schwartz, G. E. (1997). Neuroanatomical correlates of happiness, sadness, and disgust. *American Journal of Psychiatry, 154,* 926–933.

Lane, S. D., Cherek, D. R., Lieving, L. M., & Tcheremissine, O. V. (2005). Marijuana effects on human forgetting functions. *Journal of the Experimental Analysis of Behavior, 83,* 67–83.

Langer, E. (1989). *Mindlessness.* Reading, MA: Addison-Wesley.

Langlois, J. H., Kalakanis, L., Rubenstein, A. J., Larson, A., Hallam, M., & Smoot, M. (2000). Maxims or myths of beauty? A meta-analytic and theoretical review. *Psychological Bulletin, 126,* 390–423.

Langlois, J. H., & Roggman, L. A. (1990). Attractive faces are only average. *Psychological Science, 1,* 115–121.

Lanier, C. A. (2001). Rape accepting attitudes: Precursors to or consequences of forced sex. *Violence Against Women, 7,* 876–885.

LaPiere, R. T. (1934). Attitudes and actions. *Social Forces, 13,* 230–237.

LaPointe, L. L. (2005). *Aphasia and related neurogenic language disorders* (3rd ed.). New York: Thieme New York.

Larivée, S., Normandeau, S., & Parent, S. (2000). The French connection: Some contributions of French language research in the post Piagetian era. *Child Development, 71,* 823–839.

Larroque, B., & Kaminski, M. (1998). Prenatal alcohol exposure and development at preschool age: Main results of a French study. *Alcoholism: Clinical and Experimental Research, 22,* 295–303.

Larsen, R., & Buss, D. M. (2002). *Personality psychology: Domains of knowledge about human nature.* Boston: McGraw-Hill.

Larsen, R., & Diener, E. (1985). A multitrait-multimethod examination of affect structure: Hedonic level and emotional intensity. *Personality and Individual Differences, 6,* 631–636.

Larson, R. W., Moneta, G., Richards, M. H., & Wilson, W. (2002). Continuity, stability, and change in daily emotional experience across adolescence. *Child Development, 73,* 1151–1165.

Lasco, M. S., Jordan, T. J., Edgar, M. A., Petito, C. K., & Byne, W. (2002). A lack of dimorphism of sex or sexual orientation in the human anterior commissure. *Brain Research, 936,* 95–98.

Lashley, K. S. (1950). In search of the engram. *Symposia of the Society for Experimental Biology, 4,* 454–482.

Latané, B., & Bourgeois, M. J. (2001). Successfully simulating dynamic social impact: Three levels of prediction. In J. P. Forgas & K. D. Williams (Eds.), *Social influence: Direct and indirect processes. The Sydney symposium of social psychology.* Philadelphia, PA: Psychology Press.

Latané, B., & Darley, J. M. (1970). *The unresponsive bystander: Why doesn't he help?* New York: Appleton-Century-Crofts.

Latané, B., & Nida, S. (1981). Ten years of research on group size and helping. *Psychological Bulletin, 89,* 308–324.

Laumann, E. O., Gagnon, J. H., Michael, R. T., & Michaels, S. (1994). *The social organization of sexuality: Sexual practices in the United States.* Chicago: University of Chicago Press.

Lavergne, G. M. (1997). *A sniper in the tower: The Charles Whitman murders.* Denton: University of North Texas Press.

Lavie, P. (2000). Sleep-wake as a biological rhythm. *Annual Review of Psychology, 52,* 277–303.

Lavigne, J. V., Gibbons, R. D., Christoffel, K. K., & Arend, R. (1996). Prevalence rates and correlates of psychiatric disorders among preschool children. *Journal of the American Academy of Child & Adolescent Psychiatry, 35,* 204–214.

Lawler, K. A., & Schmied, L. A. (1992). A prospective study of women's health: The effects of stress, hardiness, locus of control, Type A behavior, and physiological reactivity. *Women and Health, 19,* 27–41.

Lazarus, A. A. (1995). Multimodal therapy. In R. J. Corsini & D. Wedding (Eds.), *Current psychotherapies* (5th ed.). Itasca, IL: Peacock.

Lazarus, R. S. (1991). Progress on a cognitive-motivational-relational theory of emotion. *American Psychologist, 46,* 819–834.

Lazarus, R. S. (1998). *Fifty years of the research and theory of R. S. Lazarus: An analysis of historical and perennial issues.* Mahwah, NJ: Erlbaum.

Lazarus, R. S. (2001). Relational meaning and discrete emotions. In B. K. Scherer et al. (Eds.), *Appraisal processes in emotion: Theory, methods, research.* New York: Oxford University Press.

Lazarus, R. S., & Folkman, S. (1984). *Stress, appraisal, and coping.* New York: Springer.

Leary, M. R. (2004). The self we know and the self we show: Self-esteem, self-presentation, and the maintenance of interpersonal relationships. In M. B. Brewer & M. Hewstone (Eds.), *Emotion and motivation: Perspectives on social psychology.* Malden, MA: Blackwell.

Leary, M. R., Kowalski, R. M., Smith, L., & Phillips, S. (2003). Teasing, rejection, and violence: Case studies of the school shootings. *Aggressive Behavior, 29,* 202–214.

LeDoux, J. E. (1998). *The emotional brain.* New York: Simon & Schuster.

LeDoux, J. E. (2000). Emotion circuits in the brain. *Annual Review of Neuroscience, 23,* 155–184.

LeDoux, J. E., & Phelps, E. A. (2000). Emotional networks in the brain. In M. Lewis & J. M. Haviland-Jones (Eds.), *Handbook of emotions* (2nd ed.). New York: Guilford Press.

Lee, J. D. (1998). Which kids can "become" scientists? Effects of gender, self-concepts, and perceptions of scientists. *Social Psychology Quarterly, 61,* 199–219.

Lehmann-Haupt, C. (1988, August 4). Books of the times: How an actor found success, and himself. *New York Times,* p. 2.

Leichtman, M. D., & Ceci, S. J. (1995). The effects of stereotypes and suggestions on preschool-ers' reports. *Developmental Psychology, 31,* 568–578.

LeMoal, H., (1999). *Dopamine and the brain: From neurons to networks.* New York: Academic Press.

Lenzenweger, M. F., & Clarkin, J. F. (Eds.). (2005). *Major theories of personality disorder.* New York: Guilford Press.

Leon, G. R., & Roth, L. (1977). Obesity: Psychological causes, correlations, and speculations. *Psychological Bulletin, 84,* 117–139.

Leor, J., Poole, W. K., & Kloner, R. A. (1996). Sudden cardiac death triggered by an earthquake. *New England Journal of Medicine, 334(7),* 413–419.

LePage, M., Habib, R., & Tulving, E. (1998). Hippocampal PET activations of memory encoding and retrieval: The HIPER model. *Hippocampus, 8,* 313–322.

Leppämäki, S. J., Partonen, T. T., Hurme, J., Haukka, J. K., & Lönnqvist, J. K. (2002). Randomized trial of the efficacy of bright-light exposure and aerobic exercise on depressive symptoms and serum lipids. *Journal of Clinical Psychiatry, 63,* 316–321.

Leslie, J. C. (2002). *Essential behaviour analysis.* London: Arnold.

Lester, D. (1972). Voodoo death: Some new thoughts on an old phenomenon. *American Anthropologist, 74,* 386–390.

Levant, R. F. (2004). The empirically validated treatments movement: A practitioner/educator perspective. *Clinical Psychology; Science and Practice, 11,* 219–224.

Levine, R., Sato, S., Hashimoto, T., & Verma, J. (1995). Love and marriage in eleven cultures. *Journal of Cross-Cultural Psychology, 26,* 554–571.

Levinson, D. J. (1986). A conception of adult development. *American Psychologist, 41,* 3–13.

Levinson, D. J. (1990). A theory of life structure development in adulthood. In C. N. Alexander & E. J. Langer (Eds.), *Higher stages of human development: Perspectives on adult growth.* New York: Oxford University Press.

Levinson, D. J., Darow, C. N., Klein, E. B., Levinson, M. H., & McKee, B. (1978). *The seasons of a man's life.* New York: Knopf.

Levinthal, C. F. (1996). *Drugs, behavior, and modern society.* Boston: Allyn & Bacon.

Levitsky, D. A. (2002). Putting behavior back into feeding behavior: A tribute to George Collier. *Appetite, 38,* 143–148.

Levy, B. R., Slade, M. D., Kunkel, S. R., & Kasl, S. V. (2002). Longevity increased by positive self-perceptions of aging. *Journal of Personality and Social Psychology, 83,* 261–270.

Levy, S., Marrow, L., Bagley, C., & Lippman, M. (1988). Survival hazards analysis in first recurrent breast cancer patients: Seven-year follow-up. *Psychosomatic Medicine, 50,* 520–528.

Lewin, R. (1998). *The origin of modern humans.* New York: American Scientific Library.

Lewinsohn, P. M, Gotlib, I. H., Lewinsohn, M., Seeley, J. R., & Allen, N. B. (1998). Gender differences in anxiety disorders and anxiety symptoms in adolescents. *Journal of Abnormal Psychology, 107,* 109–117.

Lewinsohn, P. M., Hoberman, H., Teri, L., & Hantzinger, M. (1985). An integrative theory of depression. In S. Reiss & R. Bootzin (Eds.), *Theoretical issues in behavior therapy.* New York: Academic Press.

Lewis, M. (1999). On the development of personality. In L. A. Pervin & O. P. John (Eds.), *Handbook of personality: Theory and research.* New York: Guilford Press.

Lewis, M. (2000). The emergence of human emotions. In M. Lewis & J. M. Haviland-Jones (Eds.), *Handbook of emotions* (2nd ed.). New York: Guilford Press.

Lewis, M. J. (1996). Alcohol reinforcement and neuropharmacological therapeutics. *Alcohol and Alcoholism, 31*(Suppl. 1), 17–25.

Lewis, M. W., Misra, S., Johnson, H. L., & Rosen, T. S. (2004). Neurological and developmental outcomes of prenatally cocaine-exposed offspring from 12 to 36 months. *American Journal of Drug and Alcohol Abuse, 30,* 299–320.

Leyens, J. P., Camino, L., Parke, R. D., & Berkowitz, L. (1975). Effects of movie violence on aggression in a field setting as a function of group dominance and cohesion. *Journal of Personality and Social Psychology, 32,* 346–360.

Lezak, M. (1995). *Neuropsychological assessment* (3rd ed.). New York: Oxford University Press.

Li, S. (2001). How close is too close? A comparison of proxemic reactions of Singaporean Chinese to male intruders of four ethnicities. *Perceptual and Motor Skills, 93,* 124–126.

Lidz, C. S. (1997). Dynamic assessment approaches. In D. P. Flanagan, J. L. Genshaft, & P. L. Harrison (Eds.), *Contemporary intellectual assessment: Theories, tests, and issues.* New York: Guilford Press.

Lieb, R., Isensee, B., Hoefier, M., Pfister, H., & Wittchen, H. U. (2002). Parental major depression and the risk of depression and other mental disorders in offspring: A prospective-longitudinal community study. *Archives of General Psychiatry, 59,* 365–374.

Lieberman, J. A. (1998). *Psychiatric drugs.* Philadelphia: Saunders.

Lilienfeld, S. O., Wood, J. M., & Garb, H. N. (2000). The scientific status of projective techniques. *Psychological Science in the Public Interest, 1,* 25–62.

Linden, W. (2005). *Stress management: From basic science to better practice.* Newbury Park, CA: Sage.

Linehan, M. M. (1993). *Cognitive-behavioral treatment of borderline personality disorder.* New York: Guilford Press.

Link, B. G., & Steuve, A. (1998). New evidence on the violence risk posed by people with mental illness. *Archives of General Psychiatry, 55,* 403–404.

Linver, M. R., Brooks-Gunn, J., & Kohen, D. E. (2002). Family processes as pathways from income to young children's development. *Developmental Psychology, 38,* 719–734.

Lippa, R. A. (2005). *Gender, nature, and nurture.* Hillsdale, NJ: Erlbaum.

Lipsitt, L. P. (1990). Learning processes in the human newborn: Sensitization, habituation, and classical conditioning. *Annals of the New York Academy of Sciences, 608,* 113–127.

Litz, B. T. (2004). *Early intervention for trauma and traumatic loss.* New York: Guilford Press.

Livesley, W. J. (2003). *Practical management of personality disorder.* New York: Guilford Press.

Livingstone, M., & Hubel, D. (1994). Segregation of form, color, movement, and depth: Anatomy, physiology, and perception. In H. Gutfreund & G. Toulouse (Eds.), *Biology and computation: A physicist's choice. Advanced series in neuroscience.* Singapore: World Scientific Publishing.

Lloyd, E. A., & Feldman, M. W. (2002). Evolutionary psychology: A view from evolutionary biology. *Psychological Inquiry, 13,* 150–156.

Lobina, C., Agabio, R., Reali, R., Gessa, G. L., & Colombo, G. (1999). Contribution of GABA-sub(A) and GABA-sub(B) receptors to the

discriminative stimulus produced by gamma-hydroxybutyric acid. *Pharmacology, Biochemistry and Behavior, 64*(2), 363–365.

Locke, E. A., & Latham, G. P. (2002). Building a practically useful theory of goal setting and task motivation: A 35-year odyssey. *American Psychologist, 57,* 705–717.

Loehlin, J. C. (1992). *Genes and environment in personality development.* Newbury Park, CA: Sage.

Loehlin, J. C., Willerman, L., & Horn, J. M. (1988). Genetics and human behavior. *Annual Review of Psychology, 39,* 101–134.

Loewenstein, R. J. (1991). Psychogenic amnesia and psychogenic fugue: A comprehensive review. In A. Tasman & S. M. Goldfinger (Eds.), *American Psychiatric Press review of psychiatry* (Vol. 10). Washington, DC: American Psychiatric Association.

Loftus, E. F., & Bernstein, D. M. (2005). Rich false memories: The royal road to success. In A. Healy (Ed.), *Experimental cognitive psychology and its applications. Decade of behavior.* Washington, DC: American Psychological Association.

Loftus, E. F., & Palmer, J. C. (1974). Reconstruction of automobile destruction: An example of the interaction between language and memory. *Journal of Verbal Learning and Verbal Behavior, 13,* 585–589.

Logue, A. W. (1991). *The psychology of eating and drinking* (2nd ed.). New York: Freeman.

Lopez, S. R., & Guarnaccia, P. J. (2000). Cultural psychopathology: Uncovering the social world of mental illness. *Annual Review of Psychology, 51,* 571–598.

Lorenz, K. (1937). The companion in the bird's world. *Auk, 54,* 245–273.

Lorenzen, L. A., Grieve, F. G., & Thomas, A. (2004). Exposure to muscular male models decreases men's body satisfaction. *Sex Roles, 51,* 743–748.

Lovaas, O. I. (1977). *The autistic child.* New York: Irvington.

Lovallo, W. (Ed.). (2005). *Stress and health: Biological and psychological interactions.* Newbury Park, CA: Sage.

Lovallo, W. R., & Gerin, W. (2003). Psychophysiological reactivity: Mechanisms and pathways to cardiovascular disease. *Psychosomatic Medicine, 65,* 36–45.

Lubinski, D. (2004). Introduction to the special section on cognitive abilities: 100 years after Spearman's (1904) "'General intelligence,' objectively determined and measured." *Journal of Personality and Social Psychology, 86,* 96–111.

Luborsky, L., Rosenthal, R., Diguer, L., Andrusyna, T. P., Berman, J. S., Jeffrey, S., Levitt, J. T., Seligman, D. A., & Krause, E. D. (2002). The dodo bird verdict is alive and well—mostly. *Clinical Psychology: Science and Practice, 9,* 2–12.

Lucas, R. E., Clark, A. E., Georgellis, Y., & Diener, E. (2004). Unemployment alters the set point for life satisfaction. *Psychological Science, 15,* 8–13.

Luchins, A. J. (1942). Mechanization in problem solving: The effect of Einstellung. *Psychological Monographs, 54*(6, Whole No. 248).

Luciano, M., Wright, M. J., Smith, G. A., Geffen, G. M., Geffen, L. B., & Martin, N. G. (2001). Genetic covariance among measures of information processing speed, working memory, and IQ. *Behavior Genetics, 31,* 581–592.

Luck, S. J., & Vecera, S. P. (2002). Attention. In H. Pashler & S.Yantis (Eds.), *Steven's handbook of experimental psychology: Vol. 1. Sensation and perception* (3rd ed.). New York: Wiley.

Luna, B., Garver, K. E., Urban, T. A., Lazar, N. A., & Sweeney, J. A. (2004). Maturation of cognitive processes from late childhood to adulthood. *Child Development, 75,* 1357–1372.

Luria, A. R. (1968). *The mind of a mnemonist: A little book about a vast memory.* New York: Basic Books.

Lykken, D. T. (1981). *A tremor in the blood: Uses and abuses of the lie detector.* New York: Plenum.

Lykken, D. T. (1984). Polygraph interrogation. *Nature, 307,* 681–684.

Lykken, D. T., McGue, M., Tellegen, A., & Bouchard, T. J. (1992). Emergenesis: Genetic traits that may not run in families. *American Psychologist, 47,* 1565–1577.

Lykken, D. T., & Tellegen, A. (1996). Happiness is a stochastic phenomenon. *Psychological Science, 7,* 186–189.

Lynn, S. J., Neuschatz, J., Fite R., & Kirsch I. (2001). Hypnosis in the forensic arena. *Journal of Forensic Psychology Practice, 1,* 113–122.

Lytton, H., & Romney, D. M. (1991). Parents' differential socialization of boys and girls: A meta-analysis. *Psychological Bulletin, 109,* 267–296.

MacAndrew, C., & Edgerton, R. B. (1969). *Drunken comportment: A social explanation.* Chicago: Aldine.

Maccoby, E., & Jacklin, C. (1974). *The psychology of sex differences.* Stanford, CA: Stanford University Press.

Maccoby, E. E., & Maccoby, N. (1954). The interview: A tool of social science. In G. Lindzey (Ed.), *Handbook of social psychology.* Cambridge, MA: Addison-Wesley.

Maccoby, E. E., & Martin, J. A. (1983). Socialization in the context of the family: Parent-child interaction. In E. M. Hetherington (Ed.), *Handbook of child psychology: Socialization, personality, and social development.* New York: Wiley.

MacCoun, R. J. (1998). Toward a psychology of harm reduction. *American Psychologist, 53,* 1199–1208.

MacDonald, S., Uesiliana, K., & Hayne, H. (2000). Cross-cultural and gender differences in childhood amnesia. *Memory, 8,* 365–376.

MacDonald, T. K., Fong, G. T., Zanna, M. P., & Martineau, A. M. (2003). Alcohol myopia and condom use: Can alcohol intoxication be associated with more prudent behavior? In P. Salovey & A. J. Rothman (Eds.), *Social psychology of health. Key readings in social psychology.* New York: Psychology Press.

MacDonald, T. K., Zanna, M. P., & Fong, G. T. (1995). Decision making in altered states: Effects of alcohol on attitudes toward drinking and driving. *Journal of Personality and Social Psychology, 68,* 973–985.

Mack, A. (2003). Inattentional blindness: Looking without seeing. *Current Directions in Psychological Science, 12,* 180–184.

MacLeod, C. (1998). Implicit perception: Perceptual processing without awareness. In K. Kirsner et al. (Eds.), *Implicit and explicit mental processes.* Mahwah, NJ: Erlbaum.

Maddux, J. E. (1999). Personal efficacy. In V. J. Derlega, B. A. Winstead, & W. H. Jones (Eds.), *Personality: Contemporary theory and research.* Chicago: Nelson Hall.

Maes, H. H. M., Neale, M. C., & Eaves, L. J. (1997). Genetic and environmental factors in relative body weight and human adiposity. *Behavior Genetics, 27,* 325–351.

Magnuson, S. (1986, March 10). "A serious deficiency": The Rogers Commission faults NASA's "flawed" decision-making process. *Time* (Intl. ed.), 40–42.

Maher, B. A. (1979). *Clinical psychology and personality: The collected papers of George Kelly.* Huntington, NY: Wiley.

Mahler, M. (1968). *On human symbiosis and the vicissitudes of individuation: Infantile psychosis.* New York: Basic Books.

Maier, S. F., & Watkins, L. R. (1999). Bidirectional communication between the brain and the immune system: Implications for behaviour. *Animal Behaviour, 57*(4), 741–751.

Major, B., Spencer, S., Schmader, T., Wolfe, C., & Crocker, J. (1998). Coping with negative stereotypes about intellectual performance: The role of psychological disengagement. *Personality and Social Psychology Bulletin, 24,* 34–50.

Mäkelä, K. (1997). Drinking, the majority fallacy, cognitive dissonance and social pressure. *Addiction, 92,* 729–736.

Malamuth, N. M., Addison, T., & Koss, M. (2000). Pornography and sexual aggression: Are there reliable effects and can we understand them? *Annual Review of Sex Research, 11,* 26–91.

Maldonado, R., & Rodriguez de Fonseca, F. (2002). Cannabinoid addiction: Behavioral models and neural correlates. *Journal of Neuroscience, 22,* 3326–3331.

Mann, L. (1981). The baiting crowd in episodes of threatened suicide. *Journal of Personality and Social Psychology, 41,* 703–709.

Manson, J. E., Colditz, G. A., Stampfer, M. J., et al. (1990). A prospective study of obesity and risk of coronary heart disease in women. *New England Journal of Medicine, 322,* 882–888.

Manson, S. M. (1994). Culture and depression: Discovering variations in the experience of illness. In W. J. Lonner & R. S. Malpass (Eds.), *Psychology and culture.* Boston: Allyn & Bacon.

Mäntylä, T. (1986). Optimizing cue effectiveness: Recall of 500 and 600 incidentally learned words. *Journal of Experimental Psychology: Learning, Memory, and Cognition, 12,* 66–71.

Marangell, L. B. (2002). Concise guide to psychopharmacology. Washington, DC: American Psychiatric Publishing.

Marcia, J. E. (1966). Development and validation of ego identity status. *Journal of Personality and Social Psychology, 3,* 551–558.

Marcia, J. E. (2002). Adolescence, identity, and the Bernardone family. *Identity, 2,* 199–209.

Marian, V., Spivey, M., & Hirsch, J. (2003). Shared and separate systems in bilingual language processing: Converging evidence from eyetracking and brain imaging. *Brain & Language, 86,* 70–82.

Markey, P. M. (2000). Bystander intervention in computer mediated communication. *Computers in Human Behavior, 16,* 183–188.

Markovits, H., & Nantel, G. (1989). The belief-bias effect in the production and evaluation of logical conclusions. *Memory and Cognition, 17,* 11–17.

Marks, I. M. (1977). Phobias and obsessions: Clinical phenomena in search of laboratory models. In J. Maser & M. E. P. Seligman (Eds.), *Psychopathology: Experimental models.* San Francisco: Freeman.

Marks, I. M. (1991). Self-administered behavioural treatment. *Behavioural Psychotherapy, 19,* 42–46.

Marks, I. M. (2002). The maturing of therapy: Some brief psychotherapies help anxiety/depressive disorders but mechanisms of action are unclear. *British Journal of Psychiatry, 180,* 200–204.

Markus, H. R., & Kitayama, S. (1991). Culture and the self: Implications for cognition, emotion, and motivation. *Psychological Review, 98,* 224–253.

Marlatt, G. A. (1996). Taxonomy of high-risk situations for alcohol relapse: Evolution and development of a cognitive-behavioral model. *Addiction, 91*(Suppl.), S37–S49.

Marlatt, G. A. (Ed.). (1998). *Harm reduction: Pragmatic strategies for managing high-risk behaviors.* New York: Guilford Press.

Marlatt, G. A., Baer, J. S., Kivlahan, D. R., et al. (1998). Screening and brief intervention for high-risk college student drinkers: Results from a 2-year follow-up assessment. *Journal of Consulting and Clinical Psychology, 66,* 604–615.

Marlatt, G. A., Blume, A. W., & Parks, G. A. (2001). Integrating harm reduction therapy and traditional substance abuse treatment. *Journal of Psychoactive Drugs, 33,* 13–21.

Marlatt, G. A., & Gordon, J. R. (1985). *Relapse prevention: Maintenance strategies in the treatment of addiction.* New York: Guilford Press.

Marler, P. (1970). A comparative approach to vocal learning: Song development in white-crowned sparrows. *Journal of Comparative and Physiological Psychology, 71,* 1–25.

Marschark, M., & Mayer, T. S. (1998). Interactions of language and memory in deaf children and adults. *Scandinavian Journal of Psychology, 39,* 145–148.

Marsh, H. W. (1990). A multidimensional, hierarchical model of self-concept: Theoretical and empirical justification. *Educational Psychology Review, 2,* 77–172.

Marshall, L. H., & Magoun, H. W. (1997). *Discoveries in the human brain: Neuroscience prehistory, brain structure, and function.* New York: Humana Press.

Marshall, N. L. (2004). The quality of early child care and children's development. *Current Directions in Psychological Science, 13,* 165–168.

Marshall, P. J., & Fox, N. A. (2000). Emotion regulation, depression, and hemispheric asymmetry. In S. L. Johnson & A. M. Hayes (Eds.), *Stress, coping, and depression.* Mahwah, NJ: Erlbaum.

Marsiglio, W., Amato, P., Day, R. D., Lamb, M. E. (2000). Scholarship on fatherhood in the 1990s and beyond. *Journal of Marriage and the Family, 62,* 1173–1191.

Marsland, A. L., Cohen, S., Rabin, B. S., & Manuck, S. B. (2001). Associations between stress, trait negative affect, acute immune reactivity, and antibody response to Hepatitis B injection in healthy young adults. *Health Psychology, 20,* 4–11.

Martell, C, Addis, M., & Dimidjian, S. (2004). Finding the action in behavioral activation: The search for empirically supported interventions and mechanisms of change. In S. C. Hayes, V. M. Follette, & M. M. Linehan (Eds.), *Mindfulness and acceptance: Expanding the cognitive-behavioral tradition.* New York: Guilford Press.

Martin, C. L., & Ruble, D. (2004). Children's search for gender cues: Cognitive perspectives on gender development. *Current Directions in Psychological Science, 13,* 67–70.

Martin, J. E., & Dubbert, P. M. (1985). Adherence in exercise. In R. I. Terjung (Ed.), *Exercise and sport sciences review* (Vol. 13). New York: Macmillan.

Martinez, J. L., Jr., Barea-Rodriguez, E. J., & Derrick, B. E. (1998). Long-term potentiation, long-term depression, and learning. In J. L. Martinez, Jr., & R. P. Kesner (Eds.), *Neurobiology of learning and memory.* San Diego, CA: Academic Press.

Martinez, M., & Raul, E. (2000). Conducta sexual procesos psicologicos moduladores, en mujeres y hombres [Sexual behavior and modulating psychological processes in women and men]. *Archivos Hispanoamericanos de Sexologia, 6,* 133–152.

Mascolo, M. E., & Li, J. (Eds.). (2004). *Culture and developing selves: Beyond dichotomization.* San Francisco, CA: Jossey-Bass.

Mash, E. J., & Barkley, R. A. (2003). *Child psychopathology* (2nd ed.). New York: Guilford Press.

Maslow, A. H. (1954). *Motivation and personality.* New York: Harper.

Mason, M. F., Tatkow, E. P., & Macrae, C. N. (2005). The look of love: Gaze shifts and person perception. *Psychological Science, 16,* 236–239.

Massion, A. O., Dyck, I. R., Shea, M. T., Phillips, K. A., Warshaw, M. G., & Keller, M. B. (2002). Personality disorders and time to remission in generalized anxiety disorder, social phobia and panic disorder. *Archives of General Psychiatry, 59,* 434–440.

Masten, A. S. (2001). Ordinary magic: Resilience processes in development. *American Psychologist, 56,* 227–238.

Masten, A. S., & Coatsworth, J. D. (1998). The development of competence in favorable and unfavorable environments: Lessons from research on successful children. *American Psychologist, 53,* 205–220.

Masters, W., & Johnson, V. (1966). *Human sexual response.* London: Churchill.

Masters, W. H., Johnson, V. E., & Kolodny, R. C. (1988). *Human Sexuality* (3rd ed.). Boston: Little, Brown.

Matlin, M. W., & Stang, D. J. (1978). *The Pollyanna Principle: Selectivity in language, memory, and thought.* Cambridge, MA: Schenkman.

Matsumoto, D., & Hull, P. (1994). Cognitive development and intelligence. In D. Matsumoto (Ed.), *People: Psychology from a cultural perspective.* Pacific Grove, CA: Brooks/Cole.

Matt, G. E., & Navarro, A. M. (1997). What meta-analyses have and have not taught us about psychotherapy effects: A review and future directions. *Clinical Psychology Review, 17,* 1–32.

Matthews, G., Roberts, R. D., & Zeidner, M. (2004). Seven myths about emotional intelligence. *Psychological Inquiry, 15,* 179–196.

Mattys, S. L. (2000). The perception of primary and secondary stress in English. *Perception & Psychophysics, 62,* 253–265.

Mattys, S. L. (2004). Stress versus coarticulation: Toward an integrated approach to explicit speech segmentation. *Journal of Experimental Psychology: Human Perception & Performance, 30,* 397–408.

May, C. P., Hasher, L., & Foong, N. (2005). Implicit memory, age, and time of day: Paradoxical priming effects. *Psychological Science, 16,* 96–100.

May, J. R., & Sieb, G. E. (1987). Athletic injuries: Psychosocial factors in the onset, sequellae, rehabilitation, and prevention. In J. R. May & M. J. Asken (Eds.), *Sport psychology: The psychological health of the athlete.* New York: PMA Publishing.

May, R. (1961). The emergence of existential psychology. In R. May (Ed.), *Existential psychology.* New York: Random House.

Mayer, J. D., Salovey, P., & Caruso, D. R. (2004). Emotional intelligence: Theory, findings, and implications. *Psychological Inquiry, 15,* 197–215.

Mayer, R. E. (2000). Intelligence and education. In R. J. Sternberg (Ed.), *Handbook of intelligence.* New York: Cambridge University Press.

McAdams, D. P., & de St. Aubin, E. (Eds.). (1998). *Generativity and adult development: How and why we care for the next generation.* Washington, DC: American Psychological Association.

McAdams, S., & Drake, C. (2002). Auditory perception and cognition. In H. Pashler & S. Yantis (Eds.), *Steven's handbook of experimental psychology: Vol. 1. Sensation and perception* (3rd ed.). New York: Wiley.

McArdle, S., & Duda, J. K. (2002). Implications of the motivational climate in youth sports. In F. L. Smoll & R. E. Smith (Eds.), *Children and youth in sport: A biopsychosocial perspective.* Dubuque, IA: Kendall/Hunt.

McAuley, E. (1992). The role of efficacy cognitions in the prediction of exercise behavior in middle-aged adults. *Journal of Behavioral Medicine, 15,* 65–88.

McCall, W. V., & Edinger, J. D. (1992). Subjective total insomnia: An example of sleep state misperception. *Sleep, 15,* 71–73.

McCann, U. D., Szabo, Z., Scheffel, U., Dannals, R. F., & Ricaurte, G. A. (1998). Positron emission tomographic evidence of toxic effect of MDMA ("Ecstasy") on brain serotonin neurons in human beings. *Lancet, 352*(9138), 1433–1437.

McCarley, R. W. (1998). Dreams: Disguise of forbidden wishes or transparent reflections of a distinct brain state? In R. M. Bilder & F. F. LeFever (Eds.), *Neuroscience of the mind on the centennial of Freud's Project for a Scientific Psychology: Annals of the New York Academy of Sciences* (Vol. 843). New York: New York Academy of Sciences.

McCaul, K. D., & Malott, J. J. (1984). Distraction and coping with pain. *Psychological Bulletin, 95,* 516–533.

McClelland, D. C. (1989). *Human motivation.* New York: Cambridge University Press.

McClelland, D. C., Atkinson, J. W., Clark, R. A., & Lowell, E. L. (1953). *The achievement motive.* New York: Appleton-Century-Crofts.

McClintock, M. K. (1971). Menstrual synchrony and suppression. *Nature, 291,* 244–245.

McConnell, J. V. (1962). Memory transfer through cannibalism in planarians. *Journal of Neuropsychiatry, 3*(Suppl. 1), 542–548.

McCracken, L. M. (1998). Learning to live with pain: Acceptance of pain predicts adjustment in persons with chronic pain. *Pain, 74,* 21–27.

McCrae, R. R., & Costa, P. T. (1990). *Personality in adulthood.* New York: Guilford Press.

McCrae, R. R., & Costa, P. T. (2003). *Personality in adulthood: A Five-Factor Theory perspective.* New York: Guilford Press.

McCullough, M. E., Worthington, E. L., Jr., & Rachal, K. C. (1997). Interpersonal forgiving in close relationships. *Journal of Personality and Social Psychology, 73,* 321–336.

McDaniel, M. A., Einstein, G. O., Stout, A. C., & Morgan, Z. (2003). Aging and maintaining intentions over delays: Do it or lose it. *Psychology and Aging, 18,* 823–835.

McEwen, B. S. (2001). *Coping with the environment: Neural and endocrine mechanisms.* New York: Oxford University Press.

McFarlane, J. (1975). Olfaction in the development of social preferences in the human neonate. In M. Hofer (Ed.), *Parent-infant interaction.* Amsterdam: Elsevier.

McGaugh, J. L. (2004). The amygdala modulates the consolidation of memories of emotionally arousing experiences. *Annual Review of Neuroscience, 27,* 1–28.

McGaugh, J. L., & Roozendaal, B. (2002). Role of adrenal stress hormones in forming lasting memories in the brain. *Current Opinion in Neurobiology, 12,* 205–210.

McGinnis, M. (1994). The role of behavioral research in national health policy. In S. J. Blumenthal, K. Matthews, and S. M. Weiss (Eds.), *New research frontiers in behavioral medicine: Proceedings of the national conference.* Washington, DC: NIH Publications.

McGinty, D. (1993). Energy conservation. In M. A. Carskadon (Ed.), *Encyclopedia of sleep and dreaming.* New York: Macmillan.

McGlashan, T. H., & Fenton, W. S. (1992). The positive-negative distinction in schizophrenia: Review of natural history validators. *Archives of General Psychiatry, 49,* 63–72.

McGregor, H. A., & Elliot, A. J. (2002). Achievement goals as predictors of achievement-relevant processes prior to task engagement. *Journal of Educational Psychology, 94,* 381–395.

McGrew, W. C. (2002). The nature of culture: Prospects and pitfalls of cultural primatology. In F. B. M. de Waal (Ed.), *Tree of origin: What primate behavior can tell us about human social evolution.* Cambridge, MA: Harvard University Press.

McGuffin, P., Owen, M. J., & Gottesman, I. I. (Eds.). (2005). *Psychiatric genetics and genomics.* New York: Oxford University Press.

McIntosh, D. N., Silver, R. C., & Wortman, C. B. (1993). Religion's role in adjustment to a negative life event: Coping with the loss of a child. *Journal of Personality and Social Psychology, 65,* 812–821.

McIntyre, R. B., Paulson, R. M., & Lord, C. G. (2003). Alleviating women's mathematics stereotype threat through salience of group achievements. *Journal of Experimental Social Psychology, 39,* 83–90.

McKenna, M. C., Zevon, M. A., Corn, B., & Rounds, J. (1999). Psychological factors and the development of breast cancer: A meta-analysis. *Health Psychology, 18,* 520–531.

McKenna, P., & Oh, T. (2003). *Formal thought disorder in schizophrenia.* New York: Cambridge University Press.

McKey, R., Conndelli, L., Gansin, H., Barrett, B., McConkey, C., & Plantz, M. (1985). *The impact of Head Start on children, families and communities (Final report of the Head Start Evaluation, Synthesis and Utilization Project).* Washington, DC: CSR, Inc.

McMillan, T. M., Robertson, I. H., & Wilson, B. A. (1999). Neurogenesis after brain injury: Implications for neurorehabilitation. *Neuropsychological Rehabilitation, 9,* 129–133.

McNeil, E. B. (1967). *The quiet furies: Man and disorder.* Englewood Cliffs, NJ: Prentice Hall.

McNulty, J. K., & Karney, B. R. (2004). Positive expectations in the early years of marriage: Should couples expect the best or brace for the worst? *Journal of Personality and Social Psychology, 86,* 729–743.

McWilliams, N. (2004). *Psychoanalytic psychotherapy: A practitioner's guide.* New York: Guilford Press.

Meaney, M. J., Mitchell, J. B., Aitken, D. H., & Bhatnagar, S. (Eds.). (1991). The effects of neonatal handling on the development of the adrenocortical response to stress: Implications for neuropathology and cognitive deficits in later life. *Psychoneuroendocrinology, 16,* 85–103.

Mechan, A. O., Moran, P. M., Elliot, J. M., Young, A. M. J., Joseph, M. H., & Green, A. R. (2002). A study of the effect of a single neurotoxic dose of 3,4-methylenedioxymethamphetamine (MDMA; "ecstasy") on the subsequent long-term behaviour of rats in the plus maze and open field. *Psychopharmacology, 159,* 167–175.

Meddis, R., Pearson, A. J., & Langford, G. (1973). An extreme case of healthy insomnia. *Electroencephalography and Clinical Neurophysiology, 35,* 213–214.

Meehl, P. E. (1995). "Is psychoanalysis one science, two sciences, or no science at all? A discourse among friendly antagonists": Comment. *Journal of the American Psychoanalytic Association, 43,* 1015–1023.

Meeus, W. H. J., & Raaijmakers, Q. A. W. (1986). Administrative obedience: Carrying out orders to use psychological-administrative violence. *European Journal of Social Psychology, 16,* 311–324.

Meeus, W. H. J., & Raaijmakers, Q. A. W. (1995). Obedience in modern society: The Utrecht studies. *Journal of Social Issues, 51,* 155–175.

Megargee, E. I. (1966). Undercontrolled and overcontrolled personality types in extreme anti-social aggression. *Psychological Monographs, 80*(Whole No. 611).

Mehnert, T., Krauss, H. H., Nadler, R., & Boyd, M. (1990). Correlates of life satisfaction in those with disabling conditions. *Rehabilitation Psychology, 35,* 3–17.

Meichenbaum, D. (1985). *Stress inoculation training.* New York: Pergamon Press.

Meier, R. P. (1991). Language acquisition by deaf children. *American Scientist, 79,* 61–70.

Meleski, M. E., & Damato, E. G. (2003). HIV exposure: Neonatal considerations. *Journal of Obstetric, Gynecologic, and Neonatal Nursing. 32,* 109–116.

Meltzoff, A. N. (2002). Elements of a developmental theory of imitation. In A. N. Meltzoff, N. Andrew, & W. Prinz (Eds.), *The imitative mind: Development, evolution, and brain bases. Cambridge studies in cognitive perceptual development.* New York: Cambridge University Press.

Melzack, R. (1998). Pain and stress. Clues toward understanding chronic pain. In M. Sabourin et al. (Eds.), *Advances in psychological science.* Hove, England: Psychology Press/Erlbaum.

Melzack, R., & Wall, P. D. (1982). *The challenge of pain.* New York: Basic Books.

Menzies, R. G., & Clarke, J. C. (1995). The etiology of acrophobia and its relationship to severity and individual response patterns. *Behaviour Research and Therapy, 33,* 795–803.

Merrill, E. C., & Lookadoo, R. (2004). Selective search for conjunctively defined targets by children and young adults. *Journal of Experimental Child Psychology, 89,* 72–90.

Mersch, P. P. A., Middendorp, H. M., Bouhuys, A. L., Beersma, D. G. M., & van den Hoofdakker, R. H. (1999). Seasonal affective disorder and latitude: A review of the literature. *Journal of Affective Disorders, 53,* 35–48.

Mesquita, B., Frijda, N. H., & Scherer, K. R. (1997). Culture and emotion. In J. W. Berry et al. (Eds.), *Handbook of cross-cultural psychology: Vol. 2. Basic processes and human development* (2nd ed.). Boston: Allyn & Bacon.

Mesquita, B., & Markus, H. R. (2005). Culture and emotion: Models of agency as sources of cultural variation in emotion. In A. S. R. Manstead, N. H. Frijda, A. H. Fischer, & K. Oatley (Eds.), *Feelings and Emotions: The Amsterdam Symposium.* New York: Cambridge University Press.

Methot, L. L., & Huitema, B. E. (1998). Effects of signal probability on individual differences in vigilance. *Human Factors, 40,* 78–90.

Meyer, C. B., & Taylor, S. E. (1986). Adjustment to rape. *Journal of Personality and Social Psychology, 50,* 1226–1234.

Meyer, R. G. & Osborne, Y. H. (1987). *Case studies in abnormal behavior* (2nd ed.). Boston: Allyn & Bacon.

Meyer, T. A., Svirsky, M. A., Kirk, K. I., & Miyamoto, R. T. (1998). Improvements in speech perception by children with profound prelingual hearing loss: Effects of device, communication mode, and chronological age. *Journal of Speech, Language, and Hearing Research, 41,* 846–858.

Mezulis, A. H., Abramson, L. Y., Hyde, J. S., & Hankin, B. L. (2004). Is there a universal positivity bias in attributions? A meta-analytic review of individual, developmental, and cultural differences in the self-serving attributional bias. *Psychological Bulletin, 130,* 711–747.

Michael, R. T., Gagnon, J. H., Laumman, E. O., & Kolata, G. (1994). *Sex in America: A definitive survey.* Boston: Little, Brown.

Michaels, J. W., Blommel, J. M., Brocato, R. M., Linkous, R. A., & Rowe, J. S. (1982). Social facilitation and inhibition in a natural setting. *Replications in Social Psychology, 2,* 21–24.

Mignot, E. (1998). Genetic and familial aspects of narcolepsy. *Neurology, 50,* S16–S22.

Mikulincer, M., & Shaver, P. R. (2005). Attachment security, compassion, and altruism. *Current Directions in Psychological Science, 14,* 34–38.

Miles, C., & Hardman, E. (1998). State-dependent memory produced by aerobic exercise. *Ergonomics, 41,* 20–28.

Miles, H. L., Mitchell, R. W., & Harper, S. E. (1996). Simon says: The development of imitation in an enculturated orangutan. In A. E. Russon & K. A. Bard (Eds.), *Reaching into thought: The minds of the great apes.* Cambridge, England: Cambridge University Press.

Milgram, S. (1974). *Obedience to authority: An experimental view.* New York: Harper & Row.

Miller, A. G. (2004). What can the Milgram obedience experiments tell us about the Holocaust? Generalizing from the social psychology laboratory. In A. G. Miller (Ed.), *The social psychology of good and evil.* New York: Guilford Press.

Miller, B. C., Fan, X., Christensen, M., Grotevant, H. D., & van Dulmen, M. (2000). Comparisons of adopted and nonadopted adolescents in a large, nationally representative sample. *Child Development, 71,* 1458–1473.

Miller, G. A. (1956). The magical number seven, plus or minus two: Some limits on our capacity for processing information. *Psychological Review, 63,* 81–97.

Miller, J. G. (1984). Culture and the development of everyday social explanation. *Journal of Personality and Social Psychology, 46,* 961–978.

Miller, J. G., Bersoff, D. M., & Harwood, R. L. (1990). Perceptions of social responsibility in India and in the United States: Moral imperatives or personal decisions? *Journal of Personality and Social Psychology, 58,* 33–47.

Miller, K. E., & Rasco, L. M. (Eds.). (2004). *The mental health of refugees: Ecological approaches to healing and adaptation.* Mahwah, NJ: Erlbaum.

Miller, K. F., & Stigler, J. F. (1987). Counting in Chinese: Cultural variation in a basic cognitive skill. *Cognitive Development, 2,* 279–305.

Miller, N. E. (1944). Experimental studies of confiict. In J. McV. Hunt (Ed.), *Personality and the behavior disorders* (Vol. 1). New York: Ronald Press.

Miller, N. E., & Dollard, J. (1941). *Social learning and imitation.* New Haven, CT: Yale University Press.

Miller, S. D., Blackburn, T., Scholes, G., White, G. L., & Mamales, N. (1991). Optical differences in multiple personality disorder: A second look. *Journal of Nervous and Mental Disease, 179,* 132–135.

Miller, W. R. (1996). Motivational interviewing: Research, practice, and puzzles. *Addictive Behaviors, 21,* 835–842.

Miller, W. R., & Brown, S. A. (1997). Why psychologists should treat alcohol and drug problems. *American Psychologist, 52,* 1269–1279.

Miller, W. R., & Rollnick, S. (2002). *Motivational interviewing* (2nd ed.). New York: Guilford Press.

Millon, T., Millon, C. M., Meagher, D., Meagher, S., Grossman, S., & Ramnath, R. (2004). *Personality disorders in modern life* (2nd ed.). New York: Wiley.

Milner, A. D., & Dijkerman, H. C. (2001). Direct and indirect visuals routes to action. In B. De Gelder, E. H. F. De Haan, & C. A. Heywood (Eds.), *Out of mind: Varieties of unconscious processes*. London: Oxford University Press.

Milner, B. (1965). Memory disturbances after bilateral hippocampal lesions. In P. Milner & S. Glickman (Eds.), *Cognitive processes and the brain*. Princeton, NJ: Van Nostrand.

Milrod, B., Busch, F., Cooper, A., & Shapiro, T. (1997). *Manual of panic-focused psychodynamic psychotherapy*. Washington, DC: American Psychiatric Press.

Milton, J., & Wiseman, R. (1999). Does psi exist? Lack of replication of an anomalous process of information transfer. *Psychological Bulletin, 125,* 387–391.

Mineka, S., Watson, D., & Clark, L. A. (1998). Comorbidity of anxiety and unipolar mood disorder. *Annual Review of Psychology, 49,* 377–412.

Mintz, J., Drake, R. E., & Crits-Christoph, P. (1996). Efficacy and effectiveness of psychotherapy: Two paradigms, one science. *American Psychologist, 51,* 1084–1085.

Minuchin, S. (1974). *Families and family therapy.* Cambridge, MA: Harvard University Press.

Mischel, W. (1984). Convergences and challenges in the search for consistency. *American Psychologist, 39,* 351–364.

Mischel, W. (1999). Personality coherence and dispositions in a cognitive-affective personality system (CAPS) approach. In D. Cervone & Y. Shoda (Eds.), *The coherence of personality*. New York: Guilford Press.

Mischel, W., Shoda, Y., & Mendoza-Denton, R. (2002). Situation-behavior profiles as a locus of consistency in personality. *Current Directions in Psychological Science, 11,* 50–54.

Mischel, W., Shoda, Y., & Smith, R. E. (2004). *Introduction to personality: Toward an integration* (7th ed.). New York: Wiley.

Mishne, J. (2002). *Multiculturalism and the therapeutic process.* New York: Guilford Press.

Mistlberger, R. E., Antle, M. C., Glass, J. D., & Miller, J. D. (2000). Behavioral and serotonergic regulation of circadian rhythms. *Biological Rhythm Research, 31,* 240–283.

Mitchell, K. J., & Zaragoza, M. S. (2001). Contextual overlap and eyewitness suggestibility. *Memory and Cognition, 29,* 616–626.

Moen, P., Kim, J. E., & Hofmeister, H. (2001). Couples' work/retirement transitions, gender, and marital quality. *Social Psychology Quarterly, 64,* 55–71.

Mokdad, A. H., Marks, J. S., Stroup, D. F., & Gerberding, J. L. (2004). Actual causes of death in the United States, 2000. *Journal of American Medical Association, 291,* 1238–1245.

Molfese, D. L., & Molfese, V. J. (2002). *Developmental variations in learning: Applications to social, executive function, language, and reading skills.* Mahwah, NJ: Erlbaum.

Monahan, J. (1992). Mental disorder and violent behavior: Attitudes and evidence. *American Psychologist, 47,* 511–521.

Monk, T. H., Buysse, D. J., Welsh, D. K., Kennedy, K. S., & Rose, L. R. (2001). A sleep diary and questionnaire study of naturally short sleepers. *Journal of Sleep Research, 10,* 173–179.

Monk, T. H., Folkard, S., & Wedderburn, A. I. (1996). Maintaining safety and high performance on shiftwork. *Applied Ergonomics, 27,* 17–23.

Monroe, S. M., & Peterman, A. M. (1988). Life stress and psychopathology. In L. H. Cohen (Ed.), *Life events and psychological functioning: Theoretical and methodological issues*. Newbury Park, CA: Sage.

Montgomery, G. H., DuHamel, K. N., & Redd, W. H. (2000). A meta-analysis of hypnotically induced analgesia: How effective is hypnosis? *International Journal of Clinical and Experimental Hypnosis, 48,* 138–153.

Montgomery, H., Lipshitz, R., & Brehmer, B. (Eds.). (2005). *How professionals make decisions*. Mahwah, NJ: Erlbaum.

Moody, M. S. (1997). Changes in scores on the Mental Rotations Test during the menstrual cycle. *Perceptual and Motor Skills, 84,* 955–961.

Moon, C., & Fifer, W. P. (1990). Syllables as signals for 2-day-old infants. *Infant Behavior and Development, 13,* 377–390.

Moore, T. M., Scarpa, A., & Raine, A. (2002). A meta-analysis of serotonin metabolite 5 HIAA and antisocial behavior. *Aggressive Behavior, 28,* 299–316.

Moorey, S. (2003). *Cognitive behaviour therapy for people with cancer.* Oxford, England: Oxford University Press.

Moreland, J. L., Dansereau, D. F., & Chmielewski, T. L. (1997). Recall of descriptive information: The roles of presentation format, annotation strategy, and individual differences. *Contemporary Educational Psychology, 22,* 521–533.

Morgan, W. (1997). *Physical activity and mental health.* Philadelphia: Taylor & Francis.

Morgan, W. P., Horstman, D. H., Cymerman, A., & Stokes, J. (1983). Facilitation of physical performance by means of a cognitive strategy. *Cognitive Therapy and Research, 7,* 251–264.

Morrell, M. J., Dixen, J. M., Carter, C. S., & Davidson, J. M. (1984). The influence of age and cycling status on sexual arousability in women. *American Journal of Obstetrics and Gynecology, 148,* 66–71.

Morris, D., Collett, P., Marsh, P., & O'Shaughnessy, M. (1979). *Gestures.* New York: Stein & Day.

Morris, J., & Dolan, R. (2001). The amygdala and unconscious fear processing. In B. De Gelder, E. H. F. De Haan, & C. A. Heywood (Eds.), *Out of mind: Varieties of unconscious processes*. London: Oxford University Press.

Morris, R., & Becker, J. (2005). *Cognitive neuropsychology of Alzheimer's disease.* New York: Oxford University Press.

Morrison, A. (2005). Psychosis and the phenomena of unwanted intrusive thoughts. In D. A. Clark (Ed.), *Intrusive thoughts in clinical disorders: Theory, research, and treatment*. New York: Guilford Press.

Morrison, D. C. (1988). Marine mammals join the navy. *Science, 242,* 1503–1504.

Moscovici, S. (1985). Social influence and conformity. In G. Lindzey & E. Aronson (Eds.), *Handbook of social psychology* (3rd ed.). New York: Random House.

Moscovici, S., & Zavalloni, M. (1969). The group as a polarizer of attitudes. *Journal of Personality and Social Psychology, 12,* 124–135.

Mowrer, O. H. (1947). On the dual nature of learning: A reinterpretation of "conditioning" and "problem solving." *Harvard Educational Review, 17,* 102–150.

Muchinsky, P. M. (2000). *Psychology applied to work* (6th ed.). Pacific Grove, CA: Brooks/Cole.

Murdoch, H. (1984). Maternal rubella: The implications. *Association of Educational Psychologists Journal, 6,* 3–6.

Murphy, S. L. (2000). Deaths: Final data for 1998. *National Vital Statistics Reports* (NCHS), pp. 26, 73.

Murray, C. (1998). *Income, inequality, and IQ.* Washington, DC: American Enterprise Institute.

Murray, R., Jones, P., Van Oss, J., et al. (2003). *The epidemiology of schizophrenia.* New York: Cambridge University Press.

Myin-Germeys, I., van Os, J., Schwartz, J. E., Stone, A. A., & Delespaul, P. A. (2001). Emotional reactivity to daily life stress in psychosis. *Archives of General Psychiatry, 58,* 1137–1144.

Nadler, A., & Ben-Slushan, D. (1989). Forty years later: Long-term consequences of massive traumatization as manifested by holocaust survivors from the city and the Kibbutz. *Journal of Consulting and Clinical Psychology, 57,* 287–293.

Nakayama, K., & Tyler, C. W. (1981). Psychophysical isolation of movement sensitivity by removal of familiar position cues. *Vision Research, 21,* 427–433.

Narrow, W. E., Rae, D. S., Robins, L. N., & Regier, D. A. (2002). Revised prevalence based estimates of mental disorders in the United States: Using a clinical signficance criterion to reconcile 2 surveys' estimates. *Archives of General Psychiatry, 59,* 115–123.

Nathan, P. E. (1985). Aversion therapy in the treatment of alcoholism: Success and failure. *Annals of the New York Academy of Sciences, 443,* 357–364.

Nathan, P. E., & Lagenbucher, J. W. (1999). Psychopathology: Description and classification. *Annual Review of Psychology, 50,* 79–107.

National Center for Education Statistics. (2001). *Postsecondary institutions in the United States: Fall 2000 and degrees and other awards conferred: 1999–2000.* Available online: http://nces.ed.gov/pubsearch/pubsinfo.aspf?pubid=2002156

National Center for Health Statistics. (1995). *Healthy people 2000.* Washington, DC: Author.

National Center for Health Statistics. (2004). Health and longevity in the United States. Retrieved October 27, 2004, from http://www.cdc.gov

National Highway Traffic Safety Administration. (2002). *Traffic Safety Facts 2000: Alcohol* (DOT HS 808 950). Available online: http://ntl.bts.gov/card_view.cfm?docid=11735

National Institutes of Health. (2002). *Alzheimer's disease: Unraveling the mystery.* NIH Publication 02-3782. Bethesda, MD. Available online: http://www.alzheimers.org/unraveling/unraveling.pdf

National Safety Council. (1992). *Blood alcohol level and risk of having an automobile accident.* Washington, DC: Author.

National Sleep Foundation. (2002). *2002 omnibus sleep in America poll.* Available online: http://sleepfoundation.org/hottopics/index.php?secid=16&id=208

Natsoulas, T. (1999). An ecological and phenomenological perspective on consciousness and perception: Contact with the world at the very heart of the being of consciousness. *Review of General Psychology, 3,* 224–245.

Needham, A., Barrett, T., & Peterman, K. (2002). A pick me up for infants' exploratory skills: Early simulated experiences reaching for objects using "sticky" mittens enhances young infants' object exploration skills. *Infant Behavior and Development, 25,* 279–295.

Neisser, U., Bouchard, T. J., Jr., Boykin, A. W., Brody, N., Ceci, S. J., Halpern, D. F., Loehlin, J. C., Perloff, R., Sternberg, R. J., & Urbina, S. (1998). Intelligence: Knowns and unknowns. In M. E. Hertzig et al. (Eds.), *Annual progress in child psychiatry and child development: 1997.* Bristol, PA: Brunner/ Mazel.

Neisser, U., & Harsch, N. (1993). Phantom flashbulbs: False recollections of hearing the news about Challenger. In E. Winograd & U. Neisser (Eds.), *Affect and accuracy in recall: Studies of "flashbulb" memories.* New York: Cambridge University Press.

Nelson, C. A., & Luciana, M. (Eds.). (2001). *Handbook of developmental cognitive neuroscience.* Cambridge, MA: MIT Press.

Nemeth, C. J., & Goncalo, J. A. (2005). Influence and persuasion in small groups. In T. C. Brock & M. C. Green (Eds.), *Persuasion: Psychological insights and perspectives* (2nd ed.). Thousand Oaks, CA: Sage.

Nemiah, J. C. (1978). Psychoneurotic disorders. In A. M. Nicholi (Ed.), *Harvard guide to modern psychiatry.* Cambridge, MA: Harvard University Press.

Nesbitt, E. B. (1973). An escalator phobia overcome in one session of flooding in vivo. *Journal of Behavior Therapy and Experimental Psychiatry, 4,* 405–406.

Neugarten, B. L., & Hall, E. (1980, April). Acting one's age: New roles for old. *Psychology Today,* 66–80.

Neumäker, K. J. (2000). Mortality rates and causes of death. *European Eating Disorders Review, 8,* 181–187.

Neumeister, A. (2004). Neurotransmitter depletion and seasonal affective disorder: Relevance for the biologic effects of light therapy. *Primary Psychiatry, 11,* 44–48.

Neumeister, A., Young, T., & Stastny, J. (2004). Implications of genetic research on the role of the serotonin in depression: Emphasis on the serotonin type 1-sub(A) receptor and the serotonin transporter. *Psychopharmacology, 174,* 512–524.

Neuschatz, J. S., Lampinen, J., Preston, E. L., Hawkins, E. R., & Toglia, M. P. (2002). The effect of memory schemata on memory and the phenomenological experience of naturalistic situations. *Applied Cognitive Psychology, 16,* 687–708.

Newell, A., & Simon, H. A. (1972). *Human problem solving.* Englewood Cliffs, NJ: Prentice Hall.

Newlin, D. B., & Thomson, J. B. (1997). Alcohol challenge with sons of alcoholics: A critical review and analysis. In G. A. Marlatt & G. R. VandenBos (Eds.), *Addictive behaviors: Readings on etiology, prevention and treatment.* Washington, DC: American Psychological Association.

Newman, D. L., Caspi, A., Moffitt, T. E., & Silva, P. A. (1997). Antecedents of adult interpersonal functioning: Effects of individual differences in age 3 temperament. *Developmental Psychology, 33,* 206–217.

Newman, D. L., Moffit, T. E., Caspi, A., Silva, P. A., & Stanton, W. R. (1996). Psychiatric disorder in a birth cohort of young adults: Prevalence, comorbidity, clinical significance, and new case incidence from ages 11–21. *Journal of Consulting and Clinical Psychology, 64,* 552–562.

Newmark, C. S. (2005). *Major psychological assessment instruments.* Austin, TX: PRO-ED.

Newsweek. (2002, March 11), p. 19.

New York Times. (1986, March 18), p. C12.

Nezami, E., & Butcher, J. N. (2000). Objective personality assessment. In G. Goldstein & M. Hersen (Eds.), *Handbook of psychological assessment* (3rd ed.). New York: Elsevier.

Nezlek, J. B., Hampton, C. P., & Shean, G. (2000). Clinical depression and day-to-day social interaction in a community sample. *Journal of Abnormal Psychology, 109,* 11–19.

Nezu, A. M., Nezu, C. M., & D'Zurilla, T. (2000). Problem-solving skills training. In G. Fink (Ed.), *Encyclopedia of stress.* San Diego, CA: Academic Press.

NICHD Early Child Care Research Network. (2001a). Child care and children's peer interaction at 24 and 36 months: The NICHD study of early child care. *Child Development, 72,* 1478–1500.

NICHD Early Child Care Research Network. (2001b). Child care and family predictors of preschool attachment and stability from infancy. *Developmental Psychology, 37,* 847–862.

NICHD Early Child Care Research Network. (2002). Early child care and children's development prior to school entry: Results from the NICHD Study of Early Child Care.

Nicholls, J. (1989). *The competitive ethos and democratic education.* Cambridge, MA: Harvard University Press.

Nichols, C. D., & Sanders-Bush, E. (2002). A single dose of lysergic acid diethylamide influences gene expression patterns within the mammalian brain. *Neuropsychopharmacology, 26,* 634–642.

Nichols, P. L. (1984). Familial mental retardation. *Behavior Genetics, 14,* 161–170.

Nickerson, R. S., & Adams, M. J. (1979). Long-term memory for a common object. *Cognitive Psychology, 11,* 287–307.

Nigg, J. T., Lohr, N. E., Westen, D., & Gold, L. J. (1992). Malevolent object representation in borderline personality disorder and major depression. *Journal of Abnormal Psychology, 101,* 61–67.

Nisbett, R. E. (1998). Race, genetics, and IQ. In C. Jencks et al. (Eds.), *The Black-White test score gap.* Washington, DC: Brookings Institution.

Nisbett, R. E. (2003). *The geography of thought: How Asians and Westerners think differently . . . and why.* New York: Free Press.

Nishino, S., Mignot, E., & Dement, W. C. (2001). Sedative hypnotics. In A. F. Schatzberg & C. B. Nemeroff (Eds.), *Essentials of clinical psychopharmacology.* Washington, DC: American Psychiatric Association.

Nixon, K., & Crews, F. T. (2004). Temporally specific burst in cell proliferation increases hippocampal neurogenesis in protracted abstinence from alcohol. *Journal of Neuroscience, 24,* 9714–9722.

Noback, C. R., Strominger, N. L., & Ruggiero, D. A. (Eds.). (2005). *The human nervous system: Structure and function.* New York: Humana Press.

Noble, E. P. (1998). The D_2 dopamine receptor gene: A review of association studies in alcoholism and phenotypes. *Alcohol, 16,* 33–45.

Noice, T., & Noice, H. (2002a). The expertise of professional actors: A review of recent research. *High Ability Studies, 13,* 7–20.

Noice, T., & Noice, H. (2002b). Very long-term recall and recognition of well-learned material. *Applied Cognitive Psychology, 16,* 259–272.

Nolen-Hoeksema, S. (1990). *Sex differences in depression.* Stanford, CA: Stanford University Press.

Nolte, J. (1998). *The human brain: An introduction to its functional anatomy.* St. Louis, MO: Mosby.

Norcross, J. C. (1991). Prescriptive matching in psychotherapy: An introduction. *Psychotherapy, 28*, 439–443.

Normann, R. A., Maynard, E. M., Guillory, K. S., & Warren, D. J. (1996). Cortical implants for the blind. *IEEE Spectrum, 33*, 54–9.

Normann, R. A., Maynard, E. M., Rousche, P. J., & Warren, D. J. (1999). A neural interface for a cortical vision prosthesis. *Vision Research, 39*, 2577–2587.

Norris, J. (1994). Alcohol and female sexuality: A look at expectancies and risks. *Alcohol Health and Research World, 18*, 197–201.

Norton, G. R., Harrison, B., Haunch, J., & Rhodes, L. (1985). Characteristics of people with infrequent panic attacks. *Abnormal Psychiatry, 94*, 216–221.

Nossal, C. J. V., & Hall, E. (1995). Choices following antigen entry: Antibody formation or immunologic tolerance? *Annual Review of Immunology, 13*, 171–204.

Nourkova, V., Bernstein, D. M., & Loftus, E. F. (2004). Altering traumatic memory. *Cognition & Emotion, 18*, 575–585.

Ockene, J. K., et al. (2001). Relapse and maintenance issues for smoking cessation. *Health Psychology, 19*, 17–31.

O'Connor, D. B., Archer, J., Hair, W. M., & Wu, F. C. W. (2002). Exogenous testosterone, aggression, and mood in eugonadal and hypogonadal men. *Physiology and Behavior, 75*, 557–566.

O'Connor, S. C., & Rosenblood, L. K. (1996). Affiliation motivation in everyday experience: A theoretical comparison. *Journal of Personality and Social Psychology, 70*, 513–522.

O'Donohue, W., & Elliot, A. (1992). The current status of posttraumatic stress disorder as a diagnostic category: Problems and proposals. *Journal of Traumatic Stress, 5*, 421–439.

Oehman, A., Flykt, A., & Esteves, F. (2001). Emotion drives attention: Detecting the snake in the grass. *Journal of Experimental Psychology, 130*, 466–478.

Ohayon, M. M., Guilleminault, C., & Priest, R. G. (1999). Night terrors, sleepwalking, and confusional arousals in the general population: Their frequency and relationship to other sleep and mental disorders. *Journal of Clinical Psychiatry, 60*, 268–276.

Ohayon, M. M., & Lemoine, P. (2004). Sleep and insomnia markers in the general population. *Encephale, 30*, 135–140.

Ohayon, M. M., Priest, R. G., Zulley, J., Smirne, S., & Paiva, T. (2002). Prevalence of narcolepsy symptomatology and diagnosis in the European general population. *Neurology, 58*, 1826–1833.

Öhman, A., & Mineka, S. (2001). Fears, phobias, and preparedness: Toward an evolved module of fear and fear learning. *Pychological Review, 108*, 483–522.

Öhman, A., & Soares, J. J. F. (1998). Emotional conditioning to masked stimuli: Expectancies for aversive outcomes following nonrecognized fear-relevant stimuli. *Journal of Experimental Psychology: General, 127*, 69–82.

Öhman, A., & Wiens, S. (2005). The concept of an evolved fear. In A. S. R. Manstead, N. H. Frijda, A. H. Fischer, & K. Oatley (Eds.), *Feelings and Emotions: The Amsterdam Symposium.* New York: Cambridge University Press.

Okado, Y., & Stark, C. EL. (2005). Neural activity during encoding predicts false memories created by misinformation. *Learning & Memory, 12*, 3–11.

Olds, J. (1958). Self-stimulation of the brain. *Science, 127*, 315–324.

O'Leary, A., & The National Institute of Mental Health Multisite HIV Prevention Trial Group. (2001). Social-cognitive theory mediators of behavior change in the National Institute of Mental Health Multisite HIV Prevention Trial. *Health Psychology, 20*, 369–376.

O'Leary, K. D., & Wilson, G. T. (1987). *Behavior therapy: Application and outcome.* Englewood Cliffs, NJ: Prentice Hall.

Olek, M. (2005). *Multiple sclerosis: Etiology, diagnosis, and new treatment strategies.* Boston: Humana Press.

Oleson, T. (2002). Auriculotherapy stimulation for neuro-rehabilitation. *NeuroRehabilitation, 17*, 49–62.

Olness, K., & Ader, R. (1992). Conditioning as an adjunct in the pharmacotherapy of lupus erythematosus. *Journal of Developmental and Behavioral Pediatrics, 13*, 124–125.

Olson, M. A., & Fazio, R. H. (2003). Relations between implicit measures of prejudice: What are we measuring? *Psychological Science, 14*, 636–639.

Olsson, A., & Phelps, E. A. (2004). Learned fear of "unseen" faces after Pavlovian, observational, and instructed fear. *Psychological Science, 15*, 822–828.

Olweus, D. (2004). Bullying at school. Prevalence estimation, a useful evaluation design, and a new national initiative in Norway. *Association for Child Psychology and Psychiatry Occasional Papers, 23*, 5–17.

Orbuch, T. L., House, J. S., Mero, R. P., & Webster, P. S. (1996). Marital quality over the life course. *Social Psychology Quarterly, 59*, 162–171.

Orne, M. T. (1959). The nature of hypnosis: Artifact and essence. *Journal of Abnormal and Social Psychology, 58*, 277–299.

Orne, M. T. (1962). On the social psychology of the psychological experiment: With particular reference to demand characteristics and their implications. *American Psychologist, 17*, 776–783.

Orne, M. T., & Evans, F. J. (1965). Social control in the psychological experiment: Antisocial behavior and hypnosis. *Journal of Personality and Social Psychology, 1*, 189–200.

Ornstein, R. (1997). *Right mind.* Ft. Worth, TX: Harcourt Brace.

Ortiz, J., & Raine, A. (2004). Heart rate level and antisocial behavior in children and adolescents: A meta-analysis. *Journal of the American Academy of Child & Adolescent Psychiatry, 43*, 154–162.

Ost, J., Vrij, A., Costall, A., & Bull, R. (2002). Crashing memories and reality monitoring: Distinguishing between perceptions, imaginations and false memories. *Applied Cognitive Psychology, 16*, 125–134.

Ouellette, J. A., & Wood, W. (1998). Habit and intention in everyday life: The multiple processes by which past behavior predicts future behavior. *Psychological Bulletin, 124*, 54–74.

Ouyang, M., Hellman, K., Abel, T., & Thomas, S. A. (2004). Adrenergic signaling plays a critical role in the maintenance of waking and in the regulation of REM sleep. *Journal of Neurophysiology, 92*, 2071–2082.

Owen, P. R., & Laurel-Seller, E. (2000). Weight and shape ideals: Thin is dangerously in. *Journal of Applied Social Psychology, 30*, 979–990.

Paffenbarger, R. S., Jr., Hyde, R. T., Wing, A. L., & Hsieh, C. C. (1986). Physical activity, all-cause mortality, and longevity of college alumni. *New England Journal of Medicine, 314*, 605–613.

Paivio, A. (1969). Mental imagery is associative learning and memory. *Psychological Review, 76*, 241–263.

Paivio, A., Khan, M., & Begg, I. (2000). Concreteness of relational effects on recall of adjective noun pairs. *Canadian Journal of Experimental Psychology, 54*, 149–160.

Pajer, K. (2000). Hysteria. In G. Fink (Ed.), *Encyclopedia of stress.* San Diego, CA: Academic Press.

Palfai, T., & Jankiewicz, H. (1991). *Drugs and human behavior.* Dubuque, IA: Wm. C. Brown.

Palmer, J. (2003). ESP in the Ganzfeld: Analysis of a debate. In J. E. Alcock, J. E. Burns, & A. Freeman (Eds.), *Psi wars: Getting to grips with the paranormal.* Charlottesville, VA: Imprint Academic.

Palmer, J. A., & Palmer, L. K. (Eds.). (2002). *Evolutionary psychology: The ultimate origins of human behavior* (Vol. 15). Needham Heights, MA: Allyn & Bacon.

Palmer, S. E. (2002). Perceptual organization in vision. In H. Pashler & S. Yantis (Eds.), *Steven's handbook of experimental psychology: Vol. 1. Sensation and perception* (3rd ed.). New York: Wiley.

Palmere, M., Benton, S. L., Glover, J. A., & Ronning, R. (1983). Elaboration and recall of main ideas in prose. *Journal of Education Psychology, 75*, 898–907.

Panksepp, J. (2005). Basic affects and the instinctual emotion system of the brain: The primordial sources of sadness, joy and seeking. In A. S. R. Manstead, N. H. Frijda, A. H. Fischer, & K. Oatley (Eds.), *Feelings and emotions: The Amsterdam Symposium.* New York: Cambridge University Press.

Papanicolaou, A. C. (1989). *Emotion: A reconsideration of the somatic theory.* New York: Gordon & Breach.

Papini, M. R. (2002). Pattern and process in the evolution of learning. *Psychological Review, 109*, 186–201.

Pappagallo. M. (2005). *The neurological basis of pain.* New York: McGraw-Hill.

Parchman, S. W., Ellis, J. A., Christinaz, D., & Vogel, M. (2000). An evaluation of three computer-based instructional strategies in basic electricity and electronics training. *Military Psychology, 12,* 73–87.

Paris, J. (1993). *Borderline personality disorder.* Washington, DC: American Psychiatric Press.

Park, C. L., Armeli, S., & Tennen, H. (2004). Appraisal-coping goodness of fit: A daily internet study. *Personality and Social Psychology Bulletin, 30,* 558–569.

Park, D. C., & Gutchess, A. H. (2005). Long-term memory and aging: A cognitive neuroscience perspective. In R. Cabeza, L. Nyberg, & D. Park (Eds.), *Cognitive neuroscience of aging: Linking cognitive and cerebral aging.* London: Oxford University Press.

Park, D. C., Smith, A. D., & Cavanaugh, J. C. (1990). Metamemories of memory researchers. *Memory and Cognition, 18,* 321–327.

Parker, A. (2000). A review of the ganzfeld work at Gothenburg University. *Journal of the Society for Psychical Research, 64,* 1–15.

Parker, C. R., Bolling, M. Y., & Kohlenberg, R. J. (1998). Operant theory of personality. In D. F. Barone, M. Hersen, & V. B. Van Hasselt (Eds.), *Advanced personality.* New York: Plenum Press.

Parkinson, A. J., Parkinson, W. S., Tyler, R. S., Lowder, M. W., & Gantz, B. J. (1998). Speech perception performance in experienced cochlear-implant patients receiving the SPEAK processing strategy in the Nucleus Spectra-22 cochlear implant. *Journal of Speech, Language, and Hearing Research, 41,* 1073–1087.

Parrott, A. C. (2001). Human psychopharmacology of Ecstasy (MDMA): A review of 15 years of empirical research. *Human Psychopharmacology: Clinical and Experimental, 16,* 557–577.

Pashler, H., & Yantis, S. (Eds.). (2002). *Steven's handbook of experimental psychology: Vol. 1. Sensation and perception* (3rd ed.). New York: Wiley.

Pasupathi, M., Staudinger, U. M., & Baltes, P. B. (2001). Seeds of wisdom: Adolescents' knowledge and judgment about difficult life problems. *Developmental Psychology, 37,* 351–361.

Patterson, D. R. (2004). Treating pain with hypnosis. *Current Directions in Psychological Science, 13,* 252–255.

Patterson, G. R., Littman, R. A., & Bricker, W. (1967). Assertive behavior in children: A step toward a theory of aggression. *Monographs of the Society for Research in Child Development, 32*(Whole No. 5).

Paul, G. L. (2001). The active unconscious, symptom substitution, and other things that went 'bump' in the night. In W. T. O'Donohue et al. (Eds.), *A history of the behavioral therapies: Founders' personal histories.* New York: Guilford Press.

Paul, G. L., & Lentz, R. J. (1977). *Psychosocial treatment of chronic mental patients: Milieu versus social learning programs.* Cambridge, MA: Harvard University Press.

Paulson, T. (2004, December 14). Thought powers computer. *Seattle Post-Intelligencer*, p. A1.

Paunonen, S. V. (2003). Big Five factors of personality and replicated predictions of behavior. *Journal of Personality and Social Psychology, 84,* 411–424.

Pavlov, I. P. (1928). *Lectures on conditioned reflexes: Twenty-five years of objective study of the higher nervous activity (behaviour) of animals* (W. H. Gantt, Trans.). New York: International Publishers. (Original work published 1923)

Pearlin, L. I., & Schooler, C. (1978). The structure of coping. *Journal of Health and Social Behavior, 19,* 2–21.

Pedersen, W. C., Miller, L. C., PutchaBhagavatula, A. D., & Yang, Y. (2002). Evolved sex differences in the number of partners desired? The long and short of it. *Psychological Science, 13,* 157–161.

Pedrotti, F. L., & Pedrotti, L. S. (1997). *Optics and vision.* Englewood Cliffs, NJ: Prentice Hall.

Pelletier, D. L., & Frongillo, E. A. (2003). Changes in child survival are strongly associated with changes in malnutrition in developing countries. *Journal of Nutrition, 133,* 107–119.

Pellino, T. A., & Ward, S. E. (1998). Perceived control mediates the relationship between pain severity and patient satisfaction. *Journal of Pain and Symptom Management, 15,* 110–116.

Pennebaker, J. W. (1995). *Emotion, disclosure and health.* Washington, DC: American Psychological Association.

Pennebaker, J. W. (1997). *Opening up: The healing power of expressing emotions.* New York: Guilford Press.

Peplau, L. A., Garnets, L. D., Spalding, L. R., Conley, T. D., & Veniegas, R. C. (1998). A critique of Bem's "Exotic Becomes Erotic" theory of sexual orientation. *Psychological Review, 105,* 387–394.

Perani, D., Paulesu, E., Galles, N. S., Dupoux, E., & Dehaene, S. (1998). The bilingual brain: Proficiency and age of acquisition of the second language. *Brain, 121,* 1841–1852.

Perdue, C. W., Dovidio, J. F., Gurtman, M. B., & Tyler, R. B. (1990). Us and them: Social categorization and the process of intergroup bias. *Journal of Personality and Social Psychology, 59,* 475–486.

Perrett, D. I., Lee, K. J., Penton-Voak, I., Rowland, D., Yoshikawa, S., Burt, D. M., Henzi, S. P., Castles, D. L., & Akamatsu, S. (1998). Effects of sexual dimorphism on facial attractiveness. *Nature, 394,* 884–887.

Pert, C. B. (1986). The wisdom of the receptors: Neuropeptides, the emotions, and bodymind. *Advances, 3,* 8–16.

Pert, C. B. (1997). *Molecules of emotion: Why you feel the way you feel.* New York: Simon & Schuster.

Pervin, L. A., Cervone, D., & John, O. (2005). *Personality: Theory and research.* New York: Wiley.

Peskin, M., & Newell, F. N. (2004). Familiarity breeds attraction: Effects of exposure on the attractiveness of typical and distinctive faces. *Perception, 33,* 147–157.

Peterson, C., & Seligman, M. E. P. (1987). Explanatory style and illness. *Journal of Personality, 55,* 237–265.

Peterson, C., & Seligman, M. E. P. (2004). *Character strengths and virtues: A handbook and classification.* Washington, DC: American Psychological Association.

Peterson, C., & Whalen, N. (2001). Five years later: Children's memory for medical emergencies. *Applied Cognitive Psychology 15,* 7–24.

Peterson, L. R., & Peterson, M. J. (1959). Short-term retention of individual verbal items. *Journal of Experimental Psychology, 58,* 193–198.

Petrill, S. (2003). The development of intelligence: Behavior genetics approaches. In R. J. Sternberg, J. Lautrey, & T. I. Lubart (Eds.), *Models of intelligence: International perspectives.* Washington, DC: American Psychological Association.

Petrovic, P., & Ingvar, M. (2002). Imaging cognitive modulation of pain processing. *Pain, 95,* 1–5.

Petrovic, P., Kalso, E., Petersson, M. K., & Ingvarm, M. (2002, February). Placebo and opioid analgesia: Imaging a shared neuronal network. *Science Express Reports,* 17–22.

Petry, N., & Martin, B. (2002). Low-cost contingency management for treating cocaine- and opioid-abusing methadone patients. *Journal of Consulting and Clinical Psychology, 70,* 398–405.

Pettigrew, T. F. (1979). The ultimate attribution error: Extending Allport's cognitive analysis of prejudice. *Personality and Social Psychology Bulletin, 55,* 461–476.

Pettigrew, T. F., & Meertens, R. W. (1995). Subtle and blatant prejudice in western Europe. *European Journal of Social Psychology, 25,* 57–76.

Pettigrew, T. F., & Tropp, L. R. (2000). Does intergroup contact reduce prejudice: Recent meta-analytic findings. In S. Oskamp (Ed.), *Reducing prejudice and discrimination. The Claremont Symposium on Applied Social Psychology.* Mahwah, NJ: Erlbaum.

Petty, R. E., & Cacioppo, J. T. (1986). *Communication and persuasion: Central and peripheral routes to attitude change.* New York: Springer-Verlag.

Petty, R. E., Cacioppo, J. T., Strathman, A. J., & Priester, J. R. (2005). To think or not to think: Exploring two routes to persuasion. In T. C. Brock & M. C. Green (Eds.), *Persuasion: Psychological insights and perspectives* (2nd ed., pp. 81–116). Thousand Oaks, CA: Sage.

Petty, R. E., Fleming, M. A., Priester, J. R., Feinstein, A. H. (2001). Individual versus group interest violation: Surprise as a determinant of argument scrutiny and persuasion. *Social Cognition, 19,* 418–442.

Pezdek, K. (2003). Event memory and autobiographical memory for the events of September 11, 2001. *Applied Cognitive Psychology, 17,* 1033–1045.

Pfeifer, M., Goldsmith, H. H., & Davidson, R. R. M. (2002). Continuity and change in inhibited and uninhibited children. *Child Development, 73,* 1474–1485.

Pfiffner, L. J., McBurnett, K., & Rathouz, P. (2001). Father absence and familial antisocial characteristics. *Journal of Abnormal Child Psychology, 29,* 357–367.

Phelps, E. A. (2005). The power of the subliminal: On subliminal persuasion and other potential applications. In R. R. Hassin, J. S. Uleman, & J. A. Bargh (Eds.), *The new unconscious.* New York: Oxford University Press.

Phillips, K. A. (2001). *Somatoform and factitious disorders.* Washington, DC: American Psychiatric Association.

Phillips, M., Brooks, G. J., Duncan, G. J., Klebanov, P., & Crane, J. (1998). Family background, parenting practices, and the Black-White test score gap. In C. Jencks & M. Phillips (Eds.), *The Black-White test score gap.* Washington, DC: Brookings Institution.

Piaget, J. (1926). *The language and thought of the child.* New York: Meridian Books.

Piaget, J. (1970). Piaget's theory. In P. H. Mussen (Ed.), *Carmichael's manual of child psychology* (Vol.1). New York: Wiley.

Piaget, J. (1977). *The development of thought: Equilibration of cognitive structure.* New York: Viking.

Pickering, A. D., & Gray, J. A. (1999). The neuroscience of personality. In L. A. Pervin & O. P. John (Eds.), *Handbook of personality: Theory and research.* New York: Guilford Press.

Pickrell, J. E., Bernstein, D., & Loftus, E. F. (2003). The misinformation effect. In R. Pohl (Ed.), *Cognitive illusions: Fallacies and biases in thinking, judgment, and memory.* London: Psychology Press.

Pies, R. W. (1998). *Handbook of essential psychopharmacology.* Washington, DC: American Psychiatric Press.

Pilbeam, D. (1984). The descent of hominoids and hominids. *Scientific American, 250,* 84–97.

Pilcher, J. J., & Huffcutt, A. J. (1996). Effects of sleep deprivation on performance: A meta-analysis. *Sleep, 19,* 318–326.

Pilcher, J. J., & Walters, A. S. (1997). How sleep deprivation affects psychological variables related to college students' cognitive performance. *Journal of American College Health, 46,* 121–126.

Pinker, S. (2000). Language as an adaptation to the cognitive niche. In M. Christiansen & S. Kirby (Eds.), *Language evolution: Reports from the research frontier.* New York: Oxford University Press.

Pinquart, M., & Sörensen, S. (2003). Differences between caregivers and noncaregivers in psychological health and physical health: A meta-analysis. *Psychology & Aging, 18,* 250–267.

Pitman, R. K., Shalev, A. Y., & Orr, S. P. (2000). Posttraumatic stress disorder: Emotion, conditioning, and memory. In M. S. Gazzaniga (Ed.), *The new cognitive neurosciences* (2nd ed.). Cambridge, MA: MIT Press.

Pitz, G. F., & Sachs, N. J. (1984). Judgment and decision: Theory and application. *Annual Review of Psychology, 35,* 139–163.

Piven, J., Saliba, K., Bailey, J., & Arndt, S. (1997). An MRI study of autism: The cerebellum revisited. *Neurology, 13,* 546–551.

Plant, E. A., & Peruche, B. M. (2005). The consequences of race for police officers' responses to criminal suspects. *Psychological Science, 16,* 180–183.

Plant, E. A., Peruche, B. M., & Butz, D. A. (2005). Eliminating automatic racial bias: Making race non-diagnostic for responses to criminal suspects. *Journal of Experimental Social Psychology, 41,* 141–156.

Plomin, R. (1997). *Behavioral genetics.* New York: St. Martin's Press.

Plomin, R., & Caspi, A. (1999). Behavior genetics and personality. In L. A. Pervin & O. P. John (Eds.), *Handbook of personality: Theory and research.* New York: Guilford Press.

Plomin, R., & Craig, I. (2002). "Genetic research on cognitive ability": Author's reply. *British Journal of Psychiatry, 180,* 185–186.

Plomin, R., & DeFries, J. C. (1998). The genetics of cognitive abilities and disabilities. *Scientific American, 6,* 62–69.

Plomin, R., & Spinath, F. M. (2004). Intelligence: Genetics, genes, and genomics. *Journal of Personality and Social Psychology, 86,* 112–129.

Plous, S. (1996a). Attitudes toward the use of animals in psychological research and education: Results from a national survey of psychologists. *American Psychologist, 51,* 1167–1180.

Plous, S. (1996b). Attitudes toward the use of animals in psychological research and education: Results from a national survey of psychology majors. *Psychological Science, 7,* 352–358.

Plutchik, R. (1994). *Psychology of emotion.* Reading, MA: Addison-Wesley.

Pollack, I., & Pickett, J. M. (1964). Intelligibility of excerpts from fluent speech: Auditory vs. structural context. *Journal of Verbal Learning and Verbal Behavior, 3,* 79–84.

Pool, R. (1994). *The dynamic brain.* Washington, DC: National Academy Press.

Porter, N. P., & Geis, F. L. (1981). Women and nonverbal leadership cues: When seeing is not believing. In C. Mayo & N. M. Henley (Eds.), *Gender and nonverbal behavior.* New York: Springer-Verlag.

Posada, G., Jacobs, A., Richmond, M. K., Carbonell, O. A., Alzate, G., Bustamante, M. R., & Quiceno, J. (2002). Maternal caregiving and infant security in two cultures. *Developmental Psychology, 38,* 67–78.

Posthuma, D., Neale, M. C., Boomsma, D. I., & de Geus, E. J. C. (2001). Are smarter brains running faster? Heritability of alpha peak frequency, IQ, and their interrelation. *Behavior Genetics, 31,* 567–579.

Postman, L., & Phillips, L. W. (1965). Short-term temporal changes in free recall. *Quarterly Journal of Experimental Psychology, 17,* 132–138.

Postman, L., & Underwood, B. J. (1973). Critical issues in interference theory. *Memory and Cognition, 1,* 19–40.

Postmes, T., & Spears, R. (1998). Deindividuation and antinormative behavior: A meta-analysis. *Psychological Bulletin, 123,* 238–259.

Powell, R. W., & Curley, M. (1976). Instinctive drift in nondomesticated rodents. *Bulletin of the Psychonomic Society, 8,* 175–178.

Powley, T. L., & Keesey, R. E. (1970). Relationship of body weight to the lateral hypothalamic feeding syndrome. *Journal of Comparative and Physiological Psychology, 70,* 25–36.

Pressman, J. D. (1998). *Last resort: Psychosurgery and the limits of medicine.* New York: Cambridge University Press.

Preti, G., Cutler, W. B., Garcia, G. R., Huggins, G. R., & Lawley, J. J. (1986). Human axillary secretions influences women's menstrual cycles: The role of donor extract from females. *Hormones and Behavior, 20,* 473–480.

Prigerson, H., Maciejewski, P. K, & Rosenheck, R. A. (2002). Population attributable fractions of psychiatric disorders and behavioral outcomes associated with combat exposure among U.S. men. *American Journal of Public Health, 92*(1), 59–63.

Priluck, R., & Till, B. D. (2004). The role of contingency awareness, involvement, and need for cognition in attitude formation. *Journal of the Academy of Marketing Science, 32,* 329–344.

Pritchard, R. M. (1961, June). Stabilized images on the retina. *Scientific American,* 72–78.

Probst, L. R., Ostrom, R., Watkins, P., Dean, T., & Mashburn, D. (1992). Comparative efficacy of religious and non-religious cognitive-behavioral therapy for the treatment of clinical depression in religious individuals. *Journal of Consulting and Clinical Psychology, 60,* 94–103.

Prochaska, J., & DiClemente, C. (1984). *The transtheoretical approach: Crossing traditional boundaries of therapy.* Illinois: Down Jones-Irwin.

Prochaska, J. O., Johnson, S., & Lee, P. (1998). The transtheoretical model of behavior change. In S. A. Shumaker & E. B. Schron (Eds.), *The handbook of health behavior change* (2nd ed.). New York: Springer.

Prochaska, J. O., Norcross, J. C., & DiClemente, C. C. (1994). *Changing for good.* New York: Avon Books.

Project MATCH Research Group. (1997). Matching alcoholism treatments to client heterogeneity: Project MATCH posttreatment drinking outcomes. *Journal of Studies on Alcohol, 58,* 7–29.

Ptacek, J. T., Smith, R. E., & Zanas, J. (1992). Gender, appraisal, and coping: A longtudinal analysis. *Journal of Personality, 60,* 747–769.

Pugh, G. E. (1977). *The biological origin of human values.* New York: Basic Books.

Punamäki, R. L., & Joustie, M. (1998). The role of culture, violence, and personal factors affecting dream content. *Journal of Cross-Cultural Psychology, 29,* 320–342.

Putnam, F. W. (1989). *Diagnosis and treatment of multiple personality disorder.* New York: Guilford Press.

Putnam, F. W. (2000). Dissociative disorders. In A. J. Sameroff & M. Lewis (Eds.), *Handbook of developmental psychopathology* (2nd ed.). New York: Cambridge University Press.

Putman, P., van Honk, J., Kessels, R. P. C., Mulder, M., & Koppeschaar, H. P. F. (2004). Salivary cortisol and short and long-term memory for emotional faces in healthy young women. *Psychoneuroendocrinology, 29,* 953–960.

Pylyshyn, Z. (2003). Return of the mental image: Are there really pictures in the brain? *Trends in Cognitive Sciences, 7,* 113–118.

Qu, T., Brannen, C. L., Kim, H. M., & Sugaya, K. (2001). Human neural stem cells improve cognitive function of aged brain. *Neuroreport: For Rapid Communication of Neuroscience Research, 12*(6), 1127–1132.

Quintero, N. (1980, February). Coming of age the Apache way. *National Geographic, 157*(2), 262–271.

Quiroga, Q. R., Reddy, L., Kreiman, G., Koch, C., & Fried, I. (2005). Invariant visual representation by single neurons in the human brain. *Nature, 423,* 1102–1107.

Rachman, S. (1998). *Anxiety.* Mahwah, NJ: Erlbaum.

Rachman, S. J., & Hodgson, R. J. (1980). *Obsessions and compulsions.* Englewood Cliffs, NJ: Prentice Hall.

Rahman, Q. (2005). Fluctuating asymmetry, second to fourth finger length ratios and human sexual orientation. *Psychoneuroendocrinology, 30,* 382–391.

Raine, A. (2002). Annotation: The role of prefrontal deficits, low autonomic arousal and early health factors in the development of antisocial and aggressive behavior in children. *Journal of Child Psychology and Psychiatry and Allied Disciplines, 43,* 417–434.

Raine, A., Buchsbaum, M., & LaCasse, L. (1997). Brain abnormalities in murderers indicated by positron tomography. *Biological Psychiatry, 42,* 495–508.

Raine, A., Lencz, T., Bihrle, S., LaCasse, L., & Colletti, P. (2000). Reduced prefrontal gray matter volume and reduced autonomic activity in antisocial personality disorder. *Archives of General Psychiatry, 57,* 119–127.

Raine, A., Mellingen, K., Liu, J. Venables, P., & Mednick, S. A. (2003). Effects of environmental enrichment at ages 3–5 years on schizotypal personality and antisocial behavior at ages 17

and 23 years. *American Journal of Psychiatry, 160,* 1627–1635.

Raine, A., Venables, P. H., & Williams, M. (1996). Better autonomic conditioning and faster electrodermal half-recovery time at age 15 years as possible protective factors against crime at age 29 years. *Developmental Psychology, 32,* 624–630.

Rajah, M. N., & McIntosh, A. R. (2005). Overlap in the functional neural systems involved in semantic and episodic memory retrieval. *Journal of Cognitive Neuroscience, 17,* 470–482.

Ramey, C., & Ramey, S. (1998). Early intervention. *American Psychologist, 53,* 210–225.

Ramey, C. T., Ramey, S. L., & Lanzi, R. G. (1998). Differentiating developmental risk levels for families in poverty: Creating a family typology. In M. Lewis & C. Feiring (Eds.), *Families, risks, and competence.* Mahway, NJ: Erlbaum.

Ramsey, J. L., Langlois, J. H., Hoss, R. A., Rubenstein, A. J., & Griffin, A. M. (2004). Origins of a stereotype: Categorization of facial attractiveness by 6-month-old infants. *Developmental Science, 7,* 201–211.

Rao, R. (2001). Cannabis: Some psychiatric aspects. *Primary Care Psychiatry, 7,* 101–105.

Raudenbush, B., & Meyer, B. (2003). Muscular dissatisfaction and supplement use among male intercollegiate athletes. *Journal of Sport & Exercise Psychology, 25,* 161–170.

Raven, J. (1962). *Colored progressive matrices.* New York: Psychological Corp.

Ravussin, E., & Gautier, J. F. (1999). Metabolic predictors of weight gain. *International Journal of Obesity and Related Metabolic Disorders, 23*(Suppl. 1), 37–41.

Ray, O. S., & Ksir, C. J. (2004). *Drugs, society and human behavior* (9th ed.). Boston: McGraw-Hill.

Raz, A., & Shapiro, T. (2002). Hypnosis and neuroscience: A cross talk between clinical and cognitive research. *Archives of General Psychiatry, 59,* 85–90.

"A Recovering Patient." (1986). "Can we talk?" The schizophrenic patient in psychotherapy. *American Journal of Psychiatry, 143,* 68–70.

Regal, B. (2005). *Human evolution: A guide to the debates.* Santa Barbara, CA: ABC-CLIO, Inc.

Reich, T. W. (2006). *Personality disorders research.* London: Brunner-Routledge.

Reisberg, D. (2001). *Cognition: Exploring the science of the mind.* New York: Norton.

Rendell, P. G., & Thomson, D. M. (1999). Aging and prospective memory: Differences between naturalistic and laboratory tasks. *Journals of Gerontology: Series B: Psychological Sciences and Social Sciences, 54B*(4), 256–269.

Rensink, R. A. (2002). Change detection. *Annual Review of Psychology, 53,* 247–277.

Renzulli, J. S. (2002). Emerging conceptions of giftedness: building a bridge to the new century, *Exceptionality, 10,* 67–75.

Reppucci, N. D., Wollard, J. L., & Fried, C. S. (1999). Social, community, and preventive interventions. *Annual Review of Psychology, 1,* 387–415.

Rescorla, R. A. (1968). Probability of shock in the presence and absence of CS in fear. *Journal of Comparative and Physiological Psychology, 66,* 1–5.

Rescorla, R. A., & Solomon, R. L. (1967). Two-process learning theory: Relationships between Pavlovian conditioning and instrumental learning. *Psychological Review, 74,* 151–182.

Rescorla, R. A., & Wagner, A. R. (1972). A theory of Pavlovian conditioning: Variations in the effectiveness of reinforcement and nonreinforcement. In A. H. Black & W. F. Prokasky (Eds.), *Classical conditioning: II. Current research and theory.* New York: Appleton-Century-Crofts.

Resick, P. (2005). *Stress and trauma.* San Francisco: Taylor & Francis.

Resnick, S. M., Pham, D. L., Kraut, M. A., Zonderman, A. B., & Davatzikos, C. (2003). Longitudinal magnetic resonance imaging studies of older adults: A shrinking brain. *Journal of Neuroscience, 23,* 3295–3301.

Rey, J. M., & Walter, G. (1997). Half a century of ECT use in young people. *American Journal of Psychiatry, 154,* 595–602.

Rhodes, G., Yoshikawa, S., Clark, A., Lee, K., McKay, R., & Akamatsu, S. (2001). Attractiveness of facial averageness and symmetry in non-Western cultures: In search of biologically based standards of beauty. *Perception, 30,* 611–625.

Richard, S., Davies, D. C., & Faure, J. M. (2000). The role of fear in one-trial passive avoidance learning in Japanese quail chicks genetically selected for long or short duration of the tonic immobility reaction. *Behavioural Processes, 48,* 165–170.

Richardson, D. R. (1991). Interpersonal attraction and love. In R. M. Baron, W. G. Graziano, & C. Stangor (Eds.), *Social psychology.* Ft. Worth, TX: Holt, Rinehart & Winston.

Richter, C. P. (1957). Phenomenon of sudden death in animals and man. *Psychosomatic Medicine, 19,* 191–198.

Riesen, A. H. (1965). Effects of early deprivation of photic stimulation. In S. F. Osler & R. E. Cooke (Eds.), *The biosocial basis of mental retardation.* Baltimore, MD: Johns Hopkins University Press.

Rilling, M. (1996). The mystery of the vanished citations: James McConnell's forgotten 1960s quest for planarian learning, a biochemical engram, and celebrity. *American Psychologist, 51,* 589–598.

Rimm, D. C., & Masters, J. C. (1979). *Behavior therapy: Techniques and empirical findings* (2nd ed.). New York: Academic Press.

Rips, L. J. (1997). Goals for a theory of deduction: Reply to Johnson-Laird. *Minds and Machines, 7,* 409–424.

Ritblatt, S. N. (2000). Children's level of participation in a false-belief task, age, and theory of mind. *Journal of Genetic Psychology, 161,* 53–64.

Ritchie, C. W., Ames, D., Clayton, T., & Lai, R. (2004). Metaanalysis of randomized trials of the efficacy and safety of donepezil, galantamine, and rivastigmine for the treatment of Alzheimer disease. *American Journal of Geriatric Psychiatry, 12,* 358–369.

Roberts, B., Helson, R., & Klohnen, E. C. (2002). Personality development and growth in women across 30 years: Three perspectives. *Journal of Personality, 70,* 79–102.

Robins, L. N., & Regier, D. A. (Eds.). (1991). *Psychiatric disorders in America: The Epidemiological Catchment Area Study.* New York: Free Press.

Robins, R. W., Gosling, S. D., & Craik, K. H. (1999). An empirical analysis of trends in psychology. *American Psychologist, 54,* 117–128.

Robinson, D. (1997). *Neurobiology.* New York: Springer-Verlag.

Robinson, M. D., Vargas, P. T., Tamir, M., & Solberg, E. C. (2004). Using and being used by categories. *Psychological Science 15,* 521–526.

Robinson, S., Sandstrom, S. M., Denenberg, V. H., & Palmiter, R. D. (2005). Distinguishing whether dopamine regulates liking, wanting, and/or learning about rewards. *Behavioral Neuroscience, 119,* 5–15.

Roche, A. F. (1979). Secular trends in human growth, maturation, and development. *Monographs of the Society for Research and Child Development, 44*(3–4, Serial No. 179).

Rodin, J., Bartoshuk, L., Peterson, C., & Schank, D. (1990). Bulimia and taste: Possible interactions. *Journal of Abnormal Psychology, 99,* 32–39.

Rodin, J., & Salovey, P. (1989). Health psychology. *Annual Review of Psychology, 40,* 533–579.

Roebers, C. M. (2002). Confidence judgments in children's and adults' recall and suggestibility. *Developmental Psychology, 38,* 1052–1067.

Roediger, H. L., III, & McDermott, K. B. (1995). Creating false memories: Remembering words not presented in lists. *Journal of Experimental Psychology: Learning, Memory, and Cognition, 21,* 803–814.

Roediger, H. L., III, & McDermott, K. B. (2000). Tricks of memory. *Current Directions in Psychological Science, 9,* 123–127.

Roelofs, K., Hoogduin, K. A. L., Keijsers, G. P. J., Naering, G. W. B, Moene, F. C., & Sandijck, P. (2002). Hypnotic susceptibility in patients with conversion disorder. *Journal of Abnormal Psychology, 111,* 390–395.

Roffwarg, H. P., Muzio, J. N., & Dement, W. C. (1966). Ontogenic development of human dream-sleep cycle. *Science, 152,* 604.

Rogers, C. R. (1951). *Client-centered therapy.* Boston: Houghton Mifflin.

Rogers, C. R. (1959). A theory of therapy, personality and interpersonal relationships, as developed in the client-centered framework. In S. Koch (Ed.), *Psychology: A study of a science* (Vol. 3). New York: McGraw-Hill.

Rogers, C. R. (Ed.). (1967). *The therapeutic relationship and its impact: A study of psychotherapy with schizophrenics.* Madison: University of Wisconsin Press.

Rogers, C. R. (1980). *A way of being.* Boston: Houghton Mifflin.

Rohsenow, D. J., & Marlatt, G. A. (1981). The balanced placebo design: Methodological considerations. *Addictive Behaviors, 6,* 107–122.

Roland, P. E. (1997). *Brain activation.* New York: Wiley.

Rollman, G. (1998). Culture and pain. In S. S. Kazarian et al. (Eds.), *Cultural clinical psychology: Theory, research, and practice.* New York: Oxford University Press.

Rolls, B. J., Rolls, E. T., Rowe, E. A., & Sweeney, K. (1981). Sensory specific satiety in man. *Physiology and Behavior, 27,* 137–142.

Rolls, E. T. (2000). Memory systems in the brain. *Annual Review of Psychology, 5,* 599–630.

Rolls, E. T., & Deco, G. (2002). *Computational neuroscience of vision.* London: Oxford University Press.

Rosch, E. (1973). On the internal structure of perceptual and semantic categories. In T. E. Moore (Ed.), *Cognitive development and the acquisition of language.* New York: Academic Press.

Rosch, E. (1977). Human categorization. In N. Warren (Ed.), *Advances in cross-cultural psychology* (Vol. 1). London: Academic Press.

Rose, R. J., Viken, R. J., Dick, D. M., Bates, J. E., Pulkkinen, L., & Kaprio, J. (2003). It does take a village: Nonfamilial environments and children's behavior. *Psychological Science, 14,* 273–277.

Rosen, C. S. (2000). Integrating stage and continuum models to explain processing of exercise messages and exercise initiation among sedentary college students. *Health Psychology, 19,* 172–180.

Rosenfarb, I. S., Goldstein, M. J., Mintz, J., & Nuechterlein, K. H. (1995). Expressed emotion and subclinical psychopathology observable within the transactions between schizophrenic patients and their family members. *Journal of Abnormal Psychology, 104,* 259–267.

Rosenhan, D. L. (1973). On being sane in insane places. *Science, 179,* 250–258.

Rosenhan, D. L., & Seligman, M. E. P. (1989). *Abnormal psychology* (2nd ed.). New York: Norton.

Rosenman, R. H., Brand, R. J., Jenkins, C. D., Friedman, M., Straus, R., & Wurm, M. (1975). Coronary disease in the Western Collaborative Group Study. Final follow-up experience of 8 1/2 years. *Journal of the American Medical Association, 233,* 872–877.

Rosenthal, N. E., & Wehr, T. A. (1987). Seasonal affective disorders. *Psychiatric Annals, 17,* 670–674.

Rosenthal, R. (1985). From unconscious experimenter bias to teacher expectancy effects. In J. B. Dusek, V. C. Hall, & W. J. Meyer (Eds.), *Teacher expectancies.* Hillsdale, NJ: Erlbaum.

Rosenthal, R., Archer, D., DiMatteo, M. R., Koivumaki, J. H., & Rogers, P. L. (1974). Body talk and tone of voice: The language without words. *Psychology Today, 8,* 64–71.

Rosenzweig, M. R. (1984). Experience, memory, and the brain. *American Psychologist, 39,* 365–376.

Rosenzweig, M. R., & Bennett, E. L. (1996). Psychobiology of plasticity: Effects of training and experience on brain and behavior. *Behavioural Brain Research, 78,* 57–65.

Rosenzweig, S. (1992). Freud and experimental psychology: The emergence of idiodynamics. In S. Koch & D. E. Leary (Eds.), *A century of psychology as science.* Washington, DC: American Psychological Association.

Rosqvist, J., & Hersen, M. (2006). *Exposure treatments for anxiety disorders.* New York: Brunner-Routledge.

Ross, L. (2001). Getting down to fundamentals: Lay dispositionism and the attributions of psychologists. *Psychological Inquiry, 12,* 37–40.

Ross, L., & Nisbett, R. E. (1991). *The person and the situation: Perspectives of social psychology.* New York: McGraw-Hill.

Ross, M., & Wilson, A. E. (2003). Autobiographical memory and conceptions of self: Getting better all the time. *Current Directions in Psychological Science, 12,* 66–69.

Rossell, S. L., Bullmore, E. T., Williams, S. C. R., et al. (2002). Sex differences in functional brain activation during a lexical visual field task. *Brain and Language, 80,* 97–105.

Roth, A., & Fonagy, P. (2005). *What works for whom: A critical review of psychotherapy research* (2nd ed). New York: Guilford Press.

Rothbaum, B. O., Hodges, L., Anderson, P. L., Price, L., & Smith, S. (2002). Twelve-month follow-up of virtual reality and standard exposure therapies for the fear of flying. *Journal of Consulting and Clinical Psychology, 70,* 428–432.

Rothrauff, T., Middlemiss, W., & Jacobson, L. (2004). Comparison of American and Austrian infants' and toddlers' sleep habits: A retrospective, exploratory study. *North American Journal of Psychology, 6,* 125–144.

Rotter, J. B. (1954). *Social learning and clinical psychology.* Englewood Cliffs, NJ: Prentice Hall.

Rotter, J. B. (1966). Generalized expectancies for internal versus external control of reinforcement. *Psychological Monographs, 80*(Whole No. 609).

Rouhana, N. N., & Bar-Tal, D. (1998). Psychological dynamics of intractable ethnonational conflicts: The Israeli-Palestinian case. *American Psychologist, 53,* 761–770.

Rowe, D. C. (1999). Heredity. In V. J. Derlega, B. A. Winstead, & W. H. Jones (Eds.), *Personality: Contemporary theory and research.* Chicago: Nelson Hall.

Rowley, J. T., Stickgold, R., & Hobson, J. A. (1998). Eyelid movements and mental activity at sleep onset. *Consciousness and Cognition: An International Journal, 7,* 67–84.

Rubin, D. C., & Kozin, M. (1984). Vivid memories. *Cognition, 16*, 81–95.

Rubin, R. T. (2000). Depression and manic-depressive illness. In G. Fink (Ed.), *Encyclopedia of stress.* San Diego, CA: Academic Press.

Rubonis, A. V., & Bickman, L. (1991). Psychological impairment in the wake of disaster: The disaster-psychopathology relationship. *Psychological Bulletin, 109*, 384–399.

Ruffman, R., Perner, J., Naito, M., Parkin, L., & Clements, W. A. (1998). Older (but not younger) siblings facilitate false belief understanding. *Developmental Psychology, 34*, 161–174.

Rumbaugh, D. M. (1990). Comparative psychology and the great apes: Their competency in learning, language, and numbers. *Psychological Record, 40*, 15–39.

Rumelhart, D. E., McClelland, J. L., & the PDP Research Group. (Eds.). (1986). *Parallel distributed processing* (Vol. 1). Cambridge, MA: MIT Press.

Rumstein, M. O., & Hunsley, J. (2001). Interpersonal and family functioning of female survivors of childhood sexual abuse. *Clinical Psychology Review, 21*, 471–490.

Rushton, J. P. (1989). Genetic similarity, human altruism, and group selection. *Behavioral and Brain Sciences, 12*, 503–559.

Russell, J. A. (1994). Is there universal recognition of emotion from facial expressions? A review of the cross-cultural studies. *Psychological Bulletin, 115*, 102–141.

Rutter, M. (2000). Genetic studies of autism: From the 1970s into the millenium. *Journal of Abnormal Child Psychology, 28*, 3–14.

Rutter, M. L. (1997). Nature-nurture integration: The example of antisocial behavior. *American Psychologist, 52*, 390–398.

Ryan, R. M., & Lynch, J. (1989). Emotional autonomy versus detachment: Revisiting the vicissitudes of adolescence and young adulthood. *Child Development, 60*, 340–356.

Ryff, C. D., & Singer, B. (2003). Flourishing under fire: Resilience as a prototype of challenged thriving. In L. M. Keyes & J. Haidt (Eds.), *Flourishing: Positive psychology and the life well-lived.* Washington, DC: American Psychological Association.

Sabini, J., Siepmann, M., & Stein, J. (2001). The really fundamental attribution error in social psychological research. *Psychological Inquiry, 12*, 1–15.

Sachse, R., & Elliott, R. (2002). Process-outcome research on humanistic therapy variables. In D. J. Cain (Ed.), *Humanistic psychotherapies: Handbook of research and practice.* Washington, DC: American Psychological Association.

Sack, R. L., Hughes, R. J., Edgar, D. M., & Lewy, A. J. (1997). Sleep-promoting effects of melatonin: At what dose, in whom, under what conditions, and by what mechanisms? *Sleep, 20*, 908–915.

Sacks, O. (1985). *The man who mistook his wife for a hat and other clinical tales.* New York: Summit Books and Simon & Schuster.

Sacks, O. (1999). *Awakenings.* Westminster, MD: Knopf.

Saczynski, J. S., Willis, S. L., & Schaie, K. W. (2002). Strategy use in reasoning training with older adults. *Aging, Neuropsychology and Cognition, 9*, 48–60.

Sage, C. E., Southcott, A. M., & Brown, S. L. (2001). The health belief model and compliance with CPAP treatment for obstructive sleep apnea. *Behaviour Change, 18*, 177–185.

Salovey, P., & Pizzaro, D. A. (2003). The value of emotional intelligence. In R. J. Sternberg, J. Lautrey, & T. I. Lubart (Eds.), *Models of intelligence: International perspectives.* Washington, DC: American Psychological Association.

Salovey, P., Rothman, A. J., Detweiler, J. B., & Steward, W. T. (2000). Emotional states and physical health. *American Psychologist, 55*, 110–121.

Salthouse, T. A. (2004). What and when of cognitive aging. *Current Directions in Psychological Science, 13*, 140–144.

Saltz, B., Lieberman, J. A., Johns, C. A., et al. (1991). Prospective study of tardive dyskinesia incidence in the elderly. *Journal of the American Medical Association, 266*, 2402–2406.

Sandler, J. (1986). Aversion methods. In F. H. Kanfer & A. P. Goldstein (Eds.), *Helping people change: A textbook of methods* (3rd ed.). New York: Pergamon Press.

Saphier, D. (1992). Electrophysiological studies of the effects of interleukin-1 and interferon on the EEG and pituitary-adrenocortical activity. In J. J. Rothwell & R. D. Dantzer (Eds.), *Interleukin-1 in the brain.* Oxford, England: Pergamon Press.

Sarason, I. G., & Sarason, B. R. (1990). Test anxiety. In H. Leitenberg (Ed.), *Handbook of social and evaluation anxiety.* New York: Plenum Press.

Sarason, I. G., Sarason, B. R., Pierce, G. R., Shearin, E. N., & Sayers, M. H. (1991). A social learning approach to increasing blood donations. *Journal of Applied Social Psychology, 21*, 896–918.

Sataloff, J., & Thayer, R. (2006). *Hearing loss.* New York: Marcel Dekker.

Satcher, D. (1999). *Mental health: A report of the Surgeon General.* Washington, DC: U.S. Department of Health and Human Services.

Satir, V. (1967). *Conjoint family therapy.* Palo Alto, CA: Sciences and Behavior Books.

Savage-Rumbaugh, E. S., McDonald, K., Sevcik, R. A., Hopkins, W. D., & Rupert, E. (1986). Spontaneous symbol acquisition and communicative use by pygmy chimpanzees (*Pan paniscus*). *Journal of Experimental Psychology: General, 115*, 211–235.

Savage-Rumbaugh, E. S., Murphy, J., Sevcik, R. A., Brakke, K. E., et al. (1993). Language comprehension in ape and child. *Monographs of the Society for Research in Child Development, 58*(233), 1–254.

Scarr, S. (1992). Developmental theories for the 1990s: Development and individual differences. *Child Development, 63*, 1–19.

Scarr, S., & McCartney, K. (1983). How do people make their own environments: A theory of genotype environment effects. *Child Development, 54*, 424–435.

Scarr, S., & Weinberg, R. A. (1977). Intellectual similarities within families of both adopted and biological children. *Intelligence, 32*, 170–190.

Schachter, S. (1959). *The psychology of affiliation: Experimental studies of the sources of gregariousness.* Stanford, CA: Stanford University Press.

Schachter, S. (1966). The interaction of cognitive and physiological determinants of emotional state. In C. D. Spielberger (Ed.), *Anxiety and behavior.* New York: Academic Press.

Schachter, S. (1982). Recidivism and self-cure of smoking and obesity. *American Psychologist, 37*, 436–444.

Schachter, S., & Latané, B. (1964). Crime, cognition, and the autonomic nervous system. In D. Levine (Ed.), *Nebraska symposium on motivation: 1964.* Lincoln, NE: University of Nebraska Press.

Schachter, S., & Wheeler, L. (1962). Epinephrine, chlorpromazine, and amusement. *Journal of Abnormal and Social Psychology, 65*, 121–128.

Schacter, D. L. (1992). Understanding implicit memory: A cognitive neuroscience approach. *American Psychologist, 47*, 559–569.

Schaefer, A., & Philippot, P. (2005). Selective effects of emotion on the phenomenal characteristics of autobiographical memories. *Memory, 13*, 148–160.

Schafe, G. E., & LeDoux, J. E. (2002). Emotional plasticity. In H. Pashler & R. Gallistel, (Eds.), *Steven's handbook of experimental psychology: Vol. 3. Learning, motivation, and emotion* (3rd ed.). New York: Wiley.

Schaie, K. W. (1994). The course of adult intellectual development. *American Psychologist, 49*, 304–313.

Schaie, K. W. (1998). The Seattle Longitudinal Studies of adult intelligence. In M. Lawton & T. Salthouse (Eds.), *Essential papers on the psychology of aging.* New York: New York University Press.

Schaie, K. W. (2005). *Developmental influences on adult intelligence: The Seattle longitudinal study.* London: Oxford University Press.

Schaller, M., & Crandall, C. S. (Eds.). (2004). *The psychological foundations of culture.* Mahwah, NJ: Erlbaum.

Schanberg, S. M., Ingledue, V. F., Lee, J. Y., Hannun, Y. A., & Bartolome, J. V. (2003). PKC alpha mediates maternal touch regulation of growth-related gene expression in infant rats. *Neuropsychopharmacology, 28*, 1026–1030.

Schatzberg, A. F., Cole, J. O., & DeBattista, C. (2002). *Manual of clinical psychopharmacology.* Washington, DC: American Psychiatric Publishing.

Scheff, T. J. (1966). *Being mentally ill: A sociological theory*. Chicago: Aldine.

Scheier, M. F., & Carver, C. S. (1985). Optimism, coping, and health: Assessment and implications of generalized outcome expectancies. *Health Psychology, 4*, 219–247.

Scheier, M. F., Carver, C. S., & Bridges, M. W. (1994). Distinguishing optimism from neuroticism (and trait anxiety, self-mastery, and self-esteem): A re-evaluation of the Life Orientation Test. *Journal of Personality and Social Psychology, 67*, 1063–1078.

Schenck, C. H., Hurwitz, T. D., Bundlie, S. R., & Mahowald, M. W. (1991). Sleep-related eating disorders: Polysomnographic correlates of a heterogeneous syndrome distinct from daytime eating disorders. *Sleep: Journal of Sleep Research and Sleep Medicine, 14*, 419–431.

Schenck, C. H., Milner, D. M., Hurwitz, T. D., & Bundlie, S. R. (1989). A polysomnographic and clinical report on sleep-related injury in 100 adult patients. *American Journal of Psychiatry, 146*, 1166–1173.

Schiff, M., & Lewontin, R. (1986). *Education and class: The irrelevance of IQ genetic studies*. Oxford, England: Clarendon Press.

Schimanski, L. A., & Nguyen, P. V. (2005). Impaired fear memories are correlated with subregion-specific deficits in hippocampal and amygdalar LTP. *Behavioral Neuroscience, 119*, 38–54.

Schimmack, U., Oishi, S., Furr, M., & Funder, D. C. (2004). Personality and life satisfaction: A facet-level analysis. *Personality and Social Psychology Bulletin, 30*, 1062–1075.

Schlegel, A., & Barry, H. (1991). *Adolescence: An anthropological inquiry*. New York: Free Press.

Schmader, T., Johns, M., & Barquissau, M. (2004). The costs of accepting gender differences: The role of stereotype endorsement in women's experience in the math domain. *Sex Roles, 50*, 835–850.

Schmidt, F. L., & Hunter, J. (2004). General mental ability in the world of work: Occupational attainment and job performance. *Journal of Personality and Social Psychology, 86*, 162–173.

Schmitt, D. P., Shackelford, T. K., & Buss, D. M. (2001). Are men really more "oriented" toward short-term mating than women? A critical review of theory and research. *Psychology, Evolution and Gender, 3*, 211–239.

Schmolck, H., Buffalo, E. A., & Squire, L. R. (2000). Memory distortions develop over time: Recollections of the O. J. Simpson trial verdict after 15 and 32 months. *Psychological Science, 11*, 39–45.

Schneer, J. A., & Reitman, F. (1997). The interrupted managerial career path: A longitudinal study of MBAs. *Journal of Vocational Behavior, 51*, 411–434.

Schneider, W., Kron, V., Hunnerkopf, M., & Krajewski, K. (2004). The development of young children's memory strategies: First findings from the Wurzburg Longitudinal Memory Study. *Journal of Experimental Child Psychology, 88*, 193–209.

Schneiderman, N. (2004). Psychosocial, behavioral, and biological aspects of chronic diseases. *Current Directions in Psychological Science, 13*, 247–251.

Schnurr, P. P., Spiro, A., III, Aldwin, C. M., & Stukel, T. A. (1998). Physical symptom trajectories following trauma exposure: Longitudinal findings from the Normative Aging Study. *Journal of Nervous and Mental Disease, 186*, 522–528.

Schwartz, B. L. (1998). Illusory tip-of-the-tongue states. *Memory, 6*, 623–642.

Schwartz, B. L. (2002). The phenomenology of naturally occurring tip of the tongue states: A diary study. In S. P. Shohov (Ed.), *Advances in psychology research* (Vol. 8). New York: Nova Science.

Schwartz, C. E., Wright, C. I., Shin, L. M., Kagan, J., & Rauch, S. L. (2003). Inhibited and uninhibited children "grown up": Amygdalar responses to novelty. *Science, 300*, 1952–1953.

Schwartz, R. (1984). Body weight regulation. *University of Washington Medicine, 10*, 16–20.

Schwartz, S., & Maquet, P. (2002). Sleep imaging and the neuro-psychological assessment of dreams. *Trends in Cognitive Sciences, 6*, 23–30.

Schwarzer, R. (1998). Stress and coping from a social-cognitive perspective. *Annals of the New York Academy of Sciences, 851*, 531–537.

Schweinhart, L. J., & Weikart, D. P. (1998). High/Scope Perry Preschool Program effects at age twenty-seven. In J. Crane (Ed.), *Social programs that work*. New York: Russell Sage.

Scoboria, A., Mazzoni, G., Kirsch, I., & Milling, L. S. (2002). Immediate and persisting effects of misleading questions and hypnosis on memory reports. *Journal of Experimental Psychology: Applied, 8*, 26–32.

Scott, T. R. (1992). Taste, feeding, and pleasure. In A. N. Epstein et al. (Eds.), *Progress in psychobiology and physiological psychology*. San Diego, CA: Academic Press.

Scott, T. R., & Giza, B. K. (1993). Gustatory control of ingestion. In D. A. Booth et al. (Eds.), *Neurophysiology of ingestion. Pergamon studies in neuroscience*. Oxford, England: Pergamon Press.

Scott, W. D., & Cervone, D. (2002). The impact of negative affect on performance standards: Evidence for an affect as information mechanism. *Cognitive Therapy and Research, 26*, 9–37.

Sears, R. R. (1977). Sources of life satisfaction of the Terman gifted men. *American Psychologist, 32*, 119–128.

Seattle Times. (1997, December 11). Paralyzed woman is good Samaritan, p. B3.

Sedikides, C., Gaertner, L., & Toguchi, Y. (2003). Pancultural self-enhancement. *Journal of Personality and Social Psychology, 84*, 60–79.

Segall, M. H., Campbell, D. T., & Herskowitz, M. J. (1966). *The influence of culture on visual perception*. New York: Pergamon Press.

Segerstrom, S. C., & Miller, G. E. (2004). Psychological stress and the human immune system. A meta-analytic study of 30 years of inquiry. *Psychological Bulletin, 130*, 601–630.

Sekuler, R., Watamaniuk, S., & Blake, R. (2002). In H. Pashler & S. Yantis (Eds.), *Steven's handbook of experimental psychology: Vol. 1. Sensation and perception* (3rd ed.). New York: Wiley.

Seligman, M. E. P. (1970). On the generality of the laws of learning. *Psychological Review, 77*, 406–418.

Seligman, M. E. P. (1971). Phobias and preparedness. *Behavior Therapy, 2*, 307–320.

Seligman, M. E. P. (1975). *Helplessness: On depression, development, and death*. New York: Freeman.

Seligman, M. E. P. (1991). *Learned optimisim*. New York: Knopf.

Seligman, M. E. P. (1995). The effectiveness of psychotherapy: The *Consumer Reports* study. *American Psychologist, 50*, 965–974.

Seligman, M. E. P. (2002). *Authentic happiness: Using the new positive psychology to realize your potential for lasting fulfillment*. New York: Free Press.

Seligman, M. E. P., & Binik, Y. M. (1977). The safety signal hypothesis. In H. Davis & H. Hurvitz (Eds.), *Pavlovian-operant interactions*. Hillsdale, NJ: Erlbaum.

Seligman, M. E. P., & Isaacowitz, D. M. (2000). Learned helplessness. In G. Fink (Ed.), *Encyclopedia of stress*. San Diego, CA: Academic Press.

Seligman, M.E.P., & Peterson, C. R. (Eds.). (2004). *Human strengths: A classification manual*. New York: Oxford University Press.

Selye, H. (1975). *Stress without distress*. New York: New American Library.

Selye, H. (1976). *The stress of life* (Rev. ed.) New York: McGraw-Hill.

Senden, M. von. (1960). *Space and sight: The perception of space and shape in the congenitally blind before and after operation* (P. Heath, Trans.). New York: Free Press.

Sergios, P. A., & Cody, J. (1985–1986). Importance of physical attractiveness and social assertiveness skills in male homosexual dating behavior and partner selection. *Journal of Homosexuality, 12*, 71–84.

Serpell, R. (2000). Intelligence and culture. In R. J. Sternberg (Ed.). (2000). *Handbook of intelligence*. New York: Cambridge University Press.

Seto, M. C., & Barbaree, H. E. (1995). The role of alcohol in sexual aggression. *Clinical Psychology Review, 15*, 545–566.

Sexton, M. M. (1979). Behavioral epidemiology. In O. F. Pomerleau & J. P. Brady (Eds.), *Behavioral Medicine: Theory and Practice*. Baltimore, MD: Williams & Wilkins.

Shaffer, D. R. (1989). *Developmental psychology: Childhood and adolescence* (2nd ed.). Pacific Grove, CA: Brooks/Cole.

Shallice, T., & Burgess, P. (1991). Higher-order cognitive impairments and frontal-lobe lesions in man. In H. S. Levin, H. M. Eisenberg, & A. L. Benton (Eds.), *Frontal lobe function and dysfunction*. New York: Oxford University Press.

Shanab, M. E., & Yahya, L. A. (1977). A behavioral study of obedience in children. *Journal of Personality and Social Psychology, 35,* 530–536.

Shapiro, A. K., & Shapiro, E. (1997). *The powerful placebo: From ancient priest to modern physician.* Baltimore: Johns Hopkins University Press.

Shapiro, C. M., Bortz, R., Mitchell, D., Bartel, P., & Jooste, P. (1981). Slow-wave sleep: A recovery period after exercise. *Science, 214,* 1253–1254.

Shaver, P., Hazan, C., & Bradshaw, D. (1988). Love as attachment: The integration of three behavioral systems. In R. J. Sternberg & M. L. Barnes (Eds.), *The psychology of love.* New Haven, CT: Yale University Press.

Shaver, P. R., & Clark, C. L. (1996). Forms of adult romantic attachment and their cognitive and emotional underpinnings. In G. G. Noam et al. (Eds.), *Development and vulnerability in close relationships. The Jean Piaget symposium series.* Mahwah, NJ: Erlbaum.

Shavit, Y. (1990). Stress-induced immune modulation in animals: Opiates and endogenous opioid peptides. In R. Ader, N. Cohen, & D. L. Felten (Eds.), *Psychoneuroimmunology II.* New York: Academic Press.

Sheehan, P. W., Green, V., & Truesdale, P. (1992). Influence of rapport on hypnotically induced pseudomemory. *Journal of Abnormal Psychology, 101,* 690–700.

Shek, D. T. L. (1998). A longitudinal study of the relations between parent-adolescent conflict and adolescent psychological well-being. *Journal of Genetic Psychology, 159,* 53–67.

Sheldon, K. M, Joiner, T. E., Pettit, J. W., & Williams, G. (2003). Reconciling humanistic ideals and scientific clinical practice. *Clinical Psychology: Science and Practice, 10,* 302–315.

Sheldon, K. M., & Kasser, T. (2001). Getting older, getting better? Personal strivings and psychological maturity across the life span. *Developmental Psychology, 37,* 491–501.

Shepard, R. N., & Metzler, J. (1971). Mental rotation of three-dimensional objects. *Science, 171,* 701–703.

Shepherd, G. (1997). *The synaptic organizer of the brain.* New York: Oxford University Press.

Shepperd, J. A., Grace, J., Cole, L. J., & Kline, C. (2005). Anxiety and outcome predictions. *Personality and Social Psychology Bulletin, 31,* 267–275.

Sherif, M. (1935). A study of some social factors in perception. *Archives of Psychology* (No. 187).

Sherif, M., Harvey, O., White, B., Hood, W., & Sherif, C. (1961). *Intergroup conflict and cooperation: The Robbers Cave experiment.* Norman: University of Oklahoma Press.

Shneidman, E. S. (1976). A psychological theory of suicide. *Psychiatric Annals, 6,* 51–66.

Shneidman, E. S. (1998). *The suicidal mind.* New York: Oxford University Press.

Shoda, Y., & Mischel, W. (2000). Reconciling contextualism with the core assumptions of personality psychology. *European Journal of Personality, 14,* 407–428.

Shoda, Y., Mischel, W., & Wright, J. C. (1994). Intra-individual stability and patterning of behavior: Incorporating psychological situations into the idiographic analysis of personality. *Journal of Personality and Social Psychology, 67,* 674–687.

Shorter, E. (1998). *A history of psychiatry: From the era of the asylum to the age of Prozac.* New York: Wiley.

Shultz, K. S., Morton, K. R., & Weckerle, J. R. (1998). The influence of push and pull factors on voluntary and involuntary early retirees' retirement decision and adjustment. *Journal of Vocational Behavior, 53,* 45–57.

Sia, C. L., Tan, B. C. Y., & Wei, K. K. (2002). Group polarization and computer mediated communication: Effects of communication cues, social presence, and anonymity. *Information Systems Research, 13,* 70–90.

Siegel, A. (2005). *Neurobiology of aggression and rage.* San Francisco: Taylor & Francis.

Siegel, S. (1984). Pavlovian conditioning and heroin overdose: Reports from overdose victims. *Bulletin of the Psychonomic Society, 22,* 428–430.

Siegel, S., & Allan, L. G. (1996). The widespread influence of the Rescorla-Wagner model. *Psychonomic Bulletin and Review, 3,* 314–321.

Siegel, S., Baptista, M. A. S., Kim, J. A., McDonald, R. V., & Weise-Kelly, L. (2000). Pavlovian psychopharmacology: The associative basis of tolerance. *Experimental and Clinical Psychopharmacology, 8,* 276–293.

Siegler, R. S. (1986). *Children's thinking.* Englewood Cliffs, NJ: Prentice Hall.

Siegler, R. S. (1996). *Emerging minds: The process of change in children's thinking.* New York: Oxford University Press.

Sigala, N., & Logothetis, N. K. (2002). Visual categorization shapes feature selectivity in the primate temporal cortex. *Nature, 415,* 318–320.

Silverman, K., Wong, C. J., Grabinski, M. J., Hampton, J., Sylvest, C. E., Dillon, E. M., & Wentland, R. D. (2005). A web-based therapeutic workplace for the treatment of drug addiction and chronic unemployment. *Behavior Modification, 29,* 417–463.

Simkin, L. R., & Gross, A. M. (1994). Assessment of coping with high risk situations for exercise relapse among healthy women. *Health Psychology, 13,* 274–277.

Simon, H. A. (1990). Invariants of human behavior. *Annual Review of Psychology, 41,* 1–20.

Simons, D. J., & Chabris, C. F. (1999). Gorillas in our midst: Sustained inattentional blindness for dynamic events. *Perception, 28,* 1059–1074.

Simonton, D. K. (1999). Creativity and genius. In L. A. Pervin & O. P. John (Eds.), *Handbook of personality: Theory and research* (2nd ed). New York: Guilford Press.

Simonton, D. K. (2001). Talent development as a multidimensional, multiplicative, and dynamic process. *Current Directions in Psychological Science, 10,* 39–43.

Simpaio, E., Maris, S., & Bach-y-Rita, P. (2001). Brain plasticity: "Visual" acuity of blind persons via the tongue. *Brain Research, 908,* 204–207.

Singer, T., Seymour, B., O'Doherty, J., Kaube, H., Dolan, R. J., & Frith, C. D. (2004). Empathy for pain involves the affective but not sensory components of pain. *Science, 303,* 1157–1162.

Singer, T., Verhaeghen, P., Ghisletta, P., Lindenberger, U., & Baltes, P. B. (2003). The fate of cognition in very old age: Six-year longitudinal findings in the Berlin Aging Study (BASE). *Psychology and Aging, 18,* 318–331.

Sistler, A. B., & Moore, G. M. (1996). Cultural diversity in coping with marital stress. *Journal of Clinical Geropsychology, 2,* 77–82.

Siu, O. (2003). Job stress and job performance among employees in Hong Kong: The role of Chinese work values and organizational commitment. *International Journal of Psychology, 38,* 337–347.

Skinner, B. F. (1938). *The behavior of organisms: An experimental analysis.* New York: Appleton-Century-Crofts.

Skinner, B. F. (1948). *Walden two.* New York: Macmillan.

Skinner, B. F. (1953). *Science and human behavior.* New York: Macmillan.

Skinner, B. F. (1957). *Verbal behavior.* New York: Prentice Hall.

Skinner, B. F. (1968). *The technology of teaching.* New York: Appleton-Century-Crofts.

Skinner, B. F. (1971). *Beyond freedom and dignity.* New York: Knopf.

Skinner, B. F. (1989a). The origins of cognitive thought. *American Psychologist, 44,* 13–18.

Skinner, B. F. (1989b). Teaching machines. *Science, 243,* 1535.

Skinner, B. F. (1990). Can psychology be a science of mind? *American Psychologist, 45,* 1206–1210.

Sklar, L. S., & Anisman, H. (1981). Stress and cancer. *Psychological Bulletin, 89,* 369–406.

Skotko, B. G., Kensinger, E. A., Locascio, J. J., Einstein, G., Rubin, D. C., Tupler, L. A., Krendl, A., & Corkin, S. (2004). Puzzling thoughts for H. M.: Can new semantic information be anchored to old semantic memories? *Neuropsychology, 18,* 756–769.

Skoyles, J. R. (1997). Evolution's 'missing link': A hypothesis upon neural plasticity, prefrontal working memory and the origins of modern cognition. *Medical Hypotheses, 48,* 499–501.

Slater, C. L. (2003). Generativity versus stagnation: An elaboration of Erikson's adult stage of human development. *Journal of Adult Development, 10,* 53–65.

Sloan, D., & Marx, D. (2004). A closer examination of the structured written disclosure procedure. *Journal of Consulting and Clinical Psychology, 72,* 165–175.

Slovic, P., Fischhoff, B., & Lichtenstein, S. (1988). Response mode, framing, and information-processing effects in risk assessment. In D. E. Bell & H. Raiffa (Eds.), *Decision making:*

Descriptive, normative, and prescriptive inter-actions. New York: Cambridge University Press.

Smalley, S. L., McGough, J. J., Del'Homme, M., et al. (2000). Familial clustering of symptoms and disruptive behaviors in multiplex families with attention-deficit/hyperactivity disorder. *Journal of the American Academy of Child & Adolescent Psychiatry, 39,* 1135–1143.

Smetana, J. (1988). Adolescents' and parents' conceptions of parental authority. *Child Development, 59,* 321–335.

Smith, B. D. (1998). *Psychology: Science and understanding.* New York: McGraw-Hill.

Smith, C. A., & Kirby, L. D. (2004). Appraisal as a pervasive determinant of anger. *Emotion, 4,* 133–138.

Smith, C. S., Folkard, S., Schmieder, R. A., Parra, L. F., Spelten, E., Almiral, H., et al. (2002). Investigation of morning-evening orientation in six countries using the preferences scale. *Personality and Individual Differences, 32,* 949–968.

Smith, C. T., Nixon, M. R., Nader, R. S. (2004). Posttraining increases in REM sleep intensity implicate REM sleep in memory processing and provide a biological marker of learning potential. *Learning & Memory, 11,* 714–719.

Smith, D. (2002). The theory heard 'round the world. *Monitor on Psychology, 33,* No. 9., October. Retrieved December 18, 2004, from http://www.apa.org/monitor/oct02/theory.html

Smith, E. R., & Zarate, M. A. (1992). Exemplar-based model of social judgment. *Psychological Review, 99,* 3–21.

Smith, J. W., & Frawley, P. J. (1993). Treatment outcome of 600 chemically dependent patients treated in a multimodal inpatient program including aversion therapy and pentothal interviews. *Journal of Substance Abuse Treatment, 10,* 359–369.

Smith, M. C., & Phillips, M. R., Jr. (2001). Age differences in memory for radio adver-tisements: The role of mnemonic. *Journal of Business Research, 53,* 103–109.

Smith, M. L., & Glass, G. V. (1977). Meta-analyses of psychotherapy outcome studies. *American Psychologist, 32,* 752–760.

Smith, R. E. (1989). Effects of coping skills training on generalized self-efficacy and locus of control. *Journal of Personality and Social Psychology, 56,* 228–233.

Smith, R. E. (1996). Performance anxiety, cognitive interference, and concentration enhancement strategies in sports. In I. G. Sarason, G. R. Pierce, & B. R. Sarason (Eds.), *Cognitive interference: Theories, methods, and findings.* Mahwah, NJ: Erlbaum.

Smith, R. E., Leffingwell, T. R., & Ptacek, J. T. (1999). Can people remember how they coped? Factors associated with discordance between same-day and retrospective reports. *Journal of Personality and Social Psychology, 76,* 1050–1061.

Smith, R. E., Smoll, F. L., & Schultz, R. W. (1990). Measurement and correlates of sport-specific cognitive and somatic trait anxiety: The Sports Anxiety Scale. *Anxiety Research* [now *Anxiety, Stress, & Coping*], *2,* 263–280.

Smith, S. M., McIntosh, W. D., & Bazzini, D. G. (1999). Are the beautiful good in Hollywood? An investigation of the beauty-and-goodness stereotype on film. *Basic and Applied Social Psychology, 21,* 69–80.

Smith, S. M., & Vela, E. (2001). Environmental context dependent memory: A review and meta-analysis. *Psychonomic Bulletin and Review, 8,* 203–220.

Smithson, J., Lewis, S., Cooper, C., & Dyer, J. (2004). Flexible working and the gender pay gap in the accountancy profession. *Work, Employment and Society, 18,* 115–135.

Smoll, F. L., Smith, R. E., Barnett, N. P., & Everett, J. J. (1993). Enhancement of children's self-esteem through social support training for youth sport coaches. *Journal of Applied Psychology, 78,* 602–610.

Snow, M. E., Jacklin, C. N., & Maccoby, E. E. (1983). Sex-of-child-differences in father-child interaction at one year of age. *Child Development, 54,* 227–232.

Snyder, C. R. (Ed.). (2001). *Coping with stress: Effective people and processes.* New York: Oxford University Press.

Snyder, C. R., & Ingram, R. E. (Eds.). (2000). *Handbook of psychological change: Psycho-therapy processes & practices for the 21st century.* Mahwah, NJ: Erlbaum.

Snyder, M. (1987). *Public appearances/private realities: The psychology of self-monitoring.* New York: Freeman.

Snyder, M., Clary, E. G., & Stukas, A. A. (2000). The functional approach to volunteerism. In G. R. Maio & J. M. Olson. *Why we evaluate: Functions of attitudes.* Mahwah, NJ: Erlbaum.

Snyder, S. H. (1977). Opiate receptors and internal opiates. *Scientific American, 236,* 44–56.

Solms, M. (2002). Dreaming: Cholinergic and dopaminergic hypotheses. In E. Perry, H. Ashton, & A. Young (Eds.), *Neurochemistry of consciousness: Neurotransmitters in mind. Advances in consciousness research.* Amsterdam: Benjamins.

Solomon, R. L., & Wynne, L. C. (1953). Traumatic avoidance learning: Acquisition in normal dogs. *Journal of Abnormal and Social Psychology, 48,* 291–302.

Son, L. K., & Metcalfe, J. (2000). Metacognitive and control strategies in study-time allocation. *Journal of Experimental Psychology: Learning, Memory, and Cognition, 26,* 204–221.

Soussignan, R. (2002). Duchenne smile, emotional experience, and autonomic reactivity: A test of the facial feedback hypothesis. *Emotion, 2,* 52–74.

Sowell, E. R., Thompson, P. M., Tessner, K. D., & Toga, A. W. (2001). Mapping continued brain growth and gray matter density reduction in dorsal frontal cortex: Inverse relationships during postadolescent brain maturation. *Journal of Neuroscience, 21,* 8819–8829.

Spanos, N. P. (1986). Hypnotic behavior: A social-psychological interpretation of amnesia, analgesia, and "trance logic." *Behavioral and Brain Sciences, 9,* 449–467.

Spanos, N. P. (1991). A sociocognitive approach to hypnosis. In S. J. Lynn & J. W. Rhue (Eds.), *Theories of hypnosis: Current models and perspectives.* New York: Guilford Press.

Spanos, N. P. (1994). Multiple identity enactments and multiple personality disorder: A sociocognitive perspective. *Psychological Bulletin, 116,* 143–165.

Spanos, N. P. (1996). *Multiple identities and false memories: A sociocognitive perspective.* Washington, DC: American Psychological Association.

Spanos, N. P., & Chaves, J. F. (Eds.). (1988). *Hypnosis: The cognitive-behavioral perspective.* Buffalo, NY: Prometheus Books.

Spear, L. P. (2000). The adolescent brain and age-related behavioral manifestations. *Neuroscience & Biobehavioral Reviews, 24,* 417–463.

Spearman, C. (1923). *The nature of "intelligence" and the principles of cognition.* London: Macmillan.

Speisman, J., Lazarus, R. S., Mordkoff, A., & Davidson, L. (1964). Experimental reduction of stress based on ego-defense theory. *Journal of Abnormal and Social Psychology, 68,* 367–380.

Spelke, E. S. (1994). Initial knowledge: Six sugges-tions. *Cognition, 46,* 29–56.

Spencer, S. J., Steele, C. M., & Quinn, D. M. (1999). Stereotype threat and women's math performance. *Journal of Experimental Social Psychology, 35,* 4–28.

Sperling, G. (1960). The information available in brief visual presentations. *Psychological Monographs, 74*(Whole No. 11).

Sperling, G. (1984). A unified theory of attention and signal detection. In R. Parasuraman & D. R. Davies (Eds.), *Varieties of attention.* New York: Academic Press.

Sperry, R. W. (1970). Perception in the absence of neocortical commissures. In Association for Research in Nervous and Mental Disease, *Perception and its disorders.* New York: Williams & Wilkins.

Spiegel, D., Bloom, J. R., Kraemer, H. C., & Gottlieb, E. (1989, October 14). Effect of psychosocial treatment on survival of patients with metastatic breast cancer. *The Lancet,* 888–891.

Spiegler, M. D., & Guevremont, D. C. (2003). *Contemporary behavior therapy.* Belmont, CA: Wadsworth.

Spielberger, C. D., & DeNike, L. D. (1966). Descriptive behaviorism versus cognitive theory in verbal operant conditioning. *Psychological Review, 73,* 306–326.

Spitzer, R. L., Skodol, A. E., Gibbon, M., & Williams, J. B. W. (1983). *Psychopathology: A casebook.* New York: McGraw-Hill.

Sporting News (1985, August 19).

Sprafkin, J. N., Liebert, R. M., & Poulos, R. W. (1975). Effects of a prosocial televised example on children's helping. *Journal of Experimental Child Psychology, 20,* 119–126.

Sprecher, S. (2001). A comparison of emotional consequences of and change in equity over time using global and domain specific measures of equity. *Journal of Social and Personal Relationships, 18,* 477–501.

Sprecher, S., & Regan, P. C. (1998). Passionate and companionate love in courting and young married couples. *Sociological Inquiry, 68,* 163–185.

Springer, S. (1997). *Left brain, right brain.* San Francisco: Freeman.

Squier, L. H., & Domhoff, G. W. (1998). The presentation of dreaming and dreams in introductory psychology textbooks: A critical examination with suggestions for textbook authors and course instructors. *Dreaming: Journal of the Association for the Study of Dreams, 8,* 149–168.

Squire, L. R. (1987). *Memory and brain.* Oxford, England: Oxford University Press.

Squire, L. R., Stark, C. E. L., & Clark, R. E. (2004). The medial temporal lobe. *Annual Review of Neuroscience, 27,* 279–306.

Squire, L. R., & Zola-Morgan, S. (1991). The medial temporal lobe memory system. *Science, 253,* 1380–1386.

Sroufe, L. (2002). From infant attachment to promotion of adolescent autonomy: Prospective, longitudinal data on the role of parents in development. In J. G. Borkowski, S. L. Ramey, & M. Bristol-Power (Eds.), *Parenting and the child's world: Influences on academic, intellectual, and social-emotional development. Monographs in parenting.* Mahwah, NJ: Erlbaum.

Stahl, S. M. (1998). *Essential psychopharmacology: Neuroscientific basis and clinical applications.* New York: Cambridge University Press.

Stanley, B. G., Kyrkouli, S. E., Lampert, S., & Leibowitz, S. F. (1986). Neuropeptide Y chronically injected into the hypothalamus: A powerful neurochemical inducer of hyperphagia and obesity. *Peptides, 7,* 1189–1192.

Stanley, S. M., Whitton, S. W., & Markman, H. J. (2004). Maybe I do: Interpersonal commitment and premarital or nonmarital cohabitation. *Journal of Family Issues, 25,* 496–519.

Stark, E. (1989, May). Teen sex: Not for love. *Psychology Today,* 10–11.

Statistics Canada. (2002). English-French Bilingualism. 2001 Census (release date December 10, 2002). Retrieved April 6, 2005, from http://www12.statcan.ca/english/census01/products/analytic/companion/lang/bilingual.cfm

Steadman, H. J., Mulvey, E. P., Monahan, J., Robbins, P. C., Appelbaum, P. S., Grisso, T., Roth, L., & Silver, E. (1998). Violence by people discharged from acute inpatient facilities and by others in the same neighborhoods. *Archives of General Psychiatry, 55,* 393–401.

Stearns, S., & Hoekstra, R. (2005). *Evolution.* New York: Oxford University Press.

Steckler, T., Kalin, N. H., & Reul, J. (2005). *Handbook of stress and the brain: Part 2. Stress: integrative and clinical aspects.* Amsterdam: Elsevier Science and Technology.

Steele, C. M. (1997). A threat in the air: How stereotypes shape intellectual identity and performance. *American Psychologist, 52,* 613–629.

Steele, C. M., & Aronson, J. (1995). Stereotype threat and the intellectual test performance of African Americans. *Journal of Personality and Social Psychology, 69,* 797–811.

Steele, C. M., & Josephs, R. A. (1990). Alcohol myopia: Its prized and dangerous effects. *American Psychologist, 45,* 921–933.

Steele, J., James, J. B., & Barnett, R. C. (2002). Learning in a man's world: Examining the perceptions of undergraduate women in male-dominated academic areas. *Psychology of Women Quarterly, 26,* 46–50.

Stein, D. J., & Hollander, E. (2002). *Textbook of anxiety disorders.* Washington, DC: American Psychiatric Press.

Steinberg, L., Lamborn, S. D., Darling, N., & Mount, N. S. (1994). Over-time changes in adjustment and competence among adolescents from authoritative, authoritarian, indulgent, and neglectful families. *Child Development, 65,* 754–770.

Stephan, W. G. (1990). School desegregation: Short-term and long-term effects. In H. Knopke (Ed.), *Opening doors: An appraisal of race relations in America.* Tuscaloosa: University of Alabama Press.

Steptoe, A. (2000). Control and stress. In G. Fink (Ed.), *Encyclopedia of stress.* San Diego, CA: Academic Press.

Sternberg, K. J., Lamb, M. E., Esplin, P. W., Opbach, Y., & Hershkowitz, I. (2002). Using a structure interview protocol to improve the quality of investigative interviews. In M. L. Eisen (Ed.), *Memory and suggestibility in the forensic interview: Personality and Clinical Psychology Series.* Mahwah, NJ: Erlbaum.

Sternberg, R. J. (1988). Triangulating love. In R. J. Sternberg & M. L. Barnes (Eds.), *The psychology of love.* New Haven, CT: Yale University Press.

Sternberg, R. J. (1997). Construct validation of a triangular love scale. *European Journal of Social Psychology, 27,* 313–335.

Sternberg, R. J. (1998). A balance theory of wisdom. *Review of General Psychology, 2,* 347–365.

Sternberg, R. J. (2004). Culture and intelligence. *American Psychologist, 59,* 325–338.

Sternberg, R. J., & Davidson, J. E. (Eds.). (2005). *Conceptions of giftedness.* New York: Cambridge University Press.

Sternberg, R. J., Lautrey, J., & Lubart, T. I. (2003). *Models of intelligence: International perspectives.* Washington, DC: American Psychological Association.

Sternberg, R. J., Nokes, C., Geissler, P., Prince, R., Okatcha, F., Bundy, D. A., & Grigorenko, E. L. (2001). The relationship between academic and practical intelligence: A case study in Kenya. *Intelligence, 29,* 401–418.

Sternberg, R. J., Torff, B., & Grigorenko, E. L. (1998). Teaching triarchically improves school achievement. *Journal of Educational Psychology, 90,* 374–384.

Stetson, B. A., Rahn, J. M., Dubbert, P. M., Wilner, B. I., & Mercury, M. G. (1997). Prospective evaluation of the effects of stress on exercise adherence in community-residing women. *Health Psychology, 16,* 515–520.

Stiles, W. B., Leach, C., Barkham, M., et al. (2003). Early sudden gains in psychotherapy under routine clinic conditions: Practice-based evidence. *Journal of Consulting and Clinical Psychology, 71,* 14–21.

Stockhorst, U., Spennes-Saleh, S., Korholz, D., Gobel, U., Schneider, M. E., Steingruber, H.-J., & Klosterhalfen, S. (2000). Anticipatory symptoms and anticipatory immune responses in pediatric cancer patients receiving chemotherapy: Features of a classically conditioned response? *Brain, Behavior and Immunity, 14,* 198–218.

Stoddard, J., Raine, A., Bihrle, S., & Buchsbaum, M. (1997). Prefrontal dysfunction in murderers lacking psychosocial deficits. In A. Raine, P. A. Brennan, D. P. Farrington, & S. A. Mednick (Eds.), *Biosocial bases of violence* (pp. 301–305). New York: Plenum Press.

Stone, A. A., Shiffman, S. S., & DeVries, M. (2000). Rethinking our self-report assessment methodologies: An argument for collecting ecologically valid, momentary measurements. In D. Kahneman, E. Diener, & N. Schwarz (Eds.), *Understanding quality of life: Scientific perspectives on enjoyment and suffering.* New York: Russel Sage.

Stone, J., & Cooper, J. (2003). The effect of self-attribute relevance on how self-esteem moderates attitude change in dissonance processes. *Journal of Experimental Social Psychology, 39,* 508–515.

Stone, K., & Church, S. L. (1968). *Personality theories.* San Francisco: Jossey-Bass.

Stone, M. H. (1986). Borderline personality disorder. In R. Michels & J. O. Cavenar (Eds.), *Psychiatry* (Vol. 1). New York: Basic Books.

Stormshak, E. A., Bierman, K. L., McMahon, R. J., Lengua, L. J., & Conduct Problems Prevention Research Group. (2000). Parenting practices and child disruptive behavior problems in early elementary school. *Journal of Clinical Child Psychology, 29,* 17–29.

Stouffer, S. A., Lumsdaine, A. A., Lumsdaine, M. H., & Williams, R. M., Jr. (1949a). *The American soldier: Combat and its aftermath.* Princeton, NJ: Princeton University Press.

Stouffer, S. A., Suchman, E. A., De Vinney, L. C., Star, S. A., & Williams, R. M., Jr. (1949b). *The American soldier: Adjustments during army life.* Princeton, NJ: Princeton University Press.

Strack, F., Martin, L. L., & Stepper, S. (1988). Inhibiting and facilitating conditions of facial expressions: A non-obtrusive test of the facial feedback hypothesis. *Journal of Personality and Social Psychology, 54,* 768–777.

Straus, M. A., & Stewart, J. H. (1999). Corporal punishment by American parents: National data on prevalence, chronicity, severity, and duration, in relation to child and family characteristics. *Clinical Child and Family Psychology Review, 2*(2), 55–70.

Strawbridge, W. J., Shema, S. J., Cohen, R. D., Roberts, R. E., & Kaplan, G. A. (1998). Religion buffers effects of some stressors on depression but exacerbates others. *Journal of Gerontology, 53*, 118–126.

Streissguth, A. P. (1977). Maternal drinking and the outcome of pregnancy: Implications for child mental health. *American Journal of Orthopsychiatry, 47*, 422–431.

Streissguth, A. P. (2001). Recent advances in fetal alcohol syndrome and alcohol use in pregnancy. In D. P. Agarwal & H. K. Seitz (Eds.), *Alcohol in health and disease.* New York: Marcel Dekker.

Streissguth, A. P., Clarren, S. K., & Jones, K. L. (1985). Natural history of the fetal alcohol syndrome: A 10-year follow-up of eleven patients. *The Lancet, 2*(8446), 85–91.

Strentz, T., & Auerbach, S. M. (1988). Adjustment to the stress of simulated captivity: Effects of emotion-focused versus problem-focused preparation on hostages differing in locus of control. *Journal of Personality and Social Psychology, 55*, 652–660.

Striedter, G. F. (2005). *Principles of brain evolution.* Springfield, IL: Sinauer.

Strober, M., & Humphrey, L. L. (1987). Familial contributions to the etiology and course of anorexia nervosa and bulimia. *Journal of Consulting and Clinical Psychology, 55*, 654–659.

Stroebe, M., Stroebe, W., & Schut, H. (2001). Gender differences in adjustment to bereavement: An empirical and theoretical review. *Review of General Psychology, 5*, 62–82.

Stryer, L. (1987). The molecules of visual excitation. *Scientific American, 257*(1), 42–50.

Subramanian, K. N. S., Yoon, H., & Toral, J. C. (2002, October 31). *Extremely low birth weight infant.* Available online: http://www.emedicine.com/ped/topic2784.htm

Sue, D. W., & Sue, D. (1990). *Counseling the culturally different: Theory and practice.* New York: Wiley.

Sue, S. (1998). In search of cultural competence in psychotherapy and counseling. *American Psychologist, 53*, 440–448.

Sue, S., & Chu, J. (2003). The mental health of ethnic minority groups: Challenges posed by the U.S. Surgeon General. *Culture, Medicine and Psychiatry, 27*, 447–465.

Sue, S., Fujino, D., Hu, L., Takeuchi, D., & Zane, N. (1991). Community mental health services for ethnic minority groups: A test of the cultural responsiveness hypothesis. *Journal of Consulting and Clinical Psychology, 59*, 533–540.

Sue, S., & Zane, N. (1987). The role of culture and cultural techniques in psychotherapy. *American Psychologist, 42*, 37–45.

Sugita, Y. (2004). Experience in early infancy is indispensable for color perception. *Current Biology, 14*, 1267–1271.

Suh, E., Diener, E., Oishi, S., & Triandis, H. (1998). The shifting basis of life satisfaction judgments across cultures: Emotions versus norms. *Journal of Personality and Social Psychology, 74*, 482–493.

Suinn, R. M., Osborne, D., & Winfree, P. (1962). The self-concept and accuracy of recall of inconsistent self-related information. *Journal of Clinical Psychology, 18*, 473–474.

Sullivan, M. A., & O'Leary, S. G. (1990). Maintenance following reward and cost token programs. *Behavior Therapy, 21*, 139–149.

Suls, J. M., & Wallston, K. A. (2003). *Social psychological foundations of health and illness.* New York: Blackwell.

Sun, M.-K. (Ed.). (2005). *Cognition and mood interreactions.* Hauppauge, NY: Nova Science.

Sun, W. L., & Rebec, G. V. (2005). The role of prefrontal cortex D1-like and D2-like receptors in cocaine-seeking behavior in rats. *Psychopharmacology, 177*, 315–323.

Sunnafrank, M., Ramirez, A., Jr., & Metts, S. (Ed.). (2004). At first sight: Persistent relational effects of get-acquainted conversations. *Journal of Social and Personal Relationships, 21*, 361–379.

Super, D. E. (1957). *The psychology of careers.* New York: Harper & Row.

Sussman, N. M., & Rosenfeld, H. M. (1982). Influence of culture, language, and sex on conversational distance. *Journal of Personality and Social Psychology, 42*, 66–74.

Sutton, S. K. (2002). Incentive and threat reactivity: Relations with anterior cortical activity. In D. Cervone & W. Mischel (Eds.), *Advances in personality science.* New York: Guilford Press.

Swain, J. C., & McLaughlin, T. F. (1998). The effects of bonus contingencies in a classwide token program on math accuracy with middle-school students with behavioral disorders. *Behavioral Interventions, 13*, 11–19.

Swann, W. B., Jr., Rentfrow, P. J., & Guinn, J. S. (2002). Self-verification: The search for coherence. In C. R. Snyder & S. J. Lopez (Eds.), *Handbook of positive psychology.* New York: Oxford University Press.

Swann, W. B., Jr., Stein-Seroussi, A., & Giesler, R. B. (1992). Why people self-verify. *Journal of Personality and Social Psychology, 62*, 392–401.

Swartz, C. (1995). Setting the ECT stimulus. *Psychiatric Times, 12*(6). (Reprint addition)

Syka, J., & Merzenich, M. M. (2005). Plasticity and signal representation in the auditory system. New York: Springer.

Szasz, T. (1963). *Law, liberty, and psychiatry: An inquiry into the social uses of mental health practices.* New York: Collier Books.

Szasz, T. S. (2004). *Faith in freedom: Libertarian principles and psychiatric practices.* Somerset, NJ: Transaction Publishers.

Szkrybalo, J., & Ruble, D. N. (1999). "God made me a girl": Sex-category constancy judgments and explanations revisited. *Developmental Psychology, 35*, 392–402.

Taglialatela, J. P., Savage-Rumbaugh, S., & Baker, L. A. (2003). Vocal production by a language-competent *Pan paniscus. International Journal of Primatology, 24*, 1–17.

Tajfel, H., & Turner, J. C. (1986). The social identity theory of intergroup behavior. In S. Worchel & W. G. Austin (Eds.), *The psychology of intergroup relations* (2nd ed.). Chicago, IL: Nelson Hall.

Takahashi, H., Yahata, N., Koeda, M., Matsuda, T., Asai, K., & Okubo, Y. (2004). Brain activation associated with evaluative processes of guilt and embarrassment: An fMRI study. *Neuroimage, 23*, 967–974.

Takahashi, Y. (1990). Is multiple personality disorder really rare in Japan? *Dissociation: Progress in the Dissociative Disorders, 3*, 57–59.

Talarico, J. M., & Rubin, D. C. (2003). Confidence, not consistency, characterizes flashbulb memories. *Psychological Science, 14*, 455–461.

Tamminga, C. A. (1997). The promise of new drugs for schizophrenia treatment. *Canadian Journal of Psychiatry, 42*, 265–273.

Tanaka-Matsumi, J. (1979). Taijin Kyofushu: Diagnostic and cultural issues in Japanese psychiatry. *Culture, Medicine, and Psychiatry, 3*, 231–245.

Tanaka-Matsumi, J., & Draguns, J. G. (1997). Culture and psychopathology. In J. W. Berry, M. H. Segall, & C. Kagitçibasi (Eds.), *Handbook of cross-cultural psychology* (Vol. 3). Boston: Allyn & Bacon.

Tarr, M. J., & Vuong, Q. C. (2002). Visual object recognition. In H. Pashler & S. Yantis (Eds.), *Steven's handbook of experimental psychology: Vol. 1. Sensation and perception* (3rd ed.). New York: Wiley.

Taylor, R. D., & Wang, M. C. (Eds.). (2000). *Resilience across contexts: Family, work, culture, and community.* Mahwah, NJ: Erlbaum.

Taylor, S. (2004). Efficacy and outcome predictors for three PTSD treatments: Exposure therapy, EMDR, and relaxation training. In S. Taylor (Ed.), *Advances in the treatment of posttraumatic stress disorder: Cognitive-behavioral perspectives.* New York: Springer.

Taylor, S. E. (2003). *Health psychology* (3rd ed.). Boston: McGraw-Hill.

Taylor, S. E. (2006). *Health psychology* (4th ed.). Boston: McGraw-Hill.

Taylor, S. E., & Brown, J. D. (1988). Illusion and well-being: A social psychological perspective on mental health. *Psychological Bulletin, 103*, 193–210.

Taylor, S. E., Klein, L. C., Lewis, B., Gruenewald, T. L., Gurung, R. A. R., & Updegraff, J. A. (2000). Biobehavioral responses to stress in females: Tend-and-befriend, not fight-or-flight. *Psychological Review, 107*, 411–429.

Taylor, S. E., Lerner, J. S., Sherman, D. K., Sage, R. M., & McDowell, N. K. (2003). Portrait of the self-enhancer: Well adjusted and well liked or maladjusted and friendless? *Journal of Personality and Social Psychology, 84*, 165–176.

Teachman, B. A., Gapinski, K. D., Brownell, K. D., Rawlins, M., & Jeyaram, S. (2003). Demonstrations of implicit anti-fat bias: The impact of providing causal information and evoking empathy. *Health Psychology, 22*, 68–78.

Teachman, J. D. (2002). Childhood living arrangements and the intergenerational transmission of divorce. *Journal of Marriage and Family, 64*, 717–729.

Teghtsoonian, R. (1971). On the exponents in Stevens' law and the constant in Ekman's law. *Psychological Review, 78*, 71–80.

Tellegen, A., Lykken, D. T., Bouchard, T. J., Wilcox, K. J., Segal, N. L., & Rich, S. (1988). Personality similarity in twins reared apart and together. *Journal of Personality and Social Psychology, 54*, 1031–1039.

Ten-Berge, M. A., Maaike, A., & De-Raad, B. (2002). The structure of situations from a personality perspective. *European Journal of Personality, 16*, 81–102.

Tenenbaum, H. R., & Leaper, C. (2003). Parent-child conversations about science: The socialization of gender inequities? *Developmental Psychology, 39*, 34–47.

Terman, L. M., & Merrill, M. A. (1972). *Stanford-Binet intelligence scale, third edition, form L–M.* Boston: Houghton Mifflin.

Terrace, H. S. (1979). *Nim.* New York: Knopf.

Tesser, A. (2004). Self-esteem. In M. B. Brewer & M. Hewstone (Eds.), *Emotion and motivation. Perspectives on social psychology.* Malden, MA: Blackwell.

Tesser, A., & Shaffer, D. (1990). Attitudes and attitude change. *Annual Review of Psychology, 41*, 479–523.

Thase, M. E., Greenhouse, J. B., Frank, E., et al. (1997). Treatment of major depression with psychotherapy or psychotherapy-pharmacotherapy combinations. *Archives of General Psychiatry, 54*, 1009–1015.

Thatch, W. T., Goodkin, H. P., & Keating, J. G. (1992). The cerebellum and the adaptive coordination of movement. *Annual Review of Neuroscience, 15*, 161–182.

Thibaut, J. W., & Kelley, H. H. (1959). *The social psychology of groups.* New York: Wiley.

Thiede, K. W., & Anderson, M. C. M. (2003). Summarizing can improve metacomprehension accuracy. *Contemporary Education Psychology, 28*, 129–160.

Thoits, P. (1983). Dimensions of life events that influence psychological distress: An evaluation and synthesis of the literature. In H. B. Kaplan (Ed.), *Psychological stress: Trends in theory and research.* New York: Academic Press.

Thomas, A., & Chess, S. (1977). *Temperament and development.* New York: Brunner/Mazel.

Thomas, L. (1974). *The lives of a cell.* New York: Viking Press.

Thomas, S. A., & Palmiter, R. D. (1997). Disruption of the dopamine Beta-hydroxylase gene in mice suggests roles for norepinephrine in motor function, learning, and memory. *Behavioral Neuroscience, 111*, 579–589.

Thomas, S. L., Skitka, L. J., Christen, S., & Jurgena, M. (2002). Social facilitation and impression formation. *Basic and Applied Social Psychology, 24*, 67–70.

Thomas, W. P., & Collier, V. P. (1997). *School effectiveness for language minority students.* Washington, DC: National Clearinghouse for Bilingual Education.

Thompson, C. P., Cowan, T. M., & Frieman, J. (1993). *Memory search by a memorist.* Hillsdale, NJ: Erlbaum.

Thompson, R. F. (1985). *The brain: An introduction to neuroscience.* New York: Freeman.

Thompson-Brenner, H., Glass, S., & Westen, D. (2003). A multidimensional meta-analysis of psychotherapy for bulimia nervosa. *Clinical Psychology: Science and Practice, 10*, 269–287.

Thorndike, E. L. (1898). *Animal intelligence: An experimental study of the associative processes in animals.* New York: Macmillan.

Thorndike, E. L. (1911). *Animal intelligence: experimental studies.* New York: Macmillan.

Thurstone, L. L. (1938). *Primary mental abilities.* Chicago: University of Chicago Press.

Tilker, H. A. (1970). Socially responsible behavior as a function of observer responsibility and victim feedback. *Journal of Personality and Social Psychology, 14*, 95–100.

Tinbergen, N. (1951). *The study of instinct.* Oxford, England: Clarendon Press.

Tizard, B., & Hodges, J. (1978). The effect of early institutional rearing on the development of eight-year-old children. *Journal of Child Psychology and Psychiatry, 19*, 99–118.

Tobin, J. J., & Friedman, J. (1983). Spirits, shamans, and nightmare death: Survivor stress in a Hmong refugee. *American Journal of Orthopsychiatry, 53*, 439–448.

Todorov, A., & Bargh, J. A. (2002). Automatic sources of aggression. *Aggression and Violent Behavior, 7*, 53–68.

Tollefson, G. D. (1993). Major depression. In D. L. Dunner (Ed.), *Current psychiatric therapy.* Philadephia: Saunders.

Tollison, C. D., Satterswaithe, J. R., & Tollison, J. W. (2002). *Practical pain management.* New York: Williams & Wilkins.

Tolman, E. C. (1948). Cognitive maps in rats and men. *Psychological Review, 55*, 189–208.

Tolman, E. C., & Honzik, C. H. (1930). Introduction and removal of reward and maze performance in rats. *University of California Publications in Psychology, 4*, 257–275.

Tomarken, A. J., & Keener, A. D. (1998). Frontal brain asymmetry and depression: A self-regulatory perspective. Special Issue: Neuropsychological perspectives on affective and anxiety disorders. *Cognition & Emotion, 12*(3), 387–420.

Tomkins, S. S. (1991). *Affect, imagery, and consciousness.* New York: Springer-Verlag.

Tooby, J., & Cosmides, L. (1992). The psychological foundations of culture. In J. H. Barkow, L. Cosmides, & J. Tooby (Eds.), *The adapted mind.* New York: Oxford University Press.

Torgerson, S. (2000). Genetics of patients with borderline personality disorder. *Psychiatric Clinics of North America, 23*, 1–9.

Torgerson, S., Kringlen, E., & Cramer, V. (2001). The prevalence of personality disorders in a community sample. *Archives of General Psychiatry, 58*, 590–596.

Torrey, E. F. (1997). *Out of the shadows: Confronting America's mental illness crisis.* New York: Wiley.

Torrey, E. F., & Zdanowicz, M. (2001). Outpatient commitment: What, why, and for whom. *Psychiatric Services, 52*, 337–341.

Trae, H. C., & Deighton, R. M. (2000). Emotional inhibition. In G. Fink (Ed.), *Encyclopedia of stress.* San Diego, CA: Academic Press.

Travers, K. R., & Lyvers, M. (2005). Mood and impulsivity of recreational Ecstasy users in the week following a "rave." *Addiction Research & Theory, 13*, 43–52.

Treasure, J. (2005). *Essential handbook of eating disorders.* New York: Wiley.

Tremblay, L. K., Naranjo, C. A., Cardenas, L., Hermann, N., & Busto, U. E. (2002). Probing brain reward system function in major depressive disorder: Altered response to dextroamphetamine. *Archives of General Psychiatry, 59*, 409–417.

Triandis, H. C. (2001). Individualism-collectivism and personality. *Journal of Personality, 69*, 907–924.

Triandis, H. C., & Suh, E. M. (2002). Cultural influences on personality. *Annual Review of Psychology, 53*, 133–160.

Trimble, M. (2003). *Somatoform disorders.* New York: Cambridge University Press.

Triplett, N. (1898). The dynamogenic factors in pace-making and competition. *American Journal of Psychology, 9*, 507–533.

Trivers, R. (1971). The evolution of reciprocal altruism. *Quarterly Review of Biology, 46*, 35–57.

Trivers, R. L. (1972). Parental investment and sexual selection. In B. Campbell (Ed.), *Sexual selection and the descent of man.* Chicago: Aldine-Atherton.

Trull, T. J., & Geary, D. C. (1997). Comparison of the Big-Five Factor structure across samples of Chinese and American adults. *Journal of Personality Assessment, 69*, 324–341.

Truscott, S. D., & Frank, A. J. (2001). Does the Flynn effect affect IQ scores of students classified as LD? *Journal of School Psychology, 39*, 319–334.

Trzesniewski, K. H., Donnellan, M. B., & Robins, R. W. (2003). Stability of self-esteem across the life span. *Journal of Personality and Social Psychology, 84*, 205–220.

Tseng, W. S., Asai, M., Liu, J., Pismai, W., et al. (1990). Multi-cultural study of minor psychiatric disorders in Asia: Symptom manifestations. *International Journal of Social Psychiatry, 36*, 252–264.

Tucker, V. A. (2000). The deep fovea, sideways vision and spiral flight paths in raptors. *Journal of Experimental Biology, 203*, 3745–3754.

Tuckett, D. (2005). Psychoanalysis in Great Britain and Continental Europe. In E. S. Person, A. M. Cooper, et al. (Eds.), *The American psychiatric publishing textbook of psychoanalysis* (pp. 407–421). Washington, DC: American Psychiatric Publishing, Inc.

Tuiten, A., Van Honk, J., Koppeschaar, H., Bernaards, C., Thijssen, J., & Verbaten, R. (2000). Time course of effects of testosterone administration on sexual arousal in women. *Archives of General Psychiatry, 57,* 149–153.

Tulsky, D. S., Saklofske, D. H., Chelune, G. J., Heaton, R. K., Ivnik, R. J., Bornstein, R., Prifitera, A., & Ledbetter, M. F. (Eds.). (2003). *Clinical interpretation of the WAIS-III and WMS-III.* San Diego, CA: Academic Press.

Tulving, E. (2002). Episodic memory: From mind to brain. *Annual Review of Psychology, 53,* 1–25.

Tulving, E., & Thomson, D. M. (1973). Encoding specificity and retrieval processes in episodic memory. *Psychological Review, 80,* 359–380.

Tupala, E., & Tiihonen, J. (2004). Dopamine and alcoholism: Neurobiological basis of ethanol abuse. *Progress in Neuro-Psychopharmacology & Biological Psychiatry, 28,* 1221–1247.

Turk, D. C. (2001). Physiological and psychological bases of pain. In A. Baum & T. A. Revenson (Eds.), *Handbook of health psychology.* Mahwah, NJ; Erlbaum.

Turk, D. C., & Melzack, R. (2001). *Handbook of pain assessment* (2nd ed.). New York: Guilford Press.

Turkheimer, E., Haley, A., Waldron, N., D'Onofrio, B., & Gottesman, I. I. (2003). Socioeconomic status modifies heritability of IQ in young children. *Psychological Science, 14,* 623–628.

Turnbull, C. M. (1961). Some observations concerning the experiences and behavior of the BaMbuti Pygmies. *American Journal of Psychology, 74,* 304–308.

Turner, J. A., & Aaron, L. A. (2001). Pain-related catastrophizing: What is it? *Clinical Journal of Pain, 17,* 65–71.

Turner, J. A., Deyo, R. A., Loeser, J. D., et al. (1994). The importance of placebo effects in pain treatment and research. *Journal of the American Medical Association, 271,* 1609–1614.

Tusing, K. J., & Dillard, J. P. (2000). The psychological reality of the door-in-the-face: It's helping, not bargaining. *Journal of Language and Social Psychology, 19,* 5–25.

Tversky, A., & Kahneman, D. (1982). Judgments of and by representativeness. In D. Kahneman, P. Slovic, & A. Tversky (Eds.), *Heuristics and biases.* Cambridge University Press.

Tversky, B., & Tuchin, M. (1989). A reconciliation of the evidence on eyewitness testimony: Comments on McCloskey and Zaragoza. *Journal of Experimental Psychology: General, 118,* 86–91.

Tyrka, A. R., Waldron, I., Graber, J. A., & Brooks-Gunn, J. (2002). Prospective predictors of the onset of anorexic and bulimic syndromes. *International Journal of Eating Disorders, 32,* 282–290.

Tzeng, O. J., Hung, W., Cohen, F. J., & Wang, P. (1979). Visual lateralization effect in reading Chinese characters. *Nature, 282,* 499–501.

Tzeng, S. F. (1997). Neural progenitors isolated from newborn rat spinal cords differentiate into neurons and astroglia. *Journal of Biomedical Science, 9*(1), 10–16.

U.S. Census Bureau. (2003a). Statistical abstract of the United States: Table 4. Language spoken at home and ability to speak English for the population 5 years and over by state: 2000. Retrieved April 5, 2005, from http://www.census.gov/population/cen2000/phc-t20/tab04.pdf

U.S. Census Bureau. (2003b). Statistical abstract of the United States: Table 5. Detailed list of languages spoken at home for the population 5 years and over by state: 2000. Retrieved April 5, 2005, from http://www.census.gov/population/cen2000/phc-t20/tab05.pdf

U.S. Department of Health and Human Services. (2002). *National Comorbidity Survey, 1990–92.* Available online: http://www.icpsr.umich.edu/SAMHDA/STUDIES/ncs.html (Substance Abuse and Mental Health Data Archive [SAMHDA]).

U.S. Office of Behavior Technology. (1990). *Provision of professional services to the physically handicapped.* Washington, DC: Author.

U.S. Public Health Service. (1979). *Healthy people: The Surgeon General's report on health promotion and disease prevention.* Washington, DC: U.S. Government Printing Office.

Ungerleider, L. G., & Mishkin, M. (1982). Two cortical visual systems. In D. J. Ingle, M. A. Goodale, & R. J. W. Mansfield (Eds.), *Analysis of visual behavior.* Cambridge, MA: MIT Press.

United Nations. (2002). *Report on the global reach of AIDS.* New York: Author.

Unverzagt, F. W., Gao, S., Baiyewu, O., Ogunniyi, A. O., Gureje, O., Perkins, A., et al. (2001). Prevalence of cognitive impairment: Data from the Indianapolis Study of Health and Aging. *Neurology, 57,* 1655–1662.

Valent, P. (1998). Effects of the Holocaust on Jewish child survivors: Traumas and latent disturbances 50 years later. *Psyche: Zeitschrift fuer Psychoanalyse und ihre Anwendungen, 52,* 751–771.

Valent, P. (2000). Stress effects of the Holocaust. In G. Fink (Ed.), *Encyclopedia of stress.* San Diego, CA: Academic Press.

Vallone, R. P., Griffin, D., Lin, S., & Ross, L. (1990). Overconfident prediction of future actions and outcomes by self and others. *Journal of Personality and Social Psychology, 58,* 582–592.

Valsiner, J., & Lawrence, J. A. (1997). Human development in culture across the life span. In J. W. Berry, P. R. Dasen, & T. S. Saraswathi (Eds.), *Handbook of cross-cultural psychology* (Vol. 2). Boston: Allyn & Bacon.

Vandell, D. L., Burchinal, M. R., Belsky, J., Owen, M. T., Friedman, S. L., Clarke-Stewart, A., McCartney, K., & Weinraub, M. (2005). *Early child care and children's development in the primary grades: Follow-up results from the NICHD Study of Early Child Care.* Paper presented at the biennial meeting of the Society for Research in Child Development, Atlanta, Georgia.

Van der Borght, K., Meerlo, P., Luiten, P., Eggen, B., & Van der Zee, E. A. (2005). Effects of active shock avoidance learning on hippocampal neurogenesis and plasma levels of corticosterone. *Behavioural Brain Research, 157,* 23–30.

Van Der Werf, Y. D., Jolles, J., Witter, M. P., & Uylings, H. B. M. (2003). Contributions of thalamic nuclei to declarative memory functioning. *Cortex, 39,* 1047–1062.

van Ijzendoorn, M. (1995). Adult attachment representations, parental responsiveness, and infant attachment: A meta-analysis of the Adult Attachment Interview. *Psychological Bulletin, 117,* 387–403.

Vanman, E. J., Saltz, J. L., Nathan, L. R., & Warren, J. A. (2004). Racial discrimination by low-prejudiced Whites: Facial movements as implicit measures of attitudes related to behavior. *Psychological Science, 15,* 711–714.

van Praag, H. M. (2004). *Stress, vulnerability and depression.* New York: Cambridge University Press.

Van Zomeren, A. H., & Brouwer, W. H. (1994). *Clinical neuropsychology of attention.* New York: Oxford University Press.

Vargha-Khadem, F., Gadian, D. G., Watkins, K. E., Connelly, A., Van Paesschen, W., & Mishkin, M. (1997). Differential effects of early hippocampal pathology on episodic and semantic memory. *Science, 277,* 376–380.

Vaughan, P. W., Rogers, E. M., Singhal, A., & Swalehe, R. M. (2000). Entertainment-education and HIV/AIDS prevention: A field experiment in Tanzania. *Journal of Health Communication, 5,* 81–100.

Vaughn, C., & Leff, J. (1976). The measurement of expressed emotion in the families of psychiatric patients. *British Journal of Social and Clinical Psychology, 15,* 157–165.

Verona, E., & Carbonell, J. L. (2000). Female violence and personality: Evidence for a pattern of overcontrolled hostility among one-time violent female offenders. *Criminal Justice and Behavior, 27,* 176–195.

Verona, E., Patrick, C., Curtin, J., Bradley, M. M., & Lang, P. J. (2004). Psychopathy and physiological response to emotionally evocative sounds. *Journal of Abnormal Psychology, 113,* 99–108.

Verplanken, B., & Holland, R. W. (2002). Motivated decision making: Effects of activation and self centrality of values on choices and behavior. *Journal of Personality and Social Psychology, 82,* 434–447.

Vertes, R. P., & Eastman, K. E. (2003). The case against memory consolidation in REM sleep. In E. F. Pace-Schott, M. Solms, M. Blagrove, & S. Harnad (Eds.), *Sleep and dreaming: Scientific advances and reconsiderations.* New York: Cambridge University Press.

Vetter, H. J. (1969). *Language behavior and psychopathology.* Chicago: Rand McNally.

Victoir, A., Eertmans, A., Van den Bergh, O., & Van den Broucke, S. (2005). Learning to drive safely: Social-cognitive responses are predictive of performance rated by novice drivers and their instructors. *Transportation*

Research Part F: Traffic Psychology and Behaviour, 8, 59–71.

Villarreal, D. M., Do, V., Haddad, E., & Derrick, B. E. (2002). NMDA receptor antagonists sustain LTP and spatial memory: Active processes mediate LTP decay. *Nature Neuroscience, 5,* 48–52.

Vinden, P. G. (2002). Understanding minds and evidence for belief: A study of Mofu children in Cameroon. *International Journal of Behavioral Development, 26,* 445–452.

Virnig, B., Huang, Z., Lurie, N., Musgrave, D., McBean, M., & Dowd, B. (2004). Does Medicare managed care provide equal treatment for mental illness across races? *Archives of General Psychiatry, 61,* 201–205.

Vitaliano, P. P., Young, H. M., & Zhang, J. (2004). Is caregiving a risk factor for illness? *Current Directions in Psychological Science, 13,* 13–16.

Vogel, D. D. (2005). A neural network model of memory and higher cognitive functions. *International Journal of Psychophysiology, 55,* 3–21.

Vogels, W. W. A., Dekker, M. R., Brouwer, W. H., & deJong, R. (2002). Age-related changes in event-related prospective memory performance: A comparison of four prospective memory tasks. *Brain and Cognition, 49,* 341–362.

von Frisch, K. (1974). Decoding the language of the bee. *Science, 185,* 663–668.

Vral, A., Thierens, H., Baeyens, A., & De Ridder, L. (2002). The micronucleus and g(2)-phase assays for human blood lymphocytes as biomarkers of individual sensitivity to ionizing radiation: Limitations imposed by intraindividual variability. *Radiation Research, 157,* 472–477.

Vurpillot, E. (1968). The development of scanning strategies and their relation to visual differentiations. *Journal of Experimental Child Psychology, 6,* 632–650.

Vygotsky, L. S. (1978). *Mind in society: The development of higher psychological processes.* Cambridge, MA: Harvard University Press. (Original work published 1935)

Wadden, T. A., Brownell, K. D., & Foster, G. D. (2002). Obesity: Responding to the global epidemic. *Journal of Consulting and Clinical Psychology, 70,* 510–525.

Wadden, T. A., Vogt, R. A., Andersen, R. E., et al. (1997). Exercise in the treatment of obesity: Effects of four interventions on body composition, resting energy expenditure, appetite, and mood. *Journal of Consulting and Clinical Psychology, 654,* 269–277.

Wade, P., & Bernstein, B. (1991). Culture sensitivity training and counselor's race: Effects on Black female client's perceptions and attrition. *Journal of Counseling Psychology, 38,* 9–15.

Wagner, K. D., Ambrosini, P., Rynn, M., Wohlberg, C., Yang, R. Y., Greenbaum, M. S., et al. (2003). Efficacy of sertraline in the treatment of children and adolescents with major depressive disorder: Two randomized

controlled trials. *Journal of the American Medical Association, 290*(8), 1033–1041.

Wagstaff, G., Brunas-Wagstaff, J., Cole, J., & Wheatcroft, J. (2004). New directions in forensic hypnosis: Facilitating memory with a focused meditation technique. *Contemporary Hypnosis, 21,* 14–27.

Wahlberg, K. E., Wynne, L. C., Oja, H., Keskitalo, P., et al. (1997). Gene-environment interaction in vulnerability to schizophrenia: Findings from the Finnish Family Study of Schizophrenia. *American Journal of Psychiatry, 154,* 355–362.

Wakefield, M., Reid, Y., Roberts, L., Mullins, R., & Gillies, R. (1998). Smoking and smoking cessation among men whose partners are pregnant: A qualitative study. *Social Science Medicine, 47,* 657–664.

Walen, S. R., & Roth, D. (1987). A cognitive approach. In J. H. Geer & W. T. O'Donohue (Eds.), *Theories of human sexuality.* New York: Plenum Press.

Walker, P. L. (2001). A bioarchaeological perspective on the history of violence. *Annual Review of Anthropology, 30,* 573–596.

Walker, W. R., Skowronski, J. J., Gibbons, J. A., Vogl, R. J., & Thompson, C. P. (in press). On the emotions that accompany autobiographical memories: Dysphoria disrupts the fading affect bias. *Cognition & Emotion.*

Walker, W. R., Skowronski, J. J., & Thompson, C. P. (2003). Life is pleasant—and memory helps to keep it that way! *Review of General Psychology, 7,* 203–210.

Walker, W. R., Vogl, R. J., & Thompson, C. P. (1997). Autobiographical memory: Unpleasantness fades faster than pleasantness over time. *Applied Cognitive Psychology, 11,* 399–413.

Wallbott, H., & Scherer, K. (1988). How universal and specific is emotional experience? Evidence from 27 countries and five continents. In K. Scherer (Ed.), *Facets of emotion: Recent research.* Hillsdale, NJ: Erlbaum.

Walling, D. P., Baker, J. M., & Dott, S. G. (1998). Scope of hypnosis education in academia: Results of a national survey. *International Journal of Clinical and Experimental Hypnosis, 46,* 150–156.

Walsh, B. T., & Devlin, M. J. (1998). Eating disorders: Progress and problems. *Science, 280,* 1387–1390.

Walster, E., Aronson, V., Abrahams, D., & Rottman, L. (1966). The importance of physical attractiveness in dating behavior. *Journal of Personality and Social Psychology, 4,* 508–516.

Walter, H., Bretschneider, V., Gron, G., Zurowski, B., Wunderlich, A. P., Tomczak, R., & Spitzer, M. (2003). Evidence for quantitative domain dominance for verbal and spatial working memory in frontal and parietal cortex. *Cortex, 39,* 897–911.

Wang, A. Y., & Thomas, M. H. (2000). Looking for long-term mnemonic effects on serial recall: The legacy of Simonides. *American Journal of Psychology, 113,* 331–340.

Wang, P. S., Demler, O., & Kessler, R. C. (2002). Adequacy of treatment for serious mental

illness in the United States. *American Journal of Public Health, 92,* 92–98.

Wang, Q. (2001). Culture effects on adults' earliest childhood recollection and self-description: Implications for the relation between memory and the self. *Journal of Personality and Social Psychology, 81,* 220–233.

Wang, S., Baillargeon, R., & Paterson, S. (2005). Detecting continuity violations in infancy: A new account and new evidence from covering and tube events. *Cognition, 95,* 129–173.

Wang, T., Brownstein, R., & Katzev, R. (1989). Promoting charitable behaviour with compliance techniques. *Applied Psychology: An International Review, 38,* 165–183.

Ward, S. L., & Overton, W. F. (1990). Semantic familiarity, relevance, and the development of deductive reasoning. *Developmental Psychology, 26,* 488–493.

Warga, C. (1987). Pain's gatekeeper. *Psychology Today, 21,* 50–59.

Wasserman, D., & Wachbroit, R. (2001). *Genetics and criminal behavior.* New York: Cambridge University Press.

Waters, A., Hill, A., & Waller, G. (2001). Bulimics' responses to food cravings: Is binge-eating a product of hunger or emotional state? *Behaviour Research and Therapy, 39,* 877–886.

Watkins, L. R., & Maier, S. F. (2003) When good pain turns bad. *Current Directions in Psychological Science, 12,* 232–236.

Watson, D., & Clark, L. A. (1992). Affects separable and inseparable: On the hierarchical arrangement of the negative affects. *Journal of Personality and Social Psychology, 62,* 489–505.

Watson, D. L., & Tharp, R. G. (1997). *Self-directed behavior: Self-modification for personal adjustment* (7th ed.) Belmont, CA: Brooks/Cole.

Watson, J. B. (1924). *Behaviorism.* New York: People's Institute.

Watson, J. B., & Rayner, R. (1920). Conditioned emotional reactions. *Journal of Experimental Psychology, 3,* 1–14.

Watson, J. C., & Greenberg, L. S. (1998). The therapeutic alliance in short-term humanistic and experiential therapies. In J. D. Safran & C. J. Muran (Eds.), *The therapeutic alliance in brief psychotherapy.* Washington, DC: American Psychological Association.

Weaver, C. A., III, & Krug, K. S. (2004). Consolidation-like effects in flashbulb memories: Evidence from September 11, 2001. *American Journal of Psychology, 117,* 517–530.

Webb, W. B. (1974). Sleep as an adaptive response. *Perceptual and Motor Skills, 38,* 1023–1027.

Webb, W. B. (1992). *Sleep: The gentle tyrant* (2nd ed.). Bolton, MA: Anker.

Webb, W. B. (1994). Prediction of sleep onset. In R. D. Ogilvie & J. R. Harsh (Eds.), *Sleep onset: Normal and abnormal processes.*

Washington, DC: American Psychological Association.

Webster, D. M., Richter, L., & Kruglanski, A. W. (1996). On leaping to conclusions when feeling tired: Mental fatigue effects on impressional primacy. *Journal of Experimental Social Psychology, 32,* 181–195.

Wechsler, H., Davenport, A., Dowdall, G., Hoeykins, B., & Castillo, S. (1994). Health and behavioral consequences of binge drinking in college: A national survey of students at 140 campuses. *Journal of the American Medical Association, 272,* 1672–1677.

Weinberger, D. R., & McClure, R. K. (2002). Neurotoxicity, neuroplasticity, and magnetic resonance imaging morphometry: What is happening in the schizophrenic brain? *Archives of General Psychiatry, 59,* 553–559.

Weiner, B. (1992). *Human motivation: Metaphors, theories, and research.* Newbury Park, CA: Sage.

Weinert, F. E., & Hany, E. A. (2003). The stability of individual differences in intellectual development. In R. J. Sternberg, J. Lautrey, & T. I. Lubart (Eds.), *Models of intelligence: International perspectives.* Washington, DC: American Psychological Association.

Weingardt, K. R., & Marlatt, G. A. (1998). Harm reduction and public policy. In G. A. Marlatt (Ed.), *Harm reduction: Pragmatic strategies for managing high-risk behaviors.* New York: Guilford Press.

Weingarten, H. P. (1983). Conditioned cues elicit feeding in sated rats: A role for learning in meal initiation. *Science, 220,* 431–433.

Weiskrantz, L. (2002). Prime-sight and blindsight. *Consciousness and Cognition, 11,* 568–581.

Weissman, M. M., Bland, R. C., Canino, G. J., et al. (1994). The cross-national epidemiology of obsessive-compulsive disorder: The Cross-National Collaborative Group. *Journal of Clinical Psychiatry, 55,* 5–10.

Weissman, M. M., Geshon, E. S., Kidd, K. K., Prusoff, B. A., Leckman, J. F., Dibble, E., Hamovit, J., Thompson, W. D., Pauls, D. L., & Guroff, J. J. (1984). Psychiatric disorders in the relatives of probands with affective disorders. *Archives of General Psychiatry, 41,* 13–21.

Weissman, M. M., & Markowitz, J. C. (1994). Interpersonal psychotherapy: Current status. *Archives of General Psychiatry, 51,* 599–606.

Weitlauf, J., Smith, R. E., & Cervone, D. (2000). Generalization effects of coping skills training: Influences of self-defense training on women's efficacy beliefs, assertiveness, and aggression. *Journal of Applied Psychology, 85,* 625–633.

Weitzenhoffer, A. M., & Hilgard, E. R. (1962). *Stanford Hypnotic Susceptibility Scale: Form C.* Palo Alto, CA: Consulting Psychologists.

Weller, A., & Weller, L. (1997). Menstrual synchrony under optimal conditions: Bedouin families. *Journal of Comparative Psychology, 111,* 143–151.

Weller, L., Weller, A., Koresh, H. K., & Shoshan, B. R. (1999). Menstrual synchrony in a sample of working women. *Psychoneuro-endocrinology, 24,* 449–459.

Wender, P. H., Kety, S. S., Rosenthal, D., Schulsinger, F., Ortmann, J., & Lunde, I. (1986). Psychiatric disorders in the biological and adoptive families of adopted individuals with affective disorders. *Archives of General Psychiatry, 43,* 923–929.

Wenzlaff, R. M., Wegner, D. M., & Roper, D. W. (1988). Depression and mental control: The resurgence of unwanted negative thoughts. *Journal of Personality and Social Psychology, 55,* 882–892.

Werner, E. E., & Smith, R. S. (1982). *Vulnerable and invincible: A longitudinal study of resilient children.* New York: McGraw-Hill.

Wernig, M., & Brustle, O. (2002). Fifty ways to make a neuron: Shifts in stem cell hierarchy and their implications for neuropathology and CNS repair. *Journal of Neuropathology and Experimental Neurology, 61*(2), 101–110.

Werth, J. L., Jr., Blevins, D., Toussaint, K. L., & Durham, M. R. (2002). The influence of cultural diversity on end of life care and decisions. *American Behavioral Scientist, 46,* 204–219.

Wertheimer, M. (1912). Experimentelle studien über das Gesehen von Bewegung. *Zeitschrift fuer Psychologie, 61,* 161–265.

West, P. D., & Evans, E. F. (1990). Early detection of hearing damage in young listeners resulting from exposure to amplified music. *British Journal of Audiology, 24,* 89–103.

West, S. A., Pen, I., & Griffin, A. S. (2002). Cooperation and competition between relatives. *Science, 296,* 72–75.

Westen, D. (1998). The scientific legacy of Sigmund Freud: Toward a psychodynamically informed psychological science. *Psychological Bulletin, 24,* 333–371.

Westen, D., & Morrison, K. (2001). A multidimensional meta-analysis of treatments for depression, panic, and generalized anxiety disorder: An empirical examination of the status of empirically supported therapies. *Journal of Consulting and Clinical Psychology, 69,* 875–899.

Westen, D., Novotny, C. M., & Thompson-Brenner, H. (2004). The empirical status of empirically supported psychotherapies: Assumptions, findings, and reporting in controlled clinical trials. *Psychological Bulletin, 130,* 631–663.

Wethington, E. (2000). Expecting stress: Americans and the "midlife crisis." *Motivation and Emotion, 24,* 85–103.

Whalen, P. J. (2003). Remembering people: Neuroimaging takes on the real world. *Learning & Memory, 10,* 240–241.

Whalley, L. J., & Deary, I. J. (2001). Longitudinal cohort study of childhood IQ and survival up to age 76. *British Medical Journal, 322,* 819–822.

Wheeden, A., Scafidi, F. A., Field, T., & Ironson, G. (1993). Massage effects on cocaine-exposed preterm neonates. *Journal of Developmental and Behavioral Pediatrics, 14,* 318–322.

Wheeler, L., & Miyake, K. (1992). Social comparison in everyday life. *Journal of Personality and Social Psychology, 62,* 760–773.

Wheeler, M. E., & Fiske, S. T. (2005). Controlling racial prejudice: Social-cognitive goals affect amygdala and stereotype activation. *Psychological Science, 16,* 56–63.

Whitam, F. L., & Mathy, R. M. (1991). Childhood cross-gender behavior of homosexual females in Brazil, Peru, the Philippines, and the United States. *Archives of Sexual Behavior, 20,* 151–170.

White, K. M., Hogg, M. A., & Terry, D. J. (2002). Improving attitude behavior correspondence through exposure to normative support from a salient ingroup. *Basic and Applied Social Psychology, 24,* 91–103.

White, N. M., & Milner, P. M. (1992). The psychobiology of reinforcers. *Annual Review of Psychology, 43,* 443–472.

Whorf, B. L. (1956). Science and linguistics. In J. B. Carroll (Ed.), *Language, thought and reality: Selected writings of Benjamin Lee Whorf.* Cambridge, MA: MIT Press.

Whyte, J., & Kavey, N. B. (1990). Somnambulistic eating: A report of three cases. *International Journal of Eating Disorders, 9,* 577–581.

Widiger, T. A., & Sankis, L. M. (2000). Adult psychopathology: Issues and controversies. *Annual Review of Psychology, 51,* 377–405.

Wiedenfeld, S. A., O'Leary, A., Bandura, A., Brown, S., Levine, S., & Raska, K. (1990). Impact of perceived self-efficacy in coping with stressors on components of the immune system. *Journal of Personality and Social Psychology, 59,* 1082–1094.

Wiederhold, B. K., & Wiederhold, M. D. (2005). *Virtual reality therapy for anxiety disorders.* Washington, DC: American Psychological Association.

Wiens, A. N., & Menustik, C. E. (1983). Treatment outcome and patient characteristics in an aversion therapy program for alcoholism. *American Psychologist, 38,* 1089–1096.

Wierzbicka, A. (1986). Human emotions: Universal or culture-specific? *American Anthropologist, 52,* 759–781.

Wilcox, S., & Storandt, M. (1996). Relations among age, exercise, and psychological variables in a community sample of women. *Health Psychology, 15,* 110–113.

Willenberg, H. S., Bornstein, S. R., & Crousos, G. P. (2000). Stress-induced disease: Overview. In G. Fink (Ed.), *Encyclopedia of stress.* San Diego, CA: Academic Press.

Williams, K. D., Case, T. I., & Govan, C. L. (2003). Impact of ostracism on social judgments and decisions: Explicit and implicit responses. In J. P. Forgas, K. D. Williams et al. (Eds.), *Social judgments: Implicit and explicit processes.* New York: Cambridge University Press.

Williams, K. D., Cheung, C. K. T., & Choi, W. (2000). Cyberostracism: Effects of being ignored over the Internet. *Journal of Personality and Social Psychology, 79,* 748–762.

Williams, T. J., Pepitone, M. E., Christensen, S. E., Cooke, B. M., Huberman, A. D., &

Breedlove, N. J. (2000). Finger length patterns and human sexual orientation. *Nature, 404,* 455–456.

Williamson, P. (2006). *Mind, brain, and schizophrenia.* New York: Oxford University Press.

Willingham, W. W., Rock, D. A., & Pollack, J. (1990). Predictability of college grades: Three tests and three national samples. In W. W. Willingham & C. Lewis (Eds.), *Predicting college grades: An analysis of institutional trends over two decades.* Princeton, NJ: Educational Testing Service.

Willis, S. L., & Schaie, K. W. (1986). Training the elderly on the ability factors of spatial orientation and inductive reasoning. *Psychology and Aging, 1,* 239–247.

Wills, A. J. (2005). Association and cognition. In A. J. Wills (Ed.), *New directions in human associative learning.* Mahwah, NJ: Erlbaum.

Wilson, B. J., & Gottman, J. M. (2002). Marital conflict, repair, and parenting. In M. H. Bornstein (Ed.), *Handbook of parenting: Vol. 4. Social conditions and applied parenting* (2nd ed.). Mahwah, NJ: Erlbaum.

Wilson, D. A., Best, A. R., & Sullivan, R. M. (2004). Plasticity in the olfactory system: lessons for the neurobiology of memory. *Neuroscientist, 10,* 513–524.

Wilson, G. T., & Lawson, D. M. (1976). Expectancies, alcohol, and sexual arousal in male social drinkers. *Journal of Abnormal Psychology, 85,* 587–594.

Wilson, J. P., & Keane, T. M. (2004). *Assessing psychological trauma and PTSD.* New York: Guilford Press.

Wilson, R. S., & Bennett, D. A. (2003). Cognitive activity and risk of Alzheimer's disease. *Current Directions in Psychological Science, 12,* 87–91.

Wilson, S. C., & Barber, T. X. (1982). The fantasy-prone personality: Implications for understanding imagery, hypnosis, and parapsychological phenomena. *PSI-Research, 1,* 94–116.

Wilson, S. J., Lipsey, M. W., & Derzon, J. H. (2003). The effects of school-based intervention programs on aggressive behavior: A meta-analysis. *Journal of Consulting and Clinical Psychology, 71,* 136–149.

Wilson, S. L. (2003). Post-institutionalization: The effects of early deprivation on development of Romanian adoptees. *Child and Adolescent Social Work Journal, 20,* 473–483.

Windholz, G. (1997). Ivan P. Pavlov: An overview of his life and psychological work. *American Psychologist, 52,* 941–946.

Winkler, I., Korzyukov, O., Gumenyuk, V., Cowan, N., Linkenkaer, H. K., Ilmoniemi, R. J., Alho, K., & Naeaetaenen, R. (2002). Temporary and longer-term retention of acoustic information. *Psychophysiology, 39,* 530–534.

Winne, P. H., & Hadwin, A. F. (1998). Studying as self-regulated learning. In D. J. Hacker, J. Dunlosky, & A. C. Graesser (Eds.), *Metacognition in educational theory and practice.* Mahwah, NJ: Erlbaum.

Winnepenninckx, B., Rooms, L., & Kooy, R. F. (2003). Mental retardation: A review of the genetic causes. *British Journal of Developmental Disabilities, 49,* 29–44.

Winner, E. (2000). The origins and ends of giftedness. *American Psychologist, 55,* 159–169.

Winson, J. (1990). The meaning of dreams. *Scientific American, 260*(11), 86–96.

Winston, J. S., Strange, B. A., O'Doherty, J., & Dolan, R. J. (2002). Automatic and intentional brain responses during evaluation of trustworthiness of faces. *Nature Neuroscience, 5,* 277–283.

Witelson, S. F., Kigar, D. L., & Harvey, T. (1999). The exceptional brain of Albert Einstein. *Lancet, 353,* 2149–2153.

Witkiewicz, K., & Marlatt, G. A. (2004). Relapse prevention for alcohol and drug problems. *American Psychologist, 59,* 224–235.

Wittchen, H. U., Zhao, S., Kessler, R. C., & Eaton, W. W. (1994). DSM-III-R generalized anxiety disorder in the National Comorbidity Survey. *Archives of General Psychiatry, 51,* 355–364.

Wixted, J. T. (2005). A theory about why we forget what we once knew. *Current Directions in Psychological Science, 14,* 6–9.

Wolberg, L. R. (1967). *The technique of psychotherapy* (2nd ed.). New York: Grune & Stratton.

Woldt, A. L., & Toman, S. M. (2005). *Gestalt therapy: History, theory, and practice.* Newbury Park, CA: Sage.

Wolfe, B. (2005). *Understanding and treating anxiety disorders: An integrative approach to healing the wounded self.* Washington, DC: American Psychological Association.

Wolken, J. J. (1995). *Light detectors, photoreceptors, and imaging systems in nature.* New York: Oxford University Press.

Wolpe, J. (1958). *Psychotherapy by reciprocal inhibition.* Stanford, CA: Stanford University Press.

Wolpe, J., & Plaud, J. J. (1997). Pavlov's contributions to behavior therapy: The obvious and the not so obvious. *American Psychologist, 52,* 966–972.

Wong, D. F., Wagner, H. N., Tune, L. E., et al. (1986). Positron emission tomography reveals elevated D_2 dopamine receptors in drug-naive schizophrenics. *Science, 234,* 1558–1563.

Wong, I. C. K., Besag, F. M. C., Santosh, P. J., & Murray, M. L. (2004). Use of selective serotonin reuptake inhibitors in children and adolescents. *Drug Safety, 27*(13).

Wong, M. M., & Csikszentmihalyi, M. (1991). Affiliation motivation and daily experience: Some issues on gender differences. *Journal of Personality and Social Psychology, 60,* 154–164.

Wood, S. L., & Swait, J. (2002). Psychological indicators of innovation adoption: Cross-classification based need for cognition and need for change. *Journal of Consumer Psychology, 12,* 1–13.

Wood, W., & Eagly, A. H. (2000). A call to recognize the breadth of evolutionary perspectives: Sociocultural theories and evolutionary psychology. *Psychological Inquiry, 11,* 52–55.

Wood, W., Lundgren, S., Ouellete, J. A., Busceme, S., & Blackstone, T. (1994). Minority influence: A meta-analytic review of social influence processes. *Psychological Bulletin, 115,* 323–345.

Wood, W., Rhodes, N., & Whelan, M. (1989). Sex differences in positive well-being: A consideration of emotional style and marital status. *Psychological Bulletin, 106,* 249–264.

Woodcock, R. W. (1997). The Woodcock-Johnson Tests of Cognitive Ability-Revised. In D. P. Flanagan, J. L. Genshaft, & P. L. Harrison (Eds.), *Contemporary intellectual assessment: Theories, tests, and issues.* New York: Guilford Press.

Woodruff-Pak, D. S. (1993). Eyeblink classical conditioning in H. M.: Delay and trace paradigms. *Behavioral Neuroscience, 107,* 911–925.

Woods, S. C., & Seeley, R. J. (2002). Hunger and energy homeostasis. In H. Pashler & R. Gallistel (Eds.), *Steven's handbook of experimental psychology: Vol. 3. Learning, motivation, and emotion* (3rd ed.), New York: Wiley.

Word, C. O., Zanna, M. P., & Cooper, J. (1974). The nonverbal mediation of self-fulfilling prophecies in interracial interaction. *Journal of Experimental Social Psychology, 10,* 109–120.

Worell, J., & Remer, P. P. (2003). *Feminist perspectives in therapy: Empowering diverse women.* New York: Wiley.

World Health Organization (2004). *Global summary of the AIDS epidemic, December, 2004.* Geneva, Switzerland: Author.

Wynn, K. (1992). Addition and subtraction by human infants. *Nature, 358,* 749–750.

Wynn, K. (1998). An evolved capacity for number. In D. D. Cummins & C. Allen (Eds.), *The evolution of mind* (pp. 107–126). New York: Oxford University Press.

Yen, S., Shea, T., Pagano, M., Sanislow, C. A., Grilo, C. M., McGlashan, T., et al. (2003). Axis I and Axis II disorders as predictors of prospective suicide attempts: Findings from the Collaborative Longitudinal Personality Disorders Study. *Journal of Abnormal Psychology, 112,* 375–381.

Yerkes, R. M., & Dodson, J. D. (1908). The relation of strength of stimulus to rapidity of habit-formation. *Journal of Comparative and Physiological Psychology, 18,* 459–482.

Yin, T. C. T., & Kuwada, S. (1984). Neuronal mechanisms of binaural interaction. In G. M. Edelman, W. M. Cowan, & W. E. Gall (Eds.), *Dynamic aspects of neocortical function.* New York: Wiley.

Young, L. R., & Joffe, R. T. (1997). *Bipolar disorder: Biological models and their clinical application.* New York: Marcel Dekker.

Youngstedt, S. D., O'Connor, P. J., & Dishman, R. K. (1997). The effects of acute exercise on sleep: A quantitative synthesis. *Sleep, 20,* 203–214.

Yrizarry, N., Matsumoto, D., Imai, C., Kooken, K., & Takeuchi, S. (2001). Culture and emotion. In L. L. Adler & U. P. Gielen (Eds.), *Cross-cultural topics in psychology* (2nd ed.). Westport, CT: Praeger.

Zajonc, R. B. (1965). Social facilitation. *Science, 149*, 269–274.

Zajonc, R. B., Murphy, S. T., & Inglehart, M. (1989). Feeling and facial efference: Implications of a vascular theory of emotion. *Psychological Review, 96*, 395–416.

Zakzanis, K. K. (1998). Neuropsychological correlates of positive vs. negative schizophrenic symptomatology. *Schizophrenia Research, 29*, 227–233.

Zambelis, T., Paparrigopoulos, T., & Soldatos, C. R. (2002). REM sleep behaviour disorder associated with a neurinoma of the left pontocerebellar angle. *Journal of Neurology, Neurosurgery, & Psychiatry, 72*, 821–822.

Zatzick, D. F., & Dimsdale, J. E. (1990). Cultural variations in response to painful stimuli. *Psychosomatic Medicine, 52*, 544–557.

Zautra, A. J. (2003). *Emotions, stress, and health.* New York: Oxford University Press.

Zebrowitz, L. A., Voinescu, L., & Collins, M. A. (1996). "Wide-eyed" and "crooked-faced": Determinants of perceived and real honesty across the life span. *Personality and Social Psychology Bulletin, 22*, 1258–1269.

Zechner, U., Wilda, M., Kehrer-Sawatzki, H., Vogel, W., Fundele, R., & Hameister, H. (2001). A high density of X-linked genes for general cognitive ability: A runaway process shaping human evolution? *Trends in Genetics, 17*, 697–701.

Zhang, D., Zhang, X., Sun, X., Li, Z., Wang, Z., He, S., & Hu, X. (2004). Cross-modal temporal order memory for auditory digits and visual locations: An fMRI study. *Human Brain Mapping, 22*, 280–289.

Zhang, Y., Proenca, R., Maffei, M., Barone, M., Leopold, L., & Friedman, J. M. (1994). Positional cloning of the mouse obese gene and its human homologue. *Nature, 372*, 425–432.

Zhdanova, I. V., & Wurtman, R. J. (1997). Efficacy of melatonin as a sleep-promoting agent. *Journal of Biological Rhythms, 12*, 644–650.

Zimbardo, P. G. (2004). A situationist perspective on the psychology of evil: Understanding how good people are transformed into perpetrators. In A. G. Miller (Ed.), *The social psychology of good and evil.* New York: Guilford Press.

Zimbardo, P. G., Haney, C., Banks, W. C., & Jaffe, D. (1973, April 8). The mind is a formidable jailer: A Pirandellian prison. *New York Times Magazine*, pp. 38–60.

Zinbarg, R. E., Barlow, D. H., Brown, T. A., & Hertz, R. M. (1992). Cognitive-behavioral approaches to the nature and treatment of anxiety disorders. *Annual Review of Psychology, 43*, 235–268.

Zinovieva, I. L. (2001). Why do people work if they are not paid? An example from Eastern Europe. In D. R. Denison (Ed.), *Managing organizational change in transition economies.* Mahwah, NJ: Erlbaum.

Zubieta, J.-K., Smith, Y. R., Bueller, J. A., et al. (2001). Regional *mu* opioid receptor regulation of sensory and affective dimensions of pain. *Science, 293*, 311–315.

Zucker, T. P., Flesche, C. W., Germing, U., Schroeter, S., Willers, R., Wolf, H. H., & Heyll, A. (1998). Patient-controlled versus staff-controlled analgesia with pethidine after allogeneic bone marrow transplantation. *Pain, 75*, 305–312.

Zuckerman, M. (1991). *Psychobiology of personality.* New York: Cambridge University Press.

Zuckerman, M., Hall, J. A., DeFrank, R. S., & Rosenthal, R. (1976). Encoding and decoding of spontaneous and posed facial expressions. *Journal of Personality and Social Psychology, 34*, 966–977.

Name Index

Subject Index